RHODODENDRONS OF THE WORLD

RHODODENDRONS OF THE WORLD

and how to grow them

DAVID G. LEACH

WITH ILLUSTRATIONS BY

Edmond Amateis

ILLUSTRATIONS FOR PHYLOGENETIC CHART
AND FLOWER TRUSS TYPES BY

Dan Miller

New York

CHARLES SCRIBNER'S SONS

7 9 11 13 15 17 19 Q/C 20 18 16 14 12 10 8 6

THIS BOOK PUBLISHED SIMULTANEOUSLY IN
CANADA BY COLLIER MACMILLAN CANADA, INC.

PRINTED IN THE UNITED STATES OF AMERICA
Library of Congress Catalog Card Number 60-6330

ISBN 0-684-10351-6

PRINTED AND BOUND BY HALLIDAY LITHOGRAPH CORPORATION,
WEST HANOVER AND PLYMPTON, MASSACHUSETTS

For my Mother,
who so encouraged an interest
in a natural world that
has never lost its wonder

FOREWORD

SINCE mankind first sustained his spirit with the beauty of cultivated gardens the flowering evergreens have been treasured above all other ornamental plants, and no such shrubs and trees have captured the loyal affection of gardeners more thoroughly than have the magnificent Rhododendrons.

The plant-hunting expeditions into the interior of Asia since the turn of the century have brought back to the Western world hundreds upon hundreds of new species including many remarkable sorts which far outrank in quality of flower and in garden usefulness the Rhododendrons previously known to horticulture. These startling discoveries stimulated a tremendous wave of interest among gardeners, first in Britain, then in our Pacific Northwest and now it is about to appear in the Northeastern United States. Hybrids in hardy form with a good measure of the extraordinary beauty of the new Asian species are just starting to come from the plant breeders to usher in a new era of importance for the Rhododendron as a garden decoration in the eastern United States and in the colder parts of the British Isles.

But even without this new stimulus the public interest in Rhododendrons has never wavered. The nursery industry has not been able to produce enough plants to meet the demand for more than twenty years. The shortage of red-flowered hybrids, especially, has been so chronic that professional growers are resigned to it.

To the enthusiast, all this is merely as it should be. To the professional grower, the market seems all but insatiable. But the novice has had no means of becoming informed about Rhododendrons and the commercial nurseryman has had no access to the essential information which is a vital tool of his trade. Small handbooks of regional or specialized interest have appeared, but there have been no new comprehensive publications on Rhododendrons in either America or Great Britain since 1936.

This present book is designed to serve three sorts of readers: the amateur gardener, the professional grower and the Rhododendron student.

For the home owner who wants a summary of practical information on this great group of plants there is a comprehensive account of the sorts suitable for various climates, where to get them, how to select and use them for various garden purposes, their planting and care, the remedies for their rare ills.

For the commercial nurseryman there is extensive information on the several methods of propagation, much of it recent research published for the first time; there are the latest discoveries in nutrition and efficient methods of production in the nursery, and how to landscape most effectively with Rhododendrons. Both American and British quality and hardiness ratings are given with the descriptions of all of the hybrids and species in commerce and there are detailed accounts of diseases and pests and the most recently developed controls for them.

For the Rhododendron enthusiast and the botanist, every species important to horticulture is illustrated and described at length in 148 profiles of them which include comments on their value for various uses, peculiarities of their culture, the finest forms and how to distinguish each of them from its relatives. This material is based largely on original observations and measurements made by the author and it corrects much information and many errors in previous publications. Also for the Rhododendron hobbyist is a critique on taxonomy, general accounts of adaptations, distribution, physiology, anatomy, recommended lists of the newest hybrids, extensive information on breeding, and so on. For special readers there are chapters on the culture of Rhododendrons in uncongenial climates, on forcing Rhododendrons and on the tender sorts which are so fine in greenhouses.

Even to the most casual gardener Rhododendrons can be a fascinating subject with the almost incredible variety of character in a thousand colorful species from the wild and many thousands of beautiful garden hybrids.

These brilliant throngs await an invitation to our gardens, there to display the wonder of their flowers and foliage for whoever will provide their simple but special needs. And they extend an invitation themselves to one of the most engrossing and rewarding studies in the whole realm of nature. The aim of this book is to encompass the pleasures of the whole jostling multitude.

DAVID G. LEACH

Brookville, Pennsylvania
1959

AUTHOR'S ACKNOWLEDGMENTS

HUNDREDS of generous people in the United States and abroad have contributed to the writing of this book, and I suspect that it will be almost as much of a relief to my friends both here and overseas as it is to me, to have it finished after four years' toil. I am indebted to them in all manner of ways. Some have answered a single letter of inquiry whereas others have replied repeatedly to questions in their special fields. The British authorities on Rhododendrons have been particularly hospitable in opening to me the magnificent Rhododendron collections in England, Scotland and Wales so that I could study them at leisure. Scores of friendly gardeners in different parts of this country have taken the time to answer questionnaires concerning the adaptability of various Rhododendrons to their conditions, and others have contributed invaluable information on the culture of these plants in regions where special methods are needed.

The multitudes of wild species from Asia are much better represented in the British collections of Rhododendrons, both public and private, than they are in American gardens because they were first introduced there to the Western world and they have been grown in large numbers ever since. I have therefore made the technical measurements and botanical observations abroad for the section of this book dealing with such matters.

The ratings of the species for ease of cultivation and freedom of flowering were compiled with the help of British experts, the Messrs T. H. Findlay, Charles Puddle and H. H. Davidian, and Mr J. P. C. Russell added his valuable advice regarding superior species forms. Dr H. N. Fletcher and his colleague, Mr Davidian, at the Royal Botanic Garden contributed data on rare species which is here published for the first time, and their counsel in combination with the collection of living plants and the Herbarium at Edinburgh has been particularly helpful. The Messrs Peter Barber, Fred Wynniatt and Edmund de Rothschild could scarcely have been more generous in paving the way for a remarkably instructive and pleasantly prolonged study of the Rhododendron collection of the late and great authority, Lionel de Rothschild, at Exbury. Mr Charles Puddle at the renowned Bodnant garden in Wales; Sir Eric Saville and his superintendent, Mr Findlay, at the Windsor Great Park collection, so beautifully arranged by botanical relationships; the Earl of Stair at Lochinch, and the Duchess of Montrose at Brodick, on the Isle of Arran in Scotland; Mrs Stevenson at Tower Court; Mr Frederick Street at his nursery near Woking, and the owners of other noteworthy collections throughout the British Isles have all been helpful by sharing their expert knowledge of this enormous group of plants and by opening their gardens to me. I am grateful to them all. Mr Patrick M. Synge and the Royal Horticultural Society have been unfailingly kind and co-operative.

In this country, Joseph B. Gable's lifetime experience as a Rhododendron specialist has been placed at my disposal on the several occasions I have consulted him since I began work on the book. Dr Henry Skinner at the United States National Arboretum; Mr Brian O. Mulligan at the University of Washington Arboretum; Dr James E. Wright, Jr, at the Pennsylvania State University; Dr Richard Howard and Dr Donald Wyman at the Arnold Arboretum; Dr John Wister at the Arthur Hoyt Scott Horticultural Foundation, have all lent a hand with bits of information and sometimes with sizable chunks. The Messrs Noel C. Farr, Warren Baldsiefen, A. M. Shammarello and Dr Henry Fleming have contributed on matters of entomology; Mr Clarence Barbre, Dr M. S. Colgrove, Jr, and Dr P. P. Pirone on organic and inorganic chemistry; Dr John Creech on physiology; Dr Clyde C. Hamilton and Mr Roland de Wilde on pathology; and the Messrs Guy G. Nearing, Paul Vossberg and Warren Baldsiefen on propagation. I am indebted as well to the Messrs Arno Nehrling, S. D. Coleman, Sr, Harold Epstein, Fred Galle and Dr Thomas Wheeldon for helping to compile the list of nurserymen who specialize in Rhododendrons. Mr Henry Hohman, Dr Henry Skinner, Dr Fred Coe and Mr Frederick P. Lee furnished information on Rhododendrons suitable for the Baltimore–Washington region. The Messrs Peter Zorg and H. J. Grootendorst provided records on the parentage of some of the Dutch hybrids.

Dr Edgar T. Wherry of the University of Pennsylvania furnished the data for the acid soil map of the United States. My friend and the illustrator of this book, Mr Edmond Amateis, made many helpful suggestions in the course of our collaboration and gave much more of his interest and talents than his role demanded. Mr Bernard Harkness provided a technical Latin botanical description.

Scores of growers responded to a questionnaire intended to pinpoint the hardiness of various hybrid Rhododendrons in the northeastern United States. It is scarcely practical to mention all of them, though I am no less grateful for their help. I am emphatically indebted to my wife for indulgence and assistance beyond all reasonable marital bounds. Miss Elinor Parker of Charles Scribner's Sons has been extraordinarily perceptive and generous in the long course of preparing the book for publication. Mrs Harold Mayes helped in the secretarial work on the manuscript.

I must make special acknowledgment to the Messrs H. L. Larson, P. H. Brydon and Rudolph Henny in the Pacific Northwest, and to Dr J. Harold Clarke, Mrs E. J. Greig and to Mr Leonard Frisbie, all of whom furnished valued information in answer to my inquiries. Mr Brydon is responsible for the Pacific Northwest edition of the plant list in Chapter II. Mr Larson has been helpful in tracking down the parentage of hybrids which originated in the Tacoma–Seattle region, and in several other respects as well.

The Messrs Lester Brandt, Carl English, Jr, Leonard Frisbie, Rudolph Henny, H. L. Larson, and Brian Mulligan, all specialists of long experience in the Portland–Tacoma–Seattle district, have supplied me with their opinions as to the finest species for western Oregon and Washington.

Mr Larson, Mr Bryden, and Mr Mulligan, together with the members of the Seattle Chapter of the American Rhododendron Society, pooled their experience to make the recommendations of the best hybrids for mild climates such as that in the Pacific Northwest coastal region.

In the San Francisco district, the Messrs Maurice Sumner, Jack Osegueda, Roy Hudson, and Guy B. Johnson gave me the benefit of their advice on the special aspects of Rhododendron culture along the California coast.

I am greatly indebted to the following inland gardeners who have generously shared with me the benefits of their experience in growing Rhododendrons in uncongenial climates: Mr F. C. Oates, Jr, Mr S. D. Coleman, Sr, and the late Mr W. E. Bowers, of Georgia; Mr F. R. Murray and Mr E. E. Bruck of Indiana; Mr Harry Seevers of Kansas; Mr F. W. Case and Mr C. W. Mann of Michigan; Mr C. Barbre, Mr A. H. Schettler and Mr G. N. Keuchler of Missouri; Mr W. H. Thorne and Mr. C. A. Dewey, Jr, of North Carolina; Mr Roy H. McCluney and Mr W. J. Cummins of Ohio; Mr L. S. Randolph of Oklahoma; Mr J. M. Boyce of South Carolina; Mr R. C. Harden of Tennessee; and Mr W. W. Coates, Jr, of Texas.

Despite my earnest wish to credit every assistance, I am sure I shall shortly be thinking of a name or two whose omission I should deplore. It is almost inevitable, when so many gracious people gave help and encouragement in the course of four years of preparation. I am all the more indebted to them, and doubly grateful too for their services which may not here have the public acknowledgment they so well deserve.

DAVID G. LEACH

ILLUSTRATOR'S ACKNOWLEDGMENTS

ALMOST all of the drawings illustrating the species of Rhododendrons were made from photographs of them taken by the author of this book. In addition, I wish to gratefully acknowledge help from the following: the Messrs Rudolph Henny, Harold Epstein, John G. Bacher, Dr Paul J. Bowman, and Mr and Mrs Del James; *Gray's Anatomy*, *The Species of Rhododendron*, *The Botanical Magazine*, *Rhododendrons and the Various Hybrids*, by J. G. Millais, the works of the Hookers, both father and son, and the Herbarium of the New York Botanical Garden. The maps of Rhododendron distribution were brought to a new standard of accuracy through the generous contributions of data by Dr Henry Skinner, Leonard Frisbie, D. L. Craig and the Royal Horticultural Society. The map showing the acid soil regions of the United States was drawn exclusively from a first draft supplied by Dr Edgar T. Wherry.

EDMOND AMATEIS

CONTENTS

FOREWORD page 7

I RHODODENDRONS IN THE WILD 15

History—Distribution—Foreign Sorts for American and British Gardens—Climate—Means for Survival in the Wild—Variation—Series or Groups of Similar Species

II RHODODENDRONS IN THE GARDEN 30

Versatility—Foliage Color Effects—Interest of Indumentum—Colorful New Growths—Character—Shrub Borders—Single Plantings—Nine Months of Bloom—Color Combinations—Fragrance—Permanence—Rhododendrons as Cut Flowers—Foundation Plantings—Rock Gardens—Small Garden—Ground Covers and Edging—Formal Gardens—Hedges—Screens—Windbreaks—Woodland Rhododendrons—City Gardens and Parks—Public Buildings

III THE PLANT AND THE SITE 50

Regions in U.S. where Rhododendrons Grow Naturally—Selecting Plants for Purchase—Transplanting Seasons—Plants to Associate with Rhododendrons—Choosing Planting Site

IV PLANTING AND CARING FOR RHODODENDRONS 68

Preparation of the Rhododendron for Planting—Preparation of Site—Function of the Mulch—Woodlands and Favored Sites—Subsidence, Drainage and Planting Depths—Spacing—Mulches—Watering—Winter Protection—Removing Faded Flowers—Disbudding—Pruning—Pinching Out Terminal Growth Buds—Nutrition—Minimizing Winter Injury with Chemicals—Humus—Water and Nutrition—Fertilizers—Foliar Feeding

V RHODODENDRON SPECIES 107

Ornamental Value of Species v. *Hybrids—Recommended Sorts—Technical Considerations—Correction of Formerly Published Species Descriptions—Species Important to Horticulture—Illustrations—Ratings for Quality, Hardiness, Freedom of Bloom and Ease of Cultivation—British and American Awards—Detailed Descriptions of 148 Important Species—Drawings Illustrating 18 Basic Types of Flower Trusses—Recommended Species for Regions of the United States and Great Britain*

VI RHODODENDRON HYBRIDS 245

History of Hybrids—Named Hybrids v. *Seedlings—Catawba Hybrids for Severe Climates—Rhododendron Hybrids for Moderately Severe Climates—Dexter Hybrids—Hybrids for Regions of the United States and Great Britain*

VII RHODODENDRON HARDINESS 270

Influence of Planting Site—Value of Mulch—Diagnosing Cold Injury—Natural Hardening off—Effect of Fertilizer and Water on Hardiness—Nature of Cold Injury—Protecting Tender Plants—Coastal Climates and Hardiness—Factors Affecting Hardiness—Increasing Cold Resistance with Chemicals

VIII RHODODENDRON TROUBLES AND THEIR REMEDIES 279

First Aid for Most Common Ailments—Injuries and Physiological Disorders—Failure to Set Flower Buds—Sun Scald—Spring Frost Injury—Winter Damage—Fungus Diseases—All-purpose Preventive Sprays—Insect Pests page

IX PROPAGATION OF RHODODENDRONS 314

Superiority of Own-Root Plants—Variety of Methods—Rooting Cuttings by Cold Method—Greenhouse Rooting of Cuttings by the Warm Method—Leaf Bud Cuttings—Easy Method for Home Gardeners to Root Cutting—Grafting—Green Grafting for Amateurs and Professionals—Budding—Ground Layering—Air Layering —Propagation from Seeds

X RHODODENDRONS FOR LESS FAVORABLE CLIMATES 361

South, Midwest and Florida—Species v. *Hybrids—Sun and Shade—Wind Protection —Preparing the Beds—New Aid to Easy Culture: Iron Chelates—Mulch—Watering—Fall Chemical Conditioners—Injury from Subsidence*

XI RHODODENDRONS FOR THE COOL GREENHOUSE 370

Small Greenhouse—Larger Greenhouse—Care—Malaysian Rhododendrons—Best Sorts

XII FORCING RHODODENDRONS 377

Suitable sorts—Plants for Later Forcing—Care—Customer Satisfaction

XIII BREEDING RHODODENDRONS 383

Goal—Selection of Parents—Promising and Unpromising Prospects—Breeding for Precocious Blooming—Breeding for Hardiness in the Northeast, Mild Climates, and Heat Resistance—Obtaining Other Characteristics—Results from Reciprocal Crosses—How to Cross—Apomixis—Obtaining and Storing Pollen—Handling Tender Plants for Use as Seed Parents—Advancing and Retarding Flowering of Seed Parents—Causes and Cures for Infertility—Incompatibility and Its Cure—Minimizing Effect of Polyploidy—Irradiation—Tricks of the Trade—Methods of Arranging Crosses for Best Results—Physical Basis for Inheritance—Evaluating First Generation Results—Reaching Goal in Second Generation—Judging Results—Form for Assessing Hybrid Quality—Form of Record for Breeder's Convenience

GENE CHART SHOWING RHODODENDRON FLOWER COLOR INHERITANCE 424

APPENDIX

A *Complete Descriptive List of Rhododendron Hybrids with their Parentage and Ratings* 425

B *Rhododendron Hybridists and Introducers* 502

C *American and European Nurseries Specializing in Rhododendrons* 505

D *Alphabetical Descriptive Listing of all Rhododendron Species with their Series and Subseries Affiliations and Ratings* 508

E *The Species of Rhododendrons Listed under their Series and Subseries* 521

F *Listing of Obsolete and Invalid Species Names with their Correct Names in Current Usage* 531

BIBLIOGRAPHY 535

INDEX 537

ILLUSTRATIONS

DRAWINGS IN TEXT

	page
Variation in stature and growth habit of Rhododendrons	23
Leaf scales of R. *carolinianum*	26
Griffithianum compared with *Micranthum*	28
R. *maddenii* being trained as an espalier against a wall	43
Root ends exposed ready for planting	69
Planting completed	75
Pruning a Rhodendendron	86
Pinching growth buds produces better form and more flowers	89
Leaf variation in three important species	114
Distinctive marks of three important species	116
Flower and leaf forms of 148 species	122–233
Rhododendron leaf shapes	234
Truss Types	235–238
Winter protection for semi-hardy Rhododendrons	275
Garden Centipede	309
Stem Cutting	317
Modified Nearing Propagating Frame	323
Leaf Bud Cutting	331
Leach polyethylene-covered tent frame	333
Modified Side Graft, Veneer Graft, Saddle Graft	338
The Green Graft	342
Union covered with sphagnum and enclosed with polyethylene plastic covering	343
The Bud Graft	345
Ground Layering	347
Air Layering	350
How to cross Rhododendrons	404
The physical basis for inheritance and variation in breeding Rhododendrons	416

PHOTOGRAPHS

RR. *fortunei, fargesii, dauricum, keiskei.* *between pages* 272 *and* 273

RR. *yakusimanum, griffithianum,* (Lady Roseberry g.) 'Pink Delight'.

RR. *lacteum, augustinii,* (Loderi g.) 'White Diamond', (hybrid) 'Blue Diamond'.

RR. ciliatum 'Bergie', (hybrid) 'America'.

R. (*carolinianum* × *edgeworthii*) 'Mildred Amateis'.

Leaves of *carolinianum, edgeworthii* and the range among hybrids from a cross between the two species.

R. (Hawk g.) 'Crest'.

Four good Rhododendrons for the rock garden.

RR. *sinogrande, dalhousiae, javanicum* hybrid, *spinuliferum.*

Leaf Spotting Diseases.

Chlorosis, Wilt, Blight, Flower Galls.
Injuries caused by Rhododendron Borer, Stem Borer, Black Vine Weevil, Cranberry Root Worm.
Midge, Bud Blast, Lace Wing Fly.
Propagating Case, Winter Storage and Protection.
Preparation of Cuttings for Propagation.
E. H. Wilson with native helpers in Asia.
Rain Forest in western Yunnan.
Dwarf alpine Rhododendrons in Tibet.

MAPS

Distribution of Rhododendrons in Europe and Asia	*endpapers*
	page
Regions in America where Rhododendrons and Azaleas grow naturally	20
Acid Soil Regions of the United States	51

CHAPTER I

Rhododendrons in the Wild

HISTORY

THE story of Rhododendrons, their distinguished ancestry, and the manner of their introduction into Western civilization is one of the most fascinating sagas in the endlessly unfolding pageant of natural history. The almost unbelievable variety, from midget mats 2 inches tall to titanic trees soaring 80 feet into the air, the wild conglomeration of distinctive characters in almost 1,000 species, has created a vast storehouse of lore and legends, not only about the plants themselves, but also about the brave men whose expeditions into the remote interior of Asia brought back to the Western world the multitudes of fine sorts which have contributed beyond measure to modern gardens. The journeys of the plant explorers into the mountain wildernesses of India, Burma, Tibet, and China were high adventures of courage and endurance, of disappointment and discovery, of exalted experience and overwhelming disaster.

Rhododendrons have the most eminent of ancestors, being descended through the Camellia and Dillenia families from the Magnolias. As a genus they are unimaginably old, and the extravagant production of floral parts which so endears them to gardeners is typical of primitive plants. Fossil records show their existence in Europe and North America 50,000,000 years ago in substantially the same form as present-day wild Rhododendrons of Asia. The few American species today are survivors of a world of lush vegetation inestimable ages ago when this continent shared many sorts of plants with Asia.

In the brief flash of modern recorded time, one of the earliest mentions of Rhododendrons was by the Roman naturalist, Pliny, at the beginning of the Christian era, but he used this Greek name, meaning 'rose tree', to describe the Oleander. It was still in use for that shrub 1,500 years later when the French writer, Matthias de L'Obel, used the name Rhododendron to describe an Oleander in a book which appeared in 1576. The 'Rose of the Alps', which we today call *Rhododendron ferrugineum*, was well known to writers of the early Herbals in the sixteenth and seventeenth centuries, and it is curious that it was so seldom mentioned in them. When it did appear in works of that period it was invariably described by some name other than Rhododendron.

Rhododendrons were first recommended as plants for garden decoration by Parkinson in 1629, and in the century that followed long Latin descriptions, varied and awkward, substituted for accurate designations. The American *R. maximum* was called by one writer, 'Chamaerhododendros lauri folio, sempervirens, floribus bullatis corymbosis'. Other authors were equally prolific and the confusion in names was intolerable by the middle of the eighteenth century.

The Azaleas

Linnaeus brought order out of chaos when he established the genus Rhododendron in his monumental book published in 1753. Only nine species were known to him, including the Azaleas which he placed in a separate genus.

Thereafter Azaleas were sometimes excluded, sometimes included with the Rhododendrons. *The Species of Rhododendrons*, which was published in England in 1930, once again established Azaleas as a group or series of similar plants within the Rhododendron genus. This view was generally accepted for many years but currently there are proposals that the motley assemblage we call Rhododendrons can be separated into three, four, or five separate and distinct genera, each made up of species with a general resemblance much more close than the tremendously varied assortment which goes under one name today.

Whatever the eventual decision, one of these groups, the Azaleas, are quite unlike other plants we know as Rhododendrons and are easily distinguished from them by marked differences which set them apart. Botanists describe Azaleas as medium-sized shrubs, distinct for their hairy leaves which lack scales beneath them and are usually shed in the autumn, but which are sometimes persistent on the familiar Oriental sorts. The long, stiff hairs usually found on the leaves often clothe the branchlets as well. The flowers may or may not spring from the same buds as the leafy branchlets, but they are always produced at the ends of the branches and have five to ten stamens.

But almost any gardener distinguishes an Azalea from a Rhododendron at a glance, so distinct and different are they. This book deals with Rhododendrons, the fascinating, complex, and endlessly varied plants, *almost* all evergreens, which have been honored as garden shrubs of the highest value since first they were introduced to the Western world.

Early Rhododendron introductions

R. hirsutum, from the European Alps, was the first species of Rhododendron in cultivation when it was introduced to Britain in 1656. It was followed by the importation of the American wildlings, *R. canescens*, *R. nudiflorum*, and *R. viscosum* in 1734, and in 1736 *R. maximum* was brought to England. *R. ferrugineum*, another species from the European Alps, came along in 1752 but communications were difficult and progress was slow in introducing additional sorts. *R. ponticum* was imported from Gibraltar some time before 1763. Then came the travels of the German naturalist, Pallas, and the description of species native to eastern Europe and to Asia: *R. dauricum* in 1780, *R. flavum* in 1793, and *R. chrysanthum* in 1796.

By 1800 there were still only twelve species known in cultivation. *R. caucasicum* and *R. obtusum* arrived in England in 1803 and *R. minus* came from America in the first few years of the new century. In 1809 *R. catawbiense* was introduced from North Carolina. It later became the principal source of hardiness in the garden hybrids which have graced our gardens for generations.

The first of the vast flood of Rhododendrons which was to come later from southeastern Asia was the magnificent tree species, *R. arboreum*, with blood-red flowers, which arrived from India in 1811. In 1823 *R. molle*, destined to become famous as one of the parents of the Mollis hybrids, was introduced from China. In 1832 *R. zeylanicum* came into England from Ceylon. It was joined in 1835 by the Himalayan species, *R. campanulatum*, and the beautiful *R. barbatum*, another important species from the same region, was imported before mid-century.

The Early Explorers

Then in 1850 came the fruits of Sir Joseph Hooker's history-making expedition to the eastern Himalayas. Hooker's introductions from Sikkim encompassed forty-five new species, many of them of extraordinary value, including such luminaries as the yellow-flowered *R. campylocarpum* and *R. wightii*; the adaptable, red-flowered *R. thomsonii*; the small trees, *RR. falconeri*, *grande*, and *hodgsonii*, with their enormous leaves; the splendid epiphytes, *RR. dalhousiae* and *maddenii;* and such sorts of quality as *RR. fulgens*, *niveum*, *wallichii*, *lanatum*, *glaucum*, and *lepidotum*.

R. fortunei, the great discovery of Robert Fortune's journey to China, was sent to England as seeds in 1856 and it later became the foundation of an important race of hybrids as well as a superb ornamental in its own right, hardy in the United States as far north as Boston and almost anywhere in Great Britain.

Twenty-five years after Fortune's China journey, a new spate of species from western China became known through the activity of the French Catholic missionaries whose names are immortalized in botany by the fine Rhododendrons they discovered: *RR. delavayi, davidii, souliei, fargesii*, and others similarly distinctive. Only three or four of their species were brought into cultivation, however, and it remained for later collectors to bring their discoveries into the gardens of the Western world. At about this same time Dr Augustine Henry sent back the important species *R. augustinii*, which became famous as his namesake for its lovely blue flowers. The valuable little *R. racemosum* was introduced in 1893.

By the beginning of the twentieth century about 300 species of Rhododendrons were known to botanists. Only about thirty-five were in cultivation but almost all of the Rhododendrons of America, Europe, and India had been described and their general characteristics were well known.

The Early Hybrids

In the meantime, the first known hybrid had resulted from a rare and accidental crossing of an Azalea, *R. nudiflorum*, with a Rhododendron, *R. ponticum*, in a London nursery about 100 years earlier. By 1814 this Azaleodendron was in the collection of the Royal Botanic Garden at Edinburgh.

In 1810 the purposeful hybridizing of Rhododendrons began in England when Michael Waterer crossed a pink-flowered form of the American wildling, *R. maximum*, with another imported American native, *R. catawbiense*, and it was stimulated in 1825 by the first dazzling red blossoms of the Asian species, *R. arboreum*, which had taken fourteen years to flower from its introduction in 1811. In 1826 J. R. Gowen made the celebrated cross of (*catawbiense* × *ponticum*) × *arboreum* which produced the hybrid called 'Altaclerense'. Published accounts in England state that by 1832 Michael Waterer had raised and given the name 'Nobleanum' to the hybrids from a cross of *arboreum* with *caucasicum* which are still popular early-blooming garden Rhododendrons today. However, writing in 1814 for *Gardener's Chronicle*, Waterer stated in an article that he had not used *R. arboreum* until 'quite recently'.

Man-made crosses of other wild Rhododendrons soon forecast their future importance to horticulture. In the 1830's the breeding of Rhododendrons created such interest that gardeners flocked to see the newest hybrids exhibited at a showroom on Regent Street in London. Despite the few species available for breeding, the lists of nursery hybrids were long and involved by mid-century. *RR. ponticum, maximum, catawbiense* and *caucasicum* were excellent parents to provide in their progeny the adaptability needed for wide cultivation in England. By crossing and recrossing them with the first of the Asian species, and by crossing the hybrids among themselves, the production of new garden Rhododendrons increased enormously throughout Britain. In the 1860's 'Doncaster' came into bloom in the Knap Hill Nursery, the first hardy hybrid with deep, true red flowers, and in the same decade this nursery exported Rhododendron hybrids to landscape the Capitol in Washington, D.C. Anthony Waterer's famous Knap Hill Nursery also introduced at this time the first of the Catawba hybrids which were to become renowned garden shrubs in the United States after their importation there in 1876. They are still the standard Rhododendron hybrids of commerce in the eastern United States and some of them are popular in the colder parts of the British Isles.

With the flowering of *R. thomsonii* in 1857 and of other Sikkim Rhododendrons from the Hooker expedition, plus the occasional introduction of new species from other collectors, the hybridization of Rhododendrons continued apace throughout the years which ended the century, and many notable cultivars which are still valued in modern gardens were introduced by professional nurserymen.

The New Guinea Rhododendrons

Meanwhile, the Rhododendrons of New Guinea had been described by explorers and more than 200 species were known to be there, but none of them was in cultivation and few were likely to be hardy in English gardens. All were sorts with leaves clad underneath with scales, tiny structures just visible to the naked eye which are shaped like minute umbrellas and which help control the amount of water retained by the plant.

Twentieth-Century Plant Hunters

At the start of the new century no one suspected that a fabulous lode of Rhododendron species was awaiting discovery in China, nor did it seem likely that gallant men of intellect were ready to step on the scene to explore this wild and dangerous land for the eternal enrichment of gardens throughout the world. But the time was ripe and the talents were available in the persons of five distinguished men: E. H. Wilson, George Forrest, Reginald Farrer, J. F. Rock, and F. Kingdon-Ward. Their expeditions into the distant provinces of western China and in adjoining Tibet and Burma were marked by discoveries of unprecedented scope and importance to the world of horticulture.

Wilson started on the first of his four expeditions to China in 1899. Initially he collected for the English nursery firm of James Veitch & Sons, and later for the Arnold Arboretum of Boston, Mass. Within the first two years he had sent home about forty new species, a performance which was welcomed with incredulous delight by his sponsor. When his outstanding discoveries flowered a few years later, they created a sensation among gardeners just as their original advent had aroused the surprised botanists to a new interest in Chinese flora. Wilson pioneered a new period in the history of the Rhododendron. His work between 1902 and 1918 stimulated a period of active exploration which resulted in the astounding revelation by him and his contemporaries of more than 600 new species in the first forty years of the new century. Between 1910 and 1920 alone 312 new species were located.

Wilson's introductions were characterized by hardiness and adaptability. They included such notable species as *R. discolor*, a large shrub with enormous fragrant white blossoms, hardy to New York City; the charming dwarf *R. williamsianum*, with dense foliage and nodding pink bells; the luxuriously beautiful, late-blooming *R. auriculatum*; the useful and versatile *R. yunnanense*, *R. ambiguum*, *R. rubiginosum*, and the peerless rock garden pygmies, *RR. fastigiatum*, *intricatum* and *sargentianum*.

Wilson was followed in 1904 by George Forrest who introduced the incredible total of 260 new Rhododendron species up to the time he died in the course of his seventh expedition to the Chinese interior in 1932. His discoveries were so varied as to defy brief description. They ranged from the scarlet-flowered *R. forrestii*, several inches tall, to the tree-like *R. sinogrande*, 30 feet tall, with enormous exotic leaves sometimes 3 feet long and a foot broad. *RR. griersonianum*, *lacteum*, *oreotrephes*, *scintillans*, *megeratum*, and *russatum* are well-known examples from the legions of fine species which this peerless plant hunter gave to the Western world.

Farrer was active in China and Upper Burma, starting in 1914, and died in the course of an expedition in 1920.

Ward began collecting in western China in 1911, later turning his attention to Tibet, Burma, and Assam. His accomplishment in the exploration for Rhododendrons would be secure if his reputation rested solely on the discovery of the stunning *R. wardii* with its yellow blossoms of classic form, but he sent back as well *R. macabeanum*, the most handsome as well as the most adaptable of the primitive large-leaved Rhododendrons. The blazing scarlet-flowered *R. elliotii* was another of his finds. Admirers of the dwarf Rhododendron species remember with affection his contribution of the popular little *pemakoense*, with its pink-mauve blooms, and the rosy-flowered *imperator*. *R. leucaspis* came from him, to launch anew the Rhododendron flowering season each year in a cloud of white blossoms. Fine ornamental forms of species previously discovered flowed in to his British sponsors, and from them to gardens everywhere.

Dr Rock has been active since 1920, his most recent collections having been made with some Americans as sponsors. He has contributed a new conception of the extreme variation of the species throughout their regions of distribution in the wild. Ludlow and Sherriff added immeasurably to our gardens and to our knowledge of Rhododendrons through their collections in Bhutan and Tibet between 1933 and 1949.

The achievements of such explorers give eloquent testimony to the valiant spirit which spurred them on in the face of desperate hardship and frightful peril. Death came to two of them—Farrer and Forrest—in the wilderness and they died bravely amid the stupendous majesty of the mountain scenes they described so well. The exaltation which they felt at times in their great adventures was their reward for the matchless beauty which was their legacy to gardeners everywhere.

DISTRIBUTION

In all probability Rhododendrons originated uncounted millions of years ago in that part of Asia which extends from Nepal along the line of the Himalaya Mountains into northern Burma and continues into the Yunnan and Szechuan provinces of southwestern China. There are found the most primitive species and there Rhododendrons occur in such wild profusion and variety that 321 species grow in one limited district alone. This giant arc, the southern slopes of the most awesome mountains on earth, is the cradle and the great natural center of the genus.

Ranging in size from tiny mat-like growths a couple of inches tall to giant trees soaring up to 80 feet or more, Rhododendrons inhabit a vast section of southeastern Asia stretching from the northwestern Himalayas through eastern Tibet, upper Burma, western and central China and thence southward through Thailand and Viet Nam to the Malay States, Indonesia, and the Philippine Islands. There nine-tenths of the world's Rhododendrons are concentrated, more than 900 species.

They reach their southernmost limit in northern Australia which has one species, possibly an immigrant from a secondary concentration of about 200 species in New Guinea.

Reversing our course, Rhododendrons occur in nature in diminishing numbers in eastern China and extend their range northward into Korea. There are three species in Siberia. Off the coast of Asia, there are wild Rhododendrons on Formosa and thirty-one species are found on the Japanese Islands. Farther north, in the frozen lands which encircle the Arctic Ocean, one species rims the earth and *R. camtschaticum* links Asia with America through its distribution on both sides of the Bering Strait.

Following the course of the mountains southward from Alaska, there are seven species in the western regions of Canada and the United States, one of which, *R. albiflorum*, extends as far inland as Colorado. In the central portion of our country the genus as now constituted is represented by *R. oblongifolium*, an Azalea, in eastern Arkansas, southeastern Oklahoma, and southeastern Texas. *R. lapponicum*, a curious immigrant from the Arctic, trails down the ledges of cliffs along the Wisconsin River at Wisconsin Dells. (It is also found on Mt Washington in New Hampshire but other than in these two oddly isolated spots it is not known to occur south of Hudson Bay.) Proceeding eastward, then, another assemblage of twenty species inhabits various parts of the region stretching from Labrador to Louisiana and Florida. Optimum conditions for Rhododendrons in the eastern United States appear to be in the mountains of North Carolina, where they grow with a vigor and luxuriance not seen elsewhere in nature.

Across the ocean there are only four species in Europe and six in Asia Minor.

FOREIGN SORTS FOR AMERICAN AND BRITISH GARDENS

Almost all of the world's Rhododendrons can be grown somewhere on the west coast of the United States and in the British Isles as well. Even the exotic epiphytes which perch like orchids on tree limbs high in the green roof of the forest in the region of China's frontier

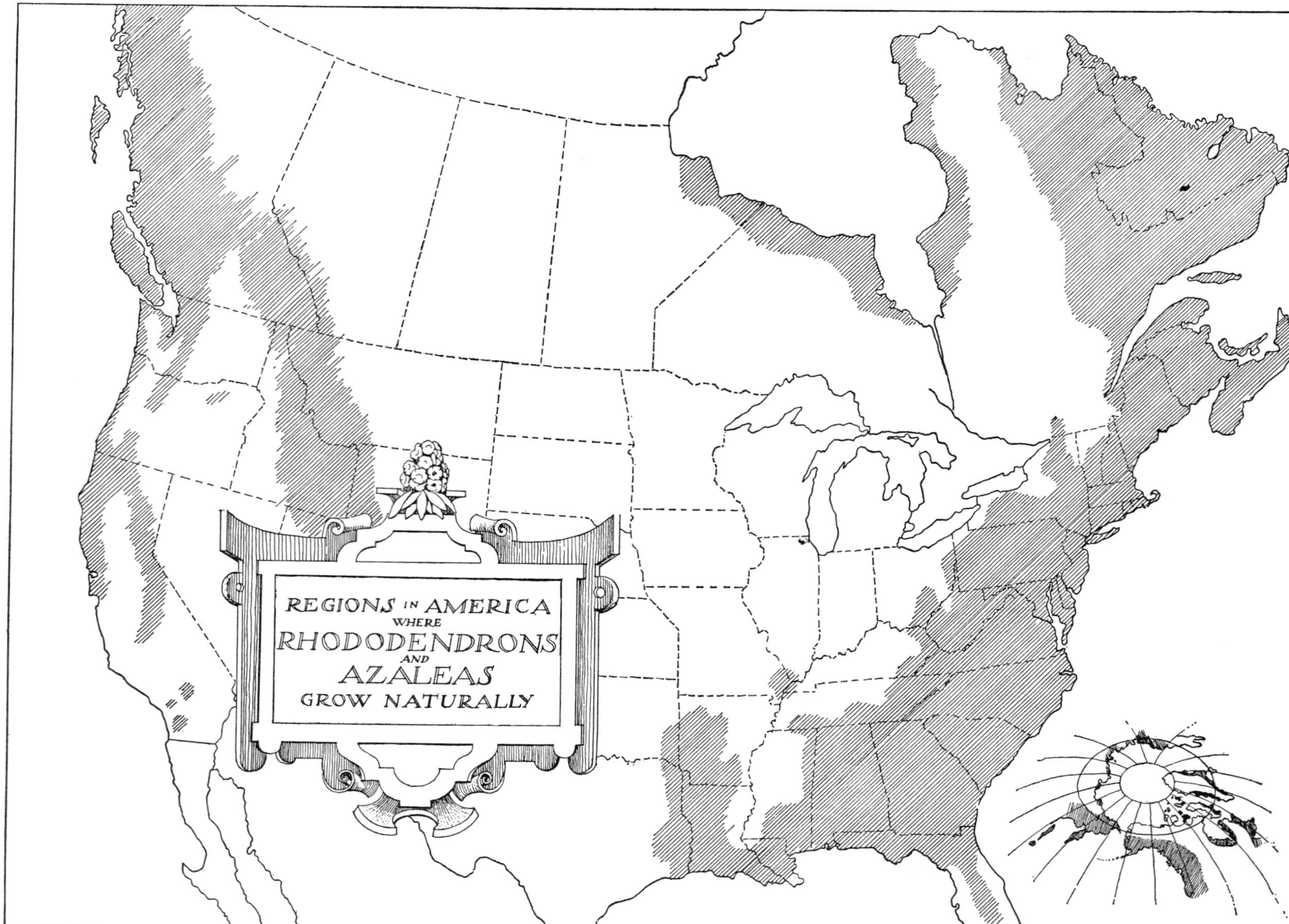
REGIONS IN AMERICA
WHERE
RHODODENDRONS
AND
AZALEAS
GROW NATURALLY

with India and Burma, flourish in the fog belt of the San Francisco district as many of them do in Cornwall and on the west coast of Scotland. In the eastern United States, however, the number of species which can be successfully cultivated is restricted to the limited few which come from regions with a climate which is roughly comparable. The species from Japan and Korea take much more kindly to our east coast than do the multitudes from southeastern Asia. Northeastern China, Manchuria, and Korea furnish some amenable sorts and in central China the 3,000 to 8,000-foot elevations of Szechuan and Hupeh provinces contributed handsome additions to the gardens of the northeast, notably the Fortunei constellation of species. The Rhododendrons of Europe and of Asia Minor can also find congenial conditions somewhere in the triangle formed by Washington, Cleveland, and Boston.

CLIMATE AND DISTRIBUTION

Captain F. Kingdon-Ward, the renowned British plant explorer, points out that in addition to the hardy and handsome Fortunei group of Rhododendrons which is found in mid-western China, other general classes of Rhododendrons can be linked with rough geographical positions. The brilliant-flowered species of the Neriiflorum type come from the wet alpine districts of western China, Burma, and Assam. The tender species of the Stenaulum series are found in the sub-tropical rain forest belt of southern China, and the medium-sized, Azalea-like Triflorum sorts, which are much more amenable in cultivation, come from the more open and dry regions of central China. The big-leaved trees of the Grande and Falconeri groups occur in the cool temperate rain forest.

The monstrous convulsions of the earth's surface—the cataclysmic upheaval of mountains and the silent encroachment of the seas—combined with rainfall and temperature variations, account for the distribution of Rhododendrons. There are none in South America, for example, because it was until recent geologic times separated by ocean from North America, and in any case there is no continuously congenial climate for Rhododendrons bridging the two continents through which the genus could have migrated from north to south.

Parenthetically, in 1957 I discovered *Rhododendron arboreum* growing in the wilderness at 6,000 feet in Jamaica, in the course of a muleback exploration of the Blue Mountain peaks. There, at Morcey's Gap on a ridge in the mist forest, in the company of orchids, gigantic ferns, and luxuriant lichens, were great old trees 25 feet tall with trunks 20 inches in diameter, blooming brilliantly half-way around the world from their relatives in southern Asia. Seedlings beneath the ancient trees gave reassuring evidence of a congenial climate, where the temperature at that altitude varies from about 50 to 70 degrees and the rainfall totals about 120 inches a year. This startling discovery creates a first-rate botanical mystery. The only plausible explanation is that the Rhododendrons were imported and established at this improbable and inaccessible location by a British colonist at least three-quarters of a century ago.

In contrast to the isolation of the two continents of the Western hemisphere, Asia, America, and Europe were once more intimately connected by land masses ages ago in a manner which permitted the spread of Rhododendrons from the one continent to the others. The United States probably received its Rhododendrons as immigrants which came from Asia by natural means across the span of the Aleutian Islands and Alaska, so long ago as to be beyond conception in time. The species which yet remain with us are relicts of a bygone epoch when Asia and North America shared many plants in addition to Rhododendrons.

With minor exceptions, then, Rhododendrons throughout the world are inhabitants of the northern hemisphere. Only in the region of Indonesia off the southeastern coast of Asia and New Guinea do they cross the equator southward. Almost always they are plants of temperate climate with high humidity. The cradle of their origin and their greatest concentration lies in the Orient in the latitude of

Texas and Suez, but the weather is neither very hot nor extremely cold at the altitudes which they find congenial, and the abundant rainfall provides the humidity in which they flourish.

The Effect of Altitude

Only rarely, and usually in arctic or temperate parts of the world, do Rhododendrons forsake the mountains for the coastal plains. In Europe they are found primarily in the Caucasus, the Alps, and the Pyrenees. In America, the evergreen species are a familiar part of the plant life of the Appalachian Mountains and their approaches in the east, and the Coast Range in the west. Across the Pacific, the Himalayas and their satellite ranges harbour myriads of species which have extended their range along the higher elevations in two great arcs, one reaching northeastward to the Japanese Islands and Siberia, the other extending into Indonesia to the southeast.

In fact, these plants are so closely allied with the mountains that the climate at the altitude where a species originates in Asia can be fairly well determined by a study of the Rhododendron population at that elevation. Not only the type of Rhododendron but the number of different species indicates the local conditions: the lighter the rainfall in summer and the lower the atmospheric humidity, the smaller is the species assortment.

The association of Rhododendrons with the mountains of the northern hemisphere is eminently practical and logical. For each increase in height of 364 feet above sea level, the average yearly temperature decreases 1° F. At the same time, the increased elevation is usually associated with higher rainfall as winds laden with moisture deposit their burdens on mountain slopes. High rainfall coupled with fairly low temperature slows the breakdown of organic matter by micro-organisms. Thus, increasing height above sea level promotes more strongly the formation of acid soils as the humus layers composed almost entirely of accumulated organic matter build up with increasing speed compared with the weathering of the basal rock. Increasing acidity in nature is accompanied by a decrease in nutrient supply and a looser, coarser soil texture as a result of the reduced breakdown of the organic matter. This describes exactly the soil conditions in which Rhododendrons flourish.

As mountain temperatures drop into the lower ranges above freezing, increasing rainfall is required for the formation of humus. At an average annual temperature of 37° F., for example, an average rainfall of 118 to 197 inches per year is essential for the accumulation of organic matter. Apply this to Rhododendrons and we find it describing the monsoon climate of the Himalayas, the great natural centre of the genus and the probable region of its birth.

A maximum summer-time temperature of 70° F., a rainfall of more than 75 inches distributed through seven or eight months of the year with a moist atmosphere the year around, and a distinct dormant period in winter, are ideal. A heavy snow cover is a welcome protection against the wintry gales which sweep the mountain passes. The more nearly these perfect conditions are approached, the greater will be the variety and number of Rhododendrons. Captain Ward reports such conditions between 10,000 and 12,000 feet in the Burmese Alps, in a region of Fir and Larch forest, where he found Rhododendron species which were trees 30 to 40 feet tall, and others which were a couple of inches tall growing moss-like on the rocks beneath them. Dwelling in happy association with the giants and the pygmies were Rhododendrons with the stature of large shrubs and species with the height and habit of heather, a couple of feet tall. Even the strange and exotic epiphytic Rhododendrons were found, clinging to moss and bits of leaf mould high on the branches of the trees in this region.

Where the misty atmosphere drips for months with fog and rain and the snow accumulates to linger long in the springtime Rhododendrons luxuriate, but conditions so nearly ideal as to provide the complete range of types and statures are not often encountered in the wild, and the different sorts normally inhabit fairly distinct climatic zones in ascending belts of increasing elevation in the Sino-Himalayan Mountains.

At 4,000 to 7,000 feet the epiphytes, with their opulent flowers deliciously scented, attach themselves to the sponge-like moss on the

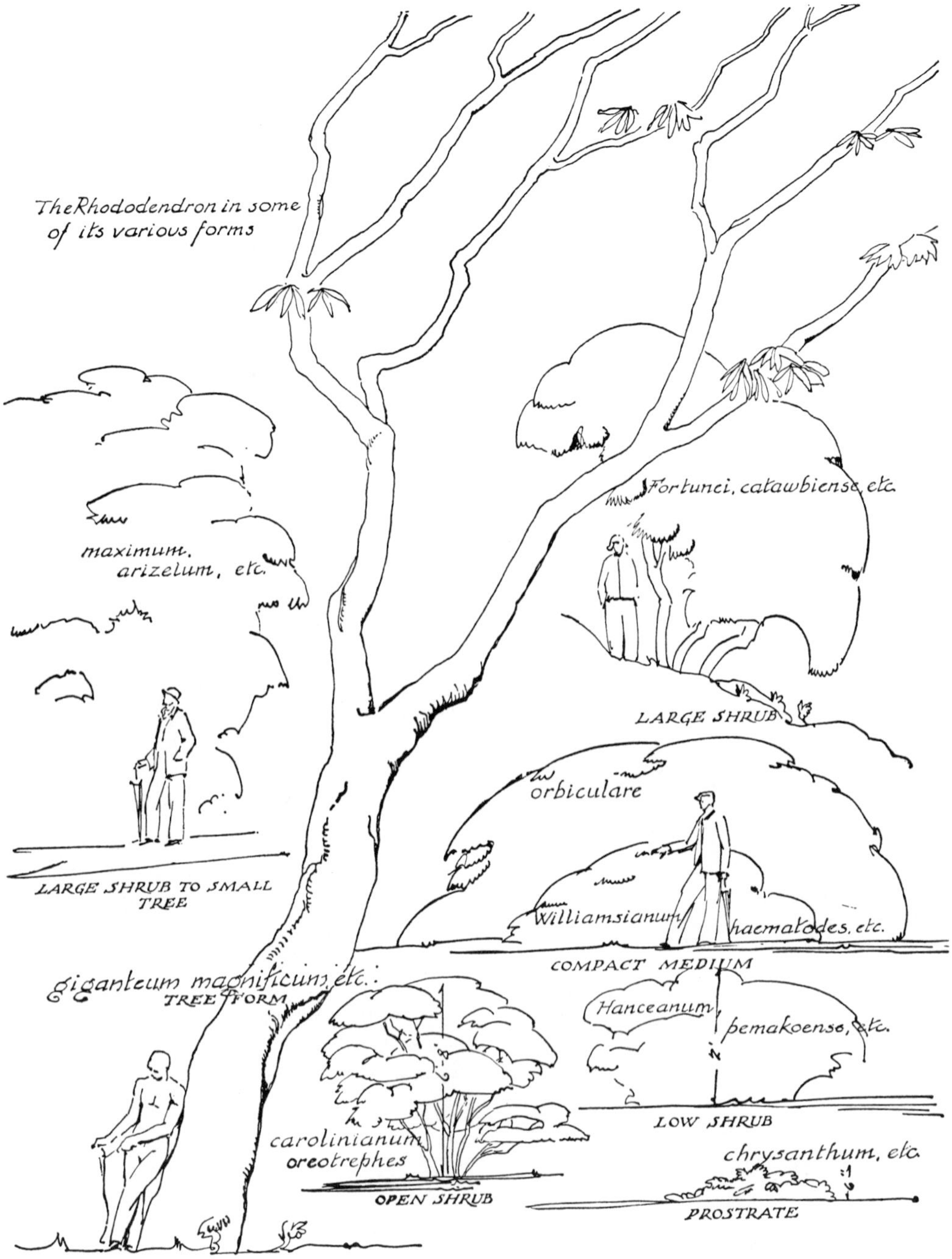

top-most tree branches or occasionally fasten a precarious hold on an exposed rock outcropping. There they revel in the months-long rain of the monsoon region which brings with it the manna of nutrients from the atmosphere, the residue from other animal and vegetable life. These exist in lonely splendor, driven by nature to a solitary aerial struggle for survival.

A little higher up most of the Rhododendrons with the stature of trees are found in the cool, temperate, evergreen rain forest zone, where frosts are rare and spring growth coincides with an inexhaustible supply of water from the snows which melt at higher elevations during February and March. Here too dwell the exotic primitive sorts, survivors not much changed since the age of the Dinosaurs, with mammoth leaves 3 feet long and a foot broad, able to support such splendid foliage because the saturated monsoon atmosphere prevents the rapid evaporation of moisture from their gigantic surfaces. The tree species may be scattered specimens or they may be social, growing in such close associations as to form dense, impenetrable secondary growths beneath the outflung branches of the giant evergreen Oaks, Chestnuts, Magnolias and other such broadleaved trees which are dispersed throughout the forest.

From moderate altitudes to a range higher than the tree sorts come most of the shrub size Rhododendrons, up to about 15 feet in stature and comprising the majority of the best-known species. Still in the region which receives the full benefit of monsoon moisture, they dwell in their homeland wilderness from the temperate forest up to the tree line in the mountains. They too are often gregarious in the mixed forest, and higher up they frequently grow in colonies among coniferous trees.

The pygmy Rhododendron species ranging from tiny mats several inches tall to more upright shrublets up to 2 or 3 feet tall, inhabit the alpine moorlands of the stupendous Himalayas, where they grow in vast associations like the heather of Scotland. Captain Ward describes the view across thousands of acres of Rhododendron heath, gleaming with purple and gold in the thin mountain air: 'Now for the first time we gaze across square miles of rock and Rhododendron, and not much else, the swirling colors of pygmy Lapponicums, Saluenenses, aromatic Anthopogons and bubbling Campylogynums making a never-to-be-forgotten picture; the whole Rhododendron sea is flecked with shimmering foam, sulphur, apricot, salmon, Tyrian purple, violet. On the sheltered side of the valley the Neriiflorums in their various crouching attitudes glow blood red against the irregular patches of snow.'

As an ascending pattern, Rhododendrons are first found at an elevation of about 4,000 to 5,000 feet in the eastern Himalayas. They populate the higher elevations in ever greater density and diversity up to about 10,000 feet, at which elevation the conifer forest usually dominates the mountain slopes. Above 10,000 feet their numbers and variety continue to increase but their stature diminishes until, above 12,000 feet, the assortment of species starts to decline as more dry and open country is approached with increasing elevation. *R. nivale* is found as high as 18,000 feet. The progressively greater profusion and luxuriance of the Rhododendrons as the altitude increases up to 12,000 feet corresponds with the greater humidity and moderating temperatures of the mountain elevations in the monsoon region.

In such a tremendous range of elevations, the genus is certain to adapt to an equally varied range of growing sites. There can be few plant groups whose members grow clinging to tree tops in evergreen rain forests; on the ground in mixed and conifer forests; on rocks in river beds and along the banks of streams; in bogs and on cliffs; in grassy pastures and on the bleak slopes of crumbled rocks left by retreating glaciers; on granite ledges and in deep ravines. The preference of the various species may range from complete shade to full and open exposure.

Rhododendrons completely dominate the plant life in some districts of the Sino-Himalayan region. In the alpine moorlands especially, they frequently form remarkable communities of as many as twenty-five different species in one mountain pass, there to provide a vast carpet of kaleidoscopic brilliance in the blooming season. At lower elevations the different species of the tree Rhododendrons often dwell together in a congenial association of the forest, forming the dominant vegetation beneath the towering Hemlocks, Spruce, and Pines.

THE MEANS FOR SURVIVAL

There is a perpetual, pitiless struggle among plants in nature for food, light, and space to grow. Why have Rhododendrons succeeded so well in the endless competition for survival? Captain Ward cites as one of the main reasons the prodigious quantities of seeds produced. In the moist mildness of the mountainsides, seeds which find a favorable lodging soon germinate, and Rhododendrons quickly take over where the forest has been burned over or the land has been cleared for roadways. The abundant seed which a mature Rhododendron produces to perpetuate the species is a familiar burden in cultivation, since the chore of removing faded blossoms is designed to prevent their formation in gardens.

The communal habit of Rhododendrons also helps them to retain the land they have dominated. Such close association not only promotes cross-pollination and the production of vast quantities of seeds; it also makes more permanent the colonies which are established in that it discourages the intrusion of competitors and provides for the perpetual renewal of the population as new plants spring up to take the place of the senile.

The massed flowers in brilliant colors, some with boldly contrasting nectar pouches deep inside, are efficient lures for the insects which pollinate them. When the blossoms are white, which is usually on species growing in isolation, they are exceptionally large, and fragrance substitutes for color to attract insects with pollen from other blossoms clinging to them.

In the very short growing season of the cold mountain passes at 16,000 to 18,000 feet, the species which flower in July have matured their seeds by September; in the benign climate at 8,000 or 9,000 feet the April-flowering species take eight months to produce ripened seeds. Then, too, Rhododendrons in the wild are even more free of disease than they are in cultivation. The plant explorers have repeatedly mentioned the absence of natural afflictions in the field, and this resistance to diseases and pests must contribute to the success of the genus.

Foliage and Climate

The foliage of Rhododendrons reflects the influences of the climate and altitude where they grow. The species with large leaves are able to endure the evaporation of moisture through such enormous surfaces only because they live in the humid mildness of the lower elevations where the atmosphere drips through much of the year and the rate of transpiration is extraordinarily low. As the altitude increases the leaves of the various species diminish in size until the scaly leaves of some of the pygmy alpines are not much larger than those of a Hemlock needle, the better to resist the drying effect of the bitter winds in the high mountain passes. Many of these rugged little Rhododendrons have managed to survive by becoming polyploids, with extra sets of chromosomes, and by so doing have acquired at the same time the late-blooming period often associated with their altered condition. Late flowering is a necessity for survival of a species at such high altitudes because the snow has not melted enough to expose the plants before June and they are covered once again by a deep blanket of it by November. The dust-like seeds are so fine and light that they must be borne for miles in the fierce winds at such heights. At lower elevations where the gentler wind is tempered even more in the forests, Rhododendron seeds have wing-like flanges to aid their flight.

Nearly everyone has noticed how Rhododendron leaves curl and droop in cold weather, an adaptation by which they conserve moisture as the cylindric shape reduces the area exposed to drying winds. Perhaps a secondary function is to shed snow which might otherwise damage the larger shrubs by its weight. But Rhododendrons also have other marvelously intricate means of regulating the absorption and the transpiration of water. Some sorts have leaves fringed with hairs. Rain water which falls on them is conducted along these hairs to the lower surface where it is absorbed. The hairs act as miniature sluices.

The Purpose of Leaf Scales and Hairs

The structures which clothe the undersides of the leaves are even more specialized in their function. In the monsoon region of southeastern Asia where most of the world's Rhododendrons are found, there are three sharply defined seasons: a cold, dry period of five months beginning in November, then two warm months when the temperature at 10,000 feet elevation may reach 70 to 80° F. in April and May, followed by a rainy season from June to October. Such extremes impose an unusual burden on the means by which Rhododendrons regulate their water supply. The stomata, tiny pores on the undersides of the leaves by which most plants control the amount of water vapor given off into the air, are in Rhododendrons unequal to the task of conserving water in time of drouth and hastening transpiration when water is present in excess. The seasons differ too much. And so Rhododendrons have developed additional structures beneath the leaves which enable them to survive the extremes of climate.

In the rainy season it is just as important for Rhododendrons to get rid of water as it is for them to conserve it at other times. At best their growing season is short. They can take advantage of it quickly only by absorbing through their roots large quantities of water and with it the dissolved minerals and other nutrients which make growth possible. The water must be conducted efficiently upward from the roots through the plants and out again rapidly through the undersides of the leaves or not enough food will be provided in such dilute solution to sustain normal growth in the brief season imposed by the climate.

This problem has been solved for Rhododendrons by the development of three different types of small structures beneath the leaves. The first are papillae, closely spaced waxy pegs which cannot be wetted. The under-surface of the leaf is therefore always dry, even in the rainy season, and water vapor continues to pass out through the stomata unhindered. The second type of water-regulating device is a coating of hairs called an indumentum. This protective woolly layer not only sheds water but it lies just enough above the under-surface of the leaf so that a sheltered air space is provided into which water vapor can be continuously exhausted by the plant during the wet months from June to October. Some glandular types of hairs are even capable of secreting water themselves as an aid to transpiration when the atmosphere is so humid that evaporation is slow.

The third of the intricate means for regulating water are the scales, minute cups with flat covers which project beyond the edges forming wide rims, the whole just visible to the naked eye as dark round dots on the leaf underside. The scales are borne on short stalks so that there is an air layer next to the nether surface into which moisture can be transpired, and the scales are often present in such numbers that they adjoin or overlap, thus forming a sheath which shields the underside of the leaf from rain water. Some types of scales have such thin walls that water can pass out directly through them, so that they serve as additional stacks through which vapor is exhausted in the race to absorb as much water as possible through the roots, extract the nutrients from it, and then pass it on out into the air during the short growing season.

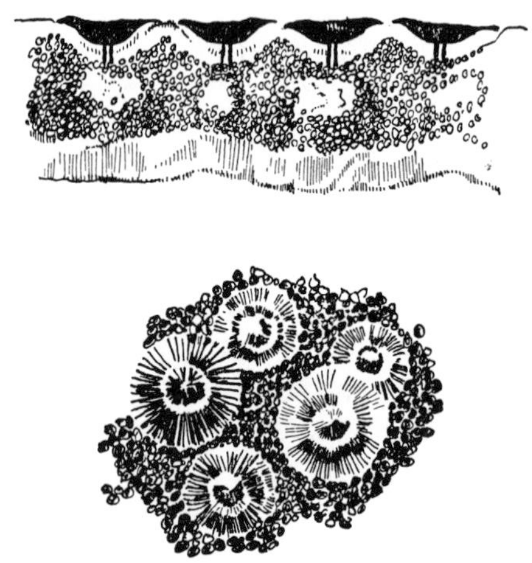

Leaf scales of *R. carolinianum*, greatly magnified, cross section (*above*) and as seen on the leaf underside through a microscope (*below*). Drawn from photomicrographs taken by the author.

But then comes the cold season, the dry period, when there is not enough water and the plants struggle to conserve every bit that they possess. Then the papillae serve a different purpose, the waxy pegs rimming the stomata forming miniature windbreaks so that the loss of water through these vapor-pores is retarded and the motionless air next to them is not continually replaced by the dry atmosphere at that season. The hairy indumentum clothing the leaf undersides of other species is then an insulating shield, reducing the loss of water by evaporation. Some sorts have hairs with glands producing a resinous secretion which forms an additional thin protective varnish-like coat embedding the surface hairs and increasing their efficiency as a screen against the transpiration of moisture. These and other hairs are even capable of catching water, conducting it to the base and there absorbing it as an additional means by which Rhododendrons survive the dry season.

At higher elevations the hairy covering seems inadequate to control the loss of water through the longer and dryer winter season and there the minute scales beneath the leaves act as marvelously efficient valves. In the Himalayas the altitude makes a tremendous difference in the conditions under which the various Rhododendrons grow in such enormous variety. At 6,000 feet a hairy indumentum provides all of the help needed in controlling the loss of water because the winter air temperature just reaches freezing and Rhododendron roots are able to absorb some additional moisture from the earth. But above 10,000 feet the ground is frozen solid for four to five months and there can be no replenishment of water through the roots. At 12,000 feet there is a winter snowfall of 3 to 4 feet; and above 14,000 feet snow covers the earth for seven months of the year.

At higher elevations the struggle for survival is bitter and the scales beneath the leaves often act as miniature sponges and reservoirs, able to absorb drops of rain or dew when there is not enough water intake through the roots to balance the loss through the leaves. Thus these marvelously made little structures, which in the rainy season hasten the transpiration of moisture, now are able in the dry period to reverse their function and absorb it. They are effective, too, in other ways. Closely spaced on their short stalks they form a screen shielding the undersides of the leaves from the play of drying winds upon them. And in many species the scales secrete in spring and summer a varnish-like film which dries by autumn to form a secondary protective barrier against the loss of moisture in winter.

Although scales are more efficient than hairs in regulating the absorption and transpiration of water, their function is identical and it is not surprising to find that their development is identical too. Both originate in a single cell in the outer layer forming the surface of the leaf underside. In the early stages of formation both hairs and scales develop in exactly the same manner from their single cell of origin. Furthermore, Dr J. M. Cowan, British Rhododendron authority, points out in his study of the leaf structures of Rhododendrons that the funnel-shaped scale and the funnel-shaped hair are so close in their resemblance that they must have had a common beginning, ages ago.

The conclusion is inescapable that scales and hairs are not really dissimilar. Though the scaly and the non-scaly Rhododendrons do not ordinarily cross for hybridists, there is no basic cleavage between them. Hairs and scales are essentially similar organs despite their distinctive appearance and their usefulness as a guide in separating the different sorts of Rhododendrons into species.

THE VARIETY IN RHODODENDRONS

Rhododendrons in nature are notorious for their variability. A single species may have numerous varieties and forms, and some of the deviations are extreme, to the consternation of taxonomists and the confusion of amateur students. The representatives of a species in one mountain valley may be substantially different from plants in another valley which none the less appear to be so clearly and closely related to them as to belong to the same species. Even in gross appearance the differences are often all but incredible. *R. campylogynum*, for example, at its tallest is 2,400 per cent greater in its stature than the height of the smallest dwarf form. In addition, one species merges into another in faithful reflection of the manner in which they progressively appeared on earth in the course of their evolution. These are reasons why there have been endless difficulties in reducing these multitudes to orderly and convenient ranks, in defining the limits of each species, and then dividing the hundreds of them into groups called series containing the sorts with a common resemblance.

For a single genus, the different species of Rhododendrons display an astounding variation in their flower parts, as in almost everything else. Most species have a five-lobed corolla (but the number of lobes may range from four to ten). The typical number of stamens is ten (but some species have as few as five or as many as twenty-eight, or a given sort will have twice as many stamens as there are lobes to the corolla of the flowers). The average Rhododendron has five chambers to the ovary (except that some have ten, or even more). The terminal style is typically straight and longer than the stamens (but some species have a very short, thick style which is bent). The calyx is normally of average size for the flower (although it is extremely large in some species and entirely absent in others). The corolla is usually bell-shaped or formed like a trumpet (although seven other shapes are known in the genus). Flowers spring from buds produced the previous growing season (except those of *R. camtschaticum*, which issue from buds on the new growth). Little wonder with these extremes and the gradations between them that Rhododendrons have resisted efforts to classify them in convenient pigeon-holes.

These and many more examples make Rhododendrons a genus of contradictions. In Asia they are still in a plastic stage of evolution and the subtle flux which creates new species and modifies the old is partly responsible for the immense difficulty of creating suitable categories into which the different sorts will fit gracefully. The jagged terrain of the Himalayas has given rise to a peculiar scattered distribution of the species in ravines and valleys often separated by towering ridges. Such a multitude of local breeds in isolated areas, each fairly uniform but differing from district to district, gives rise to the variation within the species which so plagues the taxonomist.

Rhododendrons include tiny, mat-like growths a couple of inches tall, pygmy undershrubs a foot and a half to 2 feet tall, large bushes in stature up to 15 feet or more, and giant trees which soar up to 80 feet. They may grow like orchids in tree tops or the large species may themselves serve as perches on which orchids gain a foothold. Their leaves may be a quarter of an inch long, as in the highest alpine species, or 36 inches long and 12 inches wide in the luxuriant sorts of the temperate rain forests, and they are equally varied in shape. The upper leaf surfaces are smooth in some species; in others they are rough and ridged, with the veins deeply impressed. The under-surfaces may be smooth, hairy or partially covered with very small, round scales. A few sorts are deciduous. The foliage of the massed plants may have an odor, sometimes distasteful, sometimes pleasantly

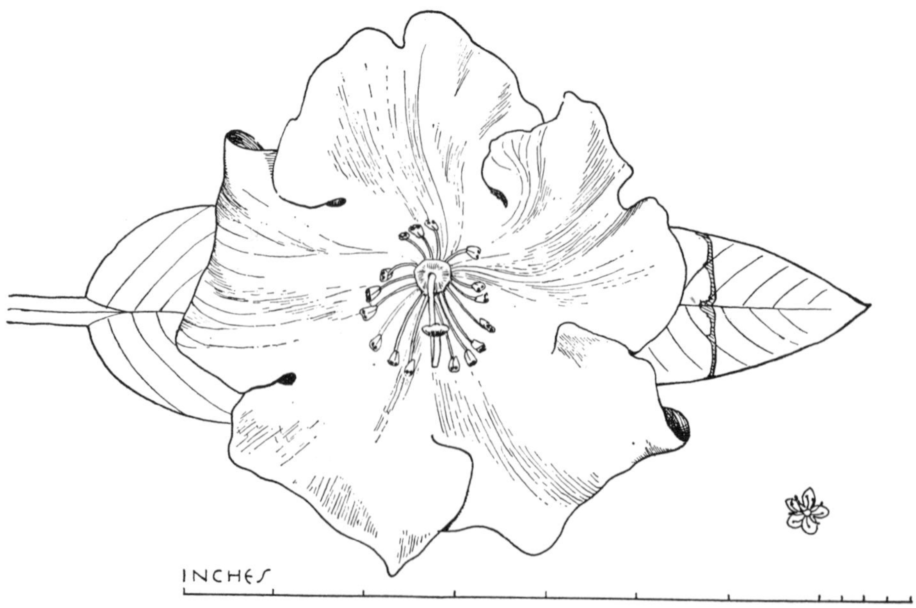

GRIFFITHIANUM COMPARED WITH MICRANTHUM

aromatic, and the natives in some districts of Sino-Himalaya believe that it causes an illness. Only one species, *R. afghanicum*, which grows, oddly, in an arid region of Afghanistan, is known to contain enough andromedotoxin in its leaves to be dangerously poisonous, however.

The colors of Rhododendron flowers range from white through pink to brilliant, blazing scarlet; from clear, soft yellow to chartreuse and orange; from pale lavender through harsh magenta shades to soft tones which are near-blue. Such an astonishing variation is due to the presence of three different pigments, two in the sap and one in the cells of the corolla. In the sap the anthocyanins are responsible for pink, red and purple flowers, and the anthoxanthins, normally colorless, can contribute yellow and orange in certain species. The carotinoids in the corolla provide the yellow, orange and scarlet shades. Individually or modified, one by the other, these pigment groups provide a range of brilliant colors and soft pastels which is probably unequalled in any other single genus. Many Rhododendron flowers have blotches of contrasting color on the upper corolla lobes to add a further decorative touch, or the nectar pouches at the base of the corolla may be intensely colored. The entire blossoms may even be striped or flecked with a contrasting color. Many species have a delicious fragrance.

In size the blossoms may be less than half an inch in diameter or more than 6 inches across. In some species they are formed into many-flowered compact trusses whereas others may bear either a single terminal bloom or a loose constellation of axillary flowers scattered along the stems. The blossoming period extends from February and March into September in the various species.

THE CLASSIFICATION OF RHODODENDRONS

Sir Isaac Bayley Balfour described and classified the discoveries from Forrest's triumphant Asian expeditions and in so doing worked out by 1920 the system of classification of Rhododendrons which is still in use today. To these shifting, elusive, and brilliant multitudes he brought an orderly index by establishing a number of groups of Rhododendrons called series, each with an outstanding species as its representative nucleus, and with its similar near relatives constituting the other species in the series. Today there are forty-three different series, each a group of related sorts with a species typical of the whole assemblage lending its name to the class. A series may contain as many as fifty or more species. Subseries are smaller, more closely related groups which share similar characteristics, and these subseries are divisions within the larger framework of the series. Thus *R. thomsonii*, for example, gives its name to a group of allied species called the Thomsonii series and it is more or less representative of all the species in the series. There are several distinct subgroups, however, which fall into this natural association and consequently the Thomsonii series has been itself divided into an equal number of smaller assemblages, each containing species which are alike in their distinctive characteristics. Thus the Thomsonii series, to continue the example, is made up of the Campylocarpum, Cerasinum, Selense, Souliei, Williamsianum, and Thomsonii subseries. About a third of the various Rhododendron series are so subdivided into subseries of even closer resemblance, and a full discussion of this and other taxonomic matters will be found on page 112.

CHAPTER II

Rhododendrons in the Garden

A BASIS FOR SELECTION

EXPERT gardeners choose Rhododendrons for their beauty the year round first, and for the unquestioned splendor of their flowers second. The emphatic form of the foliage of many sorts provides a bold strength of pattern which is present winter and summer in these superlative evergreens. Most Rhododendrons do have beautiful leaves and the sorts with larger foliage possess also an air of authority in the garden. There are both species and hybrids by the score which would still be among the finest garden plants if they did not bloom at all.

FOLIAGE COLOR EFFECTS

The foliage colors can be exploited to the taste of the gardener. The vivid blue leaves of such species as *RR. lepidostylum* and *campanulatum* var. *aeruginosum* strike a dramatic note to catch the eye and hold it. They can be the climax of an ascending scale assembled from a wide range of sorts with a frosted blue overlay on the leaves resembling the bloom on a ripened greengage plum. *R. thomsonii* and some of its close relatives, the Cinnabarinum alliance and many of the Triflorum Rhododendrons, celebrated for their beauty of flower, are also especially effective in the glaucous sheen of their leaves. The blues merge into the greys—the harmonizing foliage of the sorts with silvery or dove-grey plush beneath the leaves which often extends as well in some degree to their upper sides and spreads a thin veil of soft grey down upon them. Among the larger Rhododendrons, some of the species of the Ponticum, Campanulatum, and Arboreum series, and a few from other series as well, provide this subtle mediation for foliage colors. The little Lapponicums and some of the dwarf Saluenense series Rhododendrons offer their services in a wide range of gentle grey leaf tints for the foreground. And then the greens, the incredible greens of Rhododendrons: from the light, bright, lettuce-green of the splendid *R. auriculatum* through the bottle-greens, the bronze-greens, the soft, pleasant greens, and the acid, virulent greens, to the deep black-green of *R. crassum*, the range is made more striking by the polished highlights of some, the dull matted finish of others; and by the variety of textures, from the thick and leathery, the waxen and the hairy to the thin and papery. These are the foliage colors, the unparalleled resources within a single genus for all-season interest, which are available to bring variety to the garden winter and summer.

INTEREST OF THE INDUMENTUM

The sorts with brilliantly colored hairy coatings beneath the leaves and on the stems can often be planted where their charms can be seen the year around. So placed, they are especially enjoyed. The fiery orange foliage glow which marks sizable plants of *RR. eximium, bureavii.*

or *mallotum* is an easy match for the finest flowered sorts and these Rhododendrons are magnificently colorful, not just for several weeks but for many months.

These indumented species, scores of them, often provide stunning decorations in the brilliance of their new growths as well. As the furry shoots extend in the springtime they are feathered shafts of shining silver, rich cinnamon or soft fawn. *R. coriaceum* seems to erupt in myriads of miniature fountains of shining white kid leaves. A heavier woolly coating transforms the foliage of *R. arizelum* into lovely cockades of golden felt. Springing from purple buds, the young growth of *R. basilicum* is the color of jade with a contrasting soft silvery frosting beneath the leaves. These features are best appreciated at close range. Dramatic though they are, the intriguing texture of the living plush and the changing colors as the growths mature give a particular pleasure if they can be seen frequently and in detail. Rhododendrons of this character should be planted near a much-travelled path.

COLORFUL NEW GROWTHS

The new growths of many species are not dependent on the vivid color of a woolly indumentum to make them strongly decorative. Some sorts, such as *R. lutescens* and the tall forms of *R. keiskei* and *R. nuttallii* produce their new leaves in a springtime flush of cinnamon-red and bronzed maroon which masks their natural green. The young foliage of *R. exasperatum* is often plum-purple. The little round leaves of *R. williamsianum* are like tiers of chocolate pennies. There are many more.

Leaf Bract Brilliance

The brilliant scarlet leaf bracts which beribbon the developing shoots of some Rhododendrons are so ornamental that they are equivalent to a second period of bloom. These vivid decorations seen against the fresh green of the new growth add an extra period of spring beauty to such Rhododendrons as *hookeri, auriculatum, eclecteum*, the Loderi hybrids and many others, in addition to their splendid flowers. Such features are especially appreciated if the Rhododendron which displays them can be placed where it can be seen frequently and intimately.

The less conspicuous aspects of these extraordinary Rhododendrons are also best appreciated at close range. The sorts with peeling cinnamon-red bark provide a note of color in winter as do the geometrical patterns of scales on the floral buds which give the promise of a springtime cascade of blossoms. The diminutive rock garden Rhododendrons *en masse* and in variety create effective winter landscapes in shades of dark red, purple, bronze and smoky blue-greens.

RHODODENDRON CHARACTER

In placing Rhododendrons in the garden, thought should be given to their character. The patrician bearing of the species with large leaves, for example, should be associated with stately trees of size and importance. They demand associates of quality and distinction. Some Rhododendrons, such as *R. makinoi* and *R. roxieanum*, have about them an air of strange Oriental exoticism with their feathery masses of long narrow leaves. Others, with large, lush foliage, seem born of tropical luxuriance. It is easy to create Japanese garden effects with certain Rhododendrons. *R. pseudochrysanthum* by its perfect, mound-like growth habit and leaves borne in stiff rosettes seems to echo its Formosa homeland, and *RR. hyperythrum, degronianum* and *metternichii* give much the same picturesque impression of the Orient, especially when they are planted in association with Pines. Such Rhododendrons as *williamsianum* and *orbiculare* and others of regular growth habit and dense foliage give a strongly formal feeling. The garden which is to feature Rhododendrons will be most successful if the effect of these strong characters is judged in advance and they are planted with forethought.

SHRUB BORDERS

Not many gardeners today make the mistake of planting Rhododendrons as single specimens scattered here and there throughout the lawn as random decorations. Nowadays they are integrated into the over-all garden design, grouped into natural associations in company with other shrubs and given a background of trees in keeping with their sylvan character. The Victorian preference for awkward and arbitrary plantings in the middle of the lawn has been abandoned for shrub borders which are most often arranged around the perimeter of the property to provide privacy and at the same time form for the uncluttered lawn a natural and graceful background which will hold interest and color the year around.

The trees and shrubs and the herbaceous plants which associate well with Rhododendrons are discussed in the next chapter. Rhododendron selections for special purposes, for foundation planting, for small gardens, for the rock garden and so on, are discussed later in this chapter, and here will be found suggestions for the dwarfer sorts which are often useful as well in the forefront of shrub borders. But for the Rhododendrons of conventional size, the familiar robust hybrids so popular with the public, the reader is referred to Chapter VI which contains descriptive regional lists for every climate; and to the complete tabulation of all Rhododendron hybrids which begins on page 425, wherein they are rated for their quality and hardiness and described for their flower color. And of course anyone planting Rhododendrons should consider the species whose virtues have already been praised in the opening paragraphs of this chapter. The best of them, fully equal to any of the hybrids, are described in detail beginning on page 122.

The concern of the immediate chapter is with the principles of landscaping with Rhododendrons and the special uses to which they can be put. There are literally thousands of hybrids and species which are suitable for shrub borders but the best of them have won quality ratings from the American Rhododendron Society and the Royal Horticultural Society of England, and a selection from the multitude can be made on that basis with a good deal of confidence. The lists of sorts recommended by regional experts in Chapter VI (and on pages 239–244 for the species) should be given first consideration.

Planting in Masses

Most Rhododendrons look best in masses. The willowy species of the Triflorum, Cinnabarinum, and Heliolepis series with their slender branches and rather small leaves are particularly effective in their great banks of color when they are planted in groups. Then the gradations from violet-blue through lavender, mauve, pink, rose, ivory, and pale yellow can be combined to create color compositions of triumphant beauty. At other seasons the plants as a group have a unity in their foliage mass which together gives them importance as well as grace. Isolated single specimens on a lawn or scattered at random in a shrub border seem insecure and suffer in appearance for want of the company of their fellows. Similarly the dwarf alpines, the Lapponicums and Uniflorums, the Anthopogons and Campylogynums, are far finer in groups than as single plants. In nature they are communal and their garden value is immeasurably enhanced if at least five of a kind of these pygmies are planted together. Separately they are intrusive in bloom without being impressive, bits of scattered color breaking out in a dispersed rash. But in groups they are among the most charming and effective of all dwarf plants.

Although it is particularly important for the smaller-leaved Rhododendrons to be massed, the commercial hybrids most familiar to gardeners and nurserymen are also usually seen to best advantage when a number of them are planted together. They are strong in character, but almost equally so, and if many of them are scattered singly here and there in a garden they are warring for attention. But in groups the cumulative effect of their architectural foliage and massive clusters of flowers is enormously successful as a dominant theme to unify the garden design.

Rhododendrons in the Garden

PLANTING SINGLY

There are some exceptions to the general rule that Rhododendrons should be massed. The sorts with strongly decorative foliage which become dense mounds of symmetrical outline, such as *RR. williamsianum*, *orbiculare* and *leucaspis* should be displayed so that the luxuriant perfection of each specimen is accented by standing alone, like a solitaire gem in a ring.

The Rhododendrons with large leaves such as the Grande and Falconeri clans and the Fortunei species with long, strap-like foliage should have the space they need for perfect development, the better to exhibit their handsome habit. These Rhododendrons are only injured by crowding them together in awkward groups or unnatural banks. They are meant to be featured in the garden, loftily alone in single splendor, with lesser plants providing the contrast in form and texture which points up their massive beauty. The descriptions beginning on page 122 give the stature of the species important to horticulture and, if it is not stated in nurserymen's catalogs, it is usually possible to deduce the mature proportions of hybrids from those of their parents so that the right amount of space can be allotted to them.

NINE MONTHS OF BLOOM

Although experienced gardeners will consider foliage, habit and character first, most buyers of Rhododendrons continue to be entranced by their magnificent flowers and that will be the reason for their purchase. But the great mistake made by the uninformed public is in planting only the sorts which bloom at midseason. One of the very finest advantages of Rhododendrons as garden plants is the range of their flowering period, from January to September in mild climates, from March to July in the northeast. They are all but unique in this respect. Some of the finest sorts are a blaze of color in late winter or early spring when the garden is otherwise drab and bleak; others of special quality light up the landscape long after the flowers of other woody shrubs have passed.

Both species and hybrids are listed by their season of bloom, stature and flower color in the special regional recommended lists on pages 239–244 and pages 250–267. A study of Rhododendron catalogs from specialist-nurserymen will reveal many more of these invaluable sorts which bloom either early or late, but the average commercial grower often offers only those with flowers in midseason, known to the public and therefore in demand.

The sorts which bloom in late winter and early spring should never be planted with an eastern exposure where the rising sun strikes the flowers on frosty mornings. This is extremely important and often makes the difference between success and failure in obtaining a regular annual display. Blossoms which thaw slowly as the air temperature rises are frequently uninjured whereas others are ruined when they are quickly warmed by the morning sun. And Rhododendrons which come into flower extremely late in the season should have shade during the hottest part of the day so that the sun at its height will not prematurely shorten the life of the blossoms.

FLOWER COLOR COMBINATIONS

With their remarkable color range, Rhododendron flowers offer extraordinary landscape effects to the gardener with the perception to arrange them properly. The sultry reds are exciting, the whites cool and serene. The orange can be barbaric, the magenta boisterous and the pinks softly sentimental. The violet-blues have the candid charm of simplicity. The more urbane mauves and lavender shades seem romantic, and the deep royal purples command authority. The sorts with yellow flowers often have an incandescent glow from the play of light on the pellucid blossoms.

At close range the colors may be modified in

their effect by markings in the flowers. Some sorts are freckled or blotched or hearted deep inside with a strongly contrasting color. The shades of such markings can often be matched to good effect in the flowers of the Rhododendrons to be planted immediately adjacent.

Some gardeners profess the belief that flower colors can be mingled at random without restraint and this is no doubt a convenient principle for those unwilling or unable to discern the difference between the discipline and unity of art and the random, mindless confusion of idle chance. It is my observation that a little thoughtful planning can lift the commonplace to the distinguished and transform the unfortunate accident into a *tour de force*. Landscape architecture is an art and a fine garden is a work of art. I doubt whether an ape slinging color at a canvas will produce an effect equal to that of a man carefully placing his pigments as tellingly as his talents and experience will allow. Any aesthetic work created by design will surely be far superior if the colors which are one of its most important components are planned and executed according to the principles which have been in effective use for centuries.

With Rhododendrons, at least, the color combinations can be corrected by trial and error. The plants have such compact, fibrous root systems so close to the surface that they can be easily moved at any age with little or no injury. Even very large specimens, fully mature, can be successfully transplanted if the power from man or machine is available to lift them and take them to another site.

It is always safe to plant a group of Rhododendrons in a progression of light to dark shades in the same color but it is apt to be a little dull and lifeless if it is done on a large scale. In mild climates an exceptionally effective sequence of this sort can be created by a planting of *R. griersonianum* and some of its hybrids such as 'May Day', 'Tally Ho', 'Fusilier', and 'Day Dream' together with several forms of 'Fabia'. The result is a striking progression of shades ranging from electric geranium-red to orange-red. 'Azor', 'Azma', 'Diva', and 'Sarita Loder' offer an interesting array of salmon shades. A planting which progresses from mauve to white is easily arranged and it is coolly serene and restful.

The gardener uncertain of the effect of unusual combinations can mix several colors and keep them about equal in value, all light pastel shades, for example, or all rich, dark tones, or all intermediate, with here and there one or a few accent plants in a group either much lighter or much darker in flower color than the mass, to lend the verve and sparkle of contrast. White-flowered Rhododendrons are seldom the best choice to accent a planting of dark-flowered sorts. They seem a little too stark and startling amid the blossoms of deeper tones. Plants with ivory or pale yellow blooms are often a better selection for strongly contrasting highlights. Except for such points of accent, three or five or seven plants of a color will almost always give a much better effect than even numbers in small groups.

Their color range is so great and the flower forms in which these colors occur are so varied that Rhododendrons are uncommonly useful for the creation of distinctive effects by gardeners practiced in the arts of harmony and contrast. Deep royal purple, yellow and orange can be juxtaposed in scenes of barbaric brilliance and excitement. Heraldic scarlet, gold and blue combine in settings of regal magnificence for a spacious bay in a large garden. Soft pinks and delicate mauves, pale yellow and lavender, ivory and rose are the means to make a fairyland of almost unreal loveliness and grace. The possibilities are limited only by the imagination of the gardener.

Colors which are antagonistic in proximity may be effective separately if there is an expanse of handsome green foliage between them, and a sizable group of Rhododendrons can always be selected so that several distinct blooming periods are represented. In fact, many gardeners will prefer it so. A display can easily be arranged to cover three or four months, different portions of the group planting coming into flower in a sequence extending from March to July. The sectors which are not in bloom can separate any warring colors in those that are.

When such a group planting is made to bloom at several different periods I think the time that each portion flowers should be distinct and sharply separate from that of any other part which can be viewed from the same angle. The pleasure of seeing a group of Rhododendrons at their height of perfect flower can be marred by faded blossoms hanging forlornly on plants nearby which have just passed out of bloom. Spent blossoms are ordinarily removed but it may be inconvenient to take them off just at the time they are objectionable in appearance.

Perhaps it would be as well to warn the unwary not to order from a nursery the same Rhododendrons seen in flower together at an indoor show with the idea of duplicating the color effects in the garden. The plants exhibited at the great flower shows in March and April are forced into bloom individually at different temperatures so that they will blossom at the same time to create the exotic color effects so much admired in the displays. Outdoors in the garden these same sorts may bloom several weeks apart. The best way to achieve color combinations which are visualized in advance is to visit a nursery specializing in Rhododendrons and there select the sorts which bloom together outdoors in the desired shades. This I strongly urge.

FRAGRANCE

The fragrance of some Rhododendrons is an unexpected delight. Any planting should include some of the sorts which scent the garden air with a sweet or spicy perfume. *RR. fortunei* and *discolor* and their hybrids and, for milder climates, *R. bullatum*, and some of the Maddenii series Rhododendrons possess some of the finest floral fragrances in existence. It is a very great pleasure to lift a flower cluster to admire its form or subtlety of color and find that its beauty is projected not alone by sight but by a marvelously appealing scent as well.

PLANTING FOR PERMANENCE

Once the foliage values, the decorative aspects of the plants at different phases of growth and the flower colors are worked out so that the desired garden effects have been obtained, it is as well to remember that most Rhododendrons are long lived and that their ornamental value increases every year until they reach maturity. Some of the familar stock nurserymen's hybrids are quite likely to survive for a century or more. One of the five original plants of *R. catawbiense* imported into England in 1809 still stands where Anthony Waterer planted it in the Knap Hill Nursery. A specimen of *R. fortunei* grown from seeds sent back when this species was discovered by Robert Fortune's expedition into China in 1856 is flourishing in Windsor Great Park, west of London. Both species figure in the parentage of many popular hybrids. Plants from Hooker's mid-century discoveries in Sikkim still thrive in England a hundred years later. The large-leaved tree species of massive proportions probably survive much longer than these sorts of lesser stature.

RHODODENDRONS AS CUT FLOWERS

Many Rhododendrons are superb as cut flowers, particularly the graceful species of the Triflorum series, with their slender stems and prodigious quantities of flowers shaped like butterflies. Great arm-loads can be cut from sizable groups of older plants and the only effect on them is to improve their appearance and the quantity of their flowers by the more profuse branching which results. *R. moupinense*, *R. mucronulatum* and their hybrids make splendid bouquets for the house very early in the season when no other flowers have yet appeared in the garden. The long, tubular flowers of the Cinnabarinum clan, the interesting colors of the Boothii and Glaucum Rhododendrons and the graceful clusters of many of the Neriiflorum and Thomsonii type provide unusual, showy and long-lasting material for arrangements. The very large fragrant flowers of some of the Fortunei group can be used as the focus of floral compositions but the Rhododendrons with big formal trusses filled out with flowers to a symmetrical round or cone shape seem somewhat stiff and ungainly unless they are combined with other types of Rhododendron blossoms or with flowers of another sort to soften the regularity of their outline.

FOUNDATION PLANTINGS

Rhododendrons in a dooryard planting or at the foundation of a house have an artificial, man-made background which is, in a sense, uncongenial to their character. The sorts with larger foliage, even the familiar nurserymen's hybrids, are often so obviously out of their usual milieu of glade and glen that they appear conspicuous and ill at ease when they are planted in front of small houses. These sizable Rhododendrons need a more natural setting in garden or woodland, the companionship of other plants of similar character, to settle gracefully into their sites. They often appear awkward in foundation plantings because their texture is too coarse for the size of the structure they are meant to ornament. Their leaves are too large and their stature too great for a modest home, though they are often used with superb effect at the foundations of larger houses and they are enormously valuable for enhancing the dignity of imposing public building.

In cold climates these portly Rhododendrons so popular with the public should probably not be placed flanking the immediate entrance of a house because their leaves droop dejectedly in winter, revealing a framework of somewhat ungainly branches which are not very attractive. The color of the building material which constitutes the wall behind the plants should always be considered in choosing the flower color. All too often brilliantly scarlet flowers are seen in livid contrast against a bluish-red brick wall.

Almost all of the old standard hybrids offered by nurserymen grow too large for modern one-story homes. In a few years they cover windows, encroach on neighboring plants and unbalance the entire foundation planting by the preponderance of their size and strong character. It is the newer hybrids, those of restrained growth and moderate size foliage, and the dwarfer species, which are really suitable for this purpose.

Species

Here are a few suggestions among the species suitable for foundation planting of modern single-storey houses:

PACIFIC NORTHWEST AND GREAT BRITAIN

moupinense	pink or white
tephropeplum	pink
glaucophyllum	pink
williamsianum	pale pink
yakusimanum	pale pink and white
martinianum	white, light pink
saluenense	bright rose
haematodes	scarlet
haemaleum	dark red
scyphocalyx	orange
concatenans	apricot
impeditum	violet-blue
intricatum	violet-blue
scintillans	violet-blue
microleucum	white
leucaspis	white
calostrotum	purplish rose

NORTHEASTERN UNITED STATES

carolinianum	pink
racemosum	pink
mucronulatum	violet-pink
micranthum	white
keiskei	yellow
hippophaeoides	lilac
fastigiatum	purple-blue

Hybrids

The following hybrids are recommended for foundation planting as appropriate in stature and foliage and superior in quality. See page 426 of the Appendix for an explanation of the hardiness ratings in parentheses following their names:

PACIFIC NORTHWEST AND GREAT BRITAIN

ARTHUR J. IVENS (H-2)	pink
BOW BELLS (H-3; B)	pink
CILPINENSE (H-4; C)	pink
HUMMING BIRD (H-4; C)	pink
JOCK (H-3)	pink
RACIL (H-3; B)	pink
TEMPLE BELLE (H-3; C)	pink
TESSA	pink
BRIC-A-BRAC (H-3; C)	white
BO-PEEP (H-3; C)	cream
COWSLIP	cream
ELDORADO (H-4)	cream
MOONSTONE (H-3; C)	cream
FABIA (H-4; B)	orange
NEREID (H-3; C)	orange
ELIZABETH (H-4; B)	scarlet
LITTLE BERT (H-3)	scarlet
VENAPENS	scarlet
CARMEN (H-4; B)	dark red
BLUE BIRD (B)	blue
BLUE DIAMOND (H-3; B)	blue
BLUE TIT (H-3; B)	blue

NORTHEASTERN UNITED STATES

PIONEER	pink
WINDBEAM	pale pink
BRANDYWINE	pale pink
CONEMAUGH	rose-pink
CONESTOGA	rose-pink
CONEWAGO	rose-pink
WYANOKIE	white
CHESAPEAKE	white
MONTCHANIN	white
HOCKESSIN	white
RAMAPO	violet
LENAPE	pale yellow

ROCK GARDENS

All of the Rhododendrons of modest stature listed above are suitable for planting in a rock garden of a size and scale appropriate to shrubs up to 4 feet in height. But there are scores more of smaller dimensions, most of them species with rather awkward Latin names which are not very well known because they do not furnish immense trusses of flowers for spectacular display at indoor shows. Lacking the publicity of show awards most of them are not widely grown, but they are superbly colorful and effective as garden plants and they are slowly proving their merits as more and more venturesome growers give them a trial. There are fifty-two species in the Lapponicum series alone, all of them suitable for the rock garden.

Alpine Culture

As a group, the dwarf species are alpines and the conditions of a rock garden suit them to perfection. Volumes have been written about the requirements of various alpine Rhododendrons but most of them are alike in needs which are really very simple: they want abundant moisture at the roots and quick drainage through a porous soil, and they need the maximum exposure which will not burn the foliage at the same time that they are given shelter. Shelter is by no means the same as shade. It can be provided by planting a screen on the windward side, by placing the rock garden on a northward facing slope, if possible, and by planting the little Rhododendrons in stony crevices, miniature valleys and in the lee of rocks which shield them to some extent without appreciably reducing the amount of light that they receive. But the rocks serve a double purpose. The plants soon find beneath them the cool root run which is so congenial to their welfare. These, then, are the keys to success with alpine Rhododendrons: moisture, drainage, exposure—short of foliage burn—shelter. There are many sorts which are so tolerant that they fare well under conditions far short of the perfect site these words describe, but even the most fastidious can be grown at their best if there is a reasonable approximation of this ideal.

In the northeastern United States the arid heat of midsummer is fatal to many of the interesting alpines which are perfectly hardy to winter cold. I have had remarkable success with some of these colorful dwarfs by planting them with a ground cover of the common Hair Cap moss (*Polytrichum commune*). Presumably, the water vapor transpired by the moss, rising through the branches, and the insulating effect of the green blanket carpeting the ground, are responsible for the beneficial effect.

The rock garden Rhododendrons should be planted three or five or seven of a kind in a group. Only a few of them, used as accents or to display exceptional beauty of form, are seen to the best advantage as single specimens. Even those of upright form are far more effective in the company of their fellows, just as they grow in nature, and the sorts which extend outward horizontally as they become older soon join to make sizable blankets of good foliage and solid sheets of color in their blooming seasons. The foliage values of the rock garden Rhododendrons are good, too. There are many fine sorts among the scaly alpines with misty gray leaves. In some of them there is a blue overlay which gradually changes to gray-green as fall approaches. By mid-autumn an olive cast appears and then as the weather gets colder metallic glints quicken the deepening colors. Finally, with the advent of winter a mixed planting of alpine species presents a billowing blanket of deep red, dusky blue-greens, purple and bronze.

The listing of all Rhododendron species which begins on page 508 gives their height at maturity, their flower color and season of bloom. Still, some sorts are more choice than others, or are more easily pleased, and these have gradually become established as prime favorites among alpine gardeners.

The Best of the Dwarfs

These species are especially valued in the Pacific Northwest and in Great Britain for their fine performances in the rock garden and among them they offer three to four months of bloom:

SPECIES	HEIGHT	FLOWER COLOR	SEASON OF BLOOM	HARDINESS RATING AMERICAN	HARDINESS RATING BRITISH
anthopogon	24″	pink	April		A
apodectum	36″	orange	June	H-4	A
brachyanthum var. *hypolepidotum*	30″	lemon-yellow	June		A
calostrotum	30″	purplish-rose	May	H-3	A
campylogynum var. *myrtilloides*	8″	pink	May	H-2	A
cephalanthum	30″	white	May		B
chameunum	18″	purplish-rose	May–June		A
charitopes	30″	pink	April–May		B
chryseum	18″	yellow	April–May	H-2	A
edgarianum	30″	purplish-blue	May–June		A
*fastigiatum**	24″	purplish-blue	April-May	H-2	A
flavidum	30″	pale yellow	March	H-2	A
forrestii	8″	scarlet	April–May	H-3	B
glaucophyllum	36″	pale rose	May	H-3	B
haemaleum	36″	deep red	May–June	H-3	B
hanceanum var. *nanum*	12″	pale yellow	April		B
*hippophaeoides**	30″	lilac	April	H-3	A
horaeum	48″	orange or red	April–May		B
impeditum	18″	purplish-blue	April	H-2	A
imperator	12″	rose	May	H-3	A

SPECIES	HEIGHT	FLOWER COLOR	SEASON OF BLOOM	HARDINESS RATING AMERICAN	BRITISH
intricatum	24″	mauve	April	H-2	A
keleticum	10″	rosy purple	June	H-2	A
leucaspis	20″	white	February	H-4	C
megeratum	24″	yellow	March–April	H-4	C
microleucum	18″	white	April	H-2	A
moupinense	36″	white or pink	February–March	H-4	B
*mucronulatum**	60″	rose	February	H-2	B
nitens	12″	rosy purple	June		A
pemakoense	12″	rose	April	H-3	A
primulaeflorum	42″	yellow	April–May		A
prostratum	15″	purplish-rose	April	H-3	A
pumilum	9″	pink	June		A
racemosum	20″	pink	April	H-2	A
radicans	6″	purple	May	H-3	A
rupicola	18″	plum-purple	April		A
russatum	36″	dark blue	April	H-2	A
saluenense	36″	rose	April–May	H-3	A
sanguineum	30″	crimson	May	H-3	B
sargentianum	12″	lemon-yellow	May	H-3	B
*scintillans**	30″	blue	April	H-3	A
scyphocalyx	36″	orange	May–June	H-4	B
telmateium	30″	rose-purple	April	H-3	A
trichostomum	30″	rose	May	H-4	D
williamsianum	42″	shell pink	May	H-3	B
yakusimanum	42″	pink and white	May	H-3	B

The stature as given above is in each case a practical height to use in planning a rock garden, and is not an extreme botanical statistic. The asterisk denotes species which have been satisfactory in the eastern United States. An explanation of the hardiness ratings appears on page 120.

Almost all of these are alpine Rhododendrons with little scaly leaves, the heathers of the Himalayas, where assortments of different species cover immense slopes and form vast carpets of dazzling color. They comprise a variety of floral effects. Some produce freely large, solitary flowers atop compact tufts of foliage. Others have a number of small flowers gathered into tight little terminal trusses which are miniature editions of those on the familiar garden hybrids. Still others show several blossoms in each loose cluster. The flower shapes are equally gratifying in their variety. There are spidery, star-shaped blossoms, long, tubular blossoms, and widely open, flat blossoms. So there need be no monotony of foliage or flower when Rhododendrons are the mainstay of the rock garden. All of those recommended are extremely colorful and effective. They are not the esoteric pets of hobbyists, the unusual sorts which the public finds only eccentric.

Dwarf Hybrids

The alpine species seem so natural in rock gardens and they are so successful there that hybrids are not ordinarily used in any great quantity. There are not many hybrids which are truly miniatures in any case, less than a couple of feet tall, but I must mention here four which are only about 36 inches in height because their flowers are remarkable for the purity and intensity of their blue color. They are so free that the plants are often all but submerged beneath the clouds of them. 'Blue Bird', 'Blue Diamond', 'Blue Tit' and 'Russautini' are all about equally fine.

Permanent Effects

One of the best things about rock garden Rhododendrons is that they are not invasive and do not shortly smother their companions. The color harmonies and foliage contrasts which are planned at the beginning will be effective for a long time. These are plants of measured growth which keep their character. They will merge and mingle by design if the gardener places them close enough together, but they seem well-bred and mannerly about it even then.

The alpine gardener must visualize the mature sizes of the Rhododendrons he selects so that they will be in scale for the proportions of the rocks used in the garden. It is commonplace to see the plants just a little too large for their setting. Happily, almost all of these Rhododendrons can be sheared to restrain their height and improve the density of their growth at the same time, although most are naturally so compact that they are not in much need of improvement. The little creepers seem most at home on the exposed topmost elevations of the rock garden. The spreading hassocks and tuffets and upright shafts of foliage fit naturally below the ledges and between outcroppings of stone, just as they do in nature.

THE SMALL GARDEN

The Rhododendrons recommended for foundation and rock garden planting will suggest a variety of sorts suitable for the small garden but there are many others, among them some of the best hybrids, which are exceptionally fine though just a little too big to be classed as miniatures. The number of small gardens seems to be increasing all the time and these Rhododendrons of restrained growth are ideally suited to them. They make possible a far greater variety in a small area and after the plants have grown together their density leaves no room for weeds so that a Rhododendron garden of this sort requires little maintenance.

There are really just two problems in designing a small Rhododendron garden: how to provide variety and at the same time unity in a limited space. The variety is not hard to accomplish. The wide range of foliage textures, blossom shapes, truss formations and flower colors of Rhododendrons sustains interest almost automatically. The plants should be placed rather close together in a small garden, usually three or five of a kind, so that they will merge to form a carpet of color in their season. A pleasing variation in elevation can be arranged by planting ridges of the taller Rhododendrons and valleys of the dwarfer sorts. Accents here and there of 6-foot plants and a background of the largest size appropriate to the area complete a successful design. The whole can be interplanted with Lilies, Primroses, Ferns and berried plants to provide contrasts of form and foliage and furnish added color when the Rhododendrons are not in bloom.

Harmonious Groups

As suggested earlier in this chapter one of the most effective Rhododendron displays can be created by planting a species together with a varied group of its hybrids. The following seem to me to be especially attractive prospects for the small garden in mild climates:

forrestii and its hybrids—scarlet shades, height to about 4 feet:

Charm	Little Bert
Elizabeth	Little Joe
Ethel	Pixie
Fascinator	Rhythm
Hyperion	Yeoman
Little Ben	

williamsianum and its hybrids—neat round leaves, appealing bell-shaped flowers, compact, small shrubs:

Bow Bells—pink	Moonstone—pale yellow
Carola—pink	Pallida—pink
Cowslip—pale yellow	Temple Belle—pink
Humming Bird—red	Varna—orange

haematodes and its hybrids—brilliant red shades, height to about 5 feet:

Aspansia	May Day
Burning Bush	Phoebus
Chiron	Vega
Grosclaude	Welkin

dichroanthum and its hybrids—orange-red to orange-pink:

ARMA	FABIA
BERRYROSE	JASPER
BREAK OF DAY	KINGCUP
DIDO	NEREID

leucaspis and *moupinense* and their hybrids—very early and floriferous:

BO-PEEP—pale yellow	TESSA—pale pink
BRIC-À-BRAC—white	VALASPIS—primrose-yellow
CILPINENSE—blush white	VALPINENSE—yellow
GOLDEN ORIOLE—yellow	

Dwarf Species

There is an interesting assortment of species in the Neriiflorum series which grow slowly into dense mounds of handsome foliage often broader than their height. These have rather long, tubular flowers in loose trusses of a few blossoms and they often do not bloom freely in youth. Older plants make a vivid splash grouped in a small garden. All of these are rated hardy in the congenial climate of the Pacific Northwest down to a range of 5° below zero F. to 5° above, and they are satisfactory anywhere in the British Isles:

SPECIES	HEIGHT	FLOWER COLOR	SEASON OF BLOOM
chaetomallum	60″	crimson, dark rose, rarely cream	March–April
chamae-thomsonii	30″	red, rarely yellow, white or pink	April
didymum	36″	blackish crimson	June–July
gymnocarpum	42″	crimson	April
haemaleum	36″	blackish-crimson, rarely scarlet	May–June
herpesticum	18″	orange-red, yellow	May
microgynum	48″	rose, blackish-crimson	April
sanguineum	30″	crimson, plum-purple	April–July
scyphocalyx	36″	orange, yellow, crimson, pink	May–June
temenium	36″	crimson	May–June

A little taller than the foregoing and adding variety of foliage color and flower form are some of my favorites for small gardens in mild climates. These average about 6 feet in height:

SPECIES	FLOWER COLOR	SEASON OF BLOOM
adenopodum	pale rose, fawn indumentum beneath leaves	May
eclecteum	yellow, buff, orange, scarlet, crimson, rose, pink, yellow, ivory, white	February–March
litiense	yellow, leaves have glaucous sheen	May
meddianum	crimson, sturdy shrub with large, wide leaves	April
stewartianum	yellow, buff, orange, scarlet, crimson, rose, pink, yellow, ivory, white	February–March
wasonii	yellow, orange-brown indumentum	April

To add still another character for extra contrast I suggest some of the lesser known Triflorum species of modest stature and greater grace than the foregoing. Their slender, willowy growth, less dense, and flat flowers in informal clusters in quite another color range enliven the scene and accentuate the solid form of the others. They range in stature up to about 6 feet:

SPECIES	FLOWER COLOR	SEASON OF BLOOM	HARDINESS RATING	
			AMERICAN	BRITISH
caeruleum	rose-lavender, white	May	H-3	B
chartophyllum	white, pink	May	H-3	B
concinnum	pink, purple, rosy red	April–May	H-3	A

SPECIES	FLOWER COLOR	SEASON OF BLOOM	HARDINESS RATING AMERICAN	BRITISH
exquisitum	mauve	May	H-4	B
keiskei	lemon-yellow	April	H-2	A
searsiae	white, mauve, purplish	April–May	H-3	B
timeteum	purplish-rose	May		B

Engaging shrubs of still finer texture which are valuable for diversity in restricted space are three species from the Scabrifolium series. These have great quantities of sparkling little flowers, enormously appealing for their delicacy and airy grace:

SPECIES	FLOWER COLOR	SEASON OF BLOOM	HARDINESS RATING AMERICAN	BRITISH
hemitrichotum	white, pale pink	April	H-3	B
scabrifolium	white, pink	March–April	H-3	C
spiciferum	pink	April	H-3	C

Finally, there are three species of extraordinary foliage interest which are appropriate in stature for small gardens in mild climates:

campanulatum var. *aeruginosum*	soft metallic blue leaves, lavender flowers
concatenans	fine glaucous foliage, apricot flowers
lepidostylum	emphatically and luxuriously blue, flowers pale yellow and inconspicuous

Dwarf Sorts for the Northeastern United States

Unfortunately only a few of the treasures for small gardens described above are hardy in the cold northeast. The listing on page 239 gives the stature of all species adaptable to the climate. Among the familiar nurserymen's hybrids only 'Boule de Neige', white-flowered, is commercially available and within the size limitations, at least for a good many years. A dozen scaly-leaved hybrids suitable for the climate and recommended for foundation planting because of their small stature, are described on page 37.

GROUND COVER AND EDGING RHODODENDRONS

Any of the pygmy Rhododendrons which blanket the earth with dense mats of foliage can be used as ground covers. For the Pacific Northwest and for the British Isles the following are among the most attractive:

campylogynum var. *myrtilloides*	pink flowers in May
forrestii var. *repens*	scarlet flowers in April; F.C.C. form blooms freely
keleticum	purplish crimson flowers in June
prostratum	crimson flowers in April–May
radicans	purple flowers in May

Not quite so dense in growth are two species with startling large flowers in late April and early May. *R. imperator* is usually only about 8 or 10 inches tall, with rose blossoms. *R. patulum*, its close relative, is a little larger and its flowers are almost purple. Both are prostrate in habit and would be appealing plants to clothe a small, intimate area where they would receive good care.

Suitable both as ground covers and as edging plants are a group of species, a little more erect and emphatic in outline, which form dense mounds of attractive foliage:

SPECIES	HEIGHT	FLOWER COLOR	SEASON OF BLOOM	HARDINESS RATING AMERICAN	BRITISH
aperantum	20″	white, yellow, rose, red, orange	April–May	H-3	B
fastigiatum (dwarf form)	10″	purplish blue	April–May	H-2	A
hanceanum var. *nanum*	12″	pale yellow	April		B
herpesticum	18″	orange-red, yellow	May		B
impeditum	18″	purplish blue	April	H-2	A
keiskei (dwarf form)	24″	lemon yellow	April	H-2	A
leucaspis	20″	white	February	H-4	C
nitens	12″	rosy purple	June		A
pemakoense	12″	rose	April	H-3	A
uniflorum	12″	purple, rose	April		A

FORMAL GARDENS

The neat, firm outline of the sorts just mentioned as suitable both for edging and as ground covers also fits them for formal gardens in mild climates where dense, symmetrical plants of small stature are often needed. A bit larger but impeccably regular in its formal perfection is *R. williamsianum*, with little, rounded leaves, a height of about 4 feet and nodding pink bells in early May. *R. yakusimanum*, about the same height, is a perfect mound of gray-green foliage studded in late May with fresh pink and white flowers in dense

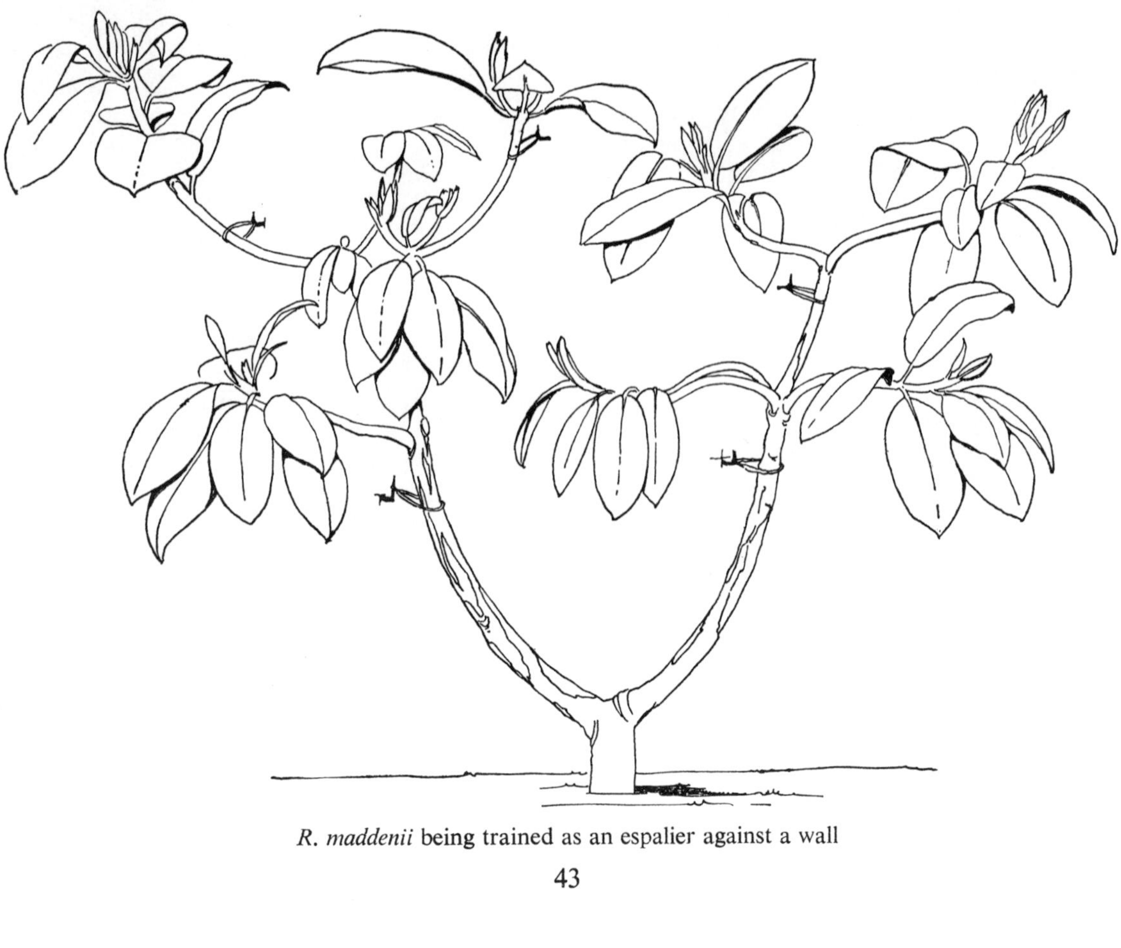

R. maddenii being trained as an espalier against a wall

clusters. All of the ten species in the Neriiflorum group listed on page 41 are suitable for the formal garden and so are many of the hybrids of *RR. forrestii*, *williamsianum*, *haematodes* and *dichroanthum* mentioned in the paragraphs immediately preceding. *R. orbiculare* is extremely formal in effect, the round leaves in measured profusion, immaculate regularity of form, and bright rose flowers in April and May all contributing to its stately distinction. It will grow eventually to a height of 10 feet but only after a great many years.

Finally, colorful formal effects can be obtained by grafting on standards some of the free blooming species and hybrids which naturally have compact, globular habits of growth. These make rounded masses of foliage poised atop bare stems, usually about 4 feet tall, which in their blooming season are reminiscent of giant bouquets. They are affected and unnatural in most settings but, like tree roses, they can be quite handsome if they are properly used in a setting of formal elegance.

HEDGES

The Rhododendrons described in the foregoing sections and recommended for their density and neatness of growth habit offer a wide assortment of plants for unusual flowering hedges. Almost any stature can be selected from the wide variety which has been mentioned. The plants in single rank, growing naturally, form continuous billowing lines of compact foliage perhaps best described as semi-formal in effect. Some of the Neriiflorum species such as *RR. scyphocalyx* and *eudoxum* are striking when an assortment of their color forms makes up the hedge. Such seedlings of a species, however, are apt to vary to some extent in their foliage, growth habit and stature. If the greatest uniformity is wanted, the plants in the hedge should be propagated as cuttings from a single good form. All will then be almost identical in height and width.

The Triflorum Rhododendrons are especially useful for hedges. Their slender, twiggy growth, small leaves and ready branching can even be turned to advantage in making hedges of clipped, angular formality. I have seen *R. lutescens* used in this fashion, sheared to symmetrical perfection with perpendicular sides and a flat top, and still with a gratifying show of pale yellow flowers produced on twigs just beneath the clipped surface. Other Rhododendrons of similar habit should be equally successful. There is a wide variety of other species in the Triflorum series with white, lavender, pink, rose and yellow flowers ranging from 6 to 15 feet in height.

These same Triflorum Rhododendrons in their natural habit of growth make delightful informal hedges of slender, graceful aspect which are great cataracts of flowing color in their season. They are among the most prolific of Rhododendrons in the production of flowers and this stunning prodigality is only augmented in effect when they are planted in line to grow naturally into a solid rank of ordered display. In single file some sorts may be a little thin in foliage if an impenetrable barrier is required, but the plants can be staggered in a double row for denser effect. A hedge-like planting of one of the good Triflorum species makes a charming informal background for dwarf Rhododendrons and other smaller shrubs in front of it. The similar Heliolepis series species, *desquamatum*, *heliolepis*, and *rubiginosum*, are other good sorts useful in the same manner.

The floriferous and adaptable *R. racemosum* can be obtained in forms which mature in almost any size from 18 inches to 15 feet, and it makes an appealing informal hedge. The small-leaved species of the Scabrifolium series, particularly *RR. pubescens* and *spiciferum*, with their delicate little white to pink flowers, are pretty in hedges 3 or 4 feet tall. *RR. tephropeplum* and *glaucophyllum*, about the same size, are more solid and stocky, with unusual pink shades of great attraction in their flowers. Finally, the American *R. carolinianum*, hardy almost anywhere, and its white-flowered variety, *album*, are first-rate for hedges if it is not required that they be densely evergreen over winter. Their habit of retaining in the autumn only the leaves produced in the current year's growth impairs their green effect through the cold months.

Gardeners who plan to use Rhododendrons for hedges should select them with special care. There ought to be at least four main branches close to ground level and the plants should be densely formed as a framework for the further profuse branching which is needed to make a good hedge clothed to the bottom with handsome foliage. Continued compact development of the large-leaved sorts can be assured while the plants are young by pinching out the small growth buds on the ends of the branches in autumn. The smaller leaved, scaly Rhododendrons can be sheared back if it is necessary to improve their form.

SCREENS

Rhododendrons make much more interesting screens than the usual conifers or deciduous shrubs which are so often used to hide an unsightly view, to provide privacy or to form a windbreak for the garden. Many plantings originally made for such purposes have become locally famous for their beauty.

Generally, the popular nurserymen's hybrids, and the more rugged species are most suitable for screens. Most of these are older sorts which have been on the market for a good many years, bred originally by professional growers in Holland and England for their vigorous growth and ease of cultivation.

Most red-flowered Rhododendrons are too sparse in foliage and gaunt in growth to make really good tall screens. There are scores of hybrids in other colors which are suitable, however, for the mild climates of the Pacific Northwest and of Great Britain:

Pink—BETTY WORMALD, COUNTESS OF DERBY, FAGGETTER'S FAVORITE, GOLDSWORTH PINK, JAN DEKENS, MARINUS KOSTER, MRS E. C. STERLING, PINK PEARL

Mauve—A. BEDFORD, MRS CHARLES PEARSON, VAN NES SENSATION

White—BEAUTY OF LITTLEWORTH, LODER'S WHITE, MRS LINDSAY SMITH

All of these are tall shrubs, with good, dense foliage.

If the site is one with a little shade and shelter the extraordinarily beautiful and free-flowering Naomi group of hybrids, especially the clones 'Glow', 'Nautilus' and 'Pink Beauty', would be fine choices to provide flowers of exceptionally high quality in unusual opalescent pink shades. All of these hybrids bloom in May. A nurseryman who specializes in Rhododendrons will be able to recommend tall sorts with good foliage adaptable to the local climate which bloom earlier or later and are suitable for screens.

WINDBREAKS

Rhododendrons are not usually plants for windswept locations but *en masse* the mutual protection of their company makes them entirely successful if the right sorts are chosen. Local conditions are so varied that it is all but impossible to recommend Rhododendrons by name for this purpose. The velocity of the wind, whether it is laden with moisture, the immediate topography of the land and many other factors must be considered to determine just how severe the conditions are. The selection anywhere rests among the most rugged sorts which are tolerant of exposure. In Europe the sturdy naturalized *R. ponticum* and some of the old Waterer English hybrids which derive their strong constitutions from *R. catawbiense* are often planted to form handsome evergreen shelter belts shielding more delicate plants from the prevailing winds.

Hedges and Screens for the Northeast

For the cold Northeast, the white-flowered hybrid 'Boule de Neige' makes a good, dense hedge or screen about 6 feet tall if it has some shade. In full exposure it is susceptible to attacks of Lace Wing Fly. 'Roseum Elegans', with lavender flowers, and the new Gable hybrid, 'Caroline', with fragrant mauve blossoms, are larger in stature, easy to maintain in their naturally dense habit in almost any reasonable site, and they make massive ribbons of color planted as screens. 'Album Elegans' is probably the best choice among the tall sorts with white flowers and 'Mrs C. S. Sargent' excels as a robust hybrid with rose-colored blossoms and good foliage. *R. catawbiense* can stand as much exposure as any Rhododendron. For those who dislike its most common flower color, a raucous magenta, there are forms with white blossoms available from specialist-nurserymen, such as variety *album*, Glass. The other large-leaved native eastern Rhododendron, *R. maximum*, makes a handsome screen the year around if it is planted with an open exposure toward the north or with about 50 per cent shade in any other position. So situated, it receives just enough shelter to thrive and enough light to encourage the fullest development of its fine foliage. Its rather small white or pale pink flowers are produced late, in early July. After many years it will ultimately grow 15 or 20 feet tall.

From Delaware northward to Boston along the coast, many of the Dexter hybrids offer good, dense foliage, large stature and flowers much finer in size and color than those of the older ironclad commercial hybrids. 'Scintillation' is now available but most of them are not yet on the market as named cultivars in any systematic way and it may take some searching to locate enough plants of a suitable sort propagated by grafting or as rooted cuttings from a fine clone. Seedlings should be avoided. Many of these Rhododendrons need a little shade to do their best and they are not hardy enough for cold inland gardens.

WOODLANDS

The gardener with an open woodland has the ideal site on which to grow to perfection the greatest possible variety of Rhododendrons. Many of the larger sorts which are only indifferent or even disappointing in the open garden burgeon forth to luxuriant splendor amid the congenial companionship of the trees. Others, dubiously hardy in open sites, are triumphantly rugged and reliable. The tempered conditions of growth reflect those of the Asian wilderness from which they sprang originally. The average maximum temperature of the air in a forest is about 4° F. lower during the summer than in the open air outside. In winter it is 2° higher. The earth is warmer by about 2° in winter and 5 to 9° cooler in summer than it is in an exposed field. The soil freezes much less deeply. Only the alpines, the pygmy sorts which come from the exposed ridges of the higher Himalayas, are not at home in the woodland.

The ideal woodlot contains mixed, deep rooting hardwood trees and conifers. Oaks and Pines are all but perfect companions because their roots go far underground. Maples and Sycamores have greedy roots which run along the surface to invade the sites where Rhododendrons are planted and rob them of food and moisture.

A woodland is the most stable and labor-saving condition in which a garden can be maintained. Once the Rhododendrons are in place, the upkeep is negligible because the only wish is to continue the natural appearance of the woodlot which is its great beauty. The annual leaf fall provides the nourishing mulch which Rhododendrons so much enjoy, and the trees themselves afford the shelter which ensures the health and welfare of their wards without further attention from the gardener. There is none of the endless weeding and fertilizing and clipping and transplanting and tidying which other sorts of gardens demand. The woodland planted to Rhododendrons offers an enormous return for very little effort. It is as nearly self-sustaining as any assemblage of plants can ever be, and nearly all of the great collections of Rhododendrons in the United States and abroad are established under woodland conditions.

A virgin woodlot is nearly always much too dense. Rhododendrons want dappled, shifting shade, or sunlight alternating with shadow. Sites are needed which will give perhaps two or three hours of shade in the heat of midday between periods of full sun in morning and afternoon. Clearings provide the pools of brighter light which the smaller sorts enjoy. The larger-leaved Rhododendrons revel in greater shelter. Places must be found for the very early blooming sorts which should be shielded from the rising sun on frosty mornings. A woodland garden which is properly planned will provide a variety of exposures and planting sites, but there are very few Rhododendrons indeed which should have more than 50 per cent shade. Most will be at their best with somewhat less.

A good deal of advance thought should be given to those trees which are to be removed in thinning a woodland. It is easy to make mistakes and they cannot be remedied for decades once the trees are felled. The light and shade should be judged not just for the various times of the day but also for the different seasons of the year. The long shadows cast northward by trees beneath the winter sun, when it is low in the southern sky, may be wanted for plants sensitive at that season which are better off without much shade a few months later. Some Rhododendrons, sorts which bloom late in the season, need shade for their flowers in the heat of summer and more sun at other seasons.

The routes the paths are to take through the woodland must also be considered before the trees are felled. They ought to be 6 or 8 feet wide, winding in gentle curves through the forest, passing from brilliant sunlight to deep shade where some of the delicate native wildlings will thrive alongside, skirting old moss-covered logs and passing sunlit glades alive with color. Such paths turn to reveal unexpected vistas of Rhododendrons abloom in sylvan splendor, massed in great banks or transfixed in solitary beauty by a golden shaft of sunlight shining down through the tree-tops. The route can cut directly through thickets of native underbrush and pass then into a glen dominated by Rhododendrons, in imitation of nature. Always, the goal should be to provide variety and natural interest, to take courses which will offer vantage-points for striking views. A natural trail must not be overplanted with Rhododendrons or it will be monotonous. Other flowering trees and shrubs, berried plants and native wild flowers and ferns vary the textures, complement the Rhododendrons, and provide interest at different seasons.

A woodland garden should not be cleared in imitation of the ordered asepsis of a public park. Some fallen trunks and stumps should remain. They will soon acquire a patina of moss and blend with the scene. Patches of underbrush which are untouched will appear more natural than the most cunning arrangement of transplanted shrubs that the gardener can devise. Most novices starting on a woodland garden take out too few trees and too much undergrowth. There is often an excess of tidiness which gives the woodlot an antiseptic, denuded look.

It can be taken as a general principle that Rhododendrons will be at their best with clear sky directly overhead. There they receive even the lightest rains which cleanse their foliage and increase the humidity about them. Most deep-rooted sheltering trees draw some moisture from the earth directly beneath them and the shade there is usually too dense as well. Great old Oaks and the Pines which also soar upward with naked trunks to heads of foliage far above the earth are exceptions. When the leafy canopy is high overhead in open woodland, Rhododendrons can be planted up to the trunks of scattered trees and they will flourish almost as well with a little extra water now and then as they do with clear sky above them.

It can also be taken as a general principle that the larger the leaves of the Rhododendrons the more shelter they will require, and the smaller the leaves, the sunnier and more exposed their planting positions should be. The primitive tree species of the Grande and Falconeri clans with their enormous tropical-looking foliage are at the one extreme in their need for protection from whipping winds and day-long sun. The uncommonly long, handsome leaves of *RR. calophytum* and *sutchuenense* characterize these species as wanting more shelter than the average. At the other end of the scale are such sorts as *RR. racemosum*, *pubescens* and *spiciferum*, which are better in foliage, habit and flower if they are given a sunny, exposed spot in the woodland.

In my opinion most of the hybrids with symmetrically round or cone-shaped trusses of large flowers are both too stiff and too gaudy to be in graceful concord with the sylvan atmosphere of a woodland. There the stocky nurserymen's hybrids seem a little synthetic, the foliage often a little out of scale for the dimensions of the plants, and the flower trusses too formal in their regularity.

In a natural setting the enthusiast can grow many of the species which have too much blue in their flowers for a cultivated garden, where they are at a disadvantage in dissonant contrast to other blossoms of clearer color. There is a wide variety of interesting Rhododendrons blooming in the purplish rose to magenta color range which are lovely as isolated groups in a wooded tract. Even the pinkish purples which seem strident in an open landscape are somehow softened and made attractive amid the quiet serenity of vaulting trees. I will make one reservation, however. I advise all readers to turn their eyes from *R. niveum* in its usual dull purple form, which is one of the most degraded, poisonously bilious colors to be found on earth. An axe, not a woodland, is the remedy for its appalling hue.

But an uncommonly fine assortment of Rhododendrons is at hand to transform a woodland in the Pacific Northwest or in Great Britain into a shining fairyland of color with the sparkling freshness which only the natural beauty of such a setting can bestow. There the white and pink blossoms of *RR. fortunei* and *discolor*, *diaprepes* and *auriculatum* put on their dazzling displays. The hosts of little Cinnabarinum trumpets glow beneath a beam of sunlight and the Triflorums are clothed with pastel butterflies. There the gilded *lacteum* flowers are poised like huge golden globes to light the way along a shadowed path and the tip of every *thomsonii* branch is aflame. The finest the genus offers, the entire resource of these incomparable compositions in color and form and texture are waiting to bestow their gifts upon the gardener who will use them in a woodland.

The hybrids of natural character are no less entrancing. The magnificent Loderis, with the largest blossoms of all, are essentially woodland Rhododendrons and their mammoth scented saucers of pink and white in loose clusters can be the dramatic climax to a wooded trail. At an earlier season 'Avalanche' and 'Red Admiral', 'Rosalind' and 'Robin Hood' light up the woodland with joyful splashes of vernal color when all else is bleak and bare. At a late season the white-flowered 'Argosy' and 'Polar Bear' are coolly beautiful and serene in the heat of midsummer. In between are endless candidates in yellow and cream, iridescent pink and rich rose, lavender and violet-blue, buff and orange, crimson and scarlet, all in an astounding array of flower shapes and sizes. Both the giant and the dwarf are represented in hybrids whose natural character and informal flower clusters fit them for a woodland setting. They are the finest in the world, for the most part creations of amateur horticulturists in the British Isles, with a quality and distinction often lacking in the portly, forthright hybrids bred by nurserymen. Most of them are now available from nurseries in the Pacific Northwest and in Great Britain which specialize in Rhododendrons. Some of them are really successful only as woodland plants, the open garden being uncongenial to their welfare. The pity is that almost none is hardy enough for the northeastern United States.

CITY GARDENS AND PUBLIC PARKS

Rhododendrons are among the most successful shrubs which can be used in tiny city gardens and in great metropolitan parks. The skyscrapers and apartment houses and other buildings crowding in from every side seem to be substitutes of glass and masonry for the trees which shield the plants from too much sun and wind in their wilderness homeland.

Even the smallest garden in the heart of a city can enjoy a few Rhododendrons, whose versatility in providing several seasons of special decorative appeal in addition to year-long attractiveness is all the more appreciated. Nor do they impose any burdensome demands in return for handsome health and vigor. They are able to get along quite well on equal terms with any other plants in the city garden. They need only the annual renewal of their mulch to thrive, and perhaps a little water and a shower to cleanse their foliage in time of drouth.

Park superintendents find Rhododendrons equally rewarding and undemanding. They are great favorites with the public, so much so that noteworthy collections have been assembled in a number of cities both in the East and in the Pacific Northwest, in response to the wide interest among those who visit the parks. Public collections are to be found even in districts with alkaline soil, such as that at Highland Park in Rochester, New York, where the Rhododendrons have become the feature of their flowering season.

As a group, the Dutch nurserymen's hybrids and the most adaptable of the English professional growers' creations are best suited for planting in public places. They are tougher, can stand more exposure and are quite content with the more or less casual care which is often the best that can be given to park plantings. The new hybrids which currently dominate the interest of Rhododendron hobbyists are, for the most part, the originations of English amateurs which often exhibit a lack of tolerance for conditions less benign than those in which they were bred.

PUBLIC BUILDINGS

No chapter on the garden uses of Rhododendrons would be complete without a note on the perfect character of the larger-leaved sorts for landscaping public buildings. Impressive structures require shrubs and trees which will enhance their dignity and there are many Rhododendrons of noble bearing suitable for the purpose. They make great mounds of greenery with massive floral displays in keeping with the grand scale of most public buildings, apartment houses and similar structures. Their strong character and the bold pattern of their foliage is appropriate to this use, and some of the most successful landscape designs for monumental buildings have featured large Rhododendrons.

CHAPTER III

The Plant and the Site

REGIONS IN THE UNITED STATES WHERE RHODODENDRONS GROW NATURALLY

RHODODENDRONS grow naturally and easily in gardens wherever the soil is acid and the temperature and humidity are a reasonable compromise with the conditions which they find congenial in the wild. In eastern North America, the growing of garden hybrids is centered in the rectangular region bounded by Cleveland, Montreal, Boston, and Washington, D.C., with an extension southwestward through West Virginia, Virginia, Tennessee, and North Carolina along the elevations of the Appalachian Mountains. *R. catawbiense* and its hybrids grow very well in Nova Scotia and in similar favored coastal climates north of Boston. Inland, the cold restricts the gardener's choice of cultivated sorts to the Catawba hybrids and a handful of wild sorts. Under the most severe conditions only the American species are successful, since they are hardier than any of the hybrids. The selected color forms of *R. catawbiense* rival some of the hybrids in their beauty, so this is no cause for discouragement, and they are available from nursery specialists for the few inland gardens which are too cold even for the familiar Catawba cultivars. The map on page 51 shows the acid soil regions of the United States.

Rhododendrons can be found thriving in Michigan, Kansas, central Georgia, Texas, and Colorado, and a separate chapter in this book is devoted to their culture in the South and in the Mid-West, but with the possible exception of parts of Michigan and Wisconsin they cannot really be said to find such climates congenial. The second center of Rhododendron culture lies in the region along the Pacific coast from San Francisco through western Oregon and Washington to Vancouver Island, and beyond. There the high humidity and benign climate provide conditions so beneficent that Rhododendrons luxuriate in a manner unequalled in the Western world. Myriads of the Asian species and of the finest hybrids thrive in the moist mildness of the climate. With the exception of a handful of species which demand precise alpine conditions, any of the world's Rhododendrons can find an agreeable *milieu* somewhere within this region.

Growing Rhododendrons in Great Britain

The climate of the British Isles is almost equally congenial. In Cornwall and on the west coast of Scotland all Rhododendrons now in cultivation are hardy except the tenderest of the exotic epiphytes. As the climate becomes progressively more severe elsewhere along the seaboard the choice is somewhat reduced, but even in the coldest inland gardens there is a tremendous assortment of both species and hybrids suitable for the climate. About 60 per cent of all of the species are rated by the Royal Horticultural Society as hardy anywhere in the British Isles. Only in the districts with alkaline soil do Rhododendrons fail to grow naturally and easily.

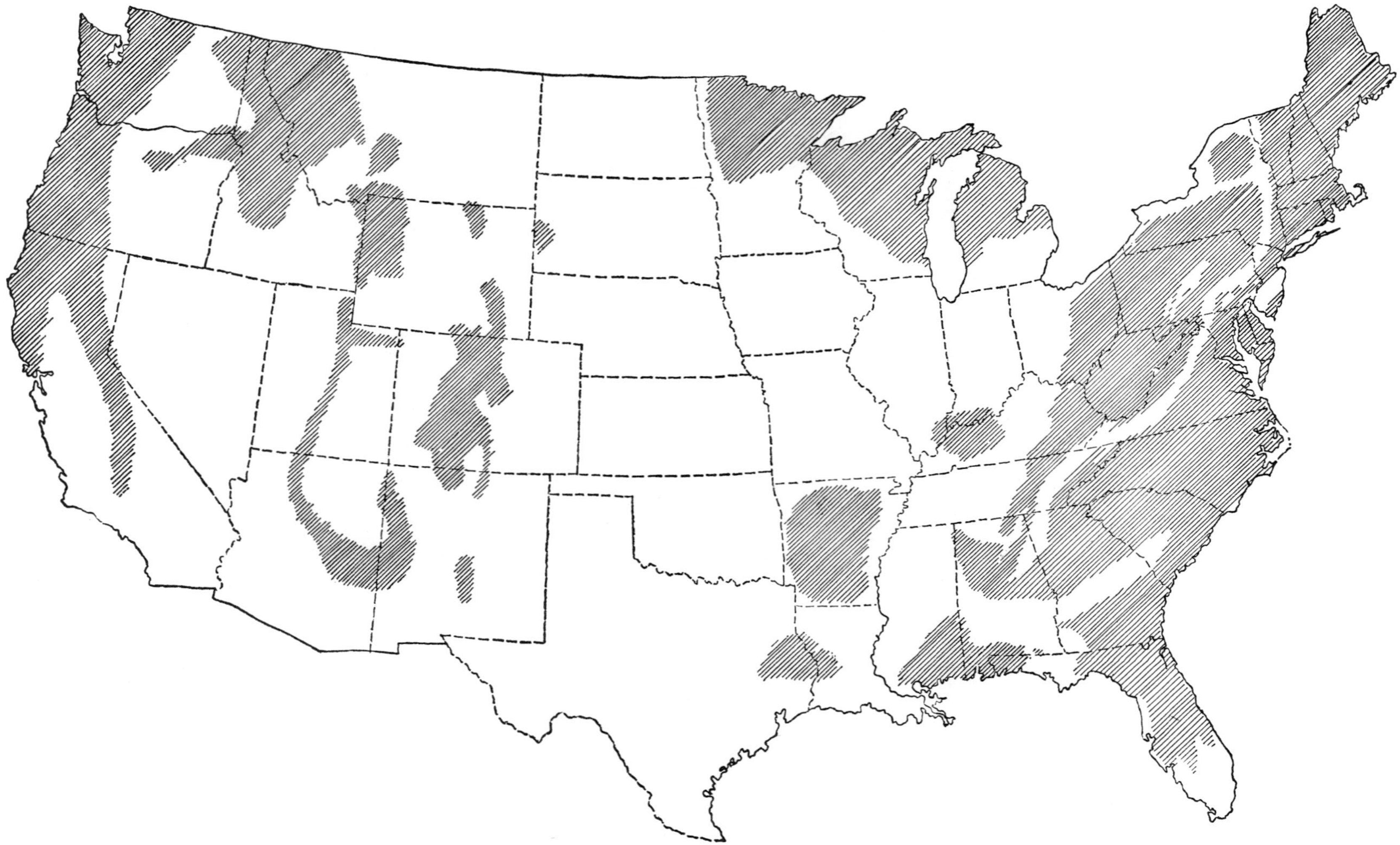

ACID SOIL REGIONS OF THE UNITED STATES

The soil is preponderantly acid in the regions shown in gray but it may be neutral in scattered local districts, too small to show at this scale, and tests at individual garden sites are usually desirable. Compare this map showing where the soil is naturally acid enough for Rhododendrons with the map on page 20 which shows their distribution in nature. Acid soil map prepared from data supplied by Dr Edgar T. Wherry, University of Pennsylvania.

SELECTING RHODODENDRONS

Gardeners with soil and climate which are suitable—and those elsewhere who are willing to make the site fit the subject—are almost certain to want to plant Rhododendrons. But buying them can be a confusing business. The size and grade vary. Grafted plants are sold by some nurseries whereas others pridefully offer Rhododendrons grown on their own roots. The catalogs offer seedlings but they may be collected from the wild in some cases, nursery-grown in others. Rhododendrons are sold in roadside markets by the colors of their blossoms. Are they as good as the named hybrids listed by the specialists?

The size of Rhododendrons to be purchased depends on the pocketbook, but it must be said that few plants will so well repay the patient gardener for his care as small Rhododendrons grown on to flowering size. Their increase in value multiplies rapidly as they progress beyond the 8 to 10-inch size. But most gardeners will probably prefer one of the three popular commercial grades of the big-leaved garden hybrids: 12 to 15-inch; 15 to 18-inch; or 18 to 24-inch. And the price of plants in each size will possibly seem a bit steep compared with the cost of ordinary deciduous shrubs.

But these are ancient aristocrats, good for a century of garden splendor. They are much harder to propagate and they grow more slowly than ordinary plants, so they are worth what the nurseryman asks. The gardener is entitled in return to good, healthy specimens with fresh green foliage which will develop into shapely shrubs of creditable appearance the year around. The most important consideration to insure such a future is to choose plants which have at least four main branches within a few inches of the ground. Unless the plant is well formed with a good branching framework in youth it will not make a trim, densely foliaged shrub in later years. Many a hopeful gardener is so dazzled by eye-filling blossoms that he buys Rhododendrons which will never be anything but lean and lanky liabilities in the landscape.

It is true that poorly branched plants can be reshaped by judicious pruning and training but in actual practice such transformations seem to be accomplished solely by experts with exceptional knowledge of their trade. It is also true that some Rhododendrons which have an open form in youth become more dense and shapely as growth slows down with approaching maturity. By that time the stems are shorter on each year's new twigs and they branch at closer intervals. But it takes the best part of a human generation for many Rhododendrons to reach maturity and effect such an improvement in their appearance. Gardeners are better advised to insist that the nurseryman provides plants properly branched close to the ground at the time they are sold. Any of the commercial hybrids, including those with red flowers, can be formed into dense young plants by appropriate management in the nursery.

Nurseries which specialize in growing Rhododendrons are the best source of supply for them. A list of such nurseries appears on page 505. The quality of the plants is likely to be superior under the most expert care, and a wider variety of different sorts and sizes offers a better selection. Plants from abroad should be avoided the first season after they are imported. They usually have beautiful glossy foliage but they also have small, compact root systems, often established in pure peat, which are scarcely adequate to support the top growth through the rigors of quarantine treatment and subsequent planting in an alien climate. Casualties may be heavy the first season for this reason, and also because plants grown in peat are reluctant to extend their roots into garden soil and become settled in a new location. After imported plants have been grown in a nursery for a year they will be as good as grafted domestic Rhododendrons because they will have developed expanded root systems and become adjusted to local growing conditions.

Grafted versus Own-Root Plants

In the past specific named Rhododendron hybrids have usually been offered as plants grafted on understocks of *R. ponticum*. More recently, advances in hormone treatments and propagation techniques have brought hybrids on their own roots to the market in increasing numbers. In my opinion they are infinitely preferable to grafted Rhododendrons.

A grafted plant can be detected by the enlarged section of the plant's main stem close to ground level where the scion was fitted to the understock. The bark on this swollen collar may be roughened or not, but the irregularity in the diameter of the trunk can still be noticed many years after the graft has been made.

Grafts can develop all sorts of troubles. There may be various degrees of incompatibility between scion and rootstock. Some Rhododendrons never really thrive until they reach a size where the accumulating mulch makes it possible for them to put out roots above the graft so that the top growth gradually acquires its own root system. For many years the stem is weak at the point where it is grafted, and it is not unusual for it to snap off under the stress of snow loads or heavy winds. Such casualties are a total loss because any new growth comes from the trash understock.

Only a small proportion of the vessels which carry sap from the understock to the scion can be matched when a graft is made and it is fairly common for grafted Rhododendrons to show distress due to inadequate translocation of fluids when top growth is active. The point where the graft is made, acting as a choke on the transmission of liquids between the rootstock and the plant above ground, may be responsible for the production of suckers, which are a nuisance in mild climates. Their foliage, different from the grafted cultivar, betrays them, and such wild growths from below the grafts should be promptly removed. In the severe climate of the northeastern United States suckers of *R. ponticum*, the most common understock, are conveniently winter-killed so they are not a garden problem.

Rhododendrons grafted on *R. ponticum* seem to be much more susceptible to the fungus disease called Rhododendron Blight (*Phytophthora cactorum*) which produces wilting and the abrupt death of branches, and subsequently of the entire shrub. Commercial growers who graft Rhododendrons operate under the constant threat of a crop failure if Wilt (*Phytophthora cinnamomi*) attacks the *ponticum* understocks in the greenhouse, and they sacrifice up to 50 per cent of the growth which can be obtained the first season from own-root plants.

It is probably true that grafted plants are a little more precocious about blooming and that they blossom more freely while they are young. In my opinion this is associated with reduced vegetative vigor of the top growth. It is also true that the robust root system of the adaptable *R. ponticum* imparts to a desirable but difficult Rhododendron an ability to grow on soil less acid and not too well suited to Rhododendrons. In fact, there are a few such as *R. lacteum*, the famous Loderi garden hybrids and some of the epiphytes which do not naturally produce vigorous root systems, and they are actually better garden plants when they are grafted on *R. ponticum*. But they are the conspicuous exceptions.

The greater vigor and vegetative growth of plants on their own roots may mean that they will not produce quite so many flowers when they are young, but this is a small sacrifice considering the many longer term advantages. The elimination of suckers is a major consideration in mild climates and there is a related advantage in the northeastern United States: own-root Rhododendrons mortally damaged by accident, disease, or insects, can often be salvaged and re-grown from sprouts which originate around the root crown. Grafted plants are a total loss in such circumstances.

Rhododendrons are produced on their own roots by layering or from cuttings. Recent advances in the use of root-forming hormones such as indolebutyric acid and 2, 4, 5-trichlorophenoxypropionic acid make the grafting of Rhododendrons obsolete and unnecessary, in my opinion. I am convinced from my experiments that any Rhododendron can be successfully produced on a commercial basis from rooted cuttings, and two different methods are described in the chapter on propagation, beginning on page 314.

The concern with the method of propagating Rhododendrons arises from the necessity of increasing a single, unique plant of superior characteristics so that there will be a great many exact duplicates of it with the same fine flowers, handsome foliage and attractive growth habit of the original. This can be done only by rooting cuttings or by grafting, layering or budding, and the entire group of identical plants is then called a clone. Either fine forms of the species or hybrids may be propagated as clones. Hybrid clones are often called cultivars. All plants with the same clone-name are identical, whether they are purchased on the West Coast or in the East, in America or in England. *R.* (hybrid) 'Pink Pearl' refers to the same Rhododendron the world over.

Seedlings

On the other hand, Rhododendrons produced from seeds often vary enormously. They may be good, bad or indifferent. And if they are seedlings of garden hybrids the chance of obtaining a first class Rhododendron by purchase is extremely small. Buyers should firmly shun Rhododendrons which are offered as 'hybrid seedlings' or perhaps 'seedlings of red-flowered hybrids'. Often the advertisements are phrased in a more subtle manner to obscure the important fact that the plants offered are seedlings and not named hybrids propagated as clones from cuttings or by grafting. The unwary gardener buys them, usually in a small size and at an attractive price, and does not discover the painful consequences until four or five years later when their blossoms appear in strident magenta shades or they lose their buds to winter cold and do not bloom at all.

Even many of the wild species vary a great deal in the quality of the plants which are produced from seeds by this, the sexual method of propagation. Many of the species which are most important as garden ornamentals have produced individual specimens of highly superior value which have been propagated as clones by cuttings, grafts, or layers, and these selected sorts are likely to yield a great deal of added satisfaction for any modest extra cost. A fine form of *R. caucasicum*, for example, is propagated asexually under the name 'Cunningham's Sulphur'. A white-flowered variety of our native Catawba Rhododendron is *R. catawbiense*, variety *album*, Glass. There appeared among numerous seedlings of this attractive variant a particularly good specimen which was named 'Catalgla' by Joseph Gable, pioneer Rhododendron authority and hybridist, and this is the choicest form of the white-flowered variety of *R. catawbiense* discovered by Mr Glass. Connoisseurs in search of a blue-flowered Rhododendron ask for "the Exbury form" or the "Tower Court form" of *R. augustinii*, knowing that the flowers are much finer than ordinary unselected seedlings of the species. Such excellent species forms, propagated not from seeds but asexually as clones, represent a standard of uniform quality and hardiness which discriminating gardeners appreciate.

A variety refers to a group of similar, distinctive plants within a wild species which usually produce seedlings resembling their parents. Varieties may be either better or worse than the typical species for garden decoration but plants of a variety grown from seeds and offered for sale by nurseries are likely to be superior to the usual run of unselected seedlings of the same species. *R. cinnabarinum* var. *roylei*, for example, is especially desirable and its superiority was formerly recognized by an extra star in its quality rating. *R. hanceanum* var. *nanum* has such a good, compact, dwarf habit that it had a quality rating of two stars a few years ago, whereas *R. hanceanum* had none.

Plants Collected from the Wild

Some nurseries advertise plants of Rhododendrons collected from the wild and such offerings can often be used advantageously. These plants are, of course, unselected seedlings as they grew in nature, but they are usually offered at attractive prices and they are certainly worth considering, especially when large numbers are to be purchased for naturalizing. Ordinarily the owner of a small garden will want to plant choice forms of the species or named garden hybrids when there is room for only a few Rhododendrons.

Collected plants should be cut back and regrown by a nursery before they are sold for landscaping use. If they are shipped directly to market from the wild, casualties will be heavy and many plants will never regain their natural vigor to become handsome, well-formed evergreens in cultivation, unless the buyer cuts them back to within several inches of the ground and regrows them.

Sometimes plants of Rhododendron species which have been raised in a nursery from seeds are available at prices comparable to the cost of collected stock, re-grown. If such a choice is available, the Rhododendrons which have been several times transplanted and cared for in a nursery from the beginning are a safer purchase.

Collected plants of the native American species are not so variable as are the Asian sorts, but some superior varieties have been found. The familiar *R. maximum* with its typical small white to pink blossoms about the first of July has three special color forms: a vinous red, a large-flowered white, and a deep pink. Only the latter is commercially available. The May-blooming *R. carolinianum* which ordinarily has mauve-pink flowers is available commercially in a white-flowered edition to those who will make the effort to locate it, and a form with blossoms of an appealing salmon-pink color is occasionally seen. Its later blooming relative, *R. minus*, seems to be more uniform, but several particularly fine expressions of it have been found. *R. macrophyllum*, the West Coast native, has a white-flowered variety which has much greater appeal for most gardeners than the common sorts with rose flowers flawed by an admixture of blue. The Catawba Rhododendron from the Blue Ridge Mountains has blossoms which are usually magenta and which seem somewhat harsh in the garden, although they are attractive in an open woodland where they are isolated from the clear, pure colors of other flowers. There are at least two forms of the white-flowered variety of this species, several vinous reds, and a pale blush-pink for the connoisseur who seeks something better than the typical magenta sort. It is always a surprise to stroll through the fields at blooming season in a nursery which specializes in re-growing collected plants of the American Rhododendron species. Specimens superior in plant habit, foliage, size, and character of flower, and in other respects can easily be isolated from the common ranks. Our Catawba Rhododendrons will flourish in a garden for a century or more. Its best forms require no more care than its worst. Discriminating buyers will take the time to visit a nursery to select such enduring companions for their gardens.

TRANSPLANTING SEASONS

Rhododendrons can be transplanted any time they are not in active growth. Being possessed of a surface root system which is compact and fibrous, they transplant easily even in large sizes. It is a great convenience to gardeners that the flowering season is a fine time to move the spring-blooming sorts. In the eastern United States I believe spring planting is preferable because it allows Rhododendrons which have been moved to extend their root systems and become established under favorable circumstances against the trying conditions of cold winters when they continue to transpire water which cannot be replaced from the frozen earth. After the season's growth has matured in August there is a second transplanting season which becomes progressively less desirable thereafter as autumn wanes and winter approaches. A thick mulch beneath fall-planted Rhododendrons is of special value because it preserves moisture and aids root development by delaying the penetration of frost into the earth.

In the Pacific Northwest and in the British Isles the transplanting season continues from the time the season's growth matures on through the fall and winter until the ground freezes or until the resumption of growth in the spring, but the early autumn is preferred since the mild humid winters encourage the root formation which prepares Rhododendrons for spring activity. Fall-planted Rhododendrons do much better in coastal regions of California which have warm weather in April and May.

Plants to Associate with Rhododendrons

The plants which associate most naturally with Rhododendrons are those which thrive under the same conditions. Unrelieved masses of Rhododendrons are inclined to have a solidity which needs to be enlivened by contrasting shrubs of lighter texture. The whole is enhanced by a setting of taller growth to provide an interesting and appropriate background. But the entire plan should be executed with trees and shrubs which grow well in acid soil.

Plants associated with Rhododendrons should not compete with them for attention during their flowering season, nor should their roots encroach to deprive them of food and moisture. They are most valuable when they provide a pleasant and unobtrusive contrast during the Rhododendron blossoming season, and then in turn furnish a period of color and interest from fruit, foliage or flower when the Rhododendrons are not in bloom. Finally, other trees and shrubs should shelter the Rhododendrons and protect them against wind, temperature extremes and excessive sun. These are the conditions, aesthetic and practical, which ought to be considered when the gardener features Rhododendrons in the landscape, and wishes to set them off to the best advantage.

Trees

Of the trees, Oaks and Pines make the best companions for Rhododendrons because their roots are deep and they do not compete with them for food and moisture. There are many excellent Pines, thirty-five species native to the United States alone. In the eastern part of the country the White Pine (*P. strobus*), is unsurpassed. The Oaks, with about seventy species in cultivation, offer an assortment equally valuable. Contrary to popular impression some of them, such as the Red Oak (*Quercus borealis*), are very fast-growing. Pine needles and Oak leaves are traditionally and justifiably first choice as a mulch and the gardener who has an open woodland of mixed Pine and Oak trees can offer most Rhododendrons an ideal association.

Hemlocks, Cedars, Spruces, Firs and False Cypresses make imposing backdrops and efficient windbreaks for Rhododendrons but their surface roots fan out in a ceaseless search for moisture. Unless they are planted at an appropriate distance from them, Rhododendrons will eventually suffer from their invading roots. Coniferous trees are natural associates of Rhododendrons in the wild, in mixed forests at intermediate elevations and in pure stands higher in the mountains. Hollies are handsome with Rhododendrons.

Birches make attractive contrasts to the heavy appearance of Rhododendron groups in the garden or in a woodland. Their light bark and delicate foliage of good color combine with a graceful habit of growth to provide just the right foil for the more assertive evergreens. But Birch roots, if not aggressive, are none the less at the surface and it is wise to keep Rhododendrons 10 or 12 feet away from the trees.

Among smaller trees, Magnolias stand supreme. They share with Rhododendrons a preference for an acid soil, their roots are docile and deep, their stature and form are a pleasing complement in the landscape and their flowers are famed for their beauty. Other good companions for Rhododendrons among the smaller trees in the northeastern United States are:

SMALL TREES

Dogwoods (*Cornus*), American and Asian—good fall foliage and fruits
Flowering Crab Apples (*Malus*)—bright fruits
Franklinia alatamaha—flowers and colorful foliage in autumn
Japanese Pagoda Tree (*Sophora japonica*)—legume, late yellow flowers
Redbud (*Cercis*)
Shadblow (*Amelanchier*)—very early flowers
Silver Bell Tree (*Halesia carolina*)
Snowbell Tree (*Styrax japonica*)
Stewartia species—bright fall foliage and midsummer flowers

LARGER TREES

Katsura Tree (*Cercidiphyllum japonicum*)—brilliant fall foliage
Sour Gum (*Nyssa sylvatica*)—brilliant fall foliage
Sour-Wood (*Oxydendron arboreum*)—brilliant fall foliage
Sweet Gum (*Liquidambar styraciflua*)—brilliant fall foliage

For milder climates the following associate with Rhododendrons to their mutual advantage:

SMALL TREES

Cotoneaster frigida
Davidia involucrata
Embothrium coccineum var. *longifolium*

Flowering Cherries: MT. FUJI, OJOCHIN and KANZAN—famous for their beauty in association with species of the Triflorum series.
Maples, Dwarf Ornamental
Parrotia persica
Pterostyrax hispida

LARGER TREES

Aesculus indica
Nothofagus antarctica
Paulownia tomentosa

Trees with low, dense heads are not especially desirable companions for Rhododendrons. Those of more open habit, higher branched and with foliage which produces a dappled, intermittent shade, are ideal. The following should generally be avoided, for the reasons noted:

Ash (*Fraxinus*)—competitive roots
Black Walnut (*Juglans nigra*)—leaves toxic to Rhododendrons
Beech (*Fagus*)—competitive roots
Elm (*Ulmus*)—competitive roots
Horse Chestnut (*Aesculus hippocastanum*)—leaves toxic
Linden (*Tilia*)—susceptible to insects which secrete injurious honeydew
Norway Maple (*Acer*)—competitive roots
Poplar (*Populus*)—competitive roots
Silver Maple (*Acer*)—competitive roots
Tulip Tree (*Liriodendron tulipifera*)—susceptible to insects which secrete injurious honeydew

There are many other trees, less commonly planted, which are quick to encroach on any favored spot where the soil is damp and friable. Rhododendrons can be protected from their invasive roots by cutting around the outside branches of the plants with a long, sharp spade at least once a year. Even so, additional irrigation will probably be required in dry weather and it is necessary to examine the beds periodically for tree roots which may have evaded the annual ringing by growing upward into the Rhododendrons from a lower level. If there is a choice, it is better to shun any planting site where there will be competition from trees known to have voracious roots.

Shrubs

There are almost 1,500 different Heaths which associate easily and naturally in acid soil with Rhododendrons. They have several unique and interesting features in common: pollen is discharged through pores at the tips of the sacs and not through slits along the sides which disperse the pollen in other families. With a magnifying glass the pollen is seen to be composed of tetrads, four grains joined into one particle, instead of the usual single grains which are formed by other plants. The seed capsules have the same number of chambers as there are lobes to the flower corolla or a greater number, whereas in most other families there are fewer compartments in the fruit than there are petals to the flower. Any gardener can tell by these tests whether a specimen under close examination is a Heath, but always with the inevitable exceptions, rather rare, by which nature resists inflexible, if convenient, man-made categories.

The evergreen Heaths are the gentry of the family, first choice as desirable associates for their relatives, the Rhododendrons. These are shrubs of universal esteem, varying in leaf texture and manner of growth, that can be used to provide a range of pleasant, lighter notes in the portly groups of broadleaved Rhododendrons:

Blueberries (*Vaccinium* species)
Dwarf Rosemary (*Andromeda polifolia*)
Fetterbush (*Leucothoë racemosa*)
Huckleberries (*Gaylussacia* species)
Lambkill (*Kalmia angustifolia*)
Leather-leaf (*Chamaedaphne calyculata*)
Ledum groenlandicum
Ledum palustre
Leucothoë axillaris
Leucothoë catesbaei
Mountain Laurel (*Kalmia latifolia*)
Pieris floribunda
Pieris japonica
Pieris taiwanensis
Sand-myrtle (*Leiophyllum buxifolium*)

These offer a complete array of shrubs of restrained growth habit, from 18 inches up to about 6 or 7 feet.

In my opinion, Azaleas are not suitable for interplanting intimately with broad-leaved Rhododendrons of the familar commercial sort. The large foliage and strong character of most garden Rhododendrons are so assertive in the landscape that Azaleas intermixed with them seem like inadequate competitors. Adroit planning and skilful execution can create mixed plantings where Azaleas and broad-leaved Rhododendrons are grown in close association, but successful examples are, to my mind, noteworthy for their rarity. In the eastern United States, most Rhododendron pinks and reds are flawed by varying taints of blue, but their lack of purity passes unnoticed unless there is nearby a similar clear color for comparison. In addition, these pinks and reds do not combine harmoniously with the salmon-pinks and orange-reds of the Azaleas. When deftly done, however, Rhododendron groups can be given a welcome note of color contrast by the addition of the clear yellow flowers of some of the deciduous Azaleas. Out of bloom, the evergreens and semi-evergreen Azaleas seem to me to be too fine and delicate in their foliage and growth to be planted immediately adjacent to broad-leaved Rhododendrons, just as conspicuous lightweights appear negative and inadequate in the company of heavy-weights. The small-leaved alpine Rhododendrons combine beautifully with the fine-textured Azaleas, however.

There is an impressive assortment of dwarf and creeping Heaths which are a great pleasure and satisfaction to gardeners who seek them out to plant at the feet of Rhododendrons. These are just a few inches high:

Alpine Azalea (*Loiseleuria procumbens*)—clusters of pink bells
Bearberry (*Arctostaphylos Uva-ursi*)—minute pink flowers, bright fruits
Cassiope species—single clusters of tiny pink trumpets
Creeping Snowberry (*Chiogenes hispidula*)—white berries
Heathers (*Calluna*)—require high humidity, somewhat special conditions
New England Mountain Heath (*Phyllodoce caerulea*)—lavender flowers
Pipsissewa (*Chimaphila umbellata* and *C. maculata*)—white or pink flowers, good evergreen ground cover
Shinleaf (*Pyrola elliptica*)—evergreen, white flowers in early July
Spike-heath (*Bruckenthalia spiculifolia*)—diminutive pink bells
Swiss Heath (*Erica carnea*)—often blossoms in midwinter
Trailing Arbutus (*Epigaea repens*)—buy nursery-grown plants in pots
Wintergreen (*Gaultheria procumbens*, *G. ovatifolia*)—white flowers, bright berries, interesting evergreen ground cover

Not Heaths but congenial miniature companions to Rhododendrons are Pyxie or Flower-moss (*Pyxidanthera barbulata*), which becomes white mats of star-like flowers in early spring, and Bunchberry (*Cornus canadensis*) whose bright clusters of red berries in summer follow dense heads of pale flowers with white bracts in mid-spring.

There is a mixed group of larger shrubs of conventional size, some of them deciduous Heaths, which combine pleasantly with Rhododendrons and thrive under the same conditions while contributing a season of ornamental interest:

American Cranberry (*Vaccinium macrocarpon*)
Barberries (*Berberis*)—several good deciduous species have bright fall fruits
Cotoneasters—bright berries in autumn
Enkianthus species—brilliant fall foliage
Firethorn (*Pyracantha coccinea* var. *lalandi*)—showy fall berries, will not thrive in soil extremely acid
Holly-barberry (*Mahonia aquifolium*)—evergreen, yellow flowers
Inkberry (*Ilex glabra*)—good summer foliage, black fall berries
Oak-leaf Hydrangea (*H. quercifolia*)—good foliage texture, white flowers
Sweet Pepperbush (*Clethra alnifolia*)—white flowers in midsummer
Sorbus species—bright fall fruits
Upright Yew (*Taxus cuspidata*)—pleasing in form but spreading, vase-shaped Yews look stilted
Winterberry (*Ilex verticillata*)—bright red berries in fall
Witch-hazel (*Hamamelis mollis*)—yellow-flowered foil for earliest lavender Rhododendrons
Zenobia (*Z. pulverulenta*)—white flowers, bluish-white foliage

Small Trees and Shrubs for the West Coast and the British Isles

Mr Brian O. Mulligan, Director of the University of Washington Arboretum at Seattle, has made below a selection of small trees and shrubs which he considers to be especially choice for association with Rhododendrons.

SMALL TREES, 20 TO 30 FEET

Acer davidii *Acer rufinerve*	For striped bark and especially for fall color
**Cornus nuttallii*	Flowers April–May; fall color
**Magnolia salicifolia* *Magnolia veitchii*	Both lovely in April
**Eucryphia nymansensis*	August flowering, evergreen
Stewartia monadelpha *Stewartia pseudocamellia*	July flowers, excellent fall color, especially of *monadelpha*
**Halesia monticola*	
Embothrium longifolium (or *lanceolatum*)	Striking May–June scarlet blossoms
**Ilex aquifolium*	Winter berries

* May reach 40 feet under favorable conditions.

LARGE SHRUBS, 10 TO 15 FEET GENERALLY

Abutilon vitifolium	Large flowers of unusual color
Acer japonicum *Acer palmatum* forms	Chiefly for fall color
**Cornus kousa*	Summer bloom and fall color
Cotoneaster henryana *Cotoneaster lactea*	For fruit in fall and early winter; evergreen
Eucryphia glutinosa	August bloom
Franklinia alatamaha	Fall color and late blooms
Hamamelis mollis	Very early flowers, fragrant
Hydrangea strigosa (or *H. viollosa*)	August flowers, handsome foliage
**Magnolia denudata* *Magnolia sieboldii* **Magnolia virginiana* **Magnolia soulangeana* vars.	Invaluable at different periods
Philadelphus delavayi (or *purpurascens*)	Fragrant, June bloom
Pieris formosa *Pieris forrestii* *Pieris japonica*	Early flowers, evergreen
Rhus Cotinus (*Cotinus coggygria*) var. *purpureus*	Foliage color
Stewartia sinensis	Striking fall color
Stranvaesia davidiana var. *salicifolia*	Fruit in fall and early winter
Styrax obassia	Handsome foliage
Viburnum betulifolium (or *V. lobophyllum*) *Viburnum prunifolium*	Berries in fall

* May reach 20 feet under favorable conditions

MEDIUM-SIZED SHRUBS 3 TO 8 FEET

Camellia sasanqua	Fall blooming, November
Camellia williamsii varieties	Early spring flowers; very promising
Clethra alnifolia var. *rosea*	Late summer flowers; fragrant
Disanthus cercidifolius	Fall coloring
**Enkianthus campanulatus*	Fall coloring
Fothergilla monticola	Fall coloring
Hydrangea arborescens	Summer flowering
Hydrangea quercifolia	Late summer bloom
Hydrangea macrophylla var. *mariesii* or var. *caerulea* **Kalmia latifolia*	Late summer bloom
Lyonia mariana	Fall color
Mahonia aquifolium	Fragrant April flowers
Pieris taiwanensis	The best small *Pieris*
Vaccinium corymbosum *Zenobia pulverulenta*	Fall color

* May exceed 8 feet in favorable locations

SHRUBS OF LESS THAN 3 FEET, AND GROUND COVERS

Calluna vulgaris 'H. E. Beale'	Flowers August–September
Cornus canadensis	An excellent ground cover
Daboecia cantabrica	Summer bloom
Erica darleyensis 'George Rendall'	Flowers February–March
Erica vagans var. *grandiflora* (or *rubra*)	August flowers; brown flower spikes through winter
Gaulthettya wisleyensis	Valuable low evergreen
Gaulthettya procumbens	An excellent ground cover
Gaulthettya miqueliana	White berries
Ledum species	Useful for wet places
Mahonia nervosa	Valuable for shady places
Pernettia mucronata	Berries ornamental until February or March
Sarcococca confusa	Fragrant February flowers; good in shade
Sarcococca humilis	Ground cover 9 to 12 inches tall
Skimmia foremanii	Berries ornamental all winter
Vaccinium vitis-idaea	Very useful ground cover

Unrelated Herbaceous Plants

A great many sorts of perennial plants, grown chiefly for their flowers, can be planted appropriately with Rhododendrons. Chief of these are the spring wild flowers, luxuriating in the cool, moist humus associated with the protecting shrubs. Often they bloom and mature their foliage before the shade of nearby deciduous trees becomes too dense. But the list can be expanded almost indefinitely. I have especially enjoyed Trilliums, Bluebells (*Mertensia*), the white-flowered evergreen Oconee Bells (*Shortia galacifolia*), various violets, Columbines, Bloodroot (*Sanguinaria canadensis*), Lady-slippers (*Cypripedium*), and Wild Phlox (*P. divaricata*). There are dozens more which can be grown. When growing wild flowers with Rhododendrons the mulch must be renewed in the autumn, not in the spring, and if it is very heavy the wildlings are planted toward the outer edges of the site where the ground covering is not so thick. But they poke their way up through many layers of leaves to give a welcome to spring in a manner which is very appealing.

Ferns are friends of Rhododendrons. With or without wild flowers, they provide an invaluable foil of gently swaying foliage of extraordinary grace and beauty which contrasts dramatically with the solidity of large evergreen leaves. Cinnamon Ferns, Interrupted Ferns, Christmas Ferns, Maidenhair Ferns, any sort of ferns enhance the woodland atmosphere in which Rhododendrons appear to such advantage. A commonplace planting of Rhododendrons can be lifted to one of remarkable effectiveness by the skilful addition of a variety of ferns and nothing else. As if in repayment to their hosts and benefactors, the fronds return to the soil as humus which Rhododendrons seem to find especially beneficial.

Primulas often flourish when they are sheltered by nearby Rhododendrons, and Violas seem to delight in their company. Low growing blue-flowered plants are often wanted to complement the delicate pastel-colored flowers of some of the best Rhododendron hybrids, and the biennial Forget-me-not, *Myosotis*, fills the need nicely. It seeds itself and spreads without being pernicious in fine-textured surface mulches such as peat, but it soon dies out if there is a dense ground covering of coarse leaves.

Among bulbous flowering plants the Lilies stand unsurpassed as natural companions which thrive in the same soil conditions as Rhododendrons. Interplanted with them, the willowy grace of Lilies stands in delightful contrast to the stout evergreen girth of the foliage through which they poke their heads. The Scillas (*S. nonscripta*), variously called Blue Squills or Wild Hyacinths (the English Bluebell), provide the low blue underplanting which seems to flatter so many Rhododendrons when in bloom. They increase rapidly by offsets, and self-sown seeds are able to fend for themselves in open woodland. Their ripening foliage is a little too conspicuous in formal beds neatly mulched with peat moss. The foliage of Daffodils also seems a bit of a problem in such surroundings, but they are an unalloyed pleasure naturalized in a woodland, flowing in rivers of gold and white beneath the lavender columns of early blooming Rhododendrons. Their foliage will have received enough sunlight by the time the deciduous trees come into leaf to insure the formation of buds for the next year's outburst of flowers. The large trumpet types become weather-beaten and their heavy blossoms bend earthward but the short cupped sorts naturalize to perfection. Crocus and many other bulbs can be used to create colorful carpets of arresting beauty in Rhododendron plantings.

For later bloom from herbaceous plants the Daylilies (*Hemerocallis*) can be put in among Rhododendrons or used as a foreplanting to fill in around their lowest branches. Undemanding and uncompetitive, they look well in neatly tended borders or as casual companions in open woodland, and a good assortment is faithful in providing color right on through the summer and early fall. Their red and pink, yellow and lavender flowers are bestowed with extraordinary freedom from plants which naturalize readily and require no care or attention whatever.

Ground Covers

Rhododendrons, having fine roots in a fibrous system close to the surface of the ground, should reasonably be expected to resent competition from the usual ground covers which form convenient mats of foliage to minimize maintenance. In actual practice the association does not seem to harm them and Myrtle (*Vinca*), Pachysandra, Ivies (*Hedera*) and *Euonymus radicans* var. *coloratus* all form familiar evergreen mats of foliage beneath Rhododendrons without adversely affecting their welfare. Wintergreen (*Gaultheria*), Pipsissewa (*Chimaphila*) and Creeping Snowberry (*Chiogenes*) are less familiar but perhaps more interesting and appropriate ground covers which are Heaths and so belong to the same family as do Rhododendrons. In a woodland several of the ferns which spread rapidly by underground rhizomes make charming ground covers for robust growing sorts which are flattered by the fresh greenery of such a foreground.

For the West Coast, Bearberry (*Arctostaphylos uva-ursi*), Mountain Boxwood (*Pachistima myrsinites*), Wintergreen (*Gaultheria humifusa*) and Cowberry (*vaccinium vitis-idaea*) are much esteemed as ground covers, and they would be equally attractive in British gardens.

CHOOSING THE PLANTING SITE

The Conditions in Nature

Nothing better prepares the gardener to locate a Rhododendron to the best advantage than an understanding of the conditions under which it, or its forebears, grows in nature. Rhododendrons are first and foremost plants of mountain elevations where the climate is cool and moist. The damp, clammy air bathes them constantly in the humidity to which their large evergreen leaves are adapted. Plant explorers in the Himalayas have often described the dramatic sight of Rhododendron blossoms standing out in sharp relief against the branches of trees laden with snow. In their native Asian homeland the southwest monsoon determines the climate and they are accustomed to prodigious rains in a long, wet season which extends from June to October. There follows then a cold season from November to March during which the temperature declines to about 32° F. at an altitude of 6,000 feet. At about 10,000 feet the earth freezes in November and does not thaw until March, but there is 3 or 4 feet of snow protection at 12,000 feet and from 14,000 feet upward the snows accumulate from October until the middle of May. The 'hot' season is April and May, when the temperature may rise to about 75° F.

In the Himalayas the southwestern slopes bear the brunt of the monsoon and the unprotected outer mountainsides may receive 200 inches of rainfall, concentrated in the four-month summer rainy season. The sheltered elevations behind the southernmost slopes receive about 100 inches of rain in this period and the vegetation luxuriates in an average relative humidity of between 90 and 97 per cent. The higher altitudes are bathed in mist much of the time, just as they are to a lesser degree in the southeastern United States where vast congregations of *R. catawbiense* cover the peaks of the Blue Ridge Mountains.

Even in the benign mildness and moisture where they originated in the heartland of Asia, Rhododendrons grow more vigorously and in greater numbers on the northern slopes of the mountains, where the sun's rays strike them at an angle, than they do in elevations which are exposed in other directions.

It is a marvel that Rhododendrons grow so well in climates which bear such slight resemblance to that of their native heaths, but still a certain amount of thoughtful attention will prompt a planting site in the garden which approaches a little more closely, even at a great distance, the ideal conditions of their homeland, and often converts misplaced shrubs of indifferent value into the shining stars of the landscape.

Sun and Shade

Most gardeners are troubled more by the amount of shade to provide for Rhododendrons than by any other single factor in choosing a place to plant them. And unfortunately no hard-and-fast rules can be given because the right course depends on the climate in which the garden is located and the sorts of Rhododendrons which are to be put into it. It is fortunate that most of these plants have an astonishing tolerance, considering the special climatic conditions from which they came originally, and they will thrive in a variety of situations with a latitude of exposure, rainfall and atmospheric humidity which is a powerful tribute to their powers of adaptation.

The amount of sunlight a Rhododendron receives has a potent bearing on how profusely it flowers, how compactly it grows and how hardy it is. If the plant is situated within its latitude of tolerance, the more exposure it receives the more flower buds will be formed, the better will be its habit of growth and the more the stem tissues will be matured to resist cold-weather injury. But most of all the amount of sun affects the general health and vigor of Rhododendrons.

Excessive exposure scorches the leaves in summer. The foliage loses its healthy green color and becomes rusty and yellowish from a reduction in the amount of chlorophyll, which in turn means a decrease in the amount of food manufactured by the plant for its own growth and vigor. The leaves which receive the sun at the most direct angle may develop irregular brown, dead areas, especially along the midribs and around their perimeters. Insects such as Thrips and the Lace Wing Fly often appear, to compound the injury. In the winter too much sunlight shining on the foliage of sorts which are at the borderline of hardiness will scald the leaves if the ground is frozen. Flowers of Rhododendrons last longer in partial shade, and those of the very late blooming sorts remain in good condition only briefly in hot weather without some protection from the sun. Shelter often means the difference between flowers ruined by frost and the escape from any damage to early-blooming Rhododendrons. And of course the more sunlight, the higher the air temperature and the lower the humidity which is so critical in the culture of Rhododendrons.

All of the foliage troubles of Rhododendrons in excessive sunlight arise from their inability to replace moisture through the roots as fast as it is lost through their leaves. The temperature of Rhododendron leaves in the sun is above that of the surrounding air and they then transpire moisture into the atmosphere even when the relative humidity is 100 per cent—complete saturation. The leaves always are at a higher temperature and therefore are losing water so long as the light strikes them, whether or not the humidity is increased by sprinkling. For this reason water loss can be more effectively controlled by shade than by any other means.

If there is a rule of thumb at all, it might be said that Rhododendrons should be grown where they have just as much sun as they can be induced to accept without foliage discoloration or other evidence of over-exposure. Obviously, plants growing in a humus-filled soil retentive of moisture and irrigated in periods of prolonged drouth will be able to endure more direct sun than will those in a sandy soil which dries out quickly and does not have the benefit of watering in dry weather. A planting site in a hot situation with a southern exposure aggravates the problem of moisture loss and makes the sun less endurable.

Fifty per cent shade lowers the temperature of the ground even 3 inches underneath the surface by 6° F., thus contributing materially to the natural preference of Rhododendrons for a cool, moist root zone.

But the question of how much shade Rhododendrons should have has still not yet been answered. Few gardeners are willing to determine by repeatedly changing the planting site just which situation provides the maximum amount of sun without causing foliage discoloration. Then, too, the brightness of the season varies from one year to the next and there are other shifting factors which make it impractical to use the suggested rule of thumb without some general indicators to approximate the desired amount of sunlight.

The broadleaved Asian species as a whole cannot stand so much sun as the garden hybrids. When many of them were first grown in the British Isles from seeds sent back by the plant collectors in the early 1900's, losses were heavy and they did not grow well because they were given the same open-field conditions under which the older cultivated hybrids throve, and this proved to be entirely too much exposure. A renowned amateur collector, Mr J. C. Williams, then demonstrated by the perfect health of the plants which he grew under partial shade from trees that shelter was necessary for the then new species, particularly the large-leaved sorts.

In China the large, broad-leaved species grow naturally in shade and the dwarf alpine sorts with scaly leaves are open to the sky in their vast associations which blanket the mountain tops. But the latter are often shrouded by mist in their lofty meadows. Full exposure there is quite a different thing compared with day-long untempered sunlight in a much brighter, clearer atmosphere, and for situations with much lower humidity even the tough little Lapponicums will grow better in the United States with some midday shade. It is still a useful rough guide to orient Rhododendrons by the size of their leaves: the larger they are, the more shade they should have; and the smaller the foliage, the more exposure they can be induced to accept. This holds true even among the native species of the eastern United States. *R. maximum*, with its long, handsome leaves, demands a planting site with a good deal of shade and shelter. *R. catawbiense*, with foliage of intermediate size, does its best in gardens with only modest protection. The small-leaved species *RR. minus* and *carolinianum* grow cheerfully in even more open situations, with very little shade and often with none at all. On the West Coast the increasingly popular small-leaved species of the Triflorum series flower equally well in full sun or in considerable shade, but the exposed plants are much more handsome in their habit of growth. The choice dwarf *R. williamsianum*, with miniature foliage, must be in as open a situation as the foliage will endure if it is to flower at all.

This matter of shade is here discussed at some length because it is debated more frequently among enthusiasts and is of more interest among novice gardeners than any other aspect of Rhododendron culture. In addition to the variations of preference among the plants themselves, the problem is complicated by the enormous differences in climate in the diverse regions of this country and abroad where Rhododendrons are grown.

The extremes are perhaps best illustrated by comparing the Seattle–Portland district with the New York–Baltimore region. The West Coast district which is so favorable to Rhododendrons has 65 per cent more cloudy days than does the coastal region between the two eastern cities. Philadelphia has 45 per cent more sunlight in spring and summer than does Seattle. To translate full exposure on the Pacific Coast or in Great Britain into a comparable amount of sun on the East Coast of the United States requires almost a 50 per cent reduction in sunlight. Eastern gardeners who read descriptions of Rhododendron culture on the Pacific Coast are often misled because they fail to take into account the enormous difference in the climate. Fortunately, the old ironclad Catawba hybrids, which are the standard Rhododendrons of commerce in the

East, can endure a great deal more exposure under the same conditions than can the most popular hybrids which are their western equivalents, and the mischief is thereby minimized. Though they cannot be said to be at their very best, most of the popular hardy commercial hybrids can endure fully exposed positions in most districts in the Northeast.

The differences in sunlight within the eastern United States, while less extreme, are still significant. Rhododendrons in New England must have almost 20 per cent less shade to receive the same amount of sunlight as they would have in Philadelphia. In Memphis and in Texas the light is so intense that enthusiasts there plant Rhododendrons where the sun never strikes them directly.

The atmospheric humidity bears importantly on the amount of exposure which Rhododendrons can be persuaded to accept. Along the coast and near inland lakes there is so much moisture in the air that many hybrids thrive in full sunlight which would grow much less vigorously inland where the humidity is a great deal lower and the atmosphere is more luminous and transparent. Coastal nurserymen often unintentionally mislead their customers with planting directions which do not take into account the drier air of gardens so far away from bodies of water as not to enjoy their beneficial effect. Inland gardeners who have planting sites alongside ponds or brooks are doubly blessed with the prospect of growing Rhododendrons with success.

That very strong light will substitute for direct sunlight is demonstrated by the universal preference among enthusiasts for planting sites which are openly exposed toward the north. On the West Coast or in the East, this is a favored situation whether it is available in a foundation planting on the north side of a house or in a position where tall evergreen and deciduous shrubs and trees are massed immediately to the south. In the eastern United States, a site with an exposure to the east is somewhat less desirable because the plants are sometimes injured by bright early morning sunlight while they are frozen. On the Pacific Coast and in the British Isles, an eastern exposure is considered very desirable for all except the sorts which bloom very early in the season, whose flowers should be shielded from the rising sun on frosty mornings so that they can thaw slowly, without injury. An exposure to the west is usually satisfactory if the screen behind the Rhododendrons is made up of tall shrubs and trees, but the western side of a house foundation is too hot unless it is partially shaded by nearby trees. For the same reason a southern exposure is usually avoided unless it is tempered even more by shade from trees. Whether the background be a house foundation or taller shrubs, open exposures to the south are undesirable, not alone for the excessive heat but also because unseasonable stimulation to growth in bright weather creates problems of winter hardiness.

Shade is most often provided for Rhododendrons by planting them near trees. The desirable and the undesirable sorts are mentioned on pages 56–59. Few gardeners realize how different the climate is beneath a high canopy of trees, and how much the right trees can contribute to the health and welfare of Rhododendrons.

The Effect of Trees

The large-leaved Rhododendrons are usually associated with trees in the wild, especially Oaks and Pines, and their benign shelter is enormously helpful in cultivation. When the brilliance of direct sunlight is 12,000 foot candles, the dappled, shifting shade beneath high deciduous trees ranges from 400 to 10,000 foot candles as the breezes create a constantly changing pattern of light intensity. Trees increase atmospheric humidity by reducing air movement and minimizing temperature fluctuations. Everyone who walks into a woodland in springtime is familiar with the peculiar, buoyant atmosphere, and this cooling moisture in the air is tremendously useful in controlling evaporation and the transpiration of water from Rhododendrons, which are in nature accustomed to a ceaselessly dripping climate from June to October in Asia.

Trees modify the temperature near the ground beneath them by preventing the loss of warmth by long-wave radiation from the earth. This is why woodlands often escape ground frosts which whiten the open fields surrounding them, and why damaging frosts occur in clear weather which are prevented by the clouds on overcast nights. Any overhead shelter, such as a canopy of high foliage or a cloudy sky, prevents the radiation which causes the earth temperature to drop rapidly below the air temperature, and thus ground frosts are avoided when it is near freezing. For Rhododendrons which bloom and start into growth early, and for those which are laggards in ripening their wood in the fall to resist cold, the advantage of tree cover may be very great.

It is surprising how much deciduous trees will temper the climate beneath them even when they are leafless in winter. By breaking the force of the cutting winds, Rhododendrons lose less water through their leaves when the ground is frozen and there is similar conservation as a result of the reduction in light intensity from the bare twigs and branches overhead. Trees will even moderate low temperatures by a few degrees despite their lack of foliage. When spring comes, the flowers of Rhododendrons so protected last longer and their evergreen leaves have a glossier color which is fresher and brighter. In the summer the soil remains cooler, more moist, and more porous. Finally, in fall the nearby guardians cast their leaves for the sustenance and protection of the Rhododendrons.

Snow Load Damage

Any site near a house foundation which is subject to avalanches of melting snow from the roof should be avoided. Many fine Rhododendron specimens have been broken and split asunder by having such burdens of snow thrust upon them. The hybrid 'America', which is highly esteemed in the eastern United States, is especially susceptible to damage from snow loads because of its spreading, somewhat pendulous growth habit.

Acidity of Disturbed Soil

The map on page 51 shows the regions of the United States where the soil is naturally acid, but it must be stressed that this refers to *undisturbed* soil. Where subsoil has been brought up from excavated basements and used for grading, or where suburban developments have been created by the massive attacks of builders who alter whole landscapes, soil tests should always be made to determine whether the acidity is suitable for Rhododendrons. A chemical treatment may be necessary to restore its original condition.

Wind Protection

As heretofore inferred, protection from wind should be an important consideration in choosing planting sites for Rhododendrons. A drafty corner of a house foundation where air currents whip and eddy is a poor choice because wind is always accompanied by the drying which Rhododendrons abhor. Some sorts can be said to be wind tender. The species of the Fortunei series, for example, although they are for the most part among the hardiest to cold of the Asian Rhododendrons, simply cannot endure strong winds. Some of the large-leaved species which are becoming more popular on the West Coast and in Great Britain can be defoliated by having their leaves twisted off in the course of a buffeting by strong winds. In fact, in the British Isles the planting of windbreaks to protect Rhododendrons is possibly the most important single consideration in their successful culture, for many gardeners. And any Rhododendron, anywhere, will be much better off out of the path of the wind than in it.

Evergreen trees and shrubs make the best windbreaks and many Rhododendrons on the borderline of hardiness can be induced to thrive and blossom freely if they are given good protection from the direction of the prevailing winds. An evergreen screen reduces the velocity of a 15-mile-per-hour wind by 70 per cent on the leeward side, to the inestimable benefit of the Rhododendrons it shelters. Dense plantings of deciduous shrubs and trees are almost equally effective in preserving atmospheric humidity and preventing the desiccating effect of winds blowing through the Rhododendron foliage. In the lee of a thick belt of mixed deciduous shrubs the velocity of a 15-mile-per-hour wind is reduced by about 40 per cent even at a distance five or six times the height of the bushes in the windbreak. In its immediate shelter the wind is reduced to about one-third of its force on the windward side. A thin screen of trees 40 feet tall reduces wind velocity by about a third at a distance of 300 feet on the leeward side.

Slopes

Slopes, except unprotected grades open to the south, are nearly always better than perfectly flat land, if a choice is available. Rhododendrons like good drainage of both air and water. The sheltered hollow is too often a frost pocket into which cold air descends, as it always does, in its movement from high ground to low. It is exactly like a liquid in this respect. As it flows downhill over irregular terrain it will fill up little valleys and depressions like water in pools, and then continue on downward. The coldest air is the heaviest and it moves ceaselessly for the lowest level.

Rhododendrons growing in a frost pocket are severely penalized. Their flowers or their spring growth may be ruined and they are likely to be much less hardy than they would be in a situation with good air drainage. North slopes are especially desirable as planting sites because they receive the sun's rays at an angle and are much cooler in summer than grades which drop in other directions.

Slopes usually imply good water drainage too, which is an absolute necessity. Rhododendrons are given lots of humus to lighten the soil and increase its porosity. This is done because the roots of Rhododendrons have an exceptionally high requirement for good aeration. But air may also be excluded from the root zone by water, and with poor drainage the plants suffer severely. Rhododendrons whose roots are immersed in water for forty-eight hours are certain to die. If standing water deprives the roots of air even for twenty-four hours, there will be many casualties and the survivors will be badly injured. A planting site can be tested by digging a flat-bottomed hole and putting two inches of water in it. If the water has drained away within 6 or 8 hours, the site should be satisfactory. If it has not, drainage tiles must be used to carry away the excess water, or a well can be dug at a lower level and filled with coarse rocks into which the surplus water can be directed. In many gardens with poor drainage, Rhododendrons are actually grown in elevated beds on top of the ground.

Woodlands

The ideal site, particularly for a collection of Rhododendrons, is an open woodland, and if the trees are Pines or Oaks, or a mixture of them, the gardener can ask for no more. Almost any untouched natural stand will require a good deal of thinning and this should, of course, be studied carefully so that it will not be necessary to cut down additional trees years later when their fall will be a major hazard to the Rhododendrons. Paths should be planned along which visitors can stroll to come unexpectedly upon the delightful surprises which await them.

The natural inclination is to leave too many trees. A solid canopy of overhead foliage casts too much shade, so the tops of the trees should not interlace. Each should stand free of its neighbors, with open sky between them which varies in amount from a few feet to rather large exposed areas. Thus is provided a variety of planting sites into which a wide range of Rhododendrons can be placed according to the amounts of sunlight which they prefer.

In planting the Rhododendrons, it is desirable not to place them right up against the tree trunks. Most of them will grow better if they are out some distance, even clear of the foliage overhead, where they will receive the benefit of light rains and will be spared the competition for moisture which even the most deep-rooted trees provide, to some extent. The amount of exposure will vary with the height of the trees, depending on the distance of the aerial roof overhead. Rhododendrons grow very well beneath great old Oaks whose lowest branches are far above them. Both the amount of natural light and of direct sunlight entering from the sides are much greater there than would be the case for plants growing beneath younger trees whose denser heads are closer than 15 feet to the ground. Then the rule should be to place the Rhododendrons clear of any overhead branches. A more extended discussion of Rhododendrons in the woodland garden and of the best sorts to use for many other such specialized purposes, appears in Chapter II.

Perfectionists Only

The urge for perfection from which plant specialists suffer encourages near-sighted concentration on refinements so small as to be imperceptible to those who are unaccountably interested only in a nice big bunch of flowers on presentable shrubs. The fact is, of course, that Rhododendrons want to grow, they want to be vigorous and handsome, and they want to flower with abandon. And they generally do. Those who wish to try the difficult sorts, and gardeners who expect the finest performances of which their plants are capable will be concerned with the finer points of placement in the garden. But the average home owner need not fret about an extra hour or two of sunlight, or a planting site which falls short of the ideal, even by a rather wide margin. Nearly every garden has at least one spot where Rhododendrons will thrive, and there are a variety of situations in most.

Summary

In summary of this discussion of planting sites, extended to resolve the uncertainty of so many gardeners on the subject, the important points can be condensed to a few simple statements:

Rhododendrons need at their planting site:

(1) Acid soil;
(2) Some shade and shelter, the amount depending on the sorts of Rhododendrons and the climate, to:
  (*a*) increase atmospheric humidity,
  (*b*) moderate high temperatures,
  (*c*) minimize winds,
  (*d*) temper frosts.

CHAPTER IV

Planting and Caring for Rhododendrons

RHODODENDRONS cannot be planted with the same ease as they transplant. They can be readily moved from one place to another at any time when they are not in active growth or the ground is not frozen, but this accommodating trait does not mean that they are equally casual about the character of the soil in which they will grow, and how they are planted in it. Many an unwary gardener has learned to his sorrow and expense that their genial tolerance about transplanting ends abruptly if they are put into heavy clay or thin sand or alkaline soil.

Of all the aspects concerned with the culture of Rhododendrons, correct planting is the most important. The site can be poorly chosen, the sunlight excessive, the soil moisture inadequate, and they will still delight the eye for generations if they can compensate below ground for the deficiencies which they encounter above it. A job of planting properly done means much less after care for a long, long time. The difference is so great that the lazy man will plant Rhododendrons with meticulous propriety in simple self-defence against any future demands on his energy.

Only at planting time can the soil be modified properly to meet the requirements of Rhododendrons. No later treatment, no surface amendment can afterward restore to healthful vigor the specimens grown lean and scrawny for lack of the right groundwork at the time they were planted. The gardener cheats only himself who tries to counterfeit a good job of soil preparation and planting. On them depend the life of the plants, their matchless beauty, and the pleasure to be received from their culture for many decades. There can be few such chores as planting a Rhododendron where a reasonable amount of thought, care and effort will so handsomely be repaid year after year in the coin of enduring satisfaction.

A Rhododendron should be transplanted within the garden by digging it so that a ball of earth protects its roots. The amount of soil depends on the dimensions of the plant. A specimen about 2 feet tall should have an earth ball about 12 or 15 inches in diameter, held together by burlap securely tied around it so that it can be safely moved from one place to another with the least possible injury to its root system. Soil which is excessively dry is hard to handle because it crumbles easily. That which is saturated falls away from the roots. But a plant with its cells plump with moisture is safer to move and easier to establish in another location, so it is a good idea to water moderately any specimen the day before it is to be transplanted.

Plants purchased from a nursery should always arrive with a good firm ball of moist earth wrapped in burlap to protect the delicate root-ends. If they are not so received, the buyer had better return the stock and transfer his patronage elsewhere. Plants supplied with peat at the roots are much harder to establish in the garden and they are so often newly imported from abroad that it is good policy to avoid them. Rhododendron roots are naturally fibrous and close to the surface. This finely divided root system holds the soil well and it is possible to dig a specimen with almost every root intact. Even large old plants can be moved readily.

PREPARATION OF THE PLANTS

If it is not possible to plant Rhododendrons promptly after they are delivered they should be well watered and set in a place which is completely shaded; or if they are not to be planted in their permanent positions for several days it will be better to heel them temporarily in the earth in a sheltered spot. The tender roots which lie just beneath the surface of the earth ball are easily injured by drying and it does not take long for the burlap and the soil just beneath it to lose moisture to a damaging extent.

When a Rhododendron is brought to the planting site the burlap should be removed before putting the plant into the ground. The perimeter of the earth ball is then carefully combed away until about an inch of the root ends is exposed without damaging them, or the soil on the outside of the ball can be washed away with a garden hose until the terminal roots are free of earth for an inch or two. The specimen is then planted immediately. If the root-ends are exposed in this manner they will almost certainly extend into the soil surrounding them at their new site. Too often Rhododendrons languish and eventually succumb because their roots are reluctant to leave the acidity and texture of the soil to which they have become accustomed. They never venture beyond the earth ball and the time comes sooner or later when they cannot obtain in such a small volume enough food and moisture to support the top growth.

root ends exposed ready for planting

PREPARATION OF THE SITE

Soil Acidity

It is not safe to assume that the soil is suitably acid for Rhododendrons even in districts where it is naturally so, if the planting site has been under cultivation or if the original topsoil has been covered or deeply disturbed by the addition of subsoil from foundations and similar excavation. At one time, the site may have been limed for lilacs, for example, or it may have been treated to make it suitable for a bluegrass lawn, or to grow the vegetables which thrive best in neutral soil. Rain water which courses down across the mortar and masonry of a house foundation may cause a gradual loss of soil acidity nearby as it seeps into the soil. Many Rhododendrons have failed in foundation plantings for this reason, which would have been great sources of satisfaction to their owners elsewhere in the garden. Water from municipal mains is often artificially stabilized at a neutral pH 7·0, or it may be alkaline, and it can cause a slow deterioration of soil acidity when it is used for irrigation during drouths over a period of time. A good many of the popular chemical fertilizers not specifically formulated for acid-soil plants leave an alkaline residue which in its cumulative effect is inimical to Rhododendrons.

There is a variety of quick and easy methods advertised in gardening publications for making soil acidity tests at home, or they will be made, usually without charge, by local county agricultural extension agents of the state universities. Rhododendrons usually thrive in any degree of acidity between pH 4·0 and pH 5·5. It is worth while to make a soil test or to have one made to confirm that the proposed planting site is sufficiently acid. The results are often an unexpected revelation, but acidity which has been lost can be quickly and conveniently restored by applying Copperas (ferrous sulphate) to the soil in the amounts recommended in the table on page 281.

Even in undisturbed soil there are local

scattered districts in which the soil acidity may vary greatly from that of the surrounding countryside. However, if members of the Heath family, such as Mountain Laurel (*Kalmia*), Huckleberries (*Gaylussacia*), Blueberries and native Cranberries (*Vaccinium*) grow naturally in the immediate vicinity of the proposed planting site, it can be assumed that the soil is suitably acid. The creeping Bearberry (*Arctostaphylos*) and Wintergreen (*Gaultheria*) are good acidity indicators.

Soil Texture

A thoughtful look at a Rhododendron in all of its parts should indicate the sort of conditions at the roots which will make it thrive. The evergreen leaves are outlets through which moisture escapes to the atmosphere day and night, winter and summer, endlessly imposing a burden of replenishment. Their task will be much harder if they are planted in a light sandy soil which dries out quickly so that the plants are constantly struggling for the moisture they need to survive. Furthermore, the most familiar Rhododendrons have large, thick heavy leaves and ripen such great quantities of seeds that they are one of the marvels of the plant kingdom. No plant which is keyed to such prodigious effort will be happy in thin, depleted soil of a sandy nature from which soluble plant food leaches quickly. Rhododendrons need the good earth, rich in food and abundantly fortified with the means to support their massive growth and flower production.

The terminal roots of Rhododendrons are so fine and delicate that a moment's reflection will convince even the most casual gardener of their inability to penetrate thick, heavy clay. Yet it is frequently their unhappy lot to be given a site with soil so stiff and dense that they can do no more than subsist miserably on the resources within their original earth ball before they finally succumb.

The ideal soil for Rhododendrons is a medium loam, acid of course, but rich and deep. It is better on the heavy side than too light and sandy. This describes the fortunate condition which exists in innumerable gardens. All that need be done to prepare it for Rhododendrons is to spread about 4 inches of coarse fibrous European peat moss on the surface of the ground and then mix it thoroughly into the top 12 inches, preferably by churning the earth with a power tiller. If a number are to be planted, it is generally easier and better to prepare a whole bed in this manner than to spade in organic matter at each spot where a Rhododendron is to be placed.

All sorts of vegetable debris can be used to provide the soil aeration and moisture retention which Rhododendron roots demand. Coarse sawdust from a forest sawmill, hardwood leaf mold, rotted wood, shredded corn cobs, bagasse, spent hops, compost, peanut hulls, old cow manure, and many other such materials have been used. However, any which are in the process of decay are likely to cause problems of balancing nitrogen depletion, and it scarcely seems worth while to cope with them for the average home owner with only a few Rhododendrons to plant. Fresh plant by-products cause a decrease in available soil nitrogen which is very rapid. When they are mixed into the soil to the extent of 10 per cent by volume, shredded corn cobs, for example, reduce the nitrates in seven days by 57 per cent. As an amendment constituting 20 per cent of the soil volume the reduction is 75 per cent. In three weeks the nitrates can be restored to their original level from the 57 per cent loss by applying 1½ pounds of ammonium sulphate per 100 square feet.

Peat moss remains first and foremost the most popular material to fit the soil for Rhododendrons, and commercial growers would not buy it in such enormous quantities if there were a more economical substitute of equal effectiveness. For outdoor use, coarse, fibrous imported peat moss is much better and longer lasting than the domestic products which are so much finer in texture. The principal difference between peat moss and most substitutes readily available is that it has already undergone the process of decay into humus.

Sawdust

Theoretically, it should be possible to balance the temporary withdrawal of nitrogen which occurs in the process of vegetative decay of sawdust and similar raw waste products in the soil, but actually it is far from simple. I have experimented extensively with sawdust and I have watched with equal interest the efforts of commercial nurserymen to use this material effectively as an economical source of humus in the growing of Rhododendrons. There are precise directions available which give the exact quantities of ammonium sulphate to be used as a nitrogen supplement for each pound or inch of sawdust layer incorporated into 100 square feet of earth.

But sawdust from forest sawmills ranges from very old and thoroughly rotted to fresh, and the intermediate stages are often hard to estimate in their degree of decay. Yet its age determines how much nitrogen to use. Further, while some sorts of sawdust decay rather rapidly the next delivery may come from another site and be predominantly from a wood which rots slowly. There is no formula for applying nitrogen which allows for such variation. Even the best calculation may be upset by the weather. If it should turn unseasonably warm for an extended period, the decay accelerates and then protracted rains may leach the nitrogen from the soil. Nitrogen chlorosis appears and the grower makes a second application of ammonium sulphate in midsummer to correct it. Should the weather then turn cool and dry, there is an excellent chance that there will be a surplus of nitrogen in the soil which will be quick to stimulate unseasonable late growth when the fall rains arrive. The plants, not ripened for the onset of cold weather, suffer severely, split their bark, and are often killed when winter arrives.

I think sawdust can be more successfully used solely as a mulch, but if it is used that way after it has already served to modify the texture of the soil there is a further problem of management. When the mulch is renewed in the spring, nitrogen must be added to compensate. At the same time, a further supplement must be provided to balance the withdrawal which takes place during the second year of decay for the sawdust mixed in the soil. The amount required to restore the nitrogen balance in the soil depends on how rapidly decay has progressed the first year. When the mulch is added as a further consideration, the calculations deteriorate into the realm of guesses. If any transplanting is done, additional sawdust from the mulch inadvertently gets mixed into the soil so the nitrogen balance is upset at that spot.

Sawdust piles are sometimes havens for grubs which are ruinous to young Rhododendrons, quickly girdling them. And some sorts of sawdust are light enough in color so that they reflect the sun's rays in exposed positions to an extent which burns very young plants.

Perhaps the worst hazard in the use of sawdust is the suspicious frequency of Rhododendron Wilt (*Phytophthera cinnamomi*) following its incorporation into the soil to supply humus. Time and again this devastating disease has appeared in Rhododendron fields where sawdust has been used to improve the texture. The coincidence would make a useful study in the plant pathology department of one of our state universities. Such a study might also include an investigation of the effect of White Pine (*Pinus strobus*) sawdust on Rhododendrons. A number of nurserymen have commented to me that it has an injurious result, unrelated to nitrogen deficiency, which is not shared by other sorts of sawdust.

I have observed with interest that a number of experienced and highly skilled commercial growers in the East have abandoned sawdust as a soil amendment after having experimented extensively with it for Rhododendron fields, and in my personal experience I have found the problems of nitrogen withdrawal extremely difficult to solve. Sometimes I have succeeded in restoring the proper balance and sometimes not, but I feel that the risk of failure is great enough, and the penalty heavy enough, so that sawdust had better be reserved for commercial growers who can incorporate it into the soil and then let it decay undisturbed for a year or two before Rhododendrons are grown on the land. Other waste vegetative by-products which are not already rotted offer the same problems in lesser degree. It is much easier to use them for surface mulches than as a means of improving soil texture.

The use of coarse sawdust in the Pacific Northwest is widespread and there are few reports from that area of injurious results. Apparently the climate or the sorts of trees sawed into rough lumber by the forest mills make its use there much safer.

Fitting Sandy Soils for Rhododendrons

Light, sandy soils are not suitable for growing Rhododendrons because they dry out so quickly that they are deficient in moisture most of the time, and dissolved plant foods drain away with the water which passes through their granular texture so rapidly. However, sandy soils can be modified for growing Rhododendrons without too much trouble. The extent of the treatment is determined by just how much sand there is in the natural soil. In some coastal regions the garden soils approach pure sand.

Where sand strongly predominates and the soil is extremely light and quick to drain, the best plan is to remove 8 inches from the surface of the area where the Rhododendrons are to be planted and lay this soil aside. Four inches of organic material are then spread over the bottom of the excavation and mixed into the foot of sandy soil directly underneath. Then a 4-inch layer of the soil previously set aside is put back into the excavation, bringing it to natural ground level or a little above it. Finally, the area is topped with another 4 inches of peat or vegetable matter which is then thoroughly mixed with 10 inches of the prepared soil beneath it. The surplus sandy topsoil remaining unused from the excavation is discarded. This method leaves the area to be planted with Rhododendrons several inches above grade level, which carries no penalty in any district and is desirable in the extremely flat regions where sandy soils usually predominate.

If a number of Rhododendrons are to be planted in a bed the preparation can be done most quickly and easily with a mechanical power tiller. If only one Rhododendron is to be planted, the ground can be prepared in this fashion with a hand spade over a circular area 36 inches in diameter.

It is my conviction that there is more latitude in the use of various organic materials in sandy soil without the unpleasant consequences which occasionally accompany some forms of undecayed vegetable matter in other types of soil. Coarse imported peat is always first choice, anywhere, but woods mold is almost as good if it comes from beneath hardwood trees or conifers, or from wild districts in which acid soil plants are conspicuous. No attempt should be made to screen this coarse black top layer, which is composed of partially rotted leaves, twigs, bits of bark and surface roots mixed with the soil. The rotten bark and wood of Hemlocks make fine humus-forming materials. Acid muck from fresh-water streams and swamps can often be used to good advantage. Pine needles and old cow manure are useful and desirable. And of course waste products such as peanut hulls, ground corn cobs, bagasse and sawdust are useful if they are already rotted. The gardener must be prepared to cope with the problem of nitrogen balance mentioned earlier if these waste materials are used fresh in any appreciable quantities. But a mixture of all sorts of vegetable debris and humus forming organic matter can usually be used to fortify sandy soils.

In the San Francisco district and northward along the California coast an esteemed soil mixture for planting Rhododendrons is made of equal parts of Pine or Redwood needles, peat, aged wood shavings, loam and sand. Many expert gardeners there prefer slightly elevated beds containing nothing but Pine needles which have previously been stored in piles to decompose for a year.

Fitting Heavy Soils for Rhododendrons

Gardens which are afflicted with dense clay soil require the greatest preparation but this is no cause for discouragement. There are probably more large and famous collections of Rhododendrons growing on soil too heavy to suit them naturally than on any other type.

Rhododendrons suffocate when they are planted in thick clay. It is one of their basic requirements that the soil be porous, with an open, loose texture which encourages the circulation of air through it. Clay is too dense to admit air. It becomes sticky and greasy and even more impenetrable when it is wet. When it is dry it bakes hard and its stony toughness precludes any possibility of ventilation.

Heavy clay is the least suitable of all soil types for Rhododendrons. Not only do roots slowly smother when they are covered by it, but they are physically unable to penetrate it. The terminal feeder roots of Rhododendrons are so thin and delicate that they cannot grow into the unyielding density of heavy clay. It is a common occurrence to find plants still entirely dependent on the earth ball in which they came from the nursery, several years after they have been planted in clay. The roots do not even attempt to force their way into such an alien medium, and such plants slowly starve to death.

Clays vary in their density, depth and where they occur in the topsoil, and the amount of treatment they require to make them suitable for Rhododendrons depends on how compact they are and how much of the clay lies in the root zone. Frequently there is a thin layer of topsoil above several feet of the thick, stiff clay which Rhododendrons abhor. There are two ways of meeting such an extreme condition.

To prepare for each specimen individually, one method is to take off the topsoil, lay it to one side, and excavate a planting hole about 30 inches in diameter and 20 inches deep to accommodate the plant of usual size purchased from a nursery. The clay which is removed is discarded and the bottom of the excavation is loosened and broken up to a depth of several inches. The topsoil previously removed is then spread over the bottom of the hole and, if the site is not in a cultivated area, additional topsoil fill is obtained from a circle extending out 3 or 4 feet in all directions from the excavation. Finally, a prepared mixture of 40 per cent topsoil, 40 per cent peat or other organic matter, and 20 per cent sand is used to fill the remainder of the hole and bring it up to 2 or 3 inches above grade level. A heavy leaf mulch is thereafter maintained over the entire area, including that which has been stripped of topsoil.

Often there will be enough topsoil taken from the planting hole and from the surface of the ground nearby to backfill the excavation to within about 4 inches of ground level. If 4 inches of coarse peat and 2 inches of sand are then added and the three layers thoroughly mixed to a depth of a foot, a good deal of labor can thereby be saved. Should the clay extend to the surface of the ground or if good acid topsoil is not available in the immediate vicinity of the planting site, the only alternative is to fill the excavation entirely with a soil mixture prepared elsewhere and brought in for the purpose. I believe it is better to prepare a planting site individually in this manner for each specimen, even when there are a number of Rhododendrons to be planted together in a group.

For less extreme conditions and in cases where considerable numbers of Rhododendrons are to be planted in sizable beds, it is usually possible to lay aside any topsoil and excavate to a depth of 6 inches. The clay which is removed is discarded, and the bottom of the excavation is then churned to a depth of 10 or 12 inches with a power tiller. Any topsoil which was saved is then spread over the bottom. Four inches of peat moss and 2 inches of sand are put on top of it and the bed is churned once again until its texture is uniform. Krilium soil conditioner, 5 pounds to a 100 square feet, can be substituted for the sand. Or, if the conditions are extreme, it can be used in addition to it.

FUNCTION OF THE MULCH

Even though clay soil has been modified to make it suitable, a mulch is especially important to Rhododendrons which are growing in it. Coarse imported European peat lasts about eight to ten years in the ground. By the end of that time it will be pretty well exhausted and the only enduring improvement will be the increased aeration which remains and the better texture created by the sand. Leaf mold is completely consumed by earthworms within a year, though the fibrous roots and coarser material in it may last somewhat longer. A mulch of hard-wood leaves which is renewed each autumn to a depth of 8 inches, or 2 inches of Pine needles, gradually decays and over a period of years accumulates as a layer of nutritious humus into which the Rhododendron roots extend more and more as the humus within the ground is gradually dissipated. I have observed that Rhododendrons in gardens with clay soil often start to deteriorate at the end of about eight years even after they have been properly planted, and this is the reason: they were not faithfully mulched each year and there was no accumulating reserve of humus on top of the ground to sustain the roots when the supply beneath it finally became exhausted.

Aged needles of coniferous trees are especially beneficial in improving the porosity of clay soil, or as a surface mulch. Almost all gardeners have had occasion at one time or another to observe the mealy, granulated texture of the soil beneath Pine trees, for example. The earth is made loose and porous by the beneficent leaching from the Pine needles which cover it. They can perform the same service as an ingredient of soil mixtures for Rhododendrons or as a blanket over the ground.

WOODLAND AND FAVORED SITES

Where large numbers of Rhododendrons are to be planted in a woodland, or on other wild land, it is quite satisfactory to blast out the planting holes with dynamite. They can be backfilled with leaves, twigs, topsoil, and leaf mold scraped from the forest floor near by. When tree stumps are blasted out, the holes which remain are often perfectly suited as planting sites for Rhododendrons.

Specialists are wryly asked if there are ever any gardens where no soil preparation is required to plant Rhododendrons. And there are, a few. Scattered throughout the coastal regions of New England and probably elsewhere, are drained peat bogs on which Rhododendrons will grow to perfection merely by spading out the soil to plant them and thereafter supplying fertilizer occasionally.

SUBSIDENCE, DRAINAGE AND PLANTING DEPTH

There is always some settling of prepared soil mixtures which have been substituted for unsuitable soil and the level at which Rhododendrons are planted may recede to their disadvantage. At a newly prepared site the soil and the plants should be elevated 2 or 3 inches above the permanent level which is planned for them so they will then gradually subside to it. Occasionally the capillarity by which water is conducted into the prepared soil mixture from the bottom and sides of the excavation is restored slowly and Rhododendrons suffer from dryness at their roots during the first summer even when the surface of the soil is superficially moist. At lower levels the roots extract all of the available moisture in the soil mixture and it is not replaced by conduction from the surrounding earth. Breaking up the subsoil at the bottom of the excavation helps in the later restoration of capillarity as the prepared mixture mingles and fuses with it, but an alert gardener will use the watering hose according to the distress of the plants and not be deceived by soil which may be moist only on the surface above the roots of newly planted Rhododendrons. Both inconveniences can be eliminated by completing the preparations well in advance of the planting so the soil mixture has settled and capillarity has been reestablished before the plants are put into the ground.

When the preparation is so important to provide good aeration of the soil it is obvious that good drainage goes hand in hand with it, since air is excluded as water accumulates in the earth. Rhododendrons are certain to die or be severely injured if their roots are submerged even for twenty-four hours by standing water which fails to drain out of their planting holes. Drainage problems and how to solve them should be considered before the planting site is selected and this matter is discussed in the preceding chapter.

Though it is of more interest to specialists than to casual gardeners, there are unusual circumstances where poor drainage and good aeration exist together. I have observed in the wild at various times that *R. maximum* grows beside ponds where the soil several inches beneath the surface is completely and permanently saturated with water to the total exclusion of air. The 3 inches or so of surface soil above water level is invariably of a loose, airy texture, but the lesson to be learned from this extraordinary situation comes from an examination of the roots. They fan out far and wide but always entirely in the thin layer of porous leaf mold above the waterlogged soil, and it is impossible to find any roots penetrating down into the saturated earth beneath. By contrast, wild Rhododendrons growing on drained peat bogs extend their roots deeply, 3 feet or more beneath the ground.

It is true that Rhododendrons are by nature surface-rooting and in the damp mildness of the climate where most of them grow in the wild there is little need for their roots to forage far down in search of moisture. It is a mistake to assume that deep preparation of the soil is wasted on Rhododendrons, yet that is a statement which is often seen in print. The fact is that Rhododendron roots will grow into the earth just as deeply as they can find congenial soil, and the depth of the soil preparation makes a tremendous difference in the performance of the plants in time of drouth. Roots will seek moisture far beneath the surface if their passage is made easy, and the resources on which they can draw there will support the top growth without irrigation in the worst of drouths. The lazy gardener who wants to plant Rhododendrons and then forget them except for the annual mulch renewal, will take the trouble to prepare the soil deeply. After having transplanted a good many Rhododendrons of all sizes I can confidently offer the observation that I have never yet seen a case where the roots had failed to exploit fully every bit of suitable soil which lay within their range.

Rhododendrons should be planted at exactly the same depth as they last grew. If they are planted too deep they will either smother or simply languish until they have generated an entirely new mat of surface roots just beneath ground level. Apparently there must be a certain minimum number of roots at the surface of the soil before others can function effectively at deeper levels. Too often gardeners will try to mask the ungainly appearance of a poor, leggy specimen by planting it a good deal deeper than it stood in the nursery. They seldom do it more than once.

It is not advisable to tramp the soil around the ball of earth when planting a Rhododendron. That is quite likely to injure the tender roots, and to make the earth so compact that its aeration is impaired. The soil should be worked around the bottom and sides of the earth ball and through the protruding roots extending from it, firming it gently with the hand as the soil mixture is filled in. After the excavation is full the plant is settled in its new location with a good watering from the hose.

The soil should never be mounded up around the trunk of a Rhododendron. In most climates the reverse is desirable and the saucer-shaped

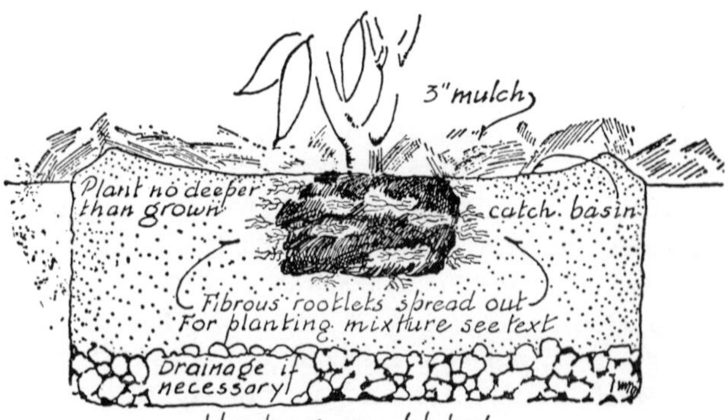

planting completed

depression serves as a catch-basin for rain and as a convenient receptacle which holds an inch or so of water from the hose until it soaks into the soil. In very severe climates I think the soil level where a Rhododendron is planted should be just even with the surrounding grade. At the time of the spring thaw it often rains heavily when the ground is still deeply frozen and then water is held in the shallow depression at the base of the plant. The standing water may then freeze overnight with the arrival of a cold snap, and possibly thaw and freeze once or twice again before it soaks away or evaporates. I have observed a number of instances where Rhododendrons in a severe climate were injured or killed in this manner.

SPACING

There are two ways of thinking about the spacing of Rhododendrons. Some gardeners like concentrated colorful effects immediately, regardless of labor or inconvenience. For them the most desirable method is to space the plants at half distance and then transplant alternate specimens elsewhere when their branches interlace and the crowding becomes injurious. Or other sorts of plants can be intermixed for quick effects and then later removed when the Rhododendrons reach dimensions which require additional space.

Where extensive soil preparation is necessary no plan is welcome which requires really extensive labor for short-term effect, and some arbitrary compromise in spacing is required. I think that the familiar, robust-growing, broad-leaved Rhododendron hybrids should be spaced about 9 feet apart. This does not provide the spacious quarters required by magnificent old specimens fifty years of age but it is a practical distance which is useful for a long, long time. With this much room, a planting of commercial Rhododendron hybrids remains in good condition even after the branches have been grown together for many years into a solid mass of foliage. Eventually, of course, even such generous spacing will be totally inadequate for these long-lived patriarchs. There are many ancient Rhododendrons in the Philadelphia district and in the region around New York and Long Island which are 15 to 20 feet in diameter and almost as tall. Any planting distance less than 20 feet apart is therefore a compromise between a practical spacing which will be attractive for many years and the ultimate needs of the plants two or three human generations hence.

A spacing of 9 feet applies only to the popular, strong-growing commercial hybrids. Those of more restrained growth are naturally planted closer together, and the giants need a great deal more room. Some of the alpines want only a few inches, other dwarf rock garden Rhododendrons a foot or a foot and a half. Considering the range in stature of Rhododendrons, from creeping mats which scarcely clear the earth to gigantic 80-foot trees, it is not possible to suggest in detail planting distances for such variety, but the stature of most hybrids can be estimated from their wild forebears and the dimensions of the species are given in the listing which begins on page 508. But it is clear that Rhododendrons are by nature gregarious and they thrive especially in the company of one another. A group of Rhododendrons will almost invariably outstrip in health and vigor of growth a single specimen planted near by. Communal by habit in the wild, they give to one another a beneficent mutual protection in the garden.

MULCHES

The earth where Rhododendrons grow in the garden should never be cultivated. The delicate roots so close to the surface of the ground are certain to be injured by a hoe or any other tool which cuts into the top of the soil. Should weeds appear, they are pulled by hand. Cultivation would disturb the mulch which is so beneficial to the welfare of the plants.

But weeds are seldom troublesome because Rhododendrons should invariably be grown with a mulch on the soil, a practice which is beneficial to them in a variety of ways. Not only does it reduce maintenance by eliminating the need for tilling the soil but it also saves a great deal of labor in time of drouth by conserving the natural moisture in the soil so that watering is greatly reduced. Tests with ground corn cobs at Michigan State College showed that surface mulches were far more effective in retaining soil moisture than mixing the material into the earth. A mulch helps to keep the earth cool in imitation of the damp chill to which most Rhododendrons are accustomed in the wild. It helps to preserve the loose, airy texture at the roots by absorbing the force of pounding rains and other natural agencies which tend to compact the soil. Water penetrates more easily into the earth so there is less run-off of rain water. And a mulch is an invaluable source of humus to the plants as it slowly decays and is renewed each year.

The insulating effect of a mulch is not the least of its virtues. The wide fluctuations in soil temperature so foreign to the natural preference of Rhododendrons are moderated under a mulch by about 50 per cent in a twenty-four-hour period. In summer the temperature of the soil is reduced by 5 or 6 degrees. In winter the earth freezes later in the season and less deeply beneath its protective covering. The plants are thereby enabled to replenish water through the roots which is transpired through the leaves. Some mulches tend to maintain the acidity of the soil, and most of them encourage the favorable activity of the invisible organisms which teem in the earth. In severe climates where even the hardiest of Rhododendrons are close to the limit of cold endurance a heavy mulch of leaves banked up around the trunks of larger Rhododendrons for a foot and a half or more will prevent the bark from splitting where it is most vulnerable near ground level. Such an extremely heavy mulch must be partially removed the following spring. It should not cover the leaves on the lower branches at any time.

Even mulches can be harmful if used indiscreetly by enthusiastic gardeners who subscribe to the notion that a recommended quantity will be twice as beneficial if twice the amount is used. The thickness of the mulch depends on the size of the plants and the nature of the mulching material. The frequent mention of the importance of aeration at the roots of Rhododendrons applies as well to any surface blanket which would deny access of air to the earth beneath it. The same amount of mulch which would be adequate for big old Rhododendrons would be a smothering blanket for small plants 12 inches tall. An inch and a half of peat moss or Pine needles are about right for a plant that size, whereas large old specimens will revel in a foot or a foot and a half of leaves. Twelve to 16 inches of Oak leaves applied in the fall will be reduced over winter to about 6 inches by spring, and this points up the adjustment of the mulch depth to the density of the material and how rapidly it decomposes. Loose, fluffy mulches can be thicker than those which are more compact. Sawdust decays slowly and 2 inches of it beneath plants which are 2 or 3 feet tall is quite enough. Maple leaves mat down quickly to form a suffocating blanket if they are used to excess. Coarse peat moss is so light in texture that 3 inches of it can be used beneath plants which are a couple of feet high. The same is true of Pine needles.

The light materials which are loose and porous always have been first choice for Rhododendron mulches and of these Oak leaves and Pine needles are unsurpassed. Coarse peat is third choice only because it tends to form a dry crust in summer which resists the penetration of rainwater, so it is therefore better used in a mixture with other organic matter or with a thin layer of other material on top of it. Hardwood leaves are generally preferred before those from trees with soft wood, but the latter can be used with complete satisfaction in moderate amounts if the soil is normally acid even though they do go through a temporary alkaline phase in their rapid decomposition. Leaves from trees growing on alkaline soil are undesirable. Coarse sawdust, of course, has been widely used and with generally better results than as a soil amendment. Then there is a long list of additional materials which make successful mulches. Wood chips, chopped tree bark, Oak and Cedar tow, rotted wood, excelsior, spent tanbark, grain straw, hay, salt hay, bracken, aged cow manure and acid sewage sludge are esteemed in varying degree by their users. Quite a number of good mulching materials are regional agricultural by-products in various parts of the country. Tobacco stems, pea pods, cotton seed hulls, tung nut and apple pomace, peanut hulls, bagasse, ground corn cobs, spent hops and many others may be available for local use at little or no cost. Of all the mulches which I have tried the only one I did not like and would not use again was buckwheat hulls. They are easily wind blown and decay so reluctantly and produce so little humus that I thought them unsuitable.

The natural time to apply mulches is in the fall and it is also the best time if the materials to be used are available then. Organic matter eventually decays into humus, goes into neutral solution and is carried out of the topsoil with the passage of water through it. Very little remains, so it is necessary to renew mulches each year. So replenished, the acidity of the soil is maintained and a layer of humus accumulates faster than it dissolves into neutral solution. Through the years this gradually increasing blanket of decayed vegetation affords a luxurious environment for the roots, and they are quick to take advantage of it to the enormous benefit of the health and beauty of the Rhododendrons.

Mulches vary widely in the amount of plant food they contain. A few, such as aged cow manure and acid sewage sludge, stimulate growth to the point where they must be used with caution lest too much nitrogen accumulates in the soil and the plants do not properly harden their tissues to resist cold weather. They are probably best used in conjunction with sawdust or other undecayed wood by-products. But many mulches contain amounts of plant food which are insignificant. Sawdust, for example, contains only 0·048 per cent nitrogen, 0·007 per cent phosphorus, and 0·0117 per cent potassium, even when it is fresh. In comparison with a familiar garden fertilizer which is 5–10–5, sawdust would be 0·05–0·01–0·01. The coarse imported peat moss which is favored for outdoor use is also practically without food value.

Nitrogen Withdrawal

As a matter of fact, most of the mulches of undecayed organic matter have a depressing effect on growth by withdrawing nutrients from the soil while they are in the process of decomposition. The big advantage of peat moss and of rotted vegetable materials is that they have already undergone the conversion into humus. In the course of decay into humus, sawdust, for example, loses about 80 per cent of its weight and in the process temporarily extracts nitrogen and phosphorus from the soil to an extent which may restrict the growth of the Rhododendrons it is designed to benefit. Decomposition of organic matter is accomplished by soil organisms, both bacteria and fungi, which are like plants in their need for food. When a mulch of fresh vegetable material is placed on the ground their activity quickens and they enter into competition with the Rhododendrons for the accumulated nitrogen reserves in the soil. As they proceed with their work of reducing the mulch to humus they win out over the plants in the struggle for nitrogen, especially in infertile soils, and the result may be a temporary reduction in growth and yellow discoloration of the Rhododendron foliage. The reduction of nitrate in the soil is rapid after the application of fresh organic matter as a surface mulch, and the extent of the reduction depends on how thickly the material is applied. A 2-inch mulch of ground corn cobs reduces soil nitrate by 72 per cent within a week after it is put in place. A 4-inch layer on top of the soil causes a reduction of 76 per cent. At the same time, the acidity is temporarily reduced by about one-half a pH unit.

I have never known a leaf mulch to cause nitrogen depletion with visible results, and most of the undecayed materials are usually used on soil which is fertile enough to provide sufficient nitrogen for their decomposition without adversely affecting plant growth to any important extent. Should the symptoms appear, they are corrected by applying ammonium sulphate, 5 ounces per estimated bushel of surface mulch, to restore the nitrogen balance.

A mulch of sawdust does not often cause trouble on a fertile soil if there is regular, routine spring fertilizing with one of the commercial formulae made especially for acid soil plants. But sawdust, wood chips, and chopped bark are much more likely to require a nitrogen supplement than the other materials and their low cost justifies a little added attention. It is advisable to apply half a pound of ammonium sulphate on top of each bushel of sawdust used as a mulch, which is equivalent to 13 pounds per cubic yard, 3,000 pounds per 2-inch layer per acre. This is a routine measure for commercial growers and the home gardener might well follow suit to forestall any untoward effects from the use of this material as a mulch.

Old, rotted sawdust and other organic materials, which have already undergone the process of decay in whole or in large part, do not present any problem of nitrogen depletion and they are always to be preferred for mulching if they are available. After decomposition, the humus residue which remains is composed of about 50 per cent carbon and the chemical combination of lignin and amino acids. The lignin comes from the mature cell walls of plant sand is the most decay-resistant constituent of them. Moist, cool conditions favor humus formation. Hot dry conditions do not.

Effect on Acidity

Mulches may themselves vary widely in acidity, but their permanent effect on the soil is generally inconsequential to Rhododendrons, which respond slowly to changes in soil acidity. Most organic materials decay rapidly. If they go through a temporary phase which is alkaline, it is usually so brief that it can be disregarded under normally acid conditions unless the soil is already so low in acidity as to be on the borderline of suitability. The alkaline phase is soon succeeded by a neutral or acid effect. Many sorts of vegetable matter, even those which are initially neutral in reaction, cause a temporary increase in soil acidity which is valuable though it eventually disappears. It is not true, for example, that sawdust and wood chips 'turn the soil sour'. They have no permanent effect whatever on acidity. Hemlock, Locust, and Elm sawdust are nearly neutral. Larch, Red and Pin Oak, White Birch, Maple, Sugar and Red Pine sawdust are moderately acid. Redwood, White and Black Oak, Spruce, and Yellow Pine produce sawdust which is strongly acid, between pH 4·0 and 5·0. And Cypress sawdust is acid in the extreme. It tests between pH 3·5 and 4·0. But all exert a temporary acidifying effect and none produces any permanent change whatever in acidity. Beech and Maple leaves from trees growing in alkaline soil will, however, deposit enough calcium from continued use as a mulch to neutralize the acidity of the soil.

An Unknown Stimulant in Sawdust

Sawdust as a mulch has a beneficial effect on the growth of ericaceous plants which has nothing to do with acidity or the familiar plant food elements. Rhododendrons treated with an extract of sawdust made by leaching it with water will produce about twice as much growth as plants given the same amount of pure water. If the extract is boiled, it has no such stimulating effect. The beneficial agent has not yet been identified, but sawdust does contain a soluble material destroyed by high temperatures, which strongly encourages growth. The experiments merely confirm a common observation which can be made wherever ericaceous plants are growing with extra vigor on the sites formerly occupied by sawdust piles near abandoned sawmills.

WATERING

Evergreen Rhododendrons are constantly losing water vapor through their leaves, day and night, the year around, and the only way it can be replaced is by absorption of water through the roots. If it is not replenished the plants soon show their distress. In winter when the temperature falls it has a drying effect on plants the colder it gets. At about 20° F. the broad evergreen leaves curl tightly inward and droop abjectly to a vertical position so that they are close to the stems. In summer Rhododendrons wilt conspicuously if they cannot obtain enough water to equalize the loss of it through their leaves, and the foliage becomes discolored if the deficiency persists. A browning of the leaves around their perimeters and along the midribs is nearly always a sign that more water in the form of vapor is going out through the foliage than can be brought in through the roots.

The requirement of Rhododendrons for water is especially high while they are in active growth. They are in themselves composed of about 55 per cent water and any increase in their stature imposes an extra burden to supply this addition to the water which is permanently retained. Only about 5 per cent of a Rhododendron is made up of the minerals which come from the soil and a prodigious amount of water must pass through the roots, up through the plant, and out through the leaves to leave a minute residue of mineral nutrients, because the food they absorb is in such exceedingly dilute solution. Water obtained from the soil and conducted upward to the foliage plays a vital part in photosynthesis, the basic process in the leaves from which the substance of the plants is formed. When transpiration is extremely active during the growing season a great deal of water is absorbed by the roots and with it the nutrients which support vigorous growth. The ability of Rhododendrons to conduct water rapidly so that their food can be obtained in adequate amounts despite its extreme dilution is the means by which they take full advantage of a very short growing season.

Rhododendrons need a great deal of water at the time they flower, too, possibly twice as much as at other times. The solid substance of the blossoms is formed in the course of the previous season and the floral buds are essentially complete for the next year by the time winter comes. With the arrival of the flowering season only water is needed to complete the process of producing their magnificent blossoms, but it must be available in quantities which would be astounding if it were measured. Fortunately nature seldom fails to provide abundant moisture in the spring, when most Rhododendrons bloom. Late blossoming sorts are almost always penalized by lack of water in the length of time their flowers remain in good condition.

But it must not be assumed that the need for water disappears with the arrival of cold weather. Evergreen leaves continue to transpire water vapor without rest and they interrupt the manufacture of food requiring water as an ingredient only when the temperature approaches 0° F. Because cold air is in itself a desiccating agent which is made all the more harmful by the blustery winds of winter, this is the season when the supply of water may well be more critical than at any other. A great deal of cold weather injury is caused, not by freezing of the tissues, but by their drying out, and experienced growers always make certain that their Rhododendrons go into the winter with abundant moisture at their roots.

The multitudes of Asian Rhododendron species which are found in the eastern Himalayas are accustomed to 100 to 200 inches of rainfall between June and October. On the Pacific Coast they receive in the three summer months 4 to 8 inches and in the northeastern United States there is a rainfall of 10 to 14 inches in this period. In Great Britain the distribution of the annual rainfall more closely approaches that to which Rhododendrons are accustomed in their Asian homeland but in most parts of the country the total for the entire year is less than half the amount they receive in four months of their native monsoon climate. It is only due to the marvelously intricate and effective system of controlling evaporation of water vapor by the hairs, scales or papillae on the leaf under-surfaces that they are able to make such heroic adaptations to a climate so different.

After they have been newly planted Rhododendrons should receive special attention for their first growing season. The soil should be kept moist by irrigation when rainfall fails to do it. In their first season the appearance of the plants is a much better indicator of water deficiency than is the surface of the ground. When special soil mixtures are used to substitute for unsuitable clay or coarse sand, it often happens that the capillarity between the mixture in the excavation and the surrounding earth is not established for a few months. Consequently the Rhododendron roots may exhaust the moisture at lower levels while the surface of the soil remains damp. The plants betray their distress by wilting and the leaves hang limply as their water content declines. Yet the bewildered gardener may withhold water because there is superficial evidence on the surface of the ground that there is sufficient moisture at lower levels.

When Rhododendrons are watered they should be given a good soaking which will moisten the soil to a depth of 18 inches at least. But once the soil is thoroughly moistened, they are only injured by additional irrigation and they should not be watered again until their supply of moisture below ground is depleted. Multitudes of Rhododendrons have been killed by overwatering in sites where the drainage has been faulty to an extent that the accumulation of water in the earth has excluded air and smothered the roots. If the soil is moist and the plants still wilt, the remedy is to spray the foliage and lightly sprinkle the ground around them in the evening with the intention, not of supplying water for root absorption, but only of increasing the atmospheric moisture. The plants respond quickly and make a surprising revival under this freshening bath. This is a useful measure to sustain newly planted Rhododendrons through exceptionally hot, prolonged dry weather. Older plants, too, relish an evening foliage spray which simulates in some small measure the frequent intermittent rainfalls of their Asian homeland, but it must never be considered a substitute for moisture needed at the roots.

It is impossible to say how often Rhododendrons should be watered. Sandy soil may contain as little as 3 per cent available water by weight whereas peat may have as much as 60 per cent of its weight in water on which the plants can draw. However, the role of organic matter as a water reservoir in the soil has been vastly over-emphasized in print. Its benefit lies much more in the improved aeration and better friability. For example, manure does not increase the amount of *available* water in the soil, despite popular belief to the contrary. It increases the amount of water retained in the ground but this increase is not available to plants so there is no benefit to them in better soil moisture. Sawdust and wood chips are only a little bit better, being intermediate in the limited range of effectiveness among organic materials. Peat moss stands at the top but even it is relatively inefficient in increasing the available moisture in heavy soils. Any organic matter benefits the dense compact soils primarily by improving their texture. However, sandy soils are always improved more than are clay soils in their capacity to retain available water when organic materials are mixed into them.

The amount of exposure at the site where the plants are growing determines how quickly the roots take moisture from the soil to replace that lost through the leaves. Sun and wind accelerate the loss. But only the most extreme conditions should make it necessary to water Rhododendrons more often than once in ten days if they are growing in soil and situation which are even approximately adapted to their needs in a congenial climate. The better the site and the soil, the less irrigation they will need.

As summer wanes Rhododendrons must harden their tissues for the cold weather ahead. Under the influence of clear, bright weather with the sun high in the sky the manufacture of food within the plant is at its peak and undesirable late season growth tends to continue if there is enough water available to support it. Without sufficient water, carbohydrates accumulate in the cells instead of going into new growth, which is exactly what is wanted. The greater the concentration, the better the cells are able to resist freezing. In normal weather and without artificial irrigation the late summer dry season halts growth and the carbohydrates are diverted in their effect to hardening the tissues for the frigid trials of winter. The gardener who upsets this natural process with excessive irrigation after the first of August is postponing the normal dormant period of his Rhododendrons by diluting with water the sugars and colloids in the cells. Freezing weather may then injure or kill them.

If newly planted Rhododendrons are properly mulched they can usually get along through any but the most extreme and prolonged drouths in late summer, but their vigor and health must not be impaired by depriving them of moisture which is urgently needed. Should their distress become acute, they must be sparingly watered, but only in the minimum amount necessary to cause a visible revival with the return of the foliage to its normal posture.

Older Rhododendrons which are not newly planted and are in good health can stand a surprising amount of drouth if they are well mulched. The foliage can furl and droop dejectedly yet the plants will resume their usual vivacity with the first natural rainfall. In my observation, much more harm is done in later winter injury by watering established plants after the first of August in cold climates than would result from normal dry weather at that time. And there are additional difficulties from excessive irrigation. Plants which should be in the process of forming flower buds divert their energy to growth under the unseasonable stimulus of abundant water supplied abruptly by the gardener. The result is a double penalty of reduced floral display and an undesirable, open, lanky extension of the branches. Sometimes this unnatural resumption of growth occurs after the flower buds have been fully formed and an occasional branch, or perhaps a tuft of foliage, grows as an extension out from the tips of the floral buds. Such buds seldom bloom and if they do, the effect is grotesque.

Unnecessary watering should be avoided too because it may result in a gradual loss of soil acidity over a period of years. Water from city mains is often standardized at neutral, pH 7·0, if it is not actually alkaline. The effect of repeatedly using such a supply is slow but insidious because it is cumulative. The alkalinity gradually builds up in the soil and the Rhododendrons as surely start to decline in health and vigor. The gardener usually reasons that he has done nothing different than in the past when he tries to account for the distressing symptoms which finally appear in the plants, and extra rations of water are often given in an effort to restore them to health. The plants may then be killed without the reason for their demise ever being realized.

An occasional watering from the city supply is not going to result quickly in the typical yellowing of the foliage which foretells lime poisoning. In regions where the soil is naturally and strongly acid many gardeners use the municipal water supply for a lifetime of watering Rhododendrons on the rather rare occasions when it is really necessary, and there are no disastrous consequences. But every specialist sees the contrary result rather frequently under less favorable circumstances. Loss of acidity due to watering from a neutral or alkaline supply is the most plausible explanation when the foliage of established Rhododendrons gradually becomes yellow without apparent cause. Gardeners alerted to the possibility can easily make a simple soil test to confirm their suspicion and apply Copperas (ferrous sulphate) in the amounts shown in the table on page 281 to restore the acidity quickly and remedy the difficulty. Shallow wells in acid soil regions usually supply acid water but deep wells should be tested. For commercial users there are devices available which acidify unsuitable water as it passes through them.

The average gardener tends to worry too much about irrigating Rhododendrons in August and September, and if water is given it is almost invariably in excessive amounts, a good deal more than is needed to restore turgidity to the tissues. With ordinary shelter from wind and sun, most older Rhododendrons will get through all but the most severe late season drouths without help from the gardener. Midday wilting need be no cause for alarm if the plants revive spontaneously in the evening, as they generally do after the heat of the day is past.

After the first killing frost it is too late in the season for growth to be stimulated by overwatering and if dry weather persists into the autumn it is not only allowable, but urgently necessary to irrigate Rhododendrons. It is a fundamental principle of their culture that they must go into the winter with the earth thoroughly moist for the cold weather trials which lie ahead, when the plants will be struggling under adverse conditions to replace the water vapor which is transpired through the leaves. In most climates nature seldom fails to provide the late autumn rains which saturate the earth. Only once in the last fifteen years has it been necessary to water the Rhododendrons in my hybridizing grounds late in the autumn, but on that occasion the plants which were watered came through an exceptionally severe winter in good condition whereas those which were beyond the convenient reach of the irrigating pipes were injured, some of them severely. In the Northeast, the time to water Rhododendrons in the fall is near Thanksgiving just before the ground freezes for the winter. If the soil is the least bit dry, they should be watered copiously then, because, after the earth is frozen, they will no longer be able to obtain moisture through their roots although they will continue to lose it through the foliage. They should be fortified for this difficult period with as much water as they can absorb.

In a group of plants so varied as Rhododendrons there are bound to be some sorts which will grow better under special conditions of culture. The little Lapponicum species, for example, are apt to thrive best in a situation which simulates the screes of their alpine homeland where there is constant and plentiful movement of water in their growing season through the coarse, quick-draining soil. Then the exotic-looking, large-leaved tree species of the Grande and Falconeri series are watered in earliest spring by melting snows from the peaks which tower above them, and later, when they unfurl their magnificent foliage their adaptation to abundant ground water and a dripping atmosphere is plainly told.

If they are to appear at their best, it is hardly practical to assemble a sizable collection of Rhododendrons in a site where water is not conveniently available. There are always the occasional cruel drouths which persist week after week beneath brazen skies, with the air so dry that eventually the plants are injured. A few specimens can be irrigated, even if it is necessary to carry the water, but a collection of Rhododendrons which is maintained for its impressive floral display needs better care. Choice plants benefit enormously from spraying the foliage occasionally in the evening with an oscillating sprinkler in dry weather, and of course a source of water near at hand is a necessity when large numbers of Rhododendrons must be irrigated in time of exceptionally severe drouth.

WINTER PROTECTION

Assuming that Rhododendrons have been given a site which offers shelter from wind and sun appropriate to their preference and the local climate, it is possible to give those of dubious hardiness additional protection which will bring them unscathed through winters which would otherwise cause their death. Most gardeners will be better served to grow sorts which are fully satisfactory without any special winter care, but specialists often take a fancy to tender sorts of rare beauty and it is surprising how much their resistance to cold can be increased by a little protection.

Essentially the aim is to give them a ventilated enclosure in which the temperature fluctuations will be more moderate than the surrounding air so that the plants will thaw slowly after they have been frozen. As plant cells freeze, they push out water into the spaces surrounding them. Then when the temperature rises again, they cannot get the water back fast enough to prevent their collapse. A shelter which slows the speed of thawing so that it does not exceed the rate at which the plant's cells can recover their lost water makes an enormous difference in their hardiness. If a suitable shelter is erected around them it is no trick to bring through the winter with floral buds intact tender plants which would normally be killed to the ground. A bushel basket or a fruit basket can be up-ended over small plants and a barrel makes a fine enclosure when Rhododendrons get a little larger. In either case, tight containers such as bushel baskets and barrels must have a hole cut near the top of them on the north side to provide ventilation. Large packing cases can be used, with similar ventilation, for older specimens of special value or closely woven cloth can be stapled to a light wood frame to make a suitable shelter when more solid enclosures become too heavy and cumbersome. Any covering which is totally enclosed may be heated by the sun in bright winter weather so that it does much more harm than good. It is absolutely necessary to provide an opening, preferably near the top on the north side, for ventilation.

Any close protection must remain throughout the winter loose and airy. Smaller plants cannot be covered by a large mound of leaves, for example. The foliage would decay and the Rhododendrons would be smothered. However, mulches are renewed annually in the fall and a second, extra ration of leaves can be heaped around the base of a borderline Rhododendron to protect the lower part of its trunk from splitting and to keep the earth from freezing deeply. Such a temporary added mulch must not be so deep as to cover the lower foliage, however, and most or all of it should be removed in the spring, leaving only the usual thickness of the permanent surface mulch which is maintained the year around.

Many fine Rhododendrons just on the borderline of hardiness need no such heroic measures but their floral displays are insured by giving them just a moderate amount of additional shade and shelter in winter. Burlap screens are effective for such purposes as are temporary fences made of the lath shades which are manufactured in rolls. Windbreaks are effective on the leeward side for a distance of about seven times their height. With the slats spaced twice their width apart, laths 6 feet in height reduce the velocity of a 15 mile-per-hour wind by more than 40 per cent at a distance of 18 to 42 feet from the windbreak. Wind barriers should be placed about three times their height away from the Rhododendrons to be shielded. If they are erected immediately adjacent their effectiveness is reduced by half because the wind tends to mount a fence and then swirl downward in whirlpools and agitated eddies which nullify much of the benefit. The effect of the shield diminishes rapidly at a distance more than seven times the height of the screen.

Discarded Christmas trees are often used to protect plants of precarious hardiness from winter wind, and cut branches of evergreen trees can be thrust into the ground at an angle so that their needles shield the tops of the Rhododendrons from the sun. Various sorts of screens can be built of burlap or other materials conveniently at hand to protect borderline Rhododendrons from their two unrelenting winter enemies: wind and sun. However, there are many sorts of Rhododendrons which require no extra winter protection whatever for almost any climate where they will grow at all. The added precautions herein described are for the enthusiast who wants to experiment with something new and rare, or of unknown hardiness; or with a particular sort whose beauty justifies a little trouble to protect it in a climate to which it is not really adapted. It is hoped also that the directions will be useful to any average home-owner who has been so unfortunate as to acquire inadvertently specimens of precarious hardiness.

REMOVING FADED FLOWERS

One of the reasons why Rhododendrons persist in the savage competition of the wilderness is the astounding number of seeds they produce. Travelers in southeastern Asia describe the unbelievable rapidity with which the Rhododendrons cover land which has been burned over or cleared. At the elevations where they thrive, they spring up wherever they can gain the slightest roothold. Such wild profusion in nature is the consequence of the prodigious fruiting.

In cultivation, however, the enormous quantities of seeds are formed at the same time that the flower buds are being developed, to the detriment of the next year's floral display. The seeds always win out in the competition between floral buds and ripening fruits, for it is thus that nature insures the perpetuation of her wards, and the flowers are only a means to that end in the wilderness.

But in our gardens we are interested in the blossoms, and the seeds are an inconvenient nuisance which must be prevented from forming, if we are to have the greatest freedom of bloom from our Rhododendrons. The best practice is to snap off the faded trusses soon after the flowers wilt, being careful to break the stalks so that the axillary growth-buds lower down on the stems are not damaged. It is important that the end of the branch from which the flower-bearing stem originates be not broken off since the loss of the growth buds will be at the cost of the next year's flowers. For a few Rhododendrons of average size it is but a matter of moments and good grooming to remove the unkempt faded flowers and there is a rich reward in the great profusion of blossoms the next year. In a large collection it becomes an exasperating chore, and in a commercial nursery it requires a great deal of labor and expense at the busiest time of the year. Yet specialists never neglect the removal of the faded blossoms regardless of the cost and inconvenience. They know how heavily the enormous crop of seeds draws on the resources of the plants, restricting their growth and reducing their display of flowers. In the wild and in gardens where the chore is neglected, Rhododendrons tend to become biennial in their blossoming, producing a really good show of flowers only in alternate years.

Eventually, of course, the commercial hybrids become so large that only the gardening perfectionists are willing to remove the wilted trusses. Fortunately, the decline of vegetative growth which is associated with maturity tends to result naturally in the production of more flower buds, so the penalty for neglect is much reduced. Some sorts of Rhododendrons bear great numbers of clusters which contain but two or three small blossoms. I know of no one who removes the faded blooms from *R. mucronulatum*, and with a few exceptions Rhododendrons of this and of the alpine type are passed by. *R. carolinianum*, however, demands this attention. Without it, this species falls so far short of its beautiful best that most gardeners resign themselves to the tiresome job of picking off the numerous small trusses which are borne on a sizable plant.

DISBUDDING

There are a few sorts of Rhododendrons which flower so profusely that they exhaust themselves even when the faded blossoms are removed to prevent the formation of seeds. Floral buds form in such prodigal numbers that the resources of the plants are taxed too heavily if they are all allowed to develop into flower trusses, and the display of poor quality blossoms is no better than fewer trusses which are well developed. *R.* (hybrid) 'China' and some of the Dexter hybrids bloom too freely for their own welfare. I have in my trial grounds a plant of *R. catawbiense* var. *album*, Glass × *R. decorum* which sets two to five buds on nearly every terminal growth. If the surplus is not removed the foliage diminishes in size and becomes sparse and yellowish in color. Growth is restricted and there is no gain in effective floral display from small, half-size blooms which wilt quickly.

All Rhododendrons occasionally set a bumper crop of flowers buds and it does no harm to allow these blossoms to develop in their extra profusion. But if any plants of the familiar broad-leaved hybrids regularly form excessive numbers of floral buds, they should be reduced in number to about one to each square foot of leaf area.

PRUNING

Rhododendrons can be pruned successfully to reduce their stature and to bring unbalanced specimens into pleasing proportions. Professional growers often cut them back to rejuvenate them, to make them more compact or to clear away branches which have been injured by accident or disease. The popular impression is that these plants do not respond well to pruning, but this is emphatically not the case. There are only a few sorts which cannot be improved in growth habit by pruning if occasion demands it.

Should a Rhododendron require pruning when its purchase is first considered the average gardener will be well advised to transfer his patronage to another nursery. Any plant which has been grown to salable size should be well-branched and compact when it leaves the grower, with three or four limbs close to the ground. Upon its training in early life depends its later outline, the density of its foliage and even the number of flowers it will produce. Only expert pruning and subsequent control can afterward correct neglect in the nursery at the time a Rhododendron is at the formative stage which will determine its habit of growth. If this important aspect of Rhododendron production has been neglected by a professional nurseryman the chances are that plants offered for sale by him may be deficient in other unseen respects.

However, even the best of young plants in after years may need pruning if they become leggy or lopsided or need to be reduced in stature. Aged Rhododendrons which have lost their vigor and beauty can be cut back to renew their top-growth with strong, healthy branches from the root crowns.

Most Rhododendrons never need pruning but when they do it is most often because they have failed to flower normally from too much shade, from surplus fertilizer, or from excessive amounts of water which have stimulated growth at the expense of flower-bud formation. When a plant forms a flower bud the effect on the branch which bears it is much the same as pinching out the terminal vegetative growth bud. As the flower truss fades several side shoots originate from immediately below the point where the cluster of blossoms sprang from the branch. There are then as many as four new branches where formerly there was but one, and this continued proliferation into several additional branches year after year, as the plant grows, maintains a compact shrub with beautiful, dense foliage.

But when there is too much water in midsummer either from rainfall or from irrigation, or when the soil has been fertilized too heavily or the plants do not have enough sunlight, they continue to grow instead of forming flower buds. This long, lanky, late-season growth gives the plants a lean appearance in itself but there is a double penalty because it seldom terminates in flower buds. The next growth then simply continues as a single extension of each branch instead of as several side branches such as would have been the case had the limb flowered. A year or two of this type of growth and a Rhododendron is well on its way toward a thin and ungainly appearance which the gardener must correct.

Rhododendrons produce their leaves in whorls or rosettes and they are clustered toward the ends of stems produced by each different cycle of growth. Depending on how long the various sorts retain their foliage it is easy to trace back for several years just how much growth was produced in each season because each tier of leaves represents the end of a growth period, and the tiers are clearly defined and spaced some distance apart. In the axil of every leaf where it joins the stem is a dormant growth bud which is capable of developing into a branch if the limb is cut off just beyond it. Below the rosette of leaves on each of the annual growths, where the stem is bare, are indentations which look as if they might be the marks left by fallen leaves. These are bud scale scars. But they do not contain dormant growth buds and they will not produce side shoots if the limb is severed just beyond them. Instead, an unsightly stub will remain, and new branches will originate lower down an the stem from the resting buds in the axils of the leaves produced in the previous growth period.

Rhododendrons which have become thin in appearance can be restored to compact habit and dense foliage by pruning the branches at a point immediately beyond the rosette of leaves terminating any of the recent growth periods. The basic cause of lanky growth should be eliminated if it is possible to do so, but in any case an entire plant can be cut over in this manner and the length of every branch reduced, if necessary, so that only the lowest rosette of leaves remains on each limb. Any single branch of recent origin which must be removed because it is dead, diseased or weakened by insects, is cut off in exactly the same manner, but remember that a whorl of leaves should remain at the very end of the limb after the unwanted portion has been pruned away.

If a plant has badly outgrown its allotted space or if it is desired to rejuvenate ancient specimens, exactly the same principle is applied to the pruning, but it is much more difficult to locate the points at which the old branches should be severed. After a sector of a limb becomes several years old the foliage drops from it and the problem then is one of distin-

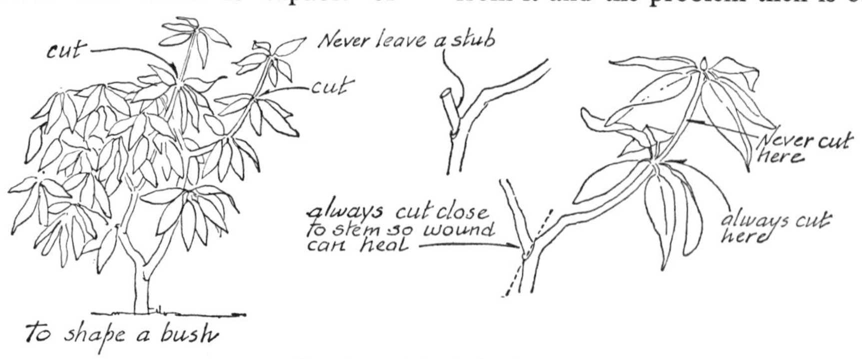

Pruning a Rhododendron

guishing between the true leaf scars, from which side shoots will originate, and the sterile bud scale scars, from which no new growth can come. Admittedly, this requires close examination, and the older the wood the sharper the observation must be. After about five years the true leaf scars can scarcely be distinguished without a magnifying lens, but patience will reveal a faint ring on the trunk which shows the termination of a growth period and there will then be seen with the aid of magnification the exceedingly small elevations caused by the growth buds resting just beneath the bark. Old branches are then severed immediately above that point and side shoots will spring from the dormant buds in the region of the cut. Big old limbs on which it is impossible to distinguish between leaf scars and bud scale scars can be pruned at random and then after the side shoots have appeared any stubs remaining above the point where the branches originate can be removed.

Rhododendrons as much as fifty years old can be rejuvenated by cutting back the trunks within a foot of ground level, but there is a minor risk that an occasional specimen, perhaps weakened by malnutrition, insects or disease, may not have the vigor to sprout again. The loss is small because such a plant would probably not have survived long in any event, and it could scarcely have been a decorative asset before it was cut back.

When one side of a large specimen has been injured it is sometimes desired to practice major surgery on that side only. This can usually be done, but not always. Occasionally the unpruned part of the shrub is then stimulated to exceptional growth by amputation of the damaged portion and the part which has been severely reduced then does not send up new shoots from below the wounds. The length of time it takes to form new shoots when big old branches are cut off near the ground varies with their diameter. Limbs up to an inch thick should show developing buds within thirty days after they would normally start into growth. Main trunks 8 or 10 feet tall which are cut off near ground level should push out side shoots within ten weeks. If no such activity is apparent by the end of this period on the portion of a large shrub which has been cut back only on one side, the remainder of the plant must be reduced in stature so that the entire specimen has been pruned uniformly by about the same amount. New branches will then originate from the base.

Many gardens now have large old plants of the vintage of *R.* (hybrid) 'Pink Pearl' which have grown up to cover windows, obstruct walks and are otherwise too big for their sites. They can be reduced to suitable dimensions by pruning, though of course a year's blossoms will be lost.

Rhododendrons should be cut back *early* in the spring. Even though the plants do not normally start growing until a good deal later the dormant axillary buds begin to mature right after the pruning and they will then break into growth much earlier once the usual growing season arrives. And they should have the longest possible time to gain in stature and strength before the advent of cold weather. Sometimes the new shoots which spring up from tough old stems will grow only a couple of inches the first season but they then progress at the normal rate in subsequent years.

Rhododendrons which have been pruned to any considerable extent should be fertilized in May and they should be watered in June and July if rains fail. A cupful of one of the commercial fertilizers formulated especially for acid soil plants is enough for a specimen 3 feet tall if it is scattered evenly over the surface of the ground beneath and a little beyond the spread of the branches. Larger plants receive an increased ration in proportion to their size.

Plants which have been neglected until they have lost their vigor will respond to pruning less satisfactorily than those which are in good condition. Plants which are failing should be examined and the remedy to correct the trouble should be applied before they have deteriorated to the point where heroic measures are necessary to salvage them. It is a great deal better to give Rhododendrons the modest care they need than to be obliged to revive ailing old specimens by such severe surgery. They cannot be expected to send up quickly a profusion of strong, vigorous new shoots as do plants which are in good health, and occasionally they fail to respond at all, to the dismay of the gardener who has been too tardily concerned with their welfare.

A few growers prune Rhododendrons systematically every couple of years in the same manner as deciduous shrubs are cut back, so that their height is restricted and they are constantly renewed by strong shoots springing up from the bases of the plants. This is done with the idea of avoiding the ills which associate more frequently with plants as they mature. Large old specimens do seem to suffer more from drouth and their more brittle limbs do break more easily beneath extraordinary burdens of snow and ice. But when they reach imposing stature they become truly magnificent spectacles, among the greatest floral showpieces in all horticulture, and not many gardeners will begrudge these patriarchs the small amount of added care which earns such a sumptuous display of beauty.

There are a few Rhododendrons which do not replace a cut branch with an increased number of new shoots, and it is hard to form them to a better habit of growth by pruning. The hybrids 'C. B. Van Nes', 'Mrs C. B. Van Nes', 'Bagshot Ruby', 'Prometheus', and 'Alice', and a few of the more tender species are rebellious to any training. Rhododendrons with very smooth bark, such as *R. thomsonii* and *R. barbatum* do not respond well to pruning. Only rarely do they produce new branches from sprouts originating on older wood.

SHAPING PLANTS BY REMOVING GROWTH BUDS

The gardener who buys a 12- to 15-inch or 15- to 18-inch Rhododendron from a nursery can improve its ultimate appearance enormously and secure a much greater number of flower trusses after a year or two by removing the terminal leaf bud which forms at the tip of each branch after every period of active growth if no flower bud is produced. This tip bud is the source of hormones which keep the side buds in the leaf axils from growing. When it is destroyed, the amount of inhibiting hormone diminishes abruptly and several shoots develop from the side buds lower on the stem, to take the place of the single shoot which would have been formed from the tip bud had it remained intact.

By pinching out the leaf buds at the tips of every branch following each cycle of active growth, a Rhododendron can be induced to form a great many extra branches. After a couple of years most of these extra branches will bear flower trusses so there results a much finer floral display in addition to the compact habit of growth and dense, handsome foliage which are thus induced.

Red-flowered Rhododendrons in particular are inclined to be sparse in their branching and may develop into ungainly specimens even though they have a good framework of branches when they come from the nursery. Practically all of the popular red-flowered hybrids grown in the eastern United States—and in milder climates the renowned 'Earl of Athlone'—tend to extend their growth into long, unbranched limbs which soon give them a thin, scrawny appearance. This can be corrected by disbudding for two or three years. There are a great many more Rhododendrons grown in benign climates which are lanky by nature, at least in youth, and specialists in the eastern United States are usually unpleasantly surprised when first they see the ungainly manner in which they are so often allowed to grow on the West Coast. The incomparable Loderi hybrids, 'Gill's Crimson', 'Mrs Lindsay Smith', 'Canary', 'Princess Elizabeth' and many of the *griersonianum* hybrids are examples of Rhododendrons which are frequently so poorly trained that they are awkward garden liabilities most of the year when their opulent flowers are not in evidence to distract and bewitch the eye.

Rhododendrons usually have two growth cycles each season and often more in mild climates. Leaf buds are usually formed at the conclusion of the first cycle and either leaf buds or flower buds appear on the branch tips at the end of the second. Flower buds can usually be distinguished because they are generally larger, and a good deal plumper than the more slim and tapering shape of the leaf buds. Even if the blossoms were not wanted there would be no point in removing flower buds because several side branches form spontaneously below them without any help from the gardener.

After a small 12- to 15-inch Rhododendron is planted in the spring, it may produce several new shoots from each of its branches. As it starts into growth, the gardener can easily tell which of the leaf buds clustered near the branch tips are elongating into new branches. Any limb which shows two or more developing shoots is passed by, but where only a single branch starts to grow as an extension of the old one this budding growth is broken off, and it will be replaced a couple of weeks later by several new shoots originating from the dormant buds where the leaf stalks join the stems. In the autumn the tip leaf buds are again removed from every branch. If this is done in the fall the dormant axillary buds will break into growth more quickly and in greater numbers the following growing season than if the disbudding is postponed until spring.

The next year in the garden there are likely to be two growth cycles. At the beginning of the second flush of growth the plants should be examined and any branches which are merely starting to extend themselves further without forming at least one additional shoot should be broken off. In the autumn there will be some flower buds which need not be removed but all of the smaller, more pointed leaf buds at the branch tips should be pinched out. This virtually completes the early training for the production of specimens of near-perfect

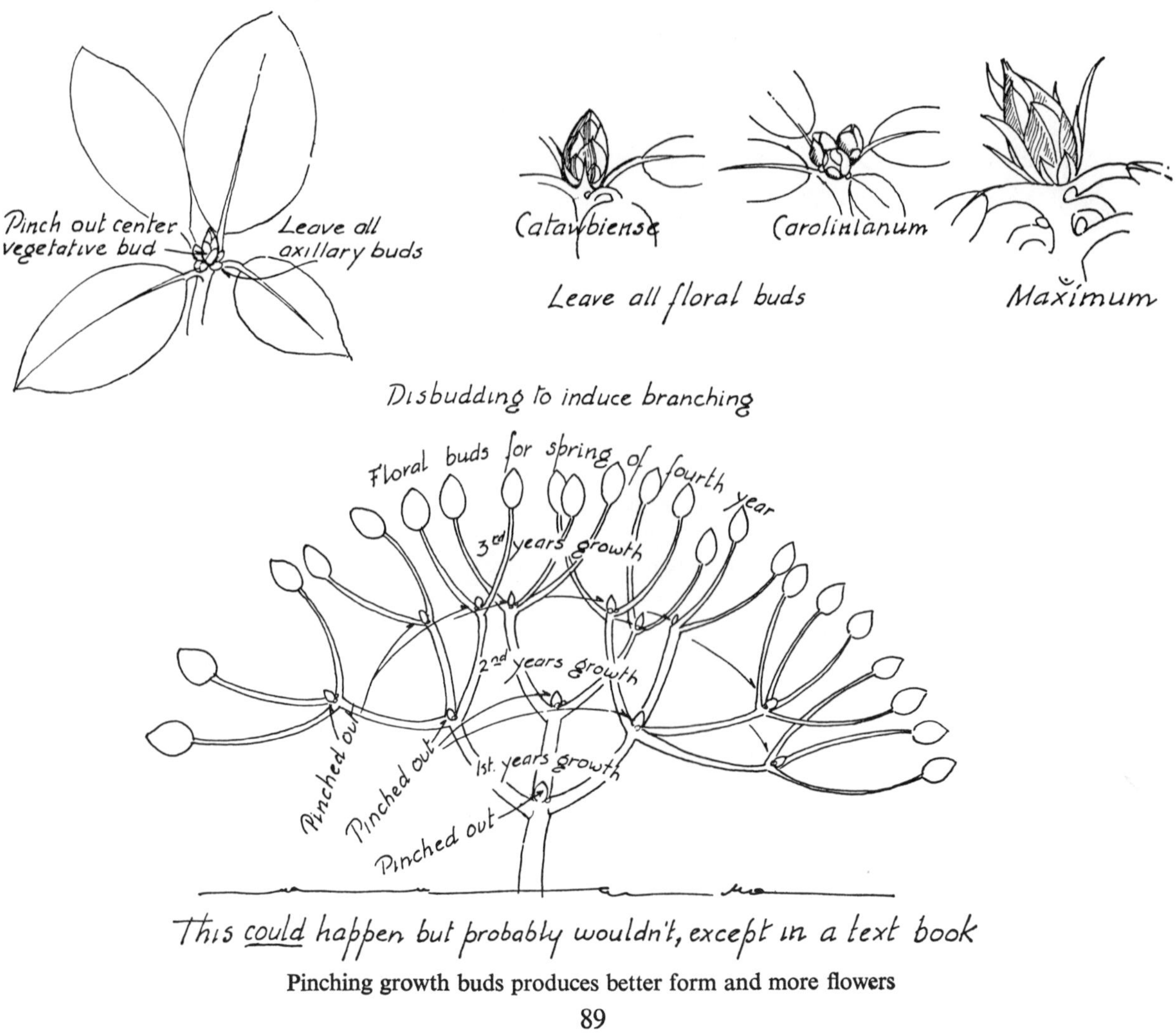

Pinching growth buds produces better form and more flowers

form and density of foliage. The next season the plant disbudded in this manner will develop into a compact Rhododendron handsomely clothed in leaves so thickly borne that it will far outshine in beauty any neighboring specimens which have not received these few minutes of attention which take so much longer in the telling than in the doing. By autumn almost every branch tip should form a flower bud. As a result of the earlier disbudding there often are as many as seventeen large flower trusses the following spring on a Rhododendron which would otherwise have had about seven.

Such early training not only makes for specimens which are immediately much more handsome but it furnishes a framework of branches which continue to benefit the appearance of the plants for decades to come. Should any sector of a specimen develop sparsely in later years it can easily be corrected by resuming disbudding on branches adjacent to the portion of thin growth, and the additional shoots then produced will quickly fill it in. There is a good deal of interest, satisfaction and pride of ownership in shaping and developing a Rhododendron to perfect blooming form. The home gardener can almost invariably grow to large size much finer specimens than those which result from large-scale production of big plants in a nursery.

There are many Rhododendrons which require no help to form good bushy plants. In the eastern United States the familiar hybrids 'Boule de Neige' and 'Roseum Elegans' are typical examples of sorts which need very little attention. In mild climates 'Bow Bells', 'Unique', 'Zuiderzee' and 'Goblin' are representative of a large group of fine hybrids which grow naturally into handsome, compact specimens.

A few Rhododendrons have practically no side buds in the axils of the leaves where they come from the branches. Their absence can be quickly detected by pressing down the leaves and noting that the usual miniature mounds which are the dormant growth buds are missing from the juncture of leaf stem and branch. These Rhododendrons, which are happily few in this deficiency, do not respond to disbudding.

NUTRITION

Leaf Analyses

Both amateur specialists and professional nurserymen are very much in need of accurate and complete information on the nutritional requirements of Rhododendrons and how to supply them. An analysis of the leaves of Rhododendron specimens which are close to the peak of health and vigor shows just what quantities of the various elements are present. Then any grower who has his soil analyzed to determine the amounts of these same elements it contains will have a basis for working out how much of each of them to apply to remedy the deficiencies.

To the best of my knowledge, this information has not been available from any source. Now, through the co-operation of the Department of Horticulture of Michigan State University, spectrographic analyses have been made of leaf samples taken from various Rhododendrons used in the course of several experiments at my trial grounds. The results are as shown at top of page 91.

The amounts present of the various elements are given on the oven-dry basis, in terms of per cent, and in the case of manganese the amounts were so large that they were obtained by extending the standard curve used in spectographic analysis.

Reviewing these results and comparing them with the amounts of the elements which promote the best growth in other sorts of plants, it seems probable that all five of the ground areas could benefit from an application of nitrogen which would bring the figure for this element up to at least 2 per cent; and that Rhododendrons growing in the last two plots could use an application of potassium to advantage. It is apparent that the heavy sawdust application brought about an undesirably high concentration of potassium in the soil, and that the level of magnesium was concurrently so lowered as to produce the leaf-yellowing deficiency symptoms which had previously been evident. The abnormally high amount of manganese found in the leaves

	PH	BORON	CALCIUM	COPPER	IRON	POTASSIUM	MAGNESIUM	MANGANESE	NITROGEN	PHOSPHORUS	ZINC
Bed, FTE-treated	4·3	0·0043	1·05	0·0010	0·014	0·640	1·13	0·0717	1·22	0·25	0·0065
Bed, untreated control	4·3	0·0040	0·94	0·0012	0·017	0·790	1·19	0·0627	1·30	0·25	0·0055
Field, 4 inch sawdust application with nitrogen supplement	4·0	0·0030	0·70	0·0012	0·011	1·33	0·11	0·0493	1·66	0·23	0·0079
Field, improved with peat and humus, no sawdust	4·4	0·0039	1·40	0·0011	0·13	0·432	0·34	0·0793	1·33	0·25	0·0070
Mature specimens in landscape	4·5	0·0037	1·22	0·0010	0·015	0·400	0·31	0·0777	1·10	0·24	0·0054

probably means only that Rhododendrons are efficient extractors of this element from the soil, since none of the plants showed any evidence of manganese poisoning. The FTE (fritted trace elements) having produced no higher concentrations in the plants in the treated bed than in the untreated, the conclusion must be that there was no response to it, and that these elements were probably already present naturally in sufficient amounts for good nutrition. Finally, it must be noted that the availability of several elements, but especially nitrogen, was probably unfavorably affected by the soil acidity, which was higher than is ideal for the best growth.

Despite these shortcomings, the Rhododendrons sampled in the last lot were growing at a rate which would be considered quite satisfactory by professional growers, and it is interesting to compare these results with tentative standards more recently established for Rhododendrons by the Farm and Garden Research Foundation, an organization sponsored by a fertilizer manufacturer in Seattle; and with the tissue analysis of Blueberries yielding satisfactory crops as reported by Michigan State University (see table below):

My results are at wide variance with those reported from the West Coast experiments. In other trials I obtained iron-manganese ratios as low as 1 : 13, with the plants growing quite satisfactorily at 0·0157 per cent iron and 0·20 per cent manganese. Except for high levels artificially induced, I have never obtained

	LEACH RHODODENDRONS IN GOOD GROWTH	FARM AND GARDEN RESEARCH RHODODENDRON STANDARDS	HIGH YIELD BLUEBERRIES
Nitrogen	1·10		2·08
Phosphorus	0·24	0·10	0·17
Potassium	0·40	1·2	0·525
Calcium	1·22	1·5	0·68
Magnesium	0·31	1·0	0·34
Manganese	0·0777	(0·005)*	0·0170
Iron	0·015	(0·01)*	0·018
Copper	0·0010		0·0009
Boron	0·0037	0·003	0·0052
Zinc	0·0054		0·0024

* In establishing their tentative minimum standards the Farm and Garden Research Foundation further specified that the ratio of iron to manganese should not drop much below 1 : 1.

any normal potassium analysis higher than 0·90 per cent, whereas 1·2 per cent is established as a tentative minimum by the West Coast organization.

Twigg and Link (1951, *Proc. Amer. Soc. Hort. Sci.*, 57: 369–375), established critical tissue levels of 0·22 per cent for calcium, 0·17 per cent for magnesium and 0·80 per cent for potassium and pointed out that these are low compared with those of many cultivated plants.

Rhododendrons do not require high nutrient salts concentrations in the soil. F. Penningsfeld (Bayr. Gartnereiverband 1952) reported that low concentrations produced compact growth and luxuriant roots. The optimum was found to be 0·05–0·10 per cent. High concentrations produced chlorosis. The latest research has shown the reason for these and similar results from experiments in earlier years: high total base salts concentration in the soil causes a reduction of acidity in the tissues of Rhododendrons, internally, so that iron is inactivated and growth is adversely affected. Professional growers and amateur enthusiasts will be quick to note that the prodigal use of standard chemical fertilizer mixtures is not a promising way to achieve maximum growth.

Fritted trace elements are undoubtedly effective in remedying existing soil deficiencies. In 1956 Appalachian Nurseries grew Rhododendron seedlings of identical parentage in flats of pure Hazleton peat, a portion of which received FTE formulation FN-501 at the rate of two grams per flat. At the end of the first season the plants in the treated flats were estimated visually to be 30 per cent larger than those in the untreated flats, and samples sent to me for tissue analysis revealed the following results:

	FTE-TREATED FLATS per cent	UNTREATED CONTROLS per cent
Nitrogen	1·63	1·27
Phosphorus	0·41	0·33
Potassium	0·908	0·596
Calcium	0·95	1·74
Magnesium	0·21	0·25
Manganese	0·20	0·20
Iron	0·0298	0·0298
Copper	0·0028	0·0028
Boron	0·0054	0·0037
Zinc	0·0020	0·0027

In 1957 I grew seedlings of identical parentage in flats containing a mixture of 40 per cent leaf mold, 40 per cent Michigan peat and 20 per cent sand. Half were treated with FTE formulation FN-501 at the rate of two grams per flat, and half received no treatment. At the end of the season it was impossible to detect visually any difference in the growth of the treated seedlings compared with the untreated, and no tissue analyses were made. The FTE produced no effect because the soil mixture already contained sufficient amounts of the elements in the frit.

The information herein provided is only a beginning but it does afford, for the first time, some basis for manipulating nutritional elements for the maximum growth of Rhododendrons. The nurseryman seeking faster growth rates and greater efficiency of production, or the grower plagued by unsatisfactory growth of field stock due to nutritional deficiencies, can now improve the conditions of growth with at least some precision by comparing the results of his soil analysis with the tissue analyses given above and providing appropriate soil treatments, possibly in consultation with his county agricultural extension agent.

There are sixteen elements generally agreed to be essential for normal plant growth. Three are obtained from water and air: carbon, hydrogen, and oxygen. Nitrogen, phosphorus, and potassium are the primary plant food elements which are the familiar ingredients of 'complete' commercial fertilizers. Calcium, magnesium, and sulphur are secondary plant food elements. Boron, manganese, copper, zinc, iron, molybdenum, and vanadium are called minor elements, not because they play a minor role, but because they need be present only in minute traces to meet the needs of plants. But their presence is vital and there is a lot of evidence to support an assumption that Rhododendrons are peculiarly dependent on ample supplies of the trace elements to utilize the three primary nutrients to the best advantage. It often happens that their growth is limited by only one mineral element which is not available in sufficient amount. A large surplus of another nutrient will not compensate for such a deficiency. Abundant nitrogen, for example, will not make up for insufficient magnesium in the soil and the latter by its absence can cause a severe restriction of growth.

Rhododendrons may be penalized by lack of the various nutrients because they are not present in the soil and probably also because they are present, but as insoluble compounds, so that they are not available in sufficient amounts to the plants, which can absorb them through the roots only when they are dissolved in water.

The nutrition of Rhododendrons is a complex subject which will be of greatest interest to specialists and to commercial nurserymen who have a particular concern with the conditions which bring about the fastest possible growth and maintain the plants in optimum condition at all seasons. Plants which are well grown in private gardens usually have good culture. They are maintained with a suitable mulch and they are watered when they need it. Rhododendrons in a garden which are growing and flowering well and have good, healthy green foliage need not be fertilized. But if they have noticeably slowed in their growth and the leaves are tending to diminish in size; if the foliage starts to lose its fresh green sheen and turns a bit rusty or acquires a faint yellowish cast, it is quite likely that the plants will benefit from a springtime application of fertilizer. Six ounces of cotton-seed meal or a cupful of one of the commercial fertilizers made especially for acid soil plants should be scattered over a square yard on top of the mulch at the base of a 3-foot Rhododendron. Larger specimens receive proportionately more in relation to their size, but excessive applications of commercial fertilizers are resented and it is best always to be cautious in their use.

The Basis for Maximum Growth

Professional growers and amateur enthusiasts interested in more detailed knowledge of Rhododendron nutrition to obtain the greatest possible rate of growth from their plants, are dealing with a subject with numerous facets. The best conditions depend, not alone on the plant nutrients in the soil, but also on the bacteria and fungi in it, on its content of moisture and organic matter, on its acidity and on the porosity which determines the penetration of water and air. It is a problem which must be viewed from all of these angles.

Acidity and Growth

One prerequisite which is usually necessary to grow Rhododendrons in any soil is acidity. Recent experiments point the way to a release from this requirement under unusual conditions but it is still generally true that Rhododendrons need an acid soil, and that they abhor lime. Under identical conditions not all Rhododendrons find the same degree of acidity to their liking, however, and the extent of soil acidity has a profound effect on their nutrition.

Acidity is measured in pH units. Between pH 7·1 and 11·0 the soil is alkaline. A pH of 7·0 is neutral. A pH of 6·0 is slightly acid. A pH of 5·0 is ten times more acid than a pH of 6·0. A pH of 4·0 is one hundred times more acid than a pH of 6·0 and a pH of 3·0 is 1,000 times more acid than a pH of 6·0. Thus the lower the pH, the higher the acidity mounts in very rapid fashion, as will be noted by the fact that a pH of 3·0, instead of being twice as acid as a pH of 6·0, has 1,000 times more capacity to neutralize alkali.

Rhododendrons grow in nature in soil which varies widely in acidity. The native American species, *R. maximum*, has been found thriving in the wild at a pH of 2·9, which is such a high concentration of acidity that it is hard to simulate it even in laboratory experiments without killing the plants with chemical salts. But *R. maximum* is also found in nature growing in soil with a pH of 5·3 and in a large number of samples the pH averaged 4·0. The Asian species vary in their preferences too. *R. lacteum*, for example, in laboratory experiments preferred very acid soil and grew poorly in soil less acid than pH 5·3. In the same soil the species of the Triflorum series, which are so useful in landscaping, were happy in a range between pH 5·0 and 6·0. Further, the various sorts in the Heliolepis series grew best between pH 4·4 and 5·7 but they were also tolerant of less acidity, even to pH 6·8. In experiments reported by Mr F. E. W. Hanger in the 1949 edition of *The Rhododendron Yearbook*, published by the Royal Horticultural Society, species of the Taliense series showed a broad range of tolerance in the acidity range but they grew best between pH 5·3 and 5·7. *R. ponticum* exhibited its well-known ability to thrive in a wide variety of soils by growing reasonably well in the entire acidity range from pH 4·0 to 6·8, thus demonstrating once again its value as a grafting rootstock for the epiphytic Rhododendrons and a few others which will not flourish on their own roots under ordinary conditions.

But we must distinguish sharply between tolerance and preference. All of the Rhododendrons in the Hanger experiments had a fairly narrow range within which they grew most lustily. An average of pH 5·3 would have come closest to suiting the majority. Mr Hanger's conclusion was that the optimum range lay between pH 4·2 and 5·5, with the large-leaved species preferring the more acid soil and the small-leaved sorts growing best toward the higher pH of the acidity range.

Authorities have differed in their views on the optimum degree of acidity for best Rhododendron growth and the latest research is showing the reason. The different sorts of Rhododendrons which have been studied not only vary in their preference but we now know that the optimum acidity depends on the chemical constitution of the soil and its porosity, the amount of rainfall and with other variables in the conditions of growth. This is a novel idea to many growers but it is extremely important. The degree of acidity which produces the best growth in one nursery may not be the most desirable for the same Rhododendrons growing in different soil and climatic conditions in another region.

Rhododendrons growing vigorously in the wild in soils with pH values substantially above 7·0 have developed acute chlorosis when they were transplanted into cultivated soils of similar or lower pH which were different in their chemical content.

Further, the temperature and rainfall have recently been shown to have a profound effect on the *tolerance* of Rhododendrons to adverse variations in the pH range. Plants growing in inland climates with limited rainfall and temperatures in the higher ranges favoring rapid breakdown of organic material are much less tolerant of deviations from optimum acidity than are those in habitats with lower temperature and high rainfall.

It is astonishing but true that only a single pH measurement of soil in which Rhododendrons are growing in the wild has been reported for the entire Asiatic continent. Dr Tod at the Edinburgh and East of Scotland College of Agriculture analyzed a soil sample sent to him by Kingdon-Ward from Upper Burma, from a stand of *R. pankimense*. It had a pH value of 4·4 and contained little potassium and very little phosphorus. Its organic matter content was 25 per cent.

In the United States Elsworth Brown, a research botanist, who investigated the growth of Rhododendrons in the wild at Little Junction, Tennessee, found a pH range of 4·5 to 5·2. In ten tests, Edgar Wherry found the optimum for one species in the wild to be pH 5·5.

I have averaged reports of numerous soil tests from the natural habitats of Rhododendrons in the United States, Europe and Japan, and the figure is pH 4·7. With present convenient methods available for tests in the field, there is probably an error range of $\pm 0 \cdot 5$ pH in the data I have accumulated, but I estimate, for a very rough and imperfect guide, that most Rhododendrons under average garden conditions will find pH 4·5 to 5·5 the most congenial acidity, with the optimum occurring at about pH 5·0.

Specialists are preoccupied with the reaction of the soil because it has such a profound effect upon the growth of Rhododendrons. For years they have been puzzled by reports from the wild of Rhododendrons growing in alkaline soils. Some of the famous plant hunters and other explorers have commented on finding Rhododendrons growing in good health in limestone districts and frequent references have been made to their presence in regions where the predominating feature is Dolomite, a rock composed largely of calcium carbonate and magnesium carbonate.

A critical examination of these reports reveals that no pH determinations were made *at the root zone*. Moderately low temperatures and high rainfall are the only requirements for acid soil to be ultimately formed from pure limestone as the decomposition of organic matter is retarded and humus accumulates on the surface. Further, the greater the annual rainfall the more rapidly is calcium leached out of the underlying rock. This probably accounts for the reports of Rhododendrons growing on Dolomite. The weathering of this rock leads first to the loss in solution of calcium carbonate, with magnesium carbonate forming an increasing proportion of the residue. This reacts slowly with water, the basicity and solubility of magnesium carbonate being much less than that of calcium carbonate.

Dr Tod of Edinburgh (*Journal* of the Scottish Rock Garden Club, Vol. V, Part 1, No. 18, April 1956) grew seedlings of *R. davidsonianum* to flowering size in five years in soil of low fertility with a pH of 8·4, the alkalinity of which was induced by magnesium carbonate and not by calcium. It was the absence of calcium which made growth possible in such alkaline soil and we can only infer that alkalinity, in itself, is not the cause of the harmful effects usually associated with it.

In other experiments, in the United States, it was the *total* concentration of base nutrient salts (calcium, magnesium, potassium) which was important. Any single one could be high if the others were low.

After carefully reviewing the evidence offered in many reports, it seems to me that there are only four proved observations of Rhododendrons growing in alkaline soil in nature. In all other cases there were other possible explanations. *R. calciphilum* has been found on pure calcareous gravel in Burma; *R. hirsutum* grows on screes in the limestone Alps which are indisputably alkaline in reaction; *R. lapponicum* inhabits calcareous cliffs in northern Scandinavia which are free of both snow and humus; and *R. occidentale* has been reported by Andrew T. Leiser (*The Rhododendron and Camellia Yearbook*, 1957, published by the Royal Horticultural Society) to be growing sixty miles north of Oakland, California, at a site where the pH values *taken at the root zone* in profiles to a depth of 2 feet ranged from 7·2 to 8·6. Interestingly, the American species was growing in low fertility serpentine soil, derived from *magnesium* iron silicate rocks, with an extremely low calcium level. Brought into the laboratory, this alkaline serpentine soil produced seedlings of an assortment of Asian and American species perfectly normal in growth and vigor.

Recent research (Technical Paper No. 953, by Colgrove and Roberts, Oregon Agricultural Experiment Station) has revealed for the first time that soil acidity is important mainly because it is one of the conditions which determine the acidity of the sap and of the internal tissues of Rhododendrons. When the acidity of the leaf tissues declines iron is inactivated and chlorotic symptoms begin to appear. The critical point appears to be about pH 4·5.

This discovery removes the emphasis from soil acidity alone and shifts attention to any condition of growth which may cause a loss of tissue acidity in Rhododendrons, such as the total base content of nutrient salts, the form of fertilizer nitrogen used in cultivation, and even the amount of light. All of these can render iron non-functional internally in Rhododendrons by reducing tissue acidity. A low soil pH is not essential if the total concentration of base nutrient salts is low, and the evidence indicates that it is the total base content of the nutrients in the soil and not that of any individual cation (calcium, magnesium, potassium) that causes a loss of tissue acidity and consequent insolubility of iron in the sap.

The pattern which emerges from this research becomes increasingly clear as does its practical application. The chemical composition of the soil is much more important than its acidity, and a desirable pH for one type of soil may be quite undesirable for another. There is some conflict in the evidence as to the detrimental effect of calcium itself, but it is certainly apparent that the requirements of Rhododendrons for calcium, magnesium, potassium, and probably phosphorus are smaller than are those of most other plants, and that the concentration of the base nutrient salts should not be high, especially in less acid soil. In nature, Rhododendrons grow in soils of low fertility, and in such circumstances they are much more tolerant of factors which would otherwise be detrimental to their welfare.

The acidity of the soil is intimately connected with Rhododendron nutrition in a variety of other ways. Both inorganic ammonia compounds and organic nitrogen are converted into usable nitrate by micro-organisms in the soil. There are many different sorts of these bacteria and molds and they also have their preferences for various ranges of acidity, moisture, aeration, and temperature just as do the plants above the ground. Below pH 5·5 the activity of the bacteria which convert nitrogen into usable form is retarded, and very acid soils are virtually bacteria-free so that the decomposition of organic material depends almost completely on the number and variety of fungi. There is in strongly acid soil a chronic shortage of nitrogen which is sequestered and unavailable in the slowly decomposing organic matter. The finding of plant and animal remains, thousands of years old, in acid peat bogs, as occasionally reported in the newspapers, is due to the slow decay of organic matter in such an infertile medium. The nurseryman who acidifies the soil more than is necessary to achieve the minimum acidity in the pH range optimum for the sorts of Rhododendrons under cultivation is needlessly sacrificing a loss of growth.

Mycorrhizae

Other soil organisms favored by acidity perform an important function in the nutrition of Rhododendrons. Fungi which are called mycorrhizae are found on or within Rhododendron roots, usually forming a covering over them which has been presumed to act as a conductor of water and nutrients from the soil into the roots in lieu of the root hairs which are normally lacking in Rhododendrons. This relay mechanism is thought to be one of mutual benefit to Rhododendrons and to the fungi which inhabit the roots. The rather formidable descriptive term for these organisms is symbiotic mycorrhizae. In addition to acting as microscopic pipelines by which water and nutrients are transported from the soil into the roots, the mycorrhizae may increase acidity, reduce organic fractions of the soil to usable form, and possibly manufacture valuable compounds from ingredients available in the earth.

Sometimes Rhododendrons which refuse to grow well can be made to thrive by inoculating the soil around them with mycorrhizae brought in with small portions of earth taken from sites where similar sorts are flourishing either in the wild or in cultivated gardens. Unless they have been suppressed by unfavorable conditions which are subsequently corrected, this is not usually justified, however, because the benign fungi should normally be in the soil ball which protects the roots of a Rhododendron when it is sold by the nursery. This is, in fact, one of the most persuasive reasons for transplanting Rhododendrons balled and burlapped.

In 1933, at the New Jersey Agricultural Experiment Station greenhouses, plants of *R. ponticum* were induced to grow 6 feet tall from seeds in only two years of year-around culture in clean coarse quartz sand which was kept moist by nutrient solution dripping on it constantly. The plant foods were supplied by mono-potassium phosphate, magnesium sulphate, ammonium sulphate and calcium nitrate, with occasional additions of ferrous sulphate to furnish iron. They were absorbed in solution by root hairs which formed in the sand.

These phenomenal results were interesting in themselves but specialists were quick to note that inasmuch as the plants were raised from seeds they attained their remarkable stature in two years despite the total absence of the benign root fungi in the sterile sand. On this basis and from the results of experiments with heather, which is an ericaceous relative of Rhododendrons, some authorities concluded that mycorrhizae were not only unnecessary, but even injurious to their hosts. Dr C. G. Bowers concluded that root fungi must be regarded as fundamentally parasitic and without benefit to Rhododendrons.

This is a conclusion with which I cannot at present agree. I have observed without exception that Rhododendron seedlings in a variety encompassing scores of species and hybrids which are grown in pure sphagnum moss develop root hairs in the absence of mycorrhizae; but when they are transplanted outdoors into suitable soil, the mycorrhizal fungus invariably soon forms and the new root development is without hairs from that time onward. It seems much more likely that the generation of root hairs under synthetic conditions of sterile culture in sand and in sphagnum moss is just another of the marvelous ways in which Rhododendrons adapt themselves to unnatural conditions in order to survive. It is probable that root fungi play a natural, beneficial role in their nutrition under normal conditions and soil acidity is one of the factors favorable to their development. The others are adequate moisture, and abundant amounts of organic matter in process of decomposition, particularly when it approaches humus.

Acidity and Nutrient Availability

Soil acidity plays a vital role in the availability of the familiar chemical elements. All of the primary, secondary, and trace elements may be present in the soil yet be of no use to Rhododendrons if they are locked up in insoluble compounds which cannot be absorbed through the roots. In an acid soil phosphorus, calcium, magnesium, and molybdenum are apt to be unavailable for assimilation, and the hydrogen ions compete with potassium, manganese, copper, zinc, and iron to affect their usefulness adversely. In addition, potassium becomes quite soluble and may be rapidly lost by leaching. The benefits which frequently result from the use of alkaline calcium and magnesium compounds in regions of very acid soil may come from remedying deficiencies of these elements at the same time that they bring about through decreased acidity a greater solubility of other elements and a larger supply of available nitrogen as a result of increased activity by the micro-organisms.

But there is a loss in the availability of other elements as acidity declines. Iron, manganese, and aluminum tend progressively to be further locked up in insoluble forms as alkalinity increases. A lack of available iron in the soil is probably very rare but it is a critical deficiency to Rhododendrons, just as it is internally in the sap if it becomes insoluble due to a loss of tissue acidity, because iron is the vital catalyst in the production of the chlorophyll which manufactures the plants' carbohydrate food in the leaves. Without iron, the foliage soon turns yellow and the Rhododendrons die.

Experimentally-minded gardeners in regions of alkaline soil will be interested in a statement issued by the Citrus Experiment Station of the University of Florida: 'They [Azaleas, Gardenias, Camellias, Rhododendrons] will grow well even on alkaline soils if supplied with sufficient iron in available form.' The best way to furnish iron to alkaline soils is in iron-EDTA-OH, an iron chelate which is about eleven times more effective than the iron-EDTA which is used on acid soil. Chelates, which have become commercially available for horticultural uses only recently, promise to become extremely important in the culture of ericaceous plants such as Rhododendrons. They have the ability to hold iron in soluble form even after absorption into the plant tissues.

The fact seems to be that Rhododendrons thrive in a low pH range not because the soil is acid but because this condition fosters proper sap acidity and provides the nutrient levels favorable to growth. The availability of plant foods in acid soil, more than anything else, controls the plants' vigor and rate of growth. Experimentally, Rhododendrons grown in pots in alkaline soil at pH 8·0, with the minor elements provided artificially by FTE (fritted trace elements), have grown just as well in a greenhouse as have other control plants in soil of normal acidity.

Under usual garden conditions all sorts of nutrition troubles arise when Rhododendrons are planted in alkaline soil or when the soil in which they have previously thriven gradually loses its acidity. Such difficulties are dramatically corrected by the use of Copperas (ferrous sulphate), and a table of the amounts to use appears on p. 281. Although it has been widely used, aluminum sulphate is not recommended as an acidifier because it is toxic in its cumulative effect. It does acidify the soil and is often mentioned in print, but it has an undesirable dual effect. The more the soil is acidified by it, the higher the solubility of the aluminum salts becomes and the more aluminum ions are present for absorption. Rhododendrons have a narrow range of tolerance to aluminum and it quickly becomes injurious as the concentration builds up from repeated applications over a period of time. Plants are killed as the pH approaches 3·4 in soil acidified with aluminum sulphate.

The availability of iron within the plants varies according to whether the soil acidifier is organic or inorganic. Since iron is the element which most frequently causes trouble by its internal absence in soluble form, this fact can be used to advantage in a good many cases. Experimentally, iron chlorosis disappeared at about pH 5·5 when the soil was naturally acid or was made so by the addition of an organic acidifier, but it was necessary to lower the pH to about 4·5 in the absence of organic matter and the acids which they produce for the iron to become soluble and available in the plants, if an inorganic chemical was the sole acidifying agent. Tannic acid is one of the organic acids most commonly offered for sale and spent tanbark is rich in it. Possibly the leaching of tannic acid from oak leaves is one of the reasons they are such favorites for use as a mulch.

It is well to keep in mind that the degree of acidity increases enormously as the pH declines, and not in proportion to a regularly graduated scale of even values. The difference between pH 5·5 and 5·0 is not very much compared with the difference between pH 4·5 and 4·0. In lowering the pH from 5·5 to 5·0 a moderate increase of acidity occurs and the concentration of positive ions increases by about 69, but in lowering the pH from 4·5 to 4·0 there is a tremendous increment in acidity and the number of positive ions mounts by about 685.

Effect of Fertilizers on Acidity

Expert growers must be aware of the effect on the acidity of the soil and on the acidity of the Rhododendron tissues of the fertilizers they use. As a source of nitrogen, for example, ammonium sulphate desirably inhibits the excessive assimilation by the plants of calcium, magnesium, and potassium, and it leaves an acid residue in the soil. Furthermore, ammonium nitrogen is absorbed equally well in a wide pH range, from soil that is very acid to that which is very alkaline. In fact, the ammonium ion is similar to the hydrogen ion, abundant in acid soils, in its congenial effect of reducing the absorption of the bases (calcium, magnesium, potassium) so that their total concentration in the plant tissues does not become excessive. When the base intake becomes high enough to reduce the internal acidity of the sap, iron becomes insoluble and therefore unavailable, and chlorosis develops. Growth is severely restricted. So superior is ammonium nitrate for Rhododendrons that Colgrove and Roberts obtained good growth and vigor from laboratory plants in sand even from a nutrient solution with pH 9·5 when the nitrogen was supplied by an ammonium compound.

In contrast, nitrate nitrogen increases the absorption of the base salts, leaves an alkaline residue in the soil, and may be highly injurious.

Specialists must be certain that the nitrogen in inorganic fertilizer they use comes from an ammonium compound, and then the best results come from small, frequent applications since there is usually a rapid conversion to nitrate in the soil. Nitrogen from an organic source is equally desirable, or perhaps even more so, because it provides a low, constant source of ammonium nitrogen.

Phosphorus is best supplied in superphosphate or ammonium phosphate. Potassium sulphate is the best source for potassium. Bone meal and wood ashes are undesirably alkaline in effect whereas cotton-seed meal and soya bean meal leave an acid residue.

Almost all fertilizers which are formulated for general garden use are undesirable for Rhododendrons and they should be avoided in favor of preparations formulated specifically for acid soil plants, with the nitrogen supplied from an organic source or by an ammonium compound. In a few districts where the soil is already below the pH range best for health and vigor, as in certain regions of the Pacific Northwest, it is not desirable to use formulations which further increase the acidity. Anyone who makes any pretence of growing Rhododendrons expertly must know the pH of his own land to manage it intelligently, and must know the effect on nutrition of any materials or treatments which are applied to the soil.

Best Results from Fertilizers

The discussions of each element which begin on page 282 give the diagnosis and treatment for every sort of common nutritional deficiency, but there are penalties for excessive amounts of these elements too. The latest research indicates that with appropriate treatment we can increase to advantage the level of plant foods which can be used by Rhododendrons. But there is always, for every set of conditions, a penalty for excessive use. Nitrogen is needed for vigorous growth, but if it is applied far in excess of the plants' requirements they may be killed or seriously injured. The amount of excess which courts disaster depends in large part upon how much organic matter is in the soil. A great deal more nitrogen can be used if the Rhododendrons are growing in a medium heavily buffered with decaying vegetable material. If nitrogen is furnished to the soil in only moderate excess the plants grow with extra vigor and produce beautiful glossy foliage, but at the expense of flowers. The stems and leaves produced by such rank growth lack stiffness and their resistance to disease, to cold, and to extreme heat is impaired. Should too much nitrogen be inadvertently supplied, the remedy is to work FTE (fritted trace elements), formulation FN–501, gently into the mulch to prevent injury to the plants, and then apply phosphorus and in acid soil potassium in a formula such as 0–10–10 or 0–12–12 at the rate of 2½ pounds per 100 square feet, to harden them off and restore the balance among the major elements.

Phosphorus helps to mature the tissues of plants so that they are protected from injury by freezing, and it makes them bloom more freely. It plays an important role in vigorous growth. Potassium fosters the development of leaves and branches, strengthening them and imparting disease resistance. It aids in the manufacture and circulation of carbohydrates within plants.

While it is true that nutritional difficulties are often caused by the lack of availability rather than the absence of the vital elements in the soil, there are none the less fairly large areas in which some necessary nutrients are actually not present. Copper is a recognized deficiency in peaty soil throughout the entire United States and zinc may be missing from some of the acid soils in the southern tier of states. Oregon soils lack boron and in Washington iron may be deficient.

The most common deficiencies for Rhododendrons, their symptoms and the best materials to correct them are discussed in detail for each element in Chapter VIII, 'Rhododendron Troubles and Their Remedies', beginning on page 282. Nurserymen will profit to keep in mind that Rhododendrons seem to be affected by inadequate supplies of the minor elements much more than are most other plants. The increase in growth, health and vigor is often astonishing when high levels of nitrogen and phosphorus and a moderate level of potassium are maintained in the presence of abundant supplies of the trace elements.

Added Growth with Fritted Trace Elements

An experiment of vital interest to professional growers and amateur enthusiasts is currently being conducted by the Charles H. Lilly Company, fertilizer manufacturers of Seattle, and a group of co-operating nurserymen in Oregon and Washington. A preliminary report in November of 1954 gave some startling indications of the probable outcome of the investigation. While the conclusions are emphatically tentative they are certainly worth local trials by everyone interested in the rapid development of Rhododendrons either in the home garden or as a matter of production efficiency in a nursery.

A brief discussion of the extraordinary value of chelated iron in the treatment of chlorosis of Rhododendrons appears on page 285. In this chelate, the iron is sequestered so that it does not combine chemically with other elements into insoluble compounds but it is held loosely so that it is available to plants even after absorption. In nature Rhododendrons are accustomed to rotting vegetation which produces organic acids, and these natural acids have the same sort of beneficial sequestering action which has enabled iron chelate to give such dramatic results. In the Lilly experiments it was assumed that inasmuch as Rhododendrons evolved in a soil environment where organic acids are natural sequesterants, they may require abnormally high proportions of such elements as iron, zinc, copper, manganese and molybdenum in their nutrition. In the experiments, the plants died when they were fed large quantities of nitrogen, phosphorus, and potassium without effective assimilation of the minor elements. But when the same amounts of these major elements which caused the death of the Rhododendrons were supplied with the addition of fritted elements of iron, zinc, copper, manganese, boron, and molybdenum, the plants thrived. If these preliminary conclusions are borne out by further investigation, as seems likely, this promises to be a discovery of first importance in the nutrition of Rhododendrons. Nutrition levels which are normally lethal can be safely reached with the use of fritted trace elements. Commercial nurserymen, amateur enthusiasts, and hybridists who are intensely interested in producing blooming size plants as quickly as possible will note the promise of repeating under their own conditions the results of the Lilly experiments. There is no point, of course, in providing nitrogen or other nutrients beyond the quantities which the plants can absorb. Although the Rhododendrons in the investigation were vigorous even at the highest feeding rates, they were actually at their optimum condition in soil containing major plant foods in amounts which would be considered moderately above usual levels in the East.

The great advantage of fritted elements, available commercially under the trade name "FTE", is that they supply the minor nutrients in a way which avoids excessive applications. The trace elements are incorporated into finely powdered glass so that they are released very slowly in rainwater. The beneficial effect persists for a long, long time and there is no injury from over-application. The formulation most congenial to Rhododendrons is designated FN–501.

It would be extremely unwise to attempt to use any other 'shotgun method' of supplying trace elements without knowledge of whether each of the various minor nutrients is needed. Excessive quantities of some, such as zinc, copper and manganese, are toxic to plants and their presence in too large amounts reacts subtly with other elements in undesirable ways. Too much copper, calcium or manganese, for example, interferes with the assimilation of iron and causes severe yellowing of the foliage.

The fact is, however, that FTE formulation FN–501 protects Rhododendrons against injury from nitrogen applications equivalent to the astounding rate of 5,000 pounds of ammonium sulphate per acre, and in the Lilly experiments it was the only form of minor element plant food to do so. Mixed fertilizers with an analysis of 4–12–8 failed to give satisfactory nitrogen feeding at the rate of one ton per acre. However, at the high level of feeding, supported by FTE, the Rhododendrons used in the experiment produced many more buds and flowers, along with great vigor of growth, and good foliage.

An interesting corollary of the Lilly experiments resulted from the inclusion of magnesium in the fertilizer mixture to the benefit of the Rhododendrons in more vigorous growth and better foliage color. The rate of application was 120 pounds per acre (5 ounces per 100 square feet). The soils used in the investigation were generally quite acid, less than pH 5·0, and such a quantity would have had a negligible alkalizing effect so it would seem that it was the increased supply of magnesium which brought about the response. It is logical to expect that assimilation of calcium and magnesium is retarded in acid soil and inasmuch as magnesium can, to some extent, function as a substitute for calcium in plant nutrition there might well have been an effect doubly beneficial. Growers in other parts of the country could well conduct a similar experiment to their own benefit, keeping in mind, however, that a high *total* concentration of calcium, magnesium and potassium is undesirable, and the less acid the soil the more undesirable the high concentration.

The result of the Lilly investigation was a tentative program of fertilizing in which the following formula is recommended as meritorious for springtime application at the rate of one ton per acre (5 pounds per 100 square feet):

4 per cent nitrogen, derived from both organic and chemical sources.

12 per cent phosphoric acid, derived from superphosphate and organic sources.

8 per cent potash, derived from sulphate of potash and organic sources.
4 per cent magnesium oxide.
2 per cent fritted trace elements, formulation FN–501.

This does not provide enough nitrogen, however, and the mixture must be supplemented with additional feeding at the rate of 100 pounds of actual nitrogen per acre, which would be equivalent to 500 pounds of ammonium sulphate ($1\frac{1}{4}$ pounds per 100 square feet).

Finally, a third application of fertilizer with a formula of 0–12–12, with 4 per cent magnesium oxide added, is made after the Rhododendrons have bloomed. This third treatment is designed to harden the plants and encourage them to set flower buds. It is made at the rate of 1,000 pounds per acre ($2\frac{1}{2}$ pounds per 100 square feet).

Any fertilizer recommendation must, of course, be modified to suit local needs, inasmuch as soils vary so widely in the nutrients which are naturally present.

I had experimented with FTE on Rhododendrons a year or so before the Lilly investigations began, and I found no benefit in the use of this material on good loam heavily enriched with humus, but without the addition of any fertilizer and without any attempt to maintain a high nutrient level. Apparently it will be principally useful when there is a deliberate effort to maintain strong concentrations of plant food in order to stimulate the most rapid growth possible, and in cases where the soil is actually deficient in some of the trace elements for the best growth at normal nutrient levels, as in sandy coastal soils in the East.

MINIMIZING WINTER INJURY

Under conditions in the northeastern United States I would be inclined to defer the application of the third treatment (0–12–12 fertilizer with 4 per cent magnesium oxide added) until several weeks before the expected first killing frost, if the principal aim of the previous intensive feeding is to obtain maximum growth. Apparently this application is made after blossoming on the West Coast to foster the production of flower buds for the next year's bloom. In the East such a soil treatment would be primarily to harden the plants after such heavy fertilization earlier in the season, so that their tissues would be matured to resist the freezing temperatures which come with the approach of winter. The primary function of the magnesium in such a case would be, not to decrease soil acidity or to remedy an actual deficiency, but to aid in the rapid diffusion throughout the plants of the phosphates which are so important in the hardening-off process.

As a matter of fact, there has been available in the East for several years a product of similar formula called Reliance Fall Conditioner, manufactured by the Reliance Fertilizer Company of Savannah, Georgia, which has been extremely effective in hardening off and saving from winter destruction plants in too active growth late in the season. If it is not locally available, potassium sulphate alone, applied at the rate of 1,000 pounds per acre, ($2\frac{1}{2}$ pounds per 100 square feet) is a good hardening-off treatment. In regions where phosphorus is deficient, superphosphate can be included also to make up a useful 0–10–10 or 0–12–12 fertilizer, or mixtures with this formula can be purchased from dealers who specialize in agricultural fertilizers. Magnesium can be added in the form of 4 pounds of magnesium oxide as an ingredient of each 100 pounds of the mixture. This late-season treatment is very valuable in protecting Rhododendrons against cold weather injury and it is surprising that so few nurserymen use it in seasons when the plants fail to harden off properly due to late summer rains. Repeated applications might be undesirable, however.

HUMUS AND NUTRITION

The amount of organic matter in the soil, and the degree to which it is decomposed, have a large bearing on the nutrition of Rhododendrons. By improving the texture of the soil and making it more porous there is a faster and more nearly complete assimilation of nutrients as a result of the better aeration provided by abundant organics in the root zone. Better aeration also means increased activity on the part of the soil organisms which convert nitrogen into usable nitrates. The value of this increase in the porosity of the soil can scarcely be over-emphasized, and there is no satisfactory substitute for it. Gardeners occasionally make the mistake of assuming that the steps they take to insure the acidity of the soil are all that is necessary to grow good Rhododendrons. Acidity is only one factor, whether it is present naturally or contrived artificially. Organic matter in the ground is also necessary and the two should never be confused.

An average garden soil contains about 5 per cent humus; 45 per cent inorganic material; 30 per cent air and 20 per cent moisture, according to soil scientists. Rhododendrons are benefited by as much as ten times more humus than the average soil contains, and many specialists routinely provide a mixture of 50 per cent peat moss and 50 per cent top soil for them. Soil can be analysed for its humus content by a laboratory but experienced gardeners can judge its texture by how it feels in the hand. If it is spongy and resilient, with a tendency to crumble when it is gently probed with a finger after it has been squeezed into a ball, it is high in humus. Heavy soil with much clay in it feels dense and unyielding when it is compressed in the hand. It gives the impression of seeming dead and inert compared with the buoyant sponginess of the earth rich in humus. Sandy soil has a lifeless, gritty feel. Its abrasive touch holds no promise of abundant life in it and it falls apart at a touch. Only a high proportion of humus imparts the sponge-like, crumbly texture when a sample of soil is compressed in the hand.

Roots cannot absorb solids. It is only when the nutrients are dissolved in soil water that they can be taken up in liquid form and used by plants. By acting as sponges which absorb water with nutrients in solution when it is available, and later release it as needed, many organics act as a storehouse to provide a more constant supply of usable plant foods.

An important function of the decay of organic materials is to provide nutrients while they are slowly converted by soil organisms into simple compounds which are taken up by plant roots to complete the endless vegetative cycle of growth, death, decay, absorption, and growth once again. Such materials as peat moss, which have already undergone some decomposition, add very little plant food to the soil, and others which are fresh or only partly decayed vary widely in their direct contribution of nutrients. Sawdust, for example, contains only 1 per cent of the nitrogen and phosphorus in the most popular formula for garden fertilizer, and only 2 per cent of the potassium. As a nutrient, aged cow manure is much more valuable. It contains ten times more nitrogen, twenty-five times more phosphorus, and fifty times more potassium than sawdust, but is still less than one-tenth as rich in nutrients as the best-selling chemical commercial fertilizer.

Organic materials which are sometimes abruptly supplied in large quantities by the grower as a measure of fitting the soil for the growth of Rhododendrons can adversely affect nutrient levels immediately after they are incorporated, independent of their long-term benefits. The micro-organisms which decompose vegetable debris also need nitrogen for their activity, and they withdraw it from the soil when they must have food to bring about the decay of organic matter. After the material has been reduced to the simple compounds which can be absorbed by plant roots the soil is the richer for the addition it has received, but the temporary withdrawal of nitrogen, and of phosphorus to a smaller extent, while decomposition is actually in process, can cause chlorosis and sharply restrict growth. A useful rule to provide enough nitrogen for both the Rhododendrons and the micro-organisms is to add 24 pounds of actual nitrogen (equivalent to 120 pounds of ammonium sulphate) for each ton of undecayed dry organic matter which is added as a soil amendment.

By stimulating the micro-organisms, both as a result of better soil aeration and of providing additional material for decomposition, organic materials increase the amount of carbon dioxide in the ground. Dissolved in soil water, such an increase means more acidity and, in turn, the dissolution of some bases which are insoluble in neutral or alkaline soil. Calcium carbonate becomes soluble calcium bicarbonate and is leached out of the soil as rainwater drains from it. The loss of lime in this fashion causes an increase in soil acidity which was brought about initially through the addition of organic matter. Leaves, wood, insects, fungi and other such organic materials also contribute additional organic acids as they decay, and as the soil becomes more acid nature's brake begins to operate because, with increasing acidity, the micro-organisms are retarded which bring about decomposition and the conversion of nitrogen into nitrates. Thus the marvelous complexity of the natural order is revealed, the cause and effect, the balance and counter-balance which provide the endless fascination of its study. By subtle controls such as this the nutrients in the soil are conserved, decomposition proceeds in moderation and acidification does not get out of hand.

In the end, of course, the organic materials exert no permanent effect on soil acidity. Their final fate eventually is to be converted into carbon dioxide and be lost to the air, or into carbonic acid, which drains from the soil with rainwater. This is the reason why organics must be renewed constantly if their value as acidifiers and sources of carbon is to be preserved.

The intermediate residue of decomposition is humus, the tough portions of lignin and carbon, much reduced in volume, which remain after the softer plant parts have decayed. Humus acts as a buffer in the soil which stabilizes its acidity and resists the influences which might otherwise cause undesirable fluctuations. It is a valuable function, another of the innumerable benefits which come from the addition of organic matter. But humus and decaying vegetation also act as buffers to prevent injury from chemical fertilizers, and much higher concentrations of them can be used in the presence of abundant organics in the soil.

WATER AND NUTRITION

The amount of water in the soil profoundly affects its fertility and even its acidity. All nutrients must first be dissolved in water before they are taken up by plants. Too little water restricts growth by limiting the amounts of plant food which can be absorbed through the roots. In addition to other undesirable effects too much water abducts with it when it drains out of the soil some of the soluble nutrients. But there is a further consideration. Water uptake and growth are practically the same. Quite aside from its function as a carrier of nutrients, water enters the plant cells and enlarges them. This increase in cell size is the basic factor in the expansion of the tissues, so it is not too much to say that, in a sense, growth and the absorption of water are essentially identical. As a building block in plant nutrition, water combines with carbon dioxide in the formation of sugar, starch, cellulose and eventually wood.

The amount of water in the soil determines its acidity, too. When there is a great deal of water the concentration of hydrogen ions must necessarily be lower and the soil will be less acid. Land which is very acid when it is drained may be neutral or perhaps even alkaline when it is saturated with water. In addition to impaired aeration, this loss of acidity may possibly be another reason why Rhododendrons are so seldom found on boggy, poorly drained soil.

KINDS AND AMOUNTS OF FERTILIZER

Since we do not have complete information on the nutrition of Rhododendrons, we are obliged to cultivate them on a trial and error basis, using watchful study and a rational approach to obtain the best possible results. The amount of help which a grower can give to his plants depends on alert observation, his knowledge of their needs, his skill, and his competence in providing the conditions in which they will thrive.

After Rhododendrons have attained some size, amateur growers and home gardeners are primarily interested in maintaining them in good condition so that they flower freely and are attractive in foliage the year around. Such a program does not usually require much more than a faithful renewal of the mulch each autumn. But professional growers are more interested in producing saleable plants quickly. Hybridists want to hasten the development of their seedlings to flowering size. Amateurs who purchase small plants may be equally concerned with fostering their growth so that they reach landscaping size as soon as possible.

There is a popular impression that it is unwise to feed Rhododendrons. It probably arose because the wrong sorts of fertilizer were used, those which were injurious on account of their alkaline residue. Actually Rhododendrons are greedy for nutrients and they respond generously to fertilizers truly appropriate to their requirements. They have an extremely high rate of cell activity and they can utilize large amounts of plant food to advantage if it is available to them. In their Asian homeland and in cultivated gardens where the climate is mild, Rhododendrons are growing in root, in branch, or both for about eight months out of the year. During that time their productivity is prodigious. An enormous amount of energy is expended on myriads of flowers which are renowned for their size and substance. Then the plants must immediately start to produce a crop of seeds so lavish that their infinite numbers are another of the remarkable features of the genus. While the seeds are being matured, an additional burden of forming the buds for next year's flowers is imposed and the normal top growth and expansion of the root system must go on.

Little wonder, then, that Rhododendrons can use fertilizers designed for their needs as advantageously as can other shrubs, and perhaps more so. In intensive cultivation it is a question of determining what kind, and how much.

Some of the reasons why ammonium sulphate is far better than any other inorganic chemical source of nitrogen have already been discussed. In addition, it becomes available more slowly, over a period of about six weeks, because organic matter in the soil helps to keep the nitrogen in the ammonium form rather than allowing bacteria to convert it rapidly to the nitrate form. This is an advantage because nitrates leach out of the soil quickly and their fertilizing value is soon lost. And of course ammonium sulphate leaves an acid residue whereas many other chemicals have an undesirably alkaline effect on the soil. It causes just about its own weight of ground limestone to go into soluble form and be washed out of the ground.

There are a number of complete inorganic chemical fertilizers commercially available which are especially formulated to leave an acid residue. One of those most widely available has an analysis of 5–10–5. Others are offered in mixtures of 4–6–8 and 3–20–3, referring to the percentages of nitrogen, phosphorus, and potassium respectively in the three figures. The source of nitrogen in inorganic fertilizers should always be an ammonium compound.

Organic fertilizers have been traditionally favored for Rhododendrons, primarily because they are safer. The nitrogen is released more slowly and the plants are almost never burned by any reasonable application. But the response to such organic sources of nitrogen as cotton-seed meal, for example, has always seemed to be somewhat more favorable than the stimulus that would reasonably be expected of the nutrients alone. We now know the reason. The additional response comes from the low, constant source of *ammonium* nitrogen which has recently been demonstrated to have an important benign collateral effect upon the nutrition of Rhododendrons, in addition to its stimulation of growth.

Cotton-seed meal, which has been a popular fertilizer for Rhododendrons for many years, contains 7 per cent nitrogen, 3 per cent phosphorus and 2 per cent potassium. Fish meal has an analysis of about 10–6–0. Castor pomace is 6–3–1. Tankage is 7–9–2. Dairy manure is 0·7–0·3–0·7. Authorities differ as to the advisability of using other waste animal products. Some experienced growers avoid the use of rabbit, poultry, horse or sheep manure whereas others have found them to be perfectly satisfactory under their conditions. Bone meal and wood ashes cause a loss of acidity.

The new urea-formaldehyde fertilizers, while providing nitrogen in the ammonium form, are not recommended for Rhododendrons because they stimulate growth over such a long period of time, much later in the season than is desirable for Rhododendrons.

Both cotton-seed meal and the popular acid soil inorganic chemical fertilizer mixtures are applied at the rate of 1,200 pounds per acre (3 pounds per 100 square feet). If nitrogen alone is wanted, ammonium sulphate is 20 per cent nitrogen and is supplied at about one-quarter that rate.

Fertilizer should be scattered evenly and thinly over the surface of the mulch beneath Rhododendrons and extending out beyond their branches because the roots normally penetrate farther than the spread of the top growth. Rainwater will carry the plant food down through the mulch to the root zone, but it is better to water it in, lest a light rainfall conduct it to the roots in excessive concentration or extended drouth defer its stimulation of growth until too late in the season. It is not necessary or desirable to disturb the mulch when applying fertilizer.

Small Rhododendron seedlings make phenomenal growth if they are watered every couple of weeks with nutrient solution. The brands which include trace elements are especially desirable providing they do not contain a sticker which leaves a tacky residue on the foliage to provide a lodging for disease fungi. Watering with nutrient solution every two weeks and supplying continuous artificial light for the first four months, I have repeatedly grown Rhododendron seedlings which were, at the end of their first year, about four times the size which is usual in good commercial practice.

When to Apply Fertilizer

No plant food should be applied so that it stimulates Rhododendrons to late growth. If the plants are caught in lush activity by temperatures of 32° F. or lower they will be killed or severely injured. In this soft condition the cells push out water when they freeze and they can not recover it fast enough when they thaw to prevent their collapse. Matured tissues are unscathed by temperatures ruinous to those in active growth which are full of water containing a low carbohydrate concentration. Rhododendrons should never have a nitrogenous fertilizer after about June 10th. Commercial growers find it advantageous to supply plant food in April and repeat the application in early June.

FOLIAR FEEDING

Rhododendrons respond well to foliar feeding. Older plants of the epiphytic sorts and young seedlings of all types luxuriate in dilute fertilizer solutions which are sprayed on their foliage. The tree-dwellers find foliar feeding similar to the manner in which they obtain their food in their lofty perches high in the green roof of the jungle forest. There every thunderstorm dissolves nitrogen in rain and with it comes in minute amounts various sorts of vegetable debris from the atmosphere and from the leaves and branches overhead. Dust in the air, decaying twigs and bits of leaves, dead insects and the dissolved droppings of birds all come to them in dilute solution with unvarying regularity in the rains which fall almost every day for at least a short period. It is this nourishing bath which provides their sustenance, and nature has made provision to take full advantage of it. Evaporation is slow in the eternally dripping atmosphere and the leaves of epiphytic Rhododendrons are designed to catch and hold the rain which brings their food.

The sorts of Rhododendrons with broad leaves present a large surface for the absorption of nutrients, and they especially appreciate showers of dilute fertilizer solution every couple of weeks. The nutrients thus provided are taken up without any complications from acidity or insoluble chemical combinations in the soil. The soluble fertilizers with trace elements seem to be especially effective in promoting growth. Foliar feeding is no substitute for adequate nutrients at the roots, however. Unless the land is reasonably well supplied with fertilizer the food may not even stay in the leaves, but may instead be absorbed from the plant tissues by the undernourished soil.

It is a good idea to put a teaspoonful of one of the synthetic detergents such as 'All', which leaves no sticky residue, into each gallon of the nutrient solution to obtain a more uniform film of liquid on the leaves and increase the efficiency of the feeding. The utilization of the elements varies. Hydrolysis begins within a few minutes and nitrogen is completely used within twelve hours. Phosphorus and potassium are entirely distributed throughout the plants within a couple of hours, at the rate of about an inch in five minutes. Calcium, on the other hand, and some other elements, stay right in the leaves where they are absorbed and are apparently incapable of downward movement. They are, of course, distributed upward when absorption is through the roots, however.

The best results come from foliar feeding when the liquid fertilizer is sprayed on the leaves in the evening or in periods of high humidity. The foliage absorbs the nutrients three to ten times more efficiently at night, probably because there is more moisture in the air. Heavy rains, excessive overhead irrigation or the application of constant mist to seedlings or cuttings means a loss of nutrients, which are then leached out of the leaves. Plant foods are absorbed as readily through the upper leaf surface as through the lower, contrary to popular belief, and they can be supplied in solution to the foliage later in the year than would be wise to apply dry fertilizer to the soil. The stimulating effect of the usual soil applications is considerably delayed by the various steps required for conversion of the chemicals to usable form and then for the movement of the food elements from the soil to the stems and leaves. Since liquid nutrients sprayed on the leaves are so quickly utilized, weak plants can be strengthened by their use later in the season without risking injury from the first killing frosts.

Injurious Growth Stimulation

Commercial nurserymen have often sustained heavy losses from the mistaken belief that the growth of Rhododendrons can be forced simply by heavy applications of nitrogenous fertilizer throughout the growing season. If weather and soil conditions do not combine to cause the death of the plants as a result of such unnatural and prolonged stimulation, the grower may achieve by autumn the added size which brings higher prices for the stock, but the penalty for such inept treatment is ruinous. There follow, either for the nurseryman or for his customers, disastrous losses from transplanting and often from winter injury as well. Plants forced in this manner may take as long as three years to resume their normal anabolism and in the meantime the production of flowers is greatly reduced or even eliminated entirely.

The efficient commercial production of Rhododendrons requires thoughtful consideration of all of the factors affecting nutrition and the supply at the right times of all of the elements needed for optimum vigor, flower production, and resistance to cold and disease. Heavy-handed applications of nitrogen throughout the season betray a totally inadequate conception of the needs of the plants and the factors which promote their welfare.

CHAPTER V

Rhododendron Species

SPECIES VERSUS HYBRIDS

MANY gardeners find after years of experience with Rhododendrons that the wild species are more interesting and attractive than the flamboyant hybrids which breeders have created by their ingenious crosses among the wildlings of America and Asia.

Rhododendron species seem to represent the clean efficiency of nature in its most appealing aspect. The natural beauty of the plants lies in the subtle balance between size of flower and leaf and in their proportions in relation to the stature, and the spread of the branches. Here is a perfect integration of plant structure which has the unity of high art. The species enthusiast believes that his Rhododendrons are modeled by nature to a higher standard of beauty than man has yet been able to accomplish with his manipulations of genes and chromosomes.

It is generally true that most species bloom a little less freely and are not so adaptable as their hybrid offspring, but this is the most that can be said against them. While scores of the wild Rhododendrons are easy to grow, others are so specialized in their cultural requirements that they demand a reasonable approximation of their natural environments to do their best. The difference between species and hybrids is vividly illustrated in the Piedmont district of Virginia and the Carolinas where most of the Asian species are a failure, but a gratifying number of hybrids can be persuaded to perform reasonably well. Hybrids are more tractable and better able to compromise with poor growing conditions because they represent a fusing of the diverse climatic conditions in which their forebears grew in the wild. As a group, they flower at an earlier age and more regularly year after year than do their natural ancestors. And it is only through the hardy commercial hybrids that gardeners in severe climates can obtain even a suggestion of the lovely clear colors and giant flowers of the tender Asian Rhododendrons.

Yet the proponents of the species are justified in holding that no man-made hybrid is superior to the wild Rhododendrons from which it is descended. For every improvement in flower size, in color or in hardiness there seems to be a loss in some other respect. The foliage often loses its natural sheen. Scarlet blossoms of intensified color are attained at a price of a gaunt and ungainly habit of growth. An over-ripe display of pinkness substitutes for the form and texture of the natural thoroughbred refined through ages of time to the distinctive quality of aristocrats of ancient lineage. No hybrid has yet matched the luminous intensity of the yellow flowers of *R. campylocarpum* nor is there a challenger for the classic purity and grace of their form.

The Rhododendron species are incomparably superior to their hybrid offspring in the quality and interest of their foliage. The thick felty indumentum beneath the leaves of some sorts is often richly colored, as is the foliage of *R. fulvum* for example. It yields easily to the wind so that delightful coppery-red ripples appear in ever-changing patterns with each passing breeze. In the large-leaved species the effect of the indumentum is dramatic. The massive leaves of *R. falconeri* are dark green up to eye level and then abruptly the tree seems almost to change color as their brilliant orange undersurface is presented to the viewer looking upward to the crown. Some species are strikingly effective in their blue-green foliage, creating refreshing contrast with the shrubs around them. *RR. lepidostylum*, and *campanulatum* var. *aeruginosum*, for example, are superb in their icy green mantles with a frosted bloom. Then there are the gay decorations of new growths, the brilliant scarlet ribbon-like bracts on the young shoots of *RR. hookeri* and *eclecteum*; the bronzed rose foliage of *R. nuttallii*; and the new leaves of *R. williamsianum* like chocolate mints, are garden attractions almost as ornamental as the flowers. The hybrids are conspicuously lacking in these added values which contribute so much to the enjoyment of Rhododendrons.

Regional Usefulness

Only a tiny fraction of the world's Rhododendron species can be grown unprotected outdoors in the northeastern United States. The sub-zero cold of the winters and the heat of the summers are too far removed from the moderate temperature range and high humidity of the mountainous elevations of southern Asia to allow the cultivation of the Oriental species in any considerable variety. Fortunately, those that do find the climate congenial include some of the most beautiful and some of the most interesting sorts in the genus. Lists of the species recommended by regional experts for the northeastern United States, for the Middle Atlantic States, for the Rhododendron belt of Washington and Oregon (which would apply as well to the British Isles), and for the San Francisco district, appear at the end of this chapter, beginning on page 239. A separate chapter deals with Rhododendrons in the South and in the Midwest.

TECHNICAL CONSIDERATIONS

Problems to be Faced

Authorities do not agree on just what constitutes a species. In such an immense and diverse group as Rhododendrons there are inevitably many differences of opinion as to exactly how much a particular sort may vary without losing its identity. Some students of the genus have tended to compress the range that each may have and so a vast array of species is created differing from one another in lesser degree. The authorities in the past who have broadened the range of permissible variation thereby decreased the number of species and the differences one from the other became greater and more distinct.

I suggest that much of the difficulty in bringing order out of the welter of species, subspecies, varieties and merging forms arises from the peculiar pattern of distribution in the Sino-Himalayas. Although a single species may inhabit a fairly wide region it is often found within its range in scattered local areas, isolated by the jagged terrain from adjacent sites where it dwells. The plants in such isolated local groups tend to become more alike and the Rhododendrons in each such tract evolve with uniform characteristics somewhat different from those of the same species which may be in another district only a few miles away but separated, perhaps, by a towering mountain ridge. It is a frequent observation among geneticists that with the passage of great spans of time, plants in an isolated and restricted area tend to become more uniform in their characteristics due to inbreeding, and the average of one such group may be appreciably different from the common run in another.

As a geneticist, I am satisfied to say that a Rhododendron species is a group of plants so constituted and so situated that its variability tends toward reduction, but having so defined a species as it is found in the wild, the problem of classifying Rhododendrons is still as far from solution as ever.

The fact is that the difficulty is basically insoluble. We want to reduce this vast, amorphous group of plants, found the world around, so that each different sort can be labeled and put into a convenient mental pigeon-hole. But the trouble is that they are often indivisible.

If we consider but a moment, it will be apparent that these Rhododendrons must have had a single, common ancestor unimaginable ages ago, and so they did, the Heath family having descended from the Magnolias through the Camellia and Dillenia families. In the course of their infinitely slow creation through the imperceptible tides of climate and geographic change there must have been originally an unbroken chain of evolving Rhododendron forms, a fluid stream of inseparable progressions differing only minutely one from the next as the plants through the millions of years adapted to gradual changes in their environment or the cataclysms of nature. New sorts probably did arise abruptly, from widely separated plants crossed by fortunate circumstance, from genetic accident, or as a result of gross mutations, but we know that they must have been inordinately rare, and then once again the inexorably slow, minute molding of the plants to their environment was resumed for aeons of time. The sorts which are alive today are those whose changes successfully kept pace with the relentless shifts in their conditions of life so that they survived the endless struggle for survival in the wild. By some rare happening, perhaps abrupt, like the transportation of seeds for long distances by animals, or as a result of natural catastrophe, perhaps timelessly deliberate, like the age-long creep of a glacier, some Rhododendrons were forced to depart from the main course of their evolution in order to survive. Thus were formed outlying colonies of new sorts which then continued their imperceptible development through time to their present appearance. Save only the gaps left by those which died out in the ages-long history of the genus, we should have today a complete, unlimited assortment of Rhododendrons progressing without any definition whatever, from the massive large-leaved primitive tree species to the highly evolved, diminutive alpines with their little scaly leaves. The probable evolution is illustrated on the folded insert.

Small wonder then that there are endless difficulties in our presumptuous efforts to pluck from this continuous cyclorama of living plants, merging one into another, a single form of Rhododendron and attempt to describe it as a species different from all others.

Newcomers to a study of the genus are invariably baffled and frustrated by the variations they encounter. It is both conventional and convenient to assume that a named species fits neatly into a rigid unique category which can be exactly described and delimited. This view is held almost universally among Rhododendron enthusiasts and it is an undeserved tribute to the prestige of the great god Science. No one who clings to it will ever enjoy or profit from the study of Rhododendrons.

The Realistic View

It is time now to fit the attitude to the facts: that there are many instances where the species merge imperceptibly one into another, and doubtless there will be many more when representatives of all the Asian forms are brought into cultivation. The only sensible conception is a fluid one, where there are an infinite number of intermediate microforms linking numerous species in uninterrupted progression. A species can be likened to a planet encircled by innumerable satellites which more or less resemble it in diminishing degree as their distance increases from it. The central planet is clearly distinguished as typical of the whole, but at some point the outer satellites intersect the orbit of an adjoining planet-species and they cannot then be identified as certainly belonging either to one species or the other.

Natural Hybrids

I am especially interested in the evolution of Rhododendrons and I am convinced that there are literally scores of natural hybrids presently enjoying an unearned distinction as species. It is no secret that plants grown from seeds sent back by explorers do not by any means always correspond in character with the herbarium specimens taken from their parents. Such is often conspicuous evidence of the natural hybridity which joins the older species with the newer in the flux of nature. As already mentioned, a segregated population of plants, whatever its origin, tends to become more uniform with each passing generation until finally all of its members acquire a common identity and their progeny resembles the parents. This is a law of genetics. Thus are new species born by the caprice of insect and geography, and the ponderous passage of the ages. But the early generation progeny of two species newly crossed in the wild are not entitled to the position of their parents.

I view with mistrust the many reports from the field that the species in the Oriental wilderness do not cross among themselves. It is incomprehensible to me why the same assortment of species which cross so readily in cultivation should not produce hybrids when they grow together in nature. On the alpine meadows the little scaly-leaved Rhododendrons dwell in communes of many species, vast associations of billowing foliage and tumultuous color which stretch for miles beneath the jagged peaks. And there must be many situations in the rougher terrain of the wild where the division into segregated local areas of distribution is not quite complete, perhaps on moderate elevations between adjoining valleys each of which may shelter distinct forms. There on the rocky cliffs a few hardy emigrants from the masses on each side below may meet and mingle to fuse a connecting link between the two.

These same species which are reported not to cross in the wild do so without assistance from man whenever they are grown in large collections, as in botanical gardens. In fact, natural hybrids occur in cultivation so readily that every specialist knows how unsatisfactory it is to collect open-pollinated seeds from species in the garden because they so often fail to duplicate the plants which bear them.

Hybridity in the wild is commonplace among the deciduous Rhododendron species of the eastern United States and it has been a subject of intensive study by Dr Henry Skinner, director of the United States National Arboretum, by Dr Fred Galle, director of horticulture for the Ida Cason Callaway Foundation, and by the author. I have in my own garden a natural hybrid between the evergreen *R. maximum* and *R. catawbiense* from the mountains of North Carolina.

Great as is our gratitude to the plant explorers, much as we admire their gallantry, force of character and strength of determination, the evidence is fatally against their views on this point. It seems certain that the imperceptible evolution of new species in Asia, as elsewhere, involves the initial appearance of natural hybrids in the primitive mountain wilderness.

Genetics Applied to the Problem

Geneticists and others interested in the fascinating detective work of reconstructing the evolution of plants and in determining the immediate forebears of existing hybrid populations, have investigated many genera which, as it is with Rhododendrons, are notorious for their variability. In every genus of variable plant species which has ever been studied, the evidence has clearly shown that the variability is due to introgression, the gradual infiltration of one species by another due to hybridization and then repeated back-crossing between the natural hybrids and the original species population.

There are really two ways of studying the imperceptible flow of plant development in its evolution. The classic approach has been to work out the influence of migration, selection, population size and mutations by applying to the analysis the proved facts of genetics in such aspects as factor segregation and mutation rates. Then, by deduction and the application of mathematical formulae, the investigators have arrived at their conclusions. More recently, in a method brought to scientific accuracy by Dr Edgar Anderson of the Missouri Botanical Garden and the University of Washington, the better approach has been to study plant population differences so carefully, using methods devised by Dr Anderson, that the patterns of character association found in them reveal their origin. The method has been so precise that, solely through the study of a hybrid population of plants, it has been possible to construct a detailed description of an unknown invading species which has later proved to be entirely accurate when it was identified from the theoretical description. This is the general approach I have used in modifying the phylogenetic chart which illustrates the probable evolution of Rhododendrons.

Genetic studies in recent years have steadily emphasized the importance of introgressive hybridization in plants. The variation within species which is characteristic of Rhododendrons can almost certainly be ascribed to the same cause with equal emphasis. Even superficial examinations of related species frequently show the patterns of character association which are a criterion of hybridity. In fact, the evidence seems so strong that I believe the Rhododendrons of Sino-Himalaya are extraordinarily dynamic in their present condition and that hybridization is taking place among them at a very high rate.

Tracing back the erroneous impression one gets from reading the scant literature on the subject, I feel that the field collectors who explored the Asian wilderness for new Rhododendron species were oriented toward the viewpoint of the systematist, who is trained to see *resemblances* among plants, and hybridization in the wild, which is primarily repeated backcrossing of natural hybrids with the original plant population, produces offspring which closely resemble the recurrent parent. Geneticists, on the other hand, are trained to see *differences* and to search for those that may even be minute, as they seek to unravel the tangled skeins which lead back to the origins of plants.

The evidence indicates to me that Rhododendrons in their Asian heartland have undergone two types of introgression: the flow of genes from one species into another inhabiting the same district has occurred sporadically as opportunities have been presented for the hybrids to find congenial ecological niches; but there must have also been gene flows between species which are natives of geographically separated areas.

Widely separated species which cross by the caprice of climate changes, insects or natural cataclysms thereby create the conditions by which a million years of evolution may be encompassed in a hundred. As the hybrids flourish in districts intermediate between the population centers of the two parental species, natural selection works quickly upon whole systems of vigorous and novel gene combinations to evolve new plant forms. The continuing chain of back crosses produces an uninterrupted series of plants intermediate between the two species forebears, linking them in fluid progression. In the Himalayas this type of introgression may have been the merging of high altitude Rhododendron species with others from lower elevations much more often than opportunity would have allowed the crossing of two different species separated by vast distances, although the geographical origin of herbarium specimens indicates that the latter occurred too.

All studies thus far made have shown that variation in plant populations is directly proportional to the opportunities for introgression, and that introgressive hybridization is far more important than all other factors (such as mutations) combined in creating the opportunities for natural selection to evolve new forms. When the contribution of foreign germ plasm to that of the original population results in new combinations which put the hybrid plants at a selective advantage, the new forms persist in nature. The floralistically active region of the Himalayas has provided the conditions conducive to the perpetuation of Rhododendrons as a genus in flux.

Collectors in Asia have sent back seeds and specimens from individual plants which apparently came from hybrid swarms, the large local populations, superficially similar, which result when an intruding immigrant species backcrosses repeatedly with the species originally at the site. Whole areas are often blanketed by such hybrid populations, particularly those which may have been burned over or otherwise disturbed by the natives at one time or another. As the progeny of two different species acquire dominance due to colonization under intermediate ecological conditions and because of their hybrid vigor, first, second and more advanced generation hybrids may build up into immense populations.

Representatives of these mixed populations should not be regarded as stable species, however, even though they have ended up in our botanical texts with that status, to perplex the gardener and confound the taxonomist. It is another factor which must be considered in attempting to arrive at a valid conception of the somewhat confused state of Rhododendron classification at the present time.

Classification

Emile Meyerson devised a neat and accurate definition when he said that science is the systematic reduction of diversity to identity. It applies with special precision to the taxonomy of Rhododendrons, the arrangement of the disorderly masses of them into related ranks and into categories for convenient identification. The job has been slow and difficult.

To classify the thousand-odd sorts into groups of related species, with their elusive differences and similarities, has been a colossal undertaking. The uniqueness of each takes its place with its likeness, and past authorities have seldom been able to agree on either their similarities or their differences in classifying this singular horde of plants. Their likeness makes them Rhododendrons (except that three groups, the Anthopogon, Cephalanthum and Camtschaticum series may not actually be Rhododendrons at all) and their uniqueness gives them the identity of species (except that many present species are not entitled to that status).

There are forty-three groups of Rhododendrons called series, each containing species which bear a common resemblance to one another and often identified by the name of a well-known species which was thought to be typical of the whole assemblage. Some series contain more than fifty species. About a third of the forty-three series are further divided into subseries, each a group of species even more closely related within the larger framework of the series.

In deciding into which categories plants should be placed, the structure of the flower is the usual basis for decision because it is the most constant: neither favorable nor unfavorable growing conditions affect the arrangement of the flower parts to any appreciable extent. But in Rhododendrons there are many sorts which have flowers so alike that the taxonomists are obliged to turn to other characteristics of the plants to establish the various groups which constitute the different species. Thus an unidentified Rhododendron may be assigned to a particular species on numerous counts other than flower structure.

Essentially, the present classification is based on the characteristics of the leaves: whether they are smooth, hairy or scaly. If hairs or scales are present, their structure has become very important in recent years as a criterion for placing a species with its nearest relatives. But the largest division of Rhododendrons is into two groups: the lepidotes, with tiny, round plate-like scales on the leaf undersurfaces; and the elepidotes, which have leaves either smooth or hairy, but never scaly. The immature leaves in the foliage buds of the scaly species roll inwards; in the non-scaly species they roll outwards.

The shape and structure of the seeds is becoming another important way of diagnosing Rhododendron relationships, and so is the number of cell layers in the leaf epidermis. Whether the flowers are borne in terminal umbels from special buds or in a multiple inflorescence scattered along the stems is an important distinction, the former being typical and the latter exceptional. There are a great many other characteristics which are used in classifying Rhododendrons and they vary enormously in their importance from one group of species to another.

The color of the flowers and the shape and size of the leaf, which have caused many errors in separating species in the past, are not as important as they once were. Floral characters, especially, present so many problems with their endless variations and intermediate gradations that minor vegetative structures have received close study and are proving to be much more reliable as a basis for classification. The structure of the hairs and scales is especially revealing in the study of the relationship of species.

Faults in the Series

There is only a limited number of series which are truly natural groups of related species. Too many of them appear to be artificial categories containing misfits for which no other place could be found. The affinities within some series are so remote that it has never been possible to organize a key of characteristics peculiar to the species in each of the series, and consequently it may be a difficult matter to place an unfamiliar species into the series to which it should belong. It is the many exceptions which invalidate the usefulness of these groupings and there are at least a dozen out of the total of forty-three series which contain such notable inconsistencies that they are badly in need of revision. The Barbatum, Neriiflorum, and Taliense series are good examples of groups of species which are confusing in their mixed characteristics. The two species of the Auriculatum series are conspicuously dissimilar. In fact, a number of species are so obviously misplaced in the series to which they have been assigned that I am making some corrections in this book, based on my own observations and on the studies of the leaf trichomes by Dr J. M. Cowan.

Despite the anomalies, the sharpest distinctions between categories of Rhododendrons are among the series into which the species are grouped by their common resemblance. On the whole, the species within a series do bear a gross similarity to each other even with the admitted exceptions and the overlapping into other series. The easiest and best way to understand the classification of Rhododendrons is to envision the typical species which represents others in the series, and to accept the existence of the numerous exceptions. The chart insert illustrates in color a species representative of each series and will enable the reader to visualize these groups of Rhododendron species and their relationship to each other much more clearly. Nature refuses to accommodate mankind with conveniently rigid categories. It abhors the straitjacket which would represent frozen immobility. The difficulty in classifying Rhododendrons is a reflection of the continuous lifestream that nature intends. We are dealing with the plastic and dynamic, with the pulse of creation, which has changed and developed unceasingly since time began. These hosts of Rhododendrons will continue to shift restlessly in the gigantic framework of evolution as long as they inhabit the earth. The wonder is, not that there are so many faults in classification, but that the botanists have done so well with the undisciplined legions of them.

Faults in the Subseries

Some large series have subseries in which are grouped species which bear a closer botanical resemblance to each other. These subseries, too, are inconsistent in their supposed uniformity of closely related species. The Caucasicum subseries of the Ponticum series; the Argyrophyllum subseries of the Arboreum series; and the Roxieanum subseries of the Taliense series are examples which come readily to mind.

The Series as Connecting Links

From gaps in the sequence of evolution, one can deduce that there are probably many Rhododendron species yet unknown to cultivation. Some may no longer survive, but there must be a considerable number yet undiscovered in the remote wildernesses of southeastern Asia which should throw new light on the relationships of the series, their sequence of evolution, and the other species which are their nearest kin. On the other hand, some groups of allied species serving as links between others more sharply defined give evidence of themselves being natural hybrids recently evolved, and it may yet be determined that these entire series are no more than the early generation progeny of accidental crosses in the wild. Elsewhere in the genus, the progression of fixed types is evident, as in the Selense subseries, which bridges the Thomsonii and Barbatum series.

The Ponticum Series

The Ponticum series is of special interest to gardeners in the northeastern United States because it contains so many species hardy there. It has been obvious for decades that this odd association has little logic. As originally envisioned, it was supposed to consist of an assemblage of Rhododendrons distinguished by flower trusses resembling candelabra. Such a vague and indefinite distinction is totally inadequate as a criterion for establishing this class of species intended to be in close relationship with each other. The two Caucasian species, *RR. smirnowii* and *ungernii* with their outlying Chinese relative, *R. adenopodum*, have only limited affinity with either the Japanese or with the American species, and it is interesting now to note the report of Dr Cowan pointing out their close relationship to the species of the Adenogynum subseries in the Taliense series. They will doubtless be placed there when next there is a major revision of these series. *R. brachycarpum* will probably go to the Lacteum series on the basis of its unique indumentum identical with the species in that group.

Merging Species

Descending to the specific level, the Rhododendron scholar finds a disconcerting lack of definition among species within a series, time and time again. *R. fictolacteum* merges imperceptibly into *R. rex* in the big-leaved species. There is a continuous progression of intermediate forms among *RR. campylocarpum*, *caloxanthum*, and *telopeum*, in the yellow-flowered shrub Rhododendrons. There is no sharp division between the popular *R. discolor* and its relative *R. houlstonii*. A complete range of intergrades connects *RR. decorum* and *diaprepes*, both splendid ornamental shrubs for the garden. The forms midway between the distinguished *R. wardii* and its ally, *R. litiense*, can be identified as either one or the other with equal accuracy. I am convinced that *RR. concatenans* and *xanthocodon* are merely two more in the swarm of varieties and natural hybrids which constitute the species we call *R. cinnabarinum*. Among the dwarfs, no distinct boundary can be found to separate *R. saluenense* from *R. chameunum*. *RR. uniflorum* and *patulum* are merely the extremes of a fluid series connected by *RR. pemakoense* and *imperator*, and no line can be drawn to distinguish any

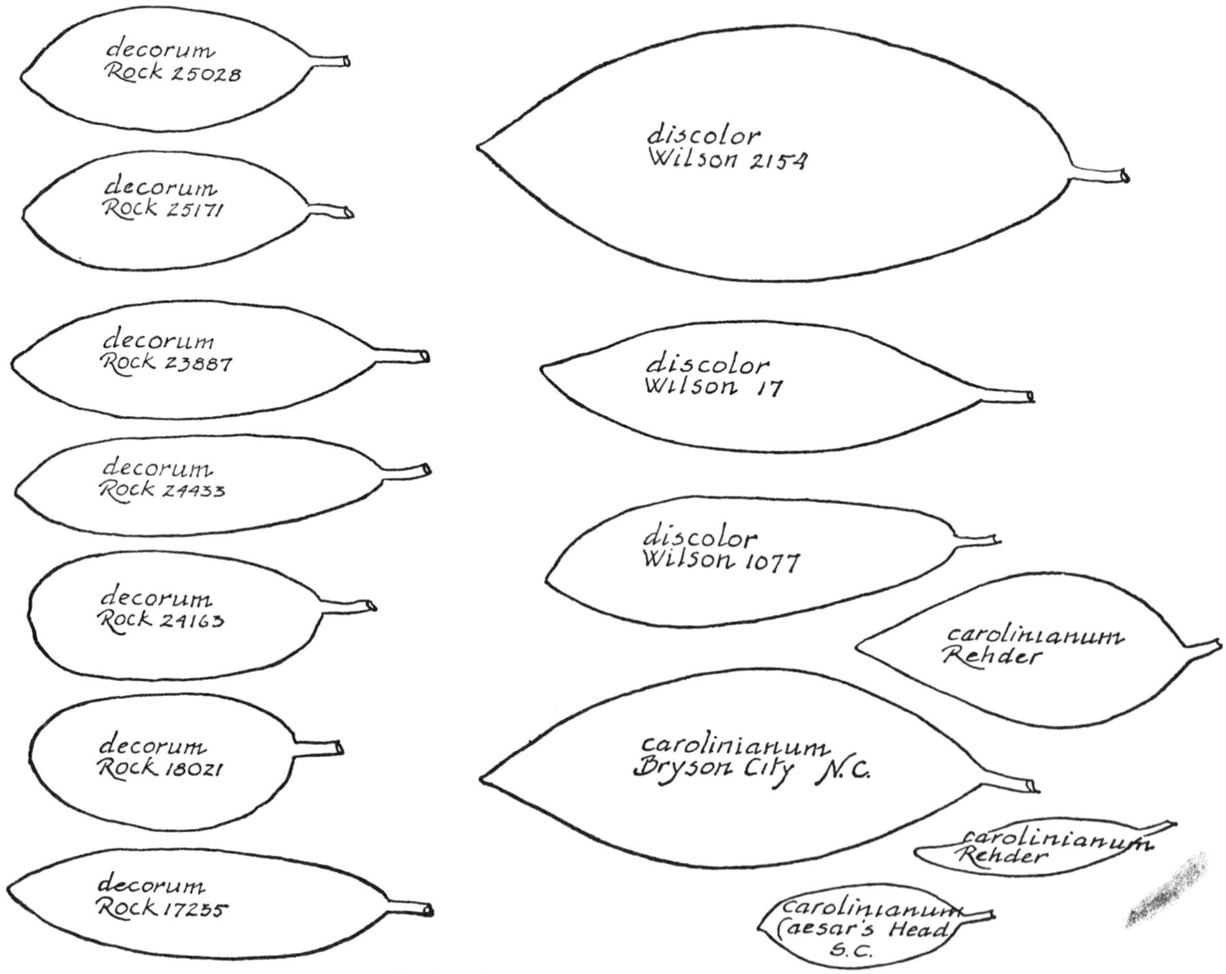

Leaf variation in three important species

one of them from its next neighbor in the range. The Triflorum, Neriiflorum, Lapponicum series and the Roxieanum subseries especially, are in chaotic condition with respect to the definition of the species within them, and the criteria by which they are purported to be recognizable. It is not that these series in a larger sense do not usually constitute related and similar plants. It is usually possible to recognize a Rhododendron as belonging to the Triflorum series at a glance. The Lapponicum species are reasonably distinct. Although some series are awkward for the lack of close relationships among some of the species in them, these are examples of other series in which the species within them lack definition, and the botanical characteristics by which their identities are diagnosed are confused.

The Technical Explanation

The imperceptible merging of one species into another indicates that the internal genetic barriers to hybridization in the wild are weak. When the internal barriers are strong, and cross-breeding occurs in spite of it, plant characteristics from the invading species are contributed to the original species in whole groups. The characteristics in a group tend to retain their association and to remain together even after many generations of back-crosses between the natural hybrids and the original species population, so that there are thus produced large numbers of more or less clearly defined subspecies. The numerous subspecies in the alliance of Rhododendron species making up the Sanguineum subseries are an example.

One of the potent cohesive forces which perpetuates the association of certain plant characteristics as a group probably results from the evolution by natural selection of these associated traits as an effective combination for the environment. This combination, perfected through aeons of time, could also operate so successfully in fitting natural hybrids to their way of life that it survives through many generations, though of course it is usually broken up gradually by repeated hybridization over a very long period of time.

Two species inhabiting the same district in the wild retain their identity because there are both external and internal forces operating to prevent indiscriminate crossing between them on a continuous and massive scale. In the first place, the established species have survived because they have been at a selective advantage in the endless process by which nature eliminates the unfit. They are adapted to their environment in the gene combinations they possess, whereas any offspring resulting from crosses between two species are endowed with new gene combinations which may not fit them so well for their conditions of life and so they perish. There are usually no ready-made, intermediate ecological niches in which first generation hybrids between two species can flourish. This is an important external barrier and it operates with considerable effectiveness, as is demonstrated by the tremendous increase in natural hybridization between species when the land is disturbed by man. By lumbering, burning underbrush, tilling the soil, pasturing animals, building roads and otherwise altering the natural condition of the land, new and unoccupied ecological niches of somewhat novel character are created into which natural hybrids can grow and remain at a selective advantage. Of course natural cataclysms such as hurricanes and floods produce the same result.

The external barriers to hybridization between species may be subtle in their influence and all but imperceptible: species may retain their identity because of their peculiar adaptation to the altitude or its temperature (there is a fall of 1° F. for each increase of 364 feet elevation in the Himalayas); to the acidity of the soil; to the amount of sunlight or shade; to moisture, or to any one of innumerable facets of their conditions of life. Their ecological preference is made up of a complex of such varying factors and with no other combination of them would they be at quite such a selective advantage in the struggle for survival. They are so perfectly adapted to their environment that an invader in the form of a natural hybrid, intermediate in its requirements, cannot compete with them and so it perishes instead of living on to infiltrate its characteristics into the original population.

Internal barriers such as sterilities between

species seem to be much less effective in preserving the purity of species in the wild. If an intermediate ecological niche is unoccupied where the progeny of two different species can survive in the wild, they seem to be produced to take advantage of it. Dr Edgar Anderson, pioneering investigator in this field, suggests that the role of sterility barriers may have been much over-emphasized by past students of the subject, and as a practising hybridist I am bound to agree. Almost every breeder is startled to learn, at some time, that someone else has unexpectedly succeeded in crossing the same two species which had previously resisted all efforts to mate them. Transferring this same experience to the wilderness, the concept of absolute sterility seems dubious. Where plants are growing by the millions and are exposed to the possibility of hybridization over millions of years, a fertility frequency as

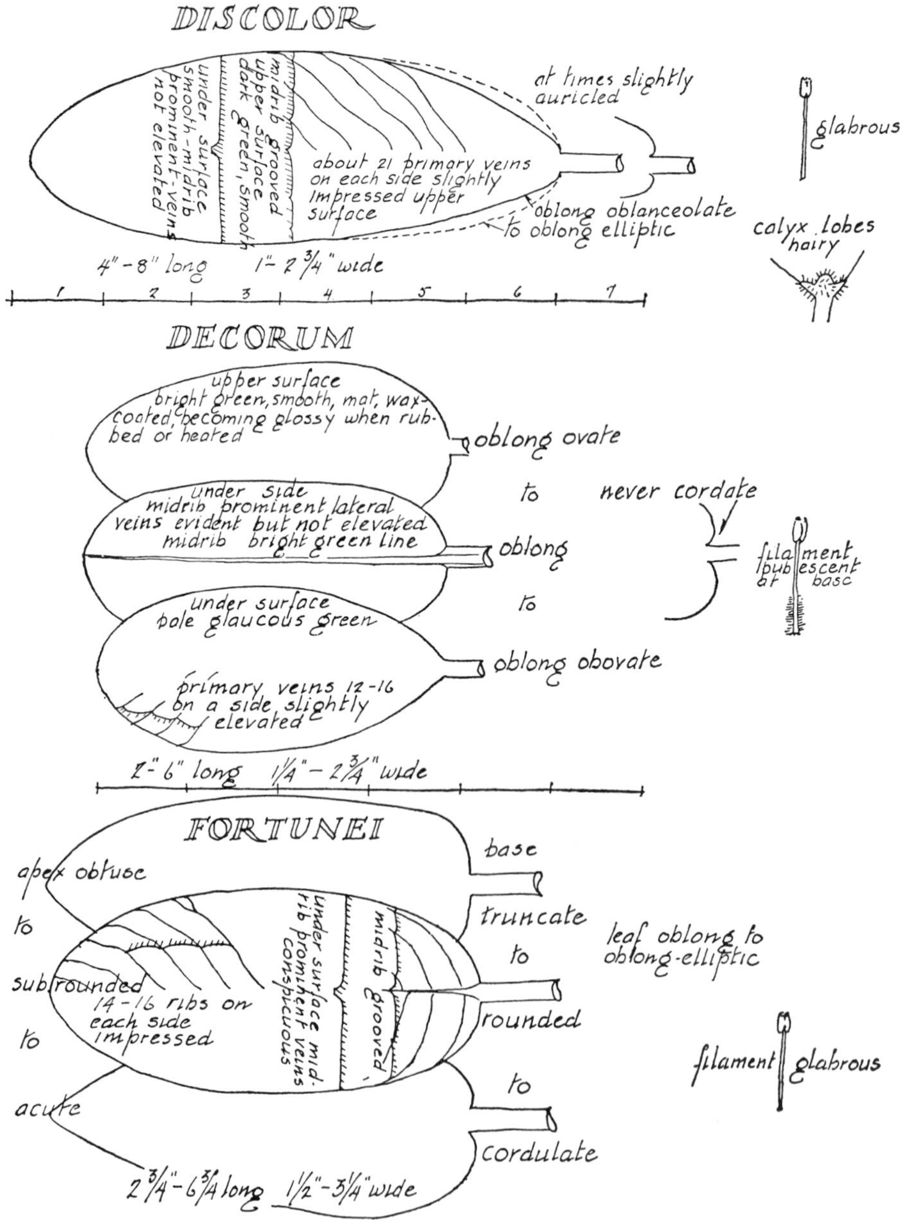

Distinctive marks of three important species

low as one in a hundred million could be extremely important. So it is that barriers arising from the interplay of germ plasm from one species upon that of another are not too well defined in their effect upon the evolution of Rhododendrons.

Identifying Unknown Specimens

Once the series affiliation of an unknown species is deduced on the basis of familiarity with the genus (since no schedule of identifying marks for each series can be drawn up), the botanical keys published in the English technical work, *The Species of Rhododendron*, are intended to make possible the identification of the unknown specimen after its series has been established. In practice, these keys are frequently inaccurate, as might inevitably be expected from the number of cases where presumably distinct species are linked by merging microforms. *The Species of Rhododendron* was a masterly work when it was produced in 1930 but much of its authority has vanished with the years and it now has many deficiencies, largely inaccuracies which are recognizable as such only in the light of our much greater current knowledge of Rhododendrons. The criteria for diagnosing the species are often untenable, the descriptions faulty. It will be retired in honor, its job well done, when the revisions of the series have been completed by the systematic botanists and a new edition appears. But it seems unrealistic to expect too much. Rhododendron species do not differ in whole sets of characters, as good species should, nor do they even differ always in one character as they are presently established. Readers are hereby warned that the identifying marks given in the descriptions of the species which follow in this chapter are the best guides we have, but they are not infallible, and experience is still the best botanical key we have at this time.

The Value of An Accurate Concept

Perhaps I have over-emphasized the exceptions, the difficulties and confusion in the classification of Rhododendrons, but I think it is important to recognize them at the outset, or else what should be a pleasant study of the genus will be a frustrating and irritating experience. Accepted, they will aid us and whet the challenge to surmount them; ignored, they will baffle and balk us until we turn away in disgust.

Accomplishment Despite Difficulties

It must not be supposed that any but the most conscientious and intelligent effort has been put on the scientific study of Rhododendrons. This work has been in the hands of the British. The technical investigations have been largely undertaken by the taxonomists at the Royal Botanic Garden in Edinburgh with their incomparable collection of herbarium specimens. The task which has confronted them has been enormous, and they have done remarkably well with what may easily be the most varied and unwieldy group of plants that exist on this earth. Only the most determined and talented effort could have reduced this massive diversity to even its present identity. Each year or two an additional series is revised in the continuing quest for an orderly and rational classification. Each year additional study reveals the relationships of the species more accurately. Undoubtedly the microscopic analysis of the leaf structures by Dr J. M. Cowan will advance the work tremendously.

The gross size and shape of Rhododendron leaves have caused many errors in classification in the past, but the taxonomist is confronted time and again with decisions on other points which have no really satisfactory solution. Many series contain species which are an awkward paradox simply because these same Rhododendrons would be even more of an anomaly if they were placed in other series. Hair structure, seed conformation and other reliable indicators of affinity may all point in the direction of different series and insoluble conflict is thus created which can be resolved only by the emphasis which the investigator chooses to place on each characteristic. And matters of opinion are sure to be matters of dispute.

Anonymous Species of the Herbarium

There are 350 or 400 species, subspecies and varieties listed in the standard reference works which are not in cultivation in the Western world. And there are a staggering number of "species" represented by herbarium specimens which have no living counterparts in our gardens or botanical institutions, and have no formal status or general recognition. If there were living representatives in the Western world of all the different herbarium specimens in the Lapponicum series, for example, the number of species in this group would multiply enormously. The same is true of many other series. This odd situation was brought about because some of the plant hunters who collected in Asia did not always send back into cultivation seeds of Rhododendrons of inferior horticultural value. Their sponsors, often amateur enthusiasts, were interested more in garden decoration than in botany. The plant hunters, on the other hand, were naturally eager to acquire the distinction of discovering new species. And so the herbarium specimens of new species multiplied enormously in the collection at Edinburgh.

There is, of course, a more or less constant divergence between the horticultural and the botanical. There are many cases where two or more Rhododendrons which seem distinct as ornamental shrubs in the garden are identical botanically. On the other hand, if the gardener could see the tremendous variation in the herbarium specimens of a species which seems to him but a single, clearly defined type, he would find it hard to believe the evidence of his eyes. For example, the gross appearance of the specimens of *R. neriiflorum* sent back from the wild fluctuates so widely that no gardener would ever recognize many of them without minute botanical analysis. Sometimes the taxonomists compromise with the gardeners (as it later usually develops, mistakenly so) by conceding specific status to an extreme Rhododendron form as a convenient identification for it, even though it deserves no such distinction. *R. litiense*, for example, is not at all distinct from *R. wardii*, but its status remains because gardeners want a separate name for the form with small, oblong leaves. The illustration on page 114 gives a small sampling of the variance within species to be found in herbarium specimens, and it conveys only minutely the scope of fluctuation to be found in the files.

CORRECTIONS OF FORMER DESCRIPTIONS

There are about 600 Rhododendron species in cultivation today. When they were described in 1930 in a comprehensive work of general distribution, the mature stature in cultivation of many of them was unknown and the extent of their variation was not realized. We have acquired an immense body of additional knowledge about Rhododendrons in the last thirty years, but unfortunately the original descriptions of them have usually been perpetuated in subsequent publications. The accounts of the species described below in detail are in good part the result of thousands of measurements and observations of living plants which I made in England, Scotland, and Wales, and of studies of herbarium specimens.

THE SPECIES IMPORTANT TO HORTICULTURE

Of the 600 species, approximately, in cultivation, about 150 are important horticulturally for their beauty of flower and foliage, and often as well for their hardiness and general adaptability. These are described below in detail from my own data, which I hope will be useful to botanists; I hope also that the manner of their description will give a clear picture of their garden virtues and aid all enthusiasts to identify them. The species given extended treatment include all of those recommended by local boards of experts in the Seattle, Portland, and San Francisco districts as being the best in each category for their stature, flower color, and season of bloom, and those most esteemed in the British Isles. The Rhododendron species hardy in the northeastern United States are described in detail, as well as those of superior quality which give preliminary evidence of being adapted to the more southerly Rhododendron belt comprised of Delaware, Maryland, Virginia and West Virginia. Finally, species prominent historically or as notable parents of hybrids are included in this group. In addition to these extended descriptions of the species important horticulturally, *a complete listing of all Rhododendron species, revised to the latest findings of botanical research and with condensed descriptions in tabular form, begins on page* 508. *Another listing of all the species, grouped by their natural relationships under the series to which they belong, begins on page* 521.

Certain obscure species which are at least precariously hardy in the milder, southern districts of the northeastern United States are omitted from detailed description below because they are so ill-adapted to the climate that successful culture is a matter of extravagant care under special conditions. Many of the Taliense group, for example, are hardy enough to New York City or even farther north in favored sites, but they grow so poorly and are so frequently afflicted with blight that they almost always die without flowering, possibly also the result of a microscopic borer which attacks them. The most tractable of the species in the lavender-flowered Lapponicum series are given extended descriptions, but there are others, more difficult, which will grow briefly and flower profusely until they suddenly and quietly collapse because of the incompatible climate. They are not ornamental plants of any permanence and few cultivators would be willing to attend their whims. *R. semibarbatum* is an example of a species which is hardy in at least a portion of the Northeast but it is omitted as its flowers are inconsequential, it is deciduous, and seems not to be commercially available.

Such things as stature and season of bloom are influenced by regional climate and local planting site. *R. ciliatum*, for example, is a shrub 3 or 4 feet tall in an average mild climate, but it becomes 9 feet high and 18 feet broad where the temperature goes a little below freezing only rarely and for brief periods. Some of the large-leaved tree species display the full splendor of their foliage solely under exceptionally benign conditions, but they grow well enough and make handsome garden subjects, even with smaller leaves, in colder climates. It is, of course, impractical to be so minutely exhaustive as to encompass in the following descriptions the multitude of effects which the immediate environment may have on the Rhododendron species, sometimes with astonishing results.

THE ILLUSTRATIONS

The drawings which accompany the discussions of the species were executed by the distinguished sculptor, Mr Edmond Amateis, who is a Rhododendron enthusiast and amateur hybridist. They are intended to give the reader a clear picture of the leaf and flower of each Rhododendron, and to emphasize the features by which each can be recognized. Close attention to the text and drawings combined should aid the reader to distinguish specimens of these species wherever they are encountered. Features conspicuously self-evident in the drawings may not be repeated by description in the text. Many Rhododendrons in gardens both public and private are unlabeled and the species, particularly, seem susceptible to a loss of identity.

THE RATINGS

In the following descriptions the species are rated for freedom of bloom, ease of cultivation, quality and hardiness. The first given rating, freedom of bloom, is in a sequence of 1 to 3 in order of decreasing floriferous character, and each such rating was determined in consultation with experts in this country and in England for the *average* of that species. There may be exceptions. For example, there is in Cairnryan, Scotland, a single specimen of *R. sinogrande* which is extraordinarily free-flowering, probably the only such example in cultivation of this normally shy-flowering species.

The second rating, ease of cultivation, is also an unofficial one devised by the author with the advice of specialists, from 1 to 3 in order of decreasing adaptability to ordinary garden conditions.

The quality ratings are those officially assigned by the American Rhododendron Society (from x to xxxx in order of increasing value); or by the Royal Horticultural Society of England (from ★ to ★★★★ in order of increasing quality). The American ratings are given for the species which have been rated in the United States. Some species, too new to cultivation in this country to be widely distributed, are still unrated here and in such cases the British rating is given. The same is true for the hardiness ratings which follow: the American system is used wherever the American Rhododendron Society has assigned symbols to indicate the hardiness of the species. A few sorts are not yet rated in the United States and in such cases only the British symbols appear. These ratings, American and British, are to be interpreted as follows:

AMERICAN RATINGS	APPLICATION	EQUIVALENT BRITISH RATING	APPLICATION
H-1	Hardy to 25 below zero F. 'These should be hardy in southern New York and New England.'		
H-2	Hardy to −15° F.	A	Hardy anywhere in the British Isles with full exposure.
H-3	Hardy to −5° F. 'These should be fairly hardy in southern Long Island and around Philadelphia.'	B	Hardy anywhere in the British Isles but requires some shade for best results.
H-4	Hardy to +5° F.	C	Hardy along the seaboard and in sheltered inland gardens.
H-5	Hardy to +15° F. 'These should be hardy during most winters in the Portland and Seattle areas.'	D	Hardy in south and west and in sheltered gardens inland.
H-6	Hardy to +25° F. 'Hardy in Pacific Northwest coastal gardens and in sheltered areas elsewhere in the region.'	E	Requires protection in even the most sheltered gardens.
H-7	Hardy to +32° F.	F	Usually a greenhouse plant.

'Hardiness' means resistance to winter cold alone. Many Asian Rhododendrons which are hardy to Philadelphia and even farther north cannot endure the heat and low humidity of summers in the eastern United States. Hardiness is determined also by the duration of cold as well as the degree. In the eastern United States tolerance of cold is not necessarily a uniform attribute throughout all of the forms of the Oriental species. Specialists have isolated hardy forms and strains of Rhododendron species which are not normally satisfactory in the cold northeastern part of the country. By allowing the rigors of the climate to take their toll of large numbers of seedlings, these nurserymen have secured from the survivors Rhododendrons which are considerably hardier than the average of the species. By using these selected plants of exceptional hardiness as parents, additional generations of Rhododendrons with unusual resistance to cold have been secured.

Further than that, the seeds sent back by the several collecting expeditions into the wild interior of Asia have varied considerably in their hardiness. For example, the form of *R. racemosum* sent back by the Forrest expedition as produced from seeds under lot #19404 is hardy at Philadelphia; the form introduced under #56363 by the Rock expedition is hopelessly tender.

Finally, some specialists have isolated single hardy plants from tender species. By propagating such hardy individuals from cuttings their floral assets combined with their exceptional resistance to cold have been made available to the gardening public.

Hardiness, then, may be an attribute of a strain created by selection; of a specific form of a species introduced by seeds from the Orient, or of an individual plant propagated commercially as a clone. It is important, therefore, that the gardener in the northeastern United States purchase his plants of the Asian mainland species from Rhododendron specialists in the East. In the list of nurseries on page 505 there are several such specialist growers who propagate and sell the selected hardy forms of the exotic species.

I feel that the system of rating resistance to cold, while it is the best available, is not very satisfactory and should be used more as a general guide than with any unqualified literal application. The reader is referred to the chapter on hardiness in this book. I am indebted to The Royal Horticultural Society's *The Rhododendron Handbook* and to *Rhododendrons*, an official publication of the American Rhododendron Society, for the ratings of quality and hardiness which are used below and in the complete tabulated descriptions of all species which starts on page 508.

For more than a hundred years the Royal Horticultural Society in England has been issuing awards to Rhododendrons as they have been exhibited in the shows and judged by committees of experts. American enthusiasts, in the absence of any comparable indications of merit in this country until very recently, have long used the British citations as evidence of superiority and have sought for their gardens plants propagated from the original award specimens. At the end of each description below there appears a note of any honors the species has received, and the year in which the citation was bestowed, A.M. for Award of Merit, and F.C.C. for the highest show citation, the First Class Certificate. In addition, there is a rare garden honor, the A.G.M., or Award of Garden Merit, given to Rhododendrons which have been carefully evaluated over a period of years for their quality as growing plants in cultivation under a variety of conditions, in contrast to the flowering branch or cut truss exhibited at a show.

These awards have often been misunderstood in the United States. It is probably true to say that as a whole they are a rough guide to superior species forms but certainly they do not invariably represent the best. *R. nuttallii*, for example, was given a First Class Certificate in 1864, and it would be strange indeed if no better form had turned up in a century than the one exhibited then. As seedlings of the species are raised year after year, extraordinarily good sorts are constantly found which supersede in quality other forms previously given awards, often only recently. Then, too, any really well-grown specimen may receive a citation. In recent years, exhibitors have assigned clone-names in order to qualify for an award a good new form of a species which has already been given a citation in years past for its quality.

The owners of extraordinarily fine examples of the species are not always interested in entering them for awards. For example, a public garden in Scotland contains a form of *R. wardii* much superior to the specimens which have competed for honors. Nor should a particular species be selected for planting on the basis of the awards it has received. Some species which have apparently never been proposed for awards are much finer ornamentals than others boasting a First Class Certificate.

American awards have recently been established, P.A. meaning Preliminary Award, given for a cut flower truss, with foliage, exhibited for appraisal by three official judges. The Award of Excellence (A.E.) is made by a panel of three judges for a complete plant exhibiting superior foliage, growth habit, and flowers. T.G.C. signifies 'Test Garden Certificate', an honor bestowed upon a Rhododendron which has been propagated vegetatively and observed in flower by three judges for at least two years in one of the recognized test gardens of the American Rhododendron Society. This award may also be given to a clone which has been judged for two years in three private gardens, each at least a mile apart.

The truss type at the end of each description refers to numbered drawings on pages 235–238 which are intended to show the arrangement of the blossoms in the inflorescence. By turning to the drawing whose number corresponds with that in the description, the general flowering effect of that species will be clear. These drawings of the complete inflorescence are not meant to portray the size and shape of the individual blossoms, but only the manner in which they are grouped in the truss, or presented singly or in pairs. Accurate conformation and dimensions of the individual flowers are shown in the drawings below, which are intended to be used as a part of the following description of each species, thereby minimizing the amount of technical botanical data required in the text.

Descriptions of all Rhododendron species in condensed tabular form, with their quality and hardiness ratings, will be found in the complete listing which begins on page 508. *The characteristics of the series and subseries, with the species in each, are described on page* 521.

R. aberconwayi (ab-er-kon′-way-i), **Cowan.** IRRORATUM SERIES, IRRORATUM SUBSERIES

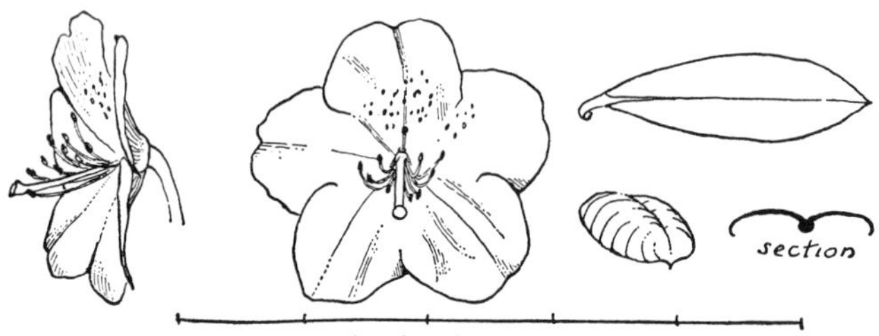

All drawings are scaled in inches.

Here is one of the newest Rhododendron species in cultivation and a unique one, so different from any heretofore found that it rests uneasily in the series to which it has been assigned, yet would be even more awkwardly placed in any other. It is a medium-sized shrub 5 to 8 feet tall with dark green, strongly veined leaves $1\frac{1}{4}$ to $2\frac{3}{4}$ inches long, $\frac{1}{2}$ to $1\frac{1}{4}$ inches wide, with downcurved margins. They are extraordinary in their stiff, leathery composition, so brittle that they crack and break if they are bent slightly. The widely open, saucer-shaped blossoms are borne in a firm, rounded racemose truss of about nine in late May, each flower usually $2\frac{1}{2}$ inches across, white or with varying suffusions of rose-pink, and lightly or conspicuously spotted dark red on the upper lobe. For the few years that this Rhododendron has been in cultivation it has found a wide acceptance. The flat blossoms with their graceful shallow outline have the same classic purity of form which makes *R. souliei* so appealing. As evergreens, the shrubs are attractive and of useful dimensions. The species is reported to be hardy and adaptable over a wide range of climates. Plants I have seen show considerable variation. *R. aberconwayi* can be instantly identified by the widely open, saucer-shaped flowers and the leathery leaves so rigid that they snap in two if slightly bent. This species is native to eastern Yunnan, where it was found by Chinese assistants to George Forrest who were retained as collectors by Lord Aberconway after Forrest's death in 1932. Seeds were sent to England in 1937 and this Rhododendron grown from them was named for the distinguished British horticulturist and Rhododendron authority who sponsored its discovery. Freedom of Flowering: 1; Ease of Cultivation: 1; American Ratings: None yet assigned; British Quality Rating: ****; British Hardiness Rating: B; Truss Type: 2; A.M., 1945.

R. adenopodum (ad-en-o-pod′-um), **Franch.** PONTICUM SERIES, CAUCASICUM SUBSERIES

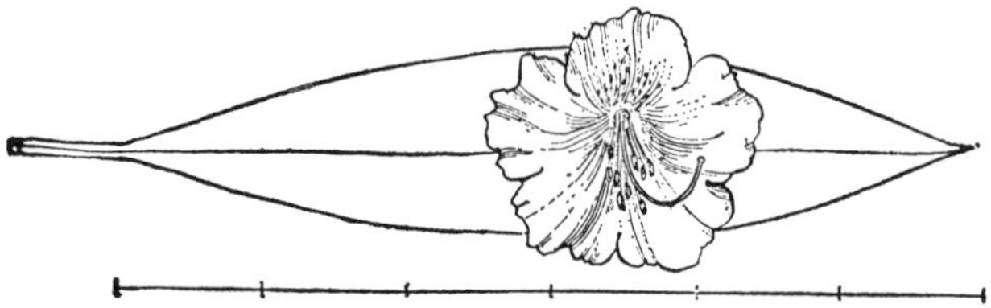

The Ponticum Series is important in cold climates and this member of it has a reputed height of 10 feet but mature specimens tend to spread as they grow older and I doubt whether plants in cultivation much exceed a height of 6 feet and a breadth of 9 feet. The dark green leaves, 3 to 8 inches long, $\frac{3}{4}$ to 2 inches broad, have a heavy felty indumentum beneath which varies from buff to cream-colored. About ten 2- to $2\frac{1}{2}$-inch translucent pale rose flowers, funnel-campanulate in shape, spotted within on the upper lobes, are borne in a loose truss. The blossoms appear in May, at about the same time as those of our native Carolina Rhododendron, and before the mid-season bloom of *R. catawbiense* and its hybrids. This good species has gained increasing admiration in recent years as it has become better known. Its profuse branching makes for a dense habit of growth to a moderate height which is especially useful in the garden. The contrast between the dark green upper surface of the leaves and the woolly fawn undersurface is particularly interesting. Altogether this is one of the loveliest and rarest of the Rhododendron clan, hardy to New York City and quite probably along the coast to Boston. It can be recognized by the comparatively loose truss in combination with flowers possessing an ovary with bristly glands and calyx of intermediate size, $\frac{1}{8}$ to $\frac{3}{16}$ inch in length. The long, oblanceolate leaves are narrow for their length, with pointed tips. Surprisingly, this species is found in eastern Szechuan and Hupeh provinces of western China, a sole representative of its series more than a thousand miles from its nearest Japanese relative in the Ponticum group. It was discovered there in thin woods at 5,000 to 7,000 feet elevation by Rev. Paul Farges who sent it to Maurice de Vilmorin at Les Barres, France, where it flowered in 1909. The name refers to the glandular flower stalks. Freedom of Flowering: 2; Ease of Cultivation: 1; American Ratings: None yet assigned; British Quality Rating: **; British Hardiness Rating: A; Truss Type: 1; A.M., 1926.

R. albiflorum (al-bif-lor′-um), **Hooker.** ALBIFLORUM SERIES

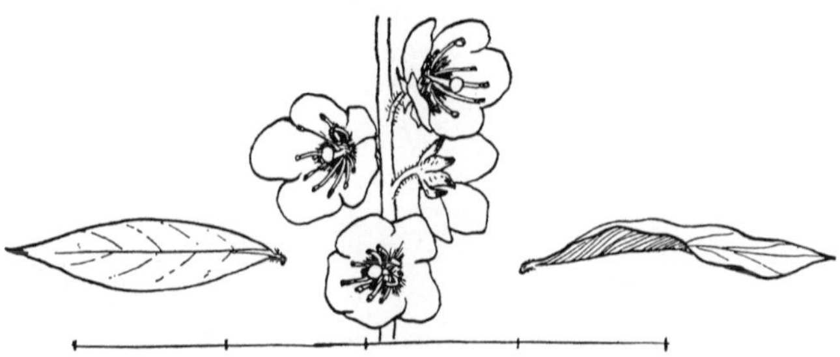

The Rhododendrons of the western United States include in *R. albiflorum* an unusual deciduous species whose only close relatives are the Chinese and Tibetan species of the Ovatum series. These Rhododendrons furnish a link with the Azaleas in their evolutionary development. The native species is an erect shrub 5 or 6 feet high in the mountain wilderness, with thin leaves 1 to $2\frac{3}{4}$ inches long, $\frac{3}{8}$ to $\frac{7}{8}$ inch wide, and dark hairs clothing the young stems. The creamy white, openly bell-shaped flowers $\frac{3}{4}$ inch across spring singly or in pairs from axillary buds scattered along the shoots of the previous year's growth, and they appear after the leaves are fully developed. In the wild *R. albiflorum* blooms in August; in cultivation at lower elevations, often in late June and early July. It is an interesting, unusual and pretty Rhododendron with the delicate white flowers nodding along the stems, one of the very few species to present its blossoms in this manner, but it seems not to take kindly to cultivation at lower elevations. I do not think that it has ever succeeded in the eastern United States. Plants which I raised from seeds grew very slowly and regularly dropped their leaves long before the end of summer. The same special cultural methods which made some of the difficult Asian species amenable brought no response from this one. In nature it is most often found in fully exposed sites with abundant moisture, frequently from melting snows. In England it is described as "not thriving", which applies as well to plants in cultivation at lower elevations on the West Coast. *R. albiflorum* is one of the most distinct species in the genus and can scarcely be confused with any other. It is found, always above 4,000 feet elevation, throughout several of the western mountain ranges. According to *Rhododendron*, the publication of the Washington Rhododendron Society, it has been observed from Colorado to Alberta, Canada, in the Rocky Mountains; in the Blue, Siskiyou and Cascade Mountains of Oregon; on Mt Angeles and on Hurricane Ridge in the Olympic Mountains and near Vancouver, B.C.; in Mt Rainier National Park, and in the region just northwest of Chinook Pass. Scouting this species in the wild, I found no stands of it south of Walden, Colorado. This may be the southern limit of its distribution in the Rocky Mountains. The name of this species refers to its white flowers. Freedom of Flowering: 2; Ease of Cultivation: 3; American Ratings: None yet assigned; British Quality Rating: None Awarded; British Hardiness Rating: A; Truss Type: 13.

R. ambiguum (am-big′-u-um), **Hemsl.** TRIFLORUM SERIES, TRIFLORUM SUBSERIES

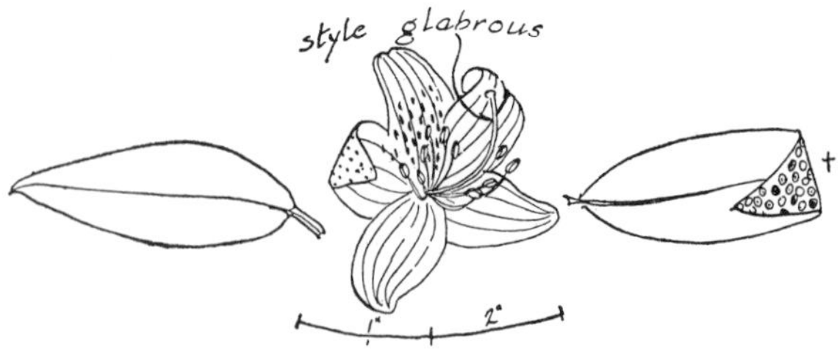

This is a 5- or 6-foot bushy shrub with aromatic olive-green leaves $1\frac{1}{2}$ to 3 inches long, $\frac{5}{8}$ to $1\frac{1}{4}$ inches broad, densely scaly underneath. It blooms in late April and early May, the pale yellow flowers spotted light green, broadly funnel-shaped and about 2 inches across, clustered in loose trusses of three to six at the ends of the branches. Here is another of the finer textured Rhododendrons of restricted growth which are so useful in providing a lighter note in the landscape than do the portly large-leaved sorts. However, to me the effect of this species in bloom is somewhat ragged and diffuse, the flowers tending to blend with the yellowish-green foliage. There are commercially available forms with blossoms a more determined yellow and also larger in size than the average. These are much more attractive. This is an adaptable Rhododendron, hardy enough to flower most years at Philadelphia but suffering occasionally in severe winters. Among other yellow-flowered species of the Triflorum Series it is characterized by minutely scalloped leaves with pointed tips, $1\frac{1}{2}$ inches long or more, with the stalks devoid of hairs. The leaf undersurface is clad in scales of various sizes, less than their own diameter apart and varying somewhat in color, the largest often being almost black. The corolla is scaly all over the outside. The style is glabrous. *R. ambiguum* was found and introduced by Wilson in 1904 from an elevation of about 11,000 feet in western Szechuan province of China. The name means "doubtful", and, for some forms at least, it is horticulturally perfectly understandable. Freedom of Flowering: 1; Ease of Cultivation: 1; American Quality Rating: x; British: **; American Hardiness Rating: H-4 (Author's dissent: H-3); British: A; Truss Type: 9.

R. aperantum (ap-er-an′-tum), **Balf. f. and Ward.** NERIIFLORUM SERIES, SANGUINEUM SUBSERIES

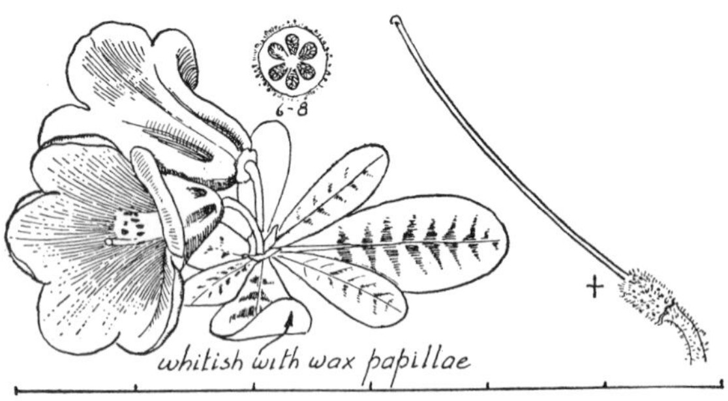

A crouching little undershrub of perfect habit for the rock garden, this Rhododendron forms spreading cushions of dense, mound-like foliage 6 to about 20 inches in height. Old plants are most often seen about 15 inches high and 3 feet across. The dark green leaves are $\frac{3}{4}$ to as much as 2 inches long, $\frac{3}{8}$ to $\frac{7}{8}$ inches wide, glaucous white beneath. In late April and early May flat-topped, lax clusters of four to six $1\frac{3}{4}$-inch flowers appear, surprisingly large for the stature of the plants which bear them. They are surprising too in their variation in color, ranging from white to rose, with yellow, orange, and crimson shades in various specimens. This might be described for garden effect as a more robust edition of the plant formerly called *R. repens*, now *R. forrestii*, and its similarity extends as well to a notorious capriciousness about flowering. A gardener for whom it does flower in perplexing freedom ascribes his success to placing the plants close together in soil which is suitable in texture but extremely low in nutrients. There this species is one of the finest features of an unusually beautiful garden, but most often this proves to be a difficult and shy-flowering Rhododendron of very slow growth. Leaves and other debris which tend to accumulate in the tangled branches beneath the top canopy of foliage should be removed occasionally lest their decay spread to the twigs and cause an unsightly rotting away of the center of the plants. The Rhododendron hunters describe colonies of plants in the wild as being packed so closely together that their tops support the weight of a man walking across them. This close communal habit may be a clue to the reproduction in cultivation of their dazzling color displays in nature. *R. aperantum* is easily recognized among species in the Sanguineum subseries by the absence of hairs or indumentum beneath the leaves, except rarely a few on the midrib, and it is more of a dwarf than its close relatives, which usually exceed its maximum height of 18 or 20 inches. The margins of the leaves are usually down-curved and the bud-scales on the young shoots are persistent. The corolla is thin, not fleshy, and the ovary is both glandular and hairy. *R. aperantum* is native to northeast Upper Burma at 12,000 to 14,000 feet, in open meadows and on rock ledges of the mountainsides. It was discovered by Ward and Farrer and introduced to cultivation by Forrest. In the wild, a single plant may eventually spread to a mat 20 feet in diameter, hence the name meaning 'limitless'. Freedom of Flowering: 3+; Ease of Cultivation: 2; American Quality Rating: x; British: **; American Hardiness Rating: H-3; British: B; Truss Type: 10; A.M., 1931.

R. apodectum (ap-o-dek′-tum), **Balf. f. and W. W. Sm.** NERIIFLORUM SERIES, SANGUINEUM SUBSERIES

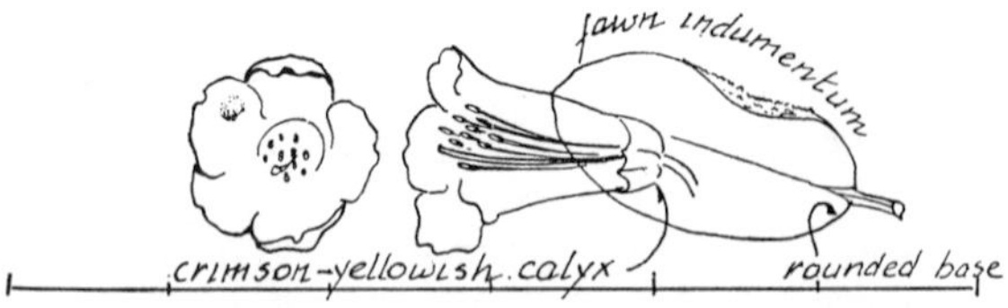

Technical references describe this subspecies as 4 to 8 feet tall, but it is usually seen as a widely spreading, dwarf, well-foliaged shrub about $2\frac{1}{2}$ feet in height, which hugs the ground and presents an exceptionally neat and attractive appearance, being densely clothed with leaves. I have measured specimens up to 11 feet in diameter which were not more than 30 inches in height. The leaves are $1\frac{1}{2}$ to 3 inches long, 1 to $1\frac{3}{8}$ inches broad, with a gray or tan downy under-surface and an odd, longitudinal ribbing above. The plants vary widely in their freedom of flowering and in the color of the blossoms, ranging from clear, bright red through crimson to dull orange. There are two to six rather long tubed, bell-shaped flowers of heavy substance, each about 1 to $1\frac{1}{4}$ inches across in a lax terminal cluster. The species blooms in late May and early June, two weeks later than *R. dichroanthum* which it otherwise resembles. It can easily be separated from it, however, by the rounded leaf base. The only place I have seen *R. apodectum* bloom *freely* is in Wales, but the Exbury orange-flowered form is especially handsome and is reputed to be more floriferous. This subspecies can be distinguished from its allies in the series by having, in addition to the leaf with rounded base, a thin indumentum underneath, and non-glandular pedicels. The ovary, also eglandular, is short, blunt, and hairy, and the seed capsule is short and straight. The leaves are ablanceolate to obovate. This subspecies of *R. dichroanthum* comes from open scrub and the edges of Rhododendron forests at 10,000 to 11,000 feet in western Yunnan province of China. Its name, meaning 'acceptable', is an amusing indication to some gardeners of its exasperating inconsistency in blooming. Freedom of Flowering: 3+; Ease of Cultivation: 2+; American Quality Rating: xx; British: **; American Hardiness Rating: H-4; British: A; Truss Type: 11.

R. arboreum (ar-bor′-ee-um), **Smith.** ARBOREUM SERIES, ARBOREUM SUBSERIES

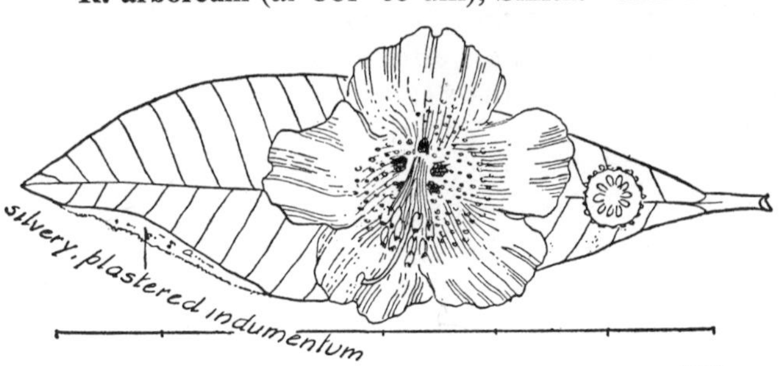

This magnificent monarch among Rhododendrons has been of the greatest importance, both horticulturally and historically, to our gardens. It was introduced into England in 1811 and flowered there for the first time in 1825. The large, rich crimson globes created a sensation when they appeared. Their size and purity of color set an entirely new standard of flower quality in the gardening world and the very next year, in 1826, the same plant which produced the beautiful blossoms was used by J. R. Gowan to cross with an earlier hybrid, *catawbiense* × *ponticum*, thus beginning the modern era of hybridizing the exotic Asian Rhododendrons with hardier sorts to capture their splendor for the harsher climate of Western gardens. Other crosses soon followed, producing such well-known Rhododendrons as *R.* (*caucasicum* × *arboreum*) 'Nobleanum' and *R.* (*catawbiense* × *arboreum*) 'Russellianum', which are still much in evidence in gardens today. Many of the red-flowered garden Rhododendrons so much admired in the northeastern United States owe their color but not their hardiness to *R. arboreum*, and this species is also important in the heritage of innumerable fine modern hybrids designed for milder climates. In itself, it is a superb tree of grandiose proportions, which can scarcely be equalled for large gardens in mild climates, covering itself in earliest spring with a flaming cascade of brilliant blossoms that constitutes one of the most impressive spectacles in horticulture. Trees of such majestic dimensions do not bloom early in life, however. In age its natural habit of growth is often an immense mound, wider than high, with the densely foliaged branches reaching down to the ground. It is popularly ascribed an ultimate height of 30 to 40 feet, but there is a mammoth old tree at Heligan in Cornwall, identified as this species by British authorities, which appears to be at least 70 feet tall. When it is aflame in March, a great billowing mass of brilliant color from top to bottom, the effect is stupendous. *R. arboreum* is, however, one of the most variable of Rhododendron species. A century-old specimen in Scotland is 42 feet tall with a trunk 72 inches in circumference. A pyramidal habit of growth is perhaps most common but columnar outlines are often seen and, in contrast to the stately proportions of most forms, variety *baileyi* is scarcely 6 feet tall. The leaves of this species are usually 4 to 8 inches long, 1 to 2½ inches wide, glossy bronze-green above with the prominent primary veins impressed enough to roughen the leaf surface. The type has a silvery, plastered indumentum beneath, but various forms and varieties have leaves clad below with indumenta which may change from thin and downy to a woolly felt, white, tan, or ruddy brown. The leaves often droop in more or less symmetrical fan-like collars on which are nestled the 5½-inch flower trusses of firmly rounded outline. There are about twelve to twenty 2-inch bell-shaped blossoms in a compact cluster, ranging in color from white through purplish-rose to blood-red. The pink-flowered *forma roseum* is usually rather heavily spotted, the white to an intermediate extent and the red much less so. This is among the earliest Rhododendron species to bloom, usually in March and sometimes as early as January in warm winters in mild climates. The variance in hardiness is evidently wide. There is general agreement that the blood-red forms are extremely tender, suitable in the United States for climates such as the Bay district of San Francisco and in Great Britain for Cornwall and the west coast of Scotland. The white subspecies, *cinnamomeum*, with woolly cinnamon-colored indumentum beneath smaller leaves, is a great deal hardier, one of the species most valued for planting throughout much of the Rhododendron belt of the northwestern Pacific coast. Opinions differ as to the pink form, *roseum*. Some growers find it to be intermediate in hardiness between the white and red sorts, whereas others rate it hardiest of all, which is usually a sign of a considerable range in cold resistance among different specimens or among groups. Among its allies, *R. arboreum* is distinguished by the typically thin indumentum which reveals the primary veins beneath the leaves, or nearly so, and lets the marginal venation remain evident. The ovary is ten-chambered. The typically tree-like growth habit with one or more boles, many-flowered, compact, globular truss, and the tubular-campanulate corolla typically deep red to magenta, with a broad base, place this species in the Arboreum subseries. In the wild, its distribution is widespread at 5,000 to 10,000 feet along a great swinging arc of the southern slopes of the outer Himalayas, from Kashmir through Nepal, Sikkim and Bhutan to Manipur, a distance of 1,500 miles. The name refers to its tree-like habit of growth.

Freedom of Bloom: 1; Ease of Cultivation: 1; American Quality Rating: xxxx; British: ★★★★; American Hardiness Rating: H-4; British: C; Truss Type: 3.

R. arizelum (ar-iz-ee′-lum), **Balf. f. and Forrest.** FALCONERI SERIES

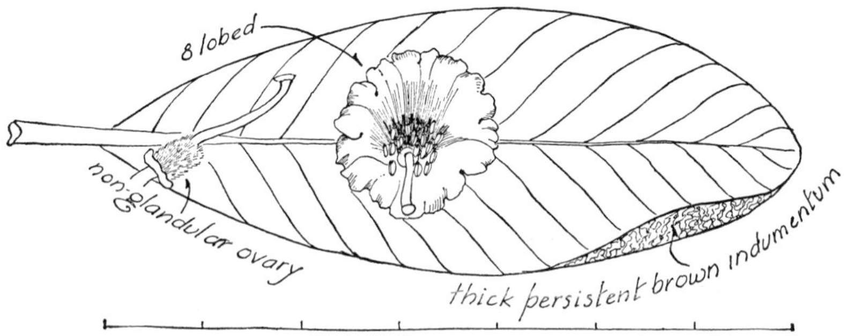

This is one of the hardiest and at the same time one of the most ornamental of the large-leaved tree Rhododendrons of the Falconeri group. In soft climates it grows eventually to a height of about 20 feet and bears in flat clusters fine, dark green veined leaves 5 to 9 inches long, $1\frac{1}{2}$ to $3\frac{1}{2}$ inches wide, with a conspicuous yellow midrib and a rich, bright orange indumentum beneath. In colder districts, it becomes an attractive spreading shrub with smaller leaves. The young shoots are coated with a soft, golden-orange down. In April tight, round 5- or 6-inch trusses appear containing about twenty bell-shaped, eight-lobed flowers $1\frac{1}{2}$ inches across. Perhaps the most common color is in the cream to yellow range, with a maroon blotch at the bottom of the blossom. There is also a white with a bold purple basal stain. The forms with yellow flowers suffused pink on the lobes are particularly attractive, but they scarcely equal the clear, unspotted brilliant crimson or the rose-red Forrest #25627 for garden effect. This is among the best large-leaved Rhododendrons, superior in foliage and in ease of cultivation to many of its allies, and more useful in its smaller size than *R. falconeri* which it otherwise resembles. Among its relatives it is characterized by the thick, ruddy indumentum beneath rugulose leaves broadest above the middle and with tapered base. The petioles are about 1 inch long, cylindric, not grooved, and clad with the velvety felt which also coats the young shoots. The ovary is non-glandular, an easy mark of distinction from *R. falconeri*, and it does not have the winged flange on the leaf stalk as does *R. basilicum*. There are sixteen stamens. *R. arizelum* was first found by Forrest in 1917 and was subsequently given its name, meaning 'notable', in anticipation of its garden value. It grows in the wild in open sites in Rhododendron forests at 10,000 to 12,000 feet in Yunnan, northeastern Upper Burma, and southeastern Tibet. Freedom of Flowering: 2; Ease of Cultivation: 2+; American Quality Rating: xx; British: ★★; American Hardiness Rating: H-4; British: B; Truss Type: 6.

R. augustinii (aw-gus-tee′-nee-i), **Hemsl.** TRIFLORUM SERIES AUGUSTINII SUBSERIES

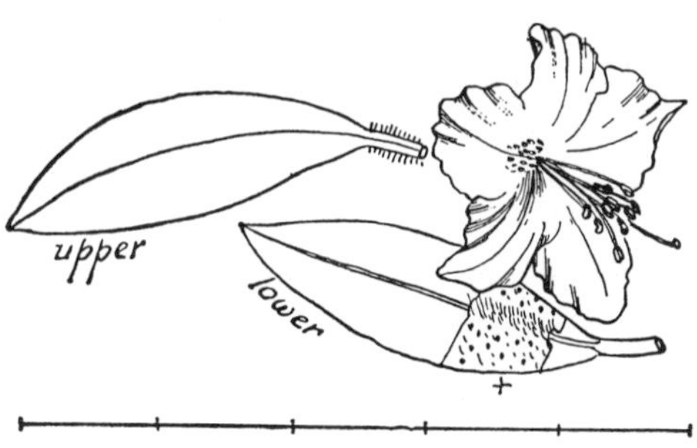

This familiar and beloved Rhododendron has been in the front rank of valuable garden species since first it became available to the public as an introduction by Maurice de Vilmorin of France. It is a bushy shrub up to 15 feet in height with pointed dark green leaves $1\frac{1}{2}$ to 4 inches long and $\frac{1}{2}$ to 1 inch broad and scaly below. In its best forms the flowers, with yellowish-green spots on the upper lobes, come gratifyingly close to blue, and various of them have been propagated from cuttings to perpetuate this color intensity. Magor's form is soft blue-mauve with a greenish center in the flower; the Tower court form is deep blue-mauve; and de Rothschild's form is deep blue-mauve with a darker flower center. 'Barto Blue'

has blue margins with the center lavender-blue. The flowers of 'Marine' are the most intense color of all. "Caeruleum" is a nurseryman's "variety", propagated from seeds, which produces plants better than the average in color. (Actually there is a separate and distinct species named, correctly, *caeruleum*.) All vary in color from year to year. A cold spring makes them conspicuously less blue and more pink. In weather warm for the season they can be very blue indeed. Some of the deeper-colored forms are a good deal more tender than those lighter in shade. Unselected seedlings which have not been seen in bloom are a hazardous purchase because this species also has flowers which range from white through shades of undistinguished pink to rather unattractive magenta. The rather large, flat, broadly funnel-shaped blossoms of *R. augustinii* resemble the shape of a butterfly in the way the widely expanded corolla lobes are held. They are 2 to 3 inches across, produced in early May up to six in a terminal cluster which measures about 3½ inches in diameter. This species is spectacularly free-flowering, and consistently so year after year, making one of the best shows in the genus. It does well all along the West Coast from San Francisco northward, and Joseph Gable has isolated some seedlings which are precariously hardy at his trial grounds at Stewartstown, Pennsylvania. The flower buds seem to be more sensitive to spring frosts than to midwinter cold. Bloom should be reasonably reliable from Philadelphia southward in the east. Out of bloom, this species with its pointed, dark green leaves gives a light and graceful effect in the garden. Among Rhododendrons of the Triflorum series with flowers which are never yellow, *R. augustinii* can usually be distinguished by the soft line of hairs on the midrib underneath the leaf. Further marks are leafy branchlets hairy as well as scaly, and the calyx lobes fringed with short hairs. The species comes from exposed hillsides up to 9,300 feet in Szechuan and western Hupeh provinces of China. It was discovered by Augustine Henry, a medical officer in the Chinese customs, whose first name it bears. Freedom of Flowering: 1; Ease of Cultivation: 1; American Quality Rating: xxxx; British: ****; American Hardiness Rating: H-3; British: B; Truss Type: 9; A.M., 1926; A.G.M., 1924.

R. auriculatum (aw-rik-u-la′-tum), **Hemsl.** AURICULATUM SERIES

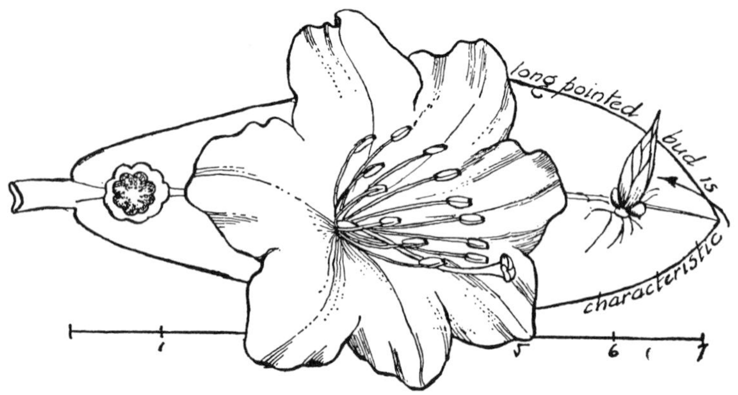

For very late bloom and fine quality of flower, this Rhododendron is invaluable. It is a large shrub or small tree, older plants 15 or so feet tall tending toward an umbrella-shaped crown and an arboreal habit. It is reputed to be 30 feet high in the wild. The heavy, leathery leaves are 6 to 13½ inches long, 2¼ to 5 inches wide, with two distinct basal lobes at either side of the midrib. They are dark green above, strongly veined, and pale green below with a thin veil of long tawny hairs which later changes to tan. The new growth appears extraordinarily late in the season, in July, and it is marked then by brilliant scarlet ribbon-like bracts which festoon the lower parts of the young shoots. Both floral and foliage buds are distinctively elongated and pointed, identical in shape, and enclosed in long, sharply tipped scales. The flowers when they appear in late July and early August are startling in their size and fragrance. They are often more than 4 inches across, with seven or eight lobes, funnel-shaped and widely expanded from a long, narrow tube. There are six to eleven blossoms in each loose cluster, sweetly scented, and white to rose-pink in color, a dramatic show so late in the summer when bold displays from other shrubs are notably lacking. This species does not flower young, but it is profuse when it fully attains flowering size. Poor forms which drop their leaves and become almost deciduous just before the new growth appears should be avoided. Protected from wind and winter sun, *R. auriculatum* is hardy with good care in a climate intermediate between that of Philadelphia and New York, but its flowers are short-lived more often than not because they so often appear in the course of a midsummer heat wave in the East. It is a remarkably beautiful Rhododendron, elsewhere doubly valued for its late season of bloom. In any climate it likes a protected site and some shade. This species is unlikely to be confused with any other. There are fourteen (rarely sixteen) stamens. The long, pointed buds and narrow, sharply tipped scales enclosing them are shared only by its ill-matched ally in the series, *R. griersonianum*, which, however, has red, five-lobed flowers in June and a dense woolly indumentum beneath leaves narrowed at both ends. *R. auriculatum* is a woodland species in western Hupeh province of China, where it grows at 5,000 to 7,000 feet elevation. It was found first by Henry and introduced by E. H. Wilson in 1900. 'Eared' is English for *auriculatum*, a reference to the two lobes at the bases of the leaves. Freedom of Flowering: 1; Ease of Cultivation: 1; American Quality Rating: xxx; British: ***; American Hardiness Rating: H-3; British: B; Truss Type: 8; A.M., 1922.

R. barbatum (bar-ba′-tum), **Wall.** BARBATUM SERIES, BARBATUM SUBSERIES

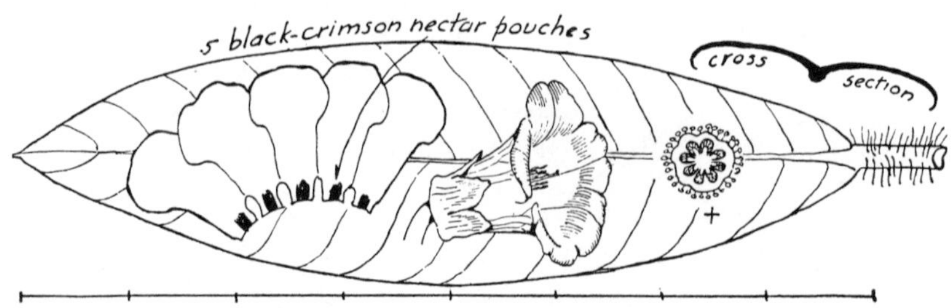

This is a tree Rhododendron, very large in the wild, sometimes as much as 60 feet in height but in cultivation ranging from a large shrub 10 feet high to a small tree 30 feet tall. It has been treasured in English gardens for more than a hundred years for the richness of its brilliant red flowers. The dark, dull green leaves are 4 to 10 inches long, $1\frac{1}{2}$ to $3\frac{1}{2}$ inches wide, strongly veined and with recurved, somewhat undulating margins. They are at first clad with a loose, woolly indumentum underneath, which later falls away leaving them pale yellowish-green. The leaf stalks and branchlets are conspicuous in bearing long, thick bristles tipped with glands. Purplish plum-colored bark is prominent and attractive. This species blooms sometimes in February but usually in March and April, the thick, waxen flowers 2 inches wide with black basal nectar pouches grouped about fourteen to a compact, globular truss frequently $4\frac{1}{2}$ inches across. The color is an incandescent scarlet, noted for its clarity and depth, and a tree in bloom is a splendid sight so early in the season with its shining red globes which are remarkably frost resistant. In age this Rhododendron is inclined to be gaunt at other seasons, the leaves too much confined to rosettes at the ends of the branches and, like other Rhododendrons with smooth bark, it does not respond to pruning with new branches originating as sprouts from older wood. It should be placed against an evergreen background, with small, more densely foliaged shrubs in front of it. Shelter for its early blossoms, especially a shield against the sun on frosty mornings, makes it much more reliable in its brilliant floral display. Among the species of its series with leaf stalks and young shoots clad with coarse bristles, this species is distinct in having leaves with pointed tips, at maturity devoid of any woolly indumentum underneath. The conspicuous calyx is $\frac{3}{8}$ to a little more than $\frac{1}{2}$ inch long. The short flower stalks, about $\frac{1}{2}$ inch long, and compact, scarlet flower truss complete the identification. This Rhododendron was introduced about 1849 from 10,000 to 12,000 feet elevation of the Himalayas in Nepal and Sikkim. The name refers to its bearded, i.e. bristly, character. Freedom of Flowering: 1;

Ease of Cultivation: 1; American Quality Rating: xxxx; British: ***; American Hardiness Rating: H-4; British: B; Truss Type: 3: A.M., 1954.

R. beanianum (bee-nee-an′-um), **Cowan.** NERIIFLORUM SERIES, HAEMATODES SUBSERIES

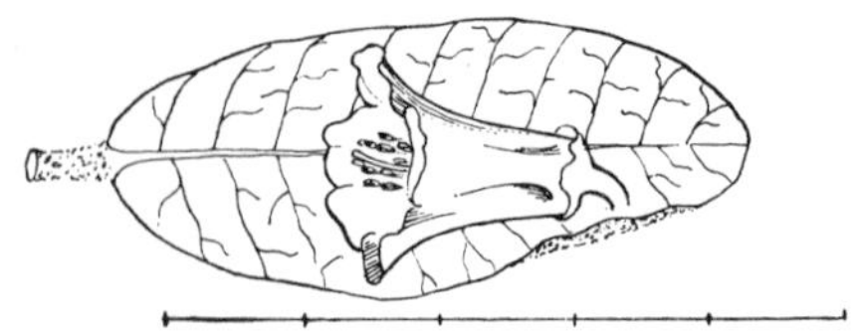

Described in the literature as a small shrub 8 feet tall, this species easily reaches 15 feet in some of its upright forms whereas others scarcely reach 6 feet, are much more spreading in habit, and have better foliage. The leaves $2\frac{1}{2}$ to 4 inches long, 1 to $1\frac{3}{4}$ inches broad, are dark green and shiny above, roughened by the conspicuous veins impressed in them, and with a rich brown indumentum below. Six to ten flowers make up the loose, flat-topped terminal clusters which appear in April. The tubular, bell-shaped blossoms are up to 2 inches in diameter and they vary in color from pink to red. A very pale pink with five conspicuous red stripes radiating from the center of the flower is a fairly common form, which tends to have larger blooms than the more popular brilliant scarlet sort. Plants of this species must be selected with care not only because of the variance in size and color of blossoms but also because some of the tall-growing forms often are sparse in foliage and lanky in habit with a distressing tendency to have rosettes of leaves only at the ends of long, naked branches. The dwarfer, more spreading plants and a more or less distinct variety, *compactum*, are extremely handsome, however, with their shining scarlet flowers appearing early in the season, and they are attractive as evergreens at other seasons too. Only one other pink-to-red-flowered species in the Haemotodes subseries, *R. mallotum*, has rugulose leaves similar to those of *R. beanianum* and it is distinct on the basis of numerous other characters. Comparing the two, *R. beanianum* has smaller leaves with the petioles reddish tomentose on the upper surface only. The young shoots are clad with a ruddy-brown wool in contrast to the greyish coating on the year-old branches of its relative. It possesses a cup-shaped calyx and a style hairy at the base as opposed to the obsolete calyx and style glabrous at the base of *R. mallotum*. *R. beanianum* has bristles on its stems and is thus easily distinguished from *R. haematodes*. It comes from an altitude of 9,000 to 11,000 feet in Tibet and Burma, and was named for W. J. Bean, former curator of the Royal Botanic Gardens at Kew, England. Freedom of Flowering: 1; Ease of Cultivation: 1; American Quality Rating: xxx; British: ***; American Hardiness Rating: H-4; British: B; Truss Type: 10; A.M., 1953. (K.W. 6805.)

R. bodinieri (bod-in-yair′-i), **Franch.** TRIFLORUM SERIES, YUNNANENSE SUBSERIES

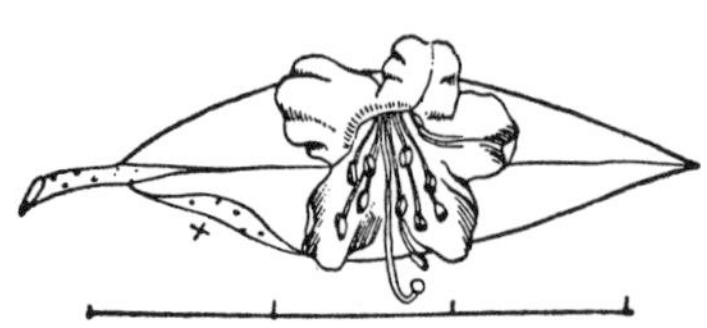

This species is much more variable than has been generally supposed and the description of it must be extensively revised. Instead of being 'a small shrub' it grows robustly to a height of 8 feet in an upright, willowy manner. The small, dull olive-green leaves are $1\frac{3}{4}$ to $3\frac{1}{4}$ inches long, $\frac{3}{4}$ to $1\frac{3}{8}$ inches broad and scaly beneath. The blossoms come in April, not only 'rose, spotted purple' but just as often pure white, $1\frac{1}{8}$ inches across, bell-shaped, about six or eight to a single-tiered, flat-topped truss 3 inches in diameter. In bloom the white form of this species is reminiscent of our native *R. carolinianum* var. *album*. This is a delicately pretty Rhododendron in flower, not bold in its floral effect but appealing none the less. The small leaves and slender branches give it a light and graceful texture in the landscape. McLaren #V-139 is a good white-flowered form and the Bodnant selection is also superior. Among species of the

Triflorum series with white to rose flowers this one is characterized by leaves acuminate at the tips, rounded to subacute at the base, with few or no hairs on the upper surface, the midrib devoid of hairs on the lower surface. The scales beneath the leaves are three to four times their own diameter apart, and the corolla tube is not scaly outside. The calyx is a minute rim with an undulating margin. The closest affinity is with *R. chartophyllum* which is, however, almost or completely deciduous. *R. bodinieri* originates in Yunnan province of China. It was named for a nineteenth century French missionary, Emile Bodinier. Freedom of Flowering: 1; Ease of Cultivation: 2+; American Ratings: None assigned. British Quality Rating: **; British Hardiness Rating: B; Truss Type: 9.

R. brachycarpum (brack-ee-kar′-pum), **D. Don ex G. Don.** PONTICUM SERIES, CAUCASICUM SUBSERIES

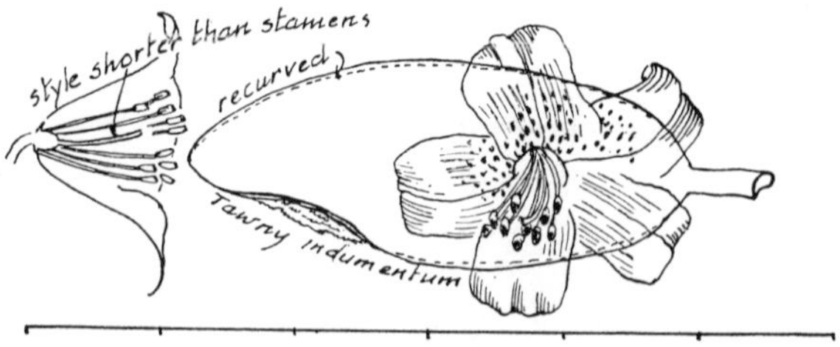

Among the hardiest of the Oriental species, *R. brachycarpum* is also among the handsomest as an evergreen shrub the year round. It grows robustly to about 8 or 10 feet in height, with a faultless habit and fine foliage 2¾ to 6 inches long, 1¼ to 2¾ inches broad, generally nearer the larger of these dimensions. The leaves are fresh, bright green above with primary veins impressed, and covered with a thin sheath of tan or whitish felt below. The broadly funnel-shaped flowers, which appear in mid-June, are distinctively colored, usually creamy white suffused pale pink and spotted green or brownish yellow on the upper lobes. As many as twenty florets up to 2 inches across make up a firm, round truss 4 inches or sometimes as much as 6 inches in diameter, although I have never seen any so large as that and I doubt whether such a fine form is in cultivation in the Occident.

Plants grown from seeds often vary greatly in stature and in freedom of flowering. Some seedlings may grow twice as tall as others from the same seed lot, and nurserymen find at times that possibly 75 per cent are barren of flowers even after many years, while a portion of the remainder bloom profusely. It is especially important, therefore, with this species, to obtain plants which have proved to be compact and free-flowering in the nursery. Balancing the fine plant habit and lustrous evergreen foliage with its interesting indumentum is a notable tendency for the leaves to curl much more readily and to roll more tightly in cold weather or in time of drouth than do those of most other Rhododendrons. The species blooms late, at a valuable period when most other Rhododendrons have gone by, and it is a rugged, adaptable shrub. *R. brachycarpum* has repeatedly endured −25° F. in my garden without injury. Most Rhododendrons with their compact masses of surface roots are easy to transplant at almost any size but nurserymen complain that this species is rather difficult to move successfully after it attains a height of about 4 feet. It is the only species outside of the Lacteum group with a radiate structure of the hairs composing the indumentum beneath the leaves, proof of relationship so close that it may be transferred to the Lacteum series when the Ponticum assemblage to which it now belongs is next critically examined for revision. Among indumented species of its series, *R. brachycarpum* is distinct because of its oblong-elliptical leaves, broad for their length and with rounded or subauricled base. The very short style, only about ⅝ inch long, is distinct in this group of shrub-like Rhododendrons. It is native to central and southern Korea, to the Kuril Islands and to mountainous northern and central parts of Japan, where it is particularly evident above the tree line on Mt Fujiyama. The name means 'short-fruited', curiously so to me, as I have never seen a specimen which was conspicuous for this reason. Freedom of Flowering: 2; Ease of Cultivation: 1; American Quality Rating: x; British: **; American Hardiness Rating: H-2 (Author's dissent: H-1); British: A; Truss Type: 1.

R. bullatum (bull-a'-tum), **Franch.** EDGEWORTHII SERIES

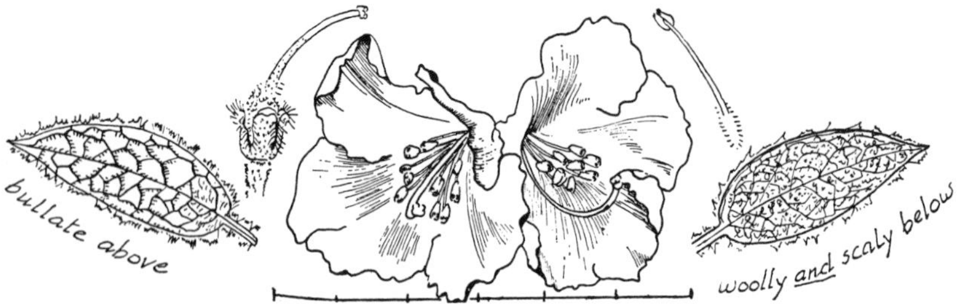

They are borne in loose terminal clusters of two to six in April and May, so wonderfully fragrant with a delightful spicy scent that they perfume the air for a long distance around. The finest form I have seen, with flowers a full 5 inches in diameter, is Rock #59202. The Exbury pink selection is also much admired. Kingdon-Ward #7137 is notably hardier than most of the other forms introduced, but this species is ordinarily suitable only for such mild climates as that of the San Francisco district; or, in the British Isles, in the Atlantic coastal climate of the west and south. There is a needless confusion with *R. edgeworthii* because it lacks the calyx lobes shaggy on the outside surface of that species. Instead, *R. bullatum* has calyx lobes covered with small scales outside and only fringed with hairs. The style is both scaly and hairy toward the base, and the strongly crinkled leaf surface gives the species its name. It was first discovered in 1886 by Delavay in Yunnan province of China growing on ledges and cliff crevices at 8,000 to 10,500 feet elevation. George Forrest immensely enriched our horticulture when he introduced it to cultivation in 1904. Freedom of Flowering: 1; Ease of Cultivation: 1; American Quality Rating: xxxx; British: ***; American Hardiness Rating: H-5; British: D; Truss Type: 12; Farrer #842, A.M., 1923; pink form, A.M., 1946; F.C.C., 1937.

This Rhododendron, now in cultivation for more than fifty years, has long held the affection of gardeners in mild climates and of those who cherish it in greenhouses. When they are well grown, younger specimens are handsome as foliage plants, but as they become older and start to reach toward their ultimate height of about 8 feet, they tend toward a somewhat thin and loose habit. Outdoors this can be remedied to some extent by placing several plants 2 or 3 feet apart and allowing them to grow together. The leaves are attractive and unusual with veins so deeply impressed that the surfaces are puckered. In their juvenile stages they are irregularly dusted with a fugitive whitish down which may disappear as they reach their mature size of $1\frac{1}{2}$ to $4\frac{1}{2}$ inches long, $\frac{3}{4}$ to 2 inches wide. The leaf undersurfaces and the young branches are thickly coated with a luxurious felty tan indumentum, and the leaves underneath are also scaly, an unusual combination. The flowers are superb, white usually flushed rose-pink in varying degree on the outside and occasionally also on the lobe tips, heavy in substance and long lasting, averaging about 4 inches in diameter.

R. burmanicum (bur-man'-ee-kum), **Hutchinson.** MADDENII SERIES, CILIICALYX SUBSERIES

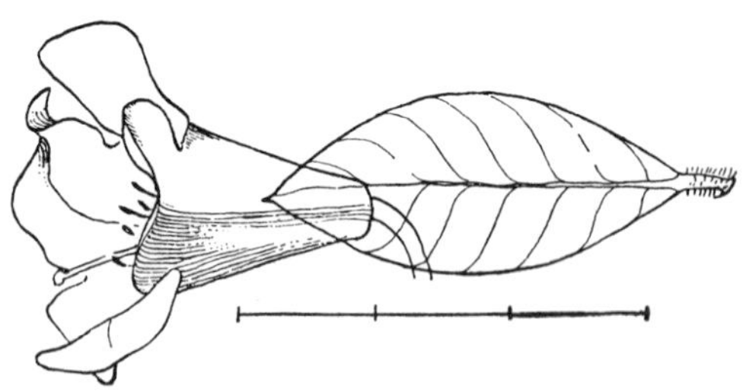

Fully grown specimens of this species are reputed to grow 8 feet tall or more but most forms, at least, are unlikely to reach that stature in cultivation and a height of about 6 feet, with a width of 8 feet, seems a realistic allowance in the garden. This is a handsome shrub at all seasons, compact in habit and dense in foliage, the burnished deep green leaves, densely scaly on both surfaces, about $2\frac{3}{4}$ inches long, $1\frac{1}{4}$ inches wide. It blooms in late April and the first part of May, and past descriptions of it seem to me to do it an injustice in describing the flowers simply as 'greenish yellow'. The fragrant blossoms are about 2½ inches wide, three to six in a single-tiered, outward-facing group. The color in the best garden forms is a strong, clear medium yellow. Even young specimens bloom profusely, the flowers often seeming extraordinarily large for the stature of the plants. For mild climates this is a Rhododendron of exceptional quality, attractive the year around and easily grown. Unselected seedlings often tend toward a greenish-gold color which fades to an ivory shade, creating a very beautiful effect, particularly when these free-blooming Rhododendrons are massed. Poor forms are occasionally greenish-white. *R. burmanicum* seems to grow to perfection in the mild moistness of the San Francisco district. It is not usually hardy enough to be a permanent garden shrub in Oregon and Washington. It is distinct from its relatives on the basis of its yellow flowers scaly all over the outside, several in each truss. The style is scaly almost half its length and there are ten stamens. The calyx is very small. The upper leaf surface is densely scaly and beneath, the leaf is vividly green between the scales. This species takes its name from Burma, where it is native to the southwestern part of the country. Freedom of Flowering: 1; Ease of Cultivation: 1; American Quality Rating: xx; British: **; American Hardiness Rating: H-5; British: F; Truss Type: 12.

R. callimorphum (kal-lee-mor′-fum), **Balf. f. and W. W. Sm.** THOMSONII SERIES, CAMPYLOCARPUM SUBSERIES

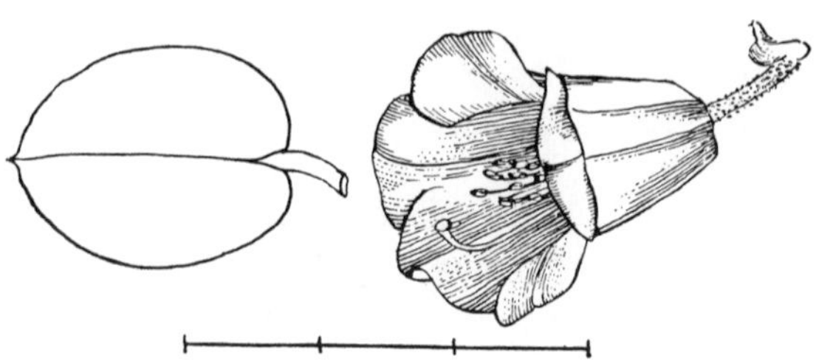

Included in this species now is the Rhododendron formerly called *R. cyclium*, and still widely offered in commerce under that name. It does not differ consistently from *R. callimorphum*, which is a shrub of rounded outline but variable height, from as little as 2 feet to as much as 11 feet tall. The dark, rounded glossy green leaves are 2 to 2¾ inches long, ¾ to 2⅛ inches broad, prominently veined, and with a striking blue bloom when first mature. In late April and early May come the soft rose to pink flowers, 1½ inches across, or up to 2 inches wide in the best forms. There are usually six or eight of them in an informally loose, outward-facing group at the ends of the branches. The color is especially attractive in its purity and delicacy, often enhanced by a bold crimson blotch, and the modeling of the flowers is particularly graceful. The growth habit of this species is neat. It presents a creditable appearance the year round. The leaves often diminish gradually in size toward the ends of the branches in a regular progression of shrinking dimensions which is notable in the species. It is a good and useful garden plant, distinct as the only pink-flowered member of the Campylocarpum subseries and easily distinguished from its closest relatives for that reason. The flowers of *R. myagrum*, its ally, are always white. The glandular ovary and style without glands or glandular only at the base; the bell-shaped corolla and minute calyx; branchlets usually glandular and not hairy; and rounded leaves, all help to identify it in the somewhat mixed lot of Rhododendrons in the Thomsonii series. *R. callimorphum* grows in the wild on exposed stony hillsides at about 10,000 feet in western Yunnan and northeast Burma. It was found by Forrest in 1912 and named for the lovely shape of the flowers. Freedom of Flowering: 2+; Ease of Cultivation: 2+; American Quality Rating: xxx; British: ****; American Hardiness Rating: H-4; British: B; Truss Type: 8.

R. calophytum (kal-o-fi′-tum), **Franch.** FORTUNEI SERIES, CALOPHYTUM SUBSERIES

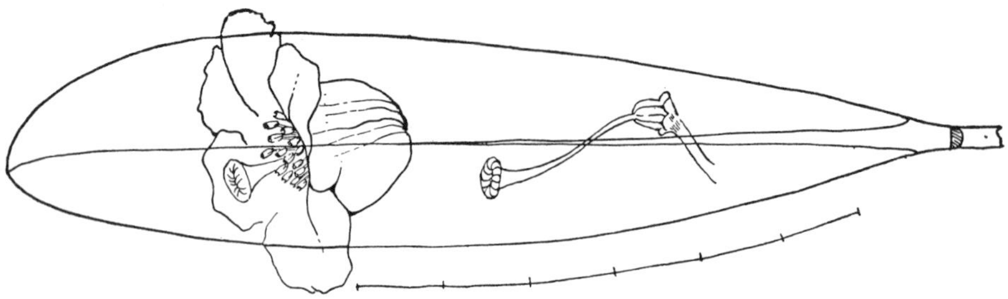

Few Rhododendrons exceed this species in its combination of large flower trusses and effective foliage. It is one of the noblest Rhododendrons, a tree 20 feet high in cultivation, twice that or more in the wild, which grows with a broad crown into an umbrella outline as it gets older. The imposing leaves, prominently veined, 8 to 16 inches long, $1\frac{1}{2}$ to $3\frac{3}{4}$ inches broad, fall in stiff collars from the large clusters of flowers produced in March and April. The fragrant blossoms, five- to seven-lobed, are 3 inches wide in good forms, about twenty or sometimes up to thirty in a many-tiered, firm terminal truss as much as 8 inches across, which is not quite full enough at the top to be completely hemispherical in shape. The flowers are most often white with a bright red blotch and a conspicuous yellow stigma, but the blush-colored forms suffused pink on the outside and those with flowers of a rosy shade are just as lovely. All have a bold red stain at the base of the upper lobe. As a large background flowering evergreen, this is superb. It is not quite hardy at Philadelphia but it does very well throughout the Rhododendron belt of the Pacific coast and in Great Britain wherever it is shielded from winds which twist and tear the large leaves. Since it blossoms in March and early April it should not be placed where the sun will strike the flowers early on frosty mornings. A form which received a F.C.C. in England is especially fine and is sparingly available in the United States. The extraordinary length of the leaves usually distinguishes this species from its allies. The corolla is bulged at the base. There are fifteen to twenty stamens and a stout, yellow style, glabrous and non-glandular, with a large disc-like stigma. *R. sutchuenense*, with leaves about 3 inches shorter, is sometimes confused with it, but it has fewer stamens, fewer flowers in the truss, a slender style and a knob-like, not a discoid, stigma. *R. calophytum* is native to the woodlands of Szechuan and Hupeh provinces of China, where it grows at 5,000 to 10,000 feet altitude. It was first found by the French missionary David, but not introduced to cultivation until Wilson sent it back in 1904. The name means 'beautiful plant'. Freedom of Flowering: 2+; Ease of Cultivation: 1; American Quality Rating: xxxx; British: ****; American Hardiness Rating: H-3; British: B; Truss Type: 6; F.C.C., 1933.

R. calostrotum (kal-os-tro′-tum), **Balf. f. and Ward.** SALUENENSE SERIES

A 15-inch, free blooming undershrub in various shades of pink, *R. calostrotum* has many uses in the rock garden or wherever an attractive dwarf plant is wanted. Occasional robust forms may grow to 4 feet. It has a gratifying disposition to succeed in any reasonable situation and it starts to bloom when it is only 3 or 4 inches high. The leaves are about an inch long and half as broad, attractive gray-green when newly opened, later turning dark green, scaly on both surfaces. Few Rhododendrons are so prodigal with their flowers and they seem extraordinarily large for the stature of the plants, about 1½ inches wide, flat, and usually borne in pairs at the end of almost every twig, in May. They vary in color from light pink to spotted crimson to a magenta-purple, with some good forms approaching a clear rose-red. The most common colors do not appear to advantage in the company of other flowers near by and they are especially jarring in proximity to the lavender- and violet-blue Lapponicums. The plant sparingly distributed as "White's Claret-colored form" is particularly attractive. This species dislikes the hot summers in the eastern United States, though it is reasonably hardy. It is distinguished from its allies in the Saluenense series by its densely scaly calyx with conspicuous hairs on the rims of the lobes; by the elliptic leaves twice as long as broad; and by the absence of bristles on flower stalks and branchlets. The base of the corolla is hairy but not scaly. *R. calostrotum* was discovered at 11,000–12,000 feet in northeastern Burma by Kingdon-Ward in 1914. Its name means 'with a beautiful covering'. Freedom of Flowering: 1; Ease of Cultivation: 1; American Quality Rating: xxx; British: ****; American Hardiness Rating: H-3; British: A; Truss Type: 14; A.M., 1935.

R. caloxanthum (kal-ox-an′-thum), **Balf. f. and Farrer.** THOMSONII SERIES, CAMPYLOCARPUM SUBSERIES

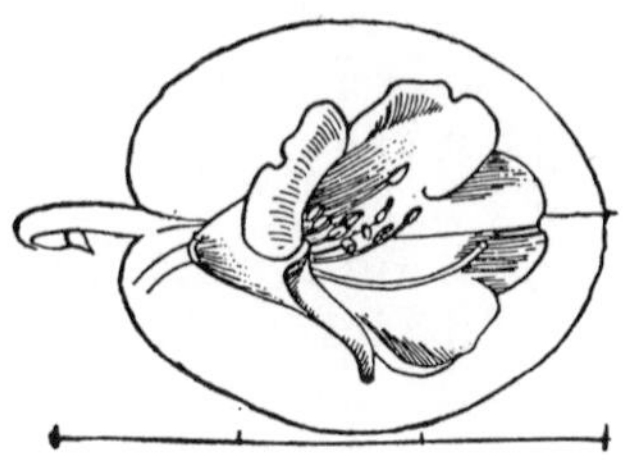

A prominent yellow-flowered Rhododendron species, this is a shrub of variable stature from 2 to 8 feet tall but usually about 6 feet, with rounded leaves 1¼ to 3¼ inches wide, pale glaucous green beneath. As the new growth matures it acquires an attractive light blue overlay. The flowers come in April and early May, about 1¾ inches in diameter, usually six or seven to a lax cluster which measures about 4 inches across. The charming light yellow bells, orange in bud, are often marked in the bottom with a red blotch. It has produced some fine forms with orange blossoms, perhaps more noteworthy than those with yellow flowers. The latter can be duplicated in other species, and in fact *R. caloxanthum* does merge imperceptibly into *RR. campylocarpum* and *telopeum*. The difference is mainly a matter of leaf shape and size. Typical *R. caloxanthum* has large (2 to 3¼ inch) round leaves, typical *R. telopeum* small (1 to 1⅝ inch) round leaves, and typical *R. campylocarpum* large (2¼ to 4 inch) oblong leaves. The flowers of *R. caloxanthum* sometimes approach the wide bowl-shaped form of those of *R. wardii* but they are normally much more bell-shaped and in any case do not have the style glandular the entire length to the tip, as do the yellow-flowered *RR. wardii* and *litiense*. In evaluating *R. caloxanthum* as a garden plant I would say that the average of this species is not quite so good as the average of either *RR. wardii* or *campylocarpum*. The flowers often do not open so fully, they tend frequently to be less strong in color, and the short, round leaf does not give it quite the foliage value. However, this is a comparison with Rhododendrons which stand at the very top in the genus for their ornamental value, and *R. caloxanthum* is still a fine shrub of extraordinary merit, an acquisition for any garden. It is usually much more restrained in growth and its flowers are often more gracefully carried. Like its relatives, it especially wants watering in time of drouth but seems equally insistent on perfect drainage. Among yellow-flowered species of the series it is more or less distinct in possessing orbicular leaves averaging about 2 inches long by 1½ inches broad, a small calyx, less than

$\frac{3}{16}$ inch in length, a style either devoid of glands or glandular only in the lower quarter, and a bell-shaped corolla. *R. caloxanthum* grows in nature at 11,000 to 12,000 feet elevation in northeast Upper Burma, in Tibet, and in Yunnan province of China. It was discovered by Farrer in 1919 and given the name meaning 'of a beautiful yellow'. Freedom of Flowering: 1; Ease of Cultivation: 1; American Quality Rating: xxx; British: ***; American Hardiness Rating: H-2; British: C; Truss Type: 8; A.M., 1934.

R. campanulatum (kam-pan-u-la'-tum), **D. Don.** CAMPANULATUM SERIES

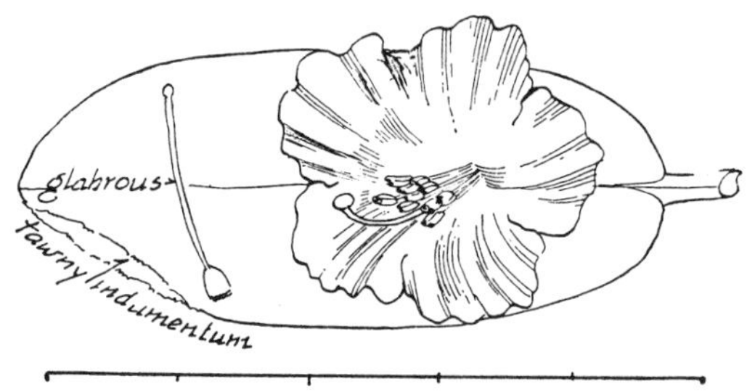

Among the best known, most useful and adaptable of Rhododendron species, this is also one of the most distinctive. The species has an air of quality about it derived from its attractive flowers and the glossy dark green leaves of flat, crisp outline which bear underneath a felty indumentum, often a rich orange but varying also to tan and brown. It is a neat shrub of rounded spreading shape with purplish-red leaf stalks and buds. The species is capable of growing 20 feet or more but older specimens are usually seen 8 to 10 feet high and a little wider, with leaves varying from 2 to 6½ inches long, 1 to 3 inches broad in various forms. The bell-shaped flowers, spotted on the upper lobes, appear in April, each 2 inches in diameter, about eight gathered into a 4½-inch truss which may vary from globular and compact to somewhat loose. The flowers range in color from almost white to deep rosy-purple. This species requires care in selection because its ornamental value in the garden is dependent upon securing a good form. Some seedlings with white flowers edged violet are very attractive, but the form sent back by Cooper under #5736, for example, has washy pale magenta flowers in a small truss. There are many others with nondescript blossoms and undistinguished indumenta. Some forms have charming flowers of a delicate shade bordering on blue and 'Knaphill' with fine brown suède beneath the leaves is so well known to be superior in foliage and flower that it was formerly awarded an extra star in its quality rating by the Royal Horticultural Society. Variety *aeruginosum*, with rather unattractive purple flowers, is one of the finest foliage plants in the entire genus, a compact dwarf with new growth metallic silver-green, later deepening to a striking soft blue. *R. campanulatum* is a sturdy shrub, easily pleased in its planting site in the Pacific Northwest. In the eastern United States it is hardy enough that at least one form will do well in sheltered garden situations as far north as Philadelphia, but its leaves roll up so tightly in cold weather that its appearance is very odd. This hardy form has clear pink flowers which fade to white as they age. Planted on an elevation, the two-tone effect of the indumented leaves seen from a lower level is striking. This is a first-rate ornamental, separated from its near relatives by possessing leaves with a continuous felty indumentum, but without metallic luster, and by its shoots and petioles usually glabrous at maturity. The rounded leaves, obtuse at the base, are widest at the middle. The seed capsule is stout, slightly curved and narrowly elongate-cylindrical or oblong. Although a lax truss is given as an identifying feature in botanical keys, this characteristic actually varies too much to be useful in this manner. Introduced in 1825, the species inhabits the Himalayas of Sikkim and Nepal. Its name refers to its bell-shaped flowers. Freedom of Flowering: 1; Ease of Cultivation: 1; American Quality Rating: xxx; British: ***; American Hardiness Rating: H-2; British: A; Truss Type: 3.

R. campylocarpum (kam-pil-o-kar′-pum), **Hook. f.** THOMSONII SERIES, CAMPYLOCARPUM SUBSERIES

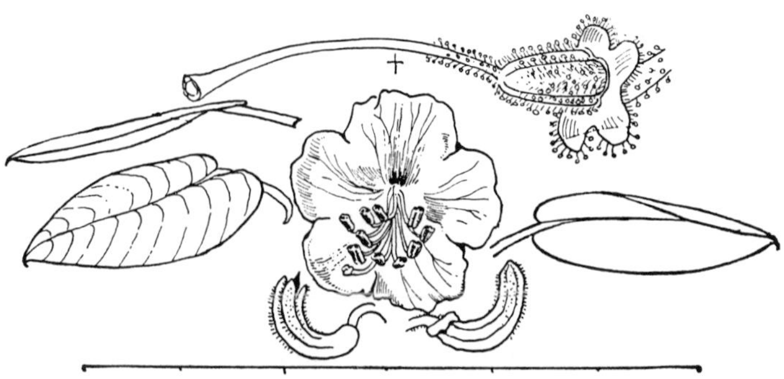

Some authorities consider this famous Rhododendron to be the best of the yellow-flowered species for general garden use. Whatever its exact position, it is certainly among the very finest in its color, a first-rate ornamental in its own right and the parent of many lovely and popular hybrids. *R. campylocarpum* is a trim, dense shrub of broad, rounded outline from 4 to as much as 12 feet tall. The dwarfer forms are mound-like in their growth habit. The largest I have seen was 9 feet tall and 13 feet wide, sheeted with sparkling yellow flowers in a dazzling display. A convention exists that there are two distinct sorts: the dwarf Hooker's variety, and the tall variety, *elatum*. Actually there is an uninterrupted series of intermediate forms linking the two and the distinction is a fiction. The dwarfer plants are the hardier. The leaves of this species are 1½ to 4 inches long, 1 to 2¼ inches wide, dark green above and pale blue-green below. The flowers vary greatly in their size, the intensity of their color and the number in the cluster. Some are so pale as to be almost cream-colored whereas the finest are a clear intense light yellow which shines forth strongly from blossoms nearly 3 inches across, about ten in loose trusses measuring up to 5 inches in diameter. More typically, the flowers would be 2¼ inches, about seven in a lax, flat-topped cluster. When they appear in late April and early May there is an engaging refinement and delicate grace in the purity of their bell-shaped form. This is one of the most popular of all Rhododendron species. It does well in a variety of garden situations and no hybrid has yet captured the luminous brilliance of its color or the elegance of the blossoms. It insists on perfect drainage but suffers if watering is neglected in dry weather. *R. campylocarpum* in its typical expression has oblong leaves 2¼ to 4 inches long but there is a progression of microforms linking it with *R. caloxanthum* (large orbicular leaves, 2 to 3¼ inches long) and continuing then in a fluid series into *R. telopeum* (small orbicular leaves, 1 to 1¼ inches long). Some of these intergrades can be assigned with as much accuracy to one species as to another. *RR. wardii* and *litiense* are easily distinguished from *R. campylocarpum* on the basis of their widely open, bowl-shaped blossoms with the style glandular all the way to the tip. The difference from *R. panteumorphum* seems to be entirely geographical, a dubious separation made by reason of their widely disjunct distribution in the wild. *R. campylocarpum* is more or less distinct within its own subseries on the basis of its oval leaves, not usually round. The bell-shaped flowers have a style glandular only at the base or up to half its length, and an ovary densely clad with short or long-stalked glands. The round, slender seed capsule is curved to some extent, and this characteristic gives the species its name referring to the bent fruits.

It has been over a hundred years since Hooker found it in Sikkim. Now it is known to grow as one of the dominant plants in extensive Rhododendron forests, in rocky valleys and clearings from 10,000 to 14,000 feet in East Nepal, Bhutan, and Tibet. Freedom of Flowering: 2+; Ease of Cultivation: 1; American Quality Rating: xxxx; British: ****; American Hardiness Rating: H-3; British: B; Truss Type: 8; F.C.C., 1892.

R. campylogynum (kam-pil-o-jin′-um), **Franch.** CAMPYLOGYNUM SERIES

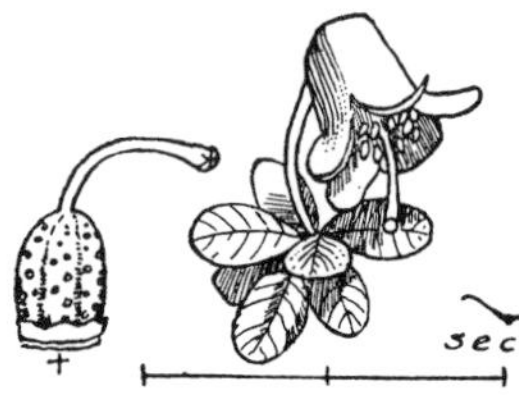

No other single Rhododendron species varies in stature so much as this, from 2 inches to 4 feet in height. It is a delightful small shrub, with leaves ¼ to 1 inch long, ⅛ to ¾ inch broad, dark bright green above and pale green below. It is a lepidote Rhododendron but the scales usually fall off the undersides of the leaves as they mature and the upper leaf surface is only rarely scaly. The flowers come in May, little nodding bells from ¼ to almost 1 inch in diameter, produced singly or two or three from each bud. They vary from fresh, clear pink through purple to crimson. In one rare form the flowers are such a deep purple that they are almost black. This is an exceptionally appealing rock garden Rhododendron in the very dwarf forms which spread widely and mold themselves to the contour of the earth in a dense blanket of fresh green foliage. The larger forms are valuable in the many situations where a neat and amenable small evergreen shrub is needed in the garden. *RR. myrtilloides*, *charopoeum*, and *cremastum*, formerly considered distinct, are now merged as varieties of this species. Var. *myrtilloides* is an especially attractive small-flowered spreading form of unusual garden value with a height to 12 inches; var. *charopoeum* is the large-flowered spreading form about 18 inches tall at maturity; and var. *cremastum*, less attractive, is the erect form with large, pale green leaves, flowers medium size, and a height to 2 feet or a little more. *R. campylogynum* is unlikely to be confused with any other species. It is the sole representative of a series allied to the Glaucophyllum group but with some resemblances to the Lepidotum and Uniflorum series. There are ten stamens, rarely eight. It was first found by Delavay in 1884, in western Yunnan, and named in an allusion to its bent ovary. Subsequently it was found in Tibet and Burma, and Forrest introduced it in 1912. This is an alpine Rhododendron which grows in the wild at altitudes up to 15,000 feet. Freedom of Flowering: 1; Ease of Cultivation: 2+; American Quality Rating: xx; British: **; American Hardiness Rating: H-2; British: A; Truss Type: 14; var. *myrtilloides*, A.M., 1925; F.C.C., 1943.

R. carolinianum (kar-o-lin-ee-a′-num), **Rehder.** CAROLINIANUM SERIES

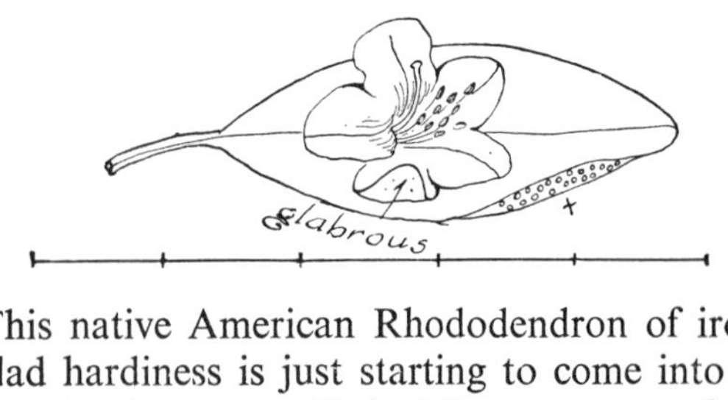

This native American Rhododendron of iron-clad hardiness is just starting to come into its own in the eastern United States as one of the best flowering evergreen shrubs in existence. It is all but unknown in mild climates where many Asian species of greater reputation but lesser value are grown instead. *R. carolinianum* usually reaches a height of 6 or 8 feet in the garden where it is one of the most useful and adaptable of all Rhododendrons, thriving in a wide variety of sites and exposures. It has a neat, attractive, broadly upright habit of growth, finer in texture and smaller in all its parts than the somewhat coarse natives, *RR. maximum* and *catawbiense*, which are inexplicably planted much more often. It is well-suited to foundation planting, where its stature is appropriate. The glossy green leaves of the Carolina Rhododendron are 1 to 3½ inches long, ½ to 1¾ inches wide, the undersides densely covered with scales which have a rusty appearance in the forms with deeper colored flowers. It is sometimes useful to know that the less rusty the leaf undersurface, the lighter will usually be the color of the flowers and the later the plant will bloom. This species typically flowers in mid-May, most often with six or seven widely bell-shaped 1½-inch flowers to a rounded compact truss, fresh pink on opening, becoming more lavender as they age and finally becoming a soft rose with a good deal of blue in it after several days. The mauve color of the typical Carolina Rhododendron's blossoms was once desirable but it is not fashionable today. The late New England Rhododendron hybridist, C. O. Dexter, had an appealing clear salmon-pink form which he raised from seeds by the hundreds. Apparently all of the plants went into the hands of non-specialists because there appears to be no source of supply for this beautiful form at the present time. It could probably be found again in the fields of any nursery which re-grows plants collected from the wild, and, as usual, discerning gardeners will be well repaid for seeking out superior forms of this fine Rhododendron. The extreme variation in flower color is variety *album*, almost a separate species with glistening white blossoms often larger than the type, produced about a week later. The leaves are often more narrow, usually much less scaly and fresh, bright green underneath. This is an extraordinarily fine ornamental, now commercially available from many nurseries. I exhibited it in a show a few years ago and it won the Silver Gilt Medal of the Royal Horticultural Society in competition with some of the best scaly-leaved Asian Rhododendron species which are much more publicized. *R. carolinianum* requires perfect drainage but is otherwise exceptionally tolerant. It naturally blooms more profusely with a full quota of sunlight but in my experience, at least, it will make a show of color and remain a presentable shrub in excessive shade longer than any other Rhododendron of iron-clad hardiness. It is particularly desirable to remove the faded flower clusters to prevent the formation of seeds. Plants with good growing conditions flower so profusely that they tend to injure themselves, and to blossom really well only in alternate years under the burden of excessive seed production. The Carolina Rhododendron is somewhat susceptible to attacks of blight (*Phytophthera cactorum*) which sometimes causes large branches to wilt and die abruptly. The control of this disease is described on page 296. A minor fault is its habit of shedding in October all leaves except those of the current season's growth, thus impairing to some extent its evergreen appearance over winter. *R. carolinianum* is found mainly in the mountains of Tennessee and of North and South Carolina. It occurs in a wide variety of exposures from woodland to unprotected upland slopes. Until it was given specific status by Rehder in 1912 it was considered to be a variety of the later-blooming and larger-growing *Rhododendron minus*. It differs also from that species, however, in having leaves less pointed; in the corolla with lobes longer than the tube, slightly or not at all scaly, usually only slightly spotted or devoid of spots. I have seen natural hybrids in the wild, intermediate between the two species, however. The botanical key to this series distinguishes the Carolina Rhododendron from its only other near relative, *R. chapmanii*, on the basis of its corolla tube less than ⅔ inch long (in contrast to a tube over ⅔ inch in length for its ally) and because its corolla lobes are not crisped, a character which seems here to me of little value in diagnosis. I have made no special study of *R. chapmanii* but I find its leaves considerably wider for their length, lighter, brighter green and conspicuously roughened on the surface, a prominent identifying mark which has thus far been constant. The name *carolinianum* refers to one of the States where it is native. Freedom of Flowering: 1; Ease of Cultivation: 1; American Quality Rating: xx; British: *; American Hardiness Rating: H-2 (Author's dissent: H-1); British: A; Truss Type: 2.

R. catawbiense (kat-aw′-bee-en-see), **Michaux.** PONTICUM SERIES, PONTICUM SUBSERIES

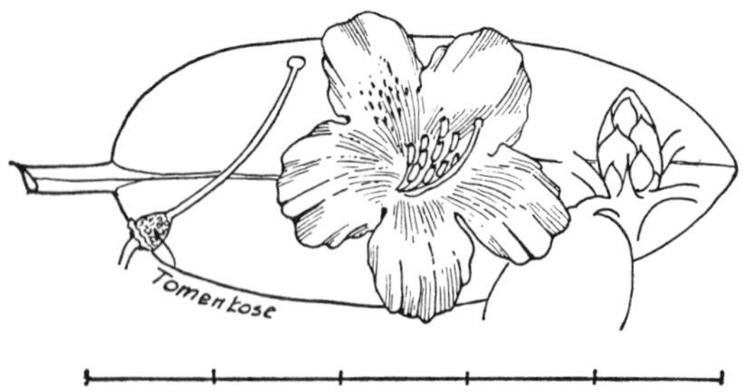

Of the American species, this is first and foremost in our gardens as an ornamental shrub in its own right, and in its priceless contribution of hardiness to its hybrids, which have brought to our eastern landscape at least a part of the Oriental splendor of the Asian Rhododendrons. Older plants of *R. catawbiense* are usually seen in gardens, about 8 or 10 feet high, possibly 12 feet broad. In the wild this species grows rarely to 20 feet or more. In cultivation, the largest specimen of established age to my knowledge is in the Knaphill Nursery in England, one of the five original plants first imported into that country in 1809. It is about 12 feet tall, 18 feet broad, still densely foliaged and attractive despite its antiquity. The leaves of this species are about 3 to 6 inches long, 1¼ to 2½ inches wide, dark, shiny green above and pale beneath. The 2¼-inch flowers come late in May and in early June, usually about fourteen to twenty in a firm, symmetrical rounded truss which may measure as much as 6 inches across. Unfortunately, it is known chiefly by its typical color form, which is also its worst. Visitors to the western mountains of North Carolina in mid-June see vast slopes of the Catawba Rhododendron in bloom, in one of the most spectacular floral displays in America. There at the top of Roan Mountain, at Craggy Gardens and at other well-known sites, whole mountain crests are transformed into vast billowing waves of lilac-magenta color in gigantic seas of Rhododendrons covering thousands of acres. Lovely in the misty violet air of the mountain wilderness, in cultivated gardens the pink is so flawed by a blue overcast that the blossoms of the typical species rest uneasily, especially where brighter, purer shades are near by, and discriminating enthusiasts have sought selected color forms which are now available through specialist-nurserymen to gardeners everywhere. There are two distinct forms with white flowers in commerce. There are at least three with blossoms approaching red, and a striking pale pink with flowers edged a deeper shade has been found. All or most of these are available from nurseries specializing in Rhododendrons and they are infinitely preferable to the ordinary magenta shade of the typical species. Interesting variations in color, size, shape and number of blossoms in the truss can be observed in a stroll through any nursery which re-grows plants collected from the wild. These better forms can often be bought in bloom at the time. The popular white-flowered Rhododendron in common commerce under the name 'Catawbiense album' has been erroneously described by past authorities as a variety of the wild species. It is not. It is a hybrid, and quite distinct from the white species variant, *catawbiense* var. *album*, an extraordinarily fine and beautiful garden Rhododendron, the first form of which was found by Powell Glass in Virginia. Of the countless plants which have been raised from seeds of this wild white Catawba Rhododendron, one of particular quality was named 'Catalgla' by Joseph Gable. It is notably superior to the average of seedlings and only this plant, or others propagated vegetatively from it, can properly be called by this name. It is much more lovely than the commercial hybrid, 'Catawbiense album'. For the most severe climates, selected forms of good color of the Catawba species will enhance the beauty of gardens too cold for commercial hybrids because they are appreciably hardier and bloom after winters so severe that the hybrids abandon their floral buds. *R. catawbiense* is hardy to −30° F. It undoubtedly is first among all species of flowering evergreen shrubs for cold sections of the country. It blooms before the new growth extends, so the blossoms are not concealed, and it is dense, neat and effective as a shrub the year around. Well-grown plants of good color forms are garden plants of the very finest quality, surpassing many of the renowned Asian sorts in the total of their merits. Early breeders, especially the Waterers in England, and later the Dutch hybridists, created from *R. catawbiense* a race of hardy hybrids which were the standard of quality throughout Europe and America and, despite the later influx of exotic sorts from the Orient, are still the dominant cultivated Rhododendrons in the colder parts of the two continents. The Catawba Rhododendron is easily distinguished from its near relative, *R. maximum*, the native Rosebay Rhododendron, because it lacks the incomplete tuft of bracts resembling miniature leaves which encircle the buds, both vegetative and floral, of the latter. The mature leaves are broadest at the middle and with a rounded base, whereas the leaves of *R. maximum* are usually broadest beyond the middle and taper gradually to the base. The minute calyx, flower stalks and ovary are all downy to some degree. In its extreme southern range this species extends into Alabama. It has been reported in the wild as far north as the Hudson River Valley, almost certainly there as an escape from cultivation. It is generally a plant of the higher elevations, up to about 6,500 feet, often occurring in immense thickets, extending southward from the uplands of West Virginia to its great concentration as the dominant shrub over many of the Appalachian mountain slopes in North Carolina and Tennessee. It is a species accustomed to wind and exposure, a valuable attribute for the gardener and for the hybridist. On Mt Mitchell a distinct crouching variety, *compactum*, has evolved, the survivors of the bitter gales which sweep that summit. Every spring collectors ship north thousands of plants which have been gathered from the wild under conditions which greatly reduce their chances of survival when they are subsequently planted in gardens. Plants which have been cut back and re-grown in a nursery are a much better choice for the gardener who finds acceptable the typical magenta-colored flowers of the wild seedlings. *R. catawbiense* was named for the district near the Catawba River where it was found in North Carolina. Freedom of Flowering: 1; Ease of Cultivation: 1; American Quality Rating: x (Author's dissent for selected color forms: xxx); British: ⋆; American Hardiness Rating: H-1; British: A; Truss Type: 1.

R. caucasicum (kaw-kas′-ik-um), **Pallas.** PONTICUM SERIES, CAUCASICUM SUBSERIES

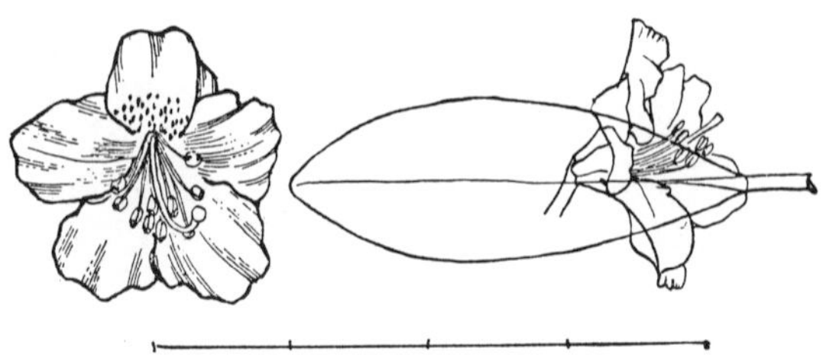

In the Western world the true *R. caucasicum* seems to be found only in the filing cases for herbarium specimens in botanical institutions. At best, it is extremely rare as a garden plant, though many other Rhododendrons masquerade under its name. This species was among the first in cultivation, however, and it has been an important influence through its hybrids on the horticulture of our time. Typical *R. caucasicum* usually grows to a height of 3 feet in cultivation but plants many years old are only 2 feet tall and 3 feet broad. Larger specimens that I have examined here and abroad were not correctly identified. The leathery, dark green leaves with grooved midrib and prominent primary veins are 2 to 4 inches long, $\frac{3}{4}$ to $1\frac{1}{2}$ inches wide, with downcurved edges and covered beneath with a tan to brownish-red felty indumentum. In May ten to fifteen 2-inch creamy white, pale rose, or yellowish flowers, spotted on the upper lobes, of somewhat papery texture, form round, firm terminal trusses of rather ragged appearance. The true *R. caucasicum* grows very slowly, blooms sparsely and forms a dense, compact, dwarf shrub. Plants which approximate the classic description have been hardy to New York City. A clone known in the trade as 'Coriaceum' (not to be confused with a species of similar name in the Falconeri series), and popularly thought to be a variety of *caucasicum*, is hardy to Boston, and freer blooming. American publications, quoting British sources, have often identified *R.* 'Cunningham's Sulphur' as a variety of *caucasicum*. Of the various so-called varieties which I have seen, all but one have been hybrids. Variety "*pictum*" is 6 feet high, 12 feet wide, and produces somewhat ragged trusses of rose-pink flowers rather freely. "*Venustum*" is 6 feet tall, 6 feet wide in older plants and produces in April rose flowers paling toward the center. It is an attractive Rhododendron but it is not a form of *R. caucasicum*. Variety *flavum*, about 18 inches high, 30 inches wide, with cream-colored flowers appears to be legitimate, but "*album*", 6 feet high, 4 feet wide, with white flowers, is not. All of these so-called varieties are to be seen so labeled in the collections of botanical institutions here and abroad, but most of them are actually hybrids, probably identical with those of similar name, bred more than a hundred years ago and described in the early literature. The classification of Rhododendrons in the Ponticum series badly needs revision, but *R. caucasicum* can be identified by its stature, less than 3 feet tall, the oblong-to-egg-shaped leaves rather wide for their length, with obtuse tips and wedge-shaped base, coated beneath with a thin indumentum. The straight style is 1¼ to 1½ inches long, and its pink color contrasts prominently against the corolla of the creamy yellow forms. Bud scales and bracts are persistent during flowering, sheathing the base of the flower stalks in an erect cluster. This species was introduced in 1803 from 6,000 to 9,000 feet elevation in the Caucasus, whence came its name. Freedom of Flowering: 3+; Ease of Cultivation: 1; American Quality Rating: x; British: ★; American Hardiness Rating: H-3 (Author's dissent: H-2); British: A; Truss Type: 1.

R. chapmanii (chap′-man-i), **Gray.** CAROLINIANUM SERIES

Here is a native American Rhododendron which is just starting to make its appearance in the milder gardens of the eastern United States. It is a 6-foot shrub with fresh, bright green, roughened leaves ¾ to 2½ inches long, ⅜ to 1⅜ inches wide, scaly beneath and often with undulating margins. The flowers, pale pink to rose-colored, about 1½ inches long overall, are widely funnel-form at the mouth, 1½ inches across, with a cylindrical tube ⅞ inch in length. There are about seven to a mound-shaped terminal truss in May. This Rhododendron is similar in appearance and in garden uses to its close relative, *R. carolinianum*, but it is a little stronger in character and possibly slightly more attractive in leaf. It blooms about the same time, with blossoms which are often superior in their clear pink effect, but I have seen some small-flowered, indeterminate faded pink forms which were vastly inferior. In my trial grounds in the mountains of northwestern Pennsylvania it is surprisingly hardy but it does not really justify itself as a satisfactory garden shrub and I estimate that a climate similar to that of Boston would be the limit of useful cultivation. If it were better known this would be an important flowering shrub for lowland southern gardens, probably the only evergreen Rhododendron which is truly heat resistant and easy to grow in the deep South. It could impart its tolerance of heat to its progeny, and hybrids of this species with its giant-flowered Asian relatives might be a richly rewarding goal for a breeder in the South. *R. chapmanii* is distinguished from its two American allies in the same series by its corolla only slightly or not at all scaly on the outside, and its blunt leaves not pointed as in *R. minus*. It differs in flower from *R. carolinianum* in its longer flower tube, over ⅔ inch. I do not believe the crisped corolla lobes given in botanical keys for *R. chapmanii* are a reliable guide to separate it from its Carolina ally, however. I find that the leaves, wider for their length than those of *R. carolinianum*, lighter, brighter green and conspicuously roughened on the surface, are quick and convenient marks for identification which have so far been reliable. *R. chapmanii* is native to the coastal plain of northwestern Florida. It was named for A. W. Chapman, the nineteenth-century American botanist. Freedom of Flowering: 1; Ease of Cultivation: 1; American Quality Rating: x; British: none: American Hardiness Rating: H-3; British: B; Truss Type: 3.

R. chartophyllum (kar-to-fi′-lum), **Franch.** TRIFLORUM SERIES, YUNNANENSE SUBSERIES

Among good species of the Triflorum group, this is distinct because it is usually at least partially deciduous and often wholly so. When mature, it is most frequently seen as a shrub of irregular growth about 6 feet tall and 8 feet broad with very pale $1\frac{1}{2}$-inch lavender pink flowers, shortly tubular at the base with five spreading lobes and conspicuously spotted on the upper one. About seven florets make up a fairly well-defined truss 3 inches in diameter. Its thin leaves are usually about 2 inches long and slightly more than $\frac{1}{2}$ inch broad, scaly on both surfaces, but it is not normally well-foliaged at blooming time in late April and early May. Like almost all of the Triflorums, this is an adaptable shrub, useful and easily pleased in a variety of situations. In my opinion, the form which is wholly deciduous is superior because it is more free-flowering and the foliage which remains over winter on plants with persistent leaves is an unattractive dull purple at blossoming time. Variety *album*, with a storm of white flowers boldly blotched with orange, is especially fine and reliable in its floral performance. This species is reputed to be somewhat lime tolerant, an attribute which has been applied to other Rhododendrons and subsequently disproved. It is distinguished from others in the same series by having sharply pointed leaves without hairs on the upper surface but with lax scales underneath three or more times their own diameter apart; by being devoid of hairs on the midrib of the leaf undersurface; and by having pale mauve flowers with the corolla tube not scaly on the outside. *R. yunnanense*, its closest relative, is evergreen and has bristles on the leaves which this species lacks, but it is otherwise very similar. The name, *chartophyllum*, refers to its paper-like leaves. It inhabits an elevation range of 6,000 to 11,000 feet in Yunnan province of southwestern China. Freedom of Flowering: 1; Ease of Cultivation: 1; American Quality Rating: xxx; British: ***; American Hardiness Rating: H-3; British: B; Truss Type: 9.

R. chasmanthum (chas-man′thum), **Diels.** TRIFLORUM SERIES, AUGUSTINII SUBSERIES

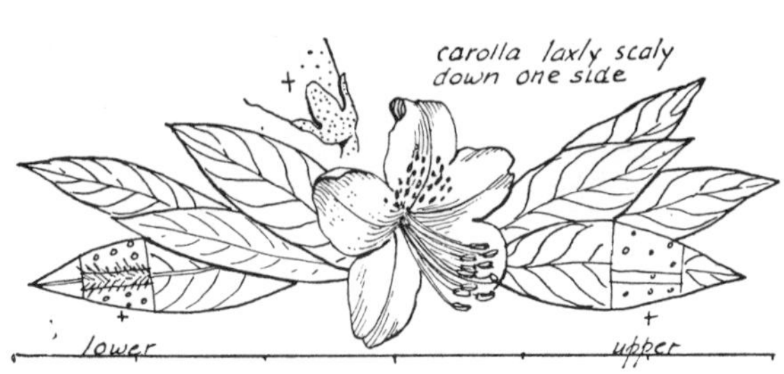

This 10-foot shrub with lance-like pointed scaly leaves 1 to $2\frac{3}{4}$ inches long and $\frac{1}{2}$ to $1\frac{1}{8}$ inches wide is universally admired for its cascades of pale to deep lavender-pink or violet flowers in May. Each blossom, with short, funnel-shaped base and five spreading lobes, is about $1\frac{3}{4}$ inches in diameter, spotted green on the upper lobe, and as many as five spring from a terminal bud.

Their number is often increased by contributions from adjacent axillary buds so that clusters of about eight or nine blooms may form a sizable truss in the best and most free-flowering forms. Plants of the pale mauve color are most often seen and they lend a light and lovely note to the landscape by their own display or in contrast with yellow-flowered Rhododendrons. They also make a handsome informal hedge, blooming about ten days after *R. augustinii*, to which this species is similar and closely related though not so hardy. The Exbury F.C.C. form is best in its violet-blue color and size of truss. Like its more famous relative, this species has a downy line along the midrib on the leaf under-surface, but it can be distinguished from *augustinii* and others of its clan with white, bluish, or pink flowers also by having leaf stalks and branchlets scaly but not hairy; scales beneath the leaves four or five times their own diameter apart; the glabrous flower stalk and ovary; and by having a scaly calyx with five lobes clearly defined. Actually it seems scarcely entitled to specific status and might be properly considered a variety of *augustinii*. The species was first found in 1893 by the Rev. J. A. Souliei. The name means 'with gaping flowers'. It grows at 10,000 feet on open mountainsides in southeast Tibet and the northwest portion of Yunnan province of China. Freedom of Flowering: 1; Ease of Cultivation: 1; American Quality Rating: xxx; British: ***; American Hardiness Rating: H-4; British: C; Truss Type: 9; A.M. 1930; F.C.C., 1932.

R. chrysanthum (kris-an'-thum), **Pallas.** PONTICUM SERIES, CAUCASICUM SUBSERIES

Until the last few years American gardeners have been obliged to obtain technical guidance and secure plants of both species and new hybrids from England, where the Rhododendrons of the Ponticum series, if not despised, are at least not admired. English indifference to this group is not matched in the United States, where the Ponticum series Rhododendrons, with their inherent hardiness, are an important contribution to the horticulture of the cold northeastern states. *R. chrysanthum* is one of the species which has evoked the curiosity of amateur enthusiasts and hybridists. It is a prostrate shrub, with an ultimate height reputed to be one foot, but scarcely reaching 6 or 8 inches as ordinarily seen in cultivation. It is extremely slow-growing. A thirty-year old specimen is possibly 6 inches tall and 30 inches wide. Some forms are matted in their spreading growth, with very short branches densely clothed with leaves. Others are a little more open and erect, with the shoots more clearly defined, but still prostrate in the procumbent extension of the stems. Leaves of this species are 1 to $3\frac{1}{4}$ inches long, $\frac{3}{8}$ to $1\frac{3}{8}$ inches wide, the upper surface dark green and conspicuously veined, the lower surface either pale green or tan, often with traces of a fugitive juvenile indumentum. Flowers appear in late April or early May, cream-color or light yellow fading to cream. They are about $1\frac{3}{4}$ inches in diameter, five to nine in a terminal truss of rounded outline, and they appear very large for the creeping plant which produces them. Unfortunately, this Rhododendron blossoms so rarely that its flowers are a great curiosity, even among specialists. Accustomed to alpine conditions in the wild, it is fastidious, but once established it continues to grow very slowly for decades. It is hardy to Boston and beyond, and its mat of green foliage tinged yellow is attractive the year around. Dr Hiroshi Hara of the University of Tokyo maintains that "variety *niko-montanum*"

is a natural hybrid, the result of a cross between *R. chrysanthum* and *R. fauriei*. However, seeds of this Rhododendron gathered from the mountains of Nikko produced plants in this country conforming to the description but entirely too uniform in every respect to be recently evolved hybrids. The undersides of the leaves appear to be glabrous to the naked eye, but there is actually an extremely scanty indumentum which can be scraped off with a blade, floated in xylene and, upon examination with a microscope, demonstrated to be identical in structure with the radiate hairs of *R. brachycarpum*. It seems much more plausible that the more free-flowering, much more erect Rhododendron originally described by Nakai as *R. niko-montanum* is entitled to distinction as a species. *R. chrysanthum* is so distinct in its prostrate posture that it can scarcely be confused with any of its relatives. There are fewer flowers in the truss and the pistil is generally about 1 inch long in contrast to a length of about $1\frac{1}{2}$ inches in its nearest relative, *R. caucasicum*, which also has larger leaves with an indumentum which is lacking or vestigial in *R. chrysanthum*. The name means 'golden-flowered', which grossly flatters the color of any that I have seen. Its dwarfness and density of growth would probably make it extremely valuable for the production of hardy hybrids of modest stature for the northeastern United States. This Rhododendron has been known to the Western world since Pallas published a description of it in 1776. It comes from the mountains of Mongolia, Siberia, Manchuria, and north and central Japan, west to Altai. Freedom of Flowering: 3; Ease of Cultivation: 3; American Quality Rating: 0; British: none; American Hardiness Rating: H-3 (Author's dissent: H-2); British: B; Truss Type: 1.

R. chryseum (kri'-see-um), **Balf. f. and Ward.** LAPPONICUM SERIES

A plant of dense, twiggy growth from 1 to 2 feet tall, this is a charming Rhododendron for the rock garden or wherever a good small undershrub is needed. The thick, aromatic leaves are $\frac{3}{8}$ to $\frac{3}{4}$ inch long, $\frac{1}{4}$ to $\frac{1}{2}$ inch wide, scaly on both surfaces. Four or five flowers about 1 inch in diameter make up miniature trusses which are usually $1\frac{1}{2}$ inches across, appearing in late April and early May. Descriptions of this species in the literature refer to its blossoms as 'bright yellow', 'golden yellow', or 'deep sulphur yellow', which would be an exaggerated courtesy to the specimens I have seen. Accuracy requires a note here that the plants usually grown in gardens are pale, creamy yellow. However, forms of more emphatic color have been isolated by connoisseurs at one time or another, and the selection commercially available under Rock #59049 is certainly much better than the average and considerably superior to *R. flavidum*, its March-flowering competitor with similarly colored flowers in the series. In any case, this species affords a delightful contrast when planted to relieve the varying mauve flowers of the great majority of dwarf alpines. It is easily recognized in its series because its yellow blossoms in a four- to five-flowered inflorescence are unique in having a glabrous style and five stamens. *R. chryseum* is native to exposed hillsides at 12,000 to 14,000 feet on the frontier between Tibet and the Chinese province of Yunnan. It was found there by Kingdon-Ward in 1912 and named for its 'golden yellow' flowers. Freedom of Flowering: 2+; Ease of Cultivation: 2+; American Quality Rating: xx; British: **; American Hardiness Rating: H-2; British: A; Truss Type: 5.

R. ciliatum (sil-ee-a′-tum), **Hooker fil.** MADDENII SERIES, CILIICALYX SUBSERIES

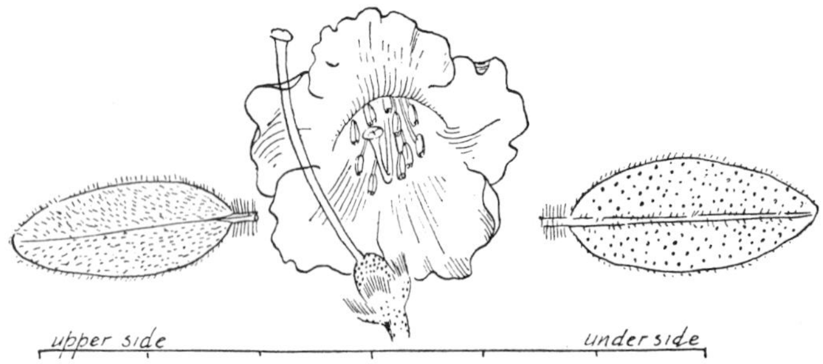

The stature of this species depends, to an unusual extent, on the climate in which it grows. It is often seen as a 5-foot shrub in climates suitable to most Rhododendrons, but it is quite capable of growing 9 feet tall and 18 feet broad where mildness and moisture combine to give it ideal conditions. Its growth habit is a little stiff, and if it is neglected it is inclined to retain its foliage only in terminal rosettes, giving the lower branches a somewhat ungainly appearance. Its dark, hairy leaves are $1\frac{1}{2}$ to 4 inches long, $\frac{3}{4}$ to $1\frac{1}{2}$ inches broad, and scaly. The branchlets are bristly. The widely bell-shaped flowers are usually very pale pink, fading to white, 2 to $2\frac{1}{2}$ inches across, borne in loose, flat-topped, outward-facing clusters of three to five, in March and early April. A $\frac{3}{8}$-inch pinkish calyx often stands out stiffly behind the blossoms. This is one of the sturdiest species of the Maddenii series, hardier than its reputation but of course not rugged enough to endure the cold winters of the northeastern United States. An especially fine form on the West Coast is available as "variety *bergii*". *R. ciliatum* differs from its relatives in the Maddenii clan in having a corolla not scaly outside and a style lacking either hairs or scales; a small calyx, $\frac{3}{8}$ inch long, with broad lobes densely fringed with long, stiff hairs; leaf stalks with a groove on the upper surface; and both leaves and branchlets clad with bristle-like hairs. There are ten stamens. The species does well over a large part of the Rhododendron belt of the West Coast. It has been in cultivation since 1850, when it was introduced from 9,000 to 11,000 feet in the Himalayan Mountains of Sikkim. The name means 'fringed', a reference to the conspicuous bristly hairs. Freedom of Flowering: 1; Ease of Cultivation: 1; American Quality Rating: xxx; British: ★★★★; American Hardiness Rating: H-4; British: C; Truss Type: 12; A.M., 1953.

R. ciliicalyx (sil-e-a-ka′-lix), **Franch.** MADDENII SERIES, CILIICALYX SUBSERIES

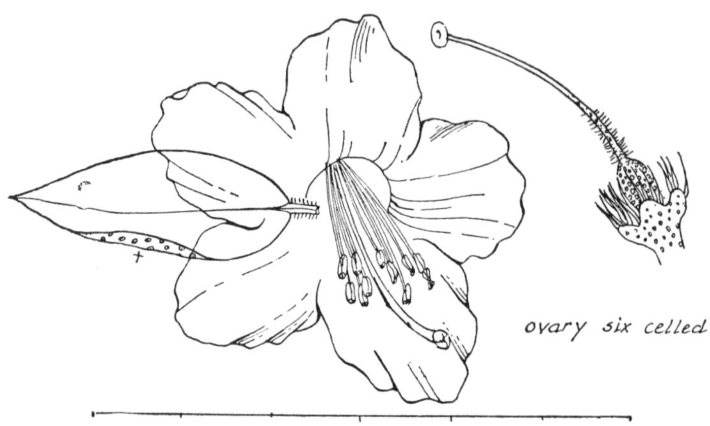

There are many beautiful species in the Maddenii series but this is among the best. It grows 8 or 10 feet tall in a somewhat open, irregular fashion and bears dark, glossy green leaves $2\frac{1}{2}$ to 4 inches long, $\frac{3}{4}$ to 2 inches wide and scaly. Sumptuous, sweet-scented, widely funnel-shaped blossoms, 4 inches across, white to pink with a yellow blotch inside the throat are borne in threes in late March and early April. It seldom fails to bloom with the utmost freedom, but it is not at all hardy, as its outdoor use is confined largely to the California coastal climate of the San Francisco district. Elsewhere it makes a fine greenhouse shrub, perhaps the best for this purpose of any of the series. This species separates from others of its kind on the base of its short, rounded calyx lobes equally separated and fringed with bristly hairs; corolla tube not scaly outside, with style both scaly and pubescent near the base; axillary leaf buds fringed with downy white hairs; leaf stalks with a V-shaped groove on the upper surface, and scales on the leaf undersides more than their own diameter apart. There are ten or eleven stamens. *R. ciliicalyx* was found by Delavay in the mountains of western Yunnan province of China in 1884. It grows at about 7,500 feet on rocky slopes there. Its name refers to the bristles fringing the calyx. Freedom of Flowering: 1; Ease of Cultivation: 1; American Quality Rating: xx; British: ****; American Hardiness Rating: H-6; British: F; Truss Type: 12; A.M., 1923.

R. cinnabarinum (sin-nab-ar-i'-num), **Hook.** CINNABARINUM SERIES

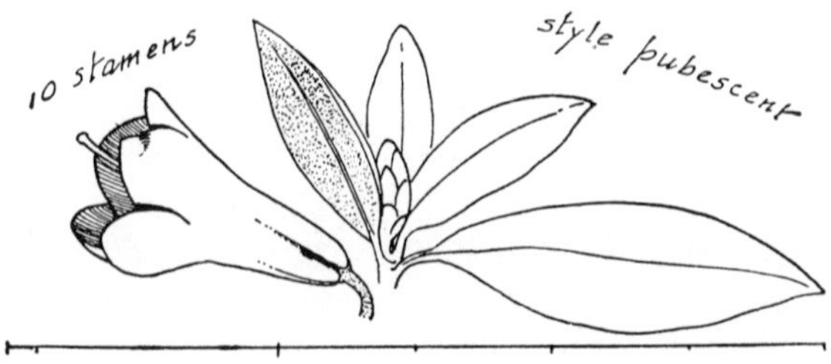

This fine species is usually seen as a shrub up to 10 feet tall with slender, pliant branches and a willowy habit of growth. Robust forms are reported to reach 15 feet. Its leaves are up to 3½ inches in length and 1¾ inches broad, glaucous and densely scaly below. The distinctive, tubular flowers of heavy substance expand rather abruptly to form elongated, pendant trumpets up to 2¾ inches long, 1¾ inches across, which hang gracefully in terminal groups of four or five on the ends of the branches in May. There is remarkable variation within this species in the size of the flowers, when they appear, how far their corollas expand, and especially in their color. I have seen specimens at various times with flowers which were deep purple, clear pink, buff, orange, yellow, brilliant red, purplish-red, and with two-toned combinations of pale orange and scarlet. The clear pink and the brilliant red forms are the most attractive. Variety *blandfordiaeflorum* has buff-yellow blossoms flushed orange-red. Variety *roylei* is much more handsome and seems to be more floriferous, with more open corollas that are brilliantly colored an incandescent red of unique quality, becoming beautifully luminous when the sun shines through them. This is a striking free-flowering Rhododendron with a unique floral effect, adaptable and useful in many garden situations. The young growth is an unusual soft blue. The species is separated from its small-flowered ally, *R. keysii*, by having blossoms more than an inch long. It allegedly differs from *R. concatenans* in the latter's broadly expanded, bell-shaped flowers of apricot color, in contrast to the tubular bell-shaped varicolored florets of this species. In my opinion, neither flower shape nor color is a reliable basis for discriminating between the two. *R. xanthocodon*, with yellow flowers, seems no more than a variety of *cinnabarinum* and I suspect that there is a fluid progression of natural hybrids linking the extreme forms of this whole group. The name refers to the cinnabar-red of its most common color form. *R. cinnabarinum* has been in cultivation since 1849, when it was introduced by Hooker. It comes from the Himalayan Mountains of Sikkim, where it grows at 10,000 to 12,000 feet. Its foliage is thought by the natives there to be poisonous to livestock. Freedom of Flowering: 1; Ease of Cultivation: 1; American Quality Rating: xxx; British: ****; American Hardiness Rating: H-3; British: B; Truss Type: 11; var. *roylei*, A.M., 1953; Var. *purpurellum*, A.M., 1951; *blandfordiaeflorum*, A.M., 1945.

R. concatenans (kon-ka′-ten-ans), **Hutchinson.** CINNABARINUM SERIES

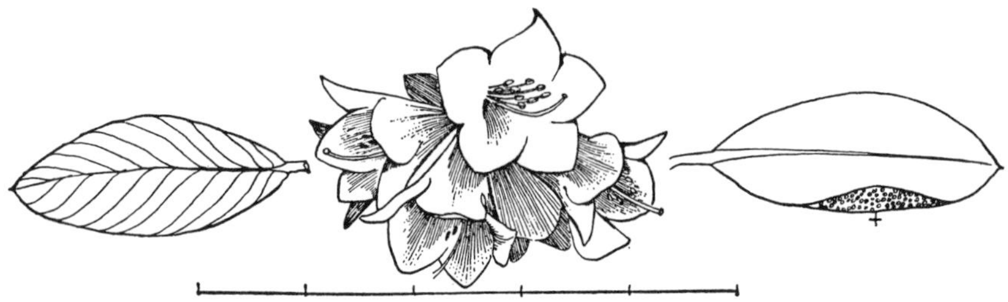

Older plants of *R. concatenans* are usually seen about 6 to 8 feet tall, well furnished with interesting glaucous-green foliage and outstanding in the garden for their distinctive attractiveness the year round. The leaves are $1\frac{1}{2}$ to 3 inches long, $\frac{3}{4}$ to $1\frac{1}{2}$ inches wide, blue-green above, either whitish or tinged with purple beneath and densely scaly. The handsome young growth is sea-green, aging to the characteristic blue-green color of the older foliage. The flowers appear in late April and early May, long, waxen, bell-shaped blossoms about $1\frac{3}{4}$ inches wide at the mouth, six or seven to a flat-topped cluster. The colors are unusual, ranging from apricot with an iridescent purple flush to clear, deep yellow with an odd, frosted mat surface. This is among the best foliage plants in the entire genus, a first-rate Rhododendron of strong and unusual character. The standard botanical reference works erroneously distinguish it from *R. xanthocodon* on the basis of apricot flowers, more widely expanded, and by the glaucous sheen of the young foliage. However, as noted above, in some forms the flowers are yellow, as they are in *R. xanthocodon*, and rarely also in *R. cinnabarinum*; in fact, this species was originally described, not from a plant in the wild, but from a living specimen grown from seeds of Kingdon-Ward's #5874, and this same number produced seedlings with yellow flowers in other gardens. Though the blossoms are often broadly bell-shaped, I do not find this characteristic constant, some forms closely approaching the tubular shape of *R. xanthocodon* and *R. cinnabarinum*. It appears to me that *R. concatenans* is no more distinct than some of the varieties of *R. cinnabarinum*, and I suggest that these two should be combined, with *R. xanthocodon*, into only one species. The presence of natural hybrids is evident in this group and the species merge imperceptibly into one another. *R. concatenans* was first described from a garden plant in 1935, and given the name meaning 'linking together' as a reference to its botanical characteristics serving as evidence of a bridge relating it to other Rhododendrons. Freedom of Flowering: 2; Ease of Cultivation: 1; American Quality Rating: xxx; British: ****; American Hardiness Rating: H-4; British: B; Truss Type: 11; F.C.C., 1935; 'Copper', A.M., 1954.

R. concinnum (kon′-sin-num), **Hemsl.** TRIFLORUM SERIES, POLYLEPIS SUBSERIES

This is a neat shrub about 8 feet tall at maturity but usually seen in gardens somewhat smaller. It is dense in growth habit, rounded and somewhat spreading in outline with leaves 1 to $3\frac{1}{2}$ inches long, $\frac{3}{8}$ to $1\frac{1}{2}$ inches wide, dark green above, grayish-green below and scaly on both sides. A Rhododendron well known and popular in gardens of the Pacific Northwest and of Great Britain, *R. pseudoyanthinum*, is only a form of the variable *R. concinnum*, and I am suppressing the name in this work. It has enjoyed its dubious status solely on the assumption that its flowers are larger and deeper in color. Since this is not the case, and it is well within the range of variation found in any sizable population of seedlings of *R. concinnum*, I see no reason for continuing the error here. Both bloom in late April and early May with funnel-shaped flowers 1½ to a little more than 2 inches across, usually about four to a loose cluster. The color most frequently seen is a distinctive purple, spotted on the upper lobe, but it varies from pale blush-pink through rather unattractive faded violet shades, to bright, rosy crimson. The dark wine-purple is unusual and appealing, probably the best in the range. Some flowers have broad, rounded lobes. Other forms produce corolla lobes narrow, sometimes twisted, with a star-like outline. This is a first-rate Rhododendron, with dense, fine-textured foliage, a convenient dwarf stature, and a reliable show of blossoms almost unique in the typical color, which is not constant enough, however, to be the accurate guide to identification suggested in botanical keys. The odd color range is handsome with yellow-flowered sorts, but there is a jarring conflict with orange-red or pink flowers near by. This species is characterized by leaves more or less elliptical in outline, shaped almost alike at each end, somewhat glaucous underneath and clad with scales about one-third their own diameter apart, but devoid of hairs on the midrib. There are no bristles on the margins of the leaf stalks. The calyx is densely scaly but not hairy. The flowers, scaly on the outside, are self-colored uniformly throughout. *R. concinnum* grows in the wild at 7,500 to 12,000 feet in the Chinese province of Szechuan, whence come some of our hardiest and most tractable Asian species. It seems likely that seedlings could be isolated which would be satisfactory at least as far north as Philadelphia. The species was first found by Rev. Ernest Faber in 1886 and given the name referring to its trim appearance. Freedom of Flowering: 1; Ease of Cultivation: 1; American Quality Rating: xx; British: ★; American Hardiness Rating: H-3; British: A; Truss Type: 9; as *pseudoyanthinum*, A.M., 1951; as *pseudoyanthinum* 'Paulina', a superior selection, P.A., 1954.

R. crassum (kraś-sum), **Franch.** MADDENII SERIES, MADDENII SUBSERIES

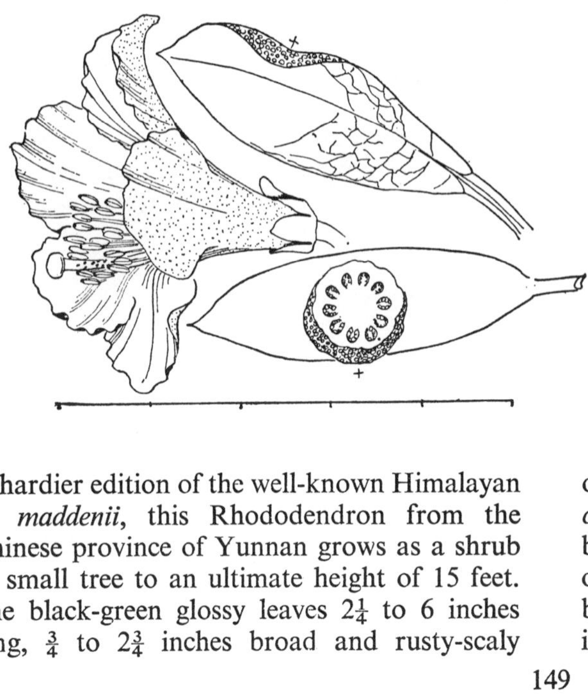

A hardier edition of the well-known Himalayan *R. maddenii*, this Rhododendron from the Chinese province of Yunnan grows as a shrub or small tree to an ultimate height of 15 feet. The black-green glossy leaves 2¼ to 6 inches long, ¾ to 2¾ inches broad and rusty-scaly below, grow close together in whorls at the ends of the branches. The richly fragrant flowers are white, up to 4 inches across, borne four or five, usually, in loose terminal clusters. They appear in June, a season when few other Rhododendrons are in bloom. Because it is so much hardier than its relatives, this lovely species can be grown outdoors in mild climates where the Maddenii Rhododendrons are ordinarily greenhouse shrubs, but there is evidently a wide variance in the cold resistance of various forms because the species has frequently been reported as unsatisfactory in Oregon. The Logan form is one of the best examples of the species. *R. crassum* is separated from its near relatives by having flowers with fifteen to twenty-one stamens, the filaments hairy toward the base, and bearing large anthers up to ¼ inch in length. The corolla tube is 2¼ to 3½ inches in length and densely scaly outside. The flower-bud scales are pubescent near their apex and the calyx is well developed, up to ½ inch in length. There are ten cells in the ovary. The leaf stalks usually have a V-shaped groove on their upper surface. *R. maddenii*, with which it is often confused, is distinct from it in possessing non-hairy stamens and a much smaller calyx, only about ⅙ inch long. *R. crassum* was discovered by Delavay about 1885 and introduced into English gardens by Forrest in 1906.

It comes from 7,500 to 12,000 feet in western Yunnan and from 8,000 to 9,000 feet elevation in Upper Burma. Its name is an allusion to the heavy substance of the flowers. Freedom of Flowering: 1; Ease of Cultivation: 1; American Quality Rating: xx; British: ***; American Hardiness Rating: H-5; British: D; Truss Type: 12; A.M., 1924 and 1928.

R. dalhousiae (dal-hous'-ee-i). **Hook, f.** MADDENII SERIES, MEGACALYX SUBSERIES

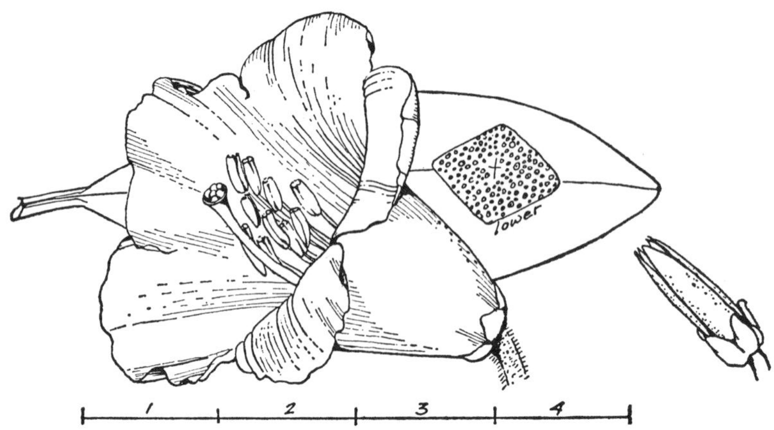

This is a famous beauty with a tender disposition and an ungainly figure. Suitable in the United States only for the mildest California climates or for the greenhouse, it is best planted with other, more densely foliaged Rhododendrons which will hide its lanky limbs while allowing full display of its magnificent, lemon-scented creamy white or pale yellow flowers resembling Easter lilies in clusters. It is reasonably satisfactory in coastal gardens of western Scotland. *R. dalhousiae* is usually seen as a thin, open shrub up to 7 or 8 feet tall, with dark green scaly leaves from 2¾ to 6 inches long and 1 to 2¼ inches wide. The flowers appear in late April and early May as trumpets 3 to 4 inches across, in terminal groups of two to four. Authorities have incorrectly described the fragrant, opulently beautiful blossoms as invariably white and this feature is even given as one of the identifying marks of the species. However, there is a form with sumptuous chamois-yellow flowers which are among the loveliest in the entire genus. The true species is rare in cultivation, many plants so labeled being actually hybrids. This Rhododendron is distinguished from its near relatives by having ten stamens, a large calyx devoid of hairs, flower stalks both scaly and hairy, and a corolla with only a few scales on the adaxial side. *R. dalhousiae* was named for the wife of the Governor-General of India when it was discovered by Hooker just a little over a hundred years ago. It comes from Sikkim and Bhutan at elevations of 6,000 to 8,000 feet, where it grows as an epiphyte on the branches of trees. Freedom of Flowering: 1; Ease of Cultivation: 2+; American Quality Rating: xxxx; British: ***; American Hardiness Rating: H-6: British: F; Truss Type: 12; A.M., 1930.

R. dauricum (daw′-rik-um), **Linn.** DAURICUM SERIES

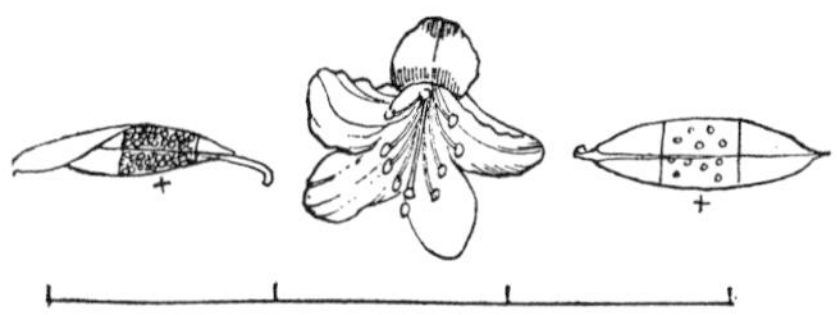

It is doubtful if *R. dauricum* in its typical form is in cultivation in the United States. There are innumerable intergrades and natural hybrids with characteristics midway between it and its near relative, *R. mucronulatum*, which pass in the trade as the species here under consideration. For an understanding of the relationship between the two, it is necessary to envision one extreme as *R. dauricum*, the many-branched shrub of compact, twiggy growth and small evergreen leaves; and the other, *R. mucronulatum*, taller and looser in growth with thin, deciduous leaves; and between the two a fluid progression of intermediate forms. The most typical specimen of *R. dauricum* that I have seen was a shrub 4 feet tall and 5 feet wide with dark evergreen leaves 1 inch long, $\frac{1}{2}$ inch broad and scaly on both surfaces. Labeled by its former name, *fittianum*, it bore freely from terminal buds in groups at the ends of the shoots bright lavender-pink flowers $\frac{13}{16}$ inch in diameter which in some cases were assembled into little round $1\frac{1}{2}$-inch trusses containing up to eighteen blossoms in various stages of development, from tight buds to blossoms fully open. It was still in bloom with such species as *RR. thomsonii* and *davidsonianum* at the end of April in an exceptionally late season. In mild climates February or March would be the usual blooming season. In its extreme form this species differs from *R. mucronulatum* for garden purposes in its heavier, darker evergreen leaves which are smaller in size and borne on a plant of better habit, closer and more twiggy in growth. It has smaller flowers more freely produced and blooms somewhat later, though within very wide limits according to the season. The literature gives a stature up to 6 feet in height, a leaf size range of $\frac{1}{2}$ to $1\frac{3}{4}$ inches, and often refers to 'a deciduous or semi-evergreen form' which is more commonly seen, though it is not as ornamental as the truly evergreen type. This is a very hardy species, perfectly satisfactory to $-25°$ F., and it is a true harbinger of spring when it comes into precocious bloom early in the year, often in February in mild climates. It should be planted where its blossoms are sheltered from frost as much as possible. *R. dauricum* is unlikely to be confused with any other species except the sole other member of the series, *R. mucronulatum*, from which it is distinct botanically in the extreme form by having smaller, heavier leaves generally less than $1\frac{1}{4}$ inches long, elliptical in shape and rounded at both ends, so scaly beneath that the scales are contiguous or overlapping. The seed capsule is straight. The rounded leaf end with a short, sharp tip is distinctive, and it is probably the easiest and quickest way to distinguish *R. dauricum* from its ally. The species was named for Dauria in northeastern Asia. It is native from Altai east to Korea with only a local distribution in Japan on some mountains in Hokkaido. Freedom of Flowering: 1; Ease of Cultivation: 1; American Quality Rating: xx; British: **; American Hardiness Rating: H-2 (Author's dissent: H-1); British: A; Truss Type: 9.

R. davidsonianum (da-vid-son-i-a′-num), **Rehd. and E. H. Wils.** TRIFLORUM SERIES, YUNNANENSE SUBSERIES

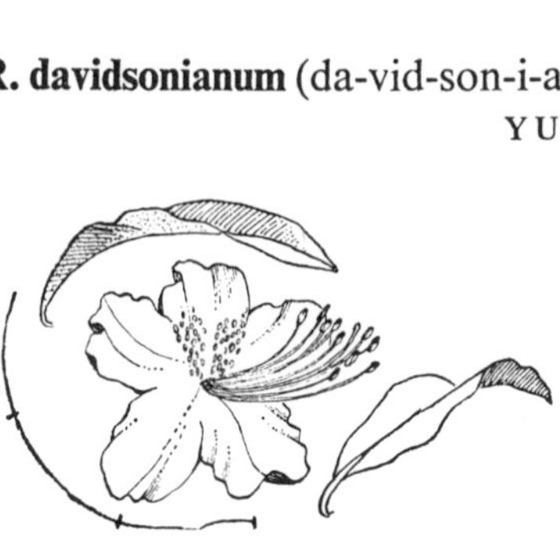

The Rhododendron often called "Pink Triflorum" is actually *R. davidsonianum*, and its popular name is a tribute to its prominence as a good garden plant. It is a 10-foot shrub in cultivation with leaves 1 to $2\frac{1}{2}$ inches long, $\frac{3}{8}$ to $\frac{7}{8}$ inch wide, shiny dark green above and dull brown below from the dense scales. The flowers with five spreading lobes from a funnel-shaped base appear in late April and early May, usually three to seven in a loose cluster, each about $1\frac{3}{4}$ inches wide, white to light pink with a few red dots on the upper lobe, or frequently deep rose. This Rhododendron varies tremendously in its ornamental effect because of the range in size and color of the flower trusses. A form sparingly distributed on the West Coast has very large, firm, rounded clusters with as many as seventeen pale pink florets in them. 'Caerhay's Pink' is the name given to a good sort with smaller trusses of luminous rose flowers, and a form popularly known as the Exbury variety is exceptionally attractive in the clarity of its deep pink blossoms. The regularity of its blooming and its versatile adaptability to a wide variety of planting sites have made this the most popular of the Triflorum Rhododendrons, valued for their lighter, more graceful note in the landscape. This species is most easily recognized amidst the welter of ill-defined Triflorums by the V-shaped leaf blade. The narrowly lanceolate to oblanceolate leaves have elevated margins and are depressed at the midrib, thus forming the distinctive V-shape in cross-section. They are pointed at the tips, subacute at the base, devoid of bristly hairs on the upper surface and on the midrib underneath; and they are much more scaly below than above, the scales only about their own diameter apart. The number of flowers in the truss, given as an identifying mark in botanical keys, is not constant enough to be a reliable guide. The blossoms are not scaly outside. They are borne on stalks about $\frac{1}{2}$ inch long and have a glabrous style, stamens pubescent in the lower part and a very small undulate calyx. This is a common Rhododendron in open sites at 6,000 to 10,000 feet in western Szechuan province of China, where it was found by Wilson and introduced by him in 1908. It was named for Dr W. H. Davidson, a Quaker missionary in China. Freedom of Flowering: 1; Ease of Cultivation: 1; American Quality Rating: xxx; British: ****; American Hardiness Rating: H-4; British: B; Truss Type: 9; A.M., 1935; pink form, F.C.C., 1955; as 'Pink Davidsonianum', a temporary name for a superior selection, P.A., 1954.

R. decorum (dek-or′-um), **Franch.** FORTUNEI SERIES, FORTUNEI SUBSERIES

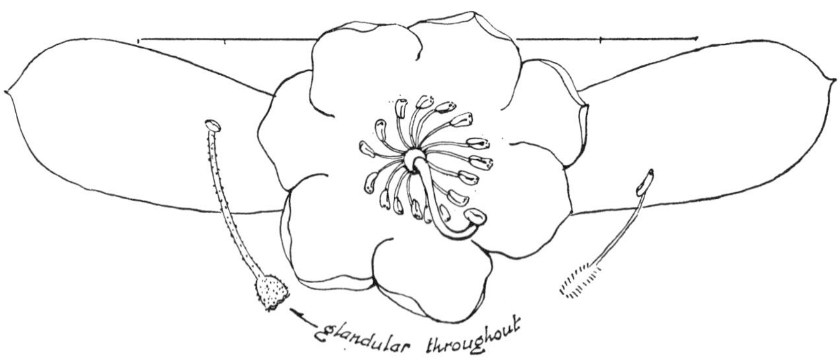

The true *R. decorum*, correctly labeled, is a rather rare plant in cultivation despite its wide distribution in western China. Many plants called in gardens "*R. fortunei*" are actually *R. decorum* or, even more frequently, hybrids of it. The authentic species is a first-rate ornamental, variable in many respects, including its height which may range from 6 to 20 feet. Most older plants tend to become rangy and tree-like as they reach skyward with the years. The leaves are 2 to 6 inches long and $1\frac{1}{4}$ to $2\frac{3}{4}$ inches broad. The white or deep pink flowers, often with yellow throats, are famous for their delicious fragrance and for their extraordinary size, up to 5 inches in diameter in the best forms, about nine of them clustered loosely in a terminal truss. There is a rare form with exotic chartreuse-colored flowers which is especially handsome. The open funnel-campanulate blossoms of this species have six to eight lobes and expand fully to a rather flat corolla when they are seen at their most attractive on specimens selected for their quality. As in so many other respects, *R. decorum* varies in its season of flowering: from early April to the latter part of May. The small-flowered forms from Yunnan and Szechuan are considerably hardier than those with enormous flowers discovered by Farrer in Upper Burma. Kingdon-Ward's late white form is particularly beautiful and it is both hardy and free blooming. Remarkable for such a large Rhododendron, this species often blooms in three years from seeds. This is a valuable garden plant, useful all along the Pacific Coast from San Francisco northward in many landscape situations where a large evergreen background shrub is wanted, and it is equally esteemed in the British Isles. Grown from seeds, it has thriven in the deep South, near Atlanta, Georgia, one of the very few Asian species to do so. It is not quite hardy enough to be thoroughly satisfactory in the collection of Joseph Gable, at Stewartstown, Pennsylvania, but the hardiest seedlings should be satisfactory in the milder climate from Philadelphia southward. *R. decorum* is often confused with *R. fortunei* from which it differs in having hairy stamens. The drawings on page 116 contrast side by side the distinguishing marks of *RR. decorum*, *fortunei*, and *discolor*. In addition to its pubescent stamen base, this species is distinct from others in the *fortunei* series by having glands white to yellow extending to the tip of the style; a minute calyx; and leaves 2 to 6 inches long. There are twelve to sixteen stamens. *R. decorum* comes from the Chinese provinces of Yunnan and Szechuan at altitudes of 8,000 to 11,000 feet, where it grows in woodlands and among hillside scrub. Its name means 'ornamental'. Freedom of Flowering: 2+; Ease of Cultivation: 1; American Quality Rating: xxx; British: ***; American Hardiness Rating: H-4; British: C; Truss Type: 8.

R. degronianum (deg-ro-nee-a′-num), **Carrière.** PONTICUM SERIES, CAUCASICUM SUBSERIES

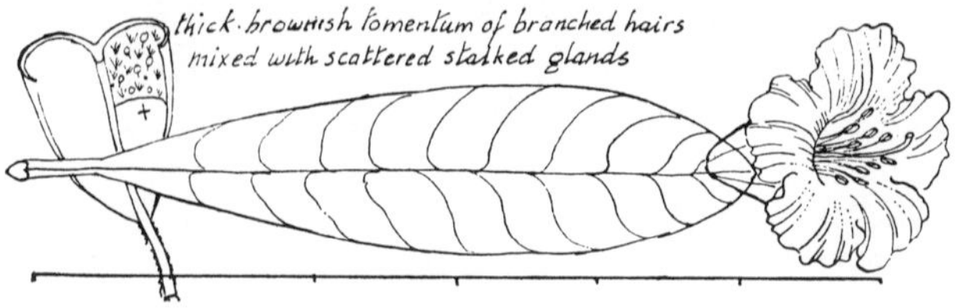

Japanese Rhododendrons seem well-adapted to conditions in the eastern United States, and *R. degronianum*, the common species in Honshu, is a horticultural asset as far north as New York City and in favored sites at Boston. It is a slow-growing shrub, very densely foliaged, usually seen about 4 feet tall and 6 feet wide, and this is a practical allowance for garden purposes, but there is a tremendous old specimen of this species at the Royal Botanic Garden in Edinburgh, identified there as a single plant, which is 6 feet tall and 22 feet in diameter. The leaves are about 3 to 6 inches long, $\frac{3}{4}$ to $1\frac{3}{4}$ inches broad, with down-curved margins, dark glossy green above and coated beneath with a buff to brownish-red sheath of branched hairs, often thick and felt-like but occasionally thin and almost plastered to the leaf undersurface. The habit of growth is frequently so perfect that the compact, mound-like shrubs seem formal in their dense symmetry. The young shoots are decoratively coated with a furry gray covering. Flowers appear in late April and early May, $1\frac{1}{2}$ to 2 inches in diameter, about twelve to a dome-shaped truss which is usually firm but in poor forms may be open and somewhat untidy as the florets bend at random to rest one on top of another. A sort sparingly in commerce in the eastern United States which otherwise corresponds botanically with the species has up to thirty flowers in a cluster. The color is most often a clear rose, occasionally light pink inside the flower and deep pink outside, or rarely almost white, just perceptibly flushed pale pink. Ordinarily the colors are notable for their delicacy, free of any taint of blue to mar their purity. This is a pretty Rhododendron, but it does not usually flower freely enough to offer a really spectacular floral display. It is none the less a fine garden plant of extraordinarily good form and restrained stature, hardy, easily pleased in its planting site and always admired by gardeners who grow it. It is especially handsome in foundation plantings. It differs botanically from *R. yakusimanum* in being less heavily indumented. It can be distinguished from *R. makinoi* by its wider leaves and earlier blooming period. The five-lobed corolla and ten stamens separate it from *R. metternichii*. It is further distinguished from its allies by the rounded, usually compact truss, with short flower stalks; the calyx less than $\frac{1}{16}$ inch long; and leaves somewhat narrow for their length, clad beneath with an indumentum usually felty and woolly in texture. *R. degronianum* was first described in 1869 and was named for M. Degron, a French civil service officer in Japan. It is native to eastern Honshu as far north as the central Tohoku district. Freedom of Flowering: 2; Ease of Cultivation: 1; American Quality Rating: xx; British: ★; American Hardiness Rating: H-3 (Author's dissent: H-2); British: A; Truss Type: 3. An exceptionally fine, dwarf compact form with light red flowers fading rose, growing in the Crystal Springs Lake Island Trial Garden of the American Rhododendron Society in Portland, received an Award of Excellence in 1956.

R. desquamatum (des-kwam-a′-tum), **Balf. f. and Forrest.** HELIOLEPIS SERIES

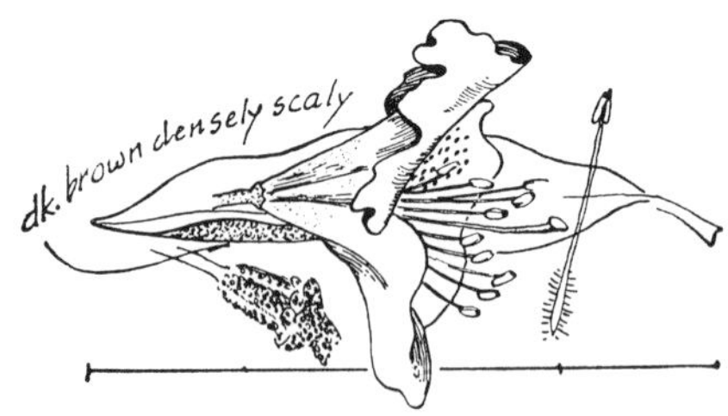

Here is an unjustly neglected species which is one of the most useful and attractive large shrubs in the genus. It is much hardier than it is presumed to be. Specimens in cultivation are seldom taller than 12 to 15 feet despite the reputed height of 25 feet. The densely scaly leaves are about $3\frac{1}{2}$ inches long, $1\frac{3}{8}$ inches broad, borne on slender branches, and the total effect in the landscape is one of lightness and grace. The flowers are unusually large for a Rhododendron of this sort, in the best forms exceeding 2 inches in diameter and borne in April in loose terminal clusters of three to five. The typical color is mauve, lightly spotted, but specimens can be selected in blossom which are lovely violet-blue or quite pure rose, varying from soft shades to bright. This species seems always to make a good show wherever it is placed in the garden. It is undemanding, extraordinarily free-flowering and even the usual mauve color form has about it an indefinable air of quality and distinction. Few Rhododendrons are more widely useful. *R. desquamatum* is distinguished on the basis of its pubescent stamens, glabrous style and oblong-elliptic leaves with unequal size scales densely covering the under-surface. It comes from 10,000 feet elevation in the Chinese province of Yunnan, and from northern Burma. Freedom of Flowering: 1; Ease of Cultivation: 1; American Quality Rating: xx; British: ★★★; American Hardiness Rating: H-3; British: B; Truss Type: 9; A.M., 1938.

R. diaprepes (di-a-pree′-pez), **Balf. f. and W. W. Sm.** FORTUNEI SERIES, FORTUNEI SUBSERIES

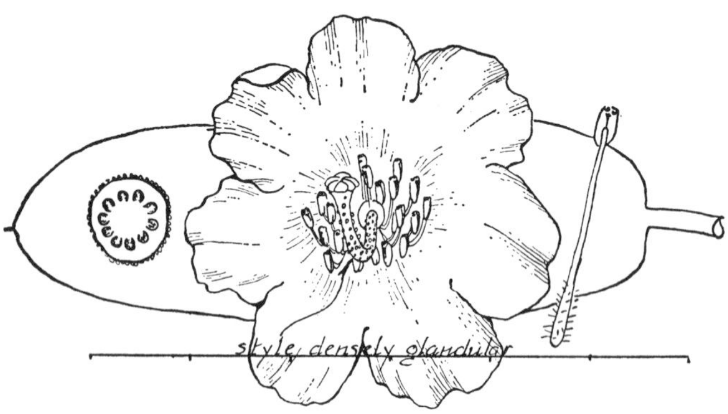

This is one of the transcendently beautiful Rhododendron species, the finest in foliage and flower of the distinguished Fortunei group. It is a robust shrub or small tree, usually seen about 15 feet tall. Some forms are reputed to reach 25 feet. The new shoots are glaucous green and the large, light green leaves are sometimes 12 inches long, usually about $7 \times 2\frac{3}{4}$ inches, with a prominent midrib and pale blue-green below. The widely open, white to pale pink flowers with seven to eight lobes are enormous, 4 to 5 inches across, funnel-shaped at the base, suffused yellow or light green in the throat. There are usually eight or nine of the giant blossoms in an open, outward-facing cluster, shedding an alluring fragrance which envelops the plant in its blooming season. This extraordinary Rhododendron has an extraordinary blossoming period, in late June and well into July. Where it is hardy, *R. diaprepes* is supremely effective in the garden, the rich foliage and opulent flowers creating a magnificent spectacle, at a season when lavish floral displays from woody shrubs are all but unknown. The best form by far is 'Gargantua', with 8-inch leaves, flowers fully 5 inches across of thick, waxen texture, and strongly scented. This is a rare triploid, with half again the usual number of chromosomes, larger in all its parts than the type and probably hardier as well. In any case, it is worth a trial in more severe climates. Forrest's #11958 has been proved to be unusually hardy. The glabrous stamens of *RR. discolor* and *fortunei* easily distinguish them from *R. diaprepes* but it is not so easy to separate it from *R. decorum*. In fact, only the size of the leaves and flowers differentiate them, and this distinction becomes fictional when the multitude of intermediates is examined. There is an uninterrupted progression of microforms which link the two, without any break whatever. *R. diaprepes* is otherwise distinct by reason of its flowers devoid of marked contrasting blotch, with eighteen to twenty pubescent stamens, and a style bearing white or yellowish glands throughout its length. The calyx is very small, only about $\frac{3}{16}$ inch in length. This species was found by Forrest in 1913 and introduced by him. It comes from clearings and the margins of forests at 10,000 to 11,000 feet in southwest Yunnan and northeast Upper Burma. The name, appropriately, means 'distinguished'. Freedom of Flowering: 2+; Ease of Cultivation: 1; American Quality Rating: xxx; British: ***; American Hardiness Rating: H-4; British: C; Truss Type: 8; A.M., 1926; 'Gargantua', A.M., 1953.

R. dichroanthum (dik-ro-an'-thum), **Diels.** NERIIFLORUM SERIES, SANGUINEUM SUBSERIES

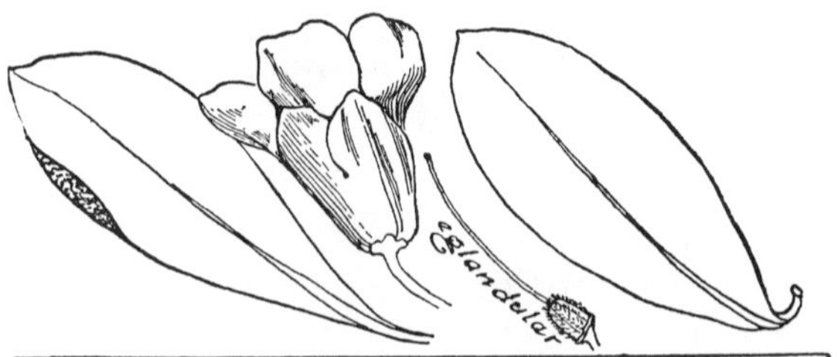

Famous as the orange-flowered Rhododendron and the parent of many hybrids, *R. dichroanthum* is a spreading, densely-foliaged shrub about 5 feet high and a little wider. Its leaves, $1\frac{1}{2}$ to 4 inches long, $\frac{3}{4}$ to $1\frac{1}{2}$ inches wide, are clad beneath with a downy whitish indumentum. Four to eight drooping, elongated, bell-shaped flowers, about 2 inches across, or a little more, and with heavy, waxen texture make up the very lax terminal truss. They appear in May, usually orange in color but varying rarely to pink, rosy and buff blends with the lobes rimmed red. This is an interesting Rhododendron with exceptionally good, dense habit of growth and a conveniently moderate stature. The flowers are striking in their unusual color but they are not well presented and it can scarcely be called spectacular in bloom with the blossoms drooping between the leaves. The form sparingly available as Forrest #11597 has blossoms of an attractive shade, and the selection made by the famous English nurseryman, Harry White, is much superior to the average of seedlings. I have seen specimens of *R. scyphocalyx*, a subspecies of *dichroanthum*, and of *R. horaeum* which were superior to the usual expressions of this species in both size and color, and it seems questionable whether this Rhododendron deserves its reputation as the best orange-flowered sort. *R. dichroanthum* separates from its allies on the basis of its non-glandular ovary and flower stalks in combination with leaves which taper very gradually at the base to the petiole. The thin, downy whitish indumentum beneath leaves not narrow for their length, thick-textured flowers orange to orange-crimson, and stature less than 6 feet identify it further. The cone-shaped ovary is blunt and hairy. This species was discovered by Forrest in 1906 in mid-western Yunnan where it grows at 11,000 to 12,000 feet in rocky clearings and in exposed sites with some shade. Its name means 'two-colored flowers', doubtless referring to the forms with red margins on the corolla lobes. Perhaps it should be only a variety of *R. apodectum* from which it differs solely in the shape of the leaf base. Freedom of Flowering: 2; Ease of Cultivation: 1; American Quality Rating: xx; British: **; American Hardiness Rating: H-4; British: B; Truss Type: 11; A.M., 1923.

R. didymum (did-i′-mum), **Balf. f. and Forrest.** NERIIFLORUM SERIES, SANGUINEUM SUBSERIES

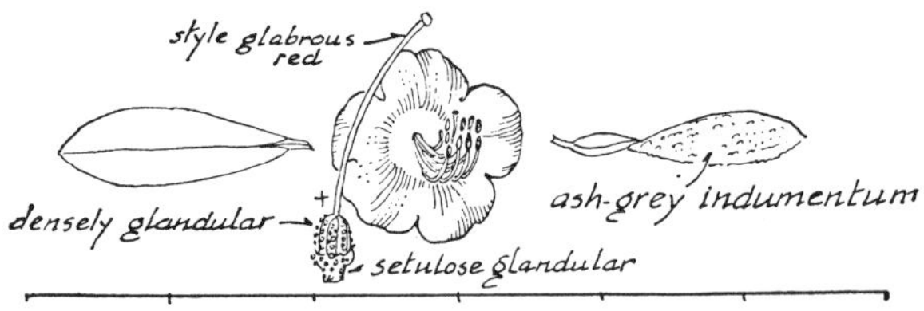

An interesting deep red-flowered, late-blooming subspecies, this Rhododendron grows from 1 to 3 feet tall. The leaves in whorls at the ends of the twigs are leathery in texture, $\frac{3}{4}$ to 2 inches long, and $\frac{3}{8}$ to 1 inch wide, clad beneath with a grayish indumentum. In late June and early July, long bell-shaped flowers of heavy, waxen substance, 1 inch in diameter, four to eight dangling in a lax, loose cluster, appear at the ends of the branches. They are an extremely dark, blackish-crimson until the sun shines through them and then they light up with a rich glow. Because of this depth of color, *R. didymum* in bloom is not a showy spectacle as are so many of its relatives. Seen at close range, this shrub excites interest for its unusual flowers, however, and its good dwarf habit is an asset. It is extremely variable in the freedom with which it produces its blossoms. Some forms are prolific whereas others are shy-blooming. The unique flower color is shared only by one other species in this series, *R. haemaleum*, from which *R. didymum* is dubiously distinct on the basis of its smaller leaves, glandular ovary and flower stalks, and glabrous stamens. This subspecies of *R. sanguineum* comes from 14,000 to 15,000 feet elevation in southeast Tibet where it grows on cliff ledges and exposed hillsides and on moist alpine moorlands. It was discovered there in 1917 by George Forrest. Its name means 'twofold'. Freedom of Flowering: 2; Ease of Cultivation: 1; American Quality Rating: xx; British: **; American Hardiness Rating: H-3; British: B; Truss Type: 11.

R. discolor (dis′-ko-lor), **Franch.** FORTUNEI SERIES, FORTUNEI SUBSERIES

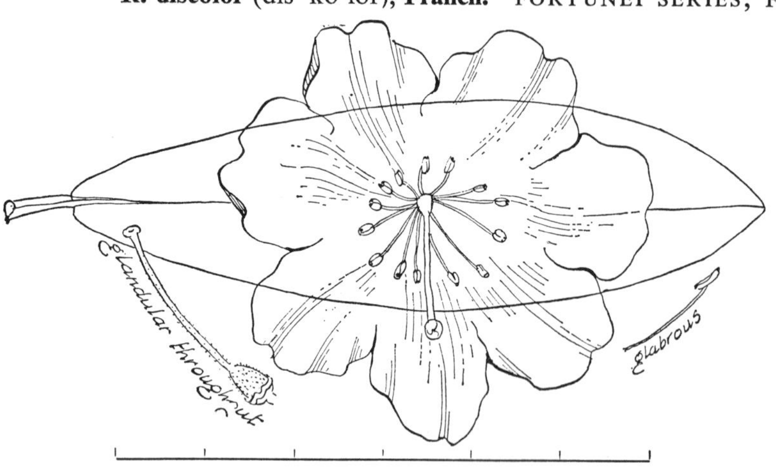

Old plants of this fine species are usually seen as large shrubs about 15 feet tall in cultivation, with attractive leaves $3\frac{1}{2}$ to 8 inches long, 1 to 3 inches wide. Young bushes often have foliage even larger, dark green above and light green beneath. The funnel-shaped flowers with six or seven lobes often exceed 4 inches in diameter and are grouped about ten in loose trusses which dress the plants in great tiers of color. They appear in early July, white to pale pink, suffused yellow in the throat, with a Gardenia-like fragrance. This is a superb Rhododendron with a strong character of dignity and opulent beauty in bloom. It is not free-flowering in youth but when it attains some size the enormous scented blossoms open prodigally with an effect of such elegance that it compensates many times over for its youthful parsimony. As it comes at a season when spectacular contributions from flowering shrubs are usually conspicuously absent, I consider *R. discolor* to be one of the most valuable and ornamental of all Rhododendron species, an opinion shared by all who grow it. Happily, it is hardy in the East to New York and along the coast in favored sites farther north. It has done well at the New York Botanical Garden but it has not been really satisfactory at the Arnold Arboretum in Boston. My experience with it has been puzzling. Several plants having failed to survive the 25-below-zero winters in the mountain climate at my home in northwestern Pennsylvania, I tried a dry site beneath tall Pines and there the replacements have thriven. One hesitates ever to recommend a dry situation for Rhododendrons but in this case possibly it aids the tissues to mature earlier, since the new growth of *R. discolor* appears exceptionally late in the season. In any case this is a good illustration of the truism that a difference of a few feet in the garden often means a planting site just enough more favorable to make a success of a Rhododendron on the borderline of hardiness which has previously failed. *R. discolor*, particularly, does need extra shade and shelter to do its best. And at its best few indeed are the flowering shrubs which can equal it. This species is often confused with *R. decorum*, from which it can easily be distinguished by its glabrous stamens. It is also confused with *R. fortunei*, but its leaves taper at the base to the petioles, instead of being rounded as they are on Fortune's Rhododendron. The drawing on page 116 illustrates the differences among these three important species of the Fortunei subseries. This group is characterized by a style glandular to the tip and a minute calyx, but *R. discolor* separates from others with non-hairy stamens on the basis of the hair-fringed calyx $\frac{1}{8}$ to $\frac{3}{16}$ inch long with distinct lobes, the corolla almost devoid of glands on the outside, and the leaf tapering toward the base. There are fourteen to sixteen stamens. The species is native to the woodlands of the Chinese provinces of Hupeh and Szechuan, at 4,000 to 7,000 feet elevation, where it was discovered by E. H. Wilson, and introduced in 1900. The name refers to its 'various colors', a puzzling designation for a species with but little variation in this respect. Freedom of Flowering: 1; Ease of Cultivation: 1; American Quality Rating: xxx; British: ***; American Hardiness Rating: H-3 (Author's dissent: H-2); British: B; Truss Type: 8; F.C.C., 1922; Pink form, A.M., 1922.

R. eclecteum (ek-leckt′-ee-um), **Balf. f. and Forrest.** THOMSONII SERIES, THOMSONII SUBSERIES

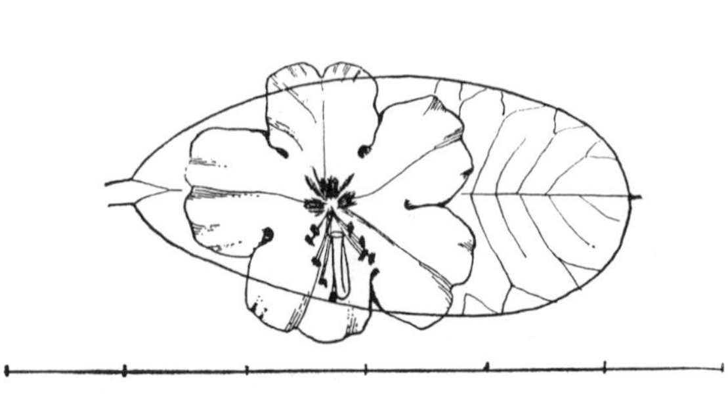

An extraordinarily fine but little-known Rhododendron, this species is the chameleon of the genus, with an astounding flower-color range.

It is usually seen as a 6-foot shrub with heavy, straight branches which are none the less well-foliaged and attractive when the plant is not in bloom. The leaves are 2 to $5\frac{3}{4}$ inches long, $\frac{3}{4}$ to $2\frac{1}{4}$ inches broad, usually with very short petioles and somewhat subject to a fungus which discolors the edges. Flowers appear among the very earliest of the season, in March, occasionally in February or even earlier depending on the season and the local climate. Because of this precocious blooming, plants should be placed in a protected spot, but not with an eastern exposure where the flowers will be exposed to the sun on frosty mornings. Choosing the right site makes the difference between a splendid and a poor garden performance. The long, bell-shaped blossoms are $2\frac{1}{2}$ inches across, six to twelve to a lax truss, with conspicuous basal nectaries and with or without spots on the upper throat varying in prominence. The remarkable thing about them is their extraordinary color range, from white and deep cream through various shades of buff to clear yellow; from palest pink through pastel salmon and coral tints to a strong, vibrant rose; from light mauve through a series of lavender gradations to violet-lilac; and from orange through unusual coppery intermediate shades to soft rose-red, brilliant scarlet, and deep crimson. The rose-red often appears also as an edging on flowers of quite another color, suffusing them to a varying extent and thus creating a multitude of entirely different effects. Out of this host of colors the buff and yellow flowers edged rose-red are among the most striking, but all are extraordinarily attractive and especially so when a considerable range is planted together. This admirable Rhododendron has another season of garden effectiveness when the new growth appears, the soft, light green leaves developing on stems often clothed with flaming scarlet ribbon-like bracts to create a dramatic contrast which is both colorful and strongly decorative. *R. eclecteum* is distinct from its allies in having, in combination, a glandular ovary and non-glandular style; bell-shaped flowers; and leaves borne on short petioles, $\frac{1}{8}$ to $\frac{3}{4}$ inch long, glabrous below except occasionally hairy on the raised midrib. There are no tufts of hair on the lateral veins, however. Var. *bellatulum* of this extremely variable species has leaves petiolate, more or less oblong and obtuse or rounded at the base. Var. *brachyandrum* is maintained for horticultural usefulness to distinguish forms with deep rose to crimson flowers and the most recent revision of the Thomsonii series, published in 1951, errs in its botanical key by excluding crimson-colored flowers from this species. *R. eclecteum* can usually be distinguished from *R. stewartianum*, which it closely resembles, by the latter's long petioles and gray-green leaf under-surface produced by a thin veil of whitish hairs. There are merging forms between the two species which are occasionally identified as accurately with one name as with the other. The species here described is native to the Chinese provinces of Yunnan and Szechuan, to Tibet and Upper Burma at 10,000 to 14,000 feet, in Rhododendron thickets. It was discovered by Forrest in 1917. The name means 'to be chosen out', an appropriate tribute to the value of this Rhododendron with its vari-colored flowers. Freedom of Flowering: 1; Ease of Cultivation: 1; American Quality Rating: None yet assigned (Author's estimate: xxx); British: **; American Hardiness Rating: H-3; British: C; Truss Type: 10; A.M., 1949.

R. edgeworthii (edge-worth′-i), **Hook. f.** EDGEWORTHII SERIES

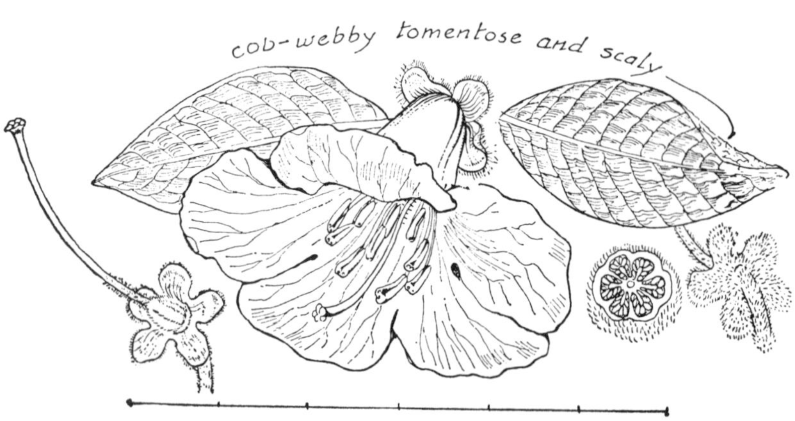

Here is another species famous for its beauty of flower, but it receives no praise for its rather loose and lanky habit of straggling growth as it grows older. It is usually seen as a thin shrub to 8 or 10 feet with leaves about $1\frac{1}{2}$ to $4\frac{1}{2}$ inches long, $\frac{3}{4}$ to 2 inches wide, most often nearer the larger of these dimensions. The leaves are strongly puckered above by the deeply impressed veins and have a tawny felted covering underneath, an unusual feature for a scaly species. The young shoots also have the densely woolly coating. The enormous, deliciously fragrant, trumpet-shaped flowers appear in late April and early May, up to 4 inches long, 4½ inches wide, waxy white, suffused yellow in the throat and often tinted rose-pink on the outside and on the tips of the corolla lobes inside. There are usually two or three to a loose terminal cluster, but exceptionally floriferous plants in good condition will often produce double that number. They disperse their rich, spicy scent widely in the garden, one of the most captivating of all floral fragrances. With good management younger plants can be maintained well clothed with foliage and reasonably compact in growth, especially in the greenhouse. Outdoors the naturally thin growth can be somewhat minimized by placing several plants 2 or 3 feet apart and allowing them to grow together. This species can also be encouraged to clamber up through a densely foliaged shrub to flaunt its splendid springtime blossoms. The selection sometimes offered as Ludlow and Sherriff's form is especially fine. Except for the Bay region of San Francisco and similar climates, this is a greenhouse shrub. It is not quite so hardy as *R. bullatum* which it closely resembles. The two are often confused but they can readily be distinguished by the style, which in *R. edgeworthii* is shaggy with hairs but not scaly toward the base, whereas its ally is scaly and only slightly hairy in the lower third; and by the calyx, which is covered with tawny down in *R. edgeworthii* in contrast to the scaly calyx of *R. bullatum*, the lobes of which are only fringed with hairs. The sole remaining species in the series with bullate leaves, *R. seinghkuense*, has a glabrous style. The combination of scales and an indumentum in these related species is unusual. *R. edgeworthii* was found by Hooker in 1849 and named for M. P. Edgeworth, then in the Bengal Civil Service. It most often grows as an epiphyte in the forks of trees in Sikkim and Bhutan at 7,000 to 10,000 feet elevation. Freedom of Flowering: 1; Ease of Cultivation: 2+; American Quality Rating: xx; British: ★★★★; American Hardiness Rating: H-6; British: F; Truss Type: 12; F.C.C., 1933.

R. elliottii (el'·lee-ot-i), **Watt.** IRRORATUM SERIES, PARISHII SUBSERIES

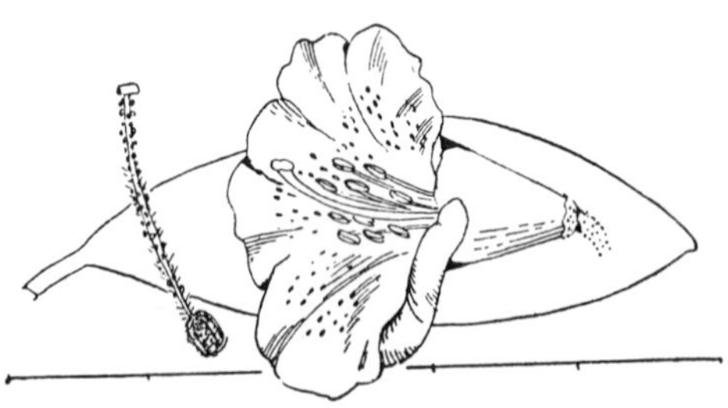

A plant of tree-like growth to a height of 10 feet or so, this is one of the most brilliant of red-flowered Rhododendrons. The leaves are 2 to 6 inches long, 1 to 2¼ inches broad, generally tending toward the larger dimensions, and with a glossy under-surface. The 2½-inch flowers, shining scarlet in color, spotted crimson, are gathered into 5-inch incandescent globes containing twelve to fifteen florets. The species blooms in late May and early June. It was originally found in 1882 and the forms first introduced had spotted rose-purple flowers, not especially attractive. With the discovery of Kingdon-Ward's #7725 in 1927, this Rhododendron came into its own as a garden plant and became well known for the burning clarity of its red flowers. It is, of course, important to secure plants propagated from one of the later introductions, of which the F.C.C. form is especially fine. Kingdon-Ward's #7725 is very good too. This is not a hardy Rhododendron and it seems doubtful if it can really be considered a permanent garden shrub in colder gardens of the Oregon and Washington Rhododendron belt. It does seem to be satisfactory in the favored coastal climate of Cornwall and of western Scotland, however. *R. elliottii* does not like transplanting in larger sizes. The species is distinct by reason of its elliptic-oblong leaves averaging about 4½ inches long with obtuse tips and glabrous under-surface, borne on leaf stalks at first bristly and glandular, but finally more or less glabrate. The flower stalks are minutely glandular and the style conspicuously so. Both style and ovary are hairy, the former sparsely, the latter to such an extent as to have a reddish woolly coating. The fugitive juvenile indumentum on the developing leaves is stellate, as are the hairs on the parts which are permanently coated with them. The species comes from Manipur at 9,000 feet where it was first discovered by Sir George Watt and named by him for a friend. Freedom of Flowering: 1; Ease of Cultivation: 1; American Quality Rating: xxxx; British: ★★★★; American Hardiness Rating: H-4; British: E; Truss Type: 3; A.M., 1934; F.C.C., 1937; as 'Warpaint', a superior selection, P.A., 1954.

R. eriogynum (er-ee-o-ji′-num), **Balf. f. and W. W. Sm.** IRRORATUM SERIES, PARISHII SUBSERIES

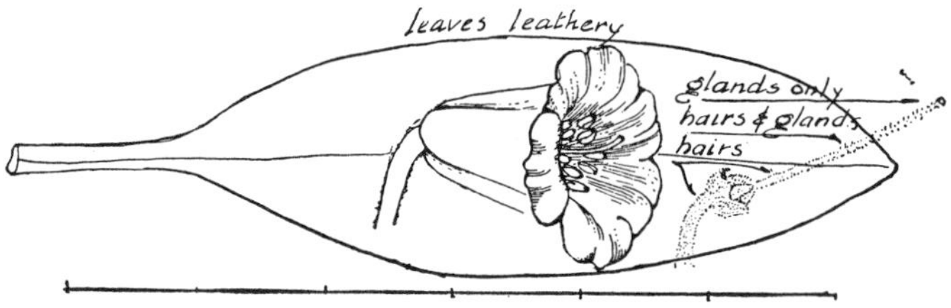

Here is another of the brilliantly beautiful, late, red-flowering Rhododendrons which extend the blossoming season so splendidly. It is a 10-foot shrub with leaves 4 to 8 inches long, $1\frac{1}{4}$ to 3 inches wide, a lively, fresh green above and with a metallic burnished sheen beneath. In late June, 2-inch wide, bright scarlet, waxy tubular flowers appear in lax terminal clusters of twelve to sixteen. They are renowned for the extraordinary purity and richness of their color. This Rhododendron starts into growth late in the season and should not be planted where tender young shoots will be exposed to early fall frosts. Even so, it is only precariously hardy north of California on the West Coast. It is reputed to resent transplanting in larger sizes, and to be hardier than *R. elliottii* and *R. kyawi*, its relatives from the same monsoon climate. It is distinguished from them and the other species in the series by the hairy ovary and style, the latter glandular as well toward the tip. The flower stalks are hairy and eglandular. The large leaves, averaging 6 inches or more in length, are leathery, with tips more or less rounded, two to four times longer than wide, with stout petioles which, like the leaves, are devoid of the bristly glands characteristic of certain of its allies. The new shoots and young leaves are coated with a whitish downy indumentum which soon disappears. *R. eriogynum* comes from 9,000 feet elevation in China's Yunnan province. It was discovered by Forrest in 1914 and named to describe its woolly ovary. Freedom of Flowering: 1; Ease of Cultivation: 1; American Quality Rating: xxxx; British: ★★★★; American Hardiness Rating: H-4; British: D; Truss Type: 7; A.M., 1924.

R. eudoxum (ew-dox′-um), **Balf. f. and Forrest.** NERIIFLORUM SERIES, SANGUINEUM SUBSERIES

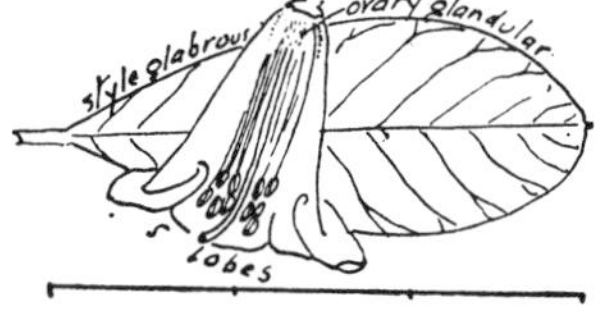

This extremely variable species is reputed to have a height of 6 feet at maturity, but even older plants are usually seen in gardens at about 4 feet. It has a good growth habit, densely clothed with dull green leaves $1\frac{1}{2}$ to 4 inches long, $\frac{3}{4}$ to $1\frac{1}{2}$ inches wide. Long, bell-shaped flowers varying from $1\frac{1}{4}$ inches, to as much as $2\frac{1}{2}$ inches wide in the best forms, hang loosely, about six in a single-tiered terminal cluster. The June blooming period which is usually given for this species must represent an early mistake copied by subsequent garden writers. Most plants, at least, blossom in April, though I have seen an unusual color form in one garden flowering in mid-May. Possibly in a species so variable as this, the blooming period could extend even further because *R. eudoxum* has an extraordinary range in the color of its flowers. Most commonly seen is a rosy crimson, but it varies also into pink, white tinted pink on the lobes, cream, and yellow, usually with red spots in broken lines on the interior of the upper lobes. In a subseries noted for its perplexing diversity this Rhododendron is distinct in having leaves with only a scant indumentum, or occasionally none at all, and in having also a thin, not a fleshy, corolla. The blunt ovary, only $\frac{3}{16}$ inch long, is both glandular and hairy. There are eight subspecies which have been distinguished, principally on the basis of being more or less indumented, or with greater or lesser glandular character than the type. *R. eudoxum* was found in open Rhododendron scrub at 11,000 to 13,000 feet altitude in northwestern Yunnan and southeastern Tibet. It was discovered by Forrest in the course of his 1917–18 expedition and given the name signifying 'of good report'. Freedom of Flowering: 2; Ease of Cultivation: 1; American Ratings: None yet assigned; British Quality Rating: None awarded; British Hardiness Rating: B; Truss Type: 10; A.M., 1960.

R. facetum (fas-ee′-tum), **Balf. f. and Ward.** IRRORATUM SERIES, PARISHII SUBSERIES

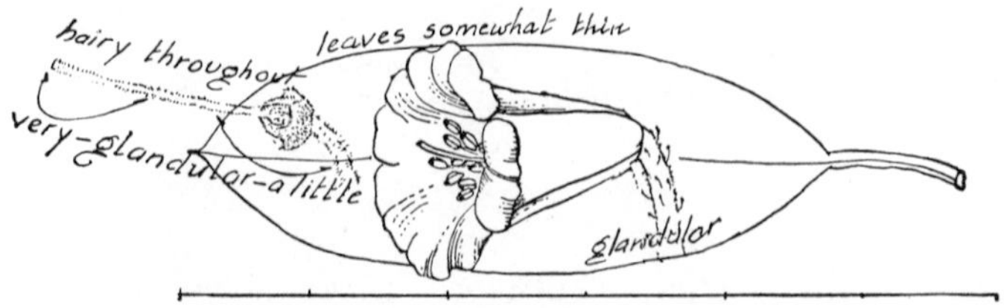

This is a magnificent, scarlet-flowered, late-blooming Rhododendron but it differs so slightly from *R. eriogynum* that the reader is referred to the comments on that species and the descriptions of it on page 160. *R. facetum* is reputed to be larger in stature with fewer flowers to the truss and with leaves of thinner texture. The foliage bud is shorter and the flower stalk is sparsely glandular in contrast to the eglandular pedicel of the typical *R. eriogynum*. Since there are many intermediate forms between the two, this species should be suppressed and the description of *R. eriogynum* altered to include *R. facetum*. For temporary garden purposes this name, meaning 'elegant', identifies a stunning Rhododendron which provides a blaze of color at a valuable season in late June when most species have gone by. The various ratings are the same as for *R. eriogynum*. A.M., 1938.

R. falconeri (fal′-kon-er-i), **Hook. f.** FALCONERI SERIES

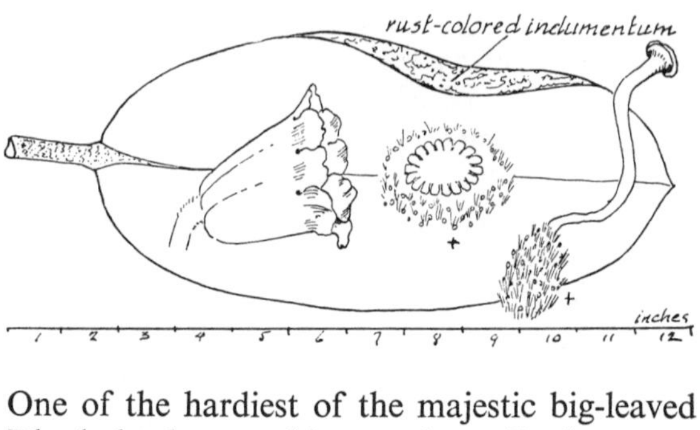

One of the hardiest of the majestic big-leaved Rhododendrons, this species affords many gardeners an opportunity to grow a small tree of great dignity and remarkable beauty. It is reputed to have an ultimate height of 50 feet, but it is rarely seen in cultivation as much as 25 feet. A tree at Stonefield, in Scotland, which is known to be more than a hundred years old, is 28 feet high, with a breadth of 30 feet. The stiff, thick limbs are inclined to branch sparsely. Huge, rich, leathery green leaves minutely wrinkled and lightly veined lemon-yellow are extraordinarily handsome and have a striking orange to reddish-brown or tan indumentum beneath, with the veins sharply outlined. They are 6 to 12 inches long, $2\frac{1}{2}$ to 6 inches wide.

The young shoots are also coated with the indumentum and are strongly decorative. The bark is burnished purplish-brown. Enormous clusters of remarkably long lasting, creamy white to pale yellow 2-inch bells with eight or, rarely, ten lobes, form a magnificent panoply on the trees in late April and early May. The globe-like trusses are often 9 inches in diameter composed of as many as twenty or more fragrant florets closely adjoining, and frequently marked with a conspicuous purple basal blotch. The yellow-flowered trees are truly beautiful. Some forms are much more floriferous than others. Like all of the large-leaved species, *R. falconeri* appreciates shelter and protection from wind. It is an exciting and exotic tree for the woodland, the largest leaved of its kind that can be grown over any great range of climatic conditions, though the leaves diminish in size in colder gardens. The great value of the species for its foliage is apparent when it reaches a size where the richly colored leaf under-surface becomes conspicuous to the viewer. Then the tree seems almost to change color looking upward from eye level to the crown. This stately Rhododendron separates from its allies on the basis of having creamy white to yellow flowers with glandular ovary. The mature leaves lack any mealy residue above from their juvenile woolly covering, but the orange indumentum beneath is persistent. The long, round petioles are clad with a thin, greyish down, and lack the wing-like flanges on either side which are characteristic of some other species. There are twelve to sixteen stamens. Native to the Himalayan Mountains at 10,000 feet from Nepal to Bhutan, *R. falconeri* was named for a superintendent of the Saharanpur Gardens in India, and introduced into cultivation about 1850. Freedom of Flowering: 2; Ease of Cultivation: 2+; American Quality Rating: xxxx; British: ****; American Hardiness Rating: H-4; British: C; Truss Type: 6; A.M., 1922.

R. fargesii (far′-ges-i), **Franch.** FORTUNEI SERIES, OREODOXA SUBSERIES

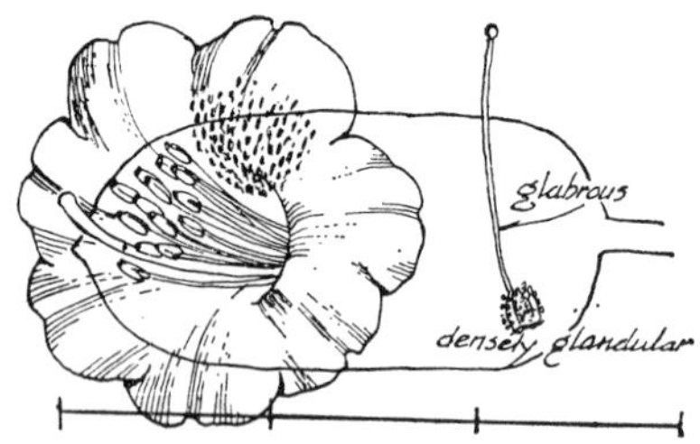

This Rhododendron with rather small leaves, 2 to 3½ inches long and 1⅜ to 1¾ inches wide, is a valuable asset in the garden for its profuse display of pink flowers early in the season, usually the first part of April. Plants forty years old are bushy shrubs 10 feet tall, and I doubt that this species often attains the height of 20 feet which is usually ascribed to it in cultivation. The open bell-shaped five- to seven-lobed blossoms are 2 to 2½ inches wide, about eight to a loose, flat-topped terminal cluster, and a bush in full bloom often gives a charming two-tone effect from the contrast between the medium pink florets just opening and the fully expanded blossoms, which are light pink. Some forms are a uniform, luminous deep rose, whereas others may have flowers with but a hint of color to warm their whiteness. These various pink shades are particularly effective planted together. Occasional plants do not expand their flowers as fully as the better forms and they should be avoided because their pinched appearance is a good deal less attractive. The selection sometimes offered as the Bodnant form is especially fine. This is a rugged, adaptable species from a part of China which has given us other Rhododendrons hardy in the Northeast, and some selected seedlings are satisfactory as far north as New York City. I have one report of plants doing well at Boston. They require a sheltered site, however, to shield from frost the prodigal flower display which comes so early in the spring. It is especially desirable to remove the faded blossoms so that the usual lavish production of seeds will not exhaust the plants. This Rhododendron is easily distinguished from its closest relatives by having a glandular ovary and non-hairy stamens. It can be assigned to its subseries on the basis of its smooth, glabrous style and by the leaves, small for the series, not more than 4 inches in length and much longer than broad. There are fourteen stamens. *R. oreodoxa*, with which it is often confused, is readily separated from it by having a glabrous ovary and more narrow leaves. Discovered by Rev. Paul Farges, for whom it was named, but not introduced into cultivation until Wilson sent it back from Asia in 1901, *R. fargesii* grows at 7,000 to 10,000 foot altitudes in the woodlands of China's Szechuan and Hupeh provinces. Freedom of Flowering: 1; Ease of Cultivation: 1; American Quality Rating: xxx; British: ***; American Hardiness Rating: H-3; British: B; Truss Type: 8; A.M., 1926.

R. fastigiatum (fas-tij-ee-a′-tum), **Franch.** LAPPONICUM SERIES

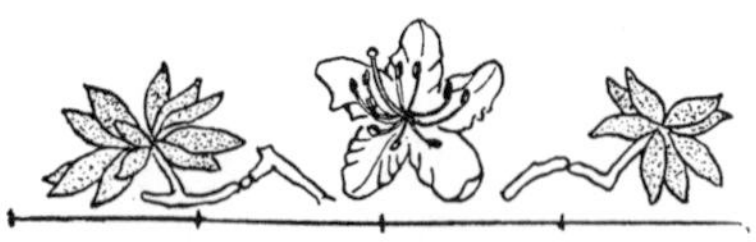

This ineptly named species is among the best of the 'blue' flowered, small-leaved alpine Rhododendrons. It is most often seen as an erect shrublet to a height of about 3 feet, with rather stiff, upright branches which frequently fan outward toward the top to form a crown on older specimens about as wide as the plant is tall. The best form, almost unknown, refutes the upright growth habit for which this species is named. It is a densely foliaged little dwarf cushion only about 10 inches tall which spreads outward and molds itself to the contour of earth or rock in a pygmy mound of perfect density and exceptional symmetry. In mid-May it is completely covered with a froth of soft mauve flowers. I count this form the finest dwarf scaly-leaved Rhododendron in the genus. It is unequalled so far as I know for the perfection of its dense foliage, faultless habit of growth and profusion of flower. The usual upright forms of *R. fastigiatum* have very small, dark, shiny green leaves, from $\frac{1}{4}$ to a little less than $\frac{1}{2}$ inch long and half as wide, densely scaly on both surfaces. The species comes into flower in late April and the first part of May, studding the tips of almost every twig with tight little trusses of four or five 1-inch, widely funnel-shaped blossoms which may be any color from light purple through pale lilac and various mauve shades to soft rose. Some of the ligher shades are wan, and care should be taken to secure a good color form. This is one of the hardiest and most useful of all the small alpine Rhododendrons. It is also among the most easily pleased. In the eastern United States where the high altitude sorts abhor the summer heat, it can often be persuaded to grow well in a sheltered but not shady spot, moist and well drained, in gardens northward to Boston and beyond, along the coast. Among Lapponicums of its flower color this species is characterized by small leaves, less than $\frac{1}{2}$ inch long with scales on the lower surface contiguous or only slightly separated. The flowers, four or five to a cluster, are neither scaly nor hairy outside; the style, as long or longer than the stamens, is glabrous; the ten stamens are hairy toward the base; and the hair-fringed, scaly calyx is only about $\frac{1}{6}$ inch long. *R. fastigiatum* is sometimes confused with *R. impeditum* but the latter can be distinguished by its larger leaves, more than $\frac{1}{2}$ inch long, the scales beneath about half their own diameter apart, and by the fewer-flowered inflorescence, generally one or two in a cluster, with longer stamens. Aside from the extremely rare dwarf forms, *R. fastigiatum* is much taller, more erect and open in habit, and has longer branchlets than *R. impeditum*. *R. fastigiatum* comes from the alpine moorlands of China's Yunnan province. The name was originally assigned to mark the erect growth habit of the first forms discovered. Freedom of Flowering: 1; Ease of Cultivation: 1; American Quality Rating: xxx; British: **; American Hardiness Rating: H-2; British: A; Truss Type: 5; A.M., 1914.

R. fauriei (for′-ee-i), **Franch.** PONTICUM SERIES, CAUCASICUM SUBSERIES

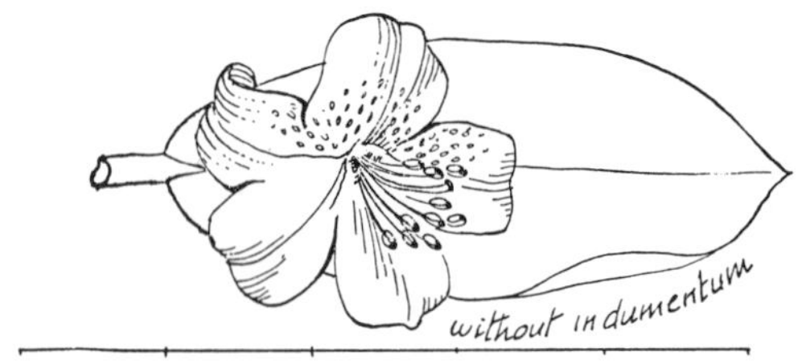

The hardiness of most species in the Ponticum Series makes them of particular interest in the eastern United States. *R. fauriei* is a very rare representative in cultivation of the Caucasicum Subseries, closely resembling *R. brachycarpum* and, in fact, Dr. Hiroshi Hara at the University of Tokyo considers the latter to be only a variety, *roseum*, of *R. fauriei*. Certainly the only difference between the two is the indumentum beneath the leaves of *R. brachycarpum*, and the leaves of young plants lack this felty coating underneath so that the two are absolutely indistinguishable until seedlings of *R. brachycarpum* develop it at a much older age than is usual with such hairy species. The Rhododendron with leaves glabrous on the undersides, *R. fauriei*, grows 8 feet tall but plants in cultivation in both England and the United States seem to be dwarfer, most often seen 3 or 4 feet high and 5 to 7 feet broad, growing in a widely spreading manner with many stems coming from the base. It is decorative as a foliage plant. The leaves are $2\frac{3}{4}$ to 6 inches long, $1\frac{1}{4}$ to $2\frac{3}{4}$ inches broad, faintly tan to pale green below and devoid of the indumentum usual in the subseries. The forms in cultivation in the West seem to be unusually shy about blooming. One would expect them to flower in early June; however, atypically, perhaps, their blossoming period is often late April and early May when twelve to fifteen florets, broadly funnel-shaped and almost 2 inches across combine to form a firm, somewhat rounded truss about $4\frac{1}{2}$ inches across. They range in color from white or rose to yellowish with green spots on the upper part, often with a faint pink suffusion in the centers of the lobes. This Rhododendron has grown very slowly, but it seems to be hardy in my garden in northwest Pennsylvania where the temperature occasionally goes to 25° or more below zero. Coming from higher, subalpine elevations, it should be hardier than its allies. Perhaps, like *R. brachycarpum*, it varies greatly in its stature and freedom of flowering and becomes more prolific as it approaches maturity. *R. fauriei* is distinct from its relatives on the basis of its leaves with rounded or subauricled base, thinner than those of its associates in the series, and broad for their length, and lacking any indumentum underneath. The style is shorter than the stamens, only about $\frac{9}{16}$ inch long. The flowers are only rarely yellowish, but this species is so much larger in stature that it is unlikely to be confused with the prostrate *R. chrysanthum*. There is a double-flowered form, rarely grown in cultivation in Japan. *R. fauriei* is native to central and southern Korea, central and northern Japan and the Kuril Islands. It was named for the Rev. L. F. Faurie, a French missionary, and described by Franchet in 1884. Freedom of Flowering: 2; Ease of Cultivation: 1; American Quality Rating: x; British: none; American Hardiness Rating: H-3 (Author's Dissent: H-1); British: B; Truss Type: 1.

R. ferrugineum (fer-ru-jin′-ee-um), **Linn.** FERRUGINEUM SERIES

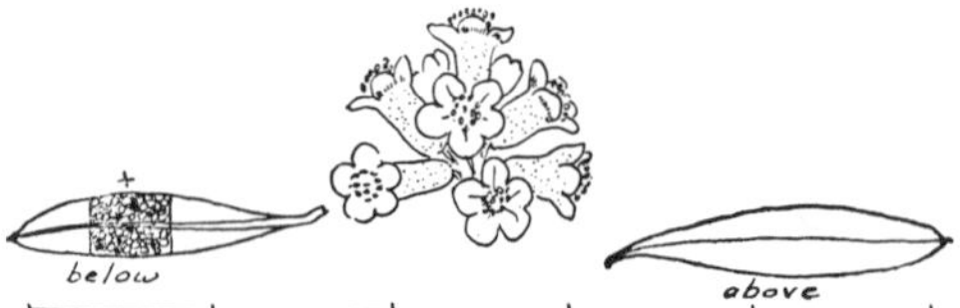

Popularly called the "Alpine Rose", this Rhododendron has been beloved by generations of tourists in Switzerland and elsewhere in the European Alps, where it erupts in massive flows of glowing rosy scarlet covering whole

mountainsides. It is a neat little rounded shrub 3 or 4 feet high, with dark, shiny leaves 1 to 1¾ inches long and ¼ to ½ inch wide, densely scaly below. At high elevations in its mountain homeland, it blooms in July but it comes into blossom in June in cultivation with six to twelve flowers, ½ to ¾ inch wide, in each terminal cluster. The color varies from deep rose to soft crimson and rarely to white. This is a pretty Rhododendron which can be used for striking landscape effects, especially in masses. Its trim, restrained growth, dense foliage and late-blooming period recommend it for almost any of the garden situations where there is seemingly an endless search for shrubs of low stature. *R. ferrugineum* cannot abide the hot, dry summers of the eastern United States, but in the Rhododendron belt of the Pacific Northwest and in Great Britain, it is vigorous, and prolific in its flowering. The white form is particularly attractive. It is distinguished from its two close relatives from southern Europe by the leaves devoid of any hairy fringe, but with scales beneath so closely placed that they overlap. The corolla tube is scaly but not hairy outside and the short stamens extend scarcely beyond the lobes. The style is only a little longer than the ovary and the calyx is minute. This species is found above 4,000 feet from the Pyrenees eastward to the Austrian Alps where it occurs in vast colonies just higher than the zone where Pines and Junipers grow. It has been in cultivation in England since 1752 and long before that on the Continent. The name refers to the rusty color of the leaf undersurface, caused by the reddish-brown scales which cover it. Freedom of Flowering: 1; Ease of Cultivation: 1; American Quality Rating: x; British: **; American Hardiness Rating: H-2; British: A; Truss Type: 9.

R. fictolacteum (fik-to-lak′-tee-um), **Balf. f.** FALCONERI SERIES

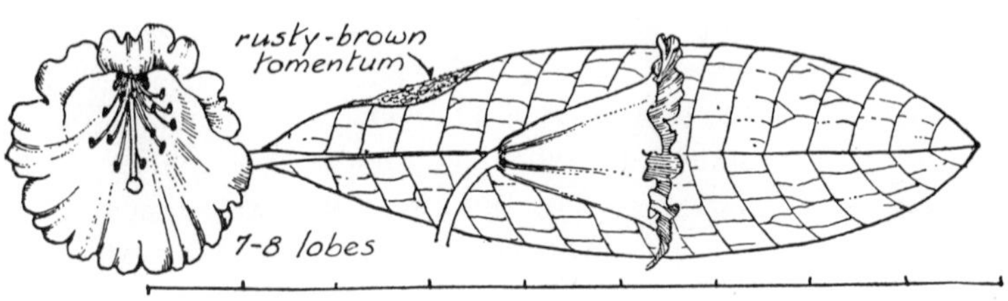

Through this species gardeners can enjoy the unique attractions of the large-leaved tree Rhododendrons in climates too cold for all others of the group. In the wild it grows to a height of 45 feet but it is normally about half that in cultivation, a tree with heavy branches and imposing appearance. The young shoots are attractively coated with a cinnamon-brown furry covering. Leaves are 5 to 12 inches long, 2 to 5 inches wide, strongly veined and dark green above, and with a handsome fawn, orange, or ruddy felted indumentum beneath. The beauty of this species as a foliage plant is multiplied many times over when it reaches a height of 8 or 10 feet. Up to eye level it then presents a picture of shining dark green foliage and as the viewer looks upward the tree suddenly and dramatically seems to change color as the brilliant undersides of the leaves are seen, with their tawny indumentum. The impressive flowers of *R. fictolacteum* appear in late April and early May, ivory or white, often suffused with rose in varying degree, with a deep red basal blotch. They are up to 3 inches wide, bell-shaped with seven or eight lobes and borne twelve to sixteen, or in the best forms as many as twenty-five, in large trusses which may be round and compact or somewhat looser and open at the top. The ornamental effect of both flowers and foliage varies a great deal. For a primitive Rhododendron there is a surprising range and of course the larger leaves and blossoms are the more desirable. In such fine expressions of the species as Kingdon-Ward #4509 and 'Cherry Tip', a named selection, the landscape effect the year round and the floral display are both spectacularly beautiful, among the very best in the genus. The best forms of *R. fictolacteum* are, in fact, actually *R. rex*, which is reputedly larger in all its parts but actually merges with its relatives in a continuous gradation of intermediates. At the present time, the identification of the species in the Falconeri series is based in large part on the color of the indumentum beneath the leaves, but this is not constant enough to be reliable. Ordinarily, however, the felty coating of this species is fairly deep in color, various shades of orange, brown, or rusty-red. The leaves, usually oblanceolate and broadest above the middle, are smooth above or only slightly rugulose, borne on round petioles 1 to 1½ inches long, not grooved. The ovary is densely tomentose but not glandular. There are fourteen to sixteen stamens. This Chinese species is native to Yunnan and Szechuan at 10,000 to 13,000 feet at the margins of the Pine forests and in protected sites on open hillsides. It was discovered by Delavay about 1884 and Balfour subsequently gave it the name meaning 'false *lacteum*' because it had been confused with *R. lacteum*. Freedom of Flowering: 1; Ease of Cultivation: 1; American Quality Rating: xxx; British: ***; American Hardiness Rating: H-3; British: B; Truss Type: 6; A.M., 1923; 'Cherry Tip', A.M., 1953; var. *roseum*, A.M., 1946; White Form (K.W. #4509), F.C.C., 1935.

R. formosum (for-mo'-sum), **Wallich.** MADDENII SERIES, CILIICALYX SUBSERIES

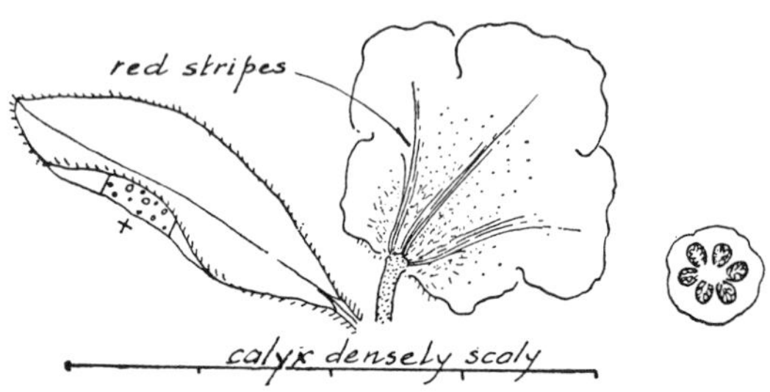

In a series renowned for the beauty of its flowers, this species is particularly good in the greenhouse or as a pot plant. In mild climates, such as the Bay district of San Francisco, *R. formosum* is a tall, rather thin, outdoor shrub up to 10 feet high, but indoors it can be made to form a nicely shaped plant which blooms young and profusely. It is not usually hardy enough to be a satisfactory garden plant in Oregon and Washington. Glossy green leaves, fringed with long white hairs, are glaucous and scaly below, 1¼ to 3 inches long, ½ to 1½ inches wide, borne on petioles which are often fringed with hairs. The young shoots are bristly. In late May or early June, two to four flowers, 3 inches or more across, are produced together in an open cluster at the ends of the branches. The blossoms are funnel-shaped, white suffused with yellow and pink, with five red stripes on the outside, and have a delightful spicy fragrance which pervades an entire room. This is among the most easily grown species of the Maddenii Series and its scented flowers are elegantly formed and exceptionally appealing. It is distinct from its allies in having flowers with a corolla generally scaly outside, pubescent toward the base, white tinged either yellow or rose and with a style scaly in the lower part. There are ten stamens. The young branchlets, leaves and the grooved leaf stalks are all hairy. The scales on the leaf under-surface are one to one and a half times their own diameter apart and the shape of the leaf, illustrated here, is diagnostic. The small calyx is densely scaly outside. The name means, appropriately, 'beautiful' and has nothing whatever to do with the island of Formosa. This species is a native of Assam at 5,000 to 5,500 feet, where it was found in 1815 and named by Wallich in 1832. Freedom of Flowering: 1; Ease of Cultivation: 1; American Ratings: None yet assigned; British Quality Rating: ***; British Hardiness Rating: D; Truss Type: 12; A.M., 1960.

R. forrestii (for′-est-i) **Balf. f.** NERIIFLORUM SERIES, FORRESTII SUBSERIES

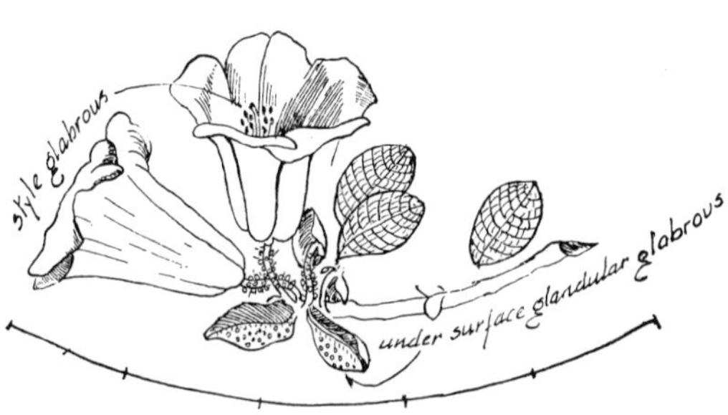

Here belongs now the prostrate Rhododendron known for many years as *R. repens*. Since there is no distinction of consequence between it and *R. forrestii*, described seven years earlier, the older name takes precedence. The plant popularly known as *R. repens* has been given a varietal status on the basis of its green underleaf and is now correctly called *R. forrestii* var. *repens*. Typical *R. forrestii* differs from var. *repens* in possessing leaves which are red beneath. It is a creeping, alpine Rhododendron which may form a mat of foliage 4 feet or more in diameter after many years. The outer branches are always prostrate, rooting as they extend outward along the ground. With age the middle of the plant may reach a height of 12 inches as the crowded stems are forced into a more erect position. The leaves have a considerable range, from ¼ up to 1¼ inches long, and a maximum width of about ¾ inch, purplish underneath. It flowers principally in April with bright scarlet bell-shaped flowers as much as 2⅜ inches across, singly or in pairs, which seem striking in their large size compared with the dwarf stature of the plants. As a species, it is very shy-flowering and I do not know of a typical form which is prolific, even moderately so. As noted above, var. *repens* differs only in the under-surface of the leaf being green. It, too, is notoriously shy-blooming as a whole, but plants propagated from a single specimen grown from seeds from Forrest #21768 are reasonably free. Other plants from this same number are worthless for bloom. For real flowering satisfaction, the gardener is obliged to turn to a clone grown from seeds of Kingdon-Ward #6832, which received a First Class Certificate in 1935 as *R. repens* and often is offered for sale commercially under its former name. This F.C.C. form is a plant about 11 inches high, 36 inches across, which should now be called *forrestii* var. *repens*. It is a stunning dwarf ornamental, very free-flowering, the large scarlet bells making a striking carpet of color year after year. So profuse is it that newly propagated rooted cuttings with just two leaves often will produce a flower which completely obscures the tiny plant supporting it. Kingdon-Ward #5845, 20 inches high, 5 feet across in the original specimen, and also available commercially, is likewise free-flowering, with three or four carmine blossoms in a cluster. It has now been assigned to *R. chamae-thomsonii* var. *chamaethauma* on the basis of its more erect growth habit. Until the revision was made, there were formerly plants of upright habit, as much as 3 feet tall, which were called *R. repens* var. *chamae-thomsonii*. All of these erect forms, regardless of their height, have been assigned to the new species, *R. chamae-thomsonii* and its smaller-leaved variety, *chamaethauma*. Only the forms of prostrate habit, with the outer branches, at least, creeping along the ground, are retained as *R. forrestii*. *R. forrestii* var. *tumescens* has larger leaves, green beneath, and a dome-shaped habit. The taxonomists have done their best but it must be admitted that *R. forrestii* var. *tumescens* does in some cases blend imperceptibly into *R. chamae-thomsonii* var. *chamaethauma* through plants of intermediate character. As a group, the flowers are not invariably scarlet or crimson. White, pink, and even pale yellow blossoms are seen occasionally. It is most important to secure plants propagated from forms known to be free-flowering, as some specimens may grow thirty years without producing a single bloom. Inasmuch as the clone formerly known as the F.C.C. form of *repens* seems to blossom prolifically wherever it is grown, I am inclined to think that inherently floriferous character is more important than the cultural conditions, but it is apparent that Rhododendrons of this group like moisture at the roots, quick drainage, and plenty of exposure. In one garden which features *R. forrestii*, the plants grow on a damp bank facing north with full exposure both east and west. This probably is ideal, but a hillside facing west with about 60 per cent of the afternoon sun screened by trees produces fine flowers in another location. I have grown flourishing specimens by sowing the seeds in common Hair Cap Moss, *Polytrichum commune*, and allowing the plants to grow on undisturbed with the mossy ground cover beneath them. Rotting leaves and other debris which lodge in the twigs supporting the top canopy of foliage must be removed periodically or else the accumulation becomes so sodden in the confined and shaded position that it causes the decay of the center of the plant. *R. forrestii* with its prostrate growth and deeply veined leaves purplish-red or pale green beneath, lacking any indumentum, can scarcely be confused with any other species. It comes from Tibet, Yunnan and Burma at 12,000 to 14,000 feet, where it grows in open moist moorlands and pastures. It was discovered by George Forrest in 1905 and its name commemorates this pioneering explorer to whom we owe the discovery of so many of our finest Rhododendron species. Freedom of Flowering: 3; Ease of Cultivation: 2+; American Quality Rating: xxxx; British: ★★★★; American Hardiness Rating: H-3; British: B; Truss Type: 15; as *R. repens* var. *chamaedoron*, A.M., 1932; as *R. repens*, F.C.C., 1935.

R. fortunei (for′-tune-i), **Lindley.** FORTUNEI SERIES, FORTUNEI SUBSERIES

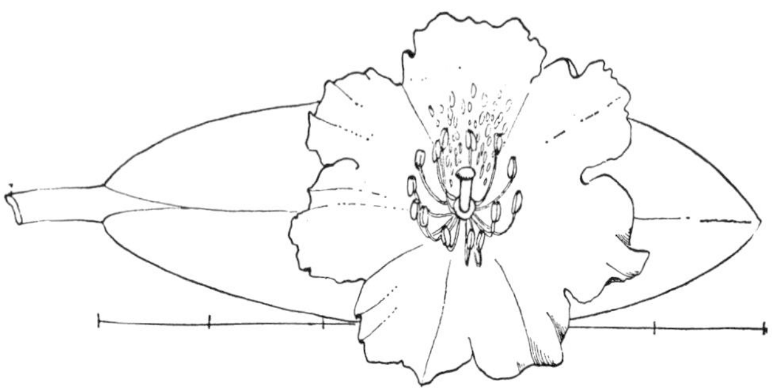

For the first true Rhododendron of the hundreds of sorts ultimately introduced from China, this species is remarkably rare today. One of the original plants from Robert Fortune's introduction in 1856 is still alive and growing in England, in Windsor Great Park, near Virginia Water, but nearly all the species labeled 'R. fortunei' which are seen in private gardens today are either *R. decorum* or hybrids of it. The authentic *R. fortunei* is a spreading, 15-foot shrub well clothed with large, handsome leaves 4 to 8 inches long, $1\frac{1}{2}$ to $3\frac{1}{2}$ inches wide, pale glaucous green beneath, which makes a rich and substantial effect in the landscape. Scarlet leaf bracts which accompany the new growth are an arresting feature in the total of its assets. In its best forms the flat, widely open flowers are more than 4 inches in diameter, deliciously fragrant, usually eight or nine to each loose terminal cluster. The sumptuous blossoms are somewhat crinkled, a lovely blush-pink on opening, fading almost white. They are unusual in having seven, sometimes eight lobes, with a yellow flare at the top of the throat which adds a piquant depth to their extraordinary beauty. *R. fortunei* flowers toward the end of May, just before the familiar Catawba hybrids in the eastern United States. Thus it serves to extend the season of Rhododendron bloom in cold climates. Both pure white and deep rose-color forms are known and a single plant with red flowers was grown from a collector's seed in England. The Rhododendron in commerce as 'Mrs Butler' is reputedly a superior form of *R. fortunei* with delicate, pearl-pink flowers. Unquestionably this is among the finest few of Rhododendron species. The enormous scented blossoms, exquisitely modeled, form a tumbling cascade of color and fragrance in a spectacle of magnificence which can scarcely be matched in the genus. In addition to its remarkable floral effect, it is exceptionally vigorous, free from pests and attractive in foliage and habit. Fortune's Rhododendron is probably the most distinguished flowering evergreen shrub that can be grown in the northeastern United States. In its hardy forms, available commercially from specialist nurserymen in Pennsylvania and New Jersey, it is satisfactory as far north as Boston and beyond. This species gains notably in hardiness with age. Small plants may be damaged by winter cold which does not affect older specimens at all, and gardeners toward the northern limit of its adaptability are advised to secure this shrub in a size 3 feet high or larger. *R. fortunei* has had a profound effect in improving the quality of garden hybrids. Beginning in 1880 with *R.* (*fortunei* × *thomsonii*) 'Luscombei', breeders have used it and its descendants continuously to this day to create many of our finest and best-known cultivars. They are generally noted for their size of blossom, hardiness, delicate coloring and often as well for a rich, spicy fragrance. An entire race of Rhododendron hybrids owes its value to this supremely beautiful species. It is distinguished from its allies on the basis of the leaf base more or less rounded, *stamens devoid of hairs* and style clad to the tip with white to yellow glands. The glandular calyx is minute. There are 14 stamens. *R. fortunei* is most often confused with *R. decorum* but the latter can be identified by its stamens pubescent at the base. The differences among *RR. fortunei, decorum* and *discolor* are illustrated by the drawings on page 116. *R. fortunei* was named for its discoverer, Robert Fortune, who first found it growing at 3,000 feet in Chekiang, in eastern China, in 1855. Freedom of Flowering: 1; Ease of Cultivation: 1; American Quality Rating: xxx; British: ***; American Hardiness Rating: H-2; British: B; Truss Type: 8.

R. fulvum (ful′-vum), **Balf. f. and W. W. Sm.** FULVUM SERIES

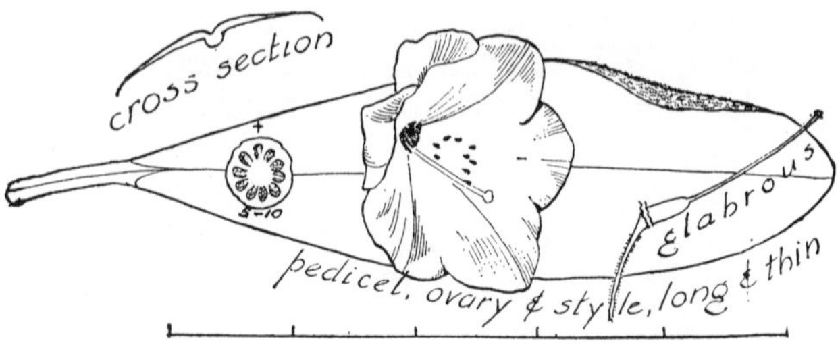

Here is a species which has enjoyed fairly wide popularity almost entirely as a foliage plant. Now, as the forms with fine flowers are slowly becoming distributed, it should take its place as one of the most versatile garden Rhododendrons in the genus. It is a large shrub or small tree, 9 to as much as 20 feet tall, with rich, lustrous dark green leaves $2\frac{1}{2}$ to as much as 11 inches long, $\frac{3}{4}$ to $3\frac{1}{2}$ inches wide, usually closer to the larger of these dimensions, coated beneath with a brilliant indumentum. Most often this felty covering gives the appearance of bright orange suède, but it varies as well to deep cinnamon, brownish-red and yellowish. The texture is soft and granular. The leaves yield readily to the wind, exposing their striking undersides in endlessly changing patterns as the shifting ripples of bold color pass over the plants with each stirring breeze. The form most often seen in gardens is Kingdon-Ward's #8300, bell-shaped white flowers with a deep crimson basal blotch, and the loose cluster of them is not particularly impressive. But there are also beautiful large-flowered silvery pink forms, free-blooming with compact globular trusses of great ornamental value. In these superior expressions of the species the blossoms often are more than 2 inches across, about twelve making up the evenly rounded inflorescence which measures almost 5 inches in diameter. Some forms are deep rose, as often without the basal blotch as with it. April is the flowering period. *R. fulvum* is easily grown and hardy, though not sufficiently cold resistant to be satisfactory in the northeastern United States. Elsewhere it is an admirable garden subject of year round interest. The Rhododendron formerly called *R. fulvoides* is now included with this species, which is unique in the genus for the indumentum of stalked hairs, much branched at the top, resembling hydrae when seen through the microscope. It is easily distinguished from the only other member of the series, *R. uvarifolium*, with a whitish or fawn, smooth, non-granular indumentum. From species of the Campanulatum series it is distinct in having oblanceolate to obovate leaves, broadest above the middle and usually tapered to the base. The seed capsule is long, thin and round, usually somewhat curved. *R. fulvum* is native to Yunnan, Szechuan, Tibet, Assam and Burma at 8,000 to 14,500 feet, in thickets and as a part of open forests. It was discovered and introduced by Forrest in 1912 and given the name referring to its tawny coating beneath the leaves. Freedom of Flowering: 2+; Ease of Cultivation: 1; American Quality Rating: x; British: ***; American Hardiness Rating: H-4; British: B; Truss Type: 3; A.M., 1933.

R. glaucophyllum (glaw-ko-fi′-lum), **Rehder.** GLAUCOPHYLLUM SERIES, GLAUCOPHYLLUM SUBSERIES

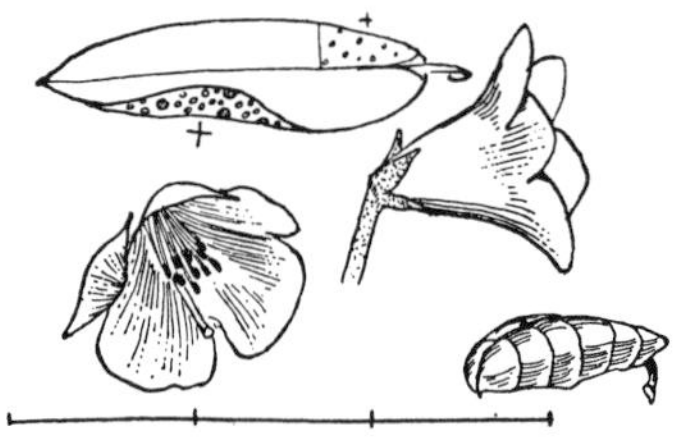

There is a considerable range of stature in this species, from 12 to 48 inches tall at maturity. It is a trim, bushy dwarf with dark, dull green leaves 1¼ to 3½ inches long, ⅜ to 1 inch wide, glaucous white and scaly underneath. The margins are often down-turned and the leaves have a strong, resinous odor when they are crushed. There are four to ten little bell-shaped flowers, about 1 inch across, in each loose cluster. When the blossoms appear in early May they are reminiscent of old-fashioned nosegays gaily bedecking the plants, fresh, clear light pink, more intense in the throats. The two shades together lend a depth of color which gives a charming effect. Some forms with darker flowers are rosy red. This is a Rhododendron with its own distinctive appeal. I have seen banks with eight or ten plants grouped together which gave a fine massed show of color, and I think that this species is most effective when several plants are used at one site. This is the Rhododendron formerly called *glaucum*. It is characterized by the lanceolate to oblanceolate leaves, often with pointed tips, which have both small, pale yellow scales and larger, brown scales underneath. The large calyx, about ¼ inch long, has lobes markedly pointed. The style may be either short, stout and bent, or long, thin and straight. This species is common in the eastern Himalayas, Sikkim and Bhutan, at 9,000 to 12,000 feet. It was found by Hooker and introduced about 1850. The name is an allusion to the bluish-gray leaf. Freedom of Flowering: 1; Ease of Cultivation: 1; American Quality Rating: x; British: **; American Hardiness Rating: H-3; British: B; Truss Type: 9; var. *luteiflorum*, A.M., 1960.

R. grande (gran′-dee), **Wight.** GRANDE SERIES

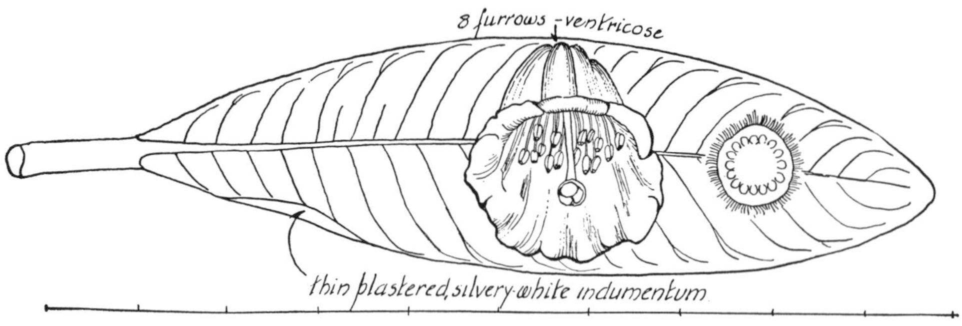

When this primitive tree flowers in earliest spring, in March, and occasionally even in February, it is one of the spectacular sights of the season. *R. grande* grows up to 30 feet tall

and has large, glossy green, decorative leaves with prominent veins and midribs. Technical sources give the leaf size range as 5½ to 12 inches in length and 3¼ to 5¼ inches in width, but I have measured leaves more than 15 inches long on several occasions, though this species never approaches the enormous broad foliage of *R. sinogrande*. The leaf under-surface is usually clad with a handsome, burnished silvery indumentum. The large truss, set in a rosette of the impressive shining leaves, is a symmetrical 7-inch globe of about twenty-five bell-shaped, eight-lobed ivory-white flowers of heavy substance, each 2½-inch blossom decorated with seven bold plum-purple rays radiating from the base and set off with a conspicuous orange-red stigma. There is a rare form with brilliant red flowers which is supremely beautiful, one of the wonders of the entire genus. This majestic tree Rhododendron demands a mild, moist climate and a sheltered site. Its impressiveness depends in large part on favorable growing conditions. I know a 100-year-old specimen grown from Hooker's original seed which is 19 feet tall and 23 feet broad. This species has usually not proved satisfactorily hardy north of California. It is separated from its relatives in the same series by having leaves averaging 3 to 5 inches wide, with a silvery, plastered indumentum and a round petiole. There are sixteen stamens. In Asia it forms forests at 8,000 to 10,000 feet in Sikkim and Bhutan, where it was found in 1849 by Joseph Hooker and named *grande* for its large size. Freedom of Flowering: 2; Ease of Cultivation: 2; American Quality Rating: xxx; British: ****; American Hardiness Rating: H-5; British: E; Truss Type: 6.

R. griersonianum (greer-son-ee-a'-num), **Balf. f. and Forrest.** AURICULATUM SERIES

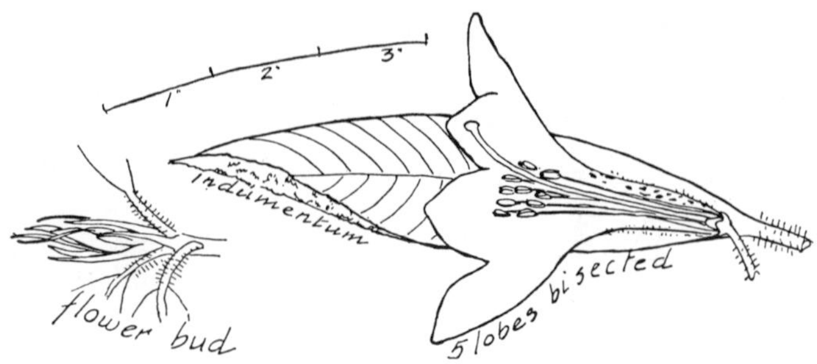

Of all the species discovered since the advent of the First World War, this, through its innumerable offspring, has had the widest influence on our gardens. By 1956 over 140 first-generation hybrids had flowered and been registered in England alone. Many more were not recorded, and the number of more advanced generation hybrids must be astronomical by now. Few species have created such interest. *R. griersonianum* is an 8-foot shrub with straight branches and an open, upright growth habit. The dull green leaves are 3½ to 7 inches long, 1 to 2 inches wide, strongly veined on the surface and coated with a buff woolly indumentum beneath. The distinctive long, pointed winter buds are enclosed by a rosette of small, elongated bracts, the effect somewhat reminiscent of the projecting bracts which encircle the buds of our native *R. maximum*. Vivid orange-scarlet, five-lobed flowers come in June, widely expanded trumpets 3 inches or more across. The corolla dilates abruptly from a narrow, fluted tube. Both style and stamens are usually crimson. There are eight or nine downy blossoms firmly and individually held in an open cluster and their peculiar, burning brilliance gives them a striking prominence in the garden. Some poor sorts, however, are somewhat thin in corolla texture and their color is diluted. The Exbury form is especially fine, a deep, vibrant crimson shade which seems to glow in the landscape. This is one of the most distinct and decorative of Rhododendron species in flower, one of Forrest's most important discoveries. It gains in hardiness with age, but I think it scarcely deserves its present American rating. Its hybrids are a great deal hardier than would be expected. While *R. griersonianum* can endure a drier site than many Rhododendrons, its foliage burns easily with too much exposure. In some climates this is such a serious fault that this species is unsatisfactory, as it is in coastal California. In the eastern counties of England, it needs a dry, shady situation. *R. griersonianum* seems oddly paired with *R. auriculatum* in the Auriculatum series. It is distinct, and not likely to be confused with any other Rhododendron, the long, pointed foliage buds, so similar in size and shape to the floral buds, making identification easy. The indumentum beneath the leaves and the peculiar flower shape with its elongated tube further distinguish it. *R. griersonianum* is native to western Yunnan province of China where it grows in thickets and in forest clearings at 7,000 to 9,000 feet altitude. It was discovered by George Forrest in 1917 and named for his friend and assistant, R. C. Grierson. Freedom of Flowering: 1; Ease of Cultivation: 1; American Quality Rating: xxx; British: ****; American Hardiness Rating: H-5; British: C; Truss Type: 4; F.C.C., 1924.

R. griffithianum (grif-fith-ee-a′-num), **Wight.** FORTUNEI SERIES, GRIFFITHIANUM SUBSERIES

This Rhododendron, formerly called *R. aucklandii*, is so distinct in the Fortunei group that it occupies its own subseries in solitary splendor. It needs no such glorification to distinguish it horticulturally, being famous in its own right for possessing the largest flowers of any of the Himalayan Rhododendrons. Mature specimens are tree-like in growth, about 20 feet tall, with an interesting trunk to which irregular patches of reddish-brown older bark adhere, in contrast to the lighter, smoother texture of the newer bark. The leaves are 4 to 12 inches long, $1\frac{1}{2}$ to 4 inches wide, but most often about 8 or 9 inches in length and $2\frac{3}{4}$ inches in width, pale green above and slightly glaucous below. The resplendent flowers are 5 or 6 inches in diameter, white or pale pink and often suffused yellow in the throat, appearing in May in loose trusses of about six, the entire cluster often presenting an expanse of color 10 inches or more across. The five-lobed blossoms are slightly fragrant, widely open and bell-shaped, with a strong, clean modeling which gives them a classic appeal. At times they are an astonishing 7 inches in diameter. In many ways they are the finest in the genus, and breeders have been quick to take advantage of their immense size, exquisite form, and delicate coloring. The magnificent Loderi hybrids and many of the most popular commercial cultivars owe the impressive dimensions of their blossoms to *R. griffithianum*. Unfortunately, this species is a greenhouse shrub in all but the mildest climates. The foliage burns even in sheltered gardens in

Cornwall, though the species blooms there. Occasionally it is grown against a wall outside in colder regions so that a canvas cover suspended from wire can be drawn in front of it to protect it in frosty weather. The radiantly beautiful flowers are worth the trouble. Where it can be grown outdoors, this Rhododendron appreciates a site sheltered from wind and too much sun. It is at its best in a woodland. *R. griffithianum* can be instantly identified by the large, saucer-shaped calyx, ⅜ to ¾ inch long, with undulating rim. The species is glabrous in all its parts and has a style glandular to the tip. There are twelve to eighteen stamens. It is native to Sikkim and Bhutan, where it grows at 7,000 to 9,000 feet. Following its introduction in 1849, it was named to honor William Griffith, superintendent of the Calcutta Botanic Garden early in the nineteenth century. Freedom of Flowering: 2+; Ease of Cultivation: 1; American Quality Rating: xxxx; British: ****; American Hardiness Rating: H-5; British: E; Truss Type: 8; F.C.C., 1866.

R. haemaleum (hem-a'-lee-um), **Balf. f. and Forrest.** NERIIFLORUM SERIES, SANGUINEUM SUBSERIES

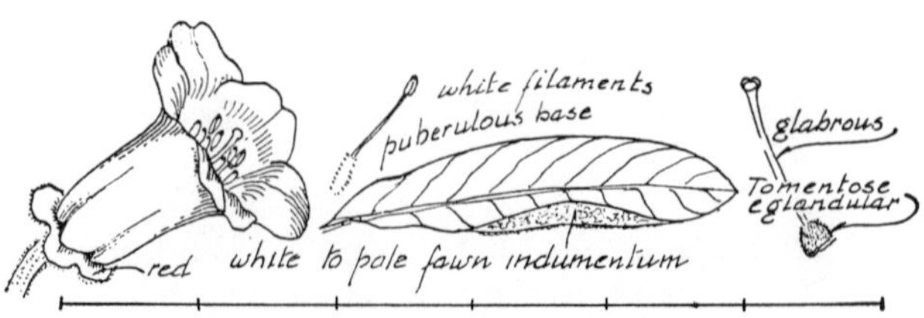

In the large and confusing Sanguineum section, as now delimited, this is a slow-growing, spreading shrub of dense foliage and mound-like habit, usually seen in mature specimens about 30 inches tall and 4½ feet broad. The leaves are 1½ to 3½ inches long, ⅝ to 1¼ inches wide, dark green above and with primary veins indented, bearing below a smooth, thin greyish-white to tan layer of down. *R. haemaleum* usually flowers in late May and early June, as stated in botanical reference works, but some forms bloom the latter part of April and others on through the first part of May, so its blossoming season actually extends over a period of six weeks or more. The flowers are 1¾ inches in diameter in the better forms, long and bell-shaped, about five pendulous in a very lax, flat-topped cluster. There is a convention that their color is black-crimson but actually it is more frequently bright red, deep red or scarlet. On the other hand, there is a form of *R. sanguineum* (Rock #59444) with flowers so deep in color that they are purplish-black. At the moment *R. haemaleum* stands as a subspecies of *R. sanguineum* but it is not distinct because of the innumerable microforms which represent all degrees of merging between the two. The garden effect of both is the same. They are useful dwarf shrubs, neat and dense, hardy enough and often remarkable for their depth of color. The forms with the very dark flowers represent interesting additions to large Rhododendron collections but they are more curious than decorative for the garden with limited space. This subspecies is very similar to *R. didymum* but the latter has smaller leaves and a densely glandular ovary almost devoid of hairs. The flowers, stalks and ovary of *R. haemaleum* are not glandular and this in combination with the thin, grey or fawn plastered indumentum and flowers of heavy, waxen texture, black-crimson to red, are aids to identification. The stamens are faintly downy toward the base. The cone-shaped ovary is densely clothed with down, the leaves are wider above the middle and the capsule is not curved. The style is glabrous, the calyx crimson. This Rhododendron was first discovered by George Forrest in 1904 growing in scrub on the margins of forests at 12,000 feet in southeast Tibet, and he introduced it thirteen years later. The name is a reference to the blood-red color of the flowers. Freedom of Flowering: 2; Ease of Cultivation: 1; American Quality Rating: xx; British: ***; American Hardiness Rating: H-3; British: B; Truss Type: 11.

R. haematodes (he-ma-to'-deez), **Franch.** NERIIFLORUM SERIES, HAEMATODES SUBSERIES

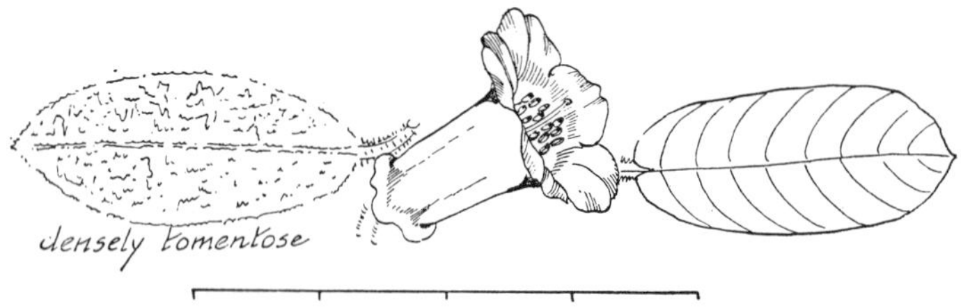

Few Asian Rhododendrons possess so many virtues as this admirable representative of a distinguished series. The literature describes *R. haematodes* as being up to 10 feet in height but it seems to be invariably a convenient little dwarf in cultivation, about 4 feet tall and spreading widely. A magnificent form (Forrest #6773) of perfect symmetry and faultless foliage is $3\frac{1}{2}$ feet tall and 10 feet broad at the present time. It is so dense in its mound-like growth as to be almost formal in effect. The leaves of this species are $1\frac{1}{2}$ to 4 inches long, $\frac{3}{4}$ to $1\frac{3}{4}$ inches broad, dark shiny green above and densely coated with a woolly reddish-brown indumentum beneath, a coating which extends attractively to the new growth. Tubular flowers expanding to bell-shaped corollas as much as 2 inches across in the best forms appear in May in lax terminal clusters of six to ten. There is a range of shades from rich, blood-red to the most brilliant scarlet, all marked by an extraordinary luminosity of color. The species is somewhat slow growing and also slow in coming into prolific flowering. Its range of leaf shape and manner of growth is much wider than is popularly appreciated. The form sent back by Kingdon-Ward under #10134, for example, has leaves almost 2 inches wide and is rather upright in growth habit. This is a fairly hardy species, satisfactory in warm sites on Cape Cod and on Long Island in the eastern United States and its dwarf, dense character and rugged constitution make it useful in a wide variety of garden situations. The rich indumentum and rather late, mid-May blossoming period are additional attractions. *R. haematodes* separates from its allies by having, in combination, waxen red flowers of heavy substance with ten to twelve stamens and a small calyx; woolly, reddish-brown shoots, leaf undersides and petioles; an ovary short, blunt and downy; and oblong to egg-shaped leaves with rounded or blunt tips. In its homeland in China's Yunnan province this species grows exposed in open meadows at 11,000 to 12,000 feet elevation. It was discovered by Delavay in 1885 but was not introduced into cultivation until Forrest sent it back to England in 1911. The name refers to the blood-like color of the flowers. Freedom of Flowering: 2; Ease of Cultivation: 1; American Quality Rating: xxxx; British: ★★★★; American Hardiness Rating: H-4; British: B; Truss Type: 10; F.C.C., 1926.

R. heliolepis (heel-ee-o-leep'-is), **Franch.** HELIOLEPIS SERIES

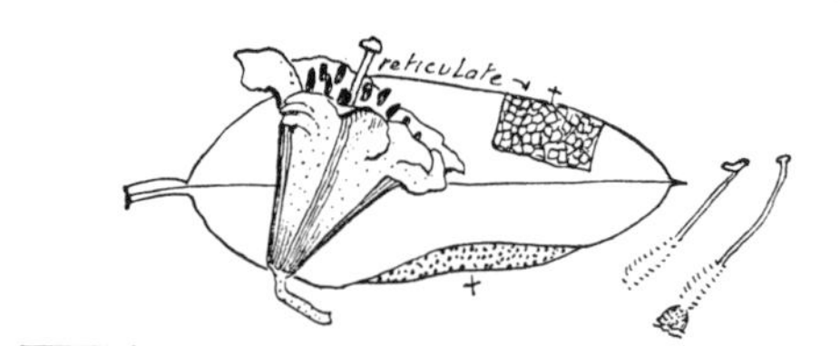

Here is one of the most versatile of all Rhododendron species for garden decoration and it has been unaccountably neglected, even by specialists. After many years it grows to a height of 8 feet or possibly a little more. The foliage is strongly aromatic, dark green above and clad with glistening scales beneath. It is often crinkled and somewhat twisted, the leaves 2 to 4 inches long, 1 to $1\frac{3}{4}$ inches broad. In good forms the flowers are $1\frac{5}{8}$ inches in diameter. They range in color from white through lavender-pinks to rose, spotted on the upper lobe and gathered into loose, $3\frac{1}{4}$-inch trusses of as many as nine, but more often four or five. They are produced with the utmost profusion. June is the usual blooming season but some early forms are in full flower at the end of April. There is a bright rose-pink which carries well in the garden and is especially attractive. The late-blooming season in a shrub which blossoms with such prodigality is invaluable, but this is a good, adaptable Rhododendron under any circumstances. It is usually densely foliaged, grows well in a wide variety of garden sites and gives an effect in the landscape which is lighter and finer in texture than do the familiar large-leaved sorts. If there is any consistent difference between it and *R. brevistylum*, I cannot detect it. The length of the style and the shape of the leaf base, purported to separate the two, are not reliable criteria. *R. heliolepis* has a corolla scaly all over the base, with a style hairy on the lower part which is as long as the stamens. The leaves, rounded at the base, bear scales underneath about 1½ times their own diameter apart, and their glittering surface gives the species its name. It is native to Yunnan province of China at 10,000 to 11,000 feet, where it was found by Delavay in 1886, but not introduced into cultivation until 1912, by Forrest. Freedom of Flowering: 1; Ease of Cultivation: 1; American Quality Rating: x; British: **; American Hardiness Rating: H-3; British: B; Truss Type: 9; Forrest #26961, A.M., 1954.

R. hippophaeoides (hip-po-fa-oy′-deez), **Balf. f. and W. W. Sm.** LAPPONICUM SERIES

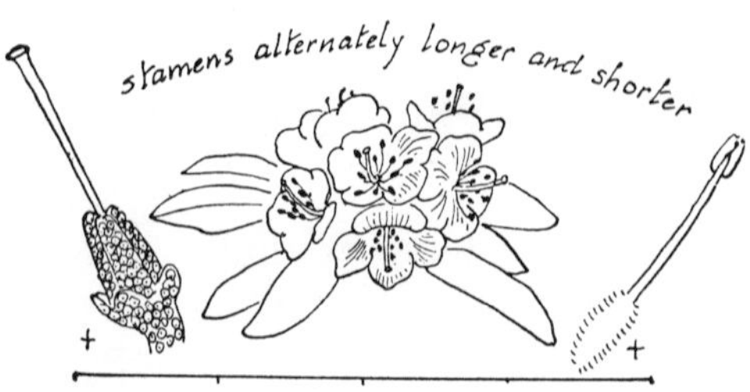

Here is the most tractable and amiable of the Lapponicum series, a 'blue'-flowered dwarf which grows to a height of about 4 feet. The acridly aromatic leaves are glossy green, ⅝ to 1½ inches long, a little less to a little more than ½ inch wide and densely scaly. The growth habit varies somewhat and is often just a little bit thin and open, especially in older specimens, whereas others are denser, due to the more twiggy branching at the ends of the limbs. In April, four to eight flowers, ⅝ to 1 inch wide, combine to form tight, diminutive terminal trusses about 1½ inches in diameter. The color of the flowers varies greatly, from quite clear light blue to deep blue through purplish, mauve, and lilac shades to pink and rose. Some of the intermediate and faded colors are much less desirable for garden purposes so plants should be selected in bloom or bought as specimens propagated from known superior forms. This is a particularly charming Rhododendron in spring flower, with tiny nosegays of color at the end of almost every twig. It is valuable for the rock garden and for many other garden uses where an amenable shrub of dwarf stature is wanted. Fine effects come from massing the plants in groups. It is almost unique among Rhododendrons in being able to grow in rather wet spots where the ground may even be boggy. Remarkably adaptable for an alpine Rhododendron, it is perfectly hardy and plants have thriven and bloomed well (occasionally out of season, in August) for years in my trial grounds in northwestern Pennsylvania, where they have endured −25° F. and lower on numerous occasions. It is reputed to suffer from the 'Victorian Vapors' and to be short-lived in the hot coastal climate of the East, but the species has been continuously represented for eight to ten years in several New Jersey gardens. An exposed but moist and sheltered site seems to suit it best. Shade accentuates a tendency toward lankiness. It presents no problems in Great Britain and in the ideal Rhododendron climate of the Pacific Coast, where the form with soft mauve flowers known as 'Haba Shan' is one of the best. Among species of the Lapponicum series with other than yellow flowers, it is distinct in possessing, in combination, leaves normally 1 inch long or more, narrowly oblanceolate, with uniform pale grey scales slightly overlapping below. The flowers, neither scaly nor hairy outside, have a glabrous style the same length as the stamens, which are hairy. The calyx is very short, scarcely $\frac{1}{8}$ inch long, fringed with scales and occasionally with a few hairs. This species comes from Yunnan province of China, at 12,000 feet, where it was discovered by Kingdon-Ward in 1913. Its name refers to its resemblance to Sea Buckthorn. Freedom of Flowering: 1; Ease of Cultivation: 1; American Quality Rating: xxx; British: ***; American Hardiness Rating: H-3 (Author's dissent: H-1); British: A; Truss Type: 5; A.M., 1927; A.G.M., 1925.

R. hirsutum (her-soo′-tum), **Linn.** FERRUGINEUM SERIES

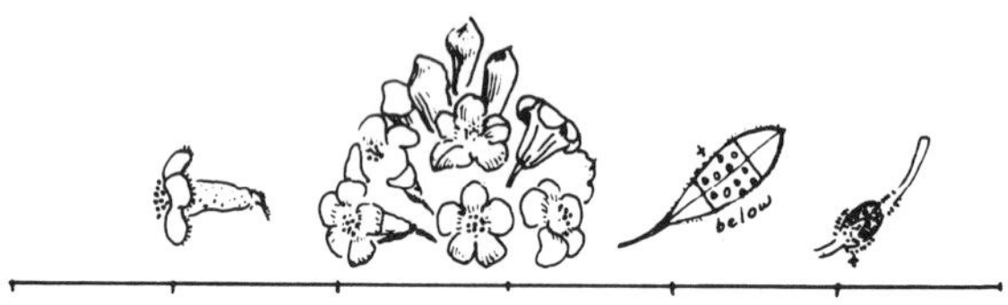

This species is so similar to *R. ferrugineum* as to have the same popular name, the "Alpine Rose". It is often a little smaller in all of its parts, about 3 feet tall, but of the same rounded outline, with leaves $\frac{1}{2}$ to 1 inch long, and $\frac{1}{4}$ to $\frac{1}{2}$ inch wide, bright green above and fringed with hairs, scaly below but less so than its relative. Occasional specimens are seen in nature as much as 5 feet high. It comes into bloom in June with flowers $\frac{1}{2}$ to $\frac{3}{4}$ inch across, deep pink to rosy scarlet, rarely white, in rounded clusters of six to twelve. This is one of only four Rhododendron species which have been *proved* to grow in alkaline soil in nature, but this unusual adaptation may be the result of a peculiar chemical constitution of the soil rather than an inherent ability of the plant to thrive in a non-acid medium. In any case, it is a rugged and adaptable dwarf Rhododendron, with trim, tailored growth habit which appears to striking advantage in foundation plantings, in the forefront of the shrub border and especially where the plants can be massed to increase the impact of their peculiarly luminous flower colors. Strangely, *R. hirsutum* seems to be better suited to the climate of the eastern United States than its close relative, *R. ferrugineum*, from the same elevations of the Alps. It has grown slowly, but it seems healthy after some years in my trial grounds in northwestern Pennsylvania. This species is distinct on the basis of the hairs fringing the leaves, the young shoots and the calyx. It is greener than its ally, the leaves only laxly scaly beneath, and both calyx lobes and flower stalks are longer. The style is $1\frac{1}{2}$ times the length of the ovary. Hybrids from natural crosses with its sister species are known to exist in the wild. This is the oldest Rhododendron in cultivation, having been introduced in 1656. It comes from above 4,000 feet in the Alps of southern Europe, extending eastward to Transylvania. The name refers to its hairy character. Freedom of Flowering: 1; Ease of Cultivation: 1; American Quality Rating: x; British: *; American Hardiness Rating: H-2; British: A; Truss Type: 9.

R. hodgsonii (hodj′-son-i), **Hooker fil.** FALCONERI SERIES

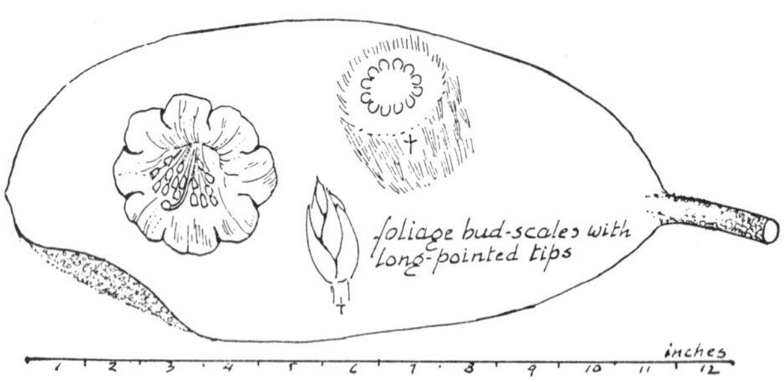

This is a small tree up to 20 feet in height with large, dark green leathery leaves 6 to 12 inches long, 3 to 5 inches wide, usually near the larger of these dimensions. There is a gray to tan, rarely rusty, indumentum beneath the leaves. The growth habit is somewhat angular and stiff, with thick, heavy branches, but the effect of older specimens in the landscape is altogether exotic and extremely handsome. A tree planted at Stonefield, Scotland, about a century ago, is 15 feet tall and 37 feet broad today. Up to twenty-five long, bell-shaped $1\frac{1}{2}$-inch rosy-lilac flowers make up firmly rounded 6-inch terminal trusses which appear in late April and early May. Some forms have blossoms of a strident, unattractive magenta. Others are beautiful pale pink deepening to rose in the center, and I have seen a single rare specimen in Scotland with extraordinary creamy yellow blossoms. Few small trees exceed this for any garden which can give it the shelter which it needs. Its noble bearing is especially effective in a woodland setting. When it starts into growth in the spring, the new leaves are covered with a silvery, downy film which adds an extra decorative note at that season. This provides one of the best marks to distinguish it from its relatives. As the leaves mature, a residue remains which results in small, irregular shiny spots on the leaf surface. The corolla of *R. hodgsonii* usually has seven or eight lobes (rarely to ten) and is normally unspotted, though there may be several small dark basal blotches. The ovary is woolly and the flowers are borne on unusually thick shoots. There are normally sixteen stamens, sometimes fifteen to eighteen. The foliage bud scales have long, pointed tips. The gray to buff indumentum, rarely rusty or reddish, combined with round petioles about 2 inches long, lacking any flange-like projections, complete the identification. This species ranges along the Himalayas at 10,000 to 12,000 feet from Nepal to Bhutan, where it is found on mountain spurs and in sheltered valleys. It was introduced by Hooker in 1849, who noted that its leaves in the wild are sometimes 18 inches long. The name derives from that of B. H. Hodgson, one-time representative of the East India Company in Nepal. Freedom of Flowering: 2; Ease of Cultivation: 2+; American Quality Rating: x; British: **; American Hardiness Rating: H-4; British: B; Truss Type: 6.

R. hookeri (hook′-er-i), **Nuttall.** THOMSONII SERIES, THOMSONII SUBSERIES

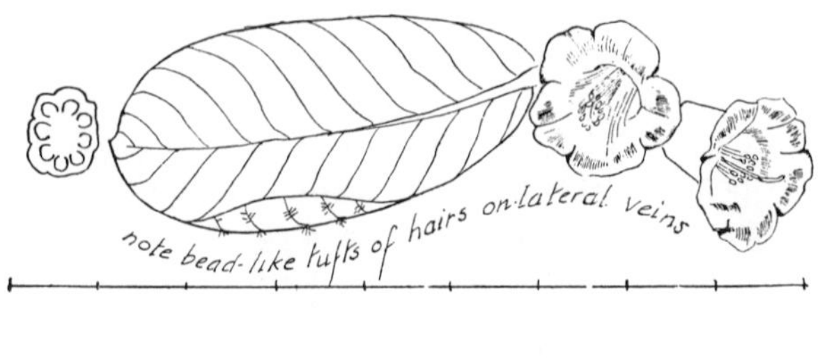

In this Rhododendron we have one of the finest of an admirable series, a superb red-flowered species which launches the blossoming season in a blaze of color. Very old plants are as much as 20 feet tall, but it is ordinarily seen in cultivation as a shrub about 10 or 12 feet high with leaves 2½ to 7 inches long, 1¼ to 3½ inches wide. The undersides are glaucous and unique in possessing, at spaced intervals along their veins, little tufts of hairs. The richly colored flowers about 2 inches wide and up to fifteen to a lax truss are pure cherry-red or deep crimson, with darker nectaries at the base. There is a waxen, burnished sheen to the bell-shaped blossoms as they appear in March or early April which gives them a singular texture. The scarlet ribbon-like bracts on the new growth in mid-May are brilliantly ornamental. An especially fine form of this species received a First Class Certificate from the Royal Horticultural Society in 1933, but the average of seedlings is extraordinarily good. This Rhododendron as grown in the United States has not been hardy enough to be regarded as a permanent garden shrub in Oregon and Washington. It seems to be a good deal hardier under the conditions of growth in the British Isles, or perhaps only the more tender forms have made their way to America. *R. hookeri* is easily distinguished from all other Rhododendrons now in cultivation by the small tufts of downy hairs spaced along the lateral veins beneath the leaves. Both style and ovary are devoid of glands. This species was found by Booth in 1852 in Bhutan and named for Sir Joseph Hooker, a pioneering explorer and plant hunter to whom we are indebted for many of our finest Rhododendron species. In the wild, it forms thickets at 8,000 to 9,000 feet and Kingdon-Ward found it in Assam at 10,000 to 12,000 feet. Freedom of Flowering: 2; Ease of Cultivation: 1; American Ratings: None yet assigned; British Quality Rating: ****; British Hardiness Rating: C; Truss Type: 8; F.C.C., 1933.

R. impeditum (im-ped-i′-tum), **Balf. f. and W. W. Sm.** LAPPONICUM SERIES

Among the best of the low undershrubs with 'blue' flowers, *R. impeditum* grows into a compact mound up to 15 or 18 inches tall when it has full exposure. In shade the densely twiggy growth becomes more open and the plant is apt to appear unkempt. The leaves are about ½ inch long and ¼ inch wide and densely scaly on both surfaces. The 1-inch flowers, either one or two from each terminal bud, range from lavender-pink to purplish-blue, and the deeper shades which tend toward blue are the more attractive. They appear at the end of April and in early May. This is an ideal species for the rock garden, in the forefront of a shrub border or as an edging for beds, anywhere on the West Coast from San Francisco northward. Planted about 15 inches apart, a number of plants will grow together to form an impenetrable ground cover, handsome at all seasons and especially effective when such an expanse becomes a blanket of blue flowers. The form sent from Asia by Dr Rock, the celebrated Rhododendron hunter of the Oriental wilderness, and offered by some nurseries as Rock #59263, is especially good in growth habit, making a perfect compact cushion. There is also an Award of Merit form of particularly fine color. The young shoots of this species are often an attractive blue-green. *R. impeditum* is hardy in most of the Northeast but it languishes in the dry heat of midsummer without special culture. I have succeeded with it and with other alpine Rhododendrons by planting them with a ground cover of the common Hair Cap Moss (*Polytrichum commune*), which seems to produce a favorable environment by the transpiration of water vapor and possibly also by acting as an insulating blanket beneath the plants. The species is separated from its relatives by its purplish-blue to mauve flowers which quickly shed their bud scales and have a glabrous style longer than the pubescent stamens; by the non-scaly corolla with corolla-tube glabrous outside; by its hair-fringed calyx less than ¼ inch long; and by its leaves about ½ inch in length. It is occasionally confused with *R. intricatum* from which it is easily distinguished by the long, protruding stamens. It is also confused with *R. fastigiatum*, possibly because the latter has an extremely rare dwarf form which is superficially similar. *R. impeditum* is so compact, with short branchlets, that it ordinarily bears little resemblance to the erect, somewhat open growth of *fastigiatum*, which also has more flowers to the truss. Forrest introduced *R. impeditum* in 1911 from the open pasture lands of Yunnan, southwest China, where it dominates large areas of the Lichiang Mountain Range at 15,000 to 16,000 feet. Its name means 'tangled', referring to its growth habit. Freedom of Flowering: 1; Ease of Cultivation: 1; American Quality Rating: xxx; British: ****; American Hardiness Rating: H-2; British: A; Truss Type: 5; A.M., 1944.

R. imperator (im-per-a′-tor), **Hutch and Ward.** UNIFLORUM SERIES

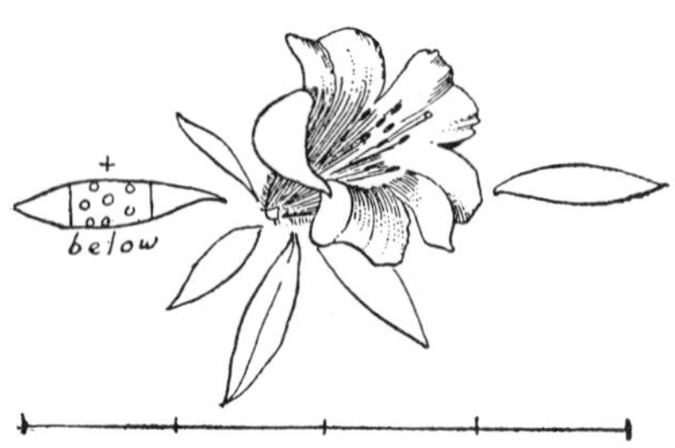

This rock garden gem is a spreading dwarf up to 12 inches high, prostrate in habit, with aromatic leaves ½ to 1½ inches long, ⅛ to ⅜ inch wide, dark green above and glaucous and slightly scaly beneath. The funnel-shaped flowers appear in late April and early May, singly or in pairs, held firmly erect. They are about 1½ inches broad and seem very large for the mat-like plants. They are light pink to deep rose with varying admixtures of blue, and the darker forms, especially, are uniquely attractive in their distinctive color. This species is considered somewhat difficult but it is so often seen smothered in flowers that it seems likely to have acquired this reputation from gardeners unfamiliar with the requirements of alpine plants. It wants the fullest possible exposure without foliage burn, shelter but no more shade than necessary, good drainage and moisture at the roots. So provided, it is an eye-catching sheet of color on a stony ledge in the rock garden. *R. imperator* is but one range of a continuous series of merging species which embraces *RR. patulum*, *pemakoense*, and *uniflorum*. When the Uniflorum series was established in 1948, the explanatory statement included the remark that 'the species are well defined'. I cannot agree. In stature, habit, leaf size, scale distribution, and in other respects, a complete progression of intermediates link them. *R. imperator* in its typical form differs from the type of *R. patulum* solely on the basis of scale distribution beneath the leaves, the scales being two to six times their own diameter apart, as against only one to one and one-half their diameter apart in *R. patulum*, a dubious and inconstant distinction. The longer, pointed leaves lanceolate or oblanceolate in shape, with entire margins; the style slightly longer than the corolla; and the spreading, prostrate habit help to distinguish it from its allies in their typical forms with wider leaves rounded at the ends and more erect habits of growth. *R. imperator* is native to Upper Burma where it was found on exposed ledges of granite cliffs at 10,000 to 11,000 feet by Kingdon-Ward. The name means 'Emperor'. Freedom of Flowering: 1; Ease of Cultivation: 1; American Quality Rating: xx; British: ****; American Hardiness Rating: H-3; British: A; Truss Type: 15; A.M., 1934.

R. insigne (in-sig'-ne), **Hemsl. and Wils.** ARBOREUM SERIES, ARGYROPHYLLUM SUBSERIES

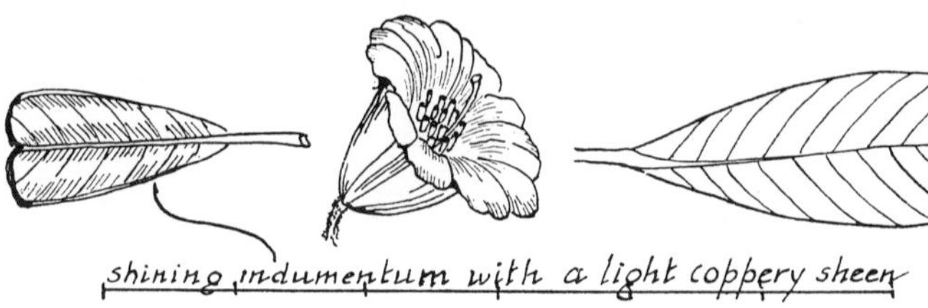

When this species was introduced from China the collector noted its height in the wild as 12 to 18 feet, but it usually reaches only half that stature in cultivation. The unfolding leaves are green with a white woolly down underneath. They are grouped in stiff rosettes and as they mature they become glossy grayish-green, 2 to 5 inches long, $\frac{3}{4}$ to 2 inches wide, with prominent veins, bearing on their nether surface a hard, plastered indumentum which has a distinctive metallic coppery sheen. The flowers are produced in the latter part of May and early June, each about 2 inches wide and uniquely colored pale to deep pink, spotted crimson on the upper lobes and often striped on the outside with rose. Some forms have firm round trusses 4 to 5 inches across of fifteen flowers or more; others are lax, containing as few as eight blossoms. This is a handsome, neat, slow-growing shrub, accepting any reasonable planting site. In its best forms the large flower trusses make an impressive display, the blossoms being both pretty and unusual in their color pattern. It flowers at an early age. The shining metallic luster of the indumentum beneath the leaf readily identifies this species. It is native to west China, Szechuan province, where it grows in woodlands at 7,000 to 10,000 feet elevation. E. H. Wilson introduced it in 1908, and it was given the name *insigne* meaning 'remarkable'. Freedom of Flowering: 2+; Ease of Cultivation: 1; American Quality Rating: xxx; British: ***; American Hardiness Rating: H-4; British: B; Truss Type: 3; A.M., 1923.

R. intricatum (in-tri-ka'-tum), **Franch.** LAPPONICUM SERIES

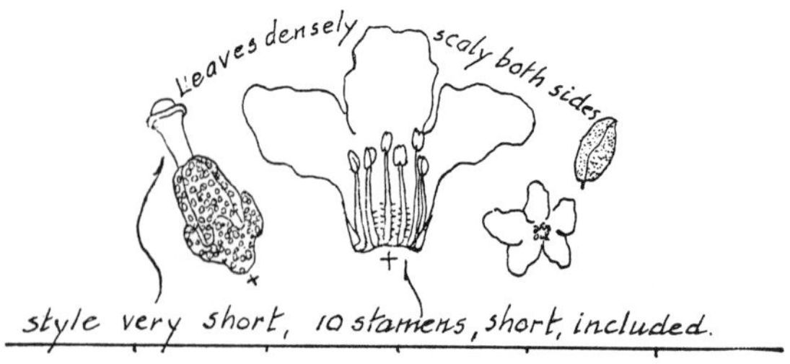

Another of the good "blue"-flowered dwarfs, this twiggy, densely branched Rhododendron seldom exceeds 24 inches in height and is often no more than 1 foot tall. The gray-green leaves are $\frac{1}{4}$ to $\frac{1}{2}$ inch long, a little more than half as wide and densely scaly both above and below. In late April and early May appear tight little terminal clusters of five or six $\frac{5}{8}$-inch flowers, violet-purple in the bud, opening to lilac. This is a slow-growing species which flowers young and profusely, so it is eminently suited for the rock garden. Its compact, rounded outline suggests its use as an edging plant as well, in the manner of dwarf Box. Like all of its relatives it varies a good deal in flower color and to a lesser degree in stature and neatness of growth habit, so it is important to secure a good form. It is hardy to New York City and beyond but it is hard to please, requiring abundant moisture, perfect drainage, and a good deal of exposure. Among its allies with mauve to purplish flowers it is distinct in having ten stamens included in the corolla tube, not exserted; a short, glabrous style; and a corolla tube devoid of hairs or scales on the outside. The scales on the lower surface of the leaves are so dense that they overlap. *R. intricatum* was first discovered by Wilson in 1904 in western Szechuan, where it grows in meadows and open grassy slopes at 11,000 to 15,000 feet. The name refers to its intricate branching habit. Freedom of Flowering: 1; Ease of Cultivation: 1; American Quality Rating: xx; British: ***; American Hardiness Rating: H-2; British: A; Truss Type: 5; F.C.C., 1907.

R. irroratum (ir-ro-ra'-tum), **Franch.** IRRORATUM SERIES, IRRORATUM SUBSERIES

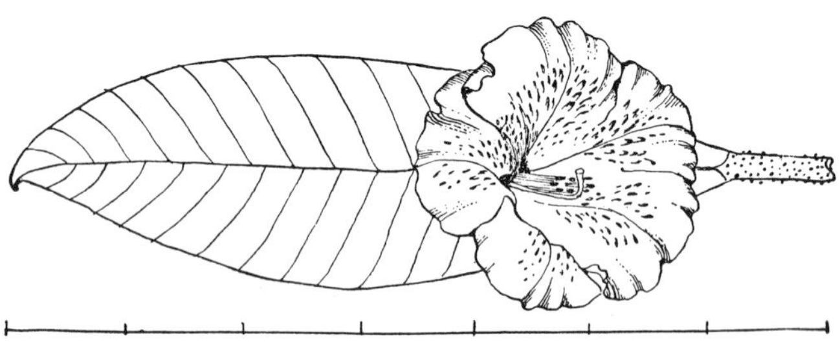

This beautiful species is a tall shrub of extraordinary character and distinction, among the loveliest of the early-blooming Rhododendrons. Older plants in cultivation are usually seen 10 to 12 feet tall, but it is reputed to reach a height of 25 feet in the wild. The leathery, prominently veined leaves are 2 to $6\frac{1}{2}$ inches long, $\frac{5}{8}$ to $2\frac{1}{4}$ inches wide, usually near the larger of these dimensions. In late March or early April twelve to fifteen $2\frac{1}{4}$-inch blossoms make up terminal trusses 5 inches or more in diameter which may be firmly rounded or loose and open at the top, depending on the quality of the form. The colors vary from white, ivory, or yellowish to rose, and they are usually spotted in varying degree. Most are attractive, some strikingly so, but there are a few nondescript sorts of indeterminate pink. A pure white-flowered form without markings is appealing and there is an attractive salmon-pink with each of the five flower lobes very heavily spotted in an identical pattern, which is a garden plant of great character and distinction. In a species so variable as this it is important to see the plants in bloom before they are bought or to obtain specimens propagated from a form known to be superior. Some forms have such small clusters of flowers as to be of little ornamental value. Because of its early flowering, *R. irroratum* should be given a spot offering some shelter from frosts, and shielded from the early sun on cold mornings. An eastern exposure is usually undesirable with species which flower early in the season because the sun shining on frozen flowers is ruinous, whereas they are often unharmed if they thaw slowly. This is one of the finest of Rhododendron species, lovely and free blooming everywhere it is seen. It can be distinguished from its allies by the flowers borne on glandular stalks about $\frac{3}{4}$ inch long with style and ovary densely glandular but not hairy. Botanical keys and descriptions note that the corolla shape is tubular-campanulate, but there are far more plants in cultivation now with bell-shaped flowers widely open and these are also the more attractive. The leaves, with pointed tips and lacking any indumentum beneath, are borne on distinctly grooved, glandular petioles. This species was discovered by Delavay in 1886, growing at 9,000 to 10,000 feet in Yunnan, where it has a wide distribution in Pine and Rhododendron forests. The name refers to the profuse spotting of the corollas in some forms. Freedom of Flowering: 1; Ease of Cultivation: 1; American Quality Rating: xx; British: ***; American Hardiness Rating: H-4; British: B; Truss Type: 3.

R. johnstoneanum (john-ston-ee-a′-num), **Watt.** MADDENII SERIES, CILIICALYX SUBSERIES

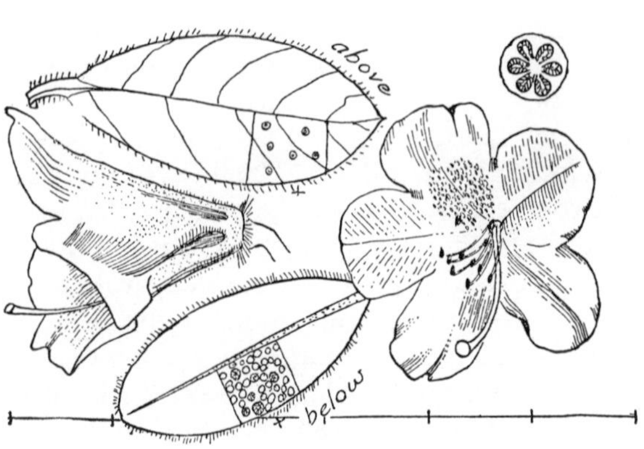

The species of the Maddenii series are not all known for their fine habit, but *R. johnstoneanum* is faultless as a densely foliaged shrub of spreading, rounded outline, often seen in gardens as a handsome mound about 6 feet high and 8 feet broad. Some less desirable forms are looser in growth, taller, and more erect in habit. In nature the species sometimes grows 15 feet tall. The hairy leaves are $1\frac{3}{4}$ inches to 4 inches long, $\frac{3}{4}$ to $1\frac{3}{4}$ inches wide, scaly on both surfaces. White or pale buff-yellow, funnel-shaped flowers with yellow throats spotted red appear in late April and early May, almost 3 inches across, intensely fragrant, and usually three or five in a loose cluster. This species is a good deal hardier than most of its relatives and in contrast to some of them it is attractive as an evergreen the year round. It comes to perfection in such mild climates as that of the San Francisco region, but it is still a charming garden subject in colder areas. It is also a fine greenhouse shrub. A very poor form with deeply cut lobes which give the flowers a ragged appearance should be avoided. A fine sort with double flowers resembling those of a Camellia is frequently available, one of the very few Rhododendrons with double flowers which are attractive. Charles Puddle, superintendent of the famed Bodnant Gardens in Wales, has told me that double flowers are produced on plants grown from seeds obtained by self-pollinating the ordinary single-flowered form of the species growing there. *R. johnstoneanum* can be identified by the flowers, three or more in a group, with ten stamens, having the lower two-thirds of the style scaly and the very short calyx densely fringed with long hairs. The broad, elliptic-obovate leaves with dense scales nearly contiguous beneath, are borne on bristly shoots. This species is native to Assam and Manipur at 6,000 to 11,000 feet elevation. It was named for the wife of the political agent in Manipur in 1882. Freedom of Flowering: 1; Ease of Cultivation: 1; American Quality Rating: xxx; British: ***; American Hardiness Rating: H-4; British: D; Truss Type: 12; A.M., 1934; var. *rubeotinctum,* A.M., 1941; double form, A.M., 1956.

R. keiskei (kis′-kee-i), **Miquel.** TRIFLORUM SERIES, TRIFLORUM SUBSERIES

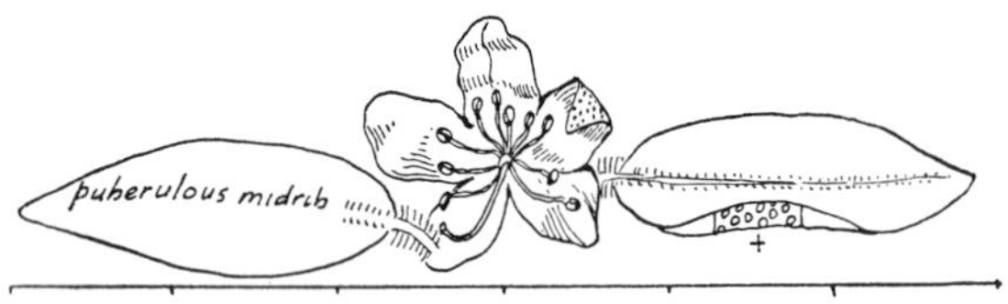

There are two forms of this popular species often seen in our gardens, one a dwarf which scarcely reaches $2\frac{1}{2}$ feet in twenty years and the other a more upright shrub of moderate growth about 8 feet tall. No doubt there are intermediates in cultivation too, since that is the case with so many other species where dwarf and tall forms are frequently and erroneously presumed to be distinct. The olive-green leaves of *R. keiskei* are $1\frac{1}{2}$ to $3\frac{1}{4}$ inches long, $\frac{1}{2}$ to $1\frac{1}{4}$ inches wide and scaly below. Two to six pale yellow flowers, broadly bell-shaped and about $1\frac{1}{2}$ inches in diameter, appear in loose clusters in April. Like so many Japanese Rhododendrons, this species is hardy and adaptable to the climate of the northeastern United States, where it should have a site which protects the early blossoms from frost as much as possible. There the tall form distributed by specialist-nurserymen is satisfactory as far north as New York City and it becomes increasingly interesting and beautiful as it approaches maturity, the only yellow-flowered Rhododendron species hardy in the Northeast. It is lighter and more graceful in texture than the familiar rotund garden hybrids with their large leaves. In the Rhododendron belt of the West Coast, and in the British Isles, the dwarf form is first choice, and it is a useful and carefree garden subject, fine for facing down larger shrubs, for low informal hedges, rock gardens and foundation plantings. Some forms of this species have flowers whose yellow shade is a good deal more showy than others which are not much more than an undistinguished cream color. All are deficient in the substance of their blossoms, which are so thin that they are rather short-lived, especially in warm weather. This is altogether better as a garden Rhododendron than *R. triflorum*, which has a similar floral effect. Among yellow-flowered species of the Triflorum group, it is identified by the leaves over $1\frac{1}{2}$ inches long with blunt, mucronate tips, a hairy midrib beneath, and scales which are about their own diameter apart. The leaf stalks on young shoots are clad with bristly hairs. The flowers in groups of two to six are scaly on the outside. *R. keiskei* is native from central Honshu south to Kyushu in Japan, on hillsides and in rocky valleys. It was introduced to cultivation in the West in 1908 and named for Ito Keisuke, a Japanese botanist. Freedom of Flowering: 1; Ease of Cultivation: 1; American Quality Rating: xxx; British: ***; American Hardiness Rating: H-2; British: A; Truss Type: 9; A.M., 1929.

R. keleticum (kel-ee′-tee-kum), **Balf. f. and Forrest.** SALUENENSE SERIES

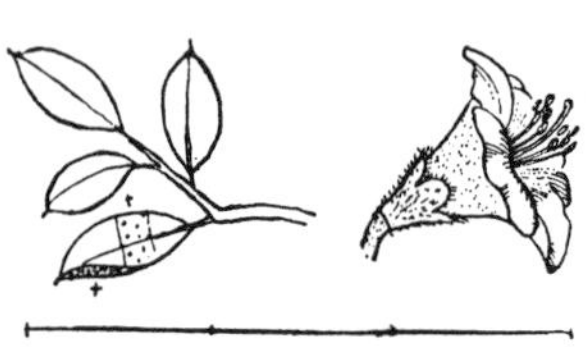

This diminutive shrub is most often seen as a rounded oval of dense, matted growth up to 12 inches high with aromatic leaves $\frac{1}{4}$ to $\frac{7}{8}$ inch long, $\frac{1}{8}$ to $\frac{3}{8}$ inch wide, shining green above, tan or brown below and densely scaly. Purplish-crimson flowers as much as $1\frac{5}{8}$ inches across with crimson flecks in the throat seem very large in relation to the size of leaf and stature of the plant when they appear from terminal buds singly, or as many as three, in early June. This is a delightful little Rhododendron for the rock garden and as a dooryard shrub, blooming late when color is especially valued. It is most easily distinguished from its allies by its semi-prostrate habit. The leaves are about twice as long as they are broad, generally not scaly above, but if scales are present they are one-half to six times their own diameter apart. The underleaf surface has so many scales that they overlap. The branchlets and petioles are devoid of bristles, or rarely with a very few.

This species is readily separated from *R. radicans*, its closest relative, because the latter is completely prostrate, with a horizontal creeping habit. *R. keleticum* comes from Tibet, Yunnan and Upper Burma where it grows in open fields, on exposed cliffs and screes. It was discovered by Forrest in 1919 and named to denote its charming character. Freedom of Flowering: 1; Ease of Cultivation: 1; American Quality Rating: xxx; British: ★★; American Hardiness Rating: H-2; British: A; Truss Type: 16; A.M., 1928.

R. kyawi (chaw′-ee), **Lace and W.W. Sm.** IRRORATUM SERIES, PARISHII SUBSERIES

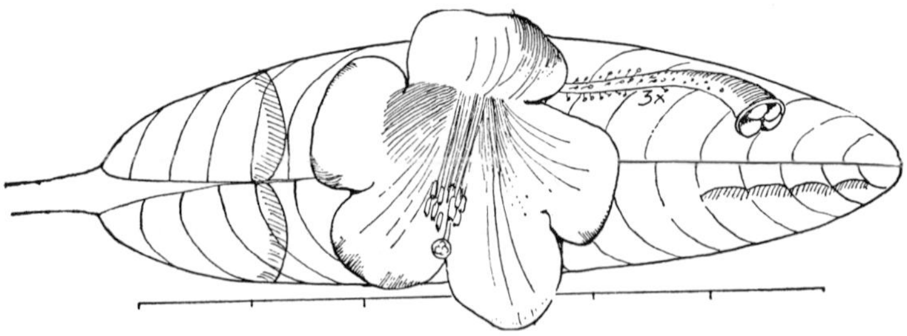

Good red-flowered Rhododendrons usher in the spring flowering season and here is one of equal distinction which marks its close in summer. With age it becomes a tall shrub 15 to 20 feet tall bearing leaves 6 to 12 inches long and 2 to 4 inches wide, with veins deeply indented, at first with hairs above and below which later fall away leaving the upper surface bright green and the under-surface an odd, burnished, pale green shade. The long, bell-shaped flowers twelve to sixteen to a loose, lax truss are 3 inches across, bright crimson-scarlet with conspicuous darker nectar pouches at the base. They appear in July at a season when they are doubly appreciated, and their size and brilliance offer midsummer color which is dramatically effective. The species is reputed to dislike transplanting in large sizes. This is a handsome foliage plant at any season and a first-class Rhododendron in favored Atlantic coastal gardens in Great Britain and in the benign California climate where it is hardy. Farrer's form is the finest. *R. kyawi* can be recognized by the leaves oblong to oval, with rounded tips, two to four times longer than wide, clad beneath with bristly glands. The flower stalks, about 1¼ inches long, are also setose-glandular. The ovary and crimson style are both glandular and softly hairy, and the fugitive indumentum is always present on the young leaves, disappearing as they mature. This Rhododendron was first discovered in 1912 by a Burmese collector, Maung Kyaw, for whom it was named. It is found in sheltered ravines at 6,000 to 9,000 feet in northeastern Upper Burma, which indicates the shade and shelter from winds it appreciates in cultivation. Protection from early fall frosts should be considered in choosing a planting site because it starts into growth late in the season. Freedom of Flowering: 2; Ease of Cultivation: 2; American Quality Rating: xxxx; British: ★★★★; American Hardiness Rating: H-6; British: E; Truss Type: 7.

R. lacteum (lak′-tee-um), **Franch.** LACTEUM SERIES

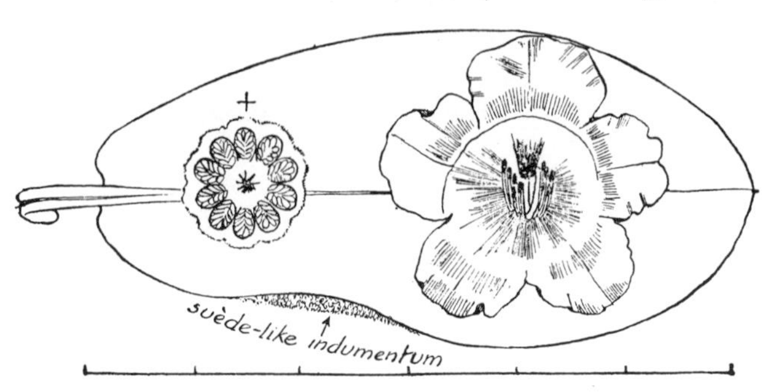

This species, famous for having the finest yellow flowers in the genus, is at the same time infamous for its temperamental disposition. In bloom it is certainly one of the most beautiful and spectacular of all Rhododendrons. Out of bloom its handsome leaves are an asset, up to 7¼ inches long and 4 inches broad. They are strongly decorative in character with a fawn-colored felty indumentum underneath, but frequently they are concentrated in terminal rosettes at the ends of the branches, leaving the stout limbs below unclothed. This may well be because plants in cultivation are seldom growing luxuriantly under the conditions which the species finds fully congenial. *R. lacteum* has a reputed height ultimately of 30 feet, but it rarely or never attains the age necessary to reach such a stature in cultivation. It is usually seen as a coarsely branched, rather stiff shrub up to 10 feet tall in older specimens, wider than high. The magnificent, clear daffodil-yellow flowers which appear in April are about $2\frac{5}{8}$ inches across, grouped into rounded, dome-shaped trusses 6 to 8 inches in diameter. The clusters vary, some containing about thirteen florets and needing perhaps one or two more to provide a perfect rounded outline, whereas other plants may produce twenty-five or more flowers to a truss almost too closely packed into a globular shape. There is a lot of difference in the intensity and attractiveness of the color and in how freely the blossoms are borne in the various forms. Some creamy-white shades are seen occasionally. The best that I have seen is in Windsor Great Park. It came originally from Werrington. The bell-shaped flowers were accented by a small red blotch deep in the throat and the huge deep yellow globes shone forth as in a mammoth illuminated candelabrum. There is also a fine form with flowers of exceptional color saturation in the collection of Mr and Mrs Del James in Oregon. Seeds of the species germinate and grow well for a year or two. The indumentum appears in the third or fourth year, at which time scions from seedlings with heavy, dark green foliage should be grafted on *R. ponticum*, this being one of the rare cases of a Rhododendron which is better grafted than growing on its own roots. The *ponticum* understock provides a sturdy, vigorous root system which makes the plants longer lived and easier pleased. *R. lacteum*, because it is hard to grow, has acquired a reputation for being tender whereas all it needs is shelter to demonstrate its cold resistance. Some specialists place perhaps half a dozen plants in various garden sites with the thought that two or three will find their situations congenial. Hot, sunny spots are never suitable. This species is distinct from its near relatives on the basis of its broad, oval to elliptical leaves with continuous indumentum composed of radiate hairs; and its yellow flowers in compact trusses, unspotted on the corolla lobes and rounded at the base, with nine- or ten-celled ovary and small stigma. It was first discovered by Delavay in 1884 but did not find its way into cultivation until Forrest introduced it in 1910. It is native to the Rhododendron forests at 12,000 feet in Yunnan. The name means 'milky', an allusion to the color of the flowers of the forms first found. Freedom of Flowering: 2; Ease of Cultivation: 3; American Ratings: None yet assigned; British Quality Rating ****; British Hardiness Rating: C; Truss Type: 3; F.C.C., 1926.

R. lepidostylum (lep-id-o-sti′-lum), **Balf. f. and Forrest.** TRICHOCLADUM SERIES

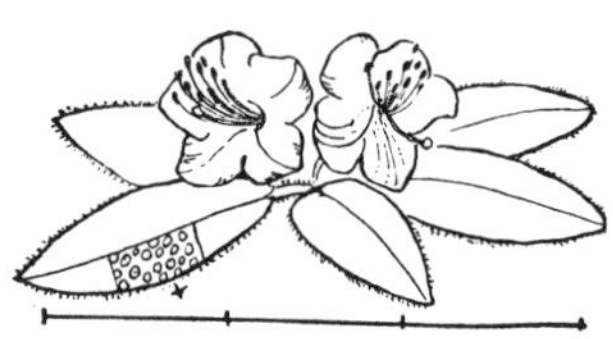

Some Rhododendrons are dramatically effective as foliage plants and this is one of them, a semi-deciduous little species which leafs out in the spring into a striking soft blue-green mound of impeccably regular outline. Descriptions ascribe a mature height of 1 foot to this Rhododendron, but I have seen it several times at least 30 inches tall and 4 to 5 feet broad. The thin leaves about $1\frac{1}{2}$ inches long and $\frac{2}{3}$ inch broad, with their icy blue bloom, are scaly below and somewhat furry in appearance from a fringe of fine white hairs encircling their margins. Flat, pale yellow flowers about 1 inch across appear in pairs in late May and early June. This unusual Rhododendron is reminiscent of an Azalea with brilliant leaves and the series of which it is a member is somewhat intermediate between a 'true' Rhododendron and that group. The selection offered in commerce as Rock's form is reputed to be especially attractive in foliage color. This and *R. campanulatum* var. *aeruginosum* undoubtedly have the bluest foliage in the genus for gardeners who are fond of such exotic color notes in the landscape. The flowers, too, are delicately pretty but not showy. *R. lepidostylum* is easily distinguished from its allies because both the ovary and style are scaly, and the ovary is also clad with bristles. It is a native of China's Yunnan province at 11,000 to 11,500 feet elevation where it grows on the exposed ledges of cliffs. The name refers to the scaly style. Freedom of Flowering: 2+; Ease of Cultivation: 1; American Ratings: None yet assigned; British Quality Rating: ★★; British Hardiness Rating: B; Truss Type: 16.

R. leucaspis (lew-kas′-pis), **Tagg.** BOOTHII SERIES, MEGERATUM SUBSERIES

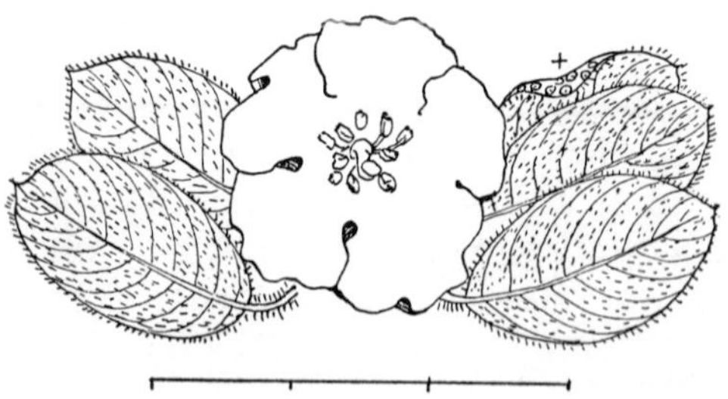

A 2-foot mound-like undershrub of attractive and distinctive character, this useful garden subject has dark green, hairy leaves from $1\frac{1}{4}$ to $2\frac{1}{2}$ inches long, $\frac{5}{8}$ to $1\frac{1}{4}$ inches wide. The tan filaments and brown anthers contrast conspicuously with the twin 2-inch flat white flowers borne on the ends of the branches in February and March in mild climates and sometimes in April. A good, dwarf ornamental, it is adaptable from San Francisco northward on the Pacific Coast, but it requires a carefully sheltered site when grown away from the Atlantic maritime climate of the British Isles. It flowers in three years from seed, but there is a fine F.C.C. form, propagated vegetatively, which is much more handsome than random seedlings. There is also a dwarf form which makes a spreading mat not more than 6 inches tall. This species is not likely to be confused with its relatives because most of them have yellow flowers, but botanically it is distinct from them in having in combination with white blossoms, only one or two (rarely three) of them from a terminal bud; a short, thick, sharply bent style; and flower stalks scaly but not bristly. Kingdon-Ward found the species at 8,000 to 10,000 feet in Tibet in 1924 and it was named *leucaspis* because of the resemblance of the flowers to a white shield. Freedom of Flowering: 1; Ease of Cultivation: 1; American Quality Rating: xxxx; British: ★★★★; American Hardiness Rating: H-4; British: C; Truss Type: 16; A.M., 1929; F.C.C., 1944.

R. lindleyi (lind′-lee-i), **T. Moore.** MADDENII SERIES, MEGACALYX SUBSERIES

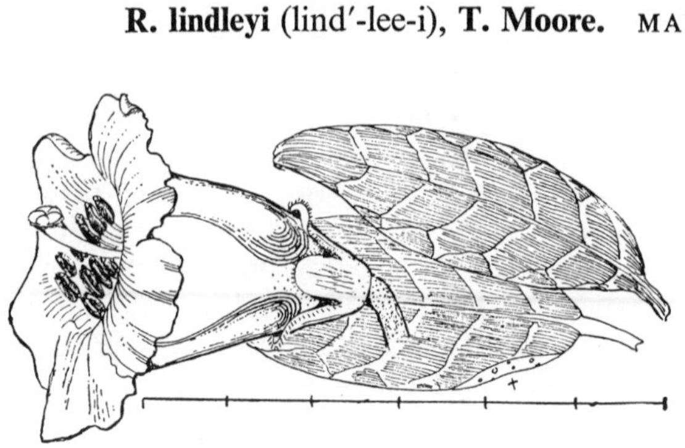

Here is a species which is usually found in the wild as an epiphyte perched high in the green canopy of the tree-tops in the forest of its homeland. In cultivation it keeps the growth habit which adapts it to aerial life, becoming a thin, lax shrub about 10 feet in height. Occasionally it is half again as tall. The leaves are $2\frac{1}{2}$ to 6 inches long, $\frac{3}{4}$ to $2\frac{1}{4}$ inches wide, scaly, prominently veined and somewhat blue-green underneath. This species is renowned for its magnificent funnel-shaped flowers, 4 inches wide and almost as long, borne in single-tiered, outward facing clusters of four to seven in late April and early May. They are white, sometimes faintly tinted rose and occasionally suffused yellow deep in the throat, with a pervading spicy fragrance. *R. lindleyi* is suitable only for the mildest climates, such as that of San Francisco, but there it becomes a thing of splendor for the garden in its blooming season. In Great Britain it requires a sheltered site even in the most favored gardens of the South and West, and even so the foliage burns at Trengwainton, in Cornwall. Several plants can be placed close together to minimize their lanky limbs or a single specimen can be situated to climb through and over more densely foliaged plants to flaunt its large scented blossoms. The species often flourishes in this manner in gardens where it languishes in an unshared growing site. This is a good greenhouse shrub in colder climates. *R. lindleyi* is often confused with *R. dalhousiae* and even its discoverer, J. D. Hooker, failed to distinguish between the two when he first found the former in 1848. They are rather easily separable, however, because *dalhousiae* has a style scaly two-thirds of its length, calyx lobes devoid of hairs, downy pedicels and young shoots bristly as well as scaly. *R. lindleyi* is characterized by a large calyx, almost $\frac{2}{3}$ inch long, densely fringed with hairs and with a few scales at the base; flower stalks scaly but devoid of hairs; corolla and style each scaly at the base only; and a 2-inch seed capsule without projecting longitudinal ridges. There are ten stamens. This species comes from 6,000 to 10,000 feet in Sikkim, Bhutan, and Manipur. It was named for Dr John Lindley, a well-known botanist in the first half of the nineteenth century. Freedom of Flowering: 1; Ease of Cultivation: 1; American Quality Rating: xxxx; British: ****; American Hardiness Rating: H-6; British: E; Truss Type: 12; A.M., 1935; F.C.C., 1937.

R. litiense (li-tee-en′-see), **Balf. f. and Forrest.** THOMSONII SERIES, SOULIEI SUBSERIES

This is one of the good yellow-flowered Rhododendrons, usually seen as an upright evergreen shrub about 6 feet tall in older specimens, but quite capable in some forms of eventually reaching almost twice that stature under good cultivation. The oblong leaves with whitish under-surfaces range in size from $1\frac{1}{2}$ to 4 inches long, and $\frac{3}{4}$ to $1\frac{3}{4}$ inches wide. When first mature they have a strongly decorative blue haze overlay. There are usually about six light yellow, bowl-shaped flowers $1\frac{3}{4}$ inches across in a lax umbel appearing in May. *R. litiense* is not quite so handsome as the superb *R. wardii*, ordinarily, though there are intermediate forms in which the two species merge. As it is usually seen, it is not so yellow and the flowers are smaller and less fully expanded. It differs too in having leaves usually smaller, which are both oblong and glaucous underneath. The style glandular to the tip distinguishes it from the yellow-flowered species of the Campylocarpum subseries. *R. litiense* comes from Yunnan province of southwest China where it grows in shady forests at an altitude of 9,000 to 13,000 feet. Its name means 'from the Li-ti-ping'. There is an Award of Merit form which is finer than the usual average of seedlings. Freedom of Flowering: 2; Ease of Cultivation: 2; American Quality Rating: xxx; British: ***; American Hardiness Rating: H-4; British: B; Truss Type: 8; A.M., 1931; F.C.C., 1953.

R. longesquamatum (long-es-kwa-ma′-tum), **Schneider.** BARBATUM SERIES, MACULIFERUM SUBSERIES

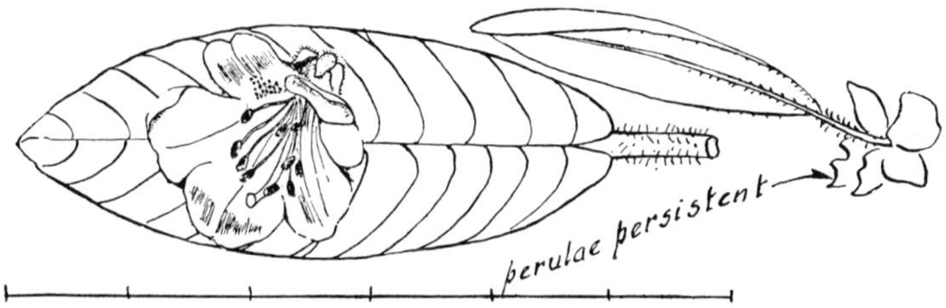

Here is a species much hardier than is generally realized and almost miraculously hardy for a Rhododendron in the Barbatum group. It is a stout, rotund shrub with heavy branches and thick, persistent leaves from 2½ to 5 inches long or more, ¾ to 1¾ inches wide, usually seen at the larger dimensions. In its ultimate height of 8 feet to possibly 10 feet it gives an appearance of shaggy strength in the landscape and bears in May attractive 2-inch bell-shaped pink flowers, with throats spotted and blotched a rich crimson. There are ten to about twelve of the openly bell-like flowers in a terminal truss. Joseph Gable at Stewartstown, Pennsylvania, has isolated plants from collectors' seeds which are hardy to New York City and doubtless farther north in warm sites. A dominant plant in the garden with distinctive flowers and habit of growth, this species is a rare and beautiful addition to the limited list of exotic Rhododendrons which are hardy in the Northeast. It has a large calyx for the subseries, about ½ inch long, which is both hairy and glandular. The young shoots and leaf petioles are densely clad with rough, bushy, branched hairs, tan later turning rusty brown. The hairs are not gland-tipped. The leaf under-surface is pale green, smooth, and somewhat glossy, but with hairy midrib, in contrast to the species of the other subseries which have indumenta ranging from dispersed and patch-like to heavy, or with scattered coarse glandular hairs. The furry coating of the young shoots is distinctive. *R. longesquamatum* was introduced by Wilson in 1904 from 10,000 to 12,000 feet in Szechuan province of China, where it grows in woodlands. Its name means 'with long scales', not an allusion to any lepidote characteristic. Freedom of Flowering: 2+; Ease of Cultivation: 2+; American Quality Rating: xx; British: none; American Hardiness Rating: H-3 (Author's dissent: H-2); British: B; Truss Type: 7.

R. lutescens (loo-tes′-sens), **Franch.** TRIFLORUM SERIES, TRIFLORUM SUBSERIES

An early-flowering Rhododendron, in the literature ascribed a height of 7 feet but actually reaching 15 feet, *R. lutescens* is a delight in its season. The new growth is an attractive, bronzy-red color, the leaves maturing to dark green, in size ranging from 1½ to 4 inches long, ½ to 1 inch wide. The foliage gives another show of good color in the fall. Pale yellow, widely funnel-shaped flowers, 1 to 1½ inches across, spotted light green, are produced from several buds at the ends of the branches, sometimes singly but often totalling seven to nine in a loose cluster. This graceful species with its willow-like leaves and light landscape effect makes an excellent foil for the early red-flowering, large-leaved Rhododendrons such as *RR. arboreum, thomsonii, hookeri* and their hybrids. It can also be clipped to make a very attractive hedge with a fair show of flowers. Its flowering season ranges from late February well into April, varying considerably with the season from year to year, and a site with some shelter from frost is highly desirable. The F.C.C. form from Exbury is especially fine but somewhat less hardy than the average. Unselected seedlings often tend to have flowers of a nondescript creamy yellow which blend with the olive-green foliage in such a manner that there is not enough contrast between the two for an effective display. Among other species with yellow flowers in the Triflorum series, it is distinct in possessing a corolla tube softly pubescent outside on the upper part; a very short calyx, less than $\frac{3}{32}$ inch long; and leaves with scales on the lower surface two or three times their own diameter apart, borne on stalks devoid of hairs along their margins. This is a common Rhododendron in Yunnan and in western Szechuan provinces of China, where it grows at elevations up to 9,000 feet in thickets and along exposed edges of forests. It has been in cultivation only since Wilson introduced it in 1904, long after it was first found in the wild by the Abbé David. The name refers to its flowers 'becoming yellow'. Freedom of Flowering: 1; Ease of Cultivation: 1; American Quality Rating: xxx; British: ****; American Hardiness Rating: H-4; British: B; Truss Type: 9; F.C.C., 1938; 'Bagshot Sands', A.M., 1953.

R. macabeanum (mk-kab′-a′-num), **Watt MS.** GRANDE SERIES

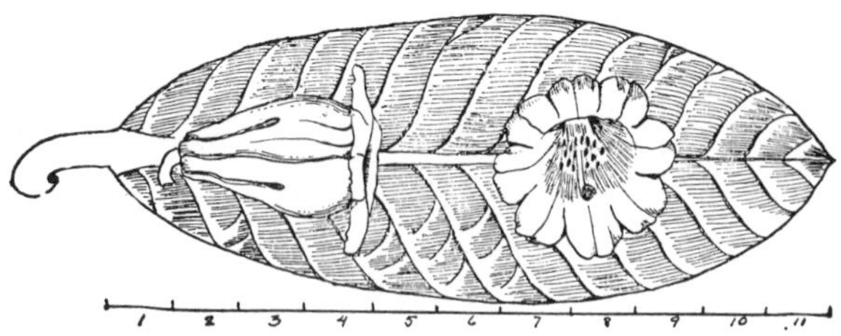

In mild climates this species is almost unique for the admiration and attention it receives from specialists. Flowers of the best forms are featured at Rhododendron shows and always become a center of public comment for their remarkable size and color. Yet this is a rare Rhododendron. Though it is the hardiest of the Grande series, it survives in Oregon and Washington by a precariously narrow margin and its special need of shelter precludes wide cultivation despite its universal appeal. Its cold resistance seems to be greater under British growing conditions. *R. macabeanum* is a small tree of stately bearing, usually seen at a height of 15 or 20 feet but apparently capable of much greater height, from its stature in the wild. In colder, drier regions close to the limit of its adaptability it is a large, spreading shrub. The species is frequently better clothed with foliage than many of its relatives, the large handsome leaves hanging in drooping collars from the ends of heavy, angular branches. They are dark, glossy green, somewhat wrinkled by the veining, about 1 foot long and up to 7 inches wide, with conspicuous midribs above and a white to light gray woolly indumentum beneath. Their huge size and leathery texture in combination with the thick branches gives the tree a massive and majestic appearance. A silvery fur coats the new shoots and their brilliant scarlet bud scales are vividly decorative when growth begins in the spring. The flowers come early, in March and the first part of April, in great yellow globes 8 or 9 inches in diameter composed of about twenty-five eight-lobed florets each a little more than 2 inches across. In the best forms the color is soft but extremely effective and peculiarly luminous, often accented by a red stigma in the center of each blossom. This is among the most free-blooming of the large-leaved Rhododendrons and it makes a fine spring spectacle when it lights up with its immense, shining heads of yellow flowers at so bleak a season. A phenomenally fine form grows at Trengwainton, in Cornwall. There are, of course, inferior forms somewhat pallid in color, and others with a purple blotch in the heart of the flower so conspicuous as to detract from its beauty, but I believe the clear, vibrant yellow *macabeanum* in its best expressions is among the most impressive of all Rhododendrons. Few equal and none excel the effectiveness of this tree in its combination of lovely flowers and splendid foliage. Because it blooms so early, it should have a sheltered site and not one facing eastward where the blossoms are exposed to morning sun in frosty weather. Like all large-leaved species, it must be shielded from wind and excessive exposure, and it produces its flowers so prodigiously that it needs fertilizing to maintain the fine appearance which comes with vigorous growth. *R. macabeanum* is characterized by bell-shaped flowers pouched at the base, which have a tomentose ovary. The unusual blossom conformation is shown in the accompanying illustration. The leaves with woolly indumentum compact, but not plastered, have cylindric petioles, not flattened, about 1 inch long where they are borne just below the flower trusses. There are sixteen stamens. This species is native to Manipur where it was found in the Naga Hills and named for Mr McCabe, the deputy commissioner there. Freedom of Flowering: 2+; Ease of Cultivation: 2; American Quality Rating: xxxx; British: ****; American Hardiness Rating: H-4; British: B; Truss Type: 6; F.C.C., 1935.

R. macrophyllum (mak-ro-fil′-um), **G. Don.** PONTICUM SERIES, PONTICUM SUBSERIES

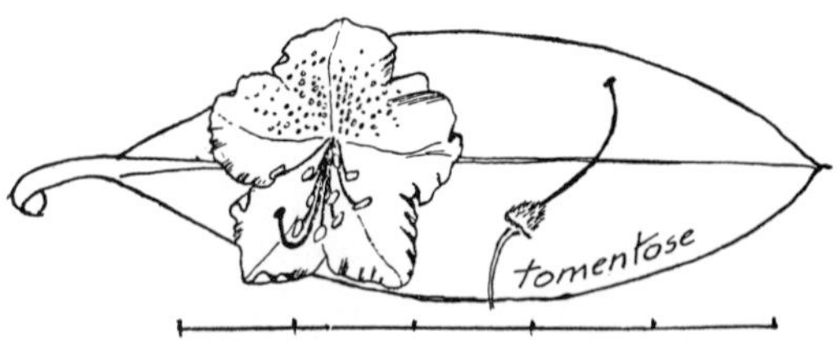

This is the West Coast native formerly called *R. californicum,* a stout shrub of erect growth to 12 feet, sometimes much more. The dark green leaves are 3 to 6 inches long, 1¼ to 2¾ inches broad, amply borne to give an attractive appearance at all seasons. The flowers come in May, about 2¼ inches across, broadly bell-shaped, about twenty in a domelike truss which is somewhat less compact and tidy than the clusters of its eastern relative, *R. catawbiense.* In color they vary from rosy purple through pink shades to white, with reddish-brown spots on the upper lobes, and the margins of the blossoms are usually crimped. This is a fine Rhododendron for woodland planting and distant effects in mild climates, handsome in leaf and effective in flower, though perhaps not suited for an intimate garden site in a climate where the world's finest species grow so well. To eyes unprejudiced by familiarity it seems always to present a pleasing appearance in cultivation wherever gardeners have been sufficiently acute to appreciate its virtues as a flowering evergreen massed in a naturalistic setting. Its habit, foliage and bearing are all exceptionally attractive, often exceeding those of more famous Asian species. Growers who do not care for the usual flower color of this Rhododendron with its admixture of blue in varying degree, should soon be able to buy the form with lovely white flowers, which, contrary to previously published descriptions, are as large as those of the type, though often a little later in their appearance. *R. macrophyllum* is the western woodland representative of *R. catawbiense* but it is not hardy in the colder parts of the northeastern United States and seems susceptible to blight from Philadelphia southward. It is easily distinguished from the eastern species by the leaf, broadest above the middle and tapered toward the base, in contrast to the rounded base of the leaf of the Catawba Rhododendron, which is widest at the middle. The flower stalks are usually, but not always, glabrous; the blossoms are normally deeper in color; and the non-glandular calyx lobes are shorter, less pointed, and not so triangular in shape as those of *R. catawbiense.* It lacks the bracts like miniature leaves which encircle the floral and foliage buds of the other American native of the Ponticum series, *R. maximum.* The ovary is densely tomentose in contrast to the glabrous ovary of *R. ponticum.* In written accounts, this species was mentioned in 1792 by Menzies in an entry in his *Journal of Vancouver's Voyage.* G. Don published in 1834 the first description, written by his brother David, from dried specimens, which was probably erroneous in calling the flowers white, since that form is rare. British records credit to W. Lobb its introduction into cultivation there in 1850. In 1855 Hooker, who had named and described many of the plants brought back from the Vancouver expedition, published an account of this Rhododendron under the designation *californicum*, and this name has been in common use for a century. However, Leonard Frisbie, on behalf of the Washington Rhododendron Society of which he is President, has pressed an investigation which has confirmed that the correct name of this Rhododendron must be *macrophyllum* under the rules of nomenclature. It occurs in nature at about 1,500 feet elevation from Vancouver Island and southern British Columbia southward in disjunct distribution along the coast of Washington and Oregon, with an outlying center at Mt Hood, into California as far as Monterey County. The name is an allusion to the size of the leaves which seemed large to Don in the days before the Asian species had been introduced. Freedom of Flowering: 1; Ease of Cultivation: 1; American Quality Rating: x; British: **; American Hardiness Rating: H-2; British: A; Truss Type: 1.

R. maddeni (mad′-den-i), **Hook. f.** MADDENII SERIES, MADDENII SUBSERIES

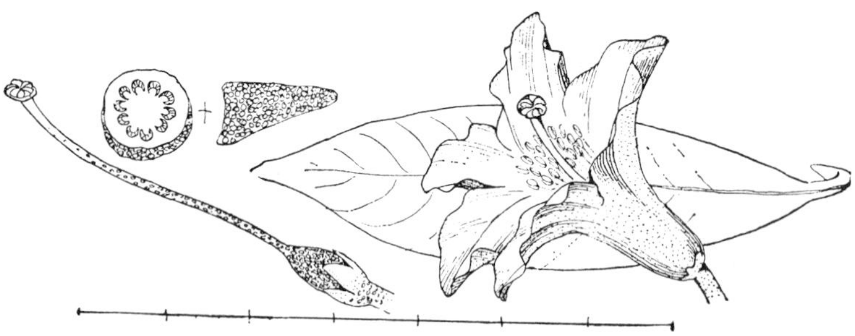

This representative Rhododendron of a series distinguished for its lovely flowers has been in cultivation for over a century now and its good qualities are more appreciated than ever in the mild climates where it is at home. It is a robust shrub of open habit growing to a height of 9 feet. Unlike some of its relatives, it is easily cultivated and the flourishing plants are well-clothed with foliage. The dull green leaves are 3 to 6 inches long, 1 to $2\frac{3}{4}$ wide, glaucous beneath but almost completely covered with reddish-brown scales. The 4-inch white flowers, flushed rose on the outside and often suffused yellow, come in June and extend into July. They are strongly fragrant, usually three or four carried firmly in an outward-facing, terminal cluster. This is a tractable Rhododendron, attractive the four seasons through, in a fine group which is not particularly noted for either of those virtues. The white scented blossoms in summer provide a note of cool distinction when they are most appreciated. *R. maddenii* does well in climates similar to that of San Francisco, in Atlantic coastal gardens of the British Isles, and in greenhouses. It is distinguished by its twenty glabrous stamens; the calyx with five unequal lobes, usually $\frac{3}{16}$ inch long but rarely as much as $\frac{5}{8}$ inch to the tips of the lobes; the ten-celled ovary; and the leaves so densely clad beneath with scales that they overlap. *R. maddenii* grows in nature at 5,000 to 9,000 feet in Sikkim and Bhutan. It was discovered and introduced about 1849 by the younger Hooker and named for Lt.-Col Madden, a member of the Bengal Civil Service at that time. Freedom of Flowering: 2+; Ease of Cultivation: 1; American Quality Rating: xxx; British: ***; American Hardiness Rating: H-6; British: E; Truss Type: 12; A.M., 1938.

R. makinoi (mak′-in-oy), **Tagg.** PONTICUM SERIES, CAUCASICUM SUBSERIES

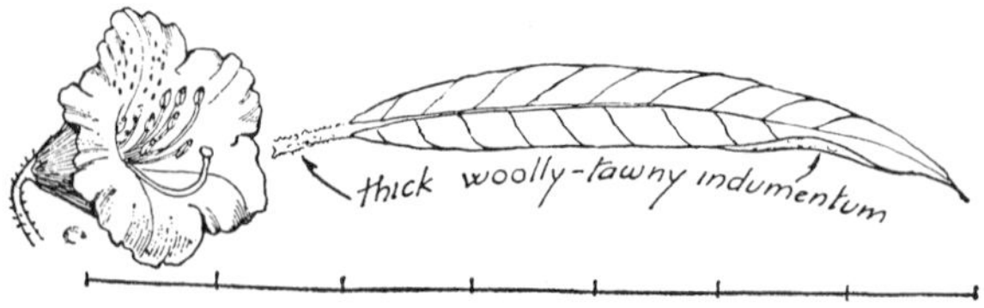

In appearance this is one of the most exotic Rhododendrons in the genus. Old specimens in cultivation are 5 or 6 feet tall and 6 feet or a little more in width, densely clothed with foliage so narrow that it gives a unique, feathery

appearance to the plants, Japanese in ornamental effect. The distinctive leaves with down-curved margins are $2\frac{3}{4}$ to $6\frac{3}{4}$ inches long, only $\frac{3}{16}$ to $\frac{3}{4}$ inch wide, bright green above and coated beneath with a woolly tan indumentum. Not only are the margins of the ribbon-like leaves rolled under, but the entire leaf describes a downward curve toward the tip, giving it the shape of a sickle. This species is usually heavily indumented, a greyish felty covering extending to the stems, leaf stalks, and floral buds. The new shoots are attractively coated with the soft silvery down, which eventually falls away from the upper surface of the roughened leaves. The flowers appear in late May and early June, about 2 inches in diameter, delightful clear shades ranging from soft rose through delicate pinks to blush white, sometimes minutely spotted but always remarkable for the purity and depth of their coloring. The trusses are firmly filled and mound-shaped, not containing six flowers as stated in botanical references, but averaging double that number and sometimes containing up to thirty florets. This is a slow-growing shrub which is interesting and conspicuous in the landscape for its strikingly unusual foliage. The new growth does not appear on the plants until late summer. *R. makinoi* is fully hardy as far north as New York City and in warm gardens at Boston. It can be considered a dwarf shrub of convenient and useful dimensions, requiring a great many years to reach its mature height of 5 feet. Like other Japanese species, it is at home in the climate of the northeastern United States, much more so than most Rhododendrons from the Asian mainland. With its dense, compact growth and unique foliage, it is an exotic acquisition for any garden. This species is so distinctive that it is unlikely to be confused with any other. Some of the narrow-leaved forms of *R. roxieanum*, of the Taliense series, may at first glance appear somewhat similar but their burnished leaves, less recurved, their heavier growth habit and thicker branches, their minute calyx and earlier flowers, usually heavily blotched or spotted crimson, distinguish them from *R. makinoi*. Leaves of some forms of *R. degronianum* approach those of *R. makinoi* but I have never observed any which matched the extreme linear narrowness of this species. In any case, *R. makinoi* is distinct in having a much larger calyx, about $\frac{1}{4}$ inch long, in blooming several weeks later, and in making its new growth late in the summer. This species grows only in a limited district in the mountains of northern Mikawa and Totomi provinces of central Honshu in Japan. It was in cultivation for many years as a narrow-leaved form of *R. degronianum* before Tagg gave it specific status and named it for T. Makino, the Japanese botanist who first described it. Freedom of Flowering: 2; Ease of Cultivation: 1; American Quality Rating: xx; British: **; American Hardiness Rating: H-3 (Author's dissent: H-2); British: B; Truss Type: 3.

R. maximum (max′-ee-mum), **Linn.** PONTICUM SERIES, PONTICUM SUBSERIES

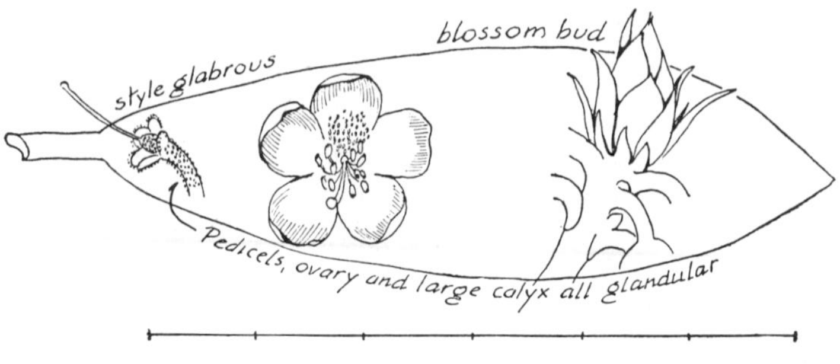

This is such a familiar feature of the native landscape that it is undoubtedly the best known, if not the most popular, of all the Rhododendrons in the eastern United States. In the extreme northern limit of its Canadian range it is only 4 feet tall at maturity, grows very slowly, and has rather small leaves. Traveling southward, it becomes increasingly luxuriant in its growth until, at Highlands, North Carolina, it seems to reach a peak of perfect growing conditions which send the plants quickly soaring skyward to the dimensions of large-leaved trees as much as 40 feet tall. When it is brought into cultivation the gardener must plan on having eventually a very large shrub with a height of 12 or 15 feet, at least. The leaves are dark green, 4 to 12 inches long, 1½ to 3 inches broad, usually glabrous beneath but not always so. Botanical reference works invariably describe this species of the Ponticum subseries as possessing leaves entirely glabrous at maturity. This is a mistake. Forms with a conspicuous, compact, plastered indumentum are fairly common, the hairy coating dense enough to give the under-surface of 2-year-old leaves a coppery color with a metallic sheen. The dark sheath can be rubbed away with the fingers. Under the microscope the hairs are shortly and intricately branched, quite unlike the long, dendroid hairs of the Japanese species of the *degronianum* group in this series. An interesting variety* of this species (var. *leachii*, described by Harkness) has been found by collectors in Greenbrier County, West Virginia. It has leaves with deeply waved margins and downcurved tips, their curly, irregular character caused by asymmetrical development when the new growth is produced. The leaves are a good deal smaller than those characteristic of *maximum* and are quite different in outline, with a cordate base and broader, obtuse apex. The floral bud is distinctive, being globular instead of conic and it lacks any acuminate tip. This variety has been propagated from seeds to become sparingly distributed among connoisseurs. Its unique appearance and restrained growth, with a mature height possibly one-fourth that of the familiar *maximum*, strike an interesting note in the garden. *R. maximum* produces flowers ordinarily pink to white, with a constellation of yellow spots on the upper lobe, in early July, and its late blooming season is one of its principal virtues. Some plants can be found in blossom even at the end of July when any flowering shrub, and particularly an evergreen, is a valuable garden asset. The flowers are about 1½ inches across, about twenty or sometimes up to thirty in a compact, firm truss which varies from round to a taller, more conical shape. Pure white blossoms are fairly common in the wild and flowers uniformly pink are often seen instead of the typical pink-margined blossoms with centers almost white. I have examined in the North Carolina wilderness a colony of extraordinary plants which were permeated in all their parts with red pigment to the extent that even the new leaves, viewed against the light, showed a bold red blotch in the center. They bore vinous red flowers. In 1953 a form with extraordinarily large white blooms was located in North Carolina by Dr W. N. Fortescue, an amateur enthusiast. Unfortunately, *R. maximum* blooms after the new growth has developed and although the flowers are not concealed, they are less effectively displayed, and this must be counted against it as an ornamental. The 3½-inch trusses seem somewhat small compared with those of the earlier blooming Catawba Rhododendron, and it does not blossom so freely. Still, it is invaluable as a woodland shrub or for tall evergreen backgrounds, particularly for large gardens, parks and estates. Its texture is much too coarse and its stature entirely too big for home foundation planting, yet uncounted thousands of plants are so misused every year, often because the unwary gardener confuses this gross, late-blooming species with the smaller, earlier and more colorful *R. catawbiense* or its hybrids. *R. maximum* is often called the Rosebay Rhododendron. Its hardiness is ironclad, but actually it is a little more sensitive to some conditions of winter cold than is the Catawba Rhododendron. On just one occasion floral buds of the northern native were ruined in my 25° F.-below-zero climate in the course of a winter which did not affect the buds of *R. catawbiense*. The Rosebay Rhododendron has only a limited use in the landscape, where it is out of scale in its texture and large dimensions for most gardens. In cold weather its large leaves curl so conspicuously as to nullify its virtues as an evergreen and reveal a framework of bare branches which are none too attractive at close quarters. The shade and shelter from winds which it demands for best appearance are missing from the average

* *Rhododendron maximum* var. *leachii*, Harkness var. nov. A typo recedit foliis brevioribus et cum basi truncatis vel leviter cordatis, margine leviter undulati; gemmae floriferae ovidea; habitu breviore. Herbarium specimens have been supplied to various herbaria, the type being in the Highland Park Herbarium at Rochester, N.Y.

garden more often than not. Collected specimens should be cut back and re-grown in a nursery before being planted in the garden. This species is most easily identified by the sparse tufts of bracts resembling miniature leaves which encircle the terminal growth and floral buds. The leaves, larger than those of any other native Rhododendron, are broadest beyond the middle and usually taper to the stalk at the base, whereas the Catawba Rhododendron has a rounded base on a leaf broadest at the middle. The viscid pedicels, large calyx about $\frac{3}{16}$ inch long, and ovary are all densely clad with short-stalked glands. There are eight to twelve stamens. *R. maximum* occurs in nature from Ontario, Quebec and Nova Scotia southward through New England and thence through New York and Pennsylvania along the Appalachian Mountains to Georgia. Along the East Coast it approaches sea level. It is the dominant shrub of the uplands in some central and southern areas of its distribution, creating impenetrable thickets in the mountain wilderness which are beloved by deer and despised by hunters. Always it seeks protection, growing in woodlands, on northern slopes and shady mountainsides, in sheltered valleys along streams and even in the few inches which are well-drained on top of bogs. It was introduced into cultivation in 1736 and given the name referring to its large size. Freedom of Flowering: 2; Ease of Cultivation: 1; American Quality Rating: x; British: none; American Hardiness Rating: H-1; British: A; Truss Type: 1.

R. meddianum (med-dee-a′-num), **G. Forrest.** THOMSONII SERIES, THOMSONII SUBSERIES

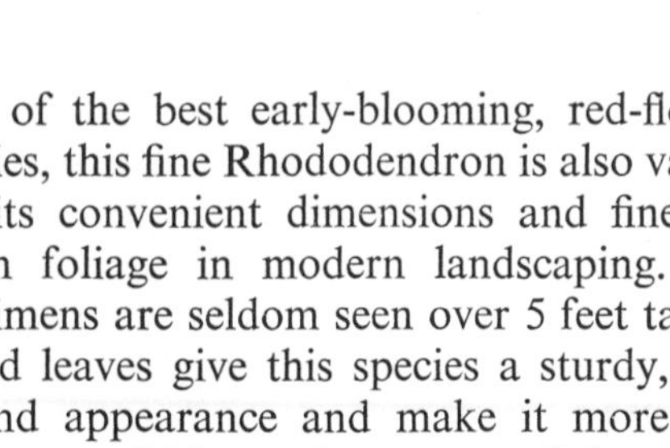

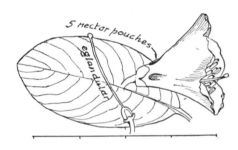

One of the best early-blooming, red-flowered species, this fine Rhododendron is also valuable for its convenient dimensions and fine, dark green foliage in modern landscaping. Older specimens are seldom seen over 5 feet tall. The broad leaves give this species a sturdy, rather rotund appearance and make it more handsome out of bloom than some of the narrow-leaved species with red flowers blooming at the same time. The leaf size is extremely variable, however, ranging from a length of $3\frac{1}{4}$ to 7 inches and a width of $1\frac{1}{4}$ to $3\frac{1}{4}$ inches. The blossoms are traditionally described as scarlet but actually they vary through rather soft shades of orange-red to cerise. They are about $2\frac{1}{2}$ inches across, about eight to a flat-topped terminal cluster, appearing in early April. Perfect, pointed, cone-shaped vegetative buds are decoratively conspicuous on some forms and also on variety *atrokermesinum*, which is usually more open and upright in growth, possesses a glandular ovary, and has a questionable reputation for bearing flowers larger and darker in color. *R. meddianum* is distinguished by its bell-shaped corolla, non-glandular ovary, glabrous style, and by its egg-shaped leaves which make it easy to separate from the round to oval leaves of *R. thomsonii*. George Forrest first found the species in 1917 growing at 10,000 to 11,000 feet in China's Yunnan province, and named it for a friend who had helped him with his explorations. Freedom of Flowering: 1; American Ratings: None yet assigned; British Quality Rating: ****; British Hardiness Rating: C; Truss Type: 7; var. *atrokermesinum*, A.M., 1954.

R. megacalyx (meg-a-ka′-lix), **Balf. f. and Ward.** MADDENII SERIES, MEGACALYX SUBSERIES

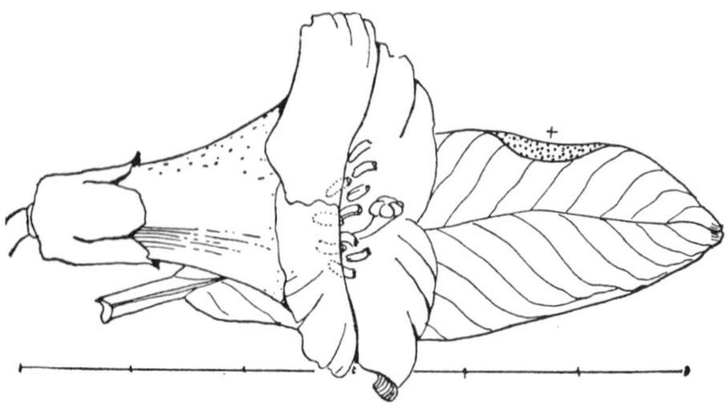

A densely foliaged small tree up to 16 feet in height, *R. megacalyx* is a valuable acquisition for greenhouses or conservatories or in mild California gardens. In Great Britain it grows well in climates such as that at Trengwainton, Cornwall, and Brodick Castle, Isle of Arran. Its dull green leaves with conspicuous veins are 4 to 6 inches long and 1 to 3 inches broad, the undersides indented with small scales. The flowers, pendant in groups of three to five, are striking 4-inch trumpets, white or faintly tinted pink, with yellow throats, and richly scented with the fragrance of nutmegs. They open in late April and early May, freely and regularly produced each year in a remarkable show of grace and elegant beauty. This is among the best of the Maddenii species famous for their sumptuous blossoms. Identification is usually easy by means of the odd stalks on which the flower buds are borne. Botanically, it is distinct by reason of the non-scaly flower stalks; the large, broad-lobed calyx without scales, divided to about the middle; and the leaf stalks grooved on the upper surface. The style is scaly only near the base and there are ten stamens. *R. megacalyx* was discovered by Kingdon-Ward growing at 7,000 to 9,000 feet in northeast Upper Burma in 1914. Its name refers to its large calyx. Freedom of Flowering: 1; Ease of Cultivation: 2; American Quality Rating: None yet assigned; British Quality Rating: ***; American Hardiness Rating: H-6; British: E; Truss Type: 12; A.M., 1937.

R. metternichii (met′-ter-nick-i), **Sieb. and Zucc.** PONTICUM SERIES, CAUCASICUM SUBSERIES

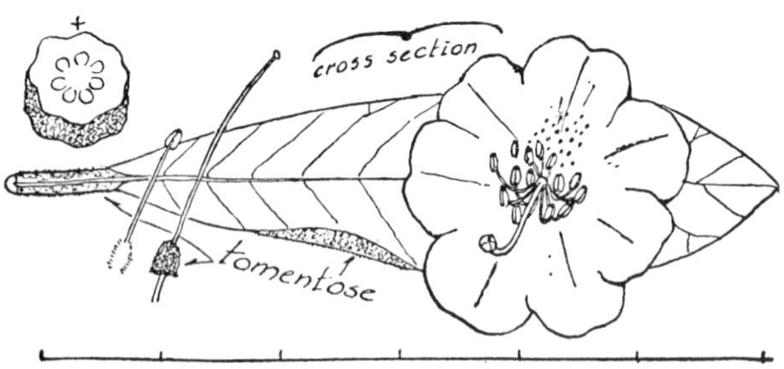

Dr Hiroshi Hara at the University of Tokyo recently described *R. metternichii* as 'the finest species among evergreen Rhododendrons in Japan', which would include such good sorts as *RR. yakusimanum*, *keiskei*, and *degronianum*, thus stimulating among specialists in the northeastern United States the lively interest which has existed for many years in the usually hardy members of the Ponticum series. *R. metternichii* has been an elusive plant for decades. Rhododendrons sold under this name in the United States have invariably proved to be some form of *degronianum*. Specimens in European botanical institutions which I have examined have produced blossoms with five lobes, not with the seven-lobed corolla which is characteristic of this Rhododendron. I doubt if the species was in cultivation anywhere in the Western world when H. L. Larson, a Pacific Coast nurseryman, imported it recently in its variety *tsukushianum* and shipped a couple of plants to growers in the East. At my trial grounds in the harsh mountain climate of northwestern Pennsylvania it appears to be at the extreme limit of its ability to endure cold and it will not bloom regularly. I estimate it to be a satisfactory garden plant as far north as New York City and possibly in favored sites to Boston, where its compact habit and serried foliage, in combination with first-rate flowers, make it an acquisition for any garden. *R. metternichii* is reputed to have a height up to 8 feet, ultimately, with a greater breadth, growing in a mound-like, spreading manner. It has leaves 4 to 6 inches long, 1 to $1\frac{5}{8}$ inches broad, with margins slightly downturned and coated beneath with a dense brownish felty indumentum. It blooms in mid-May with widely bell-shaped flowers up to 3 inches in diameter, about twelve or fourteen forming rounded, compact terminal trusses, white, pale pink or rose in color. The blossoms are unique for the Ponticum series in possessing seven lobes (except for the rare white five-lobed Mt. Amagi form) and fourteen stamens, and this species is easily distinguished from others in the group on this basis. Photographs of mature specimens show it to be a well-formed shrub with good foliage and handsome appearance out of bloom. The lovely pink and rose shades in this group of Rhododendrons are marked by exceptional clarity and delicacy. In the wild, *R. metternichii* inhabits the mountains of central and southern Japan. The name was given in honor of the famous historical figure and diplomat, Prince Metternich. Freedom of Flowering: 2; Ease of Cultivation: 1; American Ratings: None yet assigned; British Quality Rating: **; British Hardiness Rating: A; Truss Type: 1.

R. micranthum (mi-kran′-thum), **Turczaninow.** MICRANTHUM SERIES

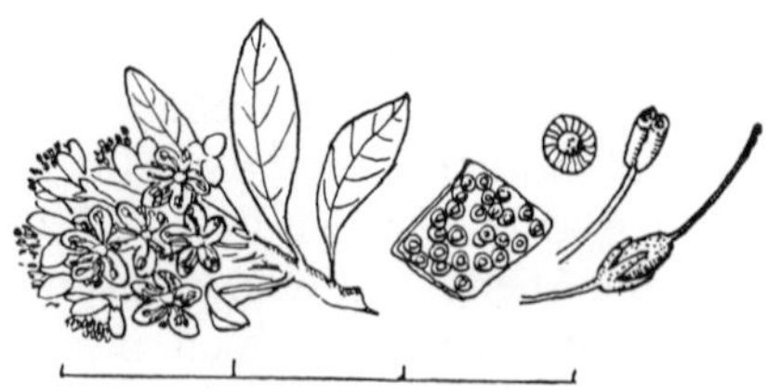

For a species which is hardy in the northeastern United States this Rhododendron is remarkably rare in our gardens. It forms a bushy shrub about 5 feet tall. The evergreen leaves are $\frac{3}{4}$ to $1\frac{3}{4}$ inches long, $\frac{1}{4}$ to $\frac{1}{2}$ inch wide, slightly scaly above and densely so below, borne on slender branches, and the light effect in the landscape affords a graceful contrast to some of the more portly large-leaved Rhododendrons. Rounded, two-inch terminal clusters contain as many as fifty or more tiny, pearly-white flowers, each little more than $\frac{1}{4}$ inch accross, unique in their floral effect when they appear in early June. Seedlings seem to vary to some extent in hardiness but this can be counted among the ironclad Rhododendrons, normally uninjured by $-25°$ F. It is adaptable and attractive as an evergreen shrub, but the public has withered its reputation by a frosty indifference to its virtues. In an effort to convey a mental impression of its unusual effect in flower, this species has been compared with a Spiraea. Since it will not sell to gardeners as a Rhododendron the thought inevitably occurs that it will probably be a sensation some day for an enterprising nurseryman who promotes it as an evergreen Spiraea. This scaly-leaved species is more likely to be confused with *Ledum latifolium* than with any other Rhododendron. It is unique in the genus. Wilson introduced *R. micranthum* in 1901 from Hupeh where he found it growing at 5,500 to 8,000 feet in elevation. It has wide distribution in western, central, and northern China and in Manchuria. Freedom of Flowering: 1; Ease of Cultivation: 1; American Quality Rating: x; British: none; American Hardiness Rating: H-1; British: A; Truss Type: 17.

R. minus (mi′-nus), **Michaux.** CAROLINIANUM SERIES

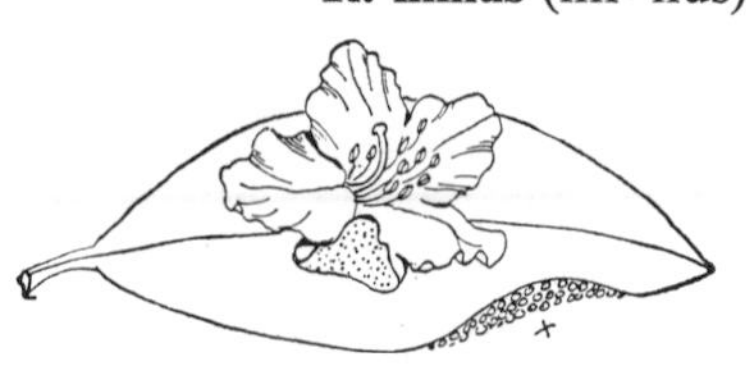

Ineptly named *R. minus*, a reference to small stature, this native American Rhododendron is actually among the largest of the species found in the United States. In the wild it grows rarely to as much as 30 feet in height, and bushes 20 feet tall are common. In cultivation the gardener must count on a shrub ultimately 12 feet in breadth and height. The leaves are $1\frac{1}{2}$ to $3\frac{1}{2}$ inches long, $\frac{1}{2}$ to $1\frac{1}{2}$ inches wide, dark green above, rusty from the scales dotting the surface beneath. Narrowly funnel-shaped flowers appear in late June, each about $1\frac{1}{2}$ inches wide, usually about seven from each bud, but the best forms produce multiple terminal flower buds which combine to make large rounded trusses containing as many as thirty florets. The blossoms are typically bright lavender-rose, lightly spotted, but occasionally white, fine clear pale pink and salmon-pink forms are found. This is a good garden Rhododendron of iron-clad hardiness, able to endure at least −25° F., which blooms at a valuable season when there is not much color from other shrubs. It should be a desirable plant too in the deep South because it is among the most tolerant to heat of all Rhododendrons. Its texture is lighter and more graceful than the rotund large-leaved sorts. The variation in *R. minus* has never been properly appreciated. In floriferousness, in color, in the way the flowers are presented, and in habit the species ranges from the ordinary to the very fine. Edmond Amateis, the illustrator of this book and an amateur enthusiast, has isolated a clear pink form with very large trusses which is extraordinarily attractive. Roland de Wilde, a professional grower, has found among his seedlings a fine form in which the blossoms are displayed to exceptional advantage before the new growth appears. Except for a rare dwarf form, *R. minus* grows too tall for foundation planting but it is useful as a robust evergreen background shrub and it tolerates even more shade than its earlier blooming relative, *R. carolinianum*. In nature it is found under less exposed conditions than that species, with which it is frequently confused, especially abroad. It is commonplace to find plants mislabeled in Europe. *R. minus* is larger in stature and looser in growth but the typical species is most easily identified by the more pointed leaves, tapering about equally at both ends. The corolla is much more densely clad with scales than that of *R. carolinianum*, but I do not find constant the crisped lobes given as an identifying mark in botanical keys and I think this is worthless as a mark of distinction. The corolla tube is longer, however, and of course it blooms much later than the Carolina Rhododendron. It appears to me that there are in nature forms of scaly-leaved Rhododendrons intermediate between *R. carolinianum* and *R. minus* in almost every degree. The latter inhabits the inland plain and on up into the lower mountain elevations from North Carolina to Alabama, generally in closer association to the shelter of woodlands than its earlier blooming relative, which also prefers higher altitudes. Where the two overlap, natural hybrids occasionally occur as they do between the high-elevation *R. catawbiense* and the lower *R. maximum*. *R. minus* was described by the pioneering explorer, Michaux, and introduced by its present identity in 1876. As noted, its name was intended as a description of its stature which we know now to be erroneous. Freedom of Flowering: 1; Ease of Cultivation: 1; American Quality Rating: x; British: **; American Hardiness Rating: H-2 (Author's dissent: H-1); British: A; Truss Type: 2.

R. moupinense (moo-pin-en′-see), **Franch.** MOUPINENSE SERIES

This is an indispensable species for early bloom all along the Pacific Coast from San Francisco northward in the Rhododendron belt, wherever its precocious blossoms can be shielded from untimely frosts. It is an adaptable little shrub, seldom more than 4 feet high, easily suited in its planting site. The thick, glossy evergreen leaves are scaly underneath, $\frac{3}{4}$ to $1\frac{1}{2}$ inches long, $\frac{1}{2}$ to 1 inch broad, borne on reddish shoots which are at first hairy and later only sparsely so. Fragrant white to rosy red, broadly funnel-shaped flowers about 2 inches across, spotted on the upper lobes, appear usually in March in terminal groups of two or three. The pure white and the deep rosy red forms are especially handsome planted together and they make an attractive show at such an early season. The darker colored selection is sometimes offered as the Exbury form. *R. moupinense* appears to advantage in rock gardens of bold scale, and it makes a fine pot-plant, one which has grown well and bloomed prodigiously for me for years, flowering in February when it is brought indoors from a deep cold frame. This species is unlikely to be confused with any other in common cultivation. The scaly flower stalks and relatively large leaves for the series, with scales on the under-surface about their own diameter apart, distinguish it from its allies. It was named for a site where it was found in China. Wilson discovered the species in 1909. It is native to Szechuan and eastern Tibet, often growing as an epiphyte in the forks of trees. Old plants tend to become sprawling and lanky. Freedom of Flowering: 1; Ease of Cultivation: 1; American Quality Rating: xxxx; British: ****; American Hardiness Rating: H-4; British: B; Truss Type: 16; A.M., 1914; pink form, A.M., 1937.

R. mucronulatum (mew-kro-nu-la′-tum), **Turcz.** DAURICUM SERIES

The gardener will regard this species as midway between a Rhododendron and an Azalea and the botanists will quite agree, but it is anticipating a few millions of years to call it an Azalea now and the writers in popular magazines who persist in doing so display a remarkable prescience. It is a deciduous Rhododendron with a mature height of about 8 feet, erect in growth habit, with slender, pliant branches and thin leaves, scaly on both surfaces, $1\frac{1}{4}$ to 4 inches long, $\frac{1}{2}$ to $1\frac{1}{4}$ inches wide. The widely funnel-shaped flowers about $1\frac{3}{4}$ inches in diameter in good forms are usually rose-purple in color, appearing singly from each of the buds grouped at the ends of the naked twigs, sometimes as many as six in a cluster. Occasionally it produces axillary flower buds. The flower season varies enormously in soft climates, from Christmas in mild winters to as late as April after a cold winter and spring. *R. mucronulatum* is perfectly hardy to −25° F. and is one of the most interesting and useful Asian species for the northeastern United States. In the harsh mountain climate of my trial grounds at Brookville in northwestern Pennsylvania it is usually in flower in April with the late yellow daffodils and the white *Magnolia stellata*, the three making a charming picture at a bleak season. At Philadelphia and southward it blooms earlier and may even be not quite so satisfactory because it is too eager about putting forth its blossoms during any period of warm weather from mid-winter onward, and they are then sometimes lost to a resumption of normal cold. The flowers are remarkably frost-resistant even so, able to endure almost to 27° F. without injury, and if the first bloom is destroyed there is often a later show from buds remaining unopened at the ends of the shoots. In milder climates a northern exposure is ideal for a planting site. Eastward facing positions should be avoided so that the flowers will be spared the early sunlight on frosty mornings. A rose-pink form, much superior in color to the typical bright mauve, is available commercially and another selection of pleasing clear shade is being propagated under the name 'Cornell Pink'. *R. mucronulatum* is valuable in climates both severe and mild. Its buoyant color display so early in the season seems to anticipate the end of winter. It grows quickly and easily in almost any planting site and it can be sheared to restrain it or to make it more compact for greater ornamental effect. Too much shade tends toward thin growth and reduces flower production, which is greatest when a twiggy, intricately branched type of growth is encouraged by exposure. The more terminal shoots there are, the greater will be the number of blossoms, and well-grown specimens make a gratifying spectacle. Evergreen forms of *R. mucronulatum* are often offered for sale in this country, evidence of the natural hybrids which exist between it and its persistent-leaved relative, *R. dauricum.* In the United States, at least, the two have so commingled that they are indistinguishable and I suspect, from observations abroad, that there exists a continuous series of intermediate forms linking these species, which are distinct only as a popular conception of their extreme expressions. Typical *R. mucronulatum* is most easily distinguished from its close ally in typical form by the pointed leaves, in contrast to the rounded leaf ends with short, sharp tips of *R. dauricum.* In addition, its leaves are larger, usually more than $1\frac{1}{4}$ inches long, and thinner, with more dispersed scales two to three times their own diameter apart. The seed capsule is curved. *R. mucronulatum* is larger in stature and looser in its growth habit. It has larger flowers and often blooms a little earlier. Of the two, typical *R. dauricum* has the better of it for its evergreen foliage and more twiggy growth which gives it a denser appearance, but *R. mucronulatum* is finer in flower. It also has a wider distribution, from north China to Korea, Tsushima Island, and in western Honshu and northern Kyushu in Japan, where it grows with full exposure or at times in thin woodland. It was introduced to cultivation in the Western world in 1907. The name is an allusion to the small sharp tips of the leaves. Freedom of Flowering: 1; Ease of Cultivation: 1; American Quality Rating: xx; British: ***; American Hardiness Rating: H-2 (Author's dissent: H-1); British: B; Truss Type: 9; A.M., 1934; var. *roseum*, A.M., 1935.

R. neriiflorum (neer-ee-flor′-um), **Franch.** NERIIFLORUM SERIES, NERIIFLORUM SUBSERIES

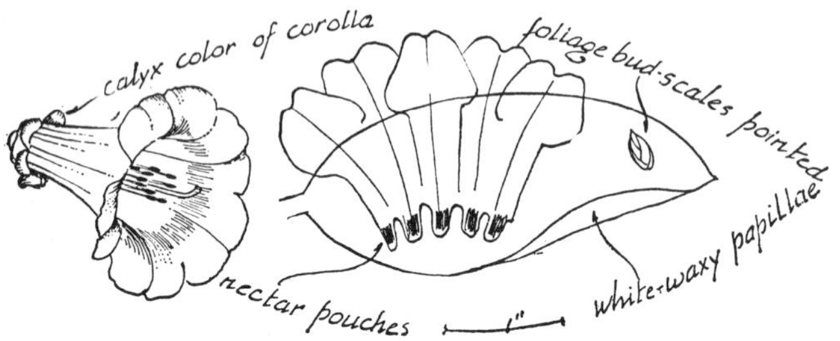

A Rhododendron important to horticulture as a garden shrub and as the parent of many hybrids, this is the central species in a series well known for its diversity and for the quality of its flowers. *R. neriiflorum* is extremely variable in habit, in stature and in almost every other respect. There are continuous gradations from spreading shrubs up to 6 feet tall and 12 feet or more broad, through intermediate forms to those of upright growth 12 feet tall. Technical botanical references describe the leaves of this species as 2 to 4 inches long, $\frac{3}{4}$ to $1\frac{3}{8}$ inches broad and even this wide range does not encompass the variety to be found. The leaves on Forrest #24091 are $3\frac{1}{4} \times 1\frac{1}{2}$ inches; on Yu #19709, $5\frac{1}{4} \times 1\frac{3}{8}$ inches; on Ludlow and Sherriff #6563, $2\frac{7}{8} \times \frac{3}{4}$ inches; on Forrest #6780, 3×1 inches. Some herbarium specimens diverge even more from the popular conception of *R. neriiflorum*, so different that few gardeners would recognize them. The leaves of all forms are glaucous-white beneath. This species is free blooming even in youth. The more erect, tall-growing forms often have larger flowers but those which are shorter and spreading in habit seem more profuse. Both make a fine show of incandescent scarlet flowers in April, a few early forms in late March. The blossoms are about 2 inches in diameter in the best expressions of the species, six to twelve in a terminal 5-inch cluster which may be lax and flat-topped or almost globular and regular in outline, depending on the number of flowers in it. Their texture is thick and waxen, with a polished sheen accentuating the burning intensity of their brilliance. They are in good bloom for an exceptionally long period in the garden. *R. neriiflorum* is in the front rank of good garden Rhododendrons, usually easily grown, reliable and profuse in bloom, but it is often difficult in the eastern counties of England. If it has a fault, it may be that the foliage is often a little sparse, and a substantial evergreen background gives it a good setting in the garden. In such a variable species it is important to obtain plants propagated from specimens known to be of superior quality. Forrest #24091 is a fine form of shapely habit, the large, glowing, scarlet flowers formed into an exceptionally good truss. The identity of subspecies *euchaites* as an upright form is a fiction. The range of intermediates between the spreading and the erect habit is complete. *Phaedropum* is a tall, narrow-leaved, sparsely indumented subspecies with lax, few-flowered trusses of buff flowers edged rose which are bizarre and unattractive. In its own subseries, *R. neriiflorum* is distinct in the absence of indumentum or at the most it has only a trace on the midrib. Perhaps the best characters to place it in its subseries are the long, narrow, hairy ovary tapered to the broad base of the style, and the narrow, sharply pointed outer scales which enclose the foliage buds. The seed capsule is long and curved. Other characters, especially leaf size and conformation, given in botanical keys, are unreliable in my experience. *R. neriiflorum* was discovered by Delavay in 1883 and introduced by Forrest in 1906. The name refers to the resemblance of the flowers to those of the Oleander. In the wild it inhabits exposed slopes, Pine forests and shaded ravines at 9,000 to 12,000 feet in China's Yunnan province. Freedom of Flowering: 1; Ease of Cultivation: 1; American Quality Rating: xxxx; British: ****; American Hardiness Rating: H-4; British: C; Truss Type: 10.

R. nuttallii (nut′-tal-i), **Booth.** MADDENII SERIES, MEGACALYX SUBSERIES

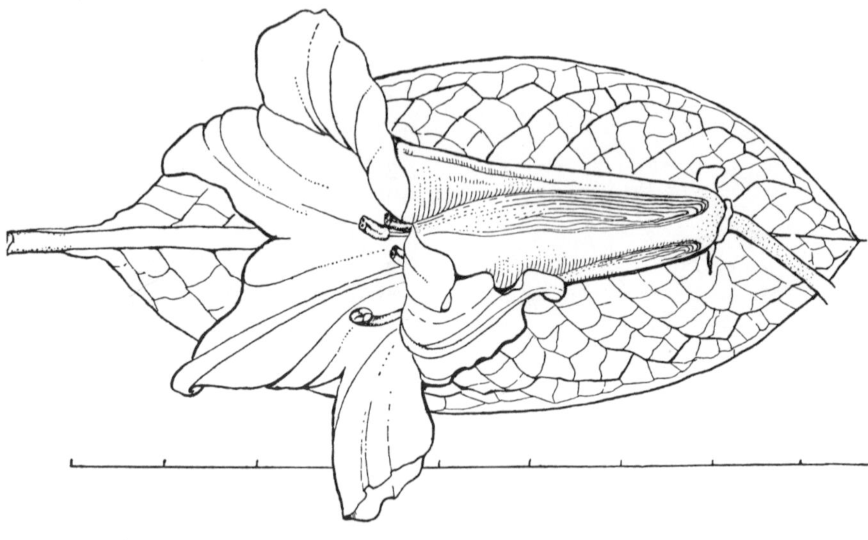

This species, famous for having the largest of Rhododendron flowers, is among the superlative spectacles of the genus when it blooms in late April and early May. In San Francisco, specimens several feet high, growing with full exposure in Golden Gate Park, are compact plants, densely furnished with the large, handsome, strongly veined leaves which are one of the attractions of *R. nuttallii*. Perhaps nowhere else in Europe or America do the species of the Maddenii series appear to such advantage. Ordinarily this Rhododendron is seen as a thin, lanky shrub or small tree 12 or 15 feet tall, to 30 feet in the wild, and straggly in habit. Its huge leaves are 5 to 12 inches long, 2¼ to 4½ inches broad, much wrinkled by the veins strongly indented on their surface, and clad with dense scales beneath. The new growth is a rather startling soft bronzed maroon color. There are usually three to six enormous, fragrant, white or pale yellow lily-like trumpets in each outward-facing cluster of flowers. The rounded lobes are often deeply separated and tend to curl along their edges, thus making of the corolla a five-pointed star, suffused within by luminous yellow rays. There is a rare form with especially broad lobes, slightly ruffled, which are flushed pink outside and faintly stained a lighter shade inside, one of the most stunning blossoms to be found anywhere. This Rhododendron blooms in late April and early May. At its best the trumpets are up to 5 inches long, flaring to a widely expanded, gracefully recurved corolla which may measure as much as 6 inches across. Their theatrical size, exquisite coloring and stately carriage make a dazzling show, one of the truly wondrous sights in horticulture. North of California and in the British Isles this sumptuous Rhododendron must be grown in a greenhouse to be really satisfactory. Coming from an extremely low altitude in Bhutan, it is probably the tenderest of the entire Maddenii series. It is not likely to be confused with any of its allies, but it can be distinguished on the basis of its flowers always in excess of 4 inches in length, scaly toward the base of the tube outside, and borne on scaly stalks without hairs. There are ten stamens. The conspicuous calyx with broad lobes is glabrous and does not have a fringe of hairs. The elliptic leaves have prominently looped and branched lateral nerves below, and are borne on stalks devoid of any V-shaped groove. *R. nuttallii* was discovered and introduced from 8,000 feet in Bhutan by T. J. Booth in 1852. It was named for a distinguished botanist, Thomas Nuttall. Freedom of Flowering: 2+; Ease of Cultivation: 2+; American Quality Rating: xxxx; British: ****; American Hardiness Rating: H-6; British: F; Truss Type: 12; F.C.C., 1864; var. *stellatum*, A.M., 1936.

R. orbiculare (or-bik-u-lar′-ee), **Decaisne.** FORTUNEI SERIES, ORBICULARE SUBSERIES

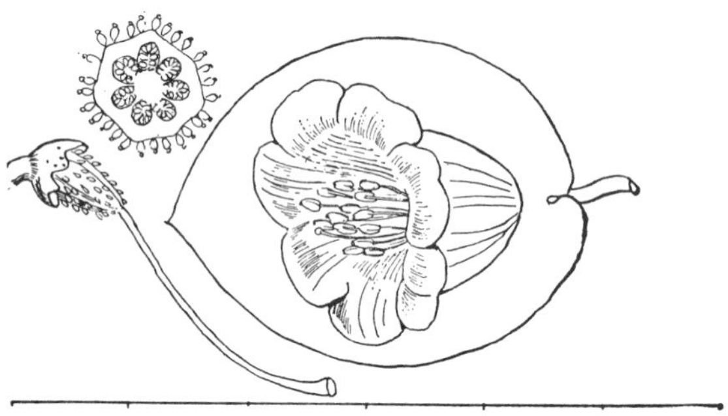

Free flowering, handsome in bloom and out, hardy and adaptable in any reasonable planting site, *R. orbiculare* is almost an ideal garden Rhododendron. Wherever it is seen, the dense, bright green foliage, impeccable growth habit, and tumbling masses of bright rose flowers make it an outstanding shrub of superlative quality. It is most often encountered as a perfectly proportioned, rounded bush, a superb foliage plant almost formal in its regularity, about 6 feet tall and about 8 feet broad in older specimens. This corresponds also with descriptions in the literature, but I have measured specimens at Caerhays in Cornwall, England, which were 10 feet tall and a great deal broader, each a mammoth cushion of faultless outline. A survivor at Bodnant from Wilson's original introduction is 20 × 20 feet. The leaves of this species are almost unique: round in shape with a heart-shaped base, 1½ to 4 inches long, 1½ to 3 inches broad, and exceptionally handsome with their polished sheen. A form not yet widely distributed, discovered by the McLaren expedition and given the number 25, has even finer foliage, the large, glossy leaves resembling lily pads. Striking, bell-shaped, seven-lobed, bright rose flowers, 2 to 2½ inches in diameter appear in late April and early May, are usually borne in loose terminal trusses of seven to twelve, which deck the plants with tiered cascades of color. This species thrives in a wide range of moderate climates and seems always to be a conspicuous asset in any garden where it grows. It is surely among the finest and most symmetrical foliage plants in the genus. *R. orbiculare* is unlikely to be confused with any other Rhododendron because of its round leaves, though a form was found a few years ago with elliptical leaves. It has a glabrous style and fourteen stamens. The species is a native of western Szechuan province in China, in woodlands and thickets at 8,000 to 10,000 feet, whence it was introduced by Wilson in 1904. The name refers to the orb-shaped leaves. Freedom of Flowering: 1; Ease of Cultivation: 1; American Quality Rating: xxx; British: ****; American Hardiness Rating: H-3; British: A; Truss Type: 4; A.M., 1922.

R. oreodoxa (or-ee-o-dox′-a), **Franch.** FORTUNEI SERIES, OREODOXA SUBSERIES

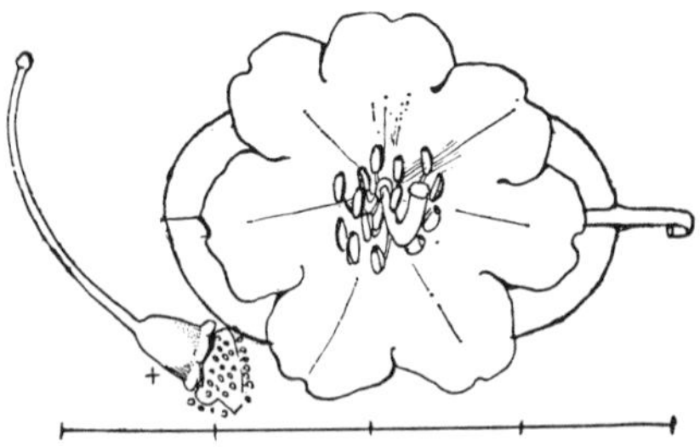

This handsome, early-blooming shrub up to about 15 feet in height has smaller leaves than its precocious flowering relative, *R. sutchuenense*, in size ranging from 2 to $4\frac{1}{2}$ inches long and $\frac{3}{4}$ to 2 inches broad. The best forms are well branched and have abundant foliage, so that they are attractive at all four seasons of the year. The species is extremely free-flowering, covering itself in late March and early April with great shelving masses of open bell-shaped blossoms ranging in color from white through lavender-pink to rose. The pink shades become paler as they age. Some authorities have described the flowers as being 4 inches in diameter, but the largest I have seen were $3\frac{1}{4}$ inches and those were on a specimen which was obviously much superior to the average. There are eight to twelve openly bell-shaped, seven- or eight-lobed florets in each flat-topped cluster. This is a rugged species which adapts itself to a wide variety of planting situations in the garden, but it flowers so early in the season that it should be placed in a protected site where the blossoms are shielded from frost. Some years ago Joseph Gable at Stewartstown, Pa., received from abroad seeds under the name *R. haematocheilum*, a geographical form of *oreodoxa*, from which hardy seedlings survived to become sparingly distributed in the northeastern United States. This form of the species seems to be tolerant of both winter cold and summer heat at New York City, and its large, light pink blossoms, remarkably frost resistant, are dramatic in their appearance so early in the year. It tends to become somewhat open and leggy as it approaches maturity, and seems to endure but not really to find congenial the high summer temperatures and aridity in the northeastern United States. As it blossoms just a few days after *R. sutchuenense* it may succeed in some gardens where its earlier blooming relative loses its display to frost. *R. oreodoxa* is distinguished by having, in combination, a seven-lobed corolla with glandular pedicels and glabrous style and ovary. *R. fargesii*, with which it is often confused, has a glandular ovary and broader leaves. The leaves of the species here described are not over $4\frac{1}{2}$ inches long, more or less elliptical in shape. It has a relatively few-flowered umbellate truss with a short axis, and the blossoms are short, up to $1\frac{3}{4}$ inches in length, compared with others in the series. There are fourteen stamens. This Chinese species was introduced to cultivation by Wilson in 1904, from Szechuan and Kansu provinces. The name, *oreodoxa*, praises the species as 'glory of the mountains', where it grows at 7,000 to 10,000 feet elevation. Freedom of Flowering: 1; Ease of Cultivation: 1; American Quality Rating: xx; British: ★★★; American Hardiness Rating: H-3; British: B; Truss Type: 10; A.M., 1937.

R. oreotrephes (or-ee-o-tref′-eez), **W. W. Smith.** TRIFLORUM SERIES, OREOTREPHES SUBSERIES

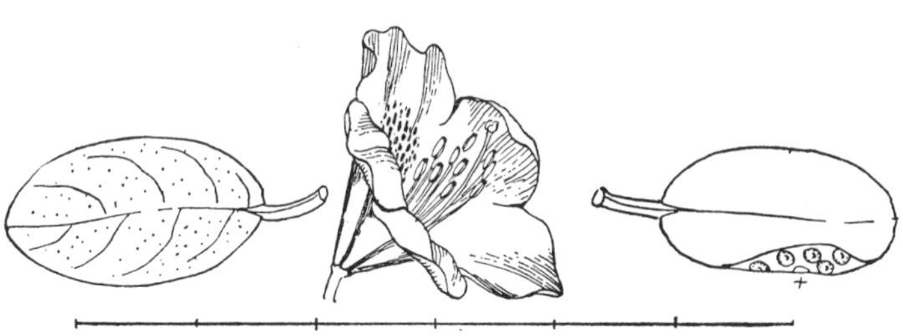

Mature plants of this valuable Rhododendron are usually about 8 feet tall, neat in outline, and exceptionally fine in foliage. The leaves, often glaucous, are $1\frac{1}{2}$ to 3 inches long, $\frac{3}{4}$ to $1\frac{1}{2}$ inches broad, blue-green as well below, and scaly. The May flowers are about $2\frac{1}{4}$ inches in diameter, four to eleven firmly carried in a terminal cluster. This species is far more variable than past descriptions in the standard reference works have indicated. The color of the flowers ranges from pale mauve with brownish-crimson spots on the upper lobe, through shades of lavender-pink to deep rosy-lilac. In addition to these colors containing more or less of a bluish admixture, there is a rarer range without it, from clear, light, soft pink to a shade so dark that it is almost a rose-red. There are two more or less distinct flowering effects, one in which the blossoms are distributed fairly uniformly over the perimeter of the plant, and the other in which the blossoms are carried in clearly defined trusses of good size (as in Forrest #15418). The color of the foliage is important horticulturally and the range here is very great. The mature leaves of many forms are a dull gray-green above, but others are among the finest foliage plants in the genus, icy blue-green in effect, with the young growth a startling bright blue-green. Some sorts have the undesirable trait of losing most of their leaves in winter. In its best expressions this is an exceptionally attractive and versatile evergreen plant of finer texture and more graceful effect than the large-leaved Rhododendrons. In some districts it bears the reputation of being a little bit hard to fit into a completely congenial site, but most gardeners find it amenable, and vigorous specimens are certainly reliable in their floral display year after year. Older plants are reputed to resent transplanting. This species is characterized by leaves about equally rounded at both ends, not hairy and almost lacking scales on the upper side, but clad beneath with dense scales only about one-half their own diameter apart. The leaf under-surface is devoid of hairs on the mid-rib. The flowers are not scaly outside. They are borne on stalks about $\frac{5}{8}$ inch long and have a minute, rim-like calyx. The style is glabrous its full length and the white stamens are downy at the base. *R. oreotrephes* grows at 10,000 to 12,000 feet in southeastern Tibet and Yunnan. It was discovered by Forrest in 1906, and given the name meaning 'mountain bred'. Freedom of Flowering: 1; Ease of Cultivation: 1; American Quality Rating: xxx; British: ****; American Hardiness Rating: H-3; British: B; Truss Type: 9.

R. ovatum (o-va'-tum), **Maxim.** OVATUM SERIES

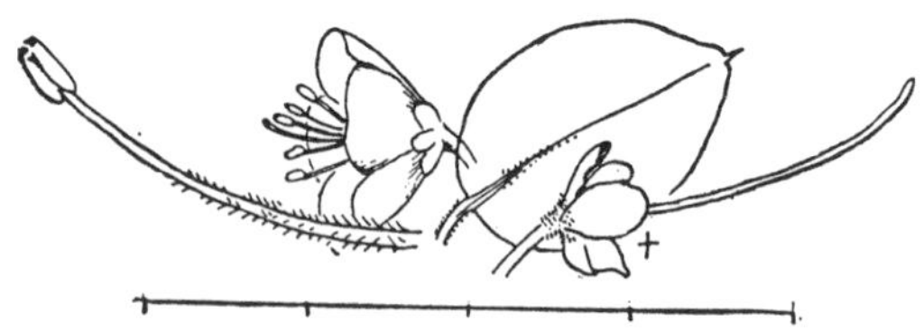

Here is a curious Azalea-like Rhododendron which comes from *eastern* China and appears to be closely related to *R. albiflorum*, our Rocky Mountain native. It is reputed to have an ultimate height of 15 feet, but it is almost invariably seen in cultivation at about 6 feet in older specimens, with leaves $\frac{3}{4}$ to $2\frac{1}{4}$ inches long and $\frac{3}{8}$ to $1\frac{1}{4}$ inches broad. The 1-inch flowers are white to pale purple or pink, spotted on the upper lobes. They are flat and open, produced singly from axillary buds at the ends of the branches in late May. *R. ovatum* is adaptable over a very wide range of climatic conditions. It does well in the deep south and some forms are hardy as far north as New York City. Reputedly tender and formerly rated 'E' in Great Britain, its hardiness in the United States is still much greater than currently indicated, so I am adding my own rating below to that of the Royal Horticultural Society. It has not yet been evaluated for hardiness by the American Rhododendron Society. This unusual plant has only five stamens and Joseph Gable has determined that it crosses readily with Azaleas of the Obtusum subseries. It is an attractive evergreen shrub the year round. The species is not likely to be confused with any other Rhododendron in common cultivation. The stamens have hairy filaments and the large calyx lobes are rounded to obovate, glabrous except at the base. The leaves are broadly egg-shaped, giving the species its name. Native of eastern China, Chekiang province and the

Chusan Islands, *R. ovatum* was originally introduced in 1844 by Robert Fortune and Wilson later found it in Hupeh province. Freedom of Flowering: 2; Ease of Cultivation: 1; American Ratings: None yet assigned; British Quality Rating: ★; British Hardiness Rating: C; (Author's dissent for the United States: A); Truss Type: 13.

R. pemakoense (pem-a-ko-en′-see), **K. Ward.** UNIFLORUM SERIES

Many Rhododendron specialists regard this as the loveliest of the dwarf Rhododendrons. It is certainly among the very best, often available in a form reaching a height of about 2 feet (despite the maximum height of 1 foot given in reference works) and also one of smaller stature, seldom exceeding 6 inches, with such large flowers that they seem startling for their size borne on such dwarf plants. Either sort grows neatly to a rounded mound of good, dense, bright green foliage frequently extending in width by underground stolons. The scaly leaves are $\frac{1}{2}$ to $1\frac{1}{4}$ inches long, $\frac{1}{4}$ to $\frac{5}{8}$ inch broad. Flowering is in April. Terminal buds may produce, singly or in pairs, as many as five or six blossoms each about $1\frac{3}{4}$ inches across, at the end of each twig. The species is remarkably floriferous, so free that the foliage can scarcely be seen between the flowers. The most common color is an attractive silvery lilac, but the forms with deeper, brighter pink blossoms are more appealing, in my opinion. An indeterminate mauve with corolla lobes so reflexed as to diminish the effectiveness of the flower is seen often enough for one to be wary of it. Though it does not have blossoms as rich in color as the very best forms, Kingdon-Ward #6301 is commercially available and is superior to the average of unselected seedlings. This stoloniferous selection grows to a height of 18 inches. *R. pemakoense* is a delightful Rhododendron in every way, presentable at all seasons, an enchanting display of color in its springtime dress. Massed plants are especially effective on banks, used as an edging for beds, or to face down larger shrubs, and of course it is superb as a rock garden Rhododendron. Of species in the Uniflorum series with entire leaves, neither undulating nor notched along their margins, *R. pemakoense* is characterized by possessing, in combination, broadly funnel-shaped flowers which are both scaly and densely hairy outside with a style about as long or a little longer than the corolla, either hairy or not, at the base. I do not find the flower color constant, nor the dimensions accurate in the description and key to this and allied species published when the Uniflorum series was established by Cowan and Davidian in 1948. In fact, *RR. uniflorum* and *patulum* are merely the extremes of a continuous series of intergrades which include *RR. pemakoense* and *imperator* as intermediates. There is an unbroken line of progression in leaf size, scale distribution and in other characters among the four. I cannot agree with Cowan and Davidian that 'the species are well defined'. In my opinion, the opposite is the case. The easiest way to distinguish typical *pemakoense* is by its erect, mound-like habit of growth, the branches neither prostrate nor sprawling, bearing small leaves usually less than 1 inch long with rounded tips ending in a fine point and clad beneath with scales of unequal size spaced half to one and a half times their own diameter apart. This species is distinct from *R. uniflorum* only on the basis of the distribution of the scales beneath the leaves, and actually is but a variety of that Rhododendron. *R. pemakoense* was discovered by Kingdon-Ward in Tibet at 10,000 feet altitude and named for Pemako province where it was first found. Freedom of Flowering: 1; Ease of Cultivation: 1; American Quality Rating: xxx; British: ★★★; American Hardiness Rating: H-3; British: A; Truss Type: 15; A.M., 1933.

R. ponticum (pon′-tik-um), **Linn.** PONTICUM SERIES, PONTICUM SUBSERIES

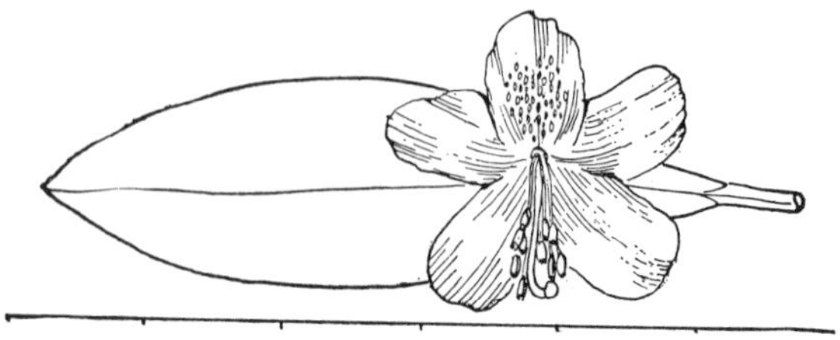

Among the best known of Rhododendrons, this species was brought into cultivation in England from Gibraltar some time before 1763. Finding the British climate ideal, it has naturalized and produced innumerable natural hybrids with imported Asian species so that the visitor today receives the impression that it is a native Rhododendron, probably the most conspicuous evergreen in the landscape. Only a rampant shrub could appropriate so much to itself and this species does grow relentlessly and luxuriantly in a congenial climate to a height of 8 to 15 feet and a width of 15 to 30 feet. The branches root quickly where they touch the earth, hastening its spread. It is an attractive evergreen with shiny, dark green leaves 4 to 8 inches long, 1 to 2½ inches wide, and when great masses of it are in bloom it can be very beautiful naturalized in the countryside. In gardens the purplish pink flowers suffer from proximity to blossoms of purer and more refined color. There are ten to fifteen 2-inch florets in firm terminal trusses which measure 4 to 6 inches across, appearing in June. This species has had a profound effect on garden Rhododendrons. It appeared as a parent in the complex pedigree of the early hybrids and those which are still the staple of commerce in the northeastern United States. Its influence in this respect has been deplorable since it is much less hardy than its reputation, has a strong susceptibility to Wilt in this country, and the dominant magenta pink has flawed the finer colors of the Asian species with which it has been crossed. The nursery industry is enormously indebted to *R. ponticum*, however, for serving as understocks for millions of grafted Rhododendrons through several generations when there was no other method of propagation available. Now that cuttings treated with modern hormones produce such superior plants on their own roots this use of the species is rapidly declining. Strangely, the true *R. ponticum* is extremely rare in the United States, despite the hosts of small plants which have been raised for understocks. Through the years the sources of seed supply have been gradually infiltrated by plants from natural crosses with other Rhododendrons until today more or less consistent minor hybrid influence is evident in nearly all seedlings used for grafting. In moderate climates, though not in the northeastern United States, this species can be extremely useful in providing dense masses of evergreen foliage which require little or no maintenance. It makes an effective windbreak. In thin woodlands and in natural settings with full exposure it finds the conditions under which it appears at its best. *R. ponticum* is too distinct to be often confused with other species in the Ponticum series. It has no indumentum. Its closest resemblance in the group is to our native *R. catawbiense* from which it differs in having a glabrous ovary and longer, narrower leaves. The corolla lobes are more deeply separated and the pedicels are glabrous. This is one of the few species from Asia Minor, the Caucasus and from that part of Armenia called Pontus in ancient times, whence comes its name. There is also an outlying European representation in the Iberian peninsula. Freedom of Flowering: 1; Ease of Cultivation: 1; American Quality Rating: 0; British: none; American Hardiness Rating: H-3; British: A; Truss Type: 1.

R. praevernum (pree-ver′-num), **Hutch.** FORTUNEI SERIES, DAVIDII SUBSERIES

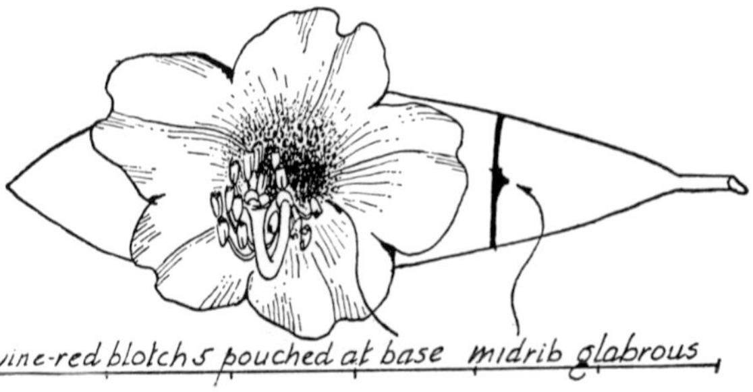

Rhododendron collectors are often annoyed by the similarity between this species and *R. sutchuenense* var. *geraldii*, and one of the distinguishing features noted in the literature is the dwarfer, more spreading habit of *R. praevernum*. This distinction, however, is not valid. Many old specimens exceed 14 feet in height, which is even in excess of the maximum stature given for *R. sutchuenense* in cultivation. The leaves are 3½ to 10 inches long, 1 to 2½ inches wide, usually about 6 × 2½ inches. About ten white to pink bell-shaped flowers 2 to 2½ inches across, with a bold maroon blotch, are produced in lax, flat-topped terminal trusses in February to April depending on the season, but usually in late March. In my judgment the best forms of this species are not so ornamental as the best forms of *R. sutchuenense* as they are commonly seen in cultivation. Since they are so similar, I would prefer the latter in a choice between the two, but *R. praevernum* is an extraordinarily attractive Rhododendron entirely on its own merits, with fine foliage and flowers. The two are easily distinguished by the glabrous midrib beneath the leaf of *R. praevernum*, which is downy in the case of its relative. This species separates from its other allies by having, in combination, a five-lobed campanulate flower with glabrous ovary and style, the latter slender and with lobulate stigma. There are fifteen stamens. The leaves are generally in excess of 4 inches in length, elliptic-oblanceolate in shape, with gradually acute apex and cuneate base. *R. praevernum* comes from 5,000 to 7,000 feet altitude of the Hupeh province of China where it was found by Wilson in 1900. Other Rhododendrons from the same region are hardy at Philadelphia and beyond, but such early-flowering species ought to have a sheltered site for frost protection. The name refers to its precocious blossoming, 'before the spring'. Freedom of Flowering: 1; Ease of Cultivation: 1; American Quality Rating: xx; British: **; American Hardiness Rating: H-3; British: B; Truss Type: 10; A.M., 1954.

R. pubescens (pew-bes′-enz), **Balf. f. and Forrest.** SCABRIFOLIUM SERIES

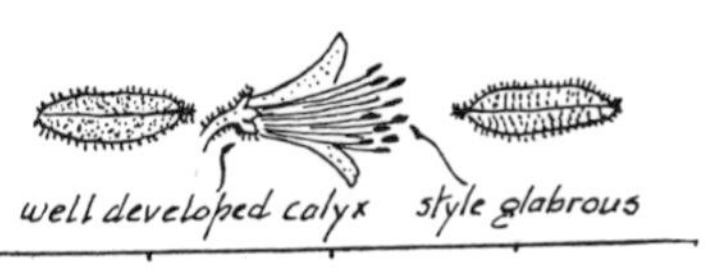

A delicately pretty little Rhododendron, airy and graceful in the landscape, this willowy shrub grows 5 or 6 feet tall in its larger edition, much less in a dwarf form sparingly distributed. The hairy and scaly leaves are about ¾ inch long, $\frac{3}{16}$ inch wide. From axillary buds clustered at the ends of the shoots single flowers appear in April which are about ⅝ inch in diameter. The best forms produce so many axillary buds that their combined effect in bloom is one of compact little flower trusses 2½ inches in diameter. Others, less free blooming, and much less colorful, have diminutive loose clusters of about four or five of the tiny blossoms. The best garden plants are those with rose-pink flowers; the more common blush-white forms are a little less effective. This Rhododendron just misses being hardy in south-central Pennsylvania and would probably be satisfactory southward of Philadelphia. It can be separated from its relatives on the basis of its widely funnel-shaped blossoms with glabrous style, eight to ten stamens pubescent toward the base, and well-developed calyx. The leaves are densely hairy on both surfaces. The flower stalks are not only hairy but scaly too, and, in fact, the generally pubescent character of this

Rhododendron gives it its name. *R. pubescens* comes from thickets and scrub at an elevation of 10,000 feet in southwestern Szechuan province of China. Freedom of Flowering: 1; Ease of Cultivation: 1; American Quality Rating: xx; British: ***; American Hardiness Rating: H-3; British: B; Truss Type: 13; A.M., 1955.

R. puralbum (pur-al′-bum), **Balf. f. and W. W. Sm.** THOMSONII SERIES, SOULIEI SUBSERIES

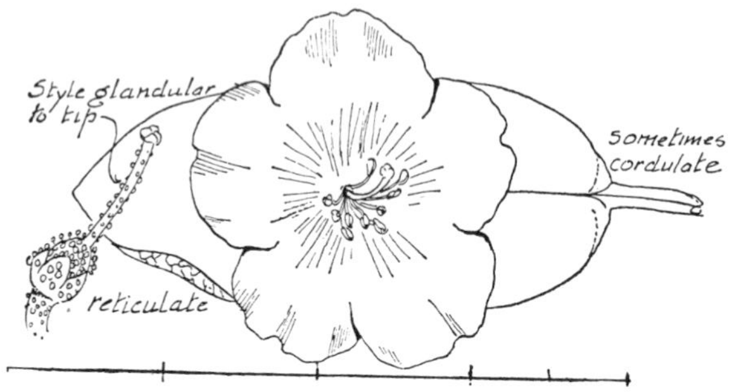

The species of the Souliei subseries are shrubs of exceptional charm and distinction, so it is something of a mystery that this Rhododendron has been neglected by gardeners. The dazzling yellow *R. wardii*, the beautiful soft rose-pink *souliei*, and the present species, *R. puralbum*, with lovely pure white flowers, are a trio of extraordinary quality from the Souliei subseries. The latter is a robust shrub 8 feet to as much as 15 feet tall with leaves 2 to 4¾ inches long, 1 to 2 inches wide, dark green with primary veins impressed above, and with a blue frosty sheen below. In May come the white flowers shaped like miniature shallow bowls, about 2¾ inches across, six or seven held firmly and individually distinct in an open cluster which shows off their classic purity of form to great advantage. This is in the front rank of Rhododendrons for garden ornament, trim in outline, handsome in foliage and effective in flower. It is presumed to be distinct from *R. souliei* by reason of its pure white flowers, whereas the paler forms of the latter are described as always suffused pink in some degree. I find this a dubious discrimination, at best, some forms of *R. souliei* being white occasionally, without perceptible pink tint. However, *R. puralbum* can easily be separated from the typical forms of its closest relatives (with the possible exception of the rare *R. wardii* var. *album*) by its color, and is otherwise distinguished by the open, bowl-shaped flowers with ten to twelve stamens, hairy at the base, style glandular to the tip, and calyx $\frac{3}{16}$ to $\frac{7}{16}$ inch long. It was first found by Forrest in 1913 at 11,000 to 14,000 feet in the mountains of China's Yunnan province. The name refers to its very white flowers. Freedom of Flowering: 2+; Ease of Cultivation: 1; American Ratings: None yet assigned; British Quality Rating: ***; British Hardiness Rating: B; Truss Type: 4.

R. racemosum (ras-ee-mo′-sum), **Hook. f.** VIRGATUM SERIES

In a genus noted for its diversity this Rhododendron probably sets a record for variance. The dwarf forms are compact, densely foliaged little plants 15 inches high. Then there are numerous forms about 5 or 6 feet tall at maturity, which correspond with the maximum height given in technical botanical works. But finally there is still a much taller sort which towers up to 14 feet in the celebrated Exbury Rhododendron collection in England, where I have measured it. The small, dark green leaves are ¾ to 2 inches long and about half that width in all forms of the species, thickly clad beneath with brown scales on the glaucous surface. In late March, April or early May, according to its origin in its mountain homeland, the flowers appear in great profusion, unbelievably varied in the prodigal manner in which they are borne. In some plants long flowering shoots are formed by the blossoms which originate from the leaf axils along the top 6 inches or foot of branches produced by the previous year's growth. Other forms, usually more twiggy in habit, have the flowers evenly distributed from lateral buds at the branch ends and these are so densely mantled with a solid sheet of color that the foliage is nearly invisible. Still others produce well-defined round or mound-shaped trusses from as many as twenty-five axillary blossoms clustered at the ends of the shoots. The flowers are about 1 inch across or a bit more, the corolla lobes often so deeply divided that they give the appearance of little five-pointed stars. They vary in color from almost white to deep rose, with many lovely, clear, luminous pink shades between. This is a charming Rhododendron, appealing in all its forms, so easily grown that it thrives in almost any garden situation. With its slender branches and small leaves it is light in texture, delicate in appearance, and irresistibly captivating when it is studded with myriads of pink puffs in springtime. The dwarf forms are unsurpassed for the rock garden and as edging plants, for foundation planting and to face down larger shrubs. They serve admirably as flowering ground covers and are particularly effective planted in masses. The intermediate and tall sorts are just as good where their stature is appropriate, and unusual informal hedges can be created in almost any size by selecting forms of the desired dimensions. In a species so variable it is necessary to buy plants of known size and superior characteristics for the greatest garden satisfaction. These can only be produced from rooted cuttings, propagated from desirable specimens. Forrest #19404, now commercially available, is one of the best dwarf sorts, compact in habit, with clear, bright pink flowers. It is satisfactory at Philadelphia. Some of the small forms of *R. racemosum* are perfectly hardy at Boston and at Cleveland; others are tender, even at Baltimore. One form, hardy at New York City, blooms in June. Specialist nurserymen offer these sorts adapted to the northeastern climate, often under the name of the 'Mayflower Rhododendron'. This species blooms so prodigiously and produces seeds in such quantity that the vitality of the older branches becomes impaired in time and they tend to die back in the Northeast. An occasional pruning of the oldest stems results in quick replacements which renew the vigor of the plant. The gardener who provides good drainage with an extra ration of water in time of midsummer drouth will be delighted with the results. This species seems to enjoy particularly an open exposure toward the north, in the climate of the northeastern United States. It is distinct from its near relatives by possessing, in combination, flower buds with scales which are glabrous outside, producing up to five flowers pink to white in color, from each bud; a corolla slightly scaly outside the lobes but not pubescent outside the tube; a glabrous style; and short leaves more or less elliptical in shape. The name refers to the manner of flowering in racemes, from axillary buds. *R. racemosum* was discovered by Delavay, who sent seeds to the Jardin des Plantes in Paris, where plants were raised in 1889. It is native to 7,000 to 9,000 feet elevation in Yunnan province of western China. Freedom of Flowering: 1; Ease of Cultivation: 1; American Quality Rating: xxxx; British: ****; American Hardiness Rating: H-2; British: A; Truss Type: 13; F.C.C., 1892; A.G.M., 1930.

R. rubiginosum (ru-bee-jin-o′-sum), **Franch.** HELIOLEPIS SERIES

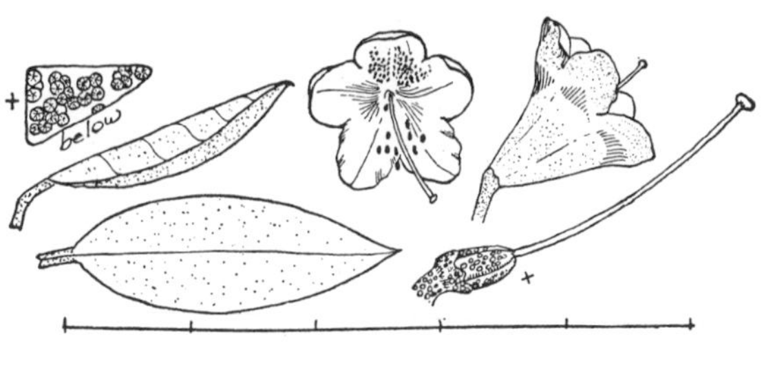

Some Rhododendrons are known for their versatility and *R. rubiginosum* is one of them, a robust shrub or small tree with warty branchlets which grows erectly to a height of 25 feet, but old specimens are usually seen in gardens about 12 feet tall. The aromatic leaves $1\frac{1}{2}$ to $3\frac{1}{2}$ inches long and $\frac{1}{2}$ to $1\frac{1}{4}$ inches broad, are dull green above and rusty beneath with reddish-brown scales. In late April and early May the funnel-shaped flowers, almost 2 inches wide, envelop the plants in sheets of pink, mauve or bright rose. The blossoms with waved margins, spotted brown on the upper lobe, are gathered into loose trusses of four to seven. This species is reminiscent of our native *R. carolinianum* except that it is taller, more erect in growth, and has flowers a little larger in size. It is much hardier than the average of the Asian species, but not quite able to survive in the northeastern United States. It is a promising prospect for experimental planting south of Washington, however. Elsewhere it already enjoys a reputation for being reliable in its floral display and easy to grow, one of those shrubs which appears to good advantage in any reasonable situation. It is easily recognized by the lance-shaped or elliptic leaves, rusty below with equal-sized scales much overlapped, and by the glabrous style and pubescent stamens. It is native to forest clearings at 7,500 to 11,000 feet in Yunnan, whence it was sent to Paris by Delavay in 1889. The name is an allusion to the brownish color of the leaf under-surface. Freedom of Flowering: 1; Ease of Cultivation: 1; American Quality Rating: xx; British: ★★★; American Hardiness Rating: H-2; British: A; Truss Type: 9; 'Wakehurst', A.M., 1960.

R. russatum (rus-sa'-tum), **Balf. f. and Forrest.** LAPPONICUM SERIES

Of species in the Lapponicum series, this is outstanding, long known for its quality and valued for its character. There are at least two forms of this Rhododendron, distinct for garden purposes. The original *R. russatum* was a 4-foot shrub with comparatively large brownish-green foliage and purple flowers somewhat diminished in their color effect by white throats. The plant formerly known as *R. cantabile* was then merged into *R. russatum* because intermediate forms were found between the two, and it is a uniform, brilliant purple with more flowers to the truss and a better, dwarfer growth habit. It seldom exceeds 2 feet and the foliage is more attractive than the older forms. The leaves of this species, rusty green in varying degree and densely scaly on both surfaces, range from $\frac{3}{4}$ to $1\frac{3}{4}$ inches long, $\frac{3}{8}$ to $\frac{7}{8}$ inch wide. The striking blue-purple flowers in late April and early May are oddly bright and the shade carries well in the garden. They are the equal of any of the dwarf alpines in their color class for their ornamental value. There are five to ten of them, about 1 inch across, in each closely packed, small, terminal cluster. This species, so useful in rock gardens, foundation plantings and the forefront of shrub borders, should be sought in superior, selected forms for best effect. The F.C.C. form, available commercially, is especially fine both in its royal purple flowers and in its habit and foliage. Rock #59211 makes an attractive, spreading shrub 30 inches tall with blossoms of a handsome shade, and good seedlings of the form still popularly called *cantabile* can often be selected to advantage if they are first seen in bloom to judge their color. Among its relatives with bluish or purple blossoms, *R. russatum* is distinct in having a style pubescent in the lower part, and an inflorescence generally four- to five-flowered or more. The calyx is glabrous outside, fringed with long hairs. Both the branchlets and leaf under-surfaces are densely scaly. This species comes from 12,000 feet elevation in northwest Yunnan province of China where it was found in 1913 by Forrest who especially noted that the stony meadows where it grows were moist. The name means 'reddened'. It is hardy enough to be grown in much of the northeastern United States, but it abhors the summer climate and requires special alpine culture to perform creditably. It is very fine in the Pacific northwest coastal region and in the British Isles. Freedom of Flowering: 1; Ease of Cultivation: 1; American Quality Rating: xxxx; British: ****; American Hardiness Rating: H-2; British: A; Truss Type: 5; A.M., 1927; A.G.M., 1938; F.C.C., 1933.

R. saluenense (sal-u-en-en′-see), **Franch.** SALUENENSE SERIES

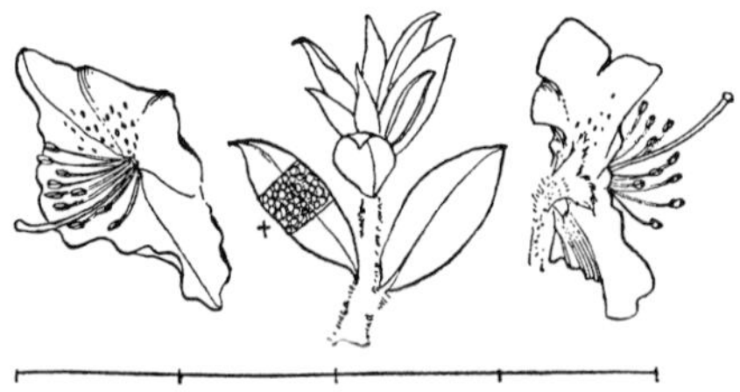

Mature plants of this fine dwarf Rhododendron are 2 to rarely 4 feet tall, with burnished green leaves about $\frac{3}{4}$ to $1\frac{3}{8}$ inches long, $\frac{3}{8}$ to 1 inch broad, scaly on both surfaces but especially beneath, where the brown scales overlap. The growth habit is often erect, and both branches and leaf stalks are clad with stout, bristle-like hairs. The widely funnel-shaped flowers come in late April and early May, about $1\frac{3}{4}$ inches across, singly or as many as seven in firm, compact clusters. They are bright rose to pinkish-purple or purplish-crimson, spotted crimson on the upper lobe, extremely variable not only in color but in size as well. This Rhododendron has been prized for rock gardens since it first became generally distributed about twenty-five years ago, and it is equally valuable for the many other situations where a fine textured shrub of restrained stature is needed in the garden, but it should not be placed where the brittle branches may have to support a snow load. The polished evergreen leaves, so densely borne, give the plants a year-round appeal, and the charming flowers in profusion make a fine show. This species merges imperceptibly into *R. chameunum*, a name retained for the convenience of gardeners to designate a smaller expression of the species with erect growth, from 1 to 2 feet tall, and dubiously reputed to be less scaly. The only other member of the series with bristly branchlets and petioles is *R. prostratum*, which is easily identified by its prostrate, spreading habit. As with so many of its alpine relatives, close and distant, this Rhododendron is hardy enough in much of the northeastern United States, but the summer climate is deadly to its welfare. It is native to the cliffs and rocky slopes at 12,000 to 13,000 feet elevation in Tibet and in China's Yunnan and Szechuan provinces, where it was found by Soulié in 1894 and subsequently introduced by Forrest in 1914. The name refers to one of its places of origin near the Salween River. Freedom of Flowering: 1; Ease of Cultivation: 1; American Quality Rating: xx; British: ***; American Hardiness Rating: H-3; British: A; Truss Type: 5; A.M., 1945.

R. sanguineum (san-gwin′-ee-um), **Franch.** NERIIFLORUM SERIES, SANGUINEUM SUBSERIES

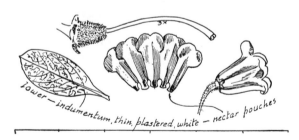

This is the Rhododendron known longest in a large and varied group of grossly similar species. It lends its name to the series of which it is typical. It is a small undershrub of serried foliage, about 3 feet tall typically, of mound-like growth habit with some forms varying to cushion shapes 15 inches tall and 36 inches in diameter. The leaves vary too within wide limits, normally $1\frac{1}{2}$ to $2\frac{1}{2}$ inches long by $\frac{1}{2}$ to 1 inch wide, coated beneath with a thin, grayish-white indumentum. The form sent back by Kingdon-Ward, however, under #6955, has leaves $4\frac{1}{4}$ inches long, $1\frac{7}{8}$ inches wide and makes a much heavier-looking plant. As many as six or more bright crimson, bell-shaped flowers, $1\frac{1}{2}$ inches across, dangle in a lax cluster. As in so many other respects, this species varies as well in flower color and season of bloom. The form in cultivation under Rock #59444 has purplish-plum-colored blossoms and the blooming season of *R. sanguineum* ranges from April to July. Rock #59083 is a good, bright crimson-flowered, April-blooming form. This is a widely useful Rhododendron suitable for the rock garden and for many other purposes where its dwarf stature and good foliage can be advantageously displayed. It does not bloom young, however, nor really prolifically even at maturity. From its allies it is usually distinct in possessing heavy, waxen flowers most frequently bright crimson, with non-glandular pedicels and ovary. The thin, grayish-white, plastered indumentum beneath leaves about two-fifths as broad as they are long, and the dwarf habit are further aids in combination to identify the species. *R. sanguineum* comes from 13,000 to 14,000 feet in western Yunnan, Szechuan and southeastern Tibet where it grows in exposed sites and on the margins of Pine forests. It was introduced to cultivation by Forrest. The name refers to its blood-red flowers. Freedom of Flowering: 2; Ease of Cultivation: 2+; American Quality Rating: xxx; British: ***; American Hardiness Rating: H-3; British: B; Truss Type: 11.

R. scintillans (sin′-til-lanz), **Balf. f. and W. W. Sm.** LAPPONICUM SERIES

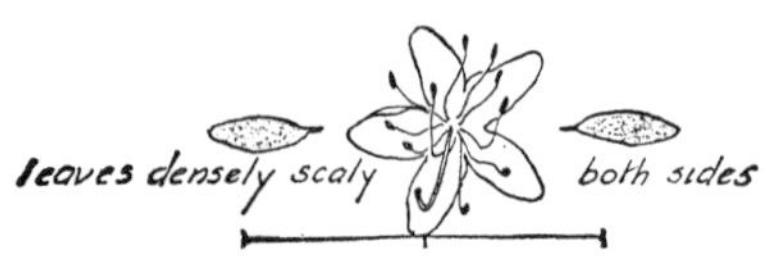

Here is another of the good, dwarf 'blue'-flowered Rhododendrons, an alpine which may eventually grow about 3 feet tall. The habit is twiggy, with slender, erect branches often somewhat lanky and bare below the terminal tufts of leaves, particularly on older specimens. The dull green leaves, crowded with scales, are $\frac{1}{4}$ to $\frac{3}{4}$ inch long, $\frac{1}{8}$ to $\frac{3}{8}$ inch wide, to some extent reminiscent of short, blunt conifer needles. The widely funnel-shaped flowers come in April, sometimes in early May, about four or five of them, each $\frac{3}{4}$ inch across or a little more, grouped into tight little terminal trusses about $1\frac{1}{4}$ inches in diameter. They vary in color from pale lavender to deep purple-blue. Forrest #20488 has good light blue blossoms. The F.C.C. form from Exbury, also commercially available, is perhaps the best, with deep, royal blue flowers. Random seedlings are apt to bloom an undistinguished pale lilac, and it is much better to secure plants propagated from specimens of known superior quality. This is a good Rhododendron for the rock garden or wherever its pygmy stature is appropriate, very attractive in flower, somewhat less so at other times. Most specialists consider its flowers to be the finest for color of any of the Lapponicum series. It seems difficult in the northeastern United States, where the high summer temperature is so foreign to its natural liking, but specialists have succeeded with it in New Jersey and southeastern New York. It has grown very slowly for me in northwestern Pennsylvania into a shapely little shrub about 10 inches tall, really more attractive in habit and foliage than it is in the mild moistness of the Pacific coastal climate. An exposed, damp site, sheltered but not shady, is needed. I consider it barely tolerant of its conditions in my trial grounds, whereas it grows easily and vigorously in the Rhododendron belt of the West Coast and in the British Isles. This species is characterized by leaves less than 1 inch long with the scales beneath contiguous or overlapping. The scaly calyx is very short, always much less than $\frac{1}{4}$ inch long, but distinctly lobed and not fringed with hairs. The corolla lacks scales or hairs on the outside but is downy in the throat. The purple, glabrous style is longer than the stamens, which are pubescent toward the base. The flower bud scales are persistent. *R. scintillans* was found and introduced by Forrest in 1913, when it was given the name meaning 'sparkling', an allusion to its gay flowers. It grows in the wild in exposed moorlands and ledges at 11,000 to 14,000 feet in China's Yunnan province. Freedom of Flowering: 1; Ease of Cultivation: 1; American Quality Rating: xx; British: ****; American Hardiness Rating: H-3; British: A; Truss Type: 5; A.M., 1924; F.C.C., 1934.

R. scyphocalyx (sky-fo-ka′-lix), **Balf. f. and Forrest.** NERIIFLORUM SERIES, SANGUINEUM SUBSERIES

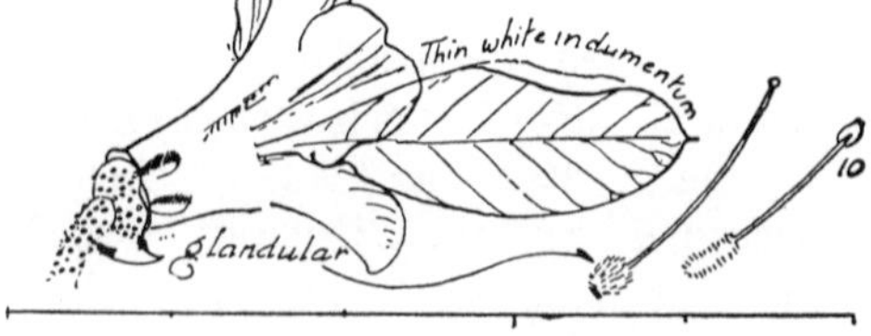

Here is a variable Rhododendron, not often seen in gardens, which possesses in some of its forms the same virtues which have made other species famous. It may reach its reputed height of 5 feet after many years, but old plants are usually observed as dwarf, mound-like shrubs of excellent habit and crowded foliage about 2 feet tall and 3½ feet broad. The prominently veined leaves are 1⅛ to 2½ inches long, ⅜ to 1 inch wide, coated beneath with a thin indumentum, white to gray, which usually drops off the midrib and lateral veins. This Rhododendron flowers in May and early June with long, trumpet-shaped flowers flaring to a diameter of about 2 inches or more in good forms, dangling in lax groups of three to seven at the ends of the branches. It has a remarkable color range, from yellow through various shades of orange and unusual, coppery rose blends to quite clear red. A hillside planted with random seedlings exhibiting the complete chromatic assortment is a striking spectacle, but some specialists find fault with the pendant posture of the flowers, which does not display them to the best advantage. I think the '0' quality rating of the American Rhododendron Society and the omission of any commendation by the Royal Horticultural Society are unjustified. Some forms produce orange flowers more intense in color than those of its recommended relatives. 'Var.' *septentrionale* is actually a subspecies of *R. dichroanthum*, the same as is *R. scyphocalyx*, but it is often erroneously offered as a form of the latter and is frequently especially attractive in color. *R. scyphocalyx* grows rather slowly. It has a fine appearance out of bloom and a stature which fits it for many uses. The unique flower colors offer interesting possibilities for unusual landscape effects. Among its closest relatives, this subspecies of *R. dichroanthum* is characterized by having a heavy, waxen corolla, orange to crimson, with five nectar pouches at the base, both flower stalks and short, blunt ovary clad with glandular hairs. The erect, colored calyx is about ¼ inch long. The thin, plastered grayish indumentum beneath obovate leaves, not narrow for their length, aids identification in a group notorious for its complexity. This subspecies seems to differ from *R. herpesticum* only in stature, and since there are intermediate forms between the two the distinction is largely a fiction. *R. scyphocalyx* was first found by Forrest in 1919 and named for its cup-shaped calyx. It grows at 10,000 to 13,000 feet in mixed scrub, on exposed stony hillsides and on the edges of taller vegetation in western Yunnan and northeast Upper Burma. Freedom of Flowering: 2; Ease of Cultivation: 1; American Quality Rating: 0; British: none; American Hardiness Rating: H-4; British: B; Truss Type: 11.

R. sinogrande (si-no-grand′-ee), **Balf. f. and W. W. Sm.** GRANDE SERIES

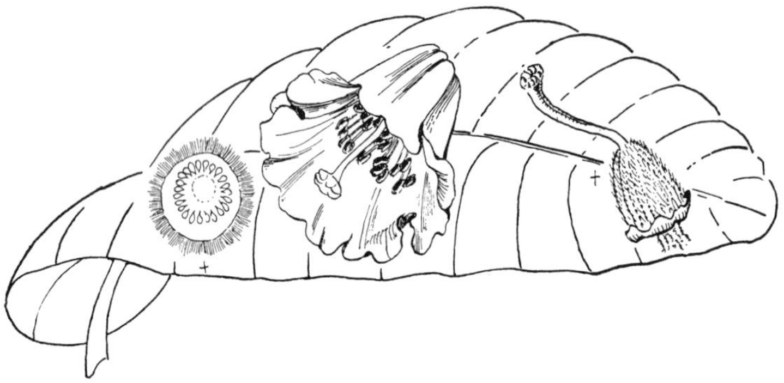

This Rhododendron is a magnificent survivor of a primitive age, come down to us in unparalleled splendor of foliage and flower from a dim time when the lushness of plants and flowers is unimaginable. The mammoth leaves, largest in the genus, are up to 3 feet long and a foot broad, set in gigantic rosettes sometimes measuring more than 2 yards across, and they create a startling effect of tropical grandeur and exotic luxuriance. A heavy, stiff-limbed tree to 30 feet, *R. sinogrande* is not often seen at its best in the Western world. The size of its striking foliage in huge, stiff collars is a good gauge of its contentment, and the variation is enormous. Perhaps the usual range would be a leaf length of 10 inches to about 2 feet on a reasonably well-grown specimen, with a width of 5 inches to 1 foot. Occasional leaves may be much larger. Juvenile leaves also often exceed the usual dimensions whereas those on older, flowering branches tend to diminish in size. Their width and shape also vary surprisingly, ranging from a rather narrow, lance-like outline to a broad, oval conformation. These amazing leaves are thick, somewhat brittle and almost metallic in substance, at first thinly coated with a silvery scurf which remains on the under-surface but disappears later on the upper side, leaving a broad expanse of deep, shining green with the veins sharply etched. Heavy, mounded trusses about 9 inches in diameter are built up of twenty to thirty thick-textured, 2-inch bell-shaped flowers with eight to ten lobes, which often lie in more or less regular tiers forming the inflorescence. They range in color from ivory-white to clear, soft yellow, often with a crimson patch in the base, and they appear in April. The deeper yellow forms are much prized by enthusiasts. This species demands shelter and protection from winds, and it resents transplanting because it is often deep-rooted, unlike most other Rhododendrons. It is invariably seen at its best growing in ravines and valleys, shielded by larger trees near by, where it is one of the most dramatic and majestically imposing sights in all horticulture. The species is only precariously hardy in Oregon and Washington. It is distinguished from its near relative, *R. grande*, by its much wider leaves, averaging 5 to 14 inches broad, and from others of the series by also possessing a silvery, plastered indumentum. It has round leaf petioles which are longer than those of many of its allies, 1¼ to 2 inches being typical, and the corollas are bell-shaped in contrast to others which are funnel-shaped. There are eighteen to twenty stamens. The name designates it as a Chinese equivalent of *R. grande*. It comes from forests at 10,000 to 14,000 feet elevation in western Yunnan province. It has also been found in southeastern Tibet and in northeastern Upper Burma. *R. sinogrande* was discovered and introduced by George Forrest in 1912–13. Although it is often somewhat shy in blossoming, this species is capable of producing its flowers in abundance as is evident from a tree growing in a private garden in Cairnryan, Scotland, which is extraordinarily floriferous. Freedom of Flowering: 2; Ease of Cultivation: 2; American Quality Rating: xxxx; British: ****; American Hardiness Rating: H-4; British: D; Truss Type: 6; A.M., 1922; F.C.C., 1926.

R. smirnowii (smir-noff′-i), **Traut.** PONTICUM SERIES, CAUCASICUM SUBSERIES

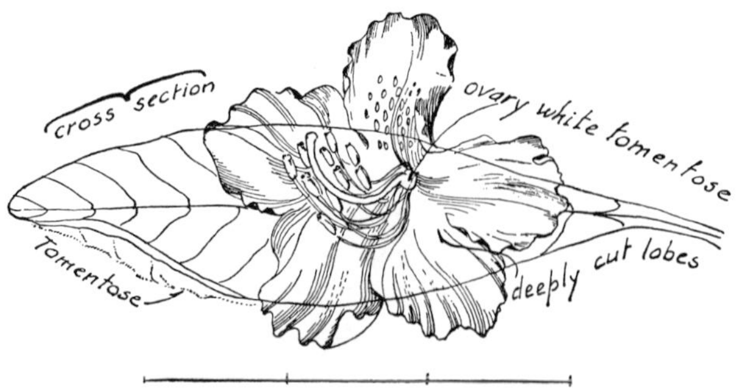

The true *R. smirnowii* is an attractive evergreen shrub 6 or 8 feet tall, usually wider than high, with dark green leaves 3 to 7 inches long, $\frac{3}{4}$ to 2 inches broad, thickly coated underneath with a soft white to fawn-colored felty indumentum. The largest specimen I have seen was 6 feet high and 14 feet wide. It produces in late May or early June rounded, $5\frac{1}{2}$-inch trusses of bright purplish-rose, broadly funnel-shaped flowers about $2\frac{1}{2}$ inches across, with frilled margins, about ten or twelve held somewhat loosely in the cluster. There is a good rose-pink form much finer in color than the average of seedlings. This handsome foliage plant, which is notably free from insect pests, bears a mixed reputation due to the paucity of plants growing in the northeastern United States which are truly representative of the species. Practically all of the specimens in collections both public and private seem to have derived directly or indirectly from seeds sent out by an American arboretum. These seeds were apparently not the result of crosses made under controlled conditions and they produced hundreds of hybrid Rhododendrons which are growing all up and down the Atlantic seaboard under the *smirnowii* label. Their progeny have further compounded the confusion. When I first obtained the authentic species from abroad I found it much more attractive than the plants in commerce in this country which showed various degrees of hybridity. Its indumentum is far heavier, the stems, dormant floral buds and leaf stalks are all covered with the soft silvery felt, and traces of it remain even on the upper leaf surfaces throughout the year. The new shoots are decoratively covered with a fresh blue-gray woolly sheath, too. The amount of indumentum does vary, of course, but generally it is much more of a conspicuous feature of the species than plants in commerce here show it to be. Plants growing under the *smirnowii* label in some fairly mild climates, close to the Pennsylvania–Maryland border, for example, open a few flowers in September and October. The balance of the florets in the clusters then fall an easy prey to subsequent winter cold, and the floral display in its proper blooming season is sharply reduced the following spring. This trait, also typical of some *caucasicum* hybrids, is much less evident in colder climates with less temperature variation in the autumn, and is not apparent at all in my garden. There is an unfortunate tendency for some plants elsewhere to open their flowers over a period so extended that the blossoms first produced are faded by the time the last florets in the truss are fully expanded. Whether these faults are really inherent in the authentic species I am unable to say. They have not been characteristic of my plants or of others on the West Coast and in England which are true to name. This is a rugged, adaptable Rhododendron, easily pleased in planting site and exposure, one of the few species from abroad which are suited to the climate of the northeastern United States. The trim, dense habit of growth, persistent foliage, and the interesting silver woolly indumentum commend it for many garden uses in climates both cold and mild. This species is hardy to Boston and beyond. It blooms at the same time as the native *R. catawbiense* but is not so decorative in flower as the finest selected color forms of the American species. *R. smirnowii* has the better of it for evergreen plant habit and garden effect, however. It has been traditional in describing *R. smirnowii* to compare it with *R. ungernii* and to state that they are hard to distinguish, with only minor differences separating them. *R. ungernii* is an extremely rare species in the United States and I think its alleged resemblance to *R. smirnowii* is nonsense. All the plants that I have ever seen either here or abroad have been distinguishable at a glance, because there is actually very little similarity between the two species, aside from the indumentum beneath their leaves. *R. ungernii* has much larger foliage, a fresh, bright green in color. It grows much more vigorously and has a texture which is a great deal coarser as a result of being larger in all its parts. It blooms six weeks later, at the end of July, and is not satisfactorily hardy at Boston. In the generally disparate botanical grouping of species in the Ponticum series, *R. smirnowii* is distinct among those with a loosely woolly indumentum on the basis of its somewhat long and narrow leaves with rounded tips lacking any short, abrupt point. The calyx is only about $\frac{1}{8}$ inch long and the ovary is coated with the characteristic white tomentum. It is native to the southern Caucasus Mountains where it was discovered by Baron Ungern-Sternberg in 1885, and named for one of his friends. Freedom of Flowering: 2+; Ease of Cultivation: 1; American Quality Rating: x; British: ★; American Hardiness Rating: H-2; British: A; Truss Type: 1.

R. souliei (soo′-lee-i), **Franch.** THOMSONII SERIES, SOULIEI SUBSERIES

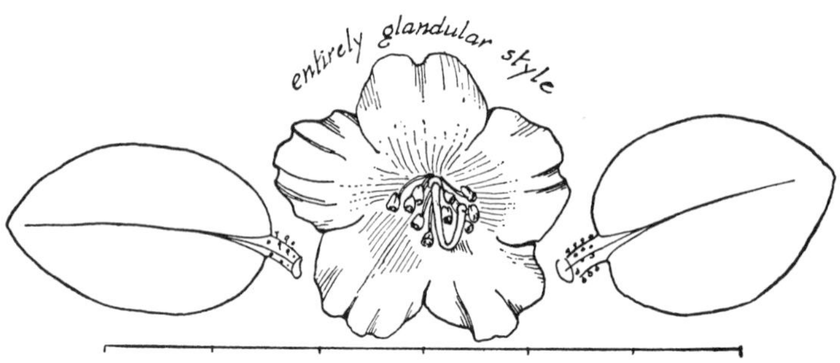

Almost every species enthusiast has a special affection for this Rhododendron, which is one of particular charm and appeal. It is restrained in growth, seldom seen more than 7 feet tall but capable of reaching 10 or 12 feet or possibly more. The glaucous leaves $1\frac{3}{8}$ to $3\frac{1}{2}$ inches long, 1 to 2 inches broad, are very distinct, with a metallic green luster. They are often heart-shaped at the base and are borne on shoots which are purplish when newly formed. The leaf base may also be rounded and occasionally the glands do not appear on the petioles as illustrated here, but the foliage in any case has an odd sheen which marks the species conspicuously. As the new leaves mature they take on an attractive blue frosty overlay which is strongly decorative. The flat, saucer-shaped flowers are beautifully modeled in shades ranging from rose to white, flushed pink, 2 to 3 inches across, appearing in May. There are six to eight blossoms held firmly in a gracefully proportioned truss, neither loose nor crowded, which shows off the florets to unusual advantage. This vivacious and delightful Rhododendron blooms in four years from seeds and is reasonably hardy. In England it grows better in the eastern counties than in the mild Cornwall climate. It should be satisfactory possibly as far north as Philadelphia in the United States in protected sites, and it is such an attractive shrub that it is well worth the trouble to find a sheltered spot for it. Three different forms of extraordinary quality have received First-Class Certificates at various times in England. It separates from its allies on the basis of its rose to faintly pink saucer-shaped flowers with style glandular to the tip. The calyx is usually $\frac{3}{16}$ to $\frac{1}{2}$ inch long. *R. souliei* was first found by Rev. R. P. Soulié in 1893, for whom it was subsequently named. It was introduced into cultivation by Wilson in 1903. It covers large areas at 9,000 to 14,000 feet elevation in western China and Tibet where it forms thickets, and also dwells in woodlands. Freedom of Flowering: 2+; Ease of Cultivation: 2+; American Quality Rating: xxx; British: ★★★★; American Hardiness Rating: H-3; British: B; Truss Type: 4. This is the most decorated Rhododendron species in the genus, having received an F.C.C. award in 1909, 1936 (for the Exbury pink form), and in 1951 (for the Windsor Park form).

R. sperabile (sper-ab′-il-lee), **Balf. f. and Farrer.** NERIIFLORUM SERIES, NERIIFLORUM SUBSERIES

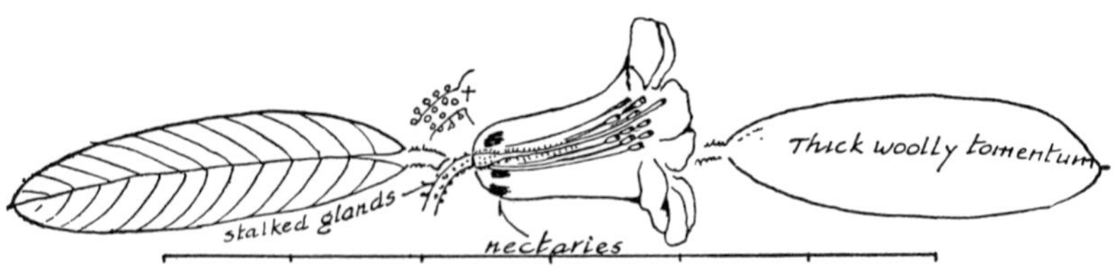

This is one of the most varied of Rhododendrons in garden value and in many other respects. At its best it is a fine ornamental. At its worst, it is drab, the inconsequential flowers drooping abjectly between small leaves so sparse that the shrub is a dispiriting sight. In habit all forms are spreading, varying in height from 18 inches to 6 feet. The dark green leaves with prominent veins and roughened surface are 2 to 4 inches long, ½ to 1¼ inches wide, covered underneath with thick tan to brown wool. The flowers appear in April, long scarlet bells about 2 inches in diameter, eight or nine to a flat-topped terminal cluster in the best forms; much smaller and fewer in number in poorer expressions of the species. The foliage tends to obscure the pendulous bells in some plants. The form sparingly available under Forrest #26478 has good foliage, and large, waxen flowers especially vivid in their scarlet brilliance, but the narrow-leaved Forrest #25569 is among those whose interest is largely botanical. Var. *weihsiense* is reputed to be distinct on the basis of thinner, lighter colored indumentum and longer narrower leaves, but there are innumerable intergrades and I think its status is not useful on the grounds of convenience or on any other. Some collectors' numbers which have been identified as this variety have produced plants with the broader, typical leaves. The best forms with larger flowers of superior color should be propagated as clones and given names to identify them. This species is distinguished from *R. floccigerum* by possessing stalked glands on petioles and stems; from *R. sperabiloides* by the absence of glands on ovary, leaf stalks and shoots of the latter. Among indumented species of the series it is distinct on the basis of the white, waxy papillate epidermis which is revealed beneath the leaf by scraping away the woolly, single-layered indumentum; by the bristly glands mixed with whitish wool on the young shoots; by the thick-textured, waxen flowers with long, curved ovary which tapers gradually into the style; and by the long, curved seed capsule. The outer scales of the foliage buds are narrow and sharply pointed. *R. sperabile* is native to the stony slopes and ravines of northeastern Upper Burma and Tibet at 10,000 to 12,000 feet elevation, where it was found by Farrer in 1919, and given the optimistic name meaning 'to be hoped for'. Freedom of Flowering: 2; Ease of Cultivation: 2+; American Quality Rating: xx; British: **; American Hardiness Rating: H-4; British: C; Truss Type: 10; A.M., 1925.

F. sperabiloides (sper-ab-il-oy′-deez), **Tagg and Forrest.** NERIIFLORUM SERIES, NERIIFLORUM SUBSERIES

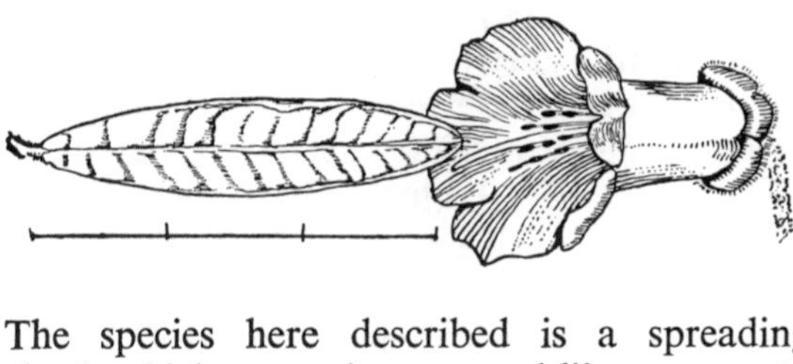

The species here described is a spreading shrub which grows in a mound-like manner to a height of about 4 feet and a width of 6 feet. The leaves, 2 to 4 inches long, ¾ to 1¼ inches broad, usually nearer the larger of these dimensions, are dull to light green above and prominently veined. Underneath they are clad in irregular patches with a dispersed, granular indumentum. They seem to be susceptible in some gardens to a fungus disease which causes a partial brownish-black discoloration. The tubular, bell-shaped flowers come in early

April, $1\frac{3}{8}$ to as much as 2 inches across in the best forms, gathered in single-tiered, flat-topped, often pendent groups of about seven at the ends of the branches. They vary in quality enormously. Some small-flowered forms such as Forrest #21824 are buff and rose, giving a nondescript two-tone effect. Others, notably Kingdon-Ward #9472, have much more impressive blossoms, burning scarlet to rich crimson. Only the best forms in flower and foliage should be grown for garden decoration. The distinctive patchy indumentum beneath long, narrow leaves separates this species from its allies in the Neriiflorum subseries. The young stems and leaf stalks are hairy but non-glandular. The long, narrow eglandular ovary tapers into the style. This species is sometimes confused with *R. sperabile*, but the latter is distinct in having stamens glabrous at the base, glands on the ovary, petioles and young shoots, and a thick, woolly, continuous indumentum beneath the leaves. The outer scales of the foliage buds are narrow and sharply pointed on *R. sperabiloides*, as they are in other species of its subseries. This Rhododendron is native to southeastern Tibet where it grows at 12,000 to 13,000 feet in mixed scrub in the valleys. It was discovered and introduced by Farrer in 1919. The name denotes its superficial resemblance to *R. sperabile*. Freedom of Flowering: 2; Ease of Cultivation: 2+; American Quality Rating: xx; British: ***; American Hardiness Rating: H-4; British: C; Truss Type: 10.

R. spinuliferum (spin-u-lif′-er-um), **Franch.** SCABRIFOLIUM SERIES

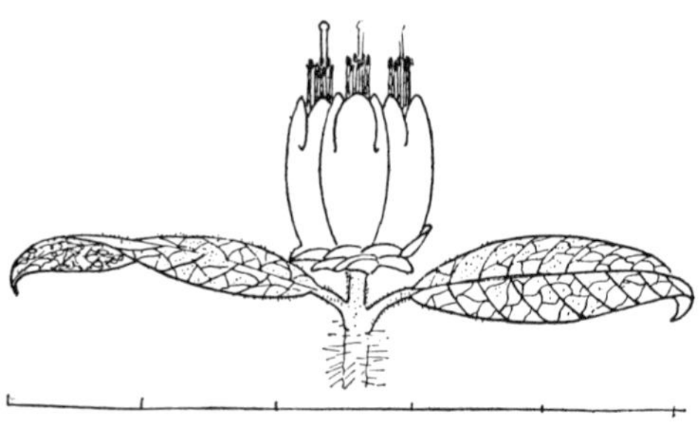

This unique, oddly pretty Rhododendron outgrows by at least 2 or 3 feet the 8 foot ultimate height usually ascribed to it in cultivation. The upright habit, slender branches and rather small leaves, $1\frac{1}{2}$ to 3 inches long, $\frac{1}{2}$ to $1\frac{1}{2}$ inches wide, fit this Rhododendron for some garden uses where the more forceful character of the large-leaved sorts would be too assertive. The leaves are puckered by indented veins and are both hairy and scaly below. The branchlets are also hairy. The peculiar, tubular flowers are about an inch long, only half an inch wide, and they become more narrow rather than expanding toward the mouth so that the corolla is dilated only enough to permit the style and stamens to protrude from the elongated tube. The blossoms are borne from axillary buds clustered near the ends of the branches, usually about five or six in a little group, often standing upright and parallel much like the candles on a birthday cake. They appear in April and range in color from pink to crimson, the orange-red forms generally being the brightest and most attractive. This Rhododendron with its blossoms of such unusual design is a good ornamental shrub. The leaves are somewhat susceptible to a spotting fungus in some climates. It blossoms early in the spring and the curious flowers always excite interest. *R. spinuliferum* can scarcely be confused with any other Rhododendron unless it would be *R. keysii* of the Cinnabarinum series. It too has a corolla constricted at both ends, but the style and stamens are pubescent toward the base and do not protrude beyond the narrow opening at the end of the tube. The flowers are smaller and any resemblance between the two species is entirely superficial in any case, because there are many points of difference between them. *R. spinuliferum* was discovered by Delavay and introduced to France in 1907. It was named for the bristly hairs which cover the young shoots and extend to the under-surfaces and margins of the leaves. Its native habitat is primarily the shady thickets at an elevation of 6,000 to 8,000 feet in Yunnan province of China. Freedom of Flowering: 2; Ease of Cultivation: 2+; American Quality Rating: xx; British: ***; American Hardiness Rating: H-4; British: D; Truss Type: 18.

R. stewartianum (stew-ar-ti-a′-num), **Diels.** THOMSONII SERIES, THOMSONII SUBSERIES

Mature plants of this species vary enormously in height from 2 to 9 feet, but it is most often seen in gardens 6 or 7 feet tall with strongly veined, bright green leaves 2 to 4¾ inches long, 1 to 2½ inches wide. The under-surface is usually, but not invariably, light grey-green from a thin veil of whitish hairs coating it. Occasionally the leaf undersides have a scant brown mealy indumentum, and rarely they are glabrous. The long, bell-shaped blossoms appear extremely early, in March and sometimes even in February in mild winters, about 2¼ inches wide and eight to a lax cluster in the best forms, with a usual count of three to six or seven. It has an outstanding color range in the flowers, from white through innumerable shades of pink and rose to scarlet and dark crimson; from ivory to yellow; and often with one of these shades rimming a corolla of another of these colors. The clear yellow forms are especially lovely, as are the cream shades suffused pink. Sometimes the blossoms are spotted. Strangely, the white flowers are often larger, frequently measuring 3 inches in diameter. This is a fine Rhododendron, perhaps with a little more tendency than most to grow lanky if neglected as it matures. The planting site often makes the difference between success and failure in its precocious blossoming. It should not be given an eastern exposure where the early sun strikes the flowers on frosty mornings. It is not true that the color of the dormant vegetative buds distinguishes this species from its close relative, *R. eclecteum*. The likeliest distinction is in the color of the leaf under-surface, usually very light gray-green and hairy in *stewartianum*, strong, dark green and glabrous in its ally, which also frequently has a much shorter leaf stalk. These differences are not invariably reliable, however, because the two species are linked by an uninterrupted progression of intermediate forms. Of the species in the Thomsonii series with flowers usually in the white-yellow-pink range, *R. stewartianum* is characterized by the ovary normally glandular, with style glabrous and non-glandular. The calyx is variable, from $\frac{1}{16}$ to $\frac{9}{16}$ inch in length, but usually conspicuous for its large size. The seed capsule is short, stout, and straight. The leaf petiole varies from ¼ to ¾ inch, but it is usually noticeably long for the size of the foliage. This species is native to southeastern Tibet, Yunnan province of China, northeastern Upper Burma, and Assam at 10,000 to 14,000 feet, in Rhododendron thickets, mixed scrub, and exposed hillsides. It was first discovered by George Forrest in 1904 and later named for L. B. Stewart, Curator of the Royal Botanic Garden at Edinburgh. Freedom of Flowering: 1; Ease of Cultivation: 1; American Quality Rating: xxx; British: ***; American Hardiness Rating: H-4; British: B; Truss Type: 10; A.M., 1934.

R. strigillosum (strij-ill-o′-sum), **Franch.** BARBATUM SERIES, GLISCHRUM SUBSERIES

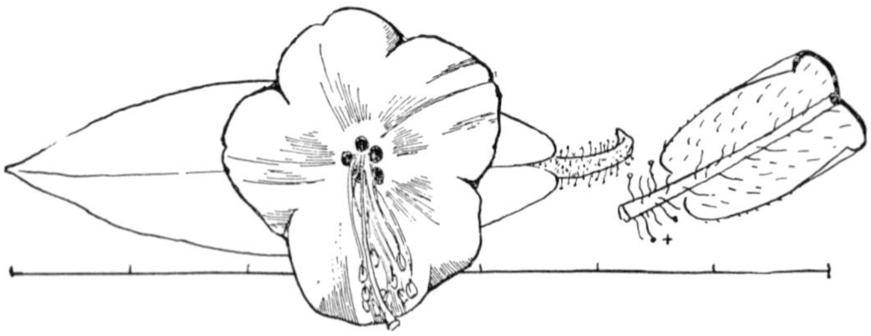

The stature of this species ranges from that of a robust shrub about 8 feet tall to a small tree as much as 20 feet high. The leaves are 3 to 7 inches long, ¾ to 1¾ inches broad, generally tending to the larger dimensions, bright green and quite attractive. The leaf stalks are thickly clad with rather stiff bristles which extend as well to the young shoots. Long, bell-shaped flowers are clear, luminous red, an exceptionally brilliant and effective shade, 1½ to 2 inches across, with conspicuous black basal nectar pouches. There are eight to twelve florets in a loose terminal cluster. As it flowers in March, this species should have a planting site shielded from frost as much as possible. It is often considered to be a Chinese counterpart of *R. barbatum*, but it has finer flowers and is reputed to be less hardy, inexplicably so considering the region and altitude where it is native. One would expect it to be a good deal more tolerant of cold and I think that it probably is hardier than its rating indicates. When Wilson introduced it from Szechuan province of China in 1904 where it grows at 7,000 to 10,000 feet in thickets and woodlands, he noted that some forms had white flowers. These seem not to occur in cultivation. The blood-red sort is a brilliantly beautiful shrub in the landscape, the sultry flowers glowing richly in the landscape at a bleak and bare season. This Rhododendron has such a strong identity, with its leaf stalks, flower stalks, calyces, young shoots and seed pods all bristly, that it is not likely to be mistaken for any other. In combination with the red flowers, small calyx, and the hairy leaf under-surface its character is distinct. *R. strigillosum* was placed in the Maculiferum subseries by British authorities but I am putting it into the Glischrum subseries, where it clearly belongs. Freedom of Flowering: 1; Ease of Cultivation: 1; American Quality Rating: xxx; British: ****; American Hardiness Rating: H-4; British: C; Truss Type: 9; A.M., 1923.

R. sulfureum (sul-fur′-yum), **Franch.** BOOTHII SERIES, BOOTHII SUBSERIES

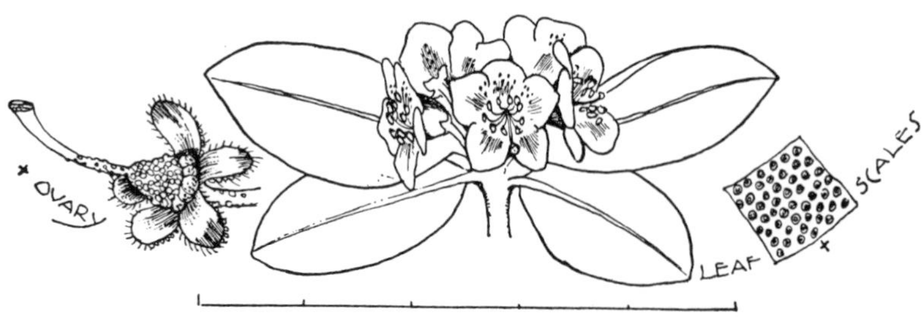

This is one of the few Rhododendron species with flowers of deep, clear yellow, an emphatic color which is rarely seen in such intensity. The blossoms are borne on a sturdy shrub which reaches 4 feet in height eventually, with thick, handsome leaves ranging in size from 1 to 3½ inches long, and ½ to 1¾ inches broad, and dotted underneath with tiny scales. The intense yellow flowers, unusual for their brilliance, with flat corollas, appear in April, each about 1¼ inches in diameter, most often borne six to a compact terminal cluster. This is an interesting species, but I do not think it can be described as beautiful because the blossoms seem inadequately small in scale placed as they are in the center of a rosette of rather large, glossy green leaves. They also seem disproportionately undersized compared with the stout, heavy limbs. However, this is an extremely variable species and some forms are much more attractive than others. It can be distinguished from other Rhododendrons of close relationship by its leaves with rounded tips and brown scales, uniform in size, on the under-surfaces, and by its flowers with short, thick sharply bent styles, borne in clusters of more than three. The calyx, about $\frac{3}{16}$ inch in length, is sparsely fringed with hairs. The species was discovered by Delavay in 1887 growing at 9,000 to 10,000 feet in damp sites shaded by ledges and has since been found in Upper Burma by other explorers. Its name means 'sulphur-colored', which falls considerably short of doing justice to the shade of the flowers. Freedom of Flowering: 1; Ease of Cultivation: 1; American Ratings: None yet assigned; British Quality Rating: ***; British Hardiness Rating: E; Truss Type: 14; A.M., 1937.

R. sutchuenense (sutch-u-en-en′-see), **Franch.** FORTUNEI SERIES, DAVIDII SUBSERIES

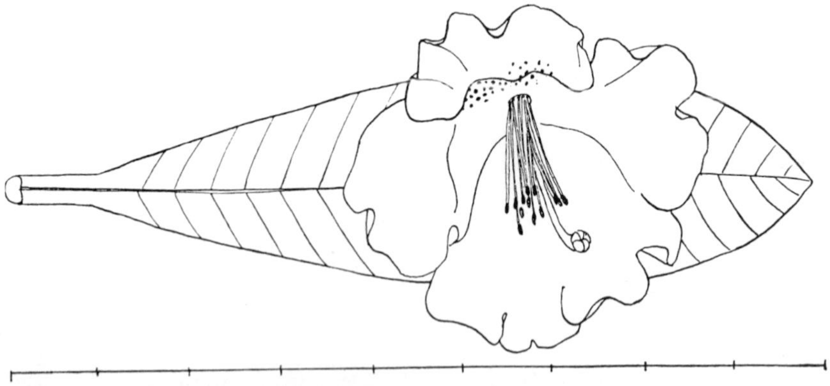

Horticultural authors have consistently understated the stature of innumerable Rhododendrons, but this beautiful species is a conspicuous example of dimensions inadequately noted in the past. *R. sutchuenense* grows in a tree-like manner in cultivation to a height of more than 25 feet and is one of the best foliage plants in the genus for fine appearance the year round. Its large, dark, mat-green leaves $4\frac{3}{4}$ to 11 inches long, $1\frac{1}{2}$ to $3\frac{1}{2}$ inches wide, usually near the greater of these dimensions, are conspicuously veined and produced in such numbers in dense rosettes that the plants seem luxuriantly clothed. The leaves often fall in a somewhat formal, drooping, fan-like arrangement. This is among the earliest species to flower, occasionally in bloom in late February. More often the delicate, light, lavender-pink blossoms come in March and make an impressive show in trusses as much as 8 inches across. The florets are widely bell-shaped, with five or six lobes, up to 3 inches across the face, spotted purple on the upper lobes and produced eight to fourteen in a loose, flat-topped terminal cluster. "Variety *geraldii*", actually a natural hybrid with *R. praevernum*, has a bold maroon blotch and the flowers are often a deeper, brighter rosy-lilac color. *R. sutchuenense* is certainly among the finest of Rhododendrons, striking at any season, and it is also among the most rugged of the Asian species. It is hardy to Boston. Its usefulness as a shrub valued for its flowers may be debatable in the northeastern United States, however, because it blossoms so early in the spring. Protected by conifers or planted near a body of water its splendid floral display is much more reliable, but with ordinary garden exposure the flowers are more or less regularly injured by frost on an average of about two years out of three in the East. Even so, the unopened buds are never harmed. They can be frozen repeatedly and still develop fully when a favorable turn in the weather allows them to demonstrate their charms. Then the huge trusses make such a brave show at the dreary end of winter that I would be quite willing to consider them a delightful, unearned bonus every two or three years, and grow this Rhododendron for its impressive value solely as a large evergreen. The literature states that *R. sutchuenense* flowers when quite small but I believe its usual disposition is quite the opposite. Plants must often be 6 feet tall and ten years old before they start to bloom. There is a form with unusually small leaves and flowers, sparingly distributed in the northeastern United States, which is somewhat less attractive than the type. This species is distinguished by the five-lobed flowers, spotted or blotched and densely puberlous inside, with glabrous ovary. The slender style is glabrous, with a knob-like, reddish stigma. There are thirteen to fifteen stamens. The large leaves, much longer than broad, have a prominent midrib which is loosely woolly beneath. There is a superficial resemblance to *R. calophytum* which has, however, three to five more stamens, flower stalks three times longer, a larger disc-like stigma and a much more pronounced bell shape to the corolla. *R. sutchuenense* comes from an altitude of 5,000 to 8,000 feet in Szechuan and Hupeh, where it grows in woodlands. It was introduced by Wilson in 1901 and named for the Chinese province of Szechuan in which it was found first. Freedom of Flowering: 1; Ease of Cultivation: 1; American Quality Rating: xxx; British: ***; American Hardiness Rating: H-3; British: B; Truss Type: 7; "var. *geraldii*", A.M., 1945.

R. taggianum (taj-je-a'-num), **Hutchinson.** MADDENII SERIES, MEGACALYX SUBSERIES

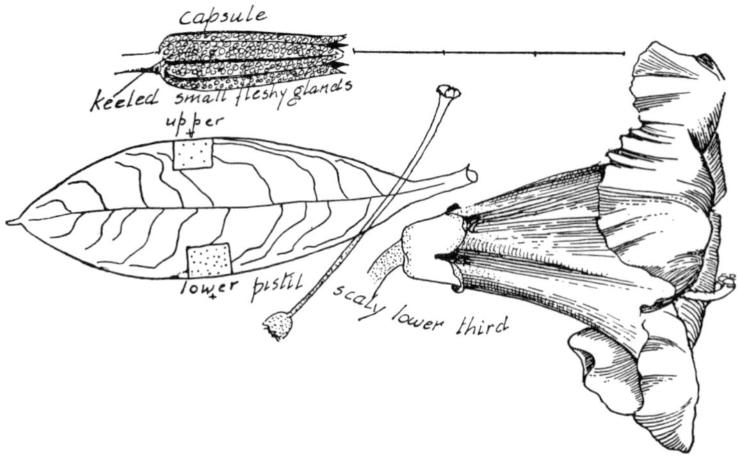

Mature specimens of this species are usually seen as thin, open shrubs 7 or 8 feet tall with dark green leaves $2\frac{1}{2}$ to 6 inches long, 1 to $2\frac{1}{4}$ inches wide, scaly on the midrib above, somewhat glaucous and dotted with many small scales beneath. It flowers in late April and the first part of May with startling, huge, white, funnel-shaped blossoms, deliciously fragrant, each fully 4 inches across and almost as long in the best forms, about four in outward facing groups at the ends of the branches. Sometimes the flowers are almost a buff color. The white forms frequently have a throat suffused yellow in varying degree. In a series noted for the remarkable quality of its flowers, this is one of the supremely beautiful species and it is the hardiest of the Megacalyx subseries. The blossoms are a stunning *tour de force*, beautifully modeled and alluringly scented.

Mr Amateis has drawn Kingdon-Ward #6808 to illustrate the flowers of *R. taggianum*. Some forms are much broader at the base of the tube, which is fluted and pinched where it issues from the calyx. Unhappily, this shrub is ungainly, inclined to be loose and straggling. Several specimens can be planted close together to minimize this fault, however, or a single plant can be placed to clamber through and over other more densely foliaged Rhododendrons.

In this country *R. taggianum* is at home outdoors only in climates similar to that of San Francisco and the west coast of Scotland. Elsewhere it is much more satisfactory as a greenhouse shrub. The species is characterized by narrowly oblong leaves faintly veined underneath (in contrast to the wider leaves with very prominent lateral nerves beneath of *R. nuttallii*). The leaf stalks are not grooved on the upper side. The non-hairy flower stalk is scaly, the corolla scaly only at the base of the tube. There are ten stamens. The large, leafy calyx about $\frac{5}{8}$ inch long, scaly on the margin and toward the base, is devoid of hairs. There are usually only three flowers to the truss whereas its close relatives, *RR. dalhousiae* and *lindleyi*, often have four, five, or six in a cluster. As if in compensation, *R. taggianum* is demonstrably hardier and succeeds where the other two fail. The straight ridged seed capsule is exceptionally long, about 2 inches, and covered with fleshy glands. This species was not found until 1925, when Forrest discovered it at 10,000 to 11,000 feet elevation growing on the edges of conifer forests and in thickets in open glades. It first flowered in cultivation at the Royal Botanic Garden in Edinburgh in 1930 when it was only 18 inches high, and was named for H. F. Tagg, a botanist there and himself the author of numerous familiar Rhododendron descriptions. Freedom of Flowering: 1; Ease of Cultivation: 2+; American Quality Rating: xxx; British: ★★★; American Hardiness Rating: H-6; British: E; Truss Type: 12; A.M., 1932; F.C.C., 1934.

R. tephropeplum (tef-ro-pep′-lum), **Balf. f. and Farrer.**

BOOTHII SERIES, TEPHROPEPLUM SUBSERIES

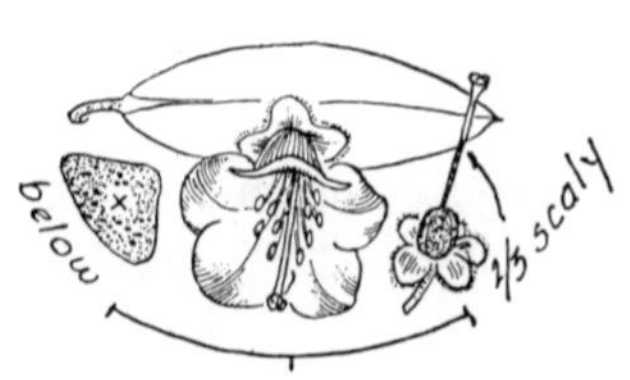

Another among the variable species, this Rhododendron is usually seen as a small shrub about 3 feet tall, 4 feet broad, with good, dense foliage and attractive habit. Some forms are reputed to reach a height of 6 feet. The leaves are 1¼ to 5 inches long, ⅜ to 1½ inches wide, glaucous and very scaly underneath. Plants can be selected to flower from late April until almost the end of May, the blossoms ranging in color from white to deep, glowing rosy-crimson with many pink shades of singular attractiveness in between. I have not seen the magenta and purplish shades mentioned in botanical references, possibly because they would be less attractive and may have dropped out of cultivation. The species is now noteworthy in gardens for the exceptional appeal of the fresh, sparkling pink and rose flowers. They have an extraordinary depth and luminosity to their color. The blossoms are about ⅞ inch across, prodigiously produced in loose little clusters of three to nine, and rarely many more. There is at Bodnant, in Wales, a form bearing the label *deleiense*, which has sixteen florets in each mound-shaped truss. This is a tractable little Rhododendron, extraordinarily free-flowering and seen always to advantage in rock gardens, facing down larger shrubs, in low, informal hedges and in foundation plantings, wherever the climate is suitable. It is one of those sorts which seem to do well and to make a brave show of color wherever they are placed. Its appeal is evident by its popularity among Rhododendron enthusiasts. Forrest collected his #20884 at 14,000 feet in Tibet but I do not know whether, as might be expected, it proved more cold resistant than his other collections or those of Kingdon-Ward and Rock. However, Kingdon-Ward's forms are superior ornamentally. Among species of the Boothii series with long, slender straight styles and tubular flowers, *R. tephropeplum* can be identified by the large calyx about ¼ inch long with spreading lobes; by the corolla not scaly on the outside, or only rarely so; and by the leaves with small scales one-half to their own diameter apart. It was first found in northeastern Upper Burma by Farrer in 1920, and later introduced to cultivation by Forrest and Kingdon-Ward, who found it also in Yunnan, Tibet, and Assam. It grows from 8,000 to 14,000 feet on ledges and rocky slopes. The name means 'with ashy-gray covering'. Freedom of Flowering: 1; Ease of Cultivation: 1; American Quality Rating: xxx; British: ★★★; American Hardiness Rating: H-4; British: B; Truss Type: 9; A.M., 1929.

R. thomsonii (tom′-son-i), **Hook. f.** THOMSONII SERIES, THOMSONII SUBSERIES

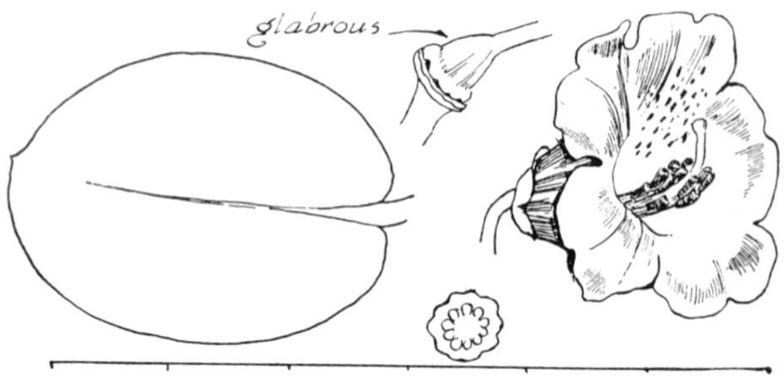

Parent of many fine hybrids and beloved for its own sake by generations of gardeners, *R. thomsonii* is in the first rank of garden ornamentals. It is among the very best Rhododendron species in the genus for its foliage, flowers, and adaptability. Long and prolific in bloom, reasonably hardy in moderate climates, with many landscape uses, *R. thomsonii* is as popular today as it was when it first became available to gardeners just about a century ago. It varies somewhat in growth habit. The finest specimen I have seen was 7 × 12 feet broad, clothed to the ground in serried leaves. Another, perhaps more common form, grows in a more open, upright manner to 15 or 20 feet. A century-old specimen in Scotland grown from seeds sent back by Hooker measures 25 feet tall. The rounded glabrous leaves, which are conspicuously blue-green above and whitish underneath, are $1\frac{1}{2}$ to 4 inches long, $1\frac{1}{4}$ to $2\frac{1}{2}$ inches wide. The soft emerald-green new growth acquires a blue haze as it matures, making the species one of the finest foliage plants to be found in the genus. Deep, blood-red, bell-shaped flowers up to 3 inches or more across in the best forms, six to ten of them gathered into large, loose clusters, spangle the tips of almost every branch in April. They bear conspicuous calyces, usually waxen, yellowish-buff but occasionally red. Rare variants have light red or even rose flowers, blotched magenta. One of the most remarkable of the many virtues of *R. thomsonii* is the length of time it remains in bloom. In a cool season the fine, clear red flowers of heavy, waxen texture remain in good condition for as long as four weeks. This species has received many awards for its tremendous horticultural value. Specimens over 100 years old are today among the garden treasures of the Western world. It is among the most versatile of Rhododendrons, useful in almost any sheltered garden position where a medium-sized shrub is wanted. The distinctively colored foliage lends a welcome note of contrast and variety against the more sober green of most other Rhododendrons. The new growth is quite noticeably blue. Faded flowers should be removed lest the plants exhaust themselves producing seeds in such prodigious quantity. This species should also probably be fertilized every year to sustain it in good health through its lavish production of blossoms since any branches which lose their vigor and die are not usually replaced by sprouts originating from older wood. It does not respond to pruning. *R. thomsonii* can be recognized by its crimson flowers in clusters of six to ten, in combination with a large calyx, $\frac{1}{4}$ inch long or more, and non-glandular ovary. The round to broadly elliptic leaves are large compared with those of most other species in the series, usually over $2\frac{1}{2}$ inches in length, and are devoid of hairs on the undersides. *R. thomsonii* is native to the eastern Himalayas at 10,000 to 14,000 feet in Sikkim, Bhutan, Nepal, and Tibet, where it grows in Rhododendron forests. It was discovered in 1849 by Hooker who named it for his travelling companion, Dr Thomas Thomson. Freedom of Flowering: 1; Ease of Cultivation: 1; American Quality Rating: xxx; British: ****; American Hardiness Rating: H-3; British: B; Truss Type: 10; A.G.M., 1925.

R. tricanthum (tri-kan′-thum), **Rehder.** TRIFLORUM SERIES, AUGUSTINII SUBSERIES

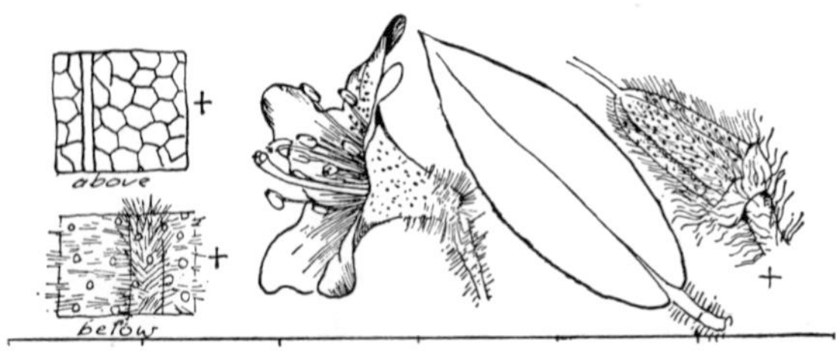

One of the hardiest of the Triflorum series Rhododendrons, older specimens of this species are most often about 8 feet tall but they are known to reach a height of 15 feet or even more. The scaly leaves are 2 to 3½ inches long, ¾ to 1¼ inches broad, conspicuously hairy and with bristles on the stalks. The young shoots are bristled as well. The mauve to dark purple flowers are borne in threes, usually, at the ends of the branches in May. They are about 1¾ inches in diameter. The darkest colored forms are striking in blossom but most unselected seedlings incline toward magenta and appear to best advantage in a woodland, isolated from other flower colors. Like its allies, *R. trichanthum* gives a light landscape effect with its willowy leaves, pliant branches and graceful growth habit. This is the Rhododendron formerly called *R. villosum*. The slate-purple Tower Court form is the one sought by specialists. The species is distinct from its relatives with white to purple flowers in the bristly character of so many of its parts. The leaf under-surface, especially the midrib, the petioles, the corolla tube, the flower stalks, and the outside of the calyx are all clad with bristles. The younger shoots are bristly with long hairs. Wilson introduced this Rhododendron in 1904 from 7,000 to 11,000 feet in the Szechuan province of China. Freedom of Flowering: 2+; Ease of Cultivation: 1; American Ratings: None yet assigned; British Quality Rating: **; British Hardiness Rating: B; Truss Type: 9.

R. triflorum (tri-flor′-um), **Hook.** TRIFLORUM SERIES, TRIFLORUM SUBSERIES

A shrub capable of reaching 10 feet in height, older specimens of *R. triflorum* are usually seen about 5 or 6 feet tall and a little wider, well foliaged with leaves 1½ to 3 inches long, ½ to 1¼ inches broad, scaly underneath. The red, peeling bark is a note of interest, perhaps the best feature of the species. The flowers are 1½ inches across with five spreading lobes springing from a funnel-shaped base. Sometimes they are as much as 2 inches in diameter, fragrant, and borne most often in threes at the ends of the branches in late April and early May. June is usually included in descriptions of the flowering period but such late blooming must be very rare. The blossoms are an odd shade of light yellow, spotted with green, in the most common form, a color which does not carry well or contrast with the olive-green foliage. There is also a dull yellow-flowered variety with conspicuous brownish-red blotch popularly called "Ward's Mahogany Triflorum". A rather clear lemon-yellow form is much more showy, but the pink-flowered species commonly called "Caerhay's Pink Triflorum" is actually *R. davidsonianum*. Many enthusiasts are fond of this species, though it is not really a colorful one. The slender branching habit and small, narrow leaves give it a note of grace against the rotund, large-leaved species. Where it is not quite hardy, *R. keiskei* is a superior substitute which offers a somewhat similar effect in flower and leaf. Among species with yellow, cream, or greenish-white flowers, *R. triflorum* is distinguished by its leaves sharply pointed at the apex, 1½ inches long or more, so thickly dotted underneath with small scales that they are less than their own diameter apart. The leaf stalks are not bristly along their margins. The usually three-flowered umbel is compact. This species comes from 8,000 to 9,500 feet in the Himalayan Mountains of Sikkim and Bhutan. It was discovered and introduced by Hooker in 1849 and its name refers to its three-flowered inflorescence. I think it is drab and commonplace as a garden shrub. Freedom of Flowering: 1; Ease of Cultivation: 1; American Quality Rating: 0; British: ★; American Hardiness Rating: H-3; British: C; Truss Type: 9.

R. ungernii (un-gern′-i), **Traut.** PONTICUM SERIES, CAUCASICUM SUBSERIES

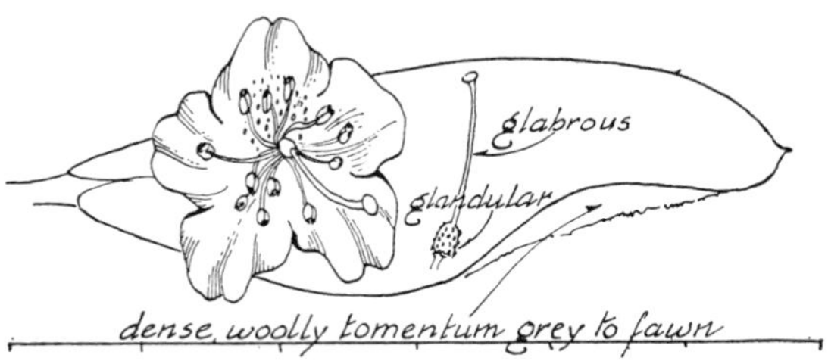

This is a handsome shrub with large, fresh green leaves coated underneath with a thick, woolly, cream-colored indumentum. Technical works note its height at 20 feet but very old specimens that I have measured were at their largest 7 feet tall and 12 feet wide. This species is probably hardy to Philadelphia and possibly also to New York City in the Northeast, though it was not a satisfactory ornamental when it was on trial at the Arnold Arboretum near Boston. *R. ungernii* leaves may vary from 4 to 8¼ inches in length and in width from 1½ to 2¾ inches. The young shoots are sheathed with a soft, silvery down. It blooms the latter part of July in a compact truss of about twenty-five white or pale pink funnel-campanulate flowers, each about 1¾ inches in diameter. I have grown this species, with protection, and it made an admirable foliage plant, attractive the year round, which bloomed prettily at a valuable time when few woody shrubs are in flower. *R. ungernii* is presented by myopic garden writers as a shrub often confused with *R. smirnowii*. Actually it is conspicuously different with much larger leaves lighter green in color, and a coarser habit of growth, heavier and larger in all its parts. It blooms a great deal later in the season too. The corolla lobes are not ruffled, as they are in *R. smirnowii*, and the flower stalks are both hairy and glandular. Botanically, it is set apart from its allies in the Ponticum series with woolly tomenta by its oblanceolate leaves with rounded ends terminating in a short, abrupt point; by its elongated truss; by its glandular ovary; and by the calyx $\frac{3}{16}$ to ¼ inch long. There are ten to twelve stamens. *R. ungernii* is one of the few European species, a native of the Caucasus Mountains where it was discovered in 1885 by Baron Ungern-Sternberg, a professor at Dorpat, and named for him. Freedom of Flowering: 3+; Ease of Cultivation: 1; American Quality Rating: x; British: ★; American Hardiness Rating: H-4 (Author's Dissent: H-2); British: A; Truss Type: 1.

R. valentinianum (val-en-tin-ee-a′-num), **Forrest.** MADDENII SERIES, CILIICALYX SUBSERIES

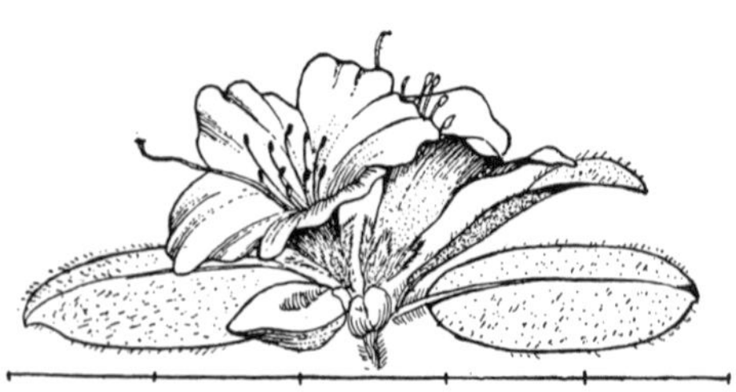

Old plants of this jaunty little Rhododendron are seldom more than 3 to 4 feet tall. The young shoots are bristly and so are the leaf stalks and the leaves, which are 1½ to 2 inches long, ¾ to 1 inch broad, are scaly underneath as well. The bright butter-yellow, funnel-campanulate flowers about 1½ inches long are startling when they appear in April grouped in firm clusters of four or five, rarely as few as two or as many as six. The color is exceptionally intense for a Rhododendron, one of the most attractive shades of all the species with yellow flowers, and the effect is quite brilliant. This is a first-rate garden plant which does well in the San Francisco district and northward. The exact limits of its hardiness are disputed by experienced amateurs, often a sign that there is a considerable range of cold resistance among various forms of the species. Some growers claim it to be as hardy as *R. ciliatum* and recommend full exposure in a lean soil mixture for best results. Others prefer shelter, especially a protected spot in a rock garden. Candor compels the notation that it has often failed to survive severe winters in Oregon and Washington. It is very successful as a small greenhouse shrub, however. Of the two distinct forms in cultivation, one has butter-yellow flowers and small leaves, rounded at the tips. The other, introduced by Rock, has blossoms of a less emphatic color and larger, more pointed leaves. This distinct, bristly species is characterized by flowers scaly on the outside with a style scaly only at the base and a scaly calyx with large lobes about $\frac{5}{16}$ inch long, densely fringed with hairs. It is native to open scrub at 11,000 feet in Yunnan, China, where it was discovered by Forrest in 1917. It was named for a French missionary in China, the Rev. S. P. Valentin. Freedom of Flowering: 2+; Ease of Cultivation: 2+; American Quality Rating: xx; British: ***; American Hardiness Rating: H-5; British: C; Truss Type: 12; A.M., 1933.

R. veitchianum (vytch-ee-a′-num), **Hook.** MADDENII SERIES, CILIICALYX SUBSERIES

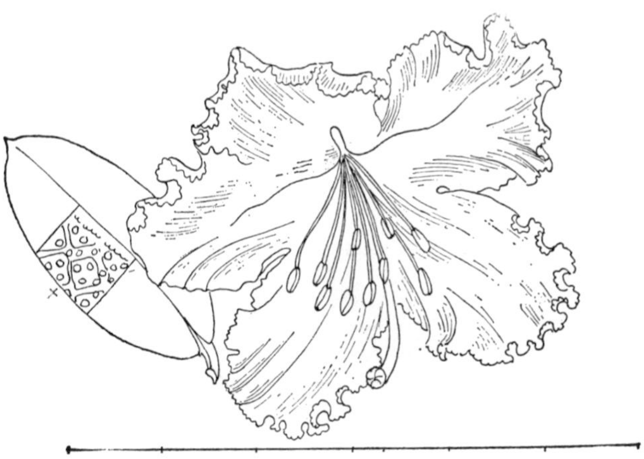

For the San Francisco district of California and for greenhouses in colder climates, this is one of the best of the small species of the Maddenii series. It reaches a height of about 8 feet but is usually much less. The scaly leaves are 2 to 4 inches long, $\frac{3}{4}$ to $1\frac{1}{2}$ inches broad. Huge, ruffled $4\frac{1}{2}$-inch white flowers are borne in groups up to five at the ends of the branches, most often in late April and early May but varying to as much as sixty days later. They are notably beautiful, the crimped edges lending an exotic note to their impressive size and stately bearing. This species separates from its allies by reason of its leaves more than $\frac{3}{4}$ to $1\frac{1}{2}$ inches broad with scales on the undersides 1 to $1\frac{1}{2}$ times their own diameter apart and V-shaped grooves on the upper sides of the stalks. Young branchlets are not bristly. There are ten stamens. The white flowers, widely funnel-shaped and faintly tinted green, three or more in a cluster, with corolla tubes scaly on the adaxial side only; the lower half of the style scaly; and the short, scaly calyx complete the identification. This epiphytic species grows on rocks or trees at 4,000 to 5,500 feet in Burma, Tenassarim and Thailand. It was named by the celebrated plant hunter, Joseph Hooker, for the famous Veitch family of nurserymen in England, following its discovery in the wild in the middle of the last century. Freedom of Flowering: 1; Ease of Cultivation: 2+; American Ratings: None yet assigned. British Quality Rating: ***; British Hardiness Rating: F; Truss Type: 12.

R. venator (ven′-a-tor), **Tagg.** IRRORATUM SERIES, PARISHII SUBSERIES

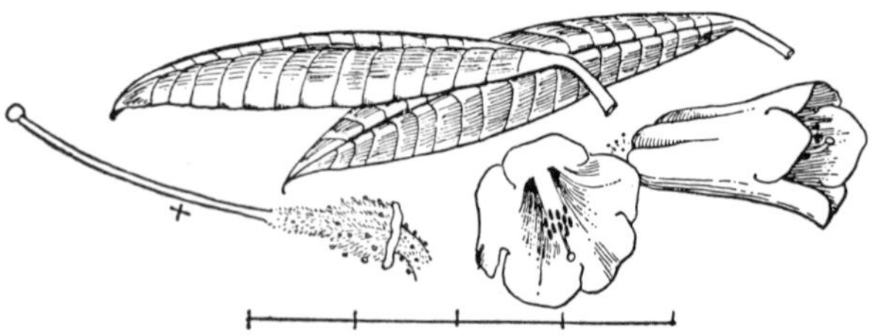

Here is a species which is oddly at variance with the other Rhododendrons in its series. It is a spreading shrub capable of a height of 8 or 9 feet but old plants are usually about 6 feet tall and 8 feet broad. The long, narrow leaves, 2¼ to 5½ inches in length and about 1 inch broad, with down-curved margins, are distinct. They are bright green and plainly veined, with a scant indumentum of star-shaped hairs underneath, so sparse that the hairs can scarcely be seen with the naked eye. It is this stellate indumentum which places *R. venator* in the Parishii subseries, despite its dissimilarity in other respects which gives it a resemblance to the Neriiflorum constellation of Rhododendrons. This species flowers in late May with about six long, bell-shaped flowers 1½ inches in diameter in a flat, single-tiered truss. The blossoms are an electric scarlet color with five dark crimson nectar pouches at the base. This is a striking Rhododendron in its season and, unlike some red-flowered sorts, it is attractive at other times throughout the year because its best forms usually have a bushy, well-branched habit and good foliage. It is much hardier than its reputation, and able to endure a great deal more cold than its relatives in the Parishii subseries. The size and shape of the long, narrow leaves easily distinguish *R. venator* from its relatives. Both the ovary and the base of the style are thickly covered with a hairy coating. It is native to southeastern Tibet at about 8,000 feet and is surprisingly hardy to originate at such a low altitude there. It was first identified in 1934 and given the name meaning 'hunter' because of its scarlet mantle in its blooming season, an association with the brilliantly garbed English foxhunters. Freedom of Flowering: 1; Ease of Cultivation: 1; American Quality Rating: xx; British: **; American Hardiness Rating: H-4; British: C; Truss Type: 10; A.M., 1933.

R. vernicosum (ver-ne-ko′-sum), **Franch.** FORTUNEI SERIES, FORTUNEI SUBSERIES

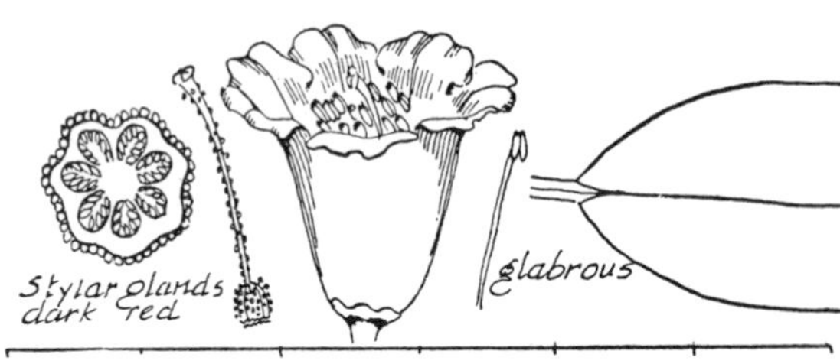

This is a species which is so varied that it has numerous geographical forms, some of which have erroneously acquired the status of species in popular conception. It is said to reach a height of about 20 feet in the wild but in gardens it is usually seen as a shrub about 8 feet tall and 6 feet broad. Some forms, mound-like in growth habit, are 6 feet high and 10 feet wide, and these spreading plants seem to have particularly good foliage as well. The leaves of the species are 2½ to 5 inches long, 1¼ to 2½ inches wide, and dull green. Flowers appear in late April and May most often but there is almost a full month between the earliest and the latest blooming forms. They vary in color from white to rose, sometimes marked with crimson, with many charming, delicate intermediate pale pink shades in between. There are about ten of the blossoms, 3 inches in diameter in the best forms, forming a truss about 5 inches across which is often rounded and well filled but may be also somewhat loose and flat-topped in the less desirable sorts. Obviously, care is necessary in selecting plants for garden use of a species so variable as this. The best examples of *R. vernicosum* are extraordinarily beautiful, especially those with pale, peach-pink blossoms, some of which are gracefully fluted and crimped around their edges, while other forms are often modeled to a classic simplicity of form which is equally pleasing. The florets are not crowded in the cluster but are held individually distinct. The form sent back by Hu under #15104 is very good and Kingdon-Ward's #5404 is fine too. Seedlings from a Rock collection proved hardy for Joseph Gable at Stewartstown, Pa., who found that they required especially good drainage and flowered poorly, possibly because, in the East, the precocious new growth was more or less regularly killed by late spring frosts. One of the hardy forms which starts into growth later in the season would be an invaluable acquisition for gardens at least as far north as Philadelphia. This species does well everywhere in the Rhododendron belt on the West Coast and in Great Britain and is easily distinguished from all of its many relatives by the unique dark red glands along the entire length of the long style. They are conspicuous and rarely any color other than red. The stamens are glabrous, the calyx is minute and there is no fragrance. This fine ornamental shrub was first found by Soulié in 1893 but was not introduced until Wilson sent it back to Western cultivation in 1904. It was called *vernicosum*, meaning 'shiny', because the leaves were inadvertently too near the fire when they were dried by the collector, and a varnish-like gloss appeared on the specimens which were first sent home to Franchet for naming. It is a misnomer because the foliage is actually dull green. This species is native to open thickets and exposed forest sites at 9,000 to 11,000 feet in Szechuan and Yunnan provinces of China. Freedom of Flowering: 2+; Ease of Cultivation: 2+; American Quality Rating: xx; British: ***; American Hardiness Rating: H-3; British: B; Truss Type: 1.

R. wardii (ward'-i), **W. W. Sm.** THOMSONII SERIES, SOULIEI SUBSERIES

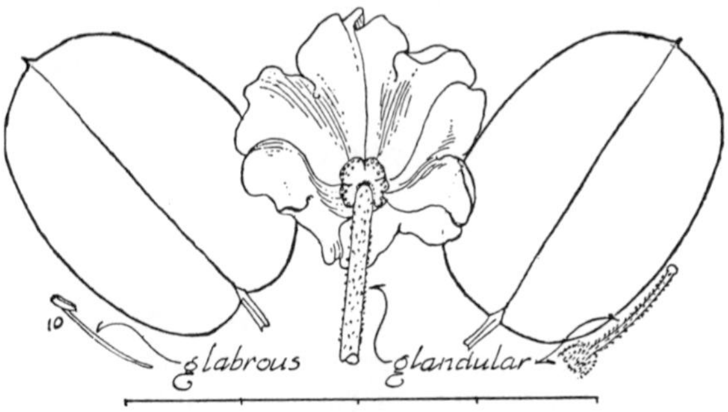

In its best forms this is the finest yellow-flowered Rhododendron species for general garden use, in my opinion. I doubt whether the most intensely colored *campylocarpums* in cultivation equal the dazzling clear yellow of such superb specimens of *R. wardii* as that at the Royal Botanic Garden in Edinburgh. The graceful flowers, more widely opened, make this a Rhododendron of incomparable quality and refinement. *R. wardii* varies enormously in its stature, from 3 to 25 feet tall at maturity, but older plants of good garden forms are mostly seen as well-formed shrubs 8 or 10 feet tall. The glossy, dark green leaves are $1\frac{1}{4}$ to $4\frac{3}{4}$ inches long, $\frac{3}{4}$ to $2\frac{1}{4}$ inches wide, glaucous or pale green underneath, rounded to oblong in shape. When the new growth first matures it has an attractive blue haze. The superlative yellow flowers are produced in late April or early May, wide, shallow, bowl-shaped blossoms about $2\frac{1}{2}$ inches across, gathered into loose terminal clusters, most often about eight to a truss measuring about $4\frac{1}{2}$ inches in diameter. Some forms have flat-topped single-tiered groups of only five or six flowers whereas others may have as many as fourteen to a firm, rounded truss. The color variance is equally great, ranging from almost white to an intense, luminous yellow with or without a red basal blotch. Apparently no nurseryman has sought the very finest expression of this species to make it available commercially, but Kingdon-Ward #4170 is sometimes offered for sale and it is extraordinarily lovely with deep yellow blossoms more widely flaring than usual, in exceptionally good, globular trusses. The buds are orange before they open. L. & S. #5679 is also exceptionally good in color. *R. wardii* follows *R. campylocarpum* in bloom, extending the season of fine, yellow-flowered species and it seems to be hardier than its earlier blossoming relative. It makes up at maturity any youthful deficiency in its freedom of bloom. The species suffers if neglected in time of drouth, but it insists on perfect drainage. No hybrid quite catches the elegance and exquisite proportions of this species in flower, a subtle symmetry which evokes the greatest admiration and affection for its patrician bearing. *R. litiense*, the only other species of the Thomsonii series with shallow, open, yellow flowers, is usually presumed to be distinct from *R. wardii* on the basis of its oblong leaves, strongly glaucous underneath, and slightly smaller flowers less widely expanded. Botanically, however, there should really be only one species. There is an unbroken procession of intermediates between *wardii* at one extreme, through the forms formerly known as *croceum*, to *R. litiense* at the other extreme. Horticulturally, gardeners want a name for the form with typically small, oblong leaves, glaucous underneath, so the name *R. litiense* apparently remains solely for their convenience. The trouble is that the merging forms with *R. wardii* become a matter of opinion as to which name should be given them. *R. wardii* easily separates from the yellow-flowered Rhododendrons of the other subseries by its widely bowl-shaped flowers with the styles glandular to the tip. The flowers of *RR. campylocarpum* and *caloxanthum*, with which it is sometimes confused, are bell-shaped, much less expanded, and with styles glandular only toward the bottom or else devoid of glands entirely. Rarely, some forms of *R. caloxanthum* have flowers approaching the openly campanulate but the style glandular to the tip remains a constant guide to *R. wardii.* This species was discovered by Rev. J. A. Soulié in 1895 and named *R. mussoti* by Franchet, but the name was never published. In 1913 Kingdon-Ward found the plant again and it was subsequently named for him. It is native to Yunnan, Szechuan and southeastern Tibet, where it grows in exposed scrub, open thickets and forests at 12,000 to 14,000 feet. Freedom of Flowering: 2+; Ease of Cultivation: 1; American Quality Rating: xxxx; British: ****; American Hardiness Rating: H-4; British: B; Truss Type: 8; A.M., 1921; A.M., 1926.

R. wasonii (wa′-son-i), **Hemsl. and Wils.** TALIENSE SERIES, WASONII SUBSERIES

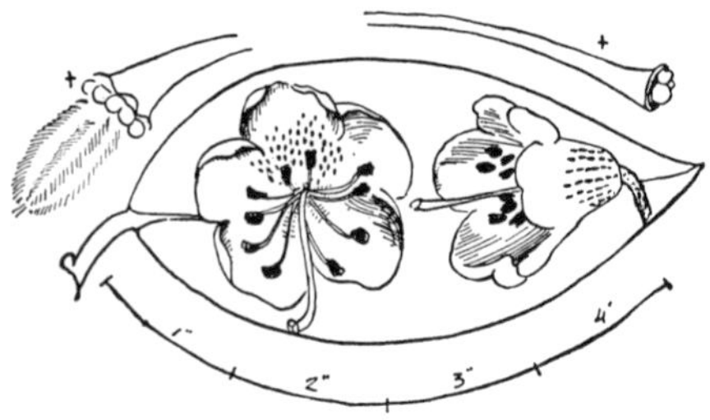

As a group the Taliense series are a mixed lot, many of them handsome in foliage and most of them exasperatingly shy about blooming. In the northeastern United States, at least, they are difficult to grow, being particularly susceptible to Rhododendron Blight (*Phytophthera cactorum*) and to a microscopic borer as well in some districts. Elsewhere there seem to be no particular difficulties in growing them, however. *R. wasonii* is among the best of the Talinsee group, and a good garden plant which is presentable at any season. Old specimens are about 5 feet tall and 6 feet wide, clothed to the ground in dark green, leathery leaves 2 to 4 inches long, 1 to 2 inches wide with an indumentum almost white at first, changing to a brilliant orange-tan, or sometimes rusty-brown, underneath. The flowers appear in April and in early May, depending on the season, about $1\frac{3}{4}$ inches wide, six to ten of them together in a loose truss measuring about $3\frac{1}{2}$ inches across. They vary in color from pure white to white faintly striped light pink, to ivory, rose and a quite clear, pretty shade of lemon-yellow. Some forms are spotted, some are not, and the sort with yellow flowers often has a small red blotch toward the base of the upper lobe. The yellow-flowered forms are the most attractive and seem to be more free-flowering. Of these, plants propagated from the specimen which received an Award of Merit are particularly colorful. The rating for floriferousness below refers, as in all cases, to the average of the species and not to any particular clone, free or shy in flower. Seen from a lower elevation, this Rhododendron is a brilliant foliage plant, the orange leaf undersurface contrasting boldly with the dark, glossy green above. It is a species hardy to Philadelphia but hard to keep in health in the Northeast. It is distinct from its allies by reason of its leaves, smooth above with the dense, felty coating below. The ⅛-inch calyx and the ovary both hairy and non-glandular; the moderate stature, neither dwarf nor prostrate; and the leaves broad for their length complete the identification within the series. *R. wasonii* is native to China's Szechuan province at 9,000 to 11,000 feet, where it grows in conifer forests. It was first found by Wilson in 1904 and named for his associate, C. R. Wason. Freedom of Flowering: 2; Ease of Cultivation: 1; American Ratings: None yet assigned; British Quality Rating: **; British Hardiness Rating: B; Truss Type: 10.

R. wightii (wit′-i), **Hook.** LACTEUM SERIES

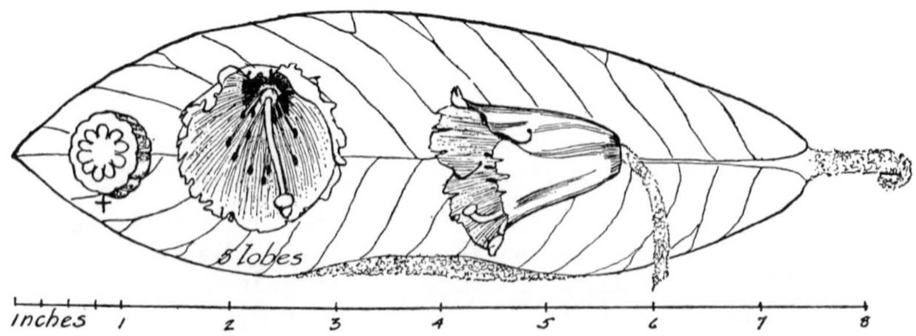

One of the most distinct and most interesting Rhododendrons, in the first rank for both flower and foliage, this species forms a bushy tree usually about 15 feet tall, 9 feet wide in older specimens. The dark green, strongly veined, leathery leaves are 5 to 9 inches long, 2½ to 3 inches wide, with an attractive tan to reddish-brown indumentum on their undersides. The terminal trusses in April and early May are about 6 inches in diameter, composed of about sixteen pale yellow bell-shaped flowers with a crimson blotch at the base. The blossoms may rarely be white, or without a blotch. Each flower is about 1½ inches wide, the edges of the lobes usually notched so that there is a distinctive, irregularly serrated outline. Some forms have brilliant red pistils in arresting contrast to the yellow flowers. The truss is peculiarly one-sided because it is not well filled with florets and they tend to fall together by their weight. Planted in a shrub border or against a dark background, however, the blossoms in the loose clusters all incline toward the front, giving the trusses a compact, rounded outline to the viewer which is extraordinarily pleasing, while the unseen backs of the trusses are vacant. This odd arrangement does not seem to belong to the Lacteum series but herbarium specimens show inflorescences which merge into the typical Lacteum type. This is a remarkably fine Rhododendron which, unaccountably, is somewhat rare in gardens. It is uniquely decorative, interesting and unusual wherever it is seen, so distinct that it is unlikely to be confused with any other species. The flowers, broad at the base and often spotted on the upper lobe with crimson, the lax inflorescence and the elongate-elliptic leaves with a continuous indumentum of ramiform hairs separate it from the only other yellow-flowered Rhododendron in the Lacteum series where, all things considered, its affinity seems dubious. It probably should be in the Taliense series or in one of its own. This species is native to the eastern Himalayan region, Sikkim, Nepal and Bhutan, from 12,000 to 14,000 feet altitude, where it grows in wooded valleys and mountain spurs. It was first found by Hooker and named for Dr Wight, a superintendent of the Madras Botanic Garden. Freedom of Flowering: 2+; Ease of Cultivation: 1; American Ratings: None yet assigned; British Quality Rating: *; British Hardiness Rating: B; Truss Type: 7; A.M., 1913.

R. williamsianum (wil-yum-see-an′-um), **Rehder and Wilson.** THOMSONII SERIES, WILLIAMSIANUM SUBSERIES

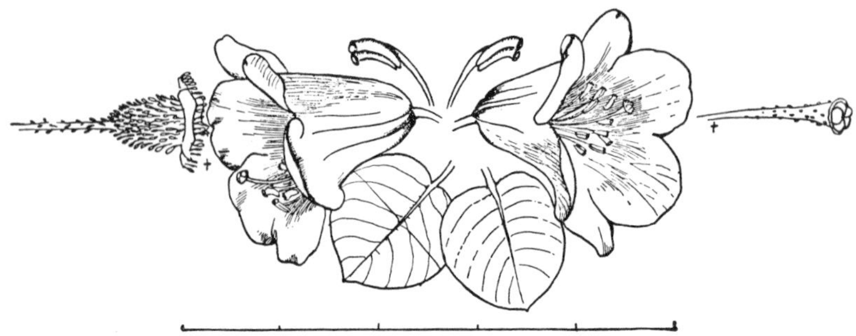

One of the most beloved of Rhododendron species and one of the most charming, *R. williamsianum* grows as a faultless mound of evergreen foliage up to 4 or 5 feet in height, densely clothed with bright green, rounded leaves ⅝ to 1¾ inches long and ½ to 1½ inches broad. Old plants are so perfect in their dome-shaped habit that they resemble clipped box-wood from a distance. The new growth provides added interest in its bronze to chocolate-colored accent against the fresh green of the older foliage. The bell-shaped pink flowers about 2¼ inches wide nod gracefully in twos and threes from the ends of the branches in April and they appear to advantage in a low hedge, rock garden or in the forefront of other, taller shrubs. This species varies a good deal in flower color. The very pale shades are not as attractive as the deeper colors, and there is a form at Bodnant in Wales with lovely clear rose blossoms conspicuously larger in size than I have seen elsewhere. In its better expressions *R. williamsianum* is utterly beguiling, the pendent, delicately pink bells dressing the round, serried leaves in a gay and festive display. It is regarded with exasperated affection in some gardens where it is reluctant to bloom freely. In an adjoining garden in full sun it may cover itself with flowers. But when the young shoots are destroyed by frost with such open exposure the replacements do not form floral buds, which is one reason plants fail to flower. Mr. H. L. Larson, a Tacoma nurseryman, has discovered that plants grafted as standards 4 or 5 feet above the ground bloom with exceptional freedom. This species seems to suffer noticeably in time of drouth, but it is equally injured by any fault in drainage. However, it grows well from San Francisco northward throughout almost all of the West Coast Rhododendron belt and in most of the British Isles. The bell-shaped blossoms with styles glandular to the tips, on low, spreading shrubs with round to oval leaves are marks which distinguish the species from its relatives. In some seed-lots corollas with six or seven lobes outnumber those with the five ascribed to this species in past descriptions. Discovered on cliffs at 8,000 to 10,000 feet in Szechuan province of central China by Wilson in 1908, it was named for J. C. Williams, a prominent British horticulturist. Freedom of Flowering: 2; Ease of Cultivation: 1; American Quality Rating: xxxx; British: ****; American Hardiness Rating: H-3; British: B; Truss Type: 15; A.M., 1938.

R. xanthocodon (zan-tho-ko′-don), **Hutchinson.** CINNABARINUM SERIES

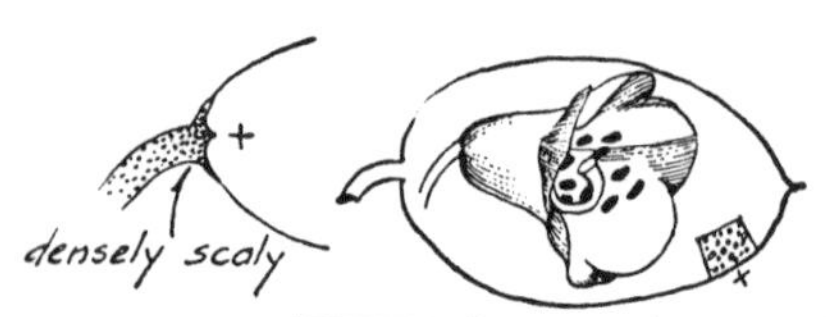

This Rhododendron grows as a large shrub usually seen in gardens about 8 feet tall or a little more but capable of reaching 15 feet. It is an attractive foliage plant. The dark green leaves 1¼ to 2¾ inches long, ¾ to 1¾ inches wide, thickly clad with scales on both surfaces, often

have a distinctive glaucous sheen, especially marked in the young growth. The waxen flowers of heavy texture are produced in May, five or six in an open, single-tiered, pendulous group. They are most often long, with a broad tube, and bell-shaped, about 1¼ or 1½ inches wide at the mouth. But this shape is not constant. Some forms have a short, narrow tube whereas others match the proportions of the flowers of *R. cinnabarinum*. The color is usually strong, clear yellow, but varying as well to lighter cream-yellow and also to dark shades verging on orange. The deep, orange-yellow Exbury form, sometimes distributed by nurseries, is much the finest in commerce for both color and size. *R. xanthocodon* is no more than a variety of *R. cinnabarinum*, which has rare yellow forms indistinguishable from it. Botanical references separate *R. xanthocodon* from *R. concatenans* on the basis of the latter's apricot-colored flowers but this distinction is also a fiction because *R. concatenans* occasionally has yellow blossoms and the flower shape is inconstant. The fact is that there are innumerable natural hybrids among the different forms in this group and that there is a regular, uninterrupted series of intergrades bridging them. All should be combined in one species. Rhododendrons of the *xanthocodon–cinnabarinum–concatenans* alliance are so distinct that they are unlikely to be confused with any others. All plants in cultivation of the species now called *R. xanthocodon* originated from a seedlot under Kingdon-Ward's #6026, collected in Tibet at 12,000 feet elevation. The name refers to the flowers, and means 'yellow bell'. Freedom of Flowering: 1; Ease of Cultivation: 1; American Quality Rating: xxx; British: ***; American Hardiness Rating: H-3; British: B; Truss Type: 11; A.M., 1935.

R. yakusimanum (yak-u-si-man′-um), **Nakai.** PONTICUM SERIES, CAUCASICUM SUBSERIES

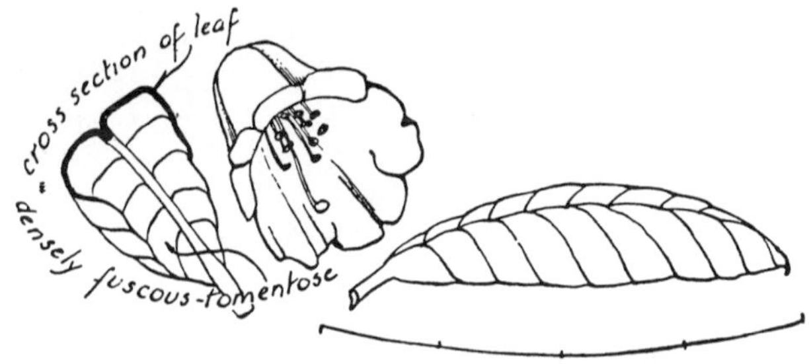

In mild climates the species of the Ponticum series have been scorned as garden Rhododendrons for so many years that the sudden recent prominence of *R. yakusimanum* has surprised professional nurserymen and created an unprecedented demand for it from amateur gardeners. The ornamental value of this extraordinary species seems to have been first appreciated at the great Rhododendron collection of the Exbury Estate in southern England, whence it found its way to the Royal Horticultural Society's gardens at Wisley. In 1947 a plant in full flower was exhibited by Wisley at the Chelsea Flower Show. It promptly received a First Class Certificate for its obvious quality and distinction, and became the sensation of the day, the Rhododendron most sought by specialists and a new-found parent of great potential usefulness in hybridizing. It has since been exhibited several times at the Chelsea shows, always to become a center of attention and admiration. *R. yakusimanum* has not been long in cultivation and it is still a very rare Rhododendron despite its present fame and the insatiable public demand for plants. It grows slowly to form a dense, spreading mound of handsome foliage, possibly 4 feet high and 6 feet wide for ordinary garden purposes. The dark glossy leaves average about 3½ inches long and 1⅛ inches broad, the edges down-curved, coated beneath with a very heavy brown woolly indumentum. Even the surface of the leaves is often irregularly dusted with a mealy whitish extension of the indumentum, which densely coats the petioles and decoratively ornaments the young shoots. In the latter part of May come the charming flowers in shades of rose, fresh pink and white, each about 1¾ inches wide, about ten to a firm, dome-shaped truss. In the F.C.C. form the buds are deep rose, the partially opened flowers a delicate pink, and the fully expanded blossoms are white so that they have much the same appeal as apple-blossoms in their lovely color phases. The widely bell-shaped flowers are cleanly and gracefully modeled, the truss in its carriage is distinguished and the whole effect, with the extraordinary color variation from deep rose to white, is one of the finest to be found in the genus. This species is very close to *R. degronianum* botanically, differing principally in its more densely indumented character, but ornamentally it is far superior, not only in the coloring of the flowers but also in the prodigious freedom of their production. Frequently every branch is studded with a flower cluster, making of the entire plant an exquisitely beautiful giant bouquet. This species is undoubtedly destined for an important place in our gardens, especially as the F.C.C. form becomes more widely available commercially. The Rhododendrons of the Ponticum series are noted for their hardiness, adaptability and tolerance of exposure, all requisites for the widest usefulness in the landscape. *R. yakusimanum*, coming from one of the southern Japanese islands, could be expected to be a little less hardy than its relatives but it seems probable that it should be satisfactory at least as far north as Boston in the East. Seedlings now five years old and about 12 inches tall in my trial grounds have survived $-24°$ F. uninjured in open frames. The faultlessly dense growth habit, restrained stature, and mound-shaped outline recommend it for many garden uses. It is characterized by a very short calyx, less than $\frac{3}{16}$ inch in length, reputedly in combination with linear-lanceolate leaves (but the linear character of which I find inconstant). The truss is dome-shaped, compact and the flower stalks are short, about $1\frac{1}{2}$ inches long. The exceptionally heavy indumentum extends even to the surface of first-year leaves and is conspicuously more dense than that on the leaves, pedicels and ovaries of *R. degronianum*. The foliage is much wider than the long, thin, scythe-shaped outline of the leaves on *R. makinoi*. *R. yakusimanum* was first described by Nakai in 1921. It was named for the Japanese Yakusima Island where it has a small, isolated distribution only in the northern part. Freedom of Flowering: 1; Ease of Cultivation: 1; American Quality Rating: xxx; British: ***; American Hardiness Rating: H-3 (Author's dissent: H-2); British: B; Truss Type: 3; F.C.C., 1947.

R. yunnanense (yu-nan-en'-see), **Franch.** TRIFLORUM SERIES, YUNNANENSE SUBSERIES

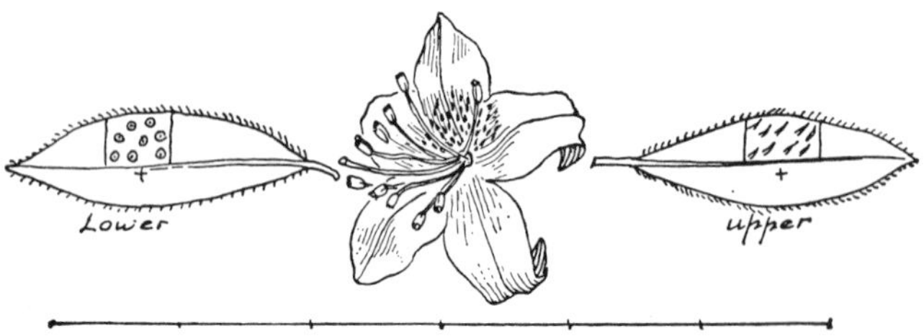

This is among the superlative Rhododendron species, one of the utmost appeal and the greatest character. It grows in a willowy fashion to as much as 12 feet with age and bears thin, bright green leaves $1\frac{1}{2}$ to 3 inches long, $\frac{1}{2}$ to 1 inch wide, which are both scaly and hairy. This is a particularly variable species from the standpoint of garden use. Some forms are mature at about 6 feet or so, whereas others are more than double that. The best foliaged plants are inclined to be a little sparse in winter and some specimens may be almost deciduous. The flat flowers, shaped like butterflies when viewed full face, are often borne in rather large, symmetrical dome-shaped trusses, but they may also be more uniformly distributed at the ends of intricately branched, twiggy stems bearing one to three or more blossoms, $1\frac{1}{2}$ to 2 inches across. The truss formation is most often seen, round or mound-shaped, containing as many as fifteen flowers, often formed from a combination of both terminal and lateral buds each producing three to five florets. When they appear in May they may be white, lavender or a clear, delicate silvery pink. All are spotted to some extent on the upper lobe but the best forms have a striking burnt-orange blotch which makes a vivid contrast with the corolla color and adds an extra accent of boldly decorative distinction to the blossoms. No Rhododendron blooms more prodigiously. The plants are usually completely smothered in a flowing mantle of color, such unbroken sheets of it that the foliage is all but invisible. Furthermore, the lavish production of blossoms seems to take place under almost any conditions, even in rather deep shade. This is an easy Rhododendron to please. It does well nearly anywhere in the garden and it thrives under a wide range of climatic conditions. Many specialists consider it to be one of the finest species of all, especially in the superior Tower Court form. It is not quite hardy at Philadelphia, but should do well in a slightly milder eastern climate. Care in selection is necessary to secure a good form. Among species of the Triflorum series with flowers in the white-mauve-rose color range, *R. yunnanense* has leaves either evergreen or partially deciduous, wedge-shaped at the base, bristly and scaly on the upper surface and with scales two to four times their own diameter apart underneath. The midrib on the leaf underside is not hairy. The flowers 1 inch long or more, not scaly on the outside, are borne on stalks $\frac{1}{2}$ inch in length or more. This species got its name from Yunnan province of China, where it grows at 9,000 feet elevation. It was introduced to cultivation first in France, about 1889, by Delavay. Freedom of Flowering: 1; Ease of Cultivation: 1; American Quality Rating: xxxx; British: ****; American Hardiness Rating: H-3; British: B; Truss Type: 9; A.M., 1903; A.G.M., 1934.

R. zeylanicum (see-lan′-ee-kum), **Hort. ex Loud Encyc Pl. (1855).** ARBOREUM SERIES, ARBOREUM SUBSERIES

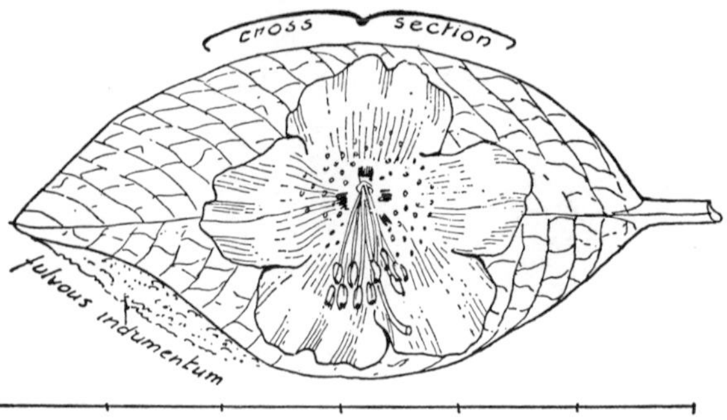

This is a small tree, 8 to rarely 30 feet tall, of rather slow growth with convex leaves usually 5 to 6 inches long and about 3 inches wide, which are much roughened on the upper surface by the indented veins and clad with a dense, felty tan to ruddy brown indumentum beneath. The 2-inch bell-shaped flowers are gathered into compact, round terminal trusses about 5 inches in diameter. There is evidently a wide range in the blooming season. Some forms come into flower in late April, others in June. The blossoms are usually deep blood-red but sometimes pink. For gardens in mild climates this fine species provides all of the virtues of one of the supremely beautiful Rhododendrons, *R. arboreum*, in a later blooming edition with better, darker green foliage. It survives outdoors in Oregon and Washington by such a narrow margin that its value as a permanent garden shrub there seems debatable. The scarlet globes nestled in terminal fans of dark glossy green leaves present a picture of extraordinary richness and character. This species is easily distinguished from *R. arboreum* by its much wider, convex leaves with margins turned downward, more puckered on the surface and with a woolly, not a plastered, silvery indumentum beneath. It has a ten-chambered ovary but the broad leaves distinguish it from the narrow-leaved *R. delavayi*. Like others of its subseries, the base of the flowers is broad and the growth is tree-like, with a main bole. Its name, meaning 'from Ceylon', indicates its origin, whence it comes from the lower, temperate elevations of the Himalayan Mountains. Now also included in this species is the Rhododendron formerly known as *R. kingianum*, Watt, from the high mountains of Manipur. Freedom of Flowering: 2; Ease of Cultivation: 2+; American Ratings: None yet assigned; British Quality Rating: ***; British Hardiness Rating: D; Truss Type: 3.

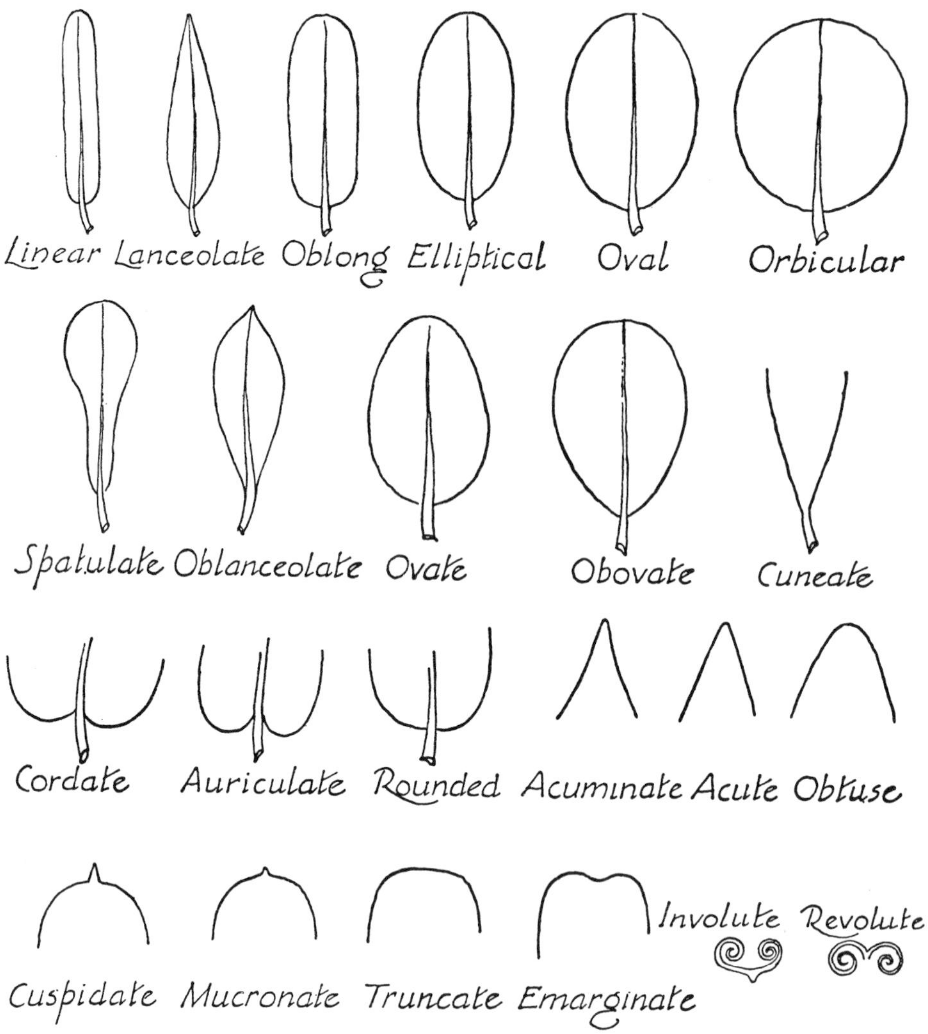

Rhododendron Leaf Shapes

TRUSS TYPES

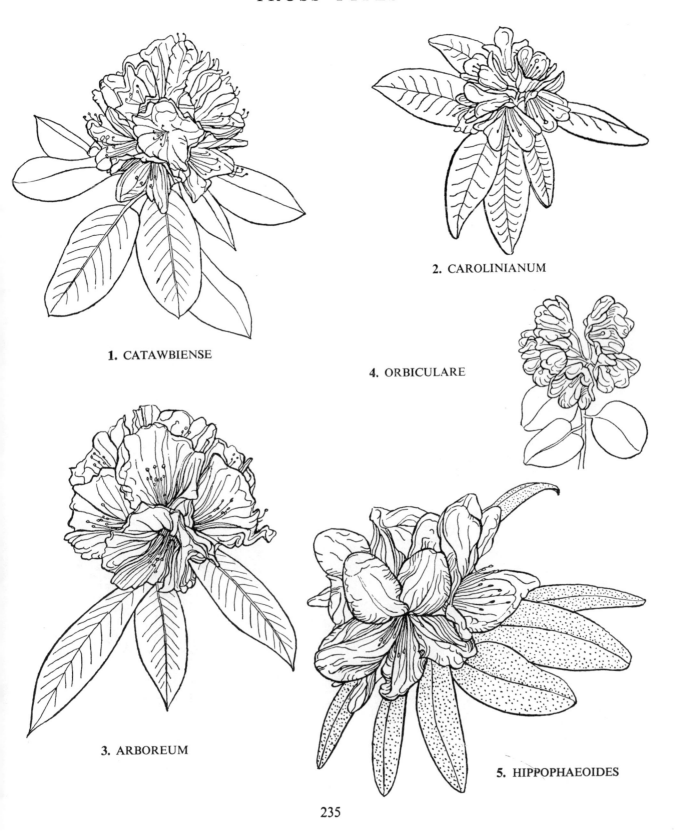

1. CATAWBIENSE

2. CAROLINIANUM

3. ARBOREUM

4. ORBICULARE

5. HIPPOPHAEOIDES

6. GRANDE

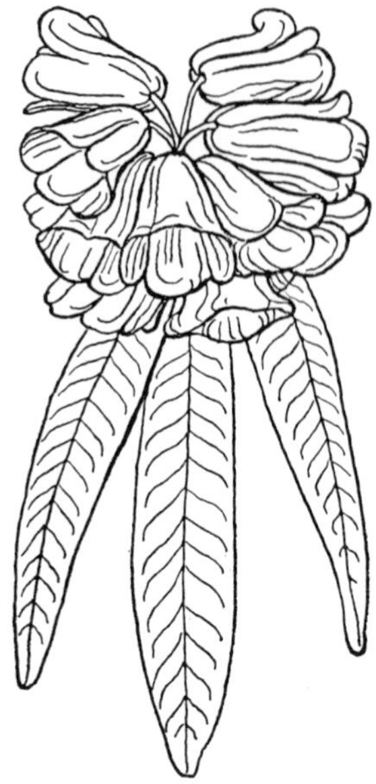

7. ARGYROPHYLLUM

8. DISCOLOR

9. DAVIDSONIANUM

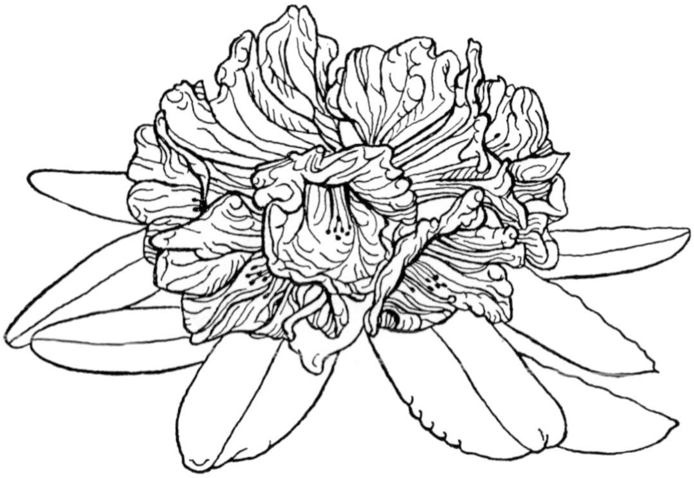

10. NERIIFLORUM

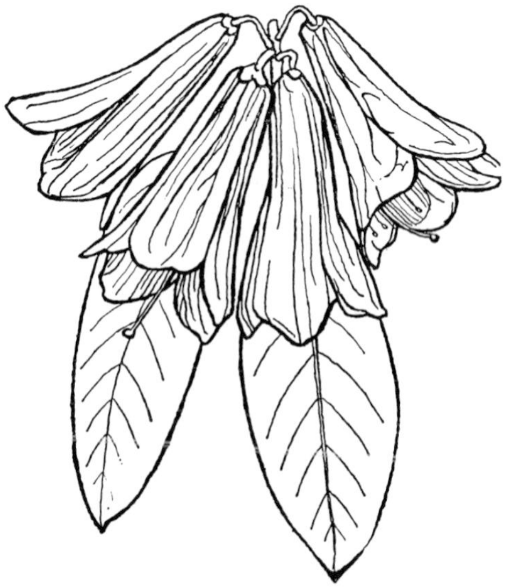

11. CINNABARINUM

12. LINDLEYI

13. ALBIFLORUM

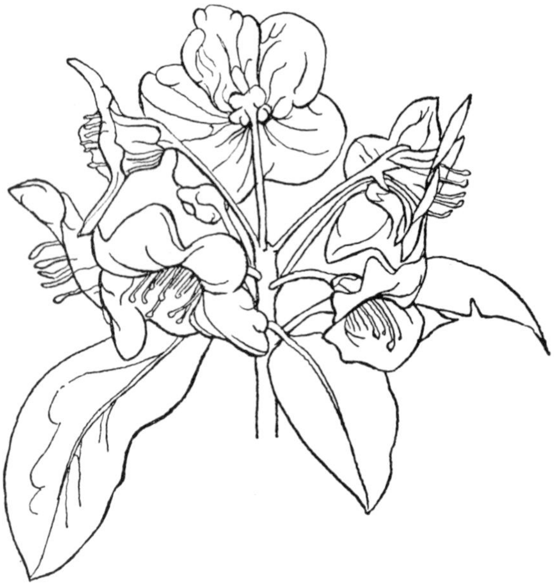

14. BAILEYI

15. FORRESTI

16. LEUCASPIS

17. MICRANTHUM

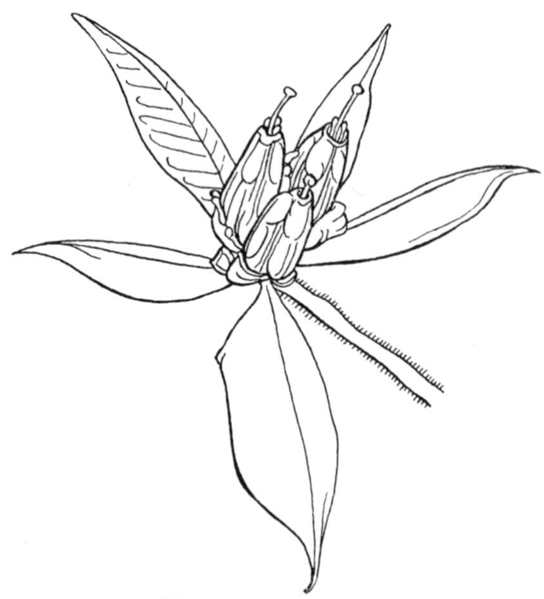

18. SPINULIFERUM

RHODODENDRON SPECIES HARDY IN THE NORTHEASTERN UNITED STATES

Where the list of hardy Rhododendrons is sharply restricted, as it is in the northeastern United States, it seems fair to evaluate the quality of those few satisfactory in the climate on a different basis than is used for the hundreds of fine species available in mild climates. I have done this below in the seventh column, from one # to four #### in order of increasing quality. For quick convenience, I have also provided in the sixth column my own hardiness ratings showing exactly how far north these Rhododendrons are satisfactory as follows:

IH—Ironclad Hardiness, to about 30° below zero F.
BH—Hardy to Boston.
NH—Hardy to New York City.
PH—Hardy to Philadelphia.

SPECIES	HEIGHT	SEASON OF BLOOM	FLOWER COLOR	LEAF SIZE	AUTHOR'S HARDINESS RATING	AUTHOR'S QUALITY RATING	REMARKS
adenopodum	6′	early May	pale rose	6″×1½″	BH	####	Good habit
brachycarpum	9′	June	cream to pink	5″×2¼″	IH	##	Dense growth
campanulatum	9′	April	white to rosy purple	4½″×2″	NH	###	Needs shelter
carolinianum	7′	mid May	white to mauve	3″×1¼″	IH	####	Deserves wider use
catawbiense	9′	late May	white, red, magenta	4½″×1½″	IH	####	Stands exposure
caucasicum	2′	May	white, yellowish, rose	3″×1¼″	NH	#	True species rare
chapmanii	6′	May	pale pink to rose	2″×1″	BH	###	Heat resistant
dauricum	6′	March–April	lavender-pink	1″×½″	IH	###	Rare true species is a gem
degronianum	4′	May	pale pink to rose	5″×1¼″	NH	###	Dense growth
discolor	15′	early July	pale pink to white	7″×2¼″	NH	####	Superb where hardy
fargesii	10′	April	white to rose	3″×1½″	NH	###	Floriferous
fastigiatum	3′	April–May	lilac	⅜″×³⁄₁₆″	BH	##	Give shelter, moisture, exposure
fortunei	15′	May	pale pink to white	7″×3″	BH	####	Very fine
hippophaeoides	4′	April	pale lilac to rose	1″×½″	BH	##	Easiest of the dwarf alpines
keiskei	8′	April	pale yellow	2¼″×1″	NH	###	Only hardy yellow-flowered species
longesquamatum	8′	May	pink	4½″×1½″	NH	###	Rugged appearance
makinoi	5′	early June	white to rose	5″×⅝″	NH	###	Exotic appearance
maximum	15′	July	pink, white, red	7″×2½″	IH	#	Coarse texture—for large backgrounds
metternichii	5′	April	white to rose	5″×1¼″	NH	###	Seven-lobed flowers

SPECIES	HEIGHT	SEASON OF BLOOM	FLOWER COLOR	LEAF SIZE	AUTHOR'S HARDINESS RATING	AUTHOR'S QUALITY RATING	REMARKS
micranthum	5′	early June	white	1½″×⅜″	IH	#	Spirea appearance
minus	15′	June	rose-pink	2½″×1″	IH	##	Large native
mucronulatum	8′	March–April	lavender-pink	2½″×1″	IH	###	Buy most evergreen form
oreodoxa forma *haematocheilum*	12′	early April	white to rose	3¾″×1¾″	NH	##	Lanky at maturity
racemosum	1½″	April	pink	1½″×¾″	BH	####	Many uses
scintillans	3′	April	lavender-blue	⅝″×¼″	NH	##	Somewhat difficult
smirnowii	7′	early June	rose	5″×1½″	IH	###	Good foliage
sutchuenense	15′	March–April	lavender-pink	5″×2″	BH	###	Early flowers need protected site
ungernii	7′	late July	pale pink to white	6½″×2¾″	PH	##	Handsome leaves
yakusimanum	4′	May	rose to white	1⅛″×3½″	BH	####	Perfect in form and flower

SPECIES FOR DELAWARE, MARYLAND, VIRGINIA AND WEST VIRGINIA

All of the species listed for the Northeast are, of course, also hardy to winter cold in the region of Wilmington, Baltimore, Washington, Richmond and on westward through much of the Rhododendron belt of West Virginia. There are also many additional species, some of them among the finest in the genus, which are sufficiently cold resistant to survive the winters but they are not all suited to the heat and drouth of summer. Consequently they are not satisfactory garden shrubs in that climate. Sometimes they exist only precariously, growing very slowly and with such scanty, stunted foliage that they are mere caricatures of the handsome lush greenness to be seen where the climate is both moist and moderate.

The culture of many Asian Rhododendron species is still experimental through much of the region from Delaware to West Virginia. On the basis of trial plantings yet too few in number, some fine sorts which are tender farther north give preliminary promise of being successful and attractive in the climate of Washington, D.C. The Asian species offer an interesting challenge to gardeners of the region, and an opportunity to determine by experiment those which could be important contributions to the horticulture of the upper South. The following seem promising on the basis of test plantings which have done well for periods ranging upwards of two years:

ambiguum, *augustinii*, *concinnum*, *yunnanense* and other species in the Triflorum series.
decorum, *diaprepes*, *praevernum*, *vernicosum* and other species in the Fortunei series.
pubescens and its allies in the Scabrifolium series.
ovatum.
haematodes and its relatives in the Haematodes subseries.
strigillosum and the other species of the Maculiferum subseries.
rubiginosum and related species in the Heliolepis series.

The species of the Lacteum, Thomsonii and Lapponicum series have generally been so difficult in the heat and atmospheric aridity of the East that they do not offer promising prospects, nor is it likely that any of the dwarf scaly-leaved alpines would find the summer conditions acceptable.

Rhododendron Species

SPECIES FOR THE PACIFIC NORTHWEST AND GREAT BRITAIN

Almost all of the native American Rhododendrons and the species from Europe and Asia can be grown somewhere in western Oregon and Washington, and in Great Britain. These are the two great centers of Rhododendron culture in the Western world and the congenial climate makes possible such a wide and bewildering selection that the amateur with an awakening interest can only rely on the guidance of expert growers who have made a specialty of the species.

The selections on page 242 were made by a group of such experts on the basis of beauty of flower, handsome plant habit, ease of culture and general garden usefulness. The species are named in the order of the frequency with which they were selected by these specialists. All are described in detail in the preceding section. The home gardener can safely choose any of the following sorts knowing that they are among the best for their height, flower color and season of bloom.

Readers will immediately note some apparent contradictions in stature, flowering period and in the color of the blossoms. The explanation is, of course, that these Rhododendrons vary considerably in all of these three respects. Some sorts may have three or four different color forms. And the different forms of *R. racemosum*, for example, may range in blooming season from March to late May. A good form of a species which differs somewhat in stature from the usual size may become established and enjoy a regional popularity. It may be widely available in nurseries in that district, and all but unknown elsewhere.

SPECIES FOR SAN FRANCISCO AND COASTAL CALIFORNIA

In the cool fog belt along the coast of California from Santa Cruz northward to Fort Bragg, almost any of the world's Rhododendrons can be grown, many of them to a state of perfection unknown elsewhere in America or in Europe. There the magnificent flowers of the Maddenii group, supreme in their immense size and sumptuous fragrance, luxuriate in the mild moistness of the climate. There too grow the exotic Edgeworthiis; the majestic trees of the Grande series with their massive leaves and huge belfries of primitive flowers; the rare Rhododendrons of the Stamineum group; the charming Boothiis; and the fine species of the Irroratum series. All seem to thrive with unsurpassed vigor along the coast, where the winter temperature seldom falls below 30° F. and the July average is 60° F.

Where the fog comes in from July to October almost all Rhododendrons can be grown in full sun. Even the Maddenii species, famous for their opulent flowers and often infamous for their gaunt lankiness, frequently are seen with full exposure as handsome, compact plants clad with dense foliage in a manner unknown in the mildest parts of the British Isles. In fact, so improved are they by the benign climate and fog-filtered sunlight that some of them would not be easily recognized by enthusiasts accustomed to their appearance in Cornwall or on the west coast of Scotland. For many years Rhododendrons were sold to gardeners near the ocean on the Pacific Coast as shade-loving plants, an erroneous conception for this climate which is still widely held by the public. With the natural reduction in sunlight by the fog in summer they failed to set flower buds properly. Now, growing in full exposure, these same sorts are spectacularly effective in both flower and foliage.

In Oakland, across the bay from San Francisco, and elsewhere inland even fifteen miles from the coast, there is an entirely different climate.

The midsummer temperatures reach 90° to 100° F. and in winter there is a drop to 18° to 22° F. The tenderest Rhododendrons are injured by frost. Some of the sturdier sorts find the heat unendurable. With no fog to filter the force of the sun and bathe the plants in the misty moistness so reminiscent of their homeland, they require a great deal of high shade. Here burning

RED

Before May 1st	dwarf	*neriiflorum*
		forrestii, KW6832
	medium	*spinuliferum*
		meddianum
	tall	*barbatum*
		thomsonii
May 1st to June 1st	dwarf	*haematodes*
		neriiflorum
	medium	*cinnabarinum*
		neriiflorum "subspecies *euchaites*"
	tall	*elliottii*, KW7725
		cinnabarinum
After June 1st	dwarf	*didymum*
	medium	*griersonianum*
	tall	*eriogynum*

PINK

Before May 1st	dwarf	*racemosum*
		williamsianum
	medium	*orbiculare*
		fargesii
	tall	*calophytum*
		sutchuenense
May 1st to June 1st	dwarf	*williamsianum*
		callimorphum
	medium	*chartophyllum*
		oreotrephes
	tall	*souliei*
		vernicosum
After June 1st	dwarf	*keleticum*
	medium	*eudoxum**
		makinoi
	tall	*heliolepis*

BLUE AND LAVENDER

Before May 1st	dwarf	*scintillans*
		impeditum
	medium	*concinnum* (selected form)
		hippophaeoides
	tall	*campanulatum*
		augustinii
May 1st to June 1st	dwarf	*russatum*, F.C.C.
		intricatum
	medium	*oreotrephes*
		chasmanthum
	tall	*augustinii*
		trichanthum
After June 1st	dwarf	*calostrotum*
	tall	*ponticum*

SHADES OF ORANGE

May 1st to June 1st	dwarf	*dichroanthum*
	medium	*concatenans*
After June 1st	dwarf	*apodectum*
		scyphocalyx
	medium	*scyphocalyx* (selected form)

CREAM TO YELLOW

Before May 1st	dwarf	*lutescens*, F.C.C.
		chryseum
	medium	*caloxanthum*
		keiskei
	tall	*stewartianum* (yellow form)
		lutescens
May 1st to June 1st	dwarf	*campylocarpum* (Hooker's form)
		caucasicum ('Cunningham's Sulphur')
	medium	*wardii*
		campylocarpum
	tall	*xanthocodon*
After June 1st	dwarf	*lepidostylum* (Rock's form)

WHITE

Before May 1st	dwarf	*leucaspis*
	medium	*eclecteum*
		irroratum
	tall	*sutchuenense*
May 1st to June 1st	dwarf	*wasonii*
	medium	*puralbum*
	tall	*arboreum* subspecies *cinnamomeum*
		decorum
After June 1st	medium	*aberconwayi*
		crassum
	tall	*discolor*

Dwarf, less than 5 feet; medium, 5 to 8 feet; tall, more than 8 feet.

* Author's note: evidently an unusual form, locally distributed. Most forms bloom much earlier.

of the foliage in clear, hot summer weather is often the main problem. Many fine Rhododendrons can be grown but the choice is naturally more restricted than in the fog belt. Shade and shelter are needed for most sorts.

A favorite planting mixture among the experts both in the fog belt and farther inland in coastal California is screened Pine needles and Redwood leaf mold. Some growers use a mixture of peat and leaf mold. Pure peat is too easily overwatered, at least in the fog belt. At Golden Gate Park the Rhododendrons are grown in a mixture of decayed Pine needles, Oak leaf mold and decayed wood shavings. When Rhododendrons are grown in a prepared mixture which replaces the natural soil in a bed or planting hole there is occasionally a problem of subsidence. As the organic material decays the plants imperceptibly sink below their original level. As mulches are renewed each year the roots may eventually fail to reach the surface for the aeration they need to survive, and the plants sometimes slowly smother. This is by far the most common cause of trouble in the Rhododendron belt of California. Any plant which languishes for no apparent cause after having previously grown satisfactorily may need only to be lifted to its original planting level, with the roots at the surface of the ground.

The water for irrigation in this region is alkaline almost everywhere. If the original planting soil is not strongly acid there may be a gradual decline in the health of the plants as the acidity at their roots is slowly neutralized by alkaline water. But when Rhododendrons are planted in the recommended mixture of Pine needles and leaf mold this problem is minimized. It is strongly acid, retentive of natural moisture and so porous that an extensive root system is soon formed to sustain the plants in dry weather and forestall foliage burn. Excessive irrigation with alkaline water is avoided and the Rhododendrons often need only overhead sprinkling in very hot weather to keep them in good condition.

A group of expert growers in the San Francisco district have named the following Rhododendrons as being among the finest species which have fully proved themselves in that region. These are all described in detail earlier in this chapter. Comparing others of similar cultural needs with those named below it is easy to deduce that in favored parts of the California Rhododendron belt the resources of almost the entire genus are open to gardeners who may wish to take advantage of them.

The apparent discrepancies in this list are due to the natural variation among the species in stature, flower color and season of bloom. Locally popular forms are sometimes considerably different from the typical species.

RED

Before May 1st	dwarf	*sperabiloides*
	medium	*neriiflorum*
	tall	*arboreum*
May 1st to June 1st	dwarf	*haemaleum*
		forrestii, KW6832
	medium	*spinuliferum*
		elliottii

PINK

Before May 1st	dwarf	*pemakoense*
	tall	*fortunei*
May 1st to June 1st	dwarf	*racemosum*, F19404
	medium	*williamsianum*
	tall	*discolor*

BLUE AND LAVENDER

Before May 1st	dwarf	*impeditum*
May 1st to June 1st	medium	*augustinii*
After June 1st	medium	*bodinieri*
		yunnanense

SHADES OF ORANGE

Before May 1st	medium	*concatenans*

CREAM TO YELLOW

Before May 1st	dwarf	*burmanicum*
	medium	*arizelum*
May 1st to June 1st	dwarf	*valentinianum*
	tall	*nuttallii*
After June 1st	medium	*wardii*

WHITE

Before May 1st	dwarf	*leucaspis*
		ciliatum
	tall	*ciliicalyx*
May 1st to June 1st	dwarf	*veitchianum*
		moupinense
	medium	*lindleyi*
	tall	*decorum*
After June 1st	medium	*maddenii*
	tall	*auriculatum*

Dwarf, less than 5 feet; medium, 5 to 8 feet; tall, more than 8 feet.

Complete Descriptive List of Species

An alphabetical listing of all Rhododendron species in the Appendix gives their series and subseries affiliations, American and British quality and hardiness ratings, flower colors, seasons of bloom, and stature. A second listing names the species which belong to each series and subseries. A third gives the obsolete and invalid names of species together with their correct names in current usage.

CHAPTER VI

Rhododendron Hybrids

HISTORY

THE parade of magnificent Rhododendron hybrids which have decorated our gardens with such distinction for a century and a half began when Michael Waterer, an English nurseryman, crossed two imported American species, *R. maximum* and *R. catawbiense*, to create the first of the hybrids made by man with the intention of producing better and more useful plants for the garden. In 1826, a year after the brilliant scarlet-flowered Asiatic import, *R. arboreum*, bloomed in England for the first time, it was crossed by J. R. Gowen with an early hybrid between *catawbiense* and *ponticum* to produce 'Altaclarense', and in 1831 *R.* (*catawbiense* × *arboreum*) 'Russellianum' made its appearance. Mammoth old plants of it are still treasured in many gardens of Britain, 30-foot umbrellas sheeted with red in May.

In the 1830's amateurs joined professionals in the production of hosts of hybrids as the stunning blood-red blossoms of the beautiful Himalayan *R. arboreum* delighted the eyes of increasing numbers of British gardeners. Too tender and too early blooming for most of Britain, there was a wild scramble to capture the purity of its flower color in hardy hybrids suitable for the climate. Rhododendrons became the sensation of the day as *ponticum*, *maximum*, *catawbiense* and *caucasicum* were all used as parents to produce in their offspring the more rugged constitution needed for general cultivation throughout the British Isles. By 1839 the interest of the gardening public there reached such a high pitch that one nurseryman found it profitable to offer the common wild Rhododendron, *ponticum*, in twenty different forms which differed from one another only in minor leaf details.

Lists of nursery hybrids were long and complicated by mid-century as the offspring of the earlier crosses were themselves recrossed or bred to the first few Asian species to reach Great Britain from the Himalayas. The hardy hybrid 'Delicatissimum' was introduced in 1848 by Standish and Noble, the predecessors of the present Sunningdale Nurseries. By 1851 'Candidissimum', 'Everestianum', and 'Purpureum grandiflorum' were on the market and they are still popular today in the northeastern United States. In 1853, Anthony Waterer, of the world-renowned Knap Hill Nursery which has so long been associated with his name, started to make numerous crosses among the same species which had been used to lesser effect by his predecessors. The glowing scarlet *R. thomsonii*, which had flowered for the first time in England in 1857, must also have been available to him in the years immediately following.

In the 1860's, Anthony Waterer's genius for breeding Rhododendrons produced the hybrids for which gardeners of the Western world will forever be in his debt. After the passage of a century the Waterer hybrids are still the most widely grown of all cultivated Rhododendrons in the northeastern United States and in the colder parts of Europe. For their time they represented a triumph of the hybridist's art: the principles of heredity in plant breeding were not then in use; there were but a handful of species available as parents; and the English climate did not test the full limit of hardiness which Waterer had imparted to his creations with such remarkable success.

This test of hardiness was to come after 1,500 of the Waterer Rhododendron hybrids were brought to America in 1876 for the great Centennial Exposition at Philadelphia. Their exhibition was an enormous success and further shipments followed quickly as the gardening public in this country clamored for the most beautiful flowering evergreen shrubs yet seen on the eastern seaboard.

Almost overnight Rhododendrons assumed a position of first importance in American horticulture and our native species, *R. catawbiense*, which had been appreciated in England since its first flowering there in 1809, at last came into its own in the land of its origin as the principal hardy parent of the hybrids which were to adorn our gardens for generations.

In the meantime, the first flowering of the incomparable *R. thomsonii* in England in 1857 and the additional startling Rhododendrons introduced from Hooker's expedition and from other early collectors stimulated a new wave of hybridizing by nurserymen and by amateur enthusiasts. As the early trickle of new species from the Himalayas grew to a freshet, interest and importance increased with the passing years, as did the opportunities for capturing their beauty in hardier form. With the turn of the century the splendid new discoveries from southeastern Asia started to pour into Britain in a flood of unparalleled beauty, first by the dozens, then by the scores, and finally by the hundreds. At one time nurserymen were so inundated by the deluge that they shoveled out whole greenhouses full of young seedlings in a frantic effort to make room for new arrivals reputed to be even finer.

As the colorful multitudes came into flower, men of talent and imagination were quick to grasp the contributions they could make and Magor, de Rothschild, and Aberconway started to hybridize the newcomers on a massive scale. Many other British breeders, both amateur gardeners and professional nurserymen, joined them in producing a tremendous roster of distinguished hybrids throughout the 1920's, '30's, and '40's.

With the advent of World War II conditions became so difficult that little hybridizing could be done in Britain and the breeding of Rhododendrons has not since regained its position there, while it has steadily increased in scope and importance in the post-war years in the United States. Parsons, Dexter, Barto, Gable, and Nearing are all American breeders who have contributed importantly to the horticulture of their country.

Hardy Hybrids versus Amateurs' Hybrids for Mild Climates

In the northwestern Pacific coastal region and in Great Britain, it is often useful to distinguish two different classes of the familiar Rhododendron hybrids—those usually robust shrubs with glossy evergreen leaves devoid of scales.

The so-called hardy hybrids have been largely created by professional nurserymen in Europe who bred them for hardiness, vigor, good foliage, and ease of cultivation and propagation. The ideal has been a firm flower truss filled out with blossoms to a symmetrical round or conical cluster of formal regularity. The blooming period is designed to be late enough to escape frosts in the colder regions but not too late for the height of garden shrub sales in the spring. As a group, these are stalwart, portly shrubs, forthright in character, hardier, more easy to care for and more reliable in the garden than the other class and frequently better in foliage as well. Most of them are complicated in their parentage and many of them have far back in their pedigrees such species as *caucasicum*, *catawbiense*, *ponticum*, and others notable for their ability to impart tolerance of exposure. The sorts most popular today have descended in large part from the nurserymen's hybrids of the late nineteenth century crossed with Rhododendrons larger in flower and better in color derived from introductions from Asia.

In England the Knap Hill Nursery, Ltd., was the scene of the first hybridizing ever done with Rhododendrons, in 1809, and the Waterer family have continued to produce fine Rhododendron hybrids. The Goldsworth Nursery of

Walter S. Slocock, Ltd., John Waterer, Sons & Crisp, Ltd., and John Waterer (& Sons) of Bagshot have also produced many currently popular hardy hybrids.

In Holland, a long roster of beloved garden Rhododendrons has come from L. J. Endtz & Co., C. B. van Nes & Sons, and M. Koster & Sons, among others who have contributed lesser numbers of prominent sorts.

In contrast to the so-called hardy hybrids are the amateurs' hybrids, most of them produced in British gardens with favored climates in the 1920's, '30's and '40's from the astounding flood of beautiful new Asian species which were introduced by the hundreds after the turn of the century. As a group, they have informal trusses of flowers loosely and gracefully held, not the firm, upstanding clusters of formal outline characteristic of the nurserymen's hardy hybrids. Their colors are purer, the scarlets brighter, the blues bluer, the whites more sparkling, the pinks more softly luminous, the oranges more intense. There are many remarkable pastel blends of great subtlety and charm.

The amateurs' hybrids are usually superior too in the modeling of the flowers, formed as they often are to an exceptionally high standard of classic elegance. These are Rhododendrons which connoisseurs admire and it is not easy to put the superiority of some of them into words. It is a matter of aesthetics, of authentic refinement and distinction. They have an elusive air of quality which derives from their perfection of form, color and proportion.

Two accomplished amateur breeders, following in the footsteps of Sir Edmund Loder, Magor and other early hybridists, have dominated the introduction of new garden Rhododendrons in Britain. Lionel de Rothschild, of the celebrated international banking family, made over 1,200 crosses at his mammoth Exbury Estate near Southampton in southern England, and hundreds of new hybrids were registered in his name with the Royal Horticultural Society throughout the 1930's and '40's. With the resources of a vast fortune he assembled the finest forms of the newly introduced Asian species and bred them on an unparalleled scale of massive diversity. A man of immaculate taste and perception, his legions of fine hybrids are world-renowned in horticulture. The Exbury Estate, open to the public at stated times in the blooming season, is incomparably the largest and finest collection of Rhododendrons in the world, with 38 miles of paths and estimated to contain more than 1,000,000 plants. Mr de Rothschild, who died in 1942, bred Rhododendrons on such a gigantic scale that it is hard to single out hybrids for mention. From the dwarf crimson-flowered 'Carmen' to the giant 'Fortune' with its enormous golden globes, the range embraces such prominent sorts as the Naomi, Lady Bessborough, Hawk, and Lady Chamberlain hybrid groups, 'Romany Chal' and innumerable others which have been honored with awards from the Royal Horticultural Society.

The late Lord Aberconway assembled at his famous garden, Bodnant, in Wales, another magnificent collection of Rhododendrons and there produced an enormous number of notable hybrids, with his talented superintendent, the late F. C. Puddle. Mr Puddle had a scientific approach to breeding, with a marked facility for correctly interpreting the results of his crosses, and the Bodnant hybrids have become the standard of quality and incandescent color in the scarlet-flowered sorts, especially. Extraordinarily fine dwarfs and some remarkable scaly-leaved hybrids have also come from Bodnant. This sumptuous garden is now open to the public as a ward of the National Trust and it contains kaleidoscopic hosts of colorful Aberconway hybrids in brilliantly landscaped array. Lord Aberconway was a contemporary of de Rochschild's. His many distinguished contributions to horticulture included a total of 298 Rhododendron hybrids which he created and registered with the Royal Horticultural Society. Many of them received awards and have become familiar to enthusiasts everywhere. 'Elizabeth', the Fabia group, 'Cilpinense', 'Welkin', 'Bluebird', and 'Vanessa' are representative of their variety and extraordinary quality.

No note on the contributions of British amateurs, however brief, could omit the names of J. C. Williams and J. B. Stevenson, two great collectors and specialists in the species, who also made some beautiful hybrids which have achieved wide popularity.

The advocates of the nurserymen's hardy hybrids criticize the amateurs' hybrids because some of them are fastidious and others are deficient in foliage. Only a minor proportion are hardy enough for the colder parts of the British Isles, but the great majority are satisfactory in the more benign coastal climate of our Pacific Northwest. The connoisseurs scorn the nurserymen's hybrids as too stolid burghers, pedestrian in bearing, often ostentatious in floral effect and a trifle gross in color. I have no intention of expressing an opinion.

In any case, the distinction between the two groups is becoming more and more blurred. There have always been some hardy hybrids of distinguished character and the amateurs have produced some rugged, adaptable Rhododendrons from their efforts. But now there seems to be a concerted effort to merge the two. Professional growers are crossing their rugged productions with the amateurs' exotic hybrids to improve the flower quality, and the amateurs are breeding their own patrician beauties to the nurserymen's stalwarts for greater hardiness and tolerance of exposure.

HYBRID CLONES VERSUS SEEDLINGS

Lest anyone misunderstand the term, hybrid Rhododendrons are the offspring which result from a cross between two species from the wild, between two other hybrids, or between a species and a hybrid. Species have been 'purified' by ages of isolation in their native wilderness and they come reasonably 'true' from seeds. Hybrids are usually the result of man-made crosses and they do not come 'true' from seeds. Because their heritage is complex and mixed, seedlings obtained from hybrids usually exhibit innumerable gradations of characteristics possessed by their ancestors, and the average of unselected seedlings is commonly far inferior to their parents in quality.

Popular gardening publications often contain advertisements for 'Rhododendron hybrids grown from seed of finest varieties' and 'Hybrid Rhododendrons! . . . A rare chance to get prized hybrid Rhododendron seedlings at a big bargain.' Such plants are usually purchased in small sizes at low prices and they are very likely to be expensive disappointments when, after years of waiting, they blossom with small flowers of an ugly magenta shade. Seedlings have no special virtue whatever merely because they are 'hybrid' seedlings, despite the popular belief to the contrary. In fact, unselected hybrid seedlings are almost certain to be less hardy, to have foliage faults, and to be vastly inferior in flower to the named nursery hybrids which are propagated by grafting or from cuttings.

The prudent gardener buys hybrids only by the exact names of the clones he wants, with the knowledge that they will then be duplicates in size and color of flower, in foliage, hardiness and stature of the original plant selected by the introducer for its superior qualities. A specific named hybrid is known as a clone, or cultivar, as it applies to Rhododendrons. The term 'cultivar' is one manufactured from two words, *cultivated variety*, by the international group authorized to determine correct usage in botany and horticulture. It denotes a single hybrid clone of constant quality. 'Variety' is reserved exclusively for the botanical usage referring to a group of more or less distinct plants which belong to a wild species.

Rhododendron clones can be propagated solely by grafting, budding, layering or from cuttings, and all other plants of the same name are then exactly like it. If a cultivar is to be increased, parts of the original plant must be removed from it and be used by the propagator to form duplicates capable of independent existence. These duplicates then furnish plant parts for further increase until finally enough identical plants have been propagated for commercial distribution. Such a group of plants, so propagated as parts of one individual, is also called a clone.

With the exception of a very few exotic hybrids which lack vigor on their own roots, Rhododendrons propagated by rooted cuttings or by layers are much to be preferred to grafted plants.

Group Names

The unwary must also beware of an unfortunate practice which afflicts the sale of Rhododendrons by the nursery industry as a result of a custom which became established in the British Isles many years ago. There the hybrids which resulted from the first recorded cross between two Rhododendron species were given a group name and all of the seedlings from the cross, regardless of their quality, were entitled to be called by this same name. The poorest Rhododendron and the finest which claimed the same two species as parents were given this common designation, regardless of when or where they were bred, or whether fine or poor forms of the species were used as parents. All of the offspring from a single, more complex cross—good, bad, or indifferent—were also given a group name. To identify the best seedlings from each cross and to separate them from the others of similar group name, the British breeders devised cultivar names in addition, which apply in each case to one distinct clone only. A Rhododendron so labeled is then propagated by grafts or cuttings so that all plants which are distributed under that cultivar name are identical with the one original seedling of unique quality which was singled out by the breeder for its superior characteristics.

Cultivar or clone names are the second names of such Rhododendrons and the group designations are the first names. They are the proper and the common names, respectively. When buying some of the most famous hybrids, it is essential to specify not only the group name but also the cultivar to identify the plant of unique quality which is desired. For example, it means nothing to ask a nurseryman for a plant of the hybrid Loderi, because there are twenty-three distinct sorts with this group name, each different from the others in varying degrees of color, flower size, fragrance, etc. If the purchaser wants the best white form he specifies the Loderi hybrid 'King George'; if he wants the deepest pink-flowered form, he must ask for 'Pink Diamond' in the Loderi hybrid group. Naomi, with nine cultivars; Hawk, with six; Mariloo, with three; Lady Chamberlain, with ten; and Fabia, with four, are typical of renowned names which designate groups without distinguishing specific individual clones. Failure to mention the cultivar in addition to the group name may even mean, as in the case of Fabia, that the purchaser will receive nondescript seedlings, in quality far below the high standard of the named cultivars.

Reputable nurserymen distinguish sharply in their catalogs between hybrid cultivars propagated as clones, with their fixed, unique qualities, and the seedlings of variable value which are offered under hybrid group names. In cases of primary crosses between two species, the system of naming legally provides a distinguished label for inferior seedlings which were produced from a mating of nondescript specimens of the same species repeated many years after the original cross was made. Such seedlings can usually be produced more cheaply than the named cultivars can be propagated by grafting or from cuttings. It is grossly misleading, in my opinion, to assign to seedlings in any commercial offering the quality ratings which have been awarded to specific cultivars meticulously selected for their outstanding quality.

Fortunately, the productions of professional breeders seem not to be burdened with the confusion which arises from group names, and most hybrids introduced by nurserymen have a name which applies solely to plants propagated from the one original introduction. Thus 'Goldsworth Orange', for example, and 'China' are English cultivar names in themselves. The hybrids of the Dutch nurseries have also been assigned one name alone, the cultivar name. For example, there is only one 'Marinus Koster', and all plants of 'Mrs C. B. van Nes' are alike in their quality.

Hybrids versus Species

Are hybrids a better choice for the garden than the unaltered species from the wild? Each has its adherents, but the unprejudiced observer will find value in both. Hybrids generally bloom more freely and are often more vigorous. They are better able to tolerate unfavorable conditions. They flower earlier in life and more consistently year after year. Indeed, it is only by an infusion of cold resistance from hardier species that the beauty of some of the tender sorts can be made available, through their hybrids, to many of our colder gardens.

CATAWBA HYBRIDS FOR SEVERE CLIMATES

Anthony Waterer's hybrids from the early importations in 1876 and shortly thereafter are still thriving in large gardens around the cities of the northeastern United States where their great size affords magnificent floral displays. At the turn of the century the largest public collection was at the Arnold Arboretum, Boston, Massachusetts, where many were eliminated through the years by winter cold. Finally, a hardy band of survivors was demonstrated to be satisfactory in their endurance of the coldest weather, and those which lived through the unprecedented temperatures of the winter of 1918 received the final seal of approval for adaptability to our climate. In 1926, the Rhododendron explorer, E. H. Wilson, published a list of these cultivars of extraordinary hardiness, which thereafter came to be known as the 'ironclad' hybrids. With one or two additions from other breeders, which also owe their hardiness to our native species, they are the mainstay of the nursery industry in the eastern United States and in the coldest parts of Europe today. As a group they are commonly called Catawba or *catawbiense* hybrids and they are propagated yearly in enormous numbers by professional growers.

The Catawba hybrids are not all equal in quality and many inferior cultivars continue to appear in catalogs for reasons entirely unrelated to their garden value. There have not been enough Rhododendrons produced by the American nursery industry to meet the demand for many years and such a situation is not conducive to the propagation of the best alone. Some sorts are apparently perpetuated solely because they are easy to propagate.

The evaluation of flowering plants is a matter of personal preference to an uncomfortable extent. The writer places what he believes to be a fair emphasis on the more subtle aesthetic values, such as the proportions of flower, leaf, and branch; the character of the plant in blossom and out of season; and the distinction which a hybrid of quality should have to lift it out of the ranks of the ordinary. Such things as flower size, color purity, floriferousness, plant habit and hardiness can be compared to determine on a factual basis the most effective hybrid Rhododendrons for the garden.

The Best of the Ironclad Group

The following clones have proved their worth for wide cultivation in the severe climate of the northeastern United States. From Philadelphia northward they are the standard hybrids of commerce and they are also extremely valuable south of the Mason and Dixon line for their ability to tolerate exposure and summer heat as well as winter cold. The superior sorts are ranked in the order of their quality, the other groups alphabetically:

RED

Superior

NOVA ZEMBLA	the best of this class
AMERICA	purest color; poor habit in youth; splits under heavy snow load
CHARLES DICKENS	difficult to propagate; slow in growth
ABE LINCOLN	difficult to propagate; color deficient
KETTLEDRUM	color varies according to location and season; scanty foliage; flowers poorly held in truss

Others

AMPHION	less hardy than those above
ATROSANGUINEUM	two hybrids by this name, one quite satisfactory
CARACTACUS	squalid color; good plant habit
CHARLES BAGLEY	good color, poor plant habit

DR H. C. DRESSELHUYS	poor color; dull foliage subject to winter injury; less hardy; grows rapidly
DR H. V. LOVINK	less hardy
DR V. H. RUTGERS	good plant habit; not ironclad in hardiness
EDWARD S. RAND	slightly less hardy
F. D. GODMAN	less hardy
GIGANTEUM	less hardy
H. W. SARGENT	slightly less hardy
MICHAEL WATERER	less hardy
MRS P. DEN OUDEN	less hardy
PROF. F. BETTEX	less hardy
VAN DEN BROEKE	less hardy
VAN WEERDEN POELMAN	less hardy

PINK

Superior

MRS C. S. SARGENT	deep reddish-rose; many specialists consider it the finest of all ironclad hybrids
ROSEUM ELEGANS	lavender-pink; fine habit; vigorous and adaptable; eight different hybrids in the trade under this name, seven of them inferior to the original; sometimes offered as 'Pink Roseum'
LADY ARMSTRONG	clear pink with paler center
EVERESTIANUM	lavender-rose, ruffled flowers

Others

CATHERINE VAN TOL	carmine-rose; less hardy
ENGLISH ROSEUM	inferior to the original, authentic 'Roseum elegans'
FASTUOSUM PLENUM	faded mauve, semi-double; less hardy (synonym:'Fastuosum flore pleno')
F. L. AMES	rosy pink; less hardy
GENERAL GRANT	rose
HENRIETTA SARGENT	rose-pink; hardy; more compact than 'Mrs C. S. Sargent'
IGNATIUS SARGENT	rose; hardy
PARSONS GRANDIFLORUM	purplish rose, small flowers; hardy
PARSONS GLORIOSUM	lavender pink; hardy
PRESIDENT LINCOLN	lavender pink
ROSEUM SUPERBUM	inferior to authentic original 'Roseum elegans'
VAN DER HOOP	dark rose; less hardy

WHITE

Superior

CATAWBIENSE ALBUM	easily the best mid-season white
BOULE DE NEIGE	early, compact, susceptible to Lace Wing Fly in full exposure
ALBUM ELEGANS	late

Others

ALBUM GRANDIFLORUM	large plant
CANDIDISSIMUM	faint lavender flush; less hardy
DELICATISSIMUM	faint pink flush; not free flowering
GOMER WATERER	faint blush; less hardy
MADAME CARVALHO	less hardy
MADAME MASSON	less hardy

LILAC

'Catawbiense Boursault' and 'Catawbiense Grandiflorum' are two Rhododendron clones with lilac-colored flowers which are sometimes offered by nurseries. They are not admired by specialists but their color is sufficiently distinct to place them in a separate group.

PURPLE

There is no Rhododendron hybrid of ironclad hardiness with dark purple flowers of first-class quality. In all of them the color is deficient in both purity and intensity. 'Purpureum Grandiflorum' is the best of those available. 'Purpureum Elegans' is equally hardy but it is not quite so desirable in other respects. 'Lee's Dark Purple' offers little improvement and a considerable sacrifice in hardiness. The standard of quality in this color is the superb 'Purple Splendour' with its flowers of deep, true royal purple. Unhappily, climates which do not exceed in severity that of Boston or the Lake Erie shore represent the extreme limit of its usefulness. It is a perennial best seller wherever it is hardy.

'Sefton' has large flowers of dark reddish plum late in the season. It is a distinct and decorative garden hybrid which has never been injured by repeated exposure to 25° below zero F. in my trial grounds. I regard it as a handsome and valuable Rhododendron for cold climates. 'Old Port' is a deep purplish red which is much less hardy.

'Cunningham's White'

'Cunningham's White' is an attractive early flowering Rhododendron with a faultless plant habit which is hardy along Lake Erie, at Boston, and in similar climates.

This hybrid originated about 1830 in the Comely Bank Nurseries of Edinburgh, Scotland, where it was thought to be a seedling of *ponticum* var. *album* crossed with *caucasicum*. It has white flowers with a greenish-yellow blotch. The leaves are without indumentum. Many authors (e.g. Bowers, *et al.*) have incorrectly considered this to be identical with 'Cunninghami', but the latter was bred by Cunningham in 1850 from *maximum* × *arboreum* var. *cinnamomeum* and described by the well-known nineteenth-century botanist, T. Moore. *R. Cunninghami* had white flowers with purple spots, not a greenish-yellow blotch, and it had a brownish indumentum beneath the leaves. It is no longer in cultivation.

This confusion between 'Cunningham's White' and 'Cunninghami' has puzzled many a nurseryman and breeder, unable to account for the hardiness of the former from the parentage of the latter. 'Cunningham's White' is reputed to be tolerant of alkaline soil, so much so that it is said to grow in districts where other hybrids perish. In my trial grounds the flowers partially open in the fall so that the remainder in the trusses are destroyed by winter cold. The hardier 'Boule de Neige' blooms a little later than 'Cunningham's White' but it is similarly compact in habit, and more reliable in its floral display.

The Parsons Hybrids

From about 1875 to 1890 a series of Rhododendron hybrids was produced by J. R. Trumpy at Kissena Nurseries in Flushing, Long Island, which subsequently came to be known as the Parsons hybrids. The following achieved the widest distribution:

Anna Parsons	Kissena
Bertha Parsons	President Lincoln
Flushing	Samuel B. Parsons
J. R. Trumpy	

'Flushing' is very similar to 'H. W. Sargent' and the others were not sufficiently distinct from or superior to the Waterer hybrids to enable them to survive the disruption to the nursery industry caused by the imposition in 1919 of Plant Quarantine No. 37. At that time, all but 'President Lincoln' disappeared from the market. This good lavender-pink hybrid is still propagated but it has been confused so often with the red-flowered 'Abraham Lincoln' that producers have become reluctant to offer it.

Ironically, the Parsons name is perpetuated solely today in two hybrids which originated at the Waterer nursery in England: 'Parsons Grandiflorum' and 'Parsons Gloriosum'. The veteran nurseryman Paul Vossberg states that Mr Parsons admired these two imported Rhododendrons and he obtained permission from Anthony Waterer to give them the names which are still familiar in the nursery industry.

Unusual Hybrids

A hybrid of an unfamiliar type in the eastern United States with small leaves and slender branching habit is available for the most severe climates through the talents of Joseph Gable, dean of American hybridists. His (*carolinianum* × *mucronulatum*) 'Conewago' bears pink flowers with a lavender undertone at an early season when it is especially valuable. Its lighter landscape effect and finer foliage texture make it blend more easily with other shrubs than do the typical large-leaved Rhododendron hybrids. 'Conewago' is successful also in many milder climates where the earlier blooming *mucronulatum* is too regularly injured by frosts. Mr Gable's more recent hybrid in this class is 'Pioneer', a phenomenally floriferous and effective dwarf evergreen shrub flowering early in the season. It is available commercially but it has not yet been tested sufficiently to confirm its preliminary promise of usefulness in the severest climates.

The foregoing recommended Rhododendrons are for the climates in the northeastern United States where the winter conditions are the coldest that the hybrids can be expected to endure. Since no Catawba hybrid is as hardy as the original species which contributed its cold resistance, a further extension northward can be made by planting *R. catawbiense*, especially the fine white and blush-pink varieties which are so much more attractive than the typical magenta color of the flowers of this species.

RHODODENDRON HYBRIDS FOR MODERATELY SEVERE CLIMATES

For the intermediate climate represented by that of New York City and along the coast farther north to Boston; for the Ohio and Pennsylvania shores of Lake Erie and for similar conditions there is a large group of satisfactory hybrids. All of the cultivars previously recommended can be grown, of course, and they should be liberally represented in any collection against the inevitable winter when unprecedented cold may decimate the ranks of hybrids whose hardiness has been less well established.

Generally, these Rhododendrons of intermediate hardiness are influenced in their adaptability by their Asian ancestors to a much greater extent than are the Catawba hybrids. They are more sensitive, not alone to winter cold, but also to other climatic conditions which are not conducive to their welfare. Thus good culture becomes increasingly important as these Rhododendrons approach the limit of their tolerance to local conditions. Their cold resistance is determined in good part by the numerous factors which affect hardiness as described in Chapter VII. Summer drouth, unfavorable soil or any other element of environment which impairs vitality will often lead to subsequent winter injury.

This increased sensitivity to growing conditions is probably responsible for the varying views held by specialists concerning the hardiness of hybrids in this group. As the tolerance toward unfavorable factors becomes more narrow their behavior in gardens becomes harder to assess. Atmospheric humidity, for example, may become the determining element in success or failure.

Some Rhododendrons in this class which are perfectly satisfactory at the Arnold Arboretum in Boston have failed in expert hands in the much milder climate of southern Pennsylvania. The reader must therefore be forewarned that some of these Rhododendrons cannot be purchased with quite the same confidence in their success as is justified with the ironclad Catawba hybrids.

In the Boston region the following Rhododendrons have been satisfactory in the collection of Walter Hunnewell. Those that Mr Hunnewell especially recommends on the basis of their performance in his garden are starred (*):

Abraham Lincoln*	red
Album elegans*	white, late, tall
Album grandiflorum*	pale mauve, fading white; spreading
Album novum	white
Alexander Dancer*	rose, light center
America	red
Amphion	red
Atrosanguineum	red
Boule de Neige*	white, early
Butlerianum	white, pink flush; late
Candidissimum	white, mauve flush
Caractacus*	dull purplish red
Caucasicum album	white, early
Charles Bagley	cherry red
Charles Dickens*	red
C. S. Sargent*	red, late
Countess of Athlone	mauve
Cunningham's White*	white, early
Doncaster	scarlet
Delicatissimum*	white, pink flush; late
Dr H. C. Dresselhuys*	red
Dr V. H. Rutgers	red
Edward S. Rand*	red, bronze center
Everestianum*	rosy lilac
F. D. Godman	dark red
F. L. Ames*	pink, light center
General Grant	rose
Giganteum	rose
Glennyanum*	light pink, early
Gloriosum* (Waterer's)	blush white

Gomer Waterer	white, pink blush; late
Hannibal	rose
Henrietta Sargent*	rose
H. H. Hunnewell	dark crimson
H. W. Sargent*	crimson
Ignatius Sargent*	rose
John Walter	crimson
Kate Waterer	deep rose, yellow center
Kettledrum*	crimson
Lady Armstrong*	rose, light center
Lady Grey-Egerton*	pale mauve
Lady Hillingdon*	pale mauve
Lady Rolle*	white, yellow blotch
Lord Roberts	dark red
Luciferum	white
Marquis of Waterford*	bright red, light center
Minnie*	white, mauve flush, orange spots
Madame Carvalho*	white
Madame Masson	white, yellow blotch
Mrs C. S. Sargent*	rose
Mrs Charles Thorold*	pink, yellow center
Mrs John Clutton*	white
Mrs Milner*	wine red
Mrs P. den Ouden	crimson
Nobleanum venustum*	rose, early
Old Port	plum color
Parsons gloriosum	rose
Parsons grandiflorum	purplish rose
Princess Mary of Cambridge*	blush, white center
Professor F. Bettex	red
Purpureum elegans	purple
Purpureum splendens	purple
Roseum elegans	lavender pink
Sultana*	white, brown blotch
Van der Broecke	carmine
Ven Weerden Poelman	crimson
Laetevirens (synonym: Wilsoni)	purplish rose

By no means are all of the ironclad cultivars displaced by hybrids of superior quality for climates similar to that of New York City. In a great many cases the gain in more attractive flowers is so slight as to be not worth the risk of an appreciable loss in hardiness. It becomes more a matter of additions to the list of recommended Rhododendrons. Hybrids which are unique in color, in stature, or in season of bloom can be grown in this milder climate which are not satisfactory farther north.

Among the red-flowered hybrids it is questionable whether any changes or additions should be made. 'Charles Bagley', 'Dr V. H. Rutgers', 'Edward S. Rand', 'Mrs P. de Ouden' and 'John Walter' can be planted by those who profess to see them as representing improvements in quality. Balancing the total of their virtues against their faults, unless a varied collection is being purposely assembled, my verdict is against making substitutions in the list of red-flowered hybrids already recommended which are ironclad in their resistance to cold.

'Lady Clementine Mitford' is a disputed candidate as an addition to the list of pink-flowered hybrids for this region. Its peach-pink blossoms with florets edged a deeper shade are not matched in the ironclad group and it has grown well at the Arnold Arboretum near Boston. 'Old Port', with unique plum-colored blossoms, is also a satisfactory ornamental shrub at the Arnold Arboretum but it has been bud tender at times along Lake Erie. It is highly regarded at the New York Botanical Garden and is well worth a trial by those who find its color attractive.

The magnificent 'Purple Splendour', with its rich diadem of imperial color, is suitable for the region under discussion, and 'Blue Peter', a pale lavender with a deeper blotch, is an addition to the lists.

In white-flowered sorts two extraordinarily fine hybrids first enter the lists for cultivation in regions of climate similar to that of New York City. 'Gomer Waterer' loses its buds a little too often at Boston to recommend it for cultivation there but it gains enough in reliability at New York to justify planting it for its exquisitely beautiful blossoms with a faint pink blush. It is one of the best hybrids ever produced. 'Mrs P. D. Williams' has demonstrated its adaptability in Westchester County, New York, long enough to warrant a cautious commendation. Its large, ivory-white flowers, boldly blotched with a brown bee, make it a Rhododendron of exceptionally strong and attractive character. No claim is made that these two hybrids can survive the bitter extremity of unprecedented cold which seems to be visited upon the Northeast about once every twenty-five years, but plants of blooming size should repay their cost and keep long before such a rare catastrophe overtakes them.

'Baroness Henry Schroeder' and 'Madame Carvalho' are white-flowered cultivars which are occasionally seen in gardens and in nursery lists. They are a little hardier than the preceding, and quite a little less beautiful.

New Introductions

Perhaps the most interesting acquisitions for this sort of climate are some new hybrids created by Guy G. Nearing from unfamiliar species of dwarf stature. 'Ramapo' is a fine, low-growing Rhododendron with neat small leaves and lavender-purple flowers produced in abundance early in the season. 'Purple Gem' is similar but much deeper in color. These resulted from a cross of *carolinianum* × *fastigiatum* and they have the convenient dwarf stature of their pollen parent, seldom exceeding 2½ feet in height and a little less in diameter. Many gardeners will find a flowering evergreen of such dimensions to be a valuable asset for foundation planting and for various other uses on the home grounds. They prefer sun and exposure.

'Windbeam' and 'Wyanokie' are a pair of dwarf hybrids whose myriad blossoms smother the plants in mantles of attractive pink and white, respectively. These too are gems for foundation planting and for other situations where restrained growth is especially desired. The former matures at 6 feet, the latter at 3 feet. Open pollinated seeds grown by Mr Nearing from a Gable hybrid (*carolinianum* × *racemosum*) 'Conestoga', gave these two good little Rhododendrons to horticulture.

The Guyencourt Rhododendrons are a group of named sorts produced by crossing *R. pubescens* with *R. keiskei*. These also are Nearing hybrids of an unfamiliar sort, quite different from the usual large-leaved Catawba cultivars. Less than 2 feet in height with narrow leaves about 2 inches long, these new sorts bloom at the beginning of May in clusters of flowers crowded near the tips of slender, arching branches. They prefer part shade.

The Guyencourt hybrids are a race of Rhododendrons which vary considerably among themselves, so readers should understand that the different cultivars must be designated by their names to secure the exact duplications of the hybrids which have been described by the originator as follows:

BRANDYWINE	pale pink, turning rose
CHESAPEAKE	apricot, fading white
DELAWARE	pinkish yellow, turning lighter
HOCKESSIN	like 'Chesapeake' but larger stature, smaller flowers
LENAPE	pale yellow
MONTCHANIN	white

Two of Joseph Gable's scaly-leaved hybrids find their northern limit of usefulness in the general region and climate under consideration. His (*racemosum* × *mucronulatum*) 'Conemaugh' is an engaging small shrub of upright habit with pink flowers produced early in the season. Its small leaves are not quite evergreen the year round: in late winter they are shed to make way for the replacements which come with the first new growth.

R. (*carolinianum* × *racemosum*) 'Conestoga', with multitudes of small pink blossoms, flowers profusely well before the midseason of Rhododendron bloom. It is a small shrub, neat in growth and attractively proportioned for the many situations appropriate to an evergreen of modest stature.

Two of Mr Gable's creations of the conventional sort with large leaves also demand attention in this climate. 'Beaufort' and 'Caroline' are the first such hybrids introduced by an American breeder since the turn of the century which promise to find commercial acceptance and general distribution. They represent the first significant advance in the quality of Rhododendrons of this type, hardy in the Northeast, since Anthony Waterer brought over his iron-clad Catawba varieties in 1876.

'Caroline' is thought to be a hybrid of *R. decorum* but no certain record of its parentage exists. Its blossoms are large and they are produced on a shapely shrub of faultless habit richly clothed with dark green foliage. In time it becomes a large specimen. The pale orchid-mauve blossoms are sweetly fragrant and this is the first hardy hybrid in commerce in the eastern United States to enjoy the heritage of scent from an Asian parent. 'Caroline' has not been injured in five years of testing in my garden, which is ordinarily suited only for Rhododendrons of the sternest hardiness.

R. ('Boule de Neige' × *fortunei*) 'Beaufort' bears white flowers just before midseason on a well-branched shrub of superior appearance which is not susceptible to attacks of Lace Wing Fly, as is its seed parent. It may be hardier than the conservative assessment inferred by its inclusion in this section.

THE DEXTER HYBRIDS

History

The late C. O. Dexter started to collect Rhododendrons for his garden in Sandwich, Massachusetts, on Cape Cod, in 1922. The collection was expanded by contributions from Leonard Ross, who had access to the foreign sources of supply of the Arnold Arboretum, and by purchases from the Farquhar Nursery, which had acquired many rare Asian Rhododendrons from the Veitch Nursery in England. Among the hardiest of these was one called 'Farquhar's Pink' which has outstanding clear pink flowers with a deeper-colored throat, and apparently Mr Dexter used it extensively as a parent. It is in itself a fine Rhododendron of considerable hardiness which has been rarely surpassed by any of its progeny of similar color and cold resistance.

The climate of Cape Cod at Sandwich is very similar to that of Long Island and the south shore of Long Island has average winter temperatures similar to those of Maryland. In addition to the moderate winter conditions, Mr Dexter's garden was favored by the high humidity and temperate summer climate of its site near the ocean.

The Farquhar Nursery had pointed the way and Mr Dexter soon demonstrated that here at last was a place in the eastern United States where many of the spectacular new Rhododendrons from Asia could be successfully grown. They had previously been a disappointing failure everywhere they had been tried.

By 1925 Mr Dexter had become engrossed in breeding Rhododendrons and Azaleas. Several years later he was growing annually 10,000 seedlings in his woodland nursery at Sandwich. In the early 1930's, through Paul Frost, his landscape architect, he became the recipient of seeds from the finest Rhododendron collections in England, and subsequently the Dexter garden at Sandwich became famous as a showplace and repository for almost all of the rare Asian Rhododendron species that could be expected to survive there. A majority of the scores of species which were tested failed to adapt to the climate but a surprising number grew well enough to serve their purpose for breeding and a modest contingent actually thrived.

The very few nurserymen who knew anything about the Asian Rhododendrons spread the word among their fellows that Mr. Dexter was using the notoriously tender *R. griffithianum* in his breeding and the professionals were wary of the Dexter hybrids for many years. They regarded them as suitable only for the mild local climate of Sandwich. Through Mr Dexter's gifts of small seedlings to other amateur gardeners, especially on Long Island, his hybrids gradually became distributed over an area wide enough to prove that they were hardier than had been previously supposed, but it is only since 1950 that an organized effort has been made to locate and to propagate the finest examples of them.

Since no details of his work are available today, it is impossible to trace back the manner in which Mr Dexter's crosses were arranged. In addition to the Fortunei clan, some seedlings show the influence of *R. haematodes*, and of the fifty or more other Asian species which he had available for use as parents a number of additional sorts were employed in his crosses as were various hybrids. Their derivation can only be surmised from the characteristics of some of the seedlings. The hybrid from Farquhar's Nursery called 'Farquhar's Pink' (unfortunately not a parent of ironclad hardiness) probably figured prominently in many crosses. From the number of hybrids with stamens hairy at the base and style glandular to the tip, it seems likely that *R. decorum*, rather than *R. fortunei* as popularly supposed, was a principal source of flower size and fragrance. Like Anthony Waterer, almost a century earlier, Mr Dexter apparently aimed only at producing hybrids which would be satisfactory for his local conditions and it is surprising that so many of his productions have proved hardy in climates much more severe.

Collections of the Dexter hybrids which are open to the public can be found at the Henry du Pont estate, Winterthur, Delaware; the Scott Horticultural Foundation at Swarthmore College; the Morris Arboretum at Chestnut Hill, Philadelphia; the New York Botanical Garden, New York City; and at the Arnold Arboretum near Boston.

Selecting the Best Dexter Hybrids

The Dexter hybrid Rhododendrons have been publicized in the last several years to the exasperation of gardeners who have avidly sought plants of the better sorts only to find them not yet available. Unfortunately, too many have compromised by purchasing seedlings of the Dexter strain and they will almost inevitably be deeply disappointed when the plants come into bloom. Such seedlings are nondescript mongrels which are not at all representative of the fine Rhododendrons selected by the late C. O. Dexter from among the tens of thousands of hybrids which he bred.

In 1950 the American Rhododendron Society sponsored a move to survey all of the Dexter hybrids in both public and private collections, and to select the best for propagation and testing on a comparative basis. I have served as a member of this Evaluating Committee, which has repeatedly visited the principal collections all the way from Winterthur, Delaware, to Newburyport, Massachusetts, observing the performance of the finest specimens and selecting those consistently superior.

Plants propagated from the most outstanding hybrids have been assembled for testing under the direction of Dr John Wister at the Arthur Hoyt Scott Horticultural Foundation of Swarthmore College. After the finest sorts from each collection have been tested side by side, the very best of each color, stature and flowering season will be named, propagated and introduced through the American Rhododendron Society and the Association of Botanical Gardens and Arboretums.

In the meantime, the market is being flooded with seedlings promoted as "Dexter Hybrids" which are a libel on the important work of a pioneering American hybridist. The species of the Fortunei series which were the dominant influence produced hosts of plants bearing fragrant blossoms of an undistinguished pale mauve shade. The coarse growth habit resembles *R. fortunei*. These are the pedestrian discards which probably would have been destroyed by Mr Dexter had he grown them to flowering size instead of having given them away as small seedlings to admiring friends.

With the exception of a group at Ipswich, Massachusetts, and a few plants on Long Island, almost all of the Rhododendrons in the various collections were grown from small plants in flats, presented by Mr Dexter as gifts. Such unselected seedlings of complex parentage inevitably produce a dominant average of indifferent value. The really fine hybrids of superior quality are very much in the minority as of course Mr Dexter knew they would be.

The "Dexter Hybrids" which are currently offered are, for the most part, offspring of these inferior discards and as such they are scarcely equal in quality to their dubious parents.

But the best of the Dexter hybrids are fine indeed, fully equal to the high standard set by modern British hybrids, and much hardier. They are characterized by large blossoms, up to 4 inches or more in diameter, which are produced about two weeks before the Catawba hybrids come into bloom. The lighter colored flowers are often fragrant and they are usually produced on plants of exceptionally strong, vigorous growth. A sizable minority produce blooms which have no stamens and these blossoms tend to have extraordinary substance and durability. The leaves are large and the trusses are often lax and somewhat open, not the formal, built-up pyramids of flowers typical of the Catawba hybrids. Most of the Dexter hybrids eventually reach generous proportions; there are few dwarfs among them.

Perhaps the greatest interest has centered in

the sorts with apricot-colored flowers, of which most collections have one or more representatives. Until Mr Dexter produced them, large flowers with this orange-yellow blend of colors were unknown on Rhododendron hybrids growing outdoors in the eastern United States, and they attracted wide attention. On Long Island a private collector tentatively named an attractive Rhododendron of this type 'C.O.D.' for Charles O. Dexter and it has attained some reputation on the strength of visits to the estate by many thousands of amateur gardeners. Unfortunately this plant suffers by having sparse foliage of poor color, as do nearly all of the other pale apricot-flowered Dexter hybrids, with the conspicuous exception of an extraordinarily fine specimen growing in a collection at Ipswich, Massachusetts.

The best Dexter hybrids with deep pink flowers are superb. One which has been named 'Mrs W. R. Coe' by its owner has a vibrant radiance in the color of its large blossoms which sets it apart from others and makes it one of the finest Rhododendron hybrids in existence anywhere. Another deep pink-flowered sort of extraordinary quality is growing in the Ipswich group and there are a fair number of good light pinks in the various collections.

White-flowered Dexter hybrids are as scarce as those with red blossoms so, of course, those that can be judged by the highest standards are even rarer. The reds which have thus far been appraised have larger blossoms of a much truer and more brilliant color than any of the Catawba hybrids, but it is a family failing of this gay tribe to bear poor foliage and many of these are no exception.

Named clones of superior Dexter hybrids became available for the first time in 1959 when the Westbury Rose Company, wholesale growers, introduced the following: 'Amethyst', lavender; 'Brookville', pink; 'Mrs W. R. Coe', deep pink; 'Scintillation', pink; 'Westbury', pink, yellow center; and 'Wheatley', light pink.

Undoubtedly the unnamed Dexter hybrids vary greatly in their hardiness, freedom and reliability of blossoming, plant habit, ease of culture and in many other important respects. The fine selections growing in the benign climate of Long Island may possibly prove to be totally unsuited to gardens in the more rigorous winter weather of the coast from New Jersey to Boston. Plants in the collections at Ipswich and at Newburyport, Massachusetts, have demonstrated their cold resistance to a greater extent, and at the Arnold Arboretum approximately fifty of the Dexter hybrids survived 30° below zero (F.) in the winter of 1934.

Super Hardy Dexter Hybrids

A special group of Dexter hybrids is in a collection open to the public at the Bosley Nursery, Mentor, Ohio. These are the survivors of a much larger number, selected by Mr Dexter as being especially suited to a severe climate. Through the years their numbers dwindled as sub-zero temperatures took their toll until there now remains a hardy band of fine pink and lavender-flowered hybrids which are superior to the Catawba clones of commerce. Many new shades of clear, true pink and some two-toned flowers with throats a deeper shade are represented here. There are no apricot-flowered hybrids, and no plants with noteworthy white or red blossoms have been able to survive the climate at Mentor.

By comparison with the old ironclad cultivars, the Dexter hybrids at Mentor have larger flowers with much more attractive colors which are pure and true, untainted by the blue undertone we have come to tolerate in the Catawba clones. A few of the Mentor specimens are slightly fragrant. Their hardiness for such a climate as that of the Lake Erie shore and Boston, Massachusetts, is unquestioned, but it is hard to fix the extreme margin of tolerance since these regions do not test the limit of cold resistance even for the older standard ironclad cultivars. The Dexter hybrids at Mentor have come through winters of extraordinary cold just as well as have the Catawba hybrids and several of the Mentor selections survived five years of 20° to 25° below zero (F.) winter weather in my garden without injury. Additional sorts are now on test and there is every possibility that some of them will prove to be fully equal in hardiness to the old Waterer cultivars.

Compared with those on the East Coast, the

Rhododendrons in the Mentor collection have smaller blossoms, but they are more free-flowering and better able to stand exposure. Some of the selections in this group are unbelievably floriferous, with flower buds on practically one hundred per cent of the terminal growths on plants growing in an open display garden without shade. On the other hand, the larger-flowered forms in the East are much more fragrant and of course in their great numbers they offer a wider variety of colors, flower shapes, and truss formations.

The Mentor selections are an important contribution to the horticulture of cold climates. Their larger flowers and lovely clear colors in shades never before seen in such hardy Rhododendrons are a milestone in the slow progress of ornamental shrub breeding. The best of the Dexter hybrids adapted to the milder climates are equally important for those regions in which they now grow. When the remainder of the finest few are eventually isolated, propagated, and introduced, all will be signal acquisitions for gardens of the East Coast.

RHODODENDRONS FOR FAVORED EASTERN CLIMATIC CONDITIONS

Philadelphia, Long Island, Cape Cod

In this region and in similar climates, the choice of adaptable Rhododendrons open to the gardener is so much wider that it is scarcely practical to discuss individually all of the candidates for consideration. It is at this point in the climatic scale that summer heat exerts an inhibiting effect which becomes increasingly important as winter cold diminishes its influence as a critical factor. Here, too, good culture has a large bearing on the success or failure of hybrids close to the limit of their climatic tolerance.

The Long Island climate in favored sites along the south shore must still be considered as atypical. Several enthusiasts are growing there collections of Rhododendrons whose roster reads like an extensive nursery list from the mildest part of England. These collections are, however, recently established. Time alone will tell whether a wind from Labrador will some day decimate their ranks. The enthusiasts alone can tell whether they have, in such an eventuality, got their money's worth in the pleasure and satisfaction of bringing to flowering such marvelous wonders as the incomparable (Loderi g.) 'King George' and the blazing 'Earl of Athlone'.

Everett Miller, former superintendent of 'Planting Fields' estate at Oyster Bay, with a Rhododendron collection which has passed through the adversities of the weather for many years, considers the following to be satisfactory there. The symbols indicate the quality ratings of the Rhododendron societies, from one x to four in order of increasing desirability for the American rating; from one star (*) to four for progressively higher value under the British system, where no American rating has been published:

AZOR	xxx	salmon pink, late
BAGSHOT RUBY#	x	blood crimson
BLACK BEAUTY	xx	dark crimson
DUKE OF YORK		rosy pink, brown spots
DUCHESS OF YORK		salmon pink, green spots
ELSIE WATERER		white, deep red blotch
GOETHE		rose
GOLDSWORTH YELLOW#	xx	apricot
GOMER WATERER#	xx	white, faint pink blush, late
KATE WATERER#		rosy crimson, yellow center
LADY CLEMENTINE MITFORD	xx	peach pink, deeper margin
LADY ELEANOR CATHCART	xx	clear pink, chocolate spots
LADY GREY-EGERTON	x	pale lilac
LADY PRIMROSE	xxx	lemon yellow, red spots
MADAME CARVALHO		white, greenish spots
MADAME DE BRUIN	xx	cerise-red
MADAME MASSON#	x	white, yellow blotch
MARQUIS OF WATERFORD		pink, light center
MARS#	xxxx	deep true red

MINNIE		white, orange spots
MRS P. D. WILLIAMS	xxx	ivory white, brown blotch
MRS R. S. HOLFORD	x	rosy salmon
Naomi (cultivars of)	xxx	pink shades with green and lilac
PRINCESS ELIZABETH	xx	crimson
PURPLE SPLENDOUR	xxxx	deep purple, black blotch
SAPPHO	xx	white, heavily blotched
SWEET SIMPLICITY	xx	white, edged pink
THE QUEEN		white, faint pink blush
UNKNOWN WARRIOR	x	bright red

The hybrids marked (#) are especially recommended by Mr Miller. This listing, from which the familiar Rhododendrons known to be hardy in much colder climates have been omitted, can be used as a rough guide for the selection of other clones of comparable hardiness for winter conditions similar to those of Oyster Bay. Most of these cultivars represent a substantial upgrading in the size of their flowers and the purity of their colors over the standard commercial Catawba hybrids. A number of entirely new colors are represented which are not at present available in the flowers of plants hardy in colder climates.

The following hybrids have proved to be satisfactory in the Philadelphia region:

ALEXANDER DANCER		bright rose, light center
AZOR	xxx	salmon pink, late
BLUE PETER	xxx	pale lavender, deeper blotch
CANDIDISSIMUM		white, faint lavender flush
GOLDSWORTH YELLOW	xx	apricot-yellow
GOMER WATERER	xx	white, slightly blushed; late
LADY GREY-EGERTON	x	pale lilac
LADY PRIMROSE	xxx	lemon yellow, red spots
MADAME CARVALHO		white, greenish spots
OLD PORT	*	plum color
PURPLE SPLENDOUR	xxxx	deep purple, black blotch
SAPPHO	xx	white, heavily blotched
SEFTON		dark maroon, late

'Goldsworth Yellow' belongs to a group of four British hybrids of distinctive clear flower color which have proved to be satisfactory in a climate intermediate between that of Philadelphia and New York. They have done well in several sites in southeastern Pennsylvania and the large stature of the specimens there attests to their contentment in that region. Several of them are growing happily in the immediate vicinity of New York City, but they have not been established there for enough years to warrant an entirely unqualified recommendation for the more severe climate. All four of these Rhododendrons are quite superior to anything of similar color and season in the ironclad lists:

CYNTHIA	xx	rosy crimson; robust; avoid full exposure
ESSEX SCARLET	xx	clear scarlet, leggy habit; avoid windy sites
GOLDSWORTH YELLOW	xx	apricot-yellow
MADAME DE BRUIN	xx	cerise red

'Madame de Bruin' is reported to be satisfactory at the New York Botanical Garden.

Of still finer quality is another group of four cultivars, probably a bit more tender than the preceding but none the less eminent subjects for experimentation in the region under consideration. Three of them are known to be satisfactory at Oyster Bay, Long Island. 'Mars' has survived several winters in southern Pennsylvania and all three can probably endure a somewhat harsher climate than that of favored sites on Long Island, but the exact limit of their tolerance to cold is unknown. These extraordinary hybrids are at or close to the finest quality of modern Rhododendrons available on our own West Coast or in England. A rich reward, of color, grace and distinction, awaits the gardener who pleases these patrician plants:

ARTHUR J. IVENS	xxx	Award of Merit winner. Pale pink, bell-shaped flowers 3 inches wide on a dwarf compact plant not over 3 to 4 feet tall. Small, rounded leaves. Early blooming

MARS	xxxx	Many flowers of true dark red make up an impressive globular truss. Universally admired. Large, dark green leaves and good habit of growth. Six feet tall at maturity
NAOMI GROUP	xxx	Rounded trusses of eight or ten large flowers, each sometimes as much as 5 inches across, in opalescent pink and cream shades. Neat, sturdy habit, with rounded leaves. Needs part shade. Conceded everywhere to be unexcelled for its type. The following clones, originally all sister seedlings, are available in the Naomi hybrid group: A.M. (Award of Merit) flowers edged pink, deeper yellow throat ASTARTE, pale pink CARISSIMA, pale pink, creamy white inside EARLY DAWN, pale pink EXBURY NAOMI, soft pink suffused pale yellow GLOW, bright pink HOPE, pink tinged mauve NAUTILUS (Award of Merit), frilled pale pink flowers, cream inside and veined rosy mauve NEREID, pink, flushed chartreuse and yellow PINK BEAUTY, deep pink STELLA MARIS (First Class Certificate), pale pink; slightly larger flowers, fuller trusses, larger leaves
PRINCESS ELIZABETH	xx	Deep crimson. Inclined to be brittle from overly vigorous growth

RHODODENDRON HYBRIDS FOR THE BALTIMORE-WASHINGTON REGION

South of the Mason and Dixon line the successful cultivation of Rhododendrons depends on the selection of sorts which can tolerate summer heat. A wide variety of hybrids of the finest quality can endure the winter cold of the Baltimore-Washington region but many of them cannot withstand the conditions in summer which are so alien to their Asian homeland. Such malcontents lose most of their foliage, fail to make proper growth and so languish as to become exasperating liabilities in the garden.

The splendid hybrids derived primarily from the fine Asian species have not been grown in variety over a period long enough to afford an accurate guide for the prospective purchaser. Reports are conflicting because cultivars which give a good account of themselves in some gardens are so close to the limit of their tolerance to the climate that they may be unsatisfactory in gardens with conditions slightly less favorable.

It is generally true that a heritage from our native Catawba Rhododendron fortifies a hybrid for resistance to exposure and to unfavorable conditions of climate and soil. The safest Rhododendrons for the Baltimore–Washington region are therefore those stand-bys of more northerly gardens described earlier in this chapter.

Even a slight contribution from *R. catawbiense* seems to bestow adaptability upon a hybrid and such better quality cultivars as 'Mars', 'Vulcan', and 'Britannia' with their fine red blossoms; the lovely white 'Sappho' and others of that general class with flowers of various colors can be recommended with some confidence.

A further clue toward a selection is the generally satisfactory performance of a half dozen species in the Fortunei series in this region, so hybrids in which *R. fortunei* and *R. discolor* predominate are promising candidates for selection. R. (*dichroanthum* × *discolor*) 'Goldsworth Orange' has done well in Washington and it brings to the East flowers of pale orange on a handsome plant. The Naomi hybrid group, derived from 'Aurora' × *fortunei*, with large pink to cream-colored blossoms in the various named cultivars, have also done well, though they require more shade. R. (*wightii* × *fortunei*) 'China', a Rhododendron with exotic-looking foliage and unique pale ochre-colored blossoms, should be a promising prospect.

R. griersonianum, though its foliage burns easily in excessive sun, is well known to be able to withstand hot, dry situations, so it is not surprising to discover that the hybrids of the Azor group are reported to be a success in central Maryland. Their tolerance of the climate there probably comes from both parents, *griersonianum* and *discolor*, and the clone which received an Award of Merit is among the best of all modern hybrids, with large salmon pink blossoms appearing late in the season when they are doubly valued. There are innumerable seedlings of varying quality which can be called Azor under the former English system of naming, so the purchaser must specify the Award of Merit cultivar to be certain of receiving the sort which has been awarded the three x rating by the American Rhododendron Society.

R. (*maximum* × *arboreum*) 'Lady Eleanor Cathcart', a large shrub with pink flowers of an admirably clear shade does well in the Washington, D.C., district.

The foregoing will give some hints for further promising trials by the experimentally minded gardener. Casting about for additional prospects with ambitions to succeed, it seems likely that hybrids of some of the better species in the Triflorum series ought to be candidates. *RR. keiskei*, *yunnanense*, *ambiguum* and *augustinii* have produced some excellent dwarf hybrids of much finer texture than the conventional large-leaved Rhododendrons and they can be used to advantage in many places in the landscape where the stronger growing sorts with coarser foliage are unsuitable.

Of course the problem of winter cold cannot be entirely disregarded in central Maryland, and the purchaser must draw a nice balance in a good many cases between the possibility of injury or loss after a rare winter of exceptional severity and the prospect of enjoying the incomparable blooms from some of the finest hybrids in existence for some years until they are put to the test.

Those who want to experiment with unproved hybrids should bear in mind the dual nature of the problems which confront them in this region. Remembering that Rhododendrons love humidity and moderate temperatures, it will be found that the degree of success and the variety of different hybrids which can be creditably grown will increase directly as cool conditions with high atmospheric moisture are approached. Since there is no prospect of attaining even an approximation of their natural environment, the wonder is that the gorgeous hybrids of the Asian species will respond so generously to so poor an imitation of it. Studied consideration in selecting the planting site is the best assurance of satisfaction with untested Rhododendrons. About 40 per cent sun and 60 per cent shade seems to be a good balance to minimize summer temperature, assure a good crop of flower buds, and avoid foliage scorch for the average hybrid.

Gardeners in the Washington-Richmond region will soon have a comprehensive and accurate guide to new Rhododendrons for their district in the performance of about 250 different hybrids which were planted in 1953 under the direction of Dr Henry Skinner at the United States National Arboretum. There can scarcely be any question that a much wider variety of Rhododendrons can be grown in central Maryland than can be successfully cultivated in Philadelphia and farther north. The problem is to determine which sorts are locally adaptable and the testing program at the United States National Arboretum will provide the answer. In the meantime the following two lists may be helpful. They have been prepared in good part from information supplied by three Rhododendron experts in the Washington region. The symbols show the quality ratings of the Rhododendron societies, from one x to four in order of increasing value for the American ratings; and from one star to four for progressively higher value under the British system in cases where no American rating has been published. With the exception of 'Prometheus', which has been passed over for a quality rating, the unrated hybrids opposite are still too new to have been evaluated:

TESTED HYBRIDS

AZMA	xx	salmon pink
Azor hybrid group	xxx	salmon pink
BRITANNIA	xxxx	crimson
CAROLINE		pale lavender
CONEMAUGH	xx	pink, dwarf
CYNTHIA	xx	rosy crimson
GLORY OF LITTLEWORTH	xx	yellow (Azalea-dendron)
GOLDSWORTH ORANGE	xx	pale orange
GOLDSWORTH YELLOW	xx	apricot-yellow
LADY ELEANOR CATHCART	xx	pink
MARS	xxxx	deep red
Naomi hybrid group	xxx	pink to cream
SAPPHO	xx	white
VULCAN	xx	brick red

HYBRIDS WHICH HAVE GROWN FOR SEVERAL YEARS UNDER TEST

AKBAR		pink
ALBATROSS	xxx	white
AVOCET		white
BUTTERFLY	xx	pale lemon
DR STOCKER	xxx	ivory
DRAGONFLY		pink
Fabia hybrid group	xx	salmon orange
IMPI	x	dark red, late
ISABELLA		white
JACKSONII	x	rosy pink
JAN DEKENS	xxx	pink
JIBUTI		scarlet
KATHERINE DALTON		pale lavender
LADY BESSBOROUGH	xxx	pale yellow
(Loderi g.) KING GEORGE	xxxx	white
LODER'S WHITE	xxxx	white
MOTHER OF PEARL	xxx	blush
PINK PEARL	xx	rose pink
PROMETHEUS		crimson
ROMANY CHAI	xx	scarlet
SIR FREDERICK MOORE	**	pink
UNIQUE	xxx	buff

The first group above includes the sorts which have been grown long enough to show that they are at home in this region from the standpoint of winter cold and summer heat. The second listing is of hybrids which have been cultivated in central Maryland for varying shorter periods and their selection must be considered a speculation in beauty for the purchaser at the present time.

HYBRIDS FOR SAN FRANCISCO AND REGIONS OF SIMILAR CLIMATE

The climate in the United States is so varied that Rhododendrons must be selected on the basis of local conditions even within a sharply restricted geographical area. It means little to recommend certain Rhododendrons for the West Coast because numerous fine sorts which are at home in San Francisco are malcontents in Seattle. It is not even correct to recommend hybrids for the San Francisco region. The cool, humid conditions of the fog belt are conducive to the health and welfare of many Rhododendrons which languish in the much warmer summer climate of adjoining Oakland. A detailed discussion of how best to grow Rhododendrons in coastal California appears in the preceding chapter on page 241. There will be found information on the amount of shade, soil planting mixtures, watering and other cultural details both for the fog belt and for gardens farther inland.

Such remarkable Rhododendrons as 'Victorianum', 'Tyermanii', 'Dr J. Hutchinson', 'Fragrantissimum' and others of the unfamiliar scaly-leaved British hybrids with astonishing qualities of size and scent to their blossoms are likely to be quite content by reason of the moist moderation of the climate in San Francisco and in warm gardens from Santa Cruz to Fort Bragg elsewhere close to the coast in California. There alone in the whole of the United States can the exotic Rhododendrons in the Maddenii and Edgeworthii groups be grown really creditably outdoors. For the typical gardener with a coastal location in this district 'Princess Alice', 'Forsterianum', and 'Countess of Haddington' are promising prospects with more than average adaptability to start an acquaintance with the hybrids. Suggestions for more extensive plantings will be found in Chapter XI on pages 375 and 376.

The English clones will no doubt be superseded in time by others such as those produced by Mr and Mrs Maurice H. Sumner, who are breeding scaly-leaved hybrids from which selections can be made with specific accommodation to local conditions.

The more familiar sort of Rhododendron hybrids, mostly somewhat portly shrubs of robust stature with large glossy evergreen leaves lacking scales beneath them, are equally at home in coastal California gardens but not all of them are equally easy to grow well. The legions of scarlet-flowered hybrids derived from *R. griersonianum* are susceptible to foliage burn which becomes progressively more severe with the distance of the garden from the coast. Inland where there is no moderation of the clarity and dryness of the atmosphere Rhododendrons derived from this species should be avoided entirely. *R.* 'Elizabeth' and *R.* 'Vulcan' are among the best in this class but even in favored sites the *griersonianum* hybrids are inclined to be scanty and yellow in foliage, the leaves too easily injured by sunlight.

It is important with the larger foliaged sorts that they be spared windy situations which seriously injure the plants by buffeting the leaves so that they cannot function properly in sustaining the vigor of the plants. Such fine hybrids as the Loderi and Naomi groups of cultivars, which are universally conceded to be among the supreme achievements of amateur breeders, do very well in coastal California if they are not placed in windswept sites. There are many other Rhododendrons which have acquired good reputations for their amiability: 'Dr Stocker', 'Azor', 'Cornish Cross', 'Moonstone', 'Temple Belle', 'Daphne' and 'Sir Frederick Moore' are examples which offer a variety in stature, foliage size and flower color. The blossoms of the late blooming sorts often tend to be somewhat hidden by new growth in the California coastal climate.

On the other hand, the early blooming sorts are especially satisfactory, the flowers sometimes lasting as long as four weeks in the damp coolness along the coast. Such fine Rhododendrons as 'Cornubia' and 'Gill's Crimson', which are not hardy farther north, provide magnificent early displays. In fact, gardeners of the coastal district from Santa Cruz to Fort Bragg see some usually tender hybrids come to a perfection of bloom there which is unknown in Oregon and Washington. *R.* (Barclayi g.) 'Helen Fox' and 'Robert Fox' and such remarkable sorts as 'Glory of Penjerrick' are typical of the tender sorts, famous for their beauty, which are uniquely at home in the benign climate.

In so far as it is possible to recommend hybrids of all types which will do well in the whole of the San Francisco region and in similar climates, the following listing represents the combined selections of three district experts:

RED

Before May 1st	dwarf	Doncaster
	medium	Felix de Sauvage
		Gill's Crimson
	tall	Cornubia
		Earl of Athlone
May 1st to June 1st	dwarf	May Day
	medium	Gill's Crimson
		Jean Marie Montague
		Lady Bligh
	tall	Princess Elizabeth
		Cynthia
After June 1st	dwarf	Elizabeth
	medium	Grenadier
	tall	Tally Ho!

PINK

Before May 1st	dwarf	Bow Bells
	medium	Corona
	tall	Pilgrim
May 1st to June 1st	dwarf	Mrs Mary Ashley
	medium	Naomi hybrid group
		Hugo de Vries
	tall	Betty Wormald
		Pink Pearl
After June 1st	dwarf	Goblin
	medium	Azor
	tall	Bonito

BLUE AND LAVENDER

Before May 1st	dwarf	Augfast
		Blue Diamond
	medium	Lavender Girl
	tall	Mrs Charles Pearson
May 1st to June 1st	dwarf	Blue Peter
	medium	Susan
	tall	Van Nes Sensation
After June 1st	medium	Purple Splendour

SHADES OF ORANGE

Before May 1st	dwarf	GOLDEN HORN
	medium	Fabia hybrid group
	tall	Lady Chamberlain hybrid group
May 1st to June 1st	dwarf	DIDO
	medium	SARITA LODER
	tall	ROYAL FLUSH
After June 1st	dwarf	MEDUSA
	medium	RADIUM

CREAM TO YELLOW

Before May 1st	dwarf	MOONSTONE
		UNIQUE
	medium	ROSA MUNDI
	tall	DR STOCKER
May 1st to June 1st	dwarf	BROUGHTONII AUREUM
		MOONSTONE
	medium	DIANE
	tall	CHINA
After June 1st	dwarf	HARVEST MOON
	medium	MARGARET DUNN
	tall	LADY BESSBOROUGH

WHITE

Before May 1st	dwarf	CILPENENSE
		FORSTERIANUM
	medium	HANDSWORTH WHITE
	tall	THE BRIDE
May 1st to June 1st	dwarf	COUNTESS OF SEFTON
	medium	BEAUTY OF LITTLEWORTH
		FRAGRANTISSIMUM
		LODER'S WHITE
	tall	(Loderi g.) KING GEORGE
		WHITE PEARL
After June 1st	medium	MOTHER OF PEARL
		SWEET SIMPLICITY
	tall	SAPPHO

Dwarf, less than 5 feet; medium, 5 to 8 feet; tall, more than 8 feet.

Readers outside California who may be puzzled by the categories into which some of the hybrids are placed must remember that Rhododendrons vary in stature, flowering period and even to some extent in flower color, according to the local growing conditions in different regions.

HYBRIDS FOR THE PORTLAND–SEATTLE REGION AND THE BRITISH ISLES

Next to the favored San Francisco district the benign climate of the Portland–Seattle region affords the successful cultivation of the widest variety of Rhododendrons in the United States. This region has become, with the British Isles, one of the two great centers of Rhododendron culture in the Western world. Its garden resources have been immeasurably enriched by the importation of innumerable British hybrids which have flourished there in response to the high humidity and moderate temperatures. In recent years fine Rhododendrons have become so widely distributed as to make the names of hybrids from the famous gardens of Britain almost as familiar to gardeners along the Northwest Coast as are the most common plants in cultivation there. The best hybrids produced by the industrious breeders of the Holland nursery industry have also been welcomed for their rugged constitutions and adaptable natures.

The culture of Rhododendrons in the Pacific Northwest and in Great Britain, the size and condition of plants to buy, where and how to plant them, and their care in garden and nursery, are described in detail earlier in this book. A list of nurseries specializing in Rhododendrons appears on page 505 and on page 425 will be found a descriptive listing, with their hardiness and quality ratings, of all Rhododendron hybrids which are thought to be in commerce now. There are so few sorts which are not suitable for the Pacific Northwest and for the British Isles among the thousands of hybrids that it is not practical to describe in detail the multitudes that are available to give endless pleasure and satisfaction in these favored climates. A selection by a board of experts of the best in each flower color and stature for each season of bloom is given later in this chapter.

The American Rhododendron Society maintains a public trial garden at Crystal Lake Springs Island in Portland which also includes a rock garden for the low-growing species and their hybrids. It has received such wide support that it is becoming a magnificent collection of unrivaled scope and beauty which any gardener can visit to inspect and to compare its multitude of Rhododendrons. There the novice has the opportunity to identify and select the most appealing hybrids of each blooming season, height and flower so that they can be specified by name when purchases are made from a commercial nursery.

In Great Britain, Windsor Great Park, the Royal Horticultural Society's gardens at Wisley, the Royal Botanic Garden at Edinburgh and Bodnant, near Tal-y-cafn, Wales, contain extensive collections of Rhododendrons which are open to the public. Such renowned private gardens as Exbury, Leonardslee and Minterne are opened to visitors on stated days during the flowering season, often for a nominal charge which goes to a charitable cause.

The Dwarf Scaly-Leaved Hybrids

Gardeners of the Pacific Northwest and Great Britain appear to have unjustly neglected the remarkable scaly-leaved hybrids, fine in texture and many of them dwarf in stature, which are the despair of growers in the eastern United States. 'Blue Diamond', for example, is surely one of the finest blue-flowering evergreen shrubs in existence and it fills a multitude of uses in the landscape with its mature height of about 3 feet. The cultivars of the Lady Chamberlain group, with slender growth habit and distinctive foliage, are attractive additions to any warm garden with a sheltered spot to display them. The dwarf, heather-like hybrids of the alpine species offer a rich variety of treasure to the rock garden enthusiast.

Selecting the Best Hybrids for the Pacific Northwest and Great Britain

There are literally hundreds upon hundreds of hybrids available in the Northwest coastal region and in the British Isles. The bewildered novice can best be guided in a selection by expert growers who have evaluated them from long experience in their own gardens and from observation elsewhere. The following represents a combined selection on the basis of beauty of flower and plant, ease of culture and general usefulness as garden ornaments, by a panel of Rhododendron specialists. Almost all of these are British hybrids, held in equal esteem by fanciers in Great Britain. Their hardiness ratings under both American and British growing conditions are in the Appendix. The selections are given in the order of their frequency of recommendation by the experts:

RED

Before May 1st	dwarf	Carmen
		Treasure
	medium	Nobleanum Coccineum
		Daphne
		Gill's Crimson
	tall	Unknown Warrior
		Queen Wilhelmina
May 1st to June 1st	dwarf	Elizabeth
		May Day
	medium	David
		Jean Marie Montague
	tall	Grenadier
		Day Dream (red form)
		Bibiani
		Cynthia
After June 1st	dwarf	Carmen
		Rubina
		Arthur Osborne
	medium	Britannia
		Fusilier
	tall	Romany Chal

PINK

Before May 1st	dwarf	Racil
		Jacksonii
		Tessa
		Harlequin
	medium	Carex Blush
		Christmas Cheer
		Nobleanum venustum
	tall	Cornish Cross
May 1st to June 1st	dwarf	Bow Bells
		Goblin, B form
		Humming Bird
	medium	Naomi hybrid group
		Goldsworth Pink
	tall	Pink Loderi hybrids
		Mrs Horace Fogg

After June 1st	dwarf	Corona
	medium	Azor hybrid group
		Jean
	tall	Aladdin

BLUE AND LAVENDER

Before May 1st	dwarf	Blue Diamond
		Impeanum
		Blue Tit
		Augfast
	medium	Praecox
	tall	Electra
May 1st to June 1st	dwarf	Sapphire
	medium	Susan
		Blue Peter
	tall	Purple Splendour
		A. Bedford

SHADES OF ORANGE

Before May 1st	dwarf	Golden Horn
	tall	(Lady Chamberlain g.) Chelsea
May 1st to June 1st	dwarf	Nereid
		Fabia hybrid group
		(Berryrose g.) Belvedere
	medium	Margaret Dunn
	tall	(Naomi g.) Nautilus
		Lady Chamberlain hybrid group
After June 1st	tall	King of Shrubs

CREAM TO YELLOW

Before May 1st	dwarf	Devonshire Cream
		Bo-Peep
		Shot Silk
	medium	Cunningham's Sulphur
		Letty Edwards
		Unique
	tall	Diane
May 1st to June 1st	dwarf	Souv. of W. C. Slocock
		Buttercup
	medium	Broughtonii aureum
		Zuider Zee
		Carita
	tall	Hawk
		Damaris
After June 1st	dwarf	Jasper
	medium	Virginia Scott
	tall	Lady Bessborough
		Inamorata

WHITE

Before May 1st	dwarf	Bric-à-Brac
		Cilpinense
	medium	Carex White
		Handsworth White
		Sir Charles Lemon
	tall	Dr Stocker
		Avalanche
May 1st to June 1st	medium	Loder's White
		Mrs P. D. Williams
	tall	(Loderi g.) King George
		(Loderi g.) White Diamond
		Beauty of Littleworth
		White Swan
After June 1st	medium	Bonito
	tall	Lodauric

Dwarf, less than 5 feet; medium, 5 to 8 feet; tall, more than 8 feet.

The Future for Rhododendron Hybrids

The era of complete dependence by American gardeners on imported Rhododendrons is coming to an end. The creation of worthy new hybrids is a painstaking process, however, and no sudden shift in the dominance of the British and Dutch productions can be expected. From the time a cross is made it takes from five to eight or more years for most seedlings to come into flower. Very frequently a second generation is required before the hybridist can hope to attain his goal, so a large part of another decade may elapse before the breeding project is completed. There follows then a period of testing for hardiness, floriferousness and so on which the conscientious breeder can scarcely limit to less than five years.

Even if propagation begins while the testing is still under way a good hybrid can hardly be increased to more than 500 or 600 plants in a period of eight years. Thereafter, progress is rapid, but it takes about ten years for a nurseryman to propagate a new Rhododendron to the best advantage for commercial introduction. Thus twenty-eight or thirty years may elapse from the time the first cross is made before the breeder sees the product of his original project ready for general distribution by the professional growers. Fifty years more may pass before the best of introductions become the standard Rhododendrons of commerce. The most popular and important Rhododendrons in commerce today are 'Pink Pearl' and the other hardy hybrids which were introduced around the turn of the century. They are yielding very slowly to the sorts which were released for sale after the First World War, such as 'Betty Wormald', 'Britannia', 'Mrs Lindsay Smith', 'Souvenir de Dr S. Endtz', and others of that period. These are just approaching their peak of popularity thirty-five years after their commercial introduction. The Rhododendrons first offered for sale in the late '30's, just before World War II, are at this time known only to specialists. It will be many, many years before they are familiar to the general public.

Few Rhododendron hybridists live long enough to see their beloved brain children become garden favorites, and this slow pace of progress places an added burden upon the breeder since it requires him to guess what the fashion will be in landscaping several decades in the future. With the present increasing popularity of one-story houses and the decline in the number of large estates, the prospects indicate a strong future demand for hybrids of dwarf stature and rugged constitution which will not require expert maintenance. American hybridists are anticipating such a preference by using in their breeding *RR. forrestii* var. *repens*, *dichroanthum*, *williamsianum*, *haematodes*, and other species, and their progeny of modest growth. With some modification, many of the Rhododendrons with scaly leaves should fit into the needs of the future and the advent of hormones which make it possible to break the old barriers of incompatibility will undoubtedly spur progress in this neglected group.

In the eastern United States, the Dexter hybrids will become gradually available in the next few years and more of Joseph Gable's pioneering productions are in the offing. 'Beaufort' and 'Caroline', already introduced by the Warren Baldsiefen nursery, are but the first of a series of his fine hybrids for cold climates now being propagated for commercial release. The creations of veteran Rhododendron authority Guy G. Nearing, which resulted from a cross of *R.* (*griffithianum* × *decorum*) 'Dorothea' with several of the popular red-flowered Catawba hybrids, seem destined for wide favor when they come on the market. A. M. Shammarello, a nurseryman in the Cleveland district, will introduce some hybrids, much finer than anything now in commerce, which are unique in being derived entirely from crosses among the standard ironclad cultivars. They are outstanding in growth habit and in their earlier season of bloom. Edmond Amateis, Joseph Casadevall, and the author are other hybridists who are working diligently to produce new and better Rhododendrons for this section of the country.

On the West Coast a new era of domestic hybrids created by breeders there promises to produce Rhododendrons of superior quality which are specifically adapted to local conditions. Such fine sorts as 'Mrs Horace Fogg', 'King of Shrubs', and 'Mrs Donald Graham' are representative of American hybrids which are not surpassed by those from any source abroad. Starting with the late James E. Barto, who pioneered in the field and made invaluable contributions to West Coast floriculture, a company of talented hybridists has arisen which seems certain to fulfill the expectations of gardeners there for new and finer Rhododendrons. The Messrs Endre Ostbo, Rudolph Henny, Lester Brandt, H. L. Larson, Halfdan Lem and B. F. Lancaster have already produced a number of noteworthy hybrids which will take pride of place among the valued garden resources of the West Coast.

European Prospects

Exbury, Bodnant, Windsor Great Park and the Royal Horticultural Society's gardens at Wisley continue to produce fine new hybrids in the great amateur tradition of Great Britain, but with more emphasis on hardiness. Such British commercial nurseries as Slocock's, Sunningdale, Knap Hill and John Waterer, Sons & Crisp are all active in the production of improved garden Rhododendrons with many breeding projects especially designed to yield hybrids of more modest stature and those with orange or yellow flowers.

In Germany Dietrich Hobbie at Linswege is breeding Rhododendrons on a large scale and will shortly have ready for introduction a distinguished series of dwarf hybrids derived in large part from crosses in which *RR. forrestii* and *williamsianum* have figured prominently.

Complete Hybrid Listing

There will be found in the Appendix on page 425 a descriptive listing of Rhododendron hybrids intended to be complete for all those introduced since 1809 which may be in commerce today. The color of their flowers, their parentage if known, their awards, and both the American and the British ratings for quality and hardiness are given.

CHAPTER VII

Rhododendron Hardiness

THE gardener who plants Rhododendrons suitable for his climate need not ordinarily be concerned about their hardiness. Local nurserymen offer foolproof sorts of stern durability which will grow lustily and bloom faithfully anywhere that Rhododendrons can be grown at all. Yet gardeners do inadvertently acquire Rhododendrons which are not quite hardy, and both specialists and venturesome novices yearn for fine but slightly tender plants which require a little extra thought and care to produce their splendid flowers and handsome foliage. It is possible for the casual grower so to mistreat even reliably hardy Rhododendrons that they will be vulnerable to winter injury. Under such circumstances the sites and conditions which favor hardiness and those which impair it may be of keen interest.

Planting Sites

In the colder parts of the northeastern United States most Rhododendrons should not be planted in a site facing East, if there is a choice, because the morning sun shining on them in winter when the temperature is far below freezing may be injurious. Some sorts of Rhododendrons are less tolerant than others to extreme temperature fluctuations and it is good practice to moderate the transition from severe cold overnight to a point above freezing during the day in a warming cycle of midwinter weather. The rapidity of temperature change often has a greater bearing on hardiness than the minimum temperature to which the plants are exposed.

A situation shielded on the north but fully open toward the south is almost always undesirable, particularly in positions where the heat of the sun's rays is reinforced by reflection from a house foundation to stimulate plant activity unseasonably early in the spring or late in the autumn. A southern exposure may be satisfactory for many Rhododendrons, however, if they are partially shielded by trees or buildings from the excessive sun and heat which are usually present at such sites. In any planting near a fence or a house foundation the distance of the plant from the reflecting surface behind it is extremely important. A small Rhododendron placed 2 feet from a wall receives only one-fourth as much radiated heat, and one placed 4 feet away receives only one-sixteenth as much as is radiated upon a plant 1 foot distant from the foundation wall.

In the Pacific Northwest and in most parts of the British Isles an eastern exposure is especially satisfactory for many Rhododendrons except that the sorts which bloom very early in the season should not be planted where the morning sun strikes them after a frosty night. These brilliant harbingers of spring with their profusion of flowers at a bleak season are often neglected because they are so frequently misplaced in the garden that they have acquired the reputation of being unreliable in their floral display. The planting position, however, may make the difference between success and failure with these colorful Rhododendrons which are so much appreciated at the end of winter. Flowers which thaw slowly as the temperature rises are frequently undamaged whereas those quickly warmed by the morning sun are ruined.

In the eastern United States, a northern exposure is usually best if there is a choice available for the few sorts, hardy in the climate, which bloom precociously in early spring. Thus shielded from the warming sun their dormant period is less likely to be ended prematurely by a few bright days only to have the flowers frosted upon the resumption of normal cold weather so early in the season. North slopes, too, are desirable because they receive the sun's rays at an angle and are much cooler than south slopes.

Plants with a northern exposure go into dormancy sooner in the fall and come out of it later in the spring. Those of precarious hardiness are greatly benefited in such a situation. Flower buds are the most susceptible to cold of any portion of the plant and the first injury is to them. Specimens which survive in the garden and set buds but do not blossom will often preserve the floral buds intact through the winter if they are moved to a situation protected from the south and openly exposed toward the north.

SITE INFLUENCE ON WATER LOSS

Rhododendrons transpire moisture through their leaves the year around but when the ground is frozen the water which is lost through the foliage cannot be freely replaced by absorption through the roots. If the loss of water is severe, leaves show a marginal browning and finally the plants may be defoliated. Sites which are especially warm and sunny should be avoided in planting Rhododendrons because they aggravate this drying-out process, which may be so damaging that it, rather than low temperature, is responsible for the loss of plants. Under the best of circumstances the atmospheric humidity in the Northeast is much lower in winter than in summer. The colder it gets, the drier the air and the more rapid becomes the evaporation of water vapor from the foliage. At about 20° F. many Rhododendrons curl their leaves to reduce the exposed surface and conserve vital water. Thus in cold weather sun pockets in the garden are a trap for Rhododendrons, accelerating the evaporation from the foliage of moisture which cannot be readily replaced from the frozen ground.

Windswept planting sites are unsuitable for most Rhododendrons for this same reason. The moving air passing over the foliage greatly increases the evaporation of water vapor at seasons when its conservation is essential to the welfare of the plants. There are a good many Rhododendrons which are not 'wind hardy', especially among the Asian species and their hybrids. These and others may succumb to excessive exposure to sweeping winds after an especially severe winter and so their loss is incorrectly blamed on low temperature when actually they died of extreme desiccation. Frequently the same sort of Rhododendron which perishes at a windy southwestern corner of a house foundation will blossom handsomely for generations if it is placed elsewhere with some thought and consideration for its welfare.

SITE INFLUENCE ON TEMPERATURE

In larger gardens Rhododendrons should not be planted on the lowest levels where there is poor air drainage. Such situations become frost pockets when the coldest air, flowing downhill, settles there and as the temperature falls is replaced constantly by still colder air which, being heavier, persistently seeks the lowest level. Plantings made in such spots may be disappointing solely because they are misplaced: if the tender young growth is frosted in the spring the second growth replacing it seldom forms flower buds; late spring or early fall frosts may kill floral buds already formed; and direct winter injury to the tissues of the plants may result from their having been placed in the coldest part of the garden.

MULCH EFFECT ON HARDINESS

A mulch helps appreciably in promoting the hardiness of Rhododendrons because it conserves moisture, minimizes the freezing and thawing which accompany extreme temperature fluctuations, and prevents the ground from freezing so deeply as to bar absorption of water through the roots. An 8- or 10-inch layer of loose litter, such as Oak leaves, placed beneath the branches, will bring many Rhododendrons of uncertain hardiness through severe winters until they have attained a size and root spread which will assure their survival. Expert growers often use such an extra-heavy mulch for newly planted specimens and then remove a part of it in the spring. Very small plants must not be smothered by covering them, however. The foliage should remain above the mulch.

Since this book is written for professional nurserymen as well as amateur gardeners I must describe here the one circumstance in which a mulch can be a lethal peril to Rhododendrons, and that is after small seedlings or rooted cuttings have been transplanted to nursery beds and are approaching their first autumn frosts outdoors. Such immature plants are especially likely not to be fully hardened off in preparation for cold weather. Early overnight freezes can be ruinous to them. A mulch blankets the earth's heat so it cannot escape to warm the night air adjacent to ground level, and early frosts can severely damage immature plants which are mulched when small Rhododendrons of similar age and conditions growing without a mulch are quite unharmed. Warren Baldsiefen, a commercial grower in New Jersey, has found in his nursery on frosty mornings a difference of 6° F. between mulched and unmulched areas in the air just above the surface of the ground. Removing the mulch from young stock which has not ripened properly by autumn may save it from destruction. Some nurserymen who are plagued by persistent frost damage year after year may minimize it by forgoing a mulch for their small seedlings and newly propagated plants.

DIAGNOSING COLD INJURY

Low winter temperature is often blamed for the loss of plants which have died primarily from disease or from insect injury. No doubt specimens which have been seriously weakened from such causes do finally succumb in the course of the extremely cold weather which is a test of their endurance, but Rhododendrons are slow about dying even when they are mortally afflicted. They are capable of making top growth after the trunk has been entirely girdled by borers, for example, and the foliage will remain firm and glossy through the autumn rains weeks after the roots have been completely killed by Wilt (*Phytophthera cinnamomi*). Only when the drying cold of the first wintry weather shrivels the leaves is there obvious evidence that something is seriously amiss, and by that time the plants may have been dead from other causes for a couple of months.

Similarly, direct injury from cold is often not diagnosed correctly because there may be no obvious symptoms of it until midsummer. The cause of foliage being discolored and burned during the winter is plain enough but it often happens that the leaves of a tender Rhododendron will be unaffected while the bark at the base of the trunk will be inconspicuously ruptured and lifted from the wood underneath it so that the plant will be completely girdled near ground level. Nevertheless, the top remains green, puts out new growth at its normal season, though perhaps not with quite the usual vigor, and the plant appears to be satisfactorily healthy until it quietly collapses in midsummer. By that time the bewildered gardener suspects every cause but the right one. Only a close examination of the trunk at ground level betrays the fatal injury from freezing.

R. fortunei at Windsor Great Park, near Virginia Water, England. One of the finest species for the Northeast, the Pacific Northwest and for the British Isles. The large fragrant flowers are blush-white. THE AUTHOR

R. fargesii at Exbury Estate in England. Some forms of this very early blooming Rhododendron with pale pink flowers are hardy as far north as New York City. THE AUTHOR

R. dauricum. This is the typical form of the species, extremely rare in cultivation, with small, dark evergreen leaves on a compact plant of twiggy growth habit. Lavender-rose flowers appear early in the season. Hardy to 25° below zero F. THE AUTHOR

R. keiskei, a yellow-flowered species hardy as far north as New York City. COURTESY OF JOHANN BERG, FROM 'FREILAND-RHODODENDRON', BY BERG AND KRUSSMAN

R. yakusimanum. Easily grown and free flowering, this species of compact growth habit is a fine garden Rhododendron. J. E. DOWNWARD, COURTESY OF THE ROYAL HORTICULTURAL SOCIETY, FROM 'THE RHODODENDRON YEARBOOK, 1950'.

R. griffithianum. Many modern hybrids owe their flower size to this magnificent species. The blossoms are sometimes 7 inches across. THE AUTHOR

R. (Lady Roseberry g.) 'Pink Delight', a beautiful hybrid originated by Lionel de Rothschild, with clear shell-pink bells shaded rose at the base. THE AUTHOR

R. lacteum. The Werrington form here pictured has superior flowers of clear, bright yellow. THE AUTHOR

R. augustinii. The best forms of this remarkably free flowering Rhododendron are a cascade of violet-blue in May. THE AUTHOR

R. (Loderi g.) 'White Diamond'. Huge pale pink to white scented flowers characterize the superb Loderi group of hybrids. THE AUTHOR

R. (hybrid) 'Blue Diamond', one of the best of the dwarf violet-blue flowered Rhododendrons. THE AUTHOR

R. ciliatum 'Bergie' in the collection of Maurice Sumner, San Francisco.
COURTESY OF CRISTOF STUDIO

R. (hybrid) 'America'. Many specialists think this is the best of the standard red-flowered Catawba hybrids for cold climates. THE AUTHOR

R. (*carolinianum* × *edgeworthii*) 'Mildred Amateis', a hybrid bred by Edmond Amateis which links the American species to this large flowered Asian series for the first time. EDMOND AMATEIS

Leaves of *carolinianum*, *edgeworthii* and the range among hybrids from a cross made by Edmond Amateis between the two species. EDMOND AMATEIS

R. (Hawk g.) 'Crest', an extraordinary hybrid with large, clear yellow flowers, the best of its color introduced to date. Bred by Lionel de Rothschild. COURTESY OF EXBURY ESTATE

FOUR GOOD RHODODENDRONS FOR THE ROCK GARDEN

R. campylogynum bears sprightly fresh pink bells from a dense carpet of foliage. THE AUTHOR

A rare dwarf, compact form of *R. fastigiatum* with lilac colored flowers. This is among the easiest to grow of all the alpine species and it is hardy as far north as Boston. THE AUTHOR

R. hanceanum var. *nanum* at Bodnant, Wales. The flowers are pale yellow. THE AUTHOR

R. saluenense. This is a good form of the species with bright rose flowers. THE AUTHOR

Leaf of *R. sinogrande*. The leaves of this species are sometimes as much as 3 feet long and 1 foot broad. THE AUTHOR

R. dalhousiae. A greenhouse Rhododendron in most climates, the enormous white trumpets are lemon scented. THE AUTHOR

R. javanicum hybrid at Bodnant, near Tal-y-cafn, Wales. This greenhouse Rhododendron with bright orange flowers is only distantly related to our garden hybrids. THE AUTHOR

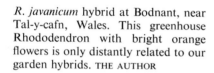

The curious tubular flowers of *R. spinuliferum* arise like clustered orange-red firecrackers. THE AUTHOR

LEAF SPOTTING DISEASES

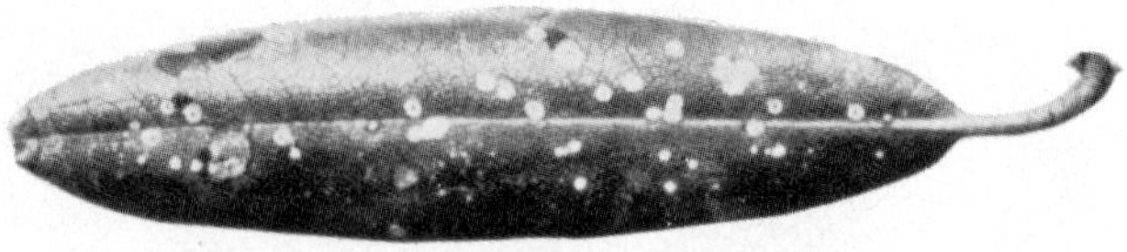

Phyllosticta sp.

Cercospora rhododendri

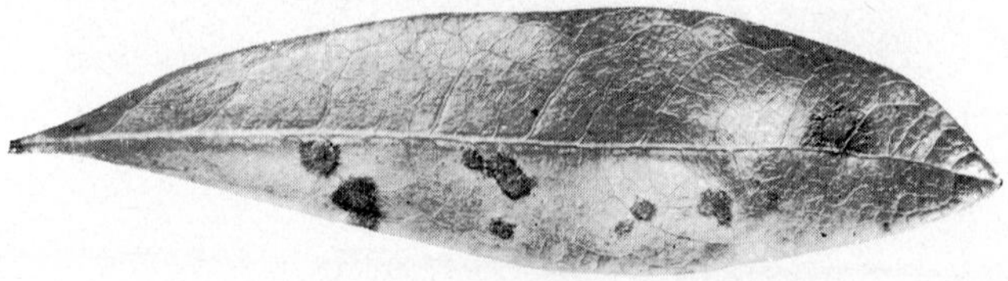

Phomopsis sp.

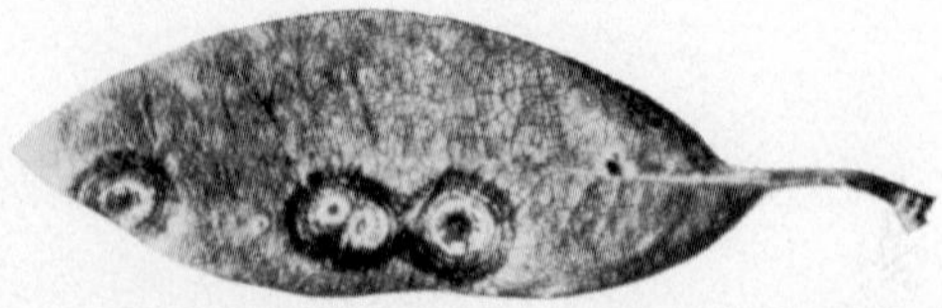

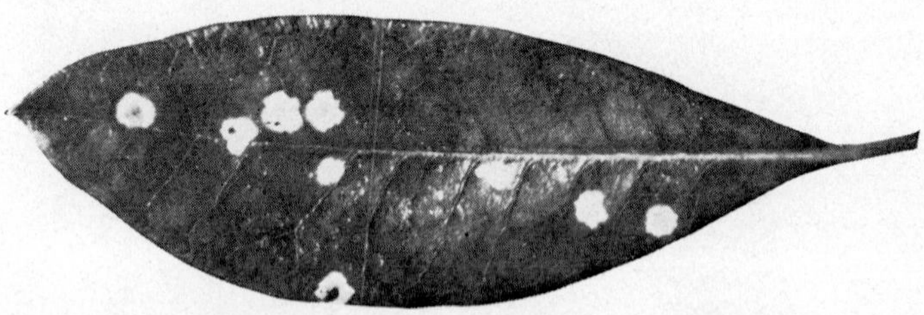

Exobasidium burtii

Rust, *Pucciniastrum myrtilli*

COURTESY OF RUTGERS UNIVERSITY

Acute Chlorosis. The dark green veins sharply outlined against yellow leaves. The plant will die unless the cause is corrected. THE AUTHOR

Wilt, *Phytophthora cinnamomi*, at an early stage. The entire plant is starting to wilt. THE AUTHOR

Blight, or Die-Back, *Phytophthora cactorum*. COURTESY OF RUTGERS UNIVERSITY

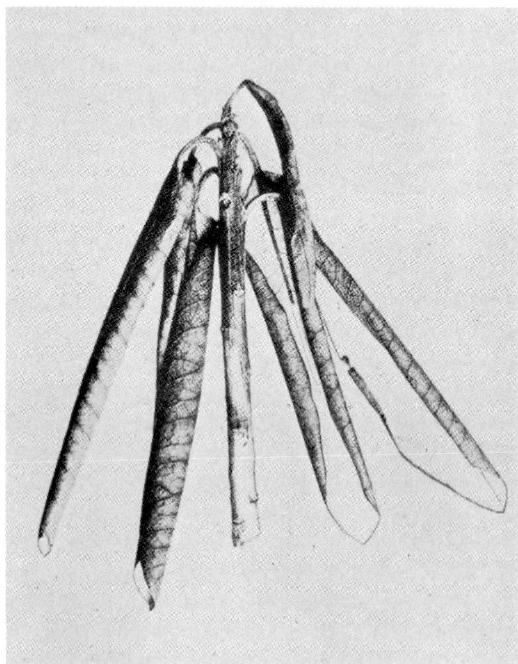

ON THE LEFT: Flower Galls, *Exobasidium vaccinii*. This grotesque disease, caused by an air-borne fungus, also deforms leaves. It is unsightly but seldom causes serious injury. COURTESY OF RUTGERS UNIVERSITY

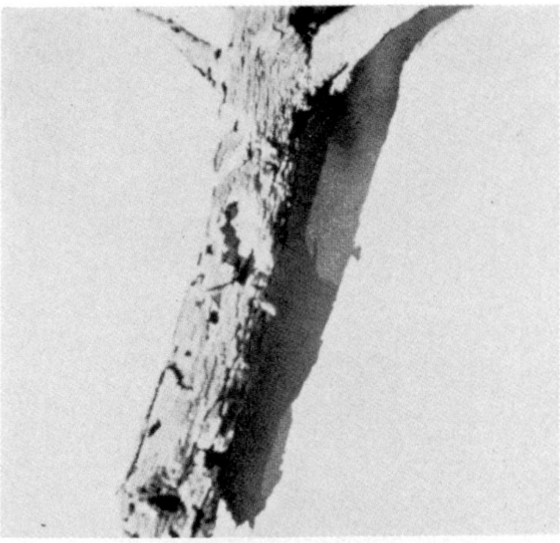

Damage to main stem near ground level by the Rhododendron Borer, *Ramosia rhododendri*. This pest is the major enemy of large specimens, destroying the trunks by tunneling near the base. THE AUTHOR

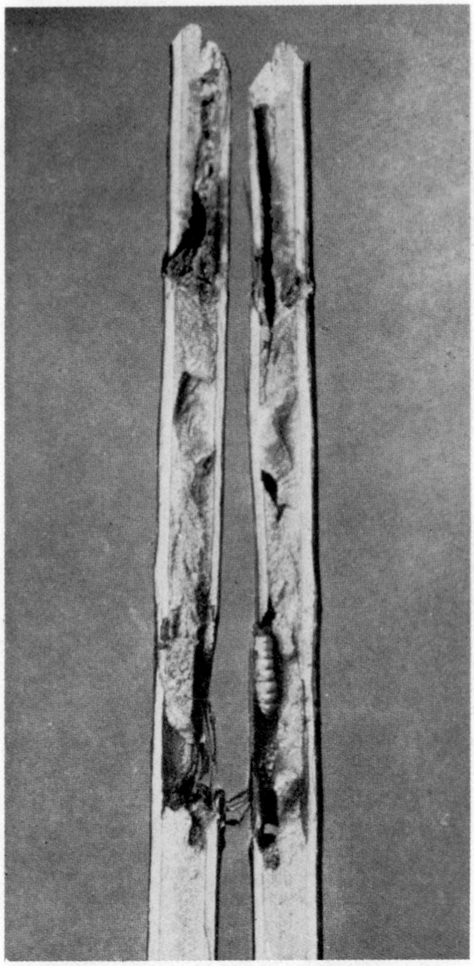

The Stem Borer, *Oberea myops*, at work. This pest is often responsible when twigs wilt abruptly. COURTESY OF AGRICULTURAL RESEARCH SERVICE, U.S. DEPARTMENT OF AGRICULTURE

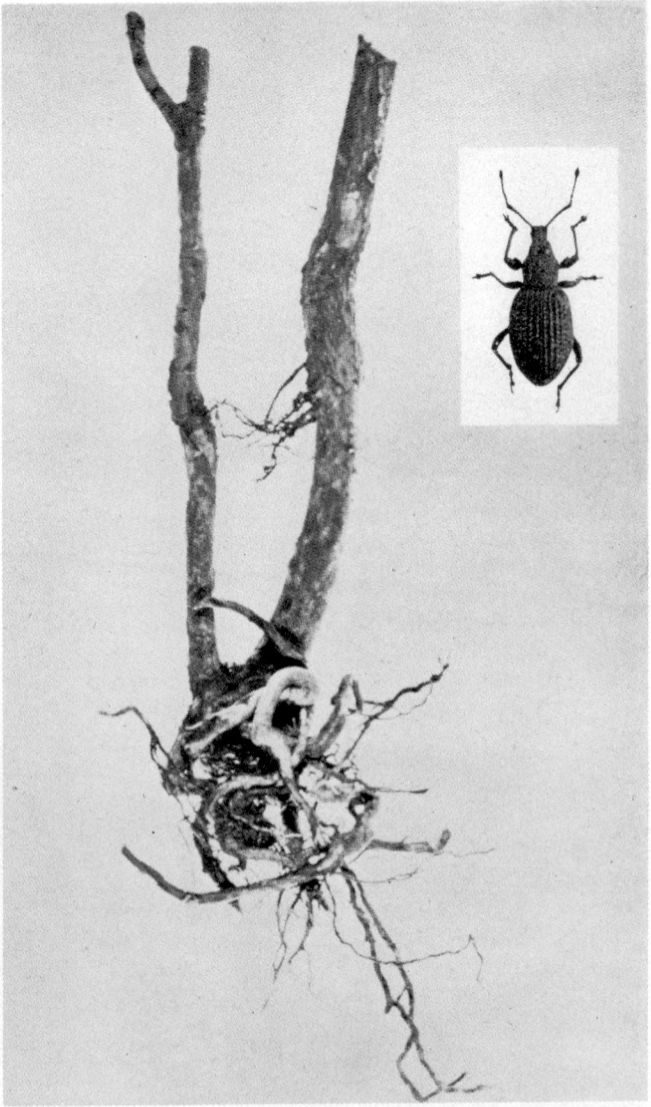

Injury to Rhododendron roots and lower stems by larvae of Black Vine Weevil, *Brachyrhinus sulcatus*. Inset, adult weevil. COURTESY OF RUTGERS UNIVERSITY

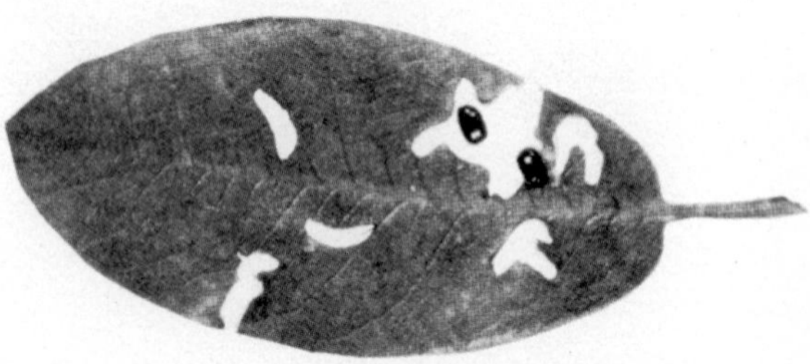

Cranberry Root Worm, *Rhabdopterus picipes*, adults feeding on Rhododendron leaves. Crescent-shaped perforations left by this small nocturnal beetle are distinctive. COURTESY OF RUTGERS UNIVERSITY

Adults of the Midge. *Giardomyia rhododendri*, on Rhododendron leaves. Their small white larvae feeding underneath the edges of the leaves may destroy the new growth entirely in severe infestations. THE AUTHOR

Lace Wing Fly, *Leptobyrsa rhododendri*, injury to upper leaf surface THE AUTHOR

Bud Blast, *Pycnostyeanus azaleae*, a fungus disease which turns the flower buds brown over winter. The dead buds are clad with multitudes of tiny black bristles. THE AUTHOR

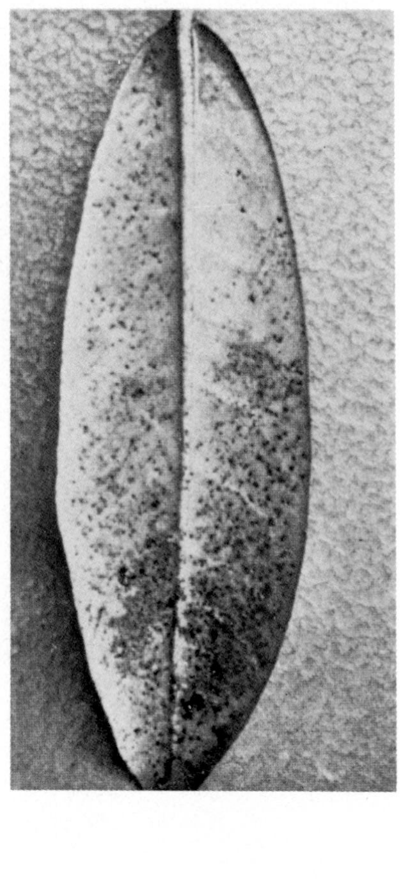

Lace Wing Fly, *Leptobyrsa rhododendri*, injury to lower leaf surface. THE AUTHOR

Glenn Dale Propagating Case. Seeds are sown in sphagnum moss in January, the seedlings grown for three to four months with liquid nutrient feeding under constant fluorescent illumination for maximum growth before transplanting. THE AUTHOR

The author's building for winter storage of plants. Seedlings in flats pass their first winter here. The double roof slopes north. There are no windows. Contents freeze slowly and stay frozen until final spring thaw. THE AUTHOR

Convenient winter protection for tender plants of large size. Board frames in sections, with short inside corner posts holding them in line, can be extended upward as plants grow. In actual use, bricks here shown separating sections are removed and roofers' felt is stapled on top of superstructure, leaving sides open at top. THE AUTHOR

Center bud starting to grow on branch of plant to be propagated. Pinched out, several branches ideal for cuttings will be formed as shown in next photograph. THE AUTHOR

Result of pinching out the center growth bud: four branches of the size and stem diameter which root best as cuttings. THE AUTHOR

Preparation of the cutting. The stem is shortened to $2\frac{1}{2}$ inches, the leaves reduced to three. THE AUTHOR

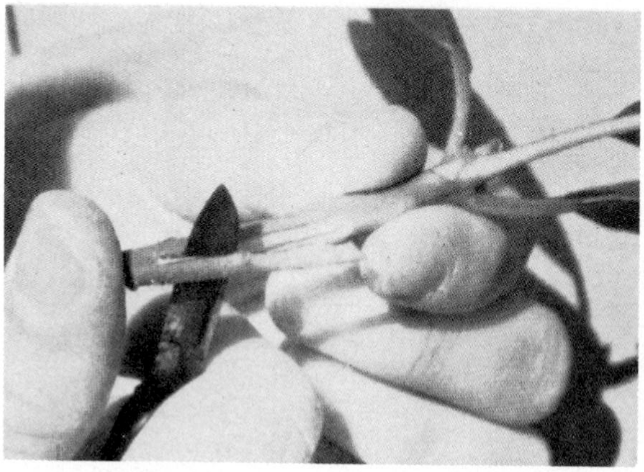

The stem of the cutting is wounded by removing a $1\frac{1}{2}$-inch slice along the side at the bottom. THE AUTHOR

The author's modified Nearing Propagating Frame. Unobstructed to the North, cuttings receive full light but no sun. THE AUTHOR

Cuttings in the Nearing Propagating Frame. More than 90 per cent usually root. THE AUTHOR

The cutting has rooted vigorously and produced some top growth in the propagating frame. It is ready for transplanting. THE AUTHOR

Rooted cutting one year later, at end of first season's growth. THE AUTHOR

Rhododendron layered in a nursery for the commercial production of new plants. COURTESY OF JOHANN BERG, FROM 'FREILAND-RHODODENDRON', BY BERG AND KRÜSSMAN

Scion with flower bud green grafted in August, crossed by hybridist the following spring, bearing normal seed capsules. THE AUTHOR

Scion with flower buds two years after green grafting as small seedling onto mature plant. THE AUTHOR

The pioneering Anglo-American plant hunter, E. H. Wilson, surrounded by his native helpers and a guard, in Asia. Wilson discovered many of the finest and hardiest Oriental Rhododendron species. COURTESY OF MRS. GEORGE L. SLATE

Above: Rain forest in western Yunnan, China. Scores of Rhododendron species form the dominant vegetation at 10,000–14,000 feet elevation, luxuriating in the monsoon mists of mountains such as these. COURTESY OF THE ROYAL HORTICULTURAL SOCIETY, FROM 'JOURNEYS AND PLANT INTRODUCTIONS OF GEORGE FORREST'.

Left: Dwarf alpine Rhododendrons at 12,000 feet elevation in Tibet. Vast carpets of variegated color are formed by a dozen or more different species covering the moorlands. F. KINGDON WARD, COURTESY OF THE ROYAL HORTICULTURAL SOCIETY

Rhododendron Hardiness

NATURAL HARDENING OFF

In the ordinary cycle of life in the wild, Rhododendrons are prepared to withstand successfully the low temperatures of winter by the dry season at the end of summer. By that time the year's growth has been completed, there being not enough rainfall then to support additional extensions of the top growth. The sun is still high in the sky, however, and the manufacture of carbohydrates in the leaves is continuing at a fast rate under the stimulus of long days of sunny weather. Since the carbohydrates are not used at that time of the year for the production of new top growth, their concentration increases in the sap. As summer wanes and frosts begin, the amount of carbohydrates in the sap has reached a peak and the freezing-point of the sap has been appreciably lowered. The plant cells also retain water better when the temperature drops so that they are not so readily injured by the loss of it.

This is the natural process of maturation, the hardening off which prepares Rhododendrons for winter. The soft new growth of springtime, at first full of water and low in carbohydrates, becomes hard and firm as the water in it diminishes and the carbohydrates increase with the season's advance. The older tissues are similarly toughened in preparation for the cold weather ahead. It should be the gardener's aim not to interfere in any way with this natural hardening by which the plants are later able to withstand cold weather.

EFFECT OF FERTILIZER AND WATER ON HARDINESS

It is poor practice to fertilize Rhododendrons after the middle of June. Innumerable specimens have been lost because gardeners have failed to consider that plants stimulated into unseasonably late growth fall an easy prey to the rupturing effect of tissues frozen when they are immature. It is possible to kill even the most reliably hardy of Rhododendrons by fertilizing them so late in the season that they are not hardened off and ready for cold weather as winter begins.

It is also poor practice to water Rhododendrons during August and September because this too results in an unnatural postponement of the maturing process. These plants can stand a surprising amount of drouth and they should be permitted to go to the full limit of their endurance in the eastern United States. Leaves can curl and droop forlornly without such symptoms of distress resulting in permanent damage to established specimens. Newly planted Rhododendrons or those weakened by disease or injury are less able to endure prolonged drouth and the gardener must relent in caring for them during late summer dry weather by irrigating them just enough to pull them through but without watering so liberally as to encourage an unnatural deferment of their seasonal maturity. Daytime wilting in hot weather is no cause for alarm if the plants revive overnight so that their leaves are in normal posture in early morning. A gallon of water applied at the base of a specimen 4 feet tall will relieve its distress for a week or more.

The aim in caring for these shrubs throughout the summer is to encourage vigorous growth early in the season and then to harden off the plants so that the tissues will be fully ripened by the advent of cold weather. A reduced supply of water in late summer is essential to prepare the plants for frigid winter temperatures. If the gardener indulges his charges too generously, the result will be bark split under the stress of freezing temperatures when the tissues are still turgid with sap of low carbohydrate content.

Having withstood the temptation to water during the dry weather of August and September the gardener must then be prepared to water lavishly in November if the autumn rains fail to saturate the earth before it finally freezes for the winter. The time to water Rhododendrons in the East is around Thanksgiving, or just before the ground becomes frozen for the season. Such irrigation so late in the year does not stimulate the plants and it is essential that it be provided when natural rainfall occasionally fails to furnish the plants with abundant moisture as they enter winter. If this chore is neglected, the damage cannot later be repaired by watering when the ground is frozen, and the Rhododendron leaves will become brown around their margins as they transpire more moisture than can be replaced. If the water deficiency becomes severe, the result is inevitably death and Taxus.

The average gardener need seldom concern himself with doubts about watering his Rhododendrons and these remarks must not be taken to mean that irrigation is a worrisome problem. After their first several years Rhododendrons can pretty well take care of themselves and the only requirement is that they enter the winter with ample moisture at their roots. But in rare seasons when nature fails to provide it, the gardener who supplies it from the hose will insure the welfare of plants which might otherwise be more or less seriously injured.

The Nature of Cold Injury

When Rhododendrons are damaged by cold, the injury becomes progressively more severe as the temperature drops and the dehydration intensifies. Ice forms within the plants' cells as the colloidal properties of the protoplasm are disorganized by low temperatures. Simultaneously the cell membranes become more permeable to fluids and they may finally collapse from loss of turgidity. So it is that cells which lose water for a prolonged period die from drying out and this explains the extra damage from cold weather which is protracted. It also explains why Rhododendrons which endure −5° F. briefly on the West Coast may be hopelessly tender in the East at the same low temperature of longer duration.

Water can freeze in the spaces between the cells without killing plants unless the ice crystals become so large as to rupture the cells. In fact, some sorts of Rhododendrons appear to be hardy because the more permeable cell membranes allow water to be drawn through them into the inter-cellular spaces where it freezes without injury to the cell protoplasm. These sorts are, however, more vulnerable to sudden cold spells than to the same low temperatures which are reached gradually. They are also more likely to be damaged by abrupt thaws.

Rhododendrons become dormant first at the tips, then progressively downward to the roots. Thus it is that early fall freezes may destroy plants by killing the bark at the base of the trunks, and temporary protection at this point is especially effective for specimens not fully matured by autumn.

When Rhododendrons unsuited to the climate are exposed to temperatures below their limit of tolerance the flower buds are destroyed first. Then the pith of the branches is killed and the wood becomes discolored. The outer bark tissues of the cambium may remain green for some time. Finally, in the usual sequence of injury from midwinter cold, the bark of the trunk ruptures just above ground level and if it splits away from the inner stem around its entire circumference the plant is girdled and it will die by August. Much of the same fatal course befalls normally hardy Rhododendrons which are not properly hardened off for winter.

Protecting Tender Plants

Hardiness appears to be much more a matter of how rapidly the temperature varies than how cold the air becomes, and shielding from drying winds may be more critical than the duration of low temperature. Proof lies in the protection afforded a tender Rhododendron by building a rough board frame around it. A box-like structure built with an opening for air circulation just below the roof will shelter a tender plant so effectively that it will retain its floral buds and blossom perfectly, whereas it would normally be killed outright with the usual planting exposure. The temperature within such an enclosure certainly falls as low in midwinter as it does elsewhere in the garden. The probable conclusion is that its beneficial effect lies in the slower *change* in temperature; in protection against dehydration from winds and winter sunshine; and in shielding the foliage from deposits of frost upon it. But the fact is that hardiness is a difficult and complex problem with many factors subtly affecting it. Sometimes certain aspects of it can be very puzzling indeed.

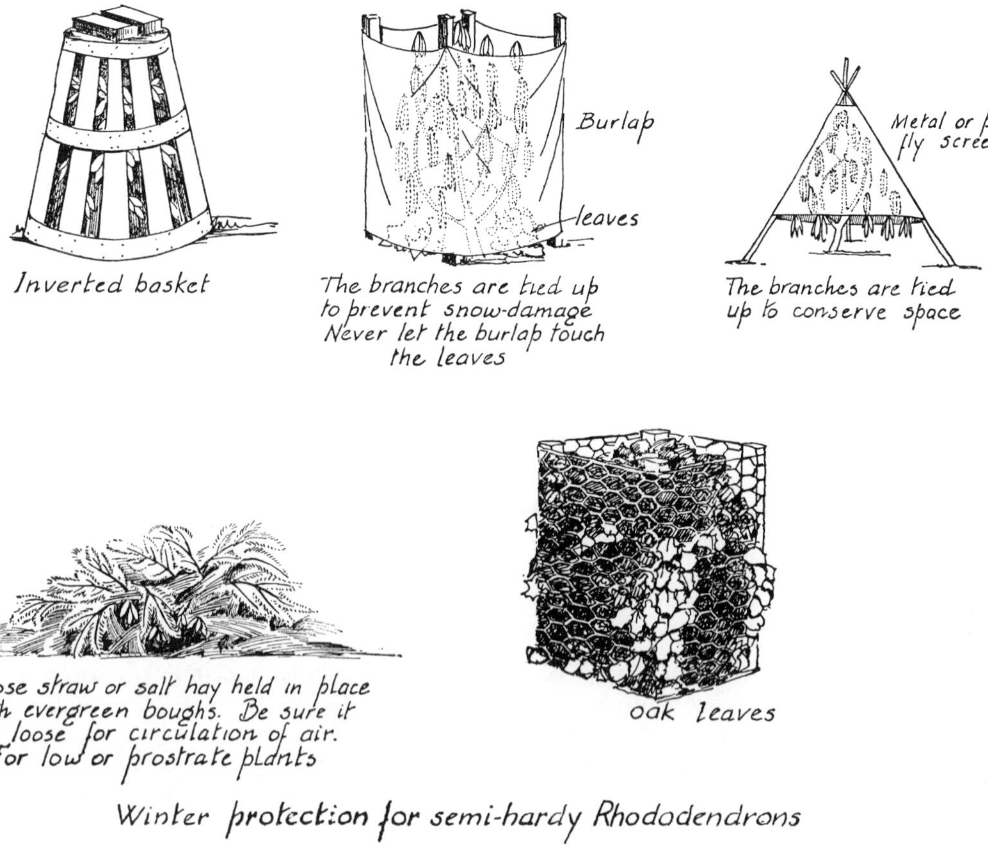
Inverted basket
Burlap
leaves
The branches are tied up to prevent snow-damage Never let the burlap touch the leaves
Metal or plastic fly screening
The branches are tied up to conserve space
Loose straw or salt hay held in place with evergreen boughs. Be sure it is loose for circulation of air. For low or prostrate plants
oak leaves
Winter protection for semi-hardy Rhododendrons

COASTAL CLIMATES AND HARDINESS

Certain it is that high humidity of the air enables these shrubs to withstand cold more successfully, and some borderline Rhododendrons are tender in a climate of moderate temperature and low humidity which are perfectly satisfactory in a colder area with higher humidity. Rarely, and contrary to expectations, the presence of large bodies of water will make it hard to grow a few sorts of Rhododendrons which do well in colder climates. High humidity combined with the prolonged autumn of lakeside gardens sometimes render an occasional species or hybrid less than normally hardy because they do not fully mature for the first cold winter weather. Usually, however, coastal gardens are favored planting sites for Rhododendrons. The moderating effect of Lake Erie, for example, is such that enthusiasts in that area grow a wide variety of superior hybrids which are completely unsatisfactory 100 miles farther south. Many tender sorts grow on Cape Cod which fail at Boston. Long Island cultivators can select from a much wider variety than can be grown in Westchester County, New York, or farther inland.

The winter of 1949–50 and the late autumn of 1955 were the most severe on record for the Rhododendron growing areas of the Pacific coast. Some gardens there recorded −18° F. in Washington and Oregon and a few were even colder. The American Rhododendron Society subsequently published hardiness ratings for many of the best-known hybrids and species, establishing seven different ranges of minimum temperatures which these various sorts survive uninjured. Professional nurserymen note these ratings in their catalogs and frequently point out in their descriptions the sorts which were not damaged in the sub-zero weather of 1949–50.

Regional Hardiness Indicators

Indicators of hardiness at low temperatures under West Coast conditions are valuable in the East but only in the broadest and most general sense. A hybrid which survives −18° F. on one or more rare and brief occasions will by no means prove equally hardy in a climate where the temperature goes to −18° F. as a routine occurrence of some duration. Innumerable sorts adaptable to the benign climate of the Pacific Northwest are little harmed there by a short exposure to very cold weather in an occasional year, but they would be killed outright under the repeated onslaughts of protracted cold of equal severity in the East. Gardeners in the Northeast cannot assume that Rhododendrons listed in nursery catalogs as having survived stated low temperatures on the West Coast will be satisfactory in an eastern climate with about the same minimum winter temperatures. The actual American and British ratings for hardiness, revised in 1956, are, however, reasonably reliable indicators. They are given starting on page 425 for the hybrids and on page 508 for the species.

FACTORS AFFECTING HARDINESS

Age and Hardiness

Rhododendrons are obviously hardier in age than they are in youth and the plants must be about four years old to give any real indication of their cold resistance at maturity. *R. fortunei* is an example representative of a number of species and hybrids which increase in hardiness with age to a noteworthy extent. The gardener who covets a Rhododendron on the borderline of hardiness for his climate is well advised to plant a vigorous specimen in a 2½- to 3-foot size. Some semi-hardy Rhododendrons which lose their buds as young plants will bloom reliably as they approach maturity, probably because growth slows down with age and vegetative activity declines.

CHEMICAL MEANS OF INCREASING HARDINESS

Hardiness can be controlled to some extent by chemical means. One of the functions of calcium is to aid in the distribution throughout the plant of the phosphates which play an important role in the maturation of tissues in preparation for cold weather. Acid soil may be deficient in calcium or may cause an impairment of its normal action but magnesium will serve in much the same way to aid the phosphates in hardening off. An application of a branded commercial formulation of magnesium, superphosphate, and potash at the rate of 25 pounds per 1,000 square feet has been demonstrated greatly to hasten the ripening of plant tissues which are in lush growth too late in the year. Such a treatment might insure the survival of many plants in a rare season when nature conspires to trick Rhododendrons into an unseasonably late growth cycle. The usefulness of this material to commercial nurserymen and hybridists is obvious.

Superphosphate alone, incorporated at the time the planting beds are prepared at the rate of 25 pounds per 1,000 square feet, has been found by one nurseryman to reduce frost damage to immature seedlings and cuttings by about 50 per cent. In the autumn of 1956, after a long, wet season, I bought 0–25–25 fertilizer, available commercially, and added to it 4 per cent of magnesium oxide. Used at the rate of 35 pounds per 1,000 square feet for specimen stock, and at half that rate for small plants, the response was both marked and gratifying.

Transplanting Effect on Hardiness

The length of time a Rhododendron has been planted has an important bearing on its hardiness. When the root system has had ample time to develop so that it can fully support a plant and replenish the loss of moisture transpired through the leaves, the endurance of a plant is enhanced. Gardeners who want to experiment with Rhododendrons of doubtful hardiness should plant them in the spring instead of in the fall. And newly planted Rhododendrons can be helped through their first winter by the application of one of the synthetic resin sprays which coat the leaves with a thin film of plastic to reduce loss of moisture.

Health and Hardiness

Specialists often note that plants which have grown lustily and are conspicuous by their vigorous health are not damaged when other Rhododendrons of the same questionable degree of hardiness are injured by winter cold. A congenial soil and the other elements of good culture often provide the extra margin of cold resistance which is needed for the success of some of the sorts which are almost at the limit of their tolerance. Conversely, plants with impaired vigor, struggling to survive under poor growing conditions, may be killed by the trials of a cold winter. The added hardiness of flourishing health extends even to individual branches. Growers often note that old limbs of declining vitality are winter-killed when young, lusty branches on the same plant are uninjured.

Effect of Short Rest Period

Some Rhododendrons are sensitive to low temperature because of their inherent response to unseasonably warm weather in the course of winter. The dormancy of these sorts which need only a short rest period before resuming activity is easily ended by a brief spell of mildness which gives a false hint of spring. Plant activity then resumes and flower buds start to expand only to be halted abruptly and injuriously by the resumption of normal cold weather. *R. mucronulatum* is an example of such species which are extraordinarily responsive to the stimulus of a few warm days. In the Northeast it gives a good account of itself in regions of sustained cold weather, but planting in a northern exposure protected from winter sun will extend its dormancy and greatly improve its performance farther south.

Seasons of Sensitivity

Rhododendrons vary greatly in their response to the *season* of cold. Some sorts which are hardy to the low temperatures of winter and late spring are tender to abrupt freezing in autumn. And others which always mature on schedule to resist the frigid weather of fall and winter are susceptible to unusual cold in springtime. *R. maximum*, for example, is generally considered to be ironclad in its hardiness but it loses its floral buds in seasons of exceptionally early severe winter weather. It can stand almost any amount of sub-zero cold later in the year. *R. poukhanense* is exactly the opposite. It is spring frosts which are responsible for the loss of its buds, according to Dr Henry Skinner, director of the United States National Arboretum. This varying susceptibility to the season of low temperatures is responsible for many of the 'mysterious' casualties among Rhododendrons. A plant may grow happily through eight or ten years of both normal and abnormal temperature variations in winter and spring only to succumb in the course of the summer following unusually cold weather the previous autumn. By the time the plant abruptly wilts and dies in August, the gardener has forgotten the extraordinary weather nine months before. No association is made between it and the subsequent death of the plant, especially since much lower temperatures can usually be recalled as having occurred later in the winter.

Hardiness can therefore mean resistance to autumn freezes; to the absolute low temperature of midwinter; or to spring frosts. A Rhododendron which is perfectly hardy to two of these seasons of cold may be sensitive to the third. To determine which season is responsible for injury to a plant which sets buds but does not bloom well, dissect several of the flower buds about two weeks after the first severe frosts of autumn; again about February 1st; and finally about a week after the late spring frosts. The first appearance of browning to the interior tissues of the buds indicates injury in the period immediately preceding.

Light and Hardiness

The day length has an important effect upon the hardiness of Rhododendrons. At Michigan State University Rhododendrons were among the most responsive in a large group of woody plants to a day length extended by artificial light to sixteen hours. *R. catawbiense* doubled its growth at Rutgers University when the lights were turned on three nights each week between May 1st and late November, but the plants did not harden off properly in preparation for winter. It would be an interesting experiment to determine whether clones which are normally tender could be made more cold resistant by artificially shortening the day length.

Variations in Hardiness

Rhododendron species, but not named hybrids propagated as clones, vary considerably in hardiness according to their inherent constitution. The same species have been represented many times in the various lots of seeds which have been sent here, often from widely separated points in the Rhododendron heartland of Asia. Some of these seed collections have produced plants much hardier than others of the same species, and only the most cold resistant of these have survived as seedlings in the nurseries of professional Rhododendron growers in the East. Such super-hardy plants, used as parents, have produced new generations of these species which are much more adaptable to the climate of the eastern United States, and some of the finest sorts are thus available from specialist-nurserymen in the eastern part of the country as selected strains to enrich the gardens of the Atlantic states and the Midwest.

The cultivation of many of the fine ornamental species from the Orient can be extended into more severe winter climates only if fanciers will grow plants from seeds of the hardiest strains available and then select the most cold-tolerant progeny to serve as parents for a locally adaptable race; or, if fully hardy individuals occur in the first generation they can be propagated as clones. Both hybrids and species must be developed by such selection for each climatic zone, providing, of course, that there is enough inherent variation in hardiness for its strongest expression to be locally satisfactory. It is not generally successful to bring individual plants of precarious hardiness into a more severe climate. Regional strains must usually evolve by selection.

It has repeatedly been demonstrated that exceptional hardiness in a species may be found solely in a single, individual plant. The prominent hybridist, Guy G. Nearing, found among his seedlings solitary specimens of *R. sanguineum* and of *R. radicans* which survived the climate of New Jersey. Both are species which are ordinarily tender in the East. Had these two plants not been accidentally destroyed by a flood they could have been propagated by cuttings to make possible a general distribution of these species in hardy forms for gardens in severe climates. The listing of nurserymen specializing in Rhododendrons on page 505 includes some growers in the East who offer extra-hardy forms of several fine Asian species.

CHAPTER VIII

Rhododendron Troubles and their Remedies

RHODODENDRONS are rarely subject to the pests and lethal diseases which afflict so many other garden plants, and the average home owner with a few specimens of them will seldom have occasion to diagnose an affliction and apply the remedy. It is conspicuously true that Rhododendrons which enjoy a suitable site and soil are unlikely to fall prey to the ills of the clan. Most of them will flourish for generations without the slightest sign of trouble whereas their brethren which are situated unhappily may give cause for concern.

Every nurseryman notices that it is the weak plants, those which have been injured or are struggling to survive unfavorable conditions, which are attacked by disease. And every professional grower notices too how Rhododendrons acquire increasing immunity with age. They are not often beset by disease after they are three or four years old.

The nurseryman who grows hundreds or thousands of Rhododendrons year after year is naturally burdened by the afflictions of his charges to an infinitely greater extent than is the home owner. There is every opportunity for pests and diseases to become established, to spread and to perpetuate themselves when large numbers of Rhododendrons are grown in close proximity.

There are countless Rhododendrons both in America and in England which are over a hundred years old. They provide their yearly festival of blossoms impervious to the onslaughts of pests and diseases. But when something does go wrong these shrubs are particularly accommodating about announcing it because they are quick to communicate symptoms of distress. In extreme drouth or sub-freezing cold their leaves are curled forlornly at half-mast as they struggle to conserve water. If the soil is too dense they will grow only 1 or 2 inches a year instead of the 6 to 12 inches of added stature to be expected each season from the sorts which aspire to the proportions of large shrubs. Any lack of soil acidity soon shows in pale green leaves with veins sharply etched a deeper color.

FIRST AID FOR THE MOST COMMON AILMENTS

The best thing that can be done for a Rhododendron with no obvious symptoms of pests or diseases which seems not to be thriving is to dig it out carefully. It has almost certainly been planted too deeply, or in soil so unsuitable that the roots have never ventured beyond the original ball of earth in which the plant was first established. So high is the requirement of Rhododendrons for a loose, well-aerated soil that they will attempt to generate an entirely new root system close to ground level if they are planted too deeply. They should always be placed at approximately the same level as they were last grown in the nursery. Many ailing plants can be cured merely by replanting them with the tops of the root balls at the surface of the surrounding earth.

Innumerable Rhododendrons have been lost because they have been placed in heavy, viscous clay, the subsoil excavated from house foundations which is often used for grading. Such an impenetrable medium is so alien to their needs that the roots will not venture beyond the earth ball which is provided by the nursery to sustain the roots during the shock of transplanting. The remedy is to remove the plant, excavate a generous planting hole well beyond the size immediately needed to accommodate the specimen, and backfill it with a combination of 50 per cent topsoil and 50 per cent peat moss, plus a couple of shovelsful of sand added to the mixture if it is conveniently available. It is also a good idea gently to scrape away an inch of soil from the perimeter of the ball so that the root-ends are exposed without damage. Replanted then, the Rhododendron soon sends out a whole new system of roots into the surrounding soil mixture and it begins to flourish once more.

Chlorosis

Most ills of Rhododendrons are cured by replanting them properly but occasionally they will suffer from chlorosis, a conspicuous condition in which the leaves become light green or yellow, with deep green veins appearing like a river with tributaries on a topographical map. Chlorosis can often be traced to a lack of sufficient acidity in the soil with the result that the plant cannot utilize all of the nutrients necessary to its health. Artificial irrigation with city water, which is usually alkaline, will cause a gradual loss of the required soil acidity. Drainage water from masonry walls or rubble remaining in the earth from construction work can have the same result. I have observed chlorosis caused by a detergent in water used for scrubbing which drained into the soil where Rhododendrons were growing in a foundation planting alongside a porch. Fertilizers not specifically formulated for acid soil plants can be equally harmful.

Other types of chlorosis which are of interest mainly to commercial growers will be discussed in detail later in this chapter but lack of acidity is by far the most common cause for the home owner and it is usually restored satisfactorily by applying Copperas (ferrous sulphate), 8 ounces scattered over a square yard of the soil, and watered in. The treatment can be repeated if a soil test shows it to be necessary. This is the quick, safe and sensible remedy. For larger areas and more exact guidance, a table is provided on page 281 giving the amounts to apply to remedy various ranges of unsatisfactorily low acidity.

Sulphur is often recommended as an acidifier but it is not consistent or predictable in the rate at which it is effective. Flowers of sulphur is a good deal more rapid in its action than is ordinary commercial ground sulphur but both acidify by first forming sulphuric acid and then a soluble calcium compound which is subsequently washed from the soil by leaching. The speed at which this conversion takes place depends so much on uncontrolled factors that sulphur is too variable to be recommended to amateur gardeners. Professional growers who require large quantities of acidifier may want to use it in preference to ferrous sulphate because of its lower cost.

Countless plants have been killed by aluminum sulphate, which is frequently recommended as an acidifying agent in popular gardening publications. The fact is that Rhododendrons have a narrow range from tolerance to toxicity of aluminum ions and there is a cumulative increase of them as the chemical further acidifies the soil. Repeated applications are especially undesirable. Practical observation amply supported by experimental evidence proves that aluminum sulphate can be extremely injurious to Rhododendrons.

INJURIES AND PHYSIOLOGICAL DISORDERS

Chlorosis and Nutrient Deficiencies

Chlorotic leaves pale progressively from their normal green to almost any shade in the range from olive to pale yellow or even white, depending upon the severity of the disorder. The foliage may be either uniformly yellow or variegated, with the veins retaining their usual green color so that they stand out sharply against the yellow background. Chlorosis in plants is comparable to anemia in animals.

There are many causes of chlorosis in Rhododendrons, but the most common is a lack of *available* iron internally. Iron acts as a catalyst in the production of the green chlorophyll which is manufactured in plant leaves as a vital part of the life process. If it is not present in usable form, the chlorophyll is not produced, the leaves turn yellow and eventually drop, and the defoliated plant dies.

A decline in the acidity of the sap is the immediate cause of chlorosis induced by a lack of available iron within the plant. Iron becomes inactivated and leaves start to turn yellow when the acidity of the leaf tissues drops to about pH 4·5.

The internal acidity of the sap is determined by the acidity of the soil, the total concentration of base nutrient salts (calcium, magnesium, potassium) in the soil and the rate of their absorption by the plant, and by the amount of light. There may be other, unknown factors but recent research indicates that a lack of available iron within the plant is far more important than any lack of iron in the soil.

Inasmuch as the reaction of the soil is one of the most important influences upon sap acidity, and can be most easily controlled by the grower, the most practical remedy for iron-induced chlorosis is to make the soil more acid. This usually results in the conversion of iron to a soluble and therefore usable form internally and the chlorosis disappears as the plants resume the production of green chlorophyll.

Soil acidity is measured by stating the hydrogen ion concentration in pH units. A pH of 7 is neutral and any reading above that figure indicates an alkaline soil. A pH of 6 is slightly acid, but not enough so for Rhododendrons. The mid-range for the best growth of most sorts is a pH of about 5·0.

There are inexpensive testing kits and paper indicators available both for home gardeners and for professional growers which determine the pH of the soil and they should be used whenever chlorosis develops in Rhododendrons. If the soil test shows that the pH is higher, or less acid, than 5·5 it will be good practice to increase the acidity with Copperas (ferrous sulphate) to about 5·0 before looking elsewhere for the cause of the difficulty. It makes the soil more acid by reacting chemically with calcium salts to make calcium sulphate, a soluble compound which leaves the soil by natural leaching. Calcium carbonate, the active ingredient in limestone, is usually responsible for a loss of acidity. Not only is it alkaline but the calcium tends to replace iron in the plant tissues, thus providing a double cause of chlorosis. If it is watered in, ferrous sulphate as an acidifier acts speedily to complete the removal of calcium from the soil in the quantity determined by the amount of its application. Twenty-four hours is ample time to allow for its full effect.

The leaching of calcium carbonate makes less difference to the pH of a heavy soil than it does to that of a light one, but Rhododendrons are not grown in clay and the following table gives the amounts of ferrous sulphate required to increase the acidity under average conditions:

TO CHANGE pH FROM	POUNDS OF FERROUS SULPHATE NEEDED PER 100 SQUARE FEET
8·0 to 7·0	9·4
8·0 to 6·5	14·1
8·0 to 6·0	18·8
8·0 to 5·5	25·9
8·0 to 5·0	32·9
7·5 to 7·0	8·2
7·5 to 6·5	9·4
7·5 to 6·0	16·5
7·5 to 5·5	23·5
7·5 to 5·0	30·6
7·0 to 6·5	7·1
7·0 to 6·0	9·4
7·0 to 5·5	16·5
7·0 to 5·0	23·5
6·5 to 6·0	7·1
6·5 to 5·5	11·8
6·5 to 5·0	18·8
6·0 to 5·5	7·1
6·0 to 5·0	14·1
5·5 to 5·0	7·1

This table has been computed on the basis of average conditions, to increase the acidity of medium loam. If the soil to be made more acid is sandy, somewhat less Copperas will be required, possibly only two-thirds as much. Should it be a heavy clay loam, up to one-third more Copperas may be required than the quantity shown in the table. Soils vary within limits as to the natural buffers they contain. These buffers resist the normal effect of chemicals used to change the acidity.

With such unknown factors affecting the results, it is best to use the table as a rough guide and to approach the goal in several steps, testing the pH of the soil after each of several chemical applications until the desired acidity is attained. A convenient method of testing is afforded by pHydrion Papers (manufactured by Micro Essential Laboratory, Brooklyn 10, New York), which are dispensed from a small plastic container in two ranges of testing papers: pH 3·0 to 5·5, and pH 6·0 to 8·0. By means of a color chart which is a part of the dispenser, the approximate acidity of the soil can be determined.

Commercial growers who may want to use sulphur because of its lower cost and are willing to wait for its slow acidifying effect, can convert the table above by multiplying the quantities by 21·3 per cent to determine the amount of sulphur needed for each step.

It is often useful to know that 2·5 pounds of ferrous sulphate nullifies the effect of 1 pound of ground limestone, and 0·41 pound of ground limestone offsets 1 pound of ferrous sulphate (Copperas). Approximately 3·1 pounds of ground limestone are needed to offset 1 pound of sulphur.

In a detailed survey of the subject it is a vast over-simplification to think of iron chlorosis as being caused by a rise in the pH of the soil. Such a loss of acidity does not necessarily cause chlorosis. Rhododendrons grow in nature in soil of iron magnesium silicate derivation with a low calcium level which tests as high as pH 8·6. They have been grown in a laboratory in low fertility soil of pH 8·4, the alkalinity of which was induced by magnesium carbonate and not by calcium. So it is not the alkalinity of the soil in itself which is harmful. This is but one factor which affects the acidity of the sap within the plant and thus the internal solubility of iron.

With a low *total* concentration of nutrient salts, and especially the base salts of potassium, calcium, and magnesium, Rhododendrons will grow without deficiency symptoms in much less acid soil than would be necessary with a high level of these nutrients. However, if nitrogen is supplied as an ammonium compound to a soil with an undesirably high total concentration of base ions their absorption by the plants is so reduced that there is no loss of sap acidity and no chlorosis appears even at the same low degree of soil acidity which would otherwise result in severe yellowing of the foliage. It is important to keep in mind that it is the chemical composition of the soil which determines how much, if any, a shift in its acidity will affect Rhododendrons.

As a matter of practical usefulness it is still true that an increase in soil acidity cures most cases of chlorosis. When it fails to do so, there are a number of other causes which may occasionally need to be studied to restore Rhododendrons to normal health.

Nitrogen Deficiency

It is characteristic of acid soils to be naturally deficient in available plant food, and when this lack becomes severe, Rhododendrons display chlorotic symptoms which reflect a serious threat to their welfare. In soil of average reaction the microbes and molds which bring about the decay of organic matter turn it into simple compounds containing nitrogen which are then available as nutrients to the plants. But with increasing acidity bacterial activity declines sharply until only molds remain to slowly reduce vegetative debris to humus. There is usually a large amount of organic matter in soil where Rhododendrons are grown and it may occasionally cause a chronic deficiency of nitrogen which is sequestered in the dead vegetative material while it is slowly being decomposed by micro-organisms. These micro-organisms, principally molds, require nitrogen just as do the plants above ground, and they have first call on it.

In commercial practice the use of sawdust, either as a soil amendment or as a mulch, often results in nitrogen deficiency unless steps are taken to prevent it. An excessively heavy sawdust mulch may also reduce the amount of oxygen in the soil to the point where nitrogen is lost by its conversion into nitrous oxide gas.

When nitrogen is lacking all of the leaves on a Rhododendron become a yellowish-green and the chlorotic foliage of the new growth does not develop to normal size. The centers of the leaves remain green longer but there is not the sharp contrast between normally green veins and a pallid yellow color between the veins which is characteristic of iron deficiency. Later the tips and outside edges become reddish or develop reddish blotches. Older leaves fade more rapidly to yellow and drop from the plants first. Growth is restricted and tends to be weak and sparse, with brittle stems. Flowers are few, small in size and deficient in substance. Nitrogen is best supplied to Rhododendrons by an application of ammonium sulphate, which is also beneficial in several collateral respects. Organic sources are also especially desirable because they supply a low constant source of the helpful *ammonium* nitrogen. Nitrate nitrogen is undesirable.

Potassium Deficiency

Insufficient potassium in the soil usually interferes with the available supply of iron so the initial effect of an inadequate supply of this element is identical with the symptoms of iron chlorosis. Interveinal yellowing begins at the leaf tips and edges, spreading until there is a strong contrast between the green veins throughout the leaf surface and the paler areas surrounding them. Dead areas and marginal scorch appear near the tips of recently matured leaves which become bronzed. The tips of the leaves roll upward and many drop from the plants. New foliage is small in size and marginal scorching and bronzing increases. Die-back is common and severe. Flowers are few, and poor in quality.

A spray of chelated iron will often temporarily cure the initial chlorosis caused by inadequate potassium, but the permanent remedy is to apply this element to the soil in the amount indicated by a soil test. Potassium is best supplied to Rhododendrons by potassium sulphate, which leaves an acid residue. The requirements of Rhododendrons for potassium are reported to be quite low compared to those of most horticultural plants. In my experiments, leaves from vigorous plants contained an average of 0·77 per cent potassium.

Phosphorus Deficiency

Bacteria use phosphorus in addition to nitrogen while they bring about the decay of organic debris which is usually abundant in Rhododendron plantings, and in any case acid soils are especially likely to be deficient in this element because of leaching.

A soil deficiency of phosphorus generally is evident in leaves which are abnormally *dark* green, at which point growth almost ceases. If a waxy sheen is characteristic of the foliage in good health, it usually disappears. Reddish purple blotches appear near the midrib of the leaf underneath, later spreading to the top surface of some of the lower leaves on vigorous branches. The lower leaves turn brown and fall from the plants, leaving reddish-bronze foliage at the ends of the branches. Flowers may be lighter in color than usual. Superphosphate or ammonium phosphate are convenient and suitable agents for correcting phosphorus deficiency. Rhododendrons are reported not to require nearly as much phosphorus as do most other cultivated plants. Leaf analyses from lusty specimens in my experiments averaged 0·24 per cent phosphorus.

Trace Element Deficiencies

Rhododendrons are especially sensitive to any lack of the principal trace elements whose presence in minute amounts is vital to their welfare. There are five which are controlled in their availability by the acidity or alkalinity of the soil and all of them are of critical consequence. They are iron, manganese, calcium, magnesium, and molybdenum. Calcium, magnesium, and molybdenum are available to plants in an alkaline soil, but iron and manganese tend to be in insoluble compounds. In an acid soil, iron and manganese are usually available for absorption through the roots, but calcium, magnesium, and molybdenum are sequestered chemically so that they are not so readily assimilated.

At first thought, it would seem that the convenient way to prevent deficiency of any of the trace elements is to apply to the soil a mixture containing all of them. But the solution is not quite that easy, because they act in an interdependent fashion when they are present in the proper proportions. An indiscriminate application of all trace elements may interfere with the absorption of some of them and perhaps make worse the one deficiency which ought to be corrected. An excess of manganese poisons the soil for many plants, although Rhododendrons were exceptionally tolerant of it in my experiments.

Trace element deficiencies may result from an actual shortage of these elements in the soil or, possibly, from their being tied up chemically in insoluble forms so that they cannot be absorbed in sufficient amounts by soil water through the roots.

No one knows exactly how much of these various nutrients are needed by Rhododendrons for optimum growth. Soil scientists can determine by tests whether a sample is deficient in the elements required for the principal agricultural crops, but the fact is that Rhododendrons require these elements in proportions quite different from those which bring about the best growth of corn, for example. Furthermore, the soil at one site may contain active compounds in excess which react chemically to make the trace elements less readily available, whereas another location may show an entirely different analysis. Since it is not desirable to adopt a shotgun method of applying all trace elements indiscriminately (unless it be in the glassy frits which are extremely slow in becoming soluble), the variable nature of the problem suggests an experimental approach.

If Rhododendrons are not growing satisfactorily and the obvious major factors have been eliminated as the cause, it will be worth while to determine by trial and error whether one or more of the trace elements may be deficient. By taking the stunted plants in groups of three and adding to each group one of the trace elements, the grower can observe from the results whether a deficiency of one of them is responsible for the unsatisfactory growth. The entire plantation can then be treated with whichever element brought about a satisfactory response in the experimental groups. The best chemical compound to supply each of the various trace elements is given under the discussion of the different deficiencies which follows.

Iron Deficiency

Contrary to popular belief, Rhododendrons do not have an exceptionally high requirement for iron, but it is critically necessary that it be soluble within the plants and available for use in the manufacture of chlorophyll. If acidifying the soil does not restore the normal green color to the foliage as suggested in the general discussion of chlorosis it is probably because the treatment failed to restore the loss of acidity which inactivated the iron already present within the plant. Deprived of this vital element, the leaves remain yellow except for the green veins. As iron starvation progresses, the color of the foliage fades to an overall cream color and finally to white before it dies. Eventually the leaves turn brown and drop. The older leaves are the last affected.

Iron is one trace element which is not normally lacking in the soil, except for the rare type which is naturally peaty. When chlorosis has appeared in Rhododendrons the conventional view has been that the iron in the earth becomes locked up in iron phosphate or other salts which do not dissolve in water and cannot therefore be taken up by the plants.

But every specialist has observed healthy green weeds growing among chlorotic Rhododendrons and wondered why the weeds obtained all the iron needed for lusty growth while the Rhododendrons did not. Now comes the further discovery from tissue analysis that the iron content of chlorotic Rhododendron leaves is just as high as that of healthy green leaves. The experiments by Colgrove and Roberts (Technical Paper No. 953, Oregon Agricultural Experiment Station) proved the close association of chlorosis with a loss of acidity of the leaf tissues. Iron becomes non-functional when sap acidity declines below about pH 4·5.

The conclusion seems inescapable that iron from the soil is equally available to all plants, Rhododendrons included. When leaves turn yellow from iron starvation, it is not because there is a lack of sufficient soluble iron in the soil. It is because the iron becomes unavailable after it is absorbed into the plant, due to a loss of sap acidity.

Fortunately, home gardeners and professional growers alike now have at their disposal a ready means of correcting the symptoms of iron chlorosis which is far superior to older methods. The new material is called chelated iron and its great virtue lies in its ability to hold iron soluble and unaffected by other chemicals even after it is absorbed and transported through the plant to its leaves. There it is held loosely enough to perform its role of catalyst in the manufacture of green chlorophyll, and it continues to remain soluble.

Foliage sprays of chelated iron are occasionally not effective, but a field of Rhododendrons sprayed with this material usually undergoes a dramatic change within four or five weeks. The usual application is at the rate of 3 pounds to 100 gallons of water (4 teaspoonsful to the gallon), with the addition of a spreader-sticker. Within a week or ten days, chlorotic foliage which is pale yellow or even cream-color exhibits scattered circular spots which are a fresh green. The moderately chlorotic leaves which are yellowish between the veins turn noticeably darker in color. By the end of several additional weeks the entire field will present a picture of healthy green foliage in which no trace of chlorosis remains.

Of course, a foliage spray is not a permanent remedy and the grower should think of it as a test to indicate by the response if a soil application of chelated iron should be made. As plants grow, their requirements for the various nutrients increase. Iron absorbed through the foliage in one season will not be enough for the additional growth the next year. A spray is the quickest way to correct iron chlorosis but as soon as the plants are obviously responding to this treatment a more permanent correction should be made by broadcasting chelated iron on the soil at the rate of 75 pounds per acre or two pounds per thousand square feet. A single plant a couple of feet tall should have about a tablespoonful, mixed with sand for even distribution, beneath the spread of its branches. For older specimens 4 feet tall or more, and of corresponding girth, nurserymen usually use three tablespoonsful per foot of height of the plant.

Manganese Deficiency

The symptoms of a manganese deficiency are initially exactly like those of an iron deficiency and it is, in fact, often the iron shortage which causes the yellowing of the leaves. In the absence of manganese, Rhododendrons are unable to assimilate iron properly, hence the appearance of chlorosis. My experiments indicate that Rhododendrons are probably exceptionally efficient extractors of manganese from the soil, and they may therefore be peculiarly sensitive to any lack of it. A deficiency first produces interveinal yellowing with the veins remaining green against the lighter background.

Spraying the foliage with a solution of chelated iron often cures the chlorosis caused by inadequate manganese, but only temporarily. Manganese sulphate supplies this element for a permanent cure but growers will be well advised to determine by experiment that it is actually needed, or to have a soil test made, so that the suspected deficiency can be confirmed. In excess, manganese displaces iron and there is a reduction in the number of effective iron-protein enzymes harmful to many sorts of cultivated plants. A five to one ratio of manganese to iron was not harmful to my experimental Rhododendrons, however, and in a few analyses the ratio reached fifteen to one without visible effect. State agricultural colleges and experiment stations will usually test soil samples for a small fee and report their mineral deficiencies.

Calcium Deficiency

Soil in which Rhododendrons grow may rarely have an insufficient supply of calcium. Under acid conditions calcium carbonate is converted into soluble calcium bicarbonate which drains from the earth by leaching. The presence of calcium is required by Rhododendrons before iron can be utilized properly, but the amount needed as determined by experiments in sand cultures is reported to be relatively small. However, the average analysis of leaves from my experimental plants growing in soil was 1·06 per cent, compared with an average of 0·77 per cent potassium, so that there was almost 40 per cent more calcium than the amount present of the major nutrient.

Inadequate calcium in the soil causes a

yellowing between the veins of new leaves, followed by tip burning as some of the new leaves expand. As the chlorosis intensifies, new terminal leaves often become twisted and the terminal buds are killed. Burning progresses toward the base of the older leaves which then curl downward in the dead areas. There may be moderate die-back of vigorous shoots.

A spray of chelated iron will often remedy, if only temporarily, chlorosis caused by insufficient calcium, but a suspected shortage should be confirmed by experiment or by a soil test and gypsum (calcium sulphate) can be applied in the amount indicated to bring about a permanent cure of the trouble.

A few nurserymen have reported good results from applications of lime to fields of Azaleas and Rhododendrons, but this is a hazardous measure because the calcium is released too quickly. Further, the temporary benefit may come from an increased supply of nutrients due to a lowered acidity which may not be permanently desirable. If calcium is needed, gypsum will supply it without risking injury to the plants and without causing a reduction of soil acidity.

Magnesium Deficiency

Magnesium is a component of chlorophyll and the yellowing between the veins of foliage caused by an inadequate supply in the soil is like iron chlorosis, appearing first at the tips of leaves located near the ends of the branches. As the bleaching progresses reddish-purple blotches appear, mostly on the upper leaves of the plants. All chlorotic leaves have slightly reddened veins on the under side. Older leaves become bronzed and curl down or die at the tips before dropping from the plants in large numbers. They do not usually remain attached long enough to develop sizable dead areas. Flowers are small, few in size and deficient in substance.

Heavy soils are more likely to be lacking in magnesium. On the basis of sand cultures, the requirement of Rhododendrons for magnesium is reported to be quite low, and experimental evidence supports the view that a high *total* concentration of magnesium, calcium and potassium salts produces chlorosis under conditions in which no yellowing appears if the total concentration is low. Tissue analysis of Rhododendrons in good growth at my trial grounds showed an average of 0·51 per cent magnesium.

Spraying the plants with a solution of Epsom Salts (magnesium sulphate), 6 pounds to 100 gallons water (2 tablespoonsful to 1 gallon) restores a healthy green to foliage made yellow by magnesium deficiency. A soil application of 10 pounds per thousand square feet will provide a more permanent remedy and at the same time increase the availability of potassium. A soil test or field experiment should, of course, confirm that it is needed before any trace element is added. I suspect that the beneficial effect of magnesium in the nutrition of Rhododendrons has been grossly undervalued.

Boron Deficiency

Boron is rarely the cause of nutritional troubles with Rhododendrons because a deficiency is nearly always associated with alkaline soils. It has been reported occasionally in the Pacific Northwest, however. A deficiency first causes a scattered sprinkling of brown dots on newly expanding leaves, which later persist as translucent flecks. As the symptoms increase, small dead spots appear on the new foliage and these spread to form larger areas, causing severe distortion of the growing leaves. Finally, the terminal buds die. Flowers may be darker in color than normal. If a suspected boron deficiency is confirmed by experiment or soil test it can be remedied by the use of borax, applied early in the season to avoid any stimulation of growth which might not be matured by the advent of cold weather.

Other Deficiencies

There are a number of other trace elements which are needed by plants in minute amounts but deficiencies of them are practically unknown by Rhododendron growers. Copper, zinc and molybdenum are needed for growth, and molybdenum is likely to be much less available in acid soils, but it is not known to be the cause of any deficiency symptoms in Rhododendrons in the nursery. Inasmuch as copper and zinc normally increase their availability in acid soils they are not responsible for any nutrition troubles.

I have experimented with FTE (an abbreviation for fritted trace elements), a material in which the minor fertilizers are imprisoned in fused glass and then ground into a very fine powder for application to the soil. Held almost insoluble by the inert glass there is little loss by leaching and the trace elements enter the plants by intimate contact through the roots. Slightly better growth was observed in the treated half than in the untreated side of some frames in which seedlings were grown, but inasmuch as the soil was not believed to be deficient in trace elements to any appreciable extent, the result indicated only that the routine use of this material is not worth while without first having the evidence of field experiment or soil test to justify its cost. I have observed dramatic improvement from applications of FTE in the growth and appearance of Rhododendrons which were planted in light, sandy coastal soil.

As an ingredient of fertilizer, FTE seems to make Rhododendrons so tolerant of nitrogen that rates of application which would ordinarily be lethal produce phenomenal growth instead. The latest research indicates that fritted trace elements may be invaluable for the production of Rhododendrons in the nursery. Their use at the rate of 2 per cent by weight of fertilizer enables the plants to sustain a surprisingly high level of feeding. The advantage in greater growth and earlier maturity is obvious to the commercial grower. A full discussion of this interesting aspect appears on page 100 of Chapter IV.

In so far as the routine maintenance of Rhododendrons in good health in the home garden is concerned, FTE can only be effective in improving their condition where a shortage already exists in the soil of one or more of the trace elements the frit contains. Ferro Corporation's formulation FN-501 has proved to be much more congenial to Rhododendrons than others which have been tried.

Other Causes of Chlorosis

There are many other causes of chlorosis besides soil deficiencies and they are reflected in the appearance of Rhododendrons by the typical yellowing of leaves which is symptomatic of a shortage of iron needed to manufacture the normal green coloring matter.

Too deep planting is often accompanied by stunted growth and yellow leaves simply because the roots suffer from lack of aeration and are unable to function properly for the absorption of iron. Planting in excessively heavy clay soil produces the same effect.

Overwatering, either from excessive rainfall or too frequent irrigation, or poor drainage, may bring about a deterioration of the roots so that they cannot fulfill their function of absorbing nutrients, including iron. Artificial irrigation may also cause chlorosis because the repeated and excessive use of city water, which is usually neutral to alkaline, brings about a gradual loss of soil acidity so that iron becomes unavailable.

Overfertilization, which burns the roots and inhibits their ability to absorb iron, can cause chlorosis. Fertilizers not specifically formulated for acid soil plants are frequent offenders. Calcium nitrate and calcium cyanamide, which may be among the ingredients of such mixtures, cause a quick loss of soil acidity by leaving a residue which is strongly alkaline. Repeated use of sodium nitrate and potassium nitrate in fertilizers can cause a more gradual loss of soil acidity, with the consequent conversion of iron to insoluble compounds within the plants. Nitrate nitrogen in any case is undesirable for Rhododendrons. Unbalanced fertilization may be responsible for yellow leaves due to the subtle interrelationship of the various elements in their assimilation.

Poor grades of peat moss may cause chlorosis while they are in the process of decomposition by soil micro-organisms tying up the nitrogen so that Rhododendrons show the symptoms of a deficiency. Sawdust, ground corn-cobs, and other vegetable waste used for its humus value or as a mulch are frequent offenders in this respect. Ammonium sulphate, applied at the rate of 2 pounds per inch of sawdust per 100 square feet (3 ounces per bushel) rectifies the shortage of nitrogen caused by incorporating sawdust into the soil to provide humus. This application is made when the sawdust is dug into the soil and another application at half this rate is usually necessary before growth starts the next spring. Used only as a mulch atop fertile soil, sawdust and other vegetable wastes do not usually require provision for a special nitrogen supplement. The acid soil fertilizers containing ammonium nitrogen, applied in the normal amounts of routine feeding, are sufficient in most cases. Some nurserymen are strongly opposed to the use of sawdust either as a mulch or as a soil amendment. They claim that the problems of soil management are theoretically simple but actually extremely difficult to solve under practical operating conditions. The maintenance of nutrients in the soil in the proper proportions is often apparently very hard to accomplish after sawdust has been incorporated.

Drouth and excessively high temperatures in summer, and very low temperatures in winter, can cause chlorosis because they result in poor root development and consequent restricted top growth which receives inadequate supplies of nutrients. The immediate effect may be that the foliage is only slightly off-color but if the roots have been seriously affected a more marked chlorosis will develop the next season, by which time the grower may have forgotten the severe conditions many months before.

Finally, yellow leaves may be caused by pests living in the soil which feed on the roots of Rhododendrons. When numerous plants with chlorosis and stunted growth occur in an irregular pattern in a block of Rhododendrons the grower should suspect that the roots are being attacked by Centipedes or by the larvae of the Black Vine Weevil or the Strawberry Root Weevil. If these pests are not checked the entire field eventually becomes infested and then, of course, the irregular pattern of unhealthy plants disappears. The entire block becomes uniformly afflicted with chlorosis, the result of the roots having been so reduced as to be inadequate to absorb the nutrients needed to support the top growth. Remedies for the various pests of Rhododendrons are given elsewhere in this chapter in the section devoted to insect enemies.

The 'Neurotic' Rhododendron

Every specialist sooner or later encounters the neurotic Rhododendron. It is usually growing next door in the yard of a neighbor who especially respects the expert's authority and ascribes to him all knowledge in human ken concerning his specialty. The Rhododendron with hypochondria has an assortment of psychosomatic symptoms which defy analysis and more often than not result from traumatic experiences with small boys and neighborhood dogs. Only the unfathomable effects of discarded experiments with home chemistry sets and Fourth of July fireworks could possibly account for the pale visage and dejected air of the neurotic Rhododendron. The ailing specimen which seems to be pining away next door is a snare which the plant doctor who values his reputation will assiduously avoid.

FAILURE TO SET FLOWER BUDS

Healthy Rhododendrons of blooming age which do not set buds for the production of flowers the next season are most commonly affected by excessive shade. All Rhododendrons need a certain minimum amount of light and a useful rough guide is the leaf size: the smaller the leaf, the more exposure the plant requires. Good strong light is just as useful as the right amount of sunshine. Rhododendrons planted with unobstructed exposure on the north side of a building usually thrive and bloom profusely, thus demonstrating that direct sunlight is not a necessity for free flowering.

In any case, pruning away the lower branches of trees to admit more light or transplanting Rhododendrons to a position with more exposure remedies most complaints of shy flowering.

Occasionally the season will be unusually cold and wet and the sky will be overcast when Rhododendrons normally form their buds in late June and July for the following year. When all of the Rhododendrons in a neighborhood fail to bloom the trouble can be traced to exceptionally dark cool weather the previous summer.

If Rhododendrons are fertilized too heavily or if the soil in which they grow is very rich, they will often make vegetative growth at the expense of flower buds. Normal flowering will resume if the roots are pruned by cutting a ring in the soil with a sharp spade just inside the circle of the outer branches. Enough roots are severed in transplanting so that overly vigorous specimens usually start to flower when they are moved to another position.

Many Rhododendrons tend to blossom only in alternate years unless the faded flowers are removed to prevent the formation of seed capsules. Some sorts bloom so prolifically that they are exhausted by the production of seeds and their vigor may be impaired for several years. All of the Rhododendrons which produce blossoms in trusses should be stripped of the faded clusters to insure full and regular flowering.

When plants produce floral buds which turn brown in the spring without flowering, injury from early autumn frosts, low midwinter temperatures, or late spring frosts is most often responsible. Bud Blast, which is described in the section on fungus diseases, is more rarely the cause. Other diseases and insect injuries which affect the general health of Rhododendrons are also quite capable of inhibiting the formation of flower buds.

SUN SCALD

Rhododendrons vary greatly in their ability to stand exposure, not only with respect to the different sorts but also in various parts of the country. With some exceptions, the larger the leaf the more shade and shelter the plant requires.

Rhododendrons which can stand full exposure in the moisture-laden air near the shore of a body of water may be injured in the clearer, brighter atmosphere of exposed plantings inland. Further than that, the same Rhododendron which is unable to withstand exposure for a year or two after it is transplanted may be able to endure the sun without injury after it has restored its root system to one which is fully able to replace water lost through the leaves by transpiration. Bright, sunny winter weather which causes increased moisture evaporation through the foliage at a time when the ground is frozen also causes damage.

Sun scald is often mistaken for a disease, perhaps because it is frequently followed by secondary fungus invasions. Generally, Rhododendrons suffering from excessive exposure have leaves of an off-color, yellowish-olive cast which may often be somewhat smaller than normal In sun scald which occurs during dry summer weather, the tips and edges of the leaves are disfigured by a pattern of round brown spots and the over-all yellowish tinge intensifies elsewhere on the leaf. Winter sun scald results in long brown patches on either side of the middle vein, caused by the added exposure of this portion of the leaf while it is curled up during cold weather.

Badly scorched leaves fall from the plants.

Sun scald is the visible effect of a simple lack of a sufficient water supply to the leaves and any measure which minimizes transpiration through the foliage or supplies additional water through the roots aids in correcting it. Naturally, transplanting to a site with increased shade is the usual remedy. Plants should be mulched and windswept positions should be avoided. Copious water when nature fails to provide it just before the advent of winter will prevent sun scald. Rhododendrons should go into the cold weather period with ample moisture at their roots.

FROST INJURY

Developing foliage is occasionally caught by frost in the spring with results that may be mistaken for disease damage. Various degrees of frost injury cause different symptoms. Very light freezing causes distorted leaves to develop with scalloped edges and roughened, uneven surfaces. Slightly lower temperatures cause an outright killing of the tissues, which turn brown along the leaf margins and at their tips as the foliage expands. Still harder freezing involves more of the leaves and in rare years the entire new growth, including the stems, may be completely destroyed.

Where partial injury has occurred its extent is determined by how far the leaves have developed at the time they are frosted. It is commonplace to see the outer ends of the leaves damaged in varying degree while the basal ends are entirely normal where they were protected by being furled within the expanding buds.

Rhododendrons which repeatedly lose their new growth to frost should be transplanted to more protected sites. Such plants do not bloom and they will eventually die from the burden of producing extra growth cycles. Protection can be gained from the nearby branches of trees and the walls of buildings, which modify the temperature near the ground more than is generally realized. Avoid low spots which become frost pockets for those Rhododendrons which start into growth early.

WINTER INJURY

Winter damage to Rhododendrons is usually noted if the foliage is affected, because it causes conspicuous water-soaked blisters along the leaf margins which turn brown with the approach of spring. More often, however, it is the floral buds or the main branches which suffer from very low temperatures.

In the case of the flower buds, winter injury is responsible when part or all of the florets fail to develop and the plant blooms sparsely or not at all. These buds are more susceptible to cold damage than any other part of the plant, and consistent injury indicates that the Rhododendron is not adapted to the climate in which it is being grown. In an exceptionally cold winter such a plant will very likely be more severely damaged. Specimens on the borderline of hardiness can often be made to retain their buds and bloom consistently if they are given a planting site shielded to the south and openly exposed toward the north.

A winter injury, often unnoticed at the time, occurs to branches or to the main stems of Rhododendrons which may be girdled when the bark splits under the stress of sub-freezing temperatures and separates from the underlying tissues. Months later, usually in late July or August and after making normal growth, the plant or a portion of it dies abruptly and disease may be blamed for its demise, because the grower does not associate such a loss with the cold weather of the previous winter after so long a time. Close examination of the main stem would show the true cause.

Winter injury frequently produces less severe damage in which a moderate splitting of the bark induces the formation of a canker which can be identified as to its cause by one or more longitudinal cracks. Such wounds heal if they are not too severe, but they also afford ready entry to disease fungi. Branches which are heavily damaged seldom regain their vigor and it is better to prune them out so that they are replaced by new, sound growth.

Winter injury may be caused by mismanagement, particularly by watering and fertilizing too late in the summer so that the plants are stimulated into unseasonable growth and the bark splits as freezing temperatures are encountered at a time when the tissues are still turgid with sap of low sugar content. Rhododendrons should not be watered in August and September unless it is absolutely necessary and then they should be given only the minimum to prevent excessive wilting. Fertilizing after early June is risky. For a full discussion of the factors which affect hardiness and, conversely, the measures that can be taken to help control winter injury, the reader is referred to Chapter VII.

Rhododendron Troubles and their Remedies

FUNGUS DISEASES OF THE ROOTS AND CROWNS

Rhododendron Wilt, Root Rot, Water Mold Root Rot (Phytophthora cinnamomi)

For the professional grower and the occasional home gardener unlucky enough to be visited by it, the most serious disease is Rhododendron Wilt, caused by the fungus *Phytophthora cinnamomi*. It attacks principally through the roots and is most often an affliction of young plants, but older Rhododendrons are infected too, usually in exceptionally rainy seasons or when they are transplanted to a site with poor drainage or with soil unsuitably dense. This is the same organism which is so destructive in the greenhouse to small plants grafted on understocks of *R. ponticum*, a species with a special susceptibility to it. *R. griersonianum* also seems to be particularly lacking in resistance to the depredations of this fungus. Its presence in the field can be detected most easily early in the morning or on cool, cloudy days when Rhododendrons are normally fresh and the foliage is turgid. At such times, plants which have been infected have a wilted look, especially the new growth. During the heat of the day all of the plants in a field block are likely to be somewhat wilted by the rapid transpiration of moisture and it is much harder to locate those which may have been stricken by the disease in its early stages.

When a Rhododendron has been attacked, the entire plant is usually affected and close observation will show that all of the foliage is slightly off-color. As the disease progresses, the leaves acquire an olive-green cast. A final diagnosis can be made by scraping away the bark near ground level. Beneath the bark at some point around its circumference the tissues of the trunk will be brown and dead, and a dark reddish band will be found ascending the main stem where the metabolite produced by the fungus has traveled along the vascular system from the roots to the body of the plant above ground. This dark band may be only the width of a thread or it may be a half-inch wide. If it happens to lead directly to a point where a branch originates from the trunk, it may initially cause the wilting of that branch alone at an early stage of infection, thus leading to a confusion of this ailment with another called Rhododendron Blight. The dead tissues beneath the bark become more extensive as more and more sap vessels are plugged and finally the brown necrotic band encircles the trunk. The actual invasion of Rhododendrons by this fungus is scant. It seems likely that an extremely potent enzyme or hormone produced by the fungus is responsible for the occlusion of the sap vessels which causes the wilting of plants and finally the death of tissues deprived of nourishment.

Rhododendron Wilt is almost invariably fatal to plants it attacks. If the dark ribbon of dead tissue is found ascending the trunk the plant should be dug immediately, and an examination of its root system before the disease has destroyed it will show a dark, dead area, usually circular, where the organism first entered. The discolored sector of the trunk is an extension of it. As it spreads throughout the entire plant the yellowing of the leaves and the wilting become progressively more acute. Brown, sunken cankers may appear on stems of the new growth, particularly on small plants newly propagated from cuttings. Eventually even the petioles and leaves are invaded. An entirely unrelated leaf spot disease may attack the weakened foliage to hasten defoliation and bring about the demise which would have occurred in any event in short order.

Rhododendron Wilt is primarily a soil-borne organism which first attacks the roots, and there is no known cure for plants already infected. In the greenhouse it spreads through the earth in a round pattern from the first focus of infection, attacking other plants as the circle of its contamination extends. In the field it seems to be more erratic, but contiguous plants are very often infected by the first specimen to be attacked.

Plants which have been attacked by Rhododendron Wilt should be dug and burned, and the soil where they were removed should be drenched with a fungicide such as Dithane D-14. This is the best treatment to prevent the spread of the disease, but it is still a great deal better to forestall its first appearance by thoughtful attention to the factors which encourage it.

Of first importance may be any lack of aeration in the soil. Rhododendrons growing in open, porous soil well fortified with humus are seldom assailed by Wilt, whereas a heavy clay soil is often associated with its appearance. A mulch too heavy or too dense, particularly sawdust in excessively heavy applications, is occasionally responsible for losses to this disease. I have observed the appearance of Wilt on a number of occasions after sawdust was mixed into the soil. The occurrence of the disease at such times is frequent enough to be suspicious. Since the fungus becomes more active as summer temperatures rise, it presumably needs a soil temperature of 70° to 85° F. to flourish.

Nurserymen often find that new plantings of young Rhododendrons are attacked by Wilt. The injured roots of the recently transplanted seedlings offer a ready entry for the fungus. Growth cracks at the soil level of second-year seedlings also provide the means of infection. Roots killed by overwatering are a pathway for entry of the pathogen.

Wilt has been controlled effectively in commercial plantings by increasing the soil acidity to pH 4·0, but care must be used at this point because many sorts of Rhododendrons are seriously affected by acidity in excess of pH 3·7. At the New Jersey Agricultural Experiment Station inoculated sulphur, applied before planting at the rate of 1,000 pounds per acre, increased soil acidity from pH 5·56 to 3·82 and controlled Rhododendron Wilt satisfactorily. The experiments resulted in a recommendation that nursery soil for young Rhododendrons be maintained at pH 4·5 and that rigid sorting be practiced.

I have successfully controlled an epidemic of *Phytophthora cinnamomi* with Dithane D-14, a commercial fungicide, applied at the rate of 2 quarts to each 1,000 square feet of soil surface. Two gallons of water are added to each 2 quarts of Dithane D-14 and the solution is then distributed over the infected plot of land through a siphoning device attached to a hose supplying an oscillating sprinkler. It is important to continue watering after the fungicide has been taken out through the hose until the earth is thoroughly soaked to a depth of 15 inches, or more if the plants in the field are large enough to have deeper roots. This remedy is best applied in late spring when the fungus is most active, but it seems to be effective in moist periods later in the season.

On a later occasion Dithane D-14 controlled the spread of this disease in ground beds containing young plants when it was applied as a drench, 1 ounce to 2 quarts of water through a siphoning device which diluted 1 : 12, thus making a final dilution of about 1 to 750.

Before the Dithane is used, any diseased Rhododendrons and the healthy plants immediately adjacent to them are removed and destroyed. No soil from the infested plot can be moved to an uninfected field, before or after the treatment. In the autumn of the year following use of the fungicide, apparently healthy plants can be moved to new ground, but they should be held there in quarantine for one more year to be certain that they are not infected before anything further is done with them. This regime seems to offer a reasonable prospect of eradicating Rhododendron Wilt from the site of an epidemic in two years.

Fortunately, this organism cannot survive sub-freezing temperature in the soil although it has rarely been known to penetrate 2½ feet below the surface, and it can usually be eradicated in fields by plowing them in the fall and allowing them to remain fallow over winter. The Wilt fungus can and does remain alive over winter in Rhododendron tissues, ready to reinfect the soil and spread to other plants, so it is necessary to examine closely the roots of new stock before a field is replanted. Any discoloration is evidence enough that the roots may be infected with Wilt and such plants should be discarded.

Frames should be rotated so that other, less susceptible nursery stock deprives the pathogen of a congenial host for its continued activity. In cold climates unused frames can be left uncovered for freezing to aid in the destruction of the fungus.

Soil fumigation is not a practical means of destroying this fungus outdoors because the fumigant evaporates rapidly and it is very difficult to obtain the penetration of it which is necessary to kill the pathogen. The fungus has a wide range of hosts in the nursery including Red Pine (*Pinus resinosa*); Japanese, English and Irish Yews (*Taxus cuspidata*, *T. baccata*, and *T. baccata stricta*); Lawson Cypress (*Chamaecyparis lawsoniana*); Heath (*Erica carnea*); and Heather (*Calluna vulgaris*). Any of these should be viewed with suspicion if unexplained recurrent infections are encountered.

In the greenhouse *Phytophthora cinnamomi* has been responsible for enormous losses of young grafted Rhododendrons because the small understocks of *R. ponticum* are especially susceptible to its inroads. Soil sterilization is a good precaution indoors and other measures to control the fungus are adaptations of those which are effective outdoors. The acidity of the soil should be increased to pH 4·5 or 4·0 and the roots of the understocks should be examined with special care so that no infected plants are carried over from one season to the next. It is quite possible for stock only slightly infected one year to carry the fungus over winter with ruinous results the following season. Grafts may be successful on understocks in which the organism has lodged with the result that the entire crop may be lost the next summer as the disease becomes virulent with the arrival of warm weather. Outdoor frames can be sterilized by allowing them to lie open and fallow over winter.

The nurseryman can be confident that his diagnosis of Wilt is accurate whenever he finds the telltale dark vertical band beneath the bark in combination with roots which are also dark and dead in one area, or entirely so in cases which are further advanced.

Phytophthora cinnamomi has world-wide distribution and is of economic importance in many temperate, tropical, and sub-tropical countries, where its depredations are usually described simply as Root Rot or Water Mold Root Rot.

Crown Rot (Phytophthora cryptogeae)

A crown decay caused by another species of *Phytophthora* has been found occasionally on collected specimens of Rhododendrons which came from the mountains of the southeastern United States. All of the native evergreen species can be afflicted by this pathogen, which is evidently harbored primarily in the soil since only the roots, crown and basal stem portions are affected. Infected branches wilt and die and if the disease is not checked the entire plant languishes and succumbs.

Crown decay has not been a problem of any consequence for Rhododendrons in cultivation so no formal treatment has been devised and the remedies are those which common sense suggests. Afflicted branches should be cut out and the crown of the plant be exposed to air and light as much as possible. A soil drench with Dithane D-14 is indicated. Badly infected plants should be dug and burned.

Damping-off and Stem Rot (Rhizoctonia species)

Rhizoctonia Rot can be a dangerous enemy of Rhododendrons from the time the seeds are sown until the plants are fully mature. Damping-off is a decay of very young seedlings caused by *Rhizoctonia solani* and other fungi which destroy the embryonic plants before they emerge from the seed coats or, at a later stage, attacking them at the soil level. Such slow germinating seeds as Rhododendrons are especially susceptible to the onslaughts of these fungi and the cumulative effect of applications of some of the older fungicidal remedies repeated over a long period of time has been injurious.

Those who insist on growing seedlings in soil mixtures have the usual remedies at their disposal. Seeds can be coated with captan or thiram dust by shaking them in a vial prior to sowing. Arasan is the name of a proprietary remedy containing thiram which is available at most stores. These chemicals also offer good control of damping-off after the seedlings are established.

It is my opinion, however, that it is infinitely better to be assured of healthy seedlings by growing them in milled sphagnum moss. I have grown thousands of seedlings in this medium without ever losing a single one to damping-off. The fungi are unable to exist in sphagnum and the tiny plants are thus isolated from their attacks. Seedlings fed with liquid nutrients make remarkable growth and I have been able to obtain larger, healthier plants in less time with this method than with any other. Milled sphagnum moss suitable for this purpose is available commercially from Mosser Lee, Millston, Wisconsin, or collected moss can be rubbed through a screen so that it is shredded to appropriate size for sowing seeds. The entire procedure for growing seedlings in it is described on page 351 of Chapter IX.

The same parasitic fungus which causes damping-off is responsible for the cobwebby growth which occasionally covers the tops of small plants and causes their decay in the stagnant, humid air of grafting chambers and propagating frames. It is also the cause of a canker at soil level on one- and two-year-old seedlings, especially those of *R. ponticum*. As these dead areas enlarge, the stems are gradually girdled, the plants become yellow and then wilt and finally die. Stems of cuttings may start to rot at the bottom as this pathogen enters the cut ends. Soil for grafts and the rooting medium for cuttings can be sterilized to prevent the appearance of the fungus. A drench of oxyquinoline sulfate, as described below, offers the best control, but I do not know if it would inhibit the rooting of cuttings.

Rhizoctonia Rot of larger plants is somewhat similar in its symptoms to Rhododendron Wilt and it is almost as common. The plants wilt as they do in time of drouth, regardless of the amount of moisture in the soil. Past authors have erroneously described the roots of older plants as unaffected by this disease, which was thought to make its entry through the trunk at soil level. The presence of dark vascular streaks beneath the bark while the roots remain in healthy condition has even been given as a means of distinguishing this malady from Rhododendron Wilt. Actually, *Rhizoctonia solani* does attack the fine roots of older plants and progressively destroys them, ultimately causing death. It rarely penetrates the bark of older stock at ground level and the loss of large branches on mature plants of *R. carolinianum* attributed to this disease is probably due instead to Rhododendron Blight (*Phytophthora cactorum*).

Overwatering, excessive humidity, crowding, lack of air drainage, and inadequate porosity of the soil are primarily responsible for the appearance of this malady among Rhododendrons. Immediate control can be obtained by treatment with oxyquinoline sulfate, as directed below, but it is essential to correct the basic conditions which favor the activity of the fungus. Young plants of *R. ponticum* are particularly susceptible to *Rhizoctonia* Rot and it is a troublesome disease in the greenhouse.

Rhizoctonia, while destroying the roots of older Rhododendrons, does *not* produce the reddish vascular streaks beneath the bark which are characteristic of Rhododendron Wilt. Plants in the field which exhibit excessive wilting for no apparent reason may usually be diagnosed on this basis. The Connecticut Agricultural Experiment Station has announced that oxyquinoline sulfate (available commercially under the trade name 'Sunox') is an effective treatment, $1\frac{1}{8}$ pints to 100 gallons of water (2 teaspoonsful to 3 gallons), used as a drench poured over the root area and applied two or three times at intervals of several days. The material has been effective in use at my trial grounds. It should be mixed in a clean container and used immediately, at least 24 hours after any rain and when no additional rainfall is expected for a day or two. Water containing dissolved limestone or other minerals which make the solution dark or cloudy is not suitable. After mixing, it should be a deep yellow color. Plants should be given as much light and air circulation and as little water as possible, following the treatment. Soil applications of oxyquinoline sulfate seem to enable Rhododendrons to produce new roots which are resistant to *Rhizoctonia* attack.

Armillaria Root Rot: Shoe String Fungus (Armillaria mellea)

The Oak-root fungus, *Armillaria*, may attack Rhododendrons whose vigor has been reduced by excessively wet or other unfavorable conditions. The leaves of infected plants turn yellow and droop. The foliage becomes sparse and a slow death ensues. The woody roots of Rhododendrons which have been affected by this pathogen often have long, black, stringy strands adhering to them, and white, fan-shaped plaques of the fungus appear beneath the loosened bark of the larger roots and of the main stems below ground level. The wet decay exudes a mushroom odor.

Shade and fruit trees as well as shrubs are the supposed hosts of this fungus, which reproduces itself by spores from toadstools on the ground and by the long, tough strands about the thickness of a matchstick which run along under the ground usually less than a foot beneath the surface. These runners are bundles of plant bodies and two different sorts may be observed: the coppery-colored elastic strands are alive and they are capable of growing dozens of feet in the course of a season; the black strands are composed of stringy fibers which are dead.

If definite evidence of infection is found, it can be controlled by phenyl-mercuric-monoethanol-ammonium-acetate, a compound which by any other name would be easier to spell, and it is available in the larger garden supply stores under several simple trade-marked names as a spray for Apple Scab. The solution, which is poisonous and must be kept away from animals and children, is prepared in the same manner as directed on the label for Scab, and then poured as a drench on the soil surface over the root area of afflicted plants.

Armillaria Root Rot is a controversial subject among plant pathologists and among commercial nurserymen. In the eastern United States, at least, the soil can be very heavily infected with *Armillaria* and healthy Rhododendrons with good growing conditions will be completely immune from attack. A New Jersey nurseryman has repeatedly demonstrated that the strands infiltrate the soil beneath his large stock of plants without attaching themselves to the roots or causing any harm whatever to the Rhododendrons. The conclusion is inescapable that *Armillaria* Rot is a secondary infection which attacks the bark of the woody roots and of the trunk at ground level of plants that have been weakened by other causes; or that it becomes virulent only when local conditions are peculiarly favorable to activate its malignancy. It is important as a destructive disease only when infected Rhododendrons with favorable conditions of growth are moved to an unfavorable situation. Nurserymen should make every effort to control it in the interest of customer satisfaction.

Crown Gall (Bacterium tumefaciens)

An enlarged, tumor-like growth occasionally develops on the main stems of Rhododendrons, usually at a point near ground level where the bark has been injured. The tissue which forms over the wound gives the appearance of proliferating much beyond the usual callus and eventually a hard, round protuberance remains. Crown Gall is of no consequence when it appears on mature plants. On young plants commercial growers usually remove the gall with a sharp knife and protect the wound with orange shellac or other dressing.

ALL-PURPOSE PREVENTIVE SPRAYS

Probably no single Rhododendron specialist has ever observed all of the parasitic fungus diseases described herein. The New Jersey Agricultural Experiment Station has published more information on this subject than has any other source and I am indebted to its research workers for essential information on some of the rarer fungi which I have not encountered at first hand.

It must be remembered that after the spores of a fungus have come to rest on a plant they sprout and penetrate into the tissues under favorable conditions. It is then too late for any spray to be effective because it is not absorbed inside the plant to kill the fungus along the path of its penetration. The fungicide must be applied before the spores alight on the plant so that they are destroyed by it before they can germinate and infect the host. Fungi are themselves minute parasitic plants without chlorophyll which prey on other plants with chlorophyll to obtain sustenance. The spores are the 'seeds' by which they reproduce and spread.

Commercial nurserymen are sometimes inclined to discount the value of a spray repeated only once or twice, since they are accustomed to thinking that the foliage must be kept constantly coated with a fungicide throughout the entire warm weather season if effective control is to be attained. It is my observation that the two- or three-time all-purpose preventive sprays are effective because they do so much toward stopping minor leaf infections and insect damage to foliage which would otherwise be followed by invasions of injurious fungi. Ruptures in the plants' tissues afford ready entry to fungi and when they are prevented, diseases are controlled. Chlorosis should be promptly corrected because the yellow leaves invite fungous invasions.

Professional growers who specialize in Rhododendrons apply all-purpose sprays with this in mind. When mechanical abrasions, lesions caused by minor infections, insects and mites are controlled, the disease problem is also minimized. A. M. Shammarello, a veteran Ohio nurseryman who specializes in Rhododendrons, uses the following spray on field stock immediately after the blossoming period, again in mid-July and in early September. Young seedlings in frames are sprayed every two to three weeks from the 1st of June to early October. The chlordane is omitted after early July.

TO 100 GALLONS OF WATER	TO 1 GALLON OF WATER
2 pounds of Fermate	2 teaspoonsful of Fermate
$1\frac{1}{2}$ pints of 50 per cent malathion emulsion	$1\frac{1}{2}$ teaspoonsful of 50 per cent malathion
2 quarts of 45 per cent chlordane emulsion	4 teaspoonsful of 45 per cent chlordane
8 ounces of DuPont spreader-sticker	12 drops of DuPont spreader-sticker

Roland de Wilde, a professional Rhododendron grower in New Jersey, applies a spray just before growth starts and again as the new growth finishes its extension and starts to mature. He has found that the following formula is adequate for the practical control of Rhododendron ills in his nursery:

TO 100 GALLONS OF WATER	TO 1 GALLON OF WATER
1 pound of Fermate	1 teaspoonful of Fermate
1 pound of 25 per cent lindane powder	1 tablespoonful of 25 per cent lindane
$1\frac{1}{2}$ pounds of Aramite powder	$1\frac{1}{2}$ tablespoonsful of Aramite
$1\frac{1}{2}$ ounces of DuPont spreader-sticker	6 drops of DuPont spreader-sticker

These sprays are also recommended to home gardeners who may have need for such chemical aids on rare occasions.

All Rhododendron sprays should contain a spreader-sticker. It is impossible to wet the waxy foliage thoroughly and to obtain uniform coverage without such an ingredient. Many growers have reported that brilliant sunshine may disfigure the foliage if a spray is applied to plants in an open field near midday in clear weather. Even water alone is alleged to bring about such spotting, so prudence suggests that sprays be applied in the morning, toward evening or on overcast days. I have never experienced this trouble, possibly because my plants are grown in partial shade.

FUNGUS DISEASES OF LEAVES, STEMS, AND BUDS

Rhododendron Blight, Die-Back (Phytophthora cactorum)

The second most important Rhododendron disease in point of its occurrence and injury is Rhododendron Blight caused by the fungus *Phytophthora cactorum*. Initially, this pathogen enters through the leaf margins, twigs, old bloom stems or seed pods on a single branch, and the first early symptom may be the appearance of conspicuous water-soaked areas on the foliage which subsequently become brown, spotted with silvery white. More often the disease is first noticed when the leaves on the branch lose their healthy sheen and start to curl and droop as they do in sub-freezing weather. A dark brown, wedge-shaped discoloration shows on the green stemwood where the fungus has caused the formation of a canker. The canker extends until it girdles the branch which then wilts abruptly, and it is at this point that the disease becomes really conspicuous. The attack is usually made on green wood or foliage of the current or previous year's growth and the infected stem at first glance seems to be changing color as it matures into the brown bark which is typical of the older wood on the plant. The normal change from green to brown which occurs on the stems of branches in the course of their second year progresses upward from the base, however. Browning caused by Die-back always proceeds downward and closer examination of an afflicted branch shows that the portions of stem below the brown cankered area are still quite green. The abnormal condition can be easily distinguished on that basis. As the disease progresses the entire stem shrivels and discolors. If it is not checked, the whole plant becomes infected in the same manner as the branch first attacked, and the over-all wilting at this late stage then becomes hard to distinguish from Rhododendron Wilt. However, in the case of the Blight, the roots are the last to be affected. They are the first to be attacked by Wilt.

Sometimes the initial wilting of a branch infected with Blight is confused with a similar effect caused by a borer, but in the latter case there is always the typical borer tunnel through the hollowed-out center of the stem as a distinguishing mark, however similar the external symptoms may be.

Rhododendron Blight can be very destructive if it is neglected. The disease is of much greater interest to the home owner because it attacks plants of all ages, whereas Rhododendron Wilt is primarily an affliction of young plants of nursery age.

This Blight is often called Die-back and any branch affected by it should be immediately cut off well below the point where evidence of the disease can be seen. Branches so removed should be burned and the pruning shears sterilized by dipping them in alcohol or other disinfectant each time they are used for this purpose. The wounds where the branches are severed should be protected against re-infection by a coating of orange shellac or other suitable wound covering. Spraying with Parzate, Phygon or with Fermate (2 pounds per 100 gallons of water; $2\frac{1}{2}$ tablespoonsful per gallon), with the addition of a spreader-sticker, immediately following the blossoming period and again ten days to two weeks later, is a good preventive measure. If the pathogen appears late in the season, two sprays spaced ten to fourteen days apart are indicated for both healthy and infected plants.

It is apparent that Blight is much worse during the summers which are exceptionally warm and humid, and I can remember seeing few exceptions to the general pattern that only plants growing in excessive shade are attacked. The precautionary measures are obvious: the amount of shade should be reduced as far as possible so that more sun is admitted and the humidity is lowered. If poor air drainage can be improved so that stagnant pools of damp air do not envelop the plants, there will be less likelihood of attacks by this pathogen. Lilacs and Dogwoods are a source of infection and Rhododendrons should not be planted in the shade near them. *R. carolinianum* is especially susceptible to injury by *P. cactorum.* Removal of the old bloom stalks after the flowers have faded is a good sanitary measure, because the developing seed pods frequently afford points of entry for the fungus. Any plant which becomes badly afflicted before the malady is discovered should be dug and burned.

The removal of infected branches accompanied by a substantial reduction in the amount of shade, either by pruning overhead tree limbs or moving the plant into a more sunny position, is generally effective in saving plants in which the disease has not progressed too far. Die-back is often responsible for the failure of Rhododendrons in climates too warm to be congenial to their welfare. Gardeners in the South should be alert for its appearance.

Leaf Spots (Botryosphaeria ribis; Cercospora rhododendri; Exobasidium burtii; Lophodermium rhododendri; Pestalotia *sp.;* Phomopsis *sp.*; Phyllosticta maxima)

Leaf Rust (Puccinastrum myrtilli; Melampsoropis piperiana; Chrysomyxa ledi *var.* rhododendri)

Leaf Scorch (Septoria solitaris)

All of the leaf-spotting fungi can be controlled by spraying with a fungicide such as Fermate or Phygon in combination with a spreader-sticker. If the injury appears on a small scale, the home owner with a few plants can deal with it most conveniently by just picking off the infected leaves and burning them. Prevention is largely a matter of avoiding winter injury, mechanical bruises, insect damage and sun scald, through which these pathogens usually gain a foothold in the hosts.

There are about eighteen different fungi which are capable of causing leaf spots on Rhododendrons and under ordinary conditions they are not very important. Under extraordinary conditions specifically favorable to their development they may require intervention to bring them under control. Commercially, any disfigurement of the foliage which impairs the salability of Rhododendrons is a matter of concern to the grower.

In addition to the pathogens listed above I have found in my own Rhododendron plantings injured stock infected with fungi which have been identified by a competent pathologist as *Mycosphaerella*, *Cryptostictis mariae* and *Gleosporium*.

Botryosphaeria ribis causes round brown spots near the leaf margin which later extend to cover all or most of the leaf. It is more of a hazard than the other leaf-spotting fungi because conditions favorable to its further development may cause a die-back of infected twigs similar to Rhododendron Blight. Such infected parts should be pruned away and burned. The minute bodies of the fungus create a surface which is rough to the touch on the leaves and stems attacked by it. Rhododendrons are often infected with *Botryosphaeria* from Currants and Roses growing nearby and these plants should be suspected of harboring the pathogen if there are unexplained recurrent attacks.

When *Cercospora* leaf spot appears it is likely to be most troublesome on the lower foliage of young seedlings or small grafted plants. Brown spots, circular on some hybrids, angular on others, form on the leaves. The spores of the fungus appear as a fine gray powdery cushion in the centers of the spots in most instances, but occasionally the leaf epidermis lifts from the tissues beneath and then the necrotic areas become silvery white in the centers. Foliage which is badly infected becomes yellow and falls from the plants.

Exobasidium Leaf Spot is conspicuous and distinct. At first the spots are very small and round. As they enlarge to about one-fourth inch in diameter their outline becomes irregular and their color is a bold, bright yellow. Their centers become brown and the scalloped margins usually have a reddish tint. The spots which penetrate through the leaves show on their undersurfaces a white fungous coating consisting of the spores. This disease rarely appears before the first of July.

Leaf Rust is normally of minor importance except on very young seedlings, when the infection may cause their death. Only the lower leaves are ordinarily affected on older stock. The disease is diagnosed by the distinct red spotting on the foliage. On the leaf undersurfaces small orange-red or golden blister-like swellings containing the spores appear. These pustules later become powdery after the spores are liberated. The alternate host is the Hemlock. Rusts do not usually kill the tissues upon which they live but in this case *Pestalotia* fungi usually enter the lesions caused by the rust and the weakened tissues are then killed. Both *Pucciniastrum myrtilli* and the Western Rust, *Melampsoropsis piperiana*, are known to afflict Rhododendrons.

Chrysomyxa ledi var. *rhododendri*, the European Rhododendron Rust, was first discovered in the United States in southwestern Washington in 1954. In 1959 it was studied intensively by the Department of Agriculture and imported Rhododendrons became subject to Federal post-entry quarantine for two growing seasons as a control measure. *Chrysomyxa* rust now occurs on *R. lapponicum* in Canada throughout almost all of its distribution range. Its injury to Spruce trees, the alternate host, is well known in both Europe and Asia but, oddly, it has never been reported on Spruce anywhere in North America. The powdery lesions of European Rust on the undersides of Rhododendron leaves are orange colored and only pin-point in size so that they are difficult to detect until they merge into clusters about a quarter of an inch in diameter. The earliest symptom on the upper leaf surfaces is the appearance of small brownish-red, reddish-violet, yellowish or dead spots. The disease first attacks the older, basal leaves and if there is a heavy infection these wither, dry and fall off. The European Rust overwinters in the vegetative stage within the Rhododendron leaf tissues, where it can remain dormant and viable for long periods. In the Seattle and Portland areas its appearance is most conspicuous from March to June, but in colder regions it does not develop extensively until midsummer. Rhododendrons have not been particularly susceptible to attacks by rust fungi but this newly imported disease should be closely watched. The Mycology and Plant Disease Reporting Section, A.R.S., U.S.D.A., Beltsville, Maryland, welcomes reports of its occurrence.

Leaf Scorch (*Septoria solitaris*) is active only in regions of exceptionally high humidity and fog. The fungus may rarely become serious because it is capable of causing defoliation of the plants. Small yellow round spots appear on the leaves. Increasing in size with age, they become dark reddish-brown and irregular or angular in shape, often with a yellow rim. The leaves fall and the fungus then produces spores which spread the disease. Destroying the fallen leaves helps to control this parasite.

Lophodermium causes spots to form up to an inch in diameter which are silvery white with reddish raised margins. Scattered over their surface are colonies of oval black spore sacs each marked by a cleft in the middle running its length which can be clearly seen with a magnifying glass. Beneath the leaves the spots on their undersides are light chocolate-brown. The destroyed tissues often fall away, leaving irregular perforations in the foliage. This ailment is usually confined to *R. maximum* and *R. catawbiense* and it is of minor consequence.

The most widespread foliage disease of Rhododendrons is caused by two species of *Pestalotia* fungi which enter leaves or stems through abrasions caused by insects, sun injury, lesions produced by other fungi, and random bruises of the foliage. Chlorotic leaves are likely to be attacked. Infections start as round brown spots on the upper leaf surface, often marked by concentric rings, yellowish around the outside perimeters. The infected tissue then becomes silvery gray in the center with a dark brown margin on the top of the leaf, and light brown underneath. As the spot enlarges, it changes to an irregular blotch and the silvery pocks may appear also on the stems. Colonies of black spores and spore-producing bodies can be easily seen with a magnifying glass. If the central leaf rib is infected, the entire leaf then becomes sun-scalded. The disease spreads from one leaf to another and my experience does not agree with published accounts which describe it as inconsequential. Under the exceptionally warm humid conditions which favor its growth, I find that it can disfigure foliage rather extensively and cause a loss of leaves which mars the appearance of the plants.

R. smirnowii and the Catawba hybrids 'Lee's Dark Purple', 'Everestianum', and 'Mrs C. S. Sargent' are reported by professional growers to be especially susceptible to attacks by this pathogen. So are hybrids of *R. caucasicum*, especially 'Cunningham's White' and 'Goldsworth Yellow', according to Roland de Wilde, a veteran nursery specialist in New Jersey.

Phomopsis Leaf Spot appears as half-inch brown areas with clearly defined, reddish-brown perimeters and silvery-white centers bearing very small spore sacs which can be seen under a magnifying glass to be arranged in circular zones in the middle. *R. maximum* is especially susceptible, as are some hybrids. This parasite is also capable of causing cankers on infected branches, which should be pruned away and burned.

Phyllosticta Leaf Spot is caused by several different fungi of this genus, and combined they are responsible for a good deal of unsightly damage to Rhododendron foliage. The dark brown circular spots usually occur at some point around the perimeter of the leaf and then spread until half of the leaf area may be involved. Under a magnifying glass the surfaces are seen to bear very small black fruiting bodies which are slightly rough to the touch. This foliage disease often follows injury by frost or drouth and it is most prevalent on plants of commercial landscaping size. *R. maximum* is occasionally afflicted by a species of *Phyllosticta* which produces spots not over $\frac{3}{8}$ inch in diameter, silvery white on the upper surface of the leaf with a few minute black fruiting bodies in the center, and light brown on the underside.

Botrytis *Blight* (Botrytis *sp.*)

Botrytis Leaf Blight attacks small seedlings in the greenhouse and sometimes it is destructive to plants in the grafting chamber or to the soft growth of rooted cuttings in propagating frames. As it is almost exclusively a disease of artificially high humidity and inadequate air circulation it is of little consequence as a hazard to Rhododendrons in the field, though leaf injuries outdoors may occasionally be followed by blotches with the peculiar wavy discolorations which are typical of *Botrytis cinerea* invasions.

Indoors, it can be ruinous to small plants in seed beds or propagating frames. Infected leaves and stems become covered with a grayish-brown mold composed of the fungus and its spores. Water-soaked areas appear briefly but the leaves soon become brown and fall from the stems, after which they are a latent source of infection because the sclerotia in them require only a recurrence of favorable conditions for this fungus to become active once again.

Botrytis Blight is not too easy to control once it becomes established in seed beds, and my experience has been that increased air and ventilation of seedlings are more effective than chemical remedies. Elimination of crowding is a great help except that infected blocks of seedlings should be transplanted with extreme care that hands and tools are disinfected after each flat is finished. Even so, the natural wilting, shock, and mechanical injuries caused by transplanting invite the invasion of the fungus.

At the first sign of *Botrytis* Blight indoors among flats of seedlings they should be dried off and thereafter watered only when wilting is apparent. If it is at all possible to transfer them outdoors where they will receive a little sun (but not enough to burn the leaves), it will be a great help. Avoid wetting the foliage when watering them. These measures, combined with a fungicide such as Fermate or Phygon, will abate the disease.

Prevention of its appearance is best achieved by strict sanitation, including the destruction of all fallen foliage in the vicinity of young plants at the end of each season. Seed beds, grafting chambers, and frames for rooting cuttings should be ventilated as much as, and as soon as, the welfare of the plants within them will permit. Precautionary sprays of one of the recommended fungicides are worth the effort.

Bud Blast (Pycnostyeanus azaleae)

A fungus which is very common in Great Britain and in the mountain stream valleys of our Southeast is the cause of Rhododendron flower buds turning brown and failing to open. Like so many other parasitic pathogens, it becomes troublesome in our gardens and nurseries only rarely, when shade, humidity, and temperature are peculiarly favorable to its development.

Flower buds become infected with *Pycnostyeanus* through the axils of the bud scales in July and August. The sap vessels of the twigs become clogged so that they cannot transport water. During the winter months the buds turn brown and are later covered with a multitude of fine black bristles about one-sixteenth of an inch long which are the spore-producing bodies responsible for later infections of the next season's buds. The dead, diseased buds cling to the plants for two or three years.

In the British Isles this pathogen appears to be spread by a Leafhopper (*Graphocephala coccinea*) through incisions in the buds made by the females just before the eggs are deposited. Control there has been achieved by a dual program of pruning away infected twigs and hand-picking the dead buds; and by spraying with fungicides such as Bordeaux (2–2–50) every two weeks from June to October. DDT was used as a spray every two or three weeks from August through October to kill the Leafhoppers.

Bees which visit the plants at flowering time are probably responsible for carrying the spores to infect other Rhododendrons.

The newer fungicides such as Fermate,

Phygon and Parzate have proved to be more effective than Bordeaux in controlling most parasitic fungi and they probably would be equally useful for this application. Spraying the plants immediately after flowering is particularly effective because it kills the spore-producing bodies. This fungus appears to have several different spore-forms.

Leaf Gall (Exobasidium vaccinii)

Under conditions particularly favorable to its development Leaf Gall can be an unsightly and superficially alarming springtime disease in which Rhododendron leaves become malformed into thickened, hard, fleshy excrescences. Rarely, the stems and floral parts become similarly deformed. *R. maximum* is particularly susceptible. These galls develop as the new growth progresses and their waxy surfaces, pale or yellowish-green, acquire a white 'bloom' of fungus spores. After the spores have been distributed by wind and insects the galls become brown and dry and fall from the plants.

For light infestations and for small gardens the most simple control is to pick the infected leaves and destroy them. For heavy infections a fungicide such as Fermate or Phygon, with a spreader-sticker, should be applied as a spray when the galls are first noticed and repeated two or three times at intervals of three weeks. This fungus does not invade mature growth. It is another of the rather rare diseases which may not be seen for many years in most Rhododendron plantings and then suddenly cause great concern by its grotesque appearance.

Powdery Mildew (Microsphaera alni)

In late summer and autumn the leaves of Rhododendrons may be attacked by Mildew which covers the foliage with a white coating. The newer organic fungicides are not effective for this parasite but it yields readily to wettable sulphur, 3 tablespoonsful to 1 gallon of spray. (*Note:* Sulphur spray must not be used on Rhododendron foliage when the temperature exceeds 85° F., or else the leaves will be severely burned.)

Witches' Broom (Exobasidium vaccinii-uliginosii)

Another alarming disease caused by a species of *Exobasidium* is Witches' Broom, in which one sector of a Rhododendron may suddenly produce an abnormally profuse branching. The mass of short twigs thus formed bears leaves much smaller than usual and of a sickly, yellowish-white color, coated with a dense white fungus. The branch bearing the brush-like cluster of stems should be pruned away and destroyed. This usually controls the disease. The native West Coast Rhododendron, *R. macrophyllum*, is reported to be especially susceptible to it.

INSECT PESTS

Insect pests, like fungous diseases, are unlikely to attack Rhododendrons which have been planted in an appropriate site with the proper soil. Vigorous plants, lusty in growth, do not seem to attract the pests which sometimes afflict those less fortunately situated. For example, it is the over-exposed plants which suffer from Lace Wing Fly.

Nevertheless, Rhododendrons are among the low maintenance plants in the home garden and most gardeners who enjoy them never have occasion to combat serious invasions of insect enemies. Commercial growers, however, usually find it a worthwhile precaution to apply several preventive sprays each season to forestall the appearance of the pests which are much more likely to be troublesome when large numbers of Rhododendrons are grown in close proximity. Professional nurserymen are referred to page 296 in the section on diseases of Rhododendrons for two all-purpose sprays which have been effective in preventing attacks of both insects and diseases for nursery specialists.

All-Purpose Sprays

All Rhododendron sprays should contain a spreader-sticker to insure thorough coverage and even distribution on the waxy foliage. Spraying should be done in early morning, late afternoon, or on overcast days to avoid the risk of having the foliage disfigured by brilliant sunlight while it is still wet.

Rhododendrons resent oil sprays and occasionally nurserymen have suffered severe losses from them, especially when young plants have been treated. Sulphur can be disastrous in its injury in very hot weather. Used as a dust, it is capable of causing the complete defoliation of Rhododendrons if the temperature goes much above 85° F. before it is washed off.

Red Spider Mites flourish if their natural enemies are destroyed as an incidental result of insecticides which are used to control other pests. For this reason I prefer malathion, which has the dual effect of killing both insects and mites.

The disadvantage of using an insecticide with a persistent residual effect is that it may destroy the several sorts of small spiders which are the enemies of the Rhododendron Midge, and thus be indirectly responsible for an enormous increase in that pest. Guy Nearing, a veteran Rhododendron hybridist and nurseryman, has reported that the Midge destroyed all of the new growth on an entire field of Rhododendrons after DDT was used as a spray for sucking insects. The old nicotine sulphate spray avoids this hazard, but apparently local conditions must be peculiarly favorable to the propagation of the Midge for it to become destructive, because most nurserymen use the newer sprays routinely without any such unwelcome consequences, and malathion in particular has the further advantage of controlling mites.

Lace Wing Fly, *Rhododendron Fly*, *Rhododendron Bug*, *Rhododendron Lace Bug* (Stephanitis rhododendri)

The presence of Lace Wing Fly is usually first noticed as a result of the whitish stippling which appears on the surfaces of Rhododendron leaves. The numerous minute discolored specks are caused by the destruction of chlorophyll by both adults and nymphs feeding on the undersides of the leaves, where will be found a residue of excreta and egg shields which appear as brown, gummy, varnish-like spots. If the foliage is suffering a severe infestation the leaves turn almost white, then brown and ultimately fall from the plant. Rhododendrons so afflicted are seriously impaired in vigor and in flowering capacity.

The Lace Wing Fly gets its name from the transparent, reticulated wings which are a conspicuous feature of its appearance when it is examined under magnification. The adults, an eighth of an inch long, lay their eggs in late summer by inserting them into the undersurfaces of Rhododendron leaves along the midribs and larger veins. The small, spiny nymphs hatch the following spring in May and are full-grown in about a month. There are then usually two additional generations throughout the warm weather months.

This is a sucking insect which is very much more damaging to Rhododendrons growing with excessive exposure to sun. It is seldom a problem when the plants have some shade, though Rhododendrons vary in their susceptibility to attacks of Lace Wing Fly. 'Boule de Neige', a popular hybrid in the eastern United States, is so prone to its disfiguring injury that it is impractical to attempt its culture in full sun. For the home owner, moving Rhododendrons which are regularly infested with Lace Wing Fly to sites with some shade is likely to be a more satisfactory and permanent remedy than combating the pest with sprays. Light attacks on a small portion of a plant may be curbed by picking and burning the affected leaves.

Until recently, the standard control for Lace Wing Fly has been nicotine sulphate, one ounce to five gallons of water, with the addition of three ounces of soap. Now some of the newer insecticides such as 25 per cent lindane (1 pound per 100 gallons of water; 1 tablespoonful to 1 gallon) or 50 per cent malathion emulsifiable solution (1 quart per 100 gallons; 2 teaspoonsful to 1 gallon), with the addition of a spreader-sticker, give better results. The spray should be directed against the undersides of the leaves and it should be applied just after the small nymphs hatch and can be seen, but before they develop into adults and start to lay eggs. This is usually about May 25th in the eastern United States. A second application about two weeks after the first is necessary to insure a thorough kill because none of these sprays affects any eggs which may already have been laid in the leaf tissues. The flies always move from the old to the new foliage to lay their eggs. Thus, if the new growth can be kept free of them for two years this insect can be practically eradicated from a Rhododendron plantation.

Midge (Giardomyia rhododendri)

Midges are first detected on Rhododendrons when the edges and the tips of the new leaves are densely spotted red or sometimes brown along their margins. The foliage is distorted in this fashion by the whitish larvae about one-twentieth of an inch long which feed beneath the edges of the leaves and are then protected when the margins roll under. In severe infestations, the new growth does not develop at all because the larvae destroy the leaves faster than they can unfurl from the buds. It is more common to see the new growth stunted and deformed. The growing tips of the leaves often are curled downward or the leaves are contorted because injury by the larvae prevents them from developing properly.

The insect passes the winter in the pupa stage and the yellowish adult flies, about one-twentieth of an inch long, appear as the buds unfurl and start into growth. Eggs are laid and soon hatch into maggots which are protected from the very beginning by the deep folds of the developing foliage, and later in the tunnels formed by the rolled leaf edges. Textbooks blandly advise the use of a contact insecticide at this stage but the fact is that it is impossible to reach the larvae with either spray or dust and in any case they are extremely hard to kill. Warren Baldsiefen, a New Jersey nurseryman, has completely eliminated the Midge from his plantings by picking and burning all new growth which showed evidence of the pest. At the end of the first year control was good. In the second year very little infestation was seen but such stems as did bear foliage showing Midge injury were once again destroyed and no further damage by this insect has since been found. Since hand-picking of infected growth has proved a practical and successful control on a commercial scale, this method is recommended to home gardeners and professional nurserymen alike.

Alternatively, a spray which kills the adult Midges has been reported successful by Dr C. C. Hamilton of the New Jersey Agricultural Experiment Station. DDT, applied at the rate of 1 quart of the 25 per cent emulsion to 100 gallons of water (2 teaspoonsful to 1 gallon), sprayed on the undersurfaces of the leaves at intervals of ten days to two weeks while the plants were in active growth gave good control. For a spray program to be successful it is essential that the minute adult flies be killed as they emerge at the time the new growth starts in the spring. The DDT, applied about every ten days, also kills the eggs. Sometimes the adults can be found on Rhododendron foliage as late as August infesting the second flush of new growth on the plants. The key to successful control by spraying lies in killing the adult flies and the eggs before the larvae follow to perpetuate the infestation.

Thrips (Thrips tabaci; Heliothrips haemorrhoidalis)

Damage by Thrips is apparent in a silver-white speckled discoloration of the upper leaf surfaces which resembles the injury caused by Lace Wing Fly, but is finer and more clearly defined in irregular diffuse blotches, not usually evenly distributed over the leaves. The leaf undersurfaces provide a more certain diagnosis. They present a glistening silvery appearance marked by minute black spots of excrement, whereas the Lace Wing Fly leaves a brownish residue of innumerable glossy, sticky spots.

Thrips are narrow, flat-bodied, black-winged insects about one-twentieth of an inch long which pass the winter in both adult and egg stages. In the spring they lay their eggs in the leaf tissues and the minute, colorless nymphs hatch in about a week to start feeding in colonies on the undersides of Rhododendron leaves. They require only about a month to mature and then reproduce another generation, so the population of this pest can be built up very rapidly under favorable conditions. The foliage discoloration is caused when the insects destroy the surface cells by rasping away the tissues to feed on the juices. Attacks are much more severe under hot dry conditions. They may cause serious injury and even defoliation, particularly when the plants are grown close together.

Rhododendrons seem to vary in their attraction to Thrips. Seedlings of *R. ponticum* are favored hosts and all greenhouse Rhododendrons are more likely to be attacked than are those grown outdoors. Under glass the pest is found on both upper and lower leaf surfaces whereas in the garden it is usually observed only on the undersurfaces.

Forty per cent nicotine sulphate has been the standard contact insecticide in the past to control Thrips, and a few growers still prefer it, 1 ounce to 5 gallons of water with the addition of 3 ounces of soap. Twenty-five per cent lindane powder (1 pound to 100 gallons of water; 1 tablespoonful to 1 gallon); or 50 per cent malathion emulsion (1 quart to 100 gallons of water; 2 teaspoonsful to 1 gallon), with the addition of a spreader-sticker, have found greater favor in recent years. The spray should be applied to the undersides of the foliage and it should be repeated a second time a week later.

Flower Thrips (Frankliniella tritici)

These insects are usually responsible for the premature wilting of flowers and a heavy infestation may completely destroy the spring display. Flower Thrips rasp the tender epidermal layers of the blossoms to obtain the plant juices which they then suck into their bodies. The corollas, deprived of sustenance, begin to collapse shortly after they open, or the flowers may not open at all if a large number of Thrips have penetrated into the developing buds.

Flower Thrips have been known as a pest of wild Rhododendrons in the Blue Ridge Mountains for many years. Their most recent appearance on these plants in cultivation was reported by nurseries along Lake Erie in 1957 and by 1959 they had become a serious problem.

This pest may appear suddenly, from no apparent source. The adults can be borne hundreds of miles by wind currents at high altitudes and then descend in large numbers to create a heavy infestation. Once established in Rhododendron plantings the population of Thrips seems to increase rapidly from one year to the next until the plants are virtually worthless in their floral display, the flowers lasting only a few hours or at best a couple of days. The insects are not easy to control because they often fly out of a cultivated area into surrounding grasslands and then return to resume their injurious feeding on ornamental plants. These are the same Thrips which infest Roses.

Eggs are laid in slits on the surface of Rhododendrons. The young are pale yellow and may be found by opening up infested buds and separating the petals. They mature quickly into the small black insects, $\frac{1}{16}$ inch long, which are more easily seen moving rapidly to seek shelter if an open wilted flower is torn quickly to reveal the base.

Control is dependent on *early* measures, taken before the blossoms develop to the point where the Flower Thrips can find protection from insecticides in the folds and fissures of unfolding buds. As the buds begin to swell, and before the unopened florets emerge, the Rhododendrons should be sprayed or dusted with malathion or DDT, repeated at intervals of five days until the plants are in bloom. Most nurseries use 1 pound of 50 per cent wettable DDT powder to 100 gallons of water (1 tablespoonful to 1 gallon) as a spray.

Black Vine Weevil, Taxus Weevil (Brachyrhinus sulcatus); *Strawberry Weevil* (Brachyrhinus ovatus); *Clay Colored Weevil* (Brachyrhinus singularis)

The Black Vine Weevil, or Taxus Weevil, is typical of the snout beetles which are enemies of Rhododendrons, and apparently it is the most widespread and destructive of these pests.

The presence of Weevils among Rhododendrons is usually first detected when the leaves are disfigured by irregular or often semicircular notches chewed in their edges by the adults. The Asiatic Beetle may occasionally cause similar damage but generally this type of injury to the foliage is distinctive with Weevils, and the semicircular holes cut from the leaf margins may be so close together as to give the appearance of a serrated edge. Rarely, the entire leaf is devoured with the exception of the midrib and large veins. Sometimes a narrow section of bark encircling new growth will be consumed late in the season so that the twig is girdled and dies during the following winter.

Damage to the foliage by the adult Weevils is not often severe but injury to the roots by their larvae can be ruinous. The first such damage is noticed as an unhealthy, starved condition of the plants. The foliage assumes an Olive-green cast as the unseen destruction of fine, water-absorbing roots proceeds. As the larvae increase in numbers and voracity they devour the bark of the larger roots and may even burrow inside them. The increasing distress of the plants causes them to shed their leaves in an effort to adjust transpiration to the restricted amount of water that can be absorbed through the reduced root system.

Rhododendrons which wilt during dry weather much more conspicuously than do others planted in the vicinity may be suspected of suffering from the loss of fine roots which absorb water, and Weevil larvae are usually responsible. At a more advanced stage of injury the plants appear to be suffering from acute drouth even during wet weather. Finally, the bark is eaten away from the crowns, the main stems are girdled, and the afflicted Rhododendrons wilt and die.

The adult beetles of the Black Vine Weevil are three-eighths of an inch long, glistening black in color, with furrows running the length of the wing covers and golden hairs interspersed over them. They cannot fly and they are nocturnal in their feeding. In clear weather they are hidden during the daytime in debris on the ground, but frequently they can be seen very early in the morning or on cloudy overcast days eating away the rounded holes along the leaf margins. When they are disturbed they feign death by drawing up their legs and falling to the ground.

The adults emerge in June and the first part of July over a period of about a month. Throughout July and August they lay white eggs on the foliage of Rhododendrons or in the ground beneath their branches. The eggs hatch in ten days to three weeks and the larvae then burrow into the ground and start to feed on the fine roots. By autumn they are half grown, about a quarter of an inch long, legless, dirty white in color and with a brownish head. The grubs hibernate over winter 6 to 14 inches underground and the next spring the serious injury is caused as they work their way toward the surface, devouring small roots and feeding on the bark of larger roots, the crowns, and even on the trunks. Reaching their full development of about half an inch, they begin to pupate late in May or the first part of June. Two to three weeks later the adults emerge to start the cycle once again. The parent beetles may live on through most of another season, going into hibernation in September. The few which survive over winter to emerge in May lay about six times more eggs than do the younger generation. No males of this beetle have ever been found. Reproduction is apparently entirely parthenogenetic.

Weevils attack many plants beside Rhododendrons, notably Yews, Hemlocks, and other needle evergreens; Blackberries, Raspberries, and Cranberries; Euonymus, Hydrangeas, Kalmias, Spiraeas, and Roses. Their depredations on the Pacific Coast have been a major problem for many years and few plantings of Rhododendrons there do not show signs of Weevil injury, possibly because the benign climate allows a longer feeding period for the larvae in the autumn. In the eastern United States Weevils have been especially injurious to Yews, but Rhododendrons appear to be subject to increasing attacks, and this insect must now be considered a major pest of Rhododendrons as well.

There are two methods of control, neither of them entirely satisfactory: the adult beetles can be attacked after they emerge and start their feeding on the leaf edges; or the larvae can be poisoned in the soil.

The adult Weevils are hidden in the ground litter during the daytime and they usually do not feed very heavily on the leaves at night, hence the difficulty of complete control by a foliage spray. However, since they emerge from the soil at least three weeks (and sometimes as much as six weeks) before they start to lay eggs, the spray can be delayed until practically all of the Weevils have reached the adult beetle stage. It is best to look for the

Weevils beneath clods and debris under the plants and make sure that they have emerged from the pupae before applying a spray. It is wasted effort to spray before the third week in June.

Lead arsenate has been the standard stomach poison spray for Weevils, but it was never effective. Twenty-five per cent dieldrin wettable powder (2 pounds to 100 gallons of water for commercial use; too hazardous for the home garden) or 45 per cent chlordane emulsion ($1\frac{1}{2}$ pints per 100 gallons of water; $1\frac{1}{2}$ teaspoonsful per gallon), with the addition of a spreader-sticker, applied at the rate of 500 gallons of the spray per acre, provides a good kill of the beetles and leaves a residual soil deposit which is effective against the newly emerging adults the next spring. On a smaller scale, calculate the amount to be received by each specimen on the basis of 1 pint of spray per 10 square feet of area occupied by the plant. The whole specimen should be sprayed, especially the branches close to the ground and the center of the plant. The remainder is used to treat the soil surface beneath the plant.

An alternative control for the adult beetles is to provide poisoned baits for them. A proprietary combination of apple pulp and sodium fluosilicate is sold under the trade name of 'Go-West' and is widely used. It is applied to the soil beneath the plants in the evening. Fresh baits should be supplied every week or ten days from the latter part of June until early August. In tests by Dr F. F. Smith, poison bran baits gave 83 per cent control and poison apple baits 57 per cent control.

Various degrees of success have been reported from applications of insecticides to the soil as a means of killing the larvae. The New York State College of Agriculture has issued a flat statement that soil treatments will not kill Black Vine Weevil grubs. On the other hand some nurserymen have had fair results from lead arsenate applied in powder form at the rate of 2 pounds per 100 square feet.

The cumulative effect of repeated soil treatments with lead arsenate or of excessive applications is extremely unfavorable to the growth of Rhododendron roots and newly planted specimens will refuse to extend their root systems into soil containing appreciable concentrations of this material.

The newer insecticides are likely to be more effective and are also available as dusts which can be applied to the soil surface for subsequent dispersion by leaching and diffusion. Five per cent chlordane dust applied at the rate of 200 pounds per acre ($4\frac{1}{2}$ pounds per 1,000 square feet) is a standard treatment for grubs and it has been reported to give good control of adult Weevils. It is as effective as any dust applied directly to the soil in an effort to poison the larvae.

In regions where the Weevils are prevalent, it is a wise precaution to mix a teaspoonful of 5 per cent chlordane dust with the soil at the bottom of the hole when planting a small Rhododendron. A tablespoonful of the dust can be used for larger plants.

A fungus attacks the margins of Rhododendron leaves, rapidly causing the death of small semicircular areas which go unnoticed until they fall away, leaving a notched outline which closely matches the injury caused by Weevils. If the recommended insecticides mysteriously fail to control this sort of foliage disfigurement, a spray of captan fungicide may be all that is needed.

Japanese Beetle (Popillia japonica); *Asiatic Garden Beetle, Brown Garden Beetle* (Autoserica castanea); *Oriental Beetle* (Phyllopertha orientalis)

The various Asian Beetles listed above are injurious to Rhododendrons in much the same way as are the Weevils, disfiguring the foliage in the adult stage and devouring the roots in the larval stage. Irregular holes are eaten in the young leaves or the Japanese Beetles may consume them entirely, leaving a skeleton of the midribs and main veins. Nurserymen often suffer considerable damage to field stock because the Japanese Beetles travel together in large numbers and are capable of quickly destroying a great deal of new growth.

The Japanese Beetle is $\frac{3}{8}$ inch long, iridescent green with bronze wings, and is active during the day. The Brown Garden Beetle, velvety chestnut-brown in color, emerges from ground litter only at night. The grubs of these beetles feed on Rhododendron roots, reducing their capacity to absorb water, and in severe infestations the crowns and main stems are girdled when the bark is eaten away below the soil level so that the foliage becomes yellow and the plants wilt and die.

Foliage sprays applied during the flight period from late June to August control the adult beetles. Two pounds of 50 per cent wettable DDT powder to 100 gallons of water (2 tablespoonsful per gallon); or 1 quart of 50 per cent malathion emulsion to 100 gallons of water (2 teaspoonsful per gallon), give good control.

The grubs can be killed in the soil by the application of 200 pounds of 5 per cent chlordane dust per acre (4½ pounds per 1,000 square feet) or by a spray of 2 pounds of 25 per cent dieldrin wettable powder per 100 gallons of water, applied at the rate of 500 gallons to the acre. Dieldrin is too hazardous to children and pets to be used in the home garden. Forty-five per cent chlordane emulsion, 1½ teaspoonsful to a gallon of water, can be sprayed on the soil at the rate of 1 pint per 10 square feet of area to be grub-proofed, if a liquid soil treatment is preferred.

Cranberry Root Worm (Rhabdopterus picipes)

The appearance in Rhododendron leaves of distinctive crescent-shaped or sharply angular holes signals the nocturnal activity of the Cranberry Root Worm. No other pest feeds in a manner which causes these characteristic holes in the shape of a thin crescent.

The adult is a brown, oval beetle about a quarter of an inch long which hides in the litter beneath Rhododendrons and comes out to feed only at night or on dark overcast days. It is not often destructive to a serious extent but the salability of nursery stock is impaired when the foliage is disfigured, and in any event the leaves are retained for several years on many sorts of Rhododendrons, so the preservation of their foliage in good condition is important to a good appearance in the home garden.

The Cranberry Root Worm can be controlled with lead arsenate spray (4 pounds to 100 gallons of water; ½ ounce to 1 gallon), for those who prefer the old remedy which has been in use for many years. Two pounds of 50 per cent wettable DDT powder to 100 gallons of water (2 tablespoonsful per gallon); or 1 quart of 50 per cent malathion emulsion to 100 gallons of water (2 teaspoonsful per gallon) are more effective. The spray should be used as needed for the six-week period between the middle of June and August 1st. Three or four applications may be needed for heavy infestations.

Rhododendron White Fly (Dialeurodes chittendeni); *Mulberry White Fly* (Tetraleurodes mori)

The White Fly causes a yellowish mottling of Rhododendron leaves and the edges curl on some sorts. The larvae secrete honeydew which falls to the foliage below the infested leaves and provides nourishment for a black, sooty mold. As the mold extends over the leaves the black coating prevents the production of carbohydrates in them and the plant is deprived of their natural function. The combination of injury from the insects feeding on the plant juices and the black mold may impair growth and flowering of Rhododendrons and in any event their ornamental value is reduced for the several years that the sooty covering disfigures the leaves.

The Rhododendron White Fly has been in the United States for only about twenty years. The adult is the shape of a flattened oval, about ⅛ inch long, winged, white, and has an unhealthy, pallid appearance under magnification. It inhabits the undersides of Rhododendron leaves but it does not appear to infest the sorts which have either scales or hairs on the leaf undersurfaces, and heavy, tough leaves are usually avoided.

Eggs are laid on the undersides of new foliage growth during May, June and July. The larvae do not develop rapidly enough or in sufficient numbers to cause any appreciable damage their first year and it is not until the following spring that the foliage is visibly injured by them. Both the nymphs and larvae produce the mottling of the leaves by the rapid consumption of plant juices as they complete their development to the adult fly stage. There is only one brood a year.

This pest can be easily killed in the adult stage while the insects are flying about. Forty per cent nicotine sulphate, 1 ounce to 5 gallons of water with the addition of 3 ounces of soap, has been an effective treatment. This, however, does not kill the eggs and nymphs. Malathion plus DDT offers a remedy of exceptional effectiveness. Four pounds of 25 per cent malathion wettable powder plus 2 pounds of 50 per cent DDT wettable powder to 100 gallons of water (4 tablespoonsful of the malathion and 2 tablespoonsful of the DDT to the gallon), with the addition of a spreader-sticker, applied as a spray to the undersides of the leaves in early May, probably gives the most complete control of any treatment now available.

Red Spider, Two-Spotted Mite (Tetranychus bimaculatus)

Spider Mites disfigure Rhododendron foliage by causing a brownish-gray or occasionally whitish stippled discoloration of the surfaces, the result of the plant juices being sucked out by Mites feeding on the undersides. As the population of this pest builds up, the diffused speckled discoloration of the foliage tends to form into irregular blotches and miniature webs appear beneath the leaves. The leaves turn brown with more extensive injury and fall to the ground and the vigor of the plants is seriously impaired. In exceptionally hot dry weather Mites may become a problem on Rhododendrons growing close together in exposed nursery fields. Ordinarily this pest, which is not a true insect, is troublesome only on Rhododendrons grown in greenhouses.

Spider Mites are usually brick-red, about $\frac{1}{32}$ inch long, and their presence can most easily be detected by drawing a leaf between thumb and forefinger. The minute crushed Mites will then appear as red streaks on the skin. They pass the cold weather in the egg stage and start to hatch early the next growing season. Under favorable dry weather conditions their increase in numbers is so rapid that they can do extensive injury before the unwary grower is aware of their unseen activity. These pests continue to multiply right on through the warm weather months into the fall unless they are checked by spraying or dusting.

Malathion is the preferred treatment for Red Spider Mites because it controls many other pests at the same time. Four pounds of 25 per cent malathion wettable powder or 1 quart of 50 per cent malathion emulsion to 100 gallons of water (2 tablespoonsful of the powder or 2 teaspoonsful of the emulsion to the gallon), with the addition of a spreader-sticker, should be applied as an early preventive spray to the undersides of the leaves before the plants come into flower, or as a control up to early June when the presence of Red Spider Mites is first detected. Later in the season, or to combat heavy infestations, Ovotran, 2 pounds of 50 per cent wettable powder to 100 gallons of water (2 tablespoonsful to the gallon), is a miticide of extraordinary effectiveness because it kills the eggs and has a residual activity. It is a more potent weapon, especially if only one spray application is to be made, but it may be somewhat risky to use it too early in the season because it will injure the tender young foliage of some evergreens under certain conditions.

Any spray for Red Spider Mites should be applied with good force to penetrate the miniature webs which shield the pests on the undersides of the leaves.

Garden Centipede (Scutigerella immaculata)

An irregular, scattered pattern of Rhododendrons in the nursery which develop yellow foliage and weak or stunted growth may be evidence of attack by the Garden Centipede, a pest which feeds on their roots and so reduces their ability to absorb water and nutrients that the plants become chlorotic and are unable to make normal growth. In severe infestations the plants may be killed, and the irregular pattern in the field of affected specimens disappears as the Centipede spreads to attack all of the Rhododendrons so that they appear to suffer from malnutrition.

This is a very serious enemy of Rhododendrons which has caused extensive losses to nurserymen in recent years. Its depredations are becoming more widespread. A prominent

New Jersey grower estimates that it has caused greater damage to field stock, without being identified as the agent, than any other pest in the state.

The Centipede is seldom observed because it is extremely agile and the largest adults are only $\frac{1}{4}$ inch long. Most of them are much smaller and they quickly seek cover between soil particles when they are exposed to light. The best method of detecting their presence is to dig a plant suspected of harboring them and dip the roots in a bucket containing about 3 inches of water. By agitating the soil ball some of the earth is washed from the roots and the Centipedes are dislodged with it. In a short time they float to the surface as minute white specks which at first are motionless but after a few moments a close examination will show them beginning to move vigorously.

Rhododendrons are usually provided with a loose, friable soil rich in humus, and the fields in which they are growing are especially likely to become infested by Centipedes because such a soil provides the crevices in which these pests can move about. It is one of their peculiarities that they are unable to tunnel their own way through the earth. They must use burrows made by earthworms and passageways left by decayed roots, or travel in the natural fissures of the soil.

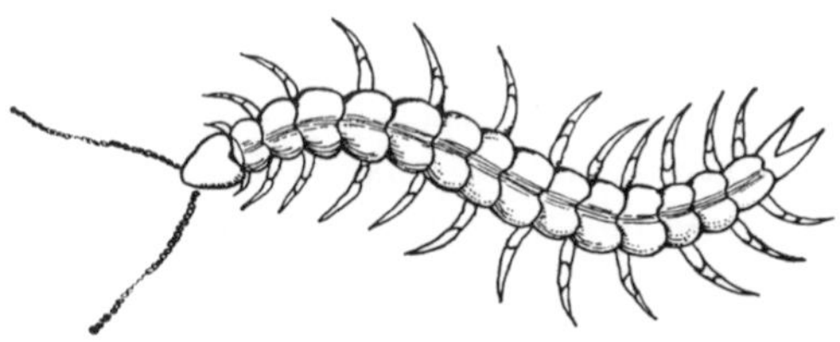

Garden Centipedes lay their eggs in the subsoil, which is ordinarily undisturbed in cultivation, and the young hatch in one to three weeks. At emergence they have six pairs of legs, eleven scuta and six antennal segments. Throughout their life span of more than four years they are thought to molt more than fifty times and reach a maximum length of a $\frac{1}{4}$ inch, but they are sexually mature after the seventh molt. The number of segments varies greatly, due to their ability to form additional ones and to regenerate replacements for those lost by injury. The white adults have twelve pairs of legs and move very quickly. In addition to devouring the fine roots which feed the plants, these pests also eat cavities into the larger roots and even into the crowns of Rhododendrons. Older plants are better able to withstand the ravages of Centipedes, and Rhododendrons which are 4 feet or more in diameter may be heavily infested without showing visible injury, probably because the root systems of larger plants are less confined and therefore less accessible; and possibly also because the growth is more rapid and extensive so that new roots are formed faster than the Centipedes devour them.

This pest can be controlled with 25 per cent wettable lindane powder, applied either as a spray to the soil ($3\frac{1}{4}$ pounds to 100 gallons of water, 500 gallons to the acre; 3 tablespoonsful to the gallon, 12 gallons to 1,000 square feet) or as a dust at the rate of 16 pounds per acre, mixed with fertilizer or other carrier. If the area to be treated is not already planted the insecticide should be disked into the upper 4 or 6 inches of soil as soon as practicable after application. If established plantings are to be treated the lindane should be thoroughly watered in.

Presumably dieldrin (for commercial use only) and chlordane, which are so effective for other pests in the soil, would also control the Garden Centipede in higher concentrations, but lindane is the only organic insecticide which I know to have given good results on soil growing Rhododendrons without injury to them. The treatment is effective for one and a half to two years.

Fumigants are not very satisfactory since they evaporate rapidly and the soil then soon becomes reinfested. An insecticide with a residual action is much more effective.

Rhododendron Borer, Clear Wing (Sesia rhododendri)

When large branches or an entire Rhododendron wilts and dies abruptly in late summer, the Rhododendron Borer is usually responsible. The wilting is often preceded by a yellowing of the foliage and the spring growth on the affected limb is short and stubby. Examination of the base of the plant will show a close pattern of many cavities eaten into the bark. Traces of fine sawdust are the borings which are pushed out as the larvae tunnel into the sapwood just beneath the bark, thus interrupting the supply of water and nutrients to the affected branches. As they mature the larvae work deeper into the main limbs, boring innumerable intricate galleries which riddle the bark with small holes where they reach the surface.

The adult is a moth with transparent wings which appears in late May or early June and lays its eggs in the Rhododendron trunks, often in wounds or branch crotches, at the soil level or within about a foot of it. By autumn the larvae are about $\frac{3}{4}$ inch to 1 inch long, white with brown heads, and they will have produced by then the typical pitted appearance of the stems near the bases of the plants. I have never seen this pest at work anywhere but in the basal portions of large branches, but entomologists say that the adult moths also lay their eggs on the new growth with resulting injury by the larvae to small twigs. I think this must be rare.

Infested branches should be pruned out and burned in the fall. The adult moths can best be killed when they are laying their eggs in the latter part of June, by spraying the stems just before that time within a couple of feet of the ground level with DDT (4 pounds of 50 per cent wettable powder per 100 gallons of water; 4 tablespoonsful per gallon). Heavy infestations should be sprayed in mid-June and again the first week of July. The DDT does not destroy the larvae in the tunnel, but after they emerge as moths the residual action prevents further infestations. Dead bark should be removed with a knife and heavily infested areas exposed, with the edges trimmed back evenly to living tissue, before spraying. A few larvae in a plant can be killed by injecting nicotine paste into the tunnels or by crushing them with a wire or small twig inserted into the burrows.

This is an important, and, in many sections of the country, the only serious enemy of mature Rhododendron specimens. The occurrence of the pest seems to be associated with the natural reduction in vigor which is characteristic of older plants. It kills them or destroys their symmetry just as they attain the imposing proportions which produce the zenith of beauty in flower and foliage.

Owners of large specimens should be alert for the symptoms of Rhododendron Borer. It is easily detected and its injury is conspicuous in the growth and foliage of afflicted limbs. Control is simple in the early stages of attack, but a season's delay can mean the disfiguring loss of a main branch and the spread of the pest to other limbs. Many magnificent old Rhododendrons have been lost because their owners neglected the initial signs of distress caused by injury from this borer.

Rhododendron Moth (Eucordylea huntella)

The Rhododendron Moth, so far confined to the West Coast, is responsible for damage to leaves and stems, but its most conspicuous injury is apparent during the blooming season when many buds on an infested plant will fail to open.

The salt-and-pepper-colored adult moth lays its eggs on the underside of a leaf or at the base of a flower bud. After they hatch the larvae tunnel into the leaves, the stems and the flower buds, preventing them from developing properly. When a plant blooms partially but some of its buds do not open, the larvae, about $\frac{7}{8}$ inch long, will be found in the undeveloped buds if this pest is responsible. They will be pink if they have been feeding on immature red flowers, or tan if they have been boring through vegetative tissues.

First reported as attacking Azaleas in California, the Rhododendron Moth has spread northward and it now appears as an enemy of evergreen Rhododendrons, especially the native *R. macrophyllum*. It is not related to the Rhododendron Borer of the East.

The Entomology Department of Oregon State College Extension Service recommends a 50 per cent wettable methoxychlor spray, applied to the leaf undersurfaces between the end of June and the middle of July, as a satisfactory control.

Stem Borer (Oberea myops)

When the Stem Borer is neglected, it is capable of causing the sudden yellowing, wilting, and death of large branches or of an entire Rhododendron in the late summer. It is only at the end of its second year that it causes such extensive destruction, however, and its depredations are usually noticed at an early stage when a twig wilts conspicuously. Examination shows one or more irregular small brown lesions on the green stems of the current year's growth, below the terminal clusters of leaves, where the adult beetle has laid the egg which hatches into the burrowing larva. If the wilted twig is cut off below this point and burned, no further harm will result. Most Rhododendron growers, as a matter of convenience, slit open the stem and kill the larva when it is located by following the tunnel in the center of the twig to its terminus near the tip. Despite published descriptions to the contrary, the larvae nearly always travel toward the tips of the twigs during their first summer. Only rarely is it necessary to prune below the green wood of current growth to locate the grub. Furthermore, I have never known the adult beetles to lay their eggs in the stem tips, as described in published accounts of this pest. In my experience they invariably lay their eggs toward the base of the new green stems formed by growth of the current year.

In any case, if the borer is neglected it does start tunneling downward through the larger branches the second summer, making holes along its course through which coarse sawdust is extruded. As it approaches the base of the plant the main trunk through which it burrows is all but severed a few inches above ground level. The plant above it then wilts and dies in the course of late summer and it may be snapped off by the wind. In the meantime, the full-grown, yellow larva, now a little more than half an inch long, will have traveled down to the base of the trunk below ground level, where it passes the winter.

This pest could no doubt be controlled by spraying with DDT during June and early July, when the adult beetles are active, but its occurrence is scattered and sporadic, its presence is easily detected at an innocuous stage by the wilted twigs, and the most convenient control is to destroy the larvae in them. A major branch can be saved by injecting nicotine paste into the tunnel. If an attack goes unnoticed and the base of a plant is invaded, it should be pulled and burned.

Pitted Ambrosia Beetle (Corthylus punctatissimus)

Plants which become chlorotic, wilt and die abruptly are occasionally found to harbor the Pitted Ambrosia Beetle which produces numerous dark burrows, crowded close together, in Rhododendron stems close to the ground. Trunks which are severely infested may be honeycombed with the level galleries containing the blackish beetles, about $\frac{1}{8}$ inch long, and their small white larvae. This pest so weakens the main stems that they readily break off in the sector where the tunnels are most numerous.

In trunks which are not too seriously invaded, the beetles and larvae can be killed by injecting a nicotine paste into their burrows. Presumably a spray made with 4 pounds of 50 per cent wettable DDT powder to 100 gallons of water (4 tablespoonsful to the gallon), such as has been found effective for other borers, should kill the insects which can be reached directly or by residual effect on the areas over which they travel. Heavily infested plants should be pulled and burned. A plant riddled by these borers may fall prey to a fungus invasion in its weakened condition but its bark is worse than its Blight. Dr C. C. Hamilton of the New Jersey Agricultural Experiment Station suggests that the most effective control results from wrapping the affected sectors of the trunks with burlap which is then sprayed with DDT. The toxic residue kills the beetles as they emerge later.

Oleander Scale, Ivy Scale (Aspidiotus hederae, Aspidiotus pseudosapinosus; Pulvinaria ericicola; Eriococcus azaleae)

A scattered yellow or reddish spotting of the foliage, coarser than the stippling caused by the Lace Wing Fly and Thrips, is usually a symptom that one of the Scales which prey on Rhododendrons is at work on the leaves and twigs. If the infestation becomes severe the vigor of the plant is noticeably reduced.

The leaf discoloration is caused by injury which the insect inflicts as it adheres to the under-surface.

Dormant oil sprays may damage Rhododendrons but Scales can be controlled very well by spraying after the young hatch and the immature crawlers, without their protective shells, are vulnerable to contact insecticides. For the two *Aspidiotus* species, which are hard Scales dull gray in color and all but impossible to distinguish without a microscope, the best time to spray in the Northeast is about June 10th. *Pulvinaria* and *Eriococcus*, both soft Scales, can best be controlled by spraying about July 15th. The former is easily recognized by the cottony oversac which it produces, and the latter is distinguished by the structure resembling a cocoon which forms around the female.

Forty per cent nicotine sulphate, 1 quart to 100 gallons of water, plus 4 pounds of soap (2 teaspoonsful to the gallon plus 3 ounces of soap) is effective when applied in a series of three treatments, each one week apart. Only two treatments a month apart are needed if a combination spray of 4 pounds of 25 per cent malathion wettable powder plus 2 pounds of 50 per cent DDT wettable powder to 100 gallons of water (4 tablespoonsful of the malathion and 2 tablespoonsful of the DDT to the gallon), with the addition of a spreader-sticker, is used.

Leaf Hopper (Graphocephala coccinea)

I have never observed any direct, visible damage caused by the Leaf Hopper, a bright green insect about a quarter of an inch long which is brilliantly striped with light blue and vermilion. It feeds by piercing the leaves and sucking out the plant juices, but it does not disfigure the foliage nor does it have any apparent effect on plant vigor.

The injury caused by the Leaf Hopper is indirect. It makes microscopic perforations in the leaves which may afford points of entry for fungus diseases. Tiny punctures are also made in the outer scales of the floral buds when the eggs are laid and these incisions have been associated with Bud Blast, which is caused by an invasion of the fungus, *Pycnostyeanus azaleae*.

The adult Leaf Hoppers appear in late July and August and start to feed at the veins of old and new leaves. Some two or three weeks later the eggs are laid by insertion in the flower-bud scales and they hatch in May of the following year. The yellowish-green nymphs then suck the sap from the undersides of the leaves as they develop through four immature stages until the adults once again appear to start breeding the next generation.

Although it is usually recommended, lindane does not control Leaf Hoppers effectively. Fifty per cent malathion emulsion, 1 quart to 100 gallons of water (2 teaspoonsful to the gallon) with the addition of a spreader-sticker, is efficient and it controls Lace Wing Fly, Mites, and several other pests at the same time. The adult Leaf Hoppers are found on the upper surfaces of the leaves at mating time in early to mid-August, but both upper- and undersides should be sprayed every two weeks from August 1st until the end of the flight period in October.

Giant Hornet (Vespa crabro germana)

When the bark is eaten away from the stems of new growth, the Giant Hornet is often responsible. Some of the twigs may suddenly die from having been girdled. The bark, which may be stripped away for 1 inch or more, or perhaps removed in a pattern of parallel vertical bands, is used by the insects to make their familiar gray paper-like nests which are seen suspended in hollow trees and from the eaves of outbuildings.

In some cases the damage may be sufficient to justify locating the nest and spraying or dusting it with DDT. The insects are then destroyed as they pick up the toxic residue upon entering and leaving the nest. Sometimes the hornets live in ground burrows which can be fumigated by placing calcium cyanide or carbon disulphite in the tunnel entrance. DDT, applied to the plants at the rate of 4 quarts of the 25 per cent emulsion to 100 gallons of water (8 teaspoonsful to the gallon) will kill the hornets as they feed, but I have never known such heroic measures to be necessary.

Other Leaf-Eating Insects

Various caterpillars, crickets, and katydids devour Rhododendron leaves but they seldom cause damage of any consequence except for very young plants and those in propagating frames where the reduction in the leaf area is sufficient to affect their welfare. Two pounds of 50 per cent wettable DDT powder to 100 gallons of water (2 tablespoonsful per gallon); or 1 quart of 50 per cent malathion emulsion to 100 gallons of water (2 teaspoonsful per gallon) give good control.

CHAPTER IX

The Propagation of Rhododendrons

THE propagation of Rhododendrons has been a subject of controversy for a great many years. The local climate, the facilities available, the skill of the propagator, and the sorts which are grown vary so much throughout the regions where Rhododendrons are cultivated that almost every nurseryman has evolved from experience methods which are successful in varying degree for the conditions which prevail.

Propagators generally have failed to take advantage of the fruits of laboratory research in the production of Rhododendrons. There has been a heavy reliance on traditional methods which have been handed down from European growers. There has been an equal reluctance to recognize the physical principles involved in propagation and to apply them to the commercial production of Rhododendrons in a manner which scientific investigation has demonstrated to be successful. Home gardeners, too, have shown little inclination to benefit from the research which has been done in this field.

SUPERIORITY OF OWN-ROOT PLANTS

It is almost universally agreed among specialists that Rhododendrons on their own roots are superior to grafted plants. There is equal agreement that own-root propagation is in the interest of the nurseryman, who is all too familiar with the ruinous losses of young grafts in the greenhouse to the lethal epidemics of Rhododendron Wilt. Furthermore, efficiency strongly favors the production of plants from rooted cuttings. It requires two years to raise an understock and an additional two years after grafting to grow a Rhododendron to the minimum size in popular demand by the trade. Plants on their own roots are ready for sale in two years of growth and a few vigorous sorts will even yield well-branched 12- to 15-inch plants in one year, with intensive cultivation.

Despite all this the great majority of Rhododendrons sold are grafted plants. But the situation is changing slowly as nursery specialists observe the successful production of Rhododendrons from rooted cuttings on a commercial scale by several pioneering growers who have profited greatly by their willingness to abandon the obsolete and adopt the modern methods devised in the laboratory and proven in practice.

I have had a special interest in the propagation of Rhododendrons and many experiments have been undertaken at my hybridizing grounds in an effort to determine the most efficient method of attaining the highest percentage of successfully rooted cuttings. Rooting media, hormones, timing and many other factors have been studied over a period of years, particularly as they apply to the "cold" method of rooting cuttings in outdoor frames without a greenhouse. The results have steadily improved until even the Rhododendrons most difficult to propagate now consistently root about 94 per cent successfully.

Propagation of Rhododendrons

VARIETY OF METHODS NEEDED

When it is considered that some Rhododendrons have leaves 3 feet long and 1 foot broad, and others are so small as to resemble the needles of a Hemlock; that some species start into growth in February in the eternally dripping atmosphere at the lower elevations of their Asian homeland, whereas others are not even freed from the snow cover until June in bleak, high mountain passes, it is apparent that there will inevitably be a tremendous difference in the conditions which foster their successful propagation.

As a very rough guide, with exceptions a little too numerous to be comfortable, it might be said that in rooting cuttings, the larger the leaves on the plants to be propagated, the earlier and the softer the cuttings should be taken and the more warmth they should have. Thus the sorts with very large foliage would be propagated with bottom heat in moist, closed conditions beginning about the end of June, whereas firm, fully matured cuttings, which may even be two years old, are usually taken from the dwarf alpines with tiny leaves late in the autumn and are rooted under rather airy conditions without heat. The Rhododendrons of intermediate character are propagated between these extremes, the time depending on whether they most resemble the lush, exotic Grande clan or the austere little Lapponicums.

It is impossible to describe in minute detail the conditions under which the thousands upon thousands of different species and hybrids are rooted from cuttings. Many root well at two different seasons. Numerous scaly-leaved Rhododendrons, for example, can be propagated about July 1st as well as in late October. The principles which apply, however, are universal in their employment, and if they are understood only a little experimenting is needed to succeed with cuttings of any type of Rhododendron. The interest in propagation for both amateurs and professionals centers in the familiar hybrids of commerce which the public recognizes as Rhododendrons, and the increase of these popular sorts from cuttings by several methods will be described in detail.

In the ensuing pages there will be given systems of propagation, small scale and large, for both amateurs and professionals. Increase by green grafting, dormant season grafting, budding, ground layering, aerial layering and by cuttings, both stem and leaf, will be considered.

ROOTED CUTTINGS

Taking the Cuttings

Cuttings are taken from the stock plants of the familiar large-leaved commercial hybrids about September 20th to the latter part of October in the northeastern United States—earlier or later in other regions, depending on the climate. It is not the time of the year which is important but the condition of the plant tissues as they mature under the influence of rainfall, temperature and their inherent constitutions. This is the factor which has been the origin of endless controversy in the propagation of Rhododendrons. It is better to err on the side of lateness than to be too early. In a typical year a hybrid which roots about 95 per cent successfully from cuttings taken in September will root less than 50 per cent from cuttings taken in mid-August.

In addition to the variation from year to year, there is a natural difference among hybrids in the time to take cuttings for the best rooting response. Those which start into growth earlier in the spring usually mature sooner and such old hybrids as 'Purpureum Elegans' and 'Lee's Dark Purple', for example, can be propagated four to five weeks before most of the Catawba cultivars are ready. It is not necessary to do so, however, and cuttings taken from September 20th to the end of October in an average year will yield gratifying results in most of the Northeast for practically all of the popular hybrids. For the Pacific Northwest, the upper South, and for the British Isles; for climates with much shorter or much longer growing seasons; for the occasional year when an exceptionally hot, dry summer hastens the maturity of the tissues or an unusually warm and moist autumn delays it, the time when the cuttings are taken will be advanced or postponed according to the condition of the plants.

If there has been any drouth it will pay to irrigate the stock plants the day before the cuttings are taken, and it is a good precaution to remove the clippings in the early morning or on an overcast day so that none of their turgidity will be lost. They should be carried from the field in covered containers which will retain humidity and keep them fresh, and the cuttings are best kept in a cool, damp cellar so that they will not start to wilt before they are prepared for hormone treatment.

The cuttings may be 4 inches long or 10 inches but they should be severed from the branches at the point where they originated from the previous growth, unless $2\frac{1}{2}$ inches can be removed from the ends and still allow a couple of leaves with resting buds in their axils to remain on the terminal shoot. It is unsightly and injurious to the stock plants to take only several inches from the end of a twig because the stub which remains has no leaf axils with dormant buds and consequently it cannot sprout anew. The next growth will originate farther back on the branch at the point where the previous growth terminated in any event, so the entire stem which provides the cutting should be removed at that juncture.

Very strong, lush stems make cuttings which are hard to root and so do growths which are conspicuously short and weak. Propagators have long noticed that cuttings from the sides of sizable plants, and particularly from the north side or from portions growing in partial shade, root most easily. These are intermediate twigs, somewhat thinner than the heavy, vigorous top growths, and there is a way to obtain them in quantity by proper management of the stock plants. By pinching out the terminal buds after the plants have flowered and are just finishing their first spring growth, each branch will produce multiple stems in its second flush of annual growth, which will be shorter and thinner than would otherwise be the case in a normal extension of the terminal buds into the next growing cycle. These several branchlets, increased in number by the pinching up to five on a stem, are just the right sort to supply the cuttings which root most heavily.

The observation that cuttings from plants making moderate growth are superior to those from stock growing with exceptional vigor is fully supported by research results which show that the accumulation of carbohydrate must be in excess of the accumulation of nitrogen for the best results.

Growths with flower buds can be used for propagating, but they do not root so readily and the buds must be removed before the cuttings are inserted in the frame. It seems illogical to break away the vegetative buds from the tips of the stems at this time with the idea of inducing branching after the cuttings root and start into growth. It is these apical buds which are the principal producers of indoleacetic acid, the rooting hormone naturally present within the stems.

Care of Stock Plants

Stock plants should not be planted in open fields without facilities for irrigation. If they can be placed in partial shade or in a lath house they will yield much better quality cuttings. Plants of moderate size set aside for the purpose provide better cuttings than do very old specimens of declining vigor or very young plants which represent a succession of quick propagations. The well-known Rhododendron authority, Guy G. Nearing, reports that a great loss of vigor results eventually from the practice of taking cuttings, year after year, from each successive generation of young plants which have themselves been propagated in this fashion only the previous season. According to Mr Nearing this chain propagation, the taking of a cutting from a newly rooted cutting, etc., is not at all desirable. Needless to say, the stock plants must be free from insects or diseases since Thrips, Lace Wing Fly or fungi can have ruinous effects later in the propagating frames. An all-purpose preventive spray, such as that suggested on page 296, is probably a worthwhile precaution, applied twice during August.

Plants can be seriously injured by taking too many cuttings from them. A good general rule is not to take more than one-third of the terminal growths from older specimens if no effort is made to increase their number by pinching the terminal buds. If the terminal growth buds are removed, however, just as a healthy, vigorous first growth is finishing, all of the smaller twigs which form from lateral buds as a second growth can then be taken from small plants without apparent injury. Such severe treatment cannot be repeated in successive years, however, without damaging the stock plants.

The aim should be to keep the available nitrogen in the stems at a low to intermediate level. It is an interesting speculation as to whether applications of potassium might help plants to produce cuttings which are especially easy to root, inasmuch as this element results in high carbohydrate production, and it is already known that rooting is associated with a high concentration of carbohydrates in the cuttings. Calcium, applied as gypsum to stock plants, has been reported to increase the percentage of successfully rooted cuttings in New Jersey.

Preparing the Cuttings

The first step in preparing the cuttings is to shorten them to about 2½ inches, making the cut directly below a node if a choice is presented. This is shorter than the length traditionally used but there is a sound reason for it: the formation of roots is greatly stimulated by a liberal supply of oxygen in the rooting medium. If the cuttings are longer the ends are too deep in the sand and peat mixture to benefit from the aeration which is naturally better toward the surface of the bed. There may also be at the ends of short cuttings a greater concentration of the natural auxin (hormone) which promotes rooting since its direction of dispersion through the plant is from the branch tips toward the roots.

The surplus leaves on each cutting should then be removed. Naturally, any leaves must be cut off which would be buried after the cuttings are inserted in the rooting medium, but beyond that the propagator must keep in mind that the rooting response is in direct proportion to the remaining leaf area and any further trimming reduces the production within the cuttings of the carbohydrates which are known to stimulate the production of roots. In addition to carbohydrates the leaves manufacture thiamine, pyridoxine and other products vital to growth. Their function in supplying nutritive factors which stimulate root formation has been conclusively demonstrated.

There are other considerations which must be taken into account in removing the leaves, however. Under some conditions the cuttings may tend to wilt because the total leaf area is so large as to allow excessive transpiration of moisture. Leaves which overlap in the propagating frames tend to decay and encourage fungous diseases. And of course space in propagating frames is conserved in commercial establishments by reducing the number of leaves and trimming them so that the cuttings can be placed closer together. It is possible to minimize the problems arising from a great deal of foliage in the frames and insure a larger leaf area by retaining all of the leaves in the terminal rosette and shortening their length by a third to a half. Thus reduced in weight, the petioles can support the five to seven trimmed leaves in a horizontal position and they do not tend to mat down and decay in the frame. However it is done, cuttings should retain three leaves as a minimum.

Next, a slice wound is made 1½ inches in length along the side at the bottom of the stem. Ideally, the sliver of stem which is removed cuts through just the cortex and cambium layers but in actual practice most cuts slice a good deal deeper and the wounds serve their purpose equally well.

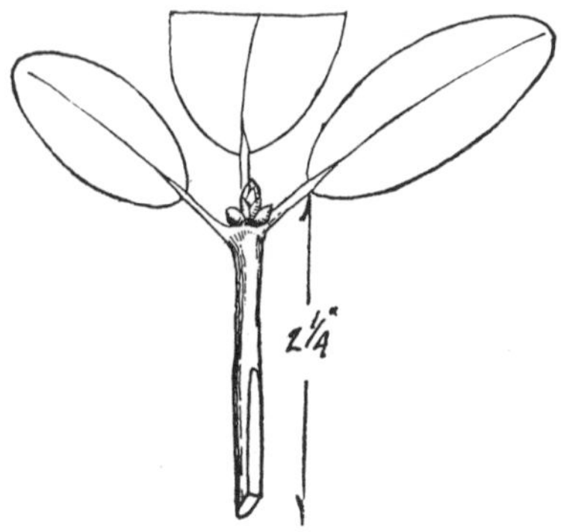

Stem cutting

When the wounding of Rhododendron cuttings was first proposed in 1939 by the well-known hybridist, Guy G. Nearing, it was with the idea that the stems would produce many more roots, thus eliminating a tendency for a single root to originate and then proliferate into an unbalanced root system which failed to anchor the plants securely. The slice wound eliminated this serious difficulty and it was an important contribution to the gradual evolution of a successful technique for the rooting of Rhododendrons from cuttings. It was not then realized just how sound the wounding of the stems would later prove to be. We now know that there is an accumulation of hormones, carbohydrates, and other root-promoting plant products in the region of an injury and as a consequence wounded cuttings require less time to root and more of them do root successfully. Respiration of the stem tissues quickens and the wound is responsible for the absorption of almost three times more water, and of hormone as well when it is used in solution by the propagator to stimulate rooting.

How Roots Form

To survive, a Rhododendron cutting is obliged to absorb through the end of the stem and through the wound the water and minerals which normally are taken into the plant through the roots. Innumerable cells are damaged where the cuts were made but in a short time they are covered with a layer of corky cells produced by the whole cells adjoining the cut surfaces. A callus forms along the injured areas by proliferation of the cells of the cambium and phloem. The callus is not essential for rooting by any means but the same conditions which promote its formation also encourage the production of roots, so most propagators welcome its appearance. Finally, root initials form inside the stem from groups of cells near the sap-conducting vessels. As they extend toward the outside of the stem the vascular portions of the developing roots connect with the vessels of the cutting. The roots then burst through the epidermal layer and assume the burden of supplying the cutting with water and nutrients.

No one knows exactly why and how a group of cells inside the stem starts to divide for the formation of a root initial. When a cutting is made the normal downward movement of the naturally occurring hormone, indoleacetic acid, is interrupted and it builds up into a stronger concentration near the end of the cut stem. This in turn causes the stem to swell as new cells form at a rapid rate under the stimulus of the concentrated auxin. Some of the newly formed cells make up the callus and others differentiate into clusters within the stem which further develop as roots. It is the apical buds at the tips of the cuttings which manufacture this natural hormone, and if they are removed, experimenters report that the formation of root initials within the stems is inhibited. It is logical, therefore, to supplement the natural supply of rooting hormone by supplying an additional amount of it through treatment by the propagator.

The basic problem in rooting cuttings is to achieve the right balance between moisture and oxygen. The rooting medium must be moist and an extremely high atmospheric humidity must be maintained within the propagating frame to keep the cuttings from wilting until they can generate the roots which will enable them to resume the normal absorption and conduction of water. But the more saturated the rooting medium the greater is the loss of aeration, and a good supply of oxygen to the zone where callus and roots are to form is essential to their rapid development. The ideal balance between moisture and oxygen levels produces the quickest and most vigorous rooting.

From the time the cuttings are removed from the stock plants until roots form on them their survival is closely linked with the maintenance of extremely high atmospheric humidity in whatever enclosures are used for them. Under normal circumstances there is a constant loss of water vapor from the surface of the leaves into the surrounding air, but the propagator knows that the more humid the air around the cuttings, the less water will be transpired by the leaves. If the atmospheric humidity can be maintained in the enclosure at a very high point, the amount of vapor passing out through the leaves will not exceed the very small volume of water which can be replaced through the rootless stem. No wilting will occur and there will be no interference with the exchange of gases on which the internal manufacture of carbohydrates for the sustenance of the cuttings depends. This is the ideal. The higher the constant atmospheric humidity in the propagating enclosure, the better the results usually are. The same principle applies to the grafting chamber.

Hormone Treatments

The Eighteen-hour Soak. From my own experiments I am convinced that soaking the stems in an aqueous solution of the hormone is a good deal more efficient than treatment with a powder in stimulating the formation of roots. This observation is well supported by the physiological processes which are involved in the absorption of the hormone. The root-inducing chemical can almost certainly be absorbed in much greater quantity through the cut end of the stem and through the wound in the course of an eighteen-hour immersion in the solution than would be possible following an application of dry powder. The material must enter the xylem of the stem in solution before it can be carried upward through the transpiration stream to serve its purpose in stimulating the metabolic changes which precede root formation. Treatment results in a mobilization of carbohydrate in the region of the wound and at the base of the stem, respiration quickens and other chemical changes associated with the activation of root initials is accelerated.

The concentration of the hormone can be profitably varied to suit the requirements of the different hybrids and species. The point to bear in mind in this respect is that the hormones are most potent in promoting roots as they approach a toxic concentration, so the aim is to use the strongest possible solution which will not be injurious. Inasmuch as Rhododendrons, both species and hybrids, vary widely in their tolerance to hormone treatments, the limits of concentration are far apart. The easily rooted hybrid 'Roseum Elegans' needs only a minimum concentration for the best response, whereas some of the red-flowered Catawba hybrids, for example, which are among the most difficult of all Rhododendrons to root from cuttings, require a stronger hormone treatment for optimum results. In fact, on an experimental basis, hormone concentrations almost forty times more potent than the strength used for easily rooted sorts have given good results on those extremely hard to root.

Skilled propagators study the Rhododendrons they are producing and determine by observation and experiment the specific concentration which yields the best results for each of the different hybrids under their care. They can be tested in small quantities, first with the weakest and then with stronger solutions until the concentration which gives the best rooting response for each different sort is discovered.

In my experiments I worked out a serviceable average which has given me 94 per cent successful rooting of a wide variety of both species and hybrids, including those most difficult to root.

Indolebutyric acid is not technically a hormone. It is one of many synthetics constructed like the natural auxin, indoleacetic acid, which has the ability to regulate plant growth, and it has been exceedingly effective as a root stimulant in my experience. After experimenting with a variety of hormones in both powder and liquid form I recommend that the stems of cuttings be soaked for eighteen hours in an aqueous solution of 3-indolebutyric acid in a concentration of 150 parts per million. The acid can be bought from Distillation Products Industries Division, Eastman Kodak Company, Rochester 3, New York. The most convenient method is to have a local druggist put it up in gelatin capsules containing 148 milligrams each. The acid in one capsule is dissolved in a teaspoonful of ethyl alcohol, since it is not soluble directly in water, and then enough water is added to make one quart of the solution. This yields a concentration of about 150 parts per million.

Larger commercial users may want to have the acid put up in capsules containing 592 milligrams each so that the solution can be prepared by the gallon. If a sizable proportion of the Rhododendrons to be propagated are difficult to root and the conditions are not too carefully controlled in the nursery, the concentration for average large-scale production can be profitably increased about 50 per cent. Capsules should then contain 888 milligrams to be dissolved in a little ethyl alcohol and then added to a gallon of water.

In any event, the cuttings are formed into bundles of twenty-five held with a rubber band and the stems are soaked for eighteen hours in the indolebutyric acid solution under ordinary room and temperature conditions. The treatment should not be in a cool, damp place because less hormone will be absorbed. The cuttings are ready for the rooting medium after they have had their eighteen-hour soak. The hormone solution can be re-used once, within several days, after which it should be discarded.

Examination of the stems through a microscope shows that more root initials are formed and at a more rapid rate following the hormone treatment and there can be no question of its tremendous help. It also retards leaf dehiscence. The assumption is that the hormones which occur naturally in hard-to-root cuttings are below the level required for successful results and that an additional infusion, artificially supplied by the propagator, increases the concentration to the point where the root initials are activated. Water absorption controls growth by the amount in which it enters and enlarges the cells and it is greatly increased by indolebutyric acid. Water uptake and growth are fundamentally the same process.

The use of hormones minimizes the need for highly skilled judgment in the timing when the cuttings are taken, and in their subsequent management. Fairly wide errors can be made and the propagation will still be successful. With this treatment sorts which usually fail to root at all produce a root system so extensive that it cannot be fitted into a 4-inch pot. Nurserymen estimate that 50 per cent successful rooting is required to make this means of propagation commercially profitable. After experimenting with a variety of methods of application and concentrations of the hormone I consistently reached more than 90 per cent of successful rooting in working out this treatment for use with the cold method of rooting cuttings in outdoor frames.

Powdered Hormones

The means of applying hormones which is in most common use consists of dipping the cut ends of the stems in a powder containing a small percentage of the growth regulator mixed with talc. In my experiments this procedure was not nearly so effective as soaking the stems in the hormone, but it is quicker and possibly more convenient. The strongest rooting powder commercially available contains 0·8 per cent indolebutyric acid and this is not potent enough for Rhododendrons with the exception of a very few, such as 'Roseum Elegans', which are easy to root. It is therefore necessary to buy indolebutyric acid and mix it to the desired strength by dissolving the hormone in enough alcohol to wet the required amount of talc. It is then mixed thoroughly and dried.

Here again the optimum results will be obtained by study and experimentation to determine the specific concentration which will yield the best results for each different Rhododendron being propagated. The most effective strength of hormone in the talc mixture is just short of toxicity in each case. As a practical compromise, a concentration of 1·6 per cent suits the greatest range of different sorts, though the propagator may prefer a larger proportion of the hormone in the mixture for the few hybrids which are extremely difficult to root. In any case, after the basal ends of the cuttings have been moistened and dipped in the powder they are ready for insertion in the rooting medium.

Some propagators report that Fermate, a fungicide, added to the rooting powder in the proportion of one to three, promotes better rooting than talc containing indolebutyric acid alone. Spraying the cuttings with a fertilizer solution would probably be beneficial since nutrients as well as auxin are needed for root formation and the amount present in the cuttings is limited.

2, 4, 5-*TP*

On June 15, 1953, the Chief of the Bureau of Plant Industry, which is a division of the Agricultural Research Administration of the United States Department of Agriculture, issued a release describing earlier experiments in which 2, 4, 5-trichlorophenoxyproprionic acid, 1 per cent concentration in a talc mixture, gave 70 to 90 per cent successful rooting of cuttings made in August of the difficult red-flowered *catawbiense* hybrids 'Dr H. C. Dresselhuys' and 'E. S. Rand'. James Wells, then propagator for a large New Jersey nursery, also experimented with this material. After preliminary trials he reported 80 per cent successful rooting of 'Dr H. C. Dresselhuys' with 4,200 cuttings taken August 27th–29th and treated with the same concentration of the material in talc as was used in the Bureau of Plant Industry experiments. He considered it to be a valuable acquisition for Rhododendrons hitherto extraordinarily difficult to root. Inasmuch as I had consistently found that soaking the stems in an aqueous solution of a hormone was superior to treatment with a powder, I soaked the stems of a variety of Dexter and *catawbiense* hybrids for eighteen hours with 2, 4, 5-TP in solutions containing 38 parts per million and 113 parts per million. Even the weaker solution proved much too strong. Of all the hybrids treated only 'America' responded and it rooted feebly despite the extensive injury from the excessive concentration. I estimated then that a further experiment with a strength of 20 parts per million might be rewarding.

ROOTING CUTTINGS BY THE COLD METHOD

The special outdoor frame used in propagating Rhododendrons by the cold method was devised by Guy G. Nearing in the course of experiments extending from 1924 to 1928. In 1932 the Nearing frame was patented by its originator who later published, in 1939, magazine articles describing his methods for using it. Years later, when Mr Nearing's nursery was so devastated by a flood that he discontinued business, Warren Baldsiefen, a New Jersey propagator, adopted the cold method and subsequently he made several significant contributions to the efficient use of the frame. The patent has now expired.

The device was successful in expert hands but it required experience and skilled judgment to use it to the best advantage. Even so, the results were occasionally erratic, especially with some of the difficult red-flowered Catawba hybrids.

My interest in the propagating frame centered in an effort to make it consistently successful for any average nursery propagator or advanced amateur who might want to use it. After experimenting extensively with hormones, both as to the method of application and the concentration adapted especially for this cold means of propagation, I believe that the remaining problems have been solved and that consistent success with the Nearing propagating frame can now be obtained by almost anyone who is willing to construct one. The hormone treatment of the cuttings as it was developed for this purpose has already been described earlier in this chapter, and it is so effective that the various elements of timing and management no longer are critical. Fine results follow the most ordinary ability and effort in the propagation of Rhododendrons. I have sent blueprints of the plan for the building of the frame, reproduced on page 323, to New Zealand, the Netherlands, England, and Germany; and in this country to propagators in New York, Pennsylvania, Ohio, South Carolina, Missouri, and Kansas, where the frames are now in use.

Anyone who is starting the propagation of Rhododendrons should consider the cold method first. It requires much less labor and it eliminates the capital investment and maintenance of expensive greenhouse space. Disease problems are minimized. Finally, it produces plants which are more rugged and which adapt to outdoor conditions a great deal better than do young plants produced from cuttings with heat in a greenhouse. Losses after rooting are less than 1 per cent compared with 15 per cent reported for young plants produced from cuttings rooted with heat under glass. Several years ago I saw a large planting of newly propagated Rhododendrons which had been set out under favorable conditions a couple of months earlier.

About half consisted of plants which had been rooted with bottom heat in a greenhouse and the remainder were the product of the cold propagating method. The portion containing the Rhododendrons from the greenhouse had suffered losses of about 40 per cent in the transition from humid protection under glass to outdoor conditions, in part due to unseasonably hot weather. The little plants produced by the cold method, however, had survived 100 per cent in so far as the eye could detect.

Building a Nearing Frame

The accompanying plans for building the Nearing propagating frame should be followed explicitly. 'Improvements' and alterations which have been attempted by several growers have produced much poorer results. Cypress, treated Fir or Redwood makes the most durable frame. The two ends can be made of wood, Celotex sheathing, outdoor plywood or similar composition material, and corrugated aluminum is a convenient material to use for the sloping back. The tongue-and-groove flooring in the bottom of the frame is not intended to be watertight and no effort should be made so to construct it. Application of the flooring in the ordinary manner retains water long enough to saturate thoroughly the bottom layer of the rooting medium, but allows it to seep away gradually at a satisfactory rate. The bottom projects beyond the walls about 8 inches, front and back, so that the weight of the earth outside anchors the frame firmly against strong winds. There will be some saving in cost if two standard 3 feet × 6 feet hotbed sashes are purchased for the tops of the bins and the frame is then made for a snug, tight fit, which is important. Cracks between the sash cover and the bin frame admit wind-blown fungus spores and result in a loss of moisture and atmospheric humidity within.

The propagating frame should be absolutely level when it is finished and in place so that there will be no trouble later in the even distribution of water to the cuttings in the two bins. It should have the lightest and brightest position available. Next, the frame is oriented so that the open front faces true North, and it is important that this be done accurately by someone who is familiar with the variation correction on the compass. It can also be done by sighting on the north star, Polaris, with three sticks in line. By daylight next day one end of the frame can be set so that it is exactly parallel to the line formed by the three sticks. If the orientation is inaccurate by only a few degrees, the device will not operate successfully.

Ten inches of earth are back-filled around the outside of the frame and some slight slope away from the structure prevents the infiltration of surface water. An inch of sand or sawdust on the earth in front of the frame prevents the glass from being spattered and provides a clean footing when it is muddy in inclement weather.

All of the wood and metal surfaces on the open north end of the frame should be painted white, not only as a preservative but primarily to reflect the maximum amount of light down into the cuttings in the bins. A light meter will show that this painting greatly increases the amount of light on the cuttings, and this is important. The aim is to eliminate direct sun but to provide the absolute maximum of light to encourage photosynthesis since it is known that a plentiful supply of carbohydrates stimulates rooting, especially when the carbohydrates occur as soluble sugars rather than as starch. This is the case when the cuttings have ample light and everything should be done to encourage it. The glass should be kept clean. If a battery of frames is built they should be lined up in single rank so that additional light can be reflected from the sloping backs into the next unit, about 6 feet behind. In this case, the outsides of the backs should be painted white, which is a good deal more efficient in reflecting value than the shiny surface of the corrugated aluminum sheets.

The Rooting Medium

For the rooting medium Mr Nearing originally used a formula incorporating fresh mushroom manure and other ingredients but I am convinced after years of trials that no complicated mixtures are necessary. Consistent success accompanies the use of the following preparation: each of the two bins receives a bottom layer of 4 bushels of European acid peat moss

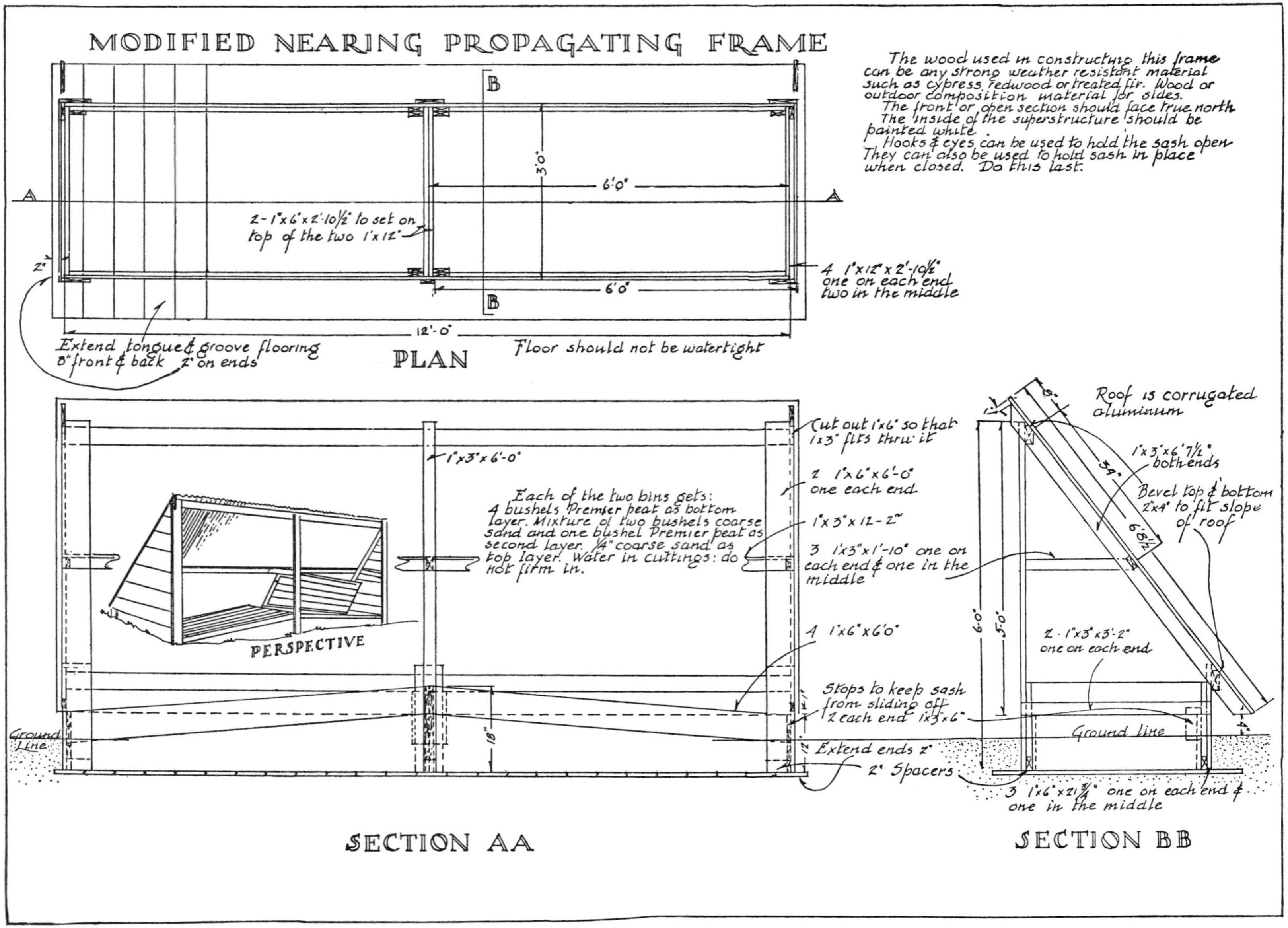
MODIFIED NEARING PROPAGATING FRAME
The wood used in constructing this frame can be any strong weather resistant material such as cypress, redwood or treated fir. Wood or outdoor composition material for sides.
The front or open section should face true north.
The inside of the superstructure should be painted white.
Hooks & eyes can be used to hold the sash open. They can also be used to hold sash in place when closed. Do this last.
3'0"
6'0"
2-1"x6"x2'-10½" to set on top of the two 1'x12"
4 1"x12"x2'-10½" one on each end two in the middle
12'-0"
Extend tongue & groove flooring 8" front & back 2" on ends
PLAN
Floor should not be watertight
1"x3"x6'-0"
Each of the two bins gets: 4 bushels Premier peat as bottom layer. Mixture of two bushels coarse sand and one bushel Premier peat as second layer. ¼" coarse sand as top layer. Water in cuttings: do not firm in.
PERSPECTIVE
Cut out 1'x6" so that 1x3" fits thru it
2 1"x6"x6'-0" one each end
1"x3"x12-2"
3 1x3"x1'-10" one on each end & one in the middle
4 1"x6"x6'0"
Stops to keep sash from sliding off 2 each end 1x3"x6"
Extend ends 2"
2" Spacers
18"
Ground Line
SECTION AA
Roof is corrugated aluminum
1"x3"x6'7½" both ends
Bevel top & bottom 2"x4" to fit slope of roof
34"
6'8½"
6'-0"
5'-0"
2 - 1"x3"x3'-2" one on each end
Ground line
3 1'x6"x21¾" one on each end & one in the middle
SECTION BB

(Premier brand, or equal), which is lightly tamped and accurately leveled. This is the reservoir which maintains a constant, uniform water supply to the next layer consisting of a mixture of 2 bushels of clean, coarse sand (100 per cent to pass through a $\frac{3}{16}$ inch screen and 80 per cent of that through a 50 mesh screen is about right if graded sand is available) and 1 bushel of Premier peat or its European equivalent. This is the layer in which the rooting takes place. It too should be smoothed to an even, flat surface with a spirit level, but it must not be tamped as the compaction will reduce the aeration required for the best rooting. Finally, $\frac{1}{4}$ inch of coarse sand is distributed on top to keep the peat in the rooting layer from flooding over the leaves of the cuttings when they are watered. The same materials make up three identical layers in the other of the two bins in the frame.

In 1956 I experimented with a middle layer consisting of 1 bushel each of shredded styrofoam, peat and sand in half of each bin and I found that the root masses were approximately 30 per cent larger on the cuttings in this mixture than they were on the control cuttings rooted in the older medium consisting of 2 parts of sand to 1 of peat. The value of this extra development added to an already sizable root system has yet to be determined.

The initial watering of the rooting medium, with a perforated rose on the hose to prevent washing away the thin top layer of sand, is continued until about a quarter of an inch of water remains momentarily on top of the sand. It is this watering which must provide the first saturation of the peat moss in the bins and it takes considerably longer than subsequent applications.

The frame is now ready to receive cuttings and up to this point the only difficulty likely to be encountered is in the quality of the sand to be used for the rooting medium. Ground sandstone of the coarse grade used for concrete work is satisfactory when it is normally clean. Plaster sand is too fine in texture. Some dredged sands which are washed before they are sold are acceptable if they do not contain salts or silt. The propagator must insist on *coarse* clean sand and experience has shown that failure often accompanies any compromise in the texture of this ingredient. Alkaline sand, of course, is unsuitable.

Inserting the Cuttings

The stems of the cuttings which have been soaked for eighteen hours in the hormone solution are inserted in the rooting medium within the frame up to the petioles supporting the terminal clusters of leaves. About 2 inches of the over-all $2\frac{1}{2}$-inch cuttings are thus thrust beneath the surface of the propagating bed. A simple device which saves a lot of time and effort makes holes in the sand with the proper spacing in straight rows to receive the cuttings. Starting $1\frac{1}{2}$ inches from one end of a $\frac{3}{4}$-inch board $2\frac{1}{2}$ inches wide and $32\frac{1}{2}$ inches long, a row of twenty-five holes $\frac{5}{32}$ inch in diameter and $1\frac{1}{4}$ inches apart is bored in a straight line $1\frac{1}{4}$ inches away from the first. Into each hole is placed a twelve-penny nail and another board $2\frac{1}{2}$ inches $\times$ $32\frac{1}{2}$ inches is then screwed over the nailheads. Two additional nails projecting out the same distance as the others, one stapled along the one side at each end in line with the first and last nails in the rows on the board, make a useful guide for placing the marks. Finally, a handle is screwed to the top of the cover board. By pressing the marker so that its projecting nails are thrust the whole way into the rooting medium and repeating the procedure along the length of the bed, a pattern of holes is quickly left which are properly spaced and efficiently arranged to receive the maximum number of cuttings. When Rhododendrons are being propagated a cutting is placed in every second hole and alternate rows, $2\frac{1}{2}$ inches apart, are used. The entire frame then accommodates 600 cuttings, 300 in each of the two bins, with a spacing of $2\frac{1}{2}$ inches $\times$ $2\frac{1}{2}$ inches. When Azaleas are being inserted, all of the holes are utilized and the frame holds a total of 1,200 cuttings with a spacing of $1\frac{1}{4}$ inches $\times$ $1\frac{1}{4}$ inches. I think the spacing for Rhododendrons could be somewhat reduced for greater production per unit of a good many hybrids with small to medium-sized leaves.

Watering

The cuttings are not firmed in or tamped. They are simply watered in with a hose on which a rose breaks the force of the stream, until about a quarter of an inch of water stands momentarily on the top sand layer of the propagating bed. Thereafter the cuttings are watered about once a week until the advent of cooler weather in late October and November, when watering every two weeks is enough. Every time the cuttings are watered the glass in the sash should be flushed clean, because maximum light encourages the plant processes which stimulate rooting. As soon as the propagating bed freezes, water is discontinued for the winter. With the spring thaw watering is resumed at two-week intervals until the weather warms up in April and then the schedule is increased to once a week. It continues at this rate throughout the warm months with sufficient water being applied so that it remains flooded momentarily on the surface of the propagating bed before the water is shut off. The weekly watering is mandatory. The bubbling water divided into fine streams by the perforated rose carries with it the oxygen which stimulates rooting as it percolates through the sand and peat mixture. From the time the cuttings are first inserted until they are rooted the frames are kept tightly closed except for watering or combating pests.

Insects and Diseases

It is probably worthwhile insurance to spray the cuttings with a fungicide, such as Bordeaux 2–2–50 or Fermate after they are first inserted and again the next spring in April and in June. If insect pests appear they can be controlled by burning in each bin a heaping teaspoonful of a proprietary fumigant sold under the name of 'Nico-Fume'. After an hour the frames are aired, and it is usually a good precaution to repeat the treatment in ten days. These details of management were worked out by Messrs Nearing and Baldsiefen for commercial use. Fungi and insects have not been troublesome for me and I do not find it necessary to observe the precautions which are desirable in a nursery.

Uses and Reliability of the Frame

I have found the frame to be just as successful for rooting other broadleaf evergreens (Pieris, Ilex, Leucothoë and the like) as it is for propagating Rhododendrons. It is not suitable for the needle evergreens but it performs admirably in rooting soft green cuttings of deciduous Azaleas.

The red-flowered Catawba hybrids such as 'Charles Dickens', 'Nova Zembla', 'Dr H. C. Dresselhuys', and 'Kettledrum' are reputed to be the hardest of all Rhododendrons to root from cuttings. Propagators have occasionally succeeded with them one year only to encounter failure the next, and every experienced nurseryman knows that to be useful a method of propagation must be consistent in its success. The Nearing propagating frame, used in conjunction with the recommended hormone soak of the cuttings, has been regularly successful for years in rooting more than 90 per cent of cuttings from these difficult red-flowered *catawbiense* hybrids.

Removing the Rooted Cuttings

By August the cuttings will be luxuriantly rooted and the frames are then ventilated in preparation for the removal of the young plants. At first the sashes are propped open just a crack and then day by day the frames are aired more and more until, in a week or ten days, the sashes are open a foot or more and the time for transplanting has arrived.

After the rooted cuttings have been transplanted from the propagating frame, the bins are emptied of the peat and sand. It is not advisable to use the rooting medium a second time because it will have lost some of its buoyant texture and would continue to lose it at a progressively faster rate. The supply of oxygen to the rooting zone is an important consideration in successful results and any lack of aeration in the peat and sand mixture should be avoided. After the bins have been emptied they are cleaned, aired and washed down with a Fermate solution. If the superstructure of the frame has lost any appreciable amount of its reflecting value, a new coat of white paint is applied. The frame is then ready for another crop of cuttings.

Aftercare

After the young plants are well rooted they can be transplanted from the propagating frame into 3-inch pots or flats or directly into beds or outdoor frames. This is ordinarily done in August but it can be done as early as July 1st, with some sacrifice in rooting percentages, if the frames are wanted for summer rooting of small scaly-leaved Rhododendrons or for the few larger-leaved hybrids such as 'Goldsworth Yellow' which root better at that time of year.

Pots are more convenient if a second transplanting is to take place the next spring but the plants will usually form better root systems and adapt better later to outdoor conditions in flats or beds. Plant bands offer a good compromise. In any case, after their removal from the propagating frame the plants should be given at least half shade, and preferably a little more. A loose soil mixture, liberally enriched with peat moss and lightened with sand is required. If it is available, leaf mold, as a base, produces better growth than does topsoil. Something like one-half leaf mold, a quarter peat moss, and a quarter sand, by volume, makes a fine mixture. A third each of topsoil, peat moss and sand produces good results. If the topsoil is already sandy the proportion of sand is reduced.

With the approach of cold weather the young plants must be protected for their first winter. After they are firmly established following the transplanting the plants are cut back to the original terminal rosette of leaves on the cuttings to induce low branching, if any growth occurred in the propagating frame. If no growth occurred, the terminal buds are removed. It is important that this be done in the fall because the dormant buds resting in the leaf axils will gradually mature over winter and be ready to start into growth on schedule in the spring. If pinching is delayed until spring several weeks of growth are lost.

When freezing weather threatens, the pots are plunged in cold frames in beds of peat so that the tops of the pots are covered with a layer of the peat and the roots of the young plants thus lie beneath it. The glass sash should be at least a foot above the plants when it is put into place so that there is no risk of overheating a too limited space in bright winter weather. Immediately the sashes are put in place they are covered with reed mats and, thus protected, the young plants pass the winter in good condition.

Plants in flats can be handled in the same manner as are those which go into pots or are placed directly in a prepared soil mixture in cold frames. In mild climates newly propagated plants 6 inches × 10 inches apart can be placed in ground beds which have vertical board sides, to remain there throughout the winter and the next growing season. They are mulched with 2 inches of Pine needles and then lath shading is put in place on wires which are supported 4 or 5 inches above the tops of the sides. When freezing weather arrives black roofer's felt is unrolled over the lath shading and stapled in place. Thus the small plants are enclosed except for several inches between the tops of the sides and the wires supporting the lath. Almost any method which guards against overheating in bright winter weather and prevents alternate freezing and thawing is satisfactory. In regions with severe winters the young plants should freeze up with the advent of cold weather and stay frozen until the spring thaw. A cold-frame, covered with glass or plastic film and shaded, is almost a necessity for this purpose. Winter losses of rooted cuttings in ground beds are often heavy in seasons when very low temperatures are encountered.

Second Year Care

When outdoor planting weather arrives the next spring it is extremely important that plants which have been overwintered in pots and flats be shifted into outdoor beds at the earliest possible moment. Rhododendrons like cool, moist conditions for root growth and young plants which are in the ground early so that the roots can develop well before the weather gets too warm will make much more progress than will those which are transplanted later.

Beds 7 feet wide and 100 feet long running east to west are prepared by the application of 4 inches of peat which is then mechanically churned into the earth with a tiller to give a proportion of about half topsoil and half peat in the root zone. If the soil is heavy 1½ inches of sand can also be incorporated to advantage.

Should the tests show any deficiency of nutrients they should be added on top of the peat before it is mixed into the soil. A full discussion of this important subject as it affects the commercial production of Rhododendrons will be found on page 93.

A large professional grower on Long Island prepares Rhododendron beds 100 feet × 7 feet by tilling in 6 bales of peat, 25 pounds of Agrinite and 3 pounds of 5 per cent chlordane dust. The amount of Agrinite is doubled for new beds in infertile soil.

An exceptionally efficient nurseryman in New Jersey incorporates in beds of this size, the autumn before they are to be planted, 1 cubic yard of aged cow manure, 2 cubic yards of commercial humus, 5 pounds of potassium sulphate, 2 pounds of magnesium oxide and 1 pound of gypsum.

If the small plants to be set out in the beds are taken from pots the root balls are gently broken enough to encourage the roots to venture out into the surrounding soil in the beds instead of remaining confined in the potting mixture. This is an important step which should not be overlooked. The plants are then set out in the beds at the same depth they grew before, with a spacing of 10 inches × 10 inches for the familiar commercial broad-leaved hybrids. A 2-inch mulch of leaves or Pineneedles is then applied and the plants are ready for shading.

Beds 7 feet wide can be shaded by two widths of standard 4-foot snow fence giving 50 per cent shade, which comes in rolls 100 feet long and is much more easily handled than wider laths. It is supported on three strands of number 8 wire on 2 inch × 4 inch stakes, two wires running the length of the bed along each edge with the third in the center. The extra foot of width of the snow fence provides some overlap on the center supporting wire and provides an overhang to shelter the plants on the south edge of the bed. This shading should be put in place quickly. Young plants are sensitive to bright sunlight when they are first exposed to outdoor conditions and their foliage is easily scorched. Facilities for irrigation must be available for the production of Rhododendrons in quantity and sprinklers are used after planting, mulching, and shading, to water in the small stock in the beds.

If this outdoor planting is done, as recommended, very early in the spring, the root system starts to extend almost immediately and the young plants will produce a gratifying size increase in their first flush of growth for the season. The terminal buds having been removed the previous autumn, the season's first growth will take place at the usual time and several branches will be produced. When these branches cease their development, which will be about the last of June for many commercial hybrids, the terminal buds on them are removed before the season's second flush of growth begins. This second pinching of the young plants results in the formation of several additional branches on each of the stems previously produced and thus a sturdy framework of eight to sixteen branches affords the basis for the later development of densely foliaged, handsome specimens of high quality. Even in climates which allow but two flushes of growth per year the popular commercial hybrids should be 12 to 15 inches tall at the end of their first growing season with good culture. The grower who keeps in mind the unwavering preference of Rhododendrons for cool, moist growing conditions will be handsomely repaid, because this is a critical point in obtaining optimum results. On very hot days the water from sprinklers falling on the lath shades is broken up into a cooling mist which envelops the plants in a temperature as much as 15° below the reading elsewhere in the vicinity. A brief sprinkling at sundown provides the high humidity overnight in which Rhododendrons luxuriate during their growing season.

Spraying

Most propagators use a preventive all-purpose spray on young Rhododendron stock two or three times, and the formulae of two successful growers are given on page 296 of the chapter concerned with pests and diseases. West Coast nurseries are obliged to use 'Go-West' or some other poisoned apple bait about twice each season to control the destructive Strawberry Weevil.

Winter Protection

In moderate climates the lath shades over the

beds provide enough protection for the plants during their second winter. Elsewhere additional lath shades can be put in place on the windward side of the beds and an additional mulch of Oak leaves can be added but not deep enough to cover the plants. Under the most severe conditions reed mats or roofer's felt can be affixed to the lath shades which cover the beds. The aim is to minimize exposure to wind and to sun; to prevent recurrent freezing and thawing; and to modify temperature changes throughout the winter so that the fluctuation in the beds occurs as slowly as possible and within the smallest practical range.

Third-Year Care

In the course of the second growing season outdoors the young Rhododendrons develop into the two-year budded plants which are the staple of the nursery trade. In the spring the beds receive a top dressing of fertilizer containing ammonium nitrogen which should be formulated specifically for acid soil plants. Experiments in the Pacific Northwest coastal region demonstrated the following mixture to be particularly effective on Rhododendrons:

Nine per cent nitrogen, derived from both ammonium sulphate and organic sources; twelve per cent phosphoric acid, from superphosphate and organic sources; eight per cent potash, from sulphate of potash and organic sources; four per cent magnesium oxide; two per cent FTE (fritted trace elements), FN-501.

This formula may need to be modified to suit local soil analyses but its components can be mixed or applied separately from ingredients readily available. In some regions an approximation of it is already available as a standard complete fertilizer formulation. The mixture is used at the rate of 50 pounds per 1,000 square feet (about one ton to the acre) and it should be emphasized that under Pacific coastal conditions, at least, the FTE was a necessary ingredient of fertilizers which provided high-level feeding. When the trace elements were added in this form the Rhododendrons throve on amounts of the major foods which would normally have been toxic.

In the presence of FTE formulation FN-501, the plants in the experiments tolerated nitrogen applications equivalent to 5,000 pounds of ammonium sulphate per acre, and made phenomenal growth. This provides an interesting prospect for the nurseryman, but the stimulation of extraordinary growth creates other problems. The appearance of the plants may be seriously affected unless the stock is faithfully pinched to encourage branching and they may not set buds. Such lush growth must be synthetically matured by the addition of chemicals in late summer so that there will be no loss of hardiness for the winter ahead.

A second application of fertilizer without nitrogen should be made as the plants are finishing their growth for the season, to harden them off and encourage the production of flower buds. This formula of elements derived from the same sources and mixed or used separately as suggested above, consists of 12 per cent phosphate, 12 per cent potash and 4 per cent magnesium oxide applied at the rate of 25 pounds per 1,000 square feet (1,000 pounds per acre).

Such a regime as this, which was successfully followed in the plantings of the Farm and Garden Research Foundation on the West Coast, points the way to cautious trials in other parts of the country. The nutrition of Rhododendrons is, however, a complex subject. The natural requirements of these plants are low for many nutrients and any substitution of a high level must provide for the solution of collateral problems which arise from such artificial stimulation.

In their second season outdoors most of the hardy commercial hybrids can stand full exposure in climates with reasonably high humidity, although growth in inland nurseries will probably be better with protection from trees yielding about 75 per cent direct sun. The lath shades are removed during overcast weather about the 1st of May, or the young plants are lined out in the open field if they have been grown the previous year in a permanent lath house. Two or three preventive sprays are again used throughout the growing season to forestall the appearance of diseases or insects which would disfigure the foliage or check the growth of the plants. The beds are kept moist by irrigation and the plants are sprinkled periodically when the atmospheric humidity falls during hot dry weather. So encouraged, the growth is prodigious and by autumn many of the most vigorous of the popular hybrids will fall into the 18 to 24-inch grade which is the most profitable commercially. The open exposure results in the formation of many flower buds and the grower's goal of producing well-budded plants of specimen quality in two years in the field will be realized.

GREENHOUSE ROOTING BY THE WARM METHOD

After cuttings have been shortened to $2\frac{1}{2}$ inches, the leaves trimmed and the stems wounded and treated with hormone either by a soak or with a powder as described earlier in this chapter, they can be rooted in a greenhouse in a considerably shorter time than is required for outdoor frames. The best and cheapest arrangement for commercial propagation in a greenhouse is simply a larger edition, adapted for use under glass, of the device which was originated at my trial grounds as a result of experiments in 1950 and 1951 designed to find a convenient method of rooting cuttings for the home gardener. It is made by erecting a light framework over a bench to support 54-inch width polyethylene film, 0·002 inch thick, which is commonly available at a cost of about 66 cents a pound. This plastic film has the unique property of acting as a barrier to water vapor while the oxygen and carbon dioxide in the air pass through it readily. The frame is made so that the plastic will be about 15 inches above the surface of the propagating bed, which contains a mixture of two-thirds clean, coarse sand and one-third acid European peat moss (Premier brand, or equal) 6 inches in depth and topped with $\frac{1}{4}$ inch of the sand alone.

Since the publication of my experiments the polyethylene enclosure has become widely used for the rooting of all sorts of cuttings, both in and out of the greenhouse. The Arnold Arboretum later publicized R. G. Coggeshall's superior results with a rooting medium composed of equal parts of sand, peat and shredded Styrofoam, a foam plastic made by the Dow Chemical Company, which increases aeration at the rooting zone. Trying their formula, I found also that such a mixture with its increased supply of oxygen gave better results than the older medium of two-thirds coarse sand and one-third peat.

Whatever rooting medium is used, the cuttings are inserted with a spacing of about $2\frac{1}{2}$ inches $\times$ $2\frac{1}{2}$ inches in the bench over which the framework has been erected. A nail-studded marker, as described on page 324 but lengthened to fit the wider dimensions of a greenhouse bench, will save a considerable amount of time and effort in spacing and inserting the cuttings. After the cuttings are in place, they are heavily watered in, without tamping. It is a mistake to settle the cuttings by pounding the rooting mixture because that tends to reduce the oxygen in it by making it denser and more compact.

After the cuttings have been watered in, the polyethylene plastic film is draped over the frame so that it is completely enclosed. Overlapping the lengths of plastic several inches makes a tight seal if the material is not under tension because the sheets adhere as they become wet from the saturated atmosphere within the frame.

Bottom heat of about 75° F. is furnished by the hot-water pipes of the regular heating system in the greenhouse or by a thermostatically controlled heating cable which is installed in the bench before the rooting mixture is put in place. After three months the bottom heat is dropped 15° if the cuttings should, by any chance, be slow about rooting. No shading is necessary to protect the cuttings inserted in October, but it may be desirable from the standpoint of reducing the air temperature in the greenhouse during very hot weather in early autumn. A maximum not exceeding 85° F. is desirable, but the maximum possible light is also desirable, so it may be necessary to reach a compromise between the two. Cold water can be run over the outside of the greenhouse glass to reduce the temperature inside without decreasing the amount of light.

If the plastic film covering the propagating frame is snug and tight it will not be necessary to syringe the cuttings or do any ventilating whatever. They need be watered only at intervals of four to six weeks, depending on the weather, and they are rooted in nine to thirteen weeks. A few hybrids may rarely take twice as long. Thus there is a very large saving in labor as well as in cost and convenience which makes the plastic-covered propagating bench far superior to the heavy, cumbersome and expensive wood and glass frames which are in common use in the greenhouse.

Constant Mist Propagation

Constant mist humidification has given good results in the propagation of Rhododendrons. Throughout the day the cuttings in the greenhouse receive a constant fog-like spray from nozzles spaced at 18-inch intervals in a waterline under 60 pounds pressure above the bench. At first thought it would seem that a peat and sand rooting mixture would be so retentive of water that its saturation would inhibit rooting. But this is not the case, probably because the finely divided water droplets carry with them a good supply of the oxygen which is needed at the rooting zone. The only necessary precaution is to use an elevated bench with good drainage and bottom heat of 75° F. Constant mist propagation outdoors in full sunlight in a protected site is another method which is economical of time and labor. The only attention required is to turn on the water in the morning and shut it off in the evening. Recently, propagation beneath mist applied automatically at pre-set periods throughout the day has given even more promising results than constant mist.

Care after Rooting

Whichever greenhouse method of propagation is used, the adjustment of the young plants to outside conditions must be tempered much more carefully than is necessary for cuttings rooted by the cold method in outdoor frames. After the young plants are lifted from the bench they go into 3-inch pots with sharp drainage in a mixture of sand, peat moss, and leaf mold or topsoil in equal parts, and they are then immediately returned to the humid atmosphere of the propagating enclosure until strong root action is evident in the pots, which will take about ten days. Then the terminal buds are pinched out so that the plants will branch freely when they are subsequently planted in outdoor beds. This operation should not be deferred or the plants will not start into growth at the normal time in the spring and some size will be lost.

Healthy, normal cuttings which have failed to root should be wounded again with a slice on the stem opposite the first wound and treated with hormone at half the original concentration. They are then re-inserted in a propagating bench which has been supplied with a fresh rooting mixture. Almost all unrooted cuttings in good condition can be salvaged if this is done.

Some propagators prefer to transplant the rooted cuttings from the propagating frame to greenhouse benches filled with pure peat instead of putting the plants in 3-inch pots, and to grow them at 55 or 60 degrees. This produces excellent growth but it has serious disadvantages. After the plants go into outdoor beds in spring, great care must be taken to be certain that the peat moss does not dry out in the course of their first growing season outside. This is a common occurrence during drouths. The peat surrounding the roots will be dry when the adjacent earth still holds some moisture. On the other hand, should the soil in the outdoor beds be a little too heavy the pockets of peat may attract excessive water which drains into them in wet weather to the injury of the plants. Finally, the roots of Rhododendrons which are grown in peat are reluctant to leave it when they are transplanted to outdoor beds. The root system does not seem to develop so extensively outside and I have observed Rhododendrons as much as 4 feet tall with underdeveloped roots which were still confined within the original ball of peat in which they were first established as very young plants. Rooted cuttings which go directly from the greenhouse to outdoor beds must be handled with the greatest care and caution or else the losses will be heavy.

In my opinion it is much better to put

greenhouse-propagated Rhododendrons in flats, preferably, or in pots, and then after they have extended their roots vigorously from having been placed back in the propagating bench, they should be hardened off and moved to sheltered outdoor cold frames. There they are plunged in peat so that if pots are used the rims are covered and the roots lie beneath a blanket of the peat. There should be at least a foot between the sash and the tops of the plants. The sashes are then replaced on the frames and they are covered with reed mats. So protected, they safely pass the balance of the winter, and thereafter the method of handling the plants to produce the greatest possible growth is the same as described under 'Second Year Care', on page 326.

Before another crop of cuttings is propagated the greenhouse should be emptied and scrupulously cleaned. All of the glass and woodwork should be washed down. Copper naphthalene stain applied to the propagating bench and to the enclosing framework destroys fungi and acts as a wood preservative. Finally, the greenhouse should be treated with a cyanide fumigant. Many crops of cuttings have been poor solely because of carelessness in greenhouse sanitation.

LEAF-BUD CUTTINGS

In the late 1930's, Dr Henry T. Skinner, then at Cornell University, demonstrated that Rhododendrons could be successfully propagated from leaf-bud cuttings. Two types of them can be made. Normally, a whole healthy leaf, with its stalk and a sliver about three-quarters of an inch long of the stem containing the resting bud in the leaf axil, is sliced from a shoot of the current year's growth with a sharp knife. Alternately, a small section of the stem is taken by cutting through the shoot immediately above and below the point where a leaf originates, so that the axillary bud is preserved intact. These leaf-bud cuttings can be taken in July or in September–October but there is probably some advantage in taking them just as soon as the leaves are mature and the stems begin to harden, because the dormant buds then break into growth more readily before winter, which is desirable though not essential.

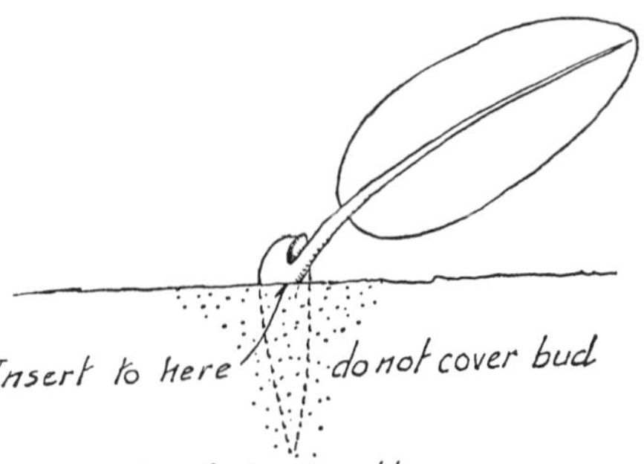

Leaf bud cutting

The cuttings can be rooted either by the cold method in outdoor frames, or in a greenhouse, by the same procedures as were described earlier in this chapter. If they are rooted under glass, it is essential that they then be given a period of normally cold winter in outdoor frames before the advent of spring so that any cuttings with resting axillary buds will break into growth at the usual time. It is equally important to avoid excessive heat in the greenhouse because the axillary buds are easily destroyed by it. Most of them, however, can usually be forced into growth after they are rooted under glass by raising the temperature to 80 degrees, after which they are hardened off in preparation for the shift to outdoor cold frames.

Whichever method is used, the cuttings may be treated with a rooting hormone, either in solution or in a powder, and the handling throughout is similar to the procedure related earlier for stem cuttings. The base of each cutting is shallowly inserted in the sand and peat rooting medium so that the leaf blade is in a vertical position and is not in contact with any other leaves surrounding it. Incidentally, the ability of the leaf blade to remain erect is a reliable indication that the cuttings are mature enough, since they will droop and bend if the petiole and the leaf it supports are too soft. The time to take cuttings of this type is as soon as they will hold their erect position.

In any case, they root in about the same length of time as do stem cuttings under comparable conditions and they are thereafter handled in the same way except that special care should be taken when they are removed from the propagating bed so that the buds in the leaf axils, if still dormant, are at the surface of the soil mixture into which they are transplanted.

At least one commercial nurseryman uses leaf-bud cuttings produced when he makes the slice wounds on his stem cuttings. Another trims the excess leaves from stem cuttings so that the axillary buds are severed with them and thus he acquires additional propagating material as a by-product of the necessary preparation. Leaf-bud cuttings taken at the same time as stem cuttings do not root in as high percentages, but these propagators regard them as useful and profitable adjuncts to their regular nursery production of Rhododendrons. Guy G. Nearing, originator of the propagating frame which bears his name, reports that the percentage of successful leaf-bud cuttings is a little less than half that of stem cuttings inserted at the same times. One professional grower finds that this type of cutting is peculiarly adapted to the production of a particular hybrid in the list which he regularly propagates, and he finds it more economical and convenient to fit his timing and handling to this method than to any other for that specific cultivar.

Advantages and Disadvantages

Generally, however, leaf-bud cuttings have not found favor in the nursery trade. I think they are valuable for special situations and that they can often be used to much better advantage than can stem cuttings if the propagator will keep them in mind and use them where experiment determines them to be suitable. Only a fraction of the number of stock plants need to be maintained to supply cuttings, and there is a substantial saving in the space and facilities required. For a new or rare hybrid, this method affords a much faster method of increase inasmuch as a single plant will yield many times more leaf-bud cuttings than it will stem cuttings.

The principal reason this sort of cutting has been avoided is that the dormant bud resting in the leaf axil is occasionally very slow to break into growth. Generally there is no trouble whatever on this score but I have known rare instances when it took just short of two years for rooted leaf cuttings to send up a shoot from the axillary bud. Almost always the cuttings will eventually develop top growth, but the time required is variable and unexpected delays in propagation are expensive in commercial operations.

It is a speculation in my mind as to whether leaf-bud cuttings should be given any hormone treatment. I have not determined by experiment whether the propagator is better off if he omits the treatment but there is a very good reason why this might well be the case. It is a peculiarity of the naturally occurring hormone, indole-3-acetic acid, that, while it promotes the growth of roots and other plant parts it actually inhibits the growth of lateral buds in the leaf axils. Auxin (hormone) is manufactured primarily in the terminal buds of the branches and every gardener is familiar with the process whereby the apical buds are pinched out to induce branching from the lateral buds farther down the stems. The lateral buds break into growth because the terminal buds are no longer producing the hormone which prevents them from growing.

When leaf cuttings are treated with indolebutyric acid, either in powder or liquid form, the propagator is supplying artificially a hormone which prevents the axillary buds from growing, yet the slow development of these buds is the principal problem encountered in this method of producing Rhododendrons. It is a speculation as to how much the stimulus to rooting outweighs the inhibition of growth in the axillary buds in net advantage to the propagator.

A METHOD OF ROOTING STEM CUTTINGS FOR THE HOME GARDENER

The familiar commercial Rhododendrons can be propagated from cuttings taken in July but it does not seem to be practical in a nursery because the results are too variable, except for a few difficult sorts which actually root better. For the home gardener whose concern with consistent percentages is much less acute, July cuttings offer a useful and convenient means of propagating a valued Rhododendron.

Rhododendrons can also be propagated right on through the winter in the greenhouse and they too will root in approximately three months, but if the cuttings are taken as late as February they will produce their first flush of growth under glass, to their ultimate disadvantage in the size they will later attain outdoors by autumn. This, too, may be of no great consequence to the amateur propagator who is not intent on producing the largest possible plants for sale at the earliest possible time.

In 1950 and 1951, when the properties of polyethylene film first became known to me, I began trials with material supplied me for experimental purposes by the Visking Corporation, producers of the plastic film, in an effort to develop a method whereby the home gardener could conveniently root cuttings of Azaleas and Rhododendrons. The procedure which evolved was very successful and in the May 1952 issue of *The Home Garden* magazine I published a description of a small home propagator which was simple but effective. The experiments were later repeated at several scientific institutions and the device was then further publicized. It has now achieved wide popularity.

In any case, the amateur who wants to propagate a limited number of Rhododendrons can easily do so. First, heavy lengths of wire, such as garden stakes, are used to form three arches which are stapled to span the width of a flat, thus making a dome-shaped framework to support a covering of polyethylene film, as shown in the accompanying drawing. The flat, about 4 inches deep, is filled with a mixture of two-thirds coarse sand and one-third European peat, and the cuttings are shortened, trimmed, and treated with hormone as described in the commercial procedure earlier in this chapter under 'The Cold Method', on page 319. They are then inserted and watered in and the flat is placed in an outdoor situation where it will receive strong light but no direct sun whatever, for instance, against the base of a north wall. It is then covered with a sheet of the plastic polyethylene film and the ends are tucked underneath so that it is totally enclosed in as snug a manner as possible. The large plastic bags which are often used as liners within burlap bags are convenient to draw over the flat with its wire superstructure, thus enclosing it in a tight covering which is tied at one end. The finished propagator then resembles a miniature Quonset hut.

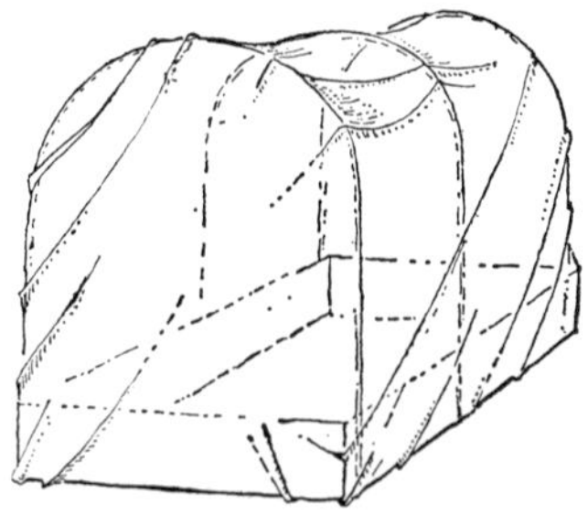

Leach polyethylene-covered tent frame enclosing flat

If the cuttings are taken in mid-July it will probably not be necessary to water them again until they are rooted, some eight or ten weeks later. The plastic which envelops the flat retains the moisture within, while allowing oxygen and carbon dioxide to pass through it. This polyethylene film is readily available at variety stores in sheets and often in bags. July cuttings will provide enough small plants to suit most amateurs even though the rooting percentages may not be consistently high.

Results which approach the professional level can be attained by taking the cuttings in mid-September. The only problem over winter is to prevent or minimize recurrent freezing and thawing. In the Northeast, if the flat is placed at the base of a north wall there will not be too much alternate freezing and thawing in most winters. Snow lingers and the ground remains frozen where the sun does not shine. Elsewhere, the gardener must use his ingenuity to solve the problem. A north-facing cold frame with a cover to prevent overheating in bright winter weather is useful.

Cuttings inserted in the fall may need to be watered once before they freeze up for the winter, depending on the weather and how tightly the flat is enclosed in plastic. No water is used while they are frozen. Several weeks after the spring thaw they may need water, and thereafter an examination about every two months will determine when they should be watered. By late August the cuttings should be heavily rooted and thereafter they are handled in the same manner as described in the commercial procedure on page 326.

Cuttings can be rooted indoors by providing 350 to 400 foot-candles of light for eighteen hours daily from two pink or daylight white fluorescent tubes suspended in a reflector above the plastic-enclosed flat.

GRAFTING

There is now general agreement that Rhododendrons on their own roots are considerably superior to those which have been propagated by grafting. The understocks of grafted plants send up suckers for twenty-five years or more and unless they are faithfully removed these unwanted trash basal shoots crowd out the desirable top growth. The union where scion and understock join is a weak spot in the trunk which may break under the stress of unusual snow loads or high winds. Occasionally incompatibility between the understock and the scion causes a reduction in vigor leading to the gradual death of the plants. More often, the point where the graft is made is a bottleneck which reduces the interchange of water and nutrients between the top growth and the roots, resulting in an enfeeblement which is reflected in poor foliage and sparse bloom. In making a graft the numerous vessels which carry the sap in the understock and in the scion can never be connected so that the flow between the two continues unimpeded. Only a portion of these conduits are matched and the circulation to the top growth is inevitably affected adversely.

When Grafting is Superior

Despite these and other disadvantages, however, there are some special situations where grafting is the best method of propagation.

A few Rhododendrons appear to have their habits of growth determined by the method used for their production in the nursery. Paul Vossberg reports that the old hybrid 'Sefton' grows in the normal, upright manner of most Catawba cultivars on its own roots but grafted on *R. ponticum* it assumes a low, spreading, even pendulous type of growth. If this is desired, grafting will naturally be the choice for propagation. Grafting on standards is the only means of achieving the decorative effects sometimes desired in formal gardens and for use in tubs and large pots.

Some of the epiphytic Rhododendron species, which grow as do orchids on aerial pavilions in the forest jungle roof, are hard to please in cultivation when they are on their own roots. But their vigor can be so enormously increased by grafting them on understocks of *R. ponticum* that they become gratifying successes in greenhouses or in gardens with suitably benign climate. The lovely yellow-flowered *R. lacteum* and some of its hybrids are lamentably fastidious, preferring soil so acid that they are rarely seen in robust good health, but they are often strong and vigorous growing on roots of *R. ponticum*. Similarly, the spectacle of enormous white blossoms enveloping a plant of *R.* (Loderi G.) 'King George' is seen at its best only when conditions are exceptionally favorable, but this hybrid performs admirably growing in ordinary or even less than average soil if it is grafted with *R. ponticum* as the understock. Some nurserymen use rootstocks of 'Cunningham's White' for a part of their propagation because its tolerance to soil which is much less acid than most Rhododendrons require enables it to support in vigorous health a number of different grafted hybrids which could not otherwise be widely grown at all on their own roots in borderline districts. Thus, grafting is justified and desirable for Rhododendrons which, for various reasons, do not develop good root systems or do not grow well on their own roots. These are distinct exceptions, however. Almost any Rhododendron can be propagated from cuttings and this method should ordinarily be used.

Selection of the Understock

R. ponticum is the favored understock for grafting the familiar Rhododendrons of commerce, both in Europe and in America. It is vigorous, has a large root system which develops well in soils varying widely in acidity, and its distinctive leaf is easy to detect when it puts forth basal suckers. Its roots are very hardy, the top growth much less so, but that represents an advantage in the northeastern United States where the suckers it produces are killed in cold weather. The great disadvantage of *R. ponticum* is its susceptibility early in life to the ruinous Rhododendron Wilt, caused by *Phytophthera cinnamomi.*

To overcome the devastating disease epidemics of *R. ponticum* some growers have turned to other rootstocks. In the eastern United States at least one nurseryman is using *R. maximum* for grafting; others are growing seedlings of *R. catawbiense* and plants raised from seeds of the popular hybrid, 'Roseum Elegans'. All have been successful, and if there is any sacrifice in the size of the plants produced it is more than offset by avoiding the losses and consequent excessive production costs caused by the lethal Wilt. *R. maximum* seedlings have served especially well as understocks for a number of years.

On the West Coast some propagators use understocks which break into active growth at about the same time as do the scions which are grafted on them. Thus *RR. decorum* and *fortunei* seedlings are used for early growing sorts; *R. ponticum* for scions of midseason Rhododendrons; and *R. discolor* for the types which produce their first flush of growth late in the season. The matching of the natural growth periods in rootstock and scion is claimed to produce exceptional vigor in the grafted plants.

For Rhododendrons of the Falconeri and Grande clans, rootstocks should be chosen from within the same series. The scaly-leaved Rhododendrons should be grafted on seedlings which are also scaly-leaved except for some of the epiphytes, particularly the Maddenii sorts, which are much better off with *ponticum* understocks. The fine, vigorous old hybrid 'Fragrantissimum' can be propagated as a rootstock for grafting the epiphytic Rhododendrons which are not compatible with *R. ponticum.*

Whichever understocks are used, they should be well grown and well cared for, because their health and vigor have an important bearing on the later success of the grafting procedure. Too often rootstocks are treated as unimportant adjuncts and the propagator eventually pays a heavy price for neglecting them.

DORMANT SEASON GRAFTING

Producing the Understock

Dormant grafting is usually done in December and January. The seedlings which are to serve as understocks are kept free of pests by periodic applications of preventive sprays such as one of those suggested on page 296. When they are brought into the greenhouse for potting in late October or early November, at the end of their second year of growth, they should have stems about $\frac{3}{8}$ inch in diameter. The production of understocks is the same as growing seedlings for any other purpose and the most efficient methods of handling them will be found described in the section devoted to propagating Rhododendrons from seeds which begins on page 351. If *R. ponticum* seedlings are being raised, however, it is essential that they be grown in soil with a pH of about 4·25 from the time they are first transplanted into flats, right on through the potting just prior to grafting, and continuing thereafter with the preparation of the outdoor beds in which the grafted plants will later be lined out. The low pH as well as constant inspection and the immediate destruction of any diseased plants, are the only effective safeguards against the ruinous epidemics of Rhododendron Wilt which can quickly decimate a complete crop of understocks or of young grafted plants. *R. ponticum* is much more susceptible to this disease than are other rootstocks.

After the understocks are brought under

glass those with multiple stems are pruned so that only the strongest remains. Leaves at the bottoms of the stems are trimmed so that they are not in the way later when the grafts are made. The understocks are then put into 3¼ to 4-inch pots, depending on the preference of the propagator, containing a loose soil mixture enriched with peat. A standard formula is two parts loam, two parts peat and one part sand. The proportion of sand is increased if the loam tends toward heaviness, because it is essential that the understock roots have a porous, quickly drained medium lest any lack of aeration encourage an attack of the Wilt. The potting soil is generally prepared some months in advance and it is mixed several times at intervals, especially if sulphur is used to reduce the pH to the required 4·25. Under ideal conditions soil sulphur exerts its acidifying effect in three to four months but the propagator should allow six months to be on the safe side. For a cubic yard of the soil mixture approximately one and a half pounds of flowers of sulphur will be needed for each full point the pH is to be lowered. Some propagators add at the same time ½ pound of 5 per cent chlordane dust and 5 pounds of high analysis balanced acid organic fertilizer to each cubic yard of the potting soil.

It is a good deal easier to adjust acidity with ferrous sulphate (Copperas) because it acts very quickly and it is possible to lower the pH more accurately by testing after each of several applications. The amount required varies with the soil mixture but about 7 pounds are required under average conditions to lower the pH of a cubic yard by one full point.

The understocks are potted firmly so that they will not be hard to handle later while the propagator is doing the grafting. A good deal of earth may need to be shaken from their roots to fit them into pots, especially if the 3¼-inch size is used, but they seem not to suffer from this crowding, which is necessary if the small pots are to be used to conserve valuable greenhouse space.

After the understocks are potted they are placed in a greenhouse at 60° F., syringed twice a day, and by the end of six weeks they should have put out new networks of fine white roots into the pot balls, indicating that they are ready for grafting.

Some propagators do not put the rootstocks into pots. Instead, they are put into enclosed benches with their roots in pure peat and gentle bottom heat is used to encourage the vigorous root action which must precede the grafting. After they are grafted they are simply returned to the peat again with the bottom heat elevated to about 70° F.

Preparing the Scions

Ideally, the scions which are selected from the current year's growth of the stock plants to be propagated should be strong and straight, and of the same diameter as the seedlings which will be used as understocks. They must be free from disease or insects, especially the eggs of the Lace Wing Fly which can later hatch in the warmth of the greenhouse to ruin the young plants in the grafting case. The scions are severed at the point where they originate from the previous growth so that no stubs without leaves remain on the stock plants.

After they are brought into the greenhouse the scions are reduced in length to about 5 inches and any leaves along the stems which will interfere with the grafting operation are removed. They are then ready to be joined to the understocks.

Why Grafting Succeeds

Grafting succeeds because of the activity of the cambium cells which encircle the stems of plants in a layer beneath the bark. They produce the growth of the plant, the inside layer dividing to increase the interior wood of the stem and the outside layer forming additions to the inner bark. The majority of the callus formation which covers injuries depends for its growth on the cambium layer.

The successful accomplishment of a graft is due to the formation of this callus by both the understock and the scion. When the two meet they fuse, and thereafter the life of the scion is sustained by the joining of their two vascular systems.

The more quickly the cambium layers of scion and understock can be induced to form the calluses which join them, the more certain will be the success of the grafting operation. The life of the scion cannot be preserved for any extended period and if it falters for any lack of atmospheric moisture there will be no union with the understock. The grafting case provides the humid conditions which preserve the wounded areas from drying out and it also controls the loss of water through the leaves of the scions so that they do not wilt. Callusing is merely the normal defense of plants whereby their wounds are healed and this process, which makes grafting possible, is accelerated within the moist protection of the grafting case.

Building a Grafting Case

A grafting case can be constructed in the greenhouse by affixing boards to extend the height of the bench sides. Glass sashes over them complete the enclosure. There must be enough clearance between the bottom of the bench and the glass cover to allow for a generous bed of peat into which the pots are plunged, plus the height of the seedling understocks before they are trimmed. A grafting case can also be constructed cheaply and quickly with polyethylene plastic film over a light wood frame in a manner similar to the propagating frame described on page 329, except that for this use provision should be made for convenient ventilation.

There are in favor three principal ways of grafting Rhododendrons and the choice seems to be influenced more by geography than by any other factor. In the eastern United States a modified side graft is popular. On the West Coast the veneer graft is most commonly used and in Great Britain the saddle graft is preferred. All three are illustrated on the next page.

The Side Graft

The modified side graft is also called a flap graft. A thin flap about 1¼ inches in length is cut from the side of the understock by slicing toward the base of the stem, but the sliver of bark is not severed at the bottom of the cut. The bottom of the scion is then cut at a 45 degree angle and a thin slice is removed from each side of its stem to a length and depth which will allow it to be fitted with the pointed end next to the understock so that the cambium layer matches that of the understock on the stem side and also on the side of the bark flap. The sliver of bark is drawn up over the outside of the wound of the scion and the whole is bound firmly with a rubber grafting strip, with twine or with grafting tape.

The Veneer Graft

In the veneer graft a cut is made which starts at about 5 inches from the base of the understock and is extended toward the roots 2½ inches, becoming gradually deeper until it ends about a third of the way through the stem. A second cut is then made on the same side of the stem, starting about ¼ inch above the bottom of the first incision and extending downward and inward until the two cuts meet. The section of the stem thus severed is removed. The scion is shaped to fit this wound in the understock by making a long tapering cut which starts about 3 inches from the bottom on one side and finishes near the base on the opposite side of the stem. A second cut is started from the opposite side of the first, ¼ inch above the bottom and angled downward to form a short wedge which will fit the notch of corresponding shape in the understock. The scion is then aligned so that its exposed cambium layer is placed in direct contact with the cambium layer of the understock in so far as possible. It is then bound in place securely.

The Saddle Graft

A saddle graft is simple and easy, made by creating a wedge-shaped point on the understock from two ¾-inch cuts angled upward from opposite sides of the stem. A single cut about 1 inch in length is then made upward from the base of the scion through the center of the stem. The wedge-shaped understock is then thrust into the split end of the scion's stem and the cambium layers are aligned, after which the two are secured in position by twine, rubber strips or tape.

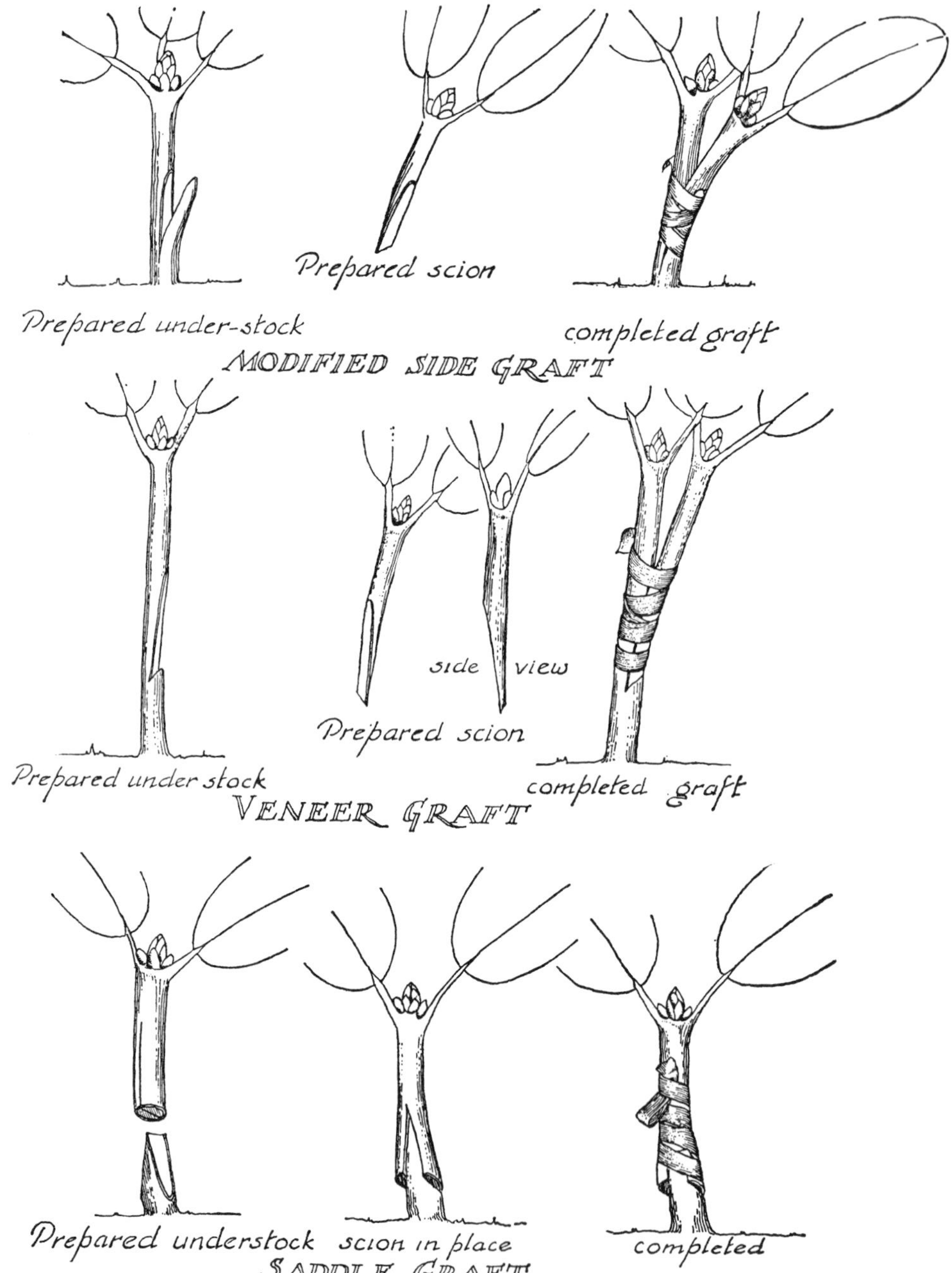

Avoiding Failures

Whichever method is selected, the grafts should be made as low on the rootstocks as it is convenient to work, thus reducing the area from which suckers can later arise and also, perhaps, eventually encouraging the plants to work on to their own roots.

In making grafts it is extremely important that the knife which is used have a thin blade and be very sharp. Bruised and torn tissues from a dull knife are responsible for many failures. If it is not possible to pair understock and scion so that the cambium layers match on both sides the fitting should be done so that they are in contact on one side and the mismatch on the other side is then disregarded. A skilled propagator uses several different types of grafts so that the maximum area of cambium contact is achieved even when the understock and scion are poorly matched in size.

Care in the Grafting Case

After the grafts have been made and bound into place the newly wounded plants are placed in the humid grafting case promptly so that the scions will not suffer from any loss of internal water through transpiration. The grafted plants should not accumulate at the work bench. As soon as there are enough to fill a tray they are transferred to the grafting case where the pots are plunged in the bed of moist peat moss, 6 inches deep, which has previously been provided for them. The peat is not saturated. It is too wet if water can be squeezed from it. The pots are buried in the peat to the point where it loosely covers the graft wounds, and the plants are set firmly in a straight vertical position. Leaning them at an angle accomplishes nothing but a loss of valuable space. After they are in place the tops of the plants are sprayed lightly and the grafting case is closed. Bottom heat of about 70° F. is provided and the healing of scions to rootstocks begins.

If the grafting case has board sides and a glass sash top, it is probably wise to open it for about half an hour each day and then lightly syringe the tops of the plants. In very bright weather the grafts must also be shaded against intense sunlight shining through the glass cover. If the case is made of polyethylene plastic film, no ventilating, spraying or shading are necessary.

It is often extremely useful to be able to anticipate with some accuracy the percentage of success which can be expected in the year's crop. This can be done by leaving stubs of the leaf stalks $\frac{1}{4}$ to $\frac{3}{8}$ inch long on the stems of a representative portion of the scions when they are trimmed. In ten or twelve days these stubs will turn yellow, loosen, and come away cleanly if sap circulation is being satisfactorily restored to the scion by a successful graft. The indicator stubs may not respond on a few red-flowered sorts for as much as three weeks, but the success of the crop can usually be determined at the end of ten days. If the prospects do not seem favorable at that time, the grafts should be watered and the temperature should be increased 5° to 10° F. to foster greater cell activity at the wounds.

At the end of three to four weeks the grafts should be callused. As soon as this is obvious, the union is gradually hardened by removing the peat in stages over a period of a few days until the point of healing is completely exposed. The plants are then removed from the case and half of the tops of the understocks are cut away with sharp pruning shears. Dead foliage and scions which are obvious failures as well as plants which show the slightest indication of disease are burned, and the peat bed is then dampened and turned over so that it will be uniformly moist. The grafts are then returned to the case, the pots plunged only to cover their rims, for the final period of hardening and healing which will require about two weeks or a little more.

Toward the end of this time the daily period of ventilation is gradually extended (or it begins, for grafts in a polyethylene case) in preparation for the transfer of the grafts out of the humid protection of their enclosure. The transition must be slow and the grafts must be watched closely, for any slight wilting of the scions is an indication that the propagator is proceeding too rapidly in airing them. The daily ventilating period can be extended and then the grafts can be aired at a slowly increasing rate around the clock until they are hardened off to the point where they can stand the removal of the grafting case without flagging. The calluses gradually turn dark brown and the plants propagated by side or veneer grafts are ready to have the remainder of the tops of the understocks pruned away, back to the point of union with the scions. At the same time any suckers coming from below the graft unions are removed, and the plants are ready for a period of rest after the long artificial stimulation of the understock.

There are always some plants which are laggards in healing so that they are not ready for full airing at the same time as are the majority of the grafts. These can be salvaged by putting them back in the enclosure and plunging the pots so deeply that the wounds are completely covered with the damp peat. The grafting case is then closed and bottom heat is increased to about 80° F. for ten days to two weeks, after which it is lowered to 70° F. This treatment usually completes the healing of the tardy grafts and they are then slowly ventilated in preparation for the shift out of the enclosure.

Care in the Greenhouse

If it is convenient, the grafting case can be dismantled and the young plants can be returned to the same peat bed in the bench from which they came, plunged only to the rims of the pots and with the greenhouse temperature reduced to about 57° F. Most propagators prefer to transfer them to a separate structure maintained as a cool greenhouse, taking care to avoid intense sunlight and excessive daytime temperatures which are injurious to the newly formed callus tissues. In either case, the young plants are sprayed frequently and every effort is made to provide a period of the cool, moist conditions which all Rhododendrons find most congenial. So treated, the plants muster new strength after resting for a few weeks and thereafter the pot balls will be found to be interlaced with new, white roots. As soon as this evidence of renewed activity is well advanced the temperature of the greenhouse is raised about 5 degrees and the scions will make their first, vigorous growth. This new growth is encouraged so that it will be fully firm and mature at the earliest moment. There is a very great gain in first-year growth in transferring the plants to outdoor beds just as early in the spring as the condition of the grafts and the state of the weather will allow. In preparation for the shift outside, the greenhouse is gradually ventilated to its open limit. After the plants are thus hardened for outdoor conditions the terminal growth buds are pinched to induce subsequent branching, the bindings, whether twine, rubber strips or tape, are removed from the wounds and the Rhododendrons are ready to be planted in outdoor beds.

The preparation of the beds and the handling of the young plants through their first two years of outdoor life are the same for grafts as they are for rooted cuttings and the reader is referred to the section entitled 'Second Year Care' on page 326 of this chapter for a description of the methods which will bring grafted plants to budded landscape size as quickly as possible.

Root Grafts for Amateurs

Amateurs often want to graft plants so that there will be no possibility of suckering, and root grafts solve this problem nicely for the cases where it is not advisable to propagate from cuttings. The method has never become popular commercially because there is an inadequate supply of suitable roots and it is a more time-consuming procedure than is stem grafting.

The understocks are pieces of Rhododendron roots about the thickness of a lead pencil and with good tufts of fibrous roots at the ends. They are brought into the congenial conditions of a greenhouse and are handled in the same manner as are the more conventional understocks. In December or January the rootstocks are shortened so that the thickened portion extends only about an inch and a half above the terminal cluster of fibrous roots. The scions are then grafted to them, using any of the popular grafting techniques described earlier, and matching the cambium layers of scion and understock in exactly the same way. The quickest and easiest method is the saddle graft, particularly if the scion and rootstock are the same size, which is especially desirable for root grafting.

After securing the scion to the rootstock with twine, rubber strips or tape, the graft is placed in a pot with the union beneath the surface of the soil mixture and the treatment thereafter is the same as for stem grafts.

GREEN GRAFTING FOR AMATEURS AND PROFESSIONALS

In 1946 Halfdan Lem, a professional West Coast nurseryman, published a method of grafting Rhododendrons during their active season of growth which aroused wide interest.

Various modifications have since been made until it now presents a simple means of propagation which holds many advantages for the commercial grower and it also provides a very easy method of increase for the home gardener who is unskilled in grafting and lacks greenhouse facilities.

Preparing the Understock

Green grafting of the popular commercial hybrids is done in early July on wood of the current year's growth, using any of the popular understocks which are employed for dormant season grafting. In early spring two-year-old seedlings are transplanted out of flats into $3\frac{1}{4}$-inch pots containing the soil mixture previously described, and the stems are cut back to within $\frac{1}{2}$ inch of the soil level. The pots are plunged in peat in shaded beds or frames where they can be conveniently watered and tended.

Not long after growth normally commences for the understocks several branches will sprout from the cut-back stubs. As soon as they are apparent the propagator goes over the potted rootstocks and rubs out all but the strongest sprout from each stub. Any additional branches which later appear are also removed. By early July the one sprout which has been allowed to remain on each understock has developed into a strong, vigorous green shoot which is in the process of maturing for the season and it is in ideal condition for green grafting.

Some propagators do not bother to cut back the rootstocks in the spring of their third year. The advantage in doing so is that the grafts can be made much lower on the understock. If the rootstocks are not cut back the best that can be done is to make the grafts on the top shoot which develops as a further extension of the second year's growth, since the union is joined only on green wood of the current year's production. While the plants are small such a graft appears to be placed rather high but after they attain a size of several feet this objection disappears and the only disadvantage probably lies in the greater area from which undesirable suckers can originate. An advantage of higher grafting is the retention of foliage on the rootstock, which aids the growth of the scion.

Making the Green Graft

The cleft graft is especially well suited to green grafting and it is a very easy one to make. The top of the understock is lopped off and the stem is split down through the center with a sharp knife a distance of an inch or a little more. Some propagators claim that the rootstock should be cut off just above the bottom pair of leaves produced on the current growth but I have never been able to observe any advantage in this position. However, if the rootstock is severed at this point it is important that a short length of stem be left above the pair of leaves for conveniently binding the scion into place.

In any event, after the split has been made down through the center of the understock stem, the scion, also green wood produced in the current year, is prepared for insertion. There is no advantage in using a scion longer than is necessary for convenient handling. Added length only makes it harder to hold the scion in the split stem until it is bound into position and thereafter it is more likely to be blown or knocked about so that the wound heals less readily.

The leaves on the scion are reduced to the top three on the stem and if they are very long they can be trimmed back to two-thirds of their length. The base of the scion is then given a long, wedge-shaped point with two $\frac{3}{4}$-inch cuts from opposite sides of the stem. This sharpened wedge is then inserted into the split end of the understock stem far enough that no exposed wound remains visible, and the union is then secured with a rubber strip or grafting tape. The length of the split should be completely enclosed in a spiral wrap of the binding. Rubber grafting strips do not remain in good condition long enough outdoors to serve their purpose with complete satisfaction. They provide an easy, convenient binding, but in the North they should be overlaid with a wrap once or twice around the stems with plastic tape. The cleft graft is shown on page 342.

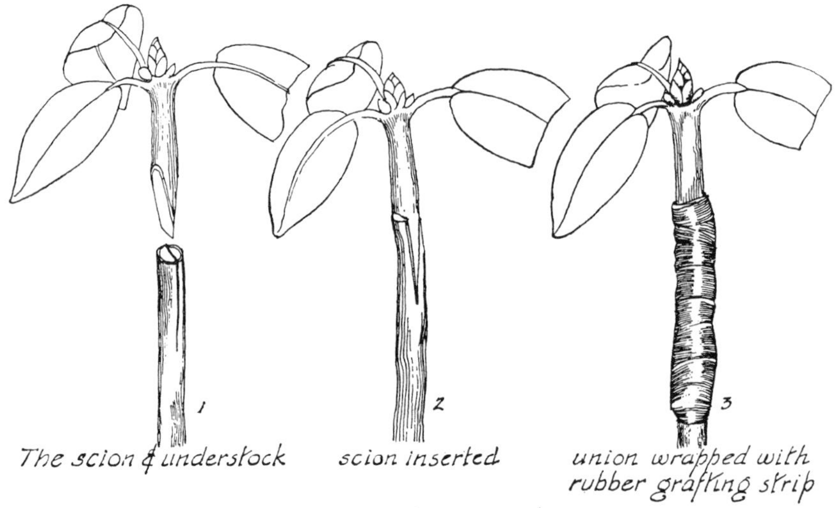

THE GREEN GRAFT

If the scion is always just a little bit larger in diameter than the understock, there will inescapably be at least four good points of cambium contact in every cleft graft and there will be few failures. Otherwise, the cambium layers of rootstock and scion should be carefully matched on at least one side. It is especially desirable for the scion to make firm contact at the bottom of the split in the understock because this is where the first healing takes place.

Aftercare

After the scions are bound into position, care being taken not to bruise the green tissues, the grafts can be plunged to the rims of the pots in a greenhouse grafting case or in shaded outdoor frames where they can be lightly sprayed once or twice a day. In my experiments, using *R. maximum* as understocks and a variety of Catawba hybrids as scions, I found that spraying the newly grafted plants with an emulsion of polyvinyl chloride plastic, sold under the name of 'Wilt Pruf', so retards transpiration of moisture from the scions that it is possible to plant the grafts out in open beds mulched with peat, if they are carefully shaded and faithfully watered. This spray coats the leaves and stems with a very thin film of plastic which prevents evaporation of water from them until it gradually erodes away over a period of several months, by which time scions and understocks have knit and it is no longer needed. Other experimenters to whom I have recommended this method of aftercare seem not to have succeeded with it under their conditions, however, and the plastic bags described below are probably better to control loss of moisture from newly grafted plants in outdoor beds.

Dr J. S. Yeates in experimenting with green grafts at the University of New Zealand covered the grafted plants with polyethylene plastic bags outdoors and had better results than were obtained in the greenhouse. A small quantity of moist sphagnum moss was tied to encircle the union of scion and rootstock, after which the plastic bags were slipped over the plants and tied just below the bottom of the wounds wrapped in moss. Such bags can be purchased in quantity at very low cost or they can be made even cheaper by heat-sealing one end of short lengths of the clear tubular polyethylene 5 inches in diameter and 2 or 3 millimeter thickness, which comes in 100-foot rolls.

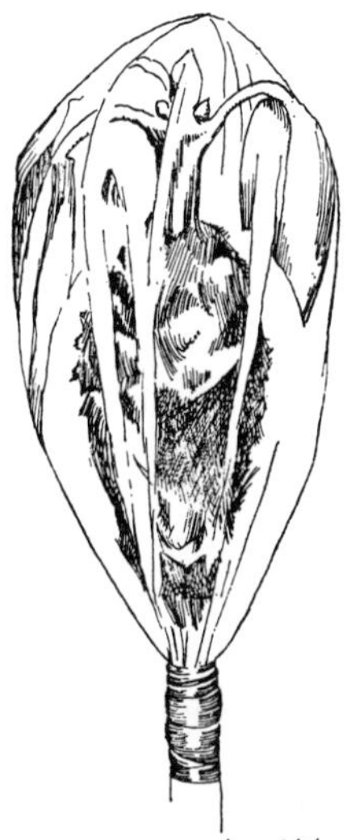

Union covered with sphagnum and all enclosed with poly-ethylene plastic covering

After the bags are secured in place the grafts are planted or plunged in peat in shaded outdoor mulched beds and no further attention is necessary other than routine watering. When the wounds have healed the bags are untied and left open at the base for a few days, after which the plastic coverings are removed entirely. Two weeks later the sphagnum moss is also removed and the grafted plants are then subsequently handled with the same care and protection as seedlings or rooted cuttings of similar size would require for the climate in which they are grown. For regions with severe winters the methods and aftercare described in the section beginning on page 326 are suggested. The binding which secures the scion in the understock is not removed until the following spring.

Whether the plants after grafting are put into frames, sprayed with plastic or enclosed in polyethylene bags, it is extremely important that they be shaded fully so that they have good light but no direct sun at all. This is a critical factor with which there can be no compromise. To allow the sun to strike the newly grafted plants before they are completely healed and hardened off is to invite failure.

Variations on the Method

All sorts of variations are possible with green grafting. The understocks can be left in flats in which they grew as seedlings and can be grafted there without transplanting, thus saving a tedious operation and affording a convenient means of winter protection. When they are moved out of the cold frames the following spring they can be lined out directly into lath-shaded beds outdoors.

In milder climates and even in severe climates, with proper protection, the understocks can be transplanted from flats into outdoor beds in the spring of their second year, spaced to remain in position for two years more. Then in July the scions can be grafted on to them right in the beds if they are subsequently shaded and protected with polyethylene bags or plastic spray.

Advantages of Green Grafting

Green grafting with the cleft method requires much less skill than does dormant season grafting. The propagator has the initial advantage in joining the wood of stock and scion when they are both the same age. The fitting of cambium layers is not nearly so critical in active, vigorous young tissues and the wounds heal more quickly. In fact, there are a number of Rhododendrons which cannot be propagated at all by dormant grafting but succeed very well as green grafts.

It is an ideal method for the amateur and there are many advantages for the professional grower. Expensive greenhouse facilities and the cost of heating them in winter can be eliminated. The saving in labor is enormous, especially if the plastic spray or polyethylene bags are used to avoid the endless syringing, shading and ventilating which are a costly feature of caring for dormant season grafts. There is much less of a disease problem in outdoor propagation and the percentage of successful grafts is very much higher. The cleft graft is faster and easier to make and the subsequent growth of the plants outstrips dormant grafts.

As it was originally published Mr Lem's method recommended that the grafting be done at the time the new leaves unfurl, and that the scion be somewhat softer than the rootstock. After making grafts at weekly intervals from mid-June to the first of September I found that scions of the familiar commercial hybrids should be at least half-ripe, with the leaves fully developed and completely firm. In my experiments I found it desirable, though not necessary, that the understocks be less mature than the scions. The more active tissues in the softer stems healed very quickly and the vigor associated with the more immature rootstocks gave results which were obviously superior. I found *R. maximum* to be ideal since it starts into growth later than many Rhododendrons and is therefore suitably softer than the scions to be grafted.

The best results came in the period between the third week in June and the end of the first week in July, and I concluded that early July represented the optimum time for making green grafts. By using the polyvinyl chloride plastic spray and providing overhead shade from burlap, the percentage of success was so nearly perfect that it was marred only by mechanical error in aligning scions which were poorly matched in size to the understocks.

Green Grafting on Older Plants

The entire process of green grafting was originally proposed as a means of top-grafting newer hybrids on sizable specimens of the older and less ornamental Rhododendrons, and for grafting several different cultivars on one shrub to suit gardeners who want variety in limited space. It is entirely successful for either purpose.

A plant 3 to 4 feet tall is moved to a sheltered, shaded location in the spring before growth starts, or a burlap screen can be erected to protect larger specimens. In early July all but one of the several terminal branches of current growth are removed from each of the limbs to be grafted. The remaining branch serves as the understock. It is lopped off, split, and the wedge-shaped base of the scion is inserted in the manner already described. Thereafter daily syringing with water for several weeks will insure a good percentage of success, but the protection of the plastic spray or the polyethylene bags previously noted should give almost perfect results in less time and with much less attention. In October the burlap screen is removed or the following spring the plant is returned to its normal exposure and any sprouts which originate from just below the graft are removed.

The effect of several different hybrids grafted on one shrub is somewhat bizarre. I have grafted as many as thirty different Rhododendrons on one 5-foot plant, not because I admired the result, but because scions cut from immature seedlings can often be induced to set buds the year after they are grafted on an older plant, and so it is possible for the hybridist thus to hasten his crosses into flower for further crossing. Thus green grafting on older plants can be extremely valuable in expediting the course of the breeder's work.

The procedure is so easy that the home gardener can convert an older specimen of indifferent quality to one of the best modern hybrids by top-grafting a few scions on it.

Green Grafting with Floral Buds

Ordinarily propagators do not choose scions with floral buds, or, if they must be taken, the buds are removed before the grafts are made. In the warm, humid atmosphere of the enclosed grafting case which must be used for dormant winter grafting the flower buds are attacked by decay fungi and they drop off. But for the hybridist green grafting in midsummer offers a valuable additional aid because the buds are unaffected.

Grafts can be made in early August using scions with floral buds and they will remain intact, ready to bloom the following spring. The flowers are somewhat undersized but they are normal in color and in the development of their floral parts. The breeder reduces their number so that only two or three florets remain in the truss and after these are crossed they will then produce normal, fully developed seed capsules.

This technique was originated by H. L. Larson, a pioneer Rhododendron specialist at Tacoma, Washington, who sent the budded grafts to me for testing in my hybridizing work, beginning in 1952. I found them enormously useful and with many advantages.

It is a simple matter to retard their flowering by placing them in cold storage at 34° F. until the pollen is available which is to be used on them. It is equally easy and convenient to force them into flower prematurely in a greenhouse or in a residence, so that pollen can be taken from them for use on a seed parent which blossoms early. Budded scions can be imported from other countries to serve as seed parents here years before mature plants of blooming age would be available.

Other advantages in using these small grafts for breeding are the saving in time, labor, expense and transportation costs as compared with using plants of blooming age. The convenience of handling a graft in a small pot as compared with a mature shrub with a heavy ball of earth is very great indeed. The small plants can be brought indoors to make the crosses under ideal conditions. Protected from the vagaries of the weather at the critical time of pollination they later yield capsules of exceptional size containing abundant quantities of seeds.

I found that the immature seed capsules on the little grafts close to ground level attracted rodents, presumably chipmunks, and it was necessary to protect them by enclosing the plants in a cage made from hardware cloth with $\frac{1}{4}$-inch mesh.

BUDDING

Rhododendrons can be propagated by budding at any time during the summer when the bark slips freely on the understock, which will be generally from the middle of June to the first of September.

A shallow incision in the shape of a T is made with a very sharp knife in the green stem which has been produced the previous year on the understock. The bark is then peeled back, thus separating the paste-like cambium layer, part of which remains attached to the wood beneath while the remainder adheres to the bark. Green wood of the previous season's growth is better for budding because the bark on the older, brown stems is too thin and fragile.

Dormant buds from the axils where the leaf stalks join the stems of the previous year's growth are carefully severed with a razor blade from the Rhododendron to be propagated. An upward slice in a shallow cut beneath the bark removes a shield-shaped portion of the stem about $\frac{3}{4}$ inch to 1 inch long with the axillary bud and leaf attached. The shield is thickest and has just a little bit of wood on its undersurface beneath the point where the leaf springs from it. It then tapers top and bottom so that it has only the thickness of the bark for most of its length.

The shield with bud and leaf is then inserted beneath the bark which has been peeled back from the T-shaped incision in the understock, so that the dormant bud is about $\frac{1}{4}$ inch below the intersection of the vertical and horizontal cuts, after it has been firmly pressed downward into position. If it is necessary to extend the vertical incision in the understock this should be done rather than trim the shield. After it is in place, the bud shield at the top should extend slightly above the level of the horizontal incision and it is then trimmed off exactly in line by drawing the razor blade lightly and carefully across it. The top tip of the shield which is thus severed is then removed. This allows the bark of the shield and that of the understock to abut in perfect alignment for the quickest healing at this point.

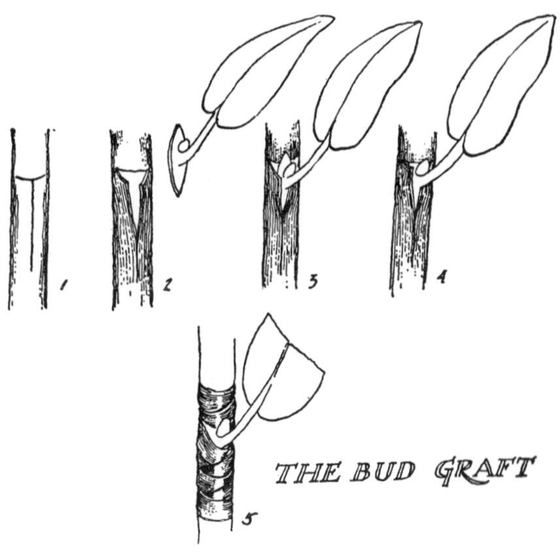

The bud shield is then secured in place by a rubber grafting strip, starting at the top and wrapping downward, with each spiral overlapping except at the point where the dormant bud and the leaf protrude. The leaf can then be trimmed to half its length if it is large or awkward to handle.

The understocks with the buds inserted are given the same protection over winter as would be dictated by the climate for seedlings or grafts of comparable size. It is especially desirable to shelter them so that water does not drain into the incisions, there to spoil the unions by freezing and thawing.

The following spring the understocks are lopped off just above the rubber grafting strips and subsequently the dormant buds in the shields inserted lower on the stems break into active growth. In midsummer any portions of the bindings which still remain are removed and thereafter the plants receive the same pinching, care and protection as have already been described for grafts or rooted cuttings of similar age.

For new hybrids or rare Rhododendrons budding provides a more rapid method of increase because a number of new plants can be created from the dormant buds on a shoot which would constitute but one scion for grafting. In this respect plants propagated from buds compare with grafts as leaf-bud cuttings do with stem cuttings. Making the lengths of the incisions in the understock to fit the dimensions of the shield containing the bud is a skill which is acquired with a little experience but the whole operation is a rather tedious one and this method of propagation is ordinarily used only for special situations. I believe the veteran hybridist, Joseph B. Gable, has experimented with it more than anyone else in the East. It is my observation that the protection of the incisions from injury over winter is an important factor in success.

LAYERING

Ground Layering

Most gardeners notice that the arching branches of old Rhododendrons which rest on the ground take root as they are covered with a gentle blanket of fallen leaves and plant debris. The limbs can then be severed to form new plants. This natural tendency of Rhododendrons to form roots in this manner can be fostered and controlled to afford a systematic method of propagation.

For the amateur it is a simple matter to scoop out a little trench about 4 inches deep and 4 inches wide and fill it with a moisture-retentive mixture of two-thirds peat and one-third sand. If the soil is naturally damp and porous beneath the plant to be propagated no prepared rooting medium need be brought in.

A low pliant branch is bent earthward so that firm growth produced in the current season or the previous year will fit into the length of the short trench. The limb is secured to the ground by fastening it with a forked branch cut from a near-by tree or by tying it to a small stake so that the stem of its terminal growth fits into the trench. Any leaves which would be buried in the trench are removed. A second peg almost at the end of the trench fastens the stem to the bottom and the remainder of the limb is thus abruptly bent and forced into a vertical position by the bank which forms the end of the miniature trench so that the protruding end of the branch is upright. It is essential that this sharp upward angle, close to 90 degrees, be forced upon the branch at the point along the one- or two-year-old wood where it is expected to root.

Old World propagators take some pride in securing an abundant root system on layers solely from the abrupt 90 degrees turn in the stems. Home gardeners are probably better advised to make a wound in the stem in the region of the upward bend. Perhaps the best and surest method for amateur and professional alike is to make a cut about 1 inch long and halfway through the *top* of the stem toward the end of the branch. The stem is likely to snap in two when it is bent to a vertical position if the wound is made on the underside of it. Therefore the cut is made on its upper surface and the branch is rotated 90 degrees as it is bent upward. This twisting leaves a flexible bridge of bark intact while the branch is partially severed so that it is easily bent into an upright position. There remains at the base of the vertical portion a 1-inch stub created by the half-severed part of the stem where it was wounded. Any leaves which would be buried are removed, the layer is pegged into position close to the wound, and the trench is filled in with soil or the prepared peat and sand mixture, packed around the stem to support it in its vertical posture. A sizable stone is then placed on the trench to mark the layer, conserve moisture and frequently to help hold the stem in position. The roots subsequently originate from the attached stub at the base of the upright branch and this makes a particularly neat new-layered plant which is convenient to transplant and to handle later.

First make incision
on upper side of stem
Rotate 90° and peg to bottom of trench
Fill trench with leafmold or peat moss, keep damp

Ground Layering

The wounding of the layer results in an increased concentration of hormone and carbohydrates in the sector where the stem is cut, so that rooting is accelerated. The sharp upward bend of the stem to a vertical position impedes the free flow of hormone downward from the branch tip so that it accumulates near the angle of the turn to promote the formation of new cells and foster the initiation of roots.

Branches can be layered at any time of the year when the ground is not frozen but the time just preceding a period of active root development is probably best. Professional growers favor August because the season's growth is then firm enough to layer and the cool, damp days of autumn lie ahead to stimulate root activity and keep the rooting medium moist in the trench where the branch is buried. Many layers are made before growth starts in the spring.

The Selection of Branches

Amateurs are often tempted to layer a large branch so that it roots well back toward its base, in the belief that this quickly provides a new plant of considerable size. The gain is illusory. The thick stems of old branches root very slowly and reluctantly. After they have finally rooted they are seldom vigorous and they often die after being severed from the parent plant. If they survive they are almost invariably so lanky and ungainly that they can be shaped into densely foliaged specimens of pleasing outline only with the greatest difficulty. It is far better to induce rooting on wood one or two years old, if the layer is made in the spring, or on firm growth of the current season or the previous year if the job is done in August. It is much easier to produce plants which are well formed even as young specimens if the branches are layered close to their tips so that they root from the most recent firm growth, with just the terminal tuft of leaves protruding above the surface of the trench. If a number of new plants are wanted a limb can be chosen with numerous terminal branches, all of which can be layered at the same time.

Time Required to Root

Rhododendrons with the familiar rough bark root much more rapidly than do those with smooth bark. Not many sorts will be rooted before eighteen months, however. At the end of that period layered branches are examined for the masses of fine white roots in the trenches which mean that they are ready to assume an independent existence. As soon as it is well rooted each layer is severed from the parent plant just back of the point on the stem where the roots originate. The small plants are then left undisturbed in the trenches for at least a month, or until the next regular transplanting season, to extend their roots still farther and adapt to life without sustenance from the mother plant. Layers which are found to be well rooted in autumn are often severed and allowed to remain in their trenches until the following spring before they are transplanted. Spring-rooted layers are probably best left undisturbed until late August.

Young layers are usually transplanted to a cold frame or to a nursery bed where they receive care and protection appropriate to their size. The terminal growth buds are removed to make them branch out, or if the familiar commercial hybrids are more than about 9 inches tall they are usually cut back to the point where the last growth originated so that they will form the branches close to the ground level which assure shapely specimens later.

The production of roots can be hastened substantially by making sure that the rooting medium in which the layer is buried is kept constantly moist. A mulch over the trench is helpful and is also useful over winter in severe climates to prevent the heaving which accompanies intermittent freezing and thawing.

The dwarf alpine Rhododendrons are easily layered by adding enough soil to cover their lower branches, leaving the growing tips exposed.

COMMERCIAL GROUND LAYERING

Layering has been used for plant propagation for more than 2,000 years and it is still widely practiced in European nurseries. It is usually associated with mild, moist climates on a commercial scale but there are at least three large professional growers in Pennsylvania who regularly and successfully propagate Rhododendrons by this method.

There are several disadvantages to commercial propagation by layering. It is slow. A considerable number of large specimens are needed to serve as mother plants and the method does not always make the most efficient use of the prime propagating wood which they produce. It is harder to make first-class shapely specimens out of young plants produced from layers. On the other hand, no special or expensive equipment is needed and once the parent plants are large enough to be brought into the regular production of layers there is not much continuing care and attention required.

For a commercial operation, deep beds are prepared in a lath house or in natural half shade, containing loam, peat moss and sand in equal proportions. It is essential that the site be supplied with water for irrigation. In August the large stock Rhododendrons are lifted from the field with good balls of earth and placed on the layering bed in a double row. Then they are turned over on their sides and planted into the prepared soil mixture, facing alternately in opposite directions so that as many as possible of the limbs can be brought to earth and there is room enough to spread them out, fan-wise, for pegging into the rooting medium. The green growths of the current season are then stripped of leaves where they will be buried. They are cut, twisted and bent sharply to a vertical position and put underground in the manner already described. For commercial purposes the branches are wounded and bent 6 to 8 inches from their tips and not much more than the ends of the stems bearing the terminal rosettes of leaves remain visible beyond the point where the branches lie buried and pegged beneath the soil. Any flower buds are removed.

With the arrival of cold weather in severe climates the propagating bed is mulched with oak leaves and pine boughs, care being taken not to cover the protruding tips of the many layered branches. The following spring the boughs are removed and about half of the mulch. Throughout the growing season the bed is kept moist by overhead sprinklers when rain fails, and in the fall the layers are severed if they are well rooted. The bed is mulched once again for the second winter, flower and terminal buds are removed, the latter to induce branching, and the following spring the young plants are transferred to shaded, prepared beds. Sometimes rooting is slow, in which case the layers may not be severed from the mother plants until early April and then transplanted several weeks later to prepared beds, before they start into growth. Some plants will be leggy and will need to be cut back.

Stock plants are heavily penalized when they are used for layering and they should be fertilized and watered as their needs may require. Practically every terminal growth can be used to form a new plant, and mother plants which are used for layering tend to branch with increasing profusion. After they have been used to produce a crop of layers the stock plants are returned to the field to recover and replacements are brought in for the next crop.

Some Rhododendrons tend to send out numerous branches from around their crowns, particularly if they are cut back. Such sorts can be conveniently propagated by building a box frame around each plant and filling it with a peat and sand mixture, into which the basal shoots are layered. When they are rooted and removed there is a tendency for even more shoots to be produced and they can in turn be layered for the production of new plants. This method of layering requires extra attention because the rooting medium in the frames above the ground tends to dry out a good deal faster than do branches which are buried underground.

AIR LAYERING

Rhododendron branches can be induced to root into damp sphagnum moss which is wrapped around them just as they will form roots when they are buried underground in a moist mixture of peat and sand. The problem has always been to find a convenient and reliable method of keeping the sphagnum moss from drying out over long periods of time.

The experiments in Florida by W. R. Grove in 1947 demonstrated that polyethylene plastic film was an ideal covering which would keep the sphagnum moss damp almost indefinitely while allowing the free passage of oxygen and carbon dioxide in and out of the wrap. The material did not deteriorate after prolonged exposure to weather.

Air layering can be done from August onward on firm wood of the current year, or the previous season's growth can be used at any time. The latter part of June seems to be favored by some propagators but I believe early spring to be the most desirable time. The selected branch should be intermediate in vigor, neither conspicuously strong in growth or noticeably weak. The stem is cut toward its tip in a slice wound about 2 inches long and a half of the way through. A small twig is inserted in the wound to keep it open and the cut surfaces are dusted with Hormodin No. 3 or one of the other hormone powders formulated for plants hard to root. A handful of moist sphagnum moss from which all free water has been squeezed is then pressed around the stem to encircle the wound, and some of it is packed between the cut surfaces.

Next, the sphagnum moss is enclosed in the polyethylene covering. An 8-inch length of tubular plastic film drawn over the end of the branch is much more convenient but if it is not available a flat sheet about 8 by 10 inches can be wrapped firmly and overlapped to form a snug, tight enclosure of the sphagnum. The

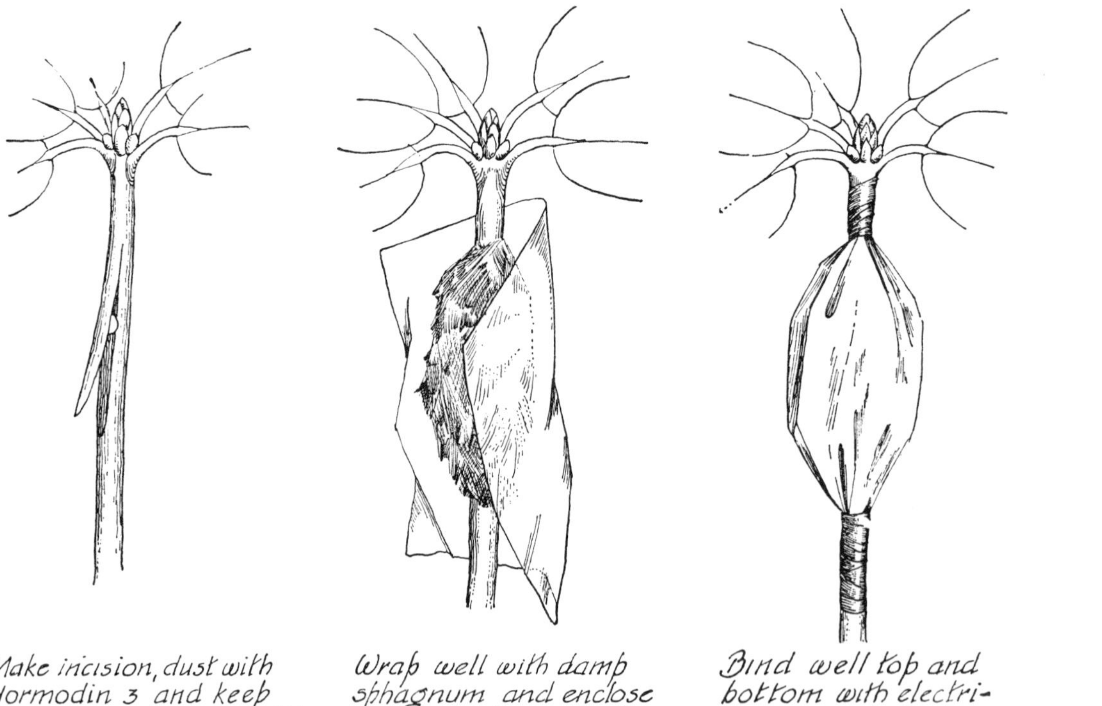

Make incision, dust with Hormodin 3 and keep open with a twig or pebble — *Wrap well with damp sphagnum and enclose in polyethylene plastic film* — *Bind well top and bottom with electricians tape*

AIR LAYERING

overlap should be on the underside of the air layer to exclude rainwater. The clear polyethylene is available in many thicknesses but the 0·004 or 0·005 inch gauge is the most often used.

Finally, the top and bottom of the plastic wrap are bound around the stem with Scotch brand waterproof electrical tape, No. 33, to form smooth, flat ends which are firmly secured in a spiral tape wrap extending to encircle the bare stem for 1 inch above and below the ends of the plastic film. There must be no collar or funnel of exposed polyethylene at either end.

Air layers prepared in this fashion in early spring are often ready to be severed from the parent plant by autumn but it makes no difference whatever if they are not. It will not harm them for the sphagnum moss to freeze solid over winter or even to remain undisturbed for a second winter if necessary because there is little deterioration in branch, moss or plastic. Whenever they are well rooted they are cut off and planted in pots, or directly in cool, shaded cold frames, where they can make a gradual transition to an independent existence on their own roots. They will need to be handled gently, to be planted in an open, porous soil enriched with humus and to be protected during their first winter.

When air layering was first publicized there was a quick rush to apply it to Rhododendrons because of the supposed difficulty of propagating them by more conventional means, and even commercial growers spent a great deal of time in an effort to exploit the new method despite its slowness. Nurseries presented a grotesque appearance as blocks of stock plants burgeoned with multitudes of dull gray excrescences where they had been air-layered. But disillusionment followed quickly, for professional and amateur alike. The method had not been fully understood and it had been improperly applied.

The failures were nearly all due to three causes:

Surplus water was not pressed out of the sphagnum moss. It must be squeezed as dry as it is possible to do so with the hand. Air layers rarely fail because they are too dry. Almost invariably those which do not root are too wet.

Grafting strips, rubber bands and even twine were used to tie the plastic wraps to the stems and very often a collar or funnel was left at the top which held water. Even if there was an initial tight seal of the plastic to the stem at the top binding, the ties deteriorated in time so that water seeped into the sphagnum and saturated it, thus preventing the formation of roots. Waterproof electrician's tape is the only satisfactory tie that I have encountered. It is sufficiently durable and it can be used as a spiral wrap extending on to the bare stem top and bottom for a full inch to insure a good, firm seal.

It was not realized that air layers which do not form roots the first year usually root luxuriantly in the course of the second season, or even later. Multitudes of spring air layers were prematurely abandoned as unsuccessful when they had not rooted by autumn. Most of them were not well prepared but in time the majority would have rooted had they not been removed.

Air layering is a reliable and consistently successful method of propagating Rhododendrons when it is properly done. Those who failed with it when the method was first publicized can be reasonably certain of success now if care is taken to avoid the pit-falls described above.

PROPAGATION FROM SEEDS

Rhododendrons are usually grown from seeds as a means of propagating the wild species, to raise understocks for grafting, or to produce new sorts after hybridists have made the crosses designed to yield superior novelties.

Reproducing Superior Sorts

Hybrids are reproduced by grafting, layering or from cuttings, and it is not ordinarily possible to obtain duplicates of a hybrid by raising plants by means of seeds taken from it.

Such seedlings may resemble any of the hybrids' parents in various respects, including their worst faults, and it is extremely unlikely that any of them in a limited group will be a replica of the fine qualities which popularized the original plants. It is not usually possible even to reproduce in quantity a particularly good specimen of a species from seeds. The progeny will show all of the variability unseen but nevertheless inherent in the parent.

By selecting the best specimens of a species and crossing them it is possible to obtain seedlings which will be somewhat above the average in quality, and by continuing to select the finest plants to use as parents in each succeeding generation a good strain of a species can be built up which will be horticulturally valuable. By similar selection through a number of generations a hardier strain can be produced from a borderline species providing, of course, that the original stock is variable in hardiness and that the climate permits a selection between the tender individuals and other, more cold-resistant plants which can be used as parents. Almost any unselected lot of seedlings of a species on the borderline of hardiness will contain a minority of plants which are appreciably more cold-resistant than the others. These have afforded the basis on which Joseph Gable's strain of *R. racemosum* and Guy Nearing's strain of *R. fortunei* have evolved with a much higher percentage of seedlings hardy in the East than these species originally produced.

When Seeds Ripen

Seeds ripen from three to ten months after Rhododendrons bloom, depending on the sorts and on the climate in which they grow. Alpines mature their seeds first. In their native mountain wilderness they may not flower until July and they are under snow again in November. The tree Rhododendrons with mammoth leaves and others with huge exotic flowers from the temperate lower valleys, such as *RR. magnificum* and *nuttallii* have in nature plenty of time to ripen their seeds and they are laggards in doing so in cultivation.

Seed capsules which are ready to be plucked from the plants in the East during the latter part of September may not be mature on identical Rhododendrons in more benign climates until November. In general, the capsules should be watched closely from mid-September onward and they should be collected as they start to turn from green to brown. Most sorts will ripen very rapidly after a hard frost or two but a few will seemingly resist any color change. In the mountains of northwestern Pennsylvania I find it advisable to collect seeds by October 20th, whether or not the pods have started to turn brown. In any event, after the capsules start to split open at the top the seeds are in danger of being lost because the sections thereafter may separate very quickly and the seeds are then scattered by the first wind.

It is just as well to distinguish between the maturity of the seeds and the ripening of the capsule. When the latter turns brown it is because the valves have dried out. When this process is almost completed the segments separate and split downward from the tip of the capsule so that the seeds are liberated. But the seeds may be mature quite some time before this takes place and I feel certain that they usually are. It is quite possible to collect the capsules in August, dry them in an oven for three days at 100° F., sow the seeds immediately and get good germination. For hybridists and others who want to gain a year in bringing seedlings into flower this is a useful technique.

Storing Seeds

Chemical changes in seeds take place under the influence of heat, moisture and oxygen. In storing them the aim is to avoid any of these stimulants to activity which destroy viability by consuming the sharply limited food reserves in such small seeds. For practical purposes, I have found that putting each sort in a small paper envelope, labeled with its parentage, and storing in a dry closet at ordinary room temperature, is quite satisfactory to preserve good germination for the two and a half months I keep the seeds before sowing. A cooler room, about 50° F., which fluctuates little in temperature or humidity would be better; and placing the seeds in sealed vials with the least possible air space and then storing them in a refrigerator at a minimum of 38° F. would be ideal.

Under ordinary room conditions seeds lose their viability at the rate of about 50 per cent a year, and those which retain their ability to germinate sprout more slowly. They are not designed by nature to endure long in good condition. Moisture and oxygen can easily penetrate the thin coat which could be no thicker in any case because the feeble embryo with its limited food supply could not burst through it. On several occasions when I held seeds over for one year, about half of them sprouted. Held over for two years at room temperature, so few germinated that the flats were discarded. I do not know how their vitality would have been had the seeds been preserved under better storage conditions.

When to Sow

There is a great difference of opinion as to when Rhododendrons should be sown, and varying climates may be responsible for the divergent views. In the East, expert propagators promote remarkable growth during the first year by sowing the seeds as early as Thanksgiving. On the West Coast the tendency is to delay sowing until about February 1st to avoid a midwinter period when the plants make little progress and are susceptible to disease. The British growers generally agree. Possibly the amount of winter sunlight determines the optimum time. Certainly the available facilities are important. If equipment is not available for indoor propagation the seeds cannot be sown in outdoor frames until April.

I sow my seeds in early January and the only reason they are not sown sooner is because the weather would not be sufficiently settled at the time of transplanting to allow shifting the flats to unheated outdoor frames. The point is to sow the seeds just as early as the propagator's conditions will allow. This is extremely important to secure maximum growth the first year. The young plants will make continuous progress up to about the middle of July but they will make very little growth after that. The longer the growing period prior to mid-July, the larger will be the seedlings at the end of the first season.

Threshing the Seeds

By the time for sowing arrives many of the capsules will have split open in their paper envelopes. Most of the seeds will fall from them and those which remain can be freed by breaking the valve walls with the point of a dull knife and shaking them loose. Some capsules may need to be crushed. The seeds should be well cleaned so that the chaff and broken bits of capsules are removed. I have found it convenient to use several kitchen sieves with meshes ranging from coarse to fine to do this threshing operation.

Germinating Media

A wide variety of materials has been used in which to sow Rhododendron seeds, including vermiculite, perlite, sawdust, peat, and, of course, soil mixtures. After having tried most of them I am convinced that nothing equals shredded sphagnum moss, which possesses a combination of virtues uniquely suited to Rhododendrons.

The leisurely germination of the seeds and the slow early growth of the seedlings make them especially susceptible to attacks of the familiar and deadly damping-off fungi. This disease is all but unknown among seedlings growing in sphagnum moss, which is sterile to such organisms. Furthermore, if the seeds have been imperfectly cleaned, it is of no consequence. Broken bits of the capsules and fine debris which would decay with disastrous results in other seeding media cause no complications in sphagnum moss. This material is naturally and suitably acid. It is so retentive of moisture that the seedlings accidentally dry out only with the grossest neglect, yet it is all but impossible to overwater them. Its spongy, yielding texture allows the release of fragile young roots with a minimum of damage. It is light and porous and it so fulfills the natural requirements of Rhododendrons in every respect that the seedlings grow more rapidly in it than in any other material.

Some growers sow Rhododendron seeds on a thin coating of sphagnum moss on top of a prepared soil mixture because they believe that the seedlings are sustained by the food in the bottom layer if they are not transplanted on schedule. Actually the young plants can be kept even better in pure sphagnum moss, and without the risk of overwatering. As an experiment, I have retained them for two years without transplanting, and this is another advantage of the material: the seedlings can be grown along to almost any desired stage and then merely by withholding nutrients they can be checked and held almost indefinitely in good condition. When it is desirable for them to progress further it is necessary only to resume feeding them or to transplant them into flats with a prepared soil mixture. Milled sphagnum moss is available in some large seed stores or by mail from Mosser Lee, Millston, Wisconsin. It can also be collected and put through a $\frac{1}{4}$-inch mesh hardware cloth. It is equally satisfactory dead or living.

Preparing for Sowing

The flats or seed pans which are to be used for sowing should be clean. They are filled to the top with slightly moist sphagnum moss which is then pressed down firmly with a brick. It will compress to about three-quarters of its original volume. A $\frac{1}{8}$-inch layer of loose sphagnum is then scattered lightly over the compressed surfaces. The containers are then liberally watered with a bulb sprayer, covered with panes of glass and set aside for twenty-four hours for the moss to become somewhat moistened so that it will later take up water readily. The next day the flats or seed pans are generously watered again and this time most of it will be absorbed. Finally, several hours later, a half-strength nutrient solution of Folium, Hyponex, Trace L, or similar commercial preparation is applied with a bulb sprayer, about a pint to each flat, and the seeds can then be sown.

Sowing the Seeds

The universal tendency is to sow the seeds too thickly. They are small and it is hard to judge their distance on the surface of the sphagnum moss, but the rate at which they are sown determines how they must be handled later, so the matter requires some thought and attention. Commercial growers usually sow about a thousand seeds to a standard size flat and then transplant the seedlings when they are very small. I believe it is better to sow them more sparsely and wait until the plants are about $\frac{3}{4}$ inch tall before transplanting them. This is done over a period of several weeks as the tallest are removed each time and new groups of the more vigorous plants quickly spring up to crowd their neighbors until they, too, are transferred out of the seed bed.

However thickly the seeds are sown, they need not be covered with sphagnum *nor should they be watered* lest they be washed too deeply into the moss. The containers are immediately covered with panes of glass and single thicknesses of newspaper. They are then set aside for the seeds to germinate.

As Rhododendrons prefer cool, moist growing conditions, the natural assumption would be that the seeds sprout most quickly in a temperature of 50° to 55° F. but this is not the case. After experimenting with various temperatures I find that 75° F. results in more rapid and vigorous germination than any lower range. In two weeks or a little more at this temperature most of the seed lots will sprout but there is always some variance and sometimes it is extreme. It is not unusual for some sorts to take an extra ten days or two weeks and for this reason it is not advisable to sow more than one kind of seed in each container since this would complicate their later care. On one occasion seeds of *R. forrestii*, which were kept moist by rainfall outdoors after the flat was set aside to be discarded, sprouted unexpectedly and vigorously for me six months after they normally should have done so.

Care After Germination

Sown in sphagnum moss and covered with glass panes, no watering is necessary under ordinary conditions until after the seeds have germinated, when the containers should be transferred to a temperature of about 60° F. and the newspaper coverings removed. At this stage the plants should have good light but no direct sun whatever. Sunlight would quickly kill the tender young seedlings beneath their glass covers.

About ten days after they have sprouted the propagator has a choice of methods for subsequent care. A considerable amount of labor can be saved by placing the seedling containers in a propagating case which can be quickly constructed of polyethylene plastic film as described on page 329. If there are enough flats or seed pans to justify this course the glass covering the flats is removed and they are placed inside the plastic enclosure. They will require no ventilation, very little watering and practically no other subsequent care until they are ready to be transplanted.

If each container is to be handled on an individual basis, ventilation begins by inserting a matchstick beneath the glass to raise it at one end. There need be no hurry about it. The seedlings should have their roots into the sphagnum and be firmly established before the airing begins. Ventilation is then gradually increased every week or ten days until the glass covers are elevated about ¾ inch at both ends, a position in which they remain until the young plants have been transferred out of the containers or until they press against the glass.

The time of germination and the first few weeks thereafter are a critical period for the young seedlings. They must be shaded from direct sunlight. The surface of the moss should not become dry even briefly and if there is any doubt they should be watered with a bulb sprayer because it is all but impossible to harm them by overwatering when they are growing in sphagnum.

The seedlings respond generously to applications of concentrated soluble fertilizers, of which there is a vast array on the market. After having tried a variety of them I have found all but one to be suitable in the strength recommended by the manufacturer. However, many of them leave a thin adhesive residue on the foliage and I believe this to be undesirable because the slightly sticky surfaces afford a ready lodging for disease fungi. It is apparent that Rhododendron seedlings find trace elements much to their liking and they seem to use nitrogenous fertilizer to greater advantage if they are present. There are a number of brands which contain these minor elements. In recent years I have been using one called Trace L alternately with half-strength Folium, with two applications of water between each feeding with a nutrient. The nitrogen in any brand which is selected should come from an ammonium compound. If the label shows that the source of nitrogen in the fertilizer is a nitrate it is not suitable for Rhododendrons. It is important to discard any undissolved residue which settles to the bottom of the solution. If it is taken up by the bulb sprayer and applied to the seed bed it will burn the seedlings and cause the rapid deterioration of the sphagnum moss.

Flats of seedlings in a polyethylene plastic propagating case will need no daily ventilating and the loss of moisture is so slight that little watering will be required, but they should nevertheless receive a generous application of nutrient solution every two or three weeks with at least one watering in between the feedings. Such a propagating case can be given just enough air to keep the moss from remaining continuously and completely saturated.

Transplanting time depends on how thickly the seeds were sown. Commercial growers transfer all of the seedlings at one time into other flats for further development just as soon as they are large enough to handle conveniently. I have found it better to sow more sparingly and to keep the seedlings in the sphagnum until they are husky young plants ¾ to 1 inch tall, which they usually are by early April. As the most vigorous seedlings are transplanted out of the sphagnum to make up a flat or two at a time, additional strong growers soon spring up and then are ready for removal. Transplanting is done periodically in this manner over a span of six weeks although it can, of course, be done all at once if it is more convenient.

The seedlings should not be allowed to become unreasonably crowded because Botrytis Blight is almost certain to appear and it is very hard to control. Infected leaves and stems become covered with a grayish-brown mold composed of the fungus and its spores. It spreads rapidly and kills the little plants as it extends across the seed bed. Further information on its diagnosis and control will be found on page 300.

Transplanting

As the time for transplanting approaches the plants are gradually given full air and a moderate amount of morning sunlight will then not harm them. After they have been fully aired for several days they are transplanted into flats and carefully labeled. Commercial growers usually put 108 seedlings to a standard flat and they use a prepared soil mixture, usually one which has been sterilized. A standard formula is 40 per cent topsoil or leaf mold, 40 per cent Michigan peat and 20 per cent sand by volume, placed over a layer of cinders to insure good drainage through the bottom of the flat. Another popular formula is made by taking one-third each of sandy loam, leaf mold, and sand and then doubling its volume by adding Michigan peat equal to the total of the three other parts. If the seedlings to be transplanted are the susceptible *R. ponticum* the acidity of the soil mixture must be adjusted to pH 4·25 by the procedure described on page 336, to minimize the risk of attack by the deadly Wilt.

The small plants should be grasped by the leaves. The sphagnum moss is loosened beneath them with a pointed stick and they will then come free without damage to their delicate roots. After each flat is filled with transplants it is gently watered with a bulb sprayer and care is taken thereafter not to compact the soil mixture by the forceful application of water at any time, even when the plants are large enough to withstand more casual watering. This is an important point which is often overlooked. Frequently the flats are later placed outdoors where the soil mixture loses its loose, porous texture under the impact of pounding rains. This brings an immediate halt to the progress of the young plants because they must have an open, well-aerated medium in which to grow.

A. M. Shammarello, a professional grower in Ohio, has had excellent results by transplanting the seedlings into flats of pure Michigan peat and fertilizing them with a nutrient solution. After experimenting for three years with the peat, plus various mixtures of it with shredded Styrofoam, I have found that growth rates of seedlings under my conditions are considerably better in a medium of 40 per cent leaf mold, 40 per cent Premier peat, and 20 per cent sand.

Putting 108 seedlings to a flat not only saves space for the commercial grower but the plants tend to be drawn up rather tall and straight from the crowding, which is desirable for the production of rootstocks. By reducing the quantity to 48 in a flat, however, much larger and sturdier plants can be obtained by the end of the first growing season and I commend this number to those who are not growing seedlings for understocks.

Starting Seedlings under Fluorescent Lights

I have found a Glenn Dale propagating case to be ideal for germinating Rhododendron seeds and growing the seedlings on until they are about 1 inch tall. This is an enclosed case about $2\frac{1}{2}$ by 6 feet and $3\frac{1}{2}$ feet tall in which fluorescent lights are suspended above the flats. The flats in turn rest on open supports beneath which an electric cable can be spread to supply bottom heat. Two large doors provide easy access and good ventilation when it is desired. The device can be built from plans provided in a leaflet entitled 'Plant Propagation Under Fluorescent Light' (November 1945), issued by the United States Department of Agriculture, Agricultural Research Administration, Bureau of Plant Industry, Beltsville, Maryland.

After some experimenting I found that a single, industrial fixture with a reflector containing two 40-watt bulbs, as recommended, did not provide quite the most desirable light intensity, but the addition of a smaller fixture containing two 20-watt bulbs at one end of the case gave the necessary level of illumination which could also then be much better distributed throughout the case from the two fixtures. Blue bulbs gave the best results for me, suspended so that they were 10 inches above the surface of the flats. They remain lighted around the clock after the seeds germinate in the sphagnum moss and this contributes materially to the phenomenal growth which the seedlings make when the light quality, heat and humidity are so closely controlled by the propagator.

It is important that the case be placed in a basement or in some other situation where the winter room temperature will not often be above 50° F. so that the temperature within the propagating case will be in the low 60's after the seeds have germinated at 75° F. and the heating cable has been switched off. The heat generated within the enclosed case by the fluorescent lights will raise the temperature about 12° above the reading in the room. If there is any tendency for the seedlings to draw up and become a bit leggy the remedy is to lower the temperature further by propping open the doors slightly at the bottom of the case. A further remedy is to increase the frequency of the feedings with nutrient solution. Contrary to popular impression, this makes for a sturdier growth of better quality and corrects a tendency toward lankiness.

Each flat is covered with its own pane of glass within the propagating case after the seeds are sown. It remains on until the last of the seeds have germinated and the seedlings show two green leaves and are definitely established with their roots running down into the moss. As soon as the first seedlings have germinated the fluorescent fixtures are switched on. It may be necessary to turn off the heating cable before the slowest seeds have sprouted to prevent the early seedlings from becoming leggy.

The plants will need to be watered every four or five days and they are generally fed and cared for as described earlier. Ventilation can start in March when the plants are about ½ inch high and gradually increase thereafter to full airing in April when the more vigorous seedlings, now 1 inch tall, are transplanted into flats and are put in shaded cold frames outdoors.

A Method for the Home Gardener

Rhododendron seedlings can be started indoors with great success by sowing the seeds in the rectangular clear plastic refrigerator dishes which are commonly available in variety stores. These containers are about 8 inches long, 4 inches wide and 3½ inches deep, with snugly fitting covers. I favor using a hot ice-pick to put four holes $\frac{1}{16}$ inch in diameter in the bottom of each container. The risk of drowning the seedlings can thus be avoided, but the holes are not strictly necessary if extreme care is used in watering.

The plastic containers are filled to about two-thirds of their depth with milled sphagnum moss which is then pressed down and moistened as described earlier in this chapter. After the moss has been wet with nutrient solution the seeds are sown sparsely and the covers are replaced. The containers can be put away in any convenient place at about 75° F. until the seeds germinate. Then they can be placed on a north windowsill where the temperature will not average much above 60° F., or in some other cool situation. It is imperative that the sunlight should never strike the closed containers for if it does the tender young seedlings will be quickly killed.

After germination has taken place the dishes can also be taken to a cool cellar and put under blue fluorescent lights delivering 350 to 400 foot-candles. Six of the plastic dishes can be satisfactorily illuminated by a fixture with a reflector containing two 20-watt bulbs suspended 10 inches above the seed beds, which remain switched on for the entire twenty-four hour period of the day.

The tightly fitting covers eliminate the need for watering and no ventilation is necessary until transplanting time approaches. As a matter of curiosity I have left seedlings in these containers for just a little less than three years. During this period they received no care whatever and were not watered once. In the absence of any further feeding the little plants remained stationary in growth, but they were in good condition when they were finally discarded.

To encourage rapid growth the home gardener will feed the seedlings with liquid fertilizer at intervals of two or three weeks. If the containers do not have holes in the bottoms the greatest care is necessary to avoid over-application of water or nutrient solutions, and it may be desirable to ventilate just a little bit at intervals to avoid continuous and excessive saturation of the sphagnum moss.

How long the seedlings can remain in the containers depends on how thickly they are sown. They must be transferred to flats before they become excessively crowded. The dishes are ventilated at a slowly increasing rate as the transplanting time approaches, until they have been given full air. During this time they must be watered more frequently, of course, but the moss should not become soggy. After the seedlings have been transplanted into flats containing the prepared soil mixture described earlier, they are given the protection of a shaded cold frame.

First Year Care of Seedlings

If transplanting is done in cold weather the seedlings must, of course, be kept in a greenhouse or under fluorescent lights at about 60° F., but as I believe that Rhododendrons grow better outdoors and are less susceptible to disease, it seems to me that seedlings should be transferred to outside frames as early as the weather will allow. The transplants cannot stand freezing. They must be protected against both frost and direct sunlight. North-facing cold frames which are shaded are ideal and if the transplanting is done in April the seedlings in the flats can be transferred directly to them and kept syringed and sheltered for a few days until they have re-established themselves. They should then be given as much air and ventilation as possible, replacing the glass or closing the frames only when cold weather threatens.

It should be the aim of the propagator to keep the seedlings moving right along without suffering any check in their growth. This continuous development is important to good results. The seedlings respond very well to applications of liquid fertilizer every two weeks, and one of the siphon devices which automatically dilutes a concentrated solution as it passes through a garden hose is a great convenience if any considerable number of flats is to be fertilized.

The seedlings make their best growth in the cool, moist weather of springtime. With periodic feeding they will progress rapidly. After danger of frost is past I put the flats on long tables where there is good light but only a little diffused sun beneath tall old White Pine trees. There they can be conveniently tended and the benign atmosphere of the open woodland seems to encourage their growth.

From early June onward commercial growers find it desirable to apply an all-purpose preventive spray, such as is recommended on page 296, at intervals of two or three weeks. As the weather becomes warmer and atmospheric humidity drops, the seedlings will benefit from a light spray which will wet their foliage, whenever it is convenient. Routine watering continues, with a rose attached to the hose to prevent compacting the growing medium, and the propagator had better be certain that his water supply is not hard or else alkaline salts will accumulate in the flats and the seedlings will suffer. This also should be suspected earlier if there is trouble while the seedlings are still in sphagnum moss. In such cases, rainwater is used for watering. Hard, driving rains falling directly on the flats will so compact the soil that growth will be radically reduced.

The last application of liquid fertilizer for the season is given in late June and the grower then allows his seedlings to come to a natural halt in growth and to begin to harden their tissues for the winter ahead. Foliage sprays to maintain humidity are discontinued by mid-July and the seedlings can be given several hours of sunlight if lath has been used so that it is convenient to adjust the shading. By early August the flats should be watered less often and the seedlings kept drier. They may wilt a bit at midday but it will not hurt them, though they should not be so dry as to wilt morning or evening.

Except for a few of the tenderest sorts suitable for the mildest climates, young plants are not injured by the first frosts of autumn. With the approach of colder weather, however, they should be protected. By this time Rhododendron seedlings of the familiar robust commercial type should average about 5 inches in height, with the earlier aid of fluorescent illumination until they were transplanted out of the sphagnum moss in which the seeds were sown. Before the flats are put away for the winter the terminal growth buds should be pinched to induce branching the next spring. Seedlings being grown for grafting understocks are not pinched, of course. The flats are given a final treatment with an all-purpose preventive spray or dust just before they are stored so that the pesticide remains on the foliage to protect the plants from insects or disease over winter.

Winter Protection

Many Rhododendrons which are perfectly hardy in larger sizes are tender in youth and propagators use different methods to protect them over their first winter. Some put them in an unheated greenhouse or a pit glasshouse. Others put them in frames about 4 feet deep with sash covers or even in conventional surface cold frames which face north. The critical point of first importance is that any structure with a glass surface which the sun strikes can heat up very quickly in bright winter weather, regardless of how cold the air temperature may be. Amateurs have lost countless multitudes of seedlings because the glass in frames and sash-covered pits was not carefully shaded to prevent overheating in winter.

In the severe climate of the northeastern United States it is harmless for the flats of seedlings to freeze solid, but once frozen they should remain so until the spring thaw, or at least they should thaw very slowly when the winter weather moderates. It is the rapid fluctuation in temperature which must be avoided. Intermittent freezing and thawing are injurious in the extreme. Rodents sometimes do extensive damage and it is good practice to set poisoned baits as a precaution.

From my experiments I am convinced that dormant Rhododendrons require neither light nor ventilation in storage over winter. After trying various types of cold weather protection I constructed a small rectangular building with a foundation size of 22 feet 6 inches × 8 feet 6 inches, built of concrete blocks, with its long axis running east and west. The south wall is 7 feet 2 inches high and the north wall is 4 feet 1 inch high, so that the roof slopes north at quite a sharp angle. The roof is a double one, with 2 × 4's bridging the short span of the building and sheathing nailed across them both top and bottom. The spaces thus formed by the boards nailed to the under and upper surfaces of the 2 × 4's are open at both ends for free air circulation so that the double roof thus forms an effective insulation. The roof is surfaced with waterproof composition asphalt material and a section is hinged at either end so that it can be lifted to provide access. Shelves for flats line the interior walls. There are no windows or any provision for ventilation in the building. A photograph appears after page 304.

This structure has been ideal for storing seedlings in flats over winter and also for protecting large Rhododendrons which are grown in pots because they are tender outdoors. In the severe mountain climate of northwestern Pennsylvania the flats are placed in the building in late October after being watered and dusted with a pesticide. By December the growing medium has frozen solid and it does not thaw until early April. From the time they are stored until they are removed the following spring it is not necessary to water the seedlings, to air them or to give them any attention whatever.

This is much more convenient and less expensive than excavating pits or deep frames and providing drainage to prevent flooding. No glass sash covers are needed nor any attention to prevent overheating. It suggests that existing facilities can be covered with solid materials, less expensive and more easily maintained than glass sash, and that unheated outbuildings which are now standing may furnish good cold weather storage.

Second and Third Year Care

From the beginning of their second year and continuing for the next two years, Rhododendron seedlings are handled so much like rooted cuttings that there is little point in repeating here the methods described under 'Second Year Care' beginning on page 326 to which the reader is referred. The growth will not be as fast so they will not achieve the size mentioned for plants propagated from rooted cuttings, and the spacing in outdoor beds need not exceed 6 inches × 8 inches for the conventional large-leaved commercial rhododendrons. Seedlings will seldom set buds in the course of their second year in the beds and they are not at this stage large enough to be grown completely unprotected in open field culture.

If the grower is raising *R. ponticum* for grafting understocks the outdoor beds must be adjusted to a pH of about 4·25 by means of the procedure given on page 281 to minimize the risk of attack from the ever-imminent Rhododendron Wilt, and since rootstocks will be taken up at the end of the first year outdoors a spacing of 3½ inches × 3½ inches in the beds is adequate.

It is assumed that a mulch is invariably beneficial to Rhododendrons but this is not always the case in the fall. By acting as a blanket which prevents heat radiated from the earth from warming the air immediately above ground level, a mulch lowers the temperature adjacent to small plants by 6°. This can be a critical consideration at the time of the first fall frosts, especially if the late summer has been wet so that the small plants have continued to grow unseasonably and their tissues are soft. The surprising disparity of 6° between mulched and unmulched ground means the difference between frost and no frost, or between a light frost and a very severe one. Growers who routinely find damage from early frosts or who anticipate it under unusual circumstances should remove the mulches in late summer.

Commercial Rhododendrons grown from rooted cuttings are usually budded and of saleable size by the end of their second year in outdoor beds. Seedlings are not, and they need the continued shelter of lath shades for their second winter in outdoor beds. The following spring they are taken up from the beds and lined out in the field, usually 15 inches apart and in rows 30 inches apart for the more vigorous sorts. Such fields have customarily been carefully prepared by plowing under cover-crops and by the incorporation of large quantities of peat or of humus-forming vegetable debris over a period of time. How long the seedlings take to bloom depends entirely on their heritage. Species of the Taliense tribe may not flower for fifteen or twenty years. Hybrids of *RR. decorum* or *griersonianum* are precocious and usually set buds their first or second year in the field. Some of the dwarf alpines will have bloomed even before they are transplanted out of the beds.

In field culture the value of a mulch can scarcely be overestimated. The importance of a cool, damp root run for Rhododendrons is well known and a mulch materially aids in the preservation of moisture and in the reduction of temperature. I am indebted to Warren Baldsiefen, a New Jersey nurseryman, for the following data which were assembled from temperature readings taken in an open Rhododendron planting in a peat bog at Macapin, New Jersey:

DATE	TIME	AIR TEMPERATURE ON PEAT BOG, FULL SUN °F.	AIR TEMPERATURE ON PEAT BOG IN SHADE °F.	3 INCHES UNDER GROUND, LATH SHADE, NO MULCH °F.	3 INCHES UNDER GROUND, FULL SUN, NO MULCH °F.	1½ INCHES SHREDDED PINE NEEDLE MULCH: 4 INCHES UNDER GROUND, 5½ INCHES UNDER MULCH °F.	3 INCHES UNDER GROUND, 4½ INCHES UNDER MULCH °F.	2 INCHES UNDER GROUND, 3½ INCHES UNDER MULCH °F.
July 7th	3 PM	108	80	74	80	72	76	78
July 21st	12 M	106	90	74	80	72	74	80
July 24th	10 AM	80	68	68	72	70	70	71
July 31st	12 M	109	82	72	78	72	74	76
Aug. 16th	10 AM	80	60	60	64	66	65	64
Aug. 30th	12 M	114	92	72	76	72	74	77
						1½ INCH HEMLOCK SAWDUST MULCH		
June 21st	2 PM	120				70	72	76
June 23rd	5 PM	100				68	70	76
June 25th	5 PM		80			67	70	76
June 28th	3 PM	112	86			69	71	75
July 7th	3 PM	108	80			70	78	82
July 21st	12 M	106	90			72	76	80
July 24th	10 AM	80	68			68	70	72
July 31st	12 M	109	82			71	74	82
Aug. 16th	10 AM	80	60			64	64	62
Aug. 30th	12 M	114	92			68	72	76

CHAPTER X

Rhododendrons for Less Favorable Climates

GARDENERS from the South and from Ohio westward through the Mississippi Valley and the Rocky Mountain states enviously renounce the prospect of growing Rhododendrons in the mistaken belief that they cannot be successfully cultivated outside the northeastern United States and the Pacific Coast. Springtime visitors from the southern states and from the Midwest to these regions favored for Rhododendrons are almost invariably entranced by their floral show, which they find one of the most beautiful and impressive features of the gardens. In New England, southward to Washington and inland to central Ohio, thence southward through West Virginia and Virginia along the slopes of the Appalachian Mountains to North Carolina and Tennessee, Rhododendrons grow naturally and exuberantly. From central California northward along the Pacific Coast is another great natural region for their culture.

In recent years a few experimentally minded gardeners have developed successful methods for growing Rhododendrons elsewhere, in climates which would normally be considered uncongenial, and they are being joined in increasing numbers by others who are ambitious to duplicate the magnificent spectacles with which they are familiar only in distant landscapes. The sorts of Rhododendrons which will grow well in less favorable climates are now better understood and there are even some recent discoveries in the nutrition of ericaceous plants which will simplify their culture in soil not to their natural liking. Of course, the needs of any plant must be met or it will not grow well, but it is often surprising to what extent the gardener can compensate for local deficiencies in the climate and satisfy his Rhododendrons by modifying the undesirable aspects of their environment.

Rhododendrons are being successfully grown in Georgia at Atlanta, Fort Gaines and Hamilton, and there is a collection of about 150 different hybrids which has been thriving at Cedartown since 1939. Sixty miles south of Atlanta another collection has been doing well since 1930. In South Carolina some sorts have grown well at Columbia. At Greensboro in North Carolina there is a twenty-five-year-old planting with many hybrid specimens 7 feet tall, and at Charlotte a similar assortment has been thriving. Farther west in the state and continuing northward through Tennessee, Virginia and West Virginia, wild Rhododendrons grow luxuriantly along the elevations of the Blue Ridge Mountains where the climate is equally suitable for many Rhododendron hybrids.

Along the Mississippi, where the climate is not congenial, Rhododendron hybrids are growing in the sultry heat of Memphis, and they are prized features of various gardens in St Louis, Florissant and Webster Groves, Missouri. Some noble old specimens there are 12 feet tall and 14 feet broad. An enthusiast at Ottawa, Kansas, has been growing them successfully for many years. At Tulsa, Oklahoma, and at Austin, Texas, Rhododendrons are beloved by the gardeners who have tended them to flowering splendor.

Farther north, Rhododendrons are prominent in gardens at Dover, Ohio, in Cincinnati and elsewhere in districts with alkaline soil. Enthusiasts at Evansville and at Hammond,

Indiana, are enthralled with their success. In Michigan there is a large collection of fine old specimens at Saginaw and commercial growers at Scotts, Saugatuck and Grosse Ile are now featuring them. Detroit has had some plantings for many years. Farther west the roll call of successful cultivators includes growers at Wheat Ridge, Colorado, and at Cheyenne, Wyoming.

This list includes only those known to me, gardeners who have participated in a survey I conducted to determine the sorts which do well in these uncongenial climates and to establish an outline of successful cultural practices. There are probably many more of these pioneering growers in the South and in the Midwest than the number I have surveyed.

One of the most interesting experiments with Rhododendrons in uncongenial climates is now taking place in central Florida near Orlando, where Edmond Amateis, an amateur hybridist and illustrator of this book, has successfully grown the Javanese epiphytic Rhododendrons outdoors for more than a year at his winter home. In that time, *R. javanicum* and the hybrid 'King Edward VII' have survived a winter temperature of 29° F. and summer heat which continued much of the time for five months between 90° and 100° F. Despite severe drouth which extended for several months and violent autumn windstorms, these exotic Rhododendrons, formerly thought to be suitable for growing only in the humid protection of warm greenhouses, have blossomed profusely. The Javanese Rhododendrons would be interesting and unusual acquisitions for the gardens of central Florida and they might prove adaptable farther south in the state. Mr Amateis is also experimenting with some of the tender lepidote species of the Maddenii and Edgeworthii series.

Factors in Success

It would be misleading to give the impression that Rhododendrons can be grown in the South and in the Midwest with the same casual attention that they receive in more favored climates where they are among the most carefree of garden subjects. But neither do they require the fussy watchfulness and constant concern which are usually associated with plants in a foreign environment. Once they are properly planted, Rhododendrons give a gratifying account of themselves as a reward for care so modest that few gardeners begrudge it.

The novice who proposes to grow these aristocrats in an uncongenial climate must acquaint himself with the routine aspects of their selection and cultivation under favorable conditions. The factors which are undesirable in regions where they grow naturally may become severe handicaps where there are additional difficulties to surmount. Conversely, the phases which are favorable deserve additional emphasis. For example, own-root plants are ordinarily much to be preferred over grafted Rhododendrons, but in the South and the Midwest they are so conspicuously superior that this fact is repeatedly mentioned in the survey by the experienced growers there. A further note of interest is the remark made on several questionnaires which I have sent to other growers, that specimens which are bushy and well-branched close to the ground seem to grow better than those which are more lanky in habit. This is undoubtedly due to the shade which is cast beneath the plants by the top-growth. Rhododendron roots lie near the surface and their liking for a cool, moist growing medium is well known. The shelter to the root zones provided by the plants themselves apparently makes a noticeable difference in their welfare when the foliage is dense and low enough to provide added shade. The atmospheric humidity may also be desirably higher immediately adjacent to the foliage of compact specimens with many leaves. So it is important to know and to understand the environmental preferences of Rhododendrons and to meet them in so far as careful observation and local conditions will permit.

SPECIES VERSUS HYBRIDS

In selecting Rhododendrons for uncongenial climates, the hybrids are a much safer choice than the species, with a few exceptions. In the deep South, the American species *R. minus* is conspicuously successful and of course *R. chapmanii*, which is native to northwestern Florida, is a natural choice for its extraordinary heat resistance. *RR. catawbiense*, *carolinianum*, and *maximum* seem to be reasonably amenable from Arkansas, Tennessee, and North Carolina northward. Among the Asian species *R. ovatum* has proved itself adaptable south of the Mason and Dixon line. *R. arboreum* has grown and bloomed well in Texas. *R. griersonianum* is not hardy in the North, but it is noted in Great Britain for its ability to thrive in hot, dry situations though its foliage is easily burned by excessive sun. *R. decorum* plants which were raised from seeds by W. E. Bowers grew well in his nursery at Stone Mountain, Georgia. But generally the species are much less flexible in adjusting to unfavorable conditions. They evolved under specific circumstances of climate through uncounted ages and they will tolerate only limited changes from their native habitats without showing meagre growth, discolored foliage, and sparse flowering. Hybrids, on the other hand, represent a blending of growing conditions which may have been quite diverse in the wild species from which they were bred. As a result of this varied ecological heritage the hybrids tend to be conspicuously more adaptable to varying conditions of climate and culture. The normal increase in thrift and vigor so often found in hybrids further fits them to a much wider range of climates.

The Sorts to Buy

In studying the survey responses a fairly consistent pattern emerges for the selection of Rhododendron hybrids suitable for uncongenial climates. Hybrids in which species of the Fortunei series figure in the parentage are likely to prove especially adaptable where they are hardy to winter cold, except that a good many sorts derived from *R. griffithianum* fail. The immediate progeny of *R. campylocarpum* are not at home inland and even advanced generation hybrids are risky. But an inheritance, in many cases a slight one, from our native *R. catawbiense* is the best possible insurance of a Rhododendron hybrid which will thrive. The old lavender-pink-flowered Catawba hybrid, 'Roseum Elegans', appears on almost every list and from the comments on its rugged durability it is safe to say that this is the cultivar which is the easiest of all to grow. The beginner should try it first.

The following tabulation consists of *catawbiense* hybrids of ironclad hardiness which consistently appear in the recommended lists prepared by successful growers in both the South and the Midwest:

x ALBUM ELEGANS, white
x BOULE DE NEIGE, white, early
x CATAWBIENSE ALBUM, white
x CHARLES DICKENS, red
o DR H. C. DRESSELHUYS, red
x EVERESTIANUM, rosy lilac
x LADY ARMSTRONG, pink
x MRS C. S. SARGENT, rose
x ROSEUM ELEGANS, lavender-pink

The symbols preceeding the names in the list above and the two following are the ratings assigned by The American Rhododendron Society, from x to xxxx in order of increasing quality.

The hybrids below are also outstanding for heat resistance, but are not so hardy as those preceding. As a group, they are of better quality though probably a little harder to please. They are recommended for growing in the latitude of Baltimore, Cincinnati, Kansas City, and southward:

x BAGSHOT RUBY, scarlet
xxx BLUE PETER, pale lavender-blue
xxx BLUE TIT, blue, dwarf
xx CYNTHIA, bright rose-red, withstands exposure
xx GOMER WATERER, white
xx LADY CLEMENTINE MITFORD, peach pink
xx MADAME B. DE BRUIN, bright red
xxxx MARS, deep true red
xxxx PURPLE SPLENDOUR, deep purple, withstands exposure
x THE BRIDE, white

The following Rhododendrons have done well in the South and in the mildest regions of the Midwest. Most of them are equal in quality to the finest modern hybrids, but they are not likely to prove hardy under average conditions north of Tulsa, Nashville, Knoxville, Winston-Salem and Durham:

- xxx BETTY WORMALD, pink
- xxxx BRITANNIA, crimson-red
- x COUNTESS OF ATHLONE, mauve
- xxx EARL OF ATHLONE, blood-red
- xxx JAN DEKENS, pink
- xxxx LODER'S WHITE, white
- xxx MARINUS KOSTER, pink
- xxx NAOMI group of hybrids, various pink shades
- xx PINK PEARL, pink
- x UNKNOWN WARRIOR, bright red

These newer hybrids are derived in whole or in large part from Asian sorts. To do their best they need somewhat more shade and shelter than do the Catawba hybrids. The more the heat and atmospheric dryness can be tempered, the better they will grow, but all have proved satisfactory with favorable humidity in various gardens in the regions for which they are recommended.

Novices will probably be best served to try first the tough *catawbiense* hybrids, even in mild climates, and then progress to the newer sorts as their experience increases.

SUN AND SHADE

In Memphis, Tennessee, and Austin, Texas, direct sunlight is so intense that growers have found it best to plant Rhododendrons with no direct sun whatever, but in good light, as in a northern exposure. Elsewhere, the recommendations in the Midwest and in the South are for 25 per cent to 40 per cent sun. High overhead shade from deep-rooting hardwood trees which are pruned annually to remove branches less than 12 feet from the ground is recommended for midday protection, with their quota of sunlight striking the plants in the morning and as little as possible in the afternoon. Honey Locusts and Oaks are mentioned in the Midwest as being especially desirable. Tall Pines and Oaks are recommended by southern gardeners. But everywhere a planting situation facing northward is mentioned as being close to ideal and many participants in the survey stated that Rhododendrons planted on the north side of a house foundation exceeded in health and beauty those planted in other situations.

WIND PROTECTION

Protection from hot drying winds is essential, and in many parts of the Midwest the north side of a building not only shields plants from sun and from radiated heat, but also shelters them against the prevailing southwesterly winds.

Some gardeners in the South have used evergreen hedges or taller deciduous plantings as shields against the wind, and a successful grower in Kansas who maintains his collection in a lath house uses laths spaced 1 inch apart on the southwest and north sides of the structure to serve as windbreaks. It is open only to the East.

PREPARING THE BEDS

The map on page 51 shows the portions of the United States where the soil is acid. In regions of alkaline soil it is not desirable to plant a Rhododendron in an isolated hole containing a prepared planting mixture. Where the earth is not naturally and suitably acid, the infiltration of water from the surrounding area can too quickly alter the acidity of a small volume of soil which is artificially maintained below pH 5·0 for the benefit of the plant. Rhododendrons should be grown in *beds* in districts where the soil is naturally alkaline and even if it is desired to plant but one specimen the minimum size of the prepared area should be 4 feet × 4 feet for permanent and practical use.

In preparing a bed it must be determined if the drainage is naturally adequate, because Rhododendron roots must have a porous growing medium which is well aerated. If it becomes waterlogged, air is excluded and the plants quickly die. A simple test can be made by digging a flat-bottomed hole 2 feet in diameter and 2 feet deep, and putting in it 2 inches of water. If it seeps away within six or eight hours, the drainage in a larger bed should be satisfactory at that location. Should the drainage not be adequate, however, one solution is to slope the bottom of the excavation to a well in one corner calculated in cubic size to hold 2 inches of water distributed over the bed, and fill it with broken bricks, coarse cinders or stones, but not limestone rocks. Excess water will drain into the well and from there gradually seep away. The recommended alternative is to build an elevated Rhododendron bed 18 inches deep above the ground level, with a retaining wall enclosing the prepared soil mixture. In no case should a planting site be lower than the surrounding terrain because alkaline surface water would then flow into it to cause a rapid loss of soil acidity.

If the soil acidity must be obtained and continued by the use of chemicals it is especially important that the beds be made up properly with an abundant supply of organic matter as a principal ingredient of the soil mixture. The welfare of Rhododendrons depends for decades on the methods used when the beds are first prepared and this step cannot be slighted without accepting the consequences later. It is laborious to do the job right but the reward is a lifetime of pleasure which continues long after the work is forgotten.

Most growers agree that beds should be excavated at least 2 feet deep. Four and a half feet is a good width if the plants are to be placed in a single row. An 8-foot width allows a more pleasing and informal arrangement of staggered spacing in two rows with open bays in which ferns, Lilies, Columbines, Mertensias, Trilliums and other wild flowers will thrive. Even if there is no apparent necessity for a well or drainage tiles it is a good idea to slope the bottom of the bed to one corner. About 4 inches of coarse rubble, stones, gravel or broken bricks, but not limestone rocks, are placed in the bottom of the excavation to interrupt the capillarity which may otherwise conduct water upward from the alkaline soil beneath the bed, and to aid drainage. On this goes the soil mixture in which the Rhododendrons will be planted.

An alternative method principally useful for commercial growers in regions of heavy clay is to churn up the topsoil to a depth of 12 inches with a mechanical tiller. To each 100 square feet is then added an eleven-bushel bale of Canadian sphagnum peat moss or fibrous European peat, five pounds of Krilium soil conditioner and three pounds of flowers of sulphur. The bed is then churned again to mix the ingredients uniformly.

The elevated bed is undoubtedly the safest and surest way to grow Rhododendrons in regions with uncongenial soil. No failures were reported in the survey with this method whereas some correspondents who failed with various subsurface soil preparation techniques reported gratifying success with enclosures 18 inches deep on top of the ground, filled with a porous, acid growing medium. At the best, a subsurface bed is only a very small island of acid soil poorly insulated from an encroaching sea of injurious elements. An elevated bed affords excellent isolation from the undesirable influence of the native soil and solves any drainage problems at the same time.

The Soil Mixture

There are almost as many different formulas for the growing medium to be used in either elevated or excavated Rhododendron beds which are recommended for amateur growers as there are gardeners who have been successful in cultivating them in different climates.

For the beginner, at least, it is probably safer to use one of the older tested formulas of which one-third each of topsoil, sand, and imported European peat is a standard mixture for regions where the natural soil is heavy clay. Domestic peats are too fine in texture and lack durability in outdoor use. Many gardeners use a mixture of old Oak leaves, Pine needles, spent tanbark, peat, or whatever organic matter is most conveniently available, with the addition of some sand to lighten the texture. In Hammond, Indiana, an experienced gardener recommends 50 per cent coarse peat, 25 per cent rotted leaves, and 25 per cent sandy topsoil. Here the soil is already light in texture and no additional sand is needed. A growing medium made up of 35 per cent leaf mold, 20 per cent peat, 15 per cent sand, and 30 per cent topsoil has worked out well at Charlotte, North Carolina. In Georgia, a half each of rotted leaves and rotted cotton-seed hulls is mixed with an equal volume of peat moss to give good results. One-half sandy loam and one-half peat moss grows good Rhododendrons in South Carolina. In Texas, pure peat moss in raised beds has been recommended and a more conventional mixture of one-third each peat moss, leaf mold, and sand is favored in the Chicago district. These various formulas have been cited to show that all of them share in common a preponderance of organic materials as the principal ingredient. The materials can be varied but every successful mixture contains a minimum of 50 per cent vegetable matter and the indications are that more than 50 per cent is desirable. The aim is always to lighten the soil and obtain good porosity.

With experience more unconventional ingredients may be successfully used in the growing medium. A veteran fancier west of the Mississippi uses 80 per cent old rotted sawdust and 20 per cent sand, and finds it so retentive of moisture that artificial irrigation is seldom necessary. In St Louis a commercial nurseryman has had fine results from a mixture of two-thirds Oak sawdust and one-third topsoil, topped with 5 pounds of Copperas (ferrous sulphate) to each 100 square feet. The sawdust mixtures have economy to recommend them, but there is some risk of disease or of nitrogen deficiency which may prove difficult to control. A few gardeners have reported severe chlorosis and problems of correcting it which persisted for several years. It is essential to add 1 pound of ammonium sulphate for each wheelbarrow load (2·5 cubic feet) of sawdust used.

The depth of the excavated bed provides a reservoir of moisture which rises through the soil mixture to sustain the plants during dry weather. At the same time it is deep enough so that the roots in the top 18 or 20 inches have good drainage even if some water does accumulate for a few hours lower down at the bottom of the bed after heavy rains.

Whatever growing medium is used, it is built up in an excavated bed to about 8 inches above the level of the ground surrounding it so that the top of the bed will be several inches above grade after the soil mixture has settled. This prevents alkaline surface water from flowing into the Rhododendrons and reducing the acidity at their roots. It also insures good aeration in the top of the bed.

Acidifying Alkaline Soil

After the level of an excavated bed has been brought above grade or the elevated bed has been filled to an 18-inch depth, Copperas (ferrous sulphate) is applied to the surface at the rate of 5 pounds per 100 square feet, if the soil is not naturally acid. It is thoroughly watered in, and after several days a soil test is made (a proprietary product called pHydrion Papers make a quick and convenient test). If it does not test between pH 4·0 and 4·5, additional applications of Copperas are watered in and a test is made after waiting for several days following each treatment, until this degree of acidity is attained. Sulphur is too slow and uncertain as an acidifier for use in the home garden and aluminum sulphate can be toxic in its cumulative effect. Copperas is the fastest and safest material for this purpose and the soil should be tested twice each year to determine what additional amounts may be needed. In most regions of alkaline soil an application of about 5 pounds per 100 square feet will be needed about twice annually if there is much irrigation with hard water.

Fertilizing

For most soil mixtures, Cotton-seed or Soya Bean meal, applied at the rate of 4 pounds per 100 square feet, is highly regarded as a spring stimulant, but many gardeners routinely use complete commercial fertilizers formulated specifically for acid soil plants. Several recommend the use of cow manure on the beds each spring. I feel that FTE (fritted trace elements), formulation FN-501, should be incorporated at the rate of $3\frac{1}{2}$ ounces per 100 square feet into the top 18 inches of Rhododendron beds at the time they are made up. All evidence indicates that the use of this material will allow considerable variation in acidity and in nutrition levels without adversely affecting the plants. It might be considered as a sort of insurance.

It is extremely important that nitrogen from any source be supplied as ammonium nitrogen and not as nitrate. Gardeners in regions of alkaline soil should examine carefully the labels of fertilizer for Rhododendrons to be certain that the nitrogen comes from ammonium sulphate or from an organic source. If ammonium sulphate is used, small frequent applications will be most beneficial to growing Rhododendrons. Organic fertilizer beneficially provides a low, constant supply of ammonium nitrogen. The ammonium form of nitrogen inhibits the absorption of the base ions which cause a loss of vital sap acidity. In laboratory experiments Rhododendrons grew quite well in alkaline sand if they were fertilized with ammonium nitrogen. They quickly started to die when a nitrate fertilizer solution was substituted.

In nature Rhododendrons are found in soil of low fertility. Under such circumstances in cultivation they are able to endure soil conditions which would normally be injurious. Evidence is accumulating that the *total* concentration in the soil of the base nutrient salts (potassium, calcium, magnesium) should be especially low in regions of alkaline soil. Rhododendrons have been grown in the laboratory and have been found in nature in infertile alkaline soil which was conspicuously low in calcium content.

Ammonium sulphate or Cotton-seed meal can be applied to new beds if they are prepared before the middle of May. The soil mixture should settle for at least a month before the beds are planted. If the Rhododendrons are to be planted after the middle of June it would be better to wait until the following spring to add the fertilizer. If the preparation can be done in the autumn and the planting the next spring, so much the better. There is then no risk of the Rhododendrons sinking below grade when the soil subsides, and capillarity between the root ball and the surrounding soil mixture is more quickly established.

The Importance of Iron

Alkaline soils are normally unsuited for Rhododendrons mainly because they cause a loss of acidity internally, within the plants, so that the iron in the sap becomes tied up in insoluble form. Deprived of iron, the foliage cannot form the green chlorophyll essential to the internal manufacture of the carbohydrates which sustain growth. The leaves become yellow while the veins remain green, later turn cream all over, then white, and finally become brown as they die and drop from the plant.

New combinations of iron with organic acids, called iron chelates, hold the element in soluble form even after absorption into the sap stream. The dry material, now available commercially, is applied around the plants at the exact rate recommended by the maker, and it seems to hold great promise for gardeners who want to grow Rhododendrons in the alkaline soil of the Midwest, in the chalk districts of Great Britain and elsewhere. In fact, the Citrus Experiment Station of the University of Florida announced after a series of experiments that, '. . . Rhododendrons will grow well even on alkaline soils if supplied with sufficient iron in available form'.

This may be a considerable oversimplification since a loss of sap acidity, which is the basic problem, probably unbalances the utilization of other nutrients. Alkaline soil in itself is not the only cause of lower sap acidity. Experimental evidence indicates that soil alkalinity may be endured if the *total* concentration of potassium, magnesium and calcium salts is low, or at least if the absorption of them can be reduced as it is, for example, in the presence of ammonium ions. Rhododendrons can be grown quite well in the laboratory in alkaline soil if the high pH is obtained with magnesium compounds and not with calcium.

A new chelate-like iron compound containing ferrous ammonium sulphate, other trace elements, and nitrogen, appears to be particularly beneficial to Rhododendrons. Careful inquiry should be made about the usefulness of any chelate on alkaline soil because some are many times more efficient than others under such circumstances. Iron-EDTA-OH, for example, is eleven times more effective than the iron-EDTA which is used on acid soil.

The value of iron chelates has been so clearly demonstrated that it should be used routinely by anyone preparing to make a Rhododendron planting in regions of lime-rich soil. It can be considered a sort of protection against injury from unnoticed loss of acidity in prepared beds.

The procedure for growing Rhododendrons in unaltered alkaline soil treated with iron chelate is still experimental, an interesting investigation for the venturesome gardener who has already succeeded with more conventional methods.

Preparing the Plants

The problems which exist for Rhododendron growers in congenial climates become accentuated in difficult climates. An important detail of successful culture inland is to prepare the plants before they are placed in the beds so that the roots will be encouraged to venture out into the prepared soil mixture. Rhododendrons are always received from the nursery with a ball of earth protecting the roots. Three inches of the root-ends should be exposed around the perimeter of the earth ball by forcefully washing away the soil with a garden hose. The plants are then immediately placed in the beds at the same depth they grew in the nursery and the roots will already then be extending out into the soil in which they are to grow. If the root-ends are not thus encouraged to penetrate the planting mixture in the new bed many Rhododendrons languish and ultimately die because the root systems fail to reach out beyond the original balls of earth in which they were first established.

THE MULCH

A good mulch to supply humus, retain moisture, and reduce the soil temperature is extremely important in uncongenial climates. Coarse imported peat, Pine needles, hardwood leaves, bagasse, rotted or fresh sawdust, wood chips, cotton-seed hulls, peanut hulls, tobacco stems, tung nut pomace, spent hops, and ground corn-cobs are variously used to a depth ranging from about 3 inches for the peat of medium density to 6 or 8 inches for the loose leaves. The mulch must be renewed each fall. In the Midwest many growers add an extra 8 inches of leaves, preferably Oak, above the permanent surface mulch in the autumn for added winter protection, and then remove three-quarters of this temporary second mulch the following spring.

Perhaps the most important function of the mulch is to supply humus after the supply in the soil is exhausted. Even the best coarse European peat incorporated at the time the beds are prepared lasts but eight years in the earth. Most other materials are much shorter lived but all eventually go into neutral solution and are leached out of the topsoil so that little or no humus remains in it. But a surface mulch which is faithfully renewed each year forms humus faster than it disintegrates so that a constantly increasing layer of decayed organic matter is built up on top of the soil into which the Rhododendron roots are gradually attracted as the underground humus in the prepared beds is slowly dissipated. This is a vital necessity for the long term health and welfare of Rhododendrons in uncongenial climates. Without it they will start to deteriorate after the humus in the earth is exhausted.

WATERING

After the Rhododendrons are planted and mulched they should be watered well and thereafter the foliage should be sprinkled and the soil kept moist until they are established.

In subsequent periods of drouth the initial care in preparing the beds will be appreciated because frequent irrigation, when the drainage is adequate, will not kill the plants by saturating the beds and displacing the oxygen in the root zone which is vital to their health. Innumerable Rhododendrons died during the summers of 1953 and 1954 in the course of the extraordinary drouths in the Midwest because their owners drowned them by constant irrigation in beds with insufficient drainage. If the soil mixture in which they are growing is moist it is harmful to flood the roots with additional water during dry weather. Should the plants still show signs of distress the foliage should be sprinkled at intervals as required, especially in the evening. A veteran grower in Indiana sprinkles the foliage of his plants twice a week in hot weather and waters them for two or three hours once a week. A Missouri gardener sprays lightly every evening and soaks the beds thoroughly every two weeks in time of drouth. Georgia Rhododendrons in a sandy soil receive water for four hours twice weekly in midsummer, with occasional foliage sprays as may be needed additionally. In Ohio and North Carolina several growers mention that they sprinkle the plants for an hour three times each week during dry weather. In any case, routine watering is discontinued in mid-August in the North so that the plants will start to mature their tissues to resist freezing temperatures in the winter ahead. The gardener must be certain that the earth is moist just before it freezes for the winter and irrigation supplies the lack if rain fails at this season.

In regions where the water supply is alkaline the grower relies on the humus in the beds to serve as a buffer and on the semi-annual soil tests to determine when additional Copperas should be applied to restore failing acidity. In one midwestern garden where Rhododendrons are watered twice each month from May to October with city water of pH 9·0, it is necessary to use an acidifier twice each year in spring and autumn, at the rate of 5 pounds per 100 square feet.

UNSEEN INJURY

Inland gardeners should note the subsidence which occurs in Rhododendron beds as the organic matter decays, especially if sawdust has been used as an important constituent of the soil mixture. In some instances plants have been gradually killed over a period of years because they sank imperceptibly with the level of the beds while new mulches were applied annually. Finally the roots were too far beneath the surface for the aeration they require and they were smothered by the yearly renewal of the mulches. Plantings should be examined with this in mind every few years and the Rhododendrons should be lifted in the beds if they do not have a vigorous root system fanning out just beneath the surface of the soil.

Rhododendrons in hot climates are more susceptible to attacks of the Blight which causes branches to wilt abruptly without apparent cause. A full discussion of this malady and its control appears on page 296 of the chapter on pests and diseases.

CHAPTER XI

Rhododendrons for the Cool Greenhouse

SOME of the most impressive of all Rhododendrons are too tender to be really satisfactory garden decorations anywhere in America except in the San Francisco region of California. Their usefulness in the British Isles is equally restricted to the most favored gardens of Cornwall and of the West. Elsewhere under glass many of them produce sumptuous flowers of luxuriant proportions and delicious fragrance. The finest forms of *R. nuttallii*, for example, bear enormous constellations of five or six marvelously scented blossoms, each 6 inches in diameter and 5 inches long, reminiscent of a mammoth white lily with luminous yellow rays in the throat. The effect of such splendid blossoms can scarcely be credited in a written description.

There is also a group of charming Rhododendrons which are hardy along the coast of Washington and Oregon but are much more attractive in the greenhouse because they are somewhat bud-tender outdoors and seldom bloom fully, or because they blossom so early that the flowers are usually disfigured by frost and inclement weather. *R. burmanicum*, for example, is an outstanding garden shrub in the Bay region of San Francisco, but farther north it is so close to the limit of its climatic range that it loses foliage in cold winters, seldom flowers freely, and is quite ordinary in its garden effect. Under glass, this same species is a triumphant success. The plants are so bedecked with trusses on the tips of almost every branch that they form a spectacular mass of gold and ivory high-lighted by glints of green from unopened buds. Compact plants handsomely clothed with foliage are attractive the year around.

R. moupinense is hardy enough outdoors along the Pacific Coast but only rarely does the weather in February treat it kindly enough for the best display of its flowers. Protected from frost and storm it too is a spendthrift of its pink or white blossoms which envelop the plant in a froth of color far superior to its garden display. *R. moupinense* bears small, shiny evergreen leaves on densely branched plants of mounded outline. It is an attractive choice for winter bloom indoors even without the facilities of a greenhouse. I have found it easy to manage by plunging the potted plants in a bed of sawdust outdoors with about 25 per cent shade in the spring, where they get along very well with routine watering and produce floral buds in prodigal numbers. In early November they are removed to a deep cold frame and from early January onward they can be induced to flower very quickly by bringing the plants indoors to a temperature of 50° or 60° F. The heavy substance of the blossoms insures a long period of bloom. When the display fades in the house the plants are returned to the deep cold frame until danger of frost is past and the time comes again to plunge the pots in the sawdust bed outdoors.

The greenhouse Rhododendrons to be discussed in this chapter are not ordinarily grown under glass to *force* them into flower. Almost all of them blossom naturally between March 1st and the middle of May and they need only a minimum night temperature of 30° F. throughout the winter to protect their floral buds from injury. In nature most of them are plants of the lower mountain ranges of southeastern Asia where many of them grow like Orchids perched high on the branches of the giant evergreen trees of the temperate jungle, or with more exposure along the edges of Pine forests and among the ledges and rocky slopes of the higher altitudes.

THE SMALL GREENHOUSE

In the small greenhouse it is better to grow Rhododendrons in pots and tubs so that they can be spared the excessive heat of a small structure in summer. With the approach of hot weather plants in containers can be moved outdoors to a lath house or to a partially shaded spot in the garden where it is convenient to water and care for them until just before the season of early frosts. The high humidity in which they luxuriate can be provided during the sojourn outdoors by frequent spraying during hot dry weather. It is better to return them to the greenhouse before they encounter any freezing whatever because the floral buds of some sorts are sensitive to even light frosts at this season outdoors.

Potting

In potting Rhododendrons, the drainage should be as nearly perfect as is possible to manage. Not less than 2 inches of rubble must be provided for the bottoms of smaller pots and one-quarter of their capacity in coarse drainage material is profitable insurance for larger containers. Any Rhododendron needs exceptional aeration at its roots, and many of the greenhouse sorts are even more demanding in this respect since they are in nature aerial acrobats clinging precariously to a bit of moss and leaf mold in the crotch of a tree top.

A standard potting mixture is 40 per cent leaf mold, 40 per cent peat, and 20 per cent coarse sand. Another formula is two parts peat, two parts coarse sand, one part leaf mold, and one part loam. Mr and Mrs D. W. James, who have grown a wide assortment of species and hybrids in their West Coast greenhouse, use a mixture composed of equal parts of peat moss and Oak leaf mold to which is added 25 per cent of sand by volume.

The species which in nature show the strongest preference for aerial perches, including some of the best of the Maddenii series, are hard to please on their own roots in the greenhouse, but there is an easy way to tame them to the amenities of cultivation under glass. Grafted on understocks of *R. ponticum* these exotic beauties display an affable disposition to grow as vigorously as any terrestrial Rhododendron. Own-root specimens are planted in a mixture of coarse peat and live sphagnum moss on an aerial platform of spaced slats and grown like orchids, preferably; or they are put in containers with special precautions against overpotting and overwatering their small root system. But when these Maddenii sorts are grafted on *R. ponticum*, the sturdy wild Rhododendron of Asia Minor and Europe, they can be easily grown in the standard potting mixture and they acquire such vigor that the flowers are larger and more freely borne on plants of superior foliage and habit. Several species which are not compatible with the Pontic Rhododendron can be grafted instead on understocks of the scaly-leaved hybrid 'Fragrantissimum'. Rhododendrons of the Maddenii group can be identified by the series affiliation given in the listing at the end of this chapter and in the complete roster of species beginning on page 524.

THE LARGER GREENHOUSE

Greenhouse Rhododendrons are really at their best in ground beds and this is the way they should be grown in larger glasshouses where the problem of minimizing midsummer heat is not so acute. Snow-fencing laid on the glass helps to support the snow load which accumulates on the roof of such slightly heated structures in severe winter climates and it provides about the right amount of shade for plants in the northeastern United States. The ideal preparation for ground beds is to provide an acid soil mixture 2 feet in depth on top of 6 inches of coarse gravel for quick drainage. A growing medium composed of two parts loam, two parts peat, and one part coarse sand is suitable. Good preparation is justified, because some of the best Rhododendrons for larger glasshouses can be expected to thrive in ground beds for a half century or more. *R. ciliicalyx* in a noted collection shows no sign of faltering after such a span of cultivation. *R. dalhousiae* after thirty-five years is 10 feet in height and as much in width; *R. nuttallii* is even larger. It is almost a necessity that most of the Maddenii species be grafted on *R. ponticum* to be permanently planted in ground beds.

CARE

A brief review of the conditions under which these Rhododendrons grow in nature will indicate the essential details of greenhouse culture. When they are dormant in midwinter their need for water is modest and any surplus is injurious, especially to the sorts whose roots are used to the instantaneous drainage of a few scraps of rotting vegetation on the limb of a tree or in a crevice of a boulder. Just enough water to prevent wilting will forestall trouble. As activity quickens with the approach of spring, watering is more liberal and the plants appreciate spraying with increasing frequency to simulate the constant quick showers and high humidity of their Asian homeland. Ventilation is given to the fullest possible extent in an effort to maintain a clean, buoyant atmosphere. As the season progresses the spraying which provides humidity also beneficially reduces the temperature in the greenhouse.

As they fade, flower trusses should be removed from Rhododendrons which show any disposition to form seed pods. Cotton-seed meal is a safe fertilizer which the plants seem to find especially congenial.

The epiphytic species did not seek their aerial perches by preference. They were forced to do so by the grim struggle for light and moisture in the temperate jungle. Through the ages they have striven toward the rain-soaked moss on the top tree branches and the life-giving gift of the sun. In the green roof of the temperate rain forests they have achieved an uneasy compromise between sustenance and light. Our summers are much clearer and brighter than any they have experienced, and these Rhododendrons must be shaded in the greenhouse as the sun mounts in the sky with the approach of warm weather.

Foliar Feeding

Epiphytic Rhododendrons respond especially well to foliar feeding because they are by nature adapted to the absorption of nutrients through their leaves. In their forest home they exist on the daily rain which brings with it the means of further life: bird guano and decayed vegetation washed down from the topmost tree branches; nitrogen-bearing dust and other food particles from the air. The nourishment raining down eternally in minute quantities is fully utilized because the high humidity of the forest retards evaporation and allows the plants to absorb it through their leaves. The greenhouse cultivator can encourage the fullest luxuriance and the most prodigious bloom on his Rhododendrons by monthly syringing with a solution containing one of the water soluble fertilizers in the concentration recommended by the maker.

Pests

The standard greenhouse spray preparations are suitable for combating the rare pests and diseases of Rhododendrons. Red spiders may be troublesome in hot weather. Parathion or malathion are effective miticides and they control many other pests as well without injuring the plants. But the greenhouse enthusiast who cultivates Rhododendrons soon comes to appreciate their health and freedom from harmful insects.

Minimum Temperature

Specialists differ as to the exact minimum temperature which these scaly-leaved Rhododendrons can endure under glass. A large collection was grown for years in the New York City district in an unheated lean-to greenhouse 17 × 40 feet and the injury to the plants was surprisingly small. However, *RR. taggianum* and *griffithianum* were killed at 14° F. when the outside temperature dropped to −20° F. in a severe winter, and other sorts such as 'Countess of Haddington' and 'Fragrantissimum' lost their buds but were otherwise uninjured. Unbudded plants of *crassum*, *maddenii*, 'Grierdal', *megacalyx*, *formosum*, and 'Lady Alice Fitzwilliam' suffered no harm. With the slow change in temperature, the protection from wind and from direct frost which a greenhouse affords, it seems apparent that these Rhododendrons can endure much more cold than is popularly believed, but the exact subfreezing degree which causes damage probably depends upon a variety of local factors.

THE MALAYSIAN RHODODENDRONS

Anyone who becomes interested in the genus sooner or later hears about a legendary race of greenhouse plants called the Javanicum Rhododendrons. Among the scores of species in this group the most attractive gave rise to innumerable hybrids in the ornate conservatories of Victorian England when glasshouses held all manner of rare and exotic tropical flowering plants. The Javanese Rhododendrons, of conservatory fame, both species and hybrids, are epiphytic and they thrive best in a mixture of one part coarse peat and one part sphagnum moss tied to a lattice platform made of spaced strips of wood, similar to the manner in which orchids are often grown. These are plants of the dripping jungle at lower elevations, accustomed to the humid warmth of the tropics, and unlike other Rhododendrons they require warmhouse conditions of shade and moisture. They are lanky shrubs up to 6 feet tall which could perhaps better be described as Malayan Rhododendrons since they are native to the region of Borneo, New Guinea, the Philippine Islands, Annam, Java, and Malaya. Their waxy, long-tubed flowers are yellow or various shades of orange and red, produced at almost any time of the year because the plants grow continuously. As warm-house subjects these plants are briefly mentioned in a chapter devoted to Rhododendrons for the cold greenhouse for lack of any better place to discuss them. Edmond Amateis, an amateur Rhododendron specialist and hybridist, has grown a number of them and through his gift I have flowered several of the leading clones in a conservatory. Although they have been glowingly described in the literature of Rhododendrons, I judged them to be stiff and ungainly in their plant habit and disappointing in their flowers.

However, only a minute proportion of the scores of species or of the hybrids which once existed are in cultivation now. There are probably scores more of species in Malaya, Indonesia and the Philippines waiting to be discovered and described. Some of them may be of dramatic beauty. An expedition from The Netherlands found a white-flowered Rhododendron in New Guinea in 1958 which was described as having flowers 7 inches in diameter. There may also be enormous variations in the hardiness and culture of this group. The mountains of Dutch New Guinea rise to 16,400 feet, with snow fields at the higher elevations, and little is known about their flora. There may be fine Rhododendrons growing there suitable for outdoor cultivation in the gardens of the Occident. Recent collections of seeds are now being grown at several European institutions.

A collection at Longwood Gardens, Kennett Square, Pennsylvania, is on public display during its blooming season in the conservatory.

See Appendix page 528 for information newly available on the "Javanicum" Rhododendrons.

Favorite Sorts

Among the Rhododendrons which are truly suited for the coolhouse, my favorite is *R. formosum*. It has large white flowers with yellow throats and a red band on the outside of each 'petal'. Seen as a pot plant about 2 feet tall it is remarkably beautiful and its pervading fragrance scents a large room. *R. scottianum*, not too different, is beloved by those with extensive experience in growing a variety of the tender scaly-leaved Rhododendrons. The hybrid 'Grierdal', which represents the result of an extraordinary mating between the scaly-leaved *R. dalhousiae* and the non-scaly *R. griersonianum*, is a fine greenhouse subject with its large, brilliant red flowers.

The Rhododendron with the largest flowers in the genus, *R. nuttallii*, belongs in this group which needs glasshouse protection and it is usually found in the collections of connoisseurs. It has sumptuous clear white or light yellow blossoms of heroic proportions. The stately candelabra of five or six funnel-shaped flowers resembling huge lilies shed a rich fragrance reminiscent of nutmegs. There are few floral treasures of the world which can equal its luster.

R. 'Tyermanii', a hybrid between *nuttallii* and *formosum*, is one of my favorites for the greenhouse. Its enormous flaring white trumpets, exquisitely ruffled and fluted around the edges and suffused with yellow in the throats, are a startling spectacle. The opulent effect of the outward-facing scented clusters is further enhanced by the stately poise of their carriage, making this one of the finest of all flowers, theatrical in size and extraordinarily beautiful in form and coloring. 'Tyermanii' appears to particular advantage trained against the wall of a conservatory or along the end of a greenhouse.

The double-flowered form of *R. johnstoneanum* is another Rhododendron which is extraordinarily effective under glass. There the handsome foliage and compact growth form an attractive background for the large white flowers of great elegance and distinction. The unique blossoms have a broad flat corolla with a spreading tuft of short waved petals in the center, the only double-flowered Rhododendron which seems to me to be intrinsically beautiful.

SELECTING THE BEST

A careful selection of species and hybrids will extend the flowering period of greenhouse Rhododendrons over a period of several months. Mr and Mrs D. W. James have prepared at my request a list, appended below, of the sorts which have given the greatest satisfaction in their extensive collection and I have added some recommendations of European experts for a wider range of flower colors at various seasons. All of these Rhododendrons bloom at some period between the first of March and the middle of May except *RR. scabrifolium* and *moupinense*, which flower in February, and *R. rhabdotum*, which blooms in July. They range from the ideal pot plant form of *R. megeratum*, bushy and compact and scarcely more than 1 foot tall, to the tall ungainly bareness of *R. dalhousiae*, a beauty with a poor figure which needs a skirt of foliage from other plants to hide its knobby knees.

The heights ascribed to the various sorts are the mature dimensions after years of growth. Many of the taller Rhododendrons blossom profusely and make attractive greenhouse subjects when they are considerably less than their maximum stature, and most of them can be severely pruned to restrain their growth. The quality ratings of the American Rhododendron Society are included with the complete listing of all species beginning on page 508 and with the list of hybrids which starts on page 425, but a number of the Rhododendrons in this restricted group for the greenhouse have not yet been evaluated in this country so the usefulness of the American ratings is limited. The quality ratings given below are therefore those of the Royal Horticultural Society of England, one to four stars in the order of increasing value, but they should be used with caution and as a basis for rough comparisons only, as they were not intended to indicate the most admirable sorts for greenhouse use. *R. scottianum* bears only one star, yet it is especially appealing when grown in the protection of a glasshouse. The hybrid 'Forsterianum' is shorn of any marks of quality but it is always greatly admired indoors. A.M. indicates that the Rhododendron has received the Award of

Merit and F.C.C. shows receipt of the First Class Certificate. The species names followed by (d) are described in detail in the descriptions which begin on page 122.

LOW GROWING (less than 5 feet)

NAME		SERIES OR PARENTAGE	COLOR
boothii	**	Boothii	yellow
bullatum (F.C.C.)	****	Edgeworthii	white or pink
burmanicum (d)	**	Maddenii	yellow
carneum (A.M.)	**	Maddenii	pink or white
CHRYCIL		*chrysodoron* × 'Cilpinense'	yellow
CHRYSASPIS (A.M.)		*chrysodoron* × *leucaspis*	yellow
chrysodoron (A.M.)	**	Boothii	yellow
CHRYSOMANICUM (A.M.)		*chrysodoron* × *burmanicum*	yellow
ciliatum (d)	****	Maddenii	pink or white
ciliicalyx (A.M.) (d)	****	Maddenii	white, pink flush
COUNTESS OF HADDINGTON (F.C.C.)	**	*ciliatum* × *dalhousiae*	white
cubittii (A.M.)	**	Maddenii	white
edgeworthii (F.C.C.) (d)	****	Edgeworthii	white
formosum (d)	***	Maddenii	white
iteophyllum		Maddenii	white
johnstoneanum (A.M.) (d)	***	Maddenii	cream
leucaspis (F.C.C.) (d)	****	Boothii	white
megeratum	**	Boothii	yellow
moupinense (A.M.) (d)	****	Moupinense	white
parryae		Maddenii	white
scabrifolium	***	Scabrifolium	white or pink
scottianum	*	Maddenii	white, fine
SETA (A.M.)	**	*spinuliferum* × *moupinense*	pink
spiciferum	***	Scabrifolium	pink
spinuliferum (d)	***	Scabrifolium	red
sulfureum (d)	***	Boothii	yellow
VALASPIS (A.M.)		*valentinianum* × *leucaspis*	yellow
valentinianum (A.M.) (d)	***	Maddenii	yellow
VALPINENSE (A.M.)		*moupinense* × *valentinianum*	yellow
veitchianum (d)	***	Maddenii	white
WHITE WINGS (A.M.)		*bullatum* × *ciliicalyx*	white
xanthostephanum	**	Boothii	yellow

MEDIUM HEIGHT (5 to 8 feet)

NAME		SERIES OR PARENTAGE	COLOR
BODNANT YELLOW (F.C.C.)		*cinnabarinum* × 'Royal Flush'	yellow
BURAMBIGUUM		*burmanicum* × *ambiguum*	yellow
COUNTESS OF SEFTON	*	*edgeworthii* × "*multiflorum*"	white
crassum (A.M.) (d)	***	Maddenii	white
dalhousiae (A.M.) (d)	***	Maddenii	cream
FORSTERIANUM		*veitchianum* × *edgeworthii*	white, fine
GRIERDAL		*dalhousiae* × *griersonianum*	red
maddenii (A.M.) (d)	***	Maddenii	white
polyandrum (A.M.)	***	Maddenii	white
rhabdotum (F.C.C.)	****	Maddenii	white, red stripes
SAFFRON QUEEN (A.M.)		*xanthostephanum* × *burmanicum*	yellow
stamineum		Stamineum	white
TYERMANNII (F.C.C.)	****	*nuttallii* × *formosum*	white

Rhododendrons

TALL (more than 8 feet)

NAME	SERIES OR PARENTAGE		COLOR
FRAGRANTISSIMUM	***	*edgeworthii* × *formosum*	white
griffithianum (F.C.C.) (d)	****	Fortunei	white or blush
LADY ALICE FITZWILLIAM (F.C.C.)	***	(Parentage unknown)	white
lindleyi (F.C.C.)	****	Maddenii	white
megacalyx (A.M.) (d)	***	Maddenii	white
nuttallii (F.C.C.) (d)	****	Maddenii	yellow
pectinatum (A.M.)	**	Stamineum	white
PRINCESS ALICE (F.C.C.)		*edgeworthii* × *ciliatum*	white
moulmainense (A.M.)	**	Stamineum	rosy mauve
taggianum (F.C.C.) (d)	***	Maddenii	white, fine
taronense (F.C.C.)	***	Maddenii	cream, pink flush
VICTORIANUM		*dalhousiae* × *nuttallii*	cream

CHAPTER XII

Forcing Rhododendrons

FORCING Rhododendrons into bloom in February, March and April is a colorful and important part of the floricultural industry of Europe but it is almost unknown among florists in America. Large specimens of Rhododendrons are occasionally brought into blossom for the great flower shows of late winter, where they invariably become a feature attraction, but otherwise these outdoor favorites are rarely seen in bloom as pot plants in the United States.

The lively interest shown in the last several years by professional growers leads to the belief that enterprising florists will inevitably take advantage of the recent information developed by European experience to create a profitable market for forced Rhododendrons in this country. The trusses in their floral effect are larger and longer lasting than are the flowers of almost any familiar florist's staple. The plants have a strong, distinct and ornamental character in themselves with their large, glossy green leaves. Their appeal to consumers for winter house decoration has already been demonstrated by the steady cold-weather sale of branches cut from Rhododendrons growing in the wild. A compact Rhododendron with its handsome foliage studded with large trusses of flowers should be a welcome improvement over the usual array of pedestrian pot plants which appear in the florist shops year after year. A further appeal to the purchaser is the acquisition of a valued and permanent ornament for his garden after the plant has served its purpose indoors.

A budded Rhododendron ready for forcing can be produced from rooted cuttings in only two years of inexpensive field culture, so the cost of acquiring plants for this purpose is much less than is generally presumed. 'Roseum Elegans', one of the best of the ironclad-hardy hybrids for forcing in the Northeast, produces handsomely formed, compact plants averaging at least 12 inches in height after one year in the field and at the end of the second year they should be 15 to 18 inches tall, well branched, and profusely budded. This clone comes into flower in seven weeks from the beginning of forcing about January 15th, and the blooms remain in good condition for almost two weeks in a cool house.

The native Rhododendron, *R. carolinianum*, forces easily. Brought into a 60° greenhouse in January it blooms in eight weeks. The typical species with rosy mauve flowers produces blossoms which are an attractive pearly white under glass. Variety *album*, with its glistening pure white flowers, is equally appealing. With due regard for the interests of conservation, plants of *R. carolinianum* can be collected from the wild, cut back, and re-grown inexpensively into small, compact specimens. Since less than two months of greenhouse care are required for even the earliest forcing, the cost of producing plants in flower is modest for such a valuable florist's novelty.

Inasmuch as its flowers do not maintain their color under glass, *R. carolinianum* is exceptional in qualifying as a good forcing Rhododendron. Fortunately, the pearly white shade produced in the greenhouse is even more attractive than the rosy-lavender color of this species as it blooms outdoors. Ordinarily any bleaching or loss of color intensity immediately eliminates a

Rhododendron from further consideration for the florist trade.

Additional requirements for forcing are shapely plants which by their nature set buds freely; blooms which open well and do not discolor; compact flower trusses of good substance which will last as long as possible; and a fast response to heat in the greenhouse so that the blossoms are produced in February and March when they have the greatest commercial value.

Turning to the familiar large-leaved Rhododendron hybrids of the nursery industry, the clones suitable for forcing have been determined by the Boskoop Growers' Association in Holland as a result of extensive trials in 1947 and 1948 and more recently, as reported by Herman J. Grootendorst. As might be expected, few red-flowered hybrids are adapted to the florist trade because the majority of them are faulty in their habit of growth and are somewhat delinquent in setting buds. The flower trusses are inclined to be lax and they do not maintain their form long enough to be satisfactory keepers.

SORTS SUITABLE FOR FORCING

Among the hybrids adapted to very cold climates outdoors, the following have proved to be satisfactory for forcing. The symbols preceding the names are the ratings of the American Rhododendron Society, from x to xxxx in order of increasing quality for outdoor use. The omission of a rating means only that the hybrid has not yet been officially evaluated for the gardens of this country. The symbols following the names are the Dutch ratings: F means good for forcing; FF, very good; and FFF, excellent:

			WEEKS REQUIRED TO FLOWER FROM START OF FORCING		
			JAN. 15TH	FEB. 1ST	MAR. 1ST
x	CATAWBIENSE ALBUM, F	white	8	7	6
	CATAWBIENSE BOURSAULT, FFF	reddish-purple	7	6–7	5
x	CATAWBIENSE GRANDIFLORUM, FFF	purple	8	7	6
	ENGLISH ROSEUM, FF	lavender pink	7	6–7	5
x	EVERESTIANUM, F	rosy lilac	9–10	8–9	7
x	LEE'S DARK PURPLE, F	purple	8	7	6
x	ROSEUM ELEGANS, F	lavender pink	7	6–7	5

The following were tested and discarded because the blossoms did not open well when forced:

AMERICA
CUNNINGHAM'S WHITE
DR H. C. DRESSELHUYS
DR H. J. LOVINK
EDWARD S. RAND
F. D. GODMAN
IGNATIUS SARGENT
LADY CLERMONT
MRS CHARLES SARGENT
MRS P. DEN OUDEN
OLD PORT
PROF. F. BETTEX
VAN DER HOOP

'Catherine van Tol', 'Van Weerden Poelman', and 'Kate Waterer' force satisfactorily and have a rating of F, but they are not quite hardy enough to be in the ironclad list.

The hybrids which are good forcers and also adapted to outdoor planting in the intermediate climates of the Philadelphia–New York region as described in Chapter VI are as follows:

			WEEKS REQUIRED TO FLOWER FROM START OF FORCING		
			JAN. 15TH	FEB. 1ST	MAR. 1ST
xx	CYNTHIA, F	rosy crimson	6–7	6	4–5
xx	GOMER WATERER, F	white	8–10	8–9	7
x	JOHN WALTER, F	crimson	8	7	6
xx	MADAME DE BRUIN, FF	cerise red	7	6–7	5
xxxx	PURPLE SPLENDOUR, F	deep purple	9–10	8–9	7

The deep, rich royal purple color which makes 'Purple Splendour' a universal favorite with both specialists and casual gardeners suggests its use as a pot plant of unique color and wide appeal.

Rhododendrons which are satisfactorily hardy along the West Coast and in the mildest climates of the East are so many that they afford a much wider selection of hybrids which are good for forcing. The huge flowers and fine colors to be found in this group may also warrant a luxury market in the cities of the Northeast for consumers who are indifferent to a later use of the plants for the outdoor garden.

The following are the best of the forcing hybrids which can also be cultivated outdoors in mild climates. The exact hardiness ratings of the sorts below which are rated for quality in the United States will be found in the complete listing of all Rhododendron hybrids which begins on page 425.

For earliest bloom, five to six weeks from January 15th; five weeks from February 1st; three to four weeks from March 1st:

x	CHEV. F. DE SAUVAGE, FFF	light red	Keeps well
	MAX SYE, FF	deep red, dark blotch	Best extra-early forcer

For early bloom, six to seven weeks from January 15th; six weeks from February 1st; four to five weeks from March 1st:

x	PETER KOSTER, FFF	crimson	Best early forcer
	SCHUBERT, FF	lilac	Large flowers; blooms keep well

For midseason bloom, seven weeks from January 15th; six to seven weeks from February 1st; four to five weeks from March 1st:

xx	DR ARNOLD W. ENDTZ, FFF	carmine	Ideal pot plant
	HOLLANDIA, FFF	deep rosy crimson	
	IRENE, FF	rose-pink	Sets buds well
	MARCEL MOSER, FF	bright red	Extra fine
	MARION, F	deep pink	Like 'Pink Pearl'
xx	MRS CHARLES E. PEARSON, F	pale blush	Large loose truss
xx	MRS E. C. STIRLING, F	blush-pink	Good keeper
xx	PINK PEARL, FF	light pink	Pale pink under glass
x	PINK PERFECTION, F	light lilac-pink	Good habit
x	PROF. J. H. ZAAYER, F	bright light red	Large flowers
x	SOUVENIR DE DR S. ENDTZ, FFF	deep pink	Compact habit

For late bloom, eight weeks from January 15th; seven weeks from February 1st; six weeks from March 1st:

xxxx	BRITANNIA, F	bright crimson-red	Truss lax; fine color
x	MARCHIONESS OF LANSDOWNE	rose, purple blotch	Distinct
	PELOPIDAS, F	dark lilac-rose	High conical truss; color lighter indoors

For very late bloom, nine to ten weeks from January 15th; eight to nine weeks from February 1st; seven weeks from March 1st:

x	BAGSHOT RUBY, F	blood-crimson	Truss slightly lax
xx	LOUIS PASTEUR, FF	pink, light center	Distinct
	SOUVENIR DE D. A. KOSTER, FF	dark scarlet	Extra fine
	VAUBAN	violet-rose blotch	Compact habit

Other popular Rhododendrons which force especially well are:

xxx	BLUE PETER, FFF	lavender-blue
	EL ALAMEIN, FF	blood-red
	KLUIS SENSATION, FF	bright scarlet
xxx	MARINUS KOSTER, FF	deep pink
xxxx	MARS, F	dark true red
	PRINSES MARIJKE, FF	deep pink
	QUEEN MARY, FF	deep pink
	WILGEN'S RUBY, FF	bright deep red

Herman J. Grootendorst of the famous Dutch nursery of similar name describes such well-known hybrids as 'Alice', 'Antoon van Welie', 'B. de Bruin', 'C. B. Van Nes', 'Countess of Athlone', 'Dr A. Blok' and 'Mrs Lindsay Smith' as being disqualified for forcing because they do not form well-shaped plants or on account of their being somewhat deficient in setting buds. 'Essex Scarlet' and 'Mrs A. T. de la Mare' are typical of clones with flower trusses too loosely built to last well. 'Hugo Koster', 'Mrs C. B. Van Nes' and 'Sweet Simplicity' are among those which fade quickly to an unattractive color. 'Unknown Warrior' cannot stand forcing heat but when placed in a cool greenhouse it is unique in blossoming earlier than any other hybrid tested.

GROWING PLANTS FOR LATER FORCING

Rhododendrons need no special field culture to be later used for forcing. The desirability of compact, well-branched plants suggests conscientious attention to the pinching of the terminal growth buds after each of the growing periods of spring and summer to induce dense branching. The maximum of sunlight and exposure consistent with good foliage color is required to promote the production of flower buds. Such open field culture also encourages the broad, bushy outline which makes good pot plants. Irrigation, fertilizing and the provision of loose, porous soil amply fortified with humus contribute to lower production costs by accelerating the growth of plants to the 15 to 18-inch and 18 to 24-inch sizes which are preferred for forcing.

Insects, such as the Lace Wing Fly, which disfigure the foliage, should be promptly controlled lest blemishes on the leaves reduce the value of the crop for use as pot plants. The first storms of early winter will often do some slight damage to the foliage of Rhododendrons in the field. Specimens so marked are perfectly satisfactory for landscape use but for close scrutiny as household decorations the preservation of the leaves in perfect condition is important and the plants should be brought under shelter in November. Rhododendrons are not so sensitive to unseasonably early and severe frosts as are Azaleas but even a remote risk of bud injury is worth avoiding where conditions allow the plants to be brought in from the field earlier in the autumn.

CARE IN THE GREENHOUSE

Forcing is done with a night temperature of 60° F. and a day temperature of 70° to 80° F. The roots are kept moist and high humidity is maintained in the greenhouse. In the absence of automatic humidifying equipment it is desirable to spray the walks and benches more than once daily during the bright weather of late winter and early spring.

Rhododendrons forced with the rootballs plunged in benches of granulated peat will blossom four to seven days sooner than the same sorts in pots. Where the earliest market is sought, potting should be deferred until the plants are coming into bloom. Then it is urgently necessary to provide perfect drainage by a layer of coarse rubble in the bottom of the pot, and to use a soil mixture of exceptional porosity, a loose texture with good aeration being vital to the later welfare of the plants until they are placed outdoors as a permanent part of the garden. Irrigation with cold water tends to delay flowering.

The water used in greenhouses in some parts of the country is always alkaline and elsewhere it is often adjusted to a neutral pH of 7·0 at the municipal filtration plant. Unless the potting mixture is already close to the limit of alkaline tolerance, or unless the water is exceptionally alkaline, there is little risk of chlorosis in the greenhouse from this cause because the budded Rhododendrons are seldom under glass more than seven or eight weeks before they move off to market. Should the telltale change in leaf color start, it can be quickly checked by the use of water containing iron sulphate at the rate of 1 ounce to the gallon. The experience of some Azalea growers suggests that it would be advantageous to collect and use rainwater where the usual supply is unsuitable for acid soil plants.

Copperas (iron sulphate) is the best acidifying agent should the necessity arise for its use. Its effect is apparent in about two weeks. About 12 pounds to 100 square feet would be an average treatment. This is the amount needed to reduce the pH of the soil from 6·5 to 5·5, as shown by the table on page 281 which gives the approximate quantities required to attain various degrees of acidity.

Leaves which fade to light green while veins remain a deeper color may be also caused by inadequate supplies of magnesium or iron. A spray to correct a deficiency of both is justified under the pressure of a forcing schedule. Three teaspoonsful of Sequestrene (iron chelate) and 2 tablespoonsful of Epsom Salts (magnesium sulphate) in 1 gallon of water sprayed on the foliage results in dramatic improvement of the deficiency symptoms within a week. More permanent correction is obtained by soil application of the dry chemicals, 1¼ ounces of the chelate and 2 pounds of the Epsom Salts to 100 square feet.

Freedom from pests and diseases is a gratifying characteristic of Rhododendrons under glass, as in the field, but any of the standard greenhouse remedies can be used if they should be required. Should Red Spider Mites become troublesome they can be easily controlled with Parathion, handled with due respect for its poisonous character. In the unlikely event that sulphur is to be employed as a fungicide or insecticide it must not be applied when the temperature is above 75° F., and to be effective against mites the temperature must be not less than 70° F. Bordeaux and lead arsenate, a standard mixture outdoors in the field, must be used immediately after mixing and only on overcast days, but this has long since been displaced by the much more effective and convenient standard sprays for the greenhouse which have the further advantage of not requiring the addition of a pigment to mask the residue on the foliage. The occasional slight burning from drops of water acting as lenses to focus sunlight of damaging intensity on the foliage of plants grown outdoors, suggests that sprays be applied cautiously in the greenhouse in bright weather in late winter and early spring. Nutrition troubles, pests, and diseases are discussed in detail in Chapter VIII.

CUSTOMER SATISFACTION

Finally, the florist who forces Rhododendrons into flower and sells them should bear in mind their second use as permanent shrubs in the garden. These plants are not by nature too well suited to pot culture for any extended period of time because of their exceptionally high requirement for aeration at the roots. Deterioration after the plants reach consumers can be avoided by insuring perfect drainage and an appropriately porous potting mix. And nothing could better promote a repeat demand for forced Rhododendrons than printed instructions with each sale, giving directions for the care of the plant between the time it flowers indoors and the arrival of frost-free weather outdoors, together with a few notes of instruction for planting in the garden.

CHAPTER XIII

Breeding Rhododendrons

RHODODENDRONS offer a dazzling prospect of achievement to both the backyard breeder and the professional hybridist. They are among the few plants important to horticulture which have scarcely been exploited in the ceaseless search for new and better garden subjects. Hundreds of the Asian species have been in cultivation so briefly that their potential contribution as parents of hybrids is unknown, and the prospects are endlessly enticing. The astounding array of breeding resources in the thousands of species and hybrids presents a panorama of unparalleled variety in stature, foliage, season of bloom, and size and color of flowers.

Almost any plant size can be obtained, from 2-inch creeping mats to trees as tall as Oaks. Foliage varies from ½ inch to 3 feet in length. The breeder can aim for any flowering period between January and September, and the resources are there to produce blossoms ranging from the size of a dime or sixpence to the size of a dinner plate. The hybridist has a full artist's palette at his disposal: red, pink, white, orange, yellow, blue, and purple, to be mixed almost at will in infinite numbers of combinations to produce better and more beautiful blossoms. The diversity in their shape and substance is almost as great, from the sorts with elongated tubular flowers of heavy, waxen texture to those flaring, flat corollas which focus a beam of color toward the viewer. The species which are hardy to as much as 30° below zero F. can impart their cold resistance to even the tenderest of the sumptuous, exotic sorts from the lower elevations of southeastern Asia. And those which are tolerant of heat can bring to the deep south through their hybrid offspring a measure of the spectacular floral show which comes from the misty coolness of the Himalaya.

BREEDING TOWARD A GOAL

Every breeder discovers sooner or later that the more carefully his crosses are considered, the more comprehensively they are planned in advance to encompass the greatest possible combination of desirable characteristics in the offspring, the fewer will be the number of failures. It may not be entirely futile to cross idly at random two familiar garden hybrids, but the chance of producing an outstanding Rhododendron from such a mating, better than either of its parents, is very much smaller than it need be.

The amateur hybridist will find his labor much more rewarding if he envisions in advance exactly what sort of hybrid he wishes to create and then combs the lists of both species and hybrids for the parents which, when combined, will contribute the most toward the realization of the goal. The stature of the proposed new hybrid, the characteristics of the foliage, the season of bloom, the size, color, fragrance and substance of the flowers, the number of florets and their arrangement in the truss, should all be visualized so that the parents can be selected which will, when merged in their offspring, come closest to the breeder's advance conception of what he wants from the cross. From the standpoint of commercial acceptance and widest usefulness, the trends in landscaping and in modern living must be anticipated so that the hybrid intended for eventual distribution by the nursery industry will be suitable in character for the needs of future gardeners.

Possibly twenty years or more elapse from the time a cross is made until the best seedling is isolated, thoroughly tested, and then propagated in sufficient numbers to be introduced commercially. In anticipating the future it must be remembered, for example, that the day of the robust hybrid which grows 15 or 20 feet tall is passing as surely as the large country estates are broken up by taxation and the spacious two-story house is abandoned for the convenience of living on one floor. It seems, therefore, that breeders should aim for compact plants of restrained growth with a mature height of 3 or 4 feet, in scale with single-story houses, and fragrant blossoms of grace and refinement for close scrutiny in the small, intimate gardens of increasing popularity. Softer, more delicate flower colors may replace the eruptions of volcanic brilliance which captivated breeders in the first half of the century. Such plants as *R. forrestii* and *R. williamsianum* and their hybrid offspring with dwarf stature and lovely flowers seemingly offer exceptional promise as parents of Rhododendrons of the future.

It is often possible to choose parents which will together impart not one, but a number of desirable characteristics to their offspring. Frequently overlooked is the importance of good foliage and dense habit of growth. Some of the popular red-flowered hybrids, especially, are ungainly in the landscape for more than eleven months in the year and it is a lamentable misdirection of effort for breeders to increase their numbers when such crosses could as well incorporate a heritage of the handsome foliage which first made Rhododendrons admired as evergreens.

Nearly all hybridizing projects involve the expectation that there will simultaneously appear in the descendants the desirable characteristics which existed separately in the two original parents. The breeder seeks to combine giant flowers with hardiness, or fragrance with dwarfness, or a certain color with a later blooming season. Usually the aim is to accomplish at one time several such transfers of good traits from each parent individually to a combined expression of them in their offspring. I suppose the consolidated goal of all breeders might be to have for every climate a complete range of fine hybrids in all useful sizes blooming from earliest spring to late summer, with the entire flower color range of the genus represented in each period of the season and for every stature. Such a goal is theoretically possible but it is a very long way from realization at the present time, and most of the cultivars which now seem so admirable in their color and season are certain to be much improved in the hands of succeeding generations of breeders.

The Rhododendron Handbook, Part Two, published in England by the Royal Horticultural Society, has in it a stud section in which is recorded the parentage of hundreds of hybrids, many of them available commercially. It is an invaluable aid to the breeder seeking parents which represent certain combinations of species and to prevent duplications of crosses already made. The earliest hybrid of known pedigree recorded therein is dated 1817. Since that time the fine Rhododendron hybrids which have appeared in our gardens have come almost entirely from amateurs or from nurserymen who have bred Rhododendrons as a self-taught art rather than from professional geneticists using the principles of science.

THE SELECTION OF PARENTS

Any discussion of Rhododendron breeding must deal to some extent with generalizations and the unhappy author is caught between the wish to be helpful in presenting the situations which usually exist, and the certain knowledge that there are an uncomfortable number of exceptions to too many statements. But it would be both tiresome and impractical to attempt an account so exhaustive as to encompass all of the qualifications which should accompany many descriptions for comprehensive, minute accuracy.

The most common hindrance to the efforts of backyard breeders is their failure to become thoroughly acquainted with the resources for hybridizing among the world's Rhododendrons. There is no substitute for a thorough knowledge of the species and their characteristics, their hardiness, stature, flower color and size, season of bloom and so on. With that knowledge, the traits of their hybrids which might also serve as parents can usually be deduced. No craftsman attempts to work without knowing the materials of his trade, yet time and again crosses are made which are only partially successful in their outcome because the breeder did not know that there existed a more suitable Rhododendron parent which exactly fitted his needs and might well have enabled him fully to achieve his goal. It takes too much effort and too many years to bring the progeny from seed to flower not to take every advance precaution against failure. Then, too, the hybridist in ignorance of the possibilities has goals which are unnecessarily limited. With the astounding variety among Rhododendron species in every conceivable respect, further extended by the vast numbers of hybrids, it is usually possible to find a parent which possesses almost any characteristic which might reasonably be desired, and pollen from it is often freely available and conveniently obtained by mail. No advice to the beginning breeder could be more useful than the suggestion that he learn what the world's Rhododendrons can offer him as raw material for his efforts.

It is almost equally important to know what crosses have already been made by other hybridists. Innumerable matings have been uselessly repeated because beginning breeders have not been aware of the stud section of Part Two of *The Rhododendron Handbook*. The primary hybrids between two species are often invaluable for use as parents and a great many such crosses have already been made. These useful primary hybrids are listed in the *Handbook* with the names that have been given to the best of them. Thus breeders the world over can avoid duplication and at the same time know that pollen of them is probably already obtainable if it is wanted to further their own hybridizing projects. Such crosses may sometimes be purposely repeated, however, when a form of a species which is hardier or finer in quality becomes available for use as a parent. Breeders will be interested in the listing of hybrid Rhododendrons which begins on page 425, where the parentage of many well-known clones is published for the first time and the derivation of the newest creations of hybridists here and abroad is given.

A gardener about to embark on some experiments in hybridizing could profitably consult other breeders, a genial and generous lot who are always eager to help new recruits. Not only is it useful to see the methods and results of colleagues in the field, but the quality of hybrids produced elsewhere will determine the wider value of the breeder's own work. It is useless to name a new hybrid and arrange for its propagation for eventual introduction if there already exists a similar Rhododendron which is superior. The appraisal of the hybridist's own productions is one of his most difficult duties in any case, calling for an objective, detached judgment which can be valid only if it is reached with full knowledge of any other Rhododendrons in the same category which have previously been created elsewhere. The American Rhododendron Society, 3514 N. Russet Street, Portland, Oregon, which exists for the encouragement of Rhododendron culture and for its service to its members, is able to provide the names and addresses of breeders in almost any section of the country where these plants are grown.

Having envisioned the sort of Rhododendron he wishes to create, and having acquainted himself with all of the species and hybrids which might serve him in the project, the breeder then makes his selection of parents and it is important that he obtain for his cross the very finest *forms* of those parents. The wild species of Rhododendrons vary enormously as do the hybrids which are bred from them, and it is only a matter of everyday observation that like begets like. The classic example to illustrate how essential it is to obtain good parents is the famed Loderi group of hybrids, the result of a cross between an extraordinarily fine form of *R. griffithianum* and an equally fine form of *R. fortunei*. These hybrids are unrivalled for their flower size, fragrance and beauty, and many gardeners have sought to duplicate them in quantity for personal garden use by repeating this simple cross. No one has ever succeeded in doing so. The offspring of the later matings have failed even to approach the quality of the original hybrids because the forms of the two species used have been inferior. Without exception the breeders who have produced noteworthy hybrids in the past have gone to great lengths to secure as parents the very finest forms available of the Rhododendrons they wished to use as parents. Where the species important to horticulture vary considerably in their quality the detailed descriptions of them which begin on page 122 give the best forms available commercially.

It is often necessary as well to select carefully the best forms of hybrids which are to be used for breeding. Novices are frequently misled by a group name which applies to both poor and fine hybrids. Clarification appears in a discussion of the naming of hybrids on pages 249 and 425.

UNPROMISING PROSPECTS

The hybridist is especially aware that Rhododendrons are divided into two great groups, those with scales (lepidote), minute structures, usually visible to the eye, found on leaf undersides and often on branches and floral parts; and those without scales (elepidote). The elepidotes, those without scales, which may have leaves smooth underneath or with a heavy woolly indumentum, are the familiar Rhododendrons with large foliage which have been popular in our gardens for a century and more, plus the addition of some sorts of shorter stature more recently discovered and introduced. The scaly lepidotes ordinarily have much smaller leaves and a more slender, willowy habit of growth, or else they are dwarf alpines. The listing which begins on page 508 tells whether each species is scaly or non-scaly.

A fact of basic importance to the breeder is that the two groups do not ordinarily cross. Almost invariably no seeds are produced; or if seeds are produced they are not generally viable; or the seedlings die in infancy if the seeds rarely do prove to be viable. There is one authenticated instance of a successful cross between a scaly and a non-scaly Rhododendron, *R.* (*dalhousiae* × *griersonianum*) 'Grierdal', but the prospect of failure is normally so certain in attempting to mate non-scaly Rhododendrons with the scaly sorts that it seems sensible to devote the major effort, at least, in more rewarding directions.

At one time it was thought that pollen from a species with a short style in germinating could not extend its tubes far enough down a long style to effect fertilization, but this seems to be unlikely. Working with Rhododendrons of the Azalea series Dr John Creech at the United States Plant Introduction Garden found that the barriers to pollen tube growth were physiological rather than structural in crosses between distantly related species with normal flowers. Embryo abortion and a lethal inheritance from the dissimilar parents were additional factors which thwarted success in some of his experiments. Whatever the reason, however, it is unlikely that crosses between scaly and non-scaly Rhododendrons will be productive.

Rhododendrons will cross much more readily with Azaleas, the non-scaly Rhododendrons with the Azaleas of the Luteum subseries, and the scaly Rhododendrons with Azaleas of the Obtusum subseries, but here too the percentage of successes is still small and the hybrids between the two groups have not been popular garden plants. Only two or three of them have ever found favor enough to become standard cultivars in commerce.

The beginning breeder, then, is most likely to be rewarded for his efforts by making his crosses within one or the other of the great groups into which Rhododendrons naturally are divided. It is interesting to note that the two are separated not only by their scaliness but by a basic difference in color as well. Scarlet, a common color in the non-scaly sorts, is lacking in the scaly Rhododendrons; blue, or a close approach to it, is common in the species with scales but lacking in the non-scaly sorts; and both colors are missing from the scaly Rhododendrons which are epiphytes in the wild, growing on trees high up in the canopy of the jungle forest.

These latter species which grow like orchids are a more or less well-defined scaly-leaved subgroup which are reluctant to hybridize with species of different habit, even though they be also scaly-leaved. The aerial dwellers include some of the most sumptuously beautiful Rhododendrons of all, but they have only occasionally been successfully bred to their lepidote relatives. The most interesting breaks linking this epiphytic group with scaly-leaved species hardy in the Northeast have been the successful crosses of several of them with our native *R. carolinianum* made by Edmond Amateis, amateur breeder and illustrator of this book.

PROMISING PROSPECTS

Within the natural limitations of botanical relationships, the choice of parents is very wide and I can only offer some suggestions which may prove useful to the gardener with an awakening interest in breeding Rhododendrons.

Breeding for Precocious Blooming

The progeny of some species are notably slow to come into flower, a characteristic which the breeder wryly avoids with greater determination as the years pass. But two species which seem always to result in bloom early in life are *RR. griersonianum* and *decorum* when they figure in the heritage. Seedlings with the influence of either one in the pedigree frequently set flower buds in three to four years. Since *R. griersonianum* is a good source for red flower color and *R. decorum* is valuable for both fragrance and flower size, one or sometimes both can be used, directly or through their hybrids, to achieve the aims which would be much slower in realization if other similar species were selected as parents.

However, *R.* (*griersonianum* × *decorum*) 'Jean' is probably not a suitable parent to produce hybrids of ironclad hardiness for New England. If the simultaneous influence of both species is sought for offspring intended to be grown in the Northeast, each had better be first combined with a hardier sort and these hybrids then used as the parents.

Breeding for Hardiness in the Northeast

A characteristic frequently sought by breeders is hardiness, because there are so many magnificent Asian Rhododendrons which are so tender that they are useful only in more benign climates. Time and again the hybridist wants to duplicate in hardier form some of the fine qualities of a Rhododendron not adaptable to his climate.

In the Northeast the most important source of hardiness by far is the white-flowered form of the Catawba Rhododendron, *catawbiense* var. *album*, Glass. A particularly fine example of this variety isolated by Joseph Gable, dean of American hybridists, is called 'Catalgla'. In itself or through its hybrid progeny this Rhododendron has been invaluable in the hands of eastern breeders because it does not usually impart a magenta taint to its offspring. The typical purplish-pink flowers of *R. catawbiense* have given a flawed inheritance of color to the efforts of Rhododendron hybridists for a century or more but this white-flowered variety, and probably also another discovered in North Carolina more recently, will almost certainly be the means of bringing to gardens of the Northeast in all their subtlety the delicately beautiful colors which are at present seen only in milder climates. Its first generation hybrids with Asian Rhododendrons will likely be even more useful as parents.

The Catawba Rhododendron transmits to its offspring a variety of valuable attributes. Its ability as a parent to pass on cold resistance to its hybrids is so marked that the most successful of them are often described as being of 'ironclad' hardiness, able to endure −20° F. without injury. But *R. catawbiense* and its white- and red-flowered varieties are also phenomenally successful in imparting tolerance of sunlight and exposure, ease of cultivation and resistance to heat. From my study of the Rhododendrons which grow well in uncongenial climates, made in the preparation of Chapter X, it is perfectly apparent that the presence of the Catawba Rhododendron in the parentage is the best possible indication that a hybrid will be able to endure heat and low humidity and be generally tolerant of both exposure and poor growing conditions.

The red-flowered variety of *R. catawbiense* var. *rubrum*, may be of great value as a source of hardiness in the production of red-flowered hybrids for severe climates, but I am less enthusiastic about it than I am about the value of 'Catalgla' because even the best forms of this red variant have a good deal of blue in them which often shows up again in their offspring. From present indications I think it likely that the ironclad hybrids which are purer in the shade of their blossoms, such as 'America', 'Nova Zembla', 'Charles Dickens', and 'Fanfare' are a better source of hardiness for the production of improved red-flowered hybrids for the severe climate of the Northeast. For the patient breeder who is willing to wait until the blooming of the second generation for his results, 'Catalgla', crossed with a scarlet-flowered Rhododendron and the progeny then backcrossed again to the red parent or crossed among themselves, should yield some plants with the purest color of all. Red-flowered Rhododendrons can sometimes dominate their progeny, even when the other parent has white blossoms, and this possibility too favors the use of 'Catalgla'.

R. maximum is much less desirable as a source of hardiness in the first generation for northeastern conditions. It is more useful for its late blooming period and also for its contribution of hardiness after it has already been combined with one of the good Asian Rhododendrons and then the hybrid used as a parent. Ordinarily, in the first generation, *R. maximum* dominates its offspring in every ornamental respect to such an extent that it is sometimes necessary to wait for the seedlings to bloom before the breeder can be certain that a true hybrid with another Rhododendron has resulted from the cross. Combined with a good Asian species such hybrids as *maximum* × *fortunei* and *maximum* × *discolor* show promise as parents for further breeding in the Northeast.

As for other sources of hardiness, the principal concern of breeders in the Northeast, I can only record the reported facts while noting my own opinion that generalizations on this subject are often extremely inaccurate. It seems to me that the value of parents is frequently inherent and unseen in individual plants which may not be at all representative of their kind. These single 'genius parents' appear to me to exist in species which are widely reputed to be useless for breeding. How frequently they occur I do not know, but I would not hesitate to experiment with any species as a parent, regardless of its reputation in this respect, if it appeared best able to contribute the characteristics sought in the offspring.

R. smirnowii as a parent has been exploited in Germany more than anywhere else. The late T. J. R. Seidel used it extensively as a source of hardiness in the production of his many hybrids, of which the best of the more advanced generation progeny is probably 'Hassan'. *R.* 'Goethe' is the most familiar in this country but for the most part the Seidel creations were distributed largely in Germany and Scandinavia and were never able to achieve popularity elsewhere. No hybrids of extraordinary beauty occurred among them and, with a few exceptions, their colors are tainted with blue. They are not noticeably superior to the older Waterer ironclad hybrids and are less hardy. The tendency of the species and of its hybrids to open some of their flowers in the autumn in intermediate climates is a serious fault. *Smirnowii* crossed with *haematodes* produced a very fine hybrid for Joseph Gable save for the fatal inheritance of precociously flowering partially in the autumn, the remainder of the exposed buds in the clusters then being lost to winter cold. *R.* (*fortunei* × *smirnowii*) 'Katherine Dalton', another Gable hybrid, is rewarding, opening pale lavender and fading to white, but it is not entirely hardy. I have several hybrids of *R. smirnowii* bred with other indumented species primarily in an effort to obtain hardy Rhododendrons brilliantly colored on the leaf undersides. They appear promising but it is too soon to evaluate them. Elsewhere I have knowledge of just two first-class hybrids which derived their hardiness from this species: one, a red-flowered sort with remarkably fine foliage inherited from *R. smirnowii* and the other with flowers of an appealing salmon-apricot color which resulted from a cross with a Dexter hybrid.

Dr Henry Skinner, director of the United States National Arboretum, produced some attractive hybrids with *R. brachycarpum* which bore double flowers, emphatically and prettily doubled, in contrast to the slightly grotesque creations which have heretofore passed as 'double'. Double-flowered forms of both *RR. brachycarpum* and *fauriei* are known in the wild in Japan. I have in my own garden a plant of *brachycarpum* × *decorum*, a dwarf, compact Rhododendron of spreading habit with clear silvery pink flowers, a gift from Joseph Gable which I value highly. *Brachycarpum* × *discolor* regularly loses its buds in the severe mountain climate here and it is not a vigorous plant. These represent my first-hand experience with this species as a source of hardiness. Mr Gable has found that an uncomfortable proportion of *brachycarpum* hybrids are lacking in vigor and have aborted flowers which do not develop, but a gratifying minority are very fine. Its ability to sire the low, compact growth habit needed for modern landscaping, and the absence of any magenta tainting the flower color of its offspring commend it to breeders. It is especially necessary to obtain a free-flowering specimen of good form for use as a parent, since *R. brachycarpum* varies so greatly both in stature and in floriferousness.

So far as I know, no hybrid in common commerce is quite so hardy as the species forebear which gave it cold resistance but some of the old Waterer hybrids derived from *R. catawbiense* have been fine parents as sources of hardy seedlings when crossed with more tender sorts. Joseph Gable has obtained several uncommonly beautiful Rhododendrons from crosses of 'Atrosanguineum' with the large-flowered Asian species. Guy G. Nearing produced a series of outstanding hybrids by mating *decorum* × *griffithianum* with such standard commercial sorts as 'Charles Dickens' and 'Kettledrum'. In Holland, the old ironclad commercial red-flowered hybrids crossed with the later cultivars of finer color but tender disposition, such as 'Earl of Athlone' and 'Jean Marie Montague' have given the most promising results for cold climates of any achieved there since the turn of the century. My own crosses of 'America' with less hardy Rhododendrons of larger flower and better color are extraordinarily encouraging.

Red-flowered ironclad hybrids have been largely used as hardy parents because those with pink blossoms have often given seedlings which bloom in bilious pale magenta shades. Exceptions there are, of course, but they are conspicuous only because they are unusual.

Since the discovery in the wild of *R. catawbiense* var. *album* Glass, few crosses have been made with the white-flowered ironclad hybrids as seed parents, perhaps unfortunately so since the most outstanding new seedling in this color class, with very large white flowers and a bold golden shield on the upper lobe, resulted from hybridizing a popular standard white-flowered cultivar with another of complex parentage which is not quite so hardy.

In the Northeast the crossing of hardy hybrids of complicated parentage among themselves to produce superior new sorts has long been a subject of controversy. Many novice hybridists have made such crosses almost at random in their first efforts at hybridizing and the results have generally been poor. On a larger scale and on a systematic basis, A. M. Shammarello, an Ohio nurseryman, has had outstanding results from these matings, however. After testing dozens of different combinations over a period of many years he has discovered a few of the standard ironclad commercial hybrids which, when bred together, yield superior seedlings. One such successful mating of two hardy red-flowered hybrids consistently gives red-flowered progeny which are remarkably constant in their color and quality. Others have produced some individual offspring which are exceptionally promising.

Few amateur breeders have the opportunity

to test many different combinations of parents from the ranks of the standard ironclad commercial hybrids to isolate the minority which give worthwhile results, and it seems that the average hybridist can work more efficiently on a smaller scale by arranging his crosses along precise lines with foreknowledge of the contribution he expects from the known heritage inherent in each parent.

In my opinion, the very best results are to be expected from using as seed parents primary hybrids between a very hardy species and an Asian Rhododendron which exhibits one or more of the qualities sought in the offspring. For example, I would consider *catawbiense* var. *album*, Glass × *fortunei* or *catawbiense* var. *album*, Glass × *discolor* to be parents of exceptional value since they would be capable of passing on simultaneously to their offspring both hardiness and large flowers. The principles of genetics support the view that such a hybrid as *brachycarpum* × *decorum* would be much superior as a parent to *R. brachycarpum* itself. If *R. brachycarpum* were crossed with *R. houlstonii*, for example, the seedlings would very likely be intermediate between the two. But if the primary hybrid *brachycarpum* × *decorum* were crossed with *R. houlstonii* there is a good prospect that the genes controlling the immense, delicately colored flowers of *R. decorum* would combine with those governing the equally fine blossoms of *R. houlstonii* to produce large-flowered offspring which inherit enough cold resistance from *R. brachycarpum* to make them satisfactory in the Northeast. This follows because *R. brachycarpum* × *houlstonii* is known to yield hardy offspring. The addition of *R. decorum* in the heritage of the seed parent is not likely to alter that result in at least a proportion of the seedlings, but it provides a prospect of much larger and finer flowers in the progeny. Exactly the same principle applies to crosses designed to achieve other goals. In the production of a hybrid with scarlet blossoms and moderate stature, for example, *catawbiense* var. *rubrum* × *haematodes* crossed with a good dwarf red *forrestii* hybrid would be much more likely to give first-rate results than if *catawbiense* var. *rubrum* alone were bred to it.

In using primary hybrids in this manner one should be able to foresee the possibility, at least, of achieving the goal through combinations which conceivably could occur in the cross. If the one hardy species which figures in the heritage of the seed parent could yield hardy seedlings in combination with either one or the other of the species in the pollen parent, as determined by experience or observation, the prospect is good for securing seedlings satisfactorily tolerant to cold. If, in addition, the other qualities sought in the offspring could result from the tender species in the seed parent in combination with one or both of the species in the pollen parent, then the chance of obtaining both hardiness and the other desired traits simultaneously in a portion of the offspring is well worth making the cross.

Hardiness in the Scaly-leaved Group

Among the scaly-leaved Rhododendrons there are four candidates in the Northeast for imparting a measure of their ironclad hardiness to the next generation: *RR. carolinianum*, *minus*, *dauricum*, and *mucronulatum*.

Of these *R. carolinianum* has been most used and it has been a good parent though not able to tip the scales, so to speak, enough to yield fully hardy progeny when it was crossed by Joseph Gable with such species as *RR. cuneatum* and *davidsonianum*. Crossed with others a little hardier, it has produced such good hybrids as *R.* (*carolinianum* × *racemosum*) 'Conestoga'. Open pollinated seedlings from this hybrid, raised by Guy Nearing, produced 'Windbeam' and 'Wyanokie', both fine garden plants. Mr Nearing also created *R.* (*carolinianum* × *fastigiatum*) 'Ramapo' which has met with such public approval that it has become a standard commercial hybrid.

In so far as my own work is concerned, I have crossed *R. carolinianum* var. *album* with such Rhododendrons as *hanceanum* var. *nanum*, *ciliatum* × *pemakoense*, *tephropeplum*, *megeratum*, *spinuliferum* × *keiskei*, and *racemosum* × *ciliatum*. It is yet too soon to evaluate the results.

It is often possible to hybridize *R. carolinianum* with a species which does not normally yield viable seeds from a mating with it, by the indirect method of making the cross with a hybrid created by mating the incompatible species with one known to be compatible. For example, many hybridists have failed to make a successful cross of *R. carolinianum* with the yellow-flowered *R. lutescens*. On the other hand *R. racemosum* crosses readily with both the Caroline Rhododendron and *R. lutescens*. By mating *carolinianum* with the hybrid (*racemosum* × *lutescens*) 'Arden Fairy' it might be possible to achieve the same goal as was intended for the ultimate outcome from the unsuccessful cross of *carolinianum* × *lutescens*. It is occasionally possible, too, by reversing the parents, to succeed in a cross which has previously failed. A species acting as a seed parent which refuses to mate with another will sometimes do so when it serves as the pollen parent.

Joseph Casadevall, a New Jersey hybridist, has experimented with *R. carolinianum* as a parent. His results seem to be typical and a summary of them will be of interest:

carolinianum

HYBRIDITY EVIDENT	HYBRIDITY NOT EVIDENT	NO SEEDS OR SEEDLINGS DIED IN INFANCY
x *burmanicum*	x *flavidum* (?)	x *chryseum*
x *keiskei*		x *davidsonianum*
x (*cinnabarinum* × *ambiguum*)*		x *pemakoense*
x (*racemosum* × *ciliatum*)		

carolinianum var. *album*

HYBRIDITY EVIDENT	HYBRIDITY NOT EVIDENT	NO SEEDS OR SEEDLINGS DIED IN INFANCY
x *chryseum*	x *burmanicum*	x (*valentinianum* × *leucaspis*)
x *moupinense*	x *keiskei* (?)	
x *ciliicalyx*	x *pemakoense* (?)	
x *nitens*	x (*lutescens* × *moupinense*)	
x *flavidum*	x (*ciliatum* × *moupinense*)	
x (*leucaspis* × *moupinense*)	x (*spinuliferum* × *lutescens*)	
x (*spinuliferum* × *keiskei*)	x (*ciliatum* × *pemakoense*)	
x 'sapphire'	x (*ciliatum* × *dauricum*) × *moupinense*	
chryseum × *carolinianum**		
calostrotum × *carolinianum**		

* Poor seed germination and weak growth.

Crosses frequently fail due to weather conditions, concealed injury to the style or ovary, and, perhaps most commonly of all, as a result of pollen which has deteriorated prior to receipt from a distant source. It is unwise to assume incompatibility on the basis of a single unproductive trial.

A development of particular interest has been the successful crosses of *R. carolinianum* with species of the Edgeworthii series by Edmond Amateis. Should these hybrids prove fertile they will open up a vast new field of promise for the Northeast, bringing to gardeners in cold climates the glowing prospect of having in hardy form the immense, scented blossoms of these patrician Asian species. The successful crossing of *R. carolinianum* with *RR. bullatum* and *edgeworthii* bridges two series which are only distantly related botanically and show little resemblance in their gross appearance. The scaly species of the Edgeworthii series bear a heavy, felty, indumentum which is almost entirely suppressed in the progeny of their mating with *R. carolinianum*. A photograph of *R.* (*carolinianum* × *edgeworthii*) 'Mildred Amateis' appears after page 304. The same hybridist has also crossed the Carolina Rhododendron with *R. ciliatum*, the first successful direct mating with *R. carolinianum* of the Maddenii series.

R. minus produces much the same results as a parent as does *R. carolinianum*, except that its hybrids are not quite so hardy and they are larger in stature and bloom later in the season, the latter along with heat tolerance being perhaps its most valuable trait for hybridizing with other scaly-leaved Rhododendrons.

R. mucronulatum is easier to use than *R. carolinianum* as a source of hardiness in breeding because it crosses more readily with a greater variety of scaly Rhododendrons and it does not tend to dominate in its offspring the inheritance from the other parent. It is also more effective in imparting hardiness to its hybrids. Its failing is that it often passes on to the progeny a tendency to be partially or sometimes even completely deciduous, and to bloom precariously early in the year in some climates. If I had available a good evergreen form of its close relative, *R. dauricum*, I would prefer it as a hardy parent to *R. mucronulatum*. An informed guess might be that it could also prove to be more fertile as a parent.

The most interesting cross that I have made with *R. mucronulatum* was with *R. ciliatum* '*Bergie*' in 1951. It gave pretty hybrids with large white flowers, very early blooming, which survive outdoors with some protection. Should any of the progeny be fertile they may provide the means of bringing hardiness to the sumptuously beautiful species of the Maddenii series.

The offspring of *R. mucronulatum* tend to bloom young in life and often set buds at the end of their second year of growth. Joseph Casadevall reports results from his crosses with *R. mucronulatum* as the seed parent which are typical of my own experience and observations elsewhere: sturdy, vigorous seedlings, obviously hybrids, result from matings with *moupinense*, *burmanicum*, *leucaspis* × *moupinense*, *ciliatum* × *moupinense*, *spinuliferum* × *lutescens*, *rubiginosum*, *valentinianum* × *leucaspis*, and ((*ciliatum* × *dauricum*) × *moupinense*). Crossed with *R. keiskei*, the seeds germinated well but the seedlings died in the course of the first season. Crossed with *R. pemakoense*, *R. flavidum* and *R. lutescens* the seeds sprouted poorly and the progeny were feeble. The mating with *R. megeratum* was sterile.

Donald L. Hardgrove, a Long Island hybridist, has also specialized in breeding scaly-leaved hybrids because of their unique possibilities of combining dwarf compact growth and small leaves; precocious blooming; blue flowers; and Azalea-like mass color effects on truly evergreen plants. He prefers *R. carolinianum* as a parent to impart hardiness although he finds that this species varies greatly in its own hardiness, habit of growth, size and color of flower and in its ability to cross with the Asian lepidotes. It is unpredictable in accepting pollen of another species, producing seeds when crossed with some specimens and failing to do so when crossed with other plants of the same species. Its progeny from matings with the Asian scaly-leaved Rhododendrons frequently seem sterile when young, but an occasional plant produces seeds when more mature; or a single fertile individual may be found among a very large number of sterile plants. After succeeding in crossing *R. carolinianum* with several species of the Boothii series, Mr Hardgrove failed to secure a desired mating of the Carolina Rhododendron with any of the giant-flowered Maddenii group. The Maddeniis do cross with the Boothii species, however, and their fine contribution was finally obtained by the indirect method of crossing *R. carolinianum* with a hybrid between a Boothii and a Maddenii species.

Information on compatibilities between scaly-leaved Rhododendrons and the outcome of crosses between them is extremely difficult to obtain. Next to nothing has been published on lepidote crosses, whereas amateur breeders have described extensively their work with non-scaly Rhododendrons. A careful study of the results thus far obtained by other hybridists can be invaluable to the beginning breeder and this additional data from Mr Hardgrove will be of interest:

HYBRIDITY EVIDENT

carolinianum
× *augustinii* (Wilson's blue form)
× *chryseum*
× (*chrysodoron* × *johnstoneanum*) 'R. W. Rye'
× (*cinnabarinum* var. *roylei* × *concatenans*) 'Conroy'
× *flavidum*
× *leucaspis*
× (*leucaspis* × *moupinense*) 'Bric-a-Brac'
× ((*intricatum* × *fastigiatum*) × *augustinii*) 'Blue Diamond'
× (*megeratum* × *mishmiense*) 'Silver Ray'
× *moupinense*
× *tephropeplum*
× (*valentinianum* × *leucaspis*) 'Valaspis'
× *russatum*

HYBRIDITY NOT EVIDENT

carolinianum
× *megeratum*
(*carolinianum* × *racemosum*)
× *nuttallii*
mucronulatum
× (*cinnarbarinum* var. *roylei* × (*cinnabarinum* × *maddenii*)) 'Lady Chamberlain'
carolinianum
× (*bullatum* × *moupinense*) 'Bulbul'

NO SEEDS OR SEEDLINGS DIED IN INFANCY

carolinianum
× *augustinii*
× (*augustinii* × *cinnabarinum* var. *roylei*)
× *aureum*
× *bullatum*
× *charitopes*
× *ciliatum*
× *ciliicalyx*
× *cinnabarinum*
× (*cinnabarinum* × *maddenii*) 'Royal Flush'
× *cinnabarinum* var. *roylei*
× (*cinnabarinum* var. *roylei* × *ambiguum*) 'Exbury Biskra'
× (*cinnabarinum* var. *roylei* × (*cinnabarinum* × *maddenii*)) 'Lady Chamberlain'
× ((*cinnabarinum* var. *roylei* × (*cinnabarinum* × *maddenii*)) × *cinnabarinum* var. *roylei*) 'Perseverance'
× 'Cunningham's Sulphur'
× *dalhousiae*
× *hanceanum* var. *nanum*
× *lindleyi*
× *nuttallii*
× *oreotrephes*
× *pemakoense*
× *taggianum*
× *russatum*
carolinianum var. *album*
× *augustinii*
× (*cinnabarinum* var. *roylei* × *concatenans*) 'Conroy'
× ((*cinnabarinum* var. *roylei* × (*cinnabarinum* × *maddenii*)) × *cinnabarinum* var. *roylei*) 'Perseverance'
(*carolinianum* × *augustinii*)
× ((*intricatum* × *fastigiatum*) × *augustinii*) 'Blue Diamond'
'Blue Tit' seedling
(*carolinianum* × *fastigiatum*)
'Ramapo'
× *carolinianum*
× *russatum*
× (*carolinianum* × *racemosum*) 'Conestoga'
× *keiskei*

HYBRIDITY EVIDENT

(*carolinianum* × *keiskei*)
× *keiskei*
(*carolinianum* × *racemosum*) 'Conestoga'
× 'Blue Tit' seedling
× (*carolinianum* × *keiskei*)
× *ciliatum*
× *leucaspis*
(*carolinianum* × *roseum*)
× (*carolinianum* × *roseum*)
(*carolinianum* × *roseum*) F_2
× ((*cinnabarinum* var. *roylei* × (*cinnabarinum* × *maddenii*)) × *cinnabarinum* var. *roylei*) 'Perseverance'
× (*cinnabarinum* var. *roylei* × *concatenans*) 'Conroy'
mucronulatum
× *taggianum*
(*ciliatum* × *dauricum*) 'Praecox'
× *carolinianum* var. *album*
× 'forsterianum'
× *taggianum*
hanceanum var. *nanum*
× *carolinianum* var. *album*
(*leucaspis* × *moupinense*) 'Bric-a-Brac'
× *carolinianum*
riparium
× *carolinianum*
× *carolinianum* var. *album*
russatum
× *carolinianum*
(*valentinianum* × *leucaspis*) 'Valaspis'
× *carolinianum* var. *album*
× *mucronulatum*
(*racemosum* × *keiskei*)
× (*carolinianum* × *keiskei*)

NO SEEDS OR SEEDLINGS DIED IN INFANCY

(*carolinianum* × *leucaspis*) 'Starlight'
× (*carolinianum* × *leucaspis*) 'Starlight'
× (*ciliatum* × *moupinense*) 'Cilpinense'
× *concatenans*
× *keiskei*
(*carolinianum* × *racemosum*) 'Conestoga'
× (*augustinii* × *cinnabarinum* var. *roylei*)
× *keleticum*
× *oreotrephes*
× *russatum*
minus
× *ciliatum*
(*minus* × *racemosum*)
× (*cinnabarinum* × (*cinnabarinum* × *maddenii*)) 'Bodnant Yellow'
× (*cinnabarinum* var. *roylei* × *concatenans*) 'Conroy'
× (*caeruleum* var. *album* × *concatenans*) 'Peace'
× (*megeratum* × *mishmiense*) 'Silver Ray'
× *taggianum*
(*augustinii* × *cinnabarinum* var. *roylei*)
× *mucronulatum*
(*ciliatum* × *moupinense*) 'Cilpinense'
× *mucronulatum*
cinnabarinum
× *carolinianum* var. *album*
(*spinuliferum* × *racemosum*) 'Spinulosum'
× *carolinianum* var. *album*
(*pemakoense* × *moupinense*)
× *carolinianum* var. *album* 'Windbeam'
× *lindleyi*

In addition to the above crosses with at least one species generally regarded as ironclad in its hardiness figuring in the parentage, the following combinations have also been tried with the results noted.

HYBRIDITY EVIDENT

hanceanum var. *nanum*
  ×*keiskei*
keiskei
  ×*leucaspis*
  ×*taggianum*
racemosum
  ×(*chrysodoron*×*johnstoneanum*) 'R. W. Rye'
  ×(*cinnabarinum* var. *roylei*× *ambiguum*) 'Exbury Biskra'
  ×*bullatum*
  ×*ciliatum*
  ×*cinnabarinum*
  ×*leucaspis*
  ×*tephropeplum*
(*racemosum*×*ciliatum*) 'Racil'
  ×(*ciliatum*×*moupinense*) 'Cilpinense'
(*racemosum*×*keiskei*)
  ×*keiskei*
  ×*leucaspis*
  ×*racemosum*
  ×(*valentinianum*×*leucaspis*) 'Valaspis'
(*racemosum*×*tephropeplum*)
  ×*leucaspis*
(*valentinianum*×*leucaspis*) 'Valaspis'
  ×*keiskei*

HYBRIDITY NOT EVIDENT

keiskei
  ×*dalhousiae*
(*racemosum*×*keiskei*)
  ×*ciliicalyx*
  ×*dalhousiae*

NO SEEDS OR SEEDLINGS DIED IN INFANCY

(*ciliatum*×*moupinense*) 'Cilpinense'
  ×*keiskei*
cinnabarinum
  ×*keiskei*
oreotrephes
  ×*scintillans*
racemosum
  ×(*caeruleum* var. *album*×*concateans*) 'Peace'
  ×(*cinnabarinum*×(*cinnabarinum*×*maddenii*)) 'Bodnant Yellow'
  ×((*cinnabarinum* var. *roylei*× (*cinnabarinum*×*maddenii*))× *cinnabarinum* var. *roylei*) 'Perseverance'
  ×(*cinnabarinum* var. *roylei*× *concatenans*) 'Conroy'
  ×*augustinii*
  ×(*augustinii*×*cinnabarinum* var. *roylei*)
  ×*ciliicalyx*
  ×*concatenans*
  ×*edgeworthii*
  ×*lindleyi*
  ×*taggianum*
(*racemosum*×*ciliatum*) 'Racil'
  ×(*mollicomum*×*spinuliferum*)
  ×(*pemakoense*×*moupinense*)
(*racemosum*×*keiskei*)
  ×*ciliatum*
  ×(*leucaspis*×*moupinense*) 'Bric-a-Brac'
  ×*megeratum*
  ×*scintillans*
  ×*taggianum*

Reviewing these results, it is evident that, with some few exceptions, *R. carolinianum* is reluctant to cross with the species of the Triflorum, Maddenii and Cinnabarinum series, whereas it seems to be moderately compatible with the Rhododendrons in the Lapponicum and Boothii series. A part of the explanation probably lies in the extra chromosome sets which are found much more consistently in the series which do not often cross with *R. carolinianum* and a way to overcome this barrier is suggested in the general discussion of this subject on pages 409 and 410.

BREEDING FOR HARDINESS IN MILD CLIMATES

The work of the hybridist in the Pacific Northwest and in the British Isles is immeasurably simplified when there is no necessity to add a very large additional measure of cold resistance to his creations. Time and again the mere increment of additional vigor and the cumulative genetic effect of greater cold resistance which often accompanies hybrids as compared with species, is enough to give sufficient tolerance of low temperatures to the seedlings. For example, *R. griffithianum* is an extremely tender species and so is *R. griersonianum*. Yet the two crossed produced the hybrid 'Sunrise' which is quite satisfactorily hardy in many gardens of the West Coast Rhododendron belt. Bred with *R.* 'Barclayi', another tender Rhododendron, the equally unsatisfactory *R. griersonianum* gave the much hardier 'Laura Aberconway'.

It is often desirable to add still more cold tolerance and in mild climates *RR. fortunei* and *discolor* have been traditionally good sources among the non-scaly species for a measure of the rugged and adaptable disposition which they display in their own right. Other species of more modest stature, or quite different in floral effect, can be profitably employed to impart cold resistance as a study of their hardiness ratings and their performance as parents for breeders elsewhere will show.

R. catawbiense var. *album*, Glass as a parent exerts such a strong influence for ease of cultivation, tolerance of wind and sun, and for wide usefulness in a variety of climatic conditions that it is surprising to find that this white form of the native Catawba Rhododendron has not been used at all by breeders in milder regions. The selected superior clone, 'Catalgla', is a stunning ornamental in its own right, much superior to many of the more famous Asian species. The refinement and purity of its flower form gives it an impeccable, chaste elegance which is enormously appealing. Considering the great numbers of fine Rhododendron hybrids which are exasperatingly lacking in resistance to exposure, even in soft climates, it is remarkable that Western breeders have not taken advantage of the ability of *catawbiense* var. *album* to erase that deficiency.

In the Pacific Northwest and in Great Britain the sources for hardiness among the hybrids number in the hundreds, probably in the thousands, and the best suggestion for selection would be that the prospective hybridist review the section of *The Rhododendron Handbook*, Part Two, which lists alphabetically both hybrids and species, and gives the names of their progeny which have been registered with the Royal Horticultural Society. Many of these hybrid descendants are widely distributed and have been assigned both British and American hardiness ratings, so the success of their parents in imparting cold resistance can often be deduced. Some hybrids, such as *R.* (*dichroanthum* × *decorum*) 'Dido', are known to be good parents. In any case, familiarity with the cold tolerance of the offspring is very useful in estimating the ability of the parents to impart this quality. The actual hardiness of the parents themselves often has no great bearing on the resistance of their offspring to low temperatures.

For the breeder in climates milder than that of the northeastern United States who does not insist on a large population of seedlings of high average quality, but would instead be content with a small proportion of extraordinarily fine hybrids in exchange for many more of indifferent quality, such Rhododendrons as the later productions of Anthony Waterer seem promising prospects for imparting their rugged constitutions to the beautiful but more delicate creations from the favored climates of the British amateurs. The white 'Mrs A. Waterer' and 'Mrs J. G. Millais'; the red 'Pygmalion' and 'Mars'; the lavender 'Mrs Davies Evans' and 'Lady Grey-Egerton'; and the pink 'Mrs Philip Martineau' and 'Mrs Furnival' seem not to have been exploited to any important extent for the contributions they could undoubtedly make toward more rugged hybrids of high quality for intermediate climates.

BREEDING FOR HEAT RESISTANCE IN THE SOUTH

The success of Edmond Amateis in crossing the spectacularly beautiful species of the Edgeworthii and Maddenii series with the American species, *R. carolinianum*, suggests that hybridists in the South might produce invaluable hybrids for hot lowland gardens by breeding the heat-resistant native, *R. chapmanii*, to some of the fragrant, giant-flowered Asian Rhododendrons in these two series. *R. minus* might also impart tolerance of heat though probably somewhat less successfully than *R. chapmanii*. Such hybrids would not likely require further development in hardiness for the South, unlike those for the North which must be fertile and able to produce a second generation to achieve the goal of combining the quality of the scaly oriental species with the cold resistance to the climate of the native Rhododendron.

OBTAINING OTHER CHARACTERISTICS

Breeding for Large Flowers

I see no reason to search further than *R.* (Loderi g.) 'King George' for a non-scaly Rhododendron parent to impart increased flower size. Its corolla is the widest of all and it tends to transmit its enormously large flowers together with a good measure of hardiness from the *R. fortunei* in its heritage. The influence of its large stature can often be minimized by an opposite inheritance from the other parent.

Breeding for Dwarf Stature

The two best sources to impart restricted growth to non-scaly Rhododendron hybrids appear to be *RR. forrestii* and *williamsianum*. The scarlet-flowered *forrestii*, often less than a foot high, is usually shy-flowering but its hybrids are just the reverse. It tends to influence its offspring strongly in their habit, stature and leaf but it does not usually dominate the size or shape of the flowers or the number of them in the truss. *R. forrestii* and its hybrids are often therefore ideally suitable as parents in the production of low-growing Rhododendrons.

R. williamsianum has fine foliage and seldom grows more than 2 or 3 feet tall. Its nodding pink bells give it an air of debonair charm. As a parent it tends to dominate in stature, leaf, and in the shape of the flowers, but not in the number of them to the truss. Its offspring are not always free blooming, especially in youth, but the springtime growth is often brilliantly colored and the parental influence it imparts is usually completely effective in restricting stature. I have crossed vigorous Rhododendrons which mature at 15 to 20 feet with pollen of *R. williamsianum* and the resulting seedlings have been almost identical in stature and leaf with the diminutive proportions of the latter. It may be that the hybrids of *R. williamsianum* will in the end prove to be more valuable as parents than the species itself.

R. haematodes is an indumented scarlet-flowered species, famous for its quality, which grows only a little larger than the foregoing. Very old plants are scarcely 5 feet tall. As a parent, this species modifies rather than dominates the stature of its offspring when it is crossed with larger Rhododendrons. However, it usually exerts the major influence on the flower shape and truss formation of the progeny.

R. orbiculare, a species with round leaves and a faultless manner of growth, would seem to be a promising parent for its compact habit and moderate dimensions but it has generally been disappointing. It seems to dominate in stature, in leaf, and in flower shape, but it also usually reproduces in its immediate descendants its own bright rose-colored flowers and their arrangement in open trusses. For mild climates, the first generation hybrids are often no appreciable improvement over the free-blooming species itself. There is an opportunity, however, to infuse additional hardiness into the species so that its virtues can be enjoyed in severe climates. Its immediate offspring have been quite tender in the Northeast. Crosses extending into the second generation would undoubtedly produce better results both for the Northeast and for the Pacific Northwest than have so far appeared in its first generation descendants.

R. aperantum is a widely spreading species seldom over 2 feet tall, with serried foliage and flowers ranging in color from white through rose and red to orange and yellow. As a parent its stature is largely reproduced in its offspring and the leaf too is dominant, but the flowers can be modified to a gratifying extent in size, in shape, and in the number of them to the truss. A shy-blooming species, its progeny are free blooming, but they are not so prolific as the hybrids descended from *R. forrestii.*

R. dichroanthum interests hybridists for its compact growth of moderate dimensions and for its orange blossoms, but unhappily it largely duplicates in its immediate descendants the drooping carriage of the flowers which dangle in partial obscurity among the leaves. The more advanced generation hybrids of this species are much more useful as parents.

Some forms of the yellow-flowered *R. wardii* are only 4 or 5 feet tall at maturity and yield fine hybrids of moderate and compact growth. *R. souliei*, with its pink blossoms of extraordinary appeal, has been an admirable parent in the production of good new sorts a little larger in stature.

The seedlings of all of the crosses I have thus far made with the newly prominent *R. yakusimanum* have closely resembled this parent in their modest dimensions and dense manner of growth and the charm of the white and rose flowers is preserved. I am also presently experimenting with the true *R. chrysanthum*, of procumbent habit, to see if it will provide dwarfness without the somewhat trashy character of its flowers. *R. catawbiense* var. *compactum* is an excellent source for hardiness combined with dwarf stature but the breeder who uses it must resign himself to a second generation cross to rid the seedlings of the magenta color it imparts to its immediate progeny.

Breeding for Fragrance

I can offer little help to the breeder searching for information on the inheritance of scent in Rhododendrons. Among species in the wild, the lighter the color of the flowers the more likely they are to be fragrant and the stronger their perfume is apt to be. Fragrance is easily bred into white-flowered Rhododendrons by design, though it may take two generations if one parent is totally lacking in it. Hybrids with pink or yellow blossoms may be fragrant, though much less commonly so and to a markedly lesser degree. I cannot remember ever having come across a scented red-flowered hybrid, though 'Ignatius Sargent' has the pleasant aroma of Raspberry jam about it. I have made no concentrated effort to impart fragrance to a Rhododendron with red flowers and I do not know whether a breeding project with this aim alone might succeed, but I suspect it would be difficult.

Breeding for Earlier and Later Blooming Seasons

Hybrids are usually intermediate between their parents in their blooming period, though not exactly so, because there is often a tendency for the midseason time of flowering to exert a somewhat stronger influence than a parent which comes into blossom either extremely early or very late. For example, a Rhododendron which blooms May 15th, when crossed with one which blooms June 15th, is likely to blossom about May 25th. There are many exceptions, however. For instance the hybrid *R.* 'Nobleanum' is a cross of *R. arboreum* with *R. caucasicum* and it blooms earlier than either of its parents.

Two late red-flowering species which are often used to extend the season are *RR. didymum* and *eriogynum*. It may be useful to know that the former usually dominates its progeny in color but not in its rather scanty flower trusses. Seedlings of the latter generally are very similar to their parent in leaf, in flower shape and in the truss. The choice of parents for extending the season both earlier and later is frequently wide enough so that the selection depends most often upon a desired flower color, stature or some other trait which is sought in addition to a specific time of bloom.

BREEDING FOR FLOWER COLOR

Red Flowers

The pursuit of red-flowered Rhododendron hybrids is probably not so keen as it was a few years ago when almost every hybridist was concentrating on their production. The northeastern United States is still notably lacking in hardy hybrids bearing blossoms with the clear scarlet and crimson shades which glow so richly on the best of the tender Asian Rhododendrons. In mild climates, however, the best hybrids today exceed the finest species in the burning intensity of their color.

For the Pacific Northwest it seems likely that the best opportunity for further advancing red-flowered hybrids lies not so much in improving their color as in perfecting the truss formation and extending the season of bloom both earlier and later in a range of plants with compact habit and moderate growth. *RR. forrestii* and *aperantum* and their hybrids seem promising prospects as parents to achieve this end.

The best garden Rhododendrons in this class intended for mild climates have so far resulted from crossing red-flowered species and hybrids over several generations and selecting from each mating for further breeding the seedlings which exhibit the greatest intensity of color. It has been a matter of the cumulative contributions of their best color from each of several species, more a case of selection than of calculated breeding programs intended to manipulate this trait according to the principles of genetics. One of the best Rhododendrons in this group is *R.* 'Billy Budd' which was created by first crossing *R. haematodes* with *R. griersonianum*. The reddest seedling from this mating was then crossed with the scarlet-flowered *R. elliottii* and the brightest of the progeny has exceptional clarity of color. *R.* 'Gretia', another hybrid with extraordinary intensity in the shade of its flowers, was bred in much the same way, the first parents in this case being *RR. strigillosum* and *neriiflorum*. Their offspring was then crossed with a third scarlet-flowered species, *R. griersonianum*. *R.* 'Review Order' came from ((*neriiflorum* × *griersonianum*) × *haematodes*) and it is a remarkably clean, smooth, crimson-flowered hybrid.

R. griersonianum has been used as a parent more than any other species in an effort to capture the brilliance of the orange-scarlet color in its flowers. Unfortunately, it imparts to its immediate descendants its own rather serious faults of foliage and habit of growth when it is crossed with other Rhododendrons of robust stature, the hybrids tending to be lanky and with leaves which sunburn easily. It strongly influences the flower shape of its offspring but not the truss formation, and although it is very tender in itself, its offspring are hardy beyond all reasonable expectation. I think its virtues can be better captured without its faults by using its hybrids as parents rather than the species itself. Such cultivars as *R.* (*griersonianum* × *forrestii*) 'Elizabeth' and *R.* (*haematodes* × *griersonianum*) 'May Day' are already known to be fine parents for the production of good red-flowered hybrids.

It frequently happens that red will act as a simple dominant, transmitted from one parent to the largest portion of the progeny even when the other parent has white flowers. This seems to be especially true of some of the Asian species and their hybrids designed for mild climates, but only rarely so of the extremely hardy hybrids grown in the Northeast.

As a group, the red-flowered cultivars have poor growth characteristics, tending toward sparse foliage, inadequate branching, and a generally lean appearance out of bloom. *RR. haematodes*, *aperantum*, and *forrestii* and their hybrids are promising prospects for remedying this deficiency.

R. 'Essex Scarlet' has proved to be a good source of color in breeding hybrids for severe climates, although my own crosses with it have usually yielded seedlings which also inherited from it the ungainly manner of growth. *R.* (*forrestii* × 'Essex Scarlet') 'Elisabeth Hobbie', a hybrid originated by Dietrich Hobbie in Germany, might as a parent eliminate this defect. However this may be, 'Essex Scarlet' transmits its color so efficiently that it often gives offspring which are red-flowered when the other parents have blossoms of another color. In Holland, 'Earl of Athlone', 'Jean Marie Montague', and 'Earl of Donoughmore' have contributed generously of their color to their offspring. There the breeders also have great confidence in *R. thomsonii* as a source of good red color, and 'Ascot Brilliant', a first generation hybrid from it, has been a successful parent. Hybridists in the Netherlands are especially partial to any Rhododendron which does not lose the intensity of its red color when it is forced into bloom in a greenhouse and they believe that such cultivars are particularly effective as parents. 'Souvenir de D. A. Koster' is an example of a parent which demonstrates this theory.

Yellow Flowers

At present, hybridists the world over are probably working more industriously on the production of yellow-flowered hybrids than on any other color class. The wild Rhododendrons with yellow blossoms have been reluctant to pass on to their hybrid offspring either the luminosity of their color or the grace of their flower form.

Flower color in Rhododendrons, as in other plants, is controlled by plastid pigments, ranging from colorless through shades of cream to yellow which are found in the tissues of the corolla and are not soluble in the sap; and by other pigments which are soluble in the cell sap: the yellow and ivory-white flavones and flavonols; and the anthocyanins, composed of red and blue coloring matter. Various mixtures of these three types of pigments give Rhododendron flowers their extraordinary range, the exact color being dependent upon the amount of each of the pigments present in the plant. The supply of two of them is not inexhaustible, incidentally; if a great deal of anthocyanin is produced there is an automatic reduction in the amount of flavone. and vice versa.

The presence or absence of these pigments, and the amounts of them, are not controlled by the same genes, the sub-microscopic bodies in the cells governing all inherited characteristics, half of which come from each parent. In Sweet Peas, for example, two different genes are known to be necessary if anthocyanin is to be produced, and at least two other genes control the production of flavone. Since the three pigment sources which determine flower color are each acquired independently it follows that the study of their behavior in inheritance and the controlled manipulation of them separately to achieve the desired effect is the best technical approach to effective breeding for flower color.

In breeding for the elusive yellow flowers we will get the greatest color intensity from a combination of yellow plastids in the cells and yellow flavones in the sap, without any anthocyanin sap pigmentation masking it. However, either one or the other alone can be effective, as is apparent in the plastid pigmentation responsible for the deep yellow Tulips and Daffodils; and by the bright yellow Dahlias and Snapdragons whose color is derived from the flavones and flavonols. The breeder who wishes to pursue further the technical approach to flower color in hybrids is referred to 'A Survey of the Interactions of Genes for Flower Color', Technical Bulletin 281, published by Michigan State University Agricultural Experiment Station, East Lansing, Mich.

Hybridists are occasionally puzzled by the unexpected appearance of yellow-flowered seedlings among the progeny of a red-flowered Rhododendron crossed with a white one. For example, *discolor* × *neriiflorum* produced 'Bobolink', a hybrid with yellow blossoms, and Joseph Gable obtained a yellow-flowered seedling from a cross of *maximum* with *haematodes*. The hybrid 'Diva', with red flowers, at times produces descendants with yellow blossoms. In such cases the colored Rhododendrons which are the parents owe their scarlet flowers to crimson anthocyanin plus yellow flavone. When yellow blooms are produced by their progeny from crosses with white-flowered Rhododendrons the plausible explanation is that the genes which control the production of crimson anthocyanin are not productive, but those which govern flavone do exercise their positive function with the result that yellow flavone pigment in the cell sap determines the flower color.

Many amateur hybridists will be interested in the simplest and most direct approach to fine yellow-flowered hybrids and one such way, at least, is the experience thus far accumulated by practiced breeders. Two of the best yellow-flowered hybrids today are unquestionably *R.* (Hawk g.) 'Crest' and *R.* (Jalisco g.) 'Goshawk'. The former was produced by crossing *R. discolor*, with its large white blossoms, with the yellow-flowered *R. campylocarpum*. The best of the offspring was then crossed with *R. wardii*, another species with yellow flowers. 'Goshawk' resulted from a mating of *discolor* (white) × *campylocarpum* (yellow) with *dichroanthum* (orange) × *decorum* (white). Orange, of course, is a mixture of red and yellow, so the success of these two new hybrids is essentially due to the same formula. They bear immense, widely open, rather flat flowers of a strong, clear yellow color with much of the unique luminosity which characterizes the species source of their color.

In the case of 'Crest' the blossom size and shape of *R. discolor* strongly dominates while the two yellow-flowered species each contributed the best of their color in interaction with each other. The capacity for producing yellow, somewhat submerged in the one parent, *discolor* × *campylocarpum*, was none the less invisibly present and capable of being once again fully expressed in the next generation when it combined with the yellow of the other parent, *R. wardii*, in a cumulative yellow effect.

Exactly the same principle applies to 'Goshawk'. In that case the yellow was largely submerged in so far as its visible effect was concerned in both of the parents, but it was none the less present. When the two parents were crossed, each with yellow in their heritage but not strongly evident in them, the hidden capacity to produce yellow flowers came out once again in pure form in combination with the large flowers inherited from the other two species in the pedigree.

It should be noted that there must be a yellow-flowered inheritance in *both* parents for such a result. Though the parents may not themselves have yellow flowers, if each contains one-half its inheritance from a yellow-flowered species there is a promising prospect that pure yellow will once again find expression in the offspring in combination with large flowers, dwarf stature or any other desired trait which is also present in the forebears. This, I think, is a practical method for the production of fine yellow-flowered hybrids. Without going into a technical explanation, it is sound genetically and it has been successful on a practical basis in the production of these, the first truly yellow-flowered hybrids of high quality. On a theoretical basis, the sibling mating of two hybrid seedlings from a cross between a yellow and a large-flowered species such as *discolor* × *campylocarpum*, might be even better. For that matter, the same method is equally successful in breeding flowers of other colors, or in the transmittal of many desirable traits from different parents which may be sought in combination in the progeny.

The best yellow-flowered parents on the basis of past performance are clearly *RR. campylocarpum* and *wardii* and their hybrids. However, the Rhododendron species with the yellowest flowers of the highest quality is *R. lacteum*. Unfortunately, this species has acquired the reputation of being worthless as a parent. I must dissent from this opinion. It is possible that *R. lacteum* may pass on a measure of its difficult disposition but that can be ameliorated should the occasion arise. The fact is that *R. lacteum* has not been really exploited at all in a manner which would be most likely to obtain the gift of its large incandescent yellow globes.

I doubt very much whether it is accurate to give a blanket dismissal to any species as 'worthless' in breeding. It is much more likely that the ability of Rhododendron parents to transmit their best traits is characteristic of individuals of a species rather than of such a great group as an entire species. Even in the present instance I can cite in disproof of its reputation as a parent such offspring as *R.* ((*caucasicum* × *griffithianum*) × *lacteum*) 'Mariloo' and *R.* (*lacteum* × *caloxanthum*) 'Joanita', both of which have flowers which are very yellow indeed.

Dr Rock's *R. vernicosum* aff. #18139 may be useful in the quest for hybrids with large yellow flowers and moderate stature suitable for the Northeast. This species form, with 4-inch apricot-yellow flowers, has survived outdoors in Joseph Gable's trial grounds for more than twenty years.

Orange Flowers

Large, bright orange flowers with the broad flat corollas preferred by most gardeners are a goal which has eluded Rhododendron breeders to this time. *R. dichroanthum* has been the usual source of this pigment in most crosses but its immediate offspring tend far too much to the drooping tubular flowers which often dangle, partially hidden, among the leaves.

The pursuit of hybrids with orange flowers has led to rather complex matings. Among the best orange-flowered hybrids to date are the Bodnant crosses derived from such matings as ((*dichroanthum* × *neriiflorum*) × *griersonianum*) × (*griffithianum* × *fortunei*); and (*griffithianum* × *fortunei*) × ((*dichroanthum* × *griersonianum*) × *dichroanthum*). The above hybrids have then been crossed with *herpesticum* × *griersonianum* in a quest for still greater intensification of the orange color.

It seems to me, however, that the introduction of additional red-flowered species is unnecessary and even undesirable, and I believe that fine hybrids with orange flowers are most likely to be produced by the same formula which has yielded the splendid new yellow-flowered hybrids described in the previous section. I suggest as a promising prospect the mating of two hybrids each of which carries a heritage of large, open flowers and orange color, regardless of whether these parents themselves are notable for their color intensity. Such a cross as (*discolor* × (*dichroanthum* × *griersonianum*)) 'Margaret Dunn' with *R.* (*dichroanthum* × *decorum*) 'Dido' ought to give good results.

Although *R. dichroanthum* and its orange-flowered hybrid offspring, the Fabia hybrid group, have been used almost entirely as a source of color for hybrids in this class, the best forms of *R. scyphocalyx* and of *R. horaeum* have flowers which exceed their species relative in color intensity.

Blue Flowers

There are no truly blue flowers among non-scaly Rhododendrons but such hybrids as 'Blue Ensign' and 'Blue Peter' and the species *R. campanulatum* offer appealing shades of violet which hold out the tantalizing prospect of more nearly approaching blue in hybrids which are so useful for planting with the yellow-flowered sorts. Breeders in mild climates are almost universal in condemning *R. campanulatum* as a parent, ascribing to its offspring flowers which they say are invariably a dingy purple. The condemnation is too inclusive, however, as the fine *campanulatum* hybrid *R.* 'Susan' demonstrates. The best form of *R. campanulatum* is 'Knaphill' and some expressions of *R. floribundum* also seem to offer interesting possibilities in breeding blue-flowered Rhododendron hybrids. These or other species with flowers in this color class, crossed among themselves or with the best of the violet-mauve hybrids, appear to hold out a reasonable prospect of improvement in this group. There are no serious faults of flower or truss, stature or habit of growth to be eliminated and the problem resolves itself to the usually rather simple one of color intensification by selection.

White Flowers

Rhododendrons are fairly typical in the manner in which white flowers are inherited. With some exceptions (as when white masks anthocyanin) a white-flowered parent crossed with another will yield seedlings with blossoms which are also white. Crossed with red, pink, yellow, or orange-flowered species, one with white blossoms will most often produce seedlings with floral colors in intermediate shades between the two parents. When white flowers are masked in the first generation after crossing with a parent of another color, they can usually be recovered in the next, in at least a portion of the seedlings, by inbreeding or by crossing with another hybrid with either an evident or unseen heritage of white flowers in its ancestry.

Pink Flowers

Pink blossoms are often, but by no means always, produced by crossing a white with a red-flowered Rhododendron. A minor portion of such crosses is characterized by red predominating in the offspring, especially when nothing but red-flowered species figure in the heritage of the one parent. When two pink-flowered sorts are crossed, at least a majority of the offspring are usually pink. Some of the yellow species, particularly a so-called variety of *campylocarpum*, *elatum*, produce pale pink shades of exceptional attractiveness when crossed with white Rhododendrons. Sorts with light pink blossoms crossed with those with yellow flowers are often noteworthy for the delicacy and subtlety of the pastel colors in the flowers of the progeny.

Double Flowers

The only species, to my knowledge, which have double flowers *in the wild* are *RR. fauriei*, *metternichii* and *brachycarpum* and these presumably would be a promising initial source for the development of this trait in hybrids. Dr Henry Skinner, director of the United States National Arboretum at Washington, produced a series of pretty double-flowered hybrids with the latter species as a parent. 'Fastuosum plenum', also called 'Fastuosum flore pleno', is a hybrid of unknown parentage which produces only a portion of its flowers partially doubled, but it is singularly unattractive in my opinion.

The most interesting instance of doubling in flowers is that of the scaly-leaved *R. johnstoneanum*. According to Charles Puddle, superintendent of the famed Bodnant gardens in Wales, when the ordinary single-flowered *R. johnstoneanum* which grows there is self-pollinated the offspring invariably have double flowers. The best of them are very beautiful, resembling large, fully double white Camellias, with the stamens converted into additional petals in the centers of the flowers.

RECIPROCAL CROSSES

Breeders are sometimes perplexed as to which of two Rhododendrons intended for cross breeding should be used as the seed parent. In practice it seems to make little difference in most cases. There is a tradition that the plant whose qualities are most urgently sought in the offspring should be selected to bear the seeds, and Dutch breeders in their search for cold resistance always try to use the hardier of the two parents as the female seed bearer. Ordinary observation does not particularly bear out this belief. There seem to be about as many exceptions as there are confirmations of the theory. I have made many crosses using pollen of hardy Rhododendrons on tender sorts and I see little difference in the cold resistance of the offspring as compared with similar matings where the hardy plant was used to bear the seeds.

Theoretically there could easily be differences in some traits of the progeny caused by reversing the roles of seed and pollen parents. It is well known among geneticists that cytoplasmic and other forms of maternal inheritance may transmit characteristics from the seed parent to the offspring which they cannot obtain from the pollen parent. Reciprocal crosses which fail because the gene complement from the pollen parent is not compatible with the cytoplasm furnished by the seed parent, may succeed when the parents are reversed. So Rhododendron hybridists do report dissimilar results from reciprocal crosses at times and this is the probable explanation. Such reports are exceptional, however. As a general rule the results are very similar regardless of which way the cross is made.

HOW TO CROSS RHODODENDRONS

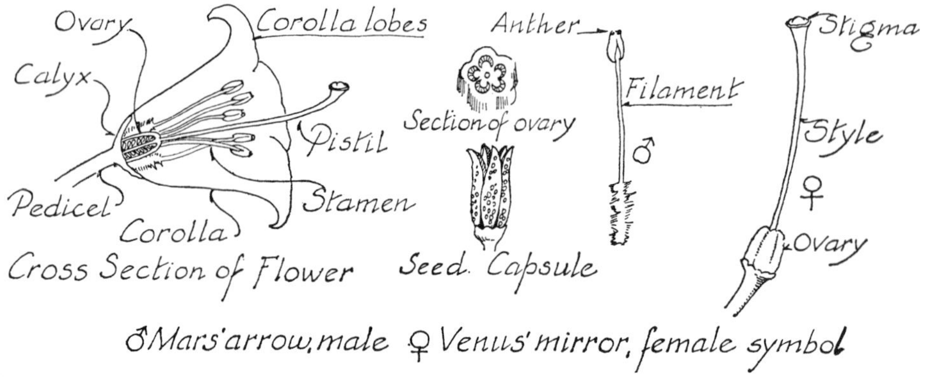

Rhododendrons are among the easiest plants to pollinate. The flower parts are large and easily accessible and no delicate or practiced technique is necessary, nor are any tools required except possibly a small pair of scissors and a pair of tweezers.

Preparing the Flowers

After the flower buds are well enough developed for easy handling and have acquired their natural color, but a day or two before they open, the corolla of a flower to be pollinated is removed so that it does not later attract bees or other insects. This is most easily accomplished by snipping through the ribs of the corolla at its base, just above the ovary, with a small pair of scissors, and the tube forming the bottom of the flower is then very easily detached. The next step is to cut away the pollen-bearing stamens by severing them at the base. There should then be no accidental self-pollination. This leaves, then, only the female flower parts, the style with the stigma at the top which is later to receive the pollen and the ovary at the bottom in which the seeds will be nurtured. The drawing below illustrates the preparation of the flower for crossing. In performing this operation of removing the unwanted floral parts the only necessary precaution is to be careful that no pollen from the anthers at the top of the stamens is accidentally brushed on to the stigma to cause an unintended self-pollination.

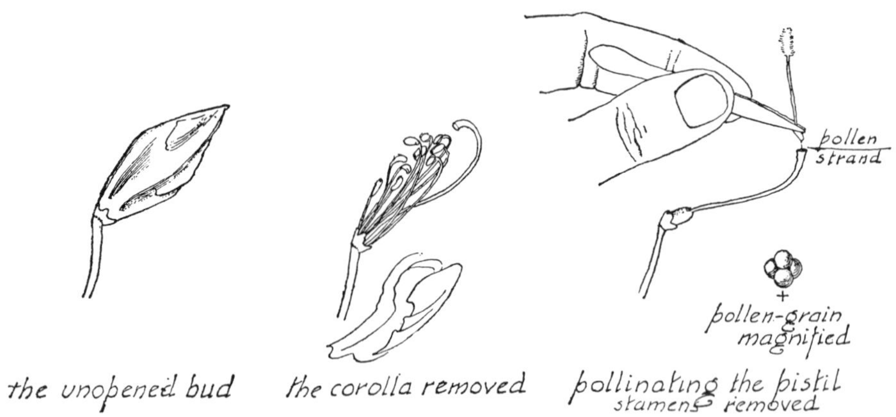

It is usually best to prepare at least eight flowers for each cross. All sorts of accidents may reduce the seed crop beyond normal expectations. Continuously wet weather or other factors may impair the effectiveness of the pollination. Insects may devour some of the capsules or they may be accidentally broken off. Partial sterility or incompatability may unexpectedly reduce the number of seeds produced. In my own work I have been thankful on a good many occasions that I had taken the few extra moments needed to emasculate and pollinate several flowers more than I thought would actually be needed. Blossoms in a cluster which are not to be used in the cross must be entirely removed at the same time the remainder are prepared for pollination.

After the corolla and stamens have been severed from the unopened flower the breeder examines carefully the stigma at the top of the style. If it is viscid with a sticky secretion designed to catch and hold the pollen, the cross can be made at once. Stamens containing the pollen in the anthers, the little sacs poised at the ends of the stalks, are removed from flowers about to open on the other plant which is to serve as a parent. Holding them in the fingers or in tweezers, they are brushed lightly over the sticky surface of the stigma in such a manner that the soft, stringy pollen which protrudes from two tiny holes in the anthers is caught in the adhesive secretion and distributed in a visibly uniform coating. Occasionally Rhododendrons produce only scanty pollen, or stamens which have been stored for later use do not release it properly. It may then be necessary to split open the anthers or even to pulverize them to make use of the pollen they contain.

If the stigma does not exhibit the glistening viscous coating at the time the corolla and stamens are removed from the flower it will be necessary to defer pollination until this evidence of a receptive condition can be seen. In some cases it may be three or four days before the sticky secretion appears and the cross can be made.

In the meantime it is not usually necessary to cover the naked styles in the cluster with any sort of a bag while they are waiting to be pollinated. Insects are not normally attracted in the absence of conspicuous floral parts and enclosures designed to give protection from them often overheat in sunlight or become excessively humid from condensation within them. A hybridist can test his local conditions by preparing some marked flowers in the usual manner but without making any crosses on them. If seeds do not later develop it can be assumed that insects at that site are not carrying unwanted pollen to contaminate flowers stripped for crossing. I find no need, either, for protection against insects after the crosses have been made.

The pollen germinates very quickly after it is distributed over the top of the stigma. Tubes descend inside the style and fertilization takes place in the ovary. If the stigma is maturely receptive, two hours is more than ample time for the pollen to germinate and start its descent of the style, so there is no need for concern if it rains thereafter. Fertilization in the ovary is accomplished about twenty-four hours after the pollination takes place.

It rarely happens that a Rhododendron will be inexplicably reluctant to provide the conditions under which pollen germinates and then effects fertilization. *R. maximum* is such a parent. Despite any earlier indications of receptive maturity there is little use in pollinating it until several days after the corolla and stamens have been removed, and then it is a wise precaution to repeat the application of pollen on two or three successive days. There are probably other such parents, unknown to me, but their number cannot be very large. Pollination and subsequent fertilization is usually easily accomplished under normal circumstances.

After Pollination

Immediately the pollen has been applied, a label giving the parentage should be attached to the stem which bears the flower cluster. It is folly to trust the memory for even a few hours because the consequence of mislabeled hybrids can be a staggering amount of wasted time and effort even years later. I find it most convenient to use a permanent zinc label on which is marked with an acid etchant the parentage, the year the cross was made and any other brief note that might be wanted. This same label then is used to mark the flat in which the seeds are later sown and it is subsequently duplicated for additional flats into which the seedlings are transplanted. It is transferred then to identify the young plants as they develop in ground beds, and finally it is attached to an iron stake which marks older plants when they are lined out in rows in the field. Thus the same label follows the hybrids from the time the cross is made until the plants resulting from it come into bloom, and the possibility of error and confusion is thereby minimized.

It is usually possible to tell within a few days after making a cross whether the pollination has been successful. The normal consequence of fertilization is an expanding ovary which begins developing almost immediately. By the end of three weeks the seed-bearing vessel has so increased in size that it is almost as large as the mature capsule which is harvested in the fall. It often happens that the pollen may not be fully potent, the stigma only partially receptive or there may be a measure of incompatability and in such cases the capsules contain fewer seeds and are usually much smaller in size.

Harvesting the Seeds

With the approach of mid-autumn the seed capsules start to turn brown and they are harvested before they split open and start to scatter their contents with the advent of the first hard frosts. Generally, the small-leaved alpine species accustomed to a short season at high elevations mature their capsules very quickly, whereas the large-leaved sorts, in nature adjusted to a leisurely cycle of growth extending over many months, do not start to disperse their seeds until very late in the season. There is no point, however, in gambling on the loss of seeds by waiting for the capsules to turn brown and start to split downward from their tips. The seeds within these vessels are fully developed long before the capsules change color. Seeds gathered experimentally in August sprouted as vigorously as did others from the same plant gathered in October. Ordinarily there would be no point in risking immature seeds by needlessly gathering them so early in the season but the usual practice of waiting until the capsules turn brown is an equally useless hazard.

Sometimes a hybridist may want to accelerate a breeding program just as much as possible. A considerable gain can be made the first year by gathering the seeds in early August, drying them at 100° F. in an oven for three days, and then sowing them right away. Carried through the winter in a greenhouse, or under fluorescent lights in active growth, the seedlings attain remarkable size by the end of their first year.

In the usual course, after the capsules are gathered, those from each cross are put separately into small envelopes together with the labels recording the parentage and are stored at ordinary room temperature for a few weeks until it is time to plant the seeds. The capsules, by then fully dried and brittle, are crushed beneath almost any round object which can be rolled over them a few times with some pressure. The broken pieces are then separated from the seeds. I find it most convenient to do this with two sieves of different mesh sizes. The threshed seeds are then returned to the envelopes containing their labels and are ready for planting. The procedure for sowing them and their aftercare to maturity is described in detail in the chapter on propagation, beginning on page 352.

APOMIXIS

The sly hand of the 'little people' seems at times to be visible in the inexplicable results which occasionally perplex Rhododendron breeders. Young plants resembling the seed parent in foliage and habit will be brought to flowering size only to discover then that they are identical in blossom as well. They are exact duplicates in every respect of the plant from which they sprang as seeds.

Now it rarely happens that such a situation results from the complete and absolute dominance of one of the parents in every respect, but normally some evidence of dual parental influence can be found even in those disappointing progeny which so strongly mirror one of the parents. However, when the resemblance of the offspring to the seed parent is absolute and complete the chances are the breeder has been the unfortunate victim of a phenomenon known as apomixis. Apomixis, or induced apogamy, is the production of seeds without fertilization. The female parent is stimulated to bear seeds by the application of pollen which fails actually to fuse with the ovules. In the absence of fertilization and a contribution of genes from the male parent, plants grown from such seeds can only be duplicates of the Rhododendron which bore them.

Induced apogamy has misled a good many breeders into claiming, with good faith, improbable parentages for their hybrids. When Rhododendrons are crossed which are only distantly related botanically, this strange phenomenon is more than ordinarily likely to be responsible for the production of seeds. Some of the hybrids recorded in the stud section of *The Rhododendron Handbook*, prior to the most recent edition, particularly those resulting from crosses between scaly and non-scaly Rhododendrons, are almost certainly the result of apomixis.

Certain well-known commercial cultivars have been reported to produce seeds in this manner rather than as a result of true fertilization. One of these is the old ironclad hardy hybrid 'Catawbiense Album' (not to be confused with *catawbiense* var. *album*, the white form of the wild species), but in my tests with it the influence of the male pollen parent was conspicuous in the offspring. Apparently, therefore, it is capable either of apomixis or of producing seeds in the normal manner, perhaps depending on the heritage of the male parent which is chosen to supply the pollen. Should any good Rhododendron consistently and invariably produce apomictic seeds it could be conveniently propagated in this manner because all of its diploid offspring would be genetically identical with the seed parent and this would be equivalent to asexual reproduction.

OBTAINING AND STORING POLLEN

Novice breeders sometimes waste a great deal of time and money by raising from seeds certain species which are needed for their pollen, or by buying or importing hybrid Rhododendron plants for this purpose. This is rarely, if ever, necessary. Pollen is so freely available and so readily preserved and sent through the mails that the hybridist need only grow the female seed parents, which is quite enough for the time and energies of many amateur breeders. Few indeed are the species of ornamental merit which are not somewhere represented in the Rhododendron collections of our Pacific Northwest or of Great Britain, and almost any hybrid of known parentage listed in the stud section of Part Two of *The Rhododendron Handbook* can be located either here or abroad. Owners of Rhododendron collections are invariably generous and cooperative, even eager to help the breeder who is striving to make a contribution toward the improvement of garden hybrids, and pollen seems always to be available from practically any Rhododendron which is sought as a parent.

Pollen is preserved by exactly the same conditions which conserve the viability of seeds. Heat and humidity bring about more rapid deterioration. Low temperature and dryness protect the pollen. For nearby use, stamens containing the desired pollen in the anther-sacs, taken from the flowers just before they open, can simply be placed in an envelope and held under ordinary room conditions until needed. There is a world-wide exchange of pollen through the mails in this manner. Depending on the weather, pollen so stored will remain in good condition for two weeks or more. Of course, a large number of moist stamens must not be put into a closed envelope to decay into a sodden mass. Their number must be restricted so that their storage conditions are loose and airy.

For longer periods of storage, pollen can be held in good condition for two or three months, possibly more, by putting the stamens from flowers just about to open into size 00 gelatin capsules, obtainable from any drugstore, and then placing the capsules in a small container with a little calcium chloride, which is also usually available from a drugstore. The capsules should not be filled more than half full. A long, thin ribbon of paper on which is noted the identity of the pollen can be placed between the bottom and the top of the capsule and this label will then be firmly attached to it after it is closed. A glass or plastic vial, a test tube or a small bottle is then filled about one-fifth full of coarse granular calcium chloride. On this goes some cotton to hold it in place, the capsules containing the stamens are put into the container and then it is tightly stoppered. The calcium chloride absorbs almost all of the moisture in the container, withdrawing it even from the stamens through the walls of the gelatin capsules, and in this dry atmosphere the pollen is preserved at ordinary room temperatures. This is very frequently a convenient and effective method of storing pollen from early blooming Rhododendrons for use on those which flower much later. For still longer storage, as demonstrated by Dr John Creech at the United States Plant Introduction Garden, pollen can be preserved for a full year under controlled refrigeration, with a temperature of 33° F. and relative humidity of 30 per cent.

HANDLING TENDER RHODODENDRONS AS SEED PARENTS

Sometimes the breeder wishes to use as the female parent a Rhododendron which is not satisfactorily hardy outdoors in his climate. Many such half-hardy plants can be grown outdoors in the protection of a lath house, or shielded in winter by an open barrel, in a burlap tent or by some other method suggested in the earlier chapter on the subject of hardiness. The effectiveness of these makeshift shelters is often beyond all expectation in bringing half-hardy plants through the winter uninjured.

Rhododendrons which are completely and absolutely tender can be grown in pots and wintered in a deep cold pit which need have neither light nor ventilation while the plants are dormant. In the spring they can be plunged outdoors in peat in ground frames and used as parents.

Small Grafts with Floral Buds

Even more convenient is a new technique for the production of small budded grafts devised by H. L. Larson, a nurseryman in Tacoma, Washington, in the course of a project in which I tested the results for hybridizing. Tender Rhododendrons with floral buds already formed are green-grafted in August using the method described on page 341. The flower buds will not remain intact on dormant grafts held in a humid grafting case in winter, and for this reason propagation for this special purpose can be done only in late summer.

Early in the following spring these tiny grafted plants of tender Rhododendrons, with their floral buds intact, are sent into the more severe climate where they are to be used in breeding. When they come into bloom the flowers are undersized but normal in color and in the development of their parts. Each graft, of course, consists of but a single short stem with one flower truss at the top.

In my experiments I found that only two or three flowers in the truss should be pollinated on each of the plants. So restricted, the grafts bear capsules of exceptional size which yield abundant supplies of seeds. When a larger number of blossoms is pollinated the burden of producing additional capsules seems to be too much for such small plants. After the little grafts are returned to the outdoor frame the developing seed capsules close to ground level are an attraction to rodents, so it is necessary to protect them by enclosing the plant in its pot with a cage made of quarter-inch mesh hardware cloth.

The successful grafting of scions with floral buds is an important contribution to hybridists everywhere. It is an easy matter to force these small potted plants into bloom in a greenhouse, or in a residence, to obtain pollen from them for early crosses much sooner in the season than it would normally be produced. It is equally easy to hold the grafts in cold storage so that they can be used as seed parents after pollen of later-blooming Rhododendrons becomes available. In addition to this flexibility which they provide in manipulating the blooming seasons for matings which would otherwise be impossible, the small budded plants offer a great saving in their cost, in the expense of transportation and in the time, labor, and convenience of handling them as compared with a balled and burlapped shrub of flowering age. Further than that, budded scions of new originations can be imported from abroad for use as seed parents here years before mature plants of blooming age would be available.

ADVANCING AND RETARDING THE FLOWERING OF SEED PARENTS

Many Rhododendrons can be brought into bloom in a greenhouse or in a residence for hybridizing much sooner in the season than their natural time of flowering outdoors. Generally, the early blossoming sorts can be induced to flower more quickly and farther in advance of their usual season than can the late blooming kinds. The information on forcing Rhododendrons in the preceding chapter will be useful.

When the breeder wants to hold back a plant from its usual flowering until pollen is available from the Rhododendron which is to serve as the male parent, it can be retarded by placing it in cold storage at about 34° F. For the climate of northwestern Pennsylvania I find that plants which are wanted in bloom in early June should be removed from cold storage thirty-one days before the desired blooming date.

CAUSES AND CURES FOR INFERTILITY

There is a technical difference between sterility and incompatibility, the latter being a failure of the pollen tubes to grow down the style, or to effect fertilization after they have done so, because of inherited genes which interfere with these normal processes. Sterility, on the other hand, is most often due to the death of the embryonic seeds after fertilization has taken place, as a result of the failure of the set of chromosomes contributed by the one parent to work in harmony with the set obtained from the other. The chromosomes are the minute thread-like structures in the cells which, through the genes they contain, determine every inherited characteristic of the plants. There are twenty-six of them in most Rhododendrons, one set of thirteen being in the ovule of the female seed parent and the other set of thirteen being added at the time of fertilization from the male pollen parent. The chromosomes then are in pairs which are similar, one from each parent, so that thirteen pairs are present in the fertilized ovule which is to become a seed.

If the thirteen chromosomes from one parent are too dissimilar from the thirteen contributed by the other, the embryo dies, or sometimes there is a delayed lethal effect and the seedlings die in infancy. If the chromosomes are a little more alike, the offspring may survive but be weak and slow growing. If the two sets are only slightly antagonistic the effect is often not noticed until the progeny bloom and then they are infertile, not capable of producing pollen, or of bearing seeds, or both. The more distantly related the parents are botanically, the more likely there is to be a lethal dissimilarity in the chromosomes. As the relationship of the parents becomes closer the chance of unnaturally weak seedlings diminishes and so does the likelihood of infertility in offspring of normal vigor, which is often the minimum effect of 'wide' crosses.

There is probably no remedy for crosses which fail due to the death of the embryonic seeds shortly after fertilization, but if a particularly promising mating of more or less distantly related Rhododendrons is unsuccessful because the progeny perish the first few weeks after the seeds germinate, there is a chance that it might be salvaged if the two parents are crossed once again and this time the germinating seeds are treated with a colchicine solution to double their number of chromosomes. Extreme lack of vigor may often be due to the chromosome set obtained from the one parent being too dissimilar to the set contributed from the other to work reciprocally with it. If, however, the chromosome number is doubled the otherwise weak seedlings may develop in a normal fashion instead of dying in infancy as before.

Colchicine is perhaps even more valuable as a means of overcoming sterility. Crosses which persistently fail because of dissimilarity in the gene complements of the two parents may succeed if one of them is synthetically converted into a polyploid by the use of colchicine.

The Use of Colchicine

Colchicine, a potent poison which should not come in contact with the skin, doubles the chromosome number by preventing the migration of the duplicate chromosome set which is created as each cell prepares to form another by division. When the duplicate set which is intended to go into the daughter cell is instead retained in the mother cell by the effect of the colchicine, it has double the usual number and all cells which subsequently spring from it will also have twice the normal number.

The treatment of the seeds with colchicine solution is easy. They are first germinated on a moist paper towel in a glass-covered container. Just as they are sprouting they are transferred into another shallow container lined with paper towels saturated with colchicine solution made by dissolving 1 gram of colchicine in 100 c.c. of water. One-sixth of the seedlings are removed at the end of eight hours and additional lots, each representing one-sixth of the total, are removed at intervals up to twenty-four hours. As they are taken from the colchicine saturated paper they are rinsed with water and then planted in moist sphagnum or any other medium that the breeder uses routinely for growing seedlings. Somewhere along the line, in the length of exposure to the chemical, I have found that there is usually one lot which is successfully treated. Those which are under-exposed are unaffected whereas those which are over-exposed to the colchicine are killed, but this method offers a reasonable prospect of success with at least part of the seedlings and I think it is far superior to the usually recommended procedure of treating the entire lot with a solution whose estimated strength may turn out to be either inadequate or lethal.

The use of colchicine in this manner need not be reserved alone for the purposes previously described. It should be a routine experimental tool in the hands of the Rhododendron breeder. Increased chromosome number is associated time and again with greater ornamental value in all sorts of garden plants. Greater vigor and often increased hardiness as a result of it, and larger flowers of better texture, more freely produced, are a frequent consequence of treating normal hybrids with colchicine so that their chromosome number is doubled. Even when the chromosome count is increased by genetic accident in the wild the results are valuable, as witness the case of *R. diaprepes* 'Gargantua', a form of the species which is remarkably superior to the average because of its extra complement of chromosomes.

When a normally vigorous Rhododendron proves upon flowering to be infertile as a result of chromosomes which are improperly paired it can often be salvaged for breeding by the use of colchicine applied in a different manner to double the chromosomes in a single branch which may thereafter bear fertile flowers. All too often a primary hybrid between two species is more or less intermediate between its parents and of little value in itself. Its potential value is great, however, if it could only be bred again to recover in the progeny a combination of the best characteristics of both its parents. Many a promising breeding project is stopped dead because the first generation hybrids are infertile and a second generation is needed to achieve the goal.

There is a good possibility of producing fertile flowers on a branch of an infertile hybrid Rhododendron by treating the growing tip with a lanolin salve containing 1 per cent colchicine. Cotton soaked with a 1 per cent colchicine solution can also be wrapped around the end of a twig which is in active growth. Usually a fresh application is made daily for three days and on the fourth day the treated part is washed with clear water. I have successfully used a 0·4 per cent colchicine solution in an emulsion of 'Hind's Honey and Almond

Cream', diluted with an equal part of water, sprayed on the growing buds three times a week. Treatment of this sort is effective only when the cells are dividing and the stems are in vigorous growth. The elongating main branch is temporarily checked by the colchicine application at the tip and secondary branches usually develop from the leaf axils. These must be broken off.

When the treatment is effective the branch as it further extends after resuming growth will have, from the point of treatment onward, double the usual number of chromosomes and when flowers are produced on it they may well be fertile in contrast to the infertile flowers elsewhere on the plant. Sometimes it is convenient and effective to break off the terminal bud from a developing branch, remove the leaves along its length and then apply colchicine to the axils so that one or more of the new stems which spring from these axillary buds will be rendered capable of producing fertile flowers as a result of treatment with the drug.

So it is that sterilities may be overcome when they are encountered by the hybridist in mating plants which are too dissimilar.

INCOMPATIBILITY AND ITS CURE

Incompatibility, on the other hand, arises from the failure of the pollen tubes to grow down the style or to effect fertilization after they have done so, as a result of mating two Rhododendrons which are too *similar*. This is an inherited incapacity, generally evident when two plants both contain the same incompatibility gene. The pollen is normal and the style is normal and both perform their natural function perfectly when the two parents carry different genes. It is only when both contain the same gene governing this characteristic, or when self-pollination is attempted, that the pollen fails to bring about fertilization in the ovary.

About 25 per cent of Rhododendron hybrids are self-incompatible and cannot normally be fertilized by their own pollen. This is, of course, a serious handicap to the hybridist since inbreeding hybrids by self-pollination is a useful and effective hybridizing procedure. A much smaller percentage of Rhododendrons is incompatible with others carrying the same gene, but this reluctance of one parent to breed with another in a planned cross can also be an exasperating handicap.

The breeder can try a number of different methods to overcome this incompatibility. Doubling the chromosome number, in itself, often overcomes it, as reported in Petunias and Clover. It can sometimes be circumvented by making the pollination in the bud stage a few days before the flower normally opens. Occasionally fertilization results after the stigma is rubbed abrasively so that its surface is macerated prior to the application of pollen. In other plants success has come from washing the stigma prior to applying the pollen. In the case of Rhododendrons the water used for washing probably should be acidified to a pH of 4·5 or 5·0 since this pollen requires an acid medium to germinate.

I have experimented with cutting off the style near the base, rubbing some of the stigmatic secretion on the cut surface and then applying the pollen over that. Several crosses then produced seeds after having previously failed. Fertilization might very well be accomplished by injecting the pollen directly into the ovary with a hypodermic needle. Specialists in other fields have had success in grafting styles, and in shortening their length by removing a section from the middle, holding the stigmatic portion on the base with a small bit of grass culm. The ingenuity of the breeder will suggest other experiments which may overcome incompatibility.

One of the most valuable and effective of the new techniques for overcoming incompatibility is the application of a plant hormone salve to a wound at the base of the flower, at the time of pollination. The best of these hormones for this purpose seems to be naphthalene acetamide in a 1 per cent preparation made by heating, while stirring, 1 gram of naphthalene acetamide and 3½ ounces of lanolin until the lanolin darkens slightly and the hormone is dissolved.

The salve is then stored in a refrigerator but it should be brought to room temperature before it is used.

The base of the flower is abraded in the region of the ovary with a needle and the salve is then applied on the wound, with results which have been extremely gratifying. Some crosses and self-pollinations which had failed repeatedly succeeded after such treatment but I cannot offer the evidence of control in these experiments since I did not make identical crosses at the same time, on the same plants, without the hormone treatment. None the less, it is my conviction that the hormone application at the time of pollination is an invaluable aid to the Rhododendron breeder.

POLYPLOIDY

Rhododendrons are remarkable for their diversity in almost every conceivable respect and this applies as well to the numbers of chromosomes they contain. Most species have thirteen pairs, (2n=26), but some have many more. As already discussed, the number of chromosomes can have a critical bearing on fertility and on the appearance of superior forms of special value to horticulture. Of the species particularly interesting to breeders, the following have been found to possess unusual chromosome counts as noted. Dr E. K. Janaki Ammal and her associates in England examined these and many others for their chromosome numbers and the results were reported in the 1950 issue of *The Rhododendron Yearbook*, published by the Royal Horticultural Society:

ambiguum	52
augustinii	52
calostrotum (some)	52
chameunum (some)	52
chartophyllum	78
chasmanthum	52
cinnabarinum	78
concatenans	78
concinnum	52
crassum	52 and 78
davidsonianum	78
desquamatum	52
diaprepres 'GARGANTUA'	39
edgarianum	52
fastigiatum (some)	52
flavidum (some)	78
heliolepis	78
intricatum (some)	52
lapponicum (some)	52
maddenii	52 and 78
oreotrephes	78
pemakoense (some)	52
rubiginosum (some)	52 and 78
russatum	52 and 78
saluenense (some)	52
xanthocodon	78
yunnanense	78

The number of chromosomes possessed by plants has a vital bearing on their size, fertility, and the way their traits are transmitted to their offspring. An extra number of chromosomes requires extra large cells to accommodate them and these body cells of more than ordinary dimensions form plants which are larger in all their parts, including their flowers. Rhododendrons which contain extra sets of chromosomes produce a much wider variety of traits in their progeny because of the additional ways the augmented number of chromosomes can combine to cause them.

Perhaps the most important effect, however, is on fertility. When a plant with the usual chromosome count of twenty-six is crossed with another containing extra sets, the fertilized cell may never divide to form a seed because the chromosomes from one parent cannot form pairs with those contributed by the other. Consequently crosses between species with different chromosome counts often fail; or if they succeed the progeny are usually sterile. Sometimes one or two seedlings of normal vigor occur among many more which are so feeble that they soon perish. Sterility could be turned to advantage in breeding Rhododendrons because sterile hybrids need not have the faded flowers removed to prevent seed production. They usually bloom regularly and prolifically.

If crosses fail, however, with a parent which

is a species in the Triflorum, Lapponicum, Heliolepis, Cinnabarinum, Maddenii, Glaucophyllum, Lepidotum, or Saluenense series, the cause could well be extra chromosomes which will not pair with those of the other parent. In any case, the species with the larger chromosome number should always be the pollen parent, if possible. Success may accompany a second breeding attempt with a different form of the species, originating from another geographical region, possibly through another collector. The above listing of species with extra chromosomes is valuable to breeders because it indicates where polyploidy may be encountered. It does not necessarily give the species where it is invariably found. Plants with the usual number of chromosomes and also those with extra sets are often found in the same species.

Undoubtedly there are some scaly-leaved series between which no successful crosses have been made due to polyploidy in one of them. This barrier could probably be broken by doubling with colchicine the usual chromosome number of a sterile *hybrid* between two scaly species, using one of the methods described under the preceding section of this chapter, 'Causes and Cures for Infertility'. With this artificially created tetraploid, containing double the usual complement, a successful cross could probably be accomplished between a Rhododendron which is normally a diploid and some of the scaly-leaved natural tetraploids.

It would probably not succeed to create the artificial tetraploid with colchicine in a plant of a species. The result would probably be sterility due to the competition in pairing of four identical chromosomes. The artificial polyploidy should be induced in a sterile hybrid between two species. Fertility would then result from the restoration of natural pairing between the two similar chromosomes existing one each in the two unmatched sets.

IRRADIATION

Mutations, basic changes in the genes, can sometimes be induced by irradiating seeds with X-rays or by exposing them to atomic radiation. I have had Rhododendron seeds irradiated for me at the Kerckhoff Laboratories of Biology at the California Institute of Technology. The first attempt with X-rays proved to be just about the right amount of treatment as follows:

Average target distance: 7·8 cm.
Total dosage time: 6·71 minutes
Average dosage received: 15,500 r. units
120 killivolts, 8 milliamperes, unfiltered X-rays

This produced somewhat more than 75 per cent mortality of the seeds and delayed germination of the remainder. Experiments with seeds exposed to neutron bombardment are now under way and will probably produce even better results.

When dominant changes are induced they are usually evident only in one sector of the plant raised from irradiated seeds. Concealed, recessive mutations are more likely to occur than those which are immediately evident, and it is necessary to grow the treated seedlings to flowering age and to self-pollinate with pollen *from the same blossom* to obtain an expression in the next generation of the mutation induced by the X-rays or neutrons..

There are already many cells in the irradiated seed and a given alteration in the chromosomes will be induced in only one cell. As this cell proliferates through division all of that portion of the plant derived from it can be expected to carry the mutation of the original cell in the seed. However, other cells in the seed could each carry an entirely different mutation so that the various sectors of the plant which develop from them could each have concealed mutations of widely different character.

After the treated seedlings are well started the terminal buds should be removed to induce lateral branching. All or several of the flowers ultimately produced on these lateral branches should be tested by an application of their own pollen, and there is then a good chance of any recessive mutation being evident in the resulting seedlings.

TRICKS OF THE TRADE

The hybridist's most exasperating adversary is time. In addition to selecting as parents, when possible, Rhododendrons whose progeny bloom young in life, sowing seeds early for maximum progress the first season, and thereafter practicing good cultural methods which accelerate growth and maturity, there are one or two other things which can hasten results.

The most useful is the green grafting on to a mature plant of the stems from new hybrid seedlings as soon as they are large enough to handle. They will then often set flower buds at the end of the second season of growth and the breeder can save a couple of years either in a limited evaluation of the results of the cross or in using the hybrids for further breeding. The procedure is described in the chapter on propagation, beginning on page 344.

This same green-grafting provides fine insurance for a particularly valuable Rhododendron parent which has not been otherwise propagated, and especially for one which is susceptible to bark splitting at the base in wintertime. By green-grafting one or two scions on to another mature Rhododendron the preservation of the valued plant is insured. It has twice happened that I have salvaged hybrids of unique value in this manner, once when the original plant succumbed to damage from a falling tree, and the other time when injury from cold weather killed a valuable specimen.

Other breeders have reported that a rubber grafting strip wrapped around the green stem of a Rhododendron old enough to bloom will restrict the passage of hormones in that branch and induce the formation of a flower bud on it. Although the use of these constricting strips in July has apparently been effective for others, I am obliged to report that they have not been so for me, perhaps due to some fault in the manner of their application. A suggested spray containing sugar, potassium, phosphorus and boron likewise failed to induce bud setting.

The breeder with greenhouse facilities can greatly hasten the progress of his work by accelerating the growing of Rhododendrons under artificial light. Experiments at the Laboratorium voor Tuinbouwplantenteelt, Landbouwhogeschool, Wegeningen, in the Netherlands showed that the dormancy of vegetative buds can be broken readily, without prior cold treatment, by extending the day length. Plants grown from seeds of *R. catawbiense* which were sown in February 1951, were grown in a greenhouse at 77° F. where the natural day was extended to eighteen hours with 60-watt incandescent lamps from September to May. In September 1953, the plants were placed in an unheated greenhouse with natural day length and the following spring they were transferred to the open field. By August 90 per cent of them were well budded, three and a half years from the time the seeds were sown. Under similar conditions Azaleodendrons budded two years and seven months after sowing, despite the loss of one summer's growth when the plants were transferred as an experiment to a shaded outdoor frame in their second year. The results of the Dutch investigators demonstrated that Rhododendron breeding programs can be greatly advanced, and the time between generations shortened, by growing the plants with the day length extended to eighteen hours or more. Constant, twenty-four-hour illumination produced the quickest response and the most vigorous growth of all.

Outdoors, experiments in this country have shown that the growth of Rhododendrons can be approximately trebled by extending the day length to sixteen hours with artificial illumination from May 1st onward to fall frosts. However, plants stimulated to late season growth in this manner fail to harden off properly. There must be some provision to protect them when cold weather arrives.

Most recently, experimental plants illuminated briefly once during each hour of darkness have shown greatly accelerated growth.

METHODS OF ARRANGING CROSSES

The author who describes breeding procedures is faced with an insoluble dilemma. If he simplifies the matter to make it lucid for those without any technical background whatever, his professional colleagues complain that the terminology lacks precision and the generalities are not exhaustively accurate. If, on the other hand, the subject is discussed in the jaw-breaking jargon of genetics it may be technically immaculate but it is quite probably incomprehensible to all but a few readers. As between less than perfect accuracy and obscurity, I choose the former.

Nearly all breeding projects involve the wish to combine in one plant the fine qualities which exist separately in two others. We may want to take scarlet flowers from one species and hardiness from another; or yellow flowers from one source and large flowers from the other parent; or perhaps the goal may be to combine dwarfness and a late season of bloom from one Rhododendron with the serene coolness of white blossoms from another, for the mid-summer garden.

When two such Rhododendrons are crossed the primary hybrid seedlings which result are often of indifferent quality, intermediate between the parents in most respects. They may sometimes be somewhat superior to both parents but they are usually a long way from the ideal result, the combination in one plant of the very best traits of the separate forebears. Frequently this first generation of hybrids between dissimilar parents is nondescript. They are half-hardy or half-yellow or half-dwarf; only semi-late blooming, medium in flower size or pink in color, instead of white or red. More often than not, the breeder casts a jaundiced eye on the mixed rabble and tosses them out. And he could not possibly make a worse mistake! He has but to carry on for one more cross and the prospect is bright for achieving the shining goal which he first envisioned in a speculative moment.

The first generation seedlings from a cross between a tender and a hardy Rhododendron should have winter protection, if necessary, until the best of them can be bred once again. Professional hybridists working with other garden plants often send the first generation hybrids from such crosses into a milder climate so that they can easily be brought to flowering maturity. It matters not at all whether these immediate descendants from a tender and a hardy Rhododendron are in themselves tolerant of cold. The hardiness which is sought will appear in the next generation.

The most important concept to be accepted by the amateur breeder is that the work is often only half done when the first generation seedlings are brought to flower. It makes no difference whatever if the coveted scarlet flowers or dwarf stature or late blooming season are not evident in the immediate offspring. The potentiality for the production of these traits is none the less there, even though it is invisible, and it was incurably optimistic to be confident of reaching the goal in the first generation in any event. The prize usually comes in the next generation.

Most breeders have the general idea that all of the characteristics of their seedlings are controlled by genes in a double set of thread-like chromosomes which are contained in the plant cells. One half of the set comes from the female seed parent, the other half from the male pollen parent at the moment of fusion and fertilization. The genes in the chromosomes could be likened to pearls on a string. In a typical Rhododendron there are thirteen pairs of these chromosomes resembling strung pearls in every cell, *except* the pollen cells and the ovules; there but one of each pair exists because its mate will contribute the other upon fertilization so that the full pairs are once again restored. The multitude of different combinations of the genes in the chromosomes when the pairs are reduced to one in the pollen and in the ovule and then once again combined into pairs in the progeny provides the basis for manipulating the traits of Rhododendrons in breeding. The process is illustrated on the following page.

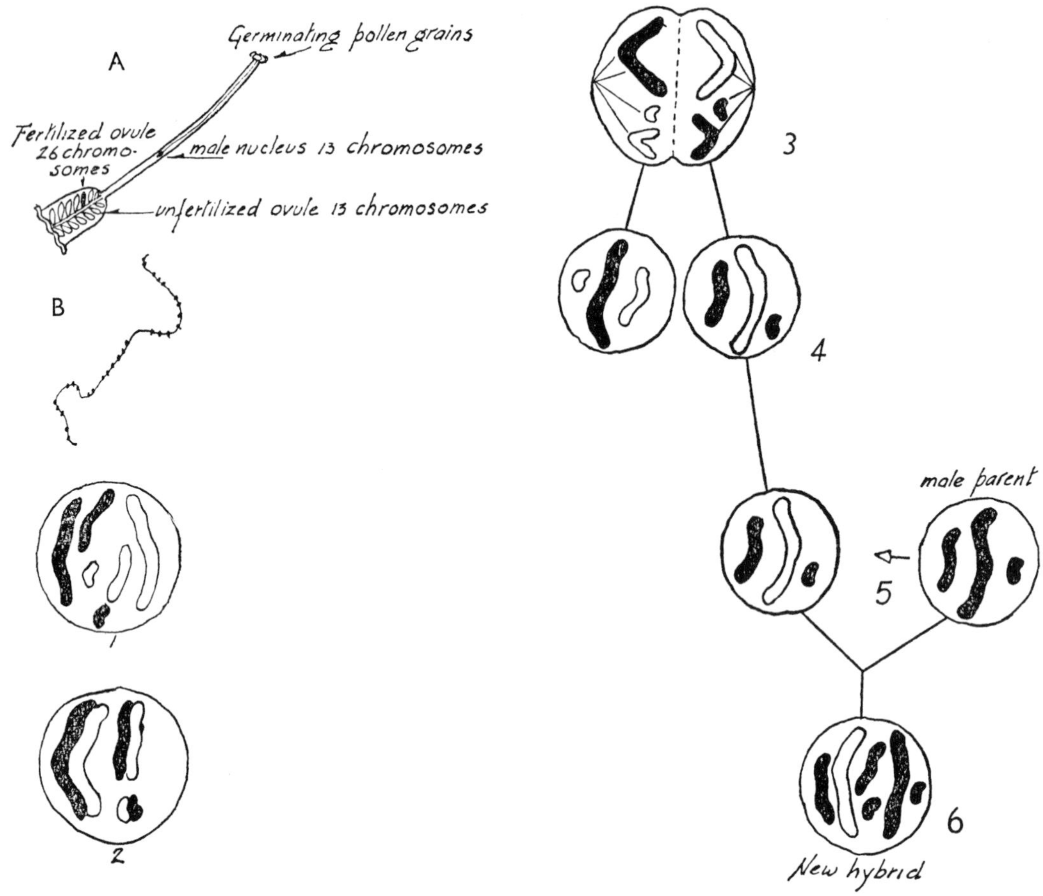

A. Pollen placed on stigma germinates, grows down style and fertilizes ovules. Up to 400 male pollen nuclei are needed to fertilize an equal number of ovules for maximum seed production. Pollen nucleus has 13 single chromosomes, as does ovule. At moment of fertilization full normal complement of 26 in 13 matching pairs is restored.

B. A single chromosome in the cell nucleus looks something like this, may contain up to 1,000 genes, each with an effect on the appearance, hardiness and vigor of the plant.

1. Preceding production of both pollen and ovules, Rhododendron cells usually have 13 pairs of chromosomes but the number in a typical cell nucleus is here reduced to 3 pairs for clarity, to show how they act in inheritance.

2. As the cell prepares to divide chromosomes thicken, contract, form into matched pairs. The black were received from one parent, the white from the other.

3. As the cell divides to form ovules, the chromosomes do not first duplicate themselves and so the daughter cells which are the ovules shown below each have only one chromosome from each pair. There may be an exchange of sections with the other in the pair, thus forming composite chromosomes. This same reduction from pairs to single chromosomes also occurs when male pollen nuclei are formed.

4. The two ovules thus formed from the mother cell above are different in the genes they contain.

5. One ovule, with a single unpaired set of chromosomes, is fertilized by a pollen nucleus, also with a single set.

6. In the resulting hybrid the full chromosome pairs are once again restored. The infinite number of possible chromosome combinations causes the variation seen in hybrid progeny.

It used to be thought that each characteristic of the plants was controlled by only one gene. Now we know that this is only rarely so. Usually many genes exert an influence. In hardiness, for example, some are acting in a plus direction toward greater hardiness whereas others are exerting a negative influence toward tenderness, and the net effect is often the production of intermediate, half-hardy plants in the first generation. In other respects as well innumerable desirable traits appear as only partially evident in the immediate offspring of two dissimilar parents. Color appears to be controlled by five genes plus a diluting gene, superficially quantitative but actually qualitative in expression.

FIRST GENERATION RESULTS

Having recognized that his work is but half finished after bringing to flower the progeny from two dissimilar Rhododendrons, the second important concept for the amateur breeder to accept is the existence, unseen, of desirable traits which are recessive, masked in whole or in part by their undesirable opposites. Thus, in a sense, scarlet may be masked by pink, yellow by pink or white or ivory, hardiness by tenderness or semi-hardiness, large flowers by small or those of intermediate size, and in fact any characteristic which is visible in one parent but not in the progeny can none the less be assumed to exist in the immediate offspring, unseen but ready to be brought to light in the next generation by proper breeding.

THE SECOND GENERATION

The classic method of securing the combination in a single plant of the very best characteristics existing separately in the two original parents is to cross two, or self-pollinate one, of the best of the first generation seedlings of intermediate character and indifferent quality which result from the initial cross. Then in the *next* generation will often be found the ideal result, the achievement of the original goal. Thus the simplest and most direct way to combine the yellow flowers of *R. wardii* with the large, widely open flowers of *R. discolor*, for example, would be to cross them and then mate two, or self-pollinate one, of the best of the progeny. Since the first cross has already been made and the best hybrid given the name 'Inamorata', it remains only for an enterprising breeder to self-pollinate it, assuming of course that it will accept its own pollen and that it is not self-incompatible. Time and again it will be found that the first cross needed for a proposed breeding project has already been made and the breeder need only obtain a plant of this initial hybrid or pollen from it to carry his program the rest of the way.

In Rhododendrons, it is probably safer to cross the two best seedlings in the first generation than to self-pollinate one of them, if there is a choice. There is often a loss of vigor in the progeny produced from self-pollination.

If the original cross to begin a breeding project must be made by the breeder, how many seedlings should be raised to flowering maturity? This depends on the 'purity' of the parents. Should this first mating of two different Rhododendrons which are to combine their best qualities in the progeny of the *second* generation be between species which are constant in their characteristics, their offspring will be much alike and I think five or ten plants would be quite enough. But many Rhododendron species are extremely variable and any single plant of such species is capable of producing a wide range of variation in its offspring. To select the best from such a range to serve as superior parents for the second generation it is necessary to grow a much larger number of seedlings.

Perhaps the best plan is to sow a full quota of seeds. If there is a good deal of variation among the little seedlings a large number of plants should then be grown to flowering maturity.

But it is in the *next* generation, from the

crossing of the two best hybrids, or the self-pollination of one of them—the generation which is to yield in one of the progeny the finest characteristics of the two original grandparents—that the population of plants raised *must* be large. Just how large? It is entirely a practical matter of space and time. Within reasonable limits the larger the better, and the greater the number of seedlings brought to flowering age the closer will probably be the best offspring to the ideal sought by the hybridist. Some breeders arbitrarily grow 100 seedlings to flowering size. Some can grow only fifty. And dumb luck always operates to upset the averages: some grow but ten and find the big prize among them. If a primary hybrid has only four unlike gene pairs controlling the characteristics important to the breeder, which is an impossibly small number, it will produce sixteen different kinds of pollen and sixteen different kinds of ovules. Self-pollinated, there will be 256 different ways in which these genes might recombine. But only one way is ideal. The minimum chance of obtaining this one truly ideal recombination is only one out of 256. This makes clear the importance of growing a relatively large number of progeny derived from the first generation hybrids to get the best possible combination in one plant of the finest traits inherent in their grandparents.

Suppose, however, that the two best plants of the first generation intermediate hybrids are self-incompatible and will not produce seeds from a cross between them or by fertilization with their own pollen? The next alternate, then, would be to choose another hybrid from a different cross as the other parent, entirely unrelated but known to contain a heritage similar to that of the self-incompatible hybrid bred originally from the two species. Continuing the example of the proposed combination of yellow color and large, widely open flowers, if the hybrid *discolor* × *wardii* refused to set seeds to its own pollen or from that taken from other seedlings of the same cross, I would then breed it to a Rhododendron such as *campylocarpum* × *fortunei*, another combination of a yellow-flowered species with one bearing large, widely open blossoms. From the cross, then, of (*discolor* × *wardii*) × (*campylocarpum* × *fortunei*) I would expect to get at least one seedling with large, widely open, truly yellow flowers. This is true even though neither of the parents, both well-known hybrids, is conspicuous for the size or color intensity of its blossoms. The ability to produce large flowers and yellow flowers is none the less inherent in them, unseen, waiting to be properly exploited by the breeder. This, in fact, is the exact method which produced one of the two best yellow-flowered hybrids in existence at the time of writing. It is often an extremely valuable way to secure the recovery in one plant of a wide variety of combinations of traits inherent in the grandparents, and some technically trained breeders working with plants other than Rhododendrons use it routinely even when other methods are open to them.

Backcrossing

In cases where it is desired to add only one or two traits (such as an improved truss, a different stature, an earlier blooming season) to an otherwise desirable Rhododendron, backcrossing is usually the most efficient procedure because it greatly reduces the number of seedlings which must be grown to secure the recovery in one plant of the desired combination of attributes. If we have a plant which is good in most respects but would be a much better and more useful sort with the addition of one or two traits now lacking, the first step, obviously, is to cross it with a Rhododendron which possesses those desirable characteristics. The next step is to backcross the intermediate seedling which best exhibits the desirable qualities to the parent to which we wish to add them. Among the offspring there is a good chance that there will appear an individual similar to the original parent but with the addition of the desirable traits which we wished it also to have.

If the attributes we seek to impart are controlled by five gene pairs, for example, it would be necessary to grow only thirty-two seedlings by the regular operation of the law of probability to secure the improved version of the original parent, whereas it would be necessary to grow 1,024 seedlings, as a theoretical calculation, to obtain the same result by inbreeding one of the intermediate progeny from the first cross.

However, there may still possibly be no escaping the necessity for inbreeding. If the desirable attributes we wish to contribute to our original parent are inherited in a recessive manner so that our ideal plant does not occur in any of the progeny resulting from the back cross of the intermediate seedling to its parent, we are then obliged to inbreed the best of the plants which are grown from this backcross, or to mate two different progeny if one will not bear seeds by its own pollen.

Linkage

The breeder seeking to recombine in one plant desirable traits which exist separately in others is sooner or later faced with a failure due to linkage, in which the genes controlling one characteristic regularly occur only in company with those governing another. Thus these two cannot be readily split apart so that the undesirable is separated from the desirable and only the latter is contributed to its descendants. Fragrance, for example, seems always to be linked to white or pastel shades in the flowers and so far, at least, the hybridist who demands strongly scented blossoms has been obliged to accept them light in color. Such linkages are not at all conspicuous by their number in the inheritance of Rhododendrons, fortunately.

The foregoing, then, are the most useful methods for breeding Rhododendrons according to the principles of genetics. Guided only by this simplified summary, a novice should be able to produce far finer hybrids than any that have yet appeared, so great are the resources for producing to order almost any combination of desired traits. Always, the theoretical possibility of success should be foreseen in the final outcome before any cross is made. The combination which is sought should be clearly within the realm of attainment in the different ways the various characteristics might recombine in the progeny to produce it.

Happy accidents do occur in crossing Rhododendrons. Genes do interact in ways which are unusual but still susceptible to rational explanation. But it takes too long to profit by mistakes and a lifetime is too short to breed Rhododendrons by the trial and error method. The sensible course is not to trust to undeserved luck but to obtain the best possible results with the greatest efficiency through familiarity with the principles of breeding which have been proven scientifically sound. Genetics is a complex science but its basic tenets are not hard to grasp and their application to the inheritance of all living things is universal. None of the amateur British and Dutch Rhododendron breeders to whom we owe nearly all of the hybrids we grow, had any formal conception of the principles of genetics. Their years of effort could have been inconceivably more productive had they taken the modest amount of time necessary to acquaint themselves with the information which would have multiplied their effectiveness a hundredfold. American hybridists who are willing to delve a bit further into genetics than the summary herein provided are urged to make at least a casual study of one of the books designed for amateur breeders. They are written with a minimum of technical jargon. The best that I know is *Plant Breeding*, by A. L. Hagedoorn, published in Great Britain by Crosby Lockwood & Son, Ltd. It can be ordered at any bookstore.

JUDGING THE RESULTS

Every father loves his own babies and breeders have an equally natural inclination to be paternally indulgent in assessing the faults of their hybrid Rhododendron creations. Both amnesia and myopia afflict the hybridist with amusing frequency when he assays the beloved seedlings that he has nursed to flowering maturity with mingled confidence and hope. Too often forgotten are the years when the blossoms were scanty in number or lost to winter cold. The lanky habit of growth or the flawed color are somehow too far out of focus to be distinguished.

Written records are objective, often disconcertingly so, and they are not subject to the gilding of wishful recollection. In my own work and in evaluating the creations of others I have a form of record which has been extremely useful in assessing the quality of Rhododendron hybrids. With the thought that it might prove useful to other breeders I am reproducing it here:

CHECK LIST FOR EVALUATION

Name of Owner..Address..

Location of Plant..Parentage..

Name of Breeder..Owner's Number for Plant..

Owner's Name for Plant..Years in Present Position..

Flower Color..R.H.S. Color #..Number of Lobes..

Blotch Color (if any)..R.H.S. Color #..for blotch.

Number of Flowers in Truss..Diameter of Florets..(spread)

Fragrant? ( )Yes ( )Slightly ( )No

Shape of Truss ( )Conical ( )Pyramidal ( )Globular ( )Flat ( )Lax, Bald

Substance of Flowers ( )Excellent ( )Good ( )Fair ( )Poor

Blooms: ( )Early ( )Early Midseason ( )Midseason ( )Late ( )Very Late

Remarks..

Owner's Estimate of Hardiness: ( )Very Hardy ( )Fairly Hardy ( )Blooms only after Mild Winters

Percent of Terminals with Flowers this Year..%..

Owner's Estimate of Floriferous Character: ( )Excellent ( )Fair
( )Good ( )Poor

Plant Outline: ( )Usual ( )Upright ( )Spreading

Present Age of Plant..Years Height.. Breadth..

New Growth tend to Conceal Flowers? ( )No ( )Yes

Foliage Color: ( )Excellent ( )Good ( )Fair ( )Poor, yellowish

Quantity of Foliage: ( )Excellent ( )Good ( )Fair ( )Poor, sparse

Habit of Growth: ( )Excellent ( )Good ( )Fair ( )Poor

Remarks..

RATING

(0 to 4 stars) Name of Evaluator..

Date..

The foregoing form has been useful for evaluating Rhododendrons of my own or other breeding which have reached flowering age and show at least some promise. The following card form has also been equally useful for recording crosses and maintaining a record of the resulting seedlings up to the time that any selections are made for naming and introduction. These cards are kept alphabetically in an indexed filing case so that comments on the hardiness, vigor, growth habit and other characteristics of each seedling lot, or individual numbered plants within the lot, can be conveniently entered on them from time to time. The reverse is printed with a somewhat different form and that side is used when the record applies to Rhododendrons acquired from other sources.

CROSS ....

.... YEAR .... POLLEN SOURCE ....

SEED PARENT CLONE-NAME ....

POLLEN PARENT CLONE-NAME ....

FIRST RESULT OF CROSS ....

SEEDLINGS IN FLATS .... IN FRAMES .... TO FIELD .... YEAR ....

....

IN FIELD AFTER 2 YEARS ....

....

EVALUATION ....

....

....

....

....

....

....

....

LOCATION ....

LOCATION ....

It may be both interesting and disconcerting for the breeder to place his own selections of good sorts where they can be seen by visitors and to keep a mental summary of their comments. Thus the future demand for his various creations can be gauged in advance of their release for sale. The connoisseur with his expert knowledge and the average gardener may be far apart in their judgments. In such cases the hybridist may be right but the public determines the issue by this forecast of the Rhododendrons it will later buy.

Any new Rhododendron hybrid developed in the United States should be registered with the American Rhododendron Society. British originations should be registered with the Royal Horticulture Society. This prevents duplication of names and subsequent confusion in the nursery industry, and provides a public record of parentage and of the hybridist who bred it. The American Rhododendron Society provides registration forms upon request to 3514 North Russet Street, Portland, Oregon.

The rewards of breeding good new Rhododendron hybrids are more spiritual than financial and it is folly to try to disseminate a clone with serious faults, or one which is not clearly superior to others already in commerce. Even the best make their way in the nursery industry with great difficulty against the inertia of professional growers and the established demand from gardeners for the tried and familiar. Breeders often do not stop to consider that the most popular nursery hybrids in mid-century are those such as 'Pink Pearl' which were introduced just as the new century began. The ironclad Waterer hybrids, so widely grown in the Northeast, were introduced in the 1860's. No hybridist who appreciates the long road ahead for his creations will want to be known by any but the very best.

By the time a seedling reaches flowering age its hardiness and habit of growth will long since have been judged with reasonable accuracy. Plants should be well clothed with foliage and much branched so that their growth habit is compact and symmetrical. Many breeders are much too indulgent on these points. Rhododendrons should be handsome garden ornaments fifty-two weeks of the year and not just for their springtime span of bloom. As evergreens, their contribution to the garden ought certainly to extend the year around but some sorts, spectacular in flower, are lean and lanky liabilities at all other seasons. The Rhododendron with a serious fault of foliage or habit must be superlatively fine in other respects to justify its introduction. And then the hybridist should still think twice before releasing it.

Ideally, flower color should be clean and pure without any admixture of purple, grey or brown. The luminosity which is so appealing in some Rhododendron flowers comes from the shifting shades which appear under the play of translucent light through the corolla. It is lost if the colors are muddy, or flawed by unwanted blue, or if the blossom tissues are opaque. Should there be a blotch or flare in the flowers, or a two-tone effect from different colors, the contrast should be emphatic.

Long, tubular flowers and those wide and flatly open both have their place in the garden. Some blossoms have crisp, sharply defined margins, others may be gracefully undulating, and still others are ruffled with an effect which is often exquisitely beautiful. Bell- and funnel-shaped blossoms which do not expand fully to their natural conformation must be faulted, presenting as they do an impression of grudgingly yielding only a stingy glimpse of their interior beauty. This failure of the flowers to open completely for a generous view of their interior may be due to a truss overcrowded with florets so that there is not room for them to expand normally.

The public loves large flowers, but Rhododendron breeders have the means for making them grotesquely large, out of all proportion to the dimensions of the leaves, branches, and stature of the plants which bear them. The marvelous power of creation which is wielded by the breeder imposes a standard of taste and judgment which ought not to be compromised by vulgarity or degraded by misguided clamor for the banal and obvious. The size of the flowers should always be in proper proportion to the other parts of the plant.

Flower texture is important, of course, as it determines how long the blossoms will remain in good condition. The crisp, heavy, waxen substance of some of the early blooming sorts, especially those with red flowers, is unhappily lacking in many of those which come into bloom later in the season. Their flaccid texture is responsible for premature browning and limp appearance, especially in warm weather, and for trusses in which the flowers at the bottom start to wilt before the topmost are fully open.

There is no rule of beauty which requires a Rhododendron truss to be a tall, cone-shaped formation filled with firmly-held flowers which give it a symmetrically perfect outline. This was Anthony Waterer's ideal and it is rather widely accepted, but only from familiarity and not by any principle of aesthetics. Surely there is room too for arrangements less stiff and formal, for the debonair lilt which makes so beguiling some of the dwarf Asian sorts with their blossoms in few-flowered clusters. The massed bells in their great round clusters on the primitive large-leaved species are enormously effective. Breeders are inclined to be provincial about the arrangement of flowers in the truss. Each type should instead be judged on its own merits, whether it is well proportioned and interesting; whether the individual flowers are displayed to good advantage; and whether the overall effect is pleasing and ornamental. These desirable characteristics are not associated exclusively with the mounded, compact trusses completely filled with flowers.

There are many other features of a Rhododendron which are valuable: ability to withstand exposure; regular and abundant production of flowers, year after year; sterility, to eliminate the chore of removing faded flowers to prevent seed formation, and a long, long, list of secondary traits which would necessarily be included in a list of specifications for the ideal garden hybrid. Ease of propagation, for example, often determines the success or failure of a plant in the nursery industry, as does its vigor and how quickly it can be grown into a salable specimen. But the novice hybridist soon acquires his own conception of the ideal Rhododendron and that is as it should be. The different tastes and standards produce the interesting variety of Rhododendron hybrids we now have, and which we will unquestionably have in ever greater profusion in the future.

SUGGESTED PLAUSIBLE DOMINANCE FOR ELEPIDOTE RHODODENDRON FLOWER COLOR INHERITANCE

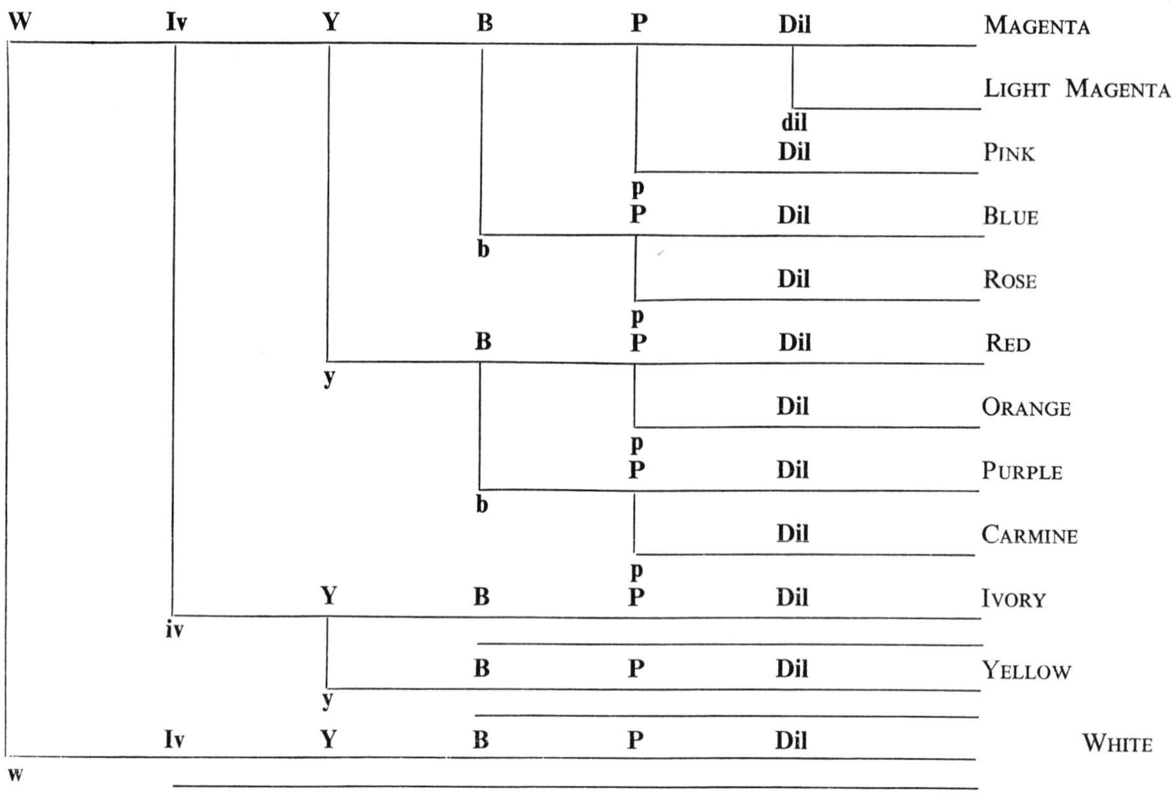

WW or **Ww**=color; ww=white

IvIv or **Iviv**=non-ivory; **iviv**=ivory

YY or **Yy**=non-yellow; **yy**=yellow or yellow co-pigmentation

BB or **Bb**=purple, magenta or violet; **bb**=blue

PP or **Pp**=purple, magenta or violet; **pp**=pink to red

DilDil or **Dildil**=intense colors; **dildil**=light colors

To find the gene status determining any given flower color, start at that color in the last column and follow the line leftward and upward until all six genes are represented. For each color the direction of the lines indicates the status of the various genes which determine it. A *horizontal* line represents dominance; a *vertical* line represents recessiveness. The action of the diluting gene is graphed only in the topmost example. For each subsequent color, dildil also acts as a diluter. Epistasis is shown by a parallel line $\frac{1}{8}''$ immediately below the main indicator line, running from the epistatic gene through the hypostatic genes to the right.

The author presents this first explanation of Rhododendron flower color inheritance as a deduction from observations for almost twenty years of the results of many hundreds of crosses, which were not made, however, specifically to prove the action of the flower color genes. The modes of inheritance shown above are proposed as a preliminary, tentative contribution toward understanding the determination of flower color in Rhododendrons.

The explanation is now apparent for yellow, red and pink flowered progeny all resulting from crosses of red with white-flowered parents. Now it can be understood how the pale yellow 'Butterfly' came from the crossing of the crimson 'Mrs. Milner' with *campylocarpum*.

This chart provides a sort of hybridizing road map which the author hopes will be useful for all Rhododendron breeders.

APPENDIX A

Complete Descriptive List of Rhododendron Hybrids

The descriptive listing of hybrids which follows is intended to be as complete as exhaustive research can make it. The aim has been to identify every hybrid which might now be in cultivation or which has been used by Rhododendron hybridists in their efforts to create better garden plants. The parents of many well-known hybrids, which were not revealed at the time the Rhododendrons were introduced, have been generously supplied by the nurseries which originated them. Color descriptions for hundreds of the British amateurs' creations, now so popular in the Pacific Northwest, have been given me by the estates of the originators.

GROUP NAMES
The letter "g." in the following listing refers to a grex, or group of hybrids of similar parentage. These collective names, used by British amateur breeders, have caused endless confusion, at least in America, because all of the progeny from a specific cross, regardless of their quality, have been identified by the same group name. In the case of a primary cross between two species the offspring from repetitions of similar crosses made many years later, even using inferior forms of these species as parents, have taken the same name assigned to the original hybrid group. This custom has not been followed in the United States and professional nurserymen abroad have generally shunned it.

Group names have recently been relegated to a position where they are merely a subsidiary convenience for identifying parentage – for those with a retentive memory. But the confusion is bound to persist because "Naomi", for example, may be either a group name applying to all of the Rhododendron hybrids obtained from 'Aurora' crossed with fortunei, or it may be a clone name, identifying a single superior selection which received an Award of Merit from the Royal Horticultural Society when it was shown in 1933 (in which case it ought always to be so designated, " 'Naomi', A.M. "). Other superior selections from the Naomi hybrid group are, fortunately, identified by the addition of a clone name so that the reader will find listed 'Naomi Nautilus', for example, and 'Naomi Stella Polaris'.

Since some careless or unscrupulous nurserymen have taken advantage of the confusion caused by group names, it must be stressed that the group name alone may be no indication of superiority and many a worthless seedling has been sold because it carried a distinguished group name. Thus it means nothing to buy a Rhododendron labeled "Loderi" but it means a great deal to own a 'Loderi King George'. The prospective purchaser should look for the addition of the clone name to the group name if he wishes to buy a Rhododendron hybrid propagated from the single plant selected by the introducer for its superior quality and conforming to the description in this listing. The Rules of Nomenclature now provide that single quotation marks enclosing a name indicate that it is a clone, not a group name.

When the nomenclature was recently revised in Great Britain some compromises had to be made in translating the old system of naming to the new. Thus the hybrid formerly known as "Fabia var. Roman Pottery" will now be found listed as 'Roman Pottery' whereas "Fabia var. Tangerine" is now correctly called 'Fabia Tangerine' and is so listed; "Hawk var. Exbury" is now 'Exbury Hawk' and "Hawk var. Crest" is presently listed 'Crest'. If a clone name was formerly associated with a group name as a "variety", cross references opposite the group name in the listing will lead the reader to its correct current designation in the event that it is no longer associated with its former group name.

Fortunately, only a minor proportion of the Rhododendrons in commerce have ever been linked with group names. 'Pink Pearl' identifies a single superior clone the world around. All clones in the following listing are specifically so designated by "cl.".

AWARDS
The American Rhododendron Society and the Royal Horticultural Society of England both have systems of honoring hybrids of outstanding quality and their awards, with the years in which they were bestowed, are given following the color descriptions. The American honors are:

P.A. — Preliminary Award, given for a cut flower truss, with foliage, exhibited at a show. This award is designed to give an early indication of the value of the hybrid and to encourage its originator to present the plant later for higher awards.

A.E. — Award of Excellence, given for a complete plant evaluated by three official judges on the basis of flowers, foliage and growth habit.

T.G.C. — Test Garden Certificate, bestowed upon a hybrid which has been seen in flower by three judges for at least two years while growing in one of the public test gardens officially designated by the American Rhododendron Society. A hybrid competing for this award may also qualify for consideration if it is grown in three private gardens at least a mile apart and there viewed in flower by the judges for two years.

The British awards given by The Royal Horticultural Society are:

A.M. — Award of Merit, granted for a cut flower truss, with foliage, exhibited at a show.

F.C.C. — First Class Certificate, a higher honor, given under the same circumstances.

A.G.M. — Award of Garden Merit, given to a hybrid which has been carefully evaluated for its quality under a wide variety of garden growing conditions over a period of many years.

S.C.C. — Second Class Certificate, in use only from 1858 to 1888.

The American awards are relatively new and their practical value to the uninitiated public largely remains to be demonstrated. It is not easy to define, exactly, the usefulness of the British awards, which have been granted for just about a hundred years. Ideas of quality have changed in the course of a century and the same hybrid which was thought to be the peak of perfection fifty years ago might be judged a gross and blatant vulgarity by some connoisseurs today. On the other hand the Loderi group of hybrids, for example, bred in 1907, have never been equalled in their class and so many unsuccessful efforts have been made to improve them that it seems unlikely that they will be replaced for another half-century. Perhaps it would be most useful to note that the year in which the awards were given has been stated in the description and those which are most recent can be considered the more meaningful as an indication of quality.

But the novice will be ill-advised to buy Rhododendrons on the basis of the British awards alone. The dwarf hybrid, 'Blue Tit', is universally regarded as among the finest of the modern hybrids with violet-blue flowers, yet it has not received a single award. And no Rhododendron is more decorated than 'Sir John Ramsden'. It received an Award of Merit in 1926, another Award of Merit in 1948 and a First Class Certificate in 1955, yet it bore a quality rating (explained below) of only one star until 1952, then two stars until 1956, when it caught up with its awards. 'Raoul Millais', which received an Award of Merit as recently as 1935, earns no quality commendation whatever in its rating today. American observers, puzzled by the mediocre performance in the United States of some hybrids bearing British honors, have concluded that the awards were not justified in some cases, or that differences between the two climates were responsible for the apparent discrepancy in quality.

QUALITY RATINGS

The American Rhododendron Society assigns quality ratings of x to xxxx in order of increasing ornamental value to Rhododendrons distributed widely enough to be rated by a sufficient number of growers in their surveys. If a hybrid merits no quality commendation whatever it is assigned a rating of "o". The omission of a rating means only that the unrated hybrid has not been grown by enough specialists to form an accurate composite judgment of its quality.

Since different clones with the same group names were imported from Great Britain to the United States and were often not further identified, the American Rhododendron Society has been obliged to assign some of its ratings to hybrid groups rather than to clones and it specifies that such ratings apply only "to the best selections of the group. In such cases it is prudent to consider the rating applicable to clones in the group which have been given awards or have been otherwise distinguished by the addition of identifying clone names. Specialist-nurserymen have re-imported by their distinguishing clone names the best out of most of the prominent hybrid groups and so list them in their catalogs.

Under the British system, the hybrid listed without any quality rating may be either unworthy of even the lowest merit status or it may mean only that it is too new or of insufficient interest to be evaluated by the committee which determines such matters. The British quality ratings are * to **** in order of increasing ornamental value.

HARDINESS RATINGS

The American and British hardiness ratings are given below in all cases where either have been assigned. The American ratings refer only to resistance to cold, but a note is required here that some hybrids which are hardy to Philadelphia and northward cannot endure the heat and atmospheric aridity of eastern summers. It should also be noted that hardiness for a rare, brief period of lower temperatures in the Pacific Northwest does not at all indicate equal cold resistance at the same temperatures under eastern conditions. The British ratings are modified by a statement that a specified amount of shelter is needed to warrant the grade given for the more tender hybrids. The two rating systems compare approximately as follows:

American Ratings	Application	British Ratings
H-1	Hardy to 25° below zero F. "These should be hardy in southern New York and southern New England." (Author's note: some hybrids with this rating are somewhat more tolerant of cold than this statement indicates.)	
H-2	Hardy to -15° F.	A
H-3	Hardy to -5° F. "These should be fairly hardy in southern Long Island and around Philadelphia."	B
H-4	Hardy to +5° F.	C
H-5	Hardy to +15° F. "These should be hardy during most winters in the Portland and Seattle areas."	D
H-6	Hardy to +25° F. "Hardy close to the coast in the Pacific Northwest and in sheltered areas elsewhere in western Washington and Oregon."	E
H-7	Hardy to +32° F.	F

The American hardiness ratings are too new to be completely accurate, having been revised but once since they were assigned following the initial survey of growers. In any case, local conditions vary so much that these ratings will never be a subject of complete agreement. 'Everestianum', for example, which is universally regarded in the East as being in a group representing the highest standard of ironclad hardiness, bears a rating of H-2. By and large, however, the American ratings have proved to be a reliable guide to hardiness. Not so the British ratings for the climatic conditions of the United States. They have been useful as general indicators but there are too many conspicuous exceptions among hybrids which have been either a good deal more tender or a good deal hardier in this country than their British ratings indicate, and the range of hardiness in American gardens among the many which are rated "A" seems to be disconcertingly wide.

COLOR DESCRIPTIONS

Wherever possible, the color descriptions of the hybrids in the following listing are those of the breeders who created them. Hundreds more have been furnished by the management of gardens, now public trusts, where they originated in Great Britain, and I have described many from personal inspection both here and abroad. The abbreviation H.C.C. refers to the Horticultural Color Chart published by the Royal Horticultural Society. N.C.F. is the abbreviation for the Nickerson Color Fan, published by the American Horticultural Society. R.C.S. identifies the Robert Ridgway Color Standard.

PARENTAGE

The parentage given for every hybrid is that which has somehow been made a matter of credible record by its originator. Private nursery records of crosses which have been made available for publication for the first time in the United States are here reproduced and ancient catalogs and periodicals have been searched in the interest of accuracy. Correspondence with breeders throughout the world has corrected or confirmed published parentages which seemed dubious. Despite all such precautions, there are undoubtedly some errors, particularly in the derivation of the older hybrids which were bred before 1900. Sometimes well-meaning breeders have been unaware that they have been deceived by a strange phenomenon called induced apogamy whereby seeds are produced but no true cross has taken place. In a few such cases I have placed a question mark following the parentage in the belief that the antecedents given are possibly not correct, but this may well be an arbitrary assumption because it is quite possible for the influence of one of the parents of a hybrid to be masked almost completely by the domination of the other.

In cases where only a single species or a hybrid is mentioned in the parentage the complete pedigree is unknown but the influence of the forebear named is evident in that hybrid, even though it may not be immediately descended from it. For example, a Rhododendron listed as "catawbiense x" is thereby designated a catawbiense hybrid because it bears the usual characteristics of Rhododendrons in this general classification, but it may be more than one generation removed from the species R. catawbiense.

Any name which is enclosed in single quotation marks is that of a hybrid clone. Group names are not so marked and are followed by the letter "g". Any name which is printed in italics or underlined is that of a species.

ORIGINATORS
The name of the breeder and, unless otherwise stated, the year in which the hybrid was first named or exhibited at a show, are given following the parentage. In a few cases it is not known whether the exhibitor was actually the hybridist. Where the hybrid was bred by one person and grown, named or introduced by another, the hybridist's name appears first, followed by a hyphen and the name of the exhibitor.

Rhododendron Hybrids

In every case where a full parentage formula is given, the first named is the FEMALE parent

		Abalone		g.	campylocarpum x callimorphum; (Rothschild 1933); cream to pink
		Abbeyi			(G. Abbey); delicate pink veined and suffused rose on exterior; A. M. 1900.
		Abbot		g.	thomsonii x delavayi; (Rothschild 1933); deep red.
xxx	H-3	A. Bedford / Arthur Bedford	*** A	cl.	mauve seedling x ponticum; (Lowinsky); pale mauve in tube, darker on lobes with dark rose madder to nearly black markings within; A.M. (R.H.S.) 1936, F.C.C., 1958.
		Abessa		g.	'Laura Aberconway' x 'Elizabeth'; (Aberconway 1946); scarlet.
		A. B. Mitford	A	cl.	(A. Waterer before 1915); crimson.
		Abraham Dixon		cl.	(A. Waterer before 1915); mauve, yellow eye.
		Abraham Lincoln		cl.	catawbiense x; (Parsons before 1875); red.
		Acidalia			'Amabile'x teysmanni; (Veitch 1891); very pale primrose.
		Acis		cl.	'Duchess of Edinburgh' x 'Princess Alexandra'; (Veitch 1891); salmon.
		A. C. Kendrick		cl.	(M. Koster & Sons); lilac rose with red purple blotch.
		Aclandianum			(A. Waterer before 1865); pink madder, scarlet or chocolate spots.
		Acutilibrum			A. Verschaffelt before 1857.
		Adalbert			Seidel 1897-1908.
		Adder		g.	thomsonii x diphrocalyx; (Rothschild 1933); deep rose.
		Adelaide		g.	'Aurora' x thomsonii; (Rothschild 1930).
		Adelaide		cl.	'Aurora' x thomsonii; (Rothschild 1930); scarlet and faintly primrose with 5 dark nectar pouches at base and lightly spotted on back of tube within; A.M.(R.H.S.) 1935.
		Adele			(Standish & Noble before 1860); deep plum color.
		Adjutant		g.	neriiflorum x sperabile; (Rothschild 1933); red to scarlet.
		Adlo		g.	'Adonis' x Loderi g.; (Aberconway 1950); pale pink.
		Admiral Piet Hein		cl.	'Mrs. Butler' x 'White Pearl'; (C. B. van Nes & Sons); light rose lilac; sweet scented; A.M. (Wisley Trials) 1957.
		Adonis		cl.	(Noble before 1850); rose, spotted.
		Adota		g.	'Adonis' x 'Coreta'; (Aberconway 1946); red.
		Adrastia		g.	williamsianum x neriiflorum; (Aberconway 1941); deep pink.
		Adrean		g.	'Adrastia' x beanianum; (Aberconway 1946); red.
		Adrian			A. Waterer before 1875.
x	H-3	Adriaan Koster	*** B	cl.	a campylocarpum hybrid x 'Mrs. Lindsay Smith'; (M. Koster & Sons 1920); creamy white, small red spot in throat.
		Advie		g.	'Cornubia' x diphrocalyx; (Rothschild 1933); deep rose.
		Affectation		cl.	ambiguum x cinnabarinum var. blandfordiaeflorum; (Sunningdale Nurseries cross 1942; flrd. 1951); pale yellow, rose at tips.
		Afghan	* B		deep blood red.
		Afghan Chief			(Davies before 1890).
		Afterglow	B	cl.	discolor x hardy hybrid; (W.C.Slocock); selected 1935; pale pink and mauve.
		Agamemnon		g.	(A.Waterer before 1875); rose crimson.
		A.Gilbert		cl.	campylocarpum x discolor; (Lowinsky); pale creamy buff, saffron rose pink; A.M. (R.H.S.) 1925.
		Aglare		cl.	'Arthur Osborn' x 'Rapture'; (Harrison 1955); deep red.
		Agleam		cl.	'Arthur Osborn' x 'Isabella'; (Harrison 1954); bright red.
		Aglow		cl.	discolor x 'Arthur Osborn'; (Harrison 1954); pink, darker center.
		Agnes		cl.	griersonianum x 'Norman Gill'; (Swaythling); bud deep pink (neyron rose H.C.C. 623), becomes paler till fully expanded; flower has deep pink color only on edges and base of tube; A.M.(R.H.S.) 1943.
		Agnes Beaufort		g.	griffithianum x ; ? (Methven of Edinburgh); ? (Mangles, Haslemere).

		Agnes Lamont			g.	'Loder's White' x thomsonii; (R.B.G., Edinburgh); various shades of pink.
		Agnes Mangles			cl.	griffithianum x ; (Mangles).
		Agricola			g.	T. Methven & Son, Edinburgh; crimson lake.
		A. G. Soames				(Van Nes before 1922); crimson red with pink interior, heavily spotted burnt umber, cream style and anthers.
		Aida			g.	'George Hardy' x auriculatum; (Rothschild 1933); white with dark markings.
		Aileen Henderson		B	cl.	griffithianum x ; (M.Koster & Sons); yellow to creamy white with brown yellow blotch.
		Ailsa Jean			g.	tephropeplum x moupinense; (Adams Acton).
		Ailsa Jean			cl.	tephropeplum x moupinense; (Adams Acton 1942); pale pink; A.M. (R.H.S.) 1946.
		Ajax		B	cl.	(G.Waterer before 1860); bright rose; A.M. 1890.
		Ajax			cl.	'Crown Princess of Germany' x javanicum; (J. Veitch); yellow to red orange; A.M. 1890.
		Akbar			g.	'Loderi King George' x discolor; (Rothschild).
		Akbar			cl.	'Loderi King George' x discolor (Rothschild 1933); rose madder (H.C.C. 23/2) with a small blotch of streaked crimson staining the throat; A.M. (R.H.S.) 1952.
xx	H-3	Aladdin			g.	griersonianum x auriculatum; (Crosfield).
		Aladdin			cl.	griersonianum x auriculatum; (Crosfield 1930); bright vermilion but with more orange hue outside, paling to a bright but soft rose pink over neck of corolla; A.M. (R.H.S.) 1935.
		Alan			g.	'Ethel' x 'F.C.Puddle'; (Aberconway 1946); blood red.
		Alane				(before 1871).
		Alaric			g.	(Methven, Edinburgh before 1871); rosy purple.
		Alarm		B	g.	(A.Waterer & Godfrey before 1867); deep crimson, white center.
		Alatum				cultivated by Noble before 1850; bright rosy lake.
		Alba Superba				Syn. of 'Blanche Superbe'.
xxx	H-3	Albatross			g.	Loderi g. x discolor; (Rothschild 1930).
		Albatross	***	B	cl.	Loderi g. x discolor; (Rothschild 1930); deep pink in bud, opening slightly bluish pink, scented; flowers white with reverse of petals slightly tinged pink. A.M. (R.H.S.) 1934; A.M.(Wisley Trials) 1953. See 'Exbury Albatross', 'Townhill Albatross'.
		Albert			cl.	'Viola' x 'Everestianum'; (Seidel in 1899); delicate lilac.
		Albert Close			cl.	maximum x macrophyllum (Fraser-Gable); rose-pink, throat spotted chocolate-red.
		Alberti				falconeri x ponticum?; bell-shaped corolla, purple magenta. Syn. 'Albertus'.
		Albertus				falconeri x ponticum? Syn. of 'Alberti'.
		Albertus Grandiflora			cl.	(T. Methven & Son, Edinburgh 1868); pink, dark spots.
		Albescens			cl.	white, large, scented, marked at base sulphur yellow.
		Albino			g.	campylocarpum x 'Loder's White'; (Stephenson Clarke); exhibited Whitaker 1935. See 'Serin'.
		Albion			cl.	(T. Methven & Son, Edinburgh 1868); rosy red, spotted; a plant under this name with red flowers recently offered by Van Veen Nursery, U. S. A.
		Albrecht Dürer			cl.	(M. Koster & Sons); bright red, fimbriated.
x	H-1	Album Elegans		A	cl.	catawbiense x ; (H.Waterer before 1876); pale mauve fading to white.
		Album Flavum				blush white, orange yellow spots.
x	H-2	Album Grandiflorum			cl.	catawbiense x ; (J.Waterer before 1851); very pale mauve fading white.
		Album Novum			cl.	catawbiense x ; (L. van Houtte); white, tinged rose lilac, greenish-yellow spots.
		Album Speciosum				(A. Verschaffelt before 1854).
		Album Triumphans			cl.	(J.Waterer before 1871); white.
		Alburtus				(Noble before 1850); white to pink, spotted.
		Alcesta			g.	lutescens x burmanicum; (Aberconway).
		Alcesta			cl.	lutescens x burmanicum; (Aberconway 1933); pale creamy yellow with darker yellow blotch at back of tube within; A.M. (R.H.S.) 1935.
		Alcibiades			g.	'Hiraethlyn' x 'F.C.Puddle'; (Aberconway 1941); turkey red.
		Alesia			g.	'Portia' x meddianum; (Aberconway 1941); crimson scarlet.
		Alexander Adie			cl.	(J.Waterer before 1871); dark pink. Syn. 'Joy Gould'.
		Alexander Dancer			cl.	catawbiense x ; (A.Waterer before 1865); reddish magenta, lighter center.
		Alexandrina			cl.	cultivated by Standish & Noble before 1860; pure white.
		Alexina			cl.	cultivated by Noble before 1850; rosy lilac, black spots.
		Alfred			cl.	'Everestianum' x 'Everestianum'; (Seidel cross in 1899); lilac.
		Algerienne			cl.	'Margaret Dunn' x 'May Day'; (Sunningdale Nursery, registered 1955); ivory flushed pale rose at tips, slight olive stain in throat.
xx	H-3	Alice	**	B	cl.	griffithianum x ; (J.Waterer); deep pink fading to pale rose; A.M. (R.H.S.) 1910.
		Alice Franklin			cl.	'Ole Olson' x 'Loderi King George'; (Lem-H. L. Larson, 1959); Naples yellow (H.C.C. 403/3), throat uranium green (H.C.C. 63/3); P.A., (A.R.S.) 1959.
		Alice Heye			cl.	(C.Frets & Sons, Boskoop); lilac red, large blackish blotch.
		Alice Mangles			cl.	griffithianum x ponticum; (Mangles); F.C.C. 1882.
		Alice Martineau	*	B	cl.	discolor x ; (W.C.Slocock); rosy crimson, dark blotch and throat; very late.
		Alice Street	*	C	cl.	'Diane' x wardii; (M. Koster & Son 1953); light yellow. Syn. 'Miss Street'.
		Alison Johnstone			g.	yunnanense x concatenans; (G.H.Johnstone).

Alison Johnstone cl. yunnanense x concatenans; (G.H.Johnstone); amber flushed with pink, no markings; A.M. (R.H.S.) 1945.

Alix g. barbatum x hookeri; (Rothschild 1930).

Alix cl. barbatum x hookeri; (Rothschild 1930); brilliant clear crimson; A.M. (R.H.S.) 1935.

Allah cl. catawbiense x ; (Seidel in 1926); light lilac rose, tinged lighter; late.

Allegro cl. 'Azor' x 'Loderi King George'; (Lancaster); yellow, flushed pink.

Alley Cat cl. (Ostbo); coral pink, darker blotch; P. A., (A.R.S.) 1960.

Allure cl. 'Fabia' x 'Dante'; (Aberconway 1942); scarlet.

Alma cl. lilac center, crimson edges.

Almond Thacker g. 'Rosy Bell' x racemosum; (Thacker 1946); deep almond pink.

Almondtime g. 'Cornubia' x sutchuenense; bright cerise pink, few dark crimson dots; A.M. (R.H.S.) 1925. See 'Cornsutch'.

Alonzo cultivated by Standish & Noble before 1860; purple lake.

Alpaca g. 'Sir Charles Lemon' x neriiflorum; (Rothschild 1933); pink; now discontinued.

Alpine Gem g. brachyanthum x ferrugineum; (Thacker 1942); yellow, shaded pink.

Alpine Glow cl. Loderi g. x calophytum (Avalanche g.); (Rothschild); delicate pale pink; A.M. (R.H.S.) 1938. Previously listed as Avalanche var. Alpine Glow.

Alpine Rose cl. Loderi g. x calophytum (Avalanche g.); delicate pink; previously known as Avalanche var. Alpine Rose.

Alre g. 'Alan' x forrestii var. repens; (Aberconway 1946); blood red.

Alstroemerioides cultivated Standish & Noble before 1860; rose, spotted on all petals.

Altaclarense (catawbiense x ponticum) x arboreum; (Gowen 1831); red or deep crimson; F.C.C. 1865.

Alvinda g. 'Ivery's Scarlet' x Loderi g.; (Aberconway 1933); pale rose pink.

Amabile g. javanicum x 'Princess Alexandra'; pinky yellow to salmon; F.C.C. 1886.

Amalfi g. 'Cornubia' x calophytum; (Rothschild).

Amalfi cl. 'Cornubia' x calophytum; (Rothschild); carmine rose (R.C.C. 621) towards the tips of corolla lobes shaded to white on tube, which is spotted dark red with a crimson splash at base within; A.M. (R.H.S.) 1939.

Amaranthora cl. catawbiense x; (Parsons).

Amaryllis g. 'Halopeanum' x haematodes; (Wallace 1934).

Amasun g. 'Amaura' x 'Sunrise'; (Aberconway 1946). pale rose.

Amata g. 'Adrastia' x 'F. C. Puddle'; (Aberconway 1941); red.

Amaura g. 'Penjerrick' x griersonianum; (Aberconway 1933); pale pink.

Amazon cl. (T.Methven & Son, Edinburgh before 1887); pink.

Amazor g. 'Amaura' x 'Azor'; (Aberconway 1946; pink.

Amba g. racemosum white form x burmanicum; (Aberconway 1934); pale yellow.

Ambient g. javanicum x 'Princess Alexandra'; cultivated Veitch 1891; pinkish yellow to salmon.

Ambrose g. 'Queen Wilhelmina' x chaetomallum; (Rothschild 1933); rose pink.

x H-1 America cl. 'Parsons Grandiflorum' x dark red hybrid; (M.Koster & Sons about 1920); dark red.

Americana cl. 'Britannia' graft sport; (Lancaster); crimson red.

Amethyst cl. Dexter fortunei ? hybrid; (Dexter-Westbury Rose Co., 1959); lavender, frilled.

Amethystina (Methven & Son); blush, tipped with puce, yellow blotch.

Amilcar Deep bright violet purple, densely spotted black; F.C.C. 1860.

Amkeys g. ambiguum x keysii; (Magor 1926); orange outside fading to yellow at mouth.

Ammerlandense B g. 'Britannia' x williamsianum; (Dietrich Hobbie 1946); coral rose.

Amoenum ciliatum x dauricum; similar to 'Praecox' but flowers larger and flowers in April.

Amor g. griersonianum x thayerianum; (Stevenson).

Amor cl. griersonianum x thayerianum; (J. B. Stevenson 1927); white tinged with pink and on outside flushed with irregular pink staining; A.M. (R.H.S.) 1951.

Amour cl. wardii x 'Lady Bessborough' (Hawk g.); (Rothschild); yellow. Previously listed as Hawk var. Amour.

o H-2 Amphion cl. catawbiense x ; (A.Waterer); red or rose pink. Syn. 'F.L.Ames'.

Amphipyros (Standish 1860); deep red with small black spots on upper segment.

Amrie catacosmum x chaetomallum; (J.B.Stevenson 1951); blackish crimson.

Amsel g. 'Burgermeester Aarts' x williamsianum; (Dietrich Hobbie 1947); clear rose, umbels 6 - 12.

x H-3 Amy ** B cl. griffithianum x ; (J.Waterer, Sons & Crisp); bright rose.

Anadyomene (Standish 1860); blush white faintly spotted yellowish brown.

Anderson (before 1871).

Androcles g. arboreum x calophytum; (Rothschild).

Androcles cl. arboreum x calophytum; (Rothschild 1933); rhodamine pink H.C.C. 527/3, with 4 lines of darker spots from the base of the tubes to the ovary; A.M. (R.H.S.) 1948.

Andromeda cl. stewartianum (scarlet form) x neriiflorum; (Reuthe 1941); crimson scarlet.

Angelina cl. cultivated Standish & Noble before 1860; clear white, yellow eye.

xx H-4 Angelo * C g. griffithianum x discolor; (Rothschild).

Angelo cl. griffithianum x discolor; (Rothschild 1930); pale blush pink outside, white with pale green spots within. A.M. (R.H.S.) 1935. See 'Exbury Angelo', 'Sheffield Park Angelo', 'Solent Queen', 'Solent Snow', 'Solent Swan'.

Angelo Diadem cl. griffithianum x discolor (Angelo g.); (Haworth-Booth.) Previously listed as Angelo var. Diadem.

Angeola (before 1857).

		Anica Bricogne			cl.	pale mauve.
		Anita			g.	campylocarpum x griersonianum; (Aberconway 1941); yellow flushed rose.
		Anna			cl.	'Norman Gill' x 'Jean Marie Montagu'; (Lem.) deep pink.
		Annabella			g.	campanulatum x Loderi g. ; (Rothschild 1933); white flushed light mauve.
		Anna Parsons			cl.	catawbiense x ; (Parsons before 1875); purplish red.
		Anna Rose Whitney			cl.	griersonianum x 'Countess of Derby'; (Whitney, 1954); P.A. (A.R.S.).
		Anne			cl.	thomsonii x ?; (Messel); pink; A.M. (R.H.S.) 1928.
		Annedore			cl.	catawbiense x ; (Seidel 1926). Syn. of 'Lady Armstrong'.
		Annette			cl.	cultivated Standish & Noble before 1860; white tinted.
		Anne Vervaef				(before 1870).
		Annie Bricogne				(Bertin before 1867).
		Annie Dixwell				(A. Waterer before 1875).
xxx	H-3	Annie E. Endtz		B	cl.	'Pink Pearl' x ; (L. J. Endtz & Co. 1939); light pink.
		Annie Dalton			cl.	(decorum x griersonianum) x 'America'; (Gable, 1960); fuchsine pink (H.C.C. 627/2), throat crimson (H.C.C. 22/1); A.E., (A.R.S.) 1960.
		Ann Rutlidge			cl.	catawbiense x ; (Stokes, Butler, Pa.).
		Ann Willis Fleming			cl.	deep pink with dark eye.
		Anstie				(C.E. Heath 1934).
		Antagonist			cl.	Standish & Noble before 1860; deep purple red.
		Anthaea } Anthea }			cl.	griffithianum x ; (Mangles).
		Anthony			cl.	'Arthur Osborn' x griffithianum; (Harrison 1952); deep red.
		Anthony Webb			cl.	'Lady Primrose' x campylocarpum; (Thacker 1938); soft yellow.
		Anton			cl.	catawbiense x ; (Seidel 1926); violet with deeper edges.
		Antonia			cl.	Standish & Noble before 1860; rosy crimson, heavy dark blotch.
		Antonio			g.	'Gill's Triumph' x discolor; (Rothschild).
		Antonio			cl.	'Gill's Triumph' x discolor; (Rothschild 1933); suffused rose pink fading with age, crimson blotched and spotted within; A.M. (R.H.S.) 1939. See 'Exbury Antonio'.
		Antonio Omega			cl.	'Gill's Triumph' x discolor (Antonio g.); (Rothschild 1933). Previously listed as Antonio var. Omega.
xx	H-3	Antoon van Welie			cl.	'Pink Pearl' hybrid; (L.J. Endtz & Co.); pure deep pink.
		Apache			g.	'Gill's Triumph' x thomsonii; (Rothschild 1933); bright rose.
		Apar			g.	aperantum x arboreum; (Aberconway 1946); deep red.
		Aperemia			g.	'Choremia' x aperantum; (Aberconway 1946); deep red.
		Aperme			g.	aperantum x meddianum; (Aberconway 1946); red.
		Apis			cl.	bullatum x nuttalii; (Stephenson Clarke 1936); pure white with canary yellow base.
		Apodeno			g.	'Eupheno' x apodectum; (Aberconway 1946); vermilion.
		Apodorum			g.	apodectum x decorum; (1942).
		Apollo				(T. Methven & Son, Edinburgh); scarlet.
		Apology				(A. Waterer); pale rose, dark blotch.
		Apple Blossom	*	B	cl.	fortunei x ; (W. C. Slocock); pink and white, yellow center.
		Apricot Lady Chamberlain			cl.	cinnabarinum var. roylei x 'Royal Flush' (orange form) (Lady Chamberlain g.); (Rothschild); apricot. Previously listed as Lady Chamberlain var. Apricot.
		Aprilis				ponticum x dauricum?; (Herbert 1843).
		Arab			g.	williamsianum x sperabile; (Rothschild 1933); pink.
		Arbad			g.	arboreum var. album x adenogynum; (Magor 1926); white shaded pink outside, boldly spotted crimson.
		Arbcalo			g.	arboreum var. album x calophytum; (Magor 1940).
		Arbcamp			g.	campylocarpum x arboreum var. album; (Magor 1928); creamy white, faint shades of crimson spots.
		Arbsutch				arboreum (pink) x sutchuenense; (Magor 1915).
		Arbutifolium			g.	minus x ferrugineum; (1917); lilac rose.
		Archiduc Etienne				(A. Verschaffelt 1866).
		Archimedes			cl.	(H. Waterer before 1851); rose, light center.
		Arden Belle			cl.	glaucophyllum x 'Rosy Bell'; (Thacker 1942); rose pink.
		Arden Fairy			cl.	racemosum x lutescens; (Thacker 1946); creamy pink.
		Arden Primrose			cl.	wardii x 'Pink Pearl'; (Thacker 1940); pale yellow.
		Ardis			g.	forrestii var. repens x arboreum var. wearii; (Aberconway 1946); bright red.
		Arena			cl.	haematodes x 'Matador'; (R.H.S. Gardens, Wisley 1953).
		Arethusa				griffithianum x ; (Waterer, Sons & Crisp Ltd.); delicate pink.
		Argiolus			g.	augustinii x concinnum; (Aberconway 1946); pale mauve. See 'Danube'.
		Argosy			g.	discolor x auriculatum; (Rothschild 1933); white, sweet scented.
x	H-3	Argosy Snow White	**	B	cl.	discolor x auriculatum (Argosy g.); white; (A.M. Waterer & Crisp 1938). Previously listed as Argosy var. Snow White.
		Argyll			cl.	'J.G. Millais' x thomsonii; (Horlick); registered Horlick 1957.
		Ariadne			cl.	griffithianum x 'Grand Duke of Würtemburg'; (G.B. van Nes & Sons); rose flowers, heavily spotted.
		Ariadne			cl.	cultivated Standish & Noble before 1860; pure white.
		Ariel			g.	discolor x 'Memoir'; (Rothschild 1933); white or pale pink.
		Ariel			cl.	Indo-Javanicum; clear yellow; A.M. 1893.
		Ariel			cl.	Standish & Noble before 1860; bright pink, yellow spots.
		Aries			g.	thomsonii x neriiflorum; (Ramsden).

		Aries			cl.	thomsonii x neriiflorum; (Ramsden 1922); deep scarlet or ruby red; A.M. (R.H.S.) 1932; F.C.C. (R.H.S.) 1938.
		Aristide Briand			cl.	'Pink Pearl' x hardy hybrid; (L. J. Endtz & Co.); carmine.
		Arma			g.	dichroanthum x forrestii var. repens; (Aberconway 1933); orange scarlet.
		Armia			g.	concatenans x lutescens; (Stevenson 1947); yellow.
o	H-3	Armistice Day		B	cl.	griffithianum hybrid x 'Maxwell T. Masters'; (C.B. van Nes & Sons 1930); scarlet red.
		Arno			cl.	catawbiense x ; (Seidel 1926); pale lilac.
		Artemis				arboreum var. album x griffithianum; (Magor 1921); white.
		Artemis				'Ophelia' x teysmannii; (Veitch 1891); primrose yellow.
		Arthuria			cl.	griersonianum x 'Master Dick'; rose madder (H.C.C. 23/1) darker throat; three upper lobes show brown spotting; A.M. (R.H.S.) 1952.
		Arthur Helps				(T. Methven & Son, Edinburgh); dark crimson.
		Arthurianum			cl.	T. Methven & Son, Edinburgh 1868; distinct light variety.
xxx	H-2	Arthur J. Ivens	*	B	cl.	williamsianum x houlstonii; (Hillier & Son); shallow, bell-shaped, Persian Rose; (H.C.C. 628/3); A.M. (R.H.S.) 1944.
xxx	H-3	Arthur Osborn	*	B	cl.	didymum x griersonianum; (Kew Gardens 1929); ruby. A.M. (R.H.S.) 1933.
		Arthur Smith			g.	wardii x decorum; (Digby 1951); See 'Ightham Yellow'.
		Artus			g.	'Amaura' x 'Fabia'; (Aberconway 1941); red.
		Aruna			g.	'Penjerrick' x wightii; (Aberconway 1933); yellow.
		Asa Gray				(van Houtte before 1874).
x	H-3	Ascot Brilliant	**	B	cl.	thomsonii x; (Standish 1861); red or deep crimson.
		Ashes of Roses			cl.	fortunei x; (Dexter?).
		Aspasia				'Maiden's Blush' x teysmanii; pure yellow; A.M. 1889.
		Aspansia			g.	'Astarte' x haematodes; (Aberconway 1932).
		Aspansia			cl.	'Astarte' x haematodes; (Aberconway 1945); brilliant red (H.C.C. 820), A.M. (R.H.S.) 1945.
		Aspansia Ruby			cl.	'Astarte' x haematodes (Aspansia g.); (Aberconway 1932); blood red. Previously listed as Aspansia var. Ruby.
		Asta			g.	forrestii var. repens x chaetomallum; (Aberconway 1941); deep red.
		Astabia			g.	'Fabia' x 'Astarte'; (Aberconway 1942); red.
		Astarte			cl.	dichroanthum x 'Penjerrick'; (Aberconway 1931); apricot or salmon pink; A.M. (R.H.S.) 1931.
		(Astarte)				See 'Naomi Astarte'
		Astel			g.	'Astarte' x 'Elizabeth'; (Aberconway 1946); red.
		Asteno			g.	'Eupheno' x 'Astarte'; (Aberconway 1946); deep red.
		Asteroid			g.	'Dr. Stocker' x thomsonii; (Rothschild 1933); rich rosy pink. See 'Crimson Banner', 'Rosy Queen'.
		Astos			g.	'Arthur Osborn' x 'Astarte'; (Aberconway 1946); brilliant scarlet.
		Asträa			g.	'Catawbiense Grandiflorum' x discolor; (Dietrich Hobbie 1948); mallow colored to violet, large.
		Astrow			g.	'Astarte' x hookeri; (Aberconway 1946); dark red.
		Atalanta			g.	'Werei' x thomsonii; (Magor 1926); geranium red with darker spots.
		Athene				(T. Methven & Son, Edinburgh); white, yellow blotch.
		Athenia				catawbiense x; blush white, stained olive, yellow blotch; commendation 1860.
		Atlas			cl.	Noble before 1850; chocolate rose, dark spots.
		Atrier			g.	'Atrosanguineum' x griersonianum; (Gable); red; exhibited 1945. See 'William Montgomery'.
		Atroflo			cl.	'Atrosanguineum' x floccigerum; (Gable); exhibited 1940; red. A.E., (A.R.S.) 1959.
		Atror			cl.	(orbiculare x williamsianum) x 'Atrosanguineum'; (Gable); pinkish crimson fading blush pink; exhibited 1945.
		Atro-rubrum			cl.	(J.Waterer 1851); rose crimson.
x	H-2	Atrosanguineum			cl.	catawbiense x ; (H. Waterer before 1851); red.
		Atsonii				'Atrosanguineum' x thomsonii; (Gable); red; exhibited 1937.
		Attila			cl.	(T. Methven & Son, Edinburgh before 1867); claret purple.
		Attraction			cl.	ponticum x ; (M. Koster & Sons); mauve, late.
		Auchati-Barbaudum			cl.	(in Cornwall?); growing at Sunningdale Nursery 1955.
		Aucubaefolium			cl.	T. Methven & Son, Edinburgh 1868.
xxx	H 3	Augfast	***	B	g.	augustinii x fastigiatum; (Magor 1921); blue. See 'Ightham'.
		August			cl.	catawbiense x ; (Seidel 1926); dark rose.
		Auguste van Geert		B	cl.	ponticum x ?; (Charles van Geert before 1867); purplish red, early.
		Auguste Lemaire			cl.	(Moser); pinkish red.
		Augustum				(Byls before 1875).
		Augustus				Standish & Noble before 1860; purplish crimson.
		Aunt Martha				(Roy W. Clark, Olympia, Wash.)
		Auredge			g.	xanthostephanum x edgeworthii; (Magor 1938).
		Aureum Punctatum				primrose, spotted orange.
		Aureum Superbum				yellow, deep orange spots.
		Auriel			g.	griersonianum x 'Polar Bear'; (Horlick 1942).

		Aurora		g.	'Kewense' x thomsonii; (Rothschild).
		Aurora	* C	cl.	'Kewense' x thomsonii; (Rothschild); soft pink; A.M. (R.H.S.) 1922.
		Aurora			'Crown Princess of Germany' x javanicum; (Veitch 1891); yellow to red and orange.
		Aurora			cultivated Standish & Noble before 1860; bright rose, yellow eye, spotted.
		Austin Layard		g.	(J. Waterer 1873); rosy crimson.
		Autumn		g.	'Fabia' x 'Clotted Cream'; (Aberconway 1950); orange.
		Autumn Gold		cl.	discolor x 'Fabia'; (Van Veen).
xxx	H-3	Avalanche		g.	Loderi g. x calophytum; (Rothschild).
		Avalanche	*** C	cl.	Loderi g. x calophytum; (Rothschild); pure white with small magenta rose blotch and 3 lines of colour inside at base; A.M. (R.H.S.) 1934; F.C.C. (R.H.S.) 1938. See 'Alpine Glow', 'Alpine Rose'.
		Avania		cl.	'Tally Ho' x 'Rapture'; (Harrison, registered 1955); geranium red.
		Avis		cl.	thomsonii x 'Glory of Penjerrick' (Barclayi g.); (Barclay Fox). Previously known as Barclayi var. Avis.
		Avocet		g.	discolor x fortunei; (Rothschild 1933); sweet scented, white.
		A. W. Coates		cl.	(Price 1948).
		Ayah		g.	discolor x eriogynum; (Rothschild 1933); pink.
		Ayesha		g.	discolor x arboreum; (Rothschild 1933); pink.
		Azamia		g.	russatum var. cantabile x augustinii; (Stevenson 1947); blue mauve.
xx	H-4	Azma		g.	griersonianum x fortunei; (Stevenson 1933); soft salmon pink.
xxx	H-4	Azor		g.	griersonianum x discolor; (Stevenson).
		Azor	*** B	cl.	griersonianum x discolor; (Stevenson 1927); clear pink with ruddy brown fleckings towards the base, A.M. (R.H.S.) 1933. See 'C.F. Wood', 'Lily Daché'.
		Azrie		g.	griersonianum x diaprepes; (Stevenson 1933); soft salmon pink.
		Aztec		g.	arboreum x irroratum; (Rothschild 1933); pink.
		Babylon		cl.	calophytum x praevernum; (Reuthe); registered Reuthe 1955; white, chocolate blotch.
		Bacchus		cl.	(A. Waterer before 1915); crimson, large truss.
		Bacher's Gold		cl.	'Unknown Warrior' x 'Fabia'; (John Bacher); edges of lobes Venetian pink (H.C.C. 420/2) shading to saffron yellow at center of lobes; P.A. from A.R.S. 1955.
x	H-3	Bagshot Ruby	** B	cl.	thomsonii x ; (J.Waterer about 1900); ruby red; A.M. (R.H.S.) 1916.
		Bagshot Sands		cl.	a form of R. lutescens; (Mrs. R. M. Stevenson); primrose yellow (H.C.C. 601/2); A.M. (R.H.S.) 1953.
		Bahram	B	cl.	(Knap Hill Nursery); blush pink fading white.
		Bai Waterer		cl.	(J. Waterer); scarlet edge, light center.
		Ballerina	B	cl.	'Alice' x discolor; (Waterer, Sons & Crisp); white with yellow flare on upper petal.
		Banshee		g.	auriculatum x 'John Tremayne'; (Rothschild 1934); white flushed pink.
xx	H-4	Barbara		g.	campylocarpum var. elatum x Loderi g.; (Rothschild 1948); cream with dark blotch. See 'Pinafore'.
		Barbara Wallace		cl.	'Queen Wilhelmina' x 'Helen Waterer'; (C.B. van Nes & Son); reddish pink with white center.
		Barbarossa		cl.	barbatum x ; (Horlick); red.
		Barbet		g.	dichroanthum x callimorphum; (Rothschild 1934); creamy pink.
		Barber of Seville		cl.	cultivated Standish & Noble before 1860; pale rose, with black spots.
		Barbsutch		g.	barbatum x sutchuenense; (Magor 1930); deep rose pink, crimson blotch.
		Barclayanum			(H. Waterer before 1851); reddish rose or crimson. Syn. 'Le Poussin'.
		Barclayi		g.	thomsonii x 'Glory of Penjerrick'; (Barclay Fox); intense crimson. See 'Romala'.
xxx	H-5	Barclayi Helen Fox	E	cl.	thomsonii x 'Glory of Penjerrick' (Barclayi g.); (Barclay Fox); deep crimson scarlet.
xxxx	H-5	Barclayi Robert Fox	****E	cl.	thomsonii x 'Glory of Penjerrick' (Barclayi g.); (Barclay Fox); deep blood red; A.M. (R.H.S.) 1921.
		Barnet Glory	B		deep rosy red. Syn. of 'Souvenir de D.A. Koster'.
		Baron Adolphe de Rothschild		cl.	(Croux between 1900 and 1915).
		Baron Alphonse Malbet		cl.	(Moser).
		Baron Chandon		cl.	(Moser).
		Baron de Bruin		cl.	(A. Waterer before 1915).
		Baron de Verdiere		cl.	(Croux between 1900 and 1913).
		Baroness Bolsover			rosy lilac, spotted.
		Baroness Henry Schröder	A	cl.	(J. Waterer); white, finely spotted, or french white; F.C.C. 1883.
		Baroness Lionel de Rothschild		g.	(J. Waterer); pale crimson center with deeper margin.
		Baroness von Panwitz			rose, deeper edging.
		Baronne Gabriel de St. Genois			(van Houtte before 1875).
		Baronne Raissa Standersfkiold		cl.	(Crous between 1900 and 1913).
		Baron Schröder	A		(J. Waterer before 1915); plum color, yellowish center.
		Bartia		g.	'Barclayi' x 'Portia'; (Aberconway).
		Bartia		cl.	'Barclayi' x 'Portia'; (Aberconway 1936); turkey red (H.C.C. 721/1); A.M. (R.H.S.) 1948.

		Barto Blue		cl.	selection of R. augustinii; (James A. Barto); lavender blue center, edged blue; named by Dr. Carl H. Phetteplace, Oregon.
		Bassano			(M. Young); red crimson, intensely blotched.
		Battle Axe		g.	'Gill's Goliath' x discolor; (Rothschild 1934); rich pink.
		Bauble	B	g.	'Dawn's Delight' x campylocarpum; (Rothschild 1934); creamy yellow, spotted.
xx	H-3	B. de Bruin / Bas de Bruin	* A	cl.	catawbiense x ; (A. Waterer); red or rich scarlet, fringed petals.
		B.B.C.		g.	'The Don' x neriiflorum var. euchaites; (Rothschild 1934); red.
x	H-4	Beacon		g.	'Fabia' x 'Arthur Osborn'; (Aberconway 1942); brilliant scarlet. See 'Fabos'.
		Beada		g.	'Ouida' x beanianum; (Aberconway 1950); pink.
		Beatrice		g.	'Choremia' x meddianum; (Aberconway 1950); pink.
		Beatrice Pierce		cl.	(decorum x griffithianum) x 'Charles Dickens'; (Nearing); exhibited 1944; rose, maroon center.
xx	H-3	Beau Brummell		g.	'Essex Scarlet' x eriogynum; (Rothschild); dark red.
		Beau Brummell	* B	cl.	'Essex Scarlet' x eriogynum; (Rothschild); clear deep red, speckled darker within, anthers black; A.M. (R.H.S.) 1938.
		Beaufort		cl.	'Boule de Neige' x fortunei; (Gable); white.
		Beaulieu	* C		griffithianum x ; (Waterer, Sons & Crisp); peach pink, whitish pink edge.
		(Beaulieu)			See 'Beaulieu Hawk'.
		Beaulieu Hawk		cl.	wardii x 'Lady Bessborough' (Hawk g.); (Rothschild); pale yellow. Formerly known as Hawk var. Beaulieu.
		Beauty			crimson, spotted all over; S.C.C. 1869.
		Beauty of Bagshot		cl.	catawbiense x ; (J. Waterer); white, soft mauve tinge, dark blotch.
		Beauty of Berry Hill		cl.	(A. Waterer); scarlet, finely spotted. Syn. of 'Beauty of Surrey'.
		Beauty of Kent			(Stanley 1860); purple tinted blush with pale edges, spotted.
xxx	H-3	Beauty of Littleworth	****B	cl.	campanulatum x griffithianum; (Miss Mangles about 1900); pure white with speckling of garnet red on upper petal at throat, buds tinged mauvy pink; F.C.C. (R.H.S.) 1904; F.C.C. (Wisley Trials) 1953.
		Beauty of Surrey			(A. Waterer); scarlet, finely spotted; F.C.C. 1872. Syn. 'Beauty of Berry Hill'.
		Beauty of Tremough		g.	griffithianum x arboreum; (R. Gill & Son); rose pink fading to pale rose; F.C.C. (R.H.S.) 1902. See 'Bodnant Beauty of Tremough', 'Glory of Penjerrick', 'Gill's Triumph', 'John Tremayne'.
		Beechwood Pink		cl.	'Atrosanguineum' x fortunei; (Gable-Herbert, 1960); fuschsine pink (H.C.C. 627/1); A.E., (A.R.S.) 1960.
		Beefeater		cl.	elliottii x 'Fusilier'; (R.H.S., Wisley, 1958); Geranium lake (H.C.C. 20/1), sparse, pale spotting; A.M. (R.H.S.) 1958; F.C.C. 1959.
		Beethoven		cl.	(M. Koster & Sons); lilac red with purple blotch.
		Belisha Beacon		g.	'Essex Scarlet' x arboreum; (Rothschild 1934); scarlet.
		Bella		g.	'Shilsonii' x griffithianum; (Aberconway 1936); pale rose.
		Belle		cl.	discolor x campylocarpum var. elatum; (Rothschild).
		Belle Heller		cl.	'Catawbiense Album' x white catawbiense seedling; (Shammarello); white, gold blotch.
		Belle of Tremeer		cl.	coeruleum var. album x augustinii ?; (natural hybrid); Harrison 1947; pale mauve;
		Bellerophon		g.	'Norman Shaw' x eriogynum; (Rothschild 1934); bright crimson red.
		Bellona		cl.	(Waterer, Sons & Crisp Ltd.) rosy pink paling at center.
		Belvedere		cl.	'Doncaster' x dichroanthum; (Rothschild); soft apricot pink.
		Bengt M. Schalin	A	g.	fortunei 'Mrs. Butler' x wardii (G. Sherriff 5679); (Dietrich Hobbie); bright yellow, red patches in throat.
		Benito		g.	discolor seedling x 'Luscombei'; white, delicately pink flushed, mingled brown and rose markings on upper side of throat; A.M. (R.H.S.) 1934.
		Benmore		cl.	a form of R. mollyanum; (Younger Botanic Garden, Benmore); a variable shade of fuchsine pink (H.C.C. 627/2) with deep pink staining and a small deep crimson blotch at base of throat; A.M; F.C.C. (R.H.S.) 1957.
		Ben Venuto		g.	seinghkuense x maddenii; (Adams-Acton 1942).
		Beranger		cl.	cultivated by Standish & Noble before 1860; white with red and brown spots.
		Bergie		cl.	a superior form of R. ciliatum; (H.L. Larson); white.
		Bern		cl.	decorum x garden hybrid; (John Bacher, Portland, Oregon); pastel mauve (H.C.C. 433) shading lighter towards center; prominent blotch on upper lobes magenta rose 027; P.A. from A.R.S. (U.S.A.) 1955.
		Bernard Crisp		cl.	'Pink Pearl' x hardy hybrid; (Waterer, Sons & Crisp 1920); pale rose pink; A.M. (R.H.S.) 1921.
		Bernard Gill		cl.	barbatum x ; (R. Gill & Son); soft rose red, few dots deeper color of carmine pink; A.M. (R.H.S.) 1925.
		Bernard Lauterback		cl.	carmine red.
		Bernard Shaw		cl.	'Pink Pearl' x calophytum; (Reuthe 1955); clear pink.
		Berryrose		g.	'Doncaster' x dichroanthum; (Rothschild).
		Berryrose	* B	cl.	'Doncaster' x dichroanthum; (Rothschild 1934); medium pink with yellow flare or apricot pink, fragrant; A.M. (R.H.S.) 1934. See 'Minterne Berryrose'.
		Bertha		cl.	catawbiense x ; (Seidel 1929); rose, marked and frilled.
		Bertha Parsons		cl.	catawbiense x ; (Parsons before 1871); rose. Syn. of 'President Lincoln'.
		Bertie Parsons		cl.	catawbiense x ; (Parsons); rose.
		Bertram Woodhouse Currie		cl.	(J. Waterer before 1922); crimson, light center.

	Beryl			dull purple; A.M. (R.H.S.) 1931.
	Berylline		g.	spinuliferum x valentinianum; (Rothschild 1934); pale yellow flushed rose.
	Betelgeuse		cl.	griersonianum x 'Madame Colijn'; (G. Reuthe Ltd. 1940); salmon pink.
	Betsy Parsons			Syn. of 'President Lincoln'.
	Betsy Trotwood			cultivated Standish & Noble before 1860; rose red.
	Betty		cl.	thomsonii x fortunei; (Loder); deep pink; A.M. (R.H.S.) 1927.
	Betty Breene		cl.	smirnowii x Dexter hybrid; (D. G. Leach 1959); pale pink flushed mauve.
	Betty King		g.	'Luscombei' x thomsonii; (Horlick 1942); red to pink.
	Betty Royal		cl.	'Luscombei' x thomsonii (Betty King g.); (Horlick).
	Betty Stewart	* B	cl.	(C.B. van Nes & Sons); cherry red, upper lobe spotted and suffused white, A.M. (R.H.S.) 1936, after trial at Exbury.
xxx H-3	Betty Wormald	*** B	cl.	'George Hardy' x red garden hybrid; (M. Koster & Sons before 1922); pink, pale center, pale purple blotch; A.M. (R.H.S.) 1935.
	B. Griffith			griffithianum x ; (Mangles).
	Bianca			salmon pink or delicate crimson; F.C.C. 1866.
	Bianchi	A		(Maurice Young); salmon pink.
	Bibber		cl.	'Mrs. Milner' x catawbiense; (Seidel cross 1900); carmine red.
xx H-4	Bibiani		g.	'Moser's Maroon' x arboreum; (Rothschild).
	Bibiani	** B	cl.	'Moser's Maroon' x arboreum; (Rothschild); bright scarlet, with few maroon spots; A.M. (R.H.S.) 1934.
	Bicolor		cl.	lilac, blush, reddish purple (in Methven cat. before 1851).
	Bidwelli			Syn. of 'Caldwelli'.
	Bijou		cl.	(Moser 1914); caucasicum hybrid.
	Bijou de Gand		cl.	raised by M. Hoenyena, Ghent Florist; introduced A. Verschaffelt 1861.
	Bilderdijk		cl.	carmine red.
	Billy Budd		cl.	'May Day' x elliottii; (R.H.S. Gardens, Wisley 1954); turkey red (H.C.C. 721/1); A.M. (R.H.S.) 1957.
	Biskra		g.	cinnabarinum var. roylei x ambiguum; (Rothschild).
	Biskra	* C	cl.	cinnabarinum var. roylei x ambiguum; (Rothschild 1934); vermilion (H.C.C. 18/2 and 18/1); A.M. (R.H.S.) 1940.
	Bismarck		cl.	'Viola' x catawbiense; (Seidel 1900); white with red lines.
xx H-3	Black Beauty	** B	cl.	(W.C.Slocock); 1930; dark velvet crimson or maroon red.
	Blackeyed Susan		cl.	(T. Methven & Son, Edinburgh); purplish lilac with black spots.
	Blackie		cl.	'Moser's Maroon' x 'Arthur Osborne'; (R. Henny, 1959); Indian lake (H.C.C. 826/3) lobes, cardinal red (H.C.C. 822/2) center.
	Black Strap		cl.	dichroanthum x didymum; (Sunningdale Nurseries 1951); deep blood red.
	Blanc de Chine		g.	'Gauntlettii' x Loderi g. (Collingwood Ingram 1939).
	Blanc-mange		g.	'Godesberg' x auriculatum; (Rothschild).
	Blanc-mange		cl.	'Godesberg' x auriculatum; (Rothschild 1934); pure white. A.M. (R.H.S.) 1947. See 'Swan Lake'.
	Blanc Superb			in nursery of T. Methven 1868; white.
o H-2	Blandyanum		cl.	'Altraclarense' x catawbiense; (Standish & Noble 1850); rosy crimson.
	Blatteum			(J. Waterer before 1871); crimson claret or rosy lilac. Syn. of 'Sir Isaac Newton'.
	Blaze		cl.	'Mars' x catawbiense var. rubrum (D. G. Leach, 1959); bright red, lighter in center.
	Blitz			haematodes x 'G. A. Sims'; (Clarke 1945).
	Blood Ruby			forrestii var. repens x 'Mandalay'; Brandt 1954; blood red.
	Blue Beard		cl.	(Davies before 1890).
	Blue Bell			(C.B. van Nes 1932).
	Bluebird		g.	intricatum x augustinii; (Aberconway 1930).
	Bluebird	*** B	cl.	intricatum x augustinii; (Aberconway 1930); blue (H.C.C. 639/1 veronica violet) or violet mauve; P.C. (R.H.S.) 1937; A.M. (R.H.S.) 1943.
	Blue Cloud		cl.	superior form of chasmanthum; (Hansen).
	Blue Danube	A		discolor x 'Purple Splendour'; (Knap Hill Nursery); deep mauve purple; H.C., (R.H.S.) 1959.
xxx H-3	Blue Diamond		g.	'Intrifast' x augustinii; (Crosfield).
	Blue Diamond	****B	cl.	'Intrifast' x augustinii (Crosfield); blue; A.M. (R.H.S.) 1935; F.C.C. (R.H.S.) 1939.
	Blue Ensign	** A	cl.	(W.C.Slocock); Slocock 1934; pale lavender blue, black spot. A.M. (R.H.S.) 1959.
	Blue Moon			'Blue Diamond' x augustinii; (Digby 1955).
xxx H-2	Blue Peter	*** A	cl.	(Waterer, Sons & Crisp); light lavender blue, purple blotch, fringed petals; A.M. (R.H.S.) 1933; F.C.C., 1958.
	Blue Ribbon		g.	'Blue Tit' x augustinii; (Johnstone); 1954. See 'Greeneye', 'Plaineye', 'Purple Eye'.
	Blue Sky			augustinii x desquamatum; (Digby 1955); blue.
	Bluestone		g.	'Bluebird' x augustinii; (Aberconway 1950); deep blue.
xxx H-3	Blue Tit	*** B	g.	impeditum x augustinii; (J. C. Williams 1933); blue.
	Bluette		cl.	impeditum x augustinii; (Lancaster).
	Blush		g.	'Ouida' x aperantum; (Aberconway 1944); pale pink.
	Blush		cl.	See 'Carex Blush'.
	Blushing Beauty			arboreum x ; (R.Gill & Son); bluish pink.
	Blushing Bride		g.	'Dawn's Delight' x discolor; (Rothschild 1934); rosy carmine.
	Boadicea		g.	thomsonii x hookeri; (Rothschild 1934).
	Bob Cherry		cl.	'Adrastia x forrestii var. repens; (Sunningdale Nurseries 1951); deep crimson red.
	Bobolink		g.	discolor x neriiflorum; (Rothschild 1934); deep yellow or apricot.

	Boddaertianum	*** A	cl.	campanulatum x arboreum; (van Houtte 1863); opens pink and fades to white, throat spotted black.
	Bodil		cl.	('Ascot Brilliant' x neriiflorum) x haematodes; exhibited M. Adams 1950.
	Bodnant Beauty of Tremough		cl.	griffithianum x arboreum (Beauty of Tremough g.); (Aberconway 1948); scented, pale rose pink. Formerly listed as Beauty of Tremough Bodnant var.
	Bodnant May Day		cl.	haematodes x griersonianum (May Day g.); (Aberconway 1939); scented, deep scarlet. Formerly listed as May Day Bodnant var.
	Bodnant Pink		cl.	form of arboreum var. album; (Aberconway).
	Bodnant Thomwilliams		cl.	thomsonii x williamsianum (Thomwilliams g.); (Aberconway 1935); waxy rose magenta; A.M. (R.H.S.) 1935. Formerly listed as Thomwilliams Bodnant var.
	Bodnant Yellow		cl.	cinnabarinum–yellow form x 'Royal Flush'–orange form; (Lady Chamberlain g.); (Aberconway); butter yellow orange buff (H.C.C. 507/1) with deeper reddish flush; F.C.C. (R.H.S.) 1944. Formerly known as Lady Chamberlain var. Bodnant Yellow.
	Bonbon		g.	maximum x souliei; (Rothschild 1934); cream.
	Bonfire	** B	cl.	(discolor x 'Mrs. R. T. Shaw') x griersonianum; (Waterer, Sons & Crisp 1928) deep red; A.M. (R.H.S.) 1933.
xxx H-3	Bonito		g.	discolor x 'Luscombei'; (Rothschild).
	Bonito	*** B	cl.	discolor x 'Luscombei'; (Rothschild 1934); white, chocolate blotch; A.M. (R.H.S.) 1934.
	Bonzo	A	cl.	(Knap Hill about 1933).
xx H-3	Bo-peep		g.	lutescens x moupinense; (Rothschild).
	Bo-peep	*** C	cl.	lutescens x moupinense; (Rothschild 1934); cream, yellow spots within at back; A.M. (R.H.S.) 1937.
xx H-3	Borde Hill	* B	cl.	'Doncaster' x 'Mrs. A.M. Williams'; (C.B. van Nes & Sons); dark scarlet red; A.M. (R.H.S. Wisley Trials) 1948.
	Borde Hill Red Cap		cl.	didymum x eriogynum (Red Cap g.); exhibited Col. S. R. Clarke. Formerly listed as Red Cap Borde Hill var.
	Borkum		g.	'America' x williamsianum; (Dietrich Hobbie 1947); clear rose.
	Botha		cl.	catawbiense x ; (Seidel cross 1900); lilac rose.
	Boule de Feu		cl.	(Davies before 1890).
x H-1	Boule de Neige		cl.	caucasicum x hardy catawbiense hybrid; (Oudieu about 1878); white.
	Boule de Rose		cl.	Red catawbiense hybrid x 'Boule de Neige' (Shammarello-D.G. Leach 1957); bright rose-pink, slight brownish flare on upper lobe; low growing, compact.
	Boule D'Or		g.	'Lord Wolseley' x teysmannii; exhibited Veitch 1891.
	Bouquet		g.	davidsonianum x 'Peace'; (Aberconway 1950); white
	Bouquet de Flore			cultivated Standish & Noble before 1860; deep purplish rose, black spots.
	Bouquet Parfait			in cultivation in nursery of T. Methven, Edinburgh 1868; pink, dark spots.
xxxxH-3	Bow Bells		g.	'Corona' x williamsianum; (Rothschild).
	Bow Bells	** B	cl.	'Corona' x williamsianum; (Rothschild 1934); bright pink, A.M. (R.H.S.) 1935.
	Brabantia		cl.	cultivated Standish & Noble before 1860; deep crimson.
	Brachbooth		g.	brachyanthum x boothii; (Magor 1926); butter yellow with green tinge and darker spots.
	Brachdis		g.	brachycarpum x discolor; (Magor 1925); blush yellow, green spotting.
	Brachlep		g.	brachyanthum x lepidotum; (Magor 1924).
	Brachsoul		g.	brachycarpum x souliei; (Magor 1927); light rose shading to white, darker outside, spotted crimson.
	Brachydum		g.	brachyanthum x flavidum; (J. Waterer 1921).
	Brachydum Primum		cl.	brachyanthum (Wilson 6771) x flavidum (Wilson 1773); pale yellow A.M. (R.H.S.) 1924.
	Brandywine		cl.	pubescens x keiskei; (Nearing 1950); rose.
	Bray		cl.	griffithianum hybrid x 'Hawk'; (Crown Estate Commissioners, 1960); Mimosa yellow (H.C.C. 602/3), upper lobes paler, (602/2), shaded pale pink outside; A.M. (R.H.S.) 1960.
	Brayanum			(H. Waterer 1851); rosy scarlet.
xx H-3	Break of Day		g.	'Dawn's Delight' x dichroanthum; (Rothschild).
	Break of Day		cl.	'Dawn's Delight' x dichroanthum; (Rothschild 1934); orange, deep orange at base A.M. (R.H.S.) 1936.
	Brebnerii			cultivated Standish & Noble before 1860; rose lake, pale center.
	Brenda		cl.	'J.H. Agnew' x griersonianum; (Rothschild 1927); pink; P.C. (R.H.S.) 1935.
	Brennus		cl.	crimson lake.
xxx H-3	Bric-à-brac		g.	leucaspis x moupinense; (Rothschild).
	Bric-à-brac	** C	cl.	leucaspis x moupinense; (Rothschild 1934); pure white with faint markings on upper lobe, chocolate anthers; A.M. (R.H.S.) 1945.
	Brickdust		cl.	williamsianum x 'Dido'; (R. Henny, 1959); rose madder (H.C.C. 32/2) shading to rhodonite red (H.C.C. 22/3); bronzy new growth.
	Bride		g.	caucasicum album x ; (Standish & Noble 1850); pure white, F.C.C. 1871. See 'The Bride'.
	Bridesmaid		cl.	cultivated Standish & Noble before 1850; pure white.
	Brigadier		g.	'Dawn's Delight' x arboreum (Rothschild 1934); pale pink.
	Bright Eyes		g.	griffithianum x diphrocalyx (Rothschild 1934); white flushed pink.
	Brilliant		cl.	thomsonii x ; (J. Waterer); bright red or intense scarlet.
	Brilliant			'Duchess of Edinburgh' x javanicum; crimson; F.C.C. 1883

	Brinco		cl.	Loderi g. x thomsonii; (Rothschild 1928); bright rose pink.
xxxxH-3	Britannia	****B	cl.	'Queen Wilhelmina' x 'Stanley Davies'; (C. B. van Nes & Sons 1921); scarlet, A.M. (R.H.S.) 1921; F.C.C. (R.H.S.) 1937,
	British Queen			(Davies before 1871).
	Briton Ferry		cl.	pink.
	Brocade	* B	g.	'Vervaeniana' x williamsianum; (Rothschild 1934); frilly peach pink.
	Brocole			(A.W. Heneage Vivian 1933).
	Brookiana			(before 1892).
	Brookville		cl.	Dexter fortunei? hybrid; (Dexter-Westbury Rose Co., 1959); delicate pink.
	Broughtonii	* B	cl.	arboreum x ; (Broughton); rosy crimson.
xxx H-3	Broughtonii Aureum	** B	cl.	Azaleodendron; (maximum x ponticum) x molle; soft yellow with orange spots at back within; F.C.C. 1935. Syn.'Norbitonense Broughtonianum'.
	Brown Eyes		cl.	fortunei hybrid; (Dexter-Bosley); pink, brown blotch.
	Brunette			javanicum x 'Princess Frederica'; exhibited Veitch 1891; yellow to yellow orange.
	Brünhilde		g.	wardii x Loderi g. ; (Stevenson 1951); pale cream.
	Brutus			cultivated Standish & Noble before 1860; purplish lake.
	Buff Lady		cl.	(dichroanthum x neriiflorum) x discolor; (Lancaster); buff, edged pink.
	Bulbul		g.	bullatum x moupinense; (Rothschild).
	Bulbul		cl.	bullatum x moupinense; (Rothschild); white with faint yellow spotting; A.M. (R.H.S.) 1949.
	Bulldog		g.	elliottii x 'Earl of Athlone'; (Bolitho 1937); deep red.
	Bulstrode / Bullstrode		g.	(van Nes before 1922); medium rosy crimson.
	Bulstrode Beauty		cl.	'Loderi King George' x 'Loder's White'; exhibited Sir J. Ramsden 1934.
	Bulstrode Belle		cl.	'Loderi King George' x 'Loder's White'; exhibited Sir J. Ramsden 1934.
xx H-3	Bulstrode Park	B	cl.	griffithianum hybrid x 'Sefton'; (C.B. van Nes & Sons); bright red, waxy.
	Bunting		cl.	'Fabia' x 'Dr. Stocker'; (R. Henny, 1959); Dresden yellow (H.C.C. 64/3), spotted uranium green.
	Burgemeester Aarts		cl.	maximum x 'L. L. Liebig'; (M. Koster & Sons 1915, introduced Aarts); dark red.
	Burgundy		cl.	'Britannia' x 'Purple Splendour'; (Lem).
	Burning Bush		g.	haematodes x dichroanthum; (Rothschild 1934); tangerine red.
	Bustard		g.	auriculatum x 'Penjerrick'; (Rothschild 1934); white.
	Busybody		cl.	(A. Waterer); white, greenish center.
	Butkew		g.	fortunei x 'Kewense'; (Magor 1929); pink.
	Butlerianum			(J. Waterer); white tinged pink.
x H-3	Buttercup	** B	cl.	campylocarpum x 'A.W.Hardy'; (Slocock about 1924); yellow, shaded apricot.
xx H-3	Butterfly	*** B	cl.	campylocarpum x 'Mrs. Milner'; (W.C.Slocock); very pale yellow, faintly spotted red; A.M. (R.H.S.) 1940.
	B.W. Elliott		cl.	(J.Waterer); clear rose, dark spots.
	Bylsianum			(J. Byls); white, margined cerise.
	Cabrera			in nursery of T. Methven & Son, Edinburgh, 1868; clear rosy crimson.
	Cadis		cl.	'Caroline' x discolor; (Gable); pink. (H.C.C. 427/2); A.E. (A.R.S.) 1959
	Caerhays		cl.	griffithianum x ; (Williams); pink.
	Caldecot Fastuosum		cl.	a form of 'Fastuosum'; (Caldecot & Claremont Nursery Co., Goffs Oak, Herts.).
	Calfort		g.	calophytum x fortunei; (Ingram).
	Calfort		cl.	calophytum x fortunei; (Ingram); flowers pink in bud, marked externally with rosy lilac; A.M. (R.H.S.) 1932. See 'Cantica'.
	Caliban			'Doncaster' x haematodes; (Rothschild 1935); red; discontinued.
	Callirhoe		g.	'Dr. Stocker' x arboreum; (Magor 1928); rose neyron red, crimson spots.
	Calomina		g.	'Queen Wilhelmina' x calophytum; (Lady Loder 1934); pink with darker blotch.
	Calotum		g.	calophytum x irroratum; (Ingram 1934).
	Calrose		g.	calophytum x griersonianum; (Aberconway 1939); cerise red.
	Calstocker		g.	calophytum x 'Dr. Stocker'; (Whittaker 1935.) See 'Exbury Calstocker'.
	Calthom		g.	calophytum x thomsonii; (Whittaker 1935).
	Calypso		g.	'Gillian' x smithii; (Magor 1934).
	Caman		g.	campylocarpum x beanianum; (Aberconway 1946); red.
	Cameronian		cl.	Azaleodendron; soft yellow pink.
	Camich		cl.	catawbiense x 'Michael Waterer'; (Gable); purplish red, spotted; exhibited 1936.
	Camilla		g.	'Penjerrick' x 'Loderi King George'; (Aberconway).
	Camilla		cl.	'Penjerrick' x 'Loderi King George'; (Aberconway 1944); white; A.M. (R.H.S.) 1944.
	Campbut		g.	campylocarpum x fortunei 'Mrs. Butler'; (Magor 1926); very pale yellow, dense spotting of crimson at base.
	Campirr		g.	campylocarpum x irroratum; (Magor 1926); pale yellow, crimson spots.
	Campkew		g.	campylocarpum x 'Kewense'; (Magor 1925); creamy white, crimson spots.
	Campxen		g.	campylocarpum x detonsum; (Magor 1940); white and pale yellow with red spots.
xx H-3	Canary		cl.	campylocarpum x caucasicum var. luteum; (M. Koster & Sons 1920); bright lemon yellow.
	Canary		cl.	(campylocarpum x discolor) x Loderi g. (Stead); pale yellow.
	Candida		g.	ambiguum x augustinii; (Rothschild 1935); blush.
	Candidissimum		cl.	catawbiense hybrid; blush-white.
	Cannizara		cl.	(M. Koster & Sons); pale lilac rose.

		Canon Furse		cl.	(J.Waterer before 1922); rose with dark spots.
		Cantatrice			cultivated Standish & Noble before 1860; white, lemon-colored spots.
		Cantica		cl.	calophytum x fortunei (Calfort g.) exhibited C.Ingram 1954. See 'Calfort'.
		Caprice		cl.	superior form of augustinii; (Hansen).
		Caprice			orchid pink, yellowish eye, frilled edge.
		Capriole		g.	'Etna' x 'Jacquetta'; (Aberconway 1942); dark red.
		Captain Beaumont		cl.	pink, white stripes and center.
		Captain Blood		cl.	griersonianum x 'Queen Wilhelmina' (Juliana g.); (Ingram 1947); claret rose (H.C.C. 021), slight spotting on upper petals, A.M. (R.H.S.) 1947. Previously known as Juliana var. Captain Blood.
		Captain Jack		cl.	'Mars' x eriogynum; (R. Henny); dark red (H.C.C. 21/13) P.A. (A.R.S.) 1956.
		Captain Kidd		cl.	'Princess Elizabeth' x 'May Day'; (R. Henny); exhibited 1956; P.A. (A.R.S.) 1960.
		Captain Webb		cl.	(Maurice Young); deep lake.
		Captivation		g.	maximum x 'Altaclarense'; (Standish & Noble before 1850); rosy crimson, black spots.
x	H-1	Caractacus		cl.	catawbiense x ; (A. Waterer); purplish red; F.C.C. 1865.
		Cardinal		g.	arboreum x 'Barclayi'; (Aberconway).
		Cardinal		cl.	arboreum x 'Barclayi'; (Aberconway 1927); flowers scarlet; F.C.C. (R.H.S.) 1937.
		Cardinale			'Duchess of Edinburgh' x javanicum; scarlet crimson; F.C.C. 1885.
		Cardinalis			cultivated Standish & Noble before 1860; purplish crimson.
		Careth		g.	'Ethel' x 'Cardinal'; (Aberconway 1946); red.
		Carex		g.	irroratum x fargesii; (Rothschild).
		Carex		cl.	irroratum x fargesii; (Rothschild 1932); rich pink, shaded outside with darker tint; A.M. (R.H.S.) 1932.
xx	H-4	Carex Blush	** C	cl.	irroratum x fargesii (Carex g.); (Rothschild); blush pink, spotted. Previously known as Carex var. Blush.
		Carex White	** C	cl.	irroratum x fargesii (Carex g.); (Rothschild); white, spotted. Previously known as Carex White var.
		Cariban		g.	'Doncaster' x haematodes; (Rothschild 1935); dark scarlet.
		(Carissima)			See 'Naomi Carissima'.
xxxx	H-3	Carita		g.	'Naomi' x campylocarpum; (Rothschild).
		Carita	** B	cl.	'Naomi' x campylocarpum; (Rothschild 1935); pale primrose (H.C.C. 64/3); A.M. (R.H.S.) 1945. See 'Carita Inchmery', 'Golden Dream'.
		Carita Inchmery		cl.	'Naomi' x camplyocarpum (Carita g.); (Rothschild); biscuit rose. Previously known as Carita var. Inchmery.
		Carlene		cl.	'Lem's Goal' x williamsianum; (Lem-Fawcett, 1960); golden yellow.
		Carl Lackner			griffithianum x ;(Otto Schulz cross 1890, purchased by J.H. van Nes 1896).
		Carl Mette		cl.	catawbiense x ; red.
		Carmania		g.	'Souvenir of Anthony Waterer' x eriogynum; (Rothschild 1935); pink.
xxx	H-4	Carmen	*** B	g.	didymum x forrestii var. repens; (Rothschild 1935); deep red.
		Carnarvonianum			(before 1843); A.M. (R.H.S.) 1927.
		Carneum Versicolor			yellow, pink edging, finely spotted.
		Carnival		g.	'May Day' x Loderi g. ; (Aberconway 1950); pink.
		Carola		g.	'Ouida' x williamsianum; (Aberconway 1941); pink.
		Carola		cl.	catawbiense x ; (Seidel 1884); pure rose with yellow markings.
		Carolid		cl.	(carolinianum x oleifolum) x davidsonianum; (Gable).
		Carolina		cl.	exhibited Crown Lands, Windsor, 1950.
		Caroline		cl.	decorum x ?; brachycarpum x ?; (Gable); orchid lavender; exhibited 1933.
		Caroline			cultivated Standish & Noble before 1860; pure white.
		Caroline Spencer		g.	fortunei x williamsianum; (Adams-Acton 1950); See 'Hubert Robert'.
		Caroline Whitner		g.	'Snow Queen' x 'Loderi Sir Edmund'; (Lady Loder); delicate pink; A.M. (R.H.S.) 1935.
		Carol Jean		cl.	'Vulcan' x 'Robin Hood'; (Joe Klupenger); carmine H.C.C. 21/1, dark blotch. P.A. (A.R.S.) 1957.
		Carolyn Grace		cl.	wardii x; (Grace, 1960); chartreuse green (H.C.C. 663/1), uranium green 63/2) in tube; A.E. (A.R.S.) 1960.
		Carpeaux		g.	cinnabarinum var. roylei x cinnabarinum var. blandfordiaeflorum; (Adams-Acton 1934); pale peach.
		Carpecio		g.	griersonianum x 'Dr. Stocker'; (Adams-Acton 1937); vermilion.
		Cartonii			Azaleodendron; nudiflorum x catawbiense; (Carton 1825).
		Cassandra			cultivated Standish & Noble before 1860; purplish lake.
		Cassiope			(Rothschild 1935).
		Castletop		g.	haematodes x 'Borde Hill'; (Clarke 1943).
		Catalgla		cl.	selected form of catawbiense var. album (Gable).
		Catalode		cl.	'Catawbiense Album' x Loderi g. ; (Gable); white; exhibited 1936. A.E. (A.R.S.) 1960
		Catanea		cl.	selected form of catawbiense var. album (Nearing).
x	H-1	Catawbiense Album		cl.	catawbiense x ; (A.Waterer); white, buds flushed pale lilac.
		Catawbiense Boursault		cl.	catawbiense x ; (Boursalt); lilac, tinged rose.
x	H-2	Catawbiense Grandiflorum		cl.	catawbiense x ; (A. Waterer); lilac.
		Cathaem		cl.	catawbiense x haematodes; (Gable); pink, hose-in-hose; exhibited 1939.

		Catharine van Tol			cl.	catawbiense x ; (J.C.van Tol, Boskoop); carmine rose.
		Cathy			cl	'Corona' x 'Dondis'; (R. Henny).
		Cato			cl.	rose, finely spotted.
		Cauapo			g.	caucasicum x apodectum; (Magor 1927); apricot.
		Caubut			g.	caucasicum x fortunei; (Magor 1926); white shaded yellow inside and spotted green.
		Caucamp			g.	caucasicum var. stramineum x campylocarpum; (Magor); light yellow spotted red.
		Caucasicum Album		A	cl.	ponticum var. album x caucasicum; white.
		Caucasicum Pictum		A	cl.	caucasicum x ; pink, prominent dark blotch, frilled.
		Caucasicum Roseum			cl.	caucasicum x ; pink.
		Caucasicum Splendidium			cl.	caucasicum x ; blush pink.
		Cauking			g.	caucasicum var. stramineum x 'Mrs. Randall Davidson'; (Magor 1928); cream with crimson spotting.
xx	H-3	Cavalcade	**	B	cl.	'Essex Scarlet' x griersonianum; (Waterer, Sons & Crisp); red. See 'Mrs. Sassoon'
		Cavalier			cl.	'Pygmalion' x 'Tally Ho'; (R. Henny).
		Cavalier				cultivated Noble in 1850; purplish rosy lilac, black spots.
		Cavalier			g.	'Radiance' x eriogynum; (Aberconway 1950); brilliant scarlet.
xx	H-4	C.B. van Nes	**	B	cl.	'Queen Wilhelmina' x 'Stanley Davies'; (C.B. van Nes & Sons); scarlet, early.
		Celebrandum			g.	maximum x 'Altraclarense'; (A.M.Waterer 1852); red or purplish crimson, dark spots.
		Celeste	**	B	cl.	'Alice' x discolor; (Waterer, Sons & Crisp); shades of solferino purple (H.C.C. 26/3 and 26/2); A.M. (R.H.S.) 1944.
		Celestrial				cultivated by Standish & Noble before 1860; fine delicate blush.
		Celia			cl.	delicate rose madder.
		Cephalus			cl.	crimson, dark spots.
		Ceramic			cl.	superior form of R. wardii; (raised and introduced by R. Henny, 1959); white, throat sap green (H.C.C. 62/1).
		Cerisette			cl.	elliottii x decorum (Sheila Moore g.); (Digby 1954); fuchsine pink (H.C.C. 627/1) with a scarlet band around the throat and limited scarlet spotting; A.M. (R.H.S.) 1954. Previously known as Sheila Moore var. Cerisette.
		Cerito				cultivated Noble in 1850; deep purplish rose.
		Cerne			cl.	'Lady Rosebery' x cinnabarinum var. roylei (Royal Beauty g.); (Digby 1954); cinnabar red. Previously known as Royal Beauty var. Cerne.
		Cervantes			cl.	(M. Koster & Sons); pink.
		Cetewayo	*	A	cl.	(A.Waterer); dark rich purple; A.M. (R.H.S.) 1958.
		C.F. Wood			cl.	griersonianum x discolor (Azor g.); exhibited Preston 1947. Previously known as Azor var. C.F.Wood.
		Chaffinch			g.	'Countess of Haddington' x ciliatum; (Rothschild); white flushed pink.
		Chalice			g.	cinnabarinum x maddenii; pendent, tubular, pale pink within, creamy white suffused rose outside; A.M. (R.H.S.) 1932.
		Challenger			g.	'Chanticleer' x 'Sunrise'; (Aberconway 1950); rose.
		Champagne			cl.	'Goldsworth Orange' x griersonianum (Tortoiseshell g.); (Slocock 1945-46); pale gold. Formerly listed as Tortoiseshell var. Champagne.
		Chan			g.	'Lady Chamberlain' x xanthocodon; (Aberconway 1946); orange yellow.
		Chancellor				cultivated Standish & Noble before 1860; pure white, yellow eye.
		Chancellor (Waterer's)			cl.	cultivated Standish & Noble before 1860; light purple, spotted.
		Chandon			g.	'Adonis' x 'Chanticleer'; (Aberconway 1946); pink.
		Chaneta			g.	'Coreta' x 'Chanticleer'; (Aberconway 1946); red.
		Changeling			cl.	'Belvedere' x decorum; (Sunningdale Nurseries 1955); rose madder outside, pale ochre inside.
xxx	H-4	Chanticleer	***	C	g.	eriogynum x thomsonii; (Rothschild 1935); large, waxy and scarlet.
		Charlemagne			cl.	in cultivation nursery of T. Methven & Son, Edinburgh, 1867; pink, spotted.
x	H-2	Charles Bagley			cl.	catawbiense x ; (A.Waterer 1865); cherry red.
x	H-1	Charles Dickens			cl.	catawbiense x ; (A.Waterer 1865); purplish crimson red, spotted; F.C.C. 1865.
		Charles H. Pattman			cl.	thomsonii hybrid x griersonianum; (Thacker 1938); rose red.
		Charles Lamont			g.	strigillosum x neriiflorum; (Royal Botanic Garden, Edinburgh, cross 1939); deep pink.
		Charles Michael			cl.	haematodes x thomsonii (Major g.); exhibited C.Williams 1948. Previously known as Major var. Charles Michael.
		Charles Noble			cl.	(C. Noble); deep red, orange yellow eye.
		Charles Thorold			cl.	(A. Waterer before 1922); purple, greenish yellow center.
		Charles Truffaut				(Bertin before 1851); crimson and white.
		Charlie Waterer			cl.	(J.Waterer before 1922); red, light center.
		Charlotte de Rothschild			cl.	discolor x 'St. Keverne' (Sir Frederick Moore g.); (exhibited E. de Rothschild, 1958); whitish pink, deep pink exterior; chocolate spotting in throat; frilled; A.M. (R.H.S.) 1958.
		Charm			g.	forrestii var. repens x 'Shilsonii'; (Aberconway 1941); blood red.

		Charmaine			g.	'Charm' x 'May Day' (Aberconway)
		Charmaine			cl.	'Charm' x 'May Day'; (Aberconway 1946); blood red (H.C.C. 820/3); A.M. (R.H.S.) 1946.
		Charmian			g.	'Vervaeniana' x callimorphum; (Rothschild 1935); rose to pale pink.
		Chaste			g.	campylocarpum x 'Queen of the May'; (Crosfield 1930); exhibited Aberconway 1939; rose.
		Chatterbox			cl.	'Arthur Osborn' x didymum; (R Henny, 1959); currant red (H.C.C. 821).
		Cheer			cl.	a red catawbiense seedling x 'Cunningham's White'; (Shammarello); exhibited 1955; rose pink.
		Cheerful			g.	'Cyclops' x 'Elizabeth'; (Crosfield 1936); exhibited Aberconway 1946; scarlet.
		Cheerio			cl.	wardii x 'Rosy Morn'; (R. Henny).
		Chelsea			cl.	cinnabarinum var. roylei x 'Royal Flush' (orange form) (Lady Chamberlain g.); (Rothschild); orange pink. Previously known as Lady Chamberlain var. Chelsea.
		Cheronia			g.	'Rose Perfection' x orbiculare; (Aberconway 1933); rose pink.
		Cherry Ripe				in cultivation Knap Hill Nursery 1955; cerise pink.
		Cherry Tip			cl.	raised from seeds of Rock 59255; a color variant of R. fictolacteum with unopened buds of a shade of bright cherry pink; A.M. (R.H.S.) 1953.
		Cherubim			g.	'Azma' x elliottii; (Bolitho 1943).
		Chesapeake			cl.	pubescens x keiskei; (Nearing); apricot, fading white; exhibited 1950.
x	H-3	Chevalier Felix de Sauvage		B	cl.	caucasicum x hardy hybrid; (Sauvage about 1870); red with dark spots.
		Chianti			cl.	auriculatum x didymum; registered by Sunningdale Nurseries 1955; deep raspberry crimson.
		Chief Paulina			cl.	a selection of R. concinnum, formerly called 'James' Purple Form'; (D. James); P.A. (A.R.S.).
		Childe Harold				cultivated Standish & Noble before 1870; deep rose with white throat.
xxx	H-3	China			g.	wightii x fortunei; (Slocock).
		China	***	B	cl.	wightii x fortunei; (Slocock 1936); creamy white with red throat; A.M. (R.H.S.) 1940 and Wisley Trials 1948.
		China 'A'			cl.	wightii x fortunei; (Slocock 1946); pale yellow.
		Chinese Pink				exhibited P.D.Williams 1935.
xx	H-3	Chintz	**	B	cl.	(A. Waterer about 1931); soft pink with ruby spots.
		Chionoides		A		ponticum hybrid; (J. Waterer); white with yellow center; exhibited before 1886.
		Chiron			g.	'Barclayi' x haematodes; (Aberconway 1946); deep red.
		Chloe				'Boddaertianum' x faberi; (Magor 1921).
		Choremia			g.	haematodes x arboreum; (Aberconway).
		Choremia			cl.	haematodes x arboreum; (Aberconway 1933); crimson scarlet, A.M. (R.H.S.) 1933; F.C.C. (R.H.S.) 1948.
		Chrissie				exhibited at R. H. S. 23rd April 1895 by T. McMeekin.
x	H-2	Christmas Cheer	*	B	cl.	caucasicum x ; (T. Methven & Son, Edinburgh); in bud pink, fading to white; on opening, blush.
		Chrycil			g.	chrysodoron x 'Cilpinense'; (Aberconway 1947); lemon to yellow.
		Chrypinense			g.	moupinense x chrysodoron; (Aberconway 1946); pale yellow.
		Chrysaspis			g.	chrysodoron x leucaspis; (Aberconway).
		Chrysaspis			cl.	chrysodoron x leucaspis; (Aberconway 1942); yellow (H.C.C. 1/3); A.M. (R.H.S.) 1942.
		Chrysomanicum			g.	chrysodoron x burmanicum; (Aberconway).
		Chrysomanicum			cl.	chrysodoron x burmanicum; (Aberconway 1947); primrose yellow (H.C.C. 601/2); A.M. (R.H.S.) 1947.
		Cilaspis				ciliatum x leucaspis; (Magor 1931); white.
		Cilbooth			g.	ciliatum x boothii; (Magor 1926).
		Ciliocale				from seed collected in China by Abbé Delavay; small, white delicatedly suffused blush pink.
		Cilkeisk			g.	ciliatum x keiskei; (Magor 1926); white tinged pink.
xxx	H-4	Cilpinense			g.	ciliatum x moupinense; (Aberconway).
		Cilpinense	***	C	cl.	ciliatum x moupinense; (Aberconway 1927); pale shell pink; A.M. (R.H.S.) 1927.
		Cincrass			g.	cinnabarinum x crassum; (Magor 1923); pure white passing to cream at the base; A.M. (R.H.S.) 1935.
		Cindy			cl.	calostrotum x ciliatum 'Bergie'; (Larson); blush pink; exhibited 1953.
		Cinnamomium Cunninghami				cultivated Standish & Noble before 1860; white and much spotted.
		Cinnandrum			g.	cinnabarinum var. roylei x polyandrum; (Aberconway 1937); pink peach.
		Cinnandrum Tangerine			cl.	cinnabarinum var. roylei x polyandrum (Cinnandrum g.); (Aberconway); pale apricot within, flushed deep rose without; A.M. (R.H.S.) 1937. Previously known as Cinnandrum var. Tangerine.
		Cinncrass			g.	cinnabarinum x crassum; (Magor).
		Cinncrass			cl.	cinnabarinum x crassum; (Magor 1935); creamy white occasionally flushed externally with rose; A.M. (R.H.S.) 1935.
		Cinnkeys			g.	cinnabarinum x keysii; (Magor).
		Cinnkeys			cl.	cinnabarinum x keysii; (Magor 1926); light clear red in tube, lobes soft yellow; A.M. (R.H.S.) 1935. See 'Minterne Cinnkeys'.
		Cinnmadd			g.	cinnabarinum x maddenii; (Magor).
		Cinzan			g.	cinnabarinum var. blandfordiaeflorum x xanthocodon; (Stevenson 1951); coral pink.
		Circe			g.	'Humming Bird' x 'F.C.Puddle'; (Aberconway 1942); bright red (H.C.C. 820/1); A.M. (R.H.S.) 1942.

	Cirrus		g.	smirnowii x arboreum; exhibited Reuthe 1926.
	C.I.S.		cl.	'Loder's White' x Fabia g. (R. Henny); orange yellow; P.A. (A.R.S.) 1952.
	Cis Grey		cl.	exhibited Milner 1953.
	Citronella		cl.	campylocarpum x 'Kewense'; (J.Waterer, Sons & Crisp); primrose yellow with red eye; form of 'Campkew'.
	Clansman		g.	'Euryalus' x zeylanicum; (Aberconway 1950); red.
	Clare Mangles		g.	griffithianum x ; (Mangles).
	Clementine Lemaire			(Moser & Fils, Versailles); bright pink, yellow blotch, late.
	Cleopatra			arboreum x (thomsonii hybrid x sutchuenense); (Magor 1931); deep satiny pink or bluish.
	Cleopatra			cultivated Standish & Noble before 1860; rosy purple, white throat.
	Cleopatra		cl.	caucasicum x ; deep satin pink, very early, compact habit.
	Climax		cl.	in cultivation in nursery of T.Methven & Son, Edinburgh, 1868; crimson.
	Clio		g.	detonsum x 'Gillian'; (Magor 1931); carmine lake.
	Clivianum			catawbiense x arboreum var. album; exhibited Iveson 1849; delicate pink spotted crimson; Knightian Medal.
	Clodion		g.	'Praecox' x cinnabarinum var. roylei; (Adams-Acton 1934); dull claret.
	Clorinda			'Jasminiflorum Carminatum' x 'Minerva'; dull rose pink; warm greenhouse cultivar, A.M.(R.H.S.) 1912.
	Cloth of Gold			A.M. (R.H.S.) 1896.
	Clotted Cream		g.	'Neda' x auriculatum; (Aberconway).
	Clotted Cream		cl.	'Neda' x auriculatum; (Aberconway 1942); deep cream (H.C.C. 503/2); A.M. (R.H.S.) 1942.
	Clove		g.	sperabile x haemaleum; (Rothschild 1935); blood crimson.
	Clowesianum			(Rollison before 1867); white, black spots.
	Clyne Blush		cl.	grande x hodgsonii (Elsae g.) (Heneage-Vivian 1933). Previously known as Elsae var. Clyne Blush.
	Clyne Cerise		cl.	grande x hodgsonii (Elsae g.); (Heneage-Vivian 1933). Previously known as Elsae var. Clyne Cerise.
	Clyne Elsae		cl.	grande x hodgsonii (Elsae g.); (Heneage-Vivian 1933); fuchsia purple (H.C.C. 28/3) edges of lobes stained deeper shade (H.C.C. 28/2); A.M. (R.H.S.) 1940. Previously known as Elsae var. Clyne.
	Clyne Pearl		cl.	grande x hodgsonii (Elsae g.) (Heneage-Vivian 1933). Previously known as Elsae var. Clyne Pearl.
	Coalition		g.	(Gill & Son); bright salmon red, paler in some forms; A.M. (R.H.S.) 1922.
	(Coccineum)			See 'Nobleanum Coccineum'.
	Cock of the Rock		cl.	cinnabarinum x 'Rose Mangles'; (Stephenson Clarke 1932); clear orange, outside suffused ruby red on orange; A.M. (R.H.S.) 1932.
	C.O.D.			decorum x ?; from the Charles O. Daxter collection; named by S.A. Everitt; pale yellow (empire yellow H. C. C. 603/3) to white, deeper (Dresden yellow H.C.C. 64/3) in throat, with deep empire yellow blotch, slight rose tinting on reverse, fragrant.
	Codorus		g.	minus x racemosum; (J.B.Gable 1934).
	Coelestinum			(A.Waterer before 1850); blush, yellow eye.
	Coelestinum Pictum		cl.	Syn. of 'Pictum'.
	Coer		cl.	'Romala' x delavayi; (J.B.Stevenson 1952); red.
	Coerulescens Daphnoides			Syn. of 'Daphnoides'.
	Colonel Coen		cl.	(Endre Ostbo).
	Colonel Lynde		g.	(Methven); pale purple.
	Colonel Rogers		g.	falconeri x niveum; (Rogers 1926); exhibited Heneage-Vivian 1933.
	Colonel Thorneycroft			cultivated Sunningdale Nurseries 1955.
	Comely		g.	'Lady Chamberlain' x concatenans; (Aberconway 1946); orange yellow.
	Comet		cl.	(Methven, Edinburgh); crimson.
	Compactum			cultivated Standish & Noble before 1860; scarlet.
	Compactum Multiflorum			white, pink flushed.
	Compeer			cultivated Noble 1850; purplish rose.
	Compton's Brow		cl.	'Magnificum' x 'Pink Pearl'; (C.B.van Nes & Sons before 1922); bright rosy pink, buds deep red.
	Compton's Scarlet		cl.	(J.Waterer); intense scarlet.
	Comte Cavour			cultivated Standish & Noble before 1870; plum color.
	Comte de Gomer		cl.	(J.Waterer); white, edged crimson.
	Comtesse de Morello		cl.	(Standish); rose.
	Concessum	A		(J. Byls before 1867); bright rose, light center.
	Concessum's Master	A	cl.	pink, darker edge.
	Conchiflorum Striatum			(Standish 1862); pale rose with numerous splashes and spots.
xx H-2	Conemaugh		g.	racemosum x mucronulatum; (Gable 1934); pink.

xx H-2 Conestoga g. carolinianum x racemosum; (Gable 1934); pink.
xx H-2 Conewago g. carolinianum x mucronulatum; (Gable 1934); rose magenta.
Conewingo g. haematodes x diphrocalyx; (Gable 1934).
Coneygar cl. 'Decsoul' x thomsonii; (Digby, registered 1955).
Coney Gar g. souliei x 'Loder's White'; (Digby 1951).
Confection cl. 'Corona' x 'Dondis'; (R. Henny); rose madder (H.C.C. 23/2); P.A. (A.R.S.) 1956.
Congestum Aureum yellow.
Congestum Roseum (J. Waterer before 1875); light rose, spotted.
Conical Kate A (J. Waterer ?); clear rosy crimson, yellow blotch.
Conoco-cheague g. catawbiense x haematodes; (Gable 1934).
Conqueror 'Duchess of Connaught' x javanicum; scarlet; F.C.C. 1884.
Conroy g. cinnabarinum var. roylei x concatenans; (Aberconway).
Conroy cl. cinnabarinum var. roylei x concatenans; (Aberconway 1937); light orange (H.C.C. 12/2) with a rosy tinge; A.M. (R.H.S.) 1950.
Conspicua Purpurea Syn. of 'Arborea Purpurea'.
Conspicuum cultivated Noble 1850; crimson, black spots.
Constance g. (arboreum var. album x griffithianum) x auriculatum; (Rothschild 1936); white
Constance Carson cl. pale pink, yellow mark.
Constance Terry cl. deep pink, fimbriated.
Constant Nymph B cl. campanulatum x 'Purple Splendour'; (Knap Hill Nursery 1955); very pale blush. Syn. 'Donum'.
Constellation cultivated Noble 1850; deep rose.
Conyan cl. concatenans x concinnum; (Stevenson 1953).
Coombe Royal g. griffithianum x ; delicate pink spotted brown on upper segment; A.M. (R.H.S.) 1900.
Copelia cl. bullatum x leucaspis; (Adams-Acton 1942); yellow.
Coplen's White cl. catawbiense x ; (Coplen-Gable); white.
Copper cl. clone of R. concatenans (L. & S. 6560); (Ingram); chinese coral (H.C.C. 614/1); suffused with shades of red and orange; A.M. (R.H.S.) 1954.
Cora g. 'Eudora' x 'Coreta'; (Aberconway 1946); red.
Coral cl. (neriiflorum x dichroanthum) x discolor F_2 ;(Ostbo); orange red; P.A. (A.R.S.) 1956.
Coralia cl. 'Loderi Pink Diamond' x 'Cornish Cross' (Ruthelma g.); (Sir E. Loder); salmon. Previously known as Ruthelma var. Coralia.
Coral Island cl. elliottii x 'Fabia'; (R.H.S. Gardens, Wisley, 1954).
Coral Reef cl. 'Fabia' x 'Goldsworth Orange' (Gloriana g.); (R.H.S. Gardens, Wisley); salmon pink fringed by rose at the margins and slightly tinged apricot at throat, upper lobe spotted apricot; A.M. (R.H.S.) 1954. Previously known as Gloriana var. Coral Reef.
Coral Star cl. white, edged pink.
Cordan g. 'Dante' x 'Coreta'; (Aberconway 1946); deep red.
Cordelia g. 'Arthur Osborne' x 'Loderi King George'; (Aberconway 1950); red.
Coreno g. 'Eupheno' x 'Coreta'; (Aberconway 1946); crimson.
Coresia g. 'Penjerrick' x 'Cornish Cross'; (Aberconway 1933); pale pink.
Coreta g. Loderi g. x zeylanicum; (Aberconway).
Coreta cl. Loderi g. x zeylanicum; (Aberconway 1935); deep crimson scarlet; F.C.C. (R.H.S.) 1935.
Coreum g. 'Cornish Cross' x arboreum; (Aberconway 1950); deep red.
Coriaceum arboreum var. album x caucasicum; (Standish & Noble 1850); white with green spots, fine foliage.
Corine cultivated Standish & Noble before 1860; white with yellow spots.
Corinne cl. 'Vulcan' selfed; (Lem-McClure); pink; petaloid stamens.
Corma g. 'Choremia' x chaetomallum; (Aberconway 1950); dark red.
Cornell Pink cl. mucronulatum form; (Skinner).
Cornish Cracker cl. campylocarpum x 'Dr. Stocker' (Damaris g.); (Harrison 1956).
Cornish Cream g. campylocarpum x 'Fortorb'; exhibited Bolitho 1937.
xxx H-4 Cornish Cross *** C g. thomsonii x griffithianum; (S. Smith); rose pink. See 'Exbury Cornish Cross', 'Pengaer'.
Cornish Early Red Syn. of 'Russellianum'.
Cornish Glow Lanarth hybrid x Lanarth hybrid; crimson in bud changing to orange yellow when open, flushed on outer lobes with rosy orange; A.M. (R.H.S.) 1947.
Cornish Loderi discolor x griffithianum; (J.C. Williams); nearly white.
Cornsutch g. 'Cornubia' x sutchuenense; (Magor 1926); carmine purple with dark blotch. See 'Almondtime' A.M. 1925).
xx H-5 Cornubia g. arboreum x 'Shilsonii'; (Barclay Fox).
Cornubia *** C cl. arboreum x 'Shilsonii' (Barclay Fox); A.M. (R.H.S.) 1912.
Coromandel cl. 'Roberte' x 'Vanessa'; (Sunningdale 1957).
xxx H-3 Corona ****B cl. (J. Waterer); coral pink or carmine pink; A.M. (R.H.S.) 1911.
Coronation g. 'Ernest Gill' x 'Kewense': R. Gill exhibited 1937.
Coronation Day ** C cl. 'Pink Shell' x Loderi g.; (Crosfield 1937); china rose (H.C.C. 24/1) with dark crimson blotch in throat; A.M. (R.H.S.) 1949.
Coronet g. 'Corona' x wardii; exhibited Wallace 1937. See 'Freckle Face', 'Panther'.
Coronis g. 'Corona' x Loderi g.; (Aberconway 1933); rose.
Corrector cl. rosy crimson, dark spots.

		Correggio			cl.	cultivated Standish & Noble before 1860; dark scarlet.
		Corros			g.	'Eros' x 'Cornish Cross' (Aberconway 1946); red.
x	H-4	Corry Koster	*	B	cl.	caucasicum x; (M. Koster & Sons 1909); light pink spotted crimson, fimbriated.
		Corsa			g.	'Choremia' x sanguineum; (Aberconway 1946); blood red.
		Cos			cl.	decorum x 'Vanessa'; registered Sunningdale Nurseries 1955; pale ivory, deepening to pale yellow in the throat, faintly spotted claret.
		Cosima			cl.	catawbiense x; (Seidel); red, yellow markings, frilled.
		Cotillon			cl.	'Fabia' x 'Naomi'; (R. Henny 1959); Mars orange (H.C.C. 013/3) inside, jasper red (H.C.C. 018/2) outside; low growing.
		Cotton Candy			cl.	'Marinus Koster' x (Loderi g.) 'Venus'; (Henny & Winnekamp 1958); pink.
		Cotterill			cl.	deep coral, fimbriated and blotched.
		Countess			cl.	delicate shell pink
		Countess de Morello				exhibited Standish 1861; soft rose, wavy edges.
		Countess Fitzwilliam			cl.	(Fisher, Son & Sibray); carmine rose, dark spots.
x	H-3	Countess of Athlone	*	B	cl.	'Geoffry Millais' x 'Catawbiense Grandiflorum'; (C. B. van Nes & Sons 1923); mauve.
		Countess of Beauchamp			cl.	blush, crimson blotch.
		Countess of Cadogan			cl.	(J. Waterer); pale pink
		Countess of Clancarty			cl.	(J. Waterer); light rosy crimson.
xx	H-3	Countess of Derby	***	B	cl.	'Pink Pearl' x 'Cynthia'; (White of Sunningdale 1913); pale rosy crimson fading to a pale pink, carmine spotting at base; A.M. (R.H.S.) 1930.
		Countess of Donoughmore			cl.	(Fischer); light center, bright pink margin.
xx	H-5	Countess of Haddington	**	F	cl.	ciliatum x dalhousiae; light pink flowers with yellow-brown markings, white flushed rose; F.C.C. 1862.
		Countess of Headfort			cl.	(J. Waterer); lilac rose, spotted.
		Countess of Ilchester			cl.	(J. Waterer); pale center, scarlet edge.
		Countess of Normanton			cl.	(J. Waterer before 1908); pale mauve fading to white, darker margin.
xx	H-5	Countess of Sefton	*	F		edgeworthii x 'Multiflorum'; (Davies 1877); exhibited 1950; white.
		Countess of Tankerville			cl.	(J. Waterer before 1922); delicate rose.
		Countess of Wharnclyffe			cl.	(Fisher, Son & Sibray); crimson.
		Countess of Wilton				(Rollison before 1874); rosy crimson.
		Cowbell			g.	ciliatum x bullatum; (Rothschild 1935); white.
		Cowslip			g.	williamsianum x wardii; (Aberconway).
		Cowslip			cl.	williamsianum x wardii; (Aberconway 1937); pale primrose, diffused pale pink or cream flushed pink; A.M. (R.H.S.) 1937.
xxx	H-4	C.P. Raffill			g.	'Britannia' x griersonianum; (at Kew); exhibited 1949; deep orange red.
		Cranbourne			cl.	'Azor' x 'Isabella'; (Crown Estate Commissioners, Windsor, Berks.) tyrian rose (H.C.C. 24/2), large red blotch in throat and reddish brown spotting on upper lobes; A.M. (R.H.S.) 1957.
		Cream Cheese			cl.	decorum x 'Margaret Dunn'; (Sunningdale Nurseries 1955) cream, banded pale pink fading white.
		Cream Cracker			cl.	campylocarpum x 'Dr. Stocker' (Damaris g.) (Harrison 1956).
		Cream Trumpet			cl.	(dalhousiae x nuttallii) (Victorianum g.)(before 1879); white, marked orange in throat; F.C.C.(R.H.S.) 1958.
		Creeping Jenny			cl.	griersonianum x forrestii var. repens, (Aberconway); red.
		Cremorne			g.	'Luscombei' x campylocarpum; (Rothschild).
		Cremorne			cl.	'Luscombei' x campylocarpum; (Rothschild); rose pink changing to soft yellow; A.M. (R.H.S.) 1947. See 'Townhill Cremorne'.
		Cresca			g.	(Aberconway 1934).
		Crest	****	C	cl.	wardii x 'Lady Bessborough' (Hawk g.); (Rothschild); yellow flowered, primrose yellow (H.C.C. 601/2-601/3) with slight darkening around the throat; F.C.C. (R.H.S.) 1953. Previously known as Hawk var. Crest.
		Cretonne			cl.	'Barclayi' x Loderi g.; (Loder); white, the lobes stained within and without rose bengal (H.C.C. 25/2); A.M. (R.H.S.) 1940.
		Crimson Banner			cl.	'Dr. Stocker' x thomsonii (Asteroid g.); (Sunningdale Nurseries 1934). Previously known as Asteroid var. Crimson Banner.
		Crimson Star			cl.	'Britannia' x 'Unknown Warrior'; (Hardgrove); exhibited 1951.
		Crossbill	**	C	g.	spinuliferum x lutescens; (J.C.Williams 1933); yellow, tinged red.
		Crown Prince			cl.	(J. Waterer); rose, yellow blotch, large truss.
		Crown Princess of Germany				brookeanum var. gracile x 'Princess Royal'; exhibited Veitch 1891; yellow.

		Cruentum			cl.	(A.Waterer before 1875); crimson lake.
		C.S. Sargent			cl.	catawbiense x ; (A.Waterer 1888); red.
		Cunninghamii				maximum x arboreum var. cinnamomeum; (Cunningham 1850); white, purple spots, brownish felt on underside of leaves. Believed not now in cultivation.
		Cunningham's Blush			cl.	(Cunningham); blush.
xx	H-3	Cunningham's Sulphur	**	B	cl.	(Cunningham); probably merely a variety of caucasicum; yellowish.
x	H-2	Cunningham's White		A	cl.	caucasicum x ponticum var. album; (Comely Bank, 1830); white, greenish yellow blotch.
		Cupid			g.	griffithianum x 'Luscombei'; (Johnstone 1926).
		Cupreum				coppery orange, suffused pink.
		Curig			g.	a cross of 'Dr. Stocker'; (Ingram 1939).
		Currieanum				(A.Waterer); dark purple or rosy lilac.
		Curtisii				form of multicolor (from Sumatra); crimson; F.C.C. 1883.
		Cutie			cl.	calostrotum ? x ?; phlox purple (H.C.C. 632/2); P.A., (A.R.S.) 1959.
		Cyaneum				(M. Young); purplish lilac.
		Cyclamen			cl.	'Earl of Athlone' x lacteum; (Horlick); violet cyclamen.
		Cyclops			g.	'F. C. Puddle' x 'Neriihaem'; (Aberconway 1941); red.
xx	H-2	Cynthia	**	B	cl.	catawbiense hybrid x griffithianum?; (Standish & Noble before 1870); rosy crimson. Syn. 'Lord Palmerston'.
		Cyrene				'Sir Charles Lemon' x lanatum; (Magor 1921); exhibited 1934; white with tinge of lemon.
		Czarina				'Princess Royal' x teysmannii; exhibited Veitch 1891; pale pinky yellow to orange.
		Dacia			g.	scyphocalyx x 'F.C.Puddle'; (Aberconway 1941); orange red.
		Dainty			g.	'May Day' x 'Elizabeth'; (Aberconway).
		Dainty			cl.	'May Day' x 'Elizabeth'; (Aberconway 1944); brilliant scarlet or currant red (H.C.C. 821); A.M. (R.H.S.) 1942; F.C.C. 1944.
xx	H-3	Dairy Maid	***	B	cl.	campylocarpum x ; (Slocock 1930) lemon primrose yellow tinged pink with pink blotch; A.M. (R.H.S.) 1934.
		Daisy			cl.	smirnowii x 'Mrs. Milner'; (Seidel cross 1902); bright carmine red.
		Daisy Rand			cl.	catawbiense x ; (Parsons); rose red.
		Dalbull			g.	dalhousiae x bullatum; (Magor 1936); white.
		(Dalmeny)				See 'Lady Rosebery Dalmeny'.
xxx	H 3	Damaris	***	C	g.	'Dr. Stocker' x campylocarpum; (Magor 1926); cream or biscuit colored or pale yellow. See 'Cornish Cracker', 'Cream Cracker', 'Logan Damaris', 'Townhill Damaris'.
		Damask			cl.	Loderi g. x eriogynum; bright rose pink; A.M. (R.H.S.) 1932.
xxx	H-3	Dame Nellie Melba	**	C	cl.	'Standishii' x arboreum; (Loder); bright pink with crimson dots; A.M. (R.H.S.) 1926.
		Damozel			g.	A.W. Bright Rose x griersonianum; (Rothschild).
		Damozel		B	cl.	A. W. Bright Rose x griersonianum; (Rothschild 1936); flowers deep rose pink with darker spotting; A.M. (R.H.S.) 1948.
		Dante				'Crown Princess of Germany' x javanicum; exhibited Veitch 1891.
		Dante			g.	dichroanthum x eriogynum; (Aberconway 1936); yellow to red orange or vermilion.
		Danube			cl.	concinnum x augustinii (Argiolus g.); (Aberconway 1950). Previously known as Argiolus var. Danube.
		Daphne			cl.	metternichii x ; (Seidel 1926); pure white spotted greenish yellow.
		Daphne				cultivated Standish & Noble before 1860; white with yellow spots.
		Daphne			cl.	'Red Admiral' x neriiflorum; (Magor 1928); bright crimson, hose-in-hose; A.M. (R.H.S.) 1933. See 'Eithne'.
		Daphne Daffarn			cl.	griffithianum x ; salmon rose.
		Daphne Millais			cl.	griffithianum x ; (Otto Schulz 1892, introduced C.B. van Nes & Sons 1896); deep pink, spotted, frilled.
		Daphnoides				virgatum x ; in cultivation T. Methven & Son, Edinburgh 1868-69; rosy lilac. Syn 'Coerulescens Daphnoides'.
		Darius			cl.	'Mrs. Milner' x smirnowii; (Seidel 1926); purplish red.
		Darlene			g.	griersonianum x 'Armistice Day'; (H. Lem, Seattle, Washington); bright red.
		Darwin			cl.	'Mrs. Lindsay Smith' x campylocarpum hybrid; (M. Koster & Sons, cross 1920); cream, brown blotch.
		Daubuzzi				griffithianum x ?; yellowish rose fading to pale pink. Syn. 'Dickson's Aucklandii'?.
xxx	H-3	David	***	B	cl.	'Hugh Koster' x neriiflorum; (Swaythling); deep blood red, slightly spotted on upper side within; F.C.C. (R.H.S.) 1939; A.M. (Wisley Trials) 1957.
		David Copperfield				cultivated Noble in 1850; rose, peach center.
		David Gable			cl.	'Atrosanguineum' x fortunei; (Gable 1960); pink, spotted throat, early; (formerly 'Pink No. 1'); A.E., (A.R.S.) 1960.
		Dawn	***	C	cl.	griffithianum x ; (Waterer, Sons & Crisp); white flushed phlox pink (H.C.C. 625/2); A.M. (R.H.S.) 1950.
xx	H-3	Dawn's Delight	***	C	cl.	griffithianum x ; (Mangles); white flowers tinged rose pink, spotted dark crimson with base of corolla bright crimson; A.M. (R.H.S.) 1911.

xxx	H-4	Day Dream	**	C	g.	'Lady Bessborough' x griersonianum; (Rothschild); deep crimson flushed and shaded without geranium lake, fading to very pale ; A.M. (R.H.S.) 1940.
		Debbie			cl.	'May Day' x 'Carmen'; (J. Henny-Prentice?).
		Decauck			g.	decorum x griffithianum; (Magor 1912); white.
		Deception				Azaleodendron; catawbiense x Ghent yellow Azalea; (Standish & Noble 1850); pink, spotted.
		Decora			g.	'Radiance' x Loderi g. ; (Aberconway 1946) pink.
		Decorator			cl.	(J. Waterer); scarlet with dark spots.
		Decsoul			cl.	decorum x souliei; (Whitaker); rosy in bud paling to almost pure white when expanded; A.M. (R.H.S.) 1937.
		Defiance			cl.	in cultivation in nursery of T. Methven & Son, Edinburgh 1868; light rose, dark spots.
		Degram			cl.	(decorum x griersonianum x 'America'; (Gable); exhibited 1946; apricot pink.
		Del			cl.	'Fabia' x wardii; (C. Thompson, 1958); amaranth rose (H.C.C. 530/1) shading white to center, chartreuse-spotted blotch.
		Delaware			cl.	pubescens x keiskei; (Nearing); apricot, fading to white; exhibited 1950.
		Delicatissimum				catawbiense x ; (J. Waterer before 1851); white tinged pale lilac.
		Delicatum				cultivated Standish & Noble before 1860; French white with maroon spots.
		Delicatum Aureum				blush pink with large blotch of orange spots.
		Delight			cl.	ciliatum x 'Praecox'; (R.Gill & Son); similar to R. ciliatum but smaller; A.M. (R.H.S.) 1929.
		Delila			cl.	smirnowii x 'Mrs. Milner'; (Seidel cross 1902); glowing red with dark markings.
		Delius			g.	'Ouida' x elliottii; (Aberconway).
		Delius			cl.	'Ouida' x elliottii; (Aberconway 1936); blood red (H.C.C. 820/3) shaded with carmine (H.C.C. 21); A.M. (R.H.S.) 1942.
		Dencombe			cl.	griersonianum x Loderi g. (Sarita Loder g.); (Loder); shrimp color. Previously known as Sarita Loder var. Dencombe.
		Denisonii			g.	dalhousiae x (edgeworthii x 'Gibsonii'); pure white flowers with lemon stain at base; F.C.C. 1862.
		Desiderius			cl.	'Mrs. Milner' x smirnowii; (Seidel cross 1902); bright carmine with lighter edges.
		Desna			g.	'Medusa' x griersonianum; (Aberconway 1946); orange red.
		Detonhaem			g.	detonsum x haematodes; (Magor 1932).
		Devagilla			g.	discolor x 'Cornubia'; (Rothschild 1936); rosy pink.
		Devaluation			g.	auriculatum x arboreum; (Rothschild 1936); white flushed pink.
xx	H-3	Devonshire Cream	**	B	cl.	A.W.Hardy Hybrid x campylocarpum; (W.C.Slocock about 1924); creamy yellow, red blotch at base; A.M. (R.H.S.) 1940.
		Dexter No. 9			cl.	fortunei x ?; (Farquhar-Dexter); pale peach-pink. Introduced by Warren Baldsiefen. Syn. 'Skyglow'.
		Dexter's Favorite			cl.	fortunei x ?; (Dexter); pale pink, greenish yellow center.
		Diadem				(T. Methven & Son, Edinburgh before 1892); white with brown blotch.
		Diadem				'Duchess of Edinburgh' x javanicum; pink, dwarf, or scarlet crimson; F.C.C. 1896.
		Diamond				brilliant scarlet; A.M. 1896.
		Diana			cl.	cultivated Standish & Noble before 1860; white with red spots.
xxx	H-3	Diane	***	B	cl.	'Mrs. Lindsay Smith' x campylocarpum hybrid; (M.Koster & Sons cross 1920); creamy white shaded primrose yellow in center; A. M. (Wisley Trials) 1948.
		Diane Titcomb			cl.	'Marinus Koster' x 'Snow Queen'; (Larson); white, edged pink; exhibited 1942.
		Dichaites			cl.	dichroanthum x neriiflorum var. euchaites; exhibited Digby 1953.
		Dicharb			g.	dichroanthum x arboreum; (Magor 1936); apricot.
		Dichdiap			g.	dichroanthum x diaprepes; (Magor 1938).
		Dichrofab			cl.	dichroanthum x 'Fabia'; (Reuthe 1940); rich orange.
		Dickson's Aucklandii				Syn. of 'Daubuzzi'; also syn. of 'Caerhays'.
		Dictator			cl.	(J. Waterer before 1875); dark crimson with a cluster of dark spots.
x	H-4	Dido	*	B	g.	dichroanthum x decorum; (Wilding 1934); orange yellow.
		Dietrich			cl.	'Mrs. Milner' x smirnowii; (Seidel cross 1952); carmine rose.
		Dignity			g.	'Glory of Leonardslee' x thomsonii; (Aberconway 1950); rose red.
		Dimidiatum			g.	callimorphum x neriiflorum; a natural hybrid.
		Dimity			g.	'F.C.Puddle x 'Penjerrick'; (Aberconway 1946); pale rose.
		Diogenes			g.	grande, red form x calophytum; (Rothschild 1936); pink with dark blotch.
		Dione			g.	neriiflorum x 'Cornsutch'; (Magor 1936); carmine lake.
		Diphole Pink	*	B	cl.	griffithianum x ; (J. Waterer, Son & Crisp Ltd.); deep rose pink or cerise pink faintly spotted brown; A.M. (R.H.S.) 1916.
		Directeur Moerlands			cl.	catawbiense x ; H. den Ouden & Son); crimson.
		Direcktor E. Hjelm				2nd generation fortunei hybrid; (D.A.Koster); dark carmine rose, bronze blotch.
		Disca			cl.	discolor x 'Caroline'; (Gable); white; exhibited 1944.
		Distinction			cl.	campanulatum x ; in cultivation in nursery of T. Methven 1868; pale lavender or light rosy crimson.
xx	H-4	Diva			g.	'Ladybird' x griersonianum; (Rothschild).
		Diva	*	C	cl.	'Ladybird' x griersonianum; (Rothschild 1937); carmine scarlet, spotted brownish within; A.M. (R.H.S.) 1937.

Doll — cl. 'Corona' x 'Dondis'; (R. Henny).

x H-5 Dolly — g. 'Dawn's Delight' x griersonianum; (Rothschild 1940); flowers rich pink flushed externally cherry red.

Domino — g. 'Barclayi' x 'Dignity'; (Aberconway 1950); red.

(Don, The) — See 'The Don'.

Donald Waterer — A cl. 'Alice' x 'Gomer Waterer'; (J. Waterer Son & Crisp Ltd.); deep rose pink fading in center; A.M. (R.H.S.) 1916.

Donar — cl. 'Jay Gould' x smirnowii; (Seidel cross 1902); light crimson with white edges and dark markings.

Dona Tizia — cl. griffithianum x 'Doncaster'; (Lowinsky); pale pink fading to white and deeper pink outside, pedicles bright red; A.M. (R.H.S.) 1921.

xx H-3 Doncaster ** B cl. arboreum x ; (A. Waterer); vivid crimson scarlet, rather dwarf.

Dondis — g. discolor x 'Doncaster'; (Kew Gardens).

Don Ernesto — cl. griffithianum x 'Doncaster' (The Don g.); (Lowinsky); rich rosy scarlet; A.M. (R.H.S.) 1920. Previously known as The Don var. Don Ernesto.

Donna Anita — cl. griffithianum x 'Doncaster' (The Don g.); (Lowinsky); shell pink; A.M. (R.H.S.) 1920. Previously known as The Don var. Donna Anita.

Donna Florenza — cl. griffithianum x 'Doncaster'; (The Don g.); (Lowinsky); deep rich rose; A.M. (R.H.S.) 1920. Previously known as The Don var. Donna Florenza.

Donum — campanulatum x 'Purple Splendour'; (Knap Hill Nursery cross 1931, introduced 1955); now called 'Constant Nymph' and on trial at Wisley.

Dora Amateis — cl. carolinianum x ciliatum; (Amateis 1955); white, lightly spotted green.

Dorcas — g. 'Bagshot Ruby' x discolor; (Rothschild 1936); rose pink.

Dorinthia — g. griersonianum x 'Hiraethlyn'; (Aberconway).

Dorinthia — cl. griersonianum x 'Hiraethlyn'; (Aberconway 1938); clear shiny red with deep wavy lobes; F.C.C. (R.H.S.) 1938.

Doris Caroline — cl. Loderi g. x 'Lady Bligh'; (R. Henny, 1960); tyrian rose (H.C.C. 24/3); P.A., (A.R.S.) 1960.

Dormouse — g. 'Dawn's Delight' x williamsianum; (Rothschild 1936); rich pink.

Dorothea ** C cl. griffithianum x decorum; (Lowinsky 1925); white with green center, sweet scented; A.M. (R.H.S.) 1925.

Dorothy Fortescue — cl. (J. Waterer before 1922); dark cherry red.

Dortmund B g. souliei x wardii, Hu 14657; (Dietrich Hobbie 1953); bright yellow flushed delicate rose.

Dot — cl. 'Mrs. Lindsay Smith' x fortunei; (Swaythling 1945); white; A.M. (R.H.S.) 1945.

Dot — Azaleodendron; rose crimson.

Douglas McEwan — cl. griffithianum hybrid x 'Monsieur Thiers'; (C.B. van Nes & Sons); rosy red.

Dragon — cl. 'F.C. Puddle' x haematodes; (Aberconway 1941). See 'Phoebus'.

Dragonfly — g. facetum x auriculatum; (Rothschild 1936); carmine red.

xxx H-3 Dr. A. Blok ** B 'Pink Pearl' x catawbiense; (L. Endtz & Co.); light rose, lighter center; A.M. (R.H.S.) 1937. Syn. 'Dr. O. Blok'. See 'Dr. Arnold W. Endtz'.

xx H-3 Dr. Arnold W. Endtz * B cl. 'Pink Pearl' x catawbiense; (L. Endtz & Co.); carmine, fimbriated; exhibited 1927. See 'Dr. A. Blok'.

Dr. C.H. Felix — cl. 'Marion' x 'Prof. C.S. Sargeant'; (Felix & Dykhuis 1951); fuchsine pink.

Dr. Ferguson — cl. (T. Methven & Son, Edinburgh); reddish purple.

o H-2 Dr. H.C. Dresselhuys — cl. 'Atrosanguineum' x 'Doncaster'; (H. den Ouden & Son 1920); aniline red. See 'Dr. H.J. Lovink'.

Dr. H.C. Karl Förster B g. 'Linswegeanum' x williamsianum; (Dietrich Hobbie 1952); deep rose to bright scarlet.

o H-2 Dr. H.J. Lovink — cl. 'Atrosanguineum' x 'Doncaster'; (H. den Ouden & Son 1929); aniline red. See 'Dr. H.C. Dresselhuys'.

Dr. Hogg — (before 1875); dark red.

Dr. Hooker — cl. cultivated Standish & Noble before 1860; rosy purple, white throat.

Dr. J. Hutchinson — g. taggianum x nuttallii; Clarke exhibited 1942.

Dr. Masters ** A cl. Azaleodendron; 'Prince Camille de Rohan' or 'Leopold' x japonicum; (G. Vander Meulen 1892); pink tinged lilac.

Dr. Mill — (Mr. Otto Schulz, Royal Porcelain Factory, Berlin, 1890); purchased by C.B. van Nes & Sons in 1896.

Dr. Muller — (Standish 1862); deep rose.

Dr. O. Blok — cl. Syn. of 'Dr. A. Blok'.

Dr. Ross — cl. griersonianum x 'Borde Hill'; (R. Henny); red.

Dr. S. Endtz — cl. rosy crimson. Syn. of 'Souvenir de Dr. S. Endtz'.

xxx H-4 Dr. Stocker ** C cl. caucasicum x griffithianum; (North); milky ivory, spotted lemon brown at base upper segment; A.M. (R.H.S.) 1900.

Dr. Torrey — cl. catawbiense x.

x H-2 Dr. V. H. Rutgers — cl. 'Charles Dickens' x 'Lord Roberts'; (H. den Ouden & Son 1925); aniline red, fringed.

Dr. W. F. Wery — cl. 'Queen Wilhelmina' x 'Stanley Davies'; (C.B. van Nes & Sons); scarlet red.

Dream Girl — g. 'Day Dream' x 'Margaret Dunn'; (L.E. Brandt).

Dream Girl — cl. 'Day Dream' x 'Margaret Dunn'; (L.E. Brandt, Tacoma); orange buff, throat blood red; exhibited 1953. See 'Gold Mohur', 'Mohur', 'Ophir'.

Dresden China — cl. ciliatum x 'Sesterianum'; (Harrison, cross 1952); white.

	Name	Rating	Class	Type	Description
	Drum Major			g.	arboreum x griersonianum; (Rothschild 1936); bright red.
	Drusilla			g.	'Essex Scarlet' x campylocarpum; (Rothschild 1936); pink.
	Dryad			g.	forrestii var. repens x hookeri; (Aberconway 1946); deep red.
	Dryope			cl.	'Latona' x 'May Day'; (Sunningdale Nurseries 1955); deep rose flushed coral red.
	Duchess of Bedford			cl.	(J. Waterer before 1922); deep rose with light marking.
	Duchess of Buccleuch			cl.	(T. Methven & Son, Edinburgh); crimson.
	Duchess of Cambridge				(J. Waterer); cerise.
	Duchess of Connaught	*	A	cl.	brookeanum var. gracile x lobbii; (J. Mason before 1892); bright scarlet crimson; F.C.C. 1881. See 'Duchess of Edinburgh'.
	Duchess of Cornwall			cl.	(R. Gill & Son); pink or salmon pink.
	Duchess of Edinburgh			cl.	brookeanum var. gracile x lobbii; (J. Waterer); light crimson, lighter center; F.C.C. 1874. See 'Duchess of Connaught'.
	Duchess of Fife			cl.	'Princess Royal' x teysmannii; large, cream color with pale red flush; A.M. 1889
	Duchess of Northumberland			cl.	(J. Waterer?); white.
	Duchess of Portland		B	cl.	barbatum x 'Handsworth Early White'; (Fisher Son & Sibray); pure white; A.M. (R.H.S.) 1903.
	Duchess of Sutherland				(J. Waterer before 1868); white or pale rose slightly spotted with margin of rosy lilac.
	Duchess of Teck	*	A	cl.	(Waterer, Sons & Crisp 1892); white deeply edged rosy mauve, bronze blotch; A.M. (R.H.S.) 1916.
	Duchess of York		B	cl.	fortunei x 'Scipio'; (G. Paul); salmon pink with green spots; A.M. (R.H.S.) 1894.
	Duet			cl.	catawbiense var. album x (dichroanthum x(griffithianum x auriculatum)); (D.G. Leach 1960); yellow, lobes edged clear bright pink; green blotch in throat.
	Duke of Cornwall			g.	arboreum x barbatum; (R. Gill & Son).
	Duke of Cornwall			cl.	arboreum x barbatum; (R. Gill & Son); crimson; A.M. (R.H.S.) 1907. See 'Trelawny', 'John Holms'.
	Duke of Malakoff			cl.	cultivated Standish & Noble before 1860; blush, large blotch of red.
	Duke of Norfolk			cl.	(before 1871); rose.
	Duke of Portland			cl.	(J. Waterer before 1875); bright scarlet, paler center.
	Duke of Teck			cl.	brookeanum var. gracile x 'Princess Royal'; (J. Waterer before 1875); rosy lilac.
	Duke of York		B	cl.	fortunei x 'Scipio'; (Paul); rosy pink with cream spots; A.M. 1894.
	Dulcibella			g.	'Diphole Pink' x eriogynum; (Rothschild 1936); bright pink.
	Dulcie Daffarn				griffithianum x ; (Mangles, Littleworth); pink.
	Duleep Singh			cl.	(J. Waterer); chocolate crimson.
	Dunlin			g.	'Dawn's Delight' x thomsonii; (Rothschild 1936); rosy red.
	Duque de San Lucar				'Marion' x 'Prof. C.S. Sargent'; (Felix & Dykhuis); pure pink.
	Dusky Maid			g.	'Moser's Maroon' x discolor; (Rothschild 1936); dark red.
xxx H-4	Earl of Athlone	***	C	cl.	'Queen Wilhelmina' x 'Stanley Davies'; (C.B. van Nes & Sons); bright blood red; F.C.C. (R.H.S.) 1933.
	Earl of Donoughmore	*	B	cl.	griersonianum x (hardy garden hybrid x 'Mrs. L. A. Dunnett'); (M. Koster & Sons 1953); bright red, orange glow.
	Earl of Haddington			cl.	(J. Waterer); clear rose.
	Earl of Morley			g.	campylocarpum x arboreum var. album; (Loder). See 'Leonardslee Primrose'.
	Earl of Selkirk			cl.	(T. Methven & Son); crimson.
	Earl of Shannon			cl.	(J. Waterer before 1867); deep crimson.
	Earlybird			cl.	williamsianum x fargesii; (R. Henny, 1959); rose madder (H.C.C. 23/1), almost white in center; very early.
	Early Brilliant			g.	'Ascot Brilliant' x barbatum; (W.C. Slocock); bright red. ? Syn. of 'Fireball' (R. Gill).
	(Early Dawn)				See 'Naomi Early Dawn'.
	Early Gem			cl.	Praecox g. x dauricum; rosy lilac; F.C.C. 1874.
	Early Stir			g.	strigillosum x irroratum; (Digby 1934); currant red.
	Easter Egg			g.	fulgens x neriiflorum; (Rothschild 1937); blood red.
	East Knoyle			cl.	griersonianum x Loderi g.; (Horlick 1930); rose.
	Echo			cl.	decorum x 'Lady Bessborough'; (Sunningdale 1955); pale cream, fading white, claret eye.
	(Eclipse)				See 'Jalisco Eclipse'.
	Ed. de Concourt			cl.	(Moser); pink.
	Edgar Stead			cl.	'Ilam Alarm' x 'Shilsonii'; (Stead).
	Edinense				nuttallii x dalhousiae; white, yellowish base.
	Edith	**	B	cl.	discolor x ; (Slocock); rich pink with carmine spots; similar to 'Alice Martineau' but richer rosy crimson, dark blotch; A.M. (R.H.S.) 1931.
	Edith A. Boulton			g.	fortunei x 'Meteor'; (at R.B.G. Kew); exhibited Kew Gardens 1894.
	Edith Berkeley			cl.	sanguineum x (auriculatum x 'Loderi King George'); (Greig).

x	H-4	Edith Mackworth Praed		cl.	'Doncaster' x; (M. Koster & Sons); bright crimson or cherry scarlet; A.M. (R.H.S.) 1934.
		Edith Preston			griffithianum x ; (Mangles).
		Edmondi		g.	arboreum x barbatum; (R. Gill 1876); orange scarlet.
		Edna McCarty		cl.	'Alice' x auriculatum #70; (Ostbo, 1959); white; P.A. (A.R.S.) 1959, as 'Lily No. 3'.
		Edouard André		cl.	Azaleodendron; 'Prince Camille de Rohan' or 'Leopard' x japonicum; (G. Van der Meulen 1892); creamy white.
		Edusa		g.	'Penjerrick' x campylocarpum; (Aberconway 1933); yellow.
		Edward Dunn		cl.	discolor x (dichroanthum x neriiflorum); (Endre Ostbo); apricot.
o	H-2	Edward S. Rand		cl.	catawbiense x ; (A. Waterer 1870); crimson red, yellow eye.
		Effner		cl.	'Alfred' x 'Everestianum'?; (Seidel cross 1903); dark violet.
		Egyptian		cl.	'Halcyone' x 'Margaret Dunn'; (Sunningdale Nurseries 1955); yellow overlaid salmon, brown eye.
		E. H. Wilding		cl.	'Troas' x 'Penjerrick' (Adams-Acton 1942); blood red.
		Eidam		cl.	metternichii x 'Alexander Adie'; (Seidel cross 1903); white flushed rose.
		Eileen	** A	cl.	(Waterer, Sons & Crisp Ltd.); blush, pink edge, yellow blotch.
		Eithne		cl.	'Red Admiral' x neriiflorum (Daphne g.) (Magor 1937); deep crimson scarlet; A.M. (R.H.S.) 1937. Known previously as Daphne var. Eithne.
		E.J.P. Magor		g.	'Campdis' x williamsianum; (Dietrich Hobbie 1954); bright rose.
		El Alamein	* B		griffithianum x ; (Kluis 1946); dark blood red (cardinal red H.C.C. 822/1), conspicuous dark brown blotch.
xx	H-4	Eldorado		g.	valentinianum x johnstoneanum; (Rothschild 1937); yellow.
		Eleanore		g.	desquamatum x augustinii; (Rothschild).
		Eleanore	** C	cl.	desquamatum x augustinii; (Rothschild 1937); amethyst violet (H.C.C. 35/3); A.M. (R.H.S.) 1943.
		(Elect)			See 'Jalisco Elect'.
		Electra		g.	chasmanthum x augustinii; (Rothschild).
		Electra	*** C	cl.	chasmanthum x augustinii; (Rothschild); violet blue (lavender blue) a shade lighter than veronica violet (H.C.C. 639/1); and marked with greenish yellow blotches at back; A.M. (R.H.S.) 1940.
		Elegans		g.	'Altaclarense' x catawbiense; (Standish & Noble before 1850); deep rose, spotted.
		Elena		g.	cinnabarinum var. blandfordiaeflorum x yunnanense; (Rothschild 1937); primrose to white.
		Elfin		cl.	'Dr. Stocker' x orbiculare; (Horlick 1933); cream flushed pink.
		Elfrida			cultivated Standish & Noble before 1860; pale rose pink with large blotch or dark spots.
		Elie		cl.	pink catawbiense seedling x pink catawbiense seedling; (Shammarello); exhibited 1955; dark pink, yellowish blotch.
		Elisabetae			caucasicum x smirnowii; rose pink.
		Elisabeth Hobbie	B	g.	'Essex Scarlet' x forrestii var. repens; (Dietrich Hobbie 1945); translucent scarlet red (cinnabar carmine).
xxx	H-4	Elizabeth		g.	forrestii var. repens x griersonianum; (Aberconway).
		Elizabeth	****B	cl.	forrestii var. repens x griersonianum; (Aberconway 1939); deep red (H.C.C. 020); A.M. (R.H.S.) 1939; F.C.C. (R.H.S.) 1943.
		Elizabethae			falconeri x 'Elsae'; (Reuthe 1926); rose pink.
		Elizabeth Blackford		cl.	(Endre Ostbo).
		Ella		g.	'General Sir John Du Cane' x griffithianum; exhibited E. de Rothschild 1951.
		Ella		cl.	dichroanthum x wardii; (R. Henny).
		Ella		cl.	smirnowii x 'Mrs. Milner'; (Seidel cross 1903); carmine red.
		Ellestee		cl.	a superior form of R. wardii; (C. Ingram, 1959); clear yellow with deep crimson blotch; A.M. (R.H.S.) 1959.
		Elna		g.	'Etna' x elliottii; (Aberconway).
		Elna		cl.	'Etna' x elliottii; (Aberconway 1949); scarlet (H.C.C. 19/1) with pronounced spotting; A.M. (R.H.S.) 1949.
		Elrise		g.	elliottii x 'Sunrise'; (Aberconway 1950); red.
		Elros		g.	'Eros' x elliottii; (Aberconway).
		Elros		cl.	'Eros' x elliottii; (Aberconway 1945); salmon pink with scattered darker spotting towards base of petal; A.M. (R.H.S.) 1948.
		Elsa Crisp	** B	cl.	a seedling from 'Mrs. E.C. Stirling'?; (Waterer, Sons & Crisp); soft pink with deeper pink margin.
		Elsae		g.	grande x hodgsonii; (Reuthe).
		Elsae	*** E	cl.	grande x hodgsonii; (Reuthe); ivory white with crimson blotch at base: A.M. (R.H.S.) 1925. See 'Clyne Blush', 'Clyne Cerise', 'Clyne Elsae', 'Clyne Pearl'.
		Elsie Phipps		g.	souliei x 'Penjerrick'; (Aberconway 1941); pale yellow flushed pink.
		Elsie Waterer		cl.	(Waterer, Sons & Crisp Ltd.); white, dark red blotch.
		Elspeth		cl.	a hybrid of 'Halopeanum'; (R. Gill & Son); pure white.
xx	H-3	Elspeth	** B	cl.	campylocarpum x hardy hybrid; (Slocock); pink in bud opening pink center fading to apricot; A.M. (R.H.S.) 1937.
		Elspeth Slocock		cl.	Syn. of 'Elspeth' (Slocock).
		Elvira			cultivated Standish & Noble before 1860; white, rich yellow blotch.
		Elvus		g.	'Venus' x elliottii; (Aberconway 1946); red.

		Emasculum		B	cl.	ciliatum x dauricum; (Waterer); pale purple, rosy lilac; without stamens; taller and later than Praecox g.
		(Emblem)				See 'Jalisco Emblem'.
		Embley Blush			cl.	thomsonii x campylocarpum (Exminster g.); (J. J. Crosfield 1935). Known previously as Exminster var. Embley Blush.
		Embley Park			cl.	thomsonii x campylocarpum (Exminster g.); (J. J. Crosfield 1936); pale rose lobes and yellowish tinged tubes; A.M. (R.H.S.) 1936. Known previously as Exminster var. Embley Park.
		Embley Pink			cl.	thomsonii x campylocarpum (Exminster g.); (J.J. Crosfield 1930); rose; A.M. (R.H.S.) 1930. Known previously as Exminster var. Embley Pink.
		Emelie				rosy crimson.
		Emeline Buckley			cl.	'Bacchus' x griffithianum hybrid; (C. B. van Nes & Sons); bright pink, dark blotch.
		Emerald Isle			g.	'Idealist' x 'Naomi'; (R.H.S. Gardens, Wisley).
		Emerald Isle			cl.	'Idealist' x 'Naomi'; (R.H.S. Wisley 1956); chartreuse green (H.C.C. 663/1). with throat stained 663/2; A.M. (R.H.S.) 1956. See 'New Comet'.
		Emil			cl.	catawbiense x ; (Seidel cross 1903); pure white.
		Emilie				cultivated Standish & Noble before 1860; rosy crimson.
		Emily Mangles			cl.	griffithianum x ; (Mangles at Littleworth); pink with crimson blotch; Syn. 'Polly Peachum'.
		Eminent				cultivated Noble 1850; rosy lilac.
		Emma			cl.	catawbiense x ; (Seidel cross 1903); bright carmine rose with few dark markings.
		Emmeline			g.	'Essex Scarlet' x haematodes; (Rothschild 1937); red.
		Empereur de Maroc			cl.	brilliant purple.
		Empire Day			cl.	'Moser's Maroon' x griersonianum (Romany Chai g.); (Knap Hill Nursery Ltd.); blood red. Previously known as Romany Chai var. Empire Day.
		Empress				cultivated Noble 1850; purplish crimson.
		Empress				'Crown Princess of Germany' x javanicum; yellow to red orange; F.C.C. 1884.
		Empress Eugenie			cl.	creamy white, finely spotted.
		Ems		C	g.	forrestii var. repens x 'Purple Splendour'; (Dietrich Hobbie 1951); purple red.
		Enchantress				cultivated Standish & Noble before 1860; white, with yellow eye.
		Endeavour			g.	arboreum var. album x lacteum; (Rothschild 1937); white to pale primrose.
		Endre Ostbo			cl.	souliei x discolor; (E. Ostbo 1958); blush-pink, fading near-white, upper tube streaked rose at base; P.A. (A.R.S.) 1954.
		Endsleigh Pink	**	C	cl.	rosy pink.
		Endymion			g.	'Lord Milner' x hookeri; (Rothschild 1937); rich red.
		English Roseum			cl.	catawbiense x ; (A. Waterer); rose. Probably seedling of 'Roseum Elegans'.
		Eos			cl.	of the 4th generation of 4 species (javanicum, jasminiflorum, lobbii, malayanum); (Mr. Heale of Veitch of Chelsea 1900).
		Erasmus			cl.	(M. Koster & Sons); dark scarlet red.
x	H-4	Erebus			g.	'Fabia' x griersonianum; (Aberconway 1936); deep scarlet.
		Erectum				(Standish before 1860); rose crimson.
		Erestium				in cultivation by T. Methven 1868; purple.
		Erich			cl.	'Mrs. Milner' x catawbiense; (Seidel cross 1903); purple red.
		Eridusa			g.	'Medusa' x eriogynum; (Aberconway 1946); deep red.
		Erika			cl.	metternichii x ; (Seidel cross 1903); carmine rose.
		Eriozor			g.	'Azor' x eriogynum; (Aberconway 1946); red.
		Ermine			cl.	'Britannia' x 'Mrs. A.T. de la Mare'; (R. Henny 1959); pure white; late.
		Erna			cl.	smirnowii x 'Mrs. Milner'; (Seidel cross 1903); carmine.
x	H-3	Ernest Gill			cl.	fortunei x arboreum; (R. Gill & Son 1918); bright cerise pink with crimson blotch at base; A.M. (R.H.S.) 1918.
		Ernestine			g.	chartophyllum x cinnabarinum var. roylei; (Rothschild 1937); lilac pink.
		Eros			g.	'Amaura' x griersonianum; (Aberconway 1936); pale pink.
		Erso			g.	'Erebus' x souliei; (Aberconway 1946).
		Esmeralda			g.	'Loderi King George' x neriiflorum; (Rothschild 1937); pale pink to deep rosy pink.
		Esmerelda			cl.	(M. Koster & Sons); light pink, deeper colored margin.
		Esoteric			cl.	(G. O. Clark); deep pink.
		Esperanza			g.	barbatum x strigillosum; (Rothschild 1937); blood red.
		Esquire			cl.	chance seedling; (Barto-James).
xx	H-3	Essex Scarlet	*	B	cl.	(G. Paul 1899); deep crimson scarlet, blackish blotch; A.M. (R.H.S.) 1899.
		Estelka Gerster			cl.	lilac rose, primrose spot.
		Estelle Gatke			cl.	'Loderi Venus' x 'Tally Ho'; (R.M. Gatke).
		Esterel			g.	arboreum var. album x meddianum; (Rothschild 1937); rose pink.
		Etandard de Flandre				Syn. of 'Lady Dorothy Neville'.
		Ethel			g.	'F. C. Puddle' x forrestii var. repens; (Aberconway).
		Ethel			cl.	'F. C. Puddle' x forrestii var. repens; (Aberconway 1940); a rich shade of light crimson scarlet; F.C.C. (R.H.S.) 1940.
		Ethel Hall				(M. Koster & Sons); white interior, white stripes and scarlet edges.
		Ethelred			g.	'Gill's Crimson' x neriiflorum; (Rothschild 1937); crimson.
		Ethel Roupe			cl.	catawbiense x ; (Stokes).
		Ethel Stocker				deep pink, buds crimson.
		Ethyl			g.	campylocarpum x orbiculare; (Rothschild 1937); pink flushed cream.
		Etna			g.	'Vanessa' x 'Fabia'; (Aberconway 1936); magenta red.

		(Etna)			See 'Lady Chamberlain Etna'.
		Etos		g.	'Eros' x thomsonii; (Aberconway 1946); deep red.
		Etzel		cl.	'Everestianum' x 'Everestianum'; (Seidel cross 1903); purplish red.
		Eucamp			campylocarpum x 'Empress Eugenie'; (Magor cross 1918); cream.
		Euchelia		cl.	forrestii var. repens x ; (Aberconway 1935); fleshy, bright deep crimson or blood red; A.M. (R.H.S.) 1935.
		Euclid			cultivated Noble 1850; rosy red.
		Eudich		cl.	dichroanthum x neriiflorum var. euchaites; (Stevenson 1953).
		Eudora		g.	'Vanessa' x facetum; (Aberconway 1936); reddish scarlet.
		Eugenie			cultivated Standish & Noble before 1860; pure white, fine spots.
		(Eugenie)			See 'Mariloo Eugenie'.
		Euking			'Empress Eugenie' x 'Mrs. Kingsmill'; (Magor 1935); clear lemon yellow, faint red spotting.
		Eulo		g.	'Eudora' x Loderi g.; (Aberconway 1941); pale pink.
x	H-3	Eupheno		g.	sperabile x griersonianum; (Aberconway 1936); deep red.
		Euphrosyne		g.	arboreum x Loderi g.; (Rothschild).
		Euphrosyne		cl.	arboreum x Loderi g.; (Rothschild 1923); bright carmine pink, spotted small crimson dots; A.M. (R.H.S.) 1923. See 'Euphrosyne Ruby'.
		Euphrosyne Ruby		cl.	arboreum (blood red form) x Loderi g. (Euphrosyne g.); exhibited Sir E. Loder; rosy red. Previously known as Euphrosyne var. Ruby.
		Eureka		g.	arboreum x hookeri; (Rothschild).
		Eureka		cl.	arboreum x hookeri; (Rothschild 1939); blood red, speckled within; A.M. (R.H.S.) 1939.
		Europa		g.	ungernii x kyawi; (Rothschild 1937); rosy lilac.
		Euryalus		g.	'Nereid' x griersonianum; (Aberconway 1936); deep red.
		Eurydice		g.	arboreum var. album x Loderi g.; (Rothschild).
		Eurydice		cl.	arboreum var. album x Loderi g.; (Rothschild 1939); delicately tinged with pale rosy pink, crimson blotch within; A.M. (R.H.S.) 1939.
		Euterpe		cl.	exquisitum x augustinii; (Reuthe 1941); rose.
		Euthom		g.	'Empress Eugenie' x thomsonii; (Magor cross 1910); light shade of carmine shading into pink, copiously spotted with crimson.
		Evelyn		g.	'Moser's Rouge Macule Noir' x griffithianum; (Standish & Noble before 1860); (also Rothschild 1937); pure white.
		Evelyn		cl.	'Loderi Venus' x 'Britannia' ; (R. Henny).
		Evening		g.	hodgsonii x 'Muriel'; (Loder).
		Evening		cl.	hodgsonii x 'Muriel'; Loder 1950. See 'Haze', 'Mist'.
		Evening Glow		cl.	discolor x 'Fabia'; (van Veen).
		Evening Star			cultivated Standish & Noble before 1860; pure white, large dark eye.
		Eventide		g.	'Sunrise' x griersonianum; (Aberconway cross 1931, introduced 1941); pale pink rose.
x	H-2	Everestianum	* A	cl.	catawbiense x ; (A. Waterer before 1850); rosy lilac, frilled edges, spotted.
		Everitt's Hardy Mauve		cl.	fortunei x ; (Dexter-Everitt); mauve.
		Ewingii			in cultivation in nursery of T. Methven & Son, Edinburgh, in 1868; white, green eye, spotted.
		Exburiense	** C	g.	didymum x kyawi; (Rothschild 1937); very dark red bell-shaped flowers; late.
		Exbury Albatross		cl.	Loderi g. x discolor (Albatross g.); (Rothschild 1935); a delicate slightly bluish pink when open, brownish red markings on back of tube within; F.C.C. (R.H.S.) 1935. Formerly listed as Albatross Exbury var.
		Exbury Angelo	****C	cl.	griffithianum x discolor (Angelo g.); (Rothschild); white with green markings; F.C.C. (R.H.S.) 1947. Formerly listed as Angelo Exbury var.
		Exbury Antonio		cl.	'Gill's Triumph' x discolor (Antonio g.); (Rothschild); white with pink markings; A.M. (R.H.S.) 1939. Formerly listed as Antonio Exbury var.
		Exbury Calstocker		cl.	calophytum x 'Dr. Stocker' (Calstocker g.); (Rothschild); white, the base of the tube marked with a maroon blotch on upper petals; buds are pink; A.M. (R.H.S.) 1948. Formerly listed as Calstocker Exbury var.
		Exbury Cornish Cross		cl.	thomsonii x griffithianum (Cornish Cross g.); (Rothschild); uniform crimson, soft bloom outside and small dark nectar pouches at base; A.M. (R.H.S.) 1935. Formerly listed as Cornish Cross Exbury var.
		Exbury Fabia			dichroanthum x griersonianum (Fabia g.); (Rothschild); apricot yellow flushed salmon pink. Formerly listed as Fabia var. Exbury.
		Exbury Hawk		cl.	wardii x 'Lady Bessborough' (Hawk g.); (Rothschild 1949); clear yellow; A.M. (R.H.S.) 1949. Formerly listed as Hawk Exbury var.
		Exbury Isabella		cl.	auriculatum x griffithianum (Isabella g.); (Rothschild 1948); late, white. Formerly listed as Isabella Exbury var.
		Exbury Lady Chamberlain		cl.	cinnabarinum var. roylei x 'Royal Flush' (orange form) (Lady Chamberlain g.); (Rothschild); orange or yellow overlaid salmon orange; F.C.C. (R.H.S.) 1931. Formerly listed as Lady Chamberlain var. Exbury.
		Exbury Matador		cl.	griersonianum x strigillosum (Matador g.); (Rothschild); brilliant scarlet. Formerly known as Matador Exbury form.
		Exbury May Day		cl.	haematodes x griersonianum (May Day g.); (Rothschild); brilliant scarlet. Formerly known as May Day, Exbury form.
		Exbury Merlin		cl.	wardii x 'Lady Bessborough' (Hawk g.); (Rothschild); deep yellow; Preliminary Commendation (R.H.S.) 1950. Formerly listed as Merlin Exbury var.

xxx	H-2	Exbury Naomi		cl.	'Aurora' x fortunei (Naomi g.); (Rothschild); lilac, tinged yellow. Formerly known as Naomi Exbury var.
		Exbury Red Cap			didymum x eriogynum; (Rothschild); deep crimson, late. Formerly known as Red Cap, Exbury form.
		Exbury Souldis		cl.	souliei x discolor (Souldis g.); (Rothschild 1948); white. Formerly known as Souldis var. Exbury.
		Exbury Spinulosum		cl.	spinuliferum x racemosum (Spinulosum g.); (Rothschild); rosy pink; A.M. (R.H.S.) 1948. Formerly known as Spinulosum Exbury var.
		Excelsior			javanicum x 'Princess Royal'; (Veitch); apple blossom; F.C.C.
		Exminster		g.	thomsonii x campylocarpum; (Barclay Fox).
		Exminster		cl.	thomsonii x campylocarpum; (Barclay Fox); exhibited 1923; pink over cream; A.M. 1923. See 'Embley Blush', 'Embley Park', 'Embley Pink', 'Leonardslee Peach', 'Little Paddocks', 'Pleasant'.
xx	H-5	Exoniense		g.	ciliatum x veitchianum; (Veitch); creamy white; F.C.C. 1881.
		Exquisite			(J.Waterer before 1875); white with buff spots.
		Exquisite		g.	javanicum x teysmanni; rich canary yellow with prominent crimson anthers; A.M. 1899.
		Fabia		g.	dichroanthum x griersonianum; (Aberconway).
		Fabia	*** B	cl.	dichroanthum x griersonianum; (Aberconway 1934); bright scarlet or orange salmon, bell-shaped; A.M. (R.H.S.) 1934. See 'Exbury Fabia', 'Fabia High Beeches', 'Fabia Tangerine', 'Fabia Tower Court', 'Minterne Apricot', 'Roman Pottery', 'Solveig'.
		Fabia High Beeches		cl.	dichroanthum x griersonianum (Fabia g.); (Loder 1937); orange. Formerly known as Fabia var. High Beeches.
xx	H-4	Fabia Tangerine		cl.	dichroanthum x griersonianum (Fabia g.); (Aberconway 1940); vermilion H.C.C. 18/1) shaded to edges of lobes geranium lake (H.C.C. 20/2) and in the throat poppy red (H.C.C. 16/1); A.M. (R.H.S.) 1940. Formerly known as Fabia var. Tangerine.
xx	H-4	Fabia Tower Court		cl.	dichroanthum x griersonianum (Fabia g.); (Stevenson 1937); very pale pink, scented. Formerly known as Fabia var. Tower Court.
		Fabiola		g.	'Fabia' x 'F.C. Puddle'; (Aberconway 1946); red.
		Fabionis		g.	'Adonis' x 'Fabia'; (Aberconway 1946); pale rose.
		Fabos		cl.	'Arthur Osborn' x 'Fabia' (Beacon g.); (Reuthe 1952); crimson. Formerly known as Beacon var. Fabos.
xxx	H-3	Faggetter's Favourite	*** B	cl.	a chance hybrid of R. fortunei, other parent unknown; (Slocock); cream, delicately flushed phlox pink (H.C.C. 625/2) upper petal at throat with slight speckling of bronze, buds spinel pink (H.C.C. 625); scented; A.M. (R.H.S.) 1933; A.M. (Wisley Trials) 1955.
		Fair Helen			(A. Waterer before 1915); white with yellow spot.
		Fair Lady		cl.	arboreum var. album x (Loderi g.) 'Venus'; (R. Henny, 1959); tyrian rose (H.C.C. 24/1), upper lobe shaded crimson (H.C.C. 22/1); P.A. (A.R.S.) 1959.
		Fair Maiden		g.	'Coreum' x griersonianum; (Aberconway 1950); red.
		Fair Rosamond			cultivated Noble before 1850; rosy pink.
		Fairy		g.	'Fabia' x 'Jacquetta'; (Aberconway 1942); bright red.
		Fairy Bell			(J.J.Crosfield 1935).
		(Fairyland)			See 'Loderi Fairyland'.
		Fairy Light		g.	'Lady Mar' x griersonianum; (Rothschild 1948); bright pink.
		Fairy Queen			cultivated Standish & Noble before 1860; white, tinged pink on margin of petals.
		(Fairy Queen)			See 'Loderi Fairy Queen'.
		Faltho		cl.	falconeri x thomsonii (Surprise g.); (Loder); rose madder (H.C.C. 23-23/1) with some faint spotting on upper lobes and dark crimson blotches at base; A.M. (R.H.S.) 1954. Previously known as Surprise var. Faltho.
		Falvia		g.	wardii x campylocarpum; (Aberconway 1933); yellow.
		Fame		g.	'Metis' x 'Fabia'; (Aberconway 1946); orange red.
		Fancy		cl.	'Mrs. Lindsay Smith' x 'Mrs. Helen Koster'; (M. Koster & Sons); pale cobalt violet (H.C.C. 637/2) fading to very pale pastel mauve (433/2) large oxblood red blotch; A.M. (Boskoop) 1955.
		Fancy Free		g.	T.L. 1690 x eriogynum; (Rothschild).
		Fancy Free		cl.	T.L. 1690 x eriogynum; (Rothschild); clear bright pink with tinge of salmon, speckled darker within; A.M. (R.H.S.) 1938.
		Fandango		g.	'Britannia' x haematodes; (Rothschild 1938); deep crimson scarlet.
		Fanfare		cl.	Red catawbiense hybrid x red catawbiense hybrid; (Shammarello-D.G. Leach 1957); bright red.
		Fantasy		g.	T.L. 1284 x griersonianum; (Rothschild 1938); pink.
		Fantin Latour		g.	cinnabarinum var. roylei x oreotrephes; (Adams-Acton 1934); mauve.
		Farall		cl.	'Moser's Maroon' x eriogynum (Romany Chal g.); (Haworth-Booth 1954).
		Fargarb		g.	fargesii x arboreum (blood red form); (Magor 1928); violet rose of deepest shade.
		Fargcalo		g.	fargesii x calophytum (Magor 1940).
		Fargsutch			fargesii x sutchuenense; (Magor 1933); blush with copious crimson spotting.
		Farnese		cl.	catawbiense x ; (Seidel 1926); white flushed lilac.
		Farola		g.	fargesii x Loderi g. ; (Loder 1940); very pale pink.
		Farquhar's Red		cl.	catawbiense x ; (Farquhar).
		Farquhar's Pink		cl.	catawbiense x ; (Farquhar).

		Fascination			cl.	pink; dwarf.
		Fascinator			g.	forrestii var. repens x 'Hiraethlyn'; (Aberconway).
		Fascinator			cl.	forrestii var. repens x 'Hiraethlyn'; (Aberconway 1950); rich carmine (H.C.C. 21) shot with turkey red (H.C.C. 721) and some faint spotting; A.M. (R.H.S.) 1950.
		Fasthip			g.	fastigiatum x hippophaeoides; (Magor 1926); palest possible lavender, almost white.
		Fastuosum Flore Pleno			cl.	Syn of 'Fastuosum Plenum'.
xx	H-2	Fastuosum Plenum	***	A	cl.	catawbiense x ponticum; (Gebr. Francoisi, Ghent, before 1846); mauve, partially double flowers; A.G.M. 1928.
		Faust			cl.	cultivated Standish & Noble before 1870; light puce, dark brown eye.
		Favourite				(before 1858); javanicum x 'Princess Alexandra'; pinky yellow to salmon; F.C.C. 1882.
		Fawn			cl.	fortunei x 'Fabia'; (James); salmon pink, yellow center; P.A.(A.R.S.) 1955.
		Fayetta			cl.	'Tally Ho' x 'Golden Horn'; (Whitney).
		F. Bettex				Syn. of 'Professor F. Bettex'.
		F.B. Hayes		A	cl.	Syn. of 'Francis B. Hayes'.
xx	H-4	F.C. Puddle			g.	neriiflorum x griersonianum; (Aberconway).
		F.C. Puddle			cl.	neriiflorum x griersonianum; (Aberconway 1932); flowers brilliant reddish scarlet, A.M. (R.H.S.) 1932.
x	H-2	F.D. Godman			cl.	catawbiense x ; (A. Waterer 1888); dark magenta red; exhibited 1888.
		Felicity			g.	'Radiance' x 'F.C. Puddle'; (Aberconway).
		Felicity			cl.	'Radiance' x 'F.C. Puddle'; (Aberconway 1942); a warm red (H.C.C. 620) amaranth rose; A.M. (R.H.S.) 1942.
		Felicity Magor			cl.	fulgens x barbatum; (Magor cross 1928); deep crimson with spots of darker shade.
		Felis	*	C	g.	dichroanthum x facetum; (Rothschild 1938); yellow to orange. Syn. 'Felix'.
		Felise			cl.	ciliatum x burmanicum; (Adams-Acton 1942); cream, fading white.
		Felix			g.	Syn. of 'Felis'.
		Festival			cl.	'Romany Chal' x griersonianum (Theresa g.) red. Previously known as Theresa var. Festival.
		Fez			g.	'King George' x haemaleum; (Rothschild 1938); crimson.
		Fiery Cross			g.	barbatum x ? griffithianum; (Hutchinson 1945).
		Fiesta			g.	'Eros' x 'F.C. Puddle'; (Aberconway 1950); red.
		Figaro			g.	'Solon' x 'Coreta'; (Aberconway 1950); red.
		Finch			cl.	a selection of R. desquamatum; (Rudolph Henny); mallow purple (H.C.C. 630/2).
		Fine Feathers			g.	'Cilpinense' x lutescens; (Aberconway 1946); white flushed pink. See 'Fine Feathers Primrose'.
		Fine Feathers Primrose			cl.	'Cilpinense' x lutescens (Fine Feathers g.); (Aberconway 1949); pale yellow. Previously known as Fine Feathers var. Primrose.
		Finesse			cl.	souliei x 'Bowbells'; (Rudolph Henny). Persian rose (H.C.C. 628/3).
		Fireball	**	B	cl.	barbatum x 'Ascot Brilliant'; (R. Gill & Son); rich carmine scarlet; A.M. (R.H.S.) 1925. ? Syn. 'Early Brilliant' (Slocock).
x	H-3	Fire Bird	**	B	g.	'Norman Shaw' x griersonianum; (Rothschild 1938); salmon red.
		Firedrake			g.	'Sardis' x kyawi; (Rothschild 1938); late, bright red.
		Firefinch			g.	'Radiance' x 'Jacquetta'; (Aberconway 1942); scarlet.
		Fire Flame			cl.	'Apodorum' x griersonianum; (Scrase-Dickins 1942); red (H.C.C. 20/1); A.M. (R.H.S.) 1942.
		Firefly			g.	'Crossbill' x spinuliferum; (Rothschild 1938); yellow to apricot.
		Fire Glow			g.	(griffithianum roseum superbum x 'H. M. Arderne') x griersonianum; (Crosfield 1935); deep scarlet; A.M. (R.H.S.) 1935.
		Fire Music			cl.	venator x dichroanthum; (Thacker 1942); fiery orange.
		Firetail			g.	'Britannia' x eriogynum; (Crosfield).
		Firetail			cl.	'Britannia' x eriogynum; (Crosfield 1937); deep scarlet, spotted brown within; A.M. (R.H.S.) 1934; F.C.C. 1937. See 'Trident'.
		Fittra			cl.	dauricum x racemosum; (Hillier); mallow purple (H.C.C. 630/1); A.M. (R.H.S.) 1949.
		Flame				javanicum x ; intensely rich orange scarlet; F.C.C. (R.H.S.) 1931.
		Flame			g.	(Loderi g. x 'Corona') x griersonianum; (Lem.).
		Flame			cl.	catawbiense x 'Mira'; (Seidel cross 1904); delicate lilac with yellow spots.
		Flameheart			cl.	auriculatum x 'Azor'; (Haworth-Booth 1955).
		F.L. Ames			cl.	catawbiense x ; A. Waterer before 1909); rosy pink, light center. Syn. of 'Amphion'.
		Flamingo			g.	'Loder's White' x griersonianum; exhibited Horlick 1941.
x	H-4	Flare	*	B	cl.	'Mrs. R.S. Holford' x (auriculatum x griersonianum); (Slocock); brilliant salmon red, late.
		Flash			g.	'Fabia' x scyphocalyx; (Aberconway 1946); orange red.
		Flashlight			g.	callimorphum x campylocarpum; (Rothschild 1938); yellow flushed pink.
		Flatterer			cl.	'Corona' x 'Lady Bessborough'; (Rudolph Henny); carmine rose (H.C.C. 621); P.A. (A.H.S.) 1957.
		(Fledgeling)				See 'Peregrine Fledgeling'.
		Fleece			cl.	Loderi g. x 'Luscombei'; (Shepherd's Delight g.) (Mrs. R.M. Stevenson, 1959); rhodomine pink (H.C.C. 527/2), flushed darker, upper lobe red spotted; A.M. (R.H.S.) 1959.
		Fleur de Roi			cl.	thomsonii x campanulatum; exhibited Wright 1903; cream suffused pink.
		Flora			cl.	(J. Waterer about 1860); rose or white striped with pale rose.
		Florence			cl.	pink.

		Florence Gill			g.	cultivar of arboreum; (R. Gill & Son); white with pink margin
		Florence Nightingale			cl.	(A. Waterer); rose, light center.
		Florence Sarah Smith			cl.	(Smith, Darley Dale); pink.
		Florescent			g.	'Oreoroyle' x xanthocodon; (Aberconway 1950); plum color.
		Floretta				cultivated Standish & Noble before 1870; cerise, white throat.
		Floretta Madame Moser				A.M. 1897.
		Florian			cl.	cultivated Standish & Noble before 1870; white, tipped with purple, yellow spots.
		Flushing			cl.	catawbiense x ; (Parsons before 1875); crimson.
		Forerunner			cl.	haematodes x 'Vanguard'; (Sunningdale Nursery 1951); glowing scarlet.
		Forest Fire			cl.	'Tally Ho' x 'Britannia'; (R. Henny).
xxx	H-5	Forsterianum				veitchianum x edgeworthii; (Forster 1917); white.
		Fortorb			g.	fortunei x orbiculare; (P.D. Williams).
		Fortune			g.	falconeri x sinogrande; (Rothschild).
		Fortune			cl.	falconeri x sinogrande; (Rothschild); creamy yellow flowers with magenta blotch; F.C.C. (R.H.S.) 1938.
		Fortune's Triumph				pink, carmine spotted; A.M. (R.H.S.) 1929.
		Fotis			cl.	'Lady Bessborough' x 'Margaret Dunn'; (Sunningdale Nurseries 1955); pale tangerine pink, fading nankeen yellow, crimson brown spotting in throat.
		Fragonard			cl.	'Betty King' x 'Cornish Cross'; (Adams-Acton 1942); Indian red.
		Fragrans	**	A	g.	Azaleodendron; catawbiense x viscosum; (Paxton of Chandler & Sons 1843); pale mauve with lighter to white tints in center.
xxx	H-5	Fragrantissimum	***	F		edgeworthii x formosum; white, tinged pink; F.C.C. 1868.
		Francis B. Hayes			cl.	(J. Waterer before 1922); white, chocolate blotch or spots.
		Francis Dickson			cl.	(A. Waterer 1865); bright red or scarlet.
xx	H-4	Francis Hanger			g.	dichroanthum x 'Isabella'; (Rothschild).
		Francis Hanger			cl.	dichroanthum x 'Isabella'; (Rothschild); chrome yellow, lobes deeply cut, margins frilled and edged delicate tinge pale rose; A.M. (R.H.S.) 1950.
		Frank Galsworthy	*	A	cl.	ponticum x ; (A. Waterer); maroon purple, yellow blotch.
		Frank LaBar			cl.	a natural hybrid of maximum x catawbiense; (LaBar's); lilac.
		Franz			cl.	catawbiense x ; (Seidel); carmine.
		Frau Minna Hartl			cl.	Azaleodendron; (Hartl 1891); acquired by crossing with Rhododendron ponticum; double, carmine rose.
		Frau Rosalie Seidel			cl.	(Seidel before 1916); white.
		Freckle Face			cl.	'Corona' x wardii (Coronet g.); (C. Ingram 1954). Previously known as Coronet var. Freckle Face.
		Freda			cl.	fortunei x ; (Paul); light pink.
		Fred Waterer / Frederick Waterer		A	cl.	catawbiense x ; (J. Waterer); crimson red.
		Friesland			cl.	'Pink Pearl' x catawbiense hybrid; (L.J. Endtz & Co.); pale lilac rose.
		Fringe			cl.	'Ascot Brilliant' x campylocarpum; (Horlick 1954).
		Fritz Henssler			g.	'Mrs. Lindsay Smith' x williamsianum; (Dietrich Hobbie 1952); bright rose.
		Fulgarb			cl.	fulgens x arboreum (blood red form); (Magor 1930); bright rosy crimson about 15 in a truss; A.M. (R.H.S.) 1937.
		Full House			g.	cinnabarinum var. blandfordiaeflorum x maddenii; (Johnstone).
		Full Moon			cl.	'Hawk' x 'Adriaan Koster'; (J. Henny); yellow; P.A. (A.R.S.) 1955.
		Fumosum				in cultivation nursery of T. Methven & Son, Edinburgh 1868; dark purple, strongly marked with dark spots.
		Furnivall's Daughter			cl.	(Knap Hill Nursery Ltd.); flower fuchsine pink (H.C.C. 627/3) veined fuchsine pink (H.C.C. 627/2), heavily spotted on upper petal with strawberry red; H.C. (Wisley Trials) 1957; A.M. 1958.
		Furore			cl.	oreotrephes x concatenans; (Harrison cross 1950); pale mauve pink.
		Furstin Bariatinsky			cl.	Azaleodendron; Indian clone x R. edgeworthii; (Schulz 1876); striped, white with purple red and rose lines and specks; broadish green crown on upper petals.
		Furvum			cl.	in cultivation in nursery of T. Methven & Son, Edinburgh 1868; very dark puce.
xxx	H-4	Fusilier			g.	elliottii x griersonianum; (Rothschild).
		Fusilier	***	C	cl.	elliottii x griersonianum; (Rothschild); brilliant red (H.C.C. 719/3); A.M. (R.H.S.) 1938; F.C.C. (R.H.S.) 1942.
		Gable's Pink No. 2			cl.	'Caroline' x discolor; (Gable); exhibited 1944; pink.
		Gabriel Liebig			cl.	griffithianum x ; (Otto Schulz 1890).
		Galatea			cl.	(Waterer, Sons & Crisp Ltd.); soft pink.
		Galathea				thomsonii x campylocarpum; yellowish rose.
		Galbannum				(M. Young); rosy crimson, pale center, with white dashes.
		Galceador	*	A		(Knap Hill Nursery); named the year that horse won Derby; lilac with gold eye.
XX	H-3	Galloper Light	**	B	cl.	Azaleodendron; (Rothschild); soft yellow pink or salmon rose, spotted deeper; Slocock–"cream with gold eye", A.M. (R.H.S.) 1927.
		Gargantua			cl.	raised by J.B. Stevenson 1923 from seed of a plant of R. diaprepes–Forrest 11958; a triploid (2n=39); larger in all its parts than R. diaprepes; A.M. (R.H.S.) 1953.

		Garibaldi	**	A	cl.	(A. Waterer before 1915); salmon red or bright light red with frilled petals.
x	H-4	Garnet			g.	griffithianum x 'Broughtonii'; (P.D. Williams 1942); red or deep salmon rose.
		Gartendirektor Glocker		B	cl.	'Doncaster' x williamsianum; (Dietrich Hobbie 1952); rose red, partly with darker margin.
x	H-3	G.A. Sims		B	cl.	(Waterer, Sons & Crisp Ltd.); dark pure scarlet; A.M. (R.H.S.) 1938.
		Gaul			g.	'Shilsonii' x elliottii; (Rothschild).
		Gaul			cl.	'Shilsonii' x elliottii; (Rothschild); deep red; A.M. (R.H.S.) 1939. See 'Gaul Mastodon'.
		Gaul Mastodon			cl.	'Shilsonii' x elliottii (Gaul g.); (Rothschild); rich deep red. Previously known as Gaul var. Mastodon.
		Gauntlettii / Gauntletii			g.	griffithianum x ; white.
		Gavotte			cl.	davidsonianum x mollicomum; (Adams-Acton 1945); pink to mauve.
		Gay Gordon			cl.	'Beau Brummel' x elliottii; (Rothschild 1939); hunting coat red.
		Gay Lady			cl.	'Cornubia' x griffithianum; deep rose; A.M. (R.H.S.) 1938.
		Gazelle				cultivated Standish & Noble before 1860; white with brown spots.
		G.B. Simpson		A	cl.	(A. Waterer, Senior, before 1915); bluish purple, light center.
		Geisha			g.	'Pineapple' x dichroanthum; (Rothschild 1939); cream.
		Gem			g.	'Halopeanum' x thomsonii; (Loder 1926); light blush or rose, deep pink edge. See 'Leonardslee Brilliant', 'Red Glow'.
		Gemmatum			cl.	(before 1874); scarlet, dark blotch.
		Gemmiferum				Azaleodendron; in cultivation T. Methven & Son, Edinburgh 1868-69; bright magenta rose.
		Gemmosum			cl.	in cultivation T. Methven & Son, Edinburgh 1868; dark scarlet rose, black spots.
		General, The				red catawbiense seedling x red catawbiense seedling; (Shammarello 1955); dark red, small dark blotch.
		General Cavendish			cl.	'Monsieur Thiers' x griffithianum hybrid; (C. B. van Nes & Sons before 1922); dark rosy pink.
		General Eisenhower		A	cl.	griffithianum x ; (Anth. Kluis 1946); deep carmine (spiraea red H.C.C. 025).
		General Grant			cl.	catawbiense x ; (Parsons before 1875); soft rose.
		General Sir John du Cane	*	B	g.	thomsonii x discolor; (Rothschild 1933); rose, dark eye.
		Geneva			cl.	'Unknown Warrior' x 'Fabia'; grown by John Bacher; inside of corolla, edge of lobes camellia rose (H.C.C. 622) shading through 622/1, 622/2 and 622/3 towards center, inconspicuously spotted on upper lobe majolica yellow (H.C.C. 09-1); P.A. (A.R.S.) 1955.
		Genoveva			cl.	catawbiense x ; (T.J.R. Seidel); pale lilac white with yellowish green blotch. Syn. 'Lucy Neal'.
		Genseric			cl.	cultivated Standish & Noble before 1860; dark claret, finely spotted.
		Geoffrey Henslow			cl.	(M. Koster & Sons); bright crimson.
		Geoffrey Millais	*	C	cl.	griffithianum x ; (Otto Schulz cross 1892, introduced C. B. van Nes & Sons); white, A.M. (R.H.S.) 1922.
		George Bennington			cl.	(Paul); pink.
		George Cunningham	*	B	cl.	arboreum x campanulatum?; the white form is similar to 'Boddaertianum'; (G. Cunningham before 1875); white with black spots.
		George Grace			cl.	Loderi g. x 'Borde Hill'; (R. Henny); light pink; P.A. (A.R.S.) 1952.
		George Hardy	*	B	cl.	griffithianum x catawbiense; (Mangles before 1922); blush fading white.
		George Paul			cl.	(A. Waterer); crimson, spotted.
		George Taylor				griffithianum x 'Luscombei'; (Adams-Acton 1942).
		(Georgette)				See 'Loderi Georgette'.
		Geraldii			g.	praevernum x sutchuenense; a natural hybrid of R. sutchuenense with praevernum, for many years erroneously thought to be a variety of sutchuenense, with deeper colored flowers (faintly mottled amaranth rose (H.C.C. 530/1), and by the purple blotch (H.C.C. 830); A.M. (R.H.S.) 1945.
		Geraldine				cultivated Standish & Noble before 1860; deep puce.
		Geranioides			cl.	cultivated Standish & Noble before 1860; pale rosy crimson with black spots in throat.
		Gertrud			cl.	catawbiense x ; (T. J. R. Seidel); carmine.
		Gertrud Schäle		B	g.	forrestii var. repens x 'Prometheus'; (Dietrich Hobbie 1951); translucent scarlet red.
		G. H. Maitland King			cl.	discolor x ; (Slocock); bright crimson pink.
		Gibraltar			g.	'Bibiani' x elliottii; (Rothschild 1939); fringed, rich orange or intense deep red.
		Gibsonii			cl.	in cultivation T. Methven & Son, Edinburgh 1868; pure white.
		Giganteum			cl.	catawbiense x ; (H. Waterer before 1851); light crimson.
		Gigha Gem			cl.	neriiflorum var. euchaites x 'Pleasant'; (Horlick 1955).
		(Gilbury)				See 'Mariloo Gilbury'.
		Gilian			cl.	campylocarpum x griffithianum; (Magor 1923); cardinal red, faintly spotted?; A.M. (R.H.S.) 1923.
		(Gillians)				See 'Gladys Gillians'.
		Gillian Spenser			g.	haematodes x ('Ascot Brilliant' x neriiflorum); (Adams-Acton 1950).
		Gillii			g.	griffithianum x arboreum (blood red form); (R. Gill & Son); soft rose; A.M. (R.H.S.) 1919.

xxx	H-5	Gill's Crimson	*** C	cl.	griffithianum x ; (R. Gill & Son); blood crimson.
		Gill's Gloriosa	** D	cl.	griffithianum x 'Pink Pearl'; R.H.S. Journal (1926) gives 'Halopeanum' x 'Luscombei Superba'; (R. Gill & Son); bright cerise; A.M. (R.H.S.) 1925.
		Gill's Goliath	* D	cl.	griffithianum x ; (R. Gill & Son); carmine pink; A.M. (R.H.S.) 1914.
		Gill's Nobleanum Album		cl.	(R. Gill & Son); pure white tinged pale green at the base; A.M. (R.H.S.) 1926.
xx	H-4	Gill's Triumph	** D	cl.	arboreum x griffithianum (Beauty of Tremough g.); (R. Gill & Son); strawberry red fading to pink; A.M. (R.H.S.) 1906.
		Gina			(T. Lowinsky); rich ruby red; A.M. (R.H.S.) 1931.
		Giorgione		cl.	rosy scarlet.
		Gipsy King		g.	'King George' x haematodes; (Rothschild 1939); deep red.
		Gipsy Maid		g.	'Sophia Gray' x Loderi g. ; (Wallace 1944).
		Gisela		cl.	'Everestianum' x 'Boule de Neige'; (Seidel cross 1905); bright lilac with darker margins and green markings..
		Gladiator		g.	'F.C. Puddle' x griersonianum; (Aberconway 1941); deep scarlet.
xxx	H-3	Gladys		g.	campylocarpum x fortunei; (Col. S.R. Clarke).
		Gladys	****B	cl.	campylocarpum x fortunei; (Clarke 1926); exhibited S.R. Clarke; cream, crimson markings; A.M. (R.H.S.) 1926; A.M. (R.H.S.) 1950. See 'Gladys Gillians', 'Mary Swaything', 'Gladys Rose'.
		Gladys Gillians		cl.	campylocarpum x fortunei (Gladys g.) exhibited Digby 1955. Formerly known as Gladys var. Gillians.
		Gladys Johnson		cl.	'Diva' x fortunei; (exhibited Mrs. E. E. Johnson); rose pink in bud, opening lighter; P.A. (A.R.S.).
		Gladys Rose		cl.	campylocarpum x fortunei (Gladys g.); (Col. S.R.Clarke); creamy white flowers with crimson blotch in throat; A.M. (R.H.S.) 1950. Formerly known as Gladys var. Rose.
		Glamour		g.	'Margaret' x griersonianum; (Rothschild).
		Glamour		cl.	'Margaret' x griersonianum; (Rothschild 1939); deep cherry red (H.C.C. 727) A.M. (R.H.S.) 1946.
		Glasgow Glow		cl.	griersonianum x 'Scarlet Lady'; (Stirling Maxwell 1953).
		Glaucoboothii		g.	glaucophyllum x boothii; (Magor 1922); closely resembles 'Lepidoboothii'; pinkish with brownish red spots.
		Glautescens		cl.	glaucophyllum x lutescens; (Reuthe 1939); yellow, suffused pink.
		Gleam		cl.	cinnabarinum var. roylei x 'Royal Flush' orange form (Lady Chamberlain g.); (Rothschild); orange yellow with crimson tipped petals. Formerly known as Lady Chamberlain var. Gleam.
		Glennyanum			light pink
		Globosum			cultivated Standish & Noble before 1860; rosy lilac.
		Gloire de Boskoop			dark crimson.
		Gloire de Gandavensis			in cultivation T. Methven & Son, Edinburgh 1868; white, spotted.
		Gloriana		cl.	'Fabia' x 'Goldsworth Orange'; (R.H.S. Gardens, Wisley); salmon orange; a variable shade between claret rose (H.C.C. 021/1) and empire rose (H.C.C. 0621/1) and suffused in the throat with an orange tinge and some spotting; A.M. (R.H.S.) 1953. See 'Coral Reef'.
		Gloriosum		cl.	(J. Waterer before 1850); blush white.
		Glorious		g.	red hybrid x thomsonii; (Smith, Penjerrick).
		Glory			Syn. of 'John Willis Fleming'.
		Glory of Athlone		cl.	'Earl of Athlone' x 'Glory of Leonardslee'; (Horlick 1954).
		Glory of Bagshot		cl.	griffithianum x ; (J. Waterer, Sons & Crisp Ltd.); pure white.
		Glory of Leonardslee		cl.	griffithianum x ; (R. Gill & Son); light strawberry red, fading.
xx	H-4	Glory of Littleworth	*** B	cl.	Azaleodendron; (Mangles); lemon color with intense orange blotch; A.M. (R.H.S.) 1911.
xx	H-4	Glory of Penjerrick	*** D	cl.	arboreum x griffithianum (Beauty of Tremough g.); (R. Gill & Son); deep strawberry red fading to pink; A.M. (R.H.S.) 1904.
		(Glow)			See 'Naomi Glow'.
		Glow		cl.	(Crosfield 1935).
		Glow		cl.	griersonianum x 'Armistice Day'; (Bovee).
		Glowing Ember			K.W. 13225 x griersonianum; (Sunningdale Nurseries 1946); vivid scarlet to bright red spotted crimson.
xx	H-3	Glowing Embers		cl.	'Romany Chal' x griersonianum; (J. Henny); scarlet.
		Glowing Star		cl.	fortunei x 'C. P. Raffill'; (Hardrove); coral rose, red throat, exhibited 1954.
		Glow Worm		cl.	dichroanthum x 'Halcyone'; (Sunningdale 1951); deep butter yellow.
		Gloxinaeflorum			See 'Gloxiniaeflorum'.
		Gloxineum		cl.	fortunei x ; (Dexter-de Wilde); pink.
		Gloxiniaeflorum			a form of arboreum; (Veitch); waxy white, purple spots.
xx	H-4	Goblin		g.	'Break of Day' x griersonianum; (Rothschild).
		Goblin		cl.	'Break of Day' x griersonianum; (Rothschild); pale salmon rose; A.M. (R.H.S.) 1939. See 'Goblin Pink'.
		Goblin Pink		cl.	'Break of Day' x griersonianum (Goblin g.); (Rothschild); soft rose pink with nankeen yellow throat.
		Godesberg		cl.	griffithianum x ; (Otto Schulz cross 1892, introduced C.B. van Nes & Sons); white flowers with brown spots.

		Goethe			cl.	catawbiense x ; (Seidel 1926); bright rose.
		Goethe			cl.	'Coombe Royal' x lilac garden hybrid; (M. Koster & Sons); pale mauve, fimbriated.
		Golconda			g.	'Beau Brummell' x dichroanthum; (Rothschild 1939); pink.
		Gold Braid			cl.	'Fabia' x 'Dondis'; (R. Henny).
		Goldbug			cl.	'Fabia' x wardii; (R. Henny).
		Golden Belle			cl.	discolor x 'Fabia' (Margaret Dunn g.); (J. Henny); similar to 'Margaret Dunn' but larger and deeper yellow in the throat. Formerly known as Margaret Dunn var. Golden Belle.
		Golden Days			cl.	'Dondis' x dichroanthum; (R. Henny, 1959); maize yellow (H.C.C. 607/2) fading straw yellow (H.C.C. 604/1), edged carrot red (H.C.C. 612/2).
		Golden Dream			cl.	campylocarpum x 'Naomi' (Carita g.); (Rothschild); deep cream, flushed and shaded pink, becoming ivory white at maturity. Previously known as Carita var. Golden Dream.
		Golden Drop			cl.	'Dr. Stocker' x campylocarpum; (Horlick 1931).
		Golden Glow			cl.	'Fabia' x 'Azor'; (B.F. Lancaster).
xx	H-4	Golden Horn			g.	dichroanthum x elliottii; (Rothschild).
		Golden Horn	**	B	cl.	dichroanthum x elliottii; (Rothschild 1939); orange-red; A.M. (R.H.S.) 1945. See 'Perisimmon'.
		Golden Oriole			cl.	moupinense x sulfureum; (P. D. Williams); Dresden yellow (H.C.C. 64/2) A.M. (R.H.S.) 1947.
		Golden Queen			cl.	cinnabarinum var. roylei x 'Royal Flush' orange var. (Lady Chamberlain g.); (Rothschild); soft salmon pink shaded with orange; F.C.C. (R.H.S.) 1947. Previously known as Lady Chamberlain var. Golden Queen.
		Golden West			cl.	fortunei x campylocarpum; (James).
		Goldfinch		A	g.	wardii x 'Mrs. P.D. Williams'; (R. Collyer, exhibited Ingram 1945); pink with gold eye.
xxx	H-3	Goldfort	***	B	cl.	'Goldsworth Yellow' x fortunei; (W.C. Slocock 1937); creamy yellow.
		Gold Mohur			cl.	'Day Dream' x 'Margaret Dunn' (Dream Girl g.); (L.E. Brandt); barium yellow (H.C.C. 503) inside and out, shading to 503/1 to 503/2, flushed and spotted greenish inside; exhibited 1956. Formerly listed as Dream Girl var. Gold Mohur.
xx	H-3	Goldsworth Crimson	**	B	cl.	griffithianum x hardy hybrid; (W.C. Slocock, selected 1926); crimson.
xx	H-3	Goldsworth Orange	**	B	cl.	dichroanthum x discolor; (W.C.Slocock 1938); low-growing shrub; pale orange tinted pink. A.M. (R.H.S.) 1959.
x	H-4	Goldsworth Pink	**	B	cl.	griffithianum x ; (W.C.Slocock 1933); light pink; A.M. (R.H.S.) 1958.
		Goldsworth Purple		A	cl.	(W.C. Slocock 1935); purple.
		Goldsworth White			cl.	griffithianum x hardy hybrid; (W.C.Slocock, selected Slocock 1926); white.
xx	H-2	Goldsworth Yellow	**	B	cl.	'Jacksonii' x campylocarpum; (W.C. Slocock 1925); apricot bud, fading pale yellow, slightly spotted green and bronze; A.M. (R.H.S.) 1925.
		Goliath			cl.	crimson.
xx	H-2	Gomer Waterer	**	A	cl.	catawbiense x ; (J. Waterer before 1900); white slightly flushed, late flowering; A.M. (R.H.S.) 1906.
		Gondolier			g.	'Lady Harcourt' x griersonianum; (Rothschild 1947); bright red.
		Good Cheer			g.	'Lord Milner' x sutchuenense; (Rothschild 1939); white with pink markings.
		(Goshawk)				See 'Jalisco Goshawk'.
		Govenianum	*	A	g.	Azaleodendron; an Azalea x (catawbiense x ponticum); in cultivation T. Methven 1868-69; fragrant, pale purplish rose.
		Grace			g.	fortunei x arboreum var. album; (Rothschild 1939); white with slight markings.
		Grace Darling				(Davies before 1890); lilac, dark spot.
		Graf Zeppelin			cl.	'Pink Pearl' x 'Mrs. C.S. Sargent'; (C.B. van Nes & Sons); bright pink.
		Granat			cl.	catawbiense x ; (Seidel 1916); crimson.
		Grand Arab			cl.	Syn. of 'Vesuvius'.
		Grandex			g.	eximium x sinogrande; (Aberconway 1950); yellow flushed pink.
		Grand Prix			cl.	grande x eximium; (Heneage-Vivian); ivory shaded without pale carmine (H.C.C. 21/3); A.M. (R.H.S.) 1940.
		Grayswood Pink			g.	williamsianum x venator; (Dowty 1949).
		Great Britain			cl.	'Britannia' x griffithianum; (Digby 1953).
		Great Lakes			cl.	catawbiense var. album x yakusimanum; (D. G. Leach 1960); fresh pink buds opening to clear light pink flowers soon aging to chalk-white; dwarf, compact; P.A. (A.R.S.) 1960.
		Greeneye			cl.	augustinii x 'Blue Tit' (Blue Ribbon g.); (Gen. Harrison 1955); mauve blue with green spots.
		Greenfinch			cl.	'Mrs. Lindsay Smith' x campylocarpum; (Zuiderzee g.) (C. Ingram 1945). Previously known as Zuiderzee var. Greenfinch.
		Greeting			g.	'Chanticleer' x Loderi g.; (Aberconway 1950); red.
		Grenada			g.	'Lady Rumbold' x griersonianum; (Rothschild 1939); red.
xxx	H-3	Grenadier			g.	'Moser's Maroon' x elliottii; (Rothschild).
		Grenadier	***	D	cl.	'Moser's Maroon' x elliottii; (Rothschild); blood red (H.C.C. 820/1); F.C.C. (R.H.S.) 1943.
		Grenadine			g.	'Pauline' x griersonianum; (Rothschild).

		Grenadine			cl.	'Pauline' x griersonianum; (Rothschild); cherry (H.C.C. 722) with deep brown spotting in the throat; A.M. (R.H.S.) 1956.
		Gretchen			cl.	(decorum x griffithianum) x 'Kettledrum'; (Nearing-Gable); pink.
		Gretchen Medlar			cl.	'Boule de Neige' x 'Henrietta Sargent'; (Skinner).
		Gretia			g.	'Portia' x griersonianum; (Aberconway).
		Gretia			cl.	'Portia' x griersonianum; (Aberconway cross 1936); blood red (H.C.C. 820/3); A.M. (R.H.S.) 1946.
		Griercalyx			g.	griersonianum x megacalyx; exhibited 1941.
x	H-5	Grierdal			g.	griersonianum x dalhousiae; (Heneage Vivian 1937); scarlet, tinged magenta. The only verified cross between a lepidote and an elepidote Rhododendron at time of publication.
		Grierocaster			g.	griersonianum x 'Doncaster'; (at Wakehurst); exhibited 1939.
		Grierosplendour			g.	griersonianum x 'Purple Splendour'; (Loder 1937).
		Griersims			g.	'G.A. Sims' x griersonianum; (Ramsden 1938).
		Grievii			g.	virgatum x ciliatum.
		Grilse			cl.	'Fusilier' x 'Jalisco Eclipse'; (Crown Estate Commissioners 1948); reddish shade of porcelain rose (H.C.C. 620-560/1), dark crimson spots in throat and on upper lobe; A.M. (R.H.S.) 1957.
		Griselda			cl.	'Fabia' x 'Margaret Dunn'; (R. Henny).
		Grisette			g.	arboreum var. album x 'Dr. Stocker'; (Rothschild 1939); pure white, with dark markings in throat.
		(Grisette Slocock)				See 'Grisette'.
xx	H-4	Grosclaude			g.	haematodes x eriogynum; (Rothschild).
		Grosclaude	***	B	cl.	haematodes x eriogynum; (Rothschild 1941); waxy blood red (H.C.C. 820/1); A.M. (R.H.S.) 1945.
		G. Streseman				Syn. of 'Hollandia' (Endtz).
		G.T. Streseman				Syn. of 'Hollandia' (Endtz).
		Guardsman			g.	'Ivery's Scarlet' x arboreum; (Loder); dark red.
		Gudrun			cl.	'Eggebrechtii' x 'Madame Linden'; (Seidel cross 1905); white with slight purple tint, red spotted.
		Guido			cl.	catawbiense x ?; (A. Waterer before 1850); crimson.
		Gulnare				(Rogers); cultivated Standish & Noble before 1870; bright rose, tipped darker pink.
		Guttatum			cl.	(Rogers?); cultivated Standish & Noble before 1860; creamy white or blush, spotted with green and red.
		Gwillt-King			cl.	griersonianum x zeylanicum; (Caton Haigh 1938); turkey red (H.C.C. 721/2) with some spotting on the upper lobe; A.M. (R.H.S.) 1952.
		Gylla MacGregor			cl.	griffithianum x ; (M. Koster & Sons); light red.
		Haembarb			g.	barbatum x haematocheilum; (Magor 1915); bright pink rose with 3 crimson blotches at base.
		Halcyon				cultivated Noble before 1850; rosy lilac.
xx	H-3	Halcyone			g.	souliei x 'Lady Bessborough'; (Rothschild 1940); deep cream. See 'Perdita'.
		Half Penny			cl.	'Anna' x 'Margaret Dunn'; (D.W. James, 1959); pink buds opening to primrose yellow (H.C.C. 601/3); large ruby red (H.C.C. 827) blotches encircling corolla.
		Hallali			g.	venator x haemaleum; exhibited Ingram 1945.
x	H-4	Halopeanum	**	B	cl.	maximum x griffithianum; (Halope, Belgium, 1896); slightly blush, changing to pure white; A.M. (R.H.S.) 1906. Syn. 'White Pearl'.
		Hamachidon				wavy edged, bright purple red; dwarf.
		Hamardor			g.	haematodes x 'Dorothea'; (Headfort 1940).
		Hamilcar			cl.	amaranth red.
		Hampreston			g.	glaucophyllum x russatum; (Marchant 1939).
		Händel			cl.	'Mrs. Lindsay Smith' x campanulatum hybrid; (M. Koster & Sons cross 1920); light yellow, flushed green with green spots on upper side, or creamy white; A.M. (R.H.S.) 1937.
		Handsworth Red			cl.	caucasicum x ; (Fisher, Son & Sibray); bright red. Syn. of 'Handsworth Scarlet'.
		Handsworth Scarlet	*	B	cl.	caucasicum x ; (Fisher, Son & Sibray before 1928); bright red. Syn. 'Handsworth Red'.
xx	H-3	Handsworth White	**	A	cl.	caucasicum x ; (Fisher, Son & Sibray before 1928); white at first with blush of pink.
		Happiness			cl.	R. fortunei seedling; (Maitland Dougall 1939).
		Happy			g.	'Pauline' x griffithianum; (Rothschild 1940); pink with darker blotch.
		Harbinger		B	cl.	pink.
		Hariet			cl.	racemosum x ciliatum; (Noble); pale pink; A.M. (R.H.S.) 1957.
		Harlequin				dichroanthum x eudoxum.
		Harmony			g.	'Vega' x Loderi g.; (Aberconway 1950); pink
		Harold Heal				('Cornish Cross' x wardii) x 'Loderi King George'; (Collingwood Ingram 1955.)
		Harrisii			g.	thomsonii x arboreum; (Harris 1880); reddish pink.
		Harrisii Superbum			cl.	thomsonii x ; deep crimson.
		Harry Bertram				cultivated Standish & Noble before 1860; deep puce, finely spotted.
		Harry Goldney			cl.	rose pink.
		Harry Tagg			cl.	'Albescens' x ciliicalyx; (Royal Botanic Gardens, Edinburgh, 1958); white, blush on exterior; faintly marked greenish-yellow on upper lobe. A.M. (R.H.S.) 1958.

		Harry White			g.	arboreum var. kermesinum x 'Ascot Brilliant'; (Loder and Rothschild 1922); scarlet or blood red.
		Hartley Luttrell			cl.	cultivated Standish & Noble before 1870; rosy red.
xxx	H-3	Harvest Moon	**	B	cl.	'Mrs. Lindsay Smith' x campylocarpum hybrid; (M. Koster & Sons); bright lemon yellow, brown-red spotting, or creamy white, carmine blotch; A.M. (R.H.S.) 1948.
		Hassan			cl.	'Carl Mette' x catawbiense; (Seidel); carmine.
xxx	H-3	Hawk			g.	wardii x 'Lady Bessborough; (Rothschild).
		Hawk	**	C	cl.	wardii x 'Lady Bessborough'; (Rothschild); a fine yellow (sulphur yellow H.C.C. 1/3); A.M. (R.H.S.) 1949. See 'Amour', 'Crest', 'Exbury Hawk', 'Beaulieu Hawk', 'Jervis Bay', 'Hawk Kestrel', 'Hawk Merlin'.
		Hawk Kestrel	**	C	cl.	wardii x 'Lady Bessborough' (Hawk g.) (Rothschild); rich yellow. Formerly known as Hawk var. Kestrel.
		Hawk Merlin			cl.	wardii x 'Lady Bessborough'(Hawk g.); (Rothschild); yellow. Formerly known as Hawk var. Merlin.
		Haydn			cl.	pink.
		Haze			cl.	hodgsonii x 'Muriel' (Evening g.); (Loder 1954); light pink mauve. Formerly known as Evening var. Haze.
		Heatherside Beauty			cl.	caucasicum x ; (Street); white.
		Hebe			g.	'Neriihaem' x williamsianum; (Magor 1927); deep rose pink.
		Heca			g.	herpesticum x campylocarpum; (Aberconway 1941); yellow.
		Hecla			g.	thomsonii x griersonianum; (Aberconway 1941); red. See 'Red Dragon'.
		Hector				(J. Waterer before 1874); bright crimson.
		Helen			cl.	campylocarpum hybrid x 'Mrs. Lindsay Smith' (Zuiderzee g.); (C. Ingram). Formerly known as Zuiderzee var. Helen.
		Helen				decorum x 'Souldis'; (Brandt 1952); white, yellow in throat.
		Helena			cl.	Syn. of 'Hellene'.
		Helena				cultivated Standish & Noble before 1870; rosy red.
xx	H-4	Hélène Schiffner	*	B		(Seidel); pure white; F.C.C. (R.H.S.) 1893.
		(Helen Fox)				See Barclayi Helen Fox.
		Helen Paul				fortunei x ; (Paul); soft pink margined rose; A.M. (R.H.S.) 1896.
		Helen Rogers			cl.	(Rogers); pink madder.
		Helen Vandevere			cl.	Azaleodendron; griersonianum x occidentale; B. C. 1939; P.C. 1939.
		Helen Waterer			cl.	(J. Waterer & Sons before 1890); red edge, white center.
		Helen Webster			cl.	discolor hybrid x 'Richard Gill'; (Commissioners of Crown Lands); Phlox pink (H.C.C. 625/3) with orange-brown spotting; A.M. (R.H.S.) 1954.
		Hellene				fortunei x ; (J. Waterer, Sons & Crisp Ltd.); white suffused and edged pale rosy lilac. Syn. 'Helena'.
		H. Elliott			g.	edgeworthii x formosum; white flowers faintly spotted pale yellow on upper segment, scented; A.M. (R.H.S.) 1900.
		Helmholtz			cl.	'Mrs. Milner' x 'Boule de Neige'; (Seidel cross 1906); purplish red.
		Hendersonii			g.	(Henderson before 1865); purple, lighter center; (Methven gives, "rosy crimson").
x	H-1	Henriette Sargent			cl.	catawbiense x ; (A. Waterer 1891); dark rose pink; much like 'Mrs. Charles Sargent' but dwarfer plant.
		Henryanum			cl.	dalhousiae x formosum; exhibited Henry 1862; white with a tinge of blush; F.C.C. 1865.
		Henry Bohn			cl.	(J. Waterer before 1875); crimson.
		Henry Drummond				(Methven); purplish crimson.
		Henry E. Burbridge			cl.	dichroanthum x 'Letty Edwards'; (Thacker 1944); apricot yellow.
		Henry Shilson			cl.	arboreum form; (R. Gill & Son); red.
		Hera			g.	haematodes x 'Jock'; (Aberconway 1941); scarlet red.
		Herbert Parsons				Syn. of 'President Lincoln'.
		Hercules			g.	javanicum x ; (Davies before 1890); apricot yellow suffused rose pink (ex Veitch); light rose, crimson spots (ex Methven); A.M. (R.H.S.) 1899.
		Hereward			g.	'Dolly' x griersonianum; (Rothschild 1940); rosy pink.
		Herga			g.	'Break of Day' x 'Lady Bessborough'; (Rothschild 1940); pale yellow with blotch.
		Her Majesty			g.	arboreum x 'Fosterianum'; soft crimson; F.C.C. 1889.
		Hermann Seidel			g.	'Eidam' x williamsianum; (Dietrich Hobbie 1952); bright rose.
		Herme			cl.	'Diadema' x 'Everestianum'; (Seidel cross 1912); pale rose with lilac edges.
		Hermes			g.	apodectum x 'Lady Bessborough'; (Rothschild 1940); orange yellow with pink markings.
		Hermia			cl.	(Rogers); rose madder, scented.
		Hermione			cl.	'Gilian' x arboreum; (Magor 1935); deep rich crimson or blood red; A.M. (R.H.S.) 1941.
		Hero			cl.	'Gloire de Gandavensis' x catawbiense; (Seidel cross 1906); pure white with yellow markings.
		Hesperia			cl.	detonsum x 'Empress Eugenie'; (Magor cross 1921).
		Hesperides			g.	'Ayah' x griersonianum; (Rothschild 1940); rose pink.
		Hester				cultivated Standish & Noble before 1860; white with brown spots.
		H. H. Hunnewell			cl.	catawbiense x; (A. Waterer); purplish red.
		Hiawatha			g.	'Adrastia' x griersonianum; (Aberconway 1941); carmine.
		(High Beeches)				See 'Fabia High Beeches'.

		High Beech Hybrid				fortunei x 'Mrs. Butler'; sweet scented; delicate salmon pink; A.M. (R.H.S.) 1894.
		Highlander			g.	'Adonis' x zeylanicum; (Aberconway 1950); rose red.
		Highland Mary				cultivated Standish & Noble before 1860; delicate blush with orange spots.
		High Noon			cl.	'Earl of Athlone' x 'Fabia'; (R. Henny).
		Hilde			cl.	fulvum x lacteum; (Stevenson 1955); yellow flushed pink.
		Hildebrand			cl.	cultivated Standish & Noble before 1870; crimson.
		Hippolyta				multicolor var. curtissii x 'Queen of the Yellows'; scarlet; F.C.C. 1888.
		Hipsal			g.	hippophaeoides x saluenense; (Magor 1926); purplish mauve.
		Hiraethlyn			g.	haematodes x griffithianum; (Aberconway 1933); rose to deep red.
		His Majesty				(R. Gill & Son); rose pink with few dots deeper shade.
		Hispaniola			cl.	'Isabella' x griersonianum (Infanta g.) (Collingwood Ingram). Formerly known as Infanta var. Hispaniola.
		H. J. Mangles				griffithianum x ; (Mangles).
		H. M. Arderne				fortunei x ; (G. Paul); pink with dark blotch; A.M. (R.H.S.) 1896.
		Hockessin			cl.	pubescens x keiskei; (Nearing); apricot, fading white.
		Hodconeri			g.	hodgsonii x falconeri; (Reuthe 1926).
		Hogarth			cl.	(A. Waterer before 1871); rosy scarlet.
		Holbein			cl.	'Alexander Adie' x 'Carl Mette'; (Seidel cross 1906); lilac rose.
		Holden			cl.	a red catawbiense seedling x 'Cunningham's White' (Shammarello); light red.
		Holger			cl.	'Madame Linden' x 'Eggebrechtii'; (Seidel cross 1906); pale violet with large dark green spots.
		Holker Hall				form of R. arboreum.
		Hollandia		B	cl.	'Pink Pearl' x 'Charles Dickens'; (L.J.Endtz & Co.); pure carmine. Syn. 'G. Streseman', 'G.T.Streseman'.
		Homer			cl.	'Kaiser Wilhelm' x 'Agnes'; (Seidel cross 1906); bright pink.
		Honey			cl.	wardii x 'Bow Bells'; (R. Henny 1960); Egyptian buff (H. C. C. 407/3), fading paler.
		Hon. John Boscawen			cl.	(J. Waterer before 1922); deep cherry red; "red edged white, yellow blotch" ex Millais.
		Hon. Mrs. Mercer Henderson			cl.	(J. Waterer); rose, black spots.
		Hoopskirt			cl.	'Rosy Morn' x 'Dido'; (R. Henny).
		(Hope)				See 'Naomi Hope'.
		Hopeful			g.	'F.C. Puddle' x hookeri; (Aberconway 1946); red.
		Horsham			cl.	griffithianum hybrid x 'Monsieur Thiers'; (C.B. van Nes & Sons before 1922); deep red.
		Hosea Waterer			cl.	in cultivation Knap Hill Nursery 1955; rich cerise pink.
		Hotshot			cl.	eriogynum x 'Mars'; (R. Henny).
		H.T.Gill				fortunei x thomsonii; (R. Gill & Son); rose; A.M. (R.H.S.) 1921.
		Hubert Robert			cl.	fortunei x williamsianum (Caroline Spencer g.); exhibited Adams-Acton 1950; shell pink. Formerly known as Caroline Spencer var. Hubert Robert.
		Hudibras				cultivated Standish & Noble before 1860; deep pink.
xx	H-4	Hugh Koster	**	B	cl.	'George Hardy' x 'Doncaster' hybrid; (M. Koster & Sons 1915); bright crimson; A.M. (R.H.S.) 1933.
		Hugh Wormald		C	cl.	(M. Koster & Sons before 1922); cerise with white stripe; striped like an Amaryllis; blotched.
		Hugo de Vries				(L.J.Endtz 1922); pink; A.M. (R.H.S.) 1921. Syn. of 'Professor Hugo de Vries'.
		Humboldt				catawbiense x ; (Seidel 1926); rose with dark markings.
		Humboldti				cultivated Standish & Noble before 1860; deep rose, white throat.
xxx	H-4	Humming Bird	**	C	g.	haematodes x williamsianum; (J.C.Williams 1933); pink shaded vermilion.
		Huntsman			g.	barbatum x campylocarpum var. elatum; exhibited Loder.
		H. Whitner			cl.	'Loderi Pink Diamond' x 'Cornish Cross' (Ruthelma g.); (Sir E. Loder); clear pink; A.M. (R.H.S.) 1935. Formerly known as Ruthelma var. H. Whitner.
		H.W.Sargent			cl.	catawbiense x ; (A. Waterer 1865); magenta crimson; F.C.C. 1865.
		Hybridum			g.	Azaleodendron; viscosum x maximum; (Herbert 1817); in cultivation T. Methven 1868-69; fragrant, edged pink, yellow spotted.
		Hyde			cl.	griffithianum x ; (C. B. van Nes & Sons); light red.
		Hymen			cl.	catawbiense x ; (Seidel 1926); light violet.
		Hypatia			g.	'Mrs. R.S. Holford' x kyawi; (Rothschild); exhibited Rothschild 1940; bright red; late.
		Hyperion			g.	'Cardinal' x forrestii var. repens; (Aberconway 1941); blood red.
x	H-3	Hyperion		A		(A. Waterer); white, chocolate blotch.
		Hyronimus Bosch			cl.	(M. Koster & Sons); light mauve.
		Iago			g.	'Romany Chai' x 'Lady Bessborough'; (Rothschild 1941); rosy crimson, large blotch of dark spots.
		Ianthe				cultivated Noble about 1885; rosy crimson.
xx	H-4	Ibex			g.	griersonianum x pocophorum; (Rothschild).
		Ibex			cl.	griersonianum x pocophorum; (Rothschild 1941); delft rose (H.C.C. 020); A.M. (R.H.S.) 1948.
		Ibis			g.	'Adelaide' x griersonianum; (Rothschild 1941); cerise pink.
		Icarus	*	B	g.	'A. Gilbert' x herpesticum; (Rothschild); deep rose pink bud opens to a flower of biscuit color shaded rose; A. M. (R. H. S.) 1947. See 'Organdie'.
		Icenia			g.	'Moser's Maroon' x 'Lady Bessborough'; (Rothschild 1941); pink.
		Ida				cultivated Standish & Noble before 1860; white with red spots.

	Ida		g.	'J.G. Millais' x neriiflorum; (Rothschild 1934); rosy red.
	Idaho		g.	'Dolly' x elliottii; (Rothschild 1941); brick red.
	Ida Waterer		cl.	(Waterer, Sons & Crisp Ltd.); violet tinted rose, greenish dots; A.M. (R.H.S.) 1925.
xxx H-3	Idealist		g.	wardii x 'Naomi'; (Rothschild).
	Idealist	*** B	cl.	wardii x 'Naomi'; (Rothschild); pale greenish yellow (H.C.C. 663/2); A.M. (R.H.S.) 1945.
	Idol		cl.	'Loderi King George' x 'Britannia'; (R. Henny); tyrian rose, lighter center. P.A. (A.R.S.) 1957.
	Ightham		cl.	augustinii (Bodnant form) x fastigiatum (Augfast g.); (G.Reuthe Ltd.) exhibited 1952. Previously known as Augfast var. Ightham.
	Ightham Yellow			wardii x decorum (Arthur Smith g.); (Reuthe 1952); yellow. Previously known as Arthur Smith var. Ightham Yellow.
x H-1	Ignatius Sargent		cl.	catawbiense x ; (A. Waterer); light rose crimson.
	Ignescens		cl.	(A. Waterer before 1850); bright red, black spots.
	Ilam Alarm		cl.	zeylanicum x griffithianum hybrid; (Stead); red, lighter center.
	Ilam Apricot		cl.	(zeylanicum x 'Pink Pearl') x dichroanthum hybrid (Stead).
	Ilam Cornubia		cl.	zeylanicum x 'Shilsonii'; (Stead).
	Ilam Orange		cl.	dichroanthum hybrid; (Stead).
	Ilam Violet		cl.	'Electra' x russatum; (Stead 1947); violet blue.
	Iliad		g.	'Nereid' x kyawi; (Rothschild).
	Iliad		cl.	'Nereid' x kyawi; (Rothschild 1949); blood red (H.C.C. 820/3); A.M. (R.H.S.) 1949.
	Illuminator			cultivated Standish & Noble before 1860; scarlet.
	Illyria		g.	'Romany Chal' x kyawi; (Rothschild 1941); rich crimson.
	Ilona		g.	valentinianum x auritum; (Rothschild 1941); pale yellow.
	Imogene		g.	'Taylori' x teysmannii; greenhouse hybrid; pale yellow; F.C.C. 1888.
xx H-3	Impeanum		g.	impeditum x hanceanum; (R.B.G.Kew).
	Impeanum	* A	cl.	impeditum x hanceanum; (R.B.G.Kew); deep lilac or blue; F.C.C. (R.H.S.) 1934.
x H-3	Impi		g.	didymum x 'Moser's Maroon'; (Rothschild).
	Impi	** B	cl.	didymum x 'Moser's Maroon'; (Rothschild); very dark red (H.C.C. 826), brilliant red when seen by transmitted light; A.M. (R.H.S.) 1945.
	Improved Parson's Grandiflorum		cl.	catawbiense x ; (Stokes); purplish rose.
	I. M. S.		cl.	Loderi g., selfed; (Stead); pink.
	Inamorata		g.	wardii x discolor; (Rothschild).
	Inamorata	** B	cl.	wardii x discolor; (Rothschild); sulphur yellow with small, spotted, crimson blotch in throat; A. M. (R. H. S.) 1950.
	Incarnatum Floribundum			'Maiden's Blush' x 'Prince Leopold'; rosy salmon; F.C.C. 1885.
	Inchmery		g.	'The Don' x eriogynum; (Rothschild 1941); deep pink, late.
	(Inchmery)			See 'Carita Inchmery'.
	Independence Day	* A	cl.	(A. Waterer about 1915); red, pale center and dark spot.
x H 5	Indiana	C	g.	scyphocalyx x kyawi; (Rothschild 1941); orange red; yellow with dark red markings.
	Indian Chief		cl.	catawbiense x ; (Stokes); red.
	Indian Yellow			'Crown Princess of Germany' x javanicum; exhibited Veitch 1891; yellow to red orange.
	Indomitable		g.	souliei x 'General Sir John du Cane'; (Rothschild 1941); white flushed pale pink.
	Infanta		cl.	'Isabella' x griersonianum; (Collingwood Ingram); light crimson (H.C.C. 22/2-3) deepening to rose madder (H.C.C. 23/1) at the base of the tube.
	Ingeborg		cl.	catawbiense x ; (T.J.R.Seidel); dark crimson.
	Ingomer			cultivated Standish & Noble before 1870; deep rose.
	Ingramii		g.	(Standish before 1860); blush white with lemon blotch; "chocolate spots" ex Methven.
	Ingre		g.	insigne x griersonianum; (Aberconway 1936); deep pink.
	Ingrid		g.	'Tally Ho' x griffithianum; (Rothschild 1941); pink.
	Insun		g.	'Ingre' x 'Sunrise'; (Aberconway 1946); pink.
	Intermedium			ferrugineum x hirsutum; natural hybrid 1891.
	Intrepid		g.	'Beau Brummell' x kyawi; (Rothschild 1941); rosy red.
	Intrifast	* B	g.	intricatum x fastigiatum; (Lowinsky); violet blue.
	Iola		g.	valentinianum x bullatum; (Rothschild 1941); primrose-cream.
	Iolanthe		g.	'Blanc-mange' x kyawi; (Rothschild 1941); late; cerise pink.
	Ione		g.	'Countess of Haddington' x bullatum; (Magor 1926); white, opens pale primrose.
	Iphigenia		g.	haematodes x 'Red Admiral'; (Magor 1934); red.
	Irene			(Gebr. Guldemond, Boskoop); pink.
	Iris Lawrence			exhibited Hugh Wormald 1941.
	Ironside		g.	'Midsummer' x kyawi; (Rothschild 1941); late; bright crimson.
	Irrifarg			irroratum x fargesii; (Magor 1926); blush with copious crimson spotting.
	Isaac Davies			(Davies before 1890); scarlet.
	Isaac Newton	B	g.	(catawbiense x thomsonii) x forrestii var. repens; (Dietrich Hobbie 1952); carmine red.
	Isabel		g.	calophyllum x maddenii; (Aberconway 1947); light rose; early.
	Isabella		g.	griffithianum x auriculatum; (Loder 1934); clear pink. See 'Exbury Isabella', 'Isabella Nevada'.
	Isabella Mangles			griffithianum x ; (Mangles); soft pink.
	Isabella Nevada		cl.	griffithianum x auriculatum (Isabella g.); exhibited C. Ingram 1936. Previously known as Isabella var. Nevada.

		Isabel Meeres		cl.	(J. Waterer); rosy crimson.
		Isis		g.	'Carex' x laxiflorum; (Rothschild 1941); spotted white.
		Islay		g.	agapetum x 'Romany Chai'; (Rothschild 1941); bright rich scarlet.
		Isme		g.	wardii x venator; (Rothschild 1941); yellow with rose markings.
		Ispahan		g.	'Fabia' x wardii; (Rothschild); exhibited Rothschild 1941; tangerine to yellow.
		Istanbul		g.	'Mrs. H. Stocker' x elliottii; (Rothschild 1941).
		Istar		g.	dichroanthum x 'Naomi'; (Rothschild 1941); yellow marked pink.
		Istria		g.	'Astarte' x griffithianum; (Aberconway 1946); pale pink.
		Italia		g.	'Duke of York' x griersonianum; (Dietrich Hobbie 1954); salmon red.
		Ithica		g.	scyphocalyx var. septentrionale x eriogynum; (Rothschild 1941).
		Ivan		g.	'B. de Bruin' x kyawi; (Rothschild 1941); bright light crimson.
		Ivanhoe			cultivated Standish & Noble before 1860; deep claret.
xx	H-3	Ivanhoe		g.	'Chanticleer' x griersonianum; (Rothschild).
		Ivanhoe		cl.	'Chanticleer' x griersonianum; (Rothschild); brilliant red (H.C.C. 020) faintly mottled on the upper petals in a darker shade of same red; A.M. (R.H.S.) 1945.
x	H-4	Ivery's Scarlet	D	cl.	blood red. Syn. 'Ivorianum'.
x	H-4	Iviza		g.	'Fabia' x 'Bustard'; (Rothschild 1941); salmon orange.
		Ivorianum			Syn. of 'Ivery's Scarlet'.
		Ivy		cl.	cinnabarinum var. roylei x 'Royal Flush' orange form (Lady Chamberlain g.); (Rothschild). Previously known as Lady Chamberlain var. Ivy).
		Izabelle			cultivated Standish & Noble before 1860; French white, bright yellow eye.
		Jackie		cl.	Azaleodendron; deep rose, spotted.
		Jack Izod		cl.	(M. Koster & Sons); pale pink.
		Jackmannii			1868-69; crimson, finely spotted.
x	H-2	Jacksonii	* A	cl.	caucasicum x 'Nobleanum'; (Herbert 1835); rosy pink with deeper pink stripe on outside of petal.
		Jack the Ripper		g.	'Erebus' x 'Jacquetta'; (Aberconway).
		Jack the Ripper		cl.	'Erebus' x 'Jacquetta'; (Aberconway 1949); blood red (H.C.C. 820/2) with faint spotting on upper three lobes; A.M. (R.H.S.) 1949.
		Jacobean		g.	'Bibiani' x haemaleum; (Rothschild 1942); deep maroon.
		Jacqueline		g.	facetum x 'Albatross'; (Rothschild 1942); late; flesh pink.
		Jacques			dichroanthum x 'Day Dream'; (Rothschild); orange pink.
		Jacquetta		g.	facetum x griersonianum; (Digby 1953). scarlet-red.
		Jade		cl.	'Fabia' x 'Corona'; (R. Henny).
		Jaipur		g.	forrestii var. repens x meddianum; (Rothschild 1942); deep crimson.
		Jalisco	** B	g.	'Lady Bessborough' x 'Dido'; (Rothschild 1942); orange. See 'Lindberg', 'Jalisco Eclipse', 'Jalisco Elect'. 'Jalisco Emblem', 'Jalisco Goshawk', 'Jalisco Janet'.
		Jalisco Eclipse	** B	cl.	'Lady Bessborough' x 'Dido' (Jalisco g.); (Rothschild); primrose yellow with a dark crimson blotch and spotting towards the base of the throat; externally streaked with crimson; A.M. (R.H.S.) 1948. Previously known as Jalisco var. Eclipse.
		Jalisco Elect	** B	cl.	'Lady Bessborough' x 'Dido' (Jalisco g.); (Rothschild); primrose yellow with paler lobes; A.M. (R.H.S.) 1948. Previously known as Jalisco var. Elect.
		Jalisco Emblem		cl.	'Lady Bessborough' x 'Dido' (Jalisco g.); (Rothschild); pale yellow with dark blotch; exhibited R.H.S. 1948. Previously known as Jalisco var. Emblem.
		Jalisco Goshawk	****B	cl.	'Lady Bessborough' x 'Dido' (Jalisco g.); (Rothschild); mimosa yellow (H.C.C. 602/1) with a dark shade on upper lobes and some crimson spotting; F.C.C. (R.H.S.) 1954. Previously known as Jalisco var. Goshawk.
		Jalisco Janet		cl.	'Lady Bessborough' x 'Dido' (Jalisco g.); (Rothschild); exhibited R.H.S. 1948; yellow. Previously known as Jalisco var. Janet.
		Jamaica		g.	'Break of Day' x eriogynum; (Rothschild 1942); orange red.
		James Barto		cl.	williamsianum x orbiculare; (James Barto); fuchsine pink (H.C.C. 627/3); P.A. (A.R.S.) 1953.
		James Bateman		cl.	(A. Waterer 1865); rosy scarlet.
		James Brigham			reddish purple.
		James Burchett	* B	cl.	discolor x ; (W.C. Slocock); white, yellow blotch.
		James Macintosh		cl.	(A. Waterer 1870); rosy scarlet.
		James Mangles			exhibited R.E. Horsfall 1934.
		James Marshall Brooks		cl.	(A. Waterer 1870); scarlet with bronze spot. Syn. 'J. Marshall Brooks'.
		James Mason		cl.	(J. Waterer before 1915); light center, bright red edging.
		James Nasmyth		cl.	(A. Waterer before 1870); rosy lilac, blotched maroon.
		Jan Baptiste		g.	eriogynum x griffithianum; (Adams-Acton 1934); coral.
xxx	H-3	Jan Dekens	B	cl.	(J. Blaauw & Co., Boskoop, 1940); rich pink, fringed.
		Jane Rogers		cl.	'Mrs. Donald Graham' x 'Mrs. R. S. Holford'; (Endre Ostbo); carmine pink, dark blotch.
		Janet		g.	'Avalanche' x 'Dr. Stocker'; (Rothschild).
		(Janet)			See 'Jalisco Janet'.
		Janet Blair		cl.	Dexter hybrid x ?; (D. G. Leach 1958); very pale pinkish mauve, golden bronze rays on upper lobes; fimbriate.
		Jan Steen		g.	'Fabia' x 'Lady Bessborough'; (Rothschild).

		Jan Steen			cl.	'Fabia' x 'Lady Bessborough'; (Rothschild); cream edge shading to pink and then to orange with a maroon splotch in throat; Preliminary Commendation (R.H.S.) 1950.
		Janus			g.	'Venus' x griersonianum; (Aberconway 1946); scarlet.
		Jaquetta / Jacquetta				facetum x griersonianum; (Digby); "scarlet-red".
		Jasminiflorum Carminatum				jasminiflorum x javanicum; approaching crimson.
		Jasminiflorum Superbum				jasminiflorum x lobbii; white; F.C.C. 1876.
		Jason			g.	lacteum x 'Penjerrick'; (Rothschild 1942); deep yellow.
x	H-3	Jasper			g.	dichroanthum x 'Lady Bessborough'; (Rothschild 1942); pale orange or cream to yellow. See 'Jasper Pimento'.
		Jasper Pimento			cl.	dichroanthum x 'Lady Bessborough' (Jasper g.) (Rothschild); orange red. Previously known as Jasper var. Pimento.
		Jay Gould				Syn. of 'Alexander Adie'.
		Jay McMartin			cl.	'C.P.Raffill' x 'Moser's Maroon'; (Lem-P.Bowman, 1949); chrysanthemum crimson (H.C.C. 824/1), heavily spotted black on upper lobe.
		J.C.Millais				Syn. of 'J.G.Millais'.
xx	H-3	Jean			g.	griersonianum x decorum; (Stirling-Maxwell 1936); pink.
		Jean Goujon			g.	'Barclayi' x 'Unknown Warrior'; (Adams-Acton 1936); vivid scarlet.
		Jeanie Deans				in cultivation with T. Methven 1868-69; deep blush, intensely spotted; syn. of 'Jennie Deans'.
		Jean Marie de Montague				See 'Jean Mary Montague'.
xxxx	H-3	Jean Mary Montague	**	B	cl.	griffithianum x ; (C.B. van Nes & Sons); bright scarlet.
		Jeanne d'Arc			cl.	(M. Koster & Sons); white.
		Jean Stearn			cl.	(J.Waterer); white with purple spots.
		J.E.Harris				falconeri x thomsonii (Surprise g.); (J.G.E.Harris 1940). Previously known as Surprise var. J.E.Harris.
		Jennifer				campylocarpum x griffithianum; (G.H.Johnstone); lemon yellow.
		Jennie Deans				cultivated Standish & Noble before 1860; deep blush, intensely spotted.
		Jeritsa			g.	griffithianum x 'Lady Bessborough'; (Rothschild).
		Jeritsa			cl.	griffithianum x 'Lady Bessborough'; (Rothschild); pale mimosa yellow (H.C.C. 602/3) darkens slightly on the 3 upper lobes, and in the base a small crimson zone and some spotting; A.M. (R.H.S.) 1951.
		Jersey Cream			cl.	'Mrs. Lindsay Smith' x campylocarpum (Zuiderzee g.); (Crosfield); cream; A.M.(R.H.S.) 1939. Previously known as Zuiderzee var. Jersey Cream.
		Jervis Bay	**	C	cl.	wardii x 'Lady Bessborough' (Hawk g.); (Rothschild); lightly frilled, sulphur yellow (H.C.C. 1/3). The throat stained with a deep red blotch and some spotting; A.M. (R.H.S.) 1951. Previously known as Hawk var. Jervis Bay.
		Jessica				cultivated Standish & Noble before 1860; with rich dark eye on lavender ground.
		Jester				dichroanthum x 'Naomi'; (Rothschild); yellow with pink markings.
		Jewess			cl.	caucasicum x ; (Liebig); cultivated by Standish & Noble before 1860; light lilac fading to almost white, early.
		Jezebel			cl.	'Fabua' x ?; (Clark).
		J. Fiala			cl.	(Belgium); blush white, spotted.
xxx	H-4	J.G.Millais	**	C	cl.	'Ascot Brilliant' x 'Pink Pearl': (J.Waterer); scarlet or deep blood red; April. Syn. 'J.C.Millais'.
xxx	H-4	J.H. van Nes	**	C	cl.	'Monsieur Thiers' x griffithianum hybrid; (C.B. van Nes & Sons); soft red.
		Jibuti			g.	griersonianum x 'Gill's Triumph'; (Rothschild).
		Jibuti			cl.	griersonianum x 'Gill's Triumph'; (Rothschild); neyron rose (H.C.C. 623/1) with a dark variation; A.M. (R.H.S.) 1949.
		Jiusepa			g.	dichroanthum x 'Day Dream'; (Rothschild); exhibited Rothschild 1942.
x	H-4	J. J. de Vink	*	C	cl.	'Doncaster' hybrid x griffithianum hybrid; (M. Koster & Sons); rose red (H.C.C. between 724, 724/1), blotched brown.
		J.Marshall Brooks			cl.	Syn. of 'James Marshall Brooks'.
		Jo			g.	'Boddaertianum' x smithii; (Magor 1920).
		Joana			g.	wardii x 'Albatross'; (Rothschild 1942); white shaded cream.
		Joanita			g.	lacteum x caloxanthum; (Rothschild); deep yellow.
		Joan of Arc				cultivated Standish & Noble before 1860; deep rosy pink.
		Jocelyne			g.	lacteum x calophytum; (Rothschild).
		Jocelyne			cl.	lacteum x calophytum; (Rothschild); white with a light cream tinge on upper lobes and a crimson blotch in throat; A.M. (R.H.S.) 1954; F.C.C. (R.H.S.) 1956.
xxx	H-3	Jock			g.	williamsianum x griersonianum; (Stirling Maxwell 1939); dark pink with a suggestion of orange in the throat.
		John Bennett Poe				fortunei x ; (Paul); crimson with olive blotch.
		John Bull			cl.	johnstoneanum x bullatum; (Noble); flowers pale pink, flushed cream.
		John Coutts			g.	('Grand Arab' x griffithianum) x griersonianum; (R.B.G. Kew); exhibited R.B.G.Kew 1946; red, dark pink in throat.
		John Gair				(Standish 1860): rose colored, paler in center, scarcely spotted.

		John Galsworthy			cl.	maroon purple, yellow blotch.
		John Henry Agnew			cl.	(J.Waterer before 1922); pink, chocolate spots.
		John Holms			cl.	arboreum x barbatum (Duke of Cornwall g.); (Gibson, Rhu); dark brilliant scarlet; A.M. (R.H.S.) 1957.
		John Keats			cl.	cinnabarinum var. roylei x augustinii; (Adams-Acton 1942); mauve, fading.
		John Marchand			cl.	moupinense x sperabile; (Ingram 1947).
		Johnnie Johnston			g.	johnstoneanum (double form) x tephropeplum; (Bolitho); variable shades of tyrian rose.
		Johnnie Johnston			cl.	johnstoneanum (double form) x tephropeplum; (Bolitho 1944); tyrian rose (H.C.C. 24/3) with staining of a darker shade (H.C.C. 24/2); A.M. (R.H.S.) 1956.
		Johnsonianum				(before 1851); in cultivation with T.Methven 1868-69; brilliant crimson.
		John Spencer			cl.	(A.Waterer); cultivated before 1870; reddish magenta.
		John Tremayne				arboreum x griffithianum (Beauty of Tremough g.); (Tremayne). Previously known as Beauty of Tremough var. John Tremayne.
x	H-2	John Walter		A	cl.	catawbiense x arboreum; (J.Waterer before 1860); crimson.
		John Waterer				catawbiense x ; (J.Waterer before 1860); purplish red; still cultivated.
		John Willis Fleming			cl.	griffithianum x ; (W.H.Rogers); rose. Syn. 'J.W.Fleming', 'Glory'.
		Jordan	**	C	g.	dichroanthum x griffithianum; (Rothschild 1942); pale orange.
		Joseph Martin			cl.	(A.Waterer); light pink.
		Joseph Martyr			cl.	(A.Waterer); light pink, yellow blotch.
		Joseph Whitworth	*	A	cl.	ponticum x ; (J.Waterer before 1867); dark purple lake, dark spots.
		Josephine			g.	wardii x 'Ayah'; (Rothschild 1942); cream.
		Josephine Everitt			cl.	fortunei x ; (Dexter); pink.
		Joyance			g.	wardii x scyphocalyx; (Rothschild); exhibited Rothschild 1942; cream with salmon pink to orange markings.
		Joyce Rickett			cl.	discolor x 'Madame Carvalho'; (Hillier 1945); white, pink edge.
		Juanita			cl.	'Isabella' x griersonianum (Infanta g.) deep pink flushed with scarlet salmon at the base of the throat. Previously known as Infanta var. Juanita.
		Jubar				cultivated Standish & Noble before 1860; light rosy crimson, dark spots.
		Jubilee				'Forsterianum' x ; exhibited Waterer, Sons & Crisp 1935.
		Jubilee				(Waterer, Sons & Crisp); recommended for trial at Exbury.
		Jubilee Queen			g.	'Loderi Venus' x 'Rose du Barri'; (Loder).
		Jubilee Queen			cl.	'Loderi Venus' x 'Rose du Barri'; (Lady Loder); pure white with the apices of lobes tinged rose at first; A.M. (R.H.S.) 1935 See 'Margaret Rose'.
		Judith			g.	Loderi g. x 'General Sir John du Cane'; (Rothschild 1942); white, flushed pink.
		Judy			g.	falconeri x pachytrichum; (Loder 1935); "now extinct" (Sir Giles Loder).
		Judy			cl.	fortunei x campylocarpum; (D.James).
		Juisepa				'Day Dream' x dichroanthum; (Rothschild); biscuit to yellow.
		Juliana			g.	griersonianum x 'Queen Wilhelmina'; (C.Ingram 1939); scarlet. See 'Captain Blood'.
		Julie			cl.	Loderi g. selfed; white suffused sulphur; A.M. (R.H.S.) 1944.
		Juliet				'Taylori' x teysmannii; (Veitch 1891); shades of primrose yellow.
		Julie Titcomb			cl.	'Marinus Koster' x 'Snow Queen'; (Larson 1942); pink.
		Julius Ruppell				(J.Waterer); rose with carmine markings.
		Juno			g.	'Amaura' x F. C. Puddle'; (Aberconway 1941); pale pink.
		Jupiter				'Mrs. E.C.Stirling' x ; (J.Waterer, Sons & Crisp Ltd.); soft lilac rose.
		Jutland			g.	elliottii x 'Bellerophon'; (Rothschild).
		Jutland			cl.	elliottii x 'Bellerophon'; (Rothschild); geranium lake (H.C.C. 20) freely flecked on the upper petals and slightly on the lower with darker red markings; A.M. (R.H.S.) 1947.
		J.W.Fleming				Syn. of 'John Willis Fleming'.
		Kaiser Wilhelm			cl.	carmine.
		Kant			cl.	(M.Koster & Sons); yellow, pink in bud.
xx	H-4	Karkov			g.	griersonianum x 'Red Admiral'; (Rothschild).
		Karkov	**	C	cl.	griersonianum x 'Red Admiral'; (Rothschild); carmine rose, faintly and evenly spotted; A.M. (R.H.S.) 1947.
		Kate Greenaway	*	A		'Mrs. E.C.Stirling' x ; (Waterer, Sons & Crisp); soft rose, veined red, fringed. Syn. 'Niobe'.
		Kate Waterer		B	cl.	(J.Waterer before 1890); pink with yellow center, late.
		Katherine Dalton			cl.	smirnowii x fortunei; (Gable); exhibited 1937; pale lavender pink.
		Katherine van Thol				Syn. of 'Catherine van Tol'.
		Kathleen Fielding			cl.	(M.Koster & Sons before 1922); red with purple blotch.
		Kathleen Wallace			cl.	(C.B.van Nes & Sons); pale pink.
		Kaulbach			cl.	catawbiense x ; (Seidel 1926); white flushed lilac with yellow marks.
		Keay Slocock	*	B	cl.	campylocarpum x hardy hybrid; (W.C.Slocock); pale yellow, flushed salmon or creamy white, slight blotch.
		Keiskarb			g.	keiskei x arboreum; (Magor cross 1918); white shaded to rose with crimson blotch at base and two short lines of crimson spots.
		Keiskrac			g.	keiskei x racemosum; (Magor 1926); pink.
		Kenlis			cl.	orbiculare x meddianum; (Headfort); neyron rose (H.C.C. 623/3): A.M. (R.H.S.) 1948.

		Kenneth		g.	'Hiraethlyn' x 'Elizabeth'; (Aberconway).
		Kenneth		cl.	'Hiraethlyn' x 'Elizabeth'; (Aberconway 1949); geranium lake (H.C.C. 20); A.M. (R.H.S.) 1949.
		Kentish Lad			'Alice' x 'Corry Koster'; (R. Wallace & Co. 1944).
		Kentucky Cardinal		cl.	brachycarpum x 'Essex Scarlet'; (Gable); exhibited 1946; deep red. Syn. 'The Cardinal'.
		Kernick Gem		cl.	barbatum x 'Luscombei'; (R. Gill & Son); rich pink with deep spots on lower segments; A.M. (R.H.S.) 1928.
		Kesselringii		g.	smirnowii x ponticum; natural hybrid 1910.
x	H-1	Kettledrum		cl.	catawbiense x ; (A. Waterer 1877); purplish crimson.
		Kewarb		g.	'Kewense' x arboreum (blood red form); (Magor cross 1918)
		Kewdec		g.	'Kewense' x decorum; (Magor cross 1913); white. See 'Kewdec White Lady'.
		Kewdec White Lady		cl.	'Kewense' x decorum (Kewdec g.); (Magor 1913); white with tinge of green within at base; A. M. (R. H. S.) 1938. Previously known as Kewdec var. White Lady.
		Kewense		g.	griffithianum x fortunei; (R. B. G. Kew before 1888); blush white. (cf. Loderi g.)
		Kewensi			griffithianum x hookeri; large, pale rosy pink. A.M. (R.H.S.) 1907.
		Kew Pearl			blush pink, edged rose.
		Kewxen		g.	'Kewense' x detonsum; (Magor 1927); violet rose with some ochre spotting.
		Kiev		g.	elliottii x 'Barclayi'; (Rothschild).
		Kiev		cl.	elliottii x 'Barclayi'; (Rothschild); deep shade of blood red (H. C. C. 820/3) which is darkened by heavy spotting with distinct basal nectaries; A.M. (R.H.S.) 1950.
		Kilimanjaro		g.	elliottii x 'Dusky Maid'; (Rothschild).
		Kilimanjaro		cl.	elliottii x 'Dusky Maid'; (Rothschild); red currant (H.C.C. 821/1); F.C.C. (R.H.S.) 1947.
		King Arthur		cl.	'Arthur Osborn' x griffithianum; (Harrison 1956).
		Kingcup		g.	dichroanthum x 'Bustard'; (Rothschild).
		Kingcup		cl.	dichroanthum x 'Bustard'; (Rothschild); Indian yellow (H.C.C. 6/2); A.M. (R.H.S.) 1943.
		King Edward VII / King Edward		g.	javanicum x teysmanni; deep yellow; similar to 'Exquisite'; A.M.(R.H.S.) 1901.
x	H-4	King George	* C	cl.	griffithianum x ; (Otto Schulz cross 1892, purchased by J.H. van Nes 1896, introduced C. B. van Nes & Sons); bright red, Gloxinia shaped flowers, not in Loderi g.
		Kingking		g.	zeylanicum x 'Mrs. Randall Davidson'; (Magor cross 1915).
xxx	H-4	King of Shrubs		cl.	discolor x 'Fabia'; (Endre Ostbo); apricot yellow at base with greenish yellow spotting in throat at base of petals, inner margin broadly banded porcelain rose (H.C.C. 620/2) outside richly flushed carmine rose (H.C.C. 6/211 to 6/212); P.A. (A.R.S.) 1950. Syn 'Orange Azor'.
		King of the Purples		cl.	(A. Waterer); deep violet purple or dark purple, spotted.
		Kingthom		g.	'Mrs. Kingsmill' x thomsonii; (Magor).
		King Tut		cl.	red catawbiense seedling x red catawbiense seedling; (Shammarello); bright red, white blotch.
		Kismet		cl.	'Grenadier' x 'Pygmalion'; (R. Henny); scarlet.
		Kissena		cl.	catawbiense x ; (Parsons); purple.
		Kittiwake		g.	lutescens x edgeworthii; (J.C.Williams 1933).
		Kluis Sensation	B	cl.	'Britannia' x an unnamed seedling; (A. Kluis 1946); bright scarlet red or turkey red, faintly spotted.
		Kluis Triumph	A	cl.	griffithianum x ; (A. Kluis); deep red.
		Knowle Brilliant		cl.	'Pygmalion' x venator; (Thacker 1942); scarlet.
		Knowle Yellow		cl.	wardii x 'Letty Edwards'; (Thacker 1940); clear yellow
		Koenig Albert			eximium x ; cream.
		Koenig Carola		g.	falconeri x ponticum; (Ludiecke 1926); lavender with purple throat.
		Koenigdis		g.	'Koenig Carola' x discolor; (Magor 1913); Heliotrope, lightest shade but one, spotted olive green, blotch at base.
		Koh-i-noor			griffithianum x ; (Otto Schulz 1892).
		Kola		g.	'Isabella' x 'Tally Ho'; (Rothschild 1947); pink.
		König Albert			eximium x ; cream. Syn. 'Koenig Albert'.
		Königdis			Syn. of 'Koenigdis'.
		Köningen Louise			'Molière' x 'Mrs. Lindsay Smith'; (M. Koster & Sons).
		Koster's Choice		cl.	fortunei x ; (Dexter); rose pink.
		Koster's Cream		cl.	campylocarpum x ; (M. Koster & Sons); creamy yellow, green blotch.
		LaBars' White		cl.	a superior form of catawbiense var. album; (LaBar, 1958); white in bud and flower, greenish-yellow markings in throat.
		La Belle			F.C.C. 1887.
		Lacs		cl.	lacteum x sinogrande; (Magor 1948); pale cream with dark crimson blotch; exhibited 1955.
		Lacsino		cl.	lacteum x sinogrande; (Magor cross 1936); white with dark splotch.
		Lactcombei		g.	'Luscombei' x lacteum; (Stevenson 1951); yellow flushed pink.
		Ladifor		cl.	'Lady Clementine Mitford' x fortunei; (Gable); pink.
xxx	H-5	Lady Alice Fitzwilliam	*** F	cl.	white with Nutmeg fragrance; F.C.C. 1881.
		Lady Alice Peel			cultivated Standish & Noble before 1870; dark rose, blotch of very dark spots.

		Lady Annette de Trafford	* A	cl.	maximum x; (A. Waterer 1874); blush pink, dark brown blotch; late.
x	H-1	Lady Armstrong		cl.	catawbiense x; (A. Waterer before 1870); carmine, lighter center. Syn. 'Annedore'.
		Lady Berry		g.	'Rosy Bell' x 'Royal Flush'; (Rothschild).
		Lady Berry	****D	cl.	'Rosy Bell' x 'Royal Flush'; (Rothschild); rose opal (H.C.C. 022/3) inside ana outside jasper red (H.C.C. 0181) gradually paling towards 5 lobed mouth; A.M. (R.H.S.) 1937; F.C.C. (R.H.S.) 1949.
xxx	H-3	Lady Bessborough		g.	discolor x campylocarpum var. elatum; (Rothschild)
		Lady Bessborough	****B	cl.	discolor x campylocarpum var. elatum; (Rothschild); stone cream or biscuit cream with maroon blotch in throat; F.C.C. (R.H.S.) 1933. See 'Montreal', 'Roberte'.
xx	H-4	Ladybird		g.	discolor x 'Corona'; (Rothschild).
		Ladybird	*** B	cl.	discolor x 'Corona'; (Rothschild); pink, freckled yellow inside: A.M. (R.H.S.) 1933.
xxx	H-3	Lady Bligh		cl.	griffithianum x; (C.B. van Nes & Sons); strawberry red fading to rich pink; A.M. (R.H.S.) 1934.
		Lady Bowring			shaded rosy pink; spotted.
		Lady Bridport			cultivated Standish & Noble before 1860; pure white.
		Lady Byng		cl.	'Lady Roseberry' x charianthum; (Thacker 1942); rose pink.
		Lady Cathcart			bright clear rose, crimson spots. Syn. of 'Lady Eleanor Cathcart'.
		Lady Catherine		cl.	auriculatum x 'Corona'; (Ramsden 1936); flushed rose with rusty speckling within; late; A.M. (R.H.S.) 1936.
		Lady Cavendish			Syn. of 'Cavendishi'.
		Lady Chamberlain		g.	cinnabarinum var. roylei x 'Royal Flush' orange form; (Rothschild).
xxxx	H-4	Lady Chamberlain	****C	cl.	cinnabarinum var. roylei x 'Royal Flush' orange form; (Rothschild 1930); salmon colored or orange red suffused with rose; F.C.C. (R.H.S.) 1931. See 'Apricot Lady Chamberlain', 'Bodnant Yellow', 'Chelsea', 'Exbury Lady Chamberlain', 'Gleam', 'Golden Queen', 'Lady Chamberlain Etna', 'Lady Chamberlain Seville', 'Oriflamme', 'Salmon Trout'.
		Lady Chamberlain Etna		cl.	cinnabarinium var. roylei x 'Royal Flush' orange form (Lady Chamberlain g.); (Rothschild). Previously known as Lady Chamberlain var. Etna.
		Lady Chamberlain Seville		cl.	cinnabarinum var. roylei x 'Royal Flush' orange form (Lady Chamberlain g.); (Rothschild); bright orange. Previously known as Lady Chamberlain var. Seville.
		Lady Clementina Mitford			
xx	H-2	Lady Clementine Mitford	** A	cl.	maximum x; (A. Waterer); exhibited 1870; soft peach pink, darker edge.
		Lady Clementine Walsh Lady C. Walsh Lady Clement Walsh		cl.	(J.Waterer); pale pink or white, spotted green on upper segment; blush edged pink. A.M. (R.H.S.) 1902.
		Lady Clermont		cl.	catawbiense x; (A. Waterer); light red or rosy red, very dark blotch; F.C.C. 1865.
		Lady Constance			deep rose; A.M. 1923
		Lady Decies	A	cl.	(J. Waterer before 1922); blush lilac or light mauve, yellow eye.
		Lady de Rothschild	B	cl.	griffithianum x 'Sappho'; (A. Waterer); white flushed blush pink and spotted crimson; A.M. (R.H.S.) 1952.
		Lady Digby		cl.	facetum x strigillosum; (Digby); blood red (H.C.C. 820) with faint spots; A.M. (R.H.S.) 1946.
		Lady Dorothy Neville		cl.	(J. Waterer before 1874); dark purple with black spots. Syn. 'Standard of Flanders', 'Etandard de Flandre'.
		Lady Dunleath		cl.	elliottii x arboreum var. kermesinum; exhibited Lord Dunleath 1954; scarlet.
		Lady Easthope		cl.	(J. Waterer before 1874); clear rose with dark spots.
xx	H-2	Lady Eleanor Cathcart	** A	cl.	maximum x arboreum; (J. Waterer before 1850); clear pale pink, with purplish red blotch; exhibited 1926. Syn. 'Lady Cathcart'.
		Lady Emily Peel		cl.	(J. Waterer before 1851); in cultivation with T. Methven 1868-9; bright rose, intensely blotched with chocolate-colored spots.
		Lady Ethel Edgar			(M. Koster & Sons); cerise red.
		Lady Ethel Hall			(M. Koster & Sons); rose pink margins, pale interior.
		Lady Falmouth		cl.	arboreum x; (J. Waterer before 1875); rose, black blotch.
		Lady Francis Crossley		cl.	(A. Waterer before 1867); rosy pink or salmon.
		Lady Galway		cl.	exhibited Mason; white, tinged mauve.
		Lady Gertrude Foljambe			pink.
		Lady Godiva		cl.	(A. Waterer before 1875); white, yellow spots.
		Lady Grenville		cl.	(J. Waterer before 1875); white center, purple edges.
x	H-2	Lady Grey Egerton	* A	cl.	catawbiense x; (A. Waterer before 1888); pale lilac, silvery blush.
		Lady Gwendoline Broderick		cl.	griffithianum hybrid x 'Bacchus'; (C.B. van Nes & Sons before 1922); dark pink, heavily overlaid with red spots.
		Lady Harcourt		cl.	(J. Waterer); pink, crimson spots.
		Lady Hillingdon		cl.	griffithianum x; (J. Waterer); pale mauve with yellow marking.

		Lady Howe			cl.	(J. Waterer); rose.
		Lady Jean			g.	diaprepes x eriogynum; (Stair 1943).
		Lady Knollys			cl.	(J. Waterer); rose.
		Lady Lawrence			cl.	'Lady Rosebery' x ambiguum; (Thacker 1942); coppery rose.
		Lady Linlithgow			g.	thomsonii x sutchuenense; (R.B.G. Edinburgh); various shades of dark pink and red.
xx	H-2	Lady Longman	**	A	cl.	(H.White); flowers clear pale pink, with chocolate eye.
		Lady Lopez				pale lilac blotched deep chocolate; commended 1862.
		Lady Malcolm Stewart			cl.	'Tally Ho' x 'Purple Splendour'; (Adams-Acton 1942); rich pink.
		Lady Mary Hood				cultivated Standish & Noble before 1860; pure white.
		Lady Mary Parker				rose, edged vivid pink.
		Lady Montagu			g.	griffithianum x thomsonii (?); (Rothschild).
xx	H-4	Lady Montagu	*	C	cl.	griffithianum x thomsonii (?); (Rothschild); pink, darker outside; A.M. (R.H.S.) 1931.
		Lady Mosley			cl.	(J. Waterer); pink, light center.
		Lady of the Lake			cl.	in cultivation with T. Methven & Son, Edinburgh 1868-69; blush, spotted.
		Lady Olive Guinness			cl.	(J. Waterer); white, dark spots.
		Lady Palmerston				(C. Noble); delicate blush, orange-yellow eye.
xxx	H-3	Lady Primrose	**	B	cl.	campylocarpum x; (Slocock); clear lemon yellow, red spots; A.M. (R.H.S.) 1933.
xxxx	H-4	Lady Rosebery			g.	cinnaba
		Lady Rosebery	****	C	cl.	cinnabarinum var. roylei x 'Royal Flush' pink form; (Rothschild); bright rosy red within, crimson outside; A.M. (R.H.S.) 1930; F.C.C. (R.H.S.) 1932.
		Lady Rosebery Dalmeny			cl.	cinnabarinum var. roylei x 'Royal Flush' pink form (Lady Rosebery g.); (Rothschild); soft pink. Previously known as Lady Rosebery var. Dalmeny.
		Lady Rosebery Etna			cl.	cinnabarinum var. roylei x 'Royal Flush' pink form (Lady Rosebery g.); (Rothschild); rosy pink. Previously known as Lady Rosebery var. Etna.
		Lady Rosebery Pink Beauty				Syn. of 'Pink Lady Rosebery'.
		Lady Rosebery Pink Dawn			cl.	cinnabarinum var. roylei x 'Royal Flush' pink form (Lady Rosebery g.); registered Digby 1954. Previously known as Lady Rosebery var. Pink Dawn.
		Lady Rosebery Pink Delight			cl.	cinnabarinum var. roylei x 'Royal Flush' pink form (Lady Rosebery g.); (Rothschild). Previously known as Lady Rosebery var. Pink Delight.
		Lady Stair			g.	griersonianum x 'Albatross'; (Stair 1939).
		Lady Strangford				(C. Noble); blush, maroon spots.
xx	H-3	Lady Stuart of Wortley	*	C	cl.	'Coombe Royal' ? x; griffithianum ? x; (M. Koster & Sons cross 1909); rosy red, A.M. (R.H.S.) 1933.
		Lady Tankerville			cl.	(J. Waterer before 1915); pink, light center.
		Lady Truro			cl.	(J. Waterer); rosy crimson.
		Lady Welch				rose lilac.
		Lady Winifred Herbert			cl.	(Young); rosy carmine, fringed.
		Laerdal			cl.	johnstonianum x dalhousiae; (Bolitho 1937 ?); pure white; exhibited 1949.
		Laetevirens		A	g.	carolinianum x ferrugineum or possibly a R. minus hybrid; magenta rose. Syn. 'Wilsoni'.
		La Fontaine				pink with brown blotch, fimbriated.
		Lagoon			cl.	augustinii x; (Wright).
		Lake Labish			cl.	'Lady Bligh' x 'Loderi Venus'; grown by Rudolph Henny; neyron rose (H.C.C.623); P.A. (A.R.S.) 1955.
		Lake Ozette			cl.	griersonianum x 'Loderi Venus'; (Clark).
		(Lamellen)				See 'Nobleanum Lamellen'.
		Lamellen			g.	campanulatum x griffithianum; (Magor 1943); pale mauve.
		Lamplighter	*	B	cl.	'Britannia' x 'Madame Fr. J. Chauvin'; (M. Koster & Sons 1955); light red (rose red H.C.C. 724) with salmon glow; F.C.C. (Boskoop) 1955.
		Lanarth Scarlet				exhibited 1934.
		Lancer			g.	griersonianum x hookeri; (Aberconway 1950); blood red.
		Landrii				cultivated Standish & Noble before 1860; white, edged with purple lake, brown spots.
xx	H-3	Langley Park	*	B	cl.	'Queen Wilhelmina' x 'Stanley Davies'; (C.B. van Nes & Sons before 1922); deep red.
		Langworth	*	B		fortunei x 'Sappho'; (W.C. Slocock); selected Slocock 1932; white, chocolate blotch, dark throat.
		Lanyon			cl.	haematodes x elliotii (Marshall g.); exhibited Col. Bolitho. Previously known as Marshall var. Lanyon.
		Largo			g.	'Astarte' x neriiflorum var. euchaites; (Aberconway 1946); red.
		Lascaux			cl.	'Fabia' x litiense; (R.H.S.Gardens, Wisley, 1954); barium yellow (H.C.C.503/2) small crimson blotch at base of throat; buds are a blended shade of red and orange; A.M. (R.H.S.) 1954.
		Last Chance			cl.	'Mars' x eriogynum; (R. Henny); claret rose H.C.C. 021/1; P.A. (A.R.S.) 1957.
		Latona			g.	souliei x dichroanthum; (Aberconway 1933); cream to pale pink.
		Laura				in cultivation with T. Methven & Son, Edinburgh 1868-69; crimson.
		Laura Aberconway			g.	griersonianum x 'Barclayi'; (Aberconway).
		Laura Aberconway			cl.	griersonianum x 'Barclayi'; (Aberconway 1944); geranium lake (H.C.C.20/1); A.M. (R.H.S.) 1944.

		Laura David		cl.	campylocarpum x ?; (Mrs. Laura David 1954).
		Lava Flow		cl.	didymum ? (K.W. 13225) x griersonianum; (Sunningdale Nurseries 1955); bright red.
x	H-3	Lavender Girl	** B	cl.	fortunei x 'Lady Grey Egerton'; (Slocock 1950); pale lavender; margins amaranth rose (H. C. C. 530/2) passing to a paler shade at center which is white; May/June; A.M. (R.H.S.) 1950.
		Lavender Princess		cl.	fortunei x; (Dexter-Bosley); lavender mauve.
		Lavender Time		cl.	discolor x 'Purple Splendour'; Harrison 1956.
		Lawsoni		cl.	Syn. of 'Broughtonii'.
		L. de Rothschild		cl.	(C. B. van Nes & Sons); rich pink fading to white.
		Leaburg		cl.	dichroanthum x 'Penjerrick'; (Phetteplace); blood red (H.C.C. 820/3); P.A. (A.R.S.) 1956.
x	H-3	Leda		g.	apodectum x griersonianum; (Aberconway 1933); vermilion.
x	H-2	Lee's Dark Purple	A	cl.	catawbiense x; (Lee before 1851); deep purple.
		Lee's Scarlet	B	cl.	caucasicum x; (Lee); rosy crimson or scarlet fading to a deep pink. Early.
		Le Fevreanum			(in Belgium); cultivated Standish & Noble before 1860; purplish crimson.
		Lemon Bells		cl.	decorum x 'Fabia'; R. Henny.
		Lemon Bill		g.	caeruleum var. album x concatenans; (Aberconway, 1943). See 'Peace'.
		Lemon Drop		cl.	'Moonstone' x ?; (R. & G. Bovee, 1960); light yellow-green (Nickerson 2·5 Gy 9/8); dwarf.
		Lem's Goal		cl.	'Ole Olson' x 'Azor'; (Lem); cream yellow.
		Lenape		cl.	pubescens x keiskei; (Nearing); exhibited 1950; pale yellow.
		Lencret		cl.	'White Wings' x ciliatum; (Adams-Acton 1942); cream, fading white.
		Leo		g.	'Britannia' x elliottii; (Rothschild).
		Leo		cl.	'Britannia' x elliottii; (Rothschild 1948); crimson scarlet or dark red; A.M. (R.H.S.) 1948.
		Leona		cl.	'Corona' x 'Dondis'; (R. Henny).
		Leonardo		cl.	'Tally Ho' x griersonianum; (Adams-Acton 1937); vermilion.
		Leonardslee Brilliant		cl.	'Halopeanum' x thomsonii (Gem g.); (Loder); deep red. Previously known as Gem var. Leonardslee Brilliant.
		Leonardslee Cream		cl.	'Halopeanum' x 'Loderi Pink Diamond' (White Lady g.); (Sir E. Loder); white flushed rose pink; "now extinct" ex Sir Giles Loder; A.M. (R.H.S.) 1930. Previously known as White Lady var. Leonardslee Cream.
		Leonardslee Flame		cl.	'Ascot Brilliant' x thomsonii (Red Star g.); Sir E. Loder. Previously known as Red Star var. Leonardslee Flame.
		Leonardslee Gem of the Woods		g.	ciliatum hybrid x virgatum; (at Leonardslee 1912); pure white; A.M. (R.H.S.) 1925.
		Leonardslee Gertrude		cl.	'Halopeanum' x 'Loderi Pink Diamond' (White Lady g.); (Sir E. Loder); white with pink markings. Previously known as White Lady var. Leonardslee Gertrude.
		Leonardslee Giles		cl.	'Standishii' x griffithianum (Sir E. Loder); buds pink, flower pale pink with a little brown spotting on upper petals, fading to white marked with darker patches externally; A.M. (R.H.S.) 1948.
		Leonardslee Peach		cl.	thomsonii x campylocarpum (Exminster g.); (Sir E. Loder); orange pink. Previously known as Exminster var. Leonardslee Peach.
		Leonardslee Primrose		cl.	campylocarpum x arboreum var. album (Earl of Morley g.); (Loder); primrose dotted on upper half with small maroon spots; A.M. (R.H.S.) 1933. Previously known as Earl of Morley var. Leonardslee Primrose.
		Leonardslee White Glory		cl.	irroratum x Loderi g. (White Glory g.); white, delicate pink outside; A. M. (R. H. S.) 1938. Previously known as White Glory Leonardslee var.
		Leonora			cultivated Standish & Noble before 1860; deep rosy pink, green spots.
		Leonore		g.	auriculatum x kyawi; (Rothschild).
		Leonore		cl.	auriculatum x kyawi; (Rothschild); crimson (H.C.C. 22/2) shaded outside carmine (H.C.C. 21/1); A.M. (R.H.S.) 1948.
		Leopardi			arboreum var. album x; in cultivation with T. Methven & Son, Edinburgh 1868-9; white with slight red tint, large brownish red spots.
		Leopold		cl.	'Mira' x catawbiense; (Seidel cross 1909); dark purple violet marked brown.
		Lepidoboothii		cl.	lepidotum x boothii (Magor 1919); yellowish white tinged pink and green; Mrs. Magor says "transparent pink, buff spottings"; A. M. (R. H. S.) 1919.
		Le Poussin			deep rose. Syn. of 'Barclayanum'.
		Le Progrès			Syn. of 'Progrès'.
		Lerigau		g.	'Duke of York' x williamsianum; (Dietrich Hobbie 1952); delicate rose.
xxxx	H-3	Letty Edwards		g.	campylocarpum var. elatum x fortunei; (Clarke).
		Letty Edwards	****B	cl.	campylocarpum var. elatum x fortunei; (Clarke); pale sulphur yellow (H.C.C. 1/3) shaded a tone darker; A.M. (R.H.S.) 1946; F.C.C. (R.H.S. Wisley Trials) 1948; (sent by Slocock).
		Lewis Carroll	** C	cl.	griffithianum x; (Waterer, Sons & Crisp); white, pink edged.
		Libelle		g.	'Faggetter's Favourite' x williamsianum; (Dietrich Hobbie 1952); bright rose.
		Liberty		g.	'Eupheno' x barbatum; (Aberconway 1950); deep red.
		Lifeguard		g.	'Lancer' x arboreum; (Aberconway 1950); deep red.
		Lilacina		cl.	catawbiense x; (Parsons).
		Lilac Time		cl.	discolor x 'Purple Splendour'; Harrison 1956.
		Lilian			griffithianum x a Mangles seedling; (W. C. Slocock); red fading to blush.
		Lilianae		g.	arboreum x 'Shilsonii'; blood red, shaded carmine; A. M. 1914.

Lily (auriculatum x 'Alice') x 'Mrs. Donald Graham'; exhibited Ostbo 1953; white; P.A. (A.R.S.) 1953.

Lily Daché cl. griersonianum x discolor (Azor g.); salmon pink.

Limbatum arboreum x; (from Belgium); cultivated Standish & Noble before 1870; white or pale blush, margined crimson.

Limerick g. 'Britannia' x dichroanthum; (Earl of Limerick 1948). See 'Margela', 'Piccaninny'.

Lindberg cl. 'Lady Bessborough' x 'Dido' (Jalisco g.); exhibited Crown Lands 1954. Previously known as Jalisco var. Lindberg.

Lindbull g. lindleyi x bullatum; (Magor 1926); white, yellow at base, sweet scented.

Lind-dal g. lindleyi x dalhousiae; (Aberconway cross 1927); white with yellowish tinge.

Lindsayi dalhousiae x formosum; (Lindsay).

Linley cl. Loderi g. x; (Messel); soft pink, blotched carmine at base; A.M. (R.H.S.) 1927.

Linley Sambourne cl. Loderi g. x; (Messel); rich pink, blotched carmine at base; A.M. (R.H.S.) 1928.

Linswegeanum B g. 'Britannia' x forrestii var. repens; (Dietrich Hobbie 1946); deep scarlet red.

Lionel cl. catawbiense x; (Parsons).

Lionel's Triumph cl. lacteum x 'Naomi'; (L. de Rothschild); Dresden yellow (H.C.C. 64/3) crimson blotch and crimson spotting in throat; A.M. (R.H.S.) 1954.

Lipstick cl. 'Fabia' x 'Dondis'; (R. Henny).

Lisa Stillman cl. griffithianum x; rosy pink.

Little Beauty malayanum x 'Monarch'; bright red or cerise or scarlet crimson; A.M. 1896.

xx H-3 Little Ben *** B cl. neriiflorum x forrestii var. repens; (Scrase-Dickins 1937); deep scarlet, dwarf; F.C.C. (R.H.S.) 1937.

xx H-3 Little Bert cl. forrestii var. repens; x neriiflorum subsp. euchaites (Scrase-Dickins 1939); shining crimson scarlet; A.M. (R.H.S.) 1939.

x H-3 Little Bill cl. williamsianum x 'Lady Stuart of Wortley'; (Wallace 1934).

Little Birdie cl. forrestii var. repens x 'Humming Bird'; (Rudolph Henny); blood red, (H.C.C. 820/3).

Little Bobbie cl. forrestii var. repens x 'Humming Bird'; exhibited R. Henny 1956.

Little Dragon cl. 'Fabia' x venator; (Lancaster); red.

Little Janet cl. forrestii var. repens x 'Humming Bird'; (R. Henny 1956).

Little Joe cl. forrestii var. repens x 'May Day'; (Lester Brandt 1951); currant red (H.C.C. 821).

Little Paddocks cl. thomsonii x campylocarpum (Exminster g.); exhibited Lt.-Col. J. N. Horlick 1940. Previously known as Exminster var. Little Paddocks.

Little Patty cl. forrestii var. repens x 'Hummingbird'; (R. Henny, 1958); Orient red (H.C.C. 819/3), dwarf.

Little Peep cl. ('Earl of Athlone' x 'Fabia') x forrestii var. repens; (R. Henny 1956).

Little Pudding cl. decorum x 'Fabia'; (R. Henny); Camellia rose (H.C.C. 622/1) on outer lobes shaded to near Chinese coral (H.C.C. 614/2) in the throat; P.A. (A.R.S.) 1953.

Little Sheba cl. ('Earl of Athlone' x 'Fabia') x forrestii var. repens; (R. Henny); P.A. (A.R.S.)

Little Winston cl. 'Cerisette' x 'Toreador'; (Digby).

Littleworth Corallina cl. (Mangles); pale lilac rose, base crimson; A.M. (R.H.S.) 1911.

Littleworth Cream exhibited R. E. Horsfall 1935.

Littleworth Hybrid resembles R. grande; (Mangles); sulphury white, purple blotch at base; A.M. (R.H.S.) 1914.

Littleworth Pearl griffithianum x; (Mangles).

Littleworth Star griffithianum x; (Mangles).

Llandaff cl. griffithianum x; (C.B. van Nes & Sons before 1923); bright red, fringed.

L.L.Liebig (Jean Bracke); carmine.

Lochinch g. 'Elsae' x eximium; (Stair 1932).

Lochinch Spinbur cl. spinuliferum x burmanicum (Spinbur g.); (Stair); pale yellow with pink staining; A.M. (R.H.S.) 1957.

Lodabia g. 'Fabia' x Loderi g.; (Aberconway 1946); rose.

xx H-3 Lodauric * B g. Loderi g. x auriculatum; (G. Taylor for Sir J. Ramsden 1922 ?); exhibited Crosfield 1939; white.

Lodauric Iceberg *** B cl. Loderi g. x auriculatum (Lodauric g.); exhibited Slocock 1946; selected Slocock 1936; white, green center. Previously known as Lodauric var. Iceberg. A.M. (R.H.S.) 1958.

Loderi ****C g. griffithianum x fortunei; bred in 1901 by Sir E. Loder from R. griffithianum plant in greenhouse of Mr. F. Godman; white or pale shell pink, sweet scented.

Loderi Cream cl. griffithianum x fortunei (Loderi g.); (Loder); blush white, sweet scented. Previously known as Loderi var. Cream.

Loderi Dairymaid cl. griffithianum x fortunei (Loderi g.); (Loder); white with green blotch. Previously known as Loderi var. Dairymaid.

Loderi Diamond cl. griffithianum x fortunei (Loderi g.); (Loder); pure white; F.C.C. (R.H.S.) 1914. Previously known as Loderi var. Diamond. Syn. Loderi White Diamond.

Loderi Fairyland cl. griffithianum x fortunei (Loderi g.); (Loder). Previously known as Loderi var. Fairyland.

Loderi Fairy Queen griffithianum x fortunei (Loderi g.); (Loder); pale pink with blotch. Previously known as Loderi var. Fairy Queen.

xxxx H-4 Loderi Game Chick cl. griffithianum x fortunei (Loderi g.); (Loder); pale pink with faint blotch. Previously known as Loderi var. Game Chick.

Loderi Georgette cl. 'Loderi King George' x 'Loderi Sir Edmund'; (Loder). Previously known as Loderi var. Georgette.

	Loderi Helen		cl.	griffithianum x fortunei (Loderi g.); (Loder); pale pink. Previously known as Loderi var. Helen.
	Loderi Irene Stead		cl.	(Stead.) Previously known as Loderi var. Irene Stead.
	Loderi Julie		cl.	griffithianum x fortunei (Loderi g.); A.M. (R.H.S.) 1944. Previously known as Loderi var. Julie.
xxxxH-4	Loderi King George		cl.	griffithianum x fortunei (Loderi g.); (Loder); blush white, fragrant. Previously known as Loderi var. King George.
	Loderi Maximus		cl.	griffithianum x fortunei (Loderi g.); Previously known as Loderi var. Maximus.
	Loderi Millais Pink		cl.	griffithianum x fortunei (Loderi g.); (Loder). Previously known as Loderi var. Millais Pink.
	Loderi Netherfield Rose		cl.	'Loderi Sir Edmund' x 'Loderi Snowdrop'; exhibited H. Heal. Previously known as Loderi var. Netherfield Rose.
xxx H-4	Loderi Patience		cl.	griffithianum x fortunei (Loderi g.); (Loder); white with crimson blotch. Previously known as Loderi var. Patience.
	Loderi Pearly Queen		cl.	'Loderi King George' x 'Loderi Sir Edmund'; (Loder); exhibited Sir Giles Loder 1949. Previously known as Loderi var. Pearly Queen.
	Loderi Pink Coral		cl.	griffithianum x fortunei (Loderi g.); (Loder); pale pink with puce blotch, scented. Previously known as Loderi var. Pink Coral.
xxxxH-4	Loderi Pink Diamond		cl.	griffithianum x fortunei (Loderi g.); (Loder); delicate pink, scented; F.C.C. (R.H.S.) 1914. Previously known as Loderi var. Pink Diamond.
	Loderi Pink Glamour		cl.	griffithianum x fortunei (Loderi g.); (Loder); very pale pink. Previously known as Loderi var. Pink Glamour.
	Loderi Pink Satin		cl.	griffithianum x fortunei (Loderi g.); exhibited J.M.Evans 1953. Previously known as Loderi var. Pink Satin.
	Loderi Pink Topaz		cl.	griffithianum x fortunei (Loderi g.); (Loder); pink with green blotch. Previously known as Loderi var. Pink Topaz.
	Loderi Pretty Polly		cl.	pink; "plant dead, no known layers" ex Sir Giles Loder.
	Loderi Princess Marina			'Loderi King George' x 'Loderi Sir Edmund'; (Loder); palest pink shading to white, often marked with deeper pink patches externally; A.M. (R.H.S.) 1948. Previously known as Loderi var. Princess Marina.
	Loderi Queen Mary		cl.	griffithianum x fortunei (Loderi g.); (Loder); pink, scented. Previously known as Loderi var. Queen Mary.
xxxxH-4	Loderi Sir Edmund		cl.	griffithianum x fortunei (Loderi g.); (Loder); waxy, blush pink, scented; A.M. (R.H.S.) 1930. Previously known as Loderi var. Sir Edmund.
xxxxH-4	Loderi Sir Joseph Hooker			griffithianum x fortunei (Loderi g.); (Loder); deep shell pink with prominent veins. Previously known as Loderi var. Sir Joseph Hooker.
	Loderi Stag's Head			griffithianum x fortunei (Loderi g.) exhibited Sir E. Loder. Previously known as Loderi var. Stag's Head.
	Loderi Sue		cl.	'Loderi King George' selfed; (James).
xxx H-4	Loderi Superlative			griffithianum x fortunei (Loderi g.); white flowers with interior flushed pale yellow, fragrant. Previously known as Loderi var. Superlative.
	Loderi Titan		cl.	griffithianum x fortunei (Loderi g.); (Reuthe Ltd.). Previously known as Loderi var. Titan.
xxxxH-4	Loderi Venus			griffithianum x fortunei (Loderi g.); (Loder); pale pink, scented. Previously known as Loderi var. Venus.
xxx H-4	Loderi White Diamond			griffithianum x fortunei (Loderi g.); (Loder); ivory to white with blotch. Syn. of 'Loderi Diamond'?
	Loder's Pink		cl.	probably seedling from 'Loder's White'; bright pink.
xxxxH-4	Loder's White	****C	cl.	arboreum var. album ? x griffithianum; (Mangles); delicate pinkish mauve at first, fading to white; A.M. (R.H.S.) 1911; A.G.M. (R.H.S.) 1931.
	Lodetta		g.	'Jacquetta' x Loderi g.; (Aberconway 1946); scarlet to rose.
	Logan Damaris	*** C	cl.	'Dr. Stocker' x campylocarpum (Damaris g.); (Stevenson 1948); Dresden yellow (H.C.C. 64/3); A.M. (R.H.S.) 1948. Previously known as Damaris Logan var.
	Loki		cl.	'Cornubia' x ; (Lady Loder); blood red; A.M. (R.H.S.) 1933.
	London		cl.	'Queen Wilhelmina' x 'Stanley Davies'; (C.B. van Nes & Sons before 1922); pink suffused bright crimson, deep crimson exterior.
	Londonense			cultivated Standish & Noble before 1860; crimson purple, finely spotted. Syn. of 'Ne Plus Ultra'.
	Lone Eagle		g.	carolinianum x 'Pink Pearl'?; exhibited Baardse (Bobbink & Atkins) 1928; pink.
	Lord Brougham			in cultivation with T. Methven 1868-69; crimson.
	Lord Byron			cultivated Standish & Noble before 1860; rosy purple, black spots.
	Lord Clyde			arboreum x ; cultivated Standish & Noble before 1860; blood red.
	Lord Eversley		cl.	(J.Waterer 1882); dark crimson, black spots.
	Lord Fairhaven	** A	cl.	(Knap Hill Nursery Co.); shrimp pink suffused yellow.
	Lord Granville		cl.	(C.Noble before 1870); scarlet tinted cerise.
	Lord John Russell		cl.	(A.Waterer before 1860); pale rose, dark blotch on upper petal.
	Lord Lambourne		cl.	griffithianum x ; (Otto Schulz cross 1892, introduced C.B. van Nes & Sons 1896); Gloxinia-shape, red.
	Lord Palmerston			Syn. of 'Cynthia'.
x H-3	Lord Roberts	A	cl.	(B.Mason); dark red, black blotch.
	Lord Selborne		cl.	(J.Waterer); crimson.
	Lord Stair		cl.	lindleyi x taggianum; (Stair 1952); white with a pale orange stain at the base of the upper two lobes; A.M. (R.H.S.) 1952.

		Lord Swaythling	*	C	cl.	griffithianum x ; (Otto Schulz cross 1890, introduced C.B. van Nes & Sons 1896); deep pink outside, rose madder (H.C.C. 23/1) fading to pale mauvy pink at margins; inside neyron rose (H.C.C. 623/1) spotted dark maroon; A.M. (R.H.S.) 1926, A.M. (R.H.S.) 1954; sent to Wisley by van Nes.
		Lord Wolseley			g.	'Duchess of Teck' x javanicum; (Noble); red orange.
		Lorenzo				cultivated Standish & Noble before 1860; white with fine yellow eye.
		Lotis			g.	'Metis' x Loderi g. ; (Aberconway 1946); orange red.
		Louis Amateis			cl.	carolinianum x bullatum; (Amateis 1955); white, tinged pink on back.
		Louisa P. Delano			cl.	fortunei x ; (Dexter); salmon pink.
		Louis Chauvin			cl.	(Moser); dark rose pink with large purple blotch.
xx	H-3	Louis Pasteur		B	cl.	'Mrs. Tritton' x 'Viscount Powerscourt'; (L.J.Endtz & Co. 1923); light red, light pink center.
		Louis Phillippe				(before 1867); crimson scarlet, black spot.
		Lovely William			cl.	neriiflorum subsp. euchaites x williamsianum; (Horlick 1940); deep rose.
		Lowi			cl.	Syn. of 'Pictum'.
		Lowinsky's White				(Lowinsky); growing in Sunningdale Nursery 1955.
		Loyalty				'Britannia' x zeylanicum; (Williams at Lanarth); red.
		Lucidum			cl.	(H. Waterer before 1857); rosy lilac.
		Lucien Linden				(Linden); crimson
		Lucifer				cultivated Noble about 1855; bright scarlet.
		Luciferum			cl.	(J. Waterer before 1875); white.
		Lucil				'Cilpinense' x lutescens; (Aberconway 1942). See 'Fine Feathers'.
		Lucky Strike			cl.	griersonianum x 'Countess of Derby'; (Van Veen).
		Lucy				cultivated Standish & Noble before 1860; blush.
		Lucy Locket				Loderi g. x ?; (Heneage-Vivian).
		Lucy Lou			cl.	leucaspis x (ciliatum x leucaspis); exhibited Larson 1956; white.
		Lucy Neal				cultivated Standish & Noble before 1860; claret, finely spotted. Syn. of 'Genseric'.
		Ludwig Leopold Liebig			cl.	Syn. of 'L.L.Liebig'.
		Luminous			g.	'Lady Rosebery' x concatenans; (Aberconway 1950); orange red.
		(Luna)				See 'Rosa Bonheur Luna'.
		Luna				pale sulphur yellow with central spot of deep red; A.M. (R.H.S.) 1930.
		(Luscombeanum)			g.	See 'Luscombei'.
		Luscombei			g.	fortunei x thomsonii; (G. Luscombe); exhibited Luscombe 1880; rose pink. See 'Pride of Leonardslee'.
		Luscombe's Red			cl.	Syn. of 'Luscombe's Scarlet'.
		Luscombe's Sanguineum			cl.	fortunei x thomsonii (Luscombei g.); (Luscombe); scarlet crimson.
		Luscombe's Scarlet			cl.	fortunei x thomsonii (Luscombei g.); (Luscombe); scarlet crimson. Syn. 'Luscombe's Red'.
		Lustre			g.	'Dante' x griersonianum; (Aberconway 1941); scarlet.
		Luteo-roseum				javanicum x 'Princess Alexandra'; pinky yellow to salmon; F.C.C. 1886.
		Lycia			g.	'Vanessa' x elliottii; (Aberconway 1942); scarlet red.
		Mabel			cl.	thomsonii x ; (R. Gill & Son); apricot.
		Mabel Parsons			cl.	catawbiense x ; (Parsons).
		McHattianum				exhibited at R.H.S. by T.Leslie, Trinity Cottage, Edinburgh, 1906.
		McNabii			g.	ciliatum x edgeworthii; (K. van Houtte before 1860); blush white; commended 1862.
		Maculatum Grandiflorum			cl.	cultivated Standish & Noble before 1850; rich plum, spotted.
		Maculatum Nigrum			cl.	cultivated Standish & Noble before 1860; deep plum, large black eye.
		Maculatum Nigrum Superbum				cultivated Standish & Noble before 1870; large flowered form of 'Malculatum Nigrum'.
		Maculatum Purpureum			cl.	in cultivation with T. Methven & Son, Edinburgh 1868-69; purple spotted.
		Maculatum Roseum			cl.	(Before 1875); rose.
		Maculosissimum				spotted all over with little dots and streaks of blackish purple on pale blush lilac ground; F.C.C. 1860.
		Madame A. Moser / Madame Albert Moser	**	B	cl.	(Moser); mauve (H.C.C. 633/2) fading to white at base of corolla, heavily spotted on upper petal Buttercup yellow (H.C.C. 5/1); buds mauve (H.C.C. 633); A.M. (R.H.S.) 1954.
		Madame Auguste Pellerin			cl.	(Moser & Fils); Cherry red, yellow eye; or pink, lighter center.
		Madame Bosio				cultivated Standish & Noble before 1870; pale blush, finely spotted
o	H-2	Madame Carvalho		A	cl.	catawbiense x ; (J. Waterer 1866); white, yellowish green spots.
		Madame Cochet			cl.	(Bertin before 1888); lilac.
xx	H-3	Madame de Bruin	**	B	cl.	'Prometheus' x 'Doncaster'; (M. Koster & Sons cross 1904); bright red.
		Madame Edward Denny				(Knap Hill Nursery); crimson, black blotch.

xx	H-3	Madame Fr. J. Chauvin	** B	cl.	fortunei x ; (M. Koster & Sons cross 1916); rosy pink, paler center, small red blotch; A.M. (R.H.S.) 1933.
		Madame Gustave Chandon			crimson.
		Madame G. Verde Delisle		g.	'Doncaster' x griffithianum; (Lowinsky); bright deep pink; A.M. (R.H.S.) 1919.
		Madame Ida Rubenstein		cl.	(Moser & Fils); bright pink.
		Madame Jean Dupuy		cl.	(Moser & Fils); very pale lilac.
		Madame Jeanne Bois		cl.	dark pink.
		Madame Jeanne Frets		cl.	caucasicum x ; (C. Frets & Son); rose, red blotch, early.
		Madame Jules Porges	** B	cl.	(Moser & Fils); pale mauve with golden blotch.
		Madame Linden		cl.	(J. Linden 1873); purplish violet.
x	H-3	Madame Mason } Madame Masson }		cl.	catawbiense hybrid x ponticum var. album; (Bertin 1849); white, yellow blotch.
		Madame Omei		g.	oreodoxa x forrestii var. repens ; (Dietrich Hobbie 1954); deep rose.
		Madame P.A. Colijn			Syn. of 'Mevrouw P.A.Colijn'.
		Madame Penco			cultivated Standish & Noble before 1870; white, finely spotted.
		Madame Sontag			cultivated Noble about 1855; white, shaded pink at edges.
		Madame van de Weyer		cl.	(J. Waterer before 1875); rosy crimson.
		Madame Wagner		cl.	caucasicum x ; (J. Macoy); white, margined rose.
		Maddchart		g.	maddenii x chartophyllum var. praecox; (Magor cross 1921); opens very pale lilac, later becomes white.
		Madeline		g.	(Aberconway 1935).
		Mademoiselle Marie Forte		cl.	(J. Bracke); pink.
		Mademoiselle Victoire Balfe			cultivated Standish & Noble before 1870; fine white, spotted with brown.
		Madonna		cl.	(decorum x griersonianum) x 'America'; (Gable); exhibited 1947; white, yellow throat.
		Madonna		g.	griffithianum x 'Mrs. Messel'; (Messel); white; A.M. (R.H.S.) 1931.
		Maggie Heywood		cl.	(J. Waterer before 1922); white, edged pink, yellow eye.
		Magnet			cultivated Noble about 1855; rosy red.
		Magnificum		cl.	(J. Waterer); crimson; early.
		Magnificum			(Byls before 1839); purple.
		Magniflorum		g.	'Countess of Haddington' x edgeworthii; exhibited Parker 1917.
		Magnum Bonum			in cultivation with T. Methven & Son, Edinburgh 1868-69.
		Mahmoud			lavender pink, large yellow eye.
		Mai		g.	decorum x campylocarpum; (Stevenson 1951); cream.
		Maiden's Blush		cl.	campylocarpum x griffithianum (Mrs. Randall Davidson g.); (Loder); pale cream edged with pink. Previously known as Mrs. Randall Davidson var. Maiden's Blush.
		Maiden's Blush		cl.	brookeanum var. gracile x 'Princess Alexandra'; cream and pink or pinky yellow; F.C.C. 1876.
		Maid of Athens			cultivated Standish & Noble before 1870; rose, pale center, brown spot.
		Maid of Kent			'Alice' x Loderi g.; exhibited R. Wallace & Co.
		Maid of Orange		cl.	dichroanthum x 'Loderi Sir Edmund'; raised and exhibited Sir Giles Loder; "extinct" –ex Sir Giles Loder.
		Majestic			in cultivation with T. Methven & Son, Edinburgh 1868-69; crimson.
		Majesticum			cultivated Standish & Noble before 1860; deep rose.
		Major		g.	haematodes x thomsonii; (Rothschild 1947); waxy deep crimson or bright red. See 'Charles Michael'.
		Major Edwards			(Methven); pale pink.
		Major Joicey			(C. Noble); dark crimson.
		Malcolm Allan		cl.	'J.G.Millais' x neriiflorum; (Col. Horlick 1931); deep red.
		Mammouth		cl.	(Rogers before 1867); rosy purple.
		Mandalay		g.	haematodes x venator; (Rothschild 1947); deep or brilliant red.
		Mandarin		cl.	'Letty Edwards' x griersonianum; (Thacker 1946); orange salmon.
		Manglesii		cl.	griffithianum x catawbiense hybrid; (Veitch); white, spotted pink; F.C.C. 1885.
		Manon		cl.	tephropeplum x ciliatum; (Adams-Acton 1942); pure white.
		Mansellii		g.	falconeri x grande; exhibited Downie 1875. See 'Muriel'.
		Marathon		g.	'Pauline' x elliottii; (Rothschild 1947); bright red.
		Marcel Moser		cl.	(Moser & Son before 1914); bright red.
		Marchioness of Downshire		cl.	exhibited Street; white spotted brown.
x	H-2	Marchioness of Lansdowne	B	cl.	maximum x ; (A. Waterer before 1915); pale violet rose, spotted black.

	Marchioness of Londonderry		cl.	(W.C.Slocock ?); pink.
	Marchioness of Tweeddale		cl.	(J. Waterer); rosy crimson, upper segments pale with yellow spots; rose pink, yellow eye; A.M. (R.H.S.) 1906.
	Marcia		cl.	campylocarpum x 'Gladys'; (Swaythling); primrose (H.C.C. 601/2); F.C.C. (R.H.S.) 1944.
	Margaret	* C		(Lowinsky); pink with dark throat.
	Margaret Bean		cl.	campylocarpum x 'Esmeralda'; (R.B.G.Kew 1935); yellow, fringed pink.
xxx H-3	Margaret Dunn		g.	discolor x 'Fabia'; (Swaythling).
	Margaret Dunn	** B	cl.	discolor x 'Fabia'; (Swaythling); apricot (H.C.C. 609) flushed shell pink (516); A.M. (R.H.S.) 1946. See 'Golden Belle', 'Margaret Dunn Talisman'.
	Margaret Dunn Talisman		cl.	discolor x 'Fabia' (Margaret Dunn g.); (R. Henny); resembling Rose 'Talisman' in color. Previously known as 'Margaret Dunn' var. 'Talisman'.
	Margaret Findlay		g.	wardii x griersonianum; (Horlick 1942); almost white with red deepening to almost port wine in the throat.
	Margaret Rose		cl.	'Loderi Venus' x 'Rose du Barri' (Jubilee Queen g.); (Loder). Previously known as Jubilee Queen var. Margaret Rose.
	Margela		cl.	'Britannia' x dichroanthum (Limerick g.); (Earl of Limerick); orange brown shading to a broad band of geranium lake (H.C.C. 20/1) round the edge of petal; A.M. (R.H.S.) 1948. Previously known as Limerick var. Margela.
	Margery Slocock		cl.	griffithianum x hardy hybrid; (Slocock 1930); deep pink.
	Margot		cl.	'Mrs. Milner' x catawbiense; (Seidel cross 1910); dark purplish red.
	Margot			mucronatum ? x micranthum; (C. Ingram 1937); vivid magenta pink.
	Marguerite		cl.	carolinianum x ; pink.
	Marguerite		cl.	catawbiense x ; exhibited Bosley; deep pink.
	Marguerite			(Methven & Son); blush, yellow spots.
	Marian			exhibited Veitch & Son 1862; French white, spotted brown.
	Maricee		cl.	selected form of sargentianum; (grown and named by Caperci, 1959); creamy white, flower 3-, 4- and 5-partite; A.E. (A.R.S.) 1959.
	Marie Antoinette		g.	'Albatross' x 'Ariel'; (Rothschild 1945); white with green markings.
	Marie Forte			crimson with dark spot. Syn. of 'Mademoiselle Marie Forte'?
	Marie Stuart	A		(A.Waterer before 1875); blush, maroon spot.
xx H-4	Mariloo	****C	g.	'Dr. Stocker' x lacteum; (Rothschild 1941); pure yellow.
	Mariloo Eugenie	** C	cl.	'Dr. Stocker' x lacteum (Mariloo g.); (Rothschild); creamy yellow, marked with small crimson spots; A.M. (R.H.S.) 1950. Previously known as Mariloo var. Eugenie.
	Mariloo Gilbury	** C	cl.	'Dr. Stocker' x lacteum (Mariloo g.); (Rothschild); pale creamy pink, dark pink stripe on back of each segment; A.M. (R.H.S.) 1943. Previously known as Mariloo var. Gilbury.
	Marine		cl.	a deep colored form of R. augustinii; (Barto–R. & G. Bovee, 1960); strong purple (Nickerson 5 P 4/9).
	Marinka		g.	'Solon' x 'Rapture'; (Aberconway 1950); pale rose.
xxx H-3	Marinus Koster	*** B	cl.	griffithianum x ; (M. Koster & Sons 1937); deep pink with lighter shadings; A.M. (R.H.S.) 1937, F.C.C. (R.H.S.) 1948.
	Marion		cl.	'Pink Pearl' x 'Catawbiense Grandiflorum'; (Felix & Dijkhuis); pink.
	Marion		cl.	raised and sent to Wisley by J. Cheal & Son Ltd.; margins frilled, tyrian rose (H.C.C. 24/3) upper petal at throat spotted with orange, reverse tyrian rose (H.C.C. 24/2); A.M. (R.H.S.) 1955.
	Marion Koster		cl.	'Mrs. L. A. Dunnett' x griersonianum; (M. Koster & Sons); red, flowering in June and July.
	Marmion			cultivated Standish & Noble before 1860; purple crimson, shaded white.
	Marmora		cl.	dichroanthum x 'Margaret Dunn'; (Sunningdale Nurseries 1955); bright orange yellow flushed rose at tips.
	Maroze		g.	'Red Admiral' x meddianum; (J.B. Stevenson 1946); waxy red, tubular.
	Marquis of Waterford		cl.	(J. Waterer before 1871); bright pink, lighter in center.
xxxxH-2	Mars	*** B	cl.	griffithianum x ; (Waterer, Sons & Crisp before 1875); deep red; A.M. (R.H.S.) 1928; F.C.C. 1935.
	Marshall		g.	haematodes x elliottii; (Rothschild 1947); bright scarlet or red. See 'Lanyon'.
	Martha Isaacson		cl.	Azaleadendron; occidentale x Ostbo seedling No. 70; (E. Ostbo, 1956); white; P.A. (A.R.S.) 1956.
	Martin Hope Sutton		cl.	(A. Waterer before 1915); red, blotched, or rich rose scarlet.
	Marwood's Caucasicum			caucasicum x ; cream and pink.
	Mary Ann		cl.	'Corona' x 'Dondis'; (R. Henny).
	Mary Blane			cultivated Standish & Noble before 1860; claret.
	Mary D. Black		cl.	fortunei x 'Madame Fr. J. Chauvin'; exhibited Larson 1956; pink, red blotch.
	Mary Fleming		cl.	racemosum x keiskei; (Nearing, 1959); bisque yellow with blotches and streaks of salmon.
	Mary Forte			dark purple.
	Mary Frances Hawkins			(J. B. Gable, 1939); pink with yellowish orange throat; very vigorous.

	Name	Rating		Description
	Mary Harmon		cl.	Azaleadendron; 'Mrs. Donald Graham' x occidentale; (E. Ostbo 1958); white, pink striped on exterior; A.E. (A.R.S.)
	Mary Mayo		cl.	'Loderi King George' x 'Ostbo Y 3'; (R. & G. Bovee 1960); shades of deep pink, strong pink and moderate pink (Nickerson 2·5 R 6/11, 2·5 R 7/8 and 2·5 R 8/5), throat suffused brilliant yellow (Nickerson 2·5 Y 9/9); frilled. P.A. (A.R.S.) 1960.
	Mary Power			exhibited R.E. Horsfall 1936.
	Mary Roxborough		cl.	discolor x 'St. Keverne' (Sir Frederick Moore g.); (Rothschild 1954). Previously known as Sir Frederick Moore var. Mary Roxborough.
	Mary Swaythling		cl.	campylocarpum x fortunei (Gladys g.); (Swaythling); soft yellow without spots or blotch; A.M. (R.H.S.) 1934. Previously known as Gladys var. Mary Swaythling.
	Mary Waterer	* B		in cultivation Knap Hill Nursery 1955; bright rich pink, paler center, buff spots.
	Master Dick		cl.	griersonianum x 'The Don'; (Crosfield); carmine scarlet with brownish speckling within; A.M. (R.H.S.) 1936.
	(Mastodon)			See 'Gaul Mastodon'.
xx H-4	Matador		g.	griersonianum x strigillosum; (Aberconway).
	Matador	*** B	cl.	griersonianum x strigillosum; (Aberconway 1945); dark orange red (H.C.C. 721/1) and tubular; A.M. (R.H.S.) 1945; F.C.C. (R.H.S.) 1946. See 'Exbury Matador'?
	Matchless			in cultivation T. Methven & Son, Edinburgh 1868-69; rosy crimson, dark blotch.
	Matilda			cultivation Standish & Noble before 1860; blush, rich brown eye.
	Mauve Queen		cl.	(M. Koster & Sons); lilac, dark blotch on upper lobe.
	Maxdis		cl.	maximum x discolor; exhibited Nearing-Gable; white.
	Maxie		cl.	maximum ? x macrophyllum; (Gable).
	Maximum Album		cl.	maximum x ; (A. Waterer before 1915); white hybrid; not true var. album.
	Maximum Roseum			Syn. of 'Ponticum Roseum'.
	Maximum Rubrum			cultivated Standish & Noble before 1860; rose.
	Maximum Superbum		cl.	maximum x ?; (Parsons).
	Maximum Triumphans			rose.
	Maximum Wellesleyanum		cl.	Syn. of 'Wellesleyanum'.
	Max Sye		cl.	'Chevalier F. de Sauvage x ?; (C. Frets & Son about 1935); dark red, black blotch, early.
	Maxwell T. Masters		cl.	(A. Waterer before 1915); rosy crimson.
	Maya		cl.	sutchuenense x ririei; (Magor 1933); very pale mauve within, spotted deep purple and blotched with intense purple at base; outside of flowers flushed a deeper shade (H.C.C. 633/3); A.M. (R.H.S.) 1940. Syn. 'Sutchrir'?
xxxxH-3	May Day		g.	haematodes x griersonianum; (A. M. Williams).
	May Day	****C	cl.	haematodes x griersonianum; (A. M. Williams 1932); cerise scarlet; A.M. (R.H.S.) 1932. See 'Bodnant May Day', 'Exbury May Day'.
	Mayflower		cl.	racemosum x carolinianum; (Gable).
	May Morn		g.	'May Day' x beanianum (pink form); (Aberconway).
	May Morn		cl.	'May Day' x beanianum (pink form); (Aberconway 1946); Azalea pink (H.C.C. 618/3) to Begonia (619/3) flushed on margins of lobes porcelain rose (H.C.C. 620/1); A.M. (R.H.S.) 1946)
	May Pink		cl.	'Cornish Loderi' x 'Loderi Sir Edmund'; (Loder 1946); fuchsine pink (H.C.C. 627/2) shaded light solferino purple (26/2); A.M. (R.H.S.) 1946.
	May Queen		g.	fortunei x ?; (Loder 1926); waxy, rich pink.
	Mayros		g.	'Eros' x 'May Day'; (Aberconway 1946).
	May Templar	** B	cl.	'Queen Wilhelmina' x 'Stanley Davies'; (C.B. van Nes & Sons); bright scarlet.
	Mayros		g.	'Eros' x 'May Day'; (Aberconway 1946); red.
	Meadowbrook		cl.	'Mrs. C. S. Sargent' x 'Everestianum'; (Paul Vossberg, U.S.A., 1928); bright pink, crenate petals.
	Mecene			A.M. 1891.
	Medea		g.	'Red Admiral' x sutchuenense; (Magor 1931); crimson rather than red.
	Medora			cultivated Noble about 1855; rose, spotted all over.
xx H-4	Medusa		g.	scyphocalyx x griersonianum; (Aberconway 1936); vermilion to orange.
	Meg Merrilees		cl.	campylocarpum x A.W. Hardy hybrid?; (Slocock 1924 approx.) apricot and yellow, red blotch; creamy white shading to yellow.
	Melanthuma		cl.	in cultivation T. Methven & Son, Edinburgh 1868-69; purplish crimson.
	Melissa		g.	'Ascot Brilliant' x arboreum; (Magor 1932); red with spotting of darker red.
	Mella		cl.	burmanicum x edgeworthii; (C. Williams); exhibited 1952.
	Mellow Gold		cl.	wardii x campylocarpum; (B. F. Lancaster).
	Melody		g.	'Loderi Venus' x 'General Sir John du Cane'; (Rothschild 1950); pale pink or creamy pink.
	Melpomene		cl.	caucasicum x ; dark rose.
	Melrose		g.	dichroanthum x 'Avocet'; (Rothschild 1947); pale pink.
	Melton		cl.	(A. Waterer before 1915); purple, dark center.
	Memoir		cl.	(A. Waterer before 1915); lilac white, yellowish green spots.
	Menippe		g.	'Erebus' x Loderi g. (Aberconway 1941); pink.

		Menziesii				cultivated Standish & Noble before 1860; rosy pink, yellow blotch.
		Mera			g.	'Ouida' x 'F.C.Puddle'; (Aberconway 1946); pale pink.
		Meridian				in cultivation T.Methven & Sons, Edinburgh 1868-69; dark crimson, black blotch.
		Meritorium				in cultivation T.Methven 1868-69; light rose, yellow spots.
		Merkur			g.	'Louis Pasteur' x williamsianum; (Dietrich Hobbie 1953); delicate rose, deeper at the edge.
		Merle Lee			cl.	'Azor' selfed; (Esch); exhibited 1954; pink; P.A. 1954.
		Merlin			g.	arboreum x 'Eupheno'; (Aberconway 1950); red.
		(Merlin)			cl.	See 'Exbury Merlin', 'Hawk Merlin'.
		Mermaid				(W.C.Slocock); coral pink.
		Merops			g.	'Cunningham's Sulphur' x lacteum; (Magor); exhibited C. Ingram 1939; sulphur yellow.
		Message of Peace			cl.	(Waterer, Sons & Crisp before 1922); white, tinged mauve.
		Messenger				cultivated Noble about 1855; purplish crimson, spotted.
		Metallicum				(Veitch & Son); dull rosy crimson.
		Metaphor				(A.Waterer); cultivated Standish & Noble before 1860; rose.
		Meteor			cl.	(R.Gill & Son); fiery red.
		Meteor				'Altaclarense' x catawbiense; (Standish & Noble before 1850); rosy crimson.
		Methven's Scarlet				(Methven); deep red.
		Metis			g.	herpesticum x griersonianum; (Aberconway 1941); orange red.
		Metternianus				form of R. metternichii?; (introduced by Wada); pink.
xx	H-3	Mevrouw P.A. Colijn	*	A	cl.	'Mrs. G. C. Stirling' x 'Madame de Bruin'; (M. Koster & Sons); dark carmine red. Syn. 'Madame P. A. Colijn'.
		Mexico			cl.	(T.J.R. Seidel); red.
x	H-2	Michael Waterer		B	cl.	ponticum x ; (J.Waterer before 1894); dark red, spotted.
		Michele			g.	griersonianum x 'Afghan'; (Rothschild 1947); red.
x	H-3	Midsummer	**	A	cl.	maximum x ; (J.Waterer, Son & Crisp); rose pink.
		Mikado			g.	griffithianum x 'Cornish Cross'; (Aberconway 1950); pale rose.
		Milady			g.	'Rosefinch' x Loderi g.; (Rothschild 1950); deep rose pink.
		Mildred Amateis			cl.	carolinianum x edgeworthii; (Amateis 1955); white flushed pink.
		Mildred Fawcett			cl.	'Faggetter's Favorite' x 'Mrs. Donald Graham'; (Fawcett 1960); blush pink, orange pink blotch; P. A. (A. R. S.) 1960.
		Militaire			g.	'Duchess of Edinburgh' x javanicum; scarlet crimson; F.C.C. 1885.
		Milkmaid				(Harry White); still grown at Sunningdale Nursery 1955.
		Mims			cl.	'Limbatum' x 'Diadema'; (T.J.R. Seidel 1910); pale carmine rose.
		Mimulus			g.	'Anita' x 'Rapture'; (Aberconway 1950); red.
		Minerva				javanicum x 'Princess Alexandra'; (before 1865); light rose, orange spots or yellow; F.C.C. 1885.
		Minerva			g.	'Sir Frederick Moore' x elliottii; (Rothschild 1945); pink.
		Ming			cl.	'Albatross' x wardii; (R. Henny 1960); uranium green (H.C.C. 63/3) with Indian lake blotch on upper lobe.
		Minne			cl.	catawbiense x ; (T.J.R.Seidel); rose, yellow markings.
		Minnehaha			g.	'Corona' x souliei; (Rothschild 1947); bright pink or white shaded pink or creamy white.
		Minnie				(Standish); exhibited Veitch & Son 1862; bluish white, chocolate blotch.
		Minnie Waterer				white, crimson edges.
		Minstrel			g.	forrestii var. repens x 'Neriihaem'; (Aberconway 1950); deep red.
		Minterne Apricot			cl.	dichroanthum x griersonianum (Fabia g.); exhibited Digby 1952. Previously known as Fabia var. Minterne Apricot.
		Minterne Berryrose			cl.	'Doncaster' x dichroanthum (Berryrose g.); exhibited Digby 1952. Previously known as Berryrose Minterne var.
		Minterne Cinnkeys			cl.	cinnabarinum x keysii (Cinnkeys g.); (Digby 1931); Nasturtium red (H.C.C. 14/2) inside and scarlet (H.C.C. 19) outside gradually paling towards the top; A.M. (R.H.S.) 1951; F.C.C. (R.H.S.) 1952. Previously known as Cinnkeys Minterne var.
		Mira			g.	beanianum x meddianum; (J.B. Stevenson 1951); reddish purple or deep red.
		Mirabile				rosy crimson. See 'Cynthia'.
		Mirage			cl.	'Fabia' x 'Margaret Dunn'; (R. Henny).
		Mirandum				(H.Waterer before 1851); light rose, spotted.
		Miss Adelaide Clow			g.	griffithianum x 'Halopeanum'; (Lowinsky 1919); white flushed pink with few chocolate spots; A.M. (R.H.S.) 1919.
		Miss Betty Stewart			cl.	vermilion red.
		Miss Butler				exhibited Veitch & Son 1863; dull purplish rose, paler at center, slightly spotted.
		Miss Edith Boscawen			cl.	(A.Waterer); white, black blotch.
		Miss Glyn				cultivated Noble about 1855; pale rose.
		Miss H. de Trafford / Miss Hilda de Trafford			cl.	(J.Waterer); pink, yellow blotch.
		Mission Bells			cl.	williamsianum x orbiculare; (Lancaster); white flushed pink.
		Miss Jekyll			cl.	(A.Waterer); blush, chocolate blotch.
		Miss Mary Ames			cl.	(A.Waterer before 1915); crimson.
		Miss Mercy Grogan				(Standish before 1875); white, spotted.

	Miss Montague			Syn. of 'Jean Marie Montague'.
	Miss Noreen Beamish		cl.	griffithianum x ; (M. Koster & Sons 1823); deep pink.
	Miss Olympia		cl.	'Loderi King George' x williamsianum (Olympic Lady g.); (Ostbo-R. Clark, 1960); blush-pink, darker throat; P.A. (A.R.S.) 1960.
	Miss Pierce			cultivated Standish & Noble before 1860; white, fine eye.
	Miss Pink		g.	'Azma' x griersonianum; exhibited Bolitho 1943.
	Miss Prim		cl.	decorum x irroratum; (R. & G. Bovee 1960); white, brilliant yellow green (Nickerson 2.5 GY 8/9) blotch.
	Miss Street			Syn. of 'Alice Street'.
	Miss Watson			(R. Gill & Son); blush, spotted pink.
	Mist		cl.	hodgsonii x 'Muriel' (Evening g.); (Loder); registered by Sir G. Loder 1954; dark pink mauve. Previously known as Evening var. Mist.
	Mistake		cl.	discolor x 'Pink Pearl'; (Brig. J.M.J. Evans); pale pink, suffused with rose madder (H.C.C. 23/3); A.M. (R.H.S.) 1956.
	Mitzi		cl.	wardii x 'Fabia'; (R. Henny).
	Mnemosyne			rose.
	Mobur		cl.	'Burgundy' x 'Moser's Maroon'; (H. Lem-P. Bowman, 1959); Dahlia purple (H.C.C. 931/3) spotted maroon (H.C.C. 1030) on upper lobes.
	Modesty			(A. Waterer); pale blush, fading.
xx H-4	Mohamet		g.	dichroanthum x 'Tally Ho'; (Rothschild).
	Mohamet	* C	cl.	dichroanthum x 'Tally Ho'; (Rothschild); red (H.C.C. 19/1); A.M. (R.H.S.) 1945.
	Mohur		cl.	'Day Dream' x 'Margaret Dunn' (Dream Girl g.); exhibited Brandt 1955; yellow, spotted green; P.A. (A.R.S.) 1955. Previously known as Dream Girl var. Mohur.
	Molière		cl.	(M. Koster & Sons); flowers a dull shade near rose red (H.C.C. 724), spotted black on upper petal at throat; A.M. (R.H.S.) 1953.
	Monarch			'Duchess of Edinburgh' x 'Princess Alexandra'; (Davies); yellow orange; F.C.C. 1882.
	Monk		cl.	thomsonii x delavayi (Horlick 1934); dark red.
	Monsieur Alfred Chauchard		cl.	(Moser & Fils); magenta, dark blotch.
	Monsieur Felix Guyon		cl.	(Moser & Fils); rose, yellow blotch.
	Monsieur Guillemot		cl.	(Moser); dark rose.
	Monsieur Thiers		cl.	(J Macoy); light red.
	Monsieur Tisserand		cl.	(Moser & Fils); red.
	Monstrous		cl.	'Mrs. E.C. Stirling' x smirnowii hybrid; (C. Waterer, Son & Crisp); rose pink or lavender pink; A.M. (R.H.S.) 1925.
	Mont Blanc			in cultivation T. Methven & Son, Edinburgh 1868-69; white, dwarf.
	Montchanin		cl.	pubescens x keiskei; (Nearing); white.
	Montreal		cl.	discolor x campylocarpum var. elatum (Lady Bessborough g.); (Rothschild); pink in bud, turning to stone cream. Previously known as Lady Bessborough var. Montreal.
	Moonbeam		g.	'Naomi' x griffithianum; (Rothschild 1947); white to light primrose.
	Moonglow		g.	'Loderi Venus' x 'Lady Bessborough'; (Rothschild 1946); pale pink.
	Moonlight		g.	exhibited at R.H.S. 23rd April 1895 by T. McMeekin, Falkland Park, East Norwood; blush, dark spots.
	Moon of Israel		cl.	(Rogers); violet rose, spotted.
	Moonrise		cl.	'Souvenir of W.C. Slocock' x 'Loderi King George'; (Wright).
	Moonrise		cl.	chasmanthum x 'Lady Chamberlain'; (Maj.-Gen. E.G.W.W. Harrison 1955); cream suffused pale lilac pink.
	Moonshine		g.	'Adriaan Koster' x litiense; (R.H.S. Gardens, Wisley).
	Moonshine		cl.	'Adriaan Koster' x litiense; (R.H.S. Gardens, Wisley 1952); primrose yellow (H.C.C. 601/2-601/3) that darkens somewhat on the upper lobe, the throat is stained a dark crimson blotch; A.M. (R.H.S.) 1952. See 'Moonshine Bright', 'Moonshine Glow', 'Moonshine Supreme'.
	Moonshine Bright		cl.	'Adriaan Koster' x litiense (Moonshine g.); (R.H.S. Gardens, Wisley).
	Moonshine Glow		cl.	'Adriaan Koster' x litiense (Moonshine g.) (R.H.S. Wisley); yellow, near uranium green (H.C.C. 63/3); H.C. (R.H.S.) 1957.
	Moonshine Supreme		cl.	'Adriaan Koster' x litiense (Moonshine g.); (R.H.S. Gardens, Wisley 1953); primrose yellow (H.C.C. 601/1-601/2) darker staining on upper segment with indistinct spotting; A.M. (R.H.S.) 1953.
xxxxH-3	Moonstone	*** C	g.	campylocarpum x williamsianum; (J.C. Williams 1933); cream, ivory and pink.
	Moontide			wardii x 'Loder's White'; (Rudolph Henny); white; P.A. (A.R.S.) 1955.
	Mooreii			arboreum x ; in cultivation T. Methven & Son, Edinburgh 1868-69; rosy crimson, spotted.
	Morawen		cl.	'Isabella' x 'Shepherd's Delight'; (Heneage-Vivian); rosy carmine or Phlox pink (H.C.C. 625/1) with upper 3 petals slightly marked dark pink spotting; A.M. (R.H.S.) 1950.
	Morfar		cl.	morii x fargesii; (Collingwood Ingram 1949); pinkish white with crimson spots.
	Morning Star			cultivated Standish & Noble before 1860; violet, tinged white.

		Morning Star		g.	'Sunrise' x williamsianum; (Aberconway 1942); pale pink.
		Morvah		cl.	elliottii x wattii; (Bolitho); turkey red (H.C.C. 721/3); spotting on upper lobes; A.M. (R.H.S.) 1956; F.C.C. 1959.
		Mosaique		g.	ambiguum x 'Cinnkeys'; (Rothschild).
		Mosaique		cl.	ambiguum x 'Cinnkeys'; (Rothschild); bright red at base (H.C.C. 020/1), lobes of pale yellow (H.C.C. 3/3); A.M. (R.H.S.) 1945.
		Moscow			raised and exhibited by Collingwood Ingram; scarlet.
x	H-3	Moser's Maroon	*** B	cl.	(Moser & Fils); red maroon flowers marked inside with darker spots; bright red young foliage; A.M. (R.H.S.) 1932.
		Moth		cl.	megeratum x mishmiense (Silver Ray g.); (Aberconway); Lemon yellow (H.C.C. 4/3-4/2) and the upper lobes are heavily spotted with brown; filaments are also yellow and the anthers dark brown; A.M. (R.H.S.) 1955. Previously known as Silver Ray var. Moth.
xxx	H-4	Mother of Pearl	*** B	cl.	'Pink Pearl' sport; (J. Waterer 1925); blush turning pearl-white; A.M. (R.H.S.) 1930.
		Mottled Aucklandii			seedling from R. griffithianum; (R. Gill & Son); shell pink.
		Moukoense		cl.	pemakoense x moupinense; (Brandt 1953); white, flushed pink.
		Mount Blanc			cultivated Standish & Noble before 1860; pure white.
xx	H-3	Mount Everest	*** B	cl.	campanulatum x ?; griffithianum x ?; (W.C. Slocock 1930); pure white speckled brown on upper petal at throat; bud white; April/May; A.M. (R.H.S.) 1953; F.C.C. 1958.
		Mouton Rothschild		cl.	'Beau Brummell' x elliottii; (exhibited E. de Rothschild, 1958); blood red (H.C.C. 820/2), heavily brown spotted; A.M. (R.H.S.) 1958.
		Mozari		g.	concatenans x ambiguum; (J.B. Stevenson 1951); pastel shades, yellow, pink etc.
		Mozart			cultivated Standish & Noble before 1860; intense crimson, finely spotted.
		Mr. W.R. Dykes		cl.	'Princess Juliana' x 'Carl Mette'; (C.B. van Nes & Sons); light red.
		Mrs. A.C. Kenrick	** B		griffithianum x ?; (M. Koster & Sons?); deep rose pink, spotted deeper shade; A.M. (R.H.S.) 1925.
		Mrs. A.F. McEwan		cl.	Loderi g. seedling; (University of Washington Arboretum); fuchsine pink (H.C.C. 627/3 to Persian rose (H.C.C. 628/3); A.E. (A.R.S.) 1956.
		Mrs. Agnew			Syn. of 'Mrs. Tom Agnew'.
		Mrs. Alistair Macintosh			(Knap Hill Nursery); soft rose mauve, fading to white.
xx	H-3	Mrs. A.M. Williams	*** B	cl.	griffithianum x ; (Otto Schulz cross 1892, introduced by C.B. van Nes & Sons 1896); cardinal red (H.C.C. 122/2) spotted dark brown; A.M. (R.H.S.) 1926; A.M.(R.H.S.) 1933; A.M. (R.H.S. Wisley Trials) 1954.
		Mrs. Anthony Waterer	* A	cl.	fortunei x ; (A. Waterer before 1915); white, yellow blotch.
		Mrs. A.R. Bede		cl.	'Doncaster' x ; (M. Koster & Sons 1923); rose scarlet.
		Mrs. Arderne		cl.	fortunei x ; (Paul); waxy cherry red.
		Mrs. Arthur Evans		cl.	(Knap Hill Nursery). Syn. of 'Mrs. Arthur Fawcus'.
		Mrs. Arthur Fawcus	A	g.	caucasicum x 'Kewense'; (Knap Hill Nursery 1946); pale yellow. Syn. 'Mrs. Arthur Evans'.
		Mrs. Arthur Hunnewell		cl.	(A. Waterer before 1915); pink, primrose center.
		Mrs. Arthur James		g.	'Essex Scarlet' x griffithianum; (Rothschild 1947); pink, now discontinued.
		Mrs. Arthur Walter		cl.	(J. Waterer); white with rose edge.
xx	H-3	Mrs. Ashley Slocock	** B		campylocarpum x hardy hybrid; (Slocock); selected 1933; cream, suffused apricot.
xx	H-3	Mrs. A.T. de la Mare	*** C	cl.	'Sir Charles Butler' x 'Halopeanum'; (C.B. van Nes & Sons); white with green spot, fragrant. A.M. (R.H.S.) 1958.
		Mrs. Bernice Baker		cl.	'Dawn's Delight' x fortunei; (Larson).
xxx	H-3	Mrs. Betty Robertson	* B	cl.	'Mrs. Lindsay Smith' x campylocarpum hybrid; (M. Koster & Sons cross 1920); pale yellow with pink flush, turning to cream, red center.
		Mrs. Byron Scott			souliei x ; seed from England, raised and distributed in U.S.A. by H.L. Larson; straw yellow.
		Mrs. Butler		cl.	(G. Paul) pale mauve; a form of R. fortunei.
		Mrs. Byrne		cl.	(M. Koster & Sons); cerise or rich salmon, heavily spotted.
		Mrs. Carter Glass		cl.	decorum x 'Catalgla'; (Gable); white.
xx	H-4	Mrs. C.B. van Nes.	* B	cl.	'Princess Juliana' x 'Florence Smith'; (C.B. van Nes & Sons); rosy red, fading to deep pink.
		Mrs. Charles Butler			See 'Mrs. Butler'.
xx	H-3	Mrs. Charles E. Pearson	****B	cl.	'George Hardy' x catawbiense; (M. Koster & Sons cross 1909); pale blush mauve, brown spots; A.M. (R.H.S.) 1933; F.C.C.(R.H.S.) 1955.
x	H-1	Mrs. Chas. S. Sargent / Mrs. C.S. Sargent		cl.	catawbiense x; (A. Waterer 1888); rosy pink or dark carmine rose, yellow spotted, margins waved.
		Mrs. Charles Thorold	A	cl.	(A. Waterer before 1915); pink, yellow center.

Mrs. C. Whitner g. 'Snow Queen' x 'Loderi Sir Edmund'; (Loder); pink.

Mrs. Davies Evans ** A cl. (A. Waterer before 1915); light mauve (imperial purple H.C.C. 33/1); H.C. (R.H.S. Wisley Trials) 1957; A.M. 1958.

xxx H-3 Mrs. Donald Graham cl. ('Corona' x griersonianum) x Loderi g.; (Rose); named by Endre Ostbo; spinel red (H.C.C. 0023/1) lobes tyrian rose (H.C.C. 24/2); P.A. (A.R.S.) 1954.

xx H-3 Mrs. E.C. Stirling * B cl. griffithianum x ; (J. Waterer); blush pink; A.M. (R.H.S.) 1906.

Mrs. Edward Denny (Knap Hill Nursery); crimson, bold black blotch.

Mrs. Edwin Hillier cl. griffithianum hybrid x 'Monsieur Thiers'; (C.B. van Nes & Sons); dark pink.

Mrs. Elizabeth Titcomb cl. 'Marinus Koster' x 'Snow Queen'; (Larson); exhibited 1942; white.

Mrs. F. Hankey cl. (A. Waterer); salmon with spots.

Mrs. Fitzgerald cl. (J. Waterer before 1867); in cultivation T. Methven & Son, Edinburgh 1868-69; bright rosy scarlet.

Mrs. F.J. Kirchner cl. (A. Waterer before 1915); cream, slightly spotted.

Mrs. Frank S. Baker cl. fortunei x 'Dawn's Delight'; exhibited Larson 1942; pink.

Mrs. Fred Paul cl. fortunei x ; (Paul); light pink.

xxxxH-3 Mrs. Furnival ****B cl. griffithianum hybrid x caucasicum hybrid; (A. Waterer); named about 1920; funnel shaped, pink heavily blotched crimson; A.M. 1933; F.C.C. (R.H.S.) 1948.

Mrs. George O. Clark cl. caroliniianum x moupinense; (G. O. Clark); pink.

Mrs. George Paul cl. griffithianum x ; (A. Waterer); blush changing to white.

Mrs. G.H.W. Heneage cl. (A. Waterer before 1871); reddish purple, white center.

Mrs. Gomer Waterer 'Corona'? x 'Strategist'?; (A. Waterer); deep pink.

Mrs. G. Reuthe edgeworthii x 'Fragrantissimum'; exhibited G. Reuthe 1935.

Mrs. Gwendoline Broderick cl. Syn. of 'Lady Gwendoline Broderick'.

xxx H-4 Mrs. G.W. Leak *** B cl. 'Coombe Royal' x 'Chevalier Felix de Sauvage' (M. Koster & Sons 1916); light pink with brown purple blotch; F.C.C. 1934.

Mrs. Hamilton (R. Gill & Son 1922); Heliotrope.

Mrs. Harold Terry cl. 'Princess Juliana' x 'Florence Smith'; (C.B. van Nes & Son); soft rose pink; A.M. (R.H.S.) 1948.

Mrs. Harry Ingersoll cl. (A. Waterer 1877); rosy lilac, greenish center.

Mrs. H.B. Gardner cl. fortunei x ; (Dexter); purplish red.

Mrs. Heal multicolor x 'Princess Beatrice'; (Veitch); white with delicate shade of pink; F.C.C. 1894.

Mrs. Helen Koster ** A cl. 'Mrs. J.J. Crosfield' x 'Catawbiense Grandiflorum'; (M. Koster & Sons); light lilac, large purplish red blotch.

Mrs. Helen Weyerhauser cl. 'Fusilier' x 'Jean'; (Larson); exhibited 1952; pink.

Mrs. Hemans cultivated Standish & Noble before 1860; pinkish white or white shaded pink, yellow spots.

x H-3 Mrs. Henry Agnew cl. grande x arboreum var. album; (Mangles); exhibited Mangles 1915; white, fringed pink.

Mrs. Henry Shilson arboreum x ; (R. Gill & Son before 1920); pink.

Mrs. Horace Fogg griersonianum x 'Loderi Venus'; (Ridgeway, Kirkland, Washington); named by H. L. Larson, Tacoma; neyron rose.

Mrs. H. Stocker cl. (M. Koster & Sons before 1923); red or brilliant scarlet, maroon blotch; A.M. (R.H.S.) 1948.

Mrs. James Horlick cl. thomsonii x 'Dr. Stocker'; (Horlick 1931); rose-pink flowers like 'Cornish Cross' but paler.

Mrs. J. Comber cl. diaprepes x decorum; (Messel); white with suggestion of yellow at base; A.M. (R.H.S.) 1932.

xx H-3 Mrs. J.C. Williams ** A cl. (A. Waterer); blush white, spotted red.

xx H-2 Mrs. J.G. Millais ** A cl. (A. Waterer); white, conspicuous yellow blotch. Syn. 'Mrs. John Millais'.

Mrs. J.H. van Nes 'Carl Mette' x 'Princess Juliana'; (C.B. van Nes & Sons); pink, spotted.

Mrs. J.J. Crosfield cl. (M. Koster & Sons); pale rose, crimson blotch.

Mrs. John Clutton A cl. maximum x ; (A. Waterer); white with small yellowish green blotch; F.C.C. 1865.

Mrs. John Kelk cl. (J. Waterer); clear rose; late.

Mrs. John Millais cl. Syn. of 'Mrs. J.G. Millais'.

Mrs. John Penn cl. (John Waterer before 1871); light red, lighter center.

Mrs. John Waterer A cl. (J. Waterer before 1865); rosy crimson.

		Mrs. Kenneth Wilson		cl.	(M. Koster & Sons); deep rose, frilled edges.
		Mrs. Kingsmill		g.	griffithianum x campylocarpum; (Mangles); yellow fading to cream; A.M. (R.H.S.) 1911. See 'Mrs. Randall Davidson'.
		Mrs. L.A. Dunnett		cl.	'Mrs. George Hardy' x ; (M. Koster & Sons cross 1909); rosy pink, lighter center, very late.
		Mrs. Leopold de Rothschild		g.	'B. de Bruin' x griersonianum; (Rothschild).
		Mrs. Leopold de Rothschild		cl.	'B. de Bruin' x griersonianum; (Rothschild); light red spotted fawn; A.M. (R.H.S.) 1933.
xx	H-3	Mrs. Lindsay Smith	** B	cl.	'George Hardy' x 'Duchess of Edinburgh'; (M. Koster & Sons cross 1910); white, slightly spotted red on upper lobe; A. M. 1933.
		Mrs. Linley Messel			orbiculare natural hybrid; (Messel 1934).
xxx	H-3	Mrs. Lionel de Rothschild	** B	cl.	(A. Waterer); bright pink, paler at maturity; A.M. (R.H.S.) 1931.
		Mrs. L. M. Hayes Palmer		cl.	(M. Koster & Sons); red, heavily blotched.
		Mrs. Loudon		g.	'Altaclarense' x maximum hybrid; (Standish & Noble 1850); carmine or pale bright rose, the whole of the petals spotted.
		Mrs. Mangles			(Mangles?); cultivated Standish & Noble before 1860; violet white, finely spotted with black.
xx	H-3	Mrs. Mary Ashley	** B	cl.	campylocarpum x ; (W.C.Slocock); salmon pink, shaded cream.
		Mrs. Matthew Rose			fortunei x ; (Paul); pink.
		Mrs. Mendel		cl.	(A. Waterer before 1871); pink rayed white, yellow center.
		Mrs. Messel		cl.	clone of R. decorum; (Messel); pure white; A.M. (R.H.S.) 1923.
		Mrs. Milner		cl.	catawbiense x ; (A. Waterer); crimson. Syn. 'Bibber'.
		Mrs. Paul B. Smith		cl.	'Albatross' x 'Pygmalion'; (Larson); opalescent pink, red throat.
o	H-2	Mrs. P. den Ouden		cl.	'Atrosanguineum' x 'Doncaster'; (H. den Ouden & Son about 1925); deep crimson.
xxx	H-2	Mrs. P.D. Williams	*** A	cl.	(A. Waterer); ivory white with browny yellow eye; A.M. (R.H.S.) 1936.
		Mrs. Peter Koster		cl.	(M. Koster & Sons); very pale pink, reverse side rose pink.
xx	H-3	Mrs. Philip Martineau	****B	cl.	(Knap Hill Nursery Co.); rose pink fading lighter, pale yellow blotch; A.M. 1933; F.C.C. (R.H.S.) 1936.
		Mrs. Powell Glass		cl.	'Catalgla' x decorum; (Gable 1949); white.
		Mrs. Prain		g.	garden hybrid x smirnowii; (Kew).
		Mrs. Randall Davidson		g.	griffithianum x campylocarpum (Hooker's form); (Mangles); exhibited Mangles 1884; white, creamy yellow or pink according to clonal variety. See 'Maiden's Blush'; 'Mrs. Kingsmill'.
		Mrs. Reuthe			bright red, fading.
		Mrs. R.G. Shaw	A	cl.	(A. Waterer before 1915); blush, dark eye.
		Mrs. Richard Gill			arboreum x ; (R. Gill & Son); bright salmon rose, blood red splashing in throat.
		Mrs. Robert W. Wallace		cl.	'Doncaster' hybrid x 'Mrs. George Hardy'; (M. Koster & Sons cross 1909); pale pink, crimson blotch.
x	H-2	Mrs. R.S. Holford	** B	cl.	(A. Waterer 1866); rosy salmon.
		Mrs. Russell Sturgis / Mrs. Russell Sturgess		cl.	(J. Waterer); white spotted chocolate.
		Mrs. Samuel Wallrock			(M. Koster & Son); white, heavily spotted red.
		Mrs. Sassoon		cl.	'Essex Scarlet' x griersonianum (Cavalcade g.); (Rothschild); brilliant scarlet. Previously known as Cavalcade var. Mrs. Sassoon.
		Mrs. Shuttleworth		cl.	(A. Waterer before 1875); scarlet, light center finely spotted.
		Mrs. Siddons			cultivated Standish & Noble before 1860; rose, white throat.
		Mrs. S. J. Beale		cl.	ponticum x ; (M. Koster & Sons); lilac.
		Mrs. S. Simpson		cl.	(A. Waterer before 1915); white, finely spotted.
		Mrs. Standish			(Standish); white, brown spots.
		Mrs. Thistleton Dyer			Syn. of 'Mrs. W. T. Thistleton-Dyer'.
		Mrs. Thomas Brassey		cl.	(J. Waterer); white, rosy purple markings.
		Mrs. Thomas Wain		cl.	(A. Waterer before 1875); pale rose, brown spots.
		Mrs. Tom Agnew	A	cl.	(J. Waterer before 1886); white with lemon blotch.
x	H-3	Mrs. Tom H. Lowinsky	** B	g.	griffithianum x 'White Pearl'; (A. Waterer-Lowinsky); blush to white, reddish brown blotch; A.M. (R.H.S.) 1919.
		Mrs. Tritton		cl.	(J. Waterer); crimson, light center.
		Mrs. T. Wezelenburg		cl.	(K. Wezelenburg & Son); dark scarlet.

xx	H-3	Mrs. Walter Burns	**	B	cl.	'Standishii' x griffithianum; (T. Lowinsky); pink with bright red blotch; A.M. (R.H.S.) 1931.
		Mrs. Wayne W. Keyes			cl.	'Earl of Athlone' x fortunei; (Larson 1956); deep red.
xxx	H-3	Mrs. W. C. Slocock	***	B	cl.	campylocarpum x ; (Slocock 1929); apricot pink shaded to yellow; A.M. (R.H.S.) 1929.
		Mrs. Webley				fortunei x ; (Paul) light rose, spotted.
		Mrs. W. H. Gaze				purplish red.
		Mrs. W. H. Gaze			cl.	(C. B. van Nes & Sons before 1922); wine red.
		Mrs. W. Agnew } Mrs. William Agnew		B	cl.	(J. Waterer before 1875); pale rose, purple blotch.
		Mrs. William Bovill			cl.	(A. Waterer & Godfrey before 1874); rosy scarlet or salmon rose.
		Mrs. Wm. R. Coe			cl.	fortunei? hybrid; (Dexter-Westbury Rose Co. 1959); dark, bright pink, crimson throat.
		Mrs. Wm. Watson	*	A	cl.	griffithianum x ; (A. Waterer); white with reddish markings on upper petals; blush fading white, violet spots; A.M. (R.H.S.) 1925.
		Mrs. Williams			cl.	(J. Waterer before 1875); light rose.
		Mrs. W. R. Coe			cl.	See 'Mrs. Wm. R. Coe'.
		Mrs. W. T. Thistleton-Dyer				fortunei x ; (George Paul); soft pink, Syn. 'Mrs. Thistleton Dyer'.
		Mt. Mitchell			cl.	maximum x catawbiense ?, a natural hybrid; named by Gable.
		Mucram			cl.	mucronulatum x ambiguum; (Gable); lavender pink.
		Mucronulatum Pink			cl.	natural hybrid; exhibited Gable 1955.
		Multiflorum				ciliatum x virgatum; (J. Waterer).
		Multimaculatum			cl.	ponticum x ; (J. Waterer before 1860); white with red spots.
		Mum		A	cl.	maximum x ; (J. Waterer 1897); white with lemon eye; compact.
		Mundulum			cl.	in cultivation T. Methven & Son, Edinburgh 1868-69; blush, pink spots.
		Mureun			g.	'F. C. Puddle' x barbatum; (Aberconway 1946); deep red.
		Muriel			cl.	falconeri x grande (Mansellii g.) (Loder); creamy white with dark crimson blotch at base; A.M. (R.H.S.) 1925. Previously known as Mansellii var. Muriel.
		Muriel Holman			g.	'Griercalyx' x maddenii; exhibited Tremayne 1941.
		Muriel Messel			cl.	Loderi g. x 'Loder's White'; (Messel); delicate pale pink, buds bright pink; A.M. (R.H.S.) 1929.
		Murillo			cl.	(M. Koster & Sons).
		Myrte			cl.	'Nigrescens' x 'Mira'; (T.J.R. Seidel 1910); purplish violet.
		Myrtifolium				minus x hirsutum; exhibited 1917 ?; lilac pink.
		Mystic			cl.	'Barclayi' x williamsianum; (Harrison cross 1950); clear pink; registered 1957.
		Nanceglos			g.	fortunei x elliottii; (Bolitho 1945). See 'Stellaby'.
		Nancy			g.	'Prometheus' x neriiflorum; (Rothschild 1931); pink.
		Nancy Hardy				Loderi g. x ?; exhibited Hardy 1954.
		Nancy Read				pemakoense x 'Racil'; exhibited Larson 1953; light pink.
		Nanette			cl.	(W.C. Slocock); blush pink with dark blotch; A.M. 1933.
		Nansen			cl.	smirnowii x ; (M. Koster & Sons); pale lilac rose.
xxx	H-2	Naomi			g.	'Aurora' x fortunei; (Rothschild).
		Naomi	***	B	cl.	'Aurora' x fortunei; (Rothschild 1926); pink, color similar to 'Mother of Pearl', with distinct yellow undertone; sweet scented; A.M. (R.H.S.) 1933. See Exbury Naomi.
xxx	H-2	Naomi Astarte			cl.	'Aurora' x fortunei (Naomi g.); (Rothschild); pink shaded yellow, yellow throat. Previously known as Naomi var. Astarte.
xxx	H-2	Naomi Carissima			cl.	'Aurora' x fortunei (Naomi g.); (Rothschild); pale pink, creamy white. Previously known as Naomi var. Carissima.
xxx	H-2	Naomi Early Dawn			cl.	'Aurora' x fortunei (Naomi g.); (Rothschild); pale pink. Previously known as Naomi var. Early Dawn.
xxx	H-2	Naomi Glow			cl.	'Aurora' x fortunei (Naomi g.); (Rothschild); bright pink. Previously known as Naomi var. Glow.
xxx	H-2	Naomi Hope			cl.	'Aurora' x fortunei (Naomi g.); (Rothschild); pink, mauve tinged. Previously known as Naomi var. Hope.
xxx	H-2	Naomi Nautilus	***	B	cl.	'Aurora' x fortunei (Naomi g.); (Rothschild); rose flushed pale orange yellow on tube within and without, soft greenish flush at throat; A.M. (R.H.S.) 1938. Previously known as Naomi var. Nautilus.
xxx	H-2	Naomi Nereid			cl.	'Aurora' x fortunei (Naomi g.); (Rothschild); lavender and yellow. Previously known as Naomi var. Nereid.
xxx	H-2	Naomi Pink Beauty			cl.	'Aurora' x fortunei (Naomi g.); (Rothschild); deep pink. Previously known as Naomi var. Pink Beauty.
xxx	H-2	Naomi Stella Maris	****	B	cl.	'Aurora' x fortunei (Naomi g.); (Rothschild). Previously known as Naomi var. Stella Maris; F.C.C. (R.H.S.) 1939.
		Napoleon Baumann			cl.	(Baumann 1867 in Belgium); in cultivation at Sunningdale Nursery before 1872; light rose, crimson spots.
		Narcissus				in cultivation T.Methven & Son, Edinburgh 1868-69; rosy red, dark spots.

	Nasturtium		cl.	griersonianum x Loderi g. (East Knoyli g.); (Horlick); Nasturtium red.
	Nausicaa		g.	calophytum x 'Gill's Triumph'; (E.J.P. Magor).
	(Nautilus)			See 'Naomi Nautilus'.
	Neapolitan		cl.	decorum x 'Fabia'; (Sunningdale Nurseries 1955); salmon pink outside, orange pink at base.
	Nectarine		g.	('Coronis' x griersonianum) x 'Margaret Dunn'; (Brandt).
	Neda		g.	dichroanthum x 'Cunningham's Sulphur'; (Aberconway 1933); orange flushed pink.
	Nehru		g.	griersonianum x 'Huntsman'; (Rothschild 1946); scarlet.
	Neilsonii		cl.	cultivated T.Methven & Son, Edinburgh 1868-69; bright cherry red.
	Nell Gwynne			(Waterer, Sons & Crisp Ltd.); cerise pink fading to pale pink with reddish brown eye.
	Nellie	B		Azaleodendron; white, yellow eye.
	Nellie Moser			(Moser); a blending of lilac, pink, yellow and white.
	Nelly de Bruin		cl.	(M. Koster & Sons); pale pink, dark red blotch.
	Nelsonii			Syn. of 'Neilsonii'.
	Ne Plus Ultra			cultivated Standish & Noble before 1860; crimson purple. Syn. 'Londonense'.
	Neptune			'Eudora' x Loderi g.; (Aberconway 1941); pale pink. See 'Eulo'.
	(Nereid)			See 'Naomi Nereid'.
xxx H-3	Nereid	** C	g.	neriiflorum x dichroanthum; (Wilding 1934); salmon orange, tabular.
	Nereus			in cultivation T. Methven & Son, Edinburgh 1868-69; purple, spotted black.
	Neriiapo		g.	apodectum x neriiflorum; (Magor 1929); orange red.
	Neriiarb		g.	neriiflorum x arboreum (blood red); (Magor 1928); clear red, inconspicuous spots of darker shade.
	Neriihaem		g.	neriiflorum x haematodes; (Magor 1927); blood red, unspotted, waxy.
	Nerissa		g.	'Choremia' x 'Neriihaem'; (Aberconway 1945); blood red.
	Nero		cl.	(A. Waterer & Godgrey before 1871); purple lake.
	Nestucca		cl.	fortunei x yakusimanum; (C. C. Smith 1960); white, compact habit; P.A.(A.R.S.) 1960.
	Netty Koster		cl.	'Mrs L. A. Dunnett' x unnamed hybrid of R. griersonianum F. 286; (M. Koster & Sons); crimson (H.C.C. 22/1) with darker spots on upper petal; A.M. (R.H.S.) 1945.
	New Comet		cl.	'Idealist' x 'Naomi' (Emerald Isle g.) (R.H.S. Gardens, Wisley); Mimosa yellow (H.C.C. 602/1) flushed pale pink; A.M. (R.H.S.) 1957.
	New Moon	*** B	cl.	'Mrs. W.C. Slocock' x fortunei; (W.C. Slocock); white flushed primrose yellow (H.C.C. 601/2) on throat and upper petal, buds cream tinged mauvy pink; A.M. (R.H.S. Wisley Trials) 1953.
	Newport		cl.	catawbiense x ; (Stokes); plum purple.
	Newton			purplish pink.
	Nigrescens		cl.	(A. Waterer; before 1871); dark plum.
	Nimbus		cl.	'Snow Queen' x 'Venus'; exhibited Knap Hill 1949; white.
	Ninette		g.	discolor x makinoi; (J. B. Stevenson 1936); clear pale pink.
	Niobe			Syn. of 'Kate Greenaway'.
	Nivaticum		cl.	(J.Waterer before 1873); white, yellow spots.
	N.N. Sherwood	** B	cl.	(Sibray); pink, gold center.
	Nobilius			javanicum x teysmanni; deep golden yellow; A.M. 1896.
	Nobleanum	** B	g.	caucasicum x arboreum; (Knap Hill Nursery, A.Waterer (1835) and at other places); rich rosy pink (damask); A.G.M. (R.H.S.) 1926.
	Nobleanum Album	*** B	cl.	caucasicum x arboreum (Nobleanum g.); white. Previously known as Nobleanum var. Album).
	Nobleanum Bicolor			'Altaclarense' x catawbiense; (Standish & Noble 1850); deep rose, white throat.
x H-3	Nobleanum Coccineum	** B	cl.	caucasicum x arboreum (Nobleanum g.); bright scarlet. Previously known as Nobleanum var. Coccineum.
	Nobleanum Lamellen		cl.	caucasicum var. stramineum x arboreum (blood red form) (Nobleanum g.); (Magor 1932); deep rose pink. Previously known as Nobleanum var. Lamellen.
	Nobleanum Silberaad's Early		cl.	caucasicum x arboreum (Nobleanum g.); start pale rose and pure white; very early. Previously known as Nobleanum var. Silberaad's Early.
x H-3	Nobleanum Venustum		cl.	caucasicum x arboreum (Nobleanum g.); (Smith); rose. Previously known as Nobleanum var. Venustum.
	Nocturne		g.	Loderi g. x 'Laura Aberconway'; (Aberconway 1950); red.
	Nonesuch		cl.	cinnabarinum var. roylei x maddenii; (Adams-Acton 1942); pale apricot, fading cream.
	Norah			(M. Koster & Son); blush, margined pale cerise.
	Norbitonense Aureum			Azaleodendron; (W. Smith, Norbiton, cross 1830); (maximum x ponticum) x molle; pale tawny yellow. Syn. 'Smithii Aureum'.
	Norbitonense Broughtonianum		cl.	Azaleodendron; (maximum x ponticum) x molle; deep yellow. Syn. of 'Broughtonii Aureum'.
	Norderney		g.	'Essex Scarlet' x williamsianum; (Dietrich Hobbie 1947); deep rose.
	Noreen Beamish		cl.	Syn. of 'Miss Noreen Beamish'.
	Norma			cultivated Standish & Noble before 1860; white shaded with pink.
	Norman Gill		cl.	'Beauty of Tremough' x griffithianum; (R. Gill & Son); pale heliotrope; A.M. (R.H.S.) 1922; A.M. (R.H.S.) 1936.

		Norman Shaw			g.	discolor x 'B. de Bruin'; (Rothschild).
		Norman Shaw	*	B	cl.	discolor x 'B. de Bruin'; (Rothschild 1919); rich pink; A.M. (R.H.S.) 1926.
		Northern Rover			cl.	venator x 'Doncaster'; (Thacker 1942); blood red.
		Notabile			cl.	(J. Waterer before 1875); bright rose.
		Nova Zembla			cl.	'Parsons Gloriosum' x ; (M. Koster & Sons cross 1902); dark red.
		Novelty			cl.	(A. Waterer); pink, edged white.
		Numa				of the 5th generation of 5 species; javanicum, jasminiflorum, brookeanum, indicum and multicolor; orange red, throat flushed deeper shade; A.M. 1895.
		Nuneham Park	*	C	cl.	griffithianum hybrid x 'Martin Hope Sutton'; (C.B. van Nes & Sons before 1922); bright red.
		Nymph			g.	forrestii var. repens x 'Largo'; (Aberconway 1946); deep red.
		Oasis			cl.	'Fawn' x 'Dido'; (D.W. James, 1959); barium yellow (H.C.C. 503/1) flushed coral pink (H.C.C. 621/2).
		Oberon			g.	'Barclayi' x 'Thomwilliams'; (Aberconway 1950); deep rose.
		Ochroleucum				caucasicum x ; (J. Waterer before 1919); semi-double; straw spotted brown (Millais); sulphur yellow or dull white, greenish center.
		Octavia			g.	'Akbar' x griersonianum; (Rothschild 1947); red.
		Octopus			g.	dichroanthum x kyawi; (Rothschild 1950); orange.
		Oculatum			cl.	(J. Waterer); pink, dark spots.
		Oculissimum			cl.	(J. Waterer before 1871); rose with dark blotches.
o	H-3	Odoratum	**	A		Azaleodendron; ponticum x nudiflorum; (at Thompson's Nursery before 1875); blush or pale lilac. The same as 'Hybridum'?
		Oedipus			g.	'Eros' x 'Jacquetta'; (Aberconway 1941); scarlet.
		Oheimb-Woislowitz			cl.	catawbiense x ; (T. J. R. Seidel); rose. Syn. of 'Von Oheimb-Woislowitz'.
		Oklahoma			g.	'Bellerophon' x 'Tally Ho'; (Rothschild 1948); waxy, bright red.
		Old Copper			cl.	'Vulcan' x 'Fabia'; (Van Veen).
		Oldenburgh			g.	discolor x williamsianum; (Dietrich Hobbie 1953); pale pink.
		Oldewig			cl.	catawbiense x ; (T. J. R. Seidel); crimson with lighter center.
		Old Olson			cl.	Syn. of 'Ole Olson'.
		Old Port	*	A	cl.	catawbiense x ; (A. Waterer 1865); deep plum color.
		Ole Olson			cl.	campylocarpum var. elatum x discolor; (Gable); light yellow.
		Olive			cl.	moupinense x dauricum; (Stirling Maxwell); mallow purple (H.C.C. 630/2) with darker scattered spots on the base of the upper lobe; A.M. (R.H.S.) 1942.
		Oliver			cl.	Loderi g. x ; (Messell); deep pink; A.M. (R.H.S.) 1933.
		Olympia			g.	'Day Dream' x elliottii; (Rothschild 1947); red.
		Olympic Blondie			cl.	'Fabia' x ?; (Clark).
		Olympic Brave			cl.	'Fabia' x ?; (Clark).
		Olympic Brownie			cl.	'Fabia' x ?; (Clark).
		Olympic Chimes			cl.	'Fabia' x ?; (Clark).
		Olympic Chinook			cl.	'Fabia' x ?; (Clark).
		Olympic Hose-in-Hose			cl.	'Fabia' x ?; (Clark).
		Olympic Hunter			cl.	'Fabia' x ?; (Clark).
		Olympic Knight			cl.	'Fabia' x ?; (Clark).
		Olympic Lady			g.	'Loderi King George' x williamsianum; (Ostbo-Clark). See 'White Olympic Lady'.
		Olympic Maid			cl.	'Fabia' x ?; (Clark).
		Olympic Miss			cl.	'Fabia' x ?; (Clark).
		Olympic Quinault			cl.	griersonianum x ; (Layritz-Clark).
		Olympic Sweetheart			cl.	'Romany Chai' x discolor; (Clark).
		Omar			g.	catacosmum x beanianum; (J. B. Stevenson 1951); deep red.
		Omar Pacha / Omar Pasha (Methven)			cl.	(J. Waterer before 1867); purple lake.
		Omega			cl.	catawbiense x ; (T. J. R. Seidel); pure carmine rose. See 'Antonio Omega'.
		Onsloweanum			cl.	(A. Waterer before 1851); delicate waxy blush, yellow eye, changing to white.
		(Opaline)				See 'Yvonne Opaline'.
		Opaline			g.	discolor x ; (Rothschild 1947).
		Operetta			g.	griersonianum x 'Ambrose'; (Rothschild 1947); crimson or bright red.
		Ophelia			g.	callimorphum x auriculatum; (Rothschild 1947); pure white.
		Ophelia			cl.	javanicum x 'Princess Alexandra'; (before 1875); creamy buff flowers margined soft pinkish mauve A.M. 1889.
		Ophir			cl.	'Day Dream' x 'Margaret Dunn' (Dream Girl g.). Previously known as Dream Girl var. Ophir.
		Oporto			cl.	haemaleum x thomsonii (Thomaleum g.); exhibited C. Ingram 1953. Previously known as Thomaleum var. Oporto.
		Optimum				in cultivation T. Methven & Son, Edinburgh 1868-69; rosy purple.
		(Orange)				See 'Tortoiseshell Orange'.
		Orange Azor				Syn. of 'King of Shrubs'.
		Orbhoulst			g.	houlstonii x orbiculare; pink; (R.H.S.) 1932.
		Orbicarb				arboreum x orbiculare; (Magor 1936); brilliant carmine, darker at base. Syn. 'Rotundarb'?

		Orchard			cl.	griersonianum x 'Ilam Alarm' (Scarlet King g.) (Stead 1950); scarlet. Previously known as Scarlet King var. Orchard.
		Oregonia			g.	'Gladys Rillstone' x griersonianum; (Rothschild 1947); rich pink.
		Oregon Queen			cl.	Azaleodendron; occidentale x macrophyllum?.
		Oreoaug			g.	oreotrephes x augustinii; (Magor 1932); palest light lilac, greenish brown spots.
x	H-3	Oreocinn			g.	oreotrephes x cinnabarinum; (Magor 1926); pale pink or violet rose with two lines of brownish pink inside.
		Orestes			g.	'Shilsonii' x griersonianum; (Aberconway 1941); blood red.
		Organdie	**	B	cl.	'A. Gilbert' x herpesticum (Icarus g.) (Rothschild); biscuit or lemon yellow with rose pink edge and a pink zone about ¼ in. deep at base of corolla; A.M. (R.H.S.) 1947. Previously known as Icarus var. Organdie.
		Oriana			g.	'F. C. Puddle' x 'Coreta'; (Aberconway 1946); red.
		Oriflamme			cl.	cinnabarinum var. roylei x 'Royal Flush' orange form (Lady Chamberlain g.); (Rothschild); orange red. Previously known as Lady Chamberlain var. Oriflamme.
		Original				caucasicum var. album selfed; (Standish & Noble 1850); pinkish white, foliage much variegated.
x	H-4	Orion	*	A	g.	'Phoebus' x Loderi g.; (Aberconway 1950); rose pink, red eye.
		Orion				discolor x 'H. M. Arden'; (Waterer, Sons & Crisp about 1920); rose pink, red eye.
		Orion			cl.	griersonianum x 'Madame P. A. Colijn'; (Reuthe).
		Ornamentum				in cultivation with T. Methven & Son, Edinburgh 1868-69; red or rosy scarlet.
		Ornatum				Azaleodendron; viscosum x ponticum; dark scarlet ex Methven; sulphur yellow, orange spots ex Millais; exhibited Gowen 1832.
		Orodes				in cultivation T. Methven & Son, Edinburgh 1868-69; red or rosy scarlet.
		Ortega			g.	'Euryalus' x 'Sunrise'; (Aberconway 1941); pale rose.
		Ortrud			cl.	catawbiense x ; (T. J. R. Seidel 1929); lilac flushed, darker edges, red in bud.
		Osbornei				(R.B.G. Kew 1933).
		Osceola			cl.	catawbiense x ; (Parsons).
		Ostbo's Copper			cl.	'Fabia' x 'Mrs. W. C. Slocock'; (Ostbo); copper red.
		Ostbo's Low Yellow			cl.	(E. Ostbo-O. Ostbo, 1960); creamy yellow; P.A. (A.R.S.) 1960.
		Ostfriesland			cl.	'Madame de Bruin' x forrestii var. repens; (Dietrich Hobbie 1949); bright scarlet red.
		Othello				cultivated by Noble before 1850; dark purple crimson.
		Othello				'Arthur Osborn' x eriogynum; (Aberconway 1941); cardinal red. See 'The Moon'
		Othello			g.	'Carmen' x ('Armistice Day' x griersonianum); registered by Brandt 1954.
		Ottawa			g.	discolor x campylocarpum var. elatum; (Rothschild); orange pink buds turning to white.
		Otto Foster			g.	griffithianum x arboreum var. album; white.
		Ouida			g.	'Astarte' x griersonianum; (Aberconway).
		Ouida			cl.	'Astarte' x griersonianum; (Aberconway cross 1930); flushed pink rose, pale on lobes and darker towards base; A.M. (R.H.S.) 1936.
		Owen Thomas			cl.	(A. Waterer before 1915); crimson, spotted.
		Oxlip			g.	williamsianum x litiense; (Rothschild 1947); cream to pink.
		Pachym				'Muriel' x pachytrichum; exhibited Loder 1954.
		(Packet)				See 'Surprise Packet'.
		Pageant			g.	'Calrose' x Loderi g.; (Aberconway 1950); pale pink.
		Painted Star			cl.	'Meadowbrook' x 'Anita'; (Hardgrove); cream, red throat.
		Palla			g.	'Pallida' x griersonianum; (Aberconway 1942); neyron rose.
		Pallida			g.	williamsianum x griffithianum; (Aberconway 1933); white flushed pink.
		Pallidum			g.	hirsutum x virgatum?; exhibited 1913.
		Pamela				cultivated Standish & Noble before 1860; deep blush.
		Pamela Fielding			cl.	griffithianum x a red hybrid; (C. B. van Nes & Sons before 1922); scarlet, exterior pale carmine pink, interior fading to white blush.
		Pamela Neve				blush, margined pale cerise.
		Pan			g.	griersonianum x crassum?; (Stirling-Maxwell 1936).
		Pandora			g.	'Fabia' x eriogynum; (Aberconway 1941); orange red.
		Panoply			g.	'G. A. Sims' x eriogynum; (Clarke).
		Panoply			cl.	'G. A. Sims' x eriogynum; (Clarke); claret (H.C.C. 021) with darker spots on upper petals; A.M. (R.H.S.) 1942. See 'Red Chief'.
		Panther			cl.	'Corona' x wardii (Coronet g.) exhibited Collingwood Ingram 1952. Previously known as Coronet var. Panther.
		Pantherinum				in cultivation T. Methven & Son, Edinburgh 1868-69; rose, dark spots.
		Papilionaceum				(J. Waterer before 1871); white with orange spots.
		Paragon			g.	'Red Ensign' x Loderi g.; (Aberconway 1950); rose.
		Pardoloton / Pardolatum			cl.	in cultivation T. Methven & Son, Edinburgh 1868-69; rosy lilac, spotted.
		Parisienne			g.	valentinianum x burmanicum; (Rothschild 1947); cream to pale yellow.
		Parkside			cl.	souliei x 'Hawk' (Peregrine g.); (Crown Lands Windsor 1954). Previously known as Peregrine var. Parkside.
		Parsons' Gloriosum			cl.	catawbiense x ; (raised by A. Waterer, introduced S. Parsons about 1860); light pink.
o	H-1	Parsons' Grandiflorum			cl.	catawbiense x ; (raised by A. Waterer, introduced S. Parsons 1875); dark purplish rose.
		(Pastel)				See 'Vanessa Pastel'.

	Pastel Star		cl.	(catawbiense var. rubrum x discolor) x 'Azor'; exhibited Hardgrove; pink, red blotch.
	Patricia		cl.	selected form of campylogynum var. charpoeum; (raised and named by Caperci, 1959); Magnolia purple (H.C.C. 030 to 030/1).
	Paulette		g.	'Bellerophon' x kyawi; (Rothschild 1950); bright crimson.
	Pauline	* C	g.	(T. Lowinsky raiser; introduced Rothschild); flowers funnel-shaped, crimson (H.C.C. 821/3), black eye; A.M. (R.H.S.) 1933; A.M. (R.H.S. Wisley Trials) 1957.
	Paxtonii			cultivated Standish & Noble in 1850; rose with chocolate spots.
	Peace		cl.	caeruleum var. album x concatenans (Lemon Bill g.); (Aberconway 1946); white faintly flushed externally with palest rose; A.M. (R.H.S.) 1946. Previously known as Lemon Bill var. Peace.
	Peach		cl.	'Vanessa' x griersonianum (Radiance g.); (Trotter 1946). Previously known as Radiance var. Peach.
	Peachblow		cl.	named by Wright; plant from Barto.
	Peach Lady		cl.	(dichroanthum x neriiflorum) x discolor; exhibited Lancaster; peach pink, edged rose.
	(Pearl)			See 'Yvonne Pearl'.
	Pearl			griffithianum x 'Princess Royal'; white flowered; F.C.C. 1885.
	Pearson's Elizabeth		cl.	in cultivation T. Methven & Son, Edinburgh 1868-69; light blush, claret spots.
	Pêche Melba			exhibited J. D. Lake, Burghfield Common, 1941.
	Peggy	** A	cl.	(Waterer, Sons & Crisp Ltd.); phlox pink (H.C.C. 625/1); A.M. (R.H.S.) 1940.
	Pelopidas		cl.	catawbiense x ; (J. Waterer); light crimson.
	Penalverne		cl.	griersonianum x 'Earl of Athlone' (Radium g.); (Bolitho). Previously known as Radium var. Penalverne.
	Penelope		g.	griersonianum x 'Dragonfly'; (Waterer, Sons & Crisp 1935); exhibited Rothschild 1950; red, dark spots.
	Penelope		g.	(R. Gill & Son); rosy carmine.
	Penelope Vesuvius		cl.	(R. Gill & Son); bright red.
	Pengaer		cl.	thomsonii x griffithianum (Cornish Cross g.); (Llewelyn 1911); crimson red; A.M. (R.H.S.) 1911. Previously known as Cornish Cross var. Pengaer.
	Penhale		g.	fortunei x eriogynum; (Bolitho 1945).
xxx H-5	Penjerrick		g.	campylocarpum var. elatum x griffithianum; (S. Smith).
	Penjerrick	****C	cl.	campylocarpum var. elatum x griffithianum; (S. Smith); pale pink campanulate flowers or cream or white; A.M. (R.H.S.) 1923.
	Penllyn		g.	orbiculare x griffithianum; (Aberconway 1933); shell pink.
	Penny		cl.	'Sarita Loder' x 'Idealist'; (D. W. James).
	Penrose Atkinson		cl.	campylocarpum x ; (Slocock); almond pink shaded orange.
	Pentilly Scarlet			red.
	Pera		g.	pemakoense x racemosum; (Lem).
	Pera		g.	'Ethel' x 'Penjerrick'; (Aberconway 1946); rose.
	Percyanum			catawbiense x ; (Iveson); pink veined deeper pink, no spots; white ex Millais; Knightian Medal 1849.
	Perdita		cl.	souliei x 'Lady Bessborough' (Halcyone g.); (Rothschild); pink, lobes fading to white; A.M. (R.H.S.) 1948. Previously known as Halcyone var. Perdita.
	Peregrine		g.	souliei x 'Hawk'; (Crown Lands).
	Peregrine		cl.	souliei x 'Hawk'; exhibited Crown Lands 1951. See 'Parkside', 'Peregrine Fledgeling'.
	Peregrine Fledgeling		cl.	souliei x 'Hawk' (Peregrine g.); exhibited Crown Lands 1953. Formerly known as Peregrine var. Fledgeling.
	Perrieanum			cultivated Standish & Noble before 1870; light rose, spotted eye.
	Persephone		g.	forrestii var. repens x floccigerum; (Aberconway 1941); orange red.
	Perseus		g.	'Vanessa' x 'Jacquetta'; (Aberconway 1941); rosy salmon pink.
	Perseverance		cl.	'Lady Chamberlain' x cinnabarinum var. roylei; (Adams-Acton 1942); apricot, fading coral.
	Persimmon		cl.	dichroanthum x elliottii (Golden Horn g.); (Rothschild 1939); light orange red. Previously known as Golden Horn var. Persimmon.
	Perspicuum		cl.	(J. Waterer before 1851); in cultivation at T. Methven & Son, Edinburgh 1868; white.
x H-3	Peter Koster	B	cl.	'George Hardy' x 'Doncaster' hybrid; (M. Koster & Sons cross 1909); bright magenta red, edged a lighter shade A.M. 1946.
	Peter Koster		cl.	fortunei x ; named by Dexter?
	Petia		cl.	'Albatross' x 'Sarita Loder'; registered by R.H.S. Gardens, Wisley, 1954.
	Petraea			exhibited Lady Martineau 1934.
	Phantasy		g.	'Eudora' x 'Erebus'; (Aberconway 1942); red.
	Phico		g.	'Phidias' x 'Cowslip'; (Aberconway 1941); cream flushed pink.
	Phidias		g.	'Astarte' x 'F. C. Puddle'; (Aberconway).
	Phidias		cl.	'Astarte' x 'F. C. Puddle'; (Aberconway 1938); clear rich red; A.M. (R.H.S.) 1938.
	Philip Waterer	* B	cl.	'Mrs. E. C. Stirling' x maximum hybrid; (J. Waterer, Sons & Crisp Ltd.); rose pink, soft rose; A.M. (R.H.S.) 1924.
	Phillida		g.	'Forsterianum' x edgeworthii; exhibited Sir John Ramsden 1934.
	Philotis			in cultivation T. Methven & Son, Edinburgh 1868-69; crimson.
	Phisun		g.	'Phidias' x 'Sunrise'; (Aberconway 1946); rose.

	Phoebus			g.	'F. C. Puddle' x haematodes; (Aberconway 1941); scarlet blood red.
	Phoenix			g.	'Dawn's Delight' x 'Tally Ho'; (Rothschild 1950); red.
	Phryne			g.	campylocarpum x Loderi g.; (Aberconway 1933); cream.
	Phyllis Ballard			cl.	(neriiflorum x dichroanthum) x discolor; (Endre Ostbo); orange-red to coral-red. P.A. (A.R.S.) 1956.
	Piccaninny			cl.	'Brittania' x dichroanthum (Limerick g.); (Earl of Limerick); orange, tinged at margin of lobes with cherry (H.C.C. 722/1); A.M. (R.H.S.) 1956. Previously known as Limerick var. Piccaninny.
	Picotee	*	A	cl.	(A. Waterer); white, picotee-edged.
	Picotee Roseum / Picotee Rosea				(Veitch); bright rose, marked intense black blotch; F.C.C. 1863.
	Pictum			cl.	maximum ? x campanulatum; (J. Waterer before 1839); pinkish white spotted. Syn. 'Lowi', 'Coelestinum Pictum'.
	Picturatum				maximum hybrid x 'Altaclarense'; (A. Waterer); Standish & Noble 1850; bright rose, much spotted crimson; or blush white with chocolate blotch?
	Picturatum Superbum				exhibited Veitch & Son 1862; blush white spotted nearly all over.
	Pierette Forestier				See 'Madame Pierette Forestier'
	Pierre Laplace			g.	'Madame Fr. J. Chauvin' x williamsianum; (Dietrich Hobbie 1952); delicate rose.
	Pierre Moser		B	cl.	caucasicum x ; (Moser & Fils 1914); light pink, early.
	Pieter de Hoogh			cl.	red, magenta tinge.
	Pilgrim			g.	fortunei x 'Gill's Triumph'; (Johnston).
xxx H-3	Pilgrim	***	B	cl.	fortunei x 'Gill's Triumph'; (Johnston); rich pink with few dark markings; A.M. (R.H.S.) 1926.
	(Pimento)				See 'Jasper Pimento'.
	Pimpernel			g.	'Eros' x arboreum; (Aberconway 1950); deep red.
	Pinafore			cl.	campylocarpum var. elatum x Loderi g. (Barbara g.); exhibited E. Rothschild 1948. Previously known as Barbara var. Pinafore.
	Pince's Victoria			cl.	in cultivation T. Methven & Son, Edinburgh 1868-69; purplish crimson.
	Pindar			cl.	catawbiense x ; (T. J. R. Seidel); purplish violet.
	Pineapple				used as a parent by L. de Rothschild. See 'Geisha'.
x H-3	Pink Beauty			cl.	griffithianum hybrid x 'John Walter'; (C. B. van Nes & Sons before 1922); pink to pale rose pink.
	(Pink Beauty)				See 'Naomi Pink Beauty'.
	Pink Bride			cl.	'Halopeanum' x griffithianum; (Loder); pale blush pink; A.M. (R.H.S.) 1931.
	Pink Cameo			cl.	'Boule de Neige' x red catawbiense seedling; exhibited Shammarello 1955; shrimp pink.
	(Pink Dawn)				See 'Lady Rosebery Pink Dawn'.
	(Pink Delight)				See 'Lady Rosebery Pink Delight'.
	Pink Delight			g.	arboreum x ?; (R. Gill & Son); clear deep pink or white, edged deep rose pink; A.M. (R.H.S.) 1926.
	Pink Domino			cl.	discolor x hardy hybrid; (Waterer, Sons & Crisp Ltd.); carmine pink spotted yellow; A.M. (R.H.S.) 1925.
	Pink Drift				calostrotum x scintillans; (H. White of Sunningdale); growing in Sunningdale Nursery 1955; magenta pink.
	Pink Flourish			cl.	catawbiense var. album x ((decorum x griffithianum) x red catawbiense hybrid); (D. G. Leach 1960); bright strong pink, boldly blotched.
	Pink Fragrance			g.	'Miss Noreen Beamish' x discolor; (Thacker 1940); shell pink.
	Pink Glory			g.	'Glory of Penjerrick' x Loderi g. ; (Heneage-Vivian 1938).
	Pink Glory			cl.	irroratum x Loderi g. (White Glory g.) (Dowager Lady Loder); blush pink stained with rose madder (H.C.C. 23/3); A. M. (R.H.S. 1940).
	Pinkie			g.	griersonianum x 'Lady G. Broderick'; (Ramsden 1938).
	Pink Lady Rosebery			cl.	cinnabarinum var. roylei x 'Royal Flush' (Lady Rosebery g.); grown at Sunningdale Nursery 1955. Syn. 'Lady Rosebery Pink Beauty'.
	Pink Mermaid			cl.	'Azor' selfed; (Esch); pink, darker edge, deep pink throat; P.A. (A.R.S.) 1954.
xx H-3	Pink Pearl	***	B	cl.	'George Hardy' x 'Broughtonii'; (J. Waterer); in bud deep pink and when open a soft pink; A.M. 1897; F.C.C. (R.H.S.) 1900; A.G.M. (R.H.S.) 1952.
	Pink Pebble			cl.	callimorphum x williamsianum; registered Harrison 1954; clear pink.
x H-3	Pink Perfection	*	B	cl.	'Duchess of Edinburgh' x 'Princess Alexandra'; (L. van Houtte); pale pink with lilac pink tinge.
	Pink Perfection			cl.	fortunei x (?) (de Wilde) rose-pink.
	Pink Rosette			cl.	fortunei x 'Mrs. E. C. Stirling'; (Evans); pinkish white suffused with fuchsine pink (H.C.C. 627/3); A.M. (R.H.S.) 1956.
	(Pink Satin)				See 'Loderi Pink Satin'.
	Pink Shell			cl.	griffithianum x 'H. M. Arderne'; (Lowinsky); pale pink; A.M. (R.H.S.) 1923.
	Pinnacle			cl.	pink catawbiense seedling x pink catawbiense seedling; exhibited Shammarello 1955; pink.
	Pioneer			g.	arboreum x 'Arthur Osborn'; (Aberconway 1942); red.
	Pioneer			cl.	(racemosum x mucronulatum) 'Conemaugh' x ?; (Gable, 1952) rose-pink, dwarf, early.
	Pirate			g.	'B. de Bruin' x meddianum; (Rothschild 1940); deep red.
	Pixie			g.	forrestii var. repens x apodectum; (Aberconway 1941); orange red.

		Pizarro			cultivated Standish & Noble before 1870; satiny rose.
		P. J. Mezzitt		cl.	carolinianum x ?; (introduced Weston Nurseries, 1959); pink. Syn. P. J. M.
		Plaineye		cl.	augustinii x 'Blue Tit' (Blue Ribbon g.); (Harrison 1956); lavender blue, unspotted. Previously known as Blue Ribbon var. Plaineye.
		Pleasant		cl.	campylocarpum x thomsonii (Exminster g.); (Horlick 1955). Previously known as Exminster var. Pleasant.
		Pleiades		g.	dichroanthum x scyphocalyx; (Reuthe 1941); orange with red.
		Plüsch		cl.	'Mrs. Milner' x catawbiense; (T. J. R. Seidel 1913); red.
		Pluto			grown by Noble about 1850; deep rose red.
		Pocahontas		cl.	catawbiense x ; (Parsons).
xx	H-3	Polar Bear		g.	diaprepes x auriculatum; (J. B. Stevenson).
		Polar Bear	****C	cl.	diaprepes x auriculatum; (Stevenson cross 1926); pure white, fragrant, with a narrow green throat; late; F.C.C. (R.H.S.) 1946.
		Polar Star		cl.	smirnowii x 'Doncaster'; (M. Koster & Sons cross 1902); red.
		Polar Sun			'Polar Bear' x facetum; (Digby 1955); pink.
		Polka Dot		cl.	clone of R. irroratum; (Rothschild 1957); white, heavily marked with spots of paeony purple (H.C.C. 729/1) suffused with pink; A. M. (R.H.S.) 1957.
		Polly Peachum		cl.	salmon to rosy pink with dark red blotches. Syn. of 'Emily Mangles'.
		Polyandrum Pink		cl.	rose pink; A.M. (R.H.S.) 1938.
		Ponticum Roseum		cl.	pinkish lilac; a hybrid; not a true variety of ponticum. Syn. 'Maximum Roseum'.
		Poot			red.
		Porpora		g.	carolinianum x polylepis.
		Portent		cl.	mucronulatum x ciliatum; exhibited D. G. Leach 1955; white.
		Portia		g.	'Taylori' x teysmannii; exhibited Veitch 1891; shades of primrose yellow.
		Portia		g.	neriiflorum subsp. euchaites x strigillosum; (Aberconway).
		Portia		cl.	neriiflorum subsp. euchaites x strigillosum; (Aberconway 1935); dark crimson scarlet with dark nectaries at base, faintly spotted within; A.M. (R.H.S.) 1935; F.C.C. (R.H.S.) 1947.
		Poussin			cultivated Standish & Noble before 1850; deep rose or crimson.
		Powell Glass		cl.	a selected form of catawbiense var. album; (grown and named by E. Amateis, 1959); white.
		Pow Wow		cl.	'Earl of Athlone' x 'Fabia'; (R. Henny).
xx	H-3	Praecox	*** B	g.	ciliatum x dauricum; exhibited Davis 1860; purple or rosy purple or rosy lilac; Commended 1861; A.G.M. 1926.
		Prelude		g.	wardii x fortunei; (Rothschild).
		Prelude	** B	cl.	wardii x fortunei; (Rothschild cross 1942); primrose yellow (H.C.C. 601/3) darkens towards base; A.M. (R.H.S.) 1951.
o	H-1	President Lincoln		cl.	catawbiense x ; (S. Parsons before 1871); mauve, bronze blotch. Syn. 'Herbert Parsons', 'Bertha Parsons', 'Betsy Parsons'.
		President Roosevelt			Petunia violet, black blotch.
		President van Den Hecke		cl.	cultivated Standish & Noble before 1870 (in Belgium); crimson, finely spotted.
		Pretty Polly			pink.
		(Pride)			See 'Yvonne Pride'.
		Pride of Cambridge			white, brownish blotch.
xx	H-3	Pride of Leonardslee	*** C	cl.	fortunei x thomsonii (Luscombei g.); (Loder); pink. Previously known as Luscombei var. Pride of Leonardslee.
		Pride of Tremough			exhibited Montiford Longfield, Penryn, 1935.
		Primrose			'Maidens Blush' x teysmannii; greenhouse hybrid; F.C.C. 1888.
		(Primrose)			See 'Fine Feathers Primrose'.
		Primulinum Elegans			light primrose, with pearl spots.
		Primulinum Formosum			primrose yellow, orange spots.
		Prince Arthur			(Davies); cultivated Standish & Noble before 1860; plum color.
		Prince Camille de Rohan / Prince C. de Rohan			caucasicum x ; (J. Verschaffelt 1865); rosy pink, frilled edge and deep brown blotch in center of dorsal petal.
		Prince Consort			exhibited Todman 1861; bright rose-colored flowers; spotted, wavy margin.
		Prince Eugene		cl.	(Rinz before 1875); rosy blush, edged with pink.
		Prince Leopold		g.	dalhousiae x formosum; exhibited J. A. Henry 1862; white suffused rose.
		Prince Leopold		g.	brookeanum var. gracile x lobbii; (Davies); red orange; F.C.C. 1876.
		Prince of Wales	** B		(J. Waterer, Sons & Crisp Ltd. before 1875); rose pink with lighter center.
		Princeps		cl.	in cultivation T. Methven 1868-69; pinkish lilac.
		Princess Alexandra		g.	jasminiflorum x 'Princess Royal'; (Veitch); white, waxy, scented; F.C.C. 1865.
		Princess Alice		cl.	edgeworthii x ciliatum; white flushed pink outside; scented; F.C.C. 1862.
		Princess Amelia		cl.	in cultivation T. Methven & Son, Edinburgh 1868-69; dark scarlet.
		Princess Beatrice		g.	'Duchess of Edinburgh' x 'Princess Alexandra'; cream and pink; F.C.C. 1884.
		Princess Christian			javanicum x 'Princess Frederica'; (J. Waterer); ?yellow to yellow orange; ?white with large orange blotch and black spots; F.C.C. 1883.

xx	H-2	Princess Elizabeth	**	B	cl.	'Bagshot Ruby' x ; (Waterer, Sons & Crisp 1928); deep crimson; strong grower; A.M. 1933.
		Princess Ena				(before 1922); mauve.
		Princess Frederica			g.	brookeanum var. gracile x 'Princess Royal'; exhibited Veitch 1891; yellow.
		Princess Frederick William			cl.	in cultivation T. Methven & Son, Edinburgh 1868-69; blush, pink spots.
		Princess Helena			g.	ciliatum x edgeworthii; exhibited J. A. Henry 1862; white, tinged rose, scented.
		Princess Helena				jasminiflorum x ; pink; F.C.C. 1865.
		Princess Hortense				(Standish before 1867); in cultivation T. Methven & Son, Edinburgh 1868; lilac rose with brown and yellow eye.
		Princess Juliana			cl.	griffithianum x ; (M. Otto Schulz cross 1890, purchased by J. H. van Nes 1896); rosy pink fading to white; A.M. (R.H.S.) 1910.
		Princess Louise			cl.	lilac white, green spot.
		Princess Margaret of Connaught			cl.	(J. Waterer); rose pink, dark blotch.
		Princess Mary of Cambridge			cl.	(J. Waterer before 1871); blush with darker edge.
		Princess of Orange				campylocarpum x 'Prince Camille de Rohan'; (Veitch); yellowish pink.
		Princess of Wales				(J. Waterer); light shade of purple, paler center and spotted; S.C.C. 1864.
		Princess Royal			g.	jasminiflorum x javanicum; exhibited Henderson & Son 1863; pale pink with yellow shading on the interior.
		Princess William of Wurtemberg				white, spotted crimson; F.C.C. 1894.
		Prinses Marijke			cl.	(Felix & Dijkhuis 1948); deep pink, light pink inside, outside of petals rose madder (H.C.C. 23/1), inside Phlox pink (H.C.C. 625/1-625/2); A.M. (Boskoop) 1948.
		Prize			cl.	red catawbiense seedling x 'Boule de Neige'; exhibited Shammarello 1955; bright pink.
		Professor Dr. Dude				lilac white, yellow blotch.
x	H-2	Professor F. Bettex			cl.	'Doncaster' x 'Atrosanguineum'; (H. den Ouden & Son cross about 1912, introduced about 1925); red.
xx	H-3	Professor Hugo de Vries	**	B	cl.	'Pink Pearl' x 'Doncaster'; (L. J. Endtz & Co.); pink.
x	H-3	Professor J. H. Zaayer	*	B	cl.	'Pink Pearl' x red catawbiense hybrid; (L. J. Endtz & Co.); light red.
		Profusion				fortunei x ; (Paul); rosy pink; A.M. 1896.
		Progrès			cl.	caucasicum x ; lilac rose, purple blotch.
		Prometheus		A	cl.	'Michael Waterer' x 'Monitor'; (C. Noble); scarlet crimson.
		Proserpine				cultivated Standish & Noble before 1870; crimson, spotted.
		Proserpine			cl.	burmanicum x tephropeplum; (Adams-Acton 1942); crimson.
		Prostigiatum			cl.	prostratum x fastigiatum; (Magor 1924); deep purple or violet purple; A.M. (R.H.S.) 1924.
		Prostsal			g.	prostratum x saluenense; (Magor 1926); pink violet slightly spotted with red.
		Psyche			g.	fortunei 'Mrs. Butler' x williamsianum; (Hobbie 1950); pink.
		Puck			cl.	racemosum x spiciferum; (Wright).
		Puget Sound			cl.	'Loderi King George' x 'Van Nes Sensation'; (R. W. Clark); pink, ruffled.
		Pulchellum			g.	catawbiense x 'Altraclarense'; (Standish & Noble 1850); rosy pink, white throat.
		Pulcherrimum				arboreum x caucasicum; (J. Waterer, Sons & Crisp Ltd.); exhibited Waterer 1835; white.
		Purity			cl.	'Taylori' x teysmannii; (Veitch 1891?); pale yellow or primrose yellow shades; A.M. 1894; A.M. 1899.
		Purity			cl.	edgeworthii x formosum; (A. Waterer before 1871) white with yellow eye; F.C.C. 1888.
xx	H-3	Purple Emperor	***	A	cl.	'Moser's Maroon' x ?; (Knap Hill Nursery Ltd. 1953); near doge purple (H.C.C. 732/3), paler towards throat, upper petal speckled black at throat; A.M. (R.H.S.) 1953.
		Purple Eye			cl.	augustinii x 'Blue Tit' (Blue Ribbon g.) (Gen. Harrison 1955); mauve blue with purple spots. Previously known as Blue Ribbon var. Purple Eye.
		Purple Fake			cl.	a superior form of concinnum; (raised and selected by R. Henny, 1959); orchid purple (H.C.C. 31), spotted crimson.
		Purple Gem			cl.	fastigiatum x carolinianum; (Nearing); purplish violet.
		Purple Prince			cl.	in cultivation Sunningdale Nurseries 1956; purple, black blotch.
xxxx	H-2	Purple Splendour	****	A	cl.	ponticum x ; (A. Waterer, Knap Hill Nursery Ltd. before 1900); deep purple, blotched darker at base; A.M. (R.H.S.) 1931.
		Purpurea Magnifica				in cultivation T. Methven 1868-69; deep purple.
		Purpurea Splendens				in cultivation T. Methven 1868-69; purple.
		Purpureum Crispum			cl.	catawbiense x ; (Parsons).
o	H-1	Purpureum Elegans			cl.	catawbiense x ; (H. Waterer before 1850); deep purple.

o	H-1	Purpureum Grandiflorum		A	cl.	catawbiense x ; (H. Waterer before 1850); purple.
xx	H-2	Pygmalion	**	B	cl.	(Waterer, Sons & Crisp Ltd.); crimson scarlet, spotted black; A.M. (R.H.S.) 1933.
		Pyramus			g.	'Doncaster' x 'Loderi'; (Aberconway 1933).
		Pyrex			cl.	haematodes x facetum; (Reuthe 1945); scarlet.
		Pyrope			g.	'Exminster' x 'Cornish Cross'; (Aberconway cross 1932); red.
		Quadrille			g.	'Sulphur Yellow' x griffithianum; (Rothschild 1950); pale cream.
		Quadroona } Quadrona }			cl.	catawbiense x ; (J. Waterer before 1874); purplish red, bronze blotch.
		Quaker Girl			g.	hyperythrum x 'Avalanche'; (Rothschild 1950); white.
		Quapp			cl.	'Limbatum' x 'Diadem'; (T. J. R. Seidel cross 1914); purplish pink.
		Quaver			g.	leucaspis x sulfureum; (Rothschild 1950); cream or primrose yellow.
		Queen				amabile x teysmannii; exhibited Veitch 1891; very pale primrose.
		Queen Alexandra				niveum x grande (argenteum); cream tinged mauve.
		Queen Bee			cl.	dichroanthum x ?; (W. Corbin, 1959); burnt orange-red.
		Queen Mary		A	cl.	'Marion' x 'Mrs. C. S. Sargent'; (Felix & Dijkhuis 1950); pink (rose bengal H.C.C. 25/2, outside 25/1); F.C.C. (Boskoop) 1948.
		Queen of Hearts			g.	meddianum x 'Moser's Maroon'; (Rothschild).
		Queen of Hearts	**	C	cl.	meddianum x 'Moser's Maroon'; (Rothschild 1949); Chrysanthemum crimson (H.C.C. 824) spotted with black on the three upper lobes; A.M. (R.H.S.) 1949.
xx	H-3	Queen o' the May	***	C	g.	'Pink Bell' x griersonianum; (C. Smith); exhibited Hamilton; white.
		Queen of the Roses				javanicum x 'Princess Alexandra'; exhibited Veitch 1891; pinky yellow to salmon.
		Queen of the Yellows				javanicum x 'Princess Frederica'; yellow to yellow orange; F.C.C. 1886.
		Queen Pomare				cultivated Standish & Noble before 1860; chocolate with white throat.
		Queen Souriya	**	B	cl.	fortunei x campylocarpum hybrid; (W. C. Slocock 1937); dusky shades sulphur and pink; pale ochre and mauve edge; A.M. (Wisley Trials) 1957.
		Queen Victoria				'Altaclarense' x ; (Standish & Noble 1850); deep claret purple; F.C.C. 1882.
		Queen Victoria				brookeanum var. gracile x lobbi; exhibited Veitch 1891; yellow orange, primrose yellow to pale salmon.
xx	H-3	Queen Wilhelmina	**	C	cl.	griffithianum x ; (Otto Schulz cross 1890, introduced C. B. van Nes & Sons 1896); scarlet fading to rosy pink.
		Quendel			cl.	catawbiense x 'Mrs. Milner'; (T. J. R. Seidel 1914); purple.
		Querele			cl.	catawbiense x ; (T. J. R. Seidel 1929); dark violet, almost without markings.
		Querida			g.	'Red Knight' x elliottii; (Rothschild).
		Querida	**	D	cl.	'Red Knight' x elliottii; (Rothschild); bright red; A.M. (R.H.S.) 1952.
		Quinella			cl.	'Britannia' x 'May Day'; (R. Henny).
		Quiver			g.	ciliatum x lutescens; (Rothschild 1950); cream.
		Rachel				cultivated Standish & Noble before 1870; white, yellow spots.
xxx	H-3	Racil	***	B	cl.	racemosum x ciliatum; exhibited N. S. Holland 1937; shell pink.
		Radiance			g.	'Vanessa' x griersonianum; (Aberconway 1936); deep rose pink. See 'Peach'.
		Radiant Morn			g.	'Fabia' x 'Sunrise'; (Aberconway 1938).
		Radiant Morn			cl.	'Fabia' x 'Sunrise'; (Aberconway cross 1938); porcelain rose (H.C.C. 620) suffused Geranium pink (H.C.C. 20/1); A.M. (R.H.S.) 1951.
xx	H-3	Radium			g.	griersonianum x 'Earl of Athlone'; (Crosfield 1936); bright Geranium scarlet. See 'Penalverne'.
		Radmosum			cl.	radicans x racemosum; exhibited Thacker 1946; rosy mauve.
		Raeanum				'Altaclarense' x maximum hybrid; exhibited Standish & Noble 1850; rosy crimson, black spots.
		Raeburn			cl.	racemosum x tephropeplum; (Collingwood Ingram 1955); yellowish copper.
		Ragged Robin				griffithianum x ; (J. Waterer, Sons & Crisp Ltd.); crimson cerise passing to lighter shade.
xx	H-3	Rainbow	**	B	cl.	'A. W. Hardy' hybrid x griffithianum; (W. C. Slocock Ltd. approximately 1928); carmine-pink with darker edged lobes.
		Ralph Sanders			cl.	(A. Waterer before 1915); purplish crimson.
		Ramapo			cl.	fastigiatum x carolinianum; (Nearing); exhibited 1940; bright light violet.
		Ramillies			g.	'Ethel' x 'Redwing'; (Aberconway 1941); blood red.
x	H-4	Raoul Millais			cl.	griffithianum x ; (M. Koster & Sons before 1922); salmon pink, light center; A.M. (R.H.S.) 1935.
		Raphael			cl.	(T. J. R. Seidel); dark lilac red.
		Raphael			cl.	(J. Waterer); cultivated Standish & Noble before 1870, and T. Methven & Son, Edinburgh 1868; rosy crimson, chocolate marks nearly covering the flower.
		Rapture			g.	griersonianum x zeylanicum; (Aberconway 1950); porcelain rose.
		Rascal			cl.	'Apache' x neriiflorum subsp. euchaites; (Harrison cross 1947); deep red; registered 1957.
		Rateph			cl.	racemosum x tephropeplum; exhibited Ingram 1955.
		Ravigo			cl.	orchid pink, yellow eye.
		Ray			cl.	fortunei x 'Idealist'; (D. W. James); Dresden yellow (H.C.C. 64/3); P.A. (A.R.S.) 1956.

		Rebecca			cultivated Standish & Noble before 1860; blush finely spotted with yellow and brown.
		Rechter		cl.	'America' x forrestii var. repens; (Dietrich Hobbie 1947); deep scarlet red.
		Red Admiral		g.	arboreum x thomsonii; (J. C. Williams); scarlet.
		Red Argenteum		g.	grande x arboreum; exhibited in 1926.
		Red Brocade		g.	'F. C. Puddle' x arboreum; (Aberconway 1943); deep red.
x	H-4	Red Cap	*** C	g.	didymum x eriogynum; (J. B. Stevenson 1935); blood red or deep plum red. See 'Borde Hill Redcap', 'Exbury Red Cap', 'Townhill Redcap'.
		Red Cat		cl.	catawbiense hybrid seedling; (Gable); red.
		Red Chief		cl.	'G. A. Sims' x eriogynum (Panoply g.); (Sir Giles Loder 1948); red. Previously known as Panoply var. Red Chief.
		Red Cloud		cl.	'Tally Ho' x 'Corona'; (R. Henny 1953); outer lobes claret rose (H.C.C. 021) inner part of tube overlaid scarlet (H.C.C. 19/1); P.A. (A.R.S.) 1953.
		Red Crown		g.	Loderi g. x thomsonii; exhibited Haworth-Booth 1948.
		Red Dragon			griersonianum x thomsonii (Hecla g.); (Aberconway 1943). Previously known as Hecla var. Red Dragon.
		Red Eagle		cl.	(Rogers); deep scarlet.
		Red Emperor			'Godesburg' x 'Meteor'; (C. B. van Nes & Son); red.
		Red Ensign		g.	'Cardinal' x griersonianum; (Aberconway 1942); rose red.
		Red Fox		g.	'Tally Ho' x 'Britannia'; (Digby 1947).
		Red Glow		cl.	'Halopeanum' x thomsonii (Gem g.); (Loder 1949); bright red. Previously known as Gem var. Red Glow.
		Red Goblin			similar to 'Goblin' but of a brilliant orange scarlet.
		Red Hackle		g.	'Chanticleer' x 'Redwing'; (Aberconway 1946); deep red.
		Redhot		cl.	'Britannia' x 'Elizabeth'; (R. Henny, 1958); Orient red (H.C.C. 819/3) shaded mandarin red (H.C.C. 17/1) in throat; low growing.
		Red Imp		cl.	haematodes x ; (R. & G. Bovee 1960); moderate red (Nickerson 2.57 4/10) outside, lighter inside; dwarf.
		Red Lamp		g.	'The Don' x facetum; (Crosfield 1936).
		Red Queen		g.	'Gill's Crimson' x 'Barclayi'; (Aberconway 1943); deep red.
xx	H-3	Red Riding Hood	** B	cl.	'Atrosanguineum' x griffithianum; (W.C.Slocock Ltd.); named 1933; bright red.
		Red Rover		g.	'J. G. Millais' x thomsonii; (Whitaker 1939); deep crimson red.
		Redskin		g.	'Dante' x 'Eudora'; (Aberconway 1950); scarlet.
		Redskin Chief		cl.	'Lady Bessborough' x 'May Day'; (Sunningdale Nurseries 1955); red.
		Red Snapper		cl.	'Azor' x griersonianum; (R. Henny).
		Red Star		g.	'Ascot Brilliant' x thomsonii; (Loder); crimson, upper petal spotted black. See 'Leonardslee Flame'.
		Red Star			'Mrs. Lindsay Smith' x 'Molière'; (M. Koster & Sons); bright scarlet.
		Redstart		g.	~~aperantum~~ x neriiflorum subsp. euchaites; (Headfort 1938).
		Red Tape		cl.	'Earl of Athlone' x 'Fabia'; (R. Henny).
		Redwax		cl.	haematodes x 'May Day'; (R. Henny). Orient red (H.C.C. 819/1); P.A. (A.R.S.) 1958.
		Redwing		g.	'Shilsonii' x 'Barclayi'; (Aberconway).
		Redwing		cl.	'Shilsonii' x 'Barclayi'; (Aberconway 1937); pale rose with darker stripe down center of each lobe; carmine lake; F.C.C. (R.H.S.) 1937.
		Reedianum		cl.	(H. Waterer before 1851); cultivated Standish & Noble before 1870; rose pink.
		Regalia			(T. Methven & Son, Edinburgh); crimson.
		Regificum			(J. Waterer before 1851); cultivated T. Methven & Son, Edinburgh 1868-69; red or rosy scarlet.
		Reginald Farrer		cl.	scyphocalyx x discolor; (Thacker 1942); apricot orange.
		Reginum			cultivated Standish & Noble before 1870; deep blush.
		Regulator			cultivated Noble before 1850; purple with red spots.
		Reine Amelie			(Byls before 1858); in cultivation T. Methven & Son, Edinburgh 1868-69; dark crimson.
		Remarkable			cultivated Standish & Noble before 1860; lilac, rich puce spots, very dark eye.
		Rembrandt		cl.	in cultivation in Nursery of T. Methven & Son, Edinburgh 1868; purple.
		Rembrandt		g.	'Dante' x 'Sunrise'; (Aberconway 1950); scarlet.
		Remo		g.	valentinianum x lutescens; (Stevenson 1943); deep yellow.
		Remus		g.	forrestii var. repens x beanianum; (Aberconway 1946); carmine.
		Renaissance			'Peter Koster' x 'Loderi King George'; (James E. Barto, Junction City, Oregon); named by Mrs. Horace Fogg; light red.
		Renata		cl.	'Annedore' x 'Mrs. Milner'; (T. J. R. Seidel 1915); dark purple.
		Rendall's Scarlet		g.	arboreum x ponticum; red; exhibited Aberconway 1946.
		Renhaven		cl.	'Umpqua Chief' x elliottii; (James); dark red; P.A. (A.R.S.) 1955.
		Renidescens		cl.	in cultivation T. Methven & Son, Edinburgh 1868-69; rosy crimson.
		Reparm		g.	forrestii var. repens x parmulatum; (Aberconway 1946); pale rose.
		Repose		g.	lacteum x discolor; (Rothschild).
		Repose	C	cl.	lacteum x discolor; (Rothschild 1950); creamy yellow; A.M. (R.H.S.) 1956.
		Resplendent			in cultivation T. Methven & Son, Edinburgh 1868-69; light pink, red spots.
		Retreat		g.	eriogynum x T. L. 3630 (Tom Lowinsky hybrid); (Rothschild cross 1936); red, tinged pink.
		Rev. R. W. Carew Hunt		cl.	griffithianum x ; (Otto Schelz cross 1890, introduced C. B. van Nes & Sons 1896); red.
		Reverie		g.	auriculatum x 'St. Keverne'; (Rothschild 1950); white, flushed pink.
		Rêve Rose		cl.	forrestii var. repens (pink form) x 'Bow Bells'; (Lester E. Brandt cross 1951) neyron rose (H.C.C. 623).

		Name	Rating		Type	Description
		Review Order			cl.	neriiflorum subsp. euchaites x 'May Day'; (Stair 1954); blood red (H.C.C. 820/2) faint brown spotting; A.M. (R.H.S.) 1954.
		Revlon			cl.	cinnabarinum var. roylei x 'Lady Chamberlain'; (Rothschild); flowers carmine (H.C.C. 21/1); A.M. (R.H.S.) 1957.
		Rhapsody			g.	'Dorinthia' x Loderi g. ; (Aberconway 1950); rose.
		Rhodoleucops			cl.	in cultivation T. Methven & Son, Edinburgh 1868-69; bright rosy crimson.
		Rhythm			g.	aperantum x forrestii var. repens; (Aberconway 1946); deep red to pale rose.
		Richard Gill				fortunei x thomsonii; (R. Gill & Son); deep rose; A.M. (R.H.S.) 1920.
		Richard Strauss			cl.	Cherry red.
		Rickshaw	*	C	g.	'Golden Horn' x 'Lady Bessborough'; (Rothschild 1950); biscuit colored with a suffusion of orange which deepens towards the throat.
		Rienzi				cultivated Standish & Noble before 1870; crimson, finely spotted.
		Rifleman			cl.	exhibited Street; crimson.
		Right Royal			cl.	'Luscombei' x thomsonii; (Horlick).
		Rima			g.	wardii x decorum; (Stevenson 1941); cream yellow.
		Rinaldo			cl.	'Mrs. Milner' x smirnowii; (T. J. R. Seidel 1915).
		Riviera Beauty				arboreum form; (R. Gill & Son); carmine pink.
		Robert Burns				cultivated Standish & Noble before 1870; crimson, white stamens, dark spots.
		Robert Croux				(Croux & Fils 1899); dark red.
		Roberte			cl.	discolor x campylocarpum var. elatum (Lady Bessborough g.); (Rothschild); rose pink speckled red within; pink in the corolla; F.C.C. 1936. Previously known as Lady Bessborough var. Roberte.
		Robert Fortune			g.	griffithianum x 'H. M. Arderne'; palest pink with crimson markings at base; A.M (R.H.S.) 1922.
		(Robert Fox)				See 'Barclayi Robert Fox'.
		Robert Keir			cl.	lacteum x 'Luscombei'; (Stevenson 1951); pale yellow, flushed with pale pink in throat and with dark pink on outside; A.M. (R.H.S.) 1957.
		Robert W. Wallace			cl.	griffithianum x ; (M. Koster & Sons 1915); rose pink.
		Robin Hood			g.	calophytum x sutchuenense; (J. C. Williams 1933).
		Robin Redbreast			g.	houlstonii x orbiculare; (Williams 1933).
		Robustum			cl.	in cultivation T. Methven & Son, Edinburgh 1868-69; lilac or sky color, dark spots.
		Robustum Catawbiense			cl.	in cultivation T. Methven & Son, Edinburgh 1868-69; light purple,spotted.
		Robustum Hybridum			cl.	in cultivation T. Methven & Son, Edinburgh 1868-69; white, spotted.
		Roc			g.	barbatum x fulgens; (Stevenson 1950); red.
		Rocket			cl.	red catawbiense seedling x 'Cunningham's White'; (Shammarello); exhibited 1955; bright red.
		Rocket			cl.	meddianum x strigillosum; (Stevenson 1954); clear shade of blood red (H.C.C. 820/2) spotted faintly brown; A.M. (R.H.S.) 1954.
		Rodeo			cl.	'Mrs. L. A. Dunnett' x griersonianum; (M. Koster & Sons); red with orange flush.
		Rokeby				cultivated Standish & Noble before 1860; rose with green spots.
		Romala			cl.	'Glory of Penjerrick' x thomsonii (Barclayi g.); (Barclay Fox); crimson. Previously known as Barclayi var. Romala.
		Romance			g.	elliottii x 'Jacquetta'; (Aberconway 1950); salmon.
xx	H-4	Roman Pottery			cl.	dichroanthum x griersonianum (Fabia g.); (exhibited J. J. Crosfield 1934); pale orange with coppery lobes. Previously known as Fabia var. Roman Pottery.
xx	H-3	Romany Chai			g.	'Moser's Maroon' x griersonianum; (Rothschild).
		Romany Chai	**	B	cl.	'Moser's Maroon' x griersonianum; (Rothschild); rich glowing reddish terra-cotta, brown spots; A.M. (R.H.S.) 1932. See 'Empire Day'.
xxx	H-3	Romany Chal			g.	'Moser's Maroon' x eriogynum; (Rothschild). See 'Farall'.
		Romany Chal	***	C	cl.	'Moser's Maroon' x eriogynum; (Rothschild); scarlet maroon with darker spots; A.M. (R.H.S.) 1932; F.C.C. (R.H.S.) 1937.
		Romarez			cl.	kyawi x griersonianum; (Stevenson 1953); Geranium lake (H.C.C. 620); A.M. (R.H.S.) 1953.
		Romari			cl.	'Coer' x meddianum; (Stevenson cross 1939); red.
		Romulus				cultivated by Noble before 1850; rosy purple.
		Rona			g.	'Cornubia' x barbatum; (Aberconway 1946); deep red.
		Ronald			cl.	hodgsonii x sinogrande; (A. C and J. F. A. Gibson, 1958); whitish, flushed pale rose-purple, darker outside; A.M. (R.H.S.) 1958.
		Ronda				(Collingwood Ingram 1944).
		Ronsdorfer Frühblühende			g.	oreodoxa x red hybrid; (G. Arends); rose to purple.
		Rosabel			cl.	'Pink Shell' x griersonianum; (A. Waterer 1865); pale pink with darker pink veining, upper lobe sparsely speckled red; A.M. (R.H.S.) 1936.
		Rosabelle				bright carmine rose-colored flowers with black spots on upper segment; commended 1860.
		Rosa Bonheur			g.	Loderi g. x 'Cornish Cross'; (Loder); deep pink.
		Rosa Bonheur Luna			cl.	Loderi g. x 'Cornish Cross' (Rosa Bonheur g.); (Sir E. Loder); "extinct" ex Sir Giles Loder. Previously known as Rosa Bonheur var. Luna.
		Rosalie				deep crimson purple; S.C.C. 1865.
		Rosalind			g.	fargesii x thomsonii; (Aberconway).

		Rosalind			cl.	fargesii x thomsonii; (Aberconway 1938); rose pink; A.M. (R.H.S.) 1938.
		Rosalind of Arden			cl.	neriiflorum subsp. phoenicodum x williamsianum; (Thacker 1946); deep rose red.
		Rosamond			g.	'Cornubia' x Loderi g. ; (Loder 1934); clear pink.
x	H-3	Rosamundii		A		caucasicum x ; (Standish & Noble); pale rose.
x	H-3	Rosamund Millais	*	B	cl.	'George Hardy' x 'Doncaster'; (M. Koster & Sons before 1922); cerise, blotched purple; A.M. 1933.
		(Rose)				See 'Gladys Rose'.
		Rose				javanicum x 'Princess Alexandra'; exhibited Veitch 1891; pinky yellow to salmon.
		Roseann			cl.	'Loderi Venus' x 'Britannia'; (R. Henny); fuchsine pink (H.C.C. 627/1) spotted crimson upper lobe; P.A. (A.R.S.) 1956.
		Rose Beauty				thomsonii x ; (R. Gill & Son); rosy pink, few markings on upper segment.
		Rose du Barri			g.	decorum x 'Standishii'; (Loder); rose.
		Rose Elf			cl.	racemosum x pemakoense; (Lancaster); white, flushed violet pink; P.A. (A.R.S.) 1954.
		Rosefinch			g.	'Bella' x griersonianum; (Aberconway).
		Rosefinch			cl.	'Bella' x griersonianium; (Aberconway 1939); deep rose with bluish tinge; calyx red; A.M. (R.H.S.) 1939.
		Rose Mangles				cinnabarinum x maddenii; (Mangles); rose pink.
		Rosemary Chipp			cl.	orbiculare x Loderi g. ; (R. B. G. Kew); pale rose pink, A.M. (R.H.S.) 1928.
		Rosemary Seys			g.	'Aries' x 'Moser's Maroon'; (Rothschild); bright crimson.
		Rosenkavalier			cl.	eriogynum x 'Tally Ho'; (R. H. S. Gardens, Wisley, 1959); scarlet (H.C.C. 19/1), sparsely red spotted on upper lobe; A.M. (R.H.S.) 1959.
		Rose Newcomb				griffithianum x ; (Mangles); white, pink edge.
		Rose of China			cl.	'Tally Ho' x discolor; (B. F. Lancaster).
		Rose Perfection	**	B		(R. Gill & Son); deep red in bud, opening clear pink.
		Rose Perfection				javanicum x 'Princess Alexandra'; rose pink; F.C.C. 1886.
		Rose Queen				rose pink tinged orange at base of tube; A.M. (R.H.S.) 1904.
		Rose Splendour			cl.	griersonianum x 'Purple Splendour'; B. F. Lancaster.
		Rosetta				cultivated Standish & Noble before 1870; bright rose, fine yellow eye.
		Roseum Argentinum				cultivated Standish & Noble before 1870; rose.
x	H-1	Roseum Elegans			cl.	catawbiense x ; (A. Waterer before 1851); rose lilac; about six clones of varying flower color in commerce under this name.
		Roseum Pictum				catawbiense x ; (H. Waterer before 1851); cultivated Standish & Noble before 1870; rose, yellow spots.
		Roseum Pink			cl.	'Roseum Elegans' x; pink.
o	H-2	Roseum Superbum			cl.	catawbiense x ; (A. Waterer before 1865); purplish rose.
xx	H-3	Rosy Bell	**	B	cl.	ciliatum x glaucophyllum; (Davies 1894); old rose or soft pink; A.M. (R.H.S.) 1894.
		Rosy Dawn			g.	thomsonii x fortunei hybrid; (Crosfield 1939).
		Rosy Fido			cl.	griersonianum x Loderi g. ; (Horlick 1930); rose.
xxx	H-3	Rosy Morn	**	C	cl.	souliei x Loderi g. ; (Rothschild); pink lightly spotted darker color; A.M. (R.H.S.) 1931.
		Rosy Queen			cl.	'Dr. Stocker' x thomsonii (Asteroid g.) exhibited Sunningdale Nurseries 1934. Previously known as Asteroid var. Rosy Queen.
		Rotundarb			g.	orbiculare x arboreum blood red; (Magor 1919); brilliant carmine, darker at base. Syn. 'Orbicarb'?
		Rouge			g.	T. L. 1249 x elliottii; (Rothschild).
		Rouge	**	C	cl.	T. L. 1249 x elliottii; (Rothschild); reddish carmine, spotted light brown in the throat; A.M. (R.H.S.) 1950.
		Rovellianum			g.	dauricum x ferrugineum; (Rovelli 1926).
		Rover			g.	'Oreoroyle' x 'Royal Flush'; (Aberconway 1946); rose pink.
		Royal Beauty			cl.	'Lady Rosebery' x cinnabarinum var. roylei; (Digby 1953); various shades of red. See 'Cerne'.
		Royal Blood			cl.	elliottii x 'Rubens'; (R.H.S. Gardens, Wisley); cardinal red (H.C.C. 822/1) with very dark blood red spotting; A.M. (R.H.S.) 1954.
		Royal Blush			cl.	'Lady Rosebery' x cinnabarinum var. blandfordiiflorum; (Adams-Acton 1935); crimson and gold.
xxx	H 4	Royal Flush	***	D	g.	cinnabarinum x maddenii; (Williams); pink and orange.
		Royal Mail			cl.	'Romany Chai' x 'Tally Ho'; (W. C. Slocock Ltd. 1946); bright scarlet.
		Royal Purple	*	A		(White); purple, yellowish blotch.
		Royalty			g.	'Yunncinn' x 'Royal Flush'; (Aberconway 1944); rose pink.
		Roylmadd				maddenii x roylei var. magnificum; (Magor cross 1920); carmine lake.
		Royyun				exhibited Hon. Mrs. Sebag-Montefiore 1935.
		(Roza)				See 'Tessa Roza'.
		Rozamarie			g.	wardii x 'Penjerrick'; (Stevenson 1951); yellow.
		Rozie			g.	'Romala' x discolor; (Stevenson cross about 1919); deep rose pink.
		R. S. Field			cl.	(A. Waterer before 1871); red or scarlet.
xx	H-2	Rubens	**	B	cl.	(A. Waterer before 1865); rich deep red.
		Rubescens				red.
xx	H-5	Rubina	**	B	g.	didymum x 'Tally Ho'; (Crosfield 1938); dark maroon red.

	Ruby		cl.	red catawbiense seedling x red catawbiense seedling; (Shammarello); exhibited 1955; Cherry red.
	Ruby			jasminiflorum var. carminatum x multicolor var. curtissii; F.C.C. 1888.
	(Ruby)			See 'Euphrosyne Ruby'.
	Ruby Bowman		cl.	fortunei x 'Lady Bligh'; (Druecker 1953); tyrian rose, blood red base.
	Ruby Gem		g.	'Charm' x haematodes; (Aberconway 1943); red.
	Ruddigore		g.	griersonianum x delavayi; (Aberconway 1948); scarlet.
	Ruddy	B		deep red.
	Rufus		g.	forrestii var. repens x sanguineum; (Aberconway 1941); red.
	Rundle's Scarlet			arboreum x.
	Russautinii		g.	russatum x augustinii; (Ramsden 1937); lavender blue.
	Russellianum			catawbiense x arboreum; (Russell 1831); pale to rosy crimson or red.
	Russellianum Album		cl.	catawbiense ? x arboreum var. album; white.
	Russellianum Superbum		cl.	arboreum hybrid; in cultivation T. Methven 1868-69; red or scarlet.
	Russellianum Tigrinum		cl.	arboreum hybrid; in cultivation T. Methven 1868-69; red, spotted.
	Rustic Maid		g.	russatum x 'Blue Diamond'; (Ingram 1945).
	Ruth		g.	'Ethel' x 'Barclayi' (Aberconway 1946); blood red.
	Ruth			cultivated Standish & Noble before 1860; bluish white, finely spotted.
	Ruthelma		g.	'Loderi Pink Diamond' x 'Cornish Cross'; (Loder); reddish pink. See 'Coralia', 'H. Whitner'.
	R. W. Rye		cl.	chrysodoron x johnstoneanum; (Stair 1951); primrose yellow (H.C.C. 601/1) gradually darkening to the throat; A.M. (R. H.S.) 1951.
	Sabrina			cultivated by Standish & Noble before 1870; rosy lilac.
	Saffron Queen		cl.	xanthostephanum x burmanicum; (C. Williams 1948); sulphur yellow with darker spotting on the upper petals; A.M. (R.H.S.) 1948.
	St. Anthony			(P. D. Williams 1935).
	St. George	*** C	g.	griffithianum hybrid x 'H. M. Arderne'; (Waterer, Sons & Crisp Ltd. 1932); in bud pale crimson (H.C.C. 22/1) fading to pale crimson (H.C.C. 22/3) distinctly veined pale crimson (H.C.C. 22/2); A.M. (R.H.S.) 1946.
	St. Keverne		cl.	zeylanicum x griffithianum; (P. D. Williams); bright red, few dark brown dots; A.M. (R.H.S.) 1922.
	St. Probus			intense crimson.
	St. Simon		cl.	(A. Waterer); rosy carmine or purplish crimson, spotted.
	St. Tudy		cl.	(Maj. -Gen. E.G.W.W. Harrison 1960); Lobelia blue (H.C.C. 41/2); A.M. (R.H.S.) 1960.
	Salm		g.	'Duke of York' x venator; (Dietrich Hobbie 1954); bright red.
	Salmon Giant			(R. Gill & Son); clear salmon pink.
	Salmon Perfection			(R. Gill & Son); deep salmon.
	Salmon Trout		cl.	cinnabarinum var. roylei x 'Royal Flush' orange form (Lady Chamberlain g.); (Rothschild); salmon-orange. Previously known as Lady Chamberlain var. Salmon Trout.
	(Salome)			See 'Tortoiseshell Salome'.
	Salome		g.	'Queen Wilhelmina' x griffithianum; (Aberconway 1950); rose red.
	Salus		g.	'Arthur Osborn' x 'Coreta'; (Aberconway 1941); deep red.
	Salutation		g.	griffithianum x lacteum; exhibited E. Rothschild 1953.
	Salvini		cl.	(Young before 1883); magenta rose.
	Samuel B. Parsons		cl.	catawbiense x ; (Parsons).
	Samuel Morley		cl.	(J. Waterer); rosy carmine with light center.
	Sandlefordianum			(J. Waterer about 1860); in cultivation T. Methven & Son, Edinburgh 1868-69; rose, well marked.
	Sangreal		g.	sanguineum x griersonianum; (Headfort 1937).
xxx H-3	Sapphire	*** A	cl.	'Blue Tit' x impeditum; (Knap Hill Nursery Ltd.); light blue.
xx H-2	Sappho	** A	cl.	(A. Waterer before 1867); white heavily spotted maroon.
	Saracen	* B		(A. Waterer); named about 1950; deep red, black blotch.
	Sardis		g.	discolor x 'C.S.Sargent'; (R.B.G. Kew).
xx H-4	Sarita Loder		g.	griersonianum x Loderi g. ; (G. H. Loder).
	Sarita Loder		cl.	griersonianum x Loderi g. ; (Loder 1934); deep crimson in bud, opens deep rose; A.M. (R.H.S.) 1934. See 'Dencombe'.
	Sarled		g.	sargentianum x trichostomum var. ledoides; (Ingram 1942); pink in bud, opening creamy white.
	Satallita / Satellite			in cultivation with T. Methven & Son, Edinburgh 1868-69; crimson.
	Satanella			(Noble before 1867); rosy red.
	Satan's Breath		g.	tephropeplum x sulfureum; (Ingram 1941).
	Satin		cl.	red catawbiense seedling x 'Boule de Neige'; (Shammarello); shrimp pink.
	Satire		g.	'Radiance' x 'Coreta'; (Aberconway 1950); bright red.
	Saturn		cl.	cerise, shading to pink, white center.
	Satyr		g.	'Choremia' x strigillosum; (Aberconway 1941); red.
	Saxa		g.	'Azor' x griersonianum; (Aberconway 1946); pale salmon rose.
	S. B. Parsons		cl.	catawbiense x ; (Parsons).

xx H-3	Scandinavia	*** B	cl.	'Betty Wormald' x 'Hugh Koster'; (M. Koster & Sons); cardinal red (H.C.C. 822) on a rose red (H.C.C. 724) base with black blotch; A.M. (R.H.S.) 1950.
	Scarlet Crown			'Duchess of Edinburgh' x javanicum; scarlet crimson; F.C.C. 1883.
	Scarlet King		g.	'Ilam Alarm' x griersonianum; (Stead 1950). See 'Orchard'.
	Scarlet Lady		cl.	'Luscombei' x haematodes; (Stirling Maxwell 1936).
	Scarlet O'Hara		g.	thomsonii x 'Langley Park'; (Horlick cross 1932); waxy light red.
	Scharnhorst		cl.	catawbiense x ; (T. J. R. Seidel); crimson.
	Schiller		cl.	'Doncaster' x 'Mrs. George Hardy'; (M. Koster & Sons cross 1909); light rose, fringed.
	Schubert		cl.	griffithianum x ; (M. Koster & Sons); pale Cattleya lilac, fringed.
	Scintillation		cl.	Dexter fortunei ? hybrid; (Dexter-Westbury Rose Co., 1957); pink.
	Scipio		cl.	catawbiense x ; (A. Waterer before 1871); purplish red.
	Scymaleum		g.	scyphocalyx x haemaleum; (Ingram).
	Seagull			(R. Gill & Son); pale lavender to almost blue.
	Seagull		g.	Loderi g. x sutchuenense; (Loder).
	Seagull		cl.	Loderi g. x sutchuenense; (Lady Loder 1938); pure white, speckled crimson within; A.M. (R.H.S.) 1938. See 'Seamew', 'Sea Mist'.
	Sealing Wax		cl.	dichroanthum x 'May Day'; (Sunningdale Nurseries 1955); vermilion.
	Seamew		cl.	Loderi g. x sutchuenense (Seagull g.); (Loder); pure white or pale pink; A.M. (R.H.S.) 1940. Previously known as Seagull var. Seamew.
	Sea Mist		cl.	Loderi g. x sutchuenense (Seagull g.); (Loder); dark pink. Previously known as Seagull var. Sea Mist.
	Sea Nymph		g.	chaetomallum x dichroanthum; (Ingram 1959).
	Sea-shell		cl.	campylocarpum x ; (W. C. Slocock Ltd.); creamy yellow, chocolate blotch.
	Seattle Gold		cl.	'Diva' x 'Lady Bessborough'; (Lem-McClure); light yellow.
	Seattle Queen		cl.	(lacteum x 'Lodauric') x campylocarpum; (Lem-McClure); ivory.
	Seattle Springtime		cl.	leucaspis x mucronulatum; (Mulligan 1954); amaranth rose (H.C.C. 530/3).
	Sefton		cl.	catawbiense x ; (A. Waterer 1881); low spreading habit; dark maroon.
	Selehurst Freak			exhibited Dame Alice Godman 1941.
	Selig		cl.	cinnabarinum var. blandfordiiflorum x calophyllum (Lady Loder 1937); pink shading to salmon pink and orange on tube; F.C.C. (R.H.S.) 1937.
	Senator Charles Sumner		cl.	catawbiense x ; (Parsons).
	Senorita		cl.	'Loderi King George' x 'Ostbo's 43 # 2'; (R. & G. Bovee 1960); reddish purple (Nickerson 2.5 RP 4/10), throat yellowish pink (7.5 R 9/3), upper lobe blotch yellowish brown.
	Sentinel		g.	'Eupheno' x 'Barclayi'; (Aberconway 1950); blood red.
	Serena		cl.	'Jalisco' x 'Vanessa'; (R.H.S. Wisley); bright carmine rose (H.C.C. 621/2), Cherry (H.C.C. 722) at base of corolla, on outside a pale shade of pink suffused with Cherry (H.C.C. 722/3); A.M. (R.H.S.) 1956.
	Serin		cl.	campylocarpum x 'Loder's White' (Albino g.); (Ingram). Previously known as Albino var. Serin.
	Sesterianum			edgeworthii x formosum?; edgeworthii x 'Gibsonii?; (Rinz before 1862); creamy white; F.C.C. 1862.
	Seta		g.	spinuliferum x moupinense; (Aberconway).
	Seta	** B	cl.	spinuliferum x moupinense; (Aberconway 1933); white suffused solferino purple (H.C.C. 26/3); A.M. (R.H.S.) 1933; F.C.C. 1960.
	(Seville)			See 'Lady Chamberlain Seville'.
	Shakespeare			'Mrs. E. C. Stirling' x 'Essex Scarlet'; (M. Koster & Sons cross 1916); bright rose pink.
	Sharon		cl.	souliei x 'Loderi King George'; (James); white, crimson blotch; P.A. (A.R.S.) 1955.
	Sheffield Park		cl.	griffithianum hybrid; (C. B. van Nes & Sons); pink, scarlet crimson edges and crimson red exterior.
	Sheffield Park Angelo	** C	cl.	griffithianum x discolor (Angelo g.); (Rothschild); pure white with faint greenish yellow blotch deep in tube base; A.M. (R.H.S.) 1950. Previously known as Angelo var. Sheffield Park.
	Sheila Moore		g.	elliottii x decorum; (Digby).
	Sheila Moore		cl.	elliottii x decorum; (Digby 1948); rose pink with darker spotting on upper lobes; A.M. (R.H.S.) 1948. See 'Cerisette'.
	Sheila Osborn		cl.	discolor x 'Strategist'; (R.B.G. Kew 1928); rose pink; A.M. (R.H.S.) 1928.
	Shellaby		cl.	elliottii x fortunei (Nanceglos g.); (R.H.S. Gardens, Wisley 1954). Previously known as Nanceglos var. Shellaby.
	Shepherdii			arboreum x ; scarlet.
	Shepherd's Delight		g.	Loderi g. x 'Luscombei'; (Heneage-Vivian 1927).
	Shepherd's Morning		cl.	'Norman Gill' x 'Naomi'; (R.H.S. Gardens, Wisley); P.C. 1956.
	Sherwoodeanum			catawbiense x arboreum var. album; (J. Waterer before 1865); in cultivation T. Methven & Son, Edinburgh 1868-69; lilac rose, much spotted.
	Shilsoneri			(Sir John Ramsden 1935).
	Shilsonii		g.	thomsonii x barbatum; (Gill).
	Shilsonii	*** C	cl.	thomsonii x barbatum; (Gill 1900); scarlet or clear crimson; A.M. (R.H.S.) 1900.
	Shot Silk		g.	campylocarpum x dichroanthum; (Ramsden 1933).

		Sidney Herbert			cl.	(J. Waterer before 1871); cultivated Standish & Noble before 1870; carmine, dark spots.
		Sidonia			g.	'Rose Perfection' x fortunei; (Aberconway 1933); rose pink.
		Sigismund Rucker			cl.	named by A. Waterer before 1871; magenta with black center; F.C.C. 1872.
		Signal			cl.	'Moser's Maroon' x 'Tally Ho'; (Lancaster); red.
		Signet				cultivated by Noble before 1850; rosy purple.
		Signor Lablanche				cultivated Standish & Noble before 1860; pale rosy purple, yellow spots.
		(Silberaad's Early)				See 'Nobleanum Silberaad's Early'.
		Silk			cl.	orbiculare x souliei; exhibited Evans 1956.
		Silkcap			cl.	leucaspis x 'Cilpinense'; (Crown Lands 1951); pure white.
		Silver Pink				(J. J. Crosfield 1935).
		Silver Ray			g.	megeratum x mishmiense; (Aberconway 1950); orange. See 'Moth'.
		Silvia			cl.	clone of R. silvaticum; (Hambro); crimson (H.C.C. 22/1); A.M. (R.H.S.) 1954.
		Silvis			cl.	(A. Waterer before 1915); purple, yellow center.
		Simplicity			g.	'Solon' x Loderi g.; (Aberconway 1950); brilliant red.
		Simsodour			g.	'G. A. Sims' x 'Purple Splendour'; (Loder 1938); deep rich purple, black blotch.
		Sinbad				cultivated Standish & Noble before 1860; purplish lake, light blotch.
		Sinbad			cl.	concinnum x 'Lady Chamberlain'; (Crown Lands); exhibited 1952.
		Sir Arthur Guiness			cl.	(J. Waterer); rose.
		Sir Charles Butler				Syn. of 'Mrs. Butler'.
xxx	H-4	Sir Charles Lemon	*	B	cl.	arboreum x ?; exhibited Lord Aberconway 1937; white; Millais says came from seed sent by Sir J. Hooker.
		Sir Colin Campbell			cl.	(J. Waterer); purplish rose, dark spots.
		Siren			g.	'Choremia' x griersonianum; (Aberconway).
		Siren			cl.	'Choremia' x griersonianum; (Aberconway 1942); brilliant red (H.C.C. 19/1) with faint darker spots on each lobe; A.M. (R.H.S.) 1942.
		Sir Frederick Moore			g.	discolor x 'St. Keverne'; (Rothschild).
		Sir Frederick Moore	**	B	cl.	discolor x 'St. Keverne'; (Rothschild); clear pink with crimson spots within at base of tube; A.M. (R.H.S.) 1937. See 'Mary Roxborough'.
		Sir George Holford				javanicum x ; orange yellow shaded red on margin of corolla; A.M. (R.H.S.) 1930.
		Sir Harry Veitch				magenta; dark eye.
		Sir Henry Havelock				(Davies before 1890); light red.
		Sir William Armstrong			cl.	(J. Waterer before 1871); dark crimson.
		Sir William Maxwell				in cultivation T. Methven & Son, Edinburgh 1868-69; pink, spotted.
		Skokomish			cl.	fortunei x 'Dr. Dresselhuys'; (Parker).
		Smirnauck			cl	smirnowii x griffithianum; (Magor 1924); pure white.
		Smithii			cl.	(before 1843); in cultivation T. Methven & Son, Edinburgh 1868-69; bright scarlet.
		Smithii Album			cl.	arboreum hybrid; white, spotted. See 'Boddaertianum'.
x	H-3	Smithii Aureum		C	cl.	Azaleodendron; (maximum x ponticum) x molle; orange yellow. See also 'Norbitonense Aureum'.
		Smithii Coccinia				parent of 'Ambrosii', etc.
		Smithii Elegans				in cultivation T. Methven & Son, Edinburgh 1868-69; crimson.
		Snowball			cl.	'Loderi Pink Diamond' x sutchuenense; (Loder?); white.
		Snowball				cultivated Standish & Noble before 1860; white.
		Snow Bunting			cl.	arboreum x sutchuenense; (J. C. Williams); white.
		Snowdon			g.	exhibited Aberconway 1935.
		Snowdrop				griffithianum x ; pure white.
		Snow Fairy			cl.	moupinense x mucronulatum(?); (Mrs. R. M. Stevenson); P.C. (R.H.S.) 1957.
		Snowflake				(A. Waterer before 1875); white, small blotch.
		Snow Lady			cl.	leucaspis x ciliatum?; (Rothschild); pure white in bud and flower; P.A. (A.R.S.) 1955.
		Snow Leopard				(Ingram).
xxx	H-3	Snow Queen			g.	'Halopeanum' x Loderi g.; (Loder).
		Snow Queen	***	B	cl.	'Halopeanum' x Loderi g.; (Loder 1926); Knap Hill Nursery Ltd.; buds neyron rose (H.C.C. 623/1) passing when fully open to pure white with very slightly red blotch at base; A.M. (R.H.S.) 1934; A.M. (Wisley Trials) 1946.
		Snow White			g.	griffithianum x fortunei; (Lowinsky); pure white; A.M. (R.H.S.) 1923.
		(Snow White)				See 'Argosy Snow White'.
		Socrates			cl.	(before 1867); rose pink, orange blotch.
		Socrianum			g.	scyphocalyx x griffithianum; (Stevenson 1951); apricot.
		Solarium			cl.	caloxanthum x 'Damaris'; (Sunningdale Nursery 1955); clear yellow, spotted crimson.
		Solent Queen	**	C	cl.	griffithianum x discolor (Angelo g.); sweet scented, very pale rose fading to almost pure white, green spotted within; A.M. (R.H.S.) 1939. Previously known as Angelo var. Solent Queen.
		Solent Snow			cl.	griffithianum x discolor (Angelo g.); (Rothschild); white with green markings. Previously known as Angelo var. Solent Snow.
		Sir Henry Mildmay			cl.	(J. Waterer before 1875); rosy crimson.

		Sir Humphrey de Trafford		cl.	(J. Waterer); rose, yellow center.
		Sir Isaac Balfour		cl.	griffithianum x ; (raised Otto Schulz 1890, introduced C. B. van Nes); reddish pink.
		Sir Isaac Newton		cl.	(A. Waterer before 1867); plum or crimson claret. Syn. 'Blatteum'.
		Sirius		cl.	crassum x cinnabarinum var. roylei magnificum; (Reuthe 1949); pink.
		Sir James		cl.	fortunei x ; (Gable); pink.
		Sir James Clark		cl.	(J. Waterer before 1871); crimson, shaded purple.
		Sir Jaspar Goldthorpe			cultivated Standish & Noble before 1870; mauve.
		Sir John Broughton			(before 1867); ponticum x ; light carmine red.
		Sir John Franklin			cultivated Standish & Noble before 1860; deep claret.
		Sir John Moore			(about 1871); crimson.
		Sir John Ramsden		g.	'Corona' x thomsonii; (Waterer, Sons & Crisp Ltd.).
		Sir John Ramsden	****B	cl.	'Corona' x thomsonii; (Waterer, Sons & Crisp Ltd. 1926); exterior carmine (H.C.C. between 21 and 21/1) changing to very pale pink at margins, midrib pencilled carmine (H.C.C. 21), interior pale Camellia rose (H.C.C. 622/3) margins slightly wavy; A.M. (R.H.S.) 1926; A.M. (R.H.S.) 1948 and F.C.C. 1955.
		Sir J. Whitworth / Sir Joseph Whitworth			(Waterer).
		Sir Laurence Peel			rosy crimson.
		Sir Philip			discolor x ; shown by Lady Martineau 1938.
		Sir Richard Carton			griffithianum hybrid x 'Rubescens'; (C. B. van Nes & Sons); crimson scarlet, cream style and stamens.
		Sir Richard Wallace			rosy, yellow center.
		Sir Robert Napier			F.C.C. 1868.
		Sir Robert Peel		cl.	(J. Waterer before 1871); crimson, dark spots.
		Sir Thomas Sebright		cl.	(A. Waterer 1865); purple, bronze blotch.
		Sir Walter Scott			cultivated Standish & Noble before 1870; lilac shading to white.
		Solent Swan		cl.	griffithianum x discolor (Angelo g.) cultivated at Sunningdale Nurseries 1955. Previously known as Angelo var. Solent Swan.
		Solitude		cl.	'Britannia' x 'Fusilier'; (R. Henny).
		Solon		g.	'Astarte' x 'Sunrise'; (Aberconway 1941); pale rose.
		Solveig		cl.	dichroanthum x griersonianum (Fabia g.); (R.H.S. Gardens, Wisley, 1954). Previously known as Fabia var. Solveig.
		Sonata		cl.	'Purple Splendour' x dichroanthum; (G. Reuthe); orange shot with purple; exhibited 1949. H.C. (R.H.S.) 1959.
		Songbird		cl.	russatum x 'Blue Tit'; (Horlick); registered Horlick 1954; violet blue; A.M. (R.H.S.) 1957.
		Songster		cl.	russatum x 'Blue Tit'; (Horlick); registered Horlick 1957.
		Sonia			white.
		Sophia Gray		cl.	caucasicum x ; (M. Koster & Sons before 1922); pink, spotted burnt umber, fimbriated.
		Sophia			cultivated Standish & Noble before 1860; pale lavender blush with yellow eye.
		Soularb		g.	souliei x arboreum blood red form; (Magor 1926); deep cerise.
		Soulbut		g.	souliei x fortunei 'Mrs. Butler'; (Magor 1926); blush white tinged pink with broad crimson spotting.
		Souldis		g.	souliei x discolor; (Magor 1927); blush pink fading to almost white with age or white with crimson blotch; P. A. (A.R.S.) 1954. See 'Exbury Souldis'.
		Soulkew		g.	souliei x 'Kewense'; (Magor 1926); blush white when open, pink outside.
		Soulking		g.	souliei x zeylanicum; (Magor 1926); crimson pink.
		Southamptonia			Syn. of 'Russellianum'.
		Souvenir de D. A. Koster	* B	cl.	'Doncaster' x 'Charlie Waterer'; (raised by D. A. Koster, introduced Wezelenberg & Son); dark scarlet, marked dark spotting; A.M. (R.H.S.) 1922. Syn. 'Barnet Glory'.
x	H-3	Souvenir de Dr. S. Endtz	* B	cl.	'Pink Pearl' x 'John Walter'; (L. J. Endtz & Co. 1927); bright rose pink, dotted dark crimson; A.M. (R.H.S.) 1924. Syn. 'Dr. S. Endtz'.
		Souvenir de G. Koster		cl.	(Ottolander & Hooftmann); lilac red.
		Souvenir de J. H. Mangles			'Crown Princess of Germany' x javanicum; chrome orange; F. C. C. 1888.
		Souvenir de Madame J. H. van Nes		cl.	griffithianum x; (raised by Otto Schulz 1890, introduced by C. B. van Nes & Sons 1896); scarlet.
		Souvenir d'un Ami			in cultivation T. Methven & Son, Edinburgh 1868-69; violet rose, semi-double.
		Souvenir of Anthony Waterer	** B	cl.	(A. Waterer); dark rosy red or salmon with yellow blotch.
xxx	H-3	Souvenir of W. C. Slocock	*** B	cl.	campylocarpum x; (W. C. Slocock & Co. Ltd.); primrose yellow; opens apricot shade fading to pale yellow ochre; A.M. (R.H.S.) 1935.
		Spanish Galleon		cl.	'Belle' x 'Margaret Dunn'; (Sunningdale Nurseries 1955); butter yellow.
		Spectabilis			exhibited Veitch & Son 1862; salmon red.

	Spectra		cl.	discolor x; (Ostbo-Fawcett 1960).
	Speculator		cl.	cultivated Standish & Noble before 1850; deep rose, throat white.
	Speculatum		cl.	in cultivation T. Methven & Son, Edinburgh 1868-69; light pink, pale center.
	Spinbur		g.	spinuliferum x burmanicum; (Stair); exhibited 1950. See 'Lochinch Spinbur'.
xx H-3	Spinulosum		g.	spinuliferum x racemosum; (R.B.G. Kew).
	Spinulosum	** C	cl.	spinuliferum x racemosum; (R.B.G. Kew); exhibited 1926; apricot pink; A. M. (R. H. S.) 1944. See 'Exbury Spinulosum'.
	Spitfire	B	cl.	griffithianum x ; (A. Kluis 1946); dark red (Chrysanthemum crimson H.C.C. 824/1) dark brown blotch.
	Spring Dance		cl.	triflorum x? (Barto-R. Bovee, 1958).
	Spring Glory		cl.	red catawbiense seedling x 'Cunningham's White'; (Shammarello); exhibited 1955; pink.
	Spring Song		cl.	(racemosum x keiskei) x keiskei; (Hardgrove); exhibited 1951; pale yellow, fading to apricot.
	Springtime		cl.	praevernum x arboreum var. album; (Gill 1945); white shading to pale greenish yellow in the throat (H.C.C. 633/3); A.M. (R.H.S.) 1945.
	Stamfordianum		cl.	in cultivation T. Methven & Son, Edinburgh 1868-69; claret, black blotch.
	Standard of Flanders			cultivated Standish & Noble before 1870; blush rose with dark eye. Syn. of 'Lady Dorothy Neville'.
	Standishi			griffithianum x; (Veitch); white, red spots.
	Standishii			maximum x 'Altaclarense'; (Standish & Noble 1850); violet crimson, black spots.
	Stanwellianum			catawbiense x caucasicum; (T. Methven & Son, Edinburgh 1917); crimson.
	Stanwellianum			(T. Methven & Son, Edinburgh before 1868); snowy white.
	Stanwellii			campanulatum x ponticum; exhibited T. Methven & Son, Edinburgh 1917.
	Starfish	** A	cl.	griffithianum x; (Waterer, Sons & Crisp Ltd. before 1922); bright pink, star-shaped.
	Starlight		cl.	carolinianum x leucaspis; (Hardgrove); exhibited 1953; white.
	Star of Ascot			(Standish before 1875); white, black spots.
	Star of Eve			tephropeplum x lindleyi.
	Star of India			'Crown Princess of Germany' x javanicum; exhibited Veitch 1891; yellow to red orange.
	Starry Eyed		cl.	(catawbiense var. rubrum x discolor) x 'Azor'; exhibited Hardgrove 1955; pink, red blotch.
	Staving			red.
	Stella		cl.	catawbiense x; (A. Waterer); lilac rose, spotted dark chocolate; F. C. C. 1865. Syn. 'Stella Waterer'.
	(Stella Maris)			See 'Naomi Stella Maris'.
	Stellata			griffithianum x; (Mangles).
	Stella Waterer			Syn. of 'Stella'.
	Stephanotum			in cultivation T. Methven & Son, Edinburgh 1868-69; crimson.
	Stephen Davies		cl.	(Davies); deep crimson.
	Stoneham Scarlet			Syn. of 'Russellianum'.
	Stoplight			griersonianum x 'Cornubia'; (R. Henny); scarlet; P.A. (A.R.S.) 1951.
	Straalstrat von Massenbach			griffithianum x; (raised Otto Schulz 1890, introduced C. B. van Nes & Sons 1896).
	Strategist	A	cl.	griffithianum x; (J. Waterer); light red.
	Strawberry			(J. J. Crosfield 1935).
	Sue		cl.	'Loderi King George' selfed; exhibited James.
	Sulfmeg		cl.	sulfureum x megeratum; (Magor 1940); pale sulphur yellow (H.C.C. 1/3); A.M. (R.H.S.) 1940.
	Sulphureum		cl.	caucasicum form; ivory yellow.
	Sulphur Yellow		g.	souliei x campylocarpum; (J. C. Williams). See 'Townhill Sulphur Yellow'.
	Sultan			cultivated Standish & Noble before 1870; rosy lake.
	Sultana		cl.	(J. Waterer before 1865); white or pale blush, brown spots.
	Summer's Dawn		g.	wardii x garden hybrid; (Ingram); exhibited 1936; yellow.
	Sun Chariot		cl.	'Solarium' x wardii; (Sunningdale Nurseries); exhibited Sunningdale 1955; yellow.
	Sundor		g.	'Dorinthia' x 'Sunrise'; (Aberconway 1946); salmon scarlet.
	Sun Glow			(J. J. Crosfield 1935).
	Sunkist		g.	'Loderi Pink Diamond' x griffithianum; (Loder); white suffused pink.
	Sunningdale Apricot		cl.	'Golden Horn' x 'Margaret Dunn'; exhibited Hamilton Smith 1955; apricot.
	Sun of Austerlitz	B		arboreum x; in cultivation T. Methven & Son, Edinburgh 1868-69; red or brilliant crimson; early.
xx H-4	Sunrise		g.	griffithianum x griersonianum; (Aberconway).
	Sunrise		cl.	griffithianum x griersonianum; (Aberconway 1933); buds deep pink (H.C.C. 21/1) opens pale pink, carmine lilac; F.C.C. (R.H.S.) 1942.
	Sunset		cl.	'Earl of Athlone' x Fabia'; (R. Henny).
	Sunset		cl.	'Queen Wilhelmina' x Loderi g.; (G. Loder); exhibited 1931; pale yellow shaded pink or white flushed pale pink; A.M. (R.H.S.) 1931.
	Sunshine		cl.	neriiflorum subsp. euchaites x beanianum; (Harrison 1955); bright dark red.
	Suomi	A	g.	'Linswegeanum' x 'Metternianus'; (Dietrich Hobbie 1953); bright red, partly deeper borders.
	Superbissimum			(before 1839); dwarf, white fragrant; F.C.C. 1897.

		Superlative			blush white.
		Surprise		g.	falconeri x thomsonii; (J. Waterer before 1867); exhibited Loder 1937; mauve, black spot. See 'Faltho', 'J. E. Harris'.
		Surprise Packet		cl.	falconeri x thomsonii (Surprise g.); (Digby 1953). Previously known as Surprise var. Packet.
xxx	H-2	Susan	****B	cl.	campanulatum x fortunei; (raised J. C. Williams, introduced W. C. Slocock Ltd.); corolla amethyst violet (H.C.C. between 35/2 and 35/3) margins and midrib amethyst violet, inside of corolla amethyst violet (H.C.C. 35/3) deepening at margin to H.C.C. 35/2, spotted on upper lobe at throat dark purple; A.M. (R.H.S.) 1930; A.M. (Wisley Trials) 1948; F.C.C. (R.H.S.) 1954.
		Susie		g.	souliei x griersonianum; (Stirling-Maxwell 1941).
		Sussex Bonfire		cl.	haematodes x 'Cornish Cross'; (Loder); deep blood red; A.M. (R.H.S.) 1934.
		Sutchbarb		g.	barbatum x sutchuenense; (Magor 1936).
		Sutchrir		g.	ririei x sutchuenense; (Magor 1919). Syn. of 'Maya'?
		Swan Lake		cl.	auriculatum x 'Godesberg' (Blanc-mange g.); (Rothschild 1955); white. Previously known as Blanc-mange var. Swan Lake.
xx	H-2	Sweet Simplicity	** A	cl.	ponticum x; (J. Waterer, Sons & Crisp Ltd. before 1922); white edged rose pink.
		Sybil			javanicum x; exhibited Rothschild 1938; rose pink, of perfect form.
		Sylph		cl.	(A. Waterer before 1915); pink.
		Symphonie		cl.	campylocarpum x; (W. C. Slocock Ltd. approximately 1930); cream center fading to white with deep almond pink edges.
		Symphony	** B	g.	'Arthur Osborn' x 'F. C. Puddle'; (Aberconway 1941); red.
		Syonense		g.	catawbiense x arboreum var. album; delicate pink spotted crimson; Knightian Medal to Iveson 1849.
		Tacoma Maiden		cl.	ciliatum x cilliicalyx; (Brandt-Fawcett 1960); white.
		Tahiti		cl.	(maximum x catawbiense) x (dichroanthum x (discolor x campylocarpum)); (D. G. Leach 1960); ivory, edged salmon-orange, darker on exterior; orange-russet blotch; conspicuous calyx.
		Talisman		cl.	'Chanticleer' x 'Ramillies'; (Aberconway 1950); blood red.
		(Talisman)			See 'Margaret Dunn Talisman'.
		Talleyrand		cl.	'G. A. Sims' x 'Tally Ho'; (Reuthe 1945); blood red.
xxxx	H-5	Tally Ho		g.	griersonianum x eriogynum.
		Tally Ho	****D	cl.	griersonianum x eriogynum; (Crosfield 1933); brilliant orange scarlet; F.C.C. (R.H.S.) 1933.
		Talvena			'Tally Ho' x venator; (Congreve 1946).
		Tamerlane		cl.	(J. Waterer before 1865); in cultivation T. Methven & Son, Edinburgh 1868-69; maroon.
		Tan		cl.	fortunei x; (Dexter).
		(Tangerine)			See 'Cinnandrum Tangerine'.
		(Tangerine)			See 'Fabia Tangerine'.
		Taranto		g.	falconeri x eximium; (Heneage-Vivian 1940).
		Tatoosh		cl.	'Britannia' x 'Venus'; (R. Henny).
		Taylori			brookeanum var. gracile x 'Princess Alexandra'; (Byls before 1874); exhibited Veitch 1891; pink; F.C.C. (R.H.S.) 1935.
		Tecumseh		cl.	catawbiense x; (Parsons).
		Ted Marchand			exhibited Collingwood Ingram.
		Ted Waterer		cl.	(J. Waterer before 1922); blush lilac, compact truss; A.M.(R.H.S.) 1925.
xxx	H-3	Temple Belle	** C	g.	orbiculare x williamsianum; raised at R.B.G. Kew 1916; soft pink; semi-dwarf.
		Tensing		cl.	'Fabia' x 'Romany Chai'; (at R.H.S. Gardens, Wisley, 1953); Camellia rose (H.C.C. 622) which merges into a tinge of orange in the throat; A.M. (R.H.S.) 1953.
		Tessa		g.	Praecox g. x moupinense; (Stevenson).
		Tessa		cl.	Praecox g. x moupinense; (Stevenson 1935); rosy lilac, A.M. (R.H.S.) 1935.
		Tessa Roza		cl.	Praecox g. x moupinense; (Tessa g.); (Stevenson 1953); shades of deep rosy pink against pale background, upper segment spotted deep carmine; A.M. (R.H.S.) 1953. Previously known as Tessa var. Roza.
		Thais		g.	'Euryalus' x Loderi g.; (Aberconway 1941); pale pink.
		Thalia			javanicum x 'Princess Royal'; exhibited Veitch 1891; ivory white or yellowish white passing to creamy pink.
		Thalia		g.	'Ascot Brilliant' x griffithianum; (Magor); mauve rose, large crimson blotch and spots.
		Thalia		cl.	ciliatum x ciliicalyx; registered by Brandt 1954.
		The Autocrat			cultivated Standish & Noble before 1870; purple with dark eye.
		The Bouncer			in cultivation T. Methven & Son, Edinburgh 1868-69; crimson scarlet, dark eye.
x	H-2	The Bride	* A	cl.	caucasicum var. album inbred; (Standish & Noble before 1850); white, greeny spots; F.C.C. 1871. See 'Bride'.
		The Cardinal		cl.	(Gable). Syn. of 'Kentucky Cardinal'.
		The Countess			(Veitch); white.
		The Czarina			cultivated Standish & Noble before 1860; delicate lavender blush.
		The Don		g.	'Doncaster' x griffithianum; (Lowinsky).
x	H-3	The Don	** C	cl.	'Doncaster' x griffithianum; (Lowinsky); intense rosy scarlet; A.M. (R.H.S.) 1920. See 'Don Ernesto', 'Donna Anita', 'Donna Florenza'.
		The Flame			'Ascot Brilliant' x thomsonii; red.
		The Gem			cultivated Standish & Noble before 1870; blush, tipped with rose.

	The General			red catawbiense seedling x red catawbiense seedling; (Shammarello); exhibited 1955; deep red, darker red blotch.
	The Giraffe			cultivated Standish & Noble before 1870; white, bold blotch.
	The Grand Arab		cl.	Syn. of 'Vesuvius'.
	The Grenadier			cultivated Standish & Noble before 1870; rose, finely spotted with red.
	The Hon. J. Boscawen			crimson
	The Hon. Jean Marie de Montague			See 'Jean Marie Montague'; Syn: 'Miss Montague'.
	The Hon. Joyce Montague	* C	cl.	griffithianum hybrid x 'Thomas Agnew'; (C. B. van Nes & Sons); scarlet after few days showing white stripes.
	The King			crimson.
	The Lynx			cultivated Standish & Noble before 1860; blush, bold blotch.
	The Maroon		cl.	(J. Waterer before 1874); purplish red, chocolate blotch.
	The Master		cl.	'China' x 'Letty Edwards'; (Slocock); selected Slocock 1948; creamy pink, dark throat.
	The Master			red catawbiense hybrid x 'Cunningham's White'; exhibited Shammarello 1955; rose pink.
	The Monitor			cultivated Standish & Noble before 1870; vermilion.
	The Moor		g.	'Arthur Osborn' x eriogynum; (Aberconway 1941); red. See 'Tremeer'.
	The Painted Lady			in cultivation T. Methven & Son, Edinburgh 1868-69; rose, blotched with chocolate.
	The Princess			cultivated Standish & Noble before 1860; pure white.
	The Queen			(C. Noble before 1871); blush, changing to white.
	The Saracen			cultivated Standish & Noble before 1870; crimson lake.
	The Saxon			(Standish 1861); rich carmine.
	The Star			cultivated Standish & Noble before 1860; white with yellow blotch.
	The Vestal			cultivated Standish & Noble before 1860; pure white.
	The Virgin			catawbiense var. album x fargesii hybrid; (Abbott); white.
	The Warrior		cl.	(J. Waterer 1867); light crimson.
	Thelma		cl.	griersonianum x 'Armistice Day' (Darlene g.); (H. Lem, 1959); Geranium lake (H.C.C. 20/1); P.A. (A.R.S.) 1959.
	Theresa		g.	'Romany Chal' x griersonianum; (Stavordale); exhibited 1950. See 'Festival'.
	Thetis			javanicum x 'Princess Frederica'; yellow to yellow orange; F.C.C. 1887.
	T. H. Kekewich		cl.	(J. Waterer); crimson.
	Thomaden		g.	thomsonii x adenogynum; (Magor 1927).
	Thomaleum		g.	haemaleum x thomsonii; (Collingwood Ingram); blackish crimson.
	Thomas Bolas		g.	decorum x fortunei; (Londonderry 1947).
	Thomasine		cl.	souliei x thomsonii; (Clarke 1931); pale pink spotted red; A.M. (R.H.S.) 1931.
	Thomas Methven			in cultivation T. Methven & Son, Edinburgh 1868-69; rosy crimson, orange spots.
	Thomdeton		g.	thomsonii x detonsum; (Magor 1941).
	Thomking		g.	thomsonii x 'Mrs. Randall Davidson'; (Magor cross 1915).
xx H-4	Thomwilliams		g.	thomsonii x williamsianum; (Magor 1927); deep shade of rose pink. See 'Bodnant Thomwilliams'.
	Three Star		cl.	(Gable).
	Thunderbolt			on trial at Wisley from Lady Martineau.
	Thunderhead		cl.	(Clark).
	Thunderstorm	** B	cl.	'Doncaster' x; (W. C. Slocock cross 1930); deep rich red near rose opal (H.C.C. 022); stamens conspicuous, white; margins slightly waved; A.M. (Wisley Trials) 1955.
	Tidbit		cl.	dichroanthum x wardii; (R. Henny); straw yellow (604/2); scarlet calyx P.A. (A.R.S.) 1957.
	Tiepolo		g.	chartophyllum x 'Clodion'; (Adams-Acton 1934); magenta.
	Timon			cultivated Standish & Noble before 1870; rosy purple.
	Timoshenko		g.	parentage uncertain; (Collingwood Ingram); exhibited 1952; scarlet.
	Tintoretto			maximum x; (C. Frets & Son); light pink, reddish blotch.
	Tipoo Sahib		cl.	(J. Waterer); in cultivation T. Methven & Son, Edinburgh 1868; dark chocolate.
	Tip-the-wink		cl.	griffithianum x 'Kewense'; (Loder); F.C.C. (R.H.S.) 1936.
	Titania			cultivated Standish & Noble before 1860; deep red, base of lobes white.
	Titian		cl.	(H. Waterer before 1851); rosy scarlet or rosy crimson.
	Titness Beauty		g.	griersonianum x Loderi g. ; (Horlick 1937).
	Titness Belle		cl.	'Countess of Derby' x Loderi g.; (Horlick 1942); deep rose fading pink.
	Titness Park		cl.	barbatum x calophytum; (Horlick 1954); pale, varying shade of Phlox pink (H.C.C. 625) with chocolate blotch in throat and some chocolate spotting; A.M. (R.H.S.) 1954.
	Titness Rose		cl.	griersonianum x Loderi g. (East Knoyle g.); Horlick.
	Titness Triumph		cl.	basilicum x mollyanum – K.W. 6261; (Horlick 1956); pink.
	Tittenhurst		cl.	wightii x barbatum; (White); primrose; A.M. (R.H.S.) 1933.
	Tittenhurst Belle		cl.	'Corona' x griffithianum; (Lowinsky); clear rose pink; A.M. (R.H.S.) 1925.
	Tolo		cl.	'Sarita Loder' x (lacteum x 'Mary Swathling'); (James).
	Tomahawk		g.	'Choremia' x hookeri; (Aberconway 1950); blood red.
	Tom Willis Flemming	* B		'Doncaster' seedling; (W. C. Slocock Ltd.); deep red.
	Tondelayo			Syn. of 'Multimaculatum'.
	Tony		cl.	red catawbiense seedling x 'Boule de Neige'; (Shammarello); exhibited 1955; bright red.

		Tony				decorum x; (Messel); white; A.M. (R.H.S.) 1930.
		Topsvoort Pearl			cl.	sport of 'Pink Pearl'; (Topsvoort Nursery, Aalsmeer, Holland); light pink with red edges, frilled.
		Torch			g.	'Ascot Brilliant' x thomsonii; red.
xx	H-4	Toreador			g.	'Arthur Osborn' x griersonianum; (Aberconway).
		Toreador			cl.	'Arthur Osborn' x griersonianum; (Aberconway 1941); dark red which changes to brilliant scarlet when light shines through. (H.C.C. 821-721); A.M. (R.H.S.) 1942.
		Torlonianum				Azaleodendron; (M. Young); light purple with yellow blotch.
		Torsun			g.	'Toreador' x 'Sunrise'; (Aberconway 1946); rose red.
		Tortoiseshell			g.	'Goldsworth Orange' x griersonianum; (Slocock); exhibited Slocock 1946. See 'Champagne'.
		Tortoiseshell Orange			cl.	'Goldsworth Orange' x griersonianum (Tortoiseshell g.); (Slocock); selected Slocock 1945; orange red. Previously known as Tortoiseshell var. Orange.
		Tortoiseshell Salome			cl.	'Goldsworth Orange' x griersonianum (Tortoiseshell g.); (Slocock 1946); biscuit and pink. Previously known as Tortoiseshell var. Salome.
		Tortoiseshell Wonder			cl.	'Goldsworth Orange' x griersonianum (Tortoiseshell g.); (Slocock); selected Slocock 1945; salmon pink, orange salmon; A.M. (R.H.S.) 1947. Previously known as Tortoiseshell var. Wonder.
		Tosca			cl.	'Exbury Naomi' x litiense; (R.H.S. Gardens, Wisley, 1959); pale pink buds opening Primrose yellow (H.C.C. 601/3); A.M. (R.H.S.) 1959.
		Toucan				eriogynum hybrid; orange red.
		Towardii / Towardianum				catawbiense x 'Altaclarense'; (Standish & Noble 1850); light rose or rosy lilac.
		(Tower Court)				See 'Fabia Tower Court'.
		Towhee			cl.	'C.P. Raffill' x ('Red Cap' x 'Tally Ho'); (James); scarlet; P.A. (A.R.S.) 1956.
		Townhill Albatross			cl.	'Loderi King George' x discolor; (Albatross g.); fuchsine pink (H. C. C. 627/3) and in fully opened flowers persists on backs and edges of lobes, center being almost white without spots; A.M. (R.H.S.) 1945. Previously known as Albatross Townhill var.
		Townhill Cremorne			cl.	'Luscombei' x campylocarpum; (Cremorne g.); bud soft pink which disperses as the flower expands to Chinese yellow (H.C.C. 606/3) flushed and margined rosy coral (about 614/2); A.M. (R.H.S.) 1947. Previously known as Cremorne Townhill var.
		Townhill Damaris			cl.	'Dr. Stocker' x campylocarpum; (Damaris g.); exhibited Swaythling 1948. Previously known as Damaris Townhill var.
		Townhill Redcap			cl.	didymum x eriogynum (Redcap g.); oxblood red (H.C.C. 00823) which lights up to scarlet against the light; A.M. (R.H.S.) 1945. Previously known as Redcap var. Townhill Park.
		Townhill Sulphur Yellow			cl.	souliei x campylocarpum; (Sulphur Yellow g.); exhibited Lord Swaythling 1939. Previously known as Sulphur Yellow Townhill var.
		Trafalgar			g.	'Eros' x 'Luscombei'; (Aberconway 1950); rose pink.
		Tranquility			cl.	'Vulcan' x 'Corona'; (Wright).
		Treasure			g.	forrestii var. repens x williamsianum; (Crosfield 1937); dark pink.
		Trebah Gem				arboreum x griffithianum; (R. Gill & Son); soft pink.
		Trebianum				arboreum x griffithianum; white, with pink flush.
		Tregedna				thomsonii x ?; red.
		Tregrehanii				exhibited Capt. Carlyon 1935.
		Trelawny			cl.	arboreum x barbatum (Duke of Cornwall g.); (R. Gill & Son); deep carmine, paler in throat with darker spots; A.M. (R.H.S.) 1936. Previously known as Duke of Cornwall var. Trelawny.
		Tremeer			cl.	'Arthur Osborn' x eriogynum (The Moor g.); (Gen. Harrison); registered Harrison 1953; bright red. Previously known as The Moor var. Tremeer.
		Trewithen Orange			cl.	'Full House' x concatenans; (Johnstone); soft orange or Carrot red (H.C.C. 612/1-612) with a faint rosy blush; F.C.C. (R.H.S.) 1950.
		Triaur			g.	triflorum x xanthostephanum; (Magor cross 1920); yellow.
		Trident			cl.	'Britannia' x eriogynum (Firetail g.); exhibited Loder 1948; dark red. Previously known as Firetail var. Trident.
x	H-2	Trilby	*	A	cl.	'Queen Wilhelmina' x 'Stanley Davies'; (C. B. van Nes & Sons); deep crimson, dark blotch.
		Tristan Thacker			g.	dichroanthum x 'G. A. Sims'; (Thacker 1944); salmon orange.
		Triton				javanicum x multicolor hybrid; salmon rose stained pale yellow in throat; A.M. (R.H.S.) 1900.
		Triumphans				'Duchess of Edinburgh' x javanicum; (Byls before 1871); scarlet crimson; F.C.C. 1883.
		Troas			g.	thomsonii x 'Cornish Cross' ; (Ramsden); exhibited 1942.
		Trojan			g.	'F. C. Puddle' x 'Shilsonii'; (Aberconway 1950); dark red.
		Troubadour			g.	'Toreador' x arboreum; (Aberconway 1950); blood red.
		Tudor Girl			cl.	(hookeri x 'Shilsonii') x Seedling 104; (Winkfield Manor Nurseries 1952).
		Tulyar		B		(A. Waterer); red, black blotch.
		Tumalo			cl.	decorum x 'Loderi King George'; (James); white, suffused; P.A. (A.R.S.) 1955.
		Twinkles			cl.	racemosum x spiciferum; (Wright).
		Tyee			cl.	'Esquire' x 'Idealist'; (D.W. James, 1960); Primrose yellow (H.C.C. 601/2), uranium green (63/2) throat; A.E. (A.R.S.) 1960.

		Tyermannii	****F	cl.	nuttallii x formosum; (Tyerman); exhibited 1925; white or cream, lily-like blooms; F.C.C. (R.H.S.) 1925.
		Tyrian Queen			(Rogers); rosy carmine.
		Umpqua Chief		cl.	'Fabia' x 'Azor'; (James).
		Una			cultivated Standish & Noble before 1860; blush, fine blotch.
x	H-4	Ungerio		g.	ungernii x eriogynum; (Magor 1933).
xxx	H-3	Unique	*** B	cl.	campylocarpum x; (W.C.Slocock Ltd.); pale ochre or yellow slightly tinged Peach color; A.M. (R.H.S.) 1934; F.C.C. (R.H.S.) 1935.
		Unique	* B	cl.	(Wallace); flesh changing to buff.
x	H-4	Unknown Warrior	* B	cl.	'Queen Wilhelmina' x 'Stanley Davies'; (C. B. van Nes & Sons before 1922); light red, early.
		Ursula Siems	B	g.	'Earl of Athlone' x forrestii var. repens; (Dietrich Hobbie 1951); scarlet-carmine, translucent.
		Valaspis		g.	valentinianum x leucaspis ; (Aberconway).
		Valaspis		cl.	valentinianum x leucaspis; (Aberconway 1935); bright yellow; A. M. (R. H. S.) 1935.
		Valda		g.	'Latona' x haematodes; (Aberconway 1941); rosy red.
		Valentina			cultivated Standish & Noble before 1860; blush, yellow eye.
		Valewood Pink		cl.	(Mangles); shell-pink, margins deeper; A.M. 1934.
		Valiant		g.	'Astarte' x chaetomallum; (Aberconway 1946); red.
		Valpinense		g.	moupinense x valentinianum; (Aberconway).
		Valpinense		cl.	moupinense x valentinianum; (Aberconway 1943); Primrose yellow (H.C.C. 601/2) deeper color in buds; A.M. (R.H.S.) 1943.
		Vampire		cl.	'Britannia' x 'Fabia'; (Wright 1951); red.
		Van den Broeke		cl.	'Charles Dickens' x 'Lord Roberts'; (H. den Ouden & Sons 1925); crimson.
		Van der Hoop		cl.	'Atrosanguineum' x 'Doncaster'; (H. den Ouden & Sons 1925); dark crimson rose.
		Van Dyck		cl.	(H. Waterer before 1851); rosy crimson.
xx	H-4	Vanessa		g.	'Soulbut' x griersonianum; (Aberconway).
		Vanessa	*** C	cl.	'Soulbut' x griersonianum; (Aberconway 1929); soft pink; F.C.C. (R.H.S.) 1929.
		Vanessa Pastel	*** C	cl.	'Soulbut' x griersonianum; (Vanessa g.); (Aberconway 1946); cream flushed shell pink (H.C.C. 516/2-3) tube stained externally scarlet (H.C.C. 19/2) and scarlet zoned at base inside; A.M. (R.H.S.) 1946. Previously known as Vanessa var. Pastel.
		Vanguard			cultivated Standish & Noble before 1870; bright crimson.
xx	H-4	Vanguard		g.	venator x griersonianum; (Lord Headfort 1940); crimson or orange red.
		Van Huysum		g.	'Chanticleer' x 'Purple Splendour'; (Adams-Acton 1935); deep red.
		Vanity		g.	'Vanessa' x 'Dante'; (Aberconway 1946); scarlet.
		Vanity Fair		g.	'Vanessa' x eriogynum; (Aberconway 1941); deep red.
		Van Nes Glory			'Queen Wilhelmina' x 'Stanley Davies'; (C. B. van Nes & Sons); red.
xxx	H-3	Van Nes Sensation	B	cl.	fortunei 'Mrs. Butler' x 'Halopeanum'; (C. B. van Nes & Sons); pale lilac, white center, fragrant.
		Vantom		cl.	thomsonii x a Van Nes hybrid; exhibited 1938; pink.
		Vanven		g.	'Vanessa' x venator; (Aberconway); deep red.
		Van Weerden Poelman		cl.	'Charles Dickens' x 'Lord Roberts'; (H. den Ouden & Son 1925); crimson.
		Varium			in cultivation Knap Hill Nursery 1955; deep pink.
		Varna		g.	'Carmen' x williamsianum; (Aberconway 1946); yellow, flushed rose.
		Vasari			(A. Waterer); in cultivation T. Methven & Son, Edinburgh 1868-69; crimson, intensely spotted.
		Vasco		g.	aperantum x stewartianum; (Aberconway 1946); red.
		Vauban		cl.	catawbiense x ; (A. Waterer); mauve, bronze yellow blotch.
		Vega		g.	'Fabia' x haematodes; (Aberconway 1941); scarlet.
		Valasquez Velazques (Methven)			in cultivation T. Methven & Son, Edinburgh 1868-69; Cherry rose.
		Velma Rozetta		cl.	Pink Beauty x (griersonianum x 'Azor'); (Whitney).
		Venapens		g.	venator x forrestii var. repens; (Ramsden 1940); scarlet.
		Venco		g.	venator x 'Coreta'; (Aberconway 1946); crimson scarlet.
		Venus		g.	'Amaura' x facetum; (Aberconway 1936); bright red or salmon red.
		Vernus		cl.	Red catawbiense hybrid x 'Cunningham's White'; (Shammarello-D. G. Leach 1957); light, clear pink; very early.
		(Venustum)			See 'Nobleanum Venustum'.
		Verrocchio		g.	campylocarpum x neriiflorum; (Adams-Acton 1936); amber.
		Verschaffeltii			'Queen Victoria' x 'Pardolatum'; in cultivation T. Methven & Son, Edinburgh 1868-69; nearly white, cluster of dark spots.
		Vesper			cultivated Noble before 1850; rosy pink, white throat.
		Vesta		g.	'Prometheus' x williamsianum; (Dietrich Hobbie 1949); deep rose.
		Vesta			cultivated Standish & Noble before 1860; white.
		Vestale		cl.	catawbiense var. album hybrid; exhibited D. G. Leach 1954; white.
		Vestris		g.	griersonianum x orbiculare; (Aberconway 1946); deep rose.
		Vesuvius		cl.	griersonianum x 'Romany Chai'; vermilion red without spotting.
		Vesuvius	B	cl.	catawbiense x arboreum; (J. Waterer before 1867); bright orange scarlet, upper segment shaded violet. Syn. 'Grand Arab'.
		Vesuvius			cultivated Standish & Noble before 1870; blood red or scarlet.

	Name	Rating		Type	Description
	Veta			g.	'Etna' x venator; (Aberconway 1946); rose.
	Vicomte Forceville			cl.	(J. Waterer); dark crimson.
	Victor Hugo				(Standish or J. Waterer); purplish crimson.
	Victoria				(Waterer before 1851); cultivated Standish & Noble before 1870; deep claret.
	Victorianum				dalhousiae x nuttallii; (Pince before 1871); exhibited 1879; creamy yellow turning white.
	Victory			g.	'Dorothea' x Loderi g.; (Loder).
	Victory			g.	'Britannia' x 'Tally Ho'; (Digby 1947).
	Viking			g.	'Solon' x 'Chanticleer'; (Aberconway 1950); rosy red.
	Village Maid			cl.	(J. Waterer); pale center, pink edges, yellow spots.
	Villager				cultivated Noble before 1850; rose.
	Vincent van Gogh			cl.	(M. Koster & Sons 1939); bright cerise red, striped white.
	Viola			cl.	caucasicum x; (Seidel before 1893); porcelain white.
	Violet Adair				griffithianum x; (Mangles).
	Violet Paget				griffithianum hybrid; (Mangles); pink.
	Violet Parsons	*	B	cl.	salmon pink.
	Virgil				'Duchess of Edinburgh' x 'Princess Alexandra'; rich creamy yellow (Primrose); A.M. 1889.
	Virgin			cl.	catawbiense album x a hybrid of fargesii; (Abbott). Syn. 'The Virgin'.
	Virginia Scott			cl.	souliei x ?; (Larson); yellow.
	Viscountess Elveden				(W. C. Slocock 1920); pink.
	Viscount Powerscourt			cl.	(J. Waterer); red, deeply spotted or purplish red with dark spots; A.M. (R.H.S.) 1906.
	Vitalio			g.	'Catherine van Tol' x discolor; (Dietrich Hobbie 1952); deep rose to bright rose,
	Vivian Grey			cl.	(J. Waterer); rose pink.
	Vivid				'Altaclarense' x maximum hybrid; (Standish & Noble 1850); rose or bright purplish rose.
	Voltaire				cultivated Standish & Noble before 1870; deep red.
	Voltaire			g.	'Eros' x Loderi g.; (Aberconway 1950); red or pink.
	Vondel			cl.	'Mrs. Lindsay Smith' x campylocarpum hybrid; (M. Koster & Sons); pale yellow.
	Von Oheimb Woislowitz			cl.	catawbiense x; (T. J. R. Seidel 1929); purplish rose. Syn. 'Oheimb-Woislowitz'.
	Voodoo			cl.	'Britannia' x 'May Day'; (R. Henny); P.A. (A.R.S.) 1952; scarlet.
xx H-3	Vulcan	**	B	cl.	'Mars' x griersonianum; (Waterer, Sons & Crisp Ltd.) exhibited 1938; bright red (H.C.C. 820/3); A.M. (R.H.S.) 1957.
	Vulcan's Flame			cl.	griersonianum x 'Mars'; (Lancaster); red.
	W. A. Dunstan				(M. Koster & Sons); creamish white.
	Waltdis			g.	'John Walter' x discolor; (Dietrich Hobbie 1952); clear deep rose.
	Walther S. Reuthe				Syn. of 'W. S. Reuthe'.
	Warbler			g.	wardii x neriiflorum; exhibited Headfort 1938.
	Wardanthum			cl.	dichroanthum x wardii; (Stevenson 1953).
	Warden Wink			cl.	'Tip-the-Wink' x wardii; (Mansfield 1939).
	Warm Spring			cl.	(D. W. James, 1959); Indian yellow (H.C.C. 6/2) flushed pink; late.
	War Paint			cl.	a selection of R. elliottii; (D. James); crimson scarlet; P.A. (A.R.S.) 1956.
	Warrior			cl.	Syn. of 'The Warrior'.
	Washington			cl.	named by B. F. Lancaster.
	Waterer's Caucasicum		B	cl.	(Waterer); caucasicum x; blush pink.
	Waterer's Hybridum	*	A	cl.	ferrugineum x; (Waterer); rose pink.
	Waterer's Victoria			cl.	in cultivation T. Methven & Son, Edinburgh 1868-69; deep claret.
	Wayfarer			g.	'Phidias' x 'Chanticleer'; (Aberconway 1950); red.
	Wayford			cl.	calophytum x 'Gill's Triumph'; (Magor); exhibited Baker 1957; flowers white with dark crimson within; A.M. (R.H.S.) 1957.
	W. Cowper				Syn. of 'William Cowper'.
	W. Downing			cl.	(A. Waterer); brownish purple or dark puce.
	Wega			g.	fortunei 'Mrs. Butler' x williamsianum; (Hobbie); pink.
	W. E. Gladstone			cl.	(J. Waterer); carmine red. Syn. of 'William Ewart Gladstone'.
	Welkin			g.	'Eros' x haematodes; (Aberconway).
	Welkin			cl.	'Eros' x haematodes; (Aberconway 1946); Geranium lake (H.C.C. 20/1) to delft rose (H.C.C. 020); A.M. (R.H.S.) 1946; F.C.C. (R.H.S.) 1951.
	Wellesleyanum				maximum x catawbiense; (A. Waterer 1880); white, tinged light rose. Syn. 'Maximum Wellesleyanum'.
	Werei		C	cl.	arboreum ? x barbatum ?; (S. Smith); rose pink; A.M. (R.H.S.) 1921.
	Werrington			cl.	'Humming Bird' x forrestii var. repens; (Williams 1953).
	Weser			g.	'Dr. V. H. Rutgers' x williamsianum; (Dietrich Hobbie 1951); rose.
	Westbury			cl.	Dexter hybrid x ?; (H. Phipps-Westbury Rose Co., 1958); pink, golden blotch in throat.
	Westward Ho	*	B	cl.	discolor x hardy hybrid; (Slocock 1932); deep pink, crimson throat.
	W. F. H.			g.	haematodes x 'Tally Ho'; (Whitaker 1941).
	Wheatley			cl.	Dexter hybrid x ?; (H. Phipps-Westbury Rose Co., 1959); light pink.
	W. H. Forster				griffithianum x; bright red.

	Whimsey		cl.	souliei x 'Bowbells'; (Henny). Camellia Rose (H.C.C. 622/3) buff inside.
	White Beauty		cl.	'Albino' x 'Loderi Pink Diamond'; pure white; A.M. (R.H.S.) 1945.
	White Cliff		cl.	griffithianum x 'Loder's White'; exhibited Digby 1953.
	White Cloud	* B	cl.	griffithianum x; (Slocock); selected Slocock 1934; pure white.
	White Ensign		g.	decorum x Loderi g.; exhibited Heneage Vivian 1937.
	White Glory		g.	irroratum x Loderi g.; (Dowager Lady Loder).
	White Glory		cl.	irroratum x Loderi g.; (Dowager Lady Loder); pure white except for pale crimson spotting within at back of corolla tube; A.M. (R.H.S.) 1937. See 'Pink Glory'.
	(White Lady)			See 'Kewdec White Lady'.
	White Lady		g.	'Halopeanum' x 'Loderi Pink Diamond'; (Loder); pure white. See 'Leonardslee Cream', 'Leonardslee Gertrude'.
	White Olympic Lady		cl.	'Loderi King George' x williamsianum (Olympic Lady g.); (Clarke); white. P.A. (A.R.S.) 1960.
	White Pearl		cl.	Syn. of 'Halopeanum'.
	White Samite	** C	cl.	'Corry Koster' x Loderi g.; white; A.M. (R.H.S.) 1932.
	White's Cunningham's Sulphur			a form of R. caucasicum raised from seed of 'Cunningham's Sulphur'; yellow; A.M. (R.H.S.) 1934.
xxx H-4	White Swan	*** C	cl.	decorum x 'Pink Pearl'; (Waterer, Sons & Crisp Ltd.); pale pink fading to white with green eye at base of upper corolla lobe; A.M. (R.H.S.) 1937; F.C.C. (R.H.S.) 1957.
	White Way		cl.	'Loder's White' x 'Mrs. Lindsay Smith'; (Digby 1952); white background with a faint, pale yellow blotch; A.M. (R.H.S.) 1952.
	White Wings		cl.	bullatum x ciliicalyx; (Scrase-Dickins); pure white with small greenish yellow blotch at base within; A.M. (R.H.S.) 1939.
	W. Hozier			pale pink.
	W. H. Punchard		cl.	(J. Waterer); Plum color, yellow center.
	Wiekhoff		g.	'Madame de Bruin' x williamsianum; (Dietrich Hobbie 1947); deep rose.
	Willamette		cl.	(D. W. James, 1960).
	Wilbar		g.	williamsianum x 'Barclayi'; (Aberconway 1946); rosy pink.
	Wilfred		g.	'Phidias' x williamsianum; (Aberconway 1946); pink.
	Wilgen's Ruby	B	cl.	(A. C. van Wilgen, Boskoop, 1951), bright deep red, outside corolla Turkish red (H.C.C. 721) towards rose red (H.C.C. 724) at edges; inside rose red (H.C.C. 724/1), dark brown blotch; F.C.C. (Boskoop) 1951.
	Wilhelm Weise		cl.	(T.J.R. Seidel); China white.
	Willem Barendtz		cl.	smirnowii x; (M. Koster & Sons); light crimson.
	Willem Vogt		cl.	griffithianum x; (C. B. van Nes & Sons); red.
	William Austin		cl.	catawbiense x; (J. Waterer before 1915); dark purplish crimson, spotted.
	William Cowper		cl.	(J. Waterer before 1922); bright scarlet. Syn. 'W. Cowper'.
	William Downing			cultivated Standish & Noble before 1870; rich puce, intense blotch.
	William Ewart Gladstone		cl.	(J. Waterer before 1882); deep rose. Syn. 'W. E. Gladstone'.
	William Godfrey			(A. Waterer); blush white, yellow spot.
	William Montgomery		cl.	'Astrosanguineum' x griersonianum (Atrier g.); (Gable); exhibited 1946; clear scarlet. Previously known as Atrier var. William Montgomery.
	William R. Coe		cl.	fortunei ? x; (Dexter); pink.
	Williamsonii			Azaleodendron; arboreum x molle; (B. S. Williams & Son); nearly white, tinted lilac; A.M. 1890.
	Williams' Seedling 'A'		cl.	'Broughtonii' x griffithianum; white.
	Williams' Seedling 'B'		cl.	'Broughtonii' x griffithianum; white, red spots.
	William Watson		cl.	'Ascot Brilliant' x griffithianum; (Gill); reddish outside, pink inside; A.M. (R.H.S.) 1925.
	William W. Drysdale		cl.	dichroanthum x 'Azor' hybrid; (Thacker 1944); orange.
	Wilsoni			Syn. of 'Laetevirens'.
	Wilsoni		g.	ciliatum x glaucum; pale rose
	Windbeam		cl.	'Conestoga' x; (Nearing); exhibited 1943; white changing to soft pale pink.
	Windsor Hawk		cl.	wardii x 'Lady Bessborough'.
	Windsori			(Reuthe Ltd. 1951).
	Windsor Lad	A		(Knap Hill Nursery); blush lilac with bold blotch.
	Winifred			exhibited Loder 1934.
	Winifred White			(W. C. Slocock 1920); pale pink, crimson edge.
	Wink		cl.	Loderi g. x 'Mrs. Mary Ashley'; (R. Henny); P.A. (A.R.S.) 1960.
	Winkfield		cl.	'Fusilier' x 'Jalisco Elect'; (Crown Estate Commissioners, Windsor Great Park, 1958); pinkish yellow flushed pink, tinged and spotted crimson in center; dorsal exterior and calyx mandarin red (H.C.C. 17); A.M. (R.H.S.) 1958.
	Winsome		g.	'Humming Bird' x griersonianum; (Aberconway).
	Winsome		cl.	'Humming Bird' x griersonianum; (Aberconway 1939); rosy cerise, neyron rose (H.C.C. 623), edges waved; A.M. (R.H.S.) 1950.
	Winston Churchill			(Kluis); scarlet.
	Withe Gem			white.
	Withe Pearl			blush pink, fading white.
	Wizard		cl.	'Catawbiense album' x 'Fabia'; (H. Lem, 1959); apricot-buff edged old rose; conspicuous apricot calyx; orange garden effect; A.E. (A.R.S.) 1959.
	W. Leith		cl.	Loderi g. x decorum; (Heneage-Vivian 1935); pale greenish cream, lobes recurved; A.M. (R.H.S.) 1935; awarded Loder Cup in 1934.

	W. Milton				(Young); dark crimson.
	Woislowitz				Syn. of 'Von Oheimb-Woislowitz'.
	(Wonder)				See 'Tortoiseshell Wonder'.
	Wonderland			cl.	(W. C. Slocock, 1958); pink buds opening white, light mustard spotting in throat; frilled; A.M. (R.H.S.) 1958.
	W. S. Reuthe		B	g.	'Staring' x williamsianum; (Dietrich Hobbie 1952); delicate rose.
	Wyanokie			cl.	'Conestoga' x; (Nearing); exhibited 1950; white.
	Xanchart			g.	trichocladum x chartophyllum;(Ingram 1935).
	Xanroy			g.	cinnabarinum var. roylei x xanthocodon; (Aberconway 1946); orange red.
	Xenarb			g.	detonsum x arboreum; (Magor 1926); deep cerise.
	Xenia			g.	'Helen Schiffner' x fortunei 'Mrs. Butler'; (Lowinsky); white with crimson lines at base; A.M. (R.H.S.) 1919.
	Yama			g.	'Yunncinn' x 'Lady Chamberlain'; (Aberconway 1946); yellowish Plum.
	Yanchart				(C. Ingram); exhibited 1935.
	Yellow Creek			cl.	'Sarita Loder' x 'Idealist'; (D.W. James, 1958); Primrose yellow (H.C.C. 601/2); P.A. (A.R.S.) 1958.
	Yellow Dwarf			g.	'Goldsworth Yellow' x dichroanthum; (Ramsden).
	Yellow Gem				Indo-Javanicum hybrid; rich yellow; A.M. 1893.
	Yellow Hammer	***	B	g.	sulfureum x flavidum (Williams); small yellow flowers.
	Yellow Jacket			cl.	wardii x 'Fabia'; (R. Henny).
	Yellow Perfection				'Lord Wolseley' x teysmannii; F. C. C. 1888.
	Yeoman			g.	forrestii var. repens x 'Choremia'; (Aberconway).
	Yeoman			cl.	forrestii var. repens. x 'Choremia'; (Aberconway 1946); turkey red (H.C.C. 721/1); A.M. (R.H.S.) 1947.
	Yolande			g.	scyphocalyx x 'Eudora'; (Aberconway 1941); rose.
	Youthful Sin			cl.	yunnanense x cinnabarinum (Yunncinn G.); (Aberconway, 1960); rhodamine purple (H.C.C. 29/2); A.M. (R.H.S.) 1960.
	Yucaba			g.	cinnabarinum x 'Yunncinn'; (Aberconway 1946); Plum.
	Yunncinn			g.	yunnanense x cinnabarinum; (Magor 1924); violet rose, darker on outside, reddish brown on interior.
	Yvonne	**	C	g.	'Aurora' x griffithianum; (Rothschild); white shaded clear pink.
	Yvonne Opaline	**	C	cl.	'Aurora' x griffithianum (Yvonne g.); (Rothschild); pink, buds darker; A.M. (R.H.S.) 1931. Previously known as Yvonne var. Opaline.
	Yvonne Pearl			cl.	'Aurora' x griffithianum (Yvonne g.) (Rothschild 1925); pale pink. Previously known as Yvonne var. Pearl.
	Yvonne Pride	**	C	cl.	'Aurora' x griffithianum (Yvonne g.); (Rothschild); pale pink fading almost white; A.M. (R.H.S.) 1948. Previously known as Yvonne var. Pride.
	Zaleutinii			cl.	augustinii x zaleucum; (Johnsone 1952).
	Zampa				cultivated Standish & Noble before 1870; deep lake, violet tinge.
	Zampa			g.	'Daphne' x 'F. C. Puddle'; (Aberconway 1941); red.
	Zanoni				cultivated Standish & Noble before 1870; crimson lake, spotted.
	Zarie			g.	catacosmum x meddianum; (J. B. Stevenson 1951); red.
	Zealander				exhibited Street; salmon pink.
	Zelenka / Zelanka				shell pink, tipped darker shade.
	Zenobia			g.	'Eros' x 'Arthur Osborn'; (Aberconway 1941); deep red.
	Zephyr			cl.	bright rosy red.
	Zora			g.	souliei x puralbum; (J. B. Stevenson 1951); white.
x H-4	Zuiderzee	**	B	cl.	'Mrs. Lindsay Smith' x campylocarpum hybrid; (M. Koster & Sons 1936); creamy yellow with small red spots on the throat; A.M. (R.H.S.) 1936. Syn. 'Zuÿder Zee'. See 'Greenfinch', 'Jersey Cream'.
	Zuyder Zee			cl.	Syn. of 'Zuiderzee'.

In every case where a full parentage formula is given, the first named is the FEMALE parent.

APPENDIX B

Rhododendron Hybridists and Introducers

ABBOTT, FRANK L., Bellows Falls, Vermont. Breeder for over 20 years.
ABERCONWAY, THE LORD. Bodnant, Tal y cafn, North Wales. (1879-1953.) Breeder, with Mr. F.C. Puddle, and species collector on a large scale for many years. Noted for red-flowered hybrids. Former owner of famed Bodnant Gardens, now open to the public under the British Trust plan. Succeeded by son.
ADAMS-ACTON, G. MURRAY, 37 Palace Gate, London, W. 8.
AMATEIS, EDMOND, Heath Haven, Brewster, N. Y. Began breeding in 1948.
BACHER, JOHN G., 1920 N. E. 7th Ave., Portland, Oregon. Started breeding in 1924, emphasizing early blooming hybrids.
BARTO, JAMES E., Junction City, Oregon. (1881-1940.) Grower and introducer of many fine species forms from 1925. Produced few hybrids.
BERTIN. Predecessor of Moser at the famous nursery at Versailles, France.
BLAAUW, J., & CO., Boskoop, Holland. Successors to C. B. van Nes. See also L. J. Endtz & Co.
BOLITHO, LIEUT.-COL. SIR EDWARD H. W., Trengwainton, Heamoor S. O., Penzance, Cornwall.
BOSLEY, PAUL, SR., Mentor, Ohio. Introducer of Dexter hybrids and breeder.
BOVEE, ROBERT M., S.W. Coronado & 16th Drive, Portland 19, Oregon. Began breeding Rhododendrons in 1950, emphasizing dwarf hybrids.
BRANDT, LESTER E., R.F.D. #5, Box 542, Tacoma, Washington. Started hybridizing in 1940 with emphasis on R. forrestii var. repens as a parent.
BYLS, J., Ghent, Belgium. Originator of arboreum hybrids about 1860-1875.
CASADEVALL, JOSEPH, 547 Newark-Pompton Tpke., Wayne, N. J. Specialist in breeding lepidote Rhododendrons.
CLARK, ROY W., 2101 Olympia Ave., Olympia, Washington. Started hybridizing in 1945.
CLARKE, COL. STEPHENSON, Borde Hill, Haywards Heath, Sussex.
CROSFIELD, THE LATE J. L., Embley Park, Hampshire.
CROWN ESTATE COMMISSIONERS, Windsor Great Park, Berkshire. Rhododendrons have been hybridized in Savill Gardens and in Valley Gardens by Sir Eric Savill and Mr. T. H. Findlay.
CUNNINGHAM. A nineteenth-century British nurseryman-breeder.
DEN OUDEN, H., & SONS, Boskoop, Holland. Nurserymen.
DE WILDE, ROLAND, Rhodo-Lake Nurseries, Bridgeton, N. J.
DEXTER, THE LATE C. O., Sandwich, Mass. Began crossing Rhododendrons on a large scale about 1925; d., 1943.
DIGBY, COL. THE LORD, Minterne, Dorchester, Dorset.
DOUGALL, CAPT. MAITLAND, R. N., Late of Lynwood, Woodham, Woking, Surrey.
EDINBURGH, ROYAL BOTANIC GARDEN, Edinburgh, Scotland.
ELLIOT, CLARENCE, Broadwell, Moreton-in-Marsh, Gloucestershire. Formerly of Six Hills Alpine Plant Nursery, Stevenage.
ENDTZ, L. J., & CO., Boskoop, Holland. Introducers of well-known hybrids; predecessors of J. Blaauw & Co.
FELIX & DIJKHUIS, Boskoop, Holland. Nurserymen.
FISHER. Owner of the Handsworth Nursery in Surrey.
FOX, THE LATE ROBERT BARCLAY, Penjerrick, Cornwall. Breeder, with Mr. Samuel Smith, of numerous well-known hybrids between 1910 and 1930.
FRANÇOIS BROS., Ghent, Belgium, Nurserymen.
FRETS, C., & SONS, Boskoop, Holland. Nurserymen.
GABLE, JOSEPH B., Stewartstown, Pa. Pioneer American species collector and hybridist; started breeding Rhododendrons about 1921.
GILL, RICHARD, & SONS, Tremough Gardens, Penryn, Cornwall. Owners of Himalayan Nurseries.
GIRARD, PETER, SR., Geneva, Ohio. Nurseryman.
GODMAN, THE LATE F. D., South Lodge, Horsham, Sussex.
GODMAN, THE MISSES EVA AND EDITH, South Lodge, Horsham, Sussex. Daughters of F. D. Godman.
GOWEN, J. R. Gardener at Highclere Castle, Newbury, Berkshire.
HALOPE. A Belgian breeder; introducer of 'Halopeanum'.
HARDGROVE, DONALD L., 100 Grace Ave., Merrick, L. I., New York.
HARDIJZER, P. W., Boskoop, Holland.
HARRISON, MAJOR-GEN. ERIC GEORGE WILLIAM WARDE, Tremeer, St. Tudy, Bodmin, Cornwall.
HAWORTH-BOOTH, MICHAEL, Farrall Nurseries, Roundhurst, Haslemere, Surrey.
HEADFORT, 4TH MARQUESS OF, Headfort, Kells, County Meath, Eire. d., 1943.
HENEAGE-VIVIAN, ADMIRAL WALKER, Clyne Castle, Blackpill, Swansea, Wales.
HENNY, RUDOLPH, Brooks, Oregon. Started hybridizing about 1940: originator of numerous new hybrid Rhododendrons.
HERBERT, THE VERY REVEREND DEAN WILLIAM. Nineteenth-century amateur British breeder.
HILLIER & SON, Winchester, Hampshire. Nurserymen.

HOBBIE, DIETRICH, Linswege, Oldenburgh, Germany. Large scale breeder, emphasizing hybrids of forrestii var. repens, williamsianum and chrysanthum.
HORLICK, COL. SIR JAMES N., BT., Isle of Gigha, Argyllshire, Scotland; formerly of Titness Farm, Sunninghill, Berkshire.
INGRAM, COLLINGWOOD, The Grange, Benenden, Kent.
JAMES, D.W., 2008 Floral Hill Drive, Eugene, Oregon.
JOHNSTONE, GEORGE H., Trewithen, Grampound Road, Cornwall. d., 1960.
KEW, THE ROYAL BOTANIC GARDENS, Richmond, Surrey.
KLUIS, ANTHONY. Nurseryman, formerly of Boskoop, Holland; in U.S.A. since 1948.
KNAP HILL NURSERY, LTD., Woking, Surrey. Producers of Rhododendron hybrids for over 150 years. (See WATERER, below.)
KOSTER, M., & SONS, Boskoop, Holland. Prominent Dutch nurserymen.
KOSTER, D.A., Boskoop, Holland. Nurserymen.
KOSTER & CO. (P. M. KOSTER), Boskoop, Holland. Now Koster Nursery at Bridgeton, N.J. (Since 1921.)
LANCASTER, B. F., R.F.D. #1, Box 20, Camas, Washington. Nurseryman breeding Rhododendrons since 1940.
LARSON, H. L., 3656 Bridgeport Way, Tacoma 66, Washington. Nurseryman.
LEACH, DAVID G., 15 Caldwell St., Brookville, Pa. Began hybridizing Rhododendrons for increased hardiness in 1945.
LEE & KENNEDY. Nurserymen in London.
LEM, HALFDAN, 19215 Aurora Ave., Seattle 33, Washington. Large scale breeder for many years.
LIMERICK, FIFTH EARL OF, Chiddinglye, West Hoathly, East Grinstead, Sussex.
LODER, SIR EDMUND G., BT., Leonardslee, Horsham, Sussex. Breeder of the Loderi group of Rhododendron hybrids. d., 1920.
LODER, SIR GILES, BT., Leonardslee, Horsham, Sussex. Grandson of Sir Edmund Loder.
LODER, LIEUT.-COL. GILES H., Dencombe, Handcross, Sussex.
LODER, THE LATE LADY. Daughter-in-law of Sir Edmund Loder.
LOWINSKY, THE LATE T. H., Tittenhurst, Sunninghill, Berkshire.
MAGOR, THE LATE E. J. P., Lamellan, St. Tudy, Cornwall. Species collector and breeder on a large scale early in twentieth century.
MANGLES, J. H., Valewood, Haslemere, Surrey. (1832-1884.)
MANGLES, THE LATE MISS CLARA, Littleworth, Farnham, Surrey. Sister of J. H. Mangles.
MASON, J. H., Liverpool.
MAXWELL, THE LATE SIR JOHN STIRLING, Pollock House, Pollokshaws, Glasgow, Scotland.
MESSEL, LIEUT.-COL. L. C. R., Nymans, Handcross, Sussex. d., 1952.
METHVEN, THOMAS & SON, Edinburgh, Scotland. Nurserymen.
MOSER ET FILS, Versailles, France. Nurserymen.
MULLIGAN, BRIAN O., Director, University of Washington Arboretum, Seattle, Washington. Started breeding Rhododendrons about 1947.
NEARING, GUY G., Box 402, Ramsey, N.J. Nurseryman, hybridist since 1928 and species collector.
NOBLE, CHARLES. A member of the firm of Standish & Noble (now Sunningdale Nurseries, Windlesham) and later an independent nurseryman.
NOBLE, MICHAEL A. C., Strone, Cairndow, Argyll, Scotland. Specializes in breeding the tender lepidote Rhododendrons.
NORTH, COL., an amateur British hybridist.
OOSTHOEK, P. J. C., & CO., Boskoop, Holland. Nurserymen.
OSTBO, THE LATE ENDRE, 2016 Lake Washington Boulevard, Bellevue, Washington. Pioneer Washington breeder and species collector.
PARKER. A British hybridist.
PARSONS, SAMUEL B., Flushing, L. I., New York. Pioneer nurseryman-breeder (1868) of Kissena Nurseries. (1819-1906.)
PAUL, GEORGE, Cheshunt, Hertfordshire. Originator of fortunei hybrids at The Old Nurseries before 1900.
PRIDE, ORLANDO S., Butler, Pa. Started hybridizing about 1934.
PUDDLE, F. C., Co-hybridist, with Lord Aberconway, at Bodnant, Tal-y-cafn, North Wales.
RAMSDEN, SIR JOHN, BT., Bullstrode, Gerrards Cross, Buckinghamshire.
REUTHE, G., LTD., Keston, Kent. Nurserymen.
ROLLISON. A British hybridist.
ROTHSCHILD, LIONEL DE, Exbury House, Exbury, Southampton. Owner of the celebrated Exbury gardens, species collector and creator of hundreds of Rhododendron hybrids from a massive breeding effort. d., 1942. Exbury Estate is now open to the public during the flowering season and one of its divisions operates a commercial nursery.
ROTHSCHILD, EDMUND DE, Exbury Estate, Exbury, Southampton. Son of Lionel de Rothschild.
ROYAL HORTICULTURAL SOCIETY'S GARDENS, Wisley, Ripley, Woking, Surrey.
RUSSELL, L. R., & CO., Richmond Nurseries, Windlesham, Surrey.
SAUVAGE. A Belgian breeder.
SCHULZ, OTTO. Head gardener at the Royal Porcelain Factory, Berlin, Germany. The griffithianum hybrids which he produced were sold in 1902 to C. B. van Nes & Sons of Boskoop for commercial introduction.
SCRASE-DICKINS, THE LATE C. R., Collhurst, Horsham, Sussex.
SEIDEL, T. J. R., Dresden en Grüngräbchen, Germany. Producer of a long list of hardy hybrids between 1880 and 1930.

SHAMMARELLO, A.M., 4590 Monticello Blvd., South Euclid 21, Ohio. A nurseryman-breeder of Rhododendrons since 1940.
SHILSON, THE LATE HENRY, Tremough, Penryn, Cornwall.
SKINNER, DR. HENRY T., Director of the United States National Arboretum, Washington, D.C.
SLOCOCK, WALTER C., Goldsworth Nurseries, Woking, Surrey.
SMITH, SAMUEL. Co-hybridist with Mr. Robert Barclay Fox of many Rhododendrons produced at Penjerrick.
SMITH, WILLIAM, Norbiton, Kingston, Surrey.
STAIR, THE EARL OF, Lochinch Castle, Stranraer, Wigtownshire, Scotland.
STANDISH. A partner, until 1857, in the firm of Standish & Noble (now Sunningdale Nurseries, Windlesham), and then operated individually as a nurseryman.
STANDISH & NOBLE. Nurserymen and hybridists prominent in Great Britain in the middle of the nineteenth century. Predecessors of Sunningdale Nurseries, Windlesham.
STAVORDALE, LORD, Abbotsbury, Dorset.
STEAD, W.T., Ilam, Ricarton Rd., Christchurch, New Zealand. Pioneer New Zealand species collector and breeder.
STEPHENSON CLARKE, COL. S.R., Borde Hill, Cuckfield, Sussex. d., 1948.
STEVENSON, JOHN B., Tower Court, Ascot, Berkshire. Species collector on a very large scale and hybridist. d., 1950.
STEVENSON, MRS. ROZA M., Tower Court, Ascot, Berkshire. Widow of John B. Stevenson.
STEWART & SON, Ferndown Nurseries, Dorset.
STIRLING-MAXWELL. A British breeder.
STOKES, WARREN E., Butler, Pa. Nurseryman.
SUNNINGDALE NURSERY, THE, Windlesham, Surrey.
SWAYTHLING, THE LORD, Bridley Manor, Worplesdon, Surrey; formerly of Townhill Park, Southampton, Hampshire, where some notable hybrids were produced.
THACKER, T.C., Knowle Nurseries, Knowle, Warwickshire.
THOMPSON. A hybridist in Great Britain.
TOPSVOORT NURSERY, Aalsmeer, Holland.
VAN NES, C.B., & SONS, Boskoop, Holland. Predecessors of J. Blaauw & Co., Boskoop nurserymen.
VAN NES, AZ. P., Boskoop, Holland. Nurseryman.
VAN NOORDT, P., & SONS, Boskoop, Holland. Nurserymen.
VAN TOL, J.C., Boskoop, Holland. Nurseryman.
VAN VEEN, THEODORE, 3127 S.E. 43rd Ave., Portland, Oregon. Nurseryman.
VEITCH, JAMES, MESSRS., & SONS, Royal Exotic Nurseries, King's Road, Chelsea, London. Active from 1792 to 1913 as Rhododendron specialists and sponsors of exploration for the discovery of new species in Asia.
VERVAENE, DOMIEN, Ghent, Belgium. Nurseryman and breeder active from 1833 to 1876.
VOSSBERG, PAUL, of Westbury Rose Co., Westbury, L.I., New York. Introducer of Dexter hybrid Rhododendrons.
VUYK VAN NES (A. VUYK), Boskoop, Holland.
WALLACE, ROBERT. d., 1954; Robert Wallace & Co., The Old Gardens, Tunbridge Wells, Kent; now Messrs. Wallace & Barr.
WATERER, MICHAEL, SR. (1745-1827), founder of Knap Hill Nursery and pioneer Rhododendron hybridist.
WATERER, MICHAEL, JR. (1770-1842), son of Michael, Sr., and inheritor of Knap Hill Nursery; founder of the Bagshot nursery.
WATERER, HOSEA (1793-1852), brother of Michael, Jr., and inheritor of Knap Hill Nursery.
WATERER, JOHN, SR. (1783-1868), brother of Michael, Jr., and inheritor of the Bagshot nursery, John Waterer (& Sons), Bagshot.
WATERER, JOHN, JR., Son of John, Sr., and inheritor of the family nursery at Bagshot.
WATERER, ANTHONY, SR. (1822-1896), nephew of Hosea Waterer, Sr., and inheritor of Knap Hill Nursery. Creator of many Rhododendron hybrids still popular today.
WATERER, ANTHONY, JR. (1848-1924), son of Anthony, Sr., and inheritor of the Knap Hill Nursery.
WATERER, HOSEA, II, brother of Anthony, Jr., and inheritor of Knap Hill Nursery, which closed in 1925.
WATERER, GOMER, son of John Waterer, Jr., originally with the Bagshot nursery. Reopened the Knap Hill Nursery in 1930. Creator of many fine hybrids in the years 1900-1939.
WATERER, JOHN, SONS & CRISP, LTD., The Nurseries, Bagshot, Surrey.
WEZELENBERG, K., & SON, Hazerswoude, Holland. Nurserymen.
WHITAKER, W.I., Pylewell Park, Lymington, Hampshire.
WHITE, HARRY G. Manager of the Sunningdale Nurseries, Windlesham, Surrey. (1897-1936.)
WHITNEY, W.E., 565 W. Third St., Camas, Washington.
WILDING, EUSTACE HENRY, Wexham Place, Stoke Poges, Buckinghamshire. d., 1939.
WILLIAMS, COMDR. ALFRED M., R.N., Werrington Park, Cornwall.
WILLIAMS, THE LATE JOHN CHARLES, Caerhays Castle, Gorran, Cornwall. d., 1939. Succeeded by the late Charles Williams and then by Julian Williams.
WILLIAMS, THE LATE PERCIVAL DACRES, Lanarth, St. Keverne, Cornwall. d., 1939. Succeeded by Michael Williams.
WRIGHT. Nurseryman at Clyne, Swansea, South Wales.
YOUNGER BOTANIC GARDEN, Ben More, Argyllshire, Scotland.

Note: The Waterers, above, are purposely out of strict alphabetical sequence for easier understanding of the complicated relationship.

APPENDIX C

Nurseries Specializing in Rhododendrons

The following nurseries offer Rhododendrons as one of their specialties and in some cases grow nothing else. This list was compiled from advertisements in trade publications and from information furnished by leading amateur specialists in each region. Some fine professional growers will inevitably be overlooked in any such nation-wide roster assembled from many sources and their inadvertent omission has no significance whatever. Each of the nurserymen below responded to a questionnaire with the information noted opposite his name.

	Number of Sorts Usually Offered	*R=Retail W=Whole-sale*	*LS=Larger Sizes for landscaping Sm=Small plants for lining out*	*Mail Orders Shipped?*	*Specialty*
New England					
Adams Nursery, Inc., Box 525, Westfield, Mass.	10	R & W	LS	No.	
Cherry Hill Nurseries, West Newbury, Mass.	15	R & W	LS	Yes.	
Little Tree Nurseries, Central St., Rowley, Mass.		R & W	Sm&LS	Yes.	
Rhode Island Nurseries, E. Main Rd., Newport, R.I.	18	W	Sm&LS		
Tumble Brook Rhododendron Nursery, 17 Simsbury Rd., West Hartford 7, Conn.	70		Sm	Yes.	Own-root liners.
Van Tol Nurseries, Box 115, Teaticket, Cape Cod, Mass.	18	R & W	Sm&LS	Yes.	
Weston Nurseries, Inc., Frankland St., Hopkinton, Mass.	40	R & W	LS	No.	
Wyman's Framingham Nurseries, Inc., Worcester Rd., Framingham, Mass.	20	W	LS	No.	
Wyman's Garden Centers, Inc., Worcester Rd., Framingham, Mass.	20	R	LS	No.	
Pennsylvania - New York - New Jersey					
Andorra Nurseries, Inc., Ridge Pike & Crescent Ave., Lafayette Hill, Pa.	18	R & W	LS	No.	
Angelica Nurseries, RFD #1, Mohnton, Pa.	100	R & W	Sm&LS	Yes.	Own-root liners.
Appalachian Nurseries, Box 87, Waynesboro, Pa.	18	W	Sm	Yes.	Own-root liners.
Backhaus Nursery, RFD #1, Renfrew, Pa.					
Warren Baldsiefen, Nurseryman, 89 Forest Place, Rochelle Park, N. J.	75	R & W	Sm&LS	Yes.	New introductions, own-root.
Bobbink Nurseries, 586 Paterson Ave., East Rutherford, N. J.	15	R & W	Sm&LS	Yes.	
Crystalaire Rhododendron Nursery, RFD #3, Slippery Rock, Pa.	25	R & W	Sm&LS	Yes.	Own-root liners.
Curtis Nurseries, Inc., Callicoon, N. Y.	7	R & W	Sm&LS	Yes.	Native species.
Dauber's Nurseries, 1705 North George St., York, Pa.		R & W	Sm&LS	No.	
Davis Mt. Airy Nurseries, Stenton & Mt. Airy Ave., Philadelphia 50	12	R	Sm&LS	No.	
deWilde's Rhodo-Lake Nurseries, RFD #1, Bridgeton, N. J.	65	R & W	LS	No.	
East Northport Nurseries, 415 Clay Pitts Rd., East Northport, N. Y.	20	W	Sm&LS	No.	Own-root liners.
William Efinger, Jr., Nurseryman, Sherwood Hill Rd., Brewster, N.Y.					
F. & F. Nurseries, 277 Milltown Road, Springfield, N.J.	20	W	Sm&LS	No.	
Fairview Evergreen Nurseries, Box E, Fairview, Pa.	20	W	LS	No.	
Joseph B. Gable, Stewartstown, Pa.	340	R & W	Sm&LS	Yes.	Species and hybrids.
Greendyke's Gardens, RFD #1, Hamburg Turnpike, Paterson, N.J.	10	R & W	LS	No.	
Green Meadow Nursery, Harriot Ave., Harrington Park, N.J.					
Heasley's Nurseries, 247 Freeport Road, Butler, Pa.	12	R & W	Sm&LS	No.	
P. D. Hileman, RFD #4, Kittanning, Pa.					
Hindla's Nursery, Bohemia, L.I., New York					Native species.
Kordus Nursery, Deer Park Ave., RFD #4, Box 152, Huntington, L.I., New York					Own-root liners.
Koster Nursery, Bridgeton, N. J.	25	W	Sm&LS	No.	Own root plants.
LaBars' Rhododendron Nursery, Stroudsburg, Pa.	30	R & W	Sm&LS	Yes.	Native species.
Levick Nursery Co., RFD #3, Bridgeton, N. J.		W	LS	Yes	
Marbarju Gardens, RFD #1, West Lake Road, Lake City, Pa.	12	R & W	Sm&LS	Yes.	
Musser Forests, Inc., Indiana, Pa.					
G. G. Nearing, Box 402, Ramsey, N. J.	50	R & W	LS	No.	Species and hybrids.
Parmentier's Roses, Grady St., Bayport, L.I., New York.					
Walter E. Peffer, Sandra Drive, Level Green, RFD #1, Trafford, Pa.	8	R & W	Sm&LS	Yes.	
Orlando S. Pride, Nurseryman, 523 5th St., Butler, Pa.	35	R & W	Sm&LS	No.	Own root plants.
Rickert Nurseries, Morrisville, Pa.					

	Number of Sorts Usually Offered	*R=Retail W=Whole-sale*	*LS=Larger Sizes for landscaping Sm=Small plants for lining out*	*Mail Orders Shipped?*	*Specialty*
Rosedale Nurseries, Inc., Saw Mill River Parkway, Eastview, N.Y.		R	LS	Yes.	
William Schlupp, Branch Pike & Church Rd., Palmyra, N.J.					Own-root liners.
Ned W. Schrope, Hegins Valley Nursery, RFD, Hegins, Pa.	10	R	LS	No.	
Sepers Nursery, N. Delsea Drive, Vineland, N.J.					
Springfield Nursery, 492 Mountain Ave., Springfield, N.J.					
Squirrel Hill Nursery, 2945 Beechwood Blvd., Pittsburgh, Pa.					
Warren E. Stokes, RFD #6, Butler, Pa.		W	LS	No.	
Thornton Nurseries, RFD #1, Conneaut Lake, Pa.	13	R & W	LS	No.	
Valley Nursery, 2951 Shadagee Rd., Eden, N.Y.	95				
Verkade's Nurseries, Wayne, N.J.	20	W	Sm	No.	
John Vermeulen & Son, Inc., Woodfern Rd., Neshanic Station, N.J.	25	W	Sm	Yes.	
James S. Wells Nursery, Box 141, Red Bank, N.J.					Own root plants.
Westbury Rose Co., Inc., Jericho Turnpike, Westbury, L.I., N.Y.	115	W	Sm&LS	No.	Own-root liners.
Wilkinson Nursery, Ambrust, Pa.					
Windy Hill Nurseries, Dr. C.R. Shuster, Saltsburg, Pa.	15	R & W	Sm&LS	Yes.	

Central States and Ohio

Edward L. Abell, 421 Moccasin Ave., Buchanan, Mich.					
Azalea Gardens, R. A. West, 9204 S. 29th St., RFD #1, Scotts, Mich.	21	R & W	LS	Yes.	
C. Barbre, 302 Hillside Ave., Webster Groves 19, Missouri	10	R & W	LS	No.	
The Bosley Nursery, Mentor Ave., Mentor, Ohio	20	R & W	Sm&LS	Yes.	
East Hill Nurseries, Chesterland, Ohio		R & W	Sm&LS	No.	
Gerard K. Klyn, Inc., Mentor, Ohio					
Girard Bros. Nurseries, RFD #4, Geneva, Ohio	18	R & W	Sm&LS	Yes.	
Green Ridge Nursery, Middle Ridge & Route 528, Madison					
Gullo Nurseries, 2221 Mentor Ave., Painesville, Ohio					
Ted Leitzell, 1735 Wesley Ave., Evanston, Ill.	7	R & W	LS	Yes.	
Lincoln Nurseries, RFD #2, Grand Rapids 4, Mich.					
Charles W. Mann, S. Maple St., Saugatuck, Mich.	13	R & W	LS	Yes.	
Northern Azalea Gardens, 823 DeGroff St., Grand Ledge, Mich.					
Red Mill Nursery, Route #20, Perry, Ohio	30	W	LS	No.	
A. Shammarello & Son Nursery, 4590 Monticello Blvd., South Euclid 21, Ohio	40	R & W	Sm&LS	No.	Shammarello hybrids.
E. Stroombeek Nursery, 278 Green Rd., North Madison, Ohio	35	R & W	Sm&LS		New introductions, own-root.
Zophar P. Warner, Willoughby, Ohio					
Westcroft Gardens, Grosse Ile, Mich.	25	R & W	Sm&LS	No.	

Middle Atlantic and Southern States

Aldridge Rhododendron Nurseries, Crossnore, N.C.	12	W	LS	No.	
Behnke Nurseries, Washington-Baltimore Blvd., Beltsville, Md.	60	R & W	LS	No.	
Cole Nurseries, Box 443 Bluefield, W. Va.		R & W	LS	Yes.	
Ellerslie Nursery, Glenwood, Md.	20	W	Sm&LS	No.	
Gladsgay Gardens, 6311 Three Chopt Rd., Richmond, Virginia		R & W	Sm&LS		
Greenbrier Farms, Inc., RFD #3, Box 52-A, Norfolk 6, Va.		R & W	LS		
Haddock Nursery, Box 603, Silver Spring, Md.	90	R			British hybrids.
Hagerstown Nursery Co., Inc., Virginia Ave. & Nursery Rd., Hagerstown, Md.	10	R		No.	
Kingsville Nursery, Kingsville, Md.		R			
Laird's Nurseries, 8900 W. Broad St. Rd., Richmond, Va.	8	R & W	Sm&LS	Yes.	
Mountain View Nurseries, Box 1144, Greenville, South Carolina		R & W	LS	No.	
E. C. Robbins, Gardens of the Blue Ridge, Ashford, North Carolina		R & W	LS	Yes	Native species.
Rock Creek Nursery, M. G. Coplen, Rockville, Md.	40	R & W	Sm&LS	Yes.	
Frank A. Smith & Co., 225 Phass Rd., N.E., Atlanta, Georgia		R & W	LS	No.	
Stone Mountain Gardens, 7400 Bowers Rd., Stone Mountain, Georgia	20	R	LS	Yes.	
Ten Oaks Nursery & Gardens, Inc., Clarksville, Md.	30	R & W	Sm&LS	Yes.	
Towson Nurseries, Inc., Paper Mill Rd., Cockeysville, Md.	40	R & W	Sm&LS	Yes.	
Vadma Nursery Agency, Inc., Hideaway Rd., Fairfax, Va.	20	R	LS	No.	
Watkins Nurseries, RFD #2, Midlothian, Va.	8	R & W	LS	Yes.	
Westminster Nurseries, Inc., Box 227, Westminster, Md.	15	W	LS	No.	
Wood-Howell Nurseries, Inc., 4473 Lee Highway, Bristol, Va.	11	R & W	LS	Yes.	

Washington - Oregon - California

Bonnell Nurseries, 14455 Rainier Ave., Renton, Wash.	55	R & W	Sm&LS	Yes.	
Bonnybrook Nursery, 14237 100th Ave., N.E., Bothell, Wash.	45	R & W	Sm&LS	Yes.	Dwarf species.
The Bovees, S.W. Coronado St. & 16th Drive, Portland, Oregon	250	R & W	Sm&LS	Yes.	Species, own-root liners.
Carlton Nursery Co., Box 8, Forest Grove, Ore.	75	R & W	LS	Yes.	

	Number of Sorts Usually Offered	R=Retail W=Wholesale	LS=Larger Sizes for landscaping Sm=Small plants for lining out	Mail Orders Shipped?	Specialty
J. Harold Clarke, Long Beach, Wash.	150	R & W	Sm&LS	Yes.	
Comerford's, Box 100, Marion, Oregon	180	R	LS	Yes.	Exbury hybrids.
Cranguyma Farms, Long Beach, Wash.	200	R & W	Sm&LS	Yes.	
F. A. Doerfler & Sons Nursery, 250 N. Lancaster Drive, Salem, Ore.	100	R & W	Sm&LS	Yes.	
John S. Druecker Nurseries, Box 511, Fort Bragg, California	150	R & W	LS	Yes.	
Esch & Seven Dees Nurseries, 6025 S. E. Powell St., Portland, Ore.	100	R & W	Sm&LS	Yes.	Own-root liners.
Flora Markeeta, 22925 102nd Place West, Edmonds, Wash.	300	R	Sm&LS	Yes.	
Floral Nursery, 17317 S.E. McLoughlin St., Portland 2, Ore.	200	R & W	Sm&LS	Yes.	
Gomes Nursery, 9875 MacArthur Blvd., Oakland 5, California	40	R	LS	No.	
Henny & Wennekamp, Inc., Box 212, Brooks, Ore.	200	R & W	Sm&LS	Yes.	
Rudolph Henny, Box 162, Brooks, Ore.	100	R & W	LS	Yes.	Species; own hybrids.
Hillside Nursery, 16809 S. E. Oatfield Rd., Milwaukie, Oregon			LS		
Homestead Nursery, Box 541, Redmond, Wash.	50	R	Sm&LS	Yes.	
Hopkins Nursery, RFD#2, Box 714, Bothell, Wash.	50	R	Sm&LS	Yes.	
Lackamas Gardens, RFD #1, Box 20, Camas, Wash.	150	R & W	Sm&LS	Yes.	
H. L. Larson, 3656 Bridgeport Way, Tacoma 66, Wash.	300	R & W	Sm&LS	Yes.	Species.
Lem Nursery, 19215 Aurora Ave., Seattle 33, Wash.	350	R & W	Sm&LS	Yes.	Species; own hybrids.
Irving B. Lincoln, 221 American Bank Bldg., Portland 5, Ore.	250	R & W	Sm&LS	Yes.	
Malmo Nurseries & Garden Store, 4700 25th Ave., N.E., Seattle, Wash.	150	R & W	LS	Yes.	
I. Owen Ostbo, 2016 Lake Washington Blvd., Bellevue, Wash.	150	R & W	LS		
Peppe's Nursery, 3616 S.E. Lake Road, Milwaukie 22, Ore.	50		Sm&LS	Yes.	
Portland Camellia Nursery, 10250 N.E. Pacific St., Portland 16, Ore.	75	R & W		Yes.	
Rainier Mt. Alpine Gardens, 2007 S. 126th St., Seattle 88, Wash.	150	R & W	Sm&LS	Yes.	Species.
Rhododendron Nursery, 4229 S.E. Division St., Portland 15, Ore.	75	R & W	Sm&LS	Yes.	
Richmond Nurseries, Richmond Beach, Wash.	65	R & W	Sm&LS	Yes.	
L.N. Roberson Co., 1539 E. 103rd St., Seattle 55, Wash.					
Seven Firs Nursery, RFD #1, Box 147, North Bend, Wash.	200	R & W	Sm&LS	Yes.	
State Flower Nursery, RFD #2, Box 5, Bothell, Wash.	60	W	Sm&LS	Yes.	
Swiss Florales, 1920 N.E. 9th Ave., Portland 12, Ore.		R & W		Yes.	Species.
Taylor Nurseries, 4647 Union Bay Place, Seattle 5, Wash.	115	R	LS	Yes.	
Van Veen Nursery, 3127 S.E. 43rd Ave., Portland 6, Ore.	70	W	Sm	Yes.	
Vic Mix Campus Nursery, 5000 25th Ave., N.E., Seattle 2, Wash.		R	Sm&LS	No.	
West Oregon Nursery, 3550 N.W. Saltzman Rd., Portland 1, Ore.	75	W	Sm&LS	Yes.	
J. B. Whalley, RFD # 2, Box 683, Troutdale, Ore.	100	W	Sm	Yes.	
Woodland Acres, 9945 S. W. Beaverton-Hillsdale Hwy., Beaverton, Ore.				No.	
Wright's Nursery, 16020 S.E. Harold Ave., Milwaukee, 22, Ore.	110	R & W	Sm&LS	Yes.	

Canada

Ancaster Nurseries, Ancaster, Ontario	20	R	LS	No.	
Layritz Nurseries, Ltd., R.R. 3, Victoria, British Columbia	500	R	Sm&LS	Yes.	
Royston Nursery, Box 228 Royston, British Columbia	200	R		Yes.	Species.
Woodland Nurseries, Cooksville, Ontario					

England

Exbury Estate, Exbury, Southampton
Hillier & Sons, Winchester
Knap Hill Nursery Ltd. Woking, Surrey
G. Reuthe Ltd., Keston, Kent
Walter C. Slocock Ltd., Woking, Surrey
Frederick Street, West End, Woking, Surrey
The Sunningdale Nurseries, Windlesham, Surrey
John Waterer, Sons & Crisp Ltd. Bagshot, Surrey

Holland

Felix & Dijkhuis, Boskoop
F. J. Grootendorst & Sons, Boskoop
The Homestead Nurseries, Boskoop
M. Koster & Zonen, Boskoop
J. Blaauw & Co., Boskoop
Vuyk van Nes, Boskoop

Germany

Dietrich Hobbie, Linswege, Oldenburgh

APPENDIX D

Alphabetical Listing of all Rhododendron Species

Readers are referred to the listing of synonyms on page 531 for the valid names of species not found below. The species listed in capital letters are described in detail among the sorts important to horticulture, beginning on page 122. A listing of the series and subseries, with the species in each, starts on page 521. Species newly described and classified by Sleumer in Section Vireya (the so-called Javanicum Rhododendrons and those added to the former Vaccinioides Series) are not included in the alphabetical listing below but will be found listed by their subsections and series beginning on page 528.

Species	*Series Affiliation*	*Subseries Affiliation*	*Scaly or Non-Scaly*	*American Quality Rating*	*British Quality Rating*	*American Hardiness Rating*	*British Hardiness Rating*	*Season of Bloom*	*Color of Flower*	*Height*
ABERCONWAYII	Irroratum	Irroratum	NS		****		B	May	white, pink	5-10'
aberrans	Lacteum		NS				B	April	white, rose	15'
achroanthum	Lapponicum		S	0		H-2	A	April, May	magenta-red	3'
adenogynum	Taliense	Adenogynum	NS	X	*	H-2	A	April	white, lavender	9'
adenophorum	Taliense	Adenogynum	NS		*		A	April	rose	8'
ADENOPODUM	Ponticum	Caucasicum	NS		**		A	May	pale rose	6'
aechmophyllum	Triflorum	Yunnanense	S				B	April	rose	10'
afghanicum	Triflorum	Hanceanum	S				A or B B	July, August	whitish-green	18'
aganniphum	Taliense	Taliense	NS				A	May, June	white, pink	15'
agapetum	Irroratum	Parishii	NS		****		F	June	scarlet	20'
agastum	Irroratum	Irroratum	NS			H-4	D		deep rose, pink	20'
agglutinatum	Lacteum		NS	X		H-3	B	April	white, pink	15'
alabamense	Azalea	Luteum	NS		**		B	April, May	white	4-5'
albertsenianum	Neriiflorum	Neriiflorum	NS				B	April	rose-crimson	7'
ALBIFLORUM	Albiflorum		NS				A	June, July	white, yellow	6'
albrechtii	Azalea	Canadense	NS		****		B	April, May	rose	10'
alpicola	Lapponicum		S				A		lavender-purple	3'
alutaceum	Taliense	Adenogynum	NS				A	April	rose	14'
amagianum	Azalea	Schlippenbachii	NS		***		A	June, July	orange-red,	12'
amandum	Maddenii	Ciliicalyx	S						pale lemon-yellow	6'
AMBIGUUM	Triflorum	Triflorum	S	X	**	H-4	A	April, May	pale yellow	10'
amesiae	Triflorum	Polylepis	S			H-4	A	May	purple	12'
amundsenianum	Lapponicum		S						flower unknown	1'
annae	Irroratum	Irroratum	NS		***		B	June, July	white flushed rose, purple spots	8'
annamense	Azalea	Obtusum	NS				F		rose-purple	6'e
anthopogon	Anthopogon		S		**		A	April	pink, yellow	2'
anthopogonoides	Anthopogon		S				A		white, whitish-pink, yellow	4
anthosphaerum	Irroratum	Irroratum	NS				C	March, April	rose-magenta to mauve	30'
anwheiense	Barbatum	Maculiferum	NS				B	April, May		12'
APERANTUM	Neriiflorum	Sanguineum	NS	X	**	H-3	B	April, May	white, rose, red orange, yellow, purple	6-20"
apiculatum	Triflorum	Oreotrephes	S				C			5'
APODECTUM (Ssp.)	Neriiflorum	Sanguineum	NS	XX	**	H-4	A	May, June	orange, crimson	$2\frac{1}{2}$'
araiophyllum	Irroratum	Irroratum	NS		***		D	April	white or white suffused rose	16'
arborescens	Azalea	Luteum	NS		***		A	June, July	white	8-18'
ARBOREUM	Arboreum	Arboreum	NS	XXXX	****	H-4	C	Jan., April	crimson, pink, white	30-40'
argipeplum	Barbatum	Barbatum	NS						crimson	15'
argyrophyllum	Arboreum	Argyrophyllum	NS	X	***	H-3	A	May	white, pink	20'
ARIZELUM	Falconeri		NS	XX	**	H-4	B	April	white, yellow, rose, crimson	20'
artosquameum	Triflorum	Oreotrephes	S	X	**		B	May	rose, purple, mauve	12'
asperulum	Vaccinioides		S				E		pink	3'e
asterochnoum									white suffused rose	14'e
atjehense	Irroratum	Irroratum	NS							

Species	Series Affiliation	Subseries Affiliation	Scaly or Non-Scaly	American Quality Rating	British Quality Rating	American Hardiness Rating	British Hardiness Rating	Season of Bloom	Color of Flower	Height
atlanticum	Azalea	Luteum	NS		***		B	May	white, pink	2-6'
atrovirens	Azalea	Obtusum	NS						red	14'e
AUGUSTINII	Triflorum	Augustinii	S	XXXX	****	H-3	B	May	lavender-rose, violet, white, pink	15'
AURICULATUM	Auriculatum		NS	XXX	***	H-3	B	July-Aug.	white, rose-pink	15'
auritum	Boothii	Tephropeplum	S	XX	**	H-5	C	April	yellow	5'
austrinum	Azalea	Luteum	NS				C	April	yellow-orange	8'
bachii	Ovatum		NS				E	April, May	rosy-lilac	6'
baileyi	Lepidotum	Baileyi	S		**	H-4	B	May	reddish-purple	6'
bainbridgeanum	Barbatum	Crinigerum	NS	0	**	H-2	B	April	white, creamy-yellow	6'
bakeri	Azalea	Luteum	NS				A	June, July	yellow, orange, scarlet	6-9'
balfourianum	Taliense	Adenogynum	NS		*		B	April	white, ivory	8'
BARBATUM	Barbatum	Barbatum	NS	XXXX	***	H-4	B	March, Apr.	crimson-scarlet	30'
basilicum	Falconeri		NS	XX	***	H-3	B	April	yellow, crimson, pink	30'
bathyphyllum	Taliense	Roxieanum	NS				A	April, May	white	5'
bauhiniiflorum	Triflorum	Triflorum	S	X	**	H-4	B	May	lemon yellow	8'
BEANIANUM	Neriiflorum	Haematodes	NS	XXX	***	H-4	B	April	scarlet, pink	8'
beesianum	Lacteum		NS	0	*	H-2	B	April	white, rose	25'
bivelatum	Triflorum	Augustinii	S						rose	6'e
blepharocalyx	Lapponicum		S				A	April, May	mauve	3'
BODINIERI	Triflorum	Yunnanense	S		**		B	April, May	rose, white	8'
boninense	Azalea	Obtusum	NS						white	6'
bonvalotii	Thomsonii	Cerasinum	NS						rose	8'e
boothii	Boothii	Boothii	S		**		F	April, May	yellow	6'
brachyanthum	Glaucophyllum	Glaucophyllum	S		*		A	June, July	yellow	3'
BRACHYCARPUM	Ponticum	Caucasicum	NS	X	**	H-2	A	June	cream, pink	9'
brachysiphon	Maddenii	Maddenii	S				F	June	pink	8'
bracteatum	Triflorum	Oreotrephes	S				B	June	white	6'
brevinerve	Irroratum	Irroratum	NS							
breviperulatum	Azalea	Obtusum	NS							
brevistylum	Heliolepis		S	0	**	H-4	A	June, July	rose	10'
brookeanum			S				F	April, May	orange, scarlet	
BULLATUM	Edgeworthii		S	XXXX	****	H-5	D	April, May	white, pink	8'
bulu	Lapponicum		S						white, mauve	5'
bureavii	Taliense	Adenogynum	NS	XX	**	H-2	B	April	rose	8'
bureavioides	Taliense	Adenogynum	NS		*		B	April	rose	8'
BURMANICUM	Maddenii	Ciliicalyx	S	XX	**	H-5	F	April, May	yellow, greenish-white	6'
caeruleum	Triflorum	Yunnanense	S	XXXX	*	H-3	B	May	rose-lavender, white	5'
caesium	Triflorum	Triflorum	S				B	May	yellow	5'e
calendulaceum	Azalea	Luteum	NS		***		A	May, June	yellow, orange, scarlet, pink	15'
CALLIMORPHUM	Thomsonii	Campylocarpum	NS	XXX	****	H-4	B	April, May	rose	2-11'
calophyllum	Maddenii	Maddenii	S				F	June	white	5'
CALOPHYTUM	Fortunei	Calophytum	NS	XXXX	****	H-3	B	Mar., April	white, pink	20'
CALOSTROTUM	Saluenense		S	XXX	****	H-3	A	May	pink, purple, rose-red	15-48"
CALOXANTHUM	Thomsonii	Campylocarpum	NS	XXX	***	H-2	C	April, May	orange, yellow	2-8'
calvescens			NS						rose	6'
camelliaeflorum	Camelliaeflorum		S				D	June, July	white tinged with pink	6'
CAMPANULATUM	Campanulatum		NS	XXX	***	H-2	A	April	white, pink, purplish blue	20'
CAMPYLOCARPUM	Thomsonii	Campylocarpum	NS	XXXX	****	H-3	B	April, May	yellow, white	4-12'
CAMPYLOGYNUM	Campylogynum		S	XX	**	H-2	A	May	pink, purple, crimson	2"-4'
camtschaticum	Camtschaticum		NS	X	**	H-2	A	May	reddish-purple	9"
canadense	Azalea	Canadense	NS		*		A	April	rose-purple, white	1-3'
canescens	Azalea	Luteum	NS		*		A	April, May	pink, white	12-15'
capitatum	Lapponicum		S				A	April, May	mauve	3'
cardiobasis	Fortunei	Orbiculare	NS	XX		H-4			white, rose	10'
carneum	Maddenii	Ciliicalyx	S	XXX	**	H-7	F	April, May	whitish-pink	8'
CAROLINIANUM	Carolinianum		S	XX	*	H-2	A	May	pink, mauve, white	7'

Species	Series Affiliation	Subseries Affiliation	Scaly or Non-Scaly	American Quality Rating	British Quality Rating	American Hardiness Rating	British Hardiness Rating	Season of Bloom	Color of Flower	Height
catacosmum	Neriiflorum	Haematodes	NS		***		B	Mar., April	crimson-rose, scarlet	9'
CATAWBIENSE	Ponticum	Ponticum	NS	X	*	H-1	A	May, June	magenta, pink, white, red	9'
CAUCASICUM	Ponticum	Caucasicum	NS	X	*	H-3	A	May	white, yellowish	2'
cavaleriei	Stamineum		NS						white, rose	9'
cephalanthum	Anathopogon		S		**		B	May	white, pink, yellow	4'
cerasinum	Thomsonii	Cerasinum	NS		***		B	May	cherry-red, creamy white	12'
cerochitum	Irroratum	Irroratum	NS				C		rose	20'
chaetomallum	Neriiflorum	Haematodes	NS	XXX	***	H-4	B	Mar., April	crimson, creamy yellow	10'
chamae-thomsonii	Neriiflorum	Forrestii	NS				B	April	red, yellow, white, pink	1-3'
chamaezelum	Lapponicum		S				A	April, May	yellow	8"
chameunum	Saluenense		S		*		A	May, June	purple-rose	2'
championae	Stamineum		NS				F	April, May	white, pink	18'
CHAPMANII	Carolinianum		S	X		H-3	B	May	rose	6'
charianthum	Triflorum	Yunnanense	S		**		B	April, May	rose	10'
charitopes	Glaucophyllum	Glaucophyllum	S		**		B	April, May	pink	4'
CHARTOPHYLLUM	Triflorum	Yunnanense	S	XXX	***	H-3	B	April, May	pink, white	6-8'
CHASMANTHUM	Triflorum	Augustinii	S	XXX	***	H-4	C	May	mauve, violet	10'
chengianum	Fortunei	Fortunei	NS						white	20'
chengshienianum	Triflorum	Triflorum	S						yellow	10'
chienianum	Arboreum	Argyrophyllum	NS						magenta, mauve	30'
chionanthum	Neriiflorum	Haematodes	NS	X		H-4	B	April	white	3'
chloranthum	Trichocladum		S		*		A	June	yellow	7'
chlorops	Fortunei	Fortunei	NS				B	May	yellow, ivory, blotched purple	10'
CHRYSANTHUM	Ponticum	Caucasicum	NS	0	*	H-3	B	April, May	ivory	8"
CHRYSEUM	Lapponicum		S	XX	**	H-2	A	April, May	yellow	1-2'
chrysodoron	Boothii	Boothii	S		**		E	Mar., April	yellow	5'
chrysolepis	Boothii	Tephropeplum	S				E	June	yellow	4'e
chunii	Azalea	Obtusum	NS						lilac-purple	6'
CILIATUM	Maddenii	Ciliicalyx	S	XXX	****	H-4	C	Mar., April	white, rose	6'
CILLIICALYX	Maddenii	Ciliicalyx	S	XX	****	H-6	F	Mar., April	white, rose	10'
ciliipes	Maddenii	Ciliicalyx	S				E		white	
CINNABARINUM	Cinnabarinum		S	XXX	****	H-3	B	May	red, orange, yellow, pink, purple	15'
cinnamomeum (Ssp.)	Arboreum	Arboreum	NS		***		C	April, May	white, pale pink	25'
circinnatum	Taliense	Adenogynum	NS							20-25'
citriniflorum	Neriiflorum	Sanguineum	NS	XX	**	H-4	B	April, May	yellow, red	2-3'
clementinae	Taliense	Taliense	NS		*		A	April, May	white, rose	10'
codonanthum	Taliense	Adenogynum	NS				B		yellow	3'
coelicum	Neriiflorum	Haematodes	NS		**		B	May	scarlet	15'
coeloneurum	Taliense	Wasonii	NS							12'
collettianum	Anthopogon		S				C		pink	3'
comisteum	Neriiflorum	Sanguineum	NS						rose	3'
compactum	Lapponicum		S				A	April, May	rosy-purple	1-2'
complexum	Lapponicum		S				A	April, May	rosy-purple	2'
CONCATENANS	Cinnabarinum		S	XXX	****	H-4	B	April, May	apricot, yellow	6-8'
concinnoides	Maddenii	Ciliicalyx	S		*		C	April, May	mauve	10'
CONCINNUM	Triflorum	Polylepis	S	XX	*	H-3	A	April, May	pink, purplish, rosy-red	8'
coriaceum	Falconeri		NS	XX	***	H-4	C	April	white, pink	25'
coryanum	Arboreum	Argyrophyllum	NS		*		B	April, May	ivory	20'
coryphaeum	Grande		NS		**		C	April	ivory	20'
cowanianum	Trichocladum		S						reddish-purple	5'
CRASSUM	Maddenii	Maddenii	S	XX	***	H-5	D	June	white	15'
crenulatum	Maddenii	Ciliicalyx	S							
crinigerum	Barbatum	Crinigerum	NS	X	**	H-2	B	April	white, ivory, rose	12'
cruentum	Taliense	Adenogynum	NS						white, rose	14'e
cubittii	Maddenii	Ciliicalyx	S		**		F	Mar., April	white	8'
cuffeanum	Maddenii	Ciliicalyx	S		**		F	April, May	white	9'
cuneatum	Lapponicum		S	X	**	H-2	A	April	rose	4'
cyanocarpum	Thomsonii	Thomsonii	NS	XX	**	H-4	B	Mar., April	white, rose	20'

Species	Series Affiliation	Subseries Affiliation	Scaly or Non-Scaly	American Quality Rating	British Quality Rating	American Hardiness Rating	British Hardiness Rating	Season of Bloom	Color of Flower	Height
DALHOUSIAE	Maddenii	Megacalyx	S	XXXX	***	H-6	F	April, May	white, chamois-yellow	8'
dasycladoides	Thomsonii	Selense	NS						rose	12'
dasycladum	Thomsonii	Selense	NS				B	April, May	rose, white	8'
dasypetalum	Lapponicum		S				A	April	purplish-rose	2½'
DAURICUM	Dauricum		S	XX	**	H-2	A	Feb.-April	lavender-rose	6'
davidii	Fortunei	Davidii	NS				B	Mar., April	lilac, rose	15'
DAVIDSONIANUM	Triflorum	Yunnanense	S	XXX	****	H-4	B	April, May	white, pink, rose	10'
decipiens	Falconeri		NS				C		purplish-rose	15'e
DECORUM	Fortunei	Fortunei	NS	XXX	***	H-4	C	April, May	white, pink, chartreuse	20'
DEGRONIANUM	Ponticum	Caucasicum	NS	XX	*	H-3	A	April, May	pale pink, rose	5'
dekatanum	Boothii	Boothii	S						lemon-yellow	4'
delavayi	Arboreum	Arboreum	NS	XXX	***	H-5	E	Mar.-May	blood-red, pink, white	25'
dendricola	Maddenii	Ciliicalyx	S				F	May	white, pink	9'
dendrocharis	Moupinense		S						rosy-red	4'e
denudatum	Arboreum	Argyrophyllum	NS						rose	12'
DESQUAMATUM	Heliolepis		S	XX	***	H-3	B	April	mauve, rose, violet	15-25'
detersile	Taliense	Adenogynum	NS				B		reddish	3'
detonsum	Taliense	Adenogynum	NS				B	May	rose	12'
diacritum	Lapponicum		S	0		H-3	A	April	rose-purple	2'
DIAPREPES	Fortunei	Fortunei	NS	XXX	***	H-4	C	June-July	white, pale rose	15-25'
DICHROANTHUM	Neriiflorum	Sanguineum	NS	XX	**	H-4	B	May	orange, buff, pink	5'
dictyotum	Lacteum		NS				B	May	white, pink	12'
DIDYMUM (Ssp.)	Neriiflorum	Sanguineum	NS	XX	**	H-3	B	June-July	blackish-crimson	3'
dignabile	Lacteum		NS						ivory, pink, yellow	18'
dimitrum	Irroratum	Irroratum	NS				D	April	rose	7'
diphrocalyx	Neriiflorum	Neriiflorum	NS		*		B	April	rosy-crimson	15'
DISCOLOR	Fortunei	Fortunei	NS	XXX	****	H-3	B	early July	white, pink	15'
doshongense	Taliense	Taliense	NS				B	April, May	pink	3'
drumonium	Lapponicum		S	XX	**	H-3	B	April	mauve, magenta	2'
dryophyllum	Lacteum		NS				B	April	white, pink, ivory	25'
dumicola	Taliense	Adenogynum	NS				A	April	white, pink	4'
dumosulum	Lacteum		NS				A	April	white, pink	4'
ECLECTEUM	Thomsonii	Thomsonii	NS		**	H-3	C	Feb.-April	white, rose, yellow, red, orange	6'
edgarianum	Lapponicum		S		**		A	May-June	purplish-blue	3'
EDGEWORTHII	Edgeworthii		S	XX	****	H-6	F	April-May	white, pink	8-10'
elegantulum	Taliense	Adenogynum	NS	0		H-2			mauve	5'
ELLIOTTII	Irroratum	Parishii	NS	XXXX	****	H-4	E	May-June	crimson, magenta	10'
emarginatum	Vaccinioides		S				E		yellow	2'
epapillatum	Irroratum	Irroratum	NS						pale rose	17'
erastum	Neriiflorum	Forrestii	NS						pink	10"e
erileucum	Triflorum	Yunnanense	S				D		white	9'
ERIOGYNUM	Irroratum	Parishii	NS	XXXX	****	H-4	D	late June	scarlet	10'
eritimum	Irroratum	Irroratum	NS				C	April	crimson, pink, magenta	18'
erosum	Barbatum	Glischrum	NS				B	Mar.-April	crimson, rose	20'
erubescens	Fortunei	Oreodoxa	NS				B	April	white, rose	12'
erythrocalyx	Thomsonii	Selense	NS		*		B	April-May	ivory, white, pink	8'
esetulosum	Thomsonii	Selense	NS				B	April-May	pink, mauve, white	6'
esquirolii	Stamineum		NS						rose-violet	
euchroum	Neriiflorum	Neriiflorum	NS				C		brick-red	2'
EUDOXUM	Neriiflorum	Sanguineum	NS				B	April-May	rosy-crimson, pink, yellow, white	4'
eurysiphon	Thomsonii	Selense	NS				B	May	ivory, rose	5'
exasperatum	Barbatum	Glischrum	NS	0	**	H-4	C	April	red	10'
excellens	Maddenii	Maddenii	S						white	10'
excelsum	Irroratum	Irroratum	NS							

Species	Series Affiliation	Subseries Affiliation	Scaly or Non-Scaly	American Quality Rating	British Quality Rating	American Hardiness Rating	British Hardiness Rating	Season of Bloom	Color of Flower	Height
eximium	Falconeri		NS	XXXX	**	H-4	C	April-May	pale pink	20'
exquisitum	Triflorum	Oreotrephes	S	XXX	***	H-4	B	May	mauve	8'
faberi	Taliense	Adenogynum	NS				B	May	white	18'
faberioides	Taliense	Adenogynum	NS					May	white	18'
FACETUM	Irroratum	Parishii	NS		****		D	late June	scarlet	20'
faithae	Fortunei	Fortunei	NS						white	20'
FALCONERI	Falconeri		NS	XXXX	****	H-4	C	April-May	ivory, pale yellow	30'
FARGESII	Fortunei	Oreodoxa	NS	XXX	***	H-3	B	early Apr.	white, pink, rose	10'
farinosum	Arboreum	Argyrophyllum	NS				C		white	6'
farrerae	Azalea	Schlippenbachii	NS				F	June	pink, rose	6'e
FASTIGIATUM	Lapponicum		S	XXX	**	H-2	A	April-May	lilac, purple	10"-3'
FAURIEI	Ponticum	Caucasicum	NS	X		H-3	B	early June	ivory, pink	8'
feddei	Stamineum		NS							12'
FERRUGINEUM	Ferrugineum		S	0	**	H-2	A	June	rosy-crimson, white	4'
FICTOLACTEUM	Falconeri		NS	XXX	***	H-3	B	April-May	white, ivory, rose	25'
fimbriatum	Lapponicum		S				A	April-May	purple	2'
flammeum	Azalea	Luteum	NS		***		B	May	scarlet, orange, yellow	10'
flavantherum	Triflorum	Triflorum	S				C	May	yellow	10'
flavidum	Lapponicum		S	XX	**	H-2	A	April-May	pale yellow	2'
flavorufum	Taliense	Taliense	NS				A	April-May	white, rose	6'
flavum	Azalea	Luteum	NS		****		A	May	yellow	12'
floccigerum	Neriiflorum	Neriiflorum	NS	X	**	H-3	B	Mar.-April	crimson, rose, yellow, buff	6'
floribundum	Arboreum	Argyrophyllum	NS		*		B	early Apr.	mauve, magenta, violet-purple	15'
fokiense	Arboreum	Argyrophyllum	NS							5'e
formosanum	Arboreum	Argyrophyllum	NS						white, rose	18'
FORMOSUM	Maddenii	Ciliicalyx	S		***		D	May-June	white	10'
FORRESTII	Neriiflorum	Forrestii	NS	XXXX	****	H-3	B	April-May	red, pink, white, yellow	1'
FORTUNEI	Fortunei	Fortunei	NS	XXX	***	H-2	B	May	white, lilac-pink, red	15'
fragariflorum	Saluenense		S		**		C	May-June	purple, purplish-crimson	12"
fulgens	Campanulatum		NS	X	**	H-3	B	March-Apr.	scarlet	12'
fulvastrum	Neriiflorum	Sanguineum	NS				A	May	pale yellow	5'
FULVUM	Fulvum		NS	X	***	H-4	B	April	white, rose	9-20'
fumidum	Heliolepis		S				C		violet	6'
galactinum	Falconeri		NS	0		H-3	A	April-May	white, pink	15'
genestierianum	Glaucophyllum	Genestierianum	S				E	April	plum-purple	12'
giganteum	Grande		NS		***		E	Jan.-March	rose-crimson	80'
glanduliferum	Fortunei	Fortunei	NS						white	14'e
glandulosum	Camtschaticum		NS						rose-purple	6"e
glaucopeplum	Taliense	Taliense	NS				B	May	rose	8'
GLAUCOPHYLLUM	Glaucophyllum	Glaucophyllum	S	X	**	H-3	B	May	white, pink, rosy red	4'
glischroides	Barbatum	Glischrum	NS	**	**		C	March-Apr.	white, pink	15'
glischrum	Barbatum	Glischrum	NS	X	*	H-4	B	May	white, pink, purplish-pink	15'
globigerum	Taliense	Roxieanum	NS				B		white	6'
glomerulatum	Lapponicum		S	X		H-3	A	April-May	purplish-mauve	3'
GRANDE	Grande		NS	XXX	****	H-5	E	Feb.-April	ivory, red	30'
GRIERSONIANUM	Auriculatum		NS	XXX	****	H-5	C	June	scarlet	8'
GRIFFITHIANUM	Fortunei	Griffithianum	NS	XXXX	****	H-5	E	May	white, pink	20'
gymnocarpum	Neriiflorum	Sanguineum	NS	XX	**	H-3	B	April	crimson	4'
habrotrichum	Barbatum	Glischrum	NS	X	*	H-4	B	April	white, pale pink	10'
HAEMALEUM (Ssp.)	Neriiflorum	Sanguineum	NS	XX	***	H-3	B	April-June	scarlet, black-crimson	$2\frac{1}{2}$'
HAEMATODES	Neriiflorum	Haematodes	NS	XXXX	****	H-4	B	May	scarlet	4'
hainanence	Azalea	Obtusum	NS						red	9'
hanceanum	Triflorum	Hanceanum	S		**		B	April	pale yellow	1-4'
hancockii	Stamineum		NS				F		white	6'
hardingii	Irroratum	Irroratum	NS				E	April-May	white, pink	8'
headfortianum	Maddenii	Megacalyx	S					May-June	ivory	3'

Species	Series Affiliation	Subseries Affiliation	Scaly or Non-Scaly	American Quality Rating	British Quality Rating	American Hardiness Rating	British Hardiness Rating	Season of Bloom	Color of Flower	Height
HELIOLEPIS	Heliolepis		S	X	**	H-3	B	April-June	white, mauve, rose	8'
hemidartum	Neriiflorum	Haematodes	NS		**		B	April	crimson	6'
hemitrichotum	Scabrifolium		S	X	**	H-3	B	April	white, pale pink	4'
hemsleyanum	Fortunei	Fortunei	NS						white	18'
henryi	Stamineum		NS						pink	
herpesticum (Ssp.)	Neriiflorum	Sanguineum	NS				B	May	orange-red, yellow	2'
hesperium	Triflorum	Yunnanense	S				B	May	mauve, magenta	6'
HIPPOPHAEOIDES	Lapponicum		S	XXX	***	H-3	A	April	lilac, rose	4'
hirsuticostatum	Triflorum	Augustinii	S				D		pink	6'e
HIRSUTUM	Ferrugineum		S	X	*	H-2	A	June	white, pink, rosy-red	4'
hirtipes	Barbatum	Glischrum	NS				B	April	white, pink	25'
HODGSONII	Falconeri		NS	X	**	H-4	B	April-May	magenta, pink, ivory	20'
hongkongense	Ovatum		NS						white	5'
HOOKERI	Thomsonii	Thomsonii	NS		****		C	Mar.-April	blood-red	12'
horaeum (Ssp.)	Neriiflorum	Sanguineum	NS		**		B	April-May	crimson, orange	6'
hormophorum	Triflorum	Yunnanense	S		**		B	May	rose, crimson, white	8'
houlstonii	Fortunei	Fortunei	NS	XX	***	H-3	B	May	white, pale pink	18'
huianum	Fortunei	Davidii	NS						lilac	15'
hunnewellianum	Arboreum	Argyrophyllum	NS		*		B	Mar.-April	white, pink	16'
hylaeum	Thomsonii	Thomsonii	NS				B	April	rose	25'
hypenanthum	Anthopogon		S		*		C	April-May	yellow	2'
hyperythrum	Ponticum	Caucasicum	NS		***		B	April-May	white, mauve	5'
hypoglaucum	Arboreum	Argyrophyllum	NS		*		B	May	white, pink	20'
hypophaeum	Triflorum	Yunnanense	S				B	May	pink, white	5'
idoneum	Lapponicum		S				A	April-May	purple	1½'
igneum	Cinnabarinum		S						salmon-pink	12'
imberbe	Barbatum	Barbatum	NS				C	March	red	8'
IMPEDITUM	Lapponicum		S	XXX	****	H-2	A	April-May	mauve, purplish-blue	18"
IMPERATOR	Uniflorum		S	XX	****	H-3	A	April-May	pink, rose	1'
inaequale	Maddenii	Ciliicalyx	S		***		F	Mar.-May	white	6'
indicum	Azalea	Obtusum	NS		**		C	June	scarlet, rose-red	6'
inopinum	Taliense	Wasonii	NS				B	April-May	ivory	6'
insculptum	Vaccinioides		S				D		orange	
INSIGNE	Arboreum	Argyrophyllum	NS	XXX	***	H-4	B	May-June	pink	9'
INTRICATUM	Lapponicum		S	XX	***	H-2	A	April-May	mauve	2'
invictum	Heliolepis		S				B		purple	7'
iodes	Lacteum		NS				B	April-May	white	4'
IRRORATUM	Irroratum	Irroratum	NS	XX	***	H-4	B	Mar.-April	white, ivory, rose	12'
iteophyllum	Maddenii	Ciliicalyx	S				F	April	white, pale pink	6'
japonicum	Azalea	Luteum	NS		****		A	May	red, orange, yellow	8'
JOHNSTONEANUM	Maddenii	Ciliicalyx	S	XXX	***	H-4	D	April-May	white, buff	8'
jucundum	Thomsonii	Selense	NS				B	May	rose, pink, white	20'
kaempferi	Azalea	Obtusum	NS		***		A	May	salmon-red, pink	8'
kanehirai	Azalea	Obtusum	NS						scarlet	8'
kasoense	Triflorum	Triflorum	S				B	April	yellow	7'
kawakamii	Vaccinioides		S							5'
KEISKEI	Triflorum	Triflorum	S	XXX	***	H-2	A	April	lemon-yellow	2½-8'
KELETICUM	Saluenense		S	XXX	**	H-2	A	early June	purplish-crimson	12"
kendrickii	Irroratum	Irroratum	NS				E	April-May	pink, red	25'
keysii	Cinnabarinum		S	XX	**	H-4	B	June	red, orange	12'
kiusianum	Azalea	Obtusum	NS				A	May-June	pink, red	3'
kiyosumense	Azalea		NS							
klossii	Stamineum		NS							
kongboense	Anthopogon		S		**		A	April-May	rose	2'
kontumense	Irroratum	Irroratum	NS							
korthalsii	Irroratum	Irroratum	NS							
kotschyi	Ferruguineum		S		**		A	May-June	pink, white	2'
kwangtungense	Azalea	Obtusum	NS						white	6'e
KYAWI	Irroratum	Parishii	NS	XXXX	****	H-6	E	July	scarlet	20'

Species	Series Affiliation	Subseries Affiliation	Scaly or Non-Scaly	American Quality Rating	British Quality Rating	American Hardiness Rating	British Hardiness Rating	Season of Bloom	Color of Flower	Height
LACTEUM	Lacteum		NS		****		B	April	yellow, white	10-15'
lampropeplum	Taliense	Roxieanum	NS				A		white, pink	3'
lanatum	Campanulatum		NS		*		B	April-May	pale yellow	6'
lanigerum	Grande		NS		***		B	March-Apr.	rose-purple	15'
lapponicum	Lapponicum		S	X		H-2	A	Jan.-Apr.	purple	15"
lasipodum	Maddenii	Ciliicalyx	S				E	June	white	16'
lasiostylum	Azalea	Obtusum	NS						pink	3'
latoucheae	Stamineum		NS				F			
laudandum	Anthopogon		S				A	April	white, pink	15'
laxiflorum	Irroratum	Irroratum	NS		**		B	April	white, pink	15'
leclerei	Heliolepis		S				C		mauve, violet	15'
leilungense	Triflorum	Yunnanense	S				C		pale rose	3'
leiopodum	Stamineum		NS				F		white, pink	
LEPIDOSTYLUM	Trichocladum		S		**		B	May-June	pale yellow	30"
lepidotum	Lepidotum	Lepidotum	S	XX	*	H-3	A-C	June	yellow, pink, purple, crimson	2-4'
leptopeplum	Irroratum	Irroratum	NS				C		ivory, pink	14'
leptothrium	Ovatum		NS		**		E	April-May	magenta-rose	6'
LEUCASPIS	Boothii	Megeratum	S	XXXX	****	H-4	C	Mar.-April	white	2'
levinei	Maddenii	Megacalyx	S						white	13'
liliiflorum	Maddenii	Megacalyx	S				F		white	9'
LINDLEYI	Maddenii	Megacalyx	S	XXXX	****	H-6	E	April-May	white	10-15'
linearifolium	Azalea	Obtusum	NS				B	April-May	lilac-pink, rose	6'
litangense	Lapponicum		S	X		H-2	A	April-May	plum-purple	2'
lithophilum	Trichocladum		S				B		pale yellow	3'
LITIENSE	Thomsonii	Souliei	NS	XXX	***	H-4	B	May	yellow	12'
lochae	Javanica		S					April-May	dark red	20'
lochmium	Triflorum	Yunnanense	S				B	May	white, pale mauve	10'
LONGESQUAMATUM	Barbatum	Maculiferum	NS	XX		H-3	B	May	pink, rose	10'
longiperulatum	Azalea	Obtusum	NS						red	
longipes	Arboreum	Argyrophyllum	NS				C		pale rose	8'
longistylum	Triflorum	Yunnanense	S		*		C	April	pink	7'
lophogynum	Trichocladum		S				C	May	yellow	3'
lopsangianum	Thomsonii	Thomsonii	NS				B	April	crimson	6'
lowndesii	Lepidotum		S					July	yellow	4-6'
lucidum	Camelliaeflorum		S							5'e
ludlowi	Uniflorum		S		*		B	May	yellow	1'
ludwigianum	Maddenii	Ciliicalyx	S				F		white, rose	4½'
lukiangense	Irroratum	Irroratum	NS				B	Mar.-April	rose, magenta	12'
LUTESCENS	Triflorum	Triflorum	S	XXX	****	H-4	B	Feb.-April	pale yellow	15'
lyi	Maddenii	Ciliicalyx	S		**		D	April-June	white	6'
lysolepis	Lapponicum		S				A	April-May	violet, mauve	4'
MACABEANUM	Grande		NS	XXXX	****	H-4	B	Mar.-April	yellow, ivory	20'
mackenzianum	Stamineum		NS							
macrogemmum	Azalea	Obtusum	NS						violet	9'
MACROPHYLLUM	Ponticum	Ponticum	NS	X	**	H-2	A	May	purplish-rose, white	12'
maculiferum	Barbatum	Maculiferum	NS		**		B	April	white, pale pink	20'
MADDENII	Maddenii	Maddenii	S	XXX	***	H-6	E	June-Aug.	white	9'
magnificum	Grande		NS		**		E	Jan.-March	rosy-purple	45'
magorianum							B		white, pink	8'e
MAKINOI	Ponticum	Caucasicum	NS	XX	**	H-3	B	May-June	white, rose	6'
malayanum	Malayovireya (Ssect.)						F		scarlet	15'
mallotum	Neriiflorum	Haematodes	NS	XXX	****	H-4	B	Mar.-April	crimson	20'
manipurense	Maddenii	Maddenii	S		**		D	June	white	15'
mariae	Azalea	Obtusum	NS						lilac, pink	10'
mariesii	Azalea	Obtusum	NS				C	April	rose-purple	10'
martinianum	Thomsonii	Selense	NS		**		B	April	pink, white	6'
MAXIMUM	Ponticum	Ponticum	NS	X		H-1	A	July	white, pink purplish-red	15'
mayebarae	Azalea	Schlippenbachii	NS	X					purple	
MEDDIANUM	Thomsonii	Thomsonii	NS		****		C	early April	crimson	5'
MEGACALYX	Maddenii	Megacalyx	S		***	H-6	E	April-May	white	16'
megeratum	Boothii	Megeratum	S	XX	**	H-4	C	Mar.-April	yellow	2'
mekongense	Trichocladum		S				B	May	pale yellow	4'
melinanthum	Trichocladum		S		**		B	April-May	yellow	6-8'

Species	Series Affiliation	Subseries Affiliation	Scaly or Non-Scaly	American Quality Rating	British Quality Rating	American Hardiness Rating	British Hardiness Rating	Season of Bloom	Color of Flower	Height
mengtszense	Irroratum	Irroratum	NS				E		purplish-red	20'
METTERNICHII	Ponticum	Caucasicum	NS		**		A	May	white, rose	8'
MICRANTHUM	Micranthum		S	X		H-1	A	June	white	5'
microygynum	Neriiflorum	Sanguineum	NS		**		B	April	rose, black-crimson	4'
microleucum	Lapponicum		S	XX	***	H-2	A	April	white	1½'
micromeres	Glaucophyllum	Genestierianum	S				C		orange-yellow, ivory	6'
microphyton	Azalea	Obtusum	NS				D	April-May	white, rose	6'
mimetes	Taliense	Adenogynum	NS				B	May	white	7'
miniatum	Campanulatum		NS						rose, crimson	16'
MINUS	Carolinianum		S	X	**	H-2	A	June	rose, white	15'
minutiflorum	Azalea	Obtusum	NS						white	7'
mishmiense	Boothii	Boothii	S		**		E	April-May	lemon-yellow	4'
missionarum	Maddenii	Ciliicalyx	S				E		violet, white	6'e
miyazawae	Azalea	Obtusum	NS						mauve	6'
molle	Azalea	Luteum	NS		****		B	May	yellow	6'
mollicomum	Scabrifolium		S		**		B	April	rose, crimson	6'
mollyanum	Grande		NS				B	March	pink	25'
monanthum	Uniflorum						D		yellow	4'
monosematum	Barbatum	Maculiferum	NS				B	April	white, pink	10'
morii	Barbatum	Maculiferum	NS		**		B	April	white, pink	25'
moulmainense	Stamineum		NS				F	Mar.-April	red, white	
MOUPINENSE	Moupinense		S	XXXX	****	H-4	B	Feb.-March	white, rose	4'
mucronatum	Azalea	Obtusum	NS		****		A	May	white, pale mauve	6'
MUCRONULATUM	Dauricum		S	XX	***	H-2	B	Jan.-April	mauve, rose	8'
myiagrum	Thomsonii	Campylocarpum	NS		**		B	May	white	5'
maamkwanense	Azalea	Obtusum	NS				B	May	white	3'
nakaharai	Azalea	Obtusum	NS						dark red	4'e
nakotiltum	Lacteum		NS				C		pink	12'
nankotaisanense	Barbatum	Maculiferum	NS				C		white, pink	6'e
NERIIFLORUM	Neriiflorum	Neriiflorum	NS	XXXX	****	H-4	C	April	scarlet, rose	6-12'
nhatrangense	Lacteum		NS							
nigro-punctatum	Lapponicum		S				A	May-June	pale purple	12"
niko-montanum	Ponticum	Caucasicum	NS					May	ivory	4'
ningyuenense	Irroratum	Irroratum	NS				D		pink	8'e
nipponicum	Azalea	Nipponicum	NS				B	May-June	white	6'
nitens	Saluenense		S		**		A	June-July	magenta-pink	18"
nitidulum	Lapponicum		S				A	April	violet-purple	4'
nivale	Lapponicum		S				A	April-May	magenta, mauve	12"
niveum	Arboreum	Arboreum	NS		***		B	April-May	magenta	15'
noriakianum									rose	
notatum	Maddenii	Ciliicalyx	S				F		white	5'e
nudiflorum	Azalea	Luteum	NS		*		A	May	pale pink, rose, reddish, white	8'
NUTTALLII	Maddenii	Megacalyx	S	XXXX	****	H-6	F	April-May	white, pale yellow	15'
oblongifolium	Azalea	Luteum	NS				C	June	white	6'
obtusum	Azalea	Obtusum	NS		****		A	May	purple, red, pink, white	5'
occidentale	Azalea	Luteum	NS		***		A	April-Aug.	white, pink, pale yellow	10'
ochraceum	Barbatum	Maculiferum	NS				C		crimson	9'
odoriferum	Maddenii	Maddenii	S				E		white	7'e
oldhamii	Azalea	Obtusum	NS		***		D	May	brick-red	10'
oleifolium	Virgatum		S	XX	***	H-3	D	April-May	white, pink	7'
ombrochares	Irroratum	Irroratum	NS				E		crimson	15'e
openshawianum	Fortunei	Calophytum	NS						white	18'
oporinum	Heliolepis		S				B	June-July	rose-pink, white	10'
ORBICULARE	Fortunei	Orbiculare	NS	XXX	****	H-3	A	April-May	rose	10'
OREODOXA	Fortunei	Oreodoxa	NS	XX	***	H-3	B	March-Apr.	rose, white	15'
OREOTREPHES	Triflorum	Oreotrephes	S	XXX	****	H-3	B	May	mauve, rosy-red, purple	8'
orthocladum	Lapponicum		S		*		A	April	mauve, purple	4'
oulotrichum	Trichocladum		S		*		B	April-May	yellow	6'
ovatosepalum	Azalea	Obtusum	NS							
OVATUM	Ovatum		NS		*		C	late May	white, pale mauve	6-15'

Species	Series Affiliation	Subseries Affiliation	Scaly or Non-Scaly	American Quality Rating	British Quality Rating	American Hardiness Rating	British Hardiness Rating	Season of Bloom	Color of Flower	Height
pachypodum	Maddenii	Ciliicalyx	S		**		E	Mar.-April	yellow, white	5'
pachytrichum	Barbatum	Maculiferum	NS	XX	*	H-3	B	March	white, pink, magenta	18'
pallescens	Triflorum	Yunnanense	S		**		A	May	white, pink	7'
paludosum	Lapponicum		S				A	April-May	violet	2'e
pankimense	Irroratum	Irroratum	NS				C	April	crimson	10'
panteumorphum	Thomsonii	Campylocarpum	NS				B	April-May	yellow	10'
papillatum	Irroratum	Irroratum					D		ivory	6'e
paradoxum	Campanulatum		NS				B	April-May	white	7'
parishii	Irroratum	Parishii	NS				F		red	20'
parmulatum	Neriiflorum	Sanguineum	NS		**		B	April	ivory, white	4'
parryae	Maddenii	Ciliicalyx	S				E	April-May	white	10'
parvifolium	Lapponicum		S				A	Jan.-March	mauve, white	1½'
patulum	Uniflorum		S				B	May	purple	2'
PEMAKOENSE	Uniflorum		S	XXX	***	H-3	A	April	lilac-pink	6"-2'
pendulum	Edgeworthii		S				C	April-Maý	white	4'
pennivenium	Irroratum	Irroratum	NS				C	April-May	crimson	20'
pentaphyllum	Azalea	Canadense	NS		****		B	March-May	rose-pink	10'
peramabile	Lapponicum		S				A	April-May	purplish-rose	2½'
peramoenum	Arboreum	Arboreum	NS				E	April	scarlet	12'
peregrinum	Grande		NS				C	March-May	white, pink	15'
perulatum	Taliense	Roxieanum	NS				A		rose	4'
petrocharis	Moupinense		S						white	3'
phaeochrysum	Lacteum		NS				B	April	pink, purplish-pink	15'
pholidotum	Heliolepis		S				B	June	rose, magenta	8'
pilicalyx	Maddenii	Ciliicalyx	S				E		white, pink	4'
pingianum	Arboreum	Argyrophyllum	NS						purple	20'
planetum	Fortunei	Davidii	NS		**		B	Mar.-April	light pink	15'
platyphyllum	Anthopogon		S				B		white, pink	5'
platypodum	Fortunei	Fortunei	NS				C		pinkish-red	20'
pleistanthum	Triflorum	Yunnanense	S				B	April-May	violet, mauve	6'
pocophorum	Neriiflorum	Haematodes	NS		**		B	Mar.-April	crimson	10'
pogonophyllum	Anthopogon		S						white, pink	1-4'
pogonostylum	Irroratum	Irroratum	NS				E		pink	15'
polifolium	Lapponicum		S				A	April-May	mauve, purple	3'
polyandrum	Maddenii	Maddenii	S		***	H-6	C	May-June	white, pink, pale yellow	10'
polycladum	Lapponicum		S				A		purple	4'
polylepis	Triflorum	Polylepis	S	0	*	H-3	A	April	purplish-magenta	12'
pomense	Lacteum		NS						pink	4'
PONTICUM	Ponticum	Ponticum	NS	0		H-3	A	June	purplish-pink	15'
populare	Thomsonii	Thomsonii	NS						crimson	15'
porphyrophyllum	Neriiflorum	Forrestii	NS				A		deep rose	2'
potanini	Taliense		NS						white	15'
poukhanense	Azalea	Obtusum	NS		**		B	May	lilac-purple	5'
praestans	Grande		NS		*		C	April	magenta-rose, pink	30'
praeteritum	Fortunei	Oreodoxa	NS				B	Mar.-April	pink	15'
PRAEVERNUM	Fortunei	Davidii	NS	XX	**	H-3	B	Feb.-April	white, rose	15'
prattii	Taliense	Adenogynum	NS				B	April-May	white	10'
preptum	Falconeri		NS				D	April	ivory	8'
primulaeflorum	Anthopogon		S		*		A	April	white, yellow, pink	5'
principis	Taliense	Taliense	NS							
pronum	Taliense	Roxieanum	NS				A	April-May	pale yellow	12"
prostratum	Saluenense		S	XX	*	H-3	A	April-May	pinkish-purple, crimson	18"
proteoides	Taliense	Roxieanum	NS		**		B	April	pale yellow, white	3'
protistum	Grande		NS				E	April	ivory, pink	30'
prunifolium	Azalea	Luteum	NS		***		A	July-Aug.	yellow, orange, scarlet	12'
przewalskii	Lacteum		NS				A	April-May	white, pink	9'
pseudochrysanthum	Barbatum	Maculiferum	NS		***		B	April	pink	9'
pseudociliicalyx	Maddenii	Ciliicalyx	S				F		white, rose	10'e
PUBESCENS	Scabrifolium		S	XX	***	H-3	B	April	white, rose	6'
pudorosum	Grande		NS						mauve	25'

Species	Series Affiliation	Subseries Affiliation	Scaly or Non-Scaly	American Quality Rating	British Quality Rating	American Hardiness Rating	British Hardiness Rating	Season of Bloom	Color of Flower	Height
pulchrum	Azalea	Obtusum	NS		**		C	May	purplish-red, white, crimson	6'
pumilum	Uniflorum		S		**		A	May-July	pink	12"
PURALBUM	Thomsonii	Souliei	NS		***		B	May	white	15'
purdomii	Taliense	Taliense	NS							9'e
pyrrhoanthum	Neriiflorum(?)	Forrestii(?)	NS				C	April	crimson	10-20"
quadrasinum	Vaccinioides		S				C	April	red	4'e
quinquefolium	Azalea	Schlippenbachii	NS		****		B	April-May	white	12'
RACEMOSUM	Virgatum		S	XXXX	****	H-2	A	Mar.-May	white, rose	1½-15'
radendum	Anthopogon		S						mauve	3'
radicans	Saluenense		S	XXX	***	H-3	A	May	purple	6"
ramosissimum	Lapponicum		S				A	April-May	purple	3'
ramsdenianum	Irroratum	Irroratum	NS				C	April	scarlet, rose	30'
ravum	Lapponicum		S	X		H-2	A	May	rose, purple	6'
recurvoides	Taliense	Roxieanum	NS		**		B	April-May	white, rose	5'
reticulatum	Azalea	Schlippenbachii	NS		***		A	April-May	purple, rose	15'
rex	Falconeri		NS		****		B	April-May	rose, ivory	40'
rhabdotum	Maddenii	Megacalyx	S	XXX	****	H-6	E	May-July	ivory, striped red	12'
rigidum	Triflorum	Yunnanense	S				C	May	pale pink	7'
ririei	Arboreum	Argyrophyllum	NS	X	***	H-4	B	Feb.-March	purple	18'
rivulare	Azalea	Obtusum	NS						red	20'
rockii	Arboreum	Argyrophyllum	NS				C		rose, mauve-purple	18'
roseatum	Maddenii	Ciliicalyx	S				E		white, pink	10'
roseum	Azalea	Luteum	NS		***		A	May	pink, white, rosy-red	10'
roxieanum	Taliense	Roxieanum	NS		**		B	April-May	white, ivory, pale pink	9'
RUBIGINOSUM	Heliolepis		S	XX	***	H-2	A	April-May	pink, mauve, rose	25'
rubrolineatum	Trichocladum		S				B	May	yellow	5'
rubropilosum	Azalea	Obtusum	NS				D	May	pink	10'
rude	Barbatum	Glischrum	NS				B	May	purplish-crimson	9'
rufescens	Anthopogon		S				C		white, pale blue	2'
rufohirtum	Azalea	Obtusum	NS				E		deep rose	3'
rufosquamosum	Maddenii	Ciliicalyx	S				F		white	3'
rufum	Taliense	Wasonii	NS				B	April	white, magenta	15'
rupicola	Lapponicum		S		**		A	April-May	purplish-crimson	2'
RUSSATUM	Lapponicum		S	XXXX	****	H-2	A	April-May	blue-purple	4'
russotinctum	Taliense	Roxieanum	NS				B	April-May	white, pink	8'
saisiuense	Azalea	Obtusum	NS				B	April May	pink	1'
SALUENENSE	Saluenense		S	XX	***	H-3	A	April-May	rose, purplish-crimson	4'
sanctum	Azalea	Schlippenbachii	NS						rose	15'
SANGUINEUM	Neriiflorum	Sanguineum	NS	XXX	***	H-3	B	April-July	crimson, plum-purple	3'
sargentianum	Anthopogon		S	XXXX	***	H-3	C	May	lemon-yellow, white	12"
sasakii	Azalea	Obtusum	NS						red	6'
saxicolum	Azalea	Obtusum	NS							
scabrifolium	Scabrifolium		S	O	***	H-3	D	Mar.-April	white, pink	10'
scabrum	Azalea	Obtusum	NS		***		E	April-May	scarlet, rose-red	6'
schistocalyx	Irroratum	Parishii	NS				C	April	crimson, bright rose	20'
schizopeplum	Taliense	Taliense	NS				A	April-May	rose	6'
schlippenbachii	Azalea	Schlippenbachii	NS		****		B	April-May	rose, pale pink	15'
sciaphilum	Edgeworthii		S				F		white	2'
SCINTILLANS	Lapponicum		S	XX	****	H-3	A	April-May	lavender, purplish blue	3'
scopulorum	Maddenii	Ciliicalyx	S		**		F	April-May	white, pink	15'
scottianum	Maddenii	Ciliicalyx	S		*		F	May-June	white, pink	12'
SCYPHOCALYX (Ssp.)	Neriiflorum	Sanguineum	NS	O		H-4	B	May-June	orange, yellow, crimson, pink	5'
searsiae	Triflorum	Yunnanense	S	XX		H-3	B	April-May	white, mauve, purplish	12'
seinghkuense	Edgeworthii		S		***		F	April	yellow	3'

Species	Series Affiliation	Subseries Affiliation	Scaly or Non-Scaly	American Quality Rating	British Quality Rating	American Hardiness Rating	British Hardiness Rating	Season of Bloom	Color of Flower	Height
selense	Thomsonii	Selense	NS		**		B	April-May	pink, rose, white, crimson	9'
semibarbatum	Semibarbatum		NS				A	June	white	10'
semilunatum	Trichocladum		S			H-4	C	May	yellow	3'
semnoides	Grande		NS	XX		H-4	D	Mar. -April	white, pink	20'
seniavinii	Azalea	Obtusum	NS						white, pink	6'
serotinum	Fortunei	Fortunei	NS				B	April	white	15'
serpens	Neriiflorum	Forrestii	NS				A		rose	$1\frac{1}{2}$'
serpyllifolium	Azalea	Obtusum	NS				B	April-May	rosy-pink, white	4'
serrulatum	Azalea	Luteum	NS		*		B	July-Oct.	white	20'
setiferum	Thomsonii	Selense	NS				B	April	ivory	9'
setosum	Lapponicum		S				A	May	purplish-pink	4'
shepherdii	Irroratum	Irroratum	NS				E	Mar.- April	scarlet	12'
sherriffii			NS				B	April	carmine	12'
shimidzuanum										
shweliense	Glaucophyllum	Glaucophyllum	S			H-3	B	May	pink	$2\frac{1}{2}$'
sidereum	Grande		NS		**		D	April	ivory, yellow	30'
siderophyllum	Triflorum	Yunnanense	S		*		B	May	white, mauve, pink, purplish	12'
silvaticum	Arboreum	Arboreum	NS		***		B	April	magenta, reddish-purple	20'
simiarum	Arboreum	Argyrophyllum	NS				B	April-May	pink	8'
simsii	Azalea	Obtusum	NS		***		D	May	rose-red, crimson	6'
sino-falconeri	Falconeri		NS				D		pale yellow	20'
SINOGRANDE	Grande		NS	XXXX	****	H-4	D	April	ivory, yellow	30'
sinonuttallii	Maddenii	Megacalyx	S		****		F	April-May	white, pale yellow	15'
smilesii	Maddenii	Ciliicalyx	S				F		white	20'
SMIRNOWII	Ponticum	Caucasicum	NS	X	*	H-2	A	May-June	rose, light red	8'
smithii	Barbatum	Barbatum	NS	XXX	***	H-3	B	Mar. -April	crimson, pink	20'
SOULIEI	Thomsonii	Souliei	NS	XXX	****	H 3	B	late May	white, rose	12'
spanotrichum	Irroratum	Irroratum	NS						crimson	20'
SPERABILE	Neriiflorum	Neriiflorum	NS	XX	**	H-4	C	April-May	scarlet	6'
SPERABILOIDES	Neriiflorum	Neriiflorum	NS	XX	***	H-4	C	Mar. -April	crimson, rose, buff	6'
sphaeroblastum	Taliense	Taliense	NS				B	April	white	6'
spiciferum	Scabrifolium		S	XX	***	H-3	C	April	pink	3'
spilanthum	Lapponicum		S					May	mauve, purple	3'
spilotum	Thomsonii	Selense	NS				C	May	pink	15'
SPINULIFERUM	Scabrifolium		S	XX	***	H-4	D	April	pink, orange, crimson	10'
stamineum	Stamineum		NS				E	April-May	white	6'
stereophyllum	Triflorum	Yunnanense	S				B	May	mauve, rose	6'
STEWARTIANUM	Thomsonii	Thomsonii	NS	XXX	***	H-4	B	Feb. -March	white, pink, scarlet, yellow	9'
stictophyllum	Lapponicum		S				A	April	mauve, rose, purple	2'
STRIGILLOSUM	Barbatum	Glischrum	NS	XXX	****	H-4	C	March	scarlet	20'
suberosum	Triflorum	Yunnanense	S		**		B	May	white, pink	10'
subnikomontanum	Azalea		NS							
subsessile	Azalea	Obtusum	NS						lilac, violet-purple	
SULFUREUM	Boothii	Boothii	S		***		E	April	yellow	4'
supranubium	Maddenii	Ciliicalyx	S		**		E	April-May	white	12'
surasianum	Maddenii	Ciliicalyx	S				F	June	pale pink	12'
SUTCHUENENSE	Fortunei	Davidii	NS	XXX	***	H-3	B	Feb. -April	pale rosy-lilac rose	25'
sycanthum	Triflorum	Oreotrephes	S				B	Mar. -April	purplish-rose	9'
TAGGIANUM	Maddenii	Megacalyx	S	XXX	***	H-6	E	April-May	white	8'
taiense	Stamineum		NS							30'
taliense	Taliense	Taliense	NS				B	May	ivory, pink	10'
tamurai	Azalea	Obtusum	NS							6'
tanastylum	Irroratum	Irroratum	NS				C	April	crimson, rosy purple	20'
tapetiforme	Lapponicum		S		*		A	April	pink or purple	2'
taronense	Maddenii	Ciliicalyx	S		***		F	April	white	15'

Species	Series Affiliation	Subseries Affiliation	Scaly or Non-Scaly	American Quality Rating	British Quality Rating	American Hardiness Rating	British Hardiness Rating	Season of Bloom	Color of Flower	Height
tashiroi	Azalea	Tashiroi	NS						pale rosy-purple	15'
tatsienense	Triflorum	Yunnanense	S						purple	7'
telmateium	Lapponicum		S	XX	*	H-3	A	April	purplish-rose	3'
telopeum	Thomsonii	Campylocarpum	NS		**		B	May	yellow	10'
temenium	Neriiflorum	Sanguineum	NS				B	May-June	crimson	4'
TEPHROPEPLUM	Boothii	Tephropeplum	S	XXX	***	H-4	B	April-May	white, pink, rosy-red	3-6'
thayerianum	Arboreum	Argyrophyllum	NS		**		B	June-July	white, pink	15'
THOMSONII	Thomsonii	Thomsonii	NS	XXX	****	H-3	B	April	blood-red, rose	20'
thymifolium	Lapponicum		S				A	April	mauve	4'
timeteum	Triflorum	Oreotrephes	S		*		B	May	purplish-rose	8'
tosaense	Azalea	Obtusum	NS		*		E	April-May	lilac-purple	7'
traillianum	Lacteum		NS				B	April	white, pink, rose	30'
TRICHANTHUM	Triflorum	Augustinii	S		**		B	May	mauve, purple, rose	15'
trichocladum	Trichocladum		S	X	*	H-4	A	April-May	yellow	4'
trichophorum	Triflorum	Augustinii	S				B	May-June	mauve	10'
tricostomum	Anthopogon	Triflorum	S	XXX		H-4	D	May-June	rose, white	4'
TRIFLORUM	Triflorum	Triflorum	S	XXX	*	H-3	C	April-May	pale yellow	10'
trilectorum	Neriiflorum	Forrestii	NS						pinkish yellow	12"
triplonaevium	Taliense	Roxieanum	NS				B		white, pink	6'
tritifolium	Taliense	Roxieanum	NS				B		white, pink	6'
tsaii	Lapponicum		S						purplish-white	12"
tsangpoense	Glaucophyllum	Glaucophyllum	S		**		B	May-June	rose, rosy-crimson, pink	3'
tsariense	Campanulatum		NS				B	April	ivory, pink	5'
tschonoskii	Azalea	Obtusum	NS				A	May	white	8'
tsoi	Azalea	Obtusum	NS						pink	3'
tutcherai	Stamineum		NS				F		violet	40'
UNGERNII	Ponticum	Caucasicum	NS	X	*	H-4	A	late July	white, pale pink	7'
uniflorum	Uniflorum		S		**		B	April	pink, purplish rose, purple	1'
uvarifolium	Fulvum		NS	O		H-3	C	April	white, rose	30'
vaccinioides	Vaccinioides		S				C	April-May	white, lilac-pink	5'
VALENTINIANUM	Maddenii	Ciliicalyx	S	XX	***	H-5	C	April	bright yellow	5'
vaseyi	Azalea	Canadense	NS		****		A	April-May	white, pink, crimson	12'
VEITCHIANUM	Maddenii	Ciliicalyx	S		***		F	April-June	white	8'
vellereum	Taliense	Taliense	NS		*		B	April	white, rose	15'
VENATOR	Irroratum	Parishii	NS	XX	**	H-4	C	late May	scarlet	8'
VERNICOSUM	Fortunei	Fortunei	NS	XX	***	H-3	B	April-May	white, rose	8-20'
verruculosum	Lapponicum		S		**		A	May	purple, pink	3'
vesiculiferum	Barbatum	Glischrum	NS				B	April	purplish-rose	10'
vestitum	Thomsonii	Selense	NS				B		white, pink	5'
vialii	Ovatum		NS				E		crimson	10'
vilmorinianum	Triflorum	Yunnanense	S	XX	**	H-4	B	May	white	6'
violaceum	Lapponicum		S				A	April-May	violet-purple	4'
virgatum	Virgatum		S		**		D	April-May	mauve, purple, pink, white	6'
viridescens	Trichocladum		S				B	June	pale yellow	4'
viscistylum	Azalea	Schlippenbachii	NS						magenta	9'
viscosum	Azalea	Luteum	NS		***		A	July	white, pink	15'
wallichii	Campanulatum		NS		*		C	April	lilac	9'
walongense	Maddenii	Ciliicalyx	S						white	10'
WARDII	Thomsonii	Souliei	NS	XXXX	****	H-4	B	April-May	bright yellow	10-25'
WASONII	Taliense	Wasonii	NS		**		B	April	white, pink, yellow	6'
watsonii	Grande		NS				C	April	white, pink	20'
wattii	Arboreum	Arboreum	NS						pink, purple	20'
websterianum	Lapponicum		S				A	April	rosy-purple	3'
weldianum	Taliense	Wasonii	NS				B	April-May	white, magenta	10'
weyrichii	Azalea	Schlippenbachii	NS		***		B	April-May	brick-red	15'
WIGHTII	Lacteum		NS		*		B	April-May	yellow, pale pink	15'
WILLIAMSIANUM	Thomsonii	Williamsianum	NS	XXXX	****	H-3	B	April	pink	5'
wilsonae	Stamineum		NS	X	**	H-3	D	April	pink	6'
wiltonii	Campanulatum		NS		*		B	April-May	white, pink	10'

Species	Series Affiliation	Subseries Affiliation	Scaly or Non-Scaly	American Quality Rating	British Quality Rating	American Hardiness Rating	British Hardi-ness Rating	Season of Bloom	Color of Flower	Height
wongii	Triflorum	Triflorum	S				B		ivory	6'
wrayii	Irroratum	Irroratum	NS							
wuense	Taliense	Adenogynum	NS				B	April		18'
XANTHOCODON	Cinnabarinum		S	XXX	***	H-3	B	May	ivory, yellow	8-15'
xanthostephanum	Boothii	Tephropeplum	S	XX	**	H-4	D	April-May	yellow	9'
yakuinsulare	Azalea		S						rosy-red	6'
YAKUSIMANUM	Ponticum	Caucasicum	NS	XXX	***	H-3	B	late May	white, rose	4'
youngae	Arboreum	Argyrophyllum	NS						purple	12'
yungningense	Lapponicum		S				A	April-May	purple, rose-purple	3'
YUNNANENSE	Triflorum	Yunnanense	S	XXXX	****	H-3	B	Late May	white, lavender, pink	12'
zaleucum	Triflorum	Yunnanense	S		**		D	April	white, pink	20'
ZEYLANICUM	Arboreum	Arboreum	NS		***		D	April-June	scarlet, pink	8-30'

In the above listing (Ssp.) refers to a subspecies, its identity in cultivation sufficiently established to warrant inclusion here. All subspecies are given under the name of the species of close affinity in the listing of them by their series which begins on page 521

The letter e, where it appears following the height, indicates that the stature has been estimated to afford some idea of the mature size of a species very rare, imperfectly known or new in cultivation.

The omission of a British quality rating may mean either that the species is not well enough known to judge its value, or that it is not worthy of even one star. The omission of an American quality rating means solely that the species has not been cultivated in this country on a scale wide enough to assess its worth. A Rhododendron which does not merit any quality commendation under the American ratings is assigned a zero, (O).

APPENDIX E

The Species of Rhododendrons Listed under their Series and Subseries

The species listed in capital letters below are described in detail in Chapter V. All species are given abbreviated descriptions in the complete alphabetical listing in Appendix D, immediately preceding this section, and readers are also referred to the alphabetical listing for the correct series and subseries affiliations of species not readily located below which have been reassigned by the author. See the listing of synonyms in Appendix F, following, for the valid names of species not found below.

ALBIFLORUM SERIES A single 6-foot deciduous species from the Rocky Mountains.
ALBIFLORUM, Hook.

ANTHOPOGON SERIES Dwarf alpine scaly-leaved shrubs with tight trusses of small flowers.
anthopogon, D. Don.
anthopogonoides, Maxim.
cephalanthum, Franch.
collettianum, Aitch. et Hemsl.
hypenanthum, Balf. f.
kongboense, Hutch.
laudandum, Cowan.
platyphyllum, Balf. f. & W. W. Sm.
pogonophyllum, Cowan et Davidian.
primulaeflorum, Bur. et Franch.
radendum, Fang.
rufescens, Franch.
sargentianum, Rehd. et Wils.
trichostomum, Franch.

ARBOREUM SERIES Large, tree-like species, fine in both flower and foliage. The distribution of R. peramoenum extends into Indo-China and that of delavayi into both Thailand and Indo-China.
Arboreum Subseries.
ARBOREUM, Smith.
Subspecies:
campbelliae, Hook. f.
cinnamomeum, Wall.
nilagiricum, Zenker.
windsori, Nutt.
delavayi, Franch.
niveum, Hook. f.
peramoenum, Balf. f. et Forrest.
silvaticum, Cowan.
wattii, Cowan.
ZEYLANICUM, Hort. ex Loud.
Argyrophyllum Subseries More shrub-like than those above, with smaller flowers lighter in color and fewer to the truss.
argyrophyllum, Franch.
chienianum, Fang.
coryanum, Tagg et Forrest.
denudatum, Lévl.
farinosum, Lévl.
floribundum, Franch.
fokienense, Franch.
formosanum, Hemsl.
hunnewellianum, Rehd. et Wils.
hypoglaucum, Hemsl.
INSIGNE, Hemsl. et Wils.
longipes, Rehd. et Wils.
pingianum, Fang.
ririei, Hemsl. et Wils.
rockii. Wils.
simiarum, Hance.
thayerianum, Rehd. et Wils.
youngae, Fang.

AURICULATUM SERIES Two valuable but dissimilar species of shrub stature.
AURICULATUM, Hemsl.
GRIERSONIANUM, Balf. f. et Forrest.

AZALEA SERIES Well-known garden shrubs, formerly regarded as a separate genus.
Canadense Subseries. Deciduous species with separate floral and growth buds.
albrechtii, Maxim.
canadense, (L.) Torrey.
pentaphyllum, Maxim.
vaseyi, A. Gray.
Luteum Subseries Deciduous species, some with yellow flowers, mostly American natives.
alabamense, Rehd.
arborescens, (Pursh) Torrey.
atlanticum, (Ashe) Rehd.
austrinum, Rehd.
bakeri, Lemmon et McKay.
calendulaceum, (Michx.) Torrey.
canescens, (Michx.) Sweet.
flammeum, (Michx) Sargent.
flavum, Hoffmansegg.
japonicum, (A. Gray) Suringar.
molle, (Blume) G. Don.
nudiflorum, (L.) Torrey.
oblongifolium, (Small) Millais.
occidentale, A. Gray.
prunifolium, (Small) Millais.
roseum, (Loisel.) Rehd.
serrulatum, (Small) Millais.
viscosum, (L.) Torrey.
Nipponicum Subseries Large leaved deciduous species with long, bell-shaped flowers.
nipponicum, Matsumura.
Obtusum Subseries Popular evergreen and persistent-leaved Oriental species. The distribution of five species (mucronatum, microphyton, saxicolum, annamense, simsii) extends southward into Indo-China and/or Thailand.
annamense, Rehd.
atrovirens, Franch.
boninense, Nakai.
breviperulatum, Hayata.
chunii, Fang.
hainanense, Merrill.
indicum, (L.) Sweet.
kaempferi, Planchon.
kanehirai, Wils.
kiusianum, Makino.
kwangtungense, Merr. et Chun.
lasiostylum, Hayata.

linearifolium, Sieb. et Zucc.
longiperulatum, Hayata.
macrogemmum, Nakai.
mariae, Hance.
mariesii, Hemsl. et Wils.
microphyton, Franch
minutiflorum, Hu.
miyazawae, Nakai et Hara.
mucronatum, G. Don (ledifolium, G. Don).
naamkwanense, Merr.
nakaharai, Hayata.
obtusum, (Lindl.) Planch.
oldhamii, Maxim.
ovatosepalum, Yamam.
poukhanense, Léveillé.
pulchrum, Sweet.
rivulare, Hand.-Mazz.
rubropilosum, Hayata.
rufohirtum, Hand.-Mazz.
saisiuense, Nakai.
sasakii, Wils.
saxicolum, Sleumer.
scabrum, G. Don.
seniavinii, Maxim.
serpyllifolium, Miquel.
simsii, Planch.
subsessile, Rendle.
tamurai, Masamune.
tosaense, Makino.
tschonoskii, Maxim.
tsoi, Merrill.

Schlippenbachii Subseries Deciduous Oriental species of great ornamental merit in which the same buds produce both flowers and new shoots.
amagianum, Makino.
farrerae, Tate.
quinquefolium, Bisset et Moore.
reticulatum, D. Don (apud G. Don).
sanctum, Nakai.
schlippenbachii, Maxim.
weyrichii, Maxim.

Tashiroi Subseries In character midway between species of the Obtusum and Schlippenbachii Series.
tashiroi, Maxim.

BARBATUM SERIES Of varied stature, with bristles or long-stalked glands, conspicuous on the leaf stalks.

Barbatum Subseries Trees with tight trusses of dark red flowers.
argipeplum, Balf. f. et Cooper.
BARBATUM, Wall.
imberbe, Hutch.
smithii, Nutt. MS. (descript. Hook).

Crinigerum Subseries Indumented shrubs of moderate size with loose trusses of flowers.
bainbridgeanum, Tagg et Forrest.
crinigerum, Franch.

Glischrum Subseries Big shrubs or small trees, with large leaves coarsely bristled.
diphrocalyx, Balf. f.
erosum, Cowan.
exasperatum, Tagg.
glischroides, Tagg et Forrest.
glischrum, Balf. f. et W.W.Sm.
habrotrichum, Balf. f. et W.W.Sm.
hirtipes, Tagg.
rude, Tagg et Forrest.
STRIGILLOSUM, Franch.
vesiculiferum, Tagg.

Maculiferum Subseries Small shrubs with lax trusses smaller in size.
anwheiense, Wils.
LONGESQUAMATUM C.K. Schneid.
maculiferum, Franch.
monosematum, Hutch.
morii, Hayata.
nankotaisanense, Hayata.
ochraceum, Rehd. et Wils.
pachytrichum, Franch.
pseudochrysanthum, Hayata.

BOOTHII SERIES Small scaly-leaved shrubs of charming character.

Boothii Subseries.
boothii, Nutt.
chrysodoron, Tagg MS. (descript. Hutch).
dekatanum Cowan.
mishmiense, Hutch. et Ward.
SULFUREUM, Franch.

Megeratum Subseries.
LEUCASPIS, Tagg.
megeratum, Balf. f. et Forrest.

Tephropeplum Subseries.
auritum, Tagg.
chrysolepis, Hutch. et Ward.
TEPHROPEPLUM, Balf. f. et Farrer.
xanthostephanum, Merr.

CAMELLIAEFLORUM SERIES Small scaly-leaved shrubs mainly of botanical interest.
camelliaeflorum, Hook. f.
lucidum, Nutt.

CAMPANULATUM SERIES A mixed assemblage of richly indumented shrubs of moderate size and great garden merit.
CAMPANULATUM, D. Don.
fulgens, Hook. f.
lanatum, Hook. f.
miniatum, Cowan.
paradoxum, Balf. f.
tsariense, Cowan.
wallichii, Hook. f.
wiltonii, Hemsl. et Wils.

CAMPYLOGYNUM SERIES Delightful small scaly-leaved shrub with solitary nodding flowers.
CAMPYLOGYNUM, Franch.

CAMTSCHATICUM SERIES Deciduous undershrubs a few inches high, with flowers on shoots of the current year's growth.
camtschaticum, Pallas.
glandulosum, Standley ex Small.
redowskianum, Maxim.

CAROLINIANUM SERIES Fine native scaly-leaved shrubs of moderate size.
CAROLINIANUM, Rehd.
CHAPMANII, A. Gray.
MINUS, Michaux (punctatum, Andrews).

CINNABARINUM SERIES Medium to large scaly-leaved shrubs with fine glaucous foliage and striking tubular flowers.
CINNABARINUM, Hook. f.
CONCATENANS, Hutch.
igneum, Cowan.
keysii, Nutt.
XANTHOCODON, Hutch.

DAURICUM SERIES Early blooming, hardy, deciduous or evergreen shrubs of intermediate size.
DAURICUM, Linn.
MUCRONULATUM, Turcz.

EDGEWORTHII SERIES Usually epiphytic shrubs, densely indumented and scaly, of moderate size. Lovely flowers.
BULLATUM, Franch.
EDGEWORTHII, Hook. f.
pendulum, Hook. f.
sciaphilum, Balf f. et Ward.
seinghkuense, Ward.

FALCONERI SERIES Mostly small trees of massive appearance with immense, heavily indumented leaves.
ARIZELUM, Balf. f. et Forrest.
basilicum, Balf f. et Forrest.
coriaceum, Franch.
decipiens, Lacaita.
eximium, Nutt.
FALCONERI, Hook. f.
FICTOLACTEUM, Balf. f.
galactinum, Balf. f.
HODGSONII, Hook. f.
preptum, Balf. f. et Forrest.
rex, Lévl.
sino-falconeri, Balf. f.

FERRUGINEUM SERIES Small scaly-leaved European alpine shrubs.
FERRUGINEUM, Linn.
HIRSUTUM, Linn.
kotschyi, Simonk.

FORTUNEI SERIES Varied in stature, often superb in flower and foliage. R. serotinum extends its distribution into Indo-China.
Calophytum Subseries Small trees, large leaves and fine early flowers.
CALOPHYTUM, Franch.
openshawianum, Rehd. et Wils.
Davidii Subseries Handsome foliage and flowers on large shrubs early in the season.
davidii, Franch.
huianum, Fang.
planetum, Balf. f.
PRAEVERNUM, Hutch.
SUTCHUENENSE, Franch.
Fortunei Subseries Fine widely open flowers on large, well-foliaged shrubs.
chengianum, Fang.
chlorops, Cowan.
DECORUM, Franch.
DIAPREPES, Balf. f. et W.W. Sm.
DISCOLOR, Franch.
faithae, Chun.
FORTUNEI, Lindl.
glanduliferum, Franch.
hemsleyanum, Wils.
houlstonii, Hemsl. et Wils.
platypodum, Diels.
serotinum, Hutch.
VERNICOSUM, Franch.
geographical forms:
araliaeforme, Balf. f. et Forrest.
euanthum, Balf. f. et W.W. Sm.
rhantum, Balf. f. et W.W. Sm.
sheltonae, Hemsl. et Wils.
Griffithianum Subseries Huge flowers on a large shrub.
GRIFFITHIANUM, Wight.
Orbiculare Subseries Moderate size shrubs, free blooming, superb foliage.
cardiobasis, Sleumer.
ORBICULARE, Decaisne.
Oreodoxa Subseries Large shrubs, early blooming.
erubescens, Hutch.
FARGESII, Franch.
OREODOXA, Franch.
geographical forms:
haematocheilum, Craib.
limprichtii, Diels.
reginaldii, Balf. f.
praeteritum, Hutch.

FULVUM SERIES Small trees with outstanding foliage, brilliantly indumented.
FULVUM, Balf. f. et W. W. Sm.
uvarifolium, Diels.

GLAUCOPHYLLUM SERIES Some charming dwarf alpine shrubs with scaly leaves.
Genestierianum Subseries.
genestierianum, Forrest.
micromeres, Tagg.
Glaucophyllum Subseries.
brachyanthum, Franch.
charitopes, Balf. f. et Farrer.
GLAUCOPHYLLUM, Hook. f.
shweliense, Balf. f. et Forrest.
tsangpoense, Hutch. et Ward.

GRANDE SERIES Trees small to very large, majestic in bearing and with magnificent leaves, sometimes 3 feet long in one species.
coryphaeum, Balf. f. et Forrest.
giganteum, Forrest (descript. Tagg).
GRANDE, Wight.
lanigerum, Tagg.
MACABEANUM, Watt, MS.(descript. Balf. f.).
magnificum, Ward.
mollyanum, Cowan et Davidian.
peregrinum, Tagg.
praestans, Balf. f. et W. W. Sm.
protistum, Balf. f. et Forrest.
pudorosum, Cowan.
semnoides, Tagg et Forrest.
sidereum, Balf. f.
SINOGRANDE, Balf. f. et W. W. Sm.
watsonii, Hemsl. et Wils.

HELIOLEPIS SERIES Large shrubs with small scaly leaves, very floriferous.
brevistylum, Franch.
DESQUAMATUM, Balf. f. et Forrest.
fumidum, Balf. f. et W. W. Sm.
HELIOLEPIS, Franch.
invictum, Balf. f. et Farrer.
leclerei, Levl.
oporinum, Balf. f. et Ward.
pholidotum, Balf. f. et W. W. Sm.
RUBIGINOSUM, Franch.

IRRORATUM SERIES Robust shrubs, usually with fine flowers and often with good foliage. The distribution of this group extends down into Viet Nam and the Malay Peninsula, with two outlying species on the island of Sumatra.
Irroratum Subseries.
ABERCONWAYII, Cowan.
agastum, Balf. f. et W.W. Sm.
annae, Franch.
anthosphaerum, Diels.
araiophyllum, Balf. f. et W.W. Sm.
atjehense, Sleumer (Sumatra).
brevinerve, Chun et Fang.
cerochitum, Balf. f. et Forrest.
dimitrum, Balf. f. et Forrest.

epapillatum, Balf. f. et Cooper.
eritimum, Balf. f. et W.W.Sm.
excelsum, Cheval. (Viet Nam).
hardingii, Forrest.
IRRORATUM, Franch.
kendrickii, Nutt.
kontumense, Sleumer (Viet Nam).
korthalsii, Miq. (Sumatra).
laxiflorum, Balf. f. et Forrest.
leptopeplum, Balf. f. et Forrest.
lukiangense, Franch.
mengtszense, Balf. f. et W.W.Sm.
ningyuenense, Hand.-Mazz.
ombrochares, Balf. f. et Ward.
pankimense, Cowan et Ward.
papillatum, Balf. f. et Cooper.
pennivenium, Balf. f. et Forrest.
pogonostylum, Balf. f. et W.W.Sm.
ramsdenianum, Cowan.
shepherdii, Nutt.
spanotrichum, Balf. f. et W.W.Sm.
tanastylum, Balf. f. et Ward.
wrayi, King et Gamble (Malay Peninsula).

Parishii Subseries Some fine red-flowered species, late blooming.
agapetum, Balf. f. et Ward.
ELLIOTTII, Watt, MS. (descript. W.W.Sm.).
ERIOGYNUM, Balf. f. et W.W.Sm.
FACETUM, Balf. f. et Ward.
KYAWI, Lace et W.W.Sm.
parishii, C.B. Clarke.
schistocalyx, Balf. f. et Forrest.
VENATOR, Tagg.

LACTEUM SERIES Varied stature, dwarf shrubs to small trees, all with thin indumentum. Two extraordinary yellow-flowered species and one from Viet Nam.
aberrans, Tagg et Forrest.
agglutinatum, Balf. f. et Forrest.
beesianum, Diels.
dictyotum, Balf. f. ex Tagg.
dignabile, Cowan.
dryophyllum, Balf. f. et Forrest.
dumosulum, Balf. f. et Forrest.
iodes, Balf. f. et Forrest.
LACTEUM, Franch.
nakotiltum, Balf. f. et Forrest.
nhatrangense, Dop. (Viet Nam).
phaeochrysum, Balf. f. et W.W.Sm.
pomense, Cowan et Davidian.
przewalskii, Maxim.
traillianum, Forrest et W.W.Sm.
WIGHTII, Hook. f.

LAPPONICUM SERIES Dwarf alpine shrubs with very small scaly leaves.
achroanthum, Balf. f. et W. W. Sm.
alpicola, Rehd. et Wils.
amundsenianum, Hand.-Mazz.
blepharocalyx, Franch.
bulu, Hutch.
capitatum, Maxim.
chamaezelum, Balf. f. et Forrest.
CHRYSEUM, Balf. f. et Ward.
compactum, Hutch.
complexum, Balf. f. et W. W. Sm.
cuneatum, W. W. Sm.
dasypetalum, Balf. f. et Forrest.
diacritum, Balf. f. et W. W. Sm.
drumonium, Balf. f. et Ward.
edgarianum, Rehd. et Wils.
FASTIGIATUM, Franch.
fimbriatum, Hutch.
flavidum, Franch.
glomerulatum, Hutch.
HIPPOPHAEOIDES, Balf. f. et W.W.Sm.
idoneum, Balf. f. et W. W. Sm.
IMPEDITUM, Balf. f. et W. W. Sm.
INTRICATUM, Franch.
lapponicum, Wahl.
litangense, Balf. f. MS.
lysolepis, Hutch.
microleucum, Hutch.
nigropunctatum, Bur. et Franch.
nitidulum, Rehd. et Wils.
nivale, Hook. f.
orthocladum, Balf. f. et Forrest.
paludosum, Hutch. et Ward.
parvifolium, Adams.
peramabile, Hutch.
polifolium, Franch.
polycladum, Franch.
ramosissimum, Franch.
ravum, Balf. f. et W. W. Sm.
rupicola, W. W. Sm.
RUSSATUM, Balf. f. et Forrest.
SCINTILLANS, Balf. f. et W.W.Sm.
setosum, D. Don.
spilanthum, Hutch.
stictophyllum, Balf. f.
tapetiforme, Balf. f. et Ward.
telmateium, Balf. f. et W. W. Sm.
thymifolium, Maxim.
tsaii, Fang.
verruculosum, Rehd. et Wils.
violaceum, Rehd. et Wils.
websterianum, Rehd. et Wils.
yungningense, Balf. f. MS.

LEPIDOTUM SERIES Alpine shrubs, small in size and with scaly leaves.

Baileyi Subseries.
baileyi, Balf. f.

Lepidotum Subseries.
lepidotum, Wall.
lowndesii, Davidian.

MADDENII SERIES Scaly-leaved shrubs of moderate size, often epiphytic in nature, with very large, fragrant flowers. At least half of the 50 species in this series as distinguished by Hutchinson, largely on the basis of scale density, are not entitled to specific status. Sleumer (Blumea, Suppl. IV, Dr. H.J. Lam Jubilee Vol., 2.X. 1958) recognizes only 22 species, eight of which are found in Indo-China and/or Thailand.

Ciliicalyx Subseries.
amandum, Cowan.
BURMANICUM, Hutch.
carneum, Hutch.
CILIATUM, Hook. f.
CILIICALYX, Franch.
ciliipes, Hutch.
concinnoides, Hutch. et Ward.
crenulatum, Hutch.
cubittii, Hutch.
cuffeanum, Craib.
dendricola, Hutch.
FORMOSUM, Wall.
inaequale, Hutch.
iteophyllum, Hutch.
JOHNSTONEANUM, Watt.
lasiopodum, Hutch.
ludwigianum, Hosseus.
lyi, Lévl.
missionarum, Lévl.
notatum, Hutch.
pachypodum, Balf. f. et W. W. Sm.

parryae, Hutch.
pilicalyx, Hutch.
pseudociliicalyx, Hutch.
roseatum, Hutch.
rufosquamosum, Hutch.
scopulorum, Hutch.
scottianum, Hutch.
smilesii, Hutch.
supranubium, Hutch.
surasianum, Balf. f. et Craib.
taronense, Hutch.
VALENTINIANUM, Forrest.
VEITCHIANUM Hook.
walongense, Ward.

Maddenii Subseries.
brachysiphon, Balf. f.
calophyllum, Nutt.
CRASSUM, Franch.
excellens, Hemsl. et Wils.
MADDENII, Hook. f.
manipurense, Balf. f. et Watt.
odoriferum, Hutch.
polyandrum, Hutch.

Megacalyx Subseries.
DALHOUSIAE, Hook. f.
headfortianum, Hutch.
levinei, Merrill.
liliiflorum, Levl.
LINDLEYI, Moore.
MEGACALYX, Balf. f. et Ward.
NUTTALLII, Booth.
rhabdotum, Balf. f. et Cooper.
sinonuttallii, Balf. f. et Forrest.
TAGGIANUM, Hutch.

MICRANTHUM SERIES Scaly-leaved species of moderate stature with tiny Spirea-like flowers.
MICRANTHUM, Turcz.

MOUPINENSE SERIES Small shrubs with scaly leaves, frequently epiphytic.
dendrocharis, Franch.
MOUPINENSE, Franch.
petrocharis, Diels.

NERIIFLORUM SERIES A varied group of small to medium size shrubs, often handsomely indumented and with brilliant flowers.

Forrestii Subseries Very dwarf plants, often prostrate.
chamae-thomsonii, (Tagg et Forrest) Cowan et Davidian.
erastum, Balf. f. et Forrest.
FORRESTII, Balf. f. MS. (descript. Diels).
porphyrophyllum, Balf. f. et Forrest.
serpens, Balf. f. et Forrest.
trilectorum, Cowan.

Haematodes Subseries Medium size shrubs with red flowers; heavily indumented.
BEANIANUM, Cowan.
catocosmum, Balf. f. MS. (descript. Tagg).
chaetomallum, Balf. f. et Forrest.
chionanthum, Tagg et Forrest.
coelicum, Balf. f. et Farrer.
HAEMATODES, Franch.
hemidartum, Balf. f. MS. (descript. Tagg).
mallotum, Balf. f. et Ward.
pocophorum, Balf. f. MS. (descript. Tagg).

Neriiflorum Subseries.
albertsenianum, Forrest.
diphrocalyx, Balf. f.
euchroum, Balf. f. et Ward.
floccigerum, Franch.
NERIIFLORUM, Franch.
Subspecies:
agetum, Balf. f. et Forrest.
phaedropum, Balf. f. et Forrest.
phoenicodum, Balf. f. et Farrer.
SPERABILE, Balf. f. et Farrer.
SPERABILOIDES, Tagg et Forrest.

Sanguineum Subseries An assemblage of ill-defined species, usually 2 to 4 feet tall, with unusual flower colors.
APERANTUM, Balf. f. et Ward.
citriniflorum, Balf. f. et Forrest.
Subspecies:
aureolum, Cowan.
citriniflorum, (typical).
horaeum, Balf. f. et Forrest.
rubens, Cowan.
comisteum, Balf. f. et Forrest.
DICHROANTHUM, Diels.
Subspecies:
APODECTUM, Balf. f. et W. W. Sm.
DICHROANTHUM, (typical).
herpesticum, Balf. f. et Ward.
SCYPHOCALYX, Balf. f. et Forrest.
septentrionale, Cowan.
EUDOXUM, Balf. f. et Forrest.
Subspecies:
brunneifolium, Balf. f. et Forrest.
eudoxum, (typical).
fulvastrum, Balf. f. et Forrest.
Subspecies:
epipastum, Balf. f. et Forrest.
fulvastrum, (typical).
mesopolium, Balf. f. et Forrest.
trichmiscum, Balf. f. et Forrest.
trichophlebium, Balf. f. et Forrest.
gymnocarpum, Balf. f. (descript. Tagg).
microgynum, Balf. f. et Forrest.
parmulatum, Cowan.
SANGUINEUM, Franch.
Subspecies:
aizoides, Cowan.
atrorubrum, Cowan.
cloiphorum, Balf. f. et Forrest.
consanguineum, Cowan.
didymoides, Tagg et Forrest.
DIDYMUM, Balf. f. et Forrest.
HAEMALEUM, Balf. f. et Forrest.
himertum, Balf. f. et Forrest.
leucopetalum, Balf. f. et Forrest.
melleum, Cowan.
mesaeum, Cowan.
roseotinctum, Balf. f. et Forrest.
sanguineoides, Cowan.
SANGUINEUM, (typical).
temenium, Balf. f. et Forrest.
Subspecies:
albipetalum, Cowan.
chrysanthemum, Cowan.
dealbatum, Cowan.
gilvum, Cowan.
glaphyrum, Balf. f. et Forrest.
pothinum, Balf. f. et Forrest.
rhodanthum, Cowan.
temenium, (typical).

OVATUM SERIES Small upright, Azalea-like shrubs with single flowers from axillary buds.
bachii, Levl.
hongkongense, Hutch.
leptothrium, Balf. f. et Forrest.
OVATUM, Planchon.
vialii, Delavay et Franch.

PONTICUM SERIES Very hardy shrubs of small to large stature.

Caucasicum Subseries Dwarf to moderate in size, mostly indumented.

ADENOPODUM, Franch.
BRACHYCARPUM, D. Don et G. Don.
CAUCASICUM, Pallas.
CHRYSANTHUM, Pallas.
DEGRONIANUM, Carriere.
FAURIEI, Franch.
hyperythrum, Hayata.
MAKINOI, Tagg.
METTERNICHII, Sieb. et Zucc.
niko-montanum, Nakai.
SMIRNOWII, Trautv.
UNGERNII, Trautv.
YAKUSIMANUM, Nakai.

Ponticum Subseries Moderate to large in size, without indumentum.

CATAWBIENSE, Michaux.
MACROPHYLLUM, G. Don.
MAXIMUM, Linn.
PONTICUM, Linn.

SALUENENSE SERIES Very small shrubs, often prostrate, with scaly leaves. Alpine.

CALOSTROTUM, Balf. f. et Ward.
chameunum, Balf. f. et Ward.
fragariflorum, Ward.
KELETICUM, Balf. f. et Forrest.
nitens, Hutch.
prostratum, W. W. Sm.
radicans, Balf. f. et Forrest.
SALUENENSE, Franch.

SCABRIFOLIUM SERIES Scaly-leaved shrubs of moderate size with axillary flowers.

hemitrichotum, Balf. f. et Forrest.
mollicomum, Balf. f. et W. W. Sm.
PUBESCENS, Balf. f. et Forrest.
scabrifolium, Franch.
spiciferum Franch.
SPINULIFERUM, Franch.

SEMIBARBATUM SERIES Deciduous shrub, intermediate in size, with solitary flowers produced from lateral buds.

semibarbatum, Maxim.

STAMINEUM SERIES Mostly shrubs of small to medium size, with axillary flowers often fragrant. Distribution of this group extends southward into Thailand, Indo-China and the Malay Peninsula.

cavaleriei, Lévl. (China, Indo-China).
championae, Hook.
esquirolii, Lévl.
feddei, Lévl.
hancockii, Hemsl.
henryi, Hance
klossii, Ridl. (China, Indo-China, Malay Peninsula).
latoucheae, Franch.
leiopodum, Hayata.
mackenzianum, Forrest.
moulmainense, Hook. (China, Indo-China, Thailand, Malay Peninsula).
stamineum, Franch.
taiense, Hutch. (Thailand).
tutcherae, Hemsl. et Wils.
wilsonae, Hemsl. et Wils.

TALIENSE SERIES Shy-blooming, medium-sized shrubs with leaves heavily felted.

Adenogynum Subseries.

adenogynum, Diels.
adenophorum, Balf. f. et W. W. Sm.
alutaceum, Balf. f. et W. W. Sm.
balfourianum, Diels.
bureavii, Franch.
bureavioides, Balf. f.
circinnatum, Cowan et Ward.
codonanthum, Balf. f. et Forrest.
cruentum, Lévl.
detersile, Franch.
detonsum, Balf. f. et Forrest.
dumicola, Tagg et Forrest.
elegantulum, Tagg et Forrest.
faberi, Hemsl.
faberioides, Balf. f.
mimetes, Tagg et Forrest.
prattii, Franch.
wuense, Balf. f.

Roxieanum Subseries Small subalpine shrubs.

bathyphyllum, Balf. f. et Forrest.
globigerum, Balf. f. et Forrest.
lampropeplum, Balf. f. et Forrest.
perulatum, Balf. f. et Forrest.
pronum, Tagg et Forrest.
proteoides, Balf. f. et W. W. Sm.
recurvoides, Tagg et Ward.
roxieanum, Forrest.
russotinctum, Balf. f. et Forrest.
triplonaevium, Balf. f. et Forrest.
tritifolium Balf. f. et Forrest.

Taliense Subseries.

aganniphum, Balf. f. et Ward.
clementinae, Forrest.
doshongense, Tagg.
flavorufum, Balf. f. et Forrest.
glaucopeplum, Balf. f. et Forrest.
principis, Bur. et Franch.
purdomii, Rehd. et Wils.
schizopeplum, Balf. f. et Forrest.
sphaeroblastum, Balf. f. et Forrest.
taliense, Franch.
vellereum, Hutch. MS. (descript. Tagg).

Wasonii Subseries.

coeloneuron, Diels.
inopinum, Balf. f.
rufum, Batal.
WASONII, Hemsl. et Wils.
weldianum, Rehd. et Wils.

THOMSONII SERIES Shrubs of medium height, many with extraordinarily fine foliage and flowers.

Campylocarpum Subseries.

CALLIMORPHUM, Balf. f. et W. W. Sm.
CALOXANTHUM, Balf. f. et Farrer.
CAMPYLOCARPUM, Hook. f.
myiagrum, Balf. f. et Forrest.
panteumorphum, Balf. f. et W. W. Sm.
telopeum, Balf. f. et Forrest.

Cerasinum Subseries.

bonvalotii, Bur. et Franch.
cerasinum, Tagg.

Selense Subseries.

dasycladoides, Hand.-Mazz.
dasycladum, Balf. f. et W. W. Sm.
erythrocalyx, Balf. f. et Forrest.
esetulosum, Balf. f. et Forrest.
eurysiphon, Tagg et Forrest.
jucundum, Balf. f. et W. W. Sm.
martinianum, Balf. f. et Forrest.

selense, Franch.
setiferum, Balf. f. et Forrest.
spilotum, Balf. f. et Farrer.
vestitum, Tagg et Forrest.
Souliei Subseries Open, bowl-shaped flowers.
LITIENSE, Balf. f. et Forrest.
PURALBUM, Balf. f. et W. W. Sm.
SOULIEI, Franch.
WARDII, W. W. Sm.
Thomsonii Subseries.
cyanocarpum, (Franch.) W. W. Sm.
ECLECTEUM, Balf. f. et Forrest.
HOOKERI, Nutt.
hylaeum, Balf. f. et Farrer.
lopsangianum, Cowan.
MEDDIANUM, Forrest.
populare, Cowan.
STEWARTIANUM, Diels.
THOMSONII, Hook. f.
Williamsianum Subseries Charming dwarf with nodding pink bells.
WILLIAMSIANUM, Rehd. et Wils.

TRICHOCLADUM SERIES Shrubs small or medium size with deciduous or persistent scaly leaves.
chloranthum, Balf. f. et Forrest.
cowanianum, Davidian.
LEPIDOSTYLUM, Balf. f. et Forrest.
lithophilum, Balf. f. et Ward.
lophogynum, Balf. f. et Forrest MS.
mekongense, Franch.
melinanthum, Balf. f. et Ward.
oulotrichum, Balf. f. et Forrest.
rubrolineatum, Balf. f. et Forrest.
semilunatum, Balf. f. et Forrest.
trichocladum, Franch.
viridescens, Hutch.

TRIFLORUM SERIES Small to medium size shrubs with scaly leaves and willowy habit of growth. Floriferous and adaptable.
Augustinii Subseries.
AUGUSTINII, Hemsl.
bivelatum, Balf. f.
CHASMANTHUM, Diels.
hirsuticostatum, Hand.-Mazz.
TRICHANTHUM, Rehder.
trichophorum, Balf. f.
Hanceanum Subseries Small stature.
afghanicum, Aitch. et Hemsl.
hanceanum, Hemsl.
Oreotrephes Subseries.
apiculatum, Rehd. et Wils.
artosquameum, Balf. f. et Forrest.
bracteatum, Rehd. et Wils.
exquisitum, Hutch.
OREOTREPHES, W. W. Sm.
sycnanthum, Balf. f. et W. W. Sm.
timeteum, Balf. f. et Forrest.
Polylepis Subseries.
amesiae, Rehd. et Wils.
CONCINNUM, Hemsl.
polylepis, Franch.
Triflorum Subseries.
AMBIGUUM, Hemsl.
bauhiniiflorum, Watt MS.
caesium, Hutch.
chengshienianum, Fang.
flavantherum, Hutch. et Ward.
kasoense, Hutch et Ward.
KEISKEI, Miquel.
LUTESCENS, Franch.
TRIFLORUM, Hook. f.
wongii, Hemsl. et Wils.
Yunnanense Subseries.
aechmophyllum, Balf. f. et Forrest.
BODINIERI, Franch.
caeruleum, Lévl.
charianthum, Hutch.
CHARTOPHYLLUM, Franch.
DAVIDSONIANUM, Rehd. et Wils.
erileucum, Balf. f. et Forrest.
hesperium, Balf. f. et Forrest.
hormophorum, Balf. f. et Forrest.
hypophaeum, Balf. f. et Forrest.
leilungense, Balf. f. et Forrest.
lochmium, Balf. f.
longistylum, Rehd. et Wils.
pallescens, Hutch.
pleistanthum, Balf. f. MS.
rigidum, Franch.
searsiae, Rehd. et Wils.
siderophyllum, Franch.
stereophyllum, Balf. f. et W. W. Sm.
suberosum, Balf. f. et Forrest.
tatsienense, Franch.
vilmorinianum, Balf. f.
YUNNANENSE, Franch.
zaleucum, Balf. f. et W. W. Sm.

UNIFLORUM SERIES Small scaly-leaved alpine shrublets. Good ornamentals.
IMPERATOR, Hutch. et Ward.
ludlowii, Cowan.
monanthum, Balf. f. et W. W. Sm.
patulum, Ward.
PEMAKOENSE, Ward.
pumilum, Hook. f.
uniflorum, Hutch. et Ward.

VACCINIOIDES SERIES Small, scaly-leaved shrubs usually epiphytic.
See below, under Subsection Pseudovireya, Dr. H. Sleumer's classification of these and other related species of the Malaysian Rhododendrons.

VIRGATUM SERIES Willowy shrubs, with scaly leaves and axillary flowers, small to large in stature.
oleifolium, Franch.
RACEMOSUM, Franch.
virgatum, Hook. f.

SPECIES UNPLACED
asterochnoum, Diels.
calvescens, Balf. f. et Forrest.
dimidiatum, Balf. f.
magorianum, Balf. f.
potanini, Batalin.
pyrrhoanthum, Balf. f.
sherriffii, Cowan.
yakuinsulare, Masam -- Azalea Series.

The foregoing listing of Rhododendron species in their series uses the basic arrangement of the 1956 edition of "The Rhododendron Handbook", published by The Royal Horticultural Society, with amendments and deletions made to conform to the results of my own investigations and the findings of others working in this field.

THE "JAVANICUM" RHODODENDRONS

Dr. H. Sleumer recognizes 261 species in his classification of the Rhododendrons in section Vireya from Malaysia, as published in Reinwardtia by Herbarium Bogoriense, Kebun Raya, Indonesia, in 1960. Many of the New Guinea Rhododendrons have minute flowers less than a half-inch in length, but Dr. L. J. Brass of the Archbold expeditions reports that some of the species in this group are spectacularly beautiful. R. toverenae has fragrant white flowers seven inches in diameter and five inches in length. The blossoms of R. superbum are pink, five inches across and Carnation-scented. R. stonori is a good red. RR. zoelleri, brassii and aurigeranum (which also has a yellow form) are examples of the orange-flowered species which are highly ornamental.

The Rhododendrons in section Vireya are scaly leaved and bear seeds which have flange-like appendages at both ends, usually so extended that the projections resemble long tails. The separation into subsections is based on flower shape and on the color, conformation and density of the scales. A few originate at an altitude of 400 feet but the majority come from the middle elevations and the subalpine forests of the high mountains below 13,500 feet. R. stonori and R. saxifragoides are examples of the small group which grows on open grasslands a thousand feet or more below the snowfields and is truly alpine.

I have scouted some of these Rhododendrons in nature in Cambodia, the Indonesian Islands and Malaya. Many are epiphytic and are distinct in gross appearance from the scaly-leaved species and hybrids, both tender and hardy, which have come to our greenhouses and gardens from the centers of distribution farther to the Northwest on the Asian mainland. They encounter little seasonal variation in temperature and there is a difference of only 30 minutes in day length throughout the year. Constant temperature and even day length obtained by artificial illumination contribute importantly to their successful cultivation and flowering in the greenhouse or conservatory. They are reported to be difficult and perhaps impossible to cross with the scaly-leaved Rhododendrons from more temperate regions familiar in cultivation.

Section VIREYA (Bl.) Copel. f. Type Species: R. javanicum (Bl.) Benn. (Vireya javanica, Bl.)

Subsection PSEUDOVIREYA.

adinophyllum, Merr. (Sumatra)
asperulum, Hutch. & Ward (Tibet)
ciliilobum, Sleumer (New Guinea)
cyrtophyllum, Wernh. (New Guinea)
emarginatum, Hemsl. & Wils. (China, Indo-China)
ericoides, Low ex Hook. f. (Borneo)
erosipetalum, J. J. Sm. (New Guinea)
gaultheriifolium, J. J. Sm. (New Guinea)
hameliiflorum, Wernh. (New Guinea)
insculptum, Hutch. & Ward (Tibet)
invasorium, Sleumer (New Guinea)
kawakamii, Hayata (Formosa)
lindaueanum, Koord. (New Guinea, Celebes)
meliphagidum, J. J. Sm. (Moluccas)
nanophyton, Sleumer (Celebes)
nummatum, J. J. Sm. (New Guinea)
oreites, Sleumer (New Guinea)
perakense K. & G. (Malay Peninsula)
pulleanum, Koord. (New Guinea)
quadrasianum, Vid. (Philippines, Celebes, Borneo)
retusum, (Bl.) Benn (Sumatra, Java)
saruwagedicum, Foerster (New Guinea)
schizostigma, Sleumer (New Guinea)
scortechinii, K. & G. (Malay Peninsula)
seimundii, J. J. Sm. (Malay Peninsula)
sororium, Sleumer (Tonkin)
spathulatum, Rdl. (Malay Peninsula)
taxoides, J. J. Sm. (New Guinea)
vaccinioides, Hook. f. (China, Tibet, Burma)
vanderbiltianum, Merr. (Sumatra)

Subsection SIPHONOVIREYA.

agathodaemonis, J. J. Sm. (New Guinea)
cinchoniflorum, Sleumer (New Guinea)
habbemae, Koord. (New Guinea)
herzogii, Warb. (New Guinea)
incommodum, Sleumer (New Guinea)

Subsection PHAEOVIREYA.

asperum, J. J. Sm. (New Guinea)
beyerinckianum, Koord. (New Guinea)
bryophilum, Sleumer (New Guinea)
cyatheicolum, Sleumer (New Guinea)
delicatulum, Sleumer (New Guinea)
dielsianum, Schltr. (New Guinea)
extrorsum, J. J. Sm. (New Guinea)
eymae, Sleumer (Celebes)
gardenia, Schltr. (New Guinea)
gilliardii, Sleumer (New Guinea)
haematophthalmum, Sleumer (New Guinea)
hellwigii, Warb. (New Guinea)
hooglandii, Sleumer (New Guinea)
konori, Becc. (New Guinea)
leptanthum, F. v. M. (New Guinea)
magnificum, Sleumer (New Guinea)
melantherum, Schltr. (New Guinea)
neriifolium, Schltr. (New Guinea)
opulentum, Sleumer (New Guinea)
phaeochitum, F. v. M. (New Guinea)
phaeopeplum, Sleumer (New Guinea)
phaeops, Sleumer (New Guinea)
prainianum, Koord. (New Guinea)
psilanthum, Sleumer (Celebes)
rappardii, Sleumer (New Guinea)
rarum, Schltr. (New Guinea)
revolutum, Sleumer (Celebes)
rhodochroum, Sleumer (New Guinea)
rubellum, Sleumer (New Guinea)
spondylophyllum, F. v. M. (New Guinea)
stolleanum, Schltr. (New Guinea)
superbum, Sleumer (New Guinea)
truncicolum, Sleumer (New Guinea)
tuberculiferum, J. J. Sm. (New Guinea)
warianum, Schltr. (New Guinea)

Subsection MALAYOVIREYA.

acuminatum, Hook. f. (Borneo)
apoanum, Stein (Philippines)
durionifolium, Becc. (Borneo)
fallacinum, Sleumer (Borneo)
fortunans, J. J. Sm. (Borneo)
himantodes, Sleumer (Borneo)
*hybridogenum, Sleumer (Malay Peninsula)
*lineare, Merr. (Borneo)
malayanum, Jack (Thailand, Malay Peninsula, Sumatra, Java, Borneo, Celebes, Moluccas)
nortoniae, Merr. (Philippines)
*obscurum, Sleumer (Malay Peninsula)
*variolosum, Becc. (Borneo)
vinicolor, Sleumer (Sumatra)
*wilhelminae, Hochr. (Java)

(Those starred (*) above are presumed to be natural hybrids.)

Subsection ALBOVIREYA.

aequabile, J. J. Sm. (Sumatra)
album, Bl. (Java)
arenicolum, Sleumer (Celebes)
cernuum, Sleumer (Sumatra)
comptum, C. H. Wright New Guinea)

correoides, J. J. Sm. (New Guinea)
giulianettii, Laut. (New Guinea)
lagunculicarpum, J. J. Sm. (Celebes)
lampongum, Miq. (Sumatra)
pudorinum, Sleumer (Celebes)
versteegii, J. J. Sm. (New Guinea)
yelliotii, Warb. (New Guinea)
zollingeri, J. J. Sm. (Java, Bali, Lombok, Celebes, Philippines)

Subsection SOLENOVIREYA
amabile, Sleumer (Celebes)
archboldianum, Sleumer (New Guinea)
armittii, F. M. Bailey (New Guinea)
carrii, Sleumer (New Guinea)
caringtoniae, F. v. M. (New Guinea)
carstensense, Wernh. (New Guinea)
chamaepitys, Sleumer (Borneo)
cinerascens, Sleumer (New Guinea)
cruttwellii, Sleumer (New Guinea)
edanoi, Merr. & Quisumb. (Philippines)
goodenoughii, Sleumer (New Guinea)
jasminiflorum, Hook. (Malay Peninsula, Sumatra, Borneo, Philippines)
loranthiflorum, Sleumer (Solomon Islands)
maius, (J. J. Sm.) Sleumer (New Guinea)
multinervium, Sleumer (New Guinea)
natalicium, Sleumer (New Guinea)
oliganthum, Sleumer (New Guinea)
oreadum, Wernh. (New Guinea)
pleianthum, Sleumer (New Guinea)
pneumonanthum, Sleumer (Borneo)
pubitubum, Sleumer (Celebes)
radians, J. J. Sm. (Celebes)
ruttenii, J. J. Sm. (Ceram)
schlechteri, Laut. (New Guinea)
stapfianum, Hemsl. ex Prain (Borneo)
suaveolens, Sleumer (Borneo)
toverenae, F. v. M. (New Guinea)
trichanthum, Sleumer (Borneo)
tuba, Sleumer (New Guinea)

Subsection EUVIREYA.
Series Linnaeoidea.
anagalliflorum, Wernh. (New Guinea)
caespitosum, Sleumer (New Guinea)
coelorum, Wernh. (New Guinea)
distigerigmoides, Sleumer (New Guinea)
gracilentum, F. v. M. (New Guinea)
microphyllum, J. J. Sm. (New Guinea)
muscicola, J. J. Sm. (New Guinea)
oxycoccoides, Sleumer (New Guinea)
parvulum, Sleumer (New Guinea)
pusillum, J. J. Sm. (New Guinea)
womersleyi, Sleumer (New Guinea)
Series Saxifragoidea.
saxifragoides, J. J. Sm. (New Guinea)
Series Taxifolia.
taxifolium, Merr. (Philippines)
Series Stenophylla.
myrsinites, Sleumer (New Guinea)
purpureiflorum, J. J. Sm. (New Guinea)
stenophyllum, Hook. f. (Borneo)
subulosum, Sleumer (New Guinea)
Series Citrina.
citrinum, Hassk. (Java, Bali, Sumatra)
Series Buxifolia.
acrocline, Sleumer (New Guinea)
acrophilum, Merr. & Quisumb. (Philippines)
alternans, Sleumer (Celebes)
alticolum, Sleumer (New Guinea)
atropurpureum, Sleumer (New Guinea)
bagobonum, Copel. f. (Philippines, Borneo)
banghamiorum, (J. J. Sm.) Sleumer (Sumatra)
brassii, Sleumer (New Guinea)
buxifolium, Low ex Hook. f. (Borneo)
commonae, Foerst. (New Guinea)
cornu-bovis, Sleumer (New Guinea)
frey-wysslingii, J. J. Sm. (Sumatra)
hatamense, Becc. (New Guinea)
helodes, Sleumer (New Guinea)
inconspicuum, J. J. Sm. (New Guinea)
lamii, J. J. Sm. (New Guinea)
leptomorphum, Sleumer (Celebes)
luteosquamatum, Sleumer (New Guinea)
nieuwenhuisii, J. J. Sm. (Borneo)
nitens, Sleumer (New Guinea)
papuanum, Becc. (New Guinea)
pauciflorum, K. & G. (Malay Peninsula)
planecostatum, Sleumer (Borneo)
psammogenes, Sleumer (New Guinea)
pseudobuxifolium, Sleumer (Celebes)
pubigermen, J. J. Sm. (Sumatra)
pyrrhophorum, Sleumer (Sumatra)
rhodostomum, Sleumer (New Guinea)
ripleyi, Merr. (Sumatra)
rubrobracteatum, Sleumer (New Guinea)
scarlatinum, Sleumer (Celebes)
simulans, Sleumer (New Guinea)
stonori, Sleumer (New Guinea)
subcrenulatum, Sleumer (New Guinea)
subuliferum, Sleumer (New Guinea)
ultimum, Wernh. (New Guinea)
vidalii, Rolfe. (Philippines)
vitis-idaea, Sleumer (New Guinea)
wrightianum, Koord. (New Guinea)
Series Javanica.
angiense, J. J. Sm. (New Guinea)
angulatum, J. J. Sm. (New Guinea)
arfakianum, Becc. (New Guinea)
aurigeranum, Sleumer (New Guinea)
baenitzianum, Laut. (New Guinea)
beccarii, Sleumer (Sumatra)
bloembergenii, Sleumer (Celebes)
brachygynum, Copel. f. (Philippines)
brevipes, Sleumer (New Guinea)
brevitubum, J. J. Sm. (Borneo)
brookeanum, Low ex Lindl. (Borneo, Sumatra)
buruense, J. J. Sm. (Moluccas)
celebicum, (Bl.) DC. (Celebes)
chevalieri, Dop. (Annam)
christi, Foerster (New Guinea)
christianae, Sleumer (New Guinea)
commutatum, Sleumer (Borneo)
comparabile, Sleumer (New Guinea)
convexum, Sleumer (New Guinea)
crassifolium, Stapf (Borneo)
culminicolum, F. v. M. (New Guinea)
curviflorum, J. J. Sm. (New Guinea)
cuspidellum, Sleumer (New Guinea)
englerianum, Koord. (New Guinea)
flavoviride, J. J. Sm. (New Guinea)
glabriflorum, J. J. Sm. (New Guinea)
gregarium, Sleumer (New Guinea)
hirtolepidotum, J. J. Sm. (New Guinea)
impositum, J. J. Sm. (Celebes)
impressopunctatum, J. J. Sm. (Moluccas)
javanicum, (Bl.) Benn (Sumatra, Java, Bali, Celebes, Philippines, Malay Peninsula)
kemulense, J. J. Sm. (Borneo)
keysseri, Foerster (New Guinea)
kochii Stein (Philippines)
laetum, J. J. Sm. (New Guinea)
lanceolatum, Ridl. (Borneo)
leptobrachion, Sleumer (Celebes)
leytense, Merr. (Philippines)

loboense, Copel. f. (Philippines)
lochae, F. v. M. (Australia)
loerzingii, J. J. Sm. (Java)
lompohense, J. J. Sm. (Celebes)
longiflorum, Lindl. (Sumatra, Borneo, Malay Peninsula, Bangka)
lowii, Hook. f. (Borneo)
luraluense, Sleumer (Solomon Islands)
macgregoriae, F. v. M. (New Guinea)
maxwellii, Gibbs (Borneo)
mindanaense, Merr. (Philippines)
mollianum, Koord. (New Guinea)
moultonii, Ridl. (Borneo)
multicolor, Miq. (Sumatra)
nervulosum, Sleumer (Borneo)
orbiculatum, Ridl. (Borneo)
pachycarpon, Sleumer (New Guinea)
perplexum, Sleumer (Sumatra)
poremense, J. J. Sm. (Celebes)
pseudomurudense, Sleumer (Borneo)
rarilepidotum, J. J. Sm. (Sumatra)
renschianum, Sleumer (Flores)
retivenium, Sleumer (Borneo)
rhodopus, Sleumer (Celebes)
robinsonii, Ridl. (Malay Peninsula)
rosendahlii, Sleumer (New Guinea)
rugosum, Low ex Hook. f. (Borneo)
salicifolium, Becc. (Borneo)
sayeri, Sleumer (New Guinea)
scabridibracteum, Sleumer (New Guinea)
seranicum, J. J. Sm. (Moluccas, Celebes)
sessilifolium, J. J. Sm. (Sumatra)
stresemannii, J. J. Sm. (Moluccas)
subcordatum, Becc. (Borneo)
sumatranum, Merr. (Sumatra)
toxopei, J. J. Sm. (Moluccas)
triumphans, Yersin & Cheval. (Annam)
vanvuurenii, J. J. Sm. (Celebes)
verticillatum, Low ex Lindl. (Borneo)
villosulum, J. J. Sm. (New Guinea)
wentianum, Koord. (New Guinea)
williamsii, Merr. ex Copel. f. (Philippines)
xanthopetalum, Merr. (Philippines)
zoelleri, Warb. (Moluccas, New Guinea)

APPENDIX F

Obsolete and Invalid Names

Here will be found obsolete and invalid names of species together with their correct names in current usage under the rules of nomenclature; and, for convenience, recognized subspecies are included as well along with the names of their species of close affinity.

acraium	= primulaeflorum
acuminatum	= mucronulatum var. acuminatum
adamsii	= primulaeflorum
adenostemonum	= a form of pogonostylum
admirabile	= lukiangense
adoxum	= vernicosum
adroserum	= lukiangense
aemulorum	= mallotum
aeruginosum	= campanulatum var. aeruginosum
agetum	= neriiflorum subspecies
aiolopeplum	= dryophyllum
aiolosalpinx	= stewartianum var. aiolosalpinx
aischropeplum	= roxieanum
aizoides	= sanguineum subspecies
albicaule	= decorum
albipetalum	= temenium subspecies
album	= a form of arboreum
algarvense	= baeticum?
amaurophyllum	= saluenense
amoenum	= a form of obtusum
angustifolium	= hirsutum
araliaeforme	= vernicosum forma
argenteum	= grande
argyi	= mucronatum?
aristatum	= barbatum
aromaticum	= anthopogon
ashleyi	= maximum
asmenistum	= cloiophorum
assamicum	= formosum
asteium	= mesopolium
astrocalyx	= wardii
atentsiense	= ciliicalyx
atrorubrum	= sanguineum subspecies
atroviride	= concinnum
aucklandii	= griffithianum
aureoleum	= citriniflorum subspecies
aureum, Franch.	= xanthostephanum
aureum, Georgi	= chrysanthum
australe	= leptothrium
axium	= selense
baeticum	= ponticum
batangense	= stictophyllum
batemanii	= campanulatum
beimäense	= erythrocalyx
bellatulum	= a variety of eclecteum
benthamianum	= concinnum
bicolor	= canescens
blandfordiaeflorum	= cinnabarinum var. blandfordiaeflorum
blandulum	= a form of jucundum
blinii	= lutescens
blumei	= niveum
brachyandrum	= eclecteum var. brachyandrum
brachystylum	= trichocladum
brettii	= longesquamatum
breynii	= indicum
brunneifolium	= eudoxum subspecies
buergeri	= obtusum forma
burmannii	= mucronatum
burriflorum	= diphrocalyx
butyricum	= chrysodoron
caeruleo-glaucum	= campylogynum
calcicola	= cuneatum
calciphilum	= calostrotum var. calciphilum
californica (Azalea)	= occidentale
californicum	= macrophyllum
calleryi	= simsii
campbelliae	= arboreum subspecies
candelabrum	= thomsonii var. candelabrum
cantabile	= russatum
cardatum	= souliei
cardioeides	= artosquameum
caryophyllum	= rubropilosum
catapastum	= desquamatum
catesbaeum	= ponticum hybrid?
caucaseum	= caucasicum
cephalanthoides	= primulaeflorum var. cephalanthoides
ceraceum	= lukiangense
cerasiflorum	= campylogynum
cerinum	= sulfureum
chaffanjonii	= stamineum
chalarocladum	= selense
chamaecistus	= rhodothamnus chamaecistus
chamaetortum	= cephalanthum
chariodotes	= chameunum
charitostreptum	= brachyanthum var. hypolepidotum
charopeum	= campylogynum var. charopeum
chasmanthoides	= chasmanthum
chawchiense	= eritimum
cheilanthum	= ravum
chionophyllum	= hypoglaucum
chlanidotum	= citriniflorum
chrysanthemum	= temenium subspecies
cinereum	= ravum
clivicola	= primulaeflorum
cloiophorum	= sanguineum subspecies
coccinopeplum	= roxieanum
colletum	= beesianum
colobodes	= chameunum
commodum	= sulfureum
confertissimum	= parvifolium
consanguineum	= sanguineum subspecies
coombense	= concinnum
cooperi	= camelliaeflorum
coreanum	= poukhanense
coronarium	= flavum
cosmetum	= chameunum
costulatum	= lutescens
crebreflorum	= cephalanthum var. crebreflorum
cremastum	= campylogynum var. cremastum
cremnastes	= lepidotum
cremnophilum	= primulaeflorum
crenatum	= racemosum
crispiflora (Azalea)	= a form of indicum
croceum	= wardii

cucullatum = roxieanum
cumberlandense = bakeri
cuthbertii = minus
cyclium = callimorphum
cymbomorphum = erythrocalyx
dahuricum = dauricum
damascenum = campylogynum
danielsianum = indicum
daphniflorum = rufescens
davuricum = dauricum
dealbatum = temenium subspecies
decandrum = reticulatum
decumbens = indicum
deleinse = tephropeplum
dendritrichum = uvarifolium
depile = oreotrephes
dianthiflora (Azalea) = a double form of linearifolium var. macrosepalum
dichropeplum = phaeochrysum
didymoides = sanguineum subspecies
dilatatum = reticulatum
docimum = erythrocalyx
dolerum = selense
duclouxii = spinuliferum
dunnii = henryi
duseimatum = selense var. duseimatum
edgarii = campanulatum
elaegnoides = lepidotum
emaculatum = beesianum
epipastum = fulvastrum subspecies
eriandrum = caeruleum
eriocarpum = a variety of simsii
eriphyllum = cyanocarpum var. eriphyllum
euanthum = vernicosum forma
eucallum = erythrocalyx
euchaites = neriiflorum
euonymifolium = emarginatum
faberi = pratti
faberoides = pratti
fissotectum = schizopeplum
fittianum = dauricum
flammea (Azalea) = calendulaceum
flavum = chrysanthum
fordii = simiarum
foveolatum = coriaceum
fragrans, Maxim. = primulaeflorum
franchetianum = decorum
fuchsiaeflorum = spinuliferum
fulva (Azalea) = flammeum
fulvoides = fulvum
gibsonii = formosum
gilvum = temenium subspecies
giraudiasii = decorum
glabrius = japonicum
glaphyrum = temenium subspecies
glauco-aureum = campylogynum
glaucum = glaucophyllum
gloeoblastum = wardii
gnaphalocarpum = mariesii
gracilipes = hypoglaucum
gymnanthum = lukiangense
gymnogynum = eritimum
gymnomiscum = primulaeflorum
haematocheilum = oreodoxa forma
haemonium = anthopogon var. haemonium
hagnoense = indicum
hallaisanense = poukhanense
hannoense = indicum
harrovianum = polylepis
hedyosmum = trichostomum var. hedyosmum
hedythamnum = callimorphum
hedythamnum var. eglandulosum = cyanocarpum

helvolum = dryophyllum
heptamerum = eritimum
hexamerum = decorum
himertum = sanguineum subspecies
hispidum = a variety of viscosum
hortense = a form of linearifolium var. macrosepalum
humicola = saluenense
humifusum = chameunum
hyacinthiflorum = ponticum
hylothreptum = anthophaerum
hymenanthes = degronianum and metternichii, each in part
hypolepidotum = brachyanthum var. hypolepidotum
hypotrichotum = oreotrephes
intortum = dryophyllum
ioanthum = concinnum
ixeuticum = crinigerum
jahandiezii = siderophyllum
jangtzowense = apodectum
japonicum, Schneider = metternichii
jenkinsii = maddenii
kamtschaticum = camtschaticum
kansuense = imperfectly known species, s. Taliense?
kialense = przewalskii
kingianum = zeylanicum
kirkii = discolor
komiyamae = tosaense
laetevirens = concinnum
lagopus = reticulatum
lamprophyllum = ovatum
lancifolium, Hook. f. = barbatum (Moench=ponticum)
lateritium = indicum
latifolium = hirsutum
ledifolium = mucronatum
ledifolium var. purpureum = pulchrum var. calycinum
ledoides = trichostomum var. ledoides
lemeei = lutescens
lepidanthum = primulaeflorum var. lepidanthum
lepidotum var. chloranthum = lepidotum
leptanthum = leiopodum
leptosanthum = leiopodum
leucobotrys = moulmainense
leucandrum = siderophyllum?
leucanthum = mucronatum
leucolasium = hunnewellianum
leucopetalum = sanguineum subspecies
levistratum = dryophyllum
limprichtii = oreodoxa forma
liratum = apodectum
liukiuense = scabrum
longifolium = grande
lophophorum = phaeochrysum
lusidusculum = obtusum forma
luteum = flavum
macrantha (Azalea) = indicum
macrosepalum = linearifolium var. macrosepalum
macrostemon = obtusum forma
mairei = lacteum
malindangense = quadrasianum
mandarinorum = discolor
mannophorum = roseotinctum
manopeplum = esetulosum
matsumurai = poukhanense
maximowiczianum = non-existent
maxwellii = a variety of pulchrum
megaphyllum = basilicum
melleum = sanguineum subspecies
mesaeum = sanguineum subspecies
mesembrinum = a variety of simsii

mesopolium	= falvastrum subspecies	pritzelianium	= micranthum
messatum	= xanthostephanum	probum	= selense var. probum
metrium	= selense	procerum	= maximum
microterum	= beesianum	prophantum	= kyawi
mirabile	= genestierianum	propinquum	= achroanthum
modestum	= ciliatum ?	pruniflorum	= tsangpoense var. pruniflorum
monbeigii	= uvarifolium	pseudoyanthinum	= concinnum
morsheadianum	= imperfectly known ? Arboreum Series	pubigerum	= artosquameum
		punctatum Ker	= carolinianum (Andr. = minus.)
motsouense	= racemosum	puniceum	= pulchrum
muliense	= chryseum	purpureum	= maximum
mussoti	= wardii	purshii	= maximum
mutabile	= campanulatum	pycnocladum	= diacritum
myrtifolia (Azalea)	= hongkongense	radinum	= trichostomum var. radinum
myrtifolium, Schott	= kotschyi (Lodd = ponticum)	randaiense	= rubropilosum
myrtilloides	= campylogynum var. myrtilloides	rarosquameum	= caeruleum
nagasakianum	= reticulatum	rasile	= diaprepes
nakaii	= degronianum var.	rawsonii	= pulchrum forma
nanothamnum	= selense	recurvum	= roxieanum
nanum	= polychadum	recurvum var. oreonastes	= roxieanum var. oreonastes
narcissiflorum	= double white-flowered form of mucronatum		
		redowskianum	= camtşchaticum
nebrites	= himertum	regale	= basilicum
nepalense	= arboreum	reginaldii	= oreodoxa forma
nikoense	= pentaphyllum	repens	= forrestii or chamae-thomsonii
nilagiricum	= arboreum subspecies	repens var. chamaedoron	= chamae-thomsonii var. chamaethauma
niphargum	= uvarifolium		
niphobolum	= stewartianum	repens var. chamaethauma	= chamae-thomsonii var. chamaethauma
nitidum	= viscosum		
nmaiense	= cephalanthum var. nmaiense	repens var. chamae-thomsonii	= chamae-thomsonii
nobile	= possibly a distinct species akin to campanulatum		
		rhaibocarpum	= dasycladum
nudiflora (Azalea)	= calendulaceum or flammeum	rhantum	= vernicosum forma
nudipes	= reticulatum	rhodanthum	= temenium subspecies
nwaiense	= cephalanthum var. nmaiense	rhododactylum	= a color variation of R. wasonii
oblongum	= griffithianum	rhodora	= canadense
obovatum	= lepidotum	rhombicum	= reticulatum
obscurum	= siderophyllum	riparium	= calostrotum
officinale	= chrysanthum	ripense	= mucronatum var. ripense
oomurasaki	= pulchrum forma	rollissonii	= zeylanicum
oreinum	= alpicola	rosaeflora (Azalea)	= indicum var. balsaminaeflorum
oreonastes	= roxieanum var. oreonastes	roseotinctum	= sanguineum subspecies
oreotrephoides	= oreotrephes	rosmarinifolium	= quadrasianum var. rosmarinifolium
oresbium	= edgarianum	rosthornii	= micranthum
oresterum	= wardii	rotundifolium	= orbiculare
osakazuki	= pulchrum var.	roylei	= cinnabarinum var. roylei
osmerum	= russatum	rubens	= citriniflorum subspecies
oxyphyllum	= moulmainense	rubriflorum	= campylogynum
pachysanthum	= morii	rubropunctatum, Hayata	= hyperythrum
pagophilum	= selense var. pagophilum		
pamprotum	= chameunum	rubropunctatum, Lévl.	= bodinieri
pentamerum	= degronianum		
periclymena (Azalea)	= nudiflorum	salignum	= lepidotum
periclymenoides	= nudiflorum	sanguineoides	= sanguineum subspecies
persicinum	= eritimum	sclerocladum	= ravum
phaedropum	= neriiflorum subspecies	seguini	= bodinieri
phaeochlorum	= oreotrephes	semanteum	= impeditum
phoeniceum	= pulchrum	semnum	= coryphaeum
phoenicodum	= neriiflorum subspecies	septentrionale	= dichroanthum subspecies
pilovittatum	= delavayi	seriocalyx	= chameunum
pittosporaefolium	= stamineum	sheltonae	= vernicosum forma
planifolium	= wallichii	shikokianum	= weyrichii
plebeium	= heliolepis	shojoense	= mariesii
poecilodermum	= roxieanum	siamense	= moulmainense
poliopeplum	= himertum	sieboldii	= kaempferi ?
pontica (Azalea)	= flavum	sigillatum	= dryophyllum
porphyroblastum	= globigerum	sinense, Maxim.	= japonicum (Sweet = molle)
porrosquameum	= brevistylum	sinolepidotum	= lepidotum
pothinum	= temenium subspecies	sinovaccinioides	= vaccinioides
praeclarum	= primulaeflorum	sinovirgatum	= oleifolium
prasinocalyx	= wardii	sonomense	= occidentale var. sonomense
primulinum	= flavidum	sordidum	= tsangpoense var. pruniflorum
prinophyllum	= roseum	sparsiflorum	= camelliaeflorum

speciosum	=	flammeum
sphaeranthum	=	trichostomum
spodopeplum	=	tephropeplum
spooneri	=	decorum
squamata (Azalea)	=	farrerae
squarrosum	=	desquamatum
stenaulum	=	moulmainense
stenophyllum	=	makinoi
stenoplastum	=	desquamatum
sublanceolatum	=	scabrum
sublateritium	=	scabrum
syncollum	=	phaeochrysum
tanakai	=	stamineum series
tapeinum	=	megeratum
tapelouense	=	tatsienense
taquetii	=	mucronulatum
tebotan	=	pulchrum forma
tectum	=	obtusum forma
telopeum forma telopeoides	=	panteumorphum
theiochroum	=	sulfureum
theiophyllum	=	dryophyllum
thomsonii var. album	=	thomsonii
thomsonii var. cyanocarpum	=	cyanocarpum
thomsonii var. flocculosa	=	thomsonii
thomsonii var. grandiflorum	=	thomsonii
thunbergii	=	obtusum
thyodocum	=	baileyi
torquatum	=	roseotinctum
transiens	=	obtusum forma
trichomistum	=	fulvastrum subspecies
trichophlebium	=	fulvastrum subspecies
trichopodum	=	artosquameum
trinerve	=	tschonoskii
truncatulum	=	erythrocalyx
tsarongense	=	primulaeflorum
vaniotii	=	esquirolii
venosum	=	falconeri
venustum	=	nudiflorum
verticillata (Azalea)	=	arborescens
vicarium	=	telmateium
vicinum	=	dryophyllum
villosum	=	trichanthum
vittatum	=	simsii var. vittatum
wadanum	=	reticulatum
wallaceanum	=	Taliense series; imperfectly known
warrenii	=	albiflorum var.
westlandii	=	moulmainense
windsori	=	arboreum subspecies
xanthinum	=	trichocladum
xanthoneuron	=	denudatum
xenosporum	=	detonsum forma
yakumontanum	=	reticulatum
yanthinum	=	concinnum
yaragongense	=	ramosissimum
yedoense	=	poukhanense
yodogawa	=	poukhanense

Bibliography

Books

Care and Feeding of Garden Plants, The; The American Society for Horticultural Science and The National Fertilizer Association
Climate and Man; 1941 Yearbook of Agriculture, U.S. Dept. of Agriculture
Diseases and Pests of Ornamental Plants, Dodge & Rickett; Ronald Press
Freiland-Rhododendron, Berg & Krüssman; Eugen Ulmer, Stuttgart
Handbook of Rhododendrons, The; University of Washington Arboretum Foundation
Hardy Rhododendrons, Frederick Street; Collins, London
International Rhododendron Register, The; Royal Horticultural Society, London
Journeys and Plant Introductions of George Forrest, The; Royal Horticultural Society, London
Methods of Plant Breeding, Hayes & Immer; McGraw-Hill Book Co., Inc.
Plant Breeding, A. L. Hagedoorn; Crosby Lockwood & Son, Ltd., London
Plants, Man and Life, Edgar Anderson; Little, Brown & Co.
Rhododendron Handbook, The, 1956 Edition; Royal Horticultural Society, London
Rhododendron Leaf, The, J.M. Cowan; Oliver & Boyd, Edinburgh
Rhododendron Yearbook, The, for 1945, 1946, 1947, 1948, 1949; The American Rhododendron Society
Rhododendron Yearbook, The, for 1946, 1947, 1948, 1949, 1950, 1951-52 and 1953; Royal Horticultural Society, London
Rhododendron and Camellia Yearbook, The, for 1954, 1955, 1956, 1957, 1958, 1959 and 1960; Royal Horticultural Society, London
Rhododendron und immergrüne Laubgehölze, Jahrbuch 1953; Rhododendron-Gesellschaft, Bremen
Rhododendrons, F. Kingdon Ward; Latimer House, Ltd., London
Rhododendrons, 1956; The American Rhododendron Society
Rhododendrons and Azaleas, C.G. Bowers; Macmillan, London
Rhododendrons and the Various Hybrids, J.G. Millais; First and Second Series; Longmans, Green and Co., London
Rhododendrons en Azaleas, Herman J. Grootendorst; Vereniging voor Boskoopse Culturen
Rhododendrons of Sikkim Hamalaya, J.D. Hooker; London, 1851
Species of Rhododendron, The, Hutchinson, Rehder and Tagg; The Rhododendron Society, London
Standard Cyclopedia of Horticulture, The, L. H. Bailey; Macmillan, London
Trees and Shrubs Hardy in the British Isles, W. J. Bean, Volume 3, Seventh Ed.; John Murray, London
Winter-Hardy Azaleas and Rhododendrons, C.G. Bowers; The Massachusetts Horticultural Society

Other Publications

American Nurseryman; Articles on propagation and pathology
Botanical Magazine, The; 1787 to 1956
Deutsche Baumschule; December, 1954, Aachen
Diseases of Ornamental Shrubs and Vines; Pennsylvania State College School of Agriculture, Bulletin 508
Effects of Incorporating Large Quantities of Fresh Sawdust and Ammonium Sulphate in Nursery Soils Upon Survival and Terminal Growth of Coniferous Transplants; W. McKay Carson. Master's Thesis, College of Forestry, Syracuse University, 1954
Flower Grower; Articles by the Author and others on culture and propagation
Gardeners' Chronicle, London
Genus Rhododendron in Malaysia, The; Reinwardtia, Herbarium Bogoriense, Vol. 5, part 2, pp. 45-231, March 1960. H. Sleumer
Genus Rhododendron L. in Indochina and Siam, The; Blumea, Suppl. IV, Dr H. J. Lam Jubilee Vol., 2. X. 1958. H. Sleumer
Home Garden, The; Articles by the Author on propagation and selections for hardiness, and on plant breeding.
Horticulture; Articles by the Author and others on culture and selections for cold climates.
Journal of the Royal Horticultural Society, 1876 to 1956; London
New York Times; Articles by the Author and others on pathology and superior garden sorts.
Notes from the Royal Botanic Garden, Edinburgh; 1920 to 1956

Quarterly Bulletin, The; April, 1947, to January, 1961; The American Rhododendron Society

1954 Recommendation for Trees, Shrubs and Turf; New York State College of Agriculture, Cornell University

Symphilid or Garden Centipede, The; Pennsylvania State College School of Agriculture, Bulletin 508

Use of Sawdust for Mulches and Soil Improvement, The; U.S. Dept. of Agriculture Circular No. 891

Index

Aberconway, Lord, 122, 246, 247
Aberconway hybrids, 247
aberconwayi, 122
'Abraham Lincoln', 252
Acidity, 50, 51, 65, 69, 79, 93, 281, 366
Adenogynum subseries, 114
adenopodum, 113, 122-3
afghanicum, 29
albiflorum, 19, 123, 202
Albiflorum series, 123
'Album Elegans', 46
'Alice', 88, 380
'Altaclerense', 17, 245
Aluminum, 97
Aluminum sulphate, 97, 280, 366
Amateis, Edmond, 119, 196, 220, 268, 362, 373, 387, 390, 397
ambiguum, 18, 124, 262
'America', 65, 321, 388, 389
American Rhododendron Society, 32, 120, 121, 154, 202, 211, 257, 265, 275, 363, 374, 378, 385, 421
'Amethyst', 258
Ammal, Dr E. K. Janaki, 412
Ammonium compound, 355; ions, 367; nitrate, 98, 367; nitrogen, 104, 105, 282, 283, 288, 328, 367; phosphate, 98, 283; sulphate, 70, 71, 78, 96, 98, 100, 101, 102, 104, 105, 283, 287, 366, 367
Anderson, Dr Edgar, 110, 116
Anthopogon series, 24, 32, 112
'Antoon van Welie', 380
aperantum, 124-5, 398, 399
apodectum, 125, 156; Exbury form, 125
Appalachian Nurseries, 92
Apple Scab, 295
arboreum, 16, 17, 21, 125-7, 187, 233, 245, 262, 363, 398; forma roseum, 126; var. baileyi, 126; var. cinnamomeum, 126, 252
Arboreum series, 30, 113, 125, 179, 233
Arboreum subseries, 125, 126, 233
'Arden Fairy', 391
'Argosy', 48
Argyrophyllum subseries, 113, 179
arizelum, 31, 127
Armillaria, see Oak Root fungus
Armillaria mellea, see Armillaria Root Rot
Armillaria Root Rot: Shoe String Fungus (Armillaria mellea), 294-5
Arnold Arboretum, Boston, Mass., 18, 157, 224, 250, 253, 254, 256, 257, 258, 329
'Ascot Brilliant', 400
Asiatic Garden Beetle (Autoserica Castanea), 306-7
Aspidiotus hederae, see Oleander Scale
Aspidiotus pseudosapinosus, see Ivy Scale
Association of Botanical Gardens and Arboretums, 257
'Atrosanguineum', 389
aucklandii, see griffithianum
augustinii, 17, 127-8, 144, 262; 'Barto Blue', 127; 'Caeruleum', 128; caeruleum species, 128; de Rothschild's form, 127; Exbury form, Tower Court form, 54, 127; Magor's form, 127; 'Marine', 128
Augustinii subseries, 127, 143, 223
auriculatum, 18, 30, 31, 48, 128-9, 172
Auriculatum series, 113, 128, 171, 172
'Aurora', 261
Autoserica castanea, see Asiatic Garden Beetle, Brown Garden Beetle
'Avalanche', 48
Azalea, 15, 16, 17, 19, 21, 57, 58, 97, 123, 184, 197, 202, 286, 310, 324, 333, 380, 381, 386, 392; of the Luteum subseries, 386; of the Obtusum subseries, 202, 386
Azalea series, 386
Azaleodendron, 17, 414
'Azma', 34
'Azor', 34, 264
Azor hybrid group, 262

Bacterium tumefaciens, see Crown Gall
'Bagshot Ruby', 88
Baldsiefen, Warren, 268, 272, 303, 321, 325, 360
Balfour, Sir Isaac Bayley, 29, 124, 125, 127, 133, 134, 135, 145, 154, 156, 157, 160, 161, 165, 166, 167, 169, 171, 173, 175, 178, 182, 184, 186, 194, 205, 206, 208, 210, 211, 212, 215, 221
barbatum, 16, 88, 129-30, 218
Barbatum series, 113, 129, 187, 218
Barbatum subseries, 129
'Barclayi', 396
'Baroness Henry Schroeder', 255
Barto, James E., 246, 268
basilicum, 31, 127
'B. de Bruin', 380
Bean, W. J., 130
beanianum, 130; var. compactum, 130
'Beaufort', 255, 256, 268
'Betty Wormald', 268
'Billy Budd', 399
Black Vine Weevil (Brachyrhinus sulcatus), 288, 304-306; grubs, 306
'Blue Bird', 39, 247
'Blue Diamond', 39, 266
'Blue Ensign', 402
'Blue Peter', 254, 402
'Blue Tit', 39
'Bobolink', 400
bodinieri, 130-1; Bodnant selection, 130; McLaren # V-139, 130
Bodnant Gardens, North Wales, 181, 200, 221, 230, 247, 266, 268, 402, 403
Booth, T. J., 177, 199, 200
Boothii series, 35, 185, 218, 221, 241, 392, 395
Boothii subseries, 218
Borax, 286
Boron, 92, 99, 100
Boron deficiency, 286
Boskoop Growers' Association, Holland, 378
Bosley Nursery, Ohio, 258, 259
Botryosphaeria ribis, see Leaf Spots
Botrytis Blight (Botrytis cinerea), 300, 355
Botrytis cinerea, see Botrytis Blight
'Boule de Neige', 42, 45, 90, 252, 256, 302
'Bow Bells', 90
Bowers, Dr C. G., 96, 252
Bowers, W. E., 363
brachycarpum, 114, 131, 145, 164, 389, 390, 403
Brachyrhinus ovatus, see Strawberry Weevil
Brachyrhinus singularis, see Clay Colored Weevil
Brachyrhinus sulcatus, see Taxus Weevil, Black Vine Weevil
Brandt, Lester, 268
brevistylum, 175
'Brittania', 261, 268
Brodick Castle, Scotland, 194
'Brookville', 258
Brown, Elsworth, 94

Brown Garden Beetle (Autoserica castanea), 306-7
Bud Blast (Pycnostyeanus azaleae), 289, 300, 312
Budding, 345-6
bullatum, 35, 132, 159, 391; Exbury selection, 132
bureavii, 30
burmanicum, 132-3, 370, 390

calciphilum, 95
Calcium, 92, 95, 97, 98, 106, 276, 280, 281, 282, 283, 285, 286, 367; bicarbonate, 103, 285; carbonate, 94, 103, 281, 285; cyanamide, 287; nitrate, 96, 287; sulphate, 281, 286
Calcium deficiency, 285
Calcutta Botanical Garden, 173
californicum, see macrophyllum
callimorphum, 133
calophytum, 47, 134, 220
Calophytum subseries, 134
calostrotum, 134-5; White's Claret-colored form, 135
caloxanthum, 114, 135-6, 137, 228, 402
Camellia, 97, 181, 403; family, 15, 109
campanulatum, 16, 136, 402; 'Knaphill' form, 136, 402; var. aeruginosum, 30, 108, 136, 185
Campanulatum series, 30, 136, 169
campylocarpum, 16, 107, 114, 135, 137-8, 227, 228, 363, 401, 403, 418; Hooker's variety, 137; var. elatum, 137, 403
Campylocarpum subseries, 29, 133, 135, 137, 186
campylogynum, 24, 27, 32, 138; var. charopoeum, 138; var. cremastum, 138; var. myrtilloides, 138
Campylogynum series, 138
camtschaticum, 19, 28
Camtschaticum series, 112
'Canary', 88
'Candidissimum', 245
canescens, 16
cantabile, see russatum
'Carmen', 247
'Caroline', 46, 255, 268
carolinianum, 44, 55, 63, 85, 122, 138-9, 142, 143, 196,208, 252, 255, 294, 297, 363, 377, 387, 390, 391, 392, 395, 397; var. album, 44, 130, 139, 377, 390
Carolinianum series, 138, 142, 195
Casadevall, Joseph, 268, 391, 392
'Catalgla', 140
Catawba hybrids, 17, 50, 63, 168, 250-2, 255, 257, 258 260, 268, 299, 315, 319, 321, 325, 342, 363, 364
catawbiense, 16, 17, 35, 45, 46, 50, 55, 62, 63, 110, 122, 126, 139, 140-1, 189, 192, 193, 196, 204, 213, 245, 246, 253, 261, 278, 299, 335, 363, 387, 388, 389, 396, 414; 'Catalgla' specimen, 54, 140, 387, 388, 396; var. album, Glass, 46, 54, 85, 140, 387, 389, 390, 396, 407; var. compactum, 141, 398; var. rubrum, 388, 390
'Catawbiense album', 140, 407
'Catawbiense boursault', 251
'Catawbiense grandiflorum', 251
Caterpillars, 313
'Catherine van Tol', 378
caucasicum, 16, 17, 54, 126, 141-2, 145, 245, 246, 252, 299, 398, 402; 'Coriaceum', 141; var. "album", 142; var. flavum, 142; var. pictum, 142; var. "Venustum", 142
Caucasicum subseries, 113, 122, 131, 141, 144, 153, 164, 190, 194, 213, 224, 231
C. B. Van Nes', 88, 380
Centipedes, 288
Cephalanthum series, 112
Cerasinum subseries, 29
Cercospora rhododendri, see Leaf Spots
chamae-thomsonii, 167; var. chamaethauma, 167
chameunum, 114, 209
chapmanii, 139, 142-3, 363, 397
'Charles Bagley', 254
'Charles Dickens', 325, 388, 389
charopoeum, see campylogynum
chartophyllum, 131, 143, var. album, 143
chasmanthum, 143-4; Exbury F.C.C. form, 144
Chelsea Flower Show, 231
'China', 85, 249
Chlorosis, 92, 94, 99, 102, 280-2, 283, 285, 286, 287-8, 296, 366, 381; iron, 98, 284-5, 286
chrysanthum, 16, 144-5, 164, 398; var. niko-montanum, 144, 145
chryseum, 145
Chrysomyxa ledi var. rhododendri, see Leaf Rust
ciliatum, 119, 146, 225, 390, 391, 392; "var. bergii", 146, 392
cilliicalyx, 146-7, 372
Ciliicalyx subseries, 132, 146, 166, 181, 224, 225
'Cilpinense', 247
cinnabarinum, 114, 147, 149, 231; var. blandfordiae-florum, 147; var. purpurellum, 147; var. roylei, 54, 147
Cinnabarinum series, 30,32, 48, 147, 148, 216, 230, 395, 413
Citrus Experiment Station of the University of Florida, 97, 367
Clay Colored Weevil (Brachyrhinus singularis), 304-6
Clear Wing (Sesia rhododendri) 309-10
'C.O.D. ', 258
Coggeshall, R.G., 329
Colchicine, 410
Cold Injury, 274, 289, 290
Colgrove, 95, 98, 284
Comely Bank Nurseries of Edinburgh, 252
concatenans, 114, 147, 148, 231; 'Copper', 148
concinnum, 148-9
'Conestoga', 255 ,390
'Conewago', 252
Connecticut Agricultural Experiment Station, 294
Cooper, 136
Copper, 92, 97, 99, 100, 286
Copperas (ferrous sulphate), 69, 82, 96, 97, 280, 281, 282, 336, 366, 369, 381
coriaceum, 31
'Cornish Cross', 264
'Cornubia', 264
Corthylus punctatissimus, see Pitted Ambrosia Beetle
'Countess of Athlone' 380
'Countess of Haddington', 263, 373
Cowan, Dr J. M., 27, 113, 114, 117, 122, 130, 203
Cranberry Root Worm (Rhabdopterus picipes), 307
crassum, 30, 149-50, 373; Logan form, 149
Creech, Dr John, 386, 408
cremastum, see campylogynum
'Crest', 401
Crickets, 313
Crown Gall (Bacterium tumefaciens), 295
Crown Rot (Phytophthora cryptogeae), 293
Cryptostictis mariae, 298
Crystal Springs Lake Island Trial Garden, 154
cuneatum, 390
Cunningham, 252
'Cunninghami', 252
'Cunningham's Sulphur', 54, 142
'Cunningham's White', 252, 299, 334
Cuttings, 313-34
cyclium, 133

dalhousiae, 16, 150, 186, 220, 372, 374, 386
Damping-off fungi (Rhizoctonia solani), 293-4, 353
'Daphne', 264
dauricum, 16, 151, 198, 390, 392
Dauricum series, 151, 197

David, Abbé, 134, 188
Davidian, 203
davidii, 17
Davidii subseries, 205, 219
Davidson, Dr W. H., 152
davidsonianum, 95, 151-2, 223, 390; "Pink Triflorum" 151; 'Caerhay's Pink', 152; Exbury variety, 152; "Pink Davidsonianum", 152
'Day Dream', 34
Decaisne, 200
decorum, 85, 114, 152-3, 155, 157, 168, 169, 255, 257, 335, 360, 363, 387, 389, 390, 396, 401, 402
Deficiencies, nutritional, 280-7
degronianum, 31, 153-4, 191, 192, 194, 232
delavayi, 17, 233
Delaway, 132, 138, 147, 150, 166, 174, 175, 181, 184, 199, 207, 208, 216, 219, 233
'Delicatissimum', 245
desquamatum, 44, 154
Dexter, C. O., 139, 246, 256, 257, 258
Dexter Garden, Sandwich, 256
Dexter hybrids, 46, 85, 256-9, 268, 321, 389
Dialeurodes chittendeni, see Rhododendron White Fly
diaprepes, 48, 114, 154-5; 'Gargantua', 155, 410
dichroanthum, 41, 44, 125, 155-6, 211, 261, 268, 396 398, 401, 402
'Dido', 396, 402
didymum, 156, 173, 398
Die-Back, see Rhododendron Blight
Diels, 143, 155, 217
discolor, 18, 35, 48, 114, 153, 155, 156-7, 169, 261, 262, 335, 388, 389, 390, 396, 400, 402, 417, 418
Diseases, fungus, 291-301
'Diva', 34, 400
Don, David, 131, 136, 189
Don, G., 131, 189, 190
'Doncaster', 17
'Dorothea', 268
'Dr A. Blok', 380
'Dr H. C. Dresselhuys', 321, 325
'Dr J. Hutchinson', 263
'Dr Stocker', 264
'Dr V. H. Rutgers, 254
du Pont, Henry, Estate, 257

'Earl of Athlone', 88, 259, 389, 400
'Earl of Donoughmore', 400
eclectum, 31, 108, 157-8, 217; var. bellatulum, 158; var. brachyandrum, 158
edgeworthii, 132, 158 9, 391; Ludlow and Sherriff's form, 159
Edgeworthii series, 132, 158, 241, 263, 362, 390, 397
'Edward S. Rand', 254
'Elizabeth', 247, 264, 399
'Elisabeth Hobbie', 400
elliottii, 18, 159-60, 399; 'Warpaint' selection, 160
Endtz, L. J., & Co., 247
Eriococcus azaleae, see Scales
eriogynum, 160, 161, 398
'Essex Scarlet', 380, 400
Eucordylea huntella, see Rhododendron Moth
eudoxum, 44, 160-1
European peat moss, 70, 73, 322, 329, 333, 365, 368
European Rhododendron Rust, see Leaf Rust
'Everestianum', 245, 299
exasperatum, 31
Exbury Estate Rhododendron Collection, England, 206, 231, 247, 266, 268
eximium, 30
Exobasidium burtii, see Leaf Spots
Exobasidium vaccinii, see Leaf Gall
Exobasidium vaccinii-uliginosii, see Witches' Broom

'Fabia', 34
Fabia group, 247, 249, 402
facetum, 161
falconeri, 16, 108, 127, 161-2
Falconeri series, 21, 33, 47, 82, 127, 141, 161, 165, 166, 176, 335
'Fanfare', 388
Fargès, Rev. Paul, 123, 163
fargesii, 17, 162-63, 201; Bodnant form, 162
Farm and Garden Research Foundation, 91
Farquhar Nursery, 256
'Farquhar's Pink', 256
Farrer, Reginald, 18, 19, 125, 132, 135, 136, 153, 183, 215, 216, 221
fastigiatum, 18, 163, 178, 255, 390
'Fastuosum flore pleno', 403
fauriei, 145, 164, 389, 403; var. roseum, 164
Ferrous ammonium sulphate, 367
Ferrous sulphate, see Copperas
ferrugineum (Rose of the Alps or Alpine Rose), 15, 16, 164-5, 176
Ferrugineum series, 164, 176
Fertilizing, 273, 328, 366
fictolactum, 114, 165-6; 'Cherry Tip' selection, 165, 166; var. roseum, 166
fittianum, 151
flavidum, 145, 392
flavum, 16
floccigerum, 215
floribundum, 402
Flower Thrips (Frankliniella tritici), 304
'Flushing', 252
formosum, 166, 373, 374
Forrest, George, 18, 19, 29, 120, 122, 125, 127, 132, 133, 138, 150, 154, 155, 156, 157, 158, 160, 161, 167, 168, 170, 171, 172, 173, 174, 175, 178, 182, 183, 184, 186, 193, 198, 199, 202, 205, 206, 207, 208, 209, 210, 211, 212, 215, 216, 217, 221, 224, 225
forrestii, 18, 40, 44, 124, 167-8, 269, 354, 384, 390, 397, 398, 399, 400; var. repens, 167, 268; var. tumescens, 167
Forrestii subseries, 167
'Forsterianum', 263, 374
Fortescue, Dr W. N., 192
'Fortune', 247
Fortune, Robert, 16, 17, 35, 157, 168, 169, 203
fortunei, 16, 35, 48, 153, 155, 157, 168-9, 256, 257, 261, 262, 276, 335, 352, 386, 388, 390, 396, 397, 402, 418; 'Mrs Butler', 168; "R. fortunei", 152
Fortunei series, 65, 134, 152, 154, 156, 162, 168, 172, 200, 201, 205, 219, 226, 256, 257, 261, 363
Fortunei subseries, 152, 154, 156, 157, 168, 226
'Fragrantissimum', 263, 335, 371, 373
Franchet, 122, 130, 132, 134, 138, 143, 146, 149, 152, 156, 162, 163, 164, 174, 180, 183, 187, 196, 198, 201, 207, 209, 214, 216, 218, 219, 226, 227, 228, 232
Frankliniella tritici, see Flower Thrips
fulgens, 16
fulvoides, see fulvum
fulvum, 107, 169-70
Fulvum series, 169
Fungus, 157, 290, 316
'Fusilier', 34

Gable, Joseph, 46, 54, 128, 140, 153, 187, 201, 202, 227, 246, 252, 255, 268, 346, 352, 387, 388, 389, 390, 400, 402
Garden Centipede (Scutigerella immaculata), 308-9
Gardener's Chronicle, 17
Giardomyia rhododendri, see Rhododendron Midge
Giant Hornet (Vespa crabro germana), 312
'Gill's Crimson', 88, 264
Glass, P., 54, 140

glaucophyllum, 16, 35, 44, 170
Glaucophyllum series, 138, 170, 413
Glaucophyllum subseries, 170
glaucum, see glaucophyllum
Gleosporium, 298
Glischrum subseries, 218
'Glory of Penjerrick', 264
'Glow', 45
'Goblin', 90
'Goethe', 388
Golden Gate Park, San Francisco, 199, 243
'Goldsworth Orange', 249, 261
'Goldsworth Yellow', 260, 299, 326
'Gomer Waterer', 254
'Goshawk', 401
Gowan, J.R., 17, 126, 245
Grafting, 53, 334-5, 408
grande, 16, 170-1, 212
Grande series, 21, 33, 47, 82, 170, 188, 212, 241, 315, 335
Graphocephala coccinea, see Leaf Hopper
Gray, 142
'Gretia', 399
'Grierdal', 373, 374, 386
griersonianum, 18, 34, 88, 129, 171-2, 262, 264, 291, 363, 374, 386, 387, 396, 399, 402; Exbury form, 171
Griffith, William, 173
griffithianum, 172-3, 256, 363, 373, 386, 389, 395, 402
Griffithianum subseries, 172
Grootendorst, Herman J., 378, 380
Grove, W.R., 350
Grubs, 71, 306
Guyencourt Rhododendron Hybrids, 255
Gypsum, see Calcium sulphate

haemaleum, 156, 173
haematocheilum, 201
haematodes, 40, 44, 130, 174, 256, 268, 388, 390, 397, 399, 400
Haematodes subseries, 130, 174
Hagedoorn, A.L., 419
Hamilton, Dr C.C., 303, 311
hanceanum, 54; var. nanum, 54, 390
Hanger, F.E.W., 93, 94
Hara, Dr Hiroshi, 144, 164, 194
Hardgrove, D.L. 392
Harkness, 192
'Hassan', 388
Hawk group, 247, 249, 401
'Helen Fox', 264
heliolepis, 44, 174-5
Heliolepis series, 32, 44, 93, 154, 174, 207, 413
Heliothrips haemorrhoidalis, see Thrips
Hemsl, 124, 127, 128, 148, 179, 228
Henny, Rudolph, 268
Henry, Dr Augustine, 17, 128, 129
herpesticum, 211, 402
Highland Park Herbarjum, Rochester, N.Y., 192
hippophaeoides, 175-6; 'Haba Shan', 175
hirsutum (Alpine Rose), 16, 95, 176
Hobbie, Dietrich, 268, 400
hodgsonii, 16, 176-7
Home Garden, The, magazine, 333
Hooker, Sir Joseph, 16, 17, 35, 123, 137, 138, 147, 150, 158, 159, 161, 170, 171, 177, 186, 189, 190, 206, 222, 223, 224, 225, 229, 246
Hooker fil., 146, 176
hookeri, 31, 108, 177, 187
horaeum, 155, 402
Hormone treatments, 319
Hort. ex Loud Encyc. Pl (1855), 233
houlstonii, 114, 390
Hu, 227
'Hugo Koster', 380
Hunnewell, Walter, 253
Hunnewell, Walter, Collection, 253
Hutch., 178, 205
Hutchinson, Dr. J., 132, 148, 220, 230
'H.W. Sargent', 252
Hybrids, complete tabular listing, see Appendix
hyperythrum, 31

'Ignatius Sargent', 398
impeditum, 163, 178
imperator, 18, 42, 114, 178-9, 203
'Inamorata', 417
Indolebutyric acid, 319, 320
Insect pests, 301-13
insigne, 179
intricatum, 18, 178, 180
Iron, 91, 92, 95, 96, 97, 98, 99, 100, 281, 283, 284, 285, 287, 367-8; chelates, 97, 99, 283, 285, 286, 367, 381; magnesium silicate, 282; phosphate, 284
Iron deficiency, 284-5
irroratum, 180-1
Irroratum series, 122, 159, 160, 161, 180, 183, 226, 241
Irroratum subseries, 122, 180
Ivy Scale (Aspidiotus pseudosapinosus), 311-12

Jalisco hybrid group, 401
James, Mr and Mrs Del, 184, 374
Japanese Beetle (Popillia japonica), 306-7
Jardin des Plantes, Paris, 207
javanicum, 362, 373
'Javanicum' Rhododendrons, see Appendix
'Jean', 387
'Jean Marie Montague', 389, 400
'Joanita', 402
'John Walter', 254
johnstoneanum, 181, 374, 403; var. rubeotinctum, 181
Journal of the Scottish Rock Garden Club, 95
Journal of Vancouver's Voyage, 189

'Kate Waterer', 378
'Katherine Dalton', 388
Katydids, 313
keiskei, 31, 182, 194, 223, 255, 262, 390, 392
keleticum, 182-3
Kerckhoff Laboratories of Biology, 413
'Kettledrum', 325, 389
keysii, 147, 216
'King Edward VII', 362
'King George', 249, 259, 334, 397
'King of Shrubs', 268
Kingdon-Ward, Captain F., 18, 21, 22, 24, 94, 124, 125, 132, 134, 135, 145, 148, 153, 159, 161, 165, 167, 169, 174, 176, 177, 178, 179, 185, 194, 203, 209, 216, 220, 221, 227, 228, 231
kingianum, see zeylanicum
Kissena Nurseries, Long Island, 252
Knap Hill Nursery, 17, 35, 140, 245, 246, 252, 268
Koster, M., and Sons, 247
kyawi, 160, 183

Laboratorium voor Tuinbouwplantenteelt, Landbouwhoge-school, Wegeningen, Netherlands, 414
Lace Wing Fly, 45, 62, 256, 301, 302, 303, 311, 312, 316, 336, 380
lacteum, 18, 48, 53, 93, 166, 183-4, 334, 401, 402
Lacteum series, 114, 131, 183, 229, 240
'Lady Alice Fitzwilliam', 373
Lady Bessborough hybrid group, 247
Lady Chamberlain hybrid group, 247, 249, 266

'Lady Clementine Mitford', 254
'Lady Eleanor Cathcart', 262
'Lady Grey-Egerton', 396
lanatum, 16
Lancaster, B. F., 268
lapponicum, 19, 24, 30, 32, 63, 95, 135, 298
Lapponicum series, 37, 82, 115, 118, 119, 145, 163, 175, 178, 180, 208, 210, 240, 315, 395, 413
Larson, H. L., 194, 230, 268, 344, 408
'Laura Aberconway', 396
Layering, 346-50
Leach Polyethylene Frame, 333
Leaf Gall (Exobasidium vaccinii), 301
Leaf Hopper (Graphocephala coccinea), 300, 312
Leaf Rust, 297-300
Leaf Scorch (Septoria solitaris), 297-300
Leaf Spots, 297-300
Lee, Mosser, 294, 354
'Lee's Dark Purple', 251, 299, 315
Leiser, Andrew T., 95
Lem, Halfdan 268, 340, 343
Leonardslee Garden, 266
lepidostylum, 30, 108, 184-5
lepidotum, 16
Lepidotum series, 138, 413
leucaspis, 18, 33, 41, 185, 392
Lilly, Charles H., Company, 99, 100, 101
Lindley, Dr John, 168, 186
lindleyi, 185-6, 220
Linnaeus, 15, 151, 164, 176, 191, 204
litiense, 114, 117, 135, 137, 186, 228
Lobb, W., 189
L'Obel, Matthias de, 15
Lockwood and Son, Ltd., 419
Loder, Sir Edmund, 247
Loderi hybrid group, 31, 48, 53, 88, 172, 249, 259, 264, 334, 386, 397
longesquamatum, 187
Longwood Gardens, Penn., 373
Lophodermium rhododendri, see Leaf Spots
Ludlow, 18, 198, 227
'Luscombei', 169
lutescens, 31, 44, 187-88, 391, 392; 'Bagshot Sands', 188; F.C.C. form, Exbury, 187

macabeanum, 18, 188-9
macrophyllum, 55, 189-90, 301, 310
Maculiferum subseries, 187, 218
'Madame Carvalho', 255
'Madame de Bruin', 260
Madden, Lt.-Col., 190
maddenii, 16, 149, 150, 190, 373
Maddenii series, 35, 132, 146, 149, 150, 166, 181, 185, 190, 194, 199, 200, 220, 224, 225, 241, 263, 335, 362, 371, 372, 392, 395, 397, 413
Maddenii subseries, 149, 190
Madras Botanic Garden, 229
Magnesium, 90, 92, 93, 95, 97, 98, 101, 276, 281, 282, 286, 367; carbonate, 94, 282; oxide, 101, 276; sulphate, 96, 283, 286, 381
Magnesium deficiency, 286
magnificum, 352
Magnolia, 15, 24, 56, 109; stellata, 197
Magor, 246, 247
makinoi, 31, 154, 190-1, 232
Malaysian Rhododendrons, 373, see Appendix
mallotum, 31, 130
Manganese, 90, 91, 92, 97, 100, 283
Manganese deficiency, 285
'Margaret Dunn', 402
Mariloo hybrid group, 249
'Marinus Koster', 249
'Mars', 260, 261, 396
maximum, 15, 16, 17, 46, 55, 63, 74, 93, 110, 139, 141, 171, 189, 191-93, 196, 245, 252, 262, 277, 299, 301, 335, 342, 344, 362, 388, 400, 405; var. leachii, 192
'May Day', 34, 399
McLaren, 200
meddianum, 193; var. atrokermesinum, 193
megacalyx, 194, 373
Megacalyx subseries, 150, 185, 194, 199, 220
megeratum, 18, 374, 390, 392
Megeratum subseries, 185
Melampsoropis piperiana, see Leaf Rust
Menzies, 189
metternichii, 31, 154, 194-5, 403; var. tsukushianum, 194
Michaux, 140, 195, 196
Michigan peat, 92, 356
Michigan State University, Department of Horticulture, 90, 91
micranthum, 195
Micranthum series, 195
Microsphaera alni, see Powdery Mildew
'Mildred Amateis', 391
Miller, Everett, 259, 260
Minterne Gardens, 266
minus, 16, 55, 63, 139, 142, 195-6, 362, 390, 392
Miquel, 182
Missouri Botanical Garden, 110
molle, 16
Mollis hybrids, 16
Molybdenum, 92, 97, 100, 283, 286
Mono-potassium phosphate, 96
'Moonstone', 264
Moore, T., 185, 252
Morris Arboretum, 257
moupinense, 35, 41, 196-7, 370, 374, 392; Exbury form, 197
Moupinense series, 196
'Mrs A. T. de la Mare', 380
'Mrs A. Waterer', 396
'Mrs C. B. Van Nes', 88, 249, 380
'Mrs C. S. Sargent', 46, 299
'Mrs Davies Evans', 396
'Mrs Donald Graham', 268
'Mrs Furnival', 396
'Mrs Horace Fogg', 268
'Mrs J. G. Millais', 396
'Mrs Lindsay Smith', 88, 268, 380
'Mrs P. de Ouden', 254
'Mrs P. D. Williams', 254
'Mrs Philip Martineau', 396
'Mrs W. R. Coe', 258
mucronulatum, 35, 85, 151, 197-8, 252, 255, 277, 390, 392; 'Cornell Pink', 197; var. roseum, 198
Mulberry White Fly (Tetraleurodes mori), 307-8
Mulch, 73, 76, 272, 368
Mulligan, Brian O., 58
mussoti, see wardii
myagrum, 133
Mycorrhizae, 96-7
Mycosphaerella, 298
myrtilloides, see campylogynum

Nakai, 145, 231, 232
Naomi hybrid group, 45, 247, 249, 261, 264
'Nautilus', 45
Nearing, Guy G., 246, 255, 268, 278, 302, 316, 318, 321, 322, 325, 332, 352, 389, 390
Nearing Frame, 322
neriiflorum, 24, 118, 198-9, 399, 400, 402; euchaites subspecies, 199; phaedropum subspecies, 199

Neriiflorum series, 21, 35, 41, 44, 113,115, 124, 125 130, 155, 156, 160, 167, 173, 174, 198, 209, 211, 215, 226
Neriiflorum subseries, 198, 215, 216
New Jersey Agricultural Experiment Station, 96, 292, 295, 303, 311
New York Botanical Garden, 157, 254, 257, 260
New York State College of Agriculture, 306
Nitrate nitrogen, 287
Nitrogen deficiency, 282
nivale, 24
niveum, 16, 48
'Nobleanum', 17, 126, 398
'Nova Zembla', 325, 388
nudiflorum, 16, 17
Nurseries (Rhododendron specialists), see Appendix
Nutrient deficiencies, 280-7
Nuttall, Thomas, 177, 200
nuttallii, 31, 108, 121, 199-200, 220, 352, 370, 372, 374; var. stellatum, 200

Oak Root fungus (Armillaria), 294
Oberea myops, see Stem Borer
oblongifolium, 19
obtusum, 16
occidentale, 95
'Old Port', 252, 254
Oleander Scale (Aspidiotus hederae), 311-12
orbiculare, 31, 33, 44, 200, 397
Orbiculare subseries, 200
Oregon Agricultural Experiment Station, 95
oreodoxa, 163, 201
Oreodoxa subseries, 162, 201
oreotrephes, 18, 201-202
Oreotrephes subseries, 201
Oriental Beetle (Phyllopertha orientalis), 306-7
Ostbo, Endre, 268
ovatum, 202, 363
Ovatum series, 123, 202

Pallas, 16, 141, 144, 145
pankimense, 94
panteumorphum, 137
Parishii subseries, 159, 160, 161, 183, 226
Parkinson, 15
Parsons, 246, 252
'Parsons gloriosum' 252
'Parsons grandiflorum', 252
Parsons hybrids, 252
patulum, 42, 114, 179, 203
pemakoense, 18, 114, 179, 203, 390, 392
Penningsfeld, F., 92
Pestalotia sp., see Leaf Spots
Phomopsis sp., see Leaf Spots
Phosphorus, 78, 92, 94, 95, 97, 98, 99, 100, 101, 102, 104, 106
Phosphorus deficiency, 283
Phyllopertha orientalis, see Oriental Beetle
Phyllosticta maxima, see Leaf Spots
Phytophthora cactorum, see Rhododendron Blight
Phytophthora cinnamomi, see Rhododendron Wilt
Phytophthora cryptogeae, see Crown Rot
'Pink Beauty', 45
'Pink Diamond', 249
'Pink Pearl', 54, 87, 268, 421
'Pioneer', 252
Pitted Ambrosia Beetle (Corthylus punctatissimus), 311
Planting Fields Estate, Oyster Bay, 259
Planting situation, 33, 61-6, 364
Pliny, 15
'Polar Bear', 48
Polylepis subseries, 148
ponticum, 16, 17, 45, 52, 53, 94, 96, 126, 184, 189, 204, 245, 246, 291, 293, 294, 304, 334, 335, 356, 359, 371, 372; var. album, 252
Ponticum series, 30, 113, 122, 131, 141, 142, 144, 153, 164, 189, 190, 191, 194, 204, 213, 224, 231, 232
Ponticum subseries, 189, 191, 192, 204
Popillia japonica, see Japanese Beetle
Potassium, 90, 92, 94, 95, 97, 98, 99, 100, 102, 104, 106, 276, 281, 282, 283, 286, 367; nitrate, 287; sulphate, 98, 101, 283
Potassium deficiency, 283
Potting, 371
poukhanense, 277
Powdery Mildew (Microsphaera alni), 301
praevernum, 205
'President Lincoln', 252
'Princess Alice', 263
'Princess Elizabeth', 88
'Prometheus', 88, 262
prostratum, 209
pseudochrysanthum, 31
pseudoyanthinum, 148, 149; 'Paulina' selection, 149
pubescens, 44, 47, 205-6, 255
Puccinastrum myrtilli, see Leaf Rust
Puddle, Charles, 181, 247, 403
Pulvinaria ericicola, see Scales
puralbum, 206
'Purple Gem', 255
'Purple Splendour', 251, 254, 379
'Purpureum elegans', 251, 315
'Purpureum grandiflorum', 245, 251
Pycnostyeanus azaleae, see Bud Blast
'Pygmalion', 396

racemosum (Mayflower Rhododendron), 17, 44, 47, 120, 206-207, 241, 255, 352, 390, 391
radicans, 183, 278
'Ramapo', 255, 390
'Red Admiral', 48
Red Spider (Tetranychus bimaculatus), 302, 308, 312, 372
Rehder, 138, 139, 151, 170, 223, 230
repens, see forrestii; var. chamaedoron, see forrestii; var. chamae-thomsonii, see chamae-thomsonii
'Review Order', 399
rex, 114, 165
rhabdotum, 374
Rhabdopterus picipes, see Cranberry Root Worm
Rhizoctonia Rot, 293-4
Rhizoctonia solani, see Damping-off fungi
Rhododendron and Camellia Yearbook, The, 95
Rhododendron Blight (Phytophthora cactorum), 53, 119, 139, 228, 291, 294, 296-7, 298, 311, 369
Rhododendron Borer (Sesia rhododendri), 309-10
Rhododendron Bug (Stephanitis rhododendri), 302
Rhododendron Fly (Stephanitis rhododendri), 302
Rhododendron Handbook, The, 121, 384, 385, 396, 407
Rhododendron Lace Bug (Stephanitis rhododendri, 302
Rhododendron Midge (Giardomyia rhododendri), 302, 303
Rhododendron Moth (Eucordylea huntella), 310
Rhododendron White Fly (Dialeurodes chittendeni), 307-8
Rhododendron Wilt (Phytophthora cinnamomi), 53, 71, 272, 291-3, 294, 297, 314, 335, 336, 356, 359
Rhododendron Yearbook, The, 94, 112
'Robert Fox', 264
Roberts, 95, 98, 284
'Robin Hood', 48
Rock, Dr J. F., 18, 120, 132, 145, 173, 177, 184, 208, 210, 221, 225, 227, 402
'Romany Chal', 247
Root Rot, see Rhododendron Wilt
'Rosalind', 48

'Roseum Elegans', 45, 90, 319, 320, 363, 377
Rothschild, Lionel de, 246, 247
roxieanum, 31, 191
Roxieanum subseries, 113, 115
Royal Botanic Garden, Edinburgh, 17, 117, 153, 217, 221, 227, 266
Royal Botanic Gardens, Kew, England, 130
Royal Horticultural Society of England, 32, 50, 94, 95, 120, 121, 136, 139, 177, 202, 211, 231, 247, 374, 384, 396, 412, 421; Gardens at Wisley, 266, 268
rubiginosum, 18, 44, 207-8, 392
'Russautini', 39
russatum, 18, 208-9
'Russellianum', 126, 245

Saharanpur Gardens, India, 162
saluenense, 24, 114, 209
Saluenense series, 30, 134, 135, 182, 209, 413
sanguineum, 173, 209-10, 278
Sanguineum subseries, 115, 124, 125, 155, 156, 160, 173, 209, 211
'Sappho', 261
sargentianum, 18
'Sarita Loder', 34
Sawdust, 70-71, 72, 77, 78, 79, 81, 90, 102, 282, 287, 288, 353, 368, 370
scabrifolium, 374
Scabrifolium series, 42, 44, 205, 216
Scales, 311-12
Schneider, 187
scintillans, 18, 210-11; Exbury form, 210
'Scintillation', 46, 258
Scott Horticultural Foundation, 257
scottianum, 374
Scutigerella immaculata, see Garden Centipede
scyphocalyx, 44, 155, 211, 402; var. septentrionale, 211
Seedlings, 54, 358
Seeds, propagation from, 351-60
'Sefton', 252, 334
Seidel, T. J. R., 388
seinghkuense, 159
Selense subseries, 29, 113
semibarbatum, 119
Septoria solitaris, see Leaf Scorch
Series, Rhododendrons listed by, see Appendix
Sesia rhododendri, see Rhododendron Borer, Clear Wing
Shammarello, A. M., 268, 296, 356, 389
Sherriff, 18, 198, 227
Sieb, 194
sinogrande, 18, 119, 171, 212
'Sir Frederick Moore', 264
Skinner, Dr Henry, 110, 262, 277, 331, 389, 403
Slocock, Walter S., Ltd., Goldsworth Nursery of, 246-7, 268
smirnowii, 113, 213-14, 224, 299, 388, 389
Smith, Dr F. F., 306
Smith, W. W., 125, 133, 154, 160, 169, 175, 177, 183, 201, 206, 210, 212, 227
Sodium nitrate, 287
Soil, 365
Soulié, Rev. J. A., 144, 209, 214, 226, 228
souliei, 17, 122, 206, 214, 398; Exbury Pink form, 214; Windsor Park form, 214
Souliei subseries, 29, 186, 206, 214, 227
'Souvenir de D. A. Koster', 400
'Souvenir de Dr S. Endtz', 268
Species, complete alphabetical descriptive tabular listing, see Appendix
Species, listed by series and subseries, see Appendix
Species of Rhododendrons, The, 16, 117
sperabile, 215, 216; var. weihsiense, 215
sperabiloides, 215-16
Sphagnum moss, 293, 294, 350, 351, 353, 354, 356, 357, 358, 365, 371, 373
spiciferium, 44, 47
spinuliferum, 216-17, 390, 392
Spotting fungus, 216
Sprays, 295, 301, 327
Stamineum group, 241
Standish and Noble, 245
Stem Borer (Oberea myops), 310-11
Stem Rot (Rhizoctonia solani), 293-4
Stenaulum series, 21
Stephanitis rhododendri, see Rhododendron Lace Bug
Stevenson, J. B., 247
Stewart, L. B., 217
stewartianum, 158, 217
Strawberry Root Weevil, 288
Strawberry Weevil (Brachyrhinus ovatus), 304-6, 327
strigillosum, 218, 399
sulfureum, 218-19
Sulphur, 92, 280, 282, 301, 302, 366, 381
Sumner, Mr and Mrs Maurice H., 263
Sun Scald, 289
Sunningdale Nurseries, 245, 268
'Sunrise', 396
Superphosphate, 276, 283
'Susan', 402
sutchuenense, 47, 134, 201, 219-20; "var. geraldii", 205, 219, 220
'Sweet Simplicity', 380
Synonyms (of species names), see Appendix

Tacoma Rhododendron Society, 190
Tagg, H. F., 185, 190, 191, 215, 226
taggianum, 220-21, 373
Taliense series, 92, 113, 114, 119, 191, 228, 229, 360
'Tally Ho', 34
Taxus Weevil (Brachyrhinus sulcatus), 304-6
telopeum, 114, 135, 137
'Temple Belle', 264
tephropeplum, 44, 221, 390; deleiense form, 221
Tephropeplum subseries, 221
Tetraleurodes mori, see Mulberry White Fly
Tetranychus bimaculatus, see Red Spider, Two-Spotted Mite
Thomson, Dr Thomas, 222
thomsonii, 16, 17, 29, 30, 48, 88, 151, 169, 187, 193, 222, 245, 246, 400
Thomsonii series, 29, 113, 133, 135, 137, 157, 158, 177, 186, 193, 206, 214, 217, 222, 227, 230, 240
Thomsonii subseries, 29, 157, 177, 193, 217, 222
Thrips (Thrips tabaci; Frankliniella tritici, Heliothrips haemorrhoidalis), 62, 303-4, 311, 316
Thrips tabaci, see Thrips
Tod, Dr, 94, 95
Trace element deficiency, 283-4
Transplanting, 55
Traut., 213, 224
tricanthum, 223; Tower Court form, 223
Trichocladum series, 184
triflorum, 44, 152, 182, 223-24; "Caerhay's Pink Triflorum", 223; "Ward's Mahogany Triflorum", 223
Triflorum series, 21, 30, 32, 35, 41, 44, 48, 63, 93, 115, 124, 127, 128, 130, 131, 143, 148, 151, 182, 187, 188, 201, 223, 232, 233, 262, 395, 413
Triflorum subseries, 124, 182, 187, 223
Trumpy, J. R., 252
Turczaninow, 195, 197
Twigg and Link (Proc. Amer. Soc. Hort. Sci.), 92
Two Spotted Mite (Tetranychus bimaculatus), 308
'Tyermanii', 263, 374

Ungern-Sternberg, Baron, 214, 224
ungernii, 113, 213, 214, 224
uniflorum, 32, 114, 179, 203

Uniflorum series, 178, 179, 203
'Unique', 90
United States National Arboretum, 262, 277, 389, 403
United States Plant Introduction Garden, 386, 408
'Unknown Warrior', 380
uvarifolium, 169

valentinianum, 224-25, 390
Vanadium, 92
van Nes, C B., & Sons, 247
'Vanessa', 247
'Van Weerden Poelman', 378
Veitch, James, & Sons Nursery, 18, 256
Veitch family, 225
veitchianum, 225
venator, 226
vernicosum, 226-7, 402
Vespa crabro germana, see Giant Hornet
"Victorian Vapors", 175
'Victorianum', 263
villosum, see tricanthum
Vilmorin, Maurice de, 123, 127
Virgatum series, 206
viscosum, 16
Vossberg, Paul, 252, 334
'Vulcan', 261, 264

Wall, 129
Wallich, 166
wallichii, 16
wardii, 18, 114, 117, 121, 135, 137, 186, 206, 227-8, 398, 401, 417, 418; croceum, 228; var. album, 206
Washington Rhododendron Society, 123
Wason, C. R., 229
wasonii, 228-9
Wasonii subseries, 228
Water Mold Root Rot, see Rhododendron Wilt
Waterer, Anthony, 17, 35, 45, 141, 245, 246, 250, 252, 255, 257, 396, 422
Waterer, John, (& Sons) of Bagshot, 247
Waterer, John, Sons & Crisp, Ltd., 247, 268
Waterer, Michael, 17, 141, 245
Waterer family, 246; also see Appendix
Waterer hybrids, 245, 246, 252, 258, 388, 389, 422
Watering, 79, 273, 325, 368
Watt, Sir George, 159, 181, 233
'Welkin', 247
Wells, James, 312
'Westbury', 258
Westbury Rose Company, 258
'Wheatley', 258
Wherry, Edgar, 94
White, Harry, 155
Wight, Dr, 170, 172, 229
wightii, 16, 229, 262
Wild plants, 54
Wilde, Roland de, 196, 296, 299
Williams, J.C., 63, 230, 247
williamsianum, 18, 31, 33, 40, 43, 44, 63, 108, 230, 268, 269, 384, 397
Williamsianum subseries, 29
Wilson, E. H., 18, 124, 129, 134, 151, 152, 157, 163, 179, 180, 187, 188, 195, 197, 200, 201, 203, 205, 214, 218, 220, 223, 227, 228, 229, 230, 250
'Windbeam', 255, 390
Windsor Great Park, England, 35, 168, 184, 266, 268
Winter protection, 274, 327
Wister, Dr John, 257
Witches' Broom (Exobasidium vaccinii-uliginosii), 301
'Wyanokie', 255, 390

xanthocodon, 114, 147, 148, 230-1; Exbury form, 231

yakusimanum, 43, 154, 194, 231-32, 398; F. C. C. form, 231, 232
Yeates, Dr J. S., 342
Yu, 198
yunnanense, 18, 143, 232-3, 262; Tower Court form, 233
Yunnanense subseries, 130, 143, 151, 232

zeylanicum, 16, 233
Zinc, 92, 97, 99, 100, 286
Zucc., 194
'Zuiderzee', 90